Contents

Abbreviations

AA	Auswärtiges Amt (German Foreign Ministry)
ACC CPC	Archives of the Central Committee of the Communist Party of Czechoslovakia
ADAP	*Akten zur deutschen Auswärtigen Politik, 1918–1945*
AMFA	Archives of the Ministry of Foreign Affairs, Prague
AMI	Archives of the Ministry of Interior, Prague
ASMAE	Archivio Storico del Ministero degli Affari Esteri
BA/MA	Bundesarchiv/Militärarchiv, Freiburg im Breisgau (German Military Archive)
BA-TGM	Archives of Edvard Benes at the Institute of Tomas G. Masaryk, Invalidovna, Prague
BDRC	*Biographical Dictionary of Republican China*
CAB	Cabinet Office Papers, Public Record Office, London.
CADN	Centre des Archives Diplomatiques, Nantes
CAEF	Centre des Archives Economiques et Financières.
CHD	*Ciano's Hidden Diaries, 1937–1938.*
DAFP	*Documents on Australia Foreign Policy, 1937–1949*
DBFP	*Documents on British Foreign Policy, 1919–1939*
DCER	*Documents on Canadian External Relations*
DDF	*Documents Diplomatiques Français, 1932–1939*
DDI	*Documenti Diplomatici Italiani*
DGFP	*Documents on German Foreign Policy*
DIMK	Diplomatic Papers Relating to the Foreign Policy of Hungary
DiT	*Diariusz i Teki Jana Szembeka, 1935–1939*
FO	Foreign Office Papers, Public Record Office, London
GAB	Gabinetto
HHStA	Haus-, Hof- und Staatsarchiv, Vienna
IWM	Imperial War Museum, London
JS-CU	Archives of Jaromir Smutny, Columbia University
LNOJ	*League of Nations Official Journal*
MAE	Ministère des Affaires Etrangères archive
MOPR	The Military Office of the President of the Republic, The Castle, Prague

NA	National Archives, Washington
NC	Neville Chamberlain Papers.
OL	Országos Levéltár (National Archives of Hungary)
OO	*Opera Omnia di Benito Mussolini*
OPR	Office of the President of the Republic, The Castle, Prague
PA	Politisches Archiv, Bonn (German Foreign Ministry Archive)
PHPP	Phipps Papers, Cambridge.
PRO	Public Record Office, London
PZ	Political Correspondence, Archives of the Foreign Ministry of Czechoslovakia
RAB	Lord Butler Papers
SAP	Serie Affari Politici
SCA	State Central Archives, Loreta, Prague
SHAA	Service Historique de l'Armée de l'Air
SHAT	Service Historique de l'Armée de Terre
UC	Ufficio di Coordinamento
US	Ufficio Spagna
WCP	Waichiaopu (Archives of the Chinese Foreign Ministry, Taipei)
ZF-ANM	Zdenek Fierlinger Papers, Archives of the National Museum, Prague

Introduction

The Czechoslovak–German crisis of the 1930s began with a seemingly manageable dispute over the historical borders of Bohemia on the one hand and the ethnic composition of the population within it on the other. However, it soon escalated into the first stage of the worst conflagration of this century. The crisis and, even more so, its short-lived solution, the Four Power Act signed at Munich by Germany, Great Britain, France and Italy at the end of September 1938, are events that are firmly embedded in the intellectual vocabulary of the world. This volume commemorates their sixtieth anniversary.

Together with, for instance, 'Waterloo' and 'Versailles', the Munich Conference or simply 'Munich' belongs to the category of phenomena into which many of us, rightly or wrongly, project meanings that surpass the confines of those historical events. For instance, it is commonplace to say 'This will be another Munich!' in reference to a diplomatic venture of which we disapprove and the outcome of which, we predict, will be disastrous.

But 'Munich' has come to refer not only to ill-conceived diplomatic initiatives. Paradoxically, even use of force may trigger the application of such a label. In fact many of the post-World War II troubles prompted politicians and commentators to use 'Munich' as a term endowed with one or another political message. Such has been the case with, for instance, the French and American interventions in, and retreats from, South East Asia; the Soviet suppressions of Hungary's bid for freedom and of the 1968 Prague Spring; the Falklands/Malvinas conflict; the Iraqi occupation of Kuwait; the wars in Slovenia, Croatia, Bosnia-Herzegovina, Kosovo; and the continuing tensions between the Israelis and the Palestinians in the Middle East.

The wisdom of 'appeasement', a derivative of 'Munich', as a way of dealing with dictators was often debated during the Cold War. Recently, both 'Munich' and 'appeasement' appeared in discussions regarding Russia's possible reaction to the decision to admit Poland, the Czech Republic, and Hungary into NATO. In short, the 1930s crisis in central Europe and the Munich Agreement that was supposed to solve it have remained on the intellectual radar of the politically literate world.

The events leading up to the Four Power Act have been described and analyzed extensively. But the record of the Munich drama produced by some of the actors (for instance, Józef Beck, Edvard Benes, Winston Churchill, Édouard Daladier, Sir Nevile Henderson, Wenzel Jaksch, Maxim Litvinov, Ivan Maiski, Emanuel Moravec, Frantisek Moravec, Hubert Ripka, Michel Sturdza) is not free from politically motivated distortions. And even a cursory examination of available secondary literature reveals that, with some exceptions, most of the well-known specialized volumes were published many years ago; such is the case, for instance, with the works of Johann W. Brügel, Boris Celovsky, Keith Feiling, George E.R. Gedye, Martin Gilbert, Jan Kren, Robert Kvacek, Frantisek Lukes, Radomir Luza, Mila Lvova, Vera Olivova, Keith Robins, Edward Taborsky, A.J.P. Taylor, Telford Taylor and Sir John Wheeler-Bennett. Moreover, these authors had written prior to the collapse of the Berlin Wall and before new archival collections had become available. Consequently, they had to rely on personal recollections, memoirs of direct participants, published diplomatic documents, and archives in the west.

The gap between the publication of the standard works on 'Munich' and the present as well as the opening of archives in central Europe and greater accessibility to evidence in the west provide us with an opportunity that must not be ignored. We have therefore invited a group of authors to take a fresh look at the Munich phenomenon.

It would have been presumptuous for us to seek to replace the classical works on this topic. Such was not our intention. Instead, we sought out and here present contributions of three kinds. In the first category are those papers that propose to look at well known problems or topics from an original perspective. In the second are submissions that examine new aspects and dimensions of the crisis. Finally, this volume offers papers based on new and hitherto inaccessible or ignored archival material.

We intended to give preference to originality without providing a foundation for cheaply provocative revisionism and we stressed the need for new material so long as it was centrally relevant to the study. Such an approach to selecting contributors has necessarily resulted in the existence of lacunae in our coverage of the Munich crisis. For instance, the vitally important domestic situation in Czechoslovakia prior to the 1938 crisis is not covered in this publication because it is the subject of three recently published monographs by Antonin Klimek.

A broad scale of relevant topics has been deliberately excluded from this volume. For instance, it is too early to write about the Prague government's stormy and ultimately failed relations with the Sudeten German population. The topic is now in a state of flux as fundamentally important and previously unexamined documents keep coming out of the Czech archives. More time is needed before historians are be able to revisit this subject on a niveau that is high enough for this serious problem. If the Sudeten German issue suffers from a sudden influx of new material, other aspects of the Munich crisis, for instance, details of politics in the Kremlin, suffer from the opposite handicap. There is still not enough new material to add in any substantial way to the books published years ago by Adam B. Ulam. We have to wait for the opening of the presidential archives and the KGB records in Moscow before the issue of Soviet domestic politics and its impact on the developing Czechoslovak crisis in 1938 is addressed anew. Finally, conflicts such as the Spanish Civil War or the brewing troubles in the Far East that paralleled the Czechoslovak–German crisis were excluded from this project since, we felt, a scope so broad would have diminished the sharpness of the final product; volumes dealing with these events can be found in the bibliography.

Aware of these limitations, we trust that the volume demonstrates that important research into the 'Munich' topic has continued to advance since the classical studies were published. This was, of course, made possible by that most welcome gift, the opening of new archival resources at the end of the Cold War. But even more important has been the desire of historians to keep revisiting the Four Power Act, the crisis that produced it, and the one that followed it with such disastrous consequences.

We are happy to acknowledge our gratitude to Frank Cass and Co. for its commitment to scholarly writing and we are both grateful for the support we enjoy at Boston University, our academic home.

IGOR LUKES
ERIK GOLDSTEIN
Boston University

Reflections on Munich after 60 Years

GERHARD L. WEINBERG

In 1945, the Soviet Union annexed the easternmost portion of pre-Munich Czechoslovakia on the grounds that the people living there were akin to those in the adjacent Ukrainian SSR – the same basis on which Germany annexed what had come to be called the Sudetenland. In 1968, the army of the Soviet Union, together with units from the German Democratic Republic, Poland, Hungary and Bulgaria, occupied the remainder of Czechoslovakia. No public demand was voiced anywhere then, and to my knowledge no historian has suggested since, that the United States, Britain, France, or anyone else go to war to protect the independence of Czechoslovakia.

In 1931, Japan occupied a large portion of China – the provinces collectively called Manchuria – and in 1937 Japan initiated a long war to take effective control of the remainder of China. The League of Nations condemned the 1931 step, and there was much sympathy and a little help for China from 1937 on, but no country went to war with Japan over these issues. It was Japan itself which expanded its war with China into a general Pacific War that only the Soviet Union entered on its own initiative.

On the other hand, when Germany invaded Poland in 1939, the United Kingdom, France, Canada, Australia, New Zealand, and, after short delay, the Union of South Africa declared war on Germany although these countries were not attacked at that time. Similarly, after Iraq invaded and occupied Kuwait in 1990, a large number of countries sent military forces to drive Iraq out. Included in the list of countries in this effort were numerous states that were certainly no more within the likely range of Iraq's forces at that time than New Zealand had been within the reach of Germany's in 1939. In both of these instances there was some internal dissent in several of the countries which went to war, but there appears to have been very substantial public support for military action all the same.

When the United States and several other countries sent forces to Korea after the invasion of South Korea by North Korea in 1950, there was support for these efforts at first but some doubt thereafter; and more than 47 years later, United States soldiers remain stationed on the armistice line dividing Korea against the possibility of a second invasion. In the case of Vietnam, it is too often forgotten that much of the early criticism (and some of the later critiques as well) was to the effect that American intervention was too limited rather than too intensive; it was only after a considerable interval that criticism of the whole venture came to dominate the discussion. Certainly by the time that there was massive and obvious deployment of regular North Vietnam units to conquer the collapsing South Vietnam, few voices in the United States called for a renewal of United States intervention.

When in 1948 Arab states that were members of the United Nations acted militarily to thwart the UN decision to partition the former British Mandate of Palestine, no country acted forcibly to uphold the decision it had just voted for. Some turned a more or less blind eye to infractions of the arms embargo, but not a single state intervened with its own forces in behalf of the UN decision. It was very much a repeat of the 1933 situation when the League of Nations approved the Lytton Commission report after the seizure of Manchuria by Japan from China but no action had followed.

These recitals of events in the 60 years 1931–91 are designed to help in placing the Munich Conference of 1938 in a broader perspective. Why do, why should, countries be willing to go to war in defence of another when not attacked themselves? This issue arises in two different but intersecting contexts. One is the nature of the society involved; the other is the specific point in time and the circumstances when the question arises.

A dictatorially ruled state can go to war, or make major force reallocations during a war, more easily than a democratic one. Italy was taken into World War II by Benito Mussolini when a large portion of the Italian elite and population at large was undoubtedly opposed to that step. It is clear that the decision of Francisco Franco not to enter World War II on Germany's side as Italy had done was based on his opposition to the conditions Germany insisted upon, and not to any consideration for the likely war-weariness of a people who had just gone through three years of civil war. When the United States began to shift forces from the European to the Pacific theatre after victory over Germany in anticipation of another year and a half of fighting against Japan, there were very serious morale problems in the units scheduled for redeployment; the men believed that they had done their share and ought not to be asked to carry still another burden. A number of measures had to be taken to cope with this problem. If there were analogous difficulties in the Red Army units which were being redeployed in the summer of 1945 from the European theatre across the Soviet Union for the coming campaign in East Asia, no sign of them has as yet come to light.

This differentiation should not, however, be exaggerated. There can be little doubt that the decision of Mussolini to dispatch a substantial expeditionary force to the eastern front in 1941 and to enlarge it in 1942, with the result that some of the heaviest casualties the Italian army suffered in World War II occurred in places in the southern USSR where practically no Italian wanted them to be, contributed substantially to the loss of support for Mussolini and the whole fascist system in Italy. More recently, the Afghanistan adventure of the Soviet Union surely played a significant role in the delegitimization of the Soviet regime and its subsequent collapse.

Even the German government of the Hitler era was not without domestic constraints even if these were to a large extent self-induced by its leaders. The firm belief of the latter in the truth of the stab-in-the-back legend led them to be sensitive to the perceptions of the home front both in contemplating the initiation of war and in the conduct of some policies once they had begun hostilities. It seems very likely that their concerns in this regard were excessive, but the evidence is strong that they existed nonetheless. Hitler, but by no means only he, believed that the optical presentation of the outbreak of war in 1914 had been badly mishandled. He and his associates tried hard, in fact ridiculously hard, to remedy this deficiency as part of their effort to assure a solid home front in any new war.

In 1937–38, they thought seriously of arranging the killing of the German military attaché or ambassador in Vienna to provide a pretext for the invasion of Austria but eventually settled for a faked request for troops to march in. In 1938 they at first thought of staging the killing of the German minister in Prague to provide the proper pretext for war with Czechoslovakia – these were clearly not the most original thinkers. Instead of murdering the German minister, Ernst Eisenlohr, the Germans created a gang of Sudeten German thugs and provided them with a quota of incidents to be staged at regular intervals, with Germany picking the one that fit the timetable Berlin had decided on, but not told the thugs about, as the public excuse for the invasion. Unfortunately for the Germans, this plan misfired for reasons I have explained elsewhere.[1]

In 1939, therefore, as one of the 'lessons of Munich', the Germans decided to play it safe: they would arrange the incidents themselves and carry them out under the control of the SS and inside Germany, not Poland. The last minute change in the date of the invasion of Poland almost wrecked this scheme also, but the confusion was just barely straightened out in time, and World War II could be launched to the accompaniment of appropriate publicity about the terrible things the Poles had supposedly done inside Germany.[2] Furthermore, the German home front was to be reassured about the justice of the cause for which Germans were asked to fight by the preparation and publication of allegedly moderate demands on Poland, with the German public, naturally, not being informed that these demands had been withheld until after they expired to preclude any danger of their being accepted.[3]

If this stress on the constraints, real or imagined, on the Germans in going to war appears exaggerated, it must be seen at least in part in the context of a world in which memories of the Great War as it was called in the West and the World War as it was called in Germany were both bitter and omnipresent. If the privations that the war had imposed on the German home front, and which would hopefully be avoided in any future war by massive looting in the areas Germany planned to conquer, were very much in the memory of people in 1939, the absence of at least one member and/or the crippling wounds of another left practically every family in Germany conscious of the cost of conflict and apprehensive about any repetition. There is at least some circumstantial evidence that Hitler's decision not to go to war in 1938 was influenced by his and other nazi leaders' observation of the most unenthusiastic crowds when German units moved through Berlin before the intended invasion of Czechoslovakia. Certainly his lengthy speech to leaders of Germany's newspapers in November 1938 shows Hitler alarmed about the reluctance of many Germans at the prospect of war and insistent on the need to whip up enthusiasm the next time.[4]

If two decades after the end of the Great War the leaders of nazi Germany, a country in which all pacifist organizations had been dissolved and in which there had been a substantial effort to militarize the population and to glorify the martial spirit which had been dampened by the human and material costs of that war, were seriously concerned about obtaining public support for another war, what about the democracies? It is surely an instructive coincidence that 1937, the very year in which Hitler ordered the major air force and naval weapons systems for war with the United States, was also a year in which the Congress was debating additional possible restrictions to tighten the country's neutrality legislation passed in the immediately preceding years. In the United States, the view that entry into the Great War had been a mistake that should under no circumstances be repeated, was very much more widely and fervently held than the current public belief that the country must avoid another Vietnam.

The enormous casualties and damage suffered by France in the war, proportionately the greatest of any major participant, not only constrained military planning and preparations but dominated the thinking of leaders and public alike.[5] The message of the French government to Prague in July 1938 that France would not fight, and the information provided to the British that if it did come to war the only initiative France would undertake would be to invade the Italian colony of Lybia from Tunisia, highlight in a most dramatic way the practical implications of French sentiments, even if both communications were kept secret at the time. It was, in fact, the panic in Paris when the British government announced that war would come if Germany invaded Czechoslovakia that induced Neville Chamberlain to fly to Germany on his first trip.

This brings up a consideration of British attitudes. Here the retrospective discussion of Munich has obscured the political realities inside and outside the country. Inside the United Kingdom, the main opposition to the Chamberlain government had been accusing it of being too militaristic, not too pacifist. In the most recent election, that of 1935, political posters of the Labour opposition showed Chamberlain as a warmonger. Through 1935, Labour had voted in parliament against any army, navy or air force for Britain, and it had only moved around to the courageous stand of abstaining instead of voting NO on the military budget in 1936 because of its argument that arms should be sent to the republican side in Spain. Chamberlain's programme for rebuilding the RAF with modern fighters, the later famous Spitfire and Hurricane, was opposed as unanimously by Labour before Munich as was his introduction of conscription to create an army after Munich.

With this background in mind, it may be easier to understand why Winston Churchill, then in the political wilderness because of his opposition to the Conservative Party's willingness to make major concessions to the nationalist movement in India, explained to Benes' confidant, Hubert Ripka, when he visited in London in June 1938, that if he were in the government he would follow the same policy as Chamberlain. That would not keep Churchill from vocal criticism in parliament and written criticism in his memoirs, but he was quite responsible enough to caution the Czechoslovak government honestly at the time.[6]

If memory of the Great War with its enormous costs in lives and treasure weighed heavily on the British public, and in this context Chamberlain was generally attacked as too bellicose rather than the opposite, external constraints also bore in on the government in London. The Great War had seen a dramatic reversal in the nature of imperial military ties. Instead of armies sent out from Britain to protect and hopefully enlarge the colonial empire, armies from the empire had been needed on the battlefields of Europe and the Middle East to help defend the United Kingdom against the danger of defeat at German hands. Anzac Day in Australia and New Zealand, as well as the Vimy Ridge monument on Parliament Hill in Ottawa, symbolized the 180-degree shift in the military situation in the last – and hence in any future – major war.[7] But was there any prospect that the dominions would of their own free will join Britain if war came and could another huge army of volunteers be raised in an India wracked by nationalist agitation?

These were not idle questions. No one in London could know in 1938 that when the decisive turn in Britain's land fighting would come at El Alamein in October–November 1942, the majority of the British forces involved would come not from the United Kingdom but from the empire and commonwealth, though the general indicators were there. The warnings from the dominions in 1938 that they would not enter war on Britain's side made any decision to fight exceedingly difficult, and that even without much thought to the implications for United States policy towards a European war from which Canada had decided to abstain.

It was in this broader context that the German propaganda approach stressing the alleged mistreatment of the Sudeten Germans and their desire for self-determination was such a shrewd approach. We know today, and some guessed at the time, that this was all pretext; that Germany wanted to destroy the Czechoslovak state and saw the presence of Czechs in it as the nationality problem that Germany would resolve by Germanizing, killing or expelling the Slavic population. But this was by no means so obvious at the time, and the only way to make the realities clear to the public could conceivably have been an initiative of very extensive concessions being offered by Prague right after the May Crisis of 1938. At that time, such concessions would not have been interpreted as a sign of weakness and would, when rejected by the Sudeten Germans as instructed by Berlin, have illuminated the real as opposed to the pretended aims of German policy. Internal factors inside the country probably made such a step impossible; in any case, it was not taken.

Two instructive comparisons may help clarify the point. While the British and French governments decided in the winter after Munich that they would go to war on the next German move if that move were resisted, a decision made in January 1939 when a German invasion of the Low Countries was rumoured, the public in both countries came to change its broader views after the Germans themselves tore up the Munich agreement in March 1939. And it should be noted that an essentially analogous development took place in large portions of government and public in several of the British dominions. When it turned out that the next victim of Germany was not to be Holland or Romania but Poland, the German effort to repeat their propaganda ploy of 1938, the trumpeting of supposed mistreatment of a large German minority, fell on deaf ears. Objectively, one might argue that the Germans in Poland had more to complain about than those in Czechoslovakia, but that made no difference in the circumstances of the time: much of the public had been persuaded by the Germans themselves that they did not care about the German minority but rather wanted to repress the Slavic majority on the road to world conquest. In this new context, it made no difference whom the Germans attacked and in which direction they moved; the public in Britain, most of the dominions and France were resigned to the need for war.

The other comparison that might be made is to the Gulf War. The approximately six months which it took to gather American and allied forces in the Gulf area for a military push provided the time for the government of the United States and numerous others to explain to their peoples where and what Kuwait is and why they should fight to free it of Iraqi invaders. Having with unerring strategic insight picked the only short time in this century when the United States divisions were no longer needed in Europe but had not yet been dissolved, Saddam Hussein found himself driven out of Kuwait and reduced to hiding weapons of mass destruction in his own bathroom. But it should be noted that the early calling off of military operations by President Bush was almost certainly connected with his concern that a prolonged campaign with substantial American casualties might well erode the degree of support his policy had obtained with the public of that country, another reflection of the importance of public support for military action of any substantial kind.

These two examples testify to the enormous significance of the circumstances in which military action is considered and the perceptions of such action at the time both by those who have to make the decision and by major segments of the public that will have to bear the burdens of any war. In this context, it is surprising that in the crisis over Czechoslovakia there was any serious consideration of going to war at all in either Britain or France. The evidence convinces me that if Hitler had indeed gone forward with his plan to invade Czechoslovakia after the Bad Godesberg meeting with Chamberlain, the United Kingdom would have gone to war and so, even more reluctantly, would France. I find it impossible to say which if any of the British dominions would have joined in, and if so, when they would have done so. Whether the public in the United Kingdom would have held together in grim determination not to make peace if the circumstances of 1940 had arisen after a French defeat in 1939 and before the Germans had so dramatically shown their hand in March 1939 is surely another entirely open question.

Certainly Hitler's assertion in the winter of 1938–39 that he had been bluffed out of war was entirely mistaken; he would have had a war had he not pulled back. Whether his later expressions of regret over not having moved in 1938 on the opposite basis, that war would have been much better for Germany in 1938 than in 1939, can be accepted as accurate in its conclusion will long remain a subject for debate. There can be no debate, however, that in 1939 he was determined not to repeat what he had come to believe were the terrible mistakes which had led to the Munich settlement.[8]

One other question which does not seem to me to be open is the fate of Czechoslovakia in the case of an Allied victory over Germany, whenever and however that occurred. As London and Paris made clear to the government in Prague in 1938, and as would almost certainly have been a part of any peace settlement, the Sudeten area would not have been left with the Czechoslovak state. Some major adjustment of the boundary between Germany and Czechoslovakia, most likely going well beyond the territorial concessions Edvard Benes at various times contemplated, would have been insisted upon. With or without war, Czechoslovakia would have had new borders.

Ironically it was the destruction of the Munich agreement by the Germans that opened the way for the retention of the Sudeten area by Czechoslovakia, with the agreement of the Allies both to that and to the displacement of the Sudeten Germans. They would, with the consent of the Allies, be sent 'Home into the Reich' in a manner few had anticipated. In an age which was still dominated by the Versailles concept of adjusting boundaries to people rather than the German-sponsored alternative of adjusting people to boundaries, that possibility had at no time been seriously put forward by anyone in the 1938 debates. It is a sign of the impact of German actions on the world that a solution which almost no one even mentioned as a possible alternative in 1938 had become a widely accepted procedure by 1945.

These ruminations on the broader issues of the war option in 1938 have been presented almost entirely without reference to the Soviet Union and its possible role in any conflict at that time. When that aspect of the situation is considered, two extremely important aspects are too frequently overlooked, the military and the geographic. The military role of the Soviet Union in any war in 1938

– whichever side it might have been on – must not be seen through the perspective of later developments on the eastern front of World War II. In 1938, the Red Army was still in the throes of the later stages of the great purge. An army that turned out to have great difficulties projecting Soviet power beyond the borders of the USSR in Poland in the autumn of 1939 and in Finland later that year was in no condition to make any major contribution to hostilities outside the country in 1938. That does not mean that it would not have and could not have fought effective delaying actions against an invader – though it certainly had plenty of difficulty in doing so three years later – but what was significant in 1938 was the inability to project power into central Europe. The Red Army of 1938 was not that of 1944. If recognition of that reality helped induce Stalin to side with the Germans in 1939, what was his assessment of the situation in 1938? We really do not know, but one should not berate the military of the French and British in 1938 for assessing the Red Army in a way not especially unlike Stalin's in the following year.

The very pro-Soviet Czechoslovak minister in Moscow, Zdenek Fierlinger, in the Munich crisis cautioned Benes about counting on Soviet help.[9] That caution was related to the geographic factor in the situation. The Soviet Union had no common border with Czechoslovakia: in between lay portions of Poland that the Soviet Union hoped to annex and did annex when the opportunity offered. If the Soviet Union joined in hostilities, what would that entail? The one thing we do know is that the Germans were not the least bit worried about that particular contingency. Perhaps they should have been, but the whole problem remains wrapped in uncertainties. With most Soviet military representatives with whom the French and British had dealt in prior years shot as German agents in the intervening purge, the doubts of the Western powers should not be difficult to understand.

From the perspective of 60 years we look back on the anguished days of September 1938 with vastly increased knowledge not only of the events which followed but also of the previously secret plans and procedures of 1938. But the difficult question: when to go to war in defence of another country, remains with us today and is not likely to disappear. On the contrary, in a world beset by the rivalries of newly independent nations as well as the ambitions and aspirations of old states and emerging national and ethnic groups, this puzzle is likely to confront this and other countries in the future as in the past. When a democratically governed country does decide to take the military option even though not attacked itself, there had best be a clear recognition by a substantial portion of the people that this is indeed the correct way to move.

This issue has a most direct and current relevance for both the Czech Republic and the United States. Much of the discussion of the extension of NATO has revolved about the question of the likely reaction of the Russians. What has not received nearly enough attention is the reaction of the public in the United States. Over a period of decades, the American public became accustomed to the concept that this nation's safety was tied up with the defence of the Federal Republic of Germany, and with greater or lesser knowledge of the detailed implications of this choice, most Americans came to accept that policy. If an analogous sense of commitment toward additional countries is to be grounded in a firm public resolve in America, there surely needs to be a great deal more discussion of the issue than has taken place up to now. A promise to defend that does not have solid backing in the country making the promise is as likely to tempt as to deter a challenge. The events of 1938 ought to serve as a warning today, not in terms of the so-called lessons of Munich but in a very different way. If there is no resolve, it may be best not to issue loud resolutions.

University of North Carolina, Chapel Hill

NOTES

1. Gerhard L. Weinberg, *The Foreign Policy of Hitler's Germany: Starting World War II, 1937–1939* (Atlantic Highlands, NJ: Humanities Press, 1993), chap. 11.
2. Jürgen Runzheimer, 'Die Grenzzwischenfälle am Abend vor dem deutschen Angriff auf Polen', in Wolfgang Benz and Hermann Graml (eds.), *Sommer 1939: Die Großmächte und der Europäische Krieg* (Stuttgart: Deutsche Verlags-Anstalt, 1979), pp.107–47.
3. Important new details on this in the complete text of the von Hassel diary for 31 August 1939, in Friedrich Freiherr Hiller von Gaertringen (ed.), *Die Hassell-Tagebücher 1938–1944: Ulrich von Hassell, Aufzeichnungen vom Andern Deutschland* (Berlin: Siedler Verlag, 1988), p.121.
4. Wilhelm Treue (ed.), 'Rede Hitlers vor der deutschen Presse (10. November 1938)', *Vierteljahrshefte für Zeitgeschichte*, Vol.6, No.2 (April 1958), pp.175–91.

5. A fine new survey in Eugenia C. Kiesling, *Arming against Hitler: France and the Limits of Military Planning* (Lawrence, KS: University Press of Kansas, 1996).
6. See Ripka's memorandum of June 1938 on his meeting with Churchill in London: Vaclav Kral (ed.), *Das Abkommen von München 1938: Tschechoslowakische diplomatische Dokumente 1937–1939* (Prag: Academia, 1968), No.94.
7. Donald C. Watt was the first historian to call attention to this important but generally neglected aspect of the Munich crisis; a revised version of his 1960 article on the subject in the *Vierteljahrshefte für Zeitgeschichte* appeared as essay 8 in his *Personalities and Policies: Studies in the Formulation of British Foreign Policy in the Twentieth Century* (South Bend, IN: University of Notre Dame Press, 1964).
8. Weinberg, *The Foreign Policy of Hitler's Germany*, pp.462–3 and chap. 14.
9. Fierlinger's report is cited in Weinberg, *The Foreign Policy of Hitler's Germany*, p.416, n.170. See also Igor Lukes, *Czechoslovakia between Stalin and Hitler: The Diplomacy of Edvard Benes in the 1930s* (New York: Oxford University Press, 1996), pp.195–6, 246, 257–8.

Stalin and Czechoslovakia in 1938–39: An Autopsy of a Myth

IGOR LUKES

Before the opening of Prague archives, Joseph Stalin's policy toward Czechoslovakia during the crisis of the 1930s had been one of the most stimulating riddles of modern central European history. To many historians it seemed particularly piquant because there was reason to believe that, barring a miracle in the form of accessible eastern European archives, the puzzle would never be solved.[1]

The paucity of evidence caused diametrically different views to appear equally plausible, so one could join the debate simply to display one's analytical skills. The topic of Joseph Stalin's policy towards Czechoslovakia on the eve of World War II sometimes also served as a lumber yard where one could go for precut bits and pieces from which an ideologically inspired structure could be built. For obvious reasons, such was the case primarily with Soviet and east European authors. This has changed quite dramatically during the past decade. New archival evidence found in Prague and to a lesser extent in Moscow has helped to resolve the puzzle.

In this article I propose to analyze Stalin's attitude toward Czechoslovakia in 1938–39. It is a topic that must be engaged on two connected levels. On the first level we must examine the allegation that the Kremlin intended to provide the Prague government with effective military assistance against the Third Reich and thus to go beyond the obligations it had assumed with the Czechoslovak–Soviet Treaty on Mutual Assistance of May 1935. Was Stalin willing to assist the Prague government unilaterally, that is, without France?[2] I present decisive evidence that the answer is 'no'.

What, then, *were* Stalin's intentions at the end of the 1930s? This is a more complicated question. After all, Soviet leaders kept their plans secret and, moreover, none of them could predict what the solution of the Czechoslovak–German crisis would be. As late as 28 September 1938, well-informed people in Prague, Berlin, Paris and

London thought that a Czechoslovak–German war was likely to break out on that day at or after 2 pm. It was only around noon, two hours before the deadline, that Hitler had agreed to postpone by 24 hours a German general mobilization and seek a negotiated settlement of the crisis. (Whether the Führer in fact had intended to commence hostilities on 28 September 1938 is another matter; I happen to doubt it.) Given all this, the Kremlin had to formulate its plans with an eye to several possible developments. This factor alone must have made the task of preparing a viable long-term plan daunting.

Therefore, Moscow could not simply implement measures in pursuit of a firmly defined objective. Instead, it had to be ready to employ various more or less acceptable policies, as dictated by the developing situation. The Kremlin and leaders of the Communist International discussed – at least since the 7th Congress in the summer of 1935 – a general, strategic objective that was to be achieved, but its contours did not appear with any clarity until the Red Army drove deep into central Europe and the dust of war had settled.

I shall deal with the issue of Stalin's intentions toward Czechoslovakia in the period from the Czechoslovak–German crisis in 1938 to the outbreak of World War II in September 1939 in the second part of this article. It is here that one finds some of the blank spots in our understanding of Stalin's attitude toward the crisis of 1938–39 in central Europe. It may well turn out that the concentration of blank spots merely reflects the open-endedness of Moscow's plans and policies in that period.

II

Let me start with the first point: did the Kremlin intend to provide Czechoslovakia with militarily meaningful assistance against the Third Reich after France had made clear it would fail to do so? This question has acquired a special status in the eyes of many historians. Although the Czechoslovak–German crisis of 1938 is incomparably small when it is viewed against the background of the crisis that followed it, World War II, it has nevertheless stimulated a great deal of interest, research and speculation.[3] I am convinced that we now have enough hard evidence to conclude the debate with a firm answer.[4]

We must establish at the outset that there could have been no serious preparations for Soviet military aid to Czechoslovakia in 1938 that would have bypassed President Edvard Benes. Although the presidency was originally endowed with limited authority, the first Czechoslovak President, Tomas G. Masaryk, had successfully built up and expanded the institution. Benes, who succeeded Masaryk in 1935, strengthened the office even further. By the spring of 1938, the Czechoslovak parliament, the prime minister and the cabinet had been pushed aside by Benes. During the dramatic summer months he was – for better, or worse – the sole decisionmaker in the country.[5]

The president did not dominate only Czechoslovak political institutions. He supervised the armed and intelligence services just as firmly as the civilian sector. Benes had a keen interest in military affairs from the beginning of his political career, and when the crisis between Prague and Berlin began to escalate he started to micromanage the army. He decided which gas-mask model would be selected for mass production, he decided whether certain units should be put on alert, he decided how many reservists would be called up to the colours.[6]

Benes personally met all the highest ranking officers of the Czechoslovak army.[7] The important generals had to spend an inordinate amount of time at the Castle (*Hrad*), the presidential office and residence in Prague, consulting the president. Generals Ludvik Krejci, Jan Syrovy, Sergej Ingr, Sergej Vojcechovsky, Vojtech Luza, Bohuslav Fiala, Emil Fiala, Karel Husarek, Alois Elias, Josef Votruba, Lev Prchala, Antonin Hasal, Rudolf Viest and all the others *de facto* served at the pleasure of the president and they behaved accordingly. They respected the president as the supreme authority in all matters pertaining to national security. Characteristic of this was the visit of Generals Krejci, Luza, Prchala and Vojcechovsky at the Castle on 29 September 1938.[8] With the prospect of national surrender looming on the horizon, their message to the president was that the army was ready and eager to fight under any circumstances, with or without allies. Benes thanked them for their determination, treated them to a lecture on his geopolitics, and then he showed them the door. They left with tears in their eyes but without a peep of protest.[9]

Yet another episode can be mentioned in support of the contention that the Czechoslovak military elites respected Benes as the supreme commander without any reservations. Colonel Emanuel Moravec had been very vocal about the need for Czechoslovakia to go to war against the Third Reich, whatever the consequences. Shortly after Benes had accepted the Munich Diktat, the colonel arrived at the Castle. According to Benes' secretary, he was armed with no less than two large army pistols and he looked like a 'god of war'. He seemed so bellicose that the secretary feared violence might ensue. But nothing of that kind happened. The red-faced Moravec sat like a schoolboy through Benes' standard two-hour-long lecture on the reasons behind his decision to accept the Munich Agreement. As the generals had done before him, the colonel left the Castle peacefully and only after he had fully conceded President Benes' authority to decide on behalf of the country and its armed services.[10]

The nature of espionage is such that the president could not have been as intimately involved in the activities of Czechoslovak intelligence as he was in military affairs. But the two important services, the third section of the ministry of foreign affairs and the second bureau of the army general staff, worked very closely with Benes. This was especially true of Jan Hajek, chief of the third section, whose main mission was to implement Benes' detailed instructions.[11] The second bureau's offensive branch operated agent networks against the Third Reich, Poland and Hungary; it conducted no intelligence operations in the Soviet Union. Military counterintelligence, a subsection of the second bureau, was engaged in standard activities. It covered as much as was possible (but without causing offence) military attachés accredited in Prague, it defended vital military secrets and installations, and it investigated cases of treason among the officer corps. The second bureau's commanding officers, Colonels Frantisek Hajek, Frantisek Havel and Frantisek Moravec, were professionals who were utterly dedicated to the president. They would never have become involved in a far-reaching intelligence operation with political consequences of any sort without Benes' knowledge and approval.

In short, it can be positively ruled out that Czechoslovak military or intelligence officers would deal with the Kremlin or their Soviet opposite numbers behind Benes' back. Thus, there could have been no plans for a Soviet intervention, unilateral or otherwise, in the Czechoslovak–German crisis unless the president knew about it. Until the Prague government had officially accepted the terms of the Four Power Act signed at Munich, no political, military or intelligence scheme between Moscow and Prague could have been arranged without Edvard Benes' direct involvement. Therefore, whoever wishes to investigate the question of Soviet assistance to Czechoslovakia in 1938 must start by examining the views of Benes. His testimony is of central, indeed decisive, importance.

Benes offered his views regarding Moscow's attitude toward Prague for the first time in the evening of 19 September 1938. The Soviet minister to Czechoslovakia, Sergei Aleksandrovsky, had been to see the president. Benes wanted to know whether the Soviet Union would come to his aid under the terms of the 1935 agreement, that is, together with France, and, second, whether it would provide assistance if France decided to renege on its duty under the Franco-Czechoslovak agreement. It was the second question that mattered and here is how Benes put it: 'What will the attitude of the Soviet Union be if France refuses to fulfil its obligations?'[12] The minister noted the questions and, on his way out, stopped briefly to speak with Benes' secretary, Prokop Drtina. He told him that Prague should remain firm. Drtina reported Aleksandrovsky's message to the president only minutes later. Benes reacted with scepticism. The Russians, he warned, could not be trusted. If they get us into a shooting war against the Third Reich, Benes said to Drtina, 'they will leave us twisting in the air'.[13]

Moscow sent a reply to the questions Benes had posed to Aleksandrovsky just about 24 hours later, at 8.20 pm on 20 September 1938. In it, the second question had been turned upside down: Benes had asked about the availability of Soviet unilateral assistance and Moscow responded regarding its course of action as a member of the League of Nations. Articles 16 and 17 of the League's Charter, to which the Soviet reply referred, had to do with collective defence, not with Soviet military action on Czechoslovakia's behalf in the case of French betrayal.[14] It should be noted that the reply, albeit to a corrupted question, arrived in Prague 35 minutes after Benes had officially rejected the Franco-British proposal of 19 September 1938 that Czechoslovakia give up some territory in the Sudetenland. Therefore, contrary to claims in scores of books, the Soviet reply – even if it had answered the question Benes had posed – could have played no role in Benes' decision initially to reject the proposal.[15] The president, himself no stranger to political manipulations, saw through the trick and it affirmed him in the view he had shared with Drtina a day before: he did not believe in the possibility of Moscow's military assistance to Czechoslovakia. Such was the status of the alleged Soviet offer ten days before the end of the crisis.

When the Soviet minister came to see President Benes at the Castle on 25 September 1938, the situation had escalated considerably. With the encouragement of the British and the French, the Benes government had successfully carried out a general mobilization, but the danger of a Franco-British deal regarding Czechoslovakia had failed to disappear. The president confronted Aleksandrovsky with a flood of questions. How would the Red Army march to Czechoslovakia? How many thousands of airborne troops would it deploy? What military equipment would they bring with them? What logistical support would they need in Czechoslovakia to engage the enemy? Their arrival, Benes stressed, would have a powerful impact on Czechoslovakia's morale during the initial stages of the war against Hitler's Third Reich. Aleksandrovsky remained stone silent. He later confessed to 'having a heavy feeling because I could tell Benes nothing, especially regarding his "practical questions"'.[16] While the conversation was taking place, the Czechoslovak army was putting finishing touches to the general mobilization it had been ordered to carry out on 23 September 1938 at 10.30 pm. The country now had up to 1,500,000 men (about ten per cent of all citizens) under arms. Benes therefore was not posing any idle or abstract questions to Aleksandrovsky. He was absolutely serious but Moscow was not.

President Benes and the Soviet minister met again on 26 September 1938 at night after Hitler's speech at the Sportpalast, and on 27 September 1938 when the crisis had reached its peak. The president was convinced that the war could break out any moment. 'I sensed clearly', wrote Minister Aleksandrovsky, 'that with much nervous tension, and with the ultimate seriousness, Benes wanted to hear from us when and how we would help.' Just as had happened two days before, Aleksandrovsky said nothing to the president, but we do know what he thought. In a memorandum for Moscow, he charged that Benes had lied to him by covering up that the French had *de facto* already abandoned him. Why did he lie? asked Aleksandrovsky rhetorically. Well, in order to drag the Soviet Union into a war against Hitler without France and Great Britain. Benes was ready to do anything so that the fate of Czechoslovakia would be decided not by a conference but by 'a large-scale European war' against Hitler.[17] The Soviet diplomat found the prospect most unappealing.

Having got nowhere with Aleksandrovsky, Benes turned early in the morning of the next day, 28 September 1938, directly to the Kremlin via the Czechoslovak legation in Moscow. The reply to this approach was a cable from the Czechoslovak minister in the Soviet Union, Zdenek Fierlinger, at 4.10 pm: 'The president's request for immediate air support has been submitted.' The legation hoped it would be dealt with favourably.[18] It hoped in vain. The Kremlin replied around 10 pm the next day, but only indirectly, through the Czechoslovak legation in Moscow. It advised Prague to turn to the League of Nations and look for 'powers that would be ready to stand up to Hitler'. This was, of course, easier said than done because at that very time the British, French and Italian politicians were engaged in talks with Adolf Hitler at the Führerhaus in Munich. The Four Power Agreement was about to be signed. Paris, Czechoslovakia's sole ally in the West, was a party to the Munich deal and had no desire to bring the crisis before the League of Nations. Since everybody knew this, the Soviet 'advice' for Prague to find allies in the League of Nations on 29 September 1938 was insincere.

And what about the Soviet Union itself? The 'Soviet government', Fierlinger summed up, 'hesitated and hesitates to enter the conflict without the Western powers'. Unilateral Soviet involvement in the Czechoslovak–German war would have created another Spain, 'with all the horrible consequences for all of Europe and especially for Czechoslovakia'.[19] It may be worth noting that Fierlinger richly deserved his reputation as being a sympathetic observer of the Soviet political scene. This gives his sceptical assessment of Stalin's willingness to fight on Czechoslovakia's side against Hitler extra weight.

Benes did not give up. Although the Munich agreement had already been signed, he called the Soviet legation at 9.30 am on 30 September 1938. He told Aleksandrovsky that Great Britain and France had abandoned Czechoslovakia to Hitler. Benes now had to choose between a war with Germany or capitulation. He asked if Aleksandrovsky could quickly find out in Moscow whether the Kremlin would support him if he chose to resist the Munich *Diktat* without France.[20]

The content of Moscow's answer was hardly improvable: the Soviet Union had been ready to assist Czechoslovakia 'under any circumstances'.[21] Presumably this alluded to Soviet unilateral military assistance against Germany. The problem was with its timing. The Kremlin replied on 3 October 1938, more than 60 hours after the Munich agreement had been signed and at least 36 hours after the Czechoslovak army had retreated from its defensive positions in the Sudetenland. The whole area was now in Hitler's hands. Such an assurance was worthless and both Moscow and the president knew it.

Benes was haunted by the 1938 crisis for the rest of his life and he compulsively kept bringing it up in conversations with his friends and staff. On 22 August 1945 he picked up the topic in his conversation with Ivan Herben, the scion of a well-known Czech political family. When Benes touched upon the question whether 'the Soviet Union had been willing to assist Czechoslovakia in 1938 'his eyes lit up with hatred for the Soviets and Stalin', noted Herben and other members of his family who watched the scene, together with Mrs Hana Benes. The president became agitated; his face turned red and large veins could be seen bulging on his forehead. All became concerned for his health and Herben proposed the two walk alone in the garden and breathe some fresh air. But Benes could not be stopped:

> The president over and over repeated that he now possessed diplomatic documents proving that the Soviets betrayed us during [the] Munich [crisis], just like Daladier and Chamberlain had done, that they had no intention at all to come to our assistance, that their willingness was only a pretense, the usual communist trick. "I will prove it! I will reveal this hoax of Soviet diplomacy, this legend of our communists!" the president shouted, waving his clenched fists above his head.

Herben, who had never seen the president in such a state, recalled their earlier conversation of 12 June 1945. It was their first postwar meeting. Herben had just come back from a concentration camp, Benes from exile in England; they talked for four hours. One sentence stuck in Herben's mind: 'My task was to defeat Hitler', suggested Benes. 'The job before your generation will be to defeat the other dictator – you know who I am talking about.' The president left unexplained the method to be employed in achieving such a mighty objective. In fact, when Herben later challenged Benes to publish the documents proving the Kremlin's treachery in 1938, he replied, with his characteristically colourless voice: 'You know, colleague, that is the *absolute* truth. But the *political* truth is different. This is why I cannot publish anything at the moment.' Herben recalled pondering the discrepancy between the Czechoslovak presidential motto – 'Truth conquers' – and his claim that there existed two kinds of truth, one that was 'absolute' and the other that was 'political'. He did not think that Benes' predecessor, President Masaryk, would have accepted the validity of such a claim.[22]

Benes talked about the Munich crisis again on 21 October 1947 at the Castle with Chancellor Jaromir Smutny. The topic came up early:

> Fierlinger in his book writes complete lies and he fabricates documents.[23] He totally falsifies the possibility of Russian assistance in September 1938. The truth is that even the Soviets did not want to come to our aid ... They behaved insincerely and I believe that the truth will come out; it has to. I asked Aleksandrovsky three questions about how the Soviets would come to our assistance and I repeated them. He did not answer me, he never answered me. That was the decisive reason why I capitulated.[24]

This remarkable document and the testimony of Ivan Herben quoted above expose as politically motivated Benes' contrary assertions that the Soviet Union was Czechoslovakia's sole ally.[25]

The communist *coup d'état* of February 1948 marked a dramatic change in the political development of Czechoslovakia. On 22 February 1948 *Pravda* published an article that presented the crisis as the outcome of Western plotting. The article subtly implied that the

Kremlin would not stand idly by while Western imperialists conspired against the emerging Soviet-style government in Prague. The next day, Benes shared his views on Soviet leaders with Minister Hubert Ripka, a leading strategist of the democratic forces in Czechoslovakia. 'I know them', Benes asserted, 'I know the Muscovites. You overestimate their intelligence and their imagination. I have made the same mistake. They do not understand other nations. They think of themselves as realists but they are only fanatics. Their policy leads to war, and they will pay a heavy price for this behaviour. They are as blind as Hitler.'[26] The president was a man of considerable inner discipline; he hardly ever spoke freely even in front of his close collaborators. Therefore, Ripka, like Ivan Herben before him, was shocked to hear such harsh words from Benes. For him to compare the Kremlin leaders with the Nazis was not a mere persiflage of a tense man. From our perspective, it seems obvious that Benes' view of Stalin in 1948 would have been considerably more charitable if Moscow had in fact offered Czechoslovakia unilateral assistance against Germany a decade earlier.

On 12 March 1948, after the death of Foreign Minister Jan Masaryk, Benes, who had secluded himself at his country villa in Sezimovo Usti, received Professor Vaclav Cerny. The president's assessment of the Soviet Union, its leaders, and their Czechoslovak puppets was scathing and so harsh that Cerny thought it to be outside the realm of what could be published verbatim. On the threshold of death, Benes was troubled by the realization that Stalin had used him as an instrument to help smooth the way for the Soviet entry into Europe (1934–38) and had paid him back only with lies and deception. Cerny noted that Benes felt especially hurt by the discovery that he himself had occasionally acted harmfully towards others by helping to advance Stalin's interests in the international arena. Cerny heard not a word from Benes about the alleged Soviet offer to provide Czechoslovakia with unilateral assistance in September 1938.[27] (The president had spoken in a similar vein on a previous occasion with Ivan Herben. On 22 August 1945, Benes recalled his wartime conversation with Franklin D. Roosevelt during which the American president inquired whether the United States should prepare for a confrontation – perhaps even war – with the Soviet Union. Benes forcefully objected. He argued that the country was in the process of democratization and that it would loyally cooperate with the West. 'So, obviously, I had managed to persuade Roosevelt brilliantly', sighed Benes, and no one thought that he was bragging. On the contrary, they understood that the president wanted to apologize.[28])

On 14 August 1948, the atmosphere in Sezimovo Usti was filled with even more apprehension and anxiety than had become the norm in that crisis-ridden time. The former Czechoslovak president (Benes had resigned from office in June 1948) had just heard from the BBC that Moscow had launched a campaign against him. It charged that Benes had never been a sincere ally of the Soviet Union. To wit, he refused the offer of Soviet military assistance in September 1938. The former president was a desperately weak, dying man – he had only two difficult weeks left – and he was too tired to respond to all the critical points raised against him by many of his faultfinders, domestic and foreign; he ignored them. But he revived when he heard of the alleged offer by Moscow of military intervention on Czechoslovakia's behalf in the conflict with Adolf Hitler's Third Reich. 'He would like to know', Smutny recorded, 'when, by whom and to whom was the offer made.'[29] The laconic Benes left it at that, but his wife, Hana, was frantic. She told Smutny she had had a vision that she and her sick husband would be sent to Siberia to die in isolation like the defeated German generals.[30]

With Benes safely out of the way in Sezimovo Usti, cut off from the rest of the world by a cordon of communist secret policemen in the garden and detectives inside the house, Moscow gave the green light to a smear campaign seeking to discredit the former president.[31] It attempted to prove that in September 1938 the Kremlin had been willing to assist Czechoslovakia against nazi Germany not only together with France but even alone, and that Benes ignored the offer. This was said to have shown that he preferred the interests of his class to the interests of the state and nation. 'The Soviet Union was ready to help Czechoslovakia', the argument has been summed up, but 'Benes was afraid of the masses'.[32] This spurious campaign and, therefore, the debate regarding the Kremlin's intentions towards Prague during the crisis of 1938 have yet to run its course.

On 24 September 1948, two weeks after Benes had died, Vaclav Kopecky, the chief propagandist of the Communist Party of

Czechoslovakia (CPC), asserted that the party had for a long time had evidence of Stalin's willingness to march against Hitler in defence of Czechoslovakia with or without the French. Kopecky warned that the documents would soon be made public; they would destroy Benes' political image and ruin his legacy, predicted Kopecky.[33] That was the last to be heard from him on this topic; no evidence was ever produced.

Klement Gottwald, the first communist president of Czechoslovakia, took the next step in the campaign. Like Kopecky, he had prudently waited for Benes' death. Then he asserted that in 1938 he had had a meeting with Stalin who addressed the question of Soviet military assistance to Czechoslovakia. The Soviet leader was said to have stated that 'the Soviet Union was ready to assist Czechoslovakia unilaterally even if France did not do so ... and even if Poland or Romania refused to allow a transfer of Soviet troops ... Stalin authorized me to share the contents of our conversation with the then President Benes. I did so in January 1938'.[34]

This was entirely made up: Gottwald did not meet Benes in January 1938 and he did not bring up the alleged offer from Stalin during any of his three meetings with the president in 1938 (17, 19 and 30 September).[35] In fact, when Benes asked Gottwald directly on 19 September 1938 whether he could enlighten the Prague government regarding the Kremlin's view of the escalating crisis, the communist leader refused to oblige. He advised Benes to contact the Kremlin through regular diplomatic channels. He, Gottwald, was not in a position to speak on behalf of the Soviet Union.[36]

If the offer had existed and Gottwald had passed it on to Benes, who then ignored it and surrendered the Sudetenland with its vital defensive perimeter to Hitler, why had not the CPC boss reproved the president for this during their meeting on 30 September 1938? Gottwald spoke about the lesson Czechoslovakia should derive from the struggle of the Abyssinians against fascist Italy. Like the Czechoslovaks, they too stood alone against superior military might, and they fought nobly. Czechoslovakia needed to do the same, Gottwald insisted. But throughout the conversation he failed to make even a passing reference to the Soviet Union or the alleged message from Stalin.

Gottwald did not bring up the alleged offer of Soviet unilateral assistance to Czechoslovakia in his analysis of the crisis before the

Presidium of the Comintern of 26 December 1938. The text of his speech has 25 pages and dwells on many minute aspects of the 1938 Czechoslovak–German conflict, yet there is no indication that the Soviet Union had intended to aid Czechoslovakia without France or at all in September 1938. Gottwald was clearly trying to demonstrate the treacherousness of the Czechoslovak bourgeoisie. That its main representative, Benes, had handed the country to Hitler because he was scared to accept a Soviet offer of military assistance even after the capitalist France had betrayed him would have been an excellent way of illustrating this point, yet not a word was uttered about Stalin's offer of unilateral assistance.[37]

Nor did Gottwald bring up the alleged offer with Benes in 1943 during their talks in the Soviet Union. He was eager to use any imaginable argument to improve his and the party's negotiating position *vis-à-vis* the president and the Czechoslovak bourgeois parties in (London) exile. Why not bring up Stalin's generous proposition, especially as the Red Army had turned the nazi tide and began its victorious offensive aimed at the nazi lair in Berlin? It would have been a powerful moment: Gottwald could have shamed Benes by pointing out that the Red Army, which had beaten the Wehrmacht at Stalingrad, could have kept Hitler at bay in Czechoslovakia in 1938. But Gottwald said nothing of the kind. He and others, such as Rudolf Slansky, the CPC general secretary, or Vaclav Kopecky, could have brought up the alleged offer during the power struggle between the CPC and the democratic parties from May 1945 to February 1948. The offer from Stalin, if it had existed, would have been worth a million votes in the ballot box. But they did not so much as mention it.

Some might still argue that Moscow's offer of unilateral assistance could have come to Prague through channels that bypassed Benes, the ministry of foreign affairs, the army, intelligence, Gottwald and the CPC and all the other formal or informal means of communication between Prague and Moscow. Let us now look into that possibility. According to Bretislav Palkovsky, there in fact existed a small group of Czechoslovak intellectuals and lesser political personalities who came together after the Prague government had formally accepted the Munich Agreement. Their goal was to reverse President Benes' decision to capitulate.[38] They did not know how they were going to achieve their objective and against whom in Prague they would have to move in order to prevent the surrender. Only the ally they had counted on for their struggle against the Munich Agreement was, as far as they were concerned, obvious – the Soviet Union. Palkovsky's memorandum, written for President Benes in 1940, states that the group had approached the Soviet legation in Prague and sought to explore the possibility of working together with Moscow to stop and reverse the Czechoslovak army's retreat from the fortified positions in the Sudetenland. The group's emissary was Professor Zdenek Nejedly, an academic with political ambitions.[39] He presented the legation with two requests on behalf of his friends. First, the group asked for a 'larger number of Soviet airplanes landing in Slovakia'. Second, it demanded of the Soviet government 'an official declaration on Radio Moscow that the Soviet Union will fight [on Czechoslovakia's behalf] against Germany even if Czechoslovakia remains alone'.[40]

The request may well have had sincere motivations but it had all the signs of having been formulated in one of Prague's coffee-houses frequented by artists and intelligentsia; it was not prepared by military people with a rudimentary understanding of the political scene and military strategic options available to Czechoslovakia and the Soviet Union. Nevertheless, the Kremlin responded. It did so with a request of its own: prior to any Soviet action or declaration on behalf of embattled Czechoslovakia, there would have to be 'a change' of government in Prague. Members of the anti-Munich group were advised further that the new government, be it a 'constitutional' or 'unconstitutional' one, would have to be installed by President Benes. The 'government' would next go to Geneva and demand protection against Hitler under Article 16. The Soviet declaration of unilateral assistance would then, but not before, follow the League's ruling that Czechoslovakia was a victim of unprovoked aggression and could exercise its right to self-defence. That was the essence of the Soviet reply, as captured in the Palkovsky memorandum.

The scheme had a number of fatally weak points. For instance, Benes was a firm believer in the democratic process. Notwithstanding his behaviour ten years later, in 1938 he would never have agreed to install a 'government' that emerged as a result of a *coup d'état*.

Furthermore, he was the chief decisionmaker throughout the Czechoslovak–German crisis. It was he who chose to accept the Franco-British ultimatum and, later, the Munich Agreement. To go against the consequences of 'Munich' would therefore have required removing Benes himself. But the Kremlin made clear it would not act unless Benes remained at the Castle. Moscow was thus asking for an impossible political hybrid to emerge in Prague: it wanted an anti-Munich government ushered in by Benes, the man who had accepted the Four Power Act on Czechoslovakia's behalf. The firmness of Benes' conviction that Czechoslovakia had suffered only a temporary setback at Munich, his belief that Hitler would eventually be defeated and that the Four Power Agreement would have to be overturned by those who had just let him down (France and, to a different extent, Great Britain), the stability of Czechoslovak democratic institutions and the absolute loyalty of the army to the president and to the state condemned any prospect of a successful a *coup d'état* in Prague at the end of September or at the beginning of October 1938 into the realm of fiction. Yet Moscow insisted on it: 'The Soviet Union was ready to oblige as to the essence of the request, but it refused to abandon its demand as to the form.' Palkovsky's memorandum concluded somewhat mysteriously that the views of Moscow apparently did not correspond with the information the group had been getting about the Soviet scene in Prague. Put differently, there was a gap between the image of the Soviet Union created for the benefit of the Czechoslovak public and the cold reality of Soviet pursuit of self-interest. In the end, nothing at all came out of this informal, back-channel attempt at securing a Soviet unilateral assistance against the Third Reich.

On the basis of the evidence presented above, we can firmly conclude that the Soviet Union never offered – officially or unofficially, formally or informally – to provide unilateral assistance to Czechoslovakia. Yet many authors have built on the false foundations laid down by Soviet propaganda, by Kopecky and by Gottwald.[41] Among the first such publications of this kind was Jiri Hajek's *Mnichov*. Hajek claimed to have proven that the Soviet Union was willing to assist Czechoslovakia unilaterally.[42] Evidence? Well, Gottwald said so in December 1948. At the end of the 1950s, Prague and Moscow began publishing collections of Czech, Soviet and other diplomatic documents on the Munich crisis.[43] These claimed that the documents published therein demonstrated Stalin's willingness to help Czechoslovakia without France. However, no evidence to that effect can be found in those volumes.[44]

The absence of any proof regarding the offer of Soviet unilateral assistance was noted during the Prague Spring of 1968 when some of the Czechoslovak archives were partially opened for a few months.[45] By then, historians were no longer prepared to trust such 'evidence' as Gottwald's speech in December 1948. They began to suggest that the Soviet Union should document its claims regarding its unilateral offer in September 1938 by providing primary archival evidence, not by footnotes to Gottwald, a mouthpiece of Moscow.[46] Sir John Wheeler-Bennett asked pointedly: 'Why, when on the record, as we know it today, the USSR comes very well out of the Munich affair, have they never published the documents which could historically confirm what has been widely stated? What have they gained by not doing so? Or what have they to hide?'[47]

Not only did the partially opened archives produce no support for the existence of the offer, they also contributed to the emerging picture of Soviet deceitfulness during the crisis of 1938. It began to appear that Moscow exposed the Benes government to several years of conflicting information regarding its probable course of action in case of a Czechoslovak–German conflict. It tended to offer Prague words of support in order to strengthen its resolve to resist the Third Reich. But the assurances, such as Maxim Litvinov's speeches in Geneva, were never followed by concrete military measures to be orchestrated with Paris, first and foremost, as well as with Prague. Another problem was that Soviet assurances of support invariably arrived late, when the crises had already passed. By contrast, when tensions were high Moscow had pulled back and allowed the crisis to take its course without Soviet intervention; such was the case during the crucial days of the May crisis and in September 1938.[48]

Faith in the mythological Soviet unilateral offer was resurrected by the policy of *glasnost'* in the Soviet Union, although no supporting evidence whatsoever was uncovered in any of the Soviet archives that became accessible in the late 1980s and in the 1990s. On that front, there was no change. But the debate began to shift toward the Soviet military dimension underlining the 1938 crisis. This was made possible by the appearance of books and articles by various Soviet authors and especially by Marshal M.V. Zakharov.[49] These works have found a receptive audience in the West, where, overturning the prevailing view, no matter how well supported by hard evidence, is an (often delightful) attribute of a vibrant intellectual life.

Throughout most of his career, Zakharov was a staff officer who in the summer of 1938 witnessed the developing Czechoslovak–German crisis as an adjutant to the Red Army chief of general staff, Marshal Boris M. Shaposhnikov.[50] The political foundations of Zakharov's brief account of the 1938 crisis contain two erroneous claims. One is the marshal's tendentious charge that Benes was a defeatist who looked for ways to surrender to Hitler without losing too much face.[51] (The same assessment is commonly expressed by other Soviet writers.[52]) The other assumption is that the Soviet Union had offered Czechoslovakia military assistance on 20 September 1938.

Let us deal with the first claim. Benes was not a defeatist; he had in fact desired a war to break out. As we have seen above, such was the view of the Soviet minister in Prague, Aleksandrovsky, who warned the Kremlin that Benes had hoped to fight a 'war against the whole world' with the Soviet Union at his side, even in the face of French and British inaction, if not hostility.[53] It was confirmed by Benes' domestic political opponents, such as Rudolf Beran, who testified that 'if the Soviets had then promised their assistance the war would have taken place. I am convinced that in that case Dr. Benes would have gone to war'.[54] It was affirmed, furthermore, by Benes' political allies, such as his then secretary Drtina. Benes, he wrote, 'hoped for a military solution after it had become apparent that agreement [with the Third Reich] was unobtainable. He counted on the possibility of an armed conflict to the end and he saw in it his last hope'.[55] Finally, we have the testimony of Chancellor Smutny, who recalled that Benes expected war to break out and that he wanted it, for only a war could defeat Hitler and nazism.[56] Edvard Benes was no appeaser of fascism in any form.[57]

Second, we must consider the claim that the Soviet Union offered Czechoslovakia military assistance on 20 September 1938. This is a common theme of Soviet authors and others who quote them. Take, for instance, the authoritative Dmitri Volkoganov: 'On 20 September

Moscow replied positively to a request from Prague as to whether the
USSR was able and willing to defend Czechoslovakia from impending
invasion.'[58] It has already been shown here that this is not true. Benes
inquired as to the availability of Soviet military intervention without
France in the evening on 19 September 1938. At 7.45 pm on 20
September 1938 Prague rejected the Franco-British proposal and at
8.20 pm it received the Soviet reply that Moscow would act on
Prague's behalf in concert with other members of the League of
Nations under articles 16 and 17. This reply had nothing to do with
the question regarding Soviet military action without France.
Incidentally, the communication came to Benes from the
Czechoslovak legation in Moscow, not from Soviet diplomats in
Prague. It was decoded at the Prague ministry of foreign affairs, not
at the Soviet legation; Aleksandrovsky was kept out of the loop.
Therefore, it was not possible for the Soviet minister to read the reply
to Benes over the telephone, as claimed by Soviet ambassador, Ivan
Maiski, whose post was in London and who knew only little about
the Prague scene.[59]

   It is, however, the military dimension of Zakharov's argument
that fascinates the Western reader who doggedly searches for reasons
to believe that Stalin intended to assist Czechoslovakia. Zakharov,
Volkoganov and others do their best to provide the believer with
ammunition. They claim that not only did Moscow assert its
willingness to assist Czechoslovakia through diplomatic channels (but
see above), it even carried out large-scale military measures to
prepare for an intervention against the Third Reich. Zakharov goes
into considerable detail; he describes step by step the measures taken
during the last week of September 1938 in the Kiev, Belorussian,
Kalinin, Leningrad, Moscow, Khar'kov, Orel, Volga, Urals, North
Caucasus and Transcaucasus military districts.[60] Volkoganov sums up
the Red Army's preparations simply: on 20 September 1938, troops
were 'regrouped' in the Kiev and Belorussian military districts; anti-
aircraft defence forces were put on combat footing; the discharging
of enlisted men and junior officers was postponed and reservists were
called up. At the end of September 1938, the Red Army fielded 'more
than seventy divisions placed on combat readiness', that were 'able
and willing', as Volkoganov puts it, to intervene in Czechoslovakia
against the imminent German invasion.[61]

The books cited above have been welcomed in print as virtually groundbreaking.[62] But they do not in fact open any new vistas at all: that there were military movements in the Kiev and possibly other military districts has been known for a long time: I recall quite clearly that such measures were highlighted by my high-school history teacher in Prague in the mid-1960s. Relying on Soviet authors from the same era, Marcia Lynn Toepfer wrote in 1977 about 'the movement of 30 Soviet infantry divisions to the western frontier and the concentration of 246 bombers and 302 fighters in the Belorussian and Kiev military districts, where they could be readily sent to Czechoslovakia. Tanks and aviation divisions were also readied for possible action along the western frontier'.[63] (Military-minded readers with a good knowledge of geography can judge for themselves whether it was in fact possible in 1938 'readily' to transfer 30 divisions and hundreds of planes from the Soviet Union to Czechoslovakia.) On the basis of similar Soviet sources, the official *Vojenske dejiny Ceskoslovenska*, published in Prague under the old regime, made equally grand claims regarding Soviet military measures on behalf of Czechoslovakia in September 1938.[64] Finally, the detailed order to the Kiev district by Soviet Commissar of Defence Kliment E. Voroshilov of 21 September 1938 has been known since the 1970s.[65]

But the one crucial component that is lacking in the works of Zakharov, his countrymen and others who quote them is evidence of any link between the Red Army partial mobilization and redeployment and the Czechoslovak–German crisis. The reader who has plowed through Zakharov's report must ask: how do we know that the measures were a prelude to the Red Army's intervention in Czechoslovakia or even vaguely directed against Hitler? After all, conducting partial mobilizations and redeployments is exactly what professional military people are supposed to be doing at a time of serious political crisis, such as the one Europe was experiencing in September 1938. For instance, France, Great Britain, Belgium, the Netherlands and Switzerland had carried out partial mobilizations or large-scale manoeuvres in September 1938, and no one would argue that they were preparing for a military intervention on Czechoslovakia's behalf against the Third Reich. We know that the British and French did their very best to avoid a military confrontation with Hitler, yet they took preparatory military measures for war. *Si vis pacem, para bellum* is universally recognized as a principle of prudent policy, as is the Clausewitzian adage regarding the seamless relationship between diplomacy and the use of force. Were the measures described by Marshal Zakharov related to the Czechoslovak crisis? There is no evidence to that effect.

The well-informed German embassy in Moscow did not believe that the Kremlin ever intended the Red Army to intervene in Czechoslovakia against Hitler. Although the embassy staff were freer to move about the Soviet Union than other diplomats accredited in Moscow, they failed to observe or hear about any preparatory steps for a Soviet military deployment to Czechoslovakia. Here is a German diplomat's summary of Moscow's behaviour written just ten days after the Munich agreement had been signed: the Soviet Union 'neglected to take such preliminary measures of mobilization as was considered necessary, for instance, in Holland, Belgium and Switzerland. Considering that the Soviet Union was under an obligation to render assistance to Czechoslovakia, this attitude must seem particularly striking'.[66] The Russian-born and well-connected German military attaché in Moscow, General Ernst Köstring, shared fully this sceptical assessment of Soviet military intentions in 1938.[67] 'Throughout Europe', noted D.C. Watt, 'only the ignorant and the believers took Soviet military power seriously.'[68] This pertains to Soviet military strength, but the same could be said about the Kremlin's willingness to deploy the Red Army against Hitler in the Czechoslovak–German crisis.

During the summer and autumn of 1938 the chief Soviet diplomat, Maxim Litvinov, was often kept in the dark by the Kremlin regarding official Soviet policy: Stalin treated him with contempt and made little effort to hide it from other Soviet leaders. Undoubtedly, Litvinov found it both worrisome and humiliating. Yet when he was in Geneva at the League of Nations or commenting before the world press in Moscow, he tried to play the role of a normal professional diplomat as much as was possible, given the abnormality of the Stalinist Soviet Union in 1938–39. Similarly, the Soviet officer corps was in 1938 undergoing the purge Stalin had launched in 1937. Before the mayhem was over, some 40,000 leaders of the Red Army had been purged; the NKVD executioners shot most of them, others were sent to the Gulag. But the officers whom the purge avoided or those temporarily still in command tried their best to behave as regular soldiers would under the circumstances of the developing European crisis. Military leaders are not supposed to be passively awaiting a hostile strike, they are expected to take preparatory measures when war is on the horizon. This was especially true for the Red Army, which was governed by a doctrine that had offensive action at its core. Cynthia Roberts has observed that in 'the early 1930s it was an article of faith, operationalised in Soviet war plans, that if the Soviet Union were attacked the Red Army would not surrender "one inch" of Soviet territory to the aggressor'.[69]

During the last week of September 1938, Czechoslovakia had fully mobilized; Germany, Great Britain and France had each taken some preparatory steps toward war, as did others in Europe. The Soviet Union was involved in a shooting war in the Far East, there was the Spanish Civil War and there were serious tensions between Moscow and Warsaw as well as between Moscow and Bucharest. Viewed thus, it would be remarkable if there had been no military manoeuvres and no partial mobilizations in the Soviet Union at the time.

Most likely, the measures taken by the Red Army at the height of the 1938 crisis were motivated by caution on the part of Soviet military commanders who did not dare to allow their units to be caught sitting down when an all-out war was likely to break out not too far from Soviet territory. In any case, there is not the slightest indication that the developments in the Kiev district, whatever their scope and nature, had anything to do with an imminent Soviet action against Hitler in Czechoslovakia. One must also ask what sense it would make for the Kremlin to deploy the Red Army in an effort to aid Czechoslovakia against the Third Reich while it had instructed Aleksandrovsky to refuse to answer President Benes' 'practical questions' during their meetings in September 1938. How smart would it be for the Red Army to assist the Czechoslovak army without there having been any previous political and military coordination?

Let us revisit in this context the often debated question of Soviet air force assistance to Czechoslovakia in the crisis of 1938. With the rest of the world, Czechoslovak military specialists had been

watching closely the development and deployment of the Soviet light
bomber SB-2 (*skorostnyi bombadirovchik*), designed by the much
admired engineer A.N. Tupolev in the early 1930s, before he was
arrested by the NKVD. The plane flew for the first time in December
1934 and full production began in early 1936. It was soon observed
in Spain, where it performed remarkably well. At about that time, the
British government had failed to lift restrictions imposed upon
exports of the two-engine Bristol 'Blenheim' to Czechoslovakia and
the Prague government decided to approach the Soviets instead. A
deal was struck: Moscow would sell the Czechs the complete
documentation for and the licence to produce in Czechoslovakia 161
SB-2 (the Czech designation was B-71) as well as 61 unfinished
prototypes of the plane. Prague would pay back with cannons R-3
and C-5 and the training plane Avia Ba-122. The deal was signed on
15 April 1937.[70] A group of 20 Czechoslovak pilots, all dressed in
mufti, travelled to the Soviet Union by train (via Romania) in
October 1937; the senior commanding officer of the unit was
Colonel (later General) Vilem Stanovsky. Their mission was to get to
know the new planes and to fly them to Czechoslovakia. There were
endless delays, a very intrusive NKVD surveillance, and long periods
of bad weather.[71] Finally, on 4 April 1938, the first group of unarmed
SB-2s/B-71s with Czechoslovak instruments, engines and fuel was
flown from Kiev to Uzhorod in eastern Czechoslovakia, via
Romania.[72] Before the end of the 1938 crisis, the Czechoslovak air
force received exactly 61 such planes as part of the business
agreement of April 1937.[73] They had nothing whatsoever to do with
Soviet assistance to Czechoslovakia in the crisis of 1938.

It should be noted that there were many problems with this simple
transaction. First, there were only a few airports that could
accommodate the modern Soviet air planes because Czech runways
were short, having been designed for the obsolete Czech planes.
Altogether, the Czechoslovak air force had just 12 airfields that were
100 per cent battle-ready. Of those, only a few were long enough for
the B-71.[74] Second, Soviet planes used high-octane fuel whereas the
Czechs still flew on 'biboli', a mixture of gas made from Romanian
or Polish oil (50 per cent), alcohol (30 per cent) and benzol (20 per
cent). This allowed the Czech military to conserve the precious oil,
but their airplane engines had become obsolete as others designed for

high-octane fuel became standard.[75] Therefore, before the Soviet planes could be flown to Czechoslovakia, the Czechs had to send their own engines and biboli fuel to the Soviet manufacturer.[76] Third, the Soviet air force used a different kind of ammunition (7.62 mm) than the Czechs (7.92 mm). Fourth, the Soviet air force used ordnance (bombs and also bomb-launchers) with different parameters than the Czechs. Fifth, if the Soviet pilots had come to Czechoslovakia's assistance they would have been unable to coordinate their manoeuvres with their allies in the air because the two used non-compatible communication equipment.[77] Finally, Czech pilots were more likely to speak German, French or English than Russian; one is not inclined to believe that their Soviet colleagues were encouraged to learn any foreign languages at that time.

Consequently, any Soviet attempt to provide Czechoslovakia with combat aviation from the Kiev district would have had to be preceded by a massive predeployment of fuel, ammunition, ordnance as well as the building of new runways, and training exercises for the pilots and the support crews on the ground. Yet because the Soviet Union and Czechoslovakia did not have a common border, and because neither Poland nor Romania would have wanted (or dared, given Hitler's probable reaction) to allow a continuous stream of Soviet military material and personnel to Czechoslovakia, such coordination was hardly possible.

In the unlikely case that, say, Romania had agreed to look the other way while the Soviet air force was being predeployed in Czechoslovakia, the scope of this project was such that it would have had to be launched at least 12 months in advance of the anticipated conflict. But in September 1937 there was not enough of a political consensus in Prague, Moscow, Bucharest, Paris and London behind the view that a war with Hitler was inevitable and that a military buildup in Czechoslovakia should take place immediately. To begin with, Benes had no reason to believe himself unsafe: after all, he was an ally of France, the mightiest power in Europe, and France stood firm and tall behind Czechoslovakia at that time. Yvon Delbos, the French foreign minister, came to Czechoslovakia at the end of 1937 to reassure the whole world that France would fully honour its commitments. He stated in Prague that his country regarded its treaties with Czechoslovakia as unbreakable.[78]

Under such circumstances, Benes would never have dared to endanger his standing with France by becoming the recipient of a flow of Soviet military materiel and specialists. In 1937, such behaviour would have amounted to playing into Hitler's hands: the Prague government was trying to fight the charge of the German and Hungarian preemptive propaganda that Czechoslovakia was an aircraft carrier whence the Red air force would invade the West. The Czechs went so far as to invite German, allied and United States military attachés to inspect their military bases and airports to see for themselves that there was no Soviet military presence.[79] Czechoslovakia's isolation would have increased many fold if it had agreed to any predeployment of Soviet material, airplanes and personnel at the time. If Benes had accepted in, say, September 1937 a large-scale Soviet predeployment it would have amounted to giving up the alliance with France because no government in Paris would have remained passive while its ally, the Prague government, had opened its borders – in peacetime – to the Bolshevik menace. This is why Benes always insisted on the primacy of the relationship between Paris and Moscow. He would deal with the Kremlin only via Paris. Perforce, this changed after the Franco-British proposal of 19 September 1938 when Benes had no option but to inquire regarding Moscow's willingness to provide him with unilateral military assistance in any shape or form, even a symbolic one; see Benes' request for Soviet aerial assistance of 28 September 1938, mentioned above.

Thus, not only did Stalin not offer to provide military assistance at any time during the 1938 crisis, Benes would not have accepted it before late September 1938. It was only when the situation became desperate, that is, after the Franco-British proposal and ultimatum and the Munich *Diktat*, that the president saw no alternative to playing the Soviet card.

It is no wonder that no one can claim to have seen the alleged Soviet aerial assistance to Czechoslovakia landing anywhere in the country. It is no wonder that not even Gottwald, Kopecky and their heirs, such as Antonin Novotny and Gustav Husak, eager as they were to seize on anything to present the Soviet Union in the best light, ever dared to claim, as a Western historian has done, that 'the Soviet government supplied Czechoslovakia with approximately 300 planes, a fact substantiated in diplomatic records'.[80] No wonder Soviet and Czech communist historians restricted themselves to claiming that the Soviet air force was ready to fly 548[81] or 730[82] planes that ultimately did not leave Soviet soil. No wonder that Stalin never brought up the alleged aerial or any other kind of military assistance to Czechoslovakia while he was putting pressure on the Prague government to reject the invitation to join the Marshall plan in 1947. He did not hesitate to speak about the losses suffered by the Red Army when it liberated Czechoslovakia in 1945, but said not a word about his activities in 1938.

General Karel Husarek, who had been received by Stalin on 28 June 1938 and who had some connections among the Soviet officer corps, was asked on 29 September 1938 during the crucial meeting of the Prague government what the Red Army was going to do in case of a German attack on Czechoslovakia. 'The Soviets won't fight, they won't go to war for us', the general answered.[83] Army General Ludvik Krejci, the highest ranking officer in the country, spoke freely on television about the 1938 crisis during the Prague Spring of 1968. There was no hint that he had ever expected or heard of Soviet unilateral intervention on the side of Czechoslovakia against the Third Reich.

Why? Only one answer is possible: because Moscow never intended it and the measures taken by the Red Army in the Kiev district were not a prelude to it.[84] The Soviet Union was not prepared to provide Czechoslovakia with unilateral military assistance against the Third Reich.

III

Let me now attempt the considerably more complicated task of trying to discern what Stalin and his colleagues had been trying to achieve during the 1930s. In the wake of Adolf Hitler's seizure of power, the Kremlin, angrily denounced by the Nazis and wishing to avoid isolation, was forced to play with Paris and Prague and therefore tried cautiously to contribute to the emergence of a collective of states with an anti-Hitler agenda. Hence the Franco-Soviet and Czechoslovak–Soviet treaties of mutual assistance of 1935, hence the switch towards the popular front, as stipulated by the 7th Congress of the Comintern.

The popular front concept meant that France, Czechoslovakia and other countries had to be strengthened domestically in order for them to avoid an outright collapse because of outside pressures from the Third Reich. At the same time, opposition to Hitler was a means of accelerating the growth of civil conflicts latent within European capitalist countries. Georgii Dimitrov predicted that there would soon be a 'period of sharp clashes' among various capitalist countries, which would prepare the ground 'for the forthcoming great battles of the second round of proletarian revolutions'.[85]

Despite serious losses in Germany and a lack of progress anywhere else, the official voice of the Soviet Union was surprisingly optimistic. Soviet Commissar of Defence K.J. Voroshilov told Benes in the Kremlin on 9 June 1935: 'We're not afraid of Hitler. If he attacks you, we'll attack him because if you fall Hitler would go further. We'll rip the enemy apart!' Benes asked how this would be done, given the absence of a corridor between Czechoslovakia and the Soviet Union. Would the Red Army cross the territory of other countries? Of course, said Voroshilov. With, or without an agreement. The next day Litvinov reassured Benes that this was the official view of the Kremlin.[86]

From that day to the very end of the Czechoslovak–German crisis on 30 September 1938, the Soviet Union would offer considerable encouragement to its Czechoslovak ally.[87] But there is reason to believe that Moscow's support for Prague was motivated by the expectation that the conflict between Franco-British capitalism and German nazism over Czechoslovakia would create favourable conditions for socialist revolutions in Europe. The Kremlin held the view that Hitler's offensive could be but a prelude to a wave of socialist revolutions in Europe.

A useful insight into Soviet strategy on the eve of World War II comes from Litvinov, who met Benes' emissary, the Czechoslovak diplomat Arnost Heidrich, in May 1938 in Geneva. War was inevitable, asserted Litvinov. The West, he continued, 'wishes Stalin to destroy Hitler and Hitler to destroy Stalin'. But Moscow would not oblige its enemies. 'This time it will be the Soviets who will stand by until near the end when they will be able to step in and bring about a just and permanent peace.'[88]

The thrust of Litvinov's informal remarks to Heidrich was officially confirmed by a representative of the Comintern during his visit to

Czechoslovakia in late August 1938; the record of his presentation, deposited in the archives of the Communist Party of Czechoslovakia, identifies him as Andrei Zhdanov.[89] In a long and detailed analysis of the international situation, Zhdanov stressed that, though fascism was a threat, it also offered an opportunity. He went on to explain his point: if the war between Czechoslovakia and Germany broke out, it would be the duty of all party members to fight the fascist aggressor. At the same time, communists would 'have to try with all their might to utilize the economic and political crises caused by the war to mobilize the masses and to accelerate the downfall of capitalism in Czechoslovakia'. In their struggle against Hitler, and subsequently against capitalism, members of the CPC would be assisted by the Red Army, which would 'represent a great political factor in this conflict'.

In conclusion, Zhdanov assured his audience that the concept of 'the second wave of proletarian revolutions' was to be taken seriously. The current political situation in Czechoslovakia, stated Zhdanov, gave the CPC a means by which it could accelerate the revolution's arrival. 'Hitler's attack upon Czechoslovakia will be the beginning of the end of fascist rule', Zhdanov predicted, 'and also of the bourgeois system of exploitation in this country.' The Czechoslovak people would at first fight side-by-side with the Red Army against the Third Reich. Then, under the leadership of the CPC, they would liberate themselves from their bourgeoisie.

Such words must be evaluated cautiously. The Comintern was officially in the business of promoting a Soviet-style revolution in every country. Therefore, whether the Kremlin considered it realistic or not, that is what Comintern representatives were expected to talk about. Nevertheless, one should not automatically dismiss Zhdanov's daring words as mere propaganda. He spoke at a secret meeting before selected CPC leaders and his speech in Prague acquires clearer contours when one sees it in the light of a conversation between Benes and Gottwald in September 1945. Gottwald confessed to the president that he had been attacked by Soviet leaders for his failure to carry out a communist *coup d'état* in Prague during the September 1938 crisis.[90] He had to defend himself vigorously before his Comintern colleagues, Gottwald told Benes; they seemed ready to judge him severely.[91] Benes, of course, listened to Gottwald with interest and, as always, he scribbled notes for his own record as the

conversation progressed. After Gottwald had left, the president
summed up the meaning of his talk with the CPC leader in this way:
'Fundamentally important was for me Gottwald's confession that
they [leaders of the Communist party of Czechoslovakia] were
reprimanded in Moscow for their failure to carry out a revolution,
and that they defended themselves by using virtually the same
arguments which I used to use.'[92]

The revolutionary component of Soviet strategy in the late 1930s
is centrally important. Without it, it could be said that Stalin reacted
to the rise of Hitler much like others in Europe: he tried to avoid
isolation, he tried to postpone his entry into the war, and he tried to
manipulate the international scene so that others would have to stand
up to the Third Reich while he was free to choose when and on
whose side he would join the conflict. But while others tried to
prevent war at all cost, Stalin saw in it an opportunity.

This was made clear by Ambassador Maiski to Benes during their
conversation in London on 23 August 1939. Benes' notes reveal the
very core of Soviet strategic thinking at the time. When Benes
expressed his amazement at the Molotov–Ribbentrop pact, Maiski
replied that war would definitely break out 'in two weeks' time'. 'My
overall impression', noted Benes, is that 'the Soviets want war, they
prepared for it conscientiously and they maintain that the war will
take place – and that they have reserved some freedom of action for
themselves.' Benes added that originally he considered this to be an
exaggeration. But when he saw the text of the nazi–Soviet pact the
next day he realized it was even worse than what Maiski had outlined
on 23 August 1939. He realized that Moscow had slammed the door
on any future negotiations with the West. The pact was, Benes wrote
and underlined, 'a rather rough tactic to drive Hitler into war'. Benes
wrote in his summary of the meeting: 'the Soviets are convinced that
the time has come for a final struggle between capitalism, fascism and
nazism and that there will be a world revolution which they will
trigger at an opportune moment when others are exhausted by war'.[93]
On the eve of World War II, Benes had no reason to fabricate or
misinterpret Maiski's words. Moreover, his record of the meeting
echoes the proclamations of the VIIth congress of the Comintern of
1935, Litvinov's declaration to Heidrich in May 1938 in Geneva, and
Zhdanov's speech in Prague in August 1938.

Finally, there is an indication that the Kremlin deemed war desirable even after it had started, in November 1939. A Soviet official told a CPC delegation in Moscow that the Molotov–Ribbentrop pact was justified because 'if the USSR had concluded a treaty with the Western powers, Germany would never have unleashed a war from which will develop world revolution, the revolution we have been preparing for a long time. ... A surrounded Germany would never have entered into war.'[94] This brief outline of the long-term Soviet strategy is in harmony with all the other evidence presented so far: Litvinov's statement to Heidrich in Geneva, Zhdanov's speech in Prague, Maiski's conversation with Benes, and the declaration quoted above are characterized by a remarkable degree of internal consistency. That is what makes the message regarding the revolutionary potential detected in the crisis of 1938–39 by Stalin credible.

It was with a degree of pride that Andrei Zhdanov, in the autumn of 1947, reviewed the changes World War II brought about in Europe. He noted that the war had significantly altered the international balance of power in favour of the Soviet Union. 'The war dealt capitalism a heavy blow', Zhdanov asserted. Some of the main bastions of imperialism were defeated (Germany, Japan and Italy) and others were weakened (Great Britain and France). By contrast, the Soviet Union was greatly strengthened.[95] This was, at least superficially, true. But this analysis failed on two grounds. First, it did not take account of the long-term American resolve not to remain passive in the face of communist advances. Second, Zhdanov conveniently overlooked that the new Soviet empire in Europe did not grow out of class conflicts triggered by the Nazi aggression but had to be established from outside by Soviet troops, secret policemen and indigenous personalities trained in the Soviet Union and imported from there. As it happened, both of these factors – omitted in Zhdanov's 1947 speech – proved to have serious consequences for the survivability of the Soviet system in Europe.

Boston University

NOTES

Research and travel for this article were enabled by a fellowship from IREX that was partly supported with funds provided by the National Endowment for the Humanities. I very much appreciate the generous support of the two organizations and the faith of their administrators in my work. The article was written while I was a Senior Fellow at the Society of Fellows at Boston University. I am grateful to Provost and Dean Dennis Berkey and Professor Katherine T. O'Connor for their kindness and support.

The following abbreviations have been used throughout this paper: ACC CPC (Archives of the Central Committee of the Communist party of Czechoslovakia, Karmelitska Street, Prague); AMFA (Archives of the Ministry of Foreign Affairs, Prague); AMI (Archives of the Ministry of Interior, Prague); BA-TGM (Archives of Edvard Benes at the Institute of Tomas G. Masaryk, Invalidovna, Prague); JS-CU (Archives of Jaromir Smutny at Columbia University, New York, NY); MOPR (The Military Office of the President of the Republic, the Castle, Prague); NA (The National Archives, Maryland, United States); OPR (Office of the President of the Republic, The Castle, Prague); SCA (State Central Archives, Loreta, Prague); ZF-ANM (Papers of Zdenek Fierlinger at the Archives of the National Museum, Loreta, Prague).

1. Note that even Karel Kaplan, who had unique access to the Prague archives in the 1960s, could offer only anecdotes when it came to the issue of Soviet assistance to Czechoslovakia in 1938. See *Mocni a bezmocni* (Toronto: Sixty-Eight Publishers, 1989), p.304.
2. In addition to the Franco-Czechoslovak Treaty of Mutual Assistance of 1925, Prague also signed in 1935 the Czechoslovak–Soviet Treaty. The two documents were linked by Article II in the Protocol of Signature of the latter document. This stipulated that Czechoslovakia and the Soviet Union would come to each other's assistance only if France had moved first. An analysis of this can be found in Igor Lukes, *Czechoslovakia Between Stalin and Hitler: The Diplomacy of Edvard Benes in the Thirties* (New York: Oxford University Press, 1996), pp.46–58.
3. In addition to the well-known, classical works by Walter Laqueur, Robert C. Tucker, Adam B. Ulam, Piotr S. Wandycz, D.C. Watt and Gerhard L. Weinberg, we have J.W. Bruegel, 'Dr. Benes on the Soviet "Offer of Help" in 1938', *East Central Europe*, Vol.4, No.1 (1977); Barry Mendel Cohen, 'Moscow at Munich', *East Central European Quarterly*, Vol.12, No.3 (1978); Jonathan Haslam, 'The Soviet Union and the Czechoslovakian Crisis of 1938', *Journal of Contemporary History*, Vol.14, No.3 (1979); Milan Hauner, 'Zari 1938: Kapitulovat ci bojovat?' *Svedectvi*, 49 (1975); Frantisek Lukes, 'Poznamky k cs.-sovetskym stykum v zari 1938', *Ceskoslovensky casopis historicky*, Vol.16, No.5 (1968); Frantisek Lukes, 'Benes a SSSR', *Sesity pro mladou literaturu*, 21 (1968); Ivan Pfaff, 'Jak tomu opravdu bylo se sovetskou pomoci v mnichovske krizi?' *Svedectvi*, 56 (1978), and 57 (1979); Edward Taborsky, 'Benes and the Soviets', *Foreign Affairs*, Vol.27, No.2 (1949); William V. Wallace, 'New Documents on the History of Munich: A Selection from the Soviet and Czechoslovak Archives', *International Affairs*, Vol.35, No.4 (1959); I have also dealt with the crisis of 1938 in 'Did Stalin Desire War in 1938? A New Look at Soviet Behaviour During the May and September Crises', *Diplomacy & Statecraft*, Vol.2, No.1 (1991); 'Stalin and Benes at the End of September 1938: New Evidence from the Prague Archives', *Slavic Review*, Vol.52, No.1 (1993); 'The Czechoslovak Partial Mobilization in May 1938: A Mystery (Almost) Solved', *Journal of Contemporary History*, Vol.31, No.4 (1996); and 'Benesch, Stalin und die Komintern: Vom Münchner Abkommen zum Molotow-Ribbetrop Pakt', *Vierteljahrshefte für Zeitgeschichte*, 3 (1993), pp.325–53.
4. Some of the evidence presented below can be found in Lukes, *Czechoslovakia Between Stalin and Hitler: The Diplomacy of Edvard Benes During the Crisis of the 1930s* (New

York: Oxford University Press, 1996).

5. The early stages of this development are described in Antonin Klimek, *Boj o hrad (1). Hrad a petka. Vnitropoliticky vyvoj Ceskoslovenska 1918–1926 na pudorysu zapasu o prezidentske nastupnictvi* (Prague: PANEVROPA, 1996).

6. Documents available at MOPR show on the one hand President Benes' inability to delegate responsibility and, on the other, the inability of Czechoslovak generals to act on their own, without the president. See, for instance, MPRR, secret, 1935–1939, CPO II, 151/38. It was only on 8 June 1938, after several forceful interventions by President Benes, that the Czechoslovak army was able to solve the question of which gas-mask models to produce and at what price. MOPR, secret, 1935–1939, CPO II, 165/38 shows Benes' repeated interventions in attempts to deal with the anticipated traffic-jams in Prague during a future general mobilization and the shortage of air-raid shelters. For evidence of Benes' involvement in deciding how many reservists are to be called up, see Lukes, 'The Czechoslovak Partial Mobilization in May 1938: A Mystery (Almost) Solved', *Journal of Contemporary History*, Vol.31, No.4 (1996).

7. Prokop Drtina, *Ceskoslovensko muj osud* (Toronto: Sixty-Eight Publishers, 1982), p.205.

8. Regarding the date of the visit, see Lukes, *Czechoslovakia Between Stalin and Hitler*, p.272, n.221.

9. Ibid., p.251.

10. Drtina, *Ceskoslovensko*, pp.189–90. A more detailed and vivid version of this scene is in the manuscript of this book. It can be found in ANM-F.

11. The nature of these activities can be discerned from Rudolf Urban, *Tajne fondy III. sekce: z archivu MZ Republiky Ceskoslovenske* (Prague: Orbis, 1943).

12. Benes, *Mnichovske dny* (Prague: Svoboda, 1968), p.316.

13. Drtina, *Ceskoslovensko*, p.106.

14. AMFA, Zdenek Fierlinger, the Czechoslovak Legation, Moscow, to the Ministry of Foreign Affairs, Prague, telegrams received 857/38, 20 Sept. 1938, decoded at 8.20 pm. It should be noted that Article 16 required a unanimous agreement in the League and that was unobtainable.

15. This incorrect claim is made in, for instance, Ivan Mikhailovich Maiski, *Vospominania sovetskogo diplomata, 1925–1945* (Moscow: Nauka, 1987), pp.357–8.

16. 'Miunkhen', *Mezhdunarodnaya zhizn*, 11 (1988), pp.138–9.

17. 'Miunkhen', p.140.

18. AMFA, Zdenek Fierlinger, the Czechoslovak Legation, Moscow, to the Ministry of Foreign Affairs, Prague, telegrams received, 980/38, 28 Sept. 1938. Regarding the telegram's unquestionable authenticity, see Vera Olivova, 'Ceskoslovensko-sovetske vztahy mezi obema valkami', *50. vyroci Ceskoslovenske republiky: Materialy z vedecke konference* (Prague: Ustav dejin KSC, 1968), Vol.2, pp.183–4.

19. AMFA, Zdenek Fierlinger, the Czechoslovak Legation, Moscow, to Kamil Krofta, the Minister of Foreign Affairs, Prague, secret, 29 Sept. 1938.

20. 'Miunkhen', pp.128–42.

21. AMFA, Zdenek Fierlinger, the Czechoslovak Legation, Moscow, to the Ministry of Foreign Affairs, Prague, telegrams received 1037/38, 3 Oct. 1938.

22. Ivan Herben, 'Benes o sve navsteve u Roosevelta a o Mnichovu', in Ladislav Karel Feierabend (ed.), *Politicke vzpominky*, Vol.III (Prague: Atlantis, 1996), pp.417–19.

23. Benes meant Fierlinger's *Ve sluzbach CSR: pameti z druheho odboje* (Prague: Prace, 1947).

24. BA-TGM, notes for manuscripts, box 10a. Record of Benes' conversation with Smutny of 21 October 1947. The record was typed the next day.

25. See Benes' *Memoirs: From Munich to New War and New Victory* (Boston: Houghton Mifflin, 1954), pp.40 and 42. 'We and the Soviet Union work together to save peace' and '*In September … we were left in military, as well as in political, isolation with the*

Soviet Union to prepare our defence against a Nazi attack' [emphasis original]. Note, however, that Benes never came close in his own writings to claiming that Moscow was willing to help him unilaterally, without France. According to Sir John Wheeler-Bennett, he apparently crossed that line in his postwar conversations with the author. But Wheeler-Bennett thought the claim so suspicious that he excluded it from his *Munich: Prologue to Tragedy.* See *Knaves, Fools and Heroes: In Europe Between the Wars* (New York: Macmillan, 1974), pp.153–4. Along the same lines, see Erika Mann's interview of Benes that appeared in *The Baltimore Sun* on 19 April 1939. The interview is best read side-by-side with J.W. Bruegel's 'Dr. Benes on the Soviet "Offer of Help" in 1938'.

26. Hubert Ripka, *Unorova tragedie* (Prague, 1995), pp.233, 271.
27. Vaclav Cerny, *Vyvoj a zlociny panslavismu* (Prague: Institut pro stredoevropskou kulturu a politiku, 1995), pp.128–31.
28. Herben, 'Benes o sve navsteve u Roosevelta a o Mnichovu', in Feierabend (ed.), *Politicke vzpominky*, p.418.
29. JS-CU, Smutny's record. Jaromir Smutny was President Edvard Benes' chancellor.
30. JS-CU, Smutny's record, 14 Aug. 1948.
31. JS-CU, Smutny records the demeaning measures taken by the Czechoslovak security, the StB, to prevent the possibility of Benes' escape to the West. Despite repeated assurances that the former president's sole desire was to die peacefully at home, he was surrounded by guards he had never met before and that contributed to his sense of humiliation and despair.
32. V.I. Mikhailov, *Prolog k voine* (Moscow: Politizdat, 1964), p.57. In a similar vein, Vaclav Kopecky charged the president that he capitulated to Hitler deliberately and that 'it was dictated by class interests, by the bourgeois fear of the forces of socialism'. ACC CPC, fond 100/45, file 2, archival unit 75; see also Zdenek Fierlinger, *Zrada ceskoslovenske burzoazie a jejich spojencu* (Prague: nakladatelstvi Mir, 1951).
33. ACC CPC, fond 100/45, vol.2, archival unit 75.
34. ACC CPC, fond 100/24, vol.26, archival unit 729; Gottwald spoke in December 1948. There are two versions of the speech. The original says: 'I did so in January 1938', while the revised text says simply 'I did so'. A version appeared as 'J.V. STALIN i chekhoslovatskii narod', in *Za prochnyi mir, za narodnuyu demokratsiu*, Vol.32, No.59 (21 Dec. 1949).
35. OPR, Record of Presidential Audineces for 1937 and 1938. Igor Lukes, 'Stalin and Benes at the End of September 1938: New Evidence from the Prague Archives', *Slavic Review*, Vol.52, No.1 (1993), pp.28–48.
36. *Dokumenty k historii mnichovskeho diktatu, 1937–1939* (Prague: Svoboda, 1979), p.233.
37. ACC CPC, fond KI 20, file 85. The speech was delivered in German.
38. Bretislav Palkovsky, b.1888, was a lawyer by training and an economist by profession. In the 1930s, Palkovsky travelled to the Soviet Union and wrote about his experience there in a positive light. He was not a communist by the standard of his time, but a left-oriented liberal who took the Soviet Union to be a source of inspiration.
39. Zdenek Nejedly, b.1878, was a professor at Charles University, Prague. He was originally close to T.G. Masaryk but he abandoned Masaryk's 'realism' and shifted closer and closer toward the CPC. Although he was ready to join the party openly, he was discouraged by Gottwald and others from doing so. At a minimum, he was a fellow traveller.
40. AMI, H-664. 'General': Materials Regarding the Work of Former [Czechoslovak] Intelligence, subvolume 4. Bretislav Palkovsky, Curia, Portugal, 22 July 1940. Palkovsky names by name only Nejedly as being a participant in this scheme. Others remain anonymous under the label of 'a large number of other personalities'.
41. A review of such literature can be fond in Igor Lukes, 'Did Stalin Desire War in 1938?

A New Look at Soviet Behaviour during the May and September Crises', *Diplomacy & Statecraft*, Vol.2, No.1 (1991), pp.4–8.

42. Jiri Hajek, *Mnichov* (Prague: Statni nakladatelstvi politicke literatury, 1958).
43. V.F. Klochko *et al.* (eds.), *Nove dokumenty k historii Mnichova* (Prague: Statni nakladatelstvi politicke literatury, 1958); V.F. Klochko *et al.* (eds.), *New Documents on the History of Munich* (Prague: Statni nakladatelstvi politicke literatury, 1958); Dusan Spacil *et al.* (eds.), *Dokumenty k historii mnichovskeho diktatu, 1937–1939* (Prague: Svoboda, 1979); P.N. Pospelov *et al.* (eds.), *Dokumenty i materiali po istorii sovietsko-chekhoslovatskikh otnoshenii* (Moscow: Nauka, 1973–78); Cestmir Amort *et al.* (eds.), *Dokumenty a materialy k dejinam ceskoslovensko-sovetskych vztahu* (Prague: Academia, 1975–84); V.F. Mal'tsev (ed.), *Dokumenty po istorii miunkhenskogo sgovora, 1937–1939* (Moscow: Politizdat, 1979).
44. *New Documents on the History of Munich* (Prague: Orbis, 1958), Introduction: 'The Soviet Union was ready to offer Czechoslovakia military aid even without France participating, on the condition that Czechoslovakia would defend herself and would request Soviet assistance'.
45. The first testimony based on the partially opened Prague archives came from Ivan Pfaff, 'Jak tomu opravdu bylo se sovetskou pomoci v mnichovske krizi?'
46. See, especially, Frantisek Lukes, 'Poznamky k cs.-sovetskym stykum v zari 1938'.
47. Sir John Wheeler-Bennett, *Knaves, Fools and Heroes: In Europe Between the Wars* (London: Macmillan, 1974), p.154.
48. This is the main theme of my 'Did Stalin Desire War in 1938?'
49. Matvei Visil'evich Zakharov, *General'nyi shtab v predvoyennye gody* (Moscow: Voenizdat, 1989); V.K. Volkov *et al.*, *1939 god: uroki istorii* (Moscow: Mysl', 1990); Oleg A. Rzheshevskii, *Europe 1939: Was War Inevitable?* (Moscow: Progress Publishers, 1989); A.S. Stepanov, 'Pered Myunkhenom', *Voyenno-istoricheskii zhurnal*, 4-5 (1992); S.I. Prasolov, 'Sovietskii soyuz i Chekhoslovakia v 1938 g.', in V.K. Volkov (ed.), *Myunkhen: preddverie voiny* (Moscow: Nauka, 1988); D.A. Volkogonov, 'Drama reshenii 1939 goda', *Novaia i noveisheia istoria*, 4 (1989); relevant documents were published in *God krizisa, 1938–1939: dokumenty i materialy* (Moscow: Politizdat, 1990).
50. Boris Mikhailovich Shaposhnikov, *Vospominania: voenno-nauchnye trudy* (Moscow: Voenizdat, 1974); see the introduction by A.M. Vasilevski and M.V. Zakharov.
51. This charge was originally made by the British Minister in Prague Basil Newton. See Lukes, *Czechoslovakia Between Stalin and Hitler*, p.266, note 86.
52. For instance, see Rzheshevskii, *Europe 1939*, pp.92–3.
53. 'Miunkhen', p.140.
54. SCA, The Ministry of National Security, 109-4-227 and ACC CPC, fond 100/45, file 10, archival unit 183.
55. Drtina, *Ceskoslovensko*, p.203.
56. JS-CU, box 2, Benes and the Soviet Union.
57. Although Benes had done a great deal as foreign minister to help usher Soviet diplomacy into the League of Nations, he reaped only scorn from Soviet diplomats. See the hateful and grossly distorted portrait of Benes painted by Andrei Gromyko. 'As President of Czechoslovakia, Benes stands judged by history for having toyed with fascism ... To the end of his life, Benes remained a bourgeois politician with no conception of the real thoughts and hopes of the working people ... he took part in a reactionary conspiracy, supported by imperialism and aimed at overthrowing the people's regime, restoring capitalism and taking Czechoslovakia into NATO'. *Memoirs* (New York: Doubleday, 1989), pp.56–7. With works like these, one is nostalgic for the pre-*glasnost*' publishing policy in Moscow.
58. Dmitri Volkogonov, *Stalin: Triumph and Tragedy* (New York: Grove Weidenfeld, 1991), p.348.

59. Maiski, *Vospominaniya*, pp.357–8.
60. Zakharov, *General'nyi shtab v predvoyennye gody,* pp.112–15.
61. Volkoganov, *Stalin*, p.348.
62. G. Jukes, 'The Red Army and the Munich Crisis', *Journal of Contemporary History*, 26 (1991), pp.195–214.
63. Marcia Lynn Toepfer, 'The Soviet Role in the Munich Crisis: An Historiographical Debate', *Diplomatic History*, Vol.1, No.4 (Fall 1977), p.354. Her footnote is to S.IU. Vygodskii *et al.*, *Istoriia diplomatii* Vol.III (Moscow: 1965), p.737. I have tried (with the help of two different reference librarians in the Boston area) to find such a volume, but without success.
64. Zdenek Prochazka, *Vojenske dejiny Ceskoslovenska* Vol.III (Prague: Nase vojsko, 1987), pp.523–6.
65. P.N. Pospelov *et al.* (eds.), *Dokumenty i materiali po istorii sovietsko-chekhoslovatskikh otnoshenii* Vol.3 (Moscow: Nauka, 1973–78), pp.515–17. See also Miloslav John, *Zari 1938: II* (Brno: Nakladatelstvi Bonus A, 1997), pp.764–5.
66. *Documents on German Foreign Policy, 1918–1945*, series D, Vol.IV (Washington, DC: US Government Printing Office, 1949), document no. 477 of 10 Oct. 1938, p.606.
67. Hans Herwarth von Bittenfeld, *Against Two Evils* (New York: Rawson and Wade, 1981), p.123.
68. D.C. Watt, *How War Came: The Immediate Origins of the Second World War, 1938–1939* (New York: Pantheon Books, 1989), p.236.
69. Cynthia A. Roberts, 'Planning for War: The Red Army and the Catastrophe of 1941', *Europe–Asia Studies*, Vol.47, No.8 (Dec. 1995), p.1321.
70. A recent Czech publication states incorrectly that the agreement was signed in March 1937. See Otto Janka, *General Stanovsky: letec a gentleman* (Prague: Elka Press, 1997), p.102.
71. Ibid., pp.103–6, 110.
72. According to Janka, two SB-2s/B-71s had flown from Kiev to Prague in February 1938 and the rest followed later. Stanovsky's Sixth Air Regiment (Prague) had 22 SB-2s/B-71s (out of 53 airplanes in total) at the time of the Munich crisis. See ibid., pp.102–6, 110–11.
73. Miloslav John, *Ceskoslovenske letectvo v roce 1938* (Beroun: Baroko & Fox, 1996), pp.29–30, 89–90, 279.
74. Ibid., p.279.
75. Ibid., pp.29–30.
76. Ibid., pp.89–90.
77. I am grateful to Dr Lubor Vaclavu, Pedagogicka fakulta University Karlovy, Prague. Personal conversation, 14 July 1998, Prague.
78. Alexander Werth, *Twilight of France, 1933–1940* (New York: Harper, 1942), p.138.
79. NA, 760F.6127/18, J. Butler Wright, US Legation, Prague, to the Secretary of State, Washington, DC, 16 Jan. 1937. The US military attaché was Major John S. Winslow.
80. Toepfer, 'The Soviet Role', 351 and 357. Ms Toepfer even charges that the 'Orthodox School's' failure to acknowledge and recognize 'this actual [Soviet] military aid [to Czechoslovakia] is disingenuous'.
81. *Vojenske dejiny Ceskoslovenska*, Vol.III, p.525.
82. Ivan Pop in P. Glotz and K.H. Pollak *et al.* (eds), *München 1938: Das Ende des alten Europas* (Essen: Reimar Hobbing, 1990), pp.438–9.
83. SCA, The Ministry of National Security, 109-4-227. General Husarek was Deputy Chief of Staff of the Czechoslovak army. A record of his interview with Stalin and Molotov in June 1938 is in ZF-ANM, box 23.
84. To this day, 60 years after the 1938 crisis, there is no real evidence that Czechoslovakia and the Soviet Union had seriously attempted to persuade Romania to permit a peaceful transfer of the Red Army over its territory. I consider it an issue of marginal

importance. Because Moscow did not *intend* to come to Czechoslovakia's assistance it does not really matter whether Romania would have permitted an innocent passage of Soviet military material and troops across its territory.

85. This is described in Lukes, *Czechoslovakia Between Stalin and Hitler*, pp.33–86.
86. UTGM-B, fond 39, Soviet Union, box 5.
87. Moscow went so far as to send Nikolai I. Bukharin to Prague in February 1936 to warn Benes against underestimating the threat of German aggression. Soviet Minister Aleksandrovsky brought a similar message in August 1936. What would the Soviet Union do if Czechoslovakia were attacked by Hitler? he was asked. 'It depends', responded the minister. If it were be a localized conflict between Czechoslovakia and Germany, Moscow would be unable to do much. But if it were be a 'global' conflict, then 'the Soviets would disregard everything and march [to Czechoslovakia's assistance] through Romania as well as through Poland'. Note that Aleksandrovsky imposed a condition on Voroshilov's promise to Benes 13 months ago, in June 1935: for the Soviet Union to act on Czechoslovakia's behalf the war with Germany would have to be global.
88. Arnost Heidrich, 'International Political Causes of the Czechoslovak Tragedies' (Washington, DC: The Czechoslovak Society for Arts and Sciences in America, 1962), p.18.
89. ACC CPC, fond 100/45, Vol.10, archival unit 184. The meeting took place on the night of 20–21 August 1938. In September 1998 Professor Milan Hauner and I discussed this document at great length. The debate provided me with an opportunity to consider the possibility that the report on Zhdanov's visit was a forgery. Having given the matter serious thought I must affirm my conviction that the document from Prague archives is authentic. Importantly, I can rule out that it was fraudulently inserted into the record after the opening of the Prague archives because at least two historians had seen it already in the 1960s (Karel Kaplan and Michal Reiman). However, it is possible that the person who in 1938 came to Prague to speak on behalf of the Comintern was not the Andrei Zhdanov we know as a member of Stalin's entourage. It may have been a low-level apparatchik who happened to have the same name or it may have been a Comintern representative who used the name 'Andrei Zhdanov' as his *nom de guerre*.
90. BA-TGM, Notes for Manuscripts, box 10a.
91. ACC CPC, fond KI 20, file 85.
92. BA-TGM, Notes for Manuscripts, box 10a.
93. BA-TGM, The Second World War, box 61.
94. NA 860F.001/106, Irving N. Linnell, US Consul General, Prague, to the Secretary of State, Washington, DC, 20 Nov. 1939.
95. ACC CPC, fond 100/50, archival unit 67.

The Munich Crisis of 1938: Plans and Strategy in Warsaw in the Context of the Western Appeasement of Germany

ANNA M. CIENCIALA

Most Western historians see the Munich Crisis primarily from the perspective of British and French policy. If they read about Poland at all, it is often an unflattering mention or strong condemnation of the Polish occupation of the Cieszyn/Tesin/Teschen part of Czechoslovakia. Perhaps the best known statement about the Poles came from Winston S. Churchill: 'in 1938, over a question as minor as Teschen, they sundered themselves from ... friends in France, Great Britain and the United States. ... We see them hurrying, while the might of Germany glowered up against them, to grasp their share of the pillage and ruin of Czechoslovakia.'[1] Most other judgements of Polish foreign policy in that fateful year are also condemnatory, though for different reasons. French historians view the Polish foreign minister, Jozef Beck, much as did their diplomats and foreign ministry, that is, as a slippery character and pro-German to boot.[2] The British historian, Hugh Seton-Watson, condemned Polish policy as anti-Soviet and explained it by class interest. He claimed the Polish government of the time was afraid of revolution and land reform. It was not sympathetic to Germany, but it was ready to cooperate and aimed to seize territory from Soviet Ukraine. Seton-Watson stated later that he had changed some of his opinions since writing the book, but he did not rewrite it because he wanted it to stand as witness to the views prevalent among young Britons of his generation before and during World War II. However, this qualifier came only in the preface to the third edition and did not affect the many readers of *Eastern Europe Between the Wars* who absorbed and retained the author's negative image of this region, including Poland.[3] Of course, the view of Polish policy as based on class interest was Marxist, and was propagated by Soviet historiography for decades; it was abandoned by Russian historians after 1990, but most still condemn

Polish foreign policy of the time and consider Beck pro-German.[4] Polish historians abandoned the class interpretation after October 1956, but still condemned Beck's policy as anti-Soviet and anti-Czechoslovak; however, the period since 1989 has witnessed a trend towards a more objective evaluation.[5] The American historian, Henry L. Roberts, was near the mark when he wrote: 'Even Beck's unpleasant performance at the time of Munich was not planned in concert with the Germans ... He did not like Czechoslovakia, but he did not plot its destruction.' Roberts concluded that while Beck's policy contributed to the demise of Czechoslovakia 'the responsibility for Eastern Europe ultimately rested with the victorious powers of the first world war'.[6]

In order to understand Polish policy in 1938, one must first look at its goals and guiding principles, and then at Polish–Czechoslovak relations before that fateful year. The basic goal of Polish foreign policy was, of course, to ensure the country's security and independence. This was a daunting task since the new Poland was flanked by two out of the three great neighbours who had partitioned it between them in the late eighteenth century. Russia and Prussia – later Germany – had oppressed the Poles for over a century, and refused to accept as final their post-1919 frontiers with the reborn Polish state. Furthermore, Poland's ally, France, soon showed a desire to reduce its obligations. Thus, the Franco-Polish alliance of 1921 was much weakened by the Locarno Treaties of October 1925, whereby Germany recognized her postwar frontiers with France and Belgium – but not those with Poland and Czechoslovakia. At the same time, French military aid to Poland in case of war became dependent on League of Nations machinery. This also applied to Czechoslovakia – but unlike Poland, its security was not threatened by Germany at the time.[7]

Jozef Pilsudski (1867–1935) – who was the dominant influence on Polish political life as well as military and foreign policy from late 1918 to summer 1923, and again from May 1926 to his death nine years later – reacted to Locarno by setting Polish foreign policy the goal of restoring 'equilibrium', that is, balancing Poland's relations with Germany and the USSR. This meant good relations with both but alliance with neither: alliance with a much stronger and traditionally hostile power was seen as the first step to the loss of

Polish independence. This policy was implemented in the Polish–Soviet Nonaggression Pact of July 1932, balanced by the Polish–German Declaration of Nonaggression of January 1934, valid for ten years, after which the pact with the USSR was renewed for ten years.[8] At the same time, the Franco-Polish alliance of 1921 remained the pillar of Polish security in case of war with Germany, while the Polish–Romanian defensive alliance, signed that same year, provided some security against the Soviet Union. After Locarno, however, Pilsudski and Beck doubted that France would fulfil her obligations to Poland without British support. Therefore, they worked to achieve a *rapprochement* with Great Britain, but this policy did not yield results until late 1938.

Polish–Czechoslovak relations, though never close, were generally friendly in the years 1921–33. The high points in this relationship were the Benes–Skirmunt Pact of 6 November 1921, named after Czechoslovak Foreign Minister – later President – Edvard Benes – and Polish Foreign Minister Konstanty Skirmunt, as well as a series of treaties signed by Benes and Polish Foreign Minister Aleksander Skrzynski in April 1925. The key provisions of the Benes–Skirmunt Pact were mutual guarantees of territory; agreement to observe benevolent neutrality if one of the parties was attacked by a neighbouring state, and to ensure the passage of war supplies. Czechoslovakia declared its lack of interest in East Galicia (western Ukraine), and undertook to dissolve interned Ukrainian formations. The annex to this treaty stated that local litigations on the former plebiscite territory of Cieszyn, Spis and Orava would be resolved with the help of a special Polish–Czechoslovak delegation, while the fate of the village of Javorina (in the Spis region) would be decided in six months. The treaties signed in 1925 by Benes and Polish Foreign Minister Aleksander Skrzynski, seemed to provide for close cooperation in international affairs as well as on minority and territorial problems.[9]

However, territorial disputes were not resolved, and they remained a major stumbling bloc to closer relations. The Poles had hoped the Czechs would agree to cede Javorina to Poland and that this would blunt the widespread Polish resentment against the Czech seizure of Teschen. However, this was not to be, and a brief sketch is necessary to understand this issue. According to the Austrian census of 1910, part of the old Duchy of Teschen, just west of the Olza river, called 'Zaolzie' by the Poles – 'Trans-Olza' in English, a term which will be used in this paper – had a Polish-speaking population of about 164,000 out of a total regional population of about 230,000. In fact, on 5 November 1918, the local Polish and Czech councils had agreed on a division of the territory along ethnic lines, leaving Trans-Olza to Poland. The region was allotted a number of seats in the forthcoming elections to the Polish Constituent Assembly, scheduled for January 1919, but the Polish government decided to delay them pending an agreement on the disputed territory with the Czechoslovak government. Indeed, the Polish ethnic claim to Trans-Olza clashed with the Czech historic claim to it as part of the lands of the Bohemian Crown, for the Duchy of Teschen, at first loosely under Polish rule, had joined these lands in the mid-fourteenth century and later came under Habsburg rule along with the rest of Bohemia. In 1919–20, the Czechs also used economic arguments to back their claim to this territory, that is, that Poland would obtain Upper Silesia from Germany, so it would not need the coal and steel of Trans-Olza, also that Czechoslovakia needed the railway line joining Bohemia and Slovakia.

Jozef Pilsudski was mindful of the need for good neighbourly relations, and this is why he wanted to obtain a Polish–Czechoslovak agreement. Therefore, in December 1918, when he was Head of the Polish State (his official title pending the election of a president), he sent a small Polish delegation to Prague with a personal letter to President Tomas G. Masaryk. Pilsudski proposed the establishment of a mixed Polish–Czechoslovak commission to resolve all problems in mutual relations, though clearly Trans-Olza was the key problem. Masaryk expressed his agreement to the Polish delegation, but handed the matter over to the Czechoslovak government, which had no intention to negotiate. At the same time, Masaryk also sanctioned the seizure of the area by Czechoslovak troops in January 1919.[10]

The Poles deeply resented the Czechoslovak use of force at a time when they were facing armed Soviet expansion into Lithuania and western Belorussia and battling the Ukrainians over Lwow (Ukr. L'viv). It is true that the Western powers forced the Czechoslovak troops to withdraw, but negotiations for a plebiscite or arbitration of the dispute over Trans-Olza failed to yield agreement. Finally, in late

July 1920, a Polish delegation that had come to the Franco-British
conference at Spa to plead for Western aid against Soviet Russia,
agreed to the Czechoslovak proposal to submit the question to the
Conference of Ambassadors in Paris. The Poles expected a thorough
consideration of the problem, but the conference simply awarded
Trans-Olza to Czechoslovakia on 28 July 1920, just as the Red Army
was nearing Warsaw. It was later learned that this award resulted
from a secret deal between Edvard Benes on the one hand and French
and British officials on the other, in which Benes promised to
persuade Czech railwaymen to allow the passage of French arms and
munitions to Poland in return for the award of Trans-Olza to
Czechoslovakia.[11] It seems that he did not try very hard to fulfil this
promise because the munitions did not go through. Furthermore,
Czechoslovakia followed Germany's example by declaring its
'neutrality' on 10 August 1920, precluding the transit of any war
material to Poland. Thus Trans-Olza remained in Czech hands. The
outcome might have been different if the Poles had defeated the Red
Army in July instead of August 1920.[12]

The Trans-Olza question rankled the Poles, but it was not the
only problem in their relations with Czechoslovakia. In fact, dis-
agreements on foreign policy were equally important. In 1920, the
Czechs had opposed the award of East Galicia to Poland. They
wished it to go to Soviet Russia or to come under Czechoslovak
administration, thus establishing a common Soviet–Czechoslovak
frontier. Despite the Benes–Skirmunt treaty, Czech statesmen always
voiced their preference for an 'ethnic' Poland, meaning that eastern
Poland, especially East Galicia, should belong to Russia. As for the
Polish–German frontier, President T.G. Masaryk did not hide his
view – also widespread in western Europe and the United States –
that Danzig/Gdansk and the Polish Corridor (P. Pomorze) must return
to Germany.[13] It is true that Danzig was preponderantly German, but
as a free city it was not part of Poland, while the Polish Corridor was
preponderantly Polish – a fact little known at the time. It was strange
that these views on the desirability of an 'ethnic' Poland were
propagated by the leaders and politicians of a state that was
considerably more multi-ethnic than interwar Poland, where the
Poles formed a clear majority (68.9 per cent according to the last
interwar census of 1931). Czechoslovakia also led the 'little entente'

consisting of Czechoslovakia, Romania and Yugoslavia. This was a defensive coalition directed primarily against Hungary, while Poland maintained friendly relations with Budapest. Finally, Czechoslovakia signed an alliance with the USSR in early May 1935, complementing the Franco-Soviet alliance signed in Paris at this time. Neither could be welcome to Poland in view of its past relations with Imperial Russia and its deep distrust of Soviet Russia.

Nevertheless, as noted earlier, Polish–Czechoslovak relations were generally friendly between 1921 and 1933. There were close contacts between the two general staffs, and even talk of a military convention. However, the Czechoslovak government was not interested in an alliance or close ties with Poland.[14] Thus, T.G. Masaryk told German Foreign Minister Gustav Stresemann in March 1927 that he did not intend to take up a recent Polish suggestion for closer relations with Czechoslovakia 'for he did not want to pull Poland's chestnuts out of the fire whenever a conflict with Germany might develop'. Six years later, on 17 March 1933 in Geneva, a few days after the nazis won the elections in Germany (5 March), and the Polish government had warned the Germans against a *putsch* in Danzig by strengthening its garrison on the Westerplatte (6 March), Foreign Minister Edvard Benes told his British counterpart, Sir John Simon, that he opposed Italian revisionist claims against Yugoslavia – because he did not want Czechoslovakia to be driven into the arms of Poland. Furthermore, he claimed that he had rejected Beck's proposal of an alliance against Germany. No Polish documents have been found to confirm such a Polish offer at this time, but Beck might have proposed it, or at least sounded out Benes on such a possibility, just before Mussolini made his revisionist four power pact proposal to British Prime Minister Ramsay MacDonald and Foreign Secretary Sir John Simon in Rome on 18 March. In fact, the Polish and Czechoslovak statesmen were in Geneva in mid-March; both stayed at the hotel Beau Rivage, and each spoke with the British ministers there on the same day, 17 March, the eve of the latters' departure for Rome. Mussolini's project of a four power pact designed to carry out certain frontier revisions – which he was to propose to the British the next day – was already in the air; in fact, the Italian delegate to the League of Nations had a preliminary talk about it with MacDonald in Geneva on 14 March. It is worth noting that while Beck warned

MacDonald and Simon against tampering with the peace treaties in connection with the disarmament conference, that is, not to envisage revision of the Polish–German frontier, Benes was only concerned with Italy. Indeed, according to the British record, he told Simon on 17 March that he 'had no serious fears as regards Germany; there was no issue between the two countries'.[15]

Whether or not Beck had proposed an alliance to Benes in March 1933, he sounded him out on closer relations almost a year later. On 20 January 1934, again in Geneva, he proposed to Benes a general discussion of all outstanding problems. According to the Polish record, Benes declared that he was ready for such a discussion. He said further that since Czechoslovakia had no quarrel with Germany, it would only come into conflict with the latter in case of a Franco-German war. Thus, he was confident that Prague had nothing to fear from Berlin. He did not, however, welcome such a state of affairs in Polish–German relations. Speaking of the Polish–German Declaration of Nonaggression – signed four days after his conversation with Beck – he told the British minister in Prague, Sir Joseph Addison, that it was 'a stab in the back', that 'Poland had always been a useless country' and 'a historical nuisance'. He also declared that history would repeat itself and Poland would deserve another partition. Addison wondered whether he was listening to Benes or to Goebbels.[16]

Benes' comments stemmed from the view, shared by many contemporary observers, that the Polish–German declaration was a significant breach in the French alliance system. Few realized that the agreements signed by France with Poland and Czechoslovakia at Locarno in October 1926 had turned that system into an empty shell. Still, if Benes had really rejected a Polish offer of alliance in 1933, he missed a chance to strengthen what was left. Whatever the case may be, and setting aside the personal animosity existing between Beck and Benes as well as the general ill-feeling existing between the two countries, it is clear that Czech leaders never wanted close relations with Poland, not wishing to share the burden of that country's difficult relations with Soviet Russia, and especially the tension with Germany, though this was largely muted in the years 1934–38. In a note written in mid-June 1938, Minister Arnost Heidrich, chief of the political department in the Czechoslovak foreign ministry, wrote to Foreign Minister Kamil Krofta that in the past the Czechoslovak government had not wanted to tie itself to Poland because the latter seemed much more threatened by Germany than Czechoslovakia. Here he mentioned 'the acute danger of a conflict over the Corridor'.[17] Fundamentally, the statesmen of each country believed that if they were involved in a war with Germany, France was much more likely to come to their country's aid than to the other's. However, it was also a cardinal article of faith in each country's foreign policy that if Germany attacked the other and France declared war on Germany, they would have to align themselves with Paris, bury the hatchet, and fight alongside each other, much as both disliked such a prospect. In December 1933, Jules Laroche, the French ambassador in Warsaw, reported Beck's opinion that Austria and Czechoslovakia could not survive without the support of the Western powers, as to which they expressed great doubt. However, Laroche also expressed his belief that Pilsudski and Beck would change their minds if they saw a France determined to draw the sword. Likewise, in December 1933, Benes told a Polish diplomat that if a war should break out between France and Poland on the one side and Germany on the other, Czechoslovakia would immediately join France and Poland, for a German victory would be logically followed by the complete destruction of Czechoslovakia.[18] Thus, French policy toward Germany was the key to the policies of each state towards Berlin, as well as towards each other.

When the Czechoslovak crisis began in spring 1938, Anglo-French appeasement of Germany had already allowed Hitler to start rearming in the spring of 1935; he had abolished the demilitarized zone in the western Rhineland March in 1936, and annexed Austria in March 1938. As far as Warsaw's knowledge of British policy was concerned, the Polish government had been informed by the Germans in early December 1937 of Lord Halifax's statements to Hitler of the previous month, except for the statement on Danzig. Indeed, in November 1937 the British statesman had told the Führer that Great Britain would *not* oppose the union of Austria and the Sudetenland with Germany, or the return of Danzig to Germany, provided all this was done peacefully. In January 1938, Beck learned of German plans to destroy Czechoslovakia. At this time, he also heard from Churchill that the Western powers would not fight for

Austria, but would fight for Czechoslovakia.[19] However, Churchill's view became more than questionable in late March 1938, when British Prime Minister Neville Chamberlain declared that Great Britain would not guarantee Czechoslovakia.[20]

As the crisis intensified, Beck kept his options open. He held to the Polish position, first communicated to Prague in February 1937, that any concessions made by the Czechoslovak government to the Sudeten Germans should be followed by the same concessions to the Polish population in Trans-Olza. While the disparity in numbers between the two minorities gives this claim a demagogic appearance, it is a fact that there was an almost unanimous demand by Polish public opinion for the return of Trans-Olza to Poland. Beck's strategy was to pursue this aim without committing Poland to Germany. It is worth noting that the Polish demand of equal treatment was supported by the British and French governments in their desire to defuse Polish pressure on Prague. This pressure resulted in early May in a declaration to Beck by the Czechoslovak minister in Warsaw, Juraj Slavik, that the Polish minority would receive the same concessions as those granted to any other minority.[21] Thus Prague conceded the key Polish demand. (Other Polish grievances concerned Polish communist and Comintern activity in Czechoslovakia as well as transit difficulties).

Sometime in the late spring or early summer of 1938, Beck outlined his views to the Polish cabinet. According to his memoirs, he saw the situation as follows: The Czechs would not fight; the Western powers were unprepared to help them; and the Soviet Union would limit itself to demonstrations. He believed that the USSR preferred to compromise Czechoslovak and French relations with Germany rather than engage in any military action itself. He also noted that, though some Soviet planes had flown over Romania to Czechoslovakia, there were no visible Soviet military preparations for intervention, and, in any case, the Red Army was in a parlous state after the purge of its higher officers. Finally, Beck stated that, whatever happened, Poland should not be the first to take action against Czechoslovakia, and that if his basic hypothesis were negated by the facts Polish foreign policy would have to change radically within 24 hours, for in case of a European war against Germany Poland could not, even indirectly, side with the latter. (It should be noted that according to the Franco-

Polish military convention of March 1921, each country was to aid the other if it was attacked by Germany, though French aid sent to Poland was to be in the form of supplies and technical equipment, not troops).[22]

In this account, Beck did not spell out what Poland should do if his basic hypothesis proved correct, that is, if the Western powers abandoned Czechoslovakia without a war. His policy objectives in such a case are to be found in notes made at various times by Deputy Foreign Minister Jan Szembek and in instructions given to Polish diplomats abroad. On this basis, it clear that Beck believed Poland should use the opportunity provided by the Czechoslovak crisis to secure three objectives: (1) parlay her 'neutrality' towards Germany in return for the latter's official recognition of the Polish–German frontier as well as specific German recognition of the status of the Free City of Danzig. (2) Poland should establish a common frontier with Hungary in Subcarpathian Ruthenia as the foundation of a projected bloc called the 'Third Europe'. This was to consist of Poland, Hungary, Romania and possibly Yugoslavia; its function would be to prevent German – or Soviet – domination of eastern Europe. (Mussolini, who wished to prevent German expansion into the Balkans, favoured the project and hinted at supporting it.) Finally, if there was a peaceful settlement whereby Czechoslovakia lost the Sudetenland to Germany, objective (3) was to regain Trans-Olza. The first and third objectives were not new but were crystallized in 1938, while the second was a reformulation of the earlier Polish goal of creating an east European federation led by Poland. (This goal was shared by General Wladyslaw Sikorski, head of the Polish government-in-exile and Polish armed forces from late September 1939 until his death in July 1943, though he envisaged the first step in a federation or confederation between Poland and Czechoslovakia.)[23] A good illustration of the early stages of Beck's 'Third Europe' project is to be found in the instructions given on 18 April 1938 by Jan Szembek to the new Polish ambassador to Romania, Roger Raczynski. Szembek said he did not believe the Western powers would defend Czechoslovakia and told the ambassador to work for a Romanian–Hungarian understanding, saying a new power system needed to emerge in the region between Germany and Russia. From other documents it is clear that the Polish

government wanted to prevent a German seizure of the whole of
Czechoslovakia if, as they expected, the Western powers would not
defend it. They did not want to have German forces on Poland's
southern as well as western frontiers; rather, they wanted
Subcarpathian Ruthenia to go to Hungary so as to provide a common
Polish–Hungarian frontier. As for Slovakia, Beck first considered
independence, but later favoured extensive Slovak autonomy in
Hungary.[24]

As the crisis intensified, most of the Polish press kept up a
drumbeat of accusations against the Czechoslovak government,
alleging severe mistreatment of the Polish minority in Trans-Olza. It
is true that pressure was exerted on these people by Czech authorities
to send their children to Czech schools and to declare Czechoslovak
or 'Silesian' nationality, but assimilationist policies were common in
borderland regions at the time. Such a policy was pursued by Polish
authorities toward the Germans of Upper Silesia and by German
authorities toward the Poles on the German side of the
Polish–German border. Each of the three countries pursued this type
of policy in ethnically mixed regions in order to bolster its claims to
'self-determination'. At the same time, the anti-Czechoslovak press
campaign, which also accused Czechoslovakia of being an outpost of
Soviet communism, was used to exert pressure on Prague and
simultaneously increase public support for the government's policy.
As for Polish opposition parties that condemned Beck's Czechoslovak
policy after the partition of Poland between Germany and Russia in
1939, all of them except the Polish Communist Party, also demanded
the return of Trans-Olza at the time. A somewhat different approach
was signalled by a small political group called 'Front Morges' – so
named after Ignacy Jan Paderewski's residence in Switzerland –
which was headed by General Wladyslaw Sikorski. In the spring of
1938, a spokesman for the Front told a Czech journalist sent by
Benes to sound out Polish political parties that if it came to power it
would offer an alliance to Prague, but only in return for a Czech
promise to cede Trans-Olza to Poland. This reflected the fact that
Polish opinion was practically unanimous in demanding this region.[25]

Meanwhile, Beck refused to be drawn either into cooperation or
confrontation with Germany. He rejected both German proposals of
coordinated economic pressure on Czechoslovakia, and repeated

French proposals that Poland should warn Berlin against using force to solve the Sudeten problem. However, in late May 1938, while refusing to support the peace efforts of London and Paris with a diplomatic Polish intervention in Berlin, he confirmed to French Foreign Minister Georges Bonnet, as he had done in March 1936, Poland's readiness to fulfil its alliance obligations to France, that is, if the latter went to war with Germany. He also expressed readiness to engage in a 'friendly discussion of all new phenomena in Central Europe, based on a mutual understanding of the interests of France and Poland', but Bonnet did not take up the offer. Later, Beck tried to inform the Western powers of his policy confidentially so as not to provoke Germany, and to elicit some reply. He did this mainly through the US ambassador in Warsaw, Anthony J. Drexel Biddle, whom he trusted and considered a personal friend (the feeling was mutual). In a long report dated 18 June 1938, Biddle cited Beck as saying that Poland would not agree to a German march through Polish territory into Soviet Ukraine. On the contrary, said Beck, she would resist such a German move because it would mean the end of Polish independence. He also said that in such a conflict Poland would be defeated but France and Britain would have to fight Germany and would finally defeat it. Biddle also reported Beck as saying that the combined armies of Poland, Romania, and possibly Yugoslavia, could present a potentially effective resistance to German aggression eastward if British and French forces simultaneously engaged German forces in the west. If this happened, Beck said, 'Poland would march not for Czechoslovakia, but against Germany'. Finally, Biddle reported Polish hopes that, after exhausting all chances of reaching a settlement with Germany, Britain and France would support a neutral Baltic–Black Sea or Baltic–Aegean bloc led by Poland that would thwart any German drive eastward.[26] Two and a half months later, on 31 August, Sir Robert Vansittart, then chief diplomatic adviser to the British foreign office, took note of a statement reportedly made by a member of Marshal Edward Smigly-Rydz's entourage. (The marshal was commander-in-chief of the Polish army.) This unnamed person stated that Polish policy would depend on the Western powers: if they came to Czechoslovakia's assistance, Poland would fight on their side, but if they did not, she would annex her share of Czechoslovakia.[27] Beck's proposal to

Bonnet, his statements to Ambassador Drexel Biddle, and the statement noted by Vansittart, show that the Polish foreign minister was, indeed, prepared to carry out a radical change of policy if the Western powers decided on war with Germany. However, these proposals and statements did not elicit any reaction from British and French governments that were bent on averting war by appeasing Germany.

The Czechoslovak crisis began to intensify in mid-September. After Chamberlain's first meeting with Hitler at Berchtesgaden, the French and British governments transmitted the Führer's demands to Prague on 19 September 1938, that is, that the Sudetenland be handed over to Germany. After the Berchtesgaden meeting, the Polish and Hungarian governments demanded plebiscites for their minorities but were unsuccessful. Benes first refused the Franco-British demand, but faced an ultimatum on 21 September 1938 – either to accept or face Germany alone. He accepted.[28] At this time, a small Polish military force began to assemble on the Polish border with Trans-Olza, but it never went into action since Warsaw's demands were finally accepted by Prague. It is interesting that before this occurred there was a discussion in the Polish general staff on the possibility of using this force to support Czechoslovakia in case of war between the latter and Germany.[29] At the same time, as recent Polish publications reveal, there was another, parallel facet of Polish policy that had remained virtually unknown. The new sources show that the Polish government had pursued secret intelligence-gathering activities in Trans-Olza, made efforts to build up secret Polish organizations there since 1935, and tried to organize guerrilla groups in summer 1938. On 23–24 September 1938, orders were given to the so-called 'battle units' of Trans-Olza Poles and to the 'Trans-Olza Legion' made up of volunteers being assembled from all over the country to cross into that territory and attack Czech strong points. However, the few that did so were repulsed by well-prepared Czech troops and retreated to Poland. Sporadic attempts by local Poles to start an uprising also failed. Thus, the effort to produce a 'popular uprising' in Trans-Olza, or at least a convincing demonstration by local Poles, was a complete fiasco. This secret Polish policy, partly modelled on the methods of Konrad Henlein's Sudetendeutsche Partei (SDP), was designed to show local support for the union of

Trans-Olza with Poland. However, without the SDP's numbers and financial resources the Poles had no chance of mounting such a demonstration. Furthermore, while there had been sporadic cooperation between Polish and SDP politicians in Czechoslovakia, in September SDP propaganda was claiming the region for Germany, so there was danger of a local or even a Polish–German clash over the territory.[30]

At this critical time, President Edvard Benes undertook two diplomatic actions regarding Poland. First, he wrote a letter, dated 22 September 1938, to Polish President Ignacy Moscicki, proposing 'a frank and friendly discussion' of all mutual differences regarding the Polish population of Czechoslovakia. He stated that he wished to resolve them on the principle of frontier rectification. An agreement would, he believed, lead to a new period of mutual relations.[31] However, the letter did not reach Moscicki until 26 September 1938. It is true that on the previous day Poland had imposed a transport stoppage between the two countries but the Czechoslovak government were informed that an air courier would be admitted at any time. Thus, it would appear that Benes had decided to delay sending the letter in hopes of a change of attitude in London and Paris. Indeed, after Chamberlain's second meeting with Hitler at Bad Godesberg, the British cabinet decided that the Führer's demands were unacceptable, that is, for the German army's occupation of the Sudetenland by 1 October 1938, with a plebiscite to be held only afterwards. Therefore, on the evening of 25 September 1938, the British and French governments informed Prague that it could proceed with mobilization.[32]

Benes now took a related action: he requested Soviet support in restraining Poland. Indeed, a Soviet verbal note to Warsaw on 23 September 1938 warned that any Polish aggression against Czechoslovakia would mean the abrogation of the Polish–Soviet Nonaggression Pact.[33] It is worth noting that the Polish government had already taken steps to warn the Soviet leadership against any attempt to send the Red Army across south-eastern Poland to Czechoslovakia, for the Polish army had carried out manoeuvres in eastern Poland on 5–19 September 1938. Whether or not Benes' appeal played a role in the Soviet mobilization that followed, Russian military documents show that about 330,000 troops were mobilized

in the period 23–28 September, with a supplemental mobilization –
perhaps another 300,000 men – ordered on 29 September 1938.
They were concentrated in the western regions of Soviet Belorussia
and Soviet Ukraine. Furthermore, Marshal Kliment E. Voroshilov
reported on 28 September 1938 that a total of 548 Soviet planes
would be ready in two days to fly, if necessary, to Czechoslovakia.
However, no Russian directives for action have been found thus far,
though one Polish historian claims that the Poles managed later to
reconstruct the first move in the Soviet 'Odre de Bataille'.[34]

The Soviet mobilization might have been designed less as a means
of putting pressure on Poland than of stiffening Czechoslovak
resistance, perhaps to the point of war. Indeed, this was suggested in
both a Comintern message to the Czechoslovak Communist Party
sent in spring 1938, and by Andrei A. Zhdanov, a secretary of the
CPSU central committee and a man close to Stalin. When he met
secretly with Czech communist leaders in Prague in late August that
year, he encouraged them to avoid a peaceful solution. War, they
were told, was necessary to build a communist society in
Czechoslovakia as well as to create favourable conditions for a
communist offensive in Europe. Zhdanov also said that in the
Czechoslovak Communist Party's struggle first against Hitler and
then capitalism, they would be assisted by the Red Army, which
would 'represent a great political factor in this conflict'.[35] On the
basis of the statements reported above it is possible to speculate that
the Soviet mobilization was meant to encourage the Czechoslovak
communists to oppose a peaceful solution of the Sudeten crisis and
press the government to fight. (Indeed, they agitated strongly for
rejection of the Munich terms on 30 September.) It is also possible to
speculate that if Czechoslovakia had refused the Munich 'dictate',
thereby incurring a German attack and a Franco-German war, thus
forcing Hitler to concentrate his troops in the west, then Stalin might
have acted as he was to do in September 1939, that is, use his
mobilized forces to enter eastern Poland and annex it without
becoming involved in a war with Germany. This view finds indirect
support in some Czechoslovak documents. Thus, when Benes asked
for Soviet support of his letter to President Moscicki, the
Czechoslovak minister in the USSR, Zdenek Fierlinger, reported
Moscow advice *against* entering into negotiations with Poland. He

expected that in the event of a 'favourable development', the USSR would try to establish a common border with Czechoslovakia. He wrote that the Soviet Union was 'resolved not to leave Warsaw's behaviour toward us without punishment. They do not doubt that the hour of reckoning will arise'.[36] Finally, in view of past allegations that in 1938 Poland refused the passage of Soviet troops to aid Czechoslovakia, it is worth noting that there is no record of any official Soviet proposal or demand on Poland to this effect. There are, however, strong indications that the Romanian government and army would not have resisted such passage through part of Romania's territory in case of war, and it would be surprising if the Soviet government were unaware of this attitude.[37]

Meanwhile Benes' letter to Moscicki was delivered on 26 September 1938, preceded by a Czechoslovak offer to start immediate negotiations and accompanied by a Franco-British note expressing hope that Poland would accept his proposal. However, Warsaw viewed it as part of Benes' policy to avoid territorial losses. In fact, the Czechoslovak president was under pressure from France and Britain to secure Polish neutrality by agreeing to negotiate with Poland over Trans-Olza with the goal of territorial cession, which Benes tried to avert or at least put off as long as possible.[38] Warsaw also suspected him of inspiring the Soviet note. President Moscicki answered Benes with a courteous letter stating that the time had come for 'a courageous decision on territorial questions'.[39] At the same time, the Polish note to Prague of 27 September 1938 demanded the immediate conclusion of an agreement whereby indisputably Polish territory should be occupied by Polish troops; this was to be followed by an agreement on plebiscites in districts with a strong percentage of Polish population.[40] However, this Polish note went unanswered until 30 September 1938.

It should also be noted that the Polish government learned that the town of Bohumin with its important railway junction – the Polish claim to which was known to Hitler – was marked for cession to Germany on the map used at the Chamberlain–Hitler meeting at Godesberg (22–23 September). Furthermore, a large part of the territory in which Poland was interested was marked by the Germans for a plebiscite. Therefore, Beck instructed Ambassador Jozef Lipski to clarify the matter with the German government. He warned that this was necessary in order to avoid a political or military conflict between Poland and Germany. The result was German agreement on 28 September 1938 not to claim Bohumin, and a promise to consult Poland on eventual plebiscites in the Frydek and Moravska-Ostrava regions.[41]

As is known, France and Britain agreed to hand over the Sudetenland to Hitler at the Munich Conference held on 29 September. In the wee hours of the morning of 30 September two Czechoslovak diplomats, who had not been allowed to participate, were informed of the decision, first by members of the foreign office, and then by a sleepy Chamberlain. The Sudetenland was to be ceded immediately to Germany but the Polish and Hungarian claims were to be settled within three months. After that, what remained of Czechoslovakia would receive an international guarantee.[42] Beck's reactions to news of the Munich decisions are recounted in the unpublished memoirs of Michal Lubienski, his chef de cabinet, that is the head of his office with whom he worked most closely.

Lubienski writes:

> When the news arrived that evening Beck called me in to see him and we spent a long time discussing whether we should mobilize in defense of Czechoslovakia. Beck also discussed this matter with the chief of [the general] staff. Finally, we heard the decision: "This could have been done if there had been certainty that the Czechs wanted to fight." And yet not only was this certainty lacking, but our information led us to conclude that the Czechs would break down completely.[43]

A few years ago, I wrote that there was no corroboration of Lubienski's account, but I had overlooked the published memoirs of Beck's private secretary Pawel Starzenski.[44] In fact, except for two minor variations, the latter's account corroborates the former. Starzenski writes that when he arrived that day at Beck's apartment shortly before 9 am the minister told him: 'You see how they have treated us again. They settled German matters among themselves, without our participation. We will not wait for three months. I have just talked to Smigly. We are sending the Czechs an ultimatum.'[45] He differs from Lubienski only in stating that Beck had spoken with the commander-in-chief of the army, Marshal Edward Smigly-Rydz, and not with the chief of the general staff, General Waclaw Stachiewicz. Indeed, it would be natural for Beck to have spoken with both of them, though the marshal was clearly the more important of the two. Lubienski also writes of speaking to Beck 'that evening', but this might have been a slip of memory for the early hours of the morning. In fact, the news of the Munich agreement reached Warsaw through a broadcast by the German state radio (DNB) at 2 am on 30 September 1938, which is also how Benes learned the news in Prague, so it is likely that Lubienski was called in to see Beck in the early morning on 30 September 1938. Whatever the case may be, he probably saw the minister before Starzenski arrived. Thus the two officials closest to Beck confirm that he followed the policy he had outlined in his statements at the cabinet meeting (probably in early summer 1938), and to Anthony J. Drexel Biddle in June 1938. Finally, no special Polish military plans were needed for Poland to go to war with Germany. If Czechoslovakia had fought and France had gone to war with Germany, Poland would have gone to war with the latter according to the Franco-Polish Military Convention of February 1921. Even a Polish historian very critical of Beck's policy in 1938 admits that a complete reorientation of Polish policy in an anti-German direction was very likely if France became engaged in war with Germany.[46]

The Polish government's decision to send an ultimatum to Prague should be viewed in the context of deep resentment that Poland had not been invited to the Munich Conference although her interests were directly involved, fear that Germany would soon annex the rest of Czechoslovakia, and fear of a new four power pact on the lines proposed by Mussolini in mid-March 1933. Indeed, the Poles vividly remembered this proposal, which aimed at setting up a great power directorate to revise certain European frontiers, and which they had strongly opposed. Beck was ready for action, but waited cautiously until news came of Benes' decision to accept the Munich dictate that was announced at 12.30 pm that day. Half an hour later, Kazimienz Papée, the Polish minister in Prague, received the Czechoslovak reply to the Polish note of 27 September. He communicated it immediately to Warsaw, where it arrived at 1 pm. The Czechs proposed that negotiations begin immediately, be completed by 31 October 1938, and that the territory be handed over to Poland no later than 1

December. This was judged inadequate in Warsaw.[47] On the afternoon of 30 September 1938, a cabinet meeting was held at which Beck proposed military action. Eugeniusz Kwiatkowski, deputy premier and minister of finances, made notes of the meeting. He writes:

> [Beck] claimed – not without justice – that what had happened at Munich, and was reminiscent of the plan for a "Four Power Pact" of a few years ago, could become a very dangerous precedent also in regard to Poland's vital interests. We should – in his view – quickly and quite drastically take a stand against such methods of resolving territorial conflicts [by] evoking the phantom of a war which is not very likely [to occur] in this case. Only such a determined and courageous step by Poland can save it from a new Munich. Furthermore, the close geographic proximity of Germany forces Poland to take immediate action. If we hesitate and delay, Germany may seize this valuable and highly industrialized patch of land, eliminating Polish claims to Trans-Olza for a long time to come. Finally, said Beck, we have long been demanding, and have received, the Czechoslovak government's agreement in principle to the equal treatment of Polish claims and the rights granted by Czechoslovakia to its German minority. Today, when the Prague government is ceding to the Reich territories inhabited by Germans, and this with the approval of the Western Powers, we must resolutely demand an analogous solution to Poland's small but justified claim.

Kwiatkowski writes that all participants at the meeting agreed in principle with these arguments, but there was a sharp clash when he opposed presenting the Polish demands as an ultimatum. He argued for normal diplomatic procedures so as to prevent Poland's identification with Germany, avoid disharmony with Western friends, and avert creating a dangerous pretext for Soviet intervention. In the end, however, he was overruled.[48]

Thus, the Polish government issued an ultimatum to Prague. It was delivered by Polish Minister Papée at 11.40 pm on 30 September 1938, that is, 11 hours after the Czechoslovak government's acceptance of the Munich dictate. The Polish note rejected the Czechoslovak proposal of negotiations and demanded the immediate cession of the preponderantly Polish areas of Trans-Olza, leaving other claims to be settled by negotiation. An answer was demanded by midday on 1 October. Papée telephoned at 11.30 am that day transmitting Prague's request for a one-hour delay for the answer, which was granted. At 11.45 he telephoned again reporting the Czechoslovak acceptance of the ultimatum. At about the same time, Beck rejected the Franco-British appeal for Polish–Czechoslovak negotiations, as well as Neville Chamberlain's personal offer to him of British mediation, an offer communicated to Lubienski by British Ambassador Sir Howard Kennard at 8.30 am. At 11 am Lubienski met with the latter and with French Ambassador Leon Noël; he told them that the Polish government could not accept the British mediation offer 'as it was too late'. This bald statement was, however, soon followed by an expression of appreciation from Beck to Kennard.[49] In view of long-standing Polish efforts to achieve a *rapprochement* with Britain, it is possible to speculate that a British mediation offer might have been accepted before the Munich conference but was judged unacceptable afterwards, as was President Franklin Roosevelt's appeal to Beck that same day (1 October), to settle the dispute with Czechoslovakia through peaceful negotiations.[50] Thus it was that after agreeing to the Czech request for a 24-hour delay in evacuating the first part of the territory, Polish troops and authorities entered Trans-Olza on 2 October 1938. Later negotiations led to the cession of a few other areas in Orava, in the Beskid mountains, as well as in Spis, and Cadca in the Tatra mountains. The latter area, demanded by Poland to secure a mountain pass, was granted in protocols signed by a mixed Polish–Czechoslovak commission in Mistek on 23 November and 9 December 1939. It included three Slovak villages: Skalite, Cerne and Svercinovec, which led to great Slovak resentment. Altogether, Poland gained 869 square kilometres of land with a mixed but preponderantly Polish-speaking population of about 258,000, though some areas had Czech majorities. The economic significance of the territory can be gauged from the fact that between October 1938 and September 1939 Trans-Olza produced 52.2 per cent of Poland's coke (anthracite), 67 per cent of its pig iron, and 38 per cent of its steel.[51]

Ultimately, Beck failed to achieve any of his goals save the return of Trans-Olza to Poland. His proposed deal with Hitler, that is, Polish neutrality in a German–Czechoslovak war in exchange for Berlin's recognition of the Polish–German frontier and the status of the Free City of Danzig and the extension of the declaration of nonaggression beyond ten years, was not considered seriously in Berlin because it was quite clear that the Western powers would not fight for Czechoslovak possession of the Sudetenland.[52] As for the 'Third Europe', it failed to materialize due to a combination of factors: (1) German opposition to a common Polish–Hungarian frontier; (2) Romanian refusal to join the bloc, a refusal abetted by France but based on fear of a German-supported Hungarian attempt to regain Transylvania; (3) Mussolini's lack of resolve to support the project against German wishes; and (4) lack of support by Great Britain. Henry L. Roberts called the Third Europe a '*jejeune* [childish] project' – but was it?[53] A few months later, in spring and summer 1939, the British and French governments tried to construct an eastern bloc based on Poland and Romania in order to deter further German expansion. The British guarantee to Poland, joined by France and followed in April by guarantees to Romania and Greece, were the key elements of such a bloc. The aim of this policy, however, was not to build a barrier against German expansion, for the two powers did not even have contingency plans to give military help to the countries concerned and did not want to do so, but to deter Hitler from further aggression. This was to be achieved in return for a negotiated settlement of German demands, while also fulfilling the cardinal British requirement that this should be accomplished by peaceful means. As it turned out, however, Hitler was determined to go to war.

It is important to emphasize a key factor in appeasement that most historians seem to underestimate but which Beck always had to keep in mind. This was the British view that central and south-eastern Europe were not a sphere of vital interests; indeed, the region was viewed as the natural sphere of German interests. (The exception was Greece). Concomitant to this view, and underpinning it, was widespread sympathy for Germany, seen as most unjustly treated by the Treaty of Versailles, which in turn fuelled support for the revision of Polish–German frontiers at Poland's expense.[54] As for British military plans, they were dictated by the imperatives of defending the British Isles and the overseas empire, not central and south-eastern

Europe. In 1938, the chiefs of staff held that Britain could not fight both Italy and Germany in Europe and, simultaneously, Japan in the Far East. However, at least one historian has argued that these views, as well as those of dominion governments – which opposed war over the Sudetenland – and British unpreparedness for war were not decisive for Neville Chamberlain, whose policy was dominated by his own peace agenda.[55] However that may be, it is a fact that until late March 1939 British military leaders and politicians had always rejected the option of a peacetime alliance with France along with guarantees for its east European allies, even though such a coalition would have relieved Britain from the burden of facing Germany and Italy alone. The standard justification for rejecting this course of action was that Great Britain would lose control of its foreign policy to France. It can be argued, however, that the bedrock for this rejection was the abovementioned conviction that central and south-eastern Europe (except for Greece) was not a sphere of vital British interest. This view predated Hitler's accession to power, after which it served to underpin British appeasement policy. A good example of the prevailing British attitude is to be found in a passage of Lord Halifax's letter of 1 November 1938 to the British ambassador in Paris, Sir Eric Phipps. In outlining his – and Chamberlain's – views on post-Munich Europe, Halifax wrote: 'Henceforward, we must count with German predominance in central Europe. Incidentally, I have always felt myself that, once Germany recovered her normal strength, this predominance was inevitable for obvious geographical and economic reasons.'[56] It was, of course, on this assumption that Halifax had made his statements to Hitler in November 1937 regarding British willingness to see peaceful border changes in central Europe.

Where Britain led, France followed. It is true that most French statesmen and French public opinion did not want to fight a war with Germany over Czechoslovakia in 1938 and were lukewarm at best about fighting for Poland in 1939. Aside from the fresh memory of France's devastating loss of life in World War I, this attitude stemmed mainly from the conviction that France could not fight Germany alone, that is, without British support; such a war was ruled out by all French governments and by the French public. Thus, the policy of appeasement, led by Britain, allowed Hitler to annex Austria, the

Sudetenland, then the Czech lands, and to set up a German satellite in Slovakia, while also encouraging him to expect the 'peaceful' return of Danzig and the Polish Corridor. Indeed, Neville Chamberlain and most of his cabinet members hoped to the last that Hitler would agree to get what he wanted from Poland by 'peaceful' negotiation, assuming that Poland would give in, and thus peace would be saved, at least for a while.[57]

In following this policy toward central Europe, British statesmen and foreign office officials ignored the warning sounded in early 1925 by James W. Headlam-Morley, historical adviser to the foreign office. He had played a significant role in working out the Versailles Treaty articles on the Free City of Danzig in 1919 and always defended it, though not the division of Upper Silesia between Poland and Germany. He had much sympathy for the Germans, but always bore the balance-of-power principle in mind, along with the lessons of German expansion in World War I. In February 1925, he opposed linking the revision of the Polish–German frontier with a Western security pact guaranteeing French and Belgian frontiers with Germany, as proposed by some colleagues in the foreign office. In contrast to this project, Headlam-Morley wrote:

> Has anyone attempted to realize what would happen if there were to be a new partition of Poland, or if the Czechoslovak State were to be so curtailed and dismembered that in fact it disappeared from the face of Europe? The whole of Europe would be at once in chaos ... Imagine for instance, that under some improbable condition Austria rejoined Germany, that Germany using the discontented minority in Bohemia, demanded a new frontier far over the mountains, including Carlsbad and Pilsen, and at the same time, in alliance with Germany, the Hungarians recovered the southern slopes of the Carpathian mountains. This would be catastrophic, and even if we neglected to intervene to prevent it happening, we should be driven to intervene, probably too late.[58]

Unfortunately, the views of Headlam-Morley, who died in 1929, were shared by only a handful of prominent Englishmen, and that only after Hitler came to power. They included Neville Chamberlain's older half-brother Sir Austen Chamberlain (foreign secretary 1924–29), Winston Churchill, and Sir Robert Vansittart, permanent undersecretary of state for foreign affairs in 1930–38.[59] Churchill was out of the government from 1929 to 1939, though very vocal in warning against Germany; Sir Austen Chamberlain died in 1936, and Neville Chamberlain removed Vansittart from his post in early 1938, to be succeeded by Sir Alexander Cadogan. The latter, like the prime minister and Lord Halifax, also considered central and eastern Europe as a natural sphere of German interests, provided Britain had free access for trade, even though her trade with this part of the world was insignificant. In mid-October 1938, Cadogan wrote:

> We must cut our losses in central and Eastern Europe – let Germany, if she can, find there her 'lebensraum', and establish herself, if she can, as a powerful economic unit. I don't know that that necessarily worsens our commercial and economic outlook. I have never heard that Mr. Gordon Selfridge ruined Harrods. (Oddly enough, small shops flourish under the shadow of both of them). I know that it is said that "Mitteleuropa will turn and rend us". But many things may happen before that.[60]

Cadogan was at least aware of warnings – most probably from Vansittart – that German domination of central Europe would prove fatal both to France and Britain, but he did not see it as a real and present danger in late 1938.

The Czechoslovak crisis of 1938 demonstrated more clearly than before Britain's domination of French policy. French leaders had, in the past, fully realized the strategic importance of Czechoslovakia as part of their eastern alliance system that was designed to contain Germany. Poland was the other key pillar of this system and the cooperation of these two countries against Germany had been the perennial goal of French policy. The fact that this cooperation failed to materialize was due primarily not to the personal animosities between Benes and Beck, or the national animosities over Trans-Olza, and radically different attitudes towards the USSR, though each of these played an important part. It was primarily due to the cardinal assumption by the leaders of each country that they could not resist Germany without a guarantee of French help and that this help most likely would be given to their country, not the other. French diplomacy was unable to resolve this problem, mainly because its leaders assumed that France could not be involved in another war with Germany without British support.

When Germany threatened Czechoslovakia in 1938, Benes tried to win time with concessions to the Sudeten Germans, while banking on a French decision to fight if Germany attacked his country. Meanwhile, Beck trimmed Polish sails to follow in Germany's wake but was ready to throw the rudder hard right if Britain and France decided to stand up to Hitler. He also planned to create a new east European bloc called the 'Third Europe' – though Polish diplomats referred to it as 'the Danubian problem' – to prevent further German expansion. According to Ambassador Lipski, in early September 1938, Beck 'laid much more stress on the settlement of the Danubian problem than on the Teschen Silesia question, which he considered to be just a starting point'.[61] But here, too, success depended on Western or at least Italian support. Beck's judgement that the Soviet Union was more likely to try and compromise French and Czechoslovak relations with Germany than take any armed action itself – a view shared by Polish military experts on the USSR – seems borne out by the available evidence, though key Russian documents on the issue, such as Politburo materials on foreign policy and records of secret discussions by Stalin and his closest advisers, are still inaccessible.

In view of all that is known today about Polish, Western and Soviet policy during the Czechoslovak crisis, it is unrealistic to claim that if Beck had followed a different policy, that is, if he had supported French warnings to Berlin and had not pressed for the return of Trans-Olza, the outcome of the Czechoslovak crisis would have been very different. First, as far as Poland was concerned, it must be borne in mind that Polish public opinion and the army were unanimous in demanding Trans-Olza for Poland. It is therefore most unlikely that any other Polish government at this time, for example one led by General Wladyslaw, would have stood by Czechoslovakia without at least a solemn promise by Prague to cede Trans-Olza to Poland. Second, even if Beck had not exerted pressure on Prague to give up this territory, it is most unlikely that Hitler would have given up his goal of seizing the Sudetenland and thus crippling Czechoslovakia, for it was clear that France and Britain would not fight over this issue, and that the USSR clearly wanted to stay out of any European war. Third, if Beck or any other Polish statesman had proposed to Prague common Polish–Czechoslovak military action against Germany in 1938, regardless of French support, it is most unlikely that Benes would have accepted the offer, just as Beck rejected the option of war with Germany without a simultaneous Franco-British or at least French war with Germany in the West. Of course, in hindsight, it is clear that if Beck had agreed to negotiations with Prague, possibly mediated by Britain, then Poland would have avoided the onus of stabbing Czechoslovakia in the back, and perhaps avoided decades of ill-feeling on the part of the Czechs, to whom Stalin granted the region in 1945. In practical terms, however, it seems that a negotiated solution of this kind might have been possible only before the Munich Conference and not after it. In sum, Beck followed a pragmatic policy in the context of Western appeasement of Germany and of Poland's precarious situation *vis-à-vis* the latter, while keeping open the option of alignment with the Western powers in case of war. The results of this policy were certainly regrettable, but they did not decide the fate of Czechoslovakia. Finally, Beck's concept of an east European bloc to stem further German expansion foreshadowed British and French policy in the spring and summer of 1939, though the latter came too little and too late.

University of Kansas

NOTES

This is a revised version of the paper read on 22 November 1997 at the AAASS Convention, Seattle, WA.

1. Winston S. Churchill, *The Gathering Storm* (Boston and London, 1948, reprint 1983), p.323.
2. French historians, who rarely if ever consult Polish-language documents or studies on inter-war Polish foreign policy or Franco-Polish relations, express a uniform condemnation of the Polish foreign minister, as, for example, in the references to Beck in Jean-Baptiste Duroselle, *La Décadence. 1932–1939* (Paris, 1979), see the index. The author of a recent study based on the reports of French ambassadors in Warsaw, Jules Laroche (1926–35) and Léon Noël (1935–39), concludes that Beck had chosen Germany over the USSR, see Suzanne Champinnois, 'Le colonel Beck at la diplomatie française' [Colonel Beck and French Diplomacy], in Michal Pulaski *et al.* (eds.), Z

74 THE MUNICH CRISIS, 1938

dziejow Europy srodkowej w XX wieku. Studia ofiarowane Henrykowi Batowskiemu w 90. rocznice urodzin [From the History of Central Europe in the 20th Century. Studies offered to Henryk Batowski on his 90th birthday] (Krakow, 1997), p.82. In citing Noël's last book, Ms Champinnois does not seem to notice the malice, bordering on hatred, as well as the many factual errors in *Polonia Restituta. La Pologne entre les deux mondes* [Poland Restored. Poland Between Two Worlds] (Paris, 1984). For a critical evaluation, see Anna M. Cienciala and Piotr S. Wandycz, 'Polona Restituta – czyli Noël redivivius' [Poland Restored – or Noël Revived], *Zeszyty Historyczne*, No.72 (Paris, 1985), pp.147–59.

3. See Hugh Seton-Watson, *Eastern Europe Between the Wars, 1918–1941* (3rd edn with new preface, Hamden, CT, 1962), on Polish foreign policy, pp.387–8.

4. See Anna M. Cienciala, 'Marxism and History. Some Recent Polish and Soviet Interpretations of Polish Foreign Policy in the Era of Appeasement. An Evaluation', *East European Quarterly*, Vol.6, No.1 (1972), pp.92–117. The old negative view of Polish foreign policy in the period 1935–39, though minus the class interest, persists in a recent, short Russian history of Poland, see A.Ia. Manusevich, 'Sanatsiia bez Pilsudskogo' [Sanacja without Pilsudski], in F.G. Zuev, V.A. Svetalov and S.M. Falkovich (eds.), *Kratkaia Istoriia Pol'shi* (Moscow, 1993), ch.16, pp.291–6.

5. The most prominent Polish critic of Beck's policy over the last few decades has been the dean of Polish diplomatic historians, Professor Henryk Batowski of the Jagiellonian University, Krakow; see, for example, his *Zdrada Monachijska* [The Munich Betrayal] (Poznan, 1973), and *Rok 1938. Dwie agresje hitlerowskie* [The Year 1938. Two Nazi Aggressions] (Poznan, 1985). Batowski believes that if Beck had followed a different policy in 1938, the outcome of the Czechoslovak crisis would have been very different. Other Polish historians, while rejecting a total rehabilitation of Beck's 1938 policy, differ strongly from Czech historians who condemn Beck outright, see Tadeusz Kisielewski, 'W odpowiedzi historykowi czeskiemu. Polemika z Jaroslavem Valenta w sprawie stosunkow polsko-czeskich w latach 1938–1945' [Reply to a Czech historian. Polemic with Jaroslav Valenta on Polish–Czechoslovak Relations 1938–1945] *Dzieje Najnowsze*, Vol.25, No.2 (1993), pp.91–100.

6. Henry L. Roberts, 'The Diplomacy of Colonel Beck', in Gordon A. Craig and Felix Gilbert (eds.), *The Diplomats 1919–1939* (Princeton, 1960), pp.603, 611; for a detailed study, see Anna M. Cienciala, *Poland and the Western Powers, 1938–1939: A Study in the Interdependence of Eastern and Western Europe* (London and Toronto, 1968). (This book, a revised version of my dissertation, was based on Polish diplomatic archives available in London, also on published British, French and German sources. British and French archival documents were not accessible at the time.)

7. On Locarno, see Piotr S. Wandycz, *France and Her Eastern Allies 1919–1925: French–Czechoslovak–Polish Relations from the Paris Peace Conference to Locarno* (Minneapolis, MN, 1962), ch.13; and idem, *The Twilight of French Eastern Alliances 1926–1936: French–Czechoslovak–Polish Relations from Locarno to the Remilitarization of the Rhineland* (Princeton, NJ, 1988), ch.1, pp.19–46; each book was awarded the prestigious George Louis Beer Prize by the American Historical Association and each is still the best in its field. On French, British and German attitudes towards Poland in the making of the Locarno Treaties, see Anna M. Cienciala and Titus Komarnicki, *From Versailles to Locarno. Keys to Polish Foreign Policy 1919–1925* (Lawrence, KS, 1984), chs.9, 10, pp.233–276.

8. See Cienciala, 'Polish Foreign Policy, 1926–1939. "Equilibrium": Stereotype and Reality', *Polish Review*, Vol.30, No.1 (New York, 1975), pp.42–57.

9. On the Benes–Skirmunt Pact, see Wandycz, *France and her Eastern Allies*, pp.238–64, and appendices IV, V; on Javorina, see ibid., appendix V, and pp.265–91; on the Benes–Skrzynski treaties of April 1925, see ibid., pp.343–4. On Polish–Czechoslovak diplomatic relations in 1919–25, see Alina Szklarska-Lohmannowa, *Polsko–*

Czechoslowackie stosunki dyplomatyczne w latach 1918–1925 (Ossolineum, Wroclaw, 1967).

10. For an excellent overview of the Teschen question in 1919–20 and up to 1925, see Wandycz, *France and her Eastern Allies*, ch.3. On the Pilsudski letter to Masaryk and the Polish delegation's experiences in Prague, December 1918, see the text of the letter and the account of one of its members: Damian S. Wandycz, 'Zapomniany List Pilsudskiego do Masaryka' [Pilsudski's Forgotten Letter to Masaryk], *Orzel Bialy*, nos.32 (580)–35 (583) (London, 1953; reprint, Jozef Pilsudski Institute of America, New York, nd); English translation: 'A Forgotten Letter of Pilsudski to Masaryk', *Polish Review*, Vol.9, No.4 (1964), pp.38–54. On the agreement of 5 November 1918, see the brief statement by William J. Rose, then a Canadian YMCA official who was caught by the outbreak of World War I in Trans-Olza and who took part in working out the agreement between local Polish and Czech councils in early November 1918; he travelled to Paris to present the Polish case at the Peace Conference, see ibid., pp.168–70. For a detailed account of his activities, see *The Polish Memoirs of William John Rose*, ed. Daniel Stone (Toronto, 1975), ch.3, 'Amateur at Peace-Making', pp.58–106. W.J. Rose, 1885–1968, became a historian of Poland.

11. See Jules Laroche memoirs: *La Pologne de Pilsudski: souvenirs d'une ambassade* [Pilsudski's Poland: Memories of an Embassy] (Paris, 1953), pp.124–26, cit. Wandycz, *France and her Eastern Allies*, p.158. In the archives of the Quai d'Orsay, there is a holograph letter from Edvard Benes to Jules Laroche, dated Spa, 11 July 1920, containing this promise, see Cienciala and Komarnicki, *From Versailles to Locarno*, p.171.

12. On the war, see Norman Davies, *White Eagle, Red Star. The Polish–Soviet War, 1919–1920* (London, 1972), and reprints. On the diplomatic aspect, see Piotr S. Wandycz, *Soviet–Polish Relations, 1917–1921* (Cambridge, MA, 1969).

13. Advice to Poland to accept an 'ethnic' frontier with Russia was given by the Czechs to the Poles as early December 1918, see Damian Wandycz, 'A Forgotten Letter', p.47. Regarding Danzig and the Corridor, T.G. Masaryk told German Foreign Minister Gustav Stresemann in March 1927: 'anyone who looks at the map of Europe must realize that things cannot remain as they are. ... Poland also knows quite well that it must give way.' He thought that Poland must have an assured access to the sea, but only through railway use rights and free ports, see F. Gregory Campbell, *Confrontation in Central Europe. Weimar Germany and Czechoslovakia* (Chicago, 1975), p.183. For Benes' support of German revisionist claims against Poland in the early 1920s, see Wandycz, *France and her Eastern Allies*, pp.336–7.

14. French Marshal Ferdinand Foch proposed in 1924 that Poland and Czechoslovakia conclude a military convention. General Wladyslaw Sikorski, then Polish premier, supported the idea as did the Czechoslovak general staff, but the Czechoslovak government rejected it. See Jerzy Kozenski, *Czechoslowacja w polskiej polityce zagranicznej w latach 1932–1938* [Czechoslovakia in Polish Foreign Policy, 1932–1938] (Poznan, 1964), pp.30–31. On the question of a Polish–Czechoslovak military alliance in the period 1921–27, see Wieslaw Balcerak, 'Sprawa polsko–czechoslowackiego sojuszu wojskowego w latach 1921–1927', *Studia z Dziejow ZSRR i Europy Srodkowej*, Vol.3 (1967), pp.207–26.

15. For T.G. Masaryk to Stresemann, March 1927, see Campbell, *Confrontation*, p.183. For Beck's conversation with Ramsay MacDonald and John Simon at the Beau Rivage Hotel on 17 March, and Benes' conversation with Sir John Simon in the same place and on the same day, see *Documents on British Foreign Policy* (DBFP), 2nd series, vol.5 (London, 1956), Nos.42, 43.

16. On the Benes–Beck conversation in Geneva, January 1934, see W. Balcerak, 'Legenda bez pokrycia' [A Legend without Foundation], *Studia z Dziejow ZSRR i Europy Srodkowej*, Vol.9 (1973), pp.200–206. For Benes on Poland after the Polish–German

Declaration of Nonaggression, see Addison's report to Sir John Simon of 3 February 1934, Foreign Office (FO) 371/17744, pp.364–5, Public Record Office (PRO), London. On the Polish–German agreement, see Anna M. Cienciala, 'The Significance of the Declaration of Non-Aggression of January 24, 1934, in Polish–German and International Relations', *East European Quarterly*, Vol.1, No.1 (1967), pp.1–30, also article by same, note 8 above.

17. The Arnost Heidrich note of June 1938 was first cited by Stefania Stanislawska, *Wielka i mala polityka Jozefa Becka* [The Great and Small Policies of Jozef Beck] (Warsaw, 1962), p.12, see also Wandycz, *Twilight*, p.282, and Cienciala, *Poland and the Western Powers*, pp.14–15, notes 32, 33 For a short and perceptive study of the Beck–Benes animosity and mutual Polish–Czech dislikes, see Piotr S. Wandycz, 'Benes a Polska i Polacy' [Benes, Poland and the Poles], in M. Pulaski (ed.), *Z dziejow Europy Srodkowej w XX wieku*, pp.143–52.

18. See Jules Laroche, *La Pologne de Pilsudski*, p.74; for the full text of Laroche's report of 19 Dec. 1933, see *Documents Diplomatiques Français* (*DDF*), lst series, Vol.5, No.156 (Paris, 1970), pp.305–7. For Benes' declaration, see report by Alfred Chlapowski, Polish ambassador in Paris, December 1933, cit. Kozenski, *Czechoslowacja*, pp.70–71.

19. For Halifax's proposals to Hitler in November 1937, see his report in *DBFP*, 2nd series, Vol.19 No.336 (London, 1982), p.345; for information on the above as transmitted to the Polish government on 3 December 1937, see Z. Landau, J. Tomaszewski (eds.), *Monachium 1938. Polskie dokumenty dyplomatyczne* [Munich 1938. Polish Diplomatic Documents] (Warsaw, 1985), No.1 (henceforth: *Monachium*). For Beck's conversations in Berlin, 13–14 January 1938, see Waclaw Jedrzejewicz (ed.), *Diplomat in Berlin 1933–1939: Papers and Memoirs of Jozef o Lipski, Ambassador of Poland* (New York, 1968), pp.321–38; original Polish documents in *Diariusz i Teki Jana Szembeka 1935–1939* [Diary and Files of Jan Szembek – Deputy Foreign Minister 1935–39], Vol.4, ed. Jozef Zaranski (London, 1972), pp.424–8 (henceforth: *DiT*. IV), also *Monachium*, Nos.2–6. For Churchill's statements to Beck in January 1938, when they met on the French Riviera, see the 12 February 1938 report by the Polish ambassador to Great Britain, Edward Raczynski, cit. Cienciala, *Poland and the Western Powers*, p.41.

20. For Chamberlain's declaration of 24 March 1938, that Great Britain would not guarantee Czechoslovakia, see *Parliamentary Debates. House of Commons*, 5th series, col.1405.

21. On the Polish demand of February 1937 for equal treatment of the Polish minority with others, see reference in Kazimierz Papée report of 1 April 1938, *Monachium*, No.27; for Juraj Slavik's declaration to Beck, 4 May 1938, see Cienciala, *Poland and the Western Powers*, p.72, also *Monachium*, No.55, p.103.

22. See Jozef Beck, *Dernier Rapport. Politique Polonaise 1926–1939* (Neuchâtel, Paris, 1951), pp.162–3; English version: *Final Report* (New York, 1957). For the original, annotated Polish text, see *Polska polityka zagraniczna w latach 1926–1939. Na podstawie tekstow min. Jozefa Becka opracowala Anna M. Cienciala* [Polish Foreign Policy 1926–1939, ed. Anna M. Cienciala on the Basis of the Texts of minister Jozef Beck] (Paris, 1990), pp.217–18; also Jozef Beck, *Ostatni Raport* (Warsaw, 1987), pp.146–7. For the Polish text of the Franco-Polish Military Convention of 19 February 1921, ratified on 1 December 1921, see Halina Janowska and Tadeusz Jedruszczak (eds.), *Powstanie II Rzeczypospolitej. Wybor dokumentow 1866–1925* [The Rise of the Second Republic. Selected Documents 1866–1925] (Warsaw, 1981), doc. no.309, also Tadeusz Jedruszczak and Maria Nowak-Kielbikowa (eds.), *Dokumenty z dziejow polskiej polityki zagranicznej 1918–1939. Tom I., 1918–1932* [Documents on the History of Polish Foreign Policy, 1918–1939, Vol.I, 1918–1932] (Warsaw, 1989), doc. no.30. The full text of the convention was first published in Kazimiera Mazurowa,

'Przymierze polsko-francuskie z roku 1921', *Najnowsze Dzieje Polski*, 11 (1967), pp.214–17. Agreement on forms of military action was finally reached by the two sides in the military protocols interpreting the convention signed on 17 May 1939. However, the French government did not carry out its obligations in September of that year, see article by Cienciala in note 57 below.

23. For the evolution of Beck's policy toward Czechoslovakia, see Cienciala, 'The View from Warsaw'. *Reappraising the Munich Pact*, pp.86–7. On the 'Third Europe', see also, idem, *Poland and the Western Powers*, chs.4, 5. On Mussolini's support for the project, see Stanislaw Sierpowski, *Stosunki polsko–wloskie w latach 1918–1940* [Polish–Italian Relations in the Years 1918–1940] (Warsaw, 1975), ch.5, sec.2, 'Wizyty Becka w Rzymie' [Beck's visits to Rome], pp.506–41. On Sikorski's wartime plans and negotiations for a Polish–Czechoslovak Confederation as the basis for a central European federation, see the pioneering work of Piotr S. Wandycz, *Czechoslovak–Polish Confederation* (Bloomington, IN, 1956); also Sarah Meiklejohn Terry, *Poland's Place in Europe: General Sikorski and the Origin of the Oder–Neisse Line, 1939–1943* (Princeton, NJ, 1983), ch.5, 'Toward a New Central Europe'. For Czech and Polish documents, see Ivan Stovicek and Jaroslav Valenta (eds.), *Ceskoslovensko–polska jednani o konfederaci a spojenectvi, 1939–1944. Ceskoslovenske diplomaticke dokumenty* [Czechoslovak–Polish Negotiations on the Establishment of an Alliance and Confederation, 1939–1944. Czechoslovak documents] (Prague, 1995).

24. For the Szembek–R. Raczynski conversation of 18 April 1938, see *DiT IV*, p.133. For the evolution of Polish policy on Slovakia in 1938–39, see Ewa Orlof, *Dyplomacja polska wobec sprawy slowackiej w latach 1938–1939* (Krakow, 1980).

25. The first to cite the report of the Czech journalist, Václav Fiala on his talks with Polish political leaders, April 1938, was S. Stanislawska, *Wielka i mala polityka*, pp.110 ff., cit. Cienciala, *Poland and the Western Powers*, pp.66–9. Even the French ambassador in Warsaw, Leon Noël, formerly the French envoy in Prague, who had worked for a Polish–Czechoslovak alliance and was very hostile to Beck, reported on 24 September 1938 that Polish public opinion and the army were both unanimous in demanding the return of the disputed territory to Poland, although the army would find it most repugnant to fight in the same camp as Germany, see *DDF*, 2nd series, Vol.11, No.327 (Paris 1977), p.500.

26. For Beck's proposal to Bonnet, see his instruction of 24 May 1938 to Juliusz Lukasiewicz, the Polish ambassador in Paris, cit. Cienciala, *Poland*, p.76 and n.52; Polish text: *Monachium*, No.81; French text of note communicated by Lukasiewicz, with attributed date of 26 May 1938, *DDF*, 2nd series, Vol.9, No.458 (Paris, 1974), pp.911–12, and see Lukasiewicz reports to Beck of 24 and 28 May, English translation in Waclaw (ed.), *Diplomat in Paris. Papers and Memoirs of Juliusz Lukasiewicz Ambassador of Poland* (New York and London, 1970), pp.91–104; for the expanded, Polish edition, see Waclaw Jedrzejewicz and Henryk Bulhak (eds.), *Dyplomata w Paryzu 1936–1939. Wspomnienia i dokumenty Juliusza Lukasiewicza Ambasadora Rzeczypospolitej Polskiej* (London, 1989); on the Teschen (Trans-Olza) question, see pp.79–184. For Beck's refusal of Goering's proposal of German–Polish–Hungarian economic pressure on Prague, see Ambassador Lipski's report on his conversation with Goering of 17 June 1938; W. Jedrzejewicz (ed.), *Diplomat in Berlin*, doc. no.87; Polish text, *Monachium*, No.109. For Anthony J. Drexel Biddle's report of 19 June 1938, see Philip V. Cannistraro, Edward D. Wynot, Jr., and Theodore P. Kovaloff (eds.), *Poland and the Coming of the Second World War. The Diplomatic Papers of A.J. Drexel Biddle, Jr., United States Ambassador to Poland 1937–1939* (Columbus, OH, 1976), doc.4, pp.208 ff. For American diplomacy in face of the German threat to Czechoslovakia and Poland in 1938–1939, see Bogdan Grzelonski, *Dyplomacja Stanow Zjednoczonych wobec zagrozenia Czechoslowacji i Polski (12 marca 1938 – l wrzesnia 1939)* (Warsaw, 1995), (Szkola Glowna Handlowa, Monografie i Opracowania, nr. 402); Biddle's report is cited on pp.158–9.

27. For Vansittart's note of 31 August 1938, see Gerhard L. Weinberg, *The Foreign Policy of Hitler's Germany. Starting World War II, 1937–1939* (Chicago, 1980), p.402, n.102.

28. For a brief recent summary of this phase of the crisis, see Igor Lukes, *Czechoslovakia between Stalin and Hitler; The Diplomacy of Edvard Benes in the 1930s* (Oxford, 1996), pp.219 ff.

29. On the possibility of using the Polish military force to help Czechoslovakia in case of war, see Marian Zgorniak, *Sytuacja militarna Europy w okresie kryzysu politycznego 1938 r.* [The European Military Situation during the Political Crisis of 1938] (Warsaw, 1979), p.294, n.343. See also same on the *ad hoc* development of the Polish military force on the border of Trans-Olza, pp.284–94.

30. For the first study of secret Polish policy on Trans-Olza, based on Polish archives, see Edward Dlugajczyk, *Tajny Front na granicy cieszynskiej. Wywiad i dywersja w latach 1919–1939* [Secret Front on the Teschen Frontier. Intelligence Work and Diversion in the Years 1919–1939] (Katowice, 1993), and same on Polish military diversion in Trans-Olza in 1935–38: 'Polska dywersja wojskowa na Zaolziu w latach 1935–1938', in *Slezsky Sbornik*, Rocnik/94, No.1 (Opava, 1996), pp.37–44; see also Krzysztof Nowak's interesting article on the activity of the Polish Consulate in Moravska-Ostrava, ibid., pp.67–74. For Polish military intelligence documents (2nd section of the Polish general staff), see Kazimierz Badziak, Pawel Samus and Gennady Matviejew (eds.), *'Powstanie' na Zaolziu w 1938 r: Polska akcja specjalna w swietle dokumentow Oddzialu II Sztabu Glownego WP* ['Uprising' in Trans-Olza in 1938. Polish Special Action in the Light of Documents of the 2nd Section, General Staff, Polish Army] (Warsaw, 1997). The archives of the 2nd Section of the Polish general staff were first seized by the Gestapo in 1939, and then by the Red Army at the end of World War II. They are still in Moscow in the Tsentr Khraneniia Istoriko-Dokumental'nykh Kollektsii [Center for the Preservation of Historical-Documentary Collections], which released some of the documents for this publication.

31. Benes' letter – written in French – was first published in *DiT IV*, pp.438–9, see also Polish translation: *Monachium*, No.360. The original is in 'Collection 39, Mnichov 1b', the archives of the T.G. Masaryk Institute, Prague. Drafts of the letter in this collection show that Benes had inserted, then omitted, arbitration alongside friendly discussion. I wish to thank Mr Bruce Berglund, my doctoral student at the University of Kansas and Fulbright Fellow in the Czech Republic 1997–98, for supplying this archival information.

32. For this phase of the crisis, see Lukes, *Czechoslovakia*, pp.234 ff.

33. For the Soviet verbal note to Poland, 23 September and the Polish answer of the same day rejecting Soviet interference (Polish texts), see *DiT IV*, pp.436–7, and *Monachium*, Nos.282, 289; for the Russian text of the Soviet note, also Deputy Commissar for Foreign Affairs V. Potemkin's notes of his conversations with the Polish chargé d'affaires in Moscow, T. Jankowski on 23 September 1938, see Euzebiusz Basinski *et al.* (eds.), *Dokumenty i materialy do historii stosunkow polsko–radzieckich [Documents and Materials on the History of Polish–Soviet Relations]*, Vol.6, 1933–1938 (Warsaw, 1967), Nos.257–9 (Russian documents published in Russian); a parallel Russian series was published in Moscow.

34. See Hugh Ragsdale's paper delivered at the 1997 AAASS conference in Seattle, WA. Ragsdale's figures of 300,000 Soviet forces mobilized in late September 1938, should be compared with those cited by Zgorniak, who notes that on 29 September 1938 330,000 men were *additionally* conscripted besides those already under arms, see *Sytuacja militarna Europy*, pp.252–3. On Polish reconstruction of the first move in the Soviet O. de B., after the cancellation of Soviet mobilization orders, see ibid., p.295, 345 n., citing an unpublished work; unfortunately, the author does not detail the O. de B.

35. For the Comintern letter and statements by Andrei Zhdanov, see Lukes, *Czechoslovakia*, pp.198–9.

36. See Zdenek Fierlinger's report of 23 September 1938, cit. in Jiri Hochman, *The Soviet Union and the Failure of Collective Security, 1934–1938* (Ithaca, 1984), p.165.

37. Jiri Hochman published a note from Romanian Foreign Minister Petrescu Comnene to Soviet Foreign Commissar Maxim M. Litvinov, dated Geneva, 24 September 1939 (both ministers were then in Geneva). Comnene informed Litvinov that the Romanian government agreed, in case of war, to the passage of 100,000 Soviet troops through Romanian territory along the Romanian segment of railway line from Cernauti to Negresti and to the overflight of Soviet planes, see Hochman, *The Soviet Union*, appendix C, pp.194–201. The genuineness of the letter has been questioned by Romanian and other historians because of the many mistakes in the French text, unlikely to have been made by Minister Comnene who knew the language well. However, his letter to Litvinov accords with the findings of Larry L. Watts that the Romanian army would not have opposed the passage of Soviet troops in case of war, see Larry L. Watts' paper delivered at the 1997 AAASS conference in Seattle, WA. The details on numbers of Soviet troops and their route, as listed in the Comnene letter, seem consistent with such an attitude. Ivan Pfaff, who had provided the letter to Hochman, cites it again, along with other sources supporting it, in his book, *Die Sowjetunion und die Verteidigung der Teschoslowakei, 1934–1938: Versuch der Revision einer Legende* [The Soviet Union and the Defence of Czechoslovakia: An Attempt at Revising a Legend] (Köln, 1996), pp.397–8.

38. For the Czechoslovak note of 25 September, proposing immediate negotiations to secure a real understanding between the two countries, see Szembek *DiT IV*, pp.437–8, and *Monachium*, No.337 (in French). For the British and French ambassadors' statement to Beck on 26 September 1938 regarding the Czechoslovak government's intent to make territorial cessions to Poland, expressing hope that Poland would maintain a benevolent neutrality, see ibid., No.354. For French and British démarches on Teschen (Trans-Olza) to the Polish government throughout September 1938, see relevant documents in *Monachium*; also *DDF*, 2nd series, Vol.11 (Paris, 1977), ch.4; and *DBFP*, 3rd series, Vol.3 (London, 1950), ch.III.

39. For Moscicki's answer to Benes of 27 September 1938, see *DiT IV*, pp.439–40; *Monachium*, No.336.

40. For the Polish note to Prague, 27 September 1938, see *DiT IV*, pp.440–41; *Monachium*, No.374.

41. See Cienciala, *Poland*, pp.134–7, 150–51; for English translations of the cited Lipski reports to Beck see *Diplomat in Berlin*, pp.424–7; for Beck's instruction to Lipski of 28 September 1938 warning that clarification of German and Polish interests was very important for a clash might have disastrous consequences, see ibid., p.429, *Monachium*, No.393; for Lipski's conversation with Secretary of State, Ernst von Weizsäcker and German agreement, 28 September 1938, see *Diplomat*, pp.430–31, *Monachium*, No.403.

42. See Lukes, *Czechoslovakia*, pp.249 ff.

43. Michal Lubienski, *Refleksje i Reminiscensje* [Reflections and Reminiscences], typescript, Jozef Pilsudski Institute of America, New York (trans. A.C); cit. Cienciala, 'The View from Warsaw', in Maya Latynski (ed.), *Reappraising The Munich Pact: Continental Perspectives* (Washington, DC, Baltimore, MD, and London, 1992), p.91.

44. Ibid.

45. See Pawel Starzenski, *Trzy Lata z Beckiem* [Three Years With Beck], edited with a Foreword by Bogdan Grzelonski (Warsaw, 1991), p.94. The first edition of this book was published in London, 1972.

46. See Zgorniak, *Sytuacja militarna Europy*, p.294. For Polish military thinking and plans regarding war with Germany, see ibid., pp.254–84, also Komisja Historyczna [Historical Commission] (eds.), *Polskie sily zbrojne w drugiej wojnie swiatowej. Tom I. Kampania wrzesniowa 1939. Czesc pierwsza* [The Polish Armed Forces in the Second

World War. Vol.I. The September Campaign. Part 1] (London, 1951), ch.3B, pp.111–29, and ch.6 on the operational plan against Germany, 'Zachod' (West, pp.257–81).

47. For the Czechoslovak note of 30 September 1938, see *DiT IV*, pp.442–4; *Monachium*, No.439.

48. See Eugeniusz Kwiatkowski, 'Jozef Beck', *Arka*, No.12 (an underground publication) (Krakow, 1985), reprinted in *Zeszyty Historyczne*, No.76 (Paris, 1986), pp.14–32 (the conference date, 30 Sept., is misprinted on p.27 as 12 Sept.); cit. Cienciala, *The View*, pp.93–4. For Beck's brief accounts, see *Dernier Rapport*, pp.166–7; Cienciala (ed.), *Polska polityka zagraniczna*, p.223.

49. Polish ultimatum note, 30 Sept. 1938, *DiT IV*, pp.444–6; *Monachium*, No.449; Papée telephone information, 1 Oct. 1938, ibid., No.459; Krofta's note accepting ultimatum, ibid., No.460. For the Franco-British proposal of Polish–Czechoslovak negotiations and Neville Chamberlain's personal offer of mediation to Beck, also Polish reactions, see. *DBFP*, 3rd series, Vol.3, Nos.85, 86, 91, 93; for the Polish record of Lubienski's statements to ambassadors Kennard and Noël, 1 Oct., see *Monachium*, No.455.

50. Ambassador Biddle communicated President Roosevelt's appeal to Beck on 1 October, *Monachium*, No.458. The English text is not included in *Foreign Relations of the United States, 1938*, Vol.1 (Washington, DC, 1955), which does, however, include a note dated 1 October 1938 by the Czechoslovak minister in Washington, V.I. Hurban, stating that the Polish ultimatum was a violation of the Kellogg–Briand Pact and of the Munich Agreement, also State Department acknowledgment of same, see ibid., p.710.

51. See Piotr S. Wandycz, *The Price of Freedom. A History of East Central Europe from the Middle Ages to the Present* (London and New York, 1992), p.208. Two Polish historians point out that the union of Trans-Olza with Poland released funds earmarked for the development of steel production, so these could be used for other purposes, but that supplies of raw materials, steel, and rolled steel products from Trans-Olza exceeded Poland's needs at the time, so that markets for them had to be found elsewhere, see Z. Landau and J. Tomaszewski, *Gospodarka Polski miedzywojennej. Tom IV. 1936–1939* [The Economy of Interwar Poland. Vol.4. 1936–1939] (Warsaw, 1989), p.127. I wish to thank Dr Milan Hauner for drawing my attention to the above.

52. For Beck's instruction to Lipski in mid-September 1938, to secure German recognition of the Polish–German frontier, of the status of the Free City of Danzig, and an extension of the nonaggression declaration of 26 January 1934, see *Diplomat in Berlin*, pp.401; Lipski raised these issues in a conversation with Goering on 16 September ibid., pp.403–5; Beck's instruction of 19 September, that Lipski raise the same points in his conversation with Hitler, ibid., p.407; Lipski's report on this conversation, 20 September, ibid., pp.408–12, Polish desiderata, p.412. Hitler countered with the concept of a superhighway and railways, that is, a German extraterritorial highway and railway through the Corridor, ibid. Polish texts of Lipski's conversations, 16 and 19 September 1938, *Monachium*, Nos.201, 246. Beck made no further attempts to raise these issues during the Czechoslovak crisis.

53. Roberts, *The Diplomats*, p.611.

54. On British views of eastern Europe and Poland in the pre-Nazi period, see Cienciala, 'German Propaganda for the Revision of the Polish–German Frontier and the Corridor; Its Effects on British Opinion and the British Foreign Policy-Making Elite in the Years 1919–1933', *Antemurale*, Vol.20 (Rome, 1976), pp.77–129. For later press views, see Franklin Reid Gannon, *The British Press and Germany, 1936–1939* (Oxford, 1971).

55. For this view of Neville Chamberlain's policy, see Geoffrey Parker, *Chamberlain and Appeasement. British Policy and the Coming of the Second World War* (London, 1993). Parker believes the alternative to appeasement was Churchill's proposal of reviving the 'Triple Entente' of Great Britain, France, and Russia, 1907–17.

56. Halifax to Phipps, 1 Nov. 1938, *DBFP*, 3rd series, Vol.3, No.285, p.252.
57. See Cienciala, 'Poland in British and French Policy in 1939: Determination to Fight or Avoid War?' *Polish Review*, Vol.34, No.3 (1989), pp.199–226, partial reprint in Patrick Finney (ed.), *The Origins of the Second World War* (London, New York, Sydney and Auckland, 1997), pp.413–33.
58. James W. Headlam-Morley, 'The History of British Foreign Policy and the Geneva Protocol', 12 Feb. 1925, FO371/11064/9/W1252/98, PRO, London, pp.150 ff., cit. Cienciala and Komarnicki, *From Versailles to Locarno*, p.234.
59. For Austen Chamberlain's and Churchill's statements opposing the cession of Danzig and the Corridor to Nazi Germany, also similar statements by Col. Wedgewood, General Spears, and Clement Attlee, see *Parliamentary Debates, House of Commons*, 13 April 1933, Vol.276, 5th series, cols.2739–824. For the views of Austen Chamberlain on Poland in the years 1924–33, see Anna M. Cienciala, 'Nastawienie Austena Chamberlaina do Polski w latach 1924–1933', in Antoni Czubinski (ed.), *Polska–Niemcy–Europa* [Poland–Germany–Europe] (Poznan, 1977), pp.482–94. For an early example of Vansittart's opposition to the cession of Danzig and the Corridor to Germany, see his 'Memorandum on the Present and Future Position of Europe', 28 Aug. 1933, *DBFP*, 2nd series, Vol.5, No.371, pp.547–59.
60. Cadogan also desired an international conference to undo the 'mistakes' of the Treaty of Versailles and other peace treaties, see *The Diaries of Sir Alexander Cadogan, O.M. 1938–1945*, ed. David Dilks (London, 1971), pp.119–120. 'Mitteleuropa' refers to the concept of a German-dominated continent, based on Berlin's prior domination of central and south-eastern Europe.
61. Lipski's comment on Beck's views when the two met in Warsaw in the first days of September 1938, see *Diplomat in Berlin*, p.389 (from Lipski's personal papers).

The Munich Crisis and Hungary: The Fall of the Versailles Settlement in Central Europe

MAGDA ÁDÁM

The crisis leading up to the Munich Conference has accumulated a vast literature. However, the published sources, memoirs and secondary works share one common shortcoming. They almost exclusively deal with the policies of the great powers. They yield little information on the conduct of the states of central and eastern Europe, or on their role in making the Munich agreement possible.[1] This study considers the policies of the Hungarian governments in office during the crisis, and the behaviour of other east-central European states.

The policy of the Hungarian government at the time of the Munich crisis was fundamentally influenced by the fact that Hungary had lost substantial territories to the newly created Czechoslovak state at the end of the First World War in the north and north-east. These territories were inhabited not only by Slovaks and Ruthenes, but also by about a million Hungarians, one-third of whom lived in compact communities close to the border. At the peace conference no great power, except France, wished to include these purely Hungarian territories in the new Czechoslovakia. In the end the views of Edvard Benes prevailed, with French backing. Strategic and geographic principles triumphed over the principles of nationality and self-determination. Eventually all the great powers accepted this attitude. This became the chief source of conflict between Hungary and Czechoslovakia.

Hungary's efforts to obtain border revision failed. The Hungarian government acknowledged this fact. They did so in the hope that in a different international environment the great powers would support their plea for revised borders. In relation to Czechoslovakia, they did not exclude the possibility of revision based on direct negotiations. Such an agreement was the purpose of the negotiations held at Bruck in 1921 between the Hungarian government, represented by Prime Minister Count Pal Teleki and Foreign Minister Gusztav Gratz, and Czechoslovak Foreign Minister Edvard Benes.[2] Similar talks were held later, in 1938, by the former foreign minister, Gratz, and in 1939 by Teleki, who was once again prime minister.

The attempts made by Gratz and Teleki to achieve border revision with Czechoslovakia were in no small degree influenced by the willingness of the Czechoslovak president, Thomas Masaryk, to return purely Hungarian territories to Hungary. This was taken seriously in Budapest. However, at Bruck, Teleki came to realize that Benes disagreed with Masaryk with regard to border revision. The Czechoslovak foreign minister harboured strong reservations about Hungary. He attacked its surviving feudal features and its foreign policy aimed at the restitution of the old kingdom. Czechoslovak–Hungarian relations, therefore, did not proceed along the lines Masaryk thought possible. The maintenance of peace, and the defence of the *status quo* with Hungary was underpinned by the establishment by Benes of the 'Little Entente'.[3] The existence of the Little Entente in many ways defined Hungary's space for manoeuvre and influenced its policy towards Czechoslovakia.

Hitler's rise to power brought fundamental changes in Hungary's policy towards Czechoslovakia. The new prime minister, the pro-German Gyula Gömbös, while preserving good relations with Italy, also wished to nurture a German orientation and bring about treaty revision with the help of these two powers. He was disappointed, however, as Hitler made it clear that he did not support Gömbös' ambition. Not yet ready for war, the Führer laid emphasis on reaching his objectives regarding Austria and Czechoslovakia without armed conflict. In order to achieve this he had to keep both the Danubian states and their Western allies divided. As a result of his disruptive efforts practically all the east-central European states, with the exception of Czechoslovakia, were eager to win his favour. Hitler intended to maintain his advantageous position by not demanding the complete revision of the Versailles system in one bid. This would have strengthened the creators of the system, the entente cordiale and the Little Entente, whose links had started to weaken.

In order to disrupt the Little Entente, Hitler pursued a friendly foreign policy towards Yugoslavia and Romania. He wished first to acquire economic positions in the two countries and then tie them to Germany politically. This is why he did not support Hungarian revisionist ambitions towards these countries. He advised, and later demanded, that the Hungarian government come to an agreement with Yugoslavia, arrive at a *modus vivendi* with Romania, and concentrate every effort against Czechoslovakia. For a long time Hungarian governments did not accept Hitler's concept of partial revision (nor did Gömbös). They hoped to satisfy their territorial demands regarding the other two neighbours, that is, Yugoslavia and Romania, with the help of the Italian alliance. The leadership in Berlin was enraged by the fact that their 'advice' was disregarded by Budapest. Both Hitler and Göring remonstrated against this behaviour, criticizing Italian influence in Hungarian politics.

By having to choose between the conflicting advice of these two friendly powers the Hungarian government faced a difficult dilemma. The situation was defused by the *rapprochement* between Hitler and Mussolini. This was a dream of Gömbös, who made every effort to bring about reconciliation between Germany and Italy. After the forging of the Berlin–Rome axis Mussolini had to conform to the German policy on east-central Europe. He changed his hostile stance towards Yugoslavia, and strove to find an agreement with Belgrade. Mussolini now recommended that the Hungarians do the same. He regarded it as very important that a settlement be found for the conflict between Hungary and Romania. Czechoslovakia thus emerged as the only country where he envisaged the satisfaction of Hungary's revisionist ambitions. Eventually, the Hungarian government accepted the principle of partial revision and took steps to come to an agreement with Yugoslavia and Romania.

At the same time, Budapest feared a continued growth of German influence. Kalman Daranyi, who became prime minister after Gömbös' death, took part in negotiations between Hungary and the Little Entente. These were aimed at the normalization of Hungary's relations with its neighbours. These negotiations were initiated by Benes. The occupation of the Rhineland and the subsequent inactivity of the Western powers made him realize that he had acted under an illusion when he had entrusted the protection of

Czechoslovakia against Germany to the Western powers. In the new situation he believed that an accommodation with the Hungarians was urgent. Bilateral negotiations with Hungary started in the spring of 1937. They concerned three questions: a nonaggression treaty; the recognition of Hungary's right to rearm on an equal basis with its neighbours; and the minorities question. On the latter issue, which so far had been regarded as an internal affair by its neighbours, Hungarian diplomacy succeeded in having it discussed at an international negotiating table. Hungary was ready to sign a nonaggression treaty in return. The fact that Hungary was negotiating with Czechoslovakia, and what is more about a nonaggression treaty, infuriated the leadership in Berlin.

By the autumn of 1937 Hitler decided that the time had come to address the new direction of Hungarian foreign policy. The first version of the plan for *Fall Grün,* which allocated a role to Hungary in a war against Czechoslovakia, had been completed, and he summoned the Hungarian government to discuss Czechoslovakia. On 21 December 1937 Prime Minister Daranyi accompanied by Foreign Minister Kalman Kanya, Defence Minister Vilmos Röder and others went to Berlin. Kanya first negotiated with Göring, then with Hitler. Göring rebuked him for disregarding German advice and for not standing up against attempts to forge an alliance among the nations of the Danube valley. Their policy on the Little Entente had deviated from the course set out by the German leadership. 'The Führer has always maintained', he said, 'that the present generation in Hungary has to be content with showing an offensive attitude only in one direction, the direction of Czechoslovakia, and thus recover the Hungarian territories lost to that country.'[4] Therefore, he found it incomprehensible that, besides Yugoslavia and Romania, the Hungarian government should also negotiate with Czechoslovakia.

Kanya tried to defend the Hungarian moves by stating that the negotiations were necessitated by the objectives that the Germans were advocating. He said that Hungarian attempts to come to an agreement with Yugoslavia and Romania, with the exclusion of Czechoslovakia, had remained unsuccessful. Feeling Germany's backing behind them, the two states refused a separate deal with Hungary. 'Therefore', continued Kanya, 'if, in accordance with the German wishes, the Hungarian government desired a *rapprochement* with Yugoslavia and Romania, we also had to negotiate with Czechoslovakia.'⁵ Hitler repeated that Hungary should concentrate on Czechoslovakia. In return for Hungary's participation in an envisaged move against that country he held out the promise of the whole of Slovakia and the Sub-Carpathian region. The negotiations in Berlin resulted in an agreement for the Hungarian and German staffs to coordinate plans for the attack on Czechoslovakia.⁶

Daranyi's visit to Germany was followed by a marked turn to the right in Hungary's foreign and internal policy. The political objectives of Gömbös were restored. This happened in spite of the fact that Daranyi had been installed as prime minister in 1936 in order to put a brake on Hungary's increasing dependence on Germany and forestall the country's lurch to the right. Daranyi had done just that during the first part of his premiership, but this course was reversed after his visit to Germany.

This had an impact on the country's relations with Prague. In spite of the serious efforts of the Prague government the negotiations in Geneva between Czechoslovak Foreign Minister Kamil Krofta and Kalman Kanya were discontinued, and a long pause ensued. In these circumstances the government in Prague indicated its willingness to make a deal with Hungary alone. Budapest, however, disregarded this approach. Since his visit to Germany, Daranyi had been opposed to any agreement with Czechoslovakia. At the same time, he took steps to mend relations with Yugoslavia.

The Daranyi government also deemed it important to ascertain the position of Poland regarding Czechoslovakia. All the more so as reports arriving in the spring of 1938 indicated that the Polish political leadership had plans regarding Slovakia and Sub-Carpathia that were contrary to Hungarian designs. The Polish military leaders were ready to defy the Hungarians.⁷ The doubts could not be dispersed even after Horthy's visit to Warsaw. While on the question of Sub-Carpathian Ruthenia they managed to forge a common platform and pledged to cooperate closely, Slovakia remained a bone of contention between the two countries for some time to come. Such deadlock led the Hungarian government to initiate secret negotiations with the Slovak nationalist leader Jozef Tiso on the question of the annexation of Slovakia to Hungary. Tiso summed up his conditions for annexing his country to Hungary in the following three points: (1) a central office must be set up with executive powers regarding the administration of Slovakia, and the official use of the Slovak language must be ensured; (2) a separate national assembly had to be created with legislative powers over internal affairs and religious and public education; (3) a fixed quota for Slovakia must be allocated from the Hungarian budget.[8] The Budapest government accepted Tiso's conditions.

In the spring of 1938 the Czechoslovak government made further efforts to restart the interrupted negotiations between the Little Entente and Hungary. Because Romania acted as a brake once again, Prague was ready to make a deal with Budapest without Bucharest. This intention was communicated to the Hungarians on several occasions. The proposal was given a cool reception.

Nevertheless, many political figures in Budapest desired the normalization of relations with Prague. Gusztav Gratz, the former foreign minister, was one of them.[9] He travelled to Prague on 5 March 1938, immediately before the *Anschluss*. He held talks with President Edvard Benes, Prime Minister Milan Hodza and Foreign Minister Kamil Krofta. The negotiations centred on the danger posed by Germany, possible ways of resisting it, and the normalization of relations between Hungary and Czechoslovakia. Benes indicated that the creation of a Vienna–Budapest–Prague triangle would become an important counterbalance to Germany. Gratz agreed with him. However, he saw no means or method of a *rapprochement* between Hungary and Czechoslovakia other than the resolution of the border dispute.[10] Gratz wrote in his report that Benes, Hodza and Krofta 'replied in the negative'. The least vehement rejection came from Benes, who said: '[I]n case a really *bona fide* relationship could develop between Czechoslovakia and Hungary, possibilities may arise in the future that allow the settlement of even the most sensitive questions in a way taking into account the wishes of Hungary.' The Hungarian governments usually regarded agreement on the question of border revision as the condition of a *bona fide* relationship. Hodza, however, considered border revision as being out of the question. He argued that 'it is impossible that Czechoslovakia should cede territories to the weak Hungary, while refusing to give up the territories demanded by the great and powerful Germany'.[11] It remained the unaltered position of the Prague government that the recognition of military parity with Hungary was the only concession that it was prepared to make in the interest of a *rapprochement*. Gratz rejected this by saying that such a concession no longer had bargaining value. Benes concluded the talks by saying that if all of Gratz's prophecies concerning the German danger came true, then 'the Czech people, who have already lived for hundreds of years in the stomach of the Holy Roman Empire, will be able to endure if they had to live for a few more centuries in the stomach of another German Empire'.[12]

Gratz's negotiations in Prague did nothing to further the cause of a Hungarian–Czechoslovak understanding, even though this was the last chance for a reasonable compromise. In less than a week, Austria was annexed by Germany, creating a dangerous situation not only for Czechoslovakia but for Hungary as well. The *Anschluss* remoulded power relations in the whole region. With the exception of Czechoslovakia, the official political line promulgated by the east-central European states was that the fusion of the two brother nations did not concern them particularly. However, between the lines of felicitations sent to Berlin on the occasion, there were distinct elements of fear, especially on the part of states directly bordering on the Third Reich. Maxim Litvinov, the Soviet foreign minister, found opportune words to describe the situation: 'though Hungary and Yugoslavia may now be crying hosanna to the Reich, I am, however, convinced, that at the bottom of their hearts, both are crying for help.'[13] A similar conclusion was drawn by Milos Kobr, the Czechoslovak minister in Budapest, during his talks with Kanya: 'Kanya's self confidence is artificial, superficial, and only hides the same fear that is felt by all the small states who live in the neighbourhood of the Third Reich.'[14] Count Istvan Bethlen, the former Hungarian prime minister, voiced this fear publicly: 'Such a great power', he emphasized, 'has all the means at its disposal with which to exert economic pressure on the small states, and this may entail political dependence.'[15]

Bethlen and his circle were aware of the fact that a Czechoslovak–Hungarian border revision, carried out with the help of the Third Reich, would increase Hungary's dependence on Germany. Therefore, he wished to accomplish it, if at all possible, with Western assistance, primarily with British support. Statements made in April 1938 by the British Labour MP Arthur Henderson to Horthy and Bethlen seemed to suggest that this was possible as long as Hungary did not support Germany's designs on Czechoslovakia.[16] However, in the wake of the prime minister's visit to Berlin, Daranyi's government began to reduce Hungary's multi-pronged foreign policy to a single German orientation. Relations with the Western powers and with Italy were loosened. Budapest refused to continue the negotiations aimed at improving relations with the Little Entente that had been initiated by Czechoslovakia. It urged German–Hungarian military staff conversations and was even ready to participate in a German war against Czechoslovakia. The regent, Miklos Horthy, decided to replace Daranyi with Bela Imredy, who was open to cooperation with the West.

The new prime minister retained as foreign minister Kalman Kanya, who was known for his anti-German orientation from the previous cabinet. While Imredy emphasized in his public statements that there was to be no change in Hungarian foreign policy, significant alterations had in fact occurred before Munich. Imredy endeavoured to lean towards the southern flank of the Berlin–Rome axis. He accepted the concept of a horizontal axis put forward by Mussolini and Ciano that had been alien to Daranyi because of its basically anti-German nature.[17]

Imredy considered it important to reinforce the British orientation of Hungarian foreign policy. In addition to economic and financial factors, this was also made necessary and possible because, as Imredy put it in his inaugural speech, Great Britain had shown increasing understanding of central Europe. At the same time he observed with satisfaction that 'France has also come nearer to realising the real essence of these extremely complex problems'.[18] The new prime minister advocated improved relations with Hungary's neighbours. He suggested in his inaugural speech that conditions should be created in the Danube Basin that could guarantee the normal coexistence of the peoples inhabiting this region. Therefore Imredy wished to continue the negotiations with the Little Entente, and resume dialogue with Czechoslovakia, the country that was excluded from these negotiations by his predecessor, Daranyi. Imredy embarked on an active quest for measures to counterbalance Germany's preponderance in Hungary's foreign relations. These measures were pursued until the conclusion of the Munich agreement. They included contacts with London, Paris and the southern flank of the Berlin–Rome axis. The easing of tensions with Hungary's neighbours was also on Imredy's agenda. Nonetheless, Imredy did not abandon hope of territorial revision *vis-à-vis* Czechoslovakia either, even though he wished to accomplish it through peaceful means with the help of the Western powers.

The internal political manoeuvrings in Hungary, as well as events on the international stage, made Imredy's goals increasingly difficult to realize. Shortly after his accession to office, the so-called May Crisis erupted. It strained German–Czechoslovak relations to breaking point and it strengthened the hand of those politicians in Hungary who demanded the immediate return of regions of Czechoslovakia where Hungarians formed a majority. The fledgling Hungarian–Czechoslovak *rapprochement* suffered a serious setback as a result these developments. There are, however, many misconceptions in historiography about the nature and effects of the crisis. Historians usually seek the origins of the crisis in the German troop concentrations along the Czechoslovak border. New light has, however, been thrown recently on this event in Igor Lukes' book *Czechoslovakia between Stalin and Hitler: The Diplomacy of Edvard Benes.*[19] According to Lukes, Benes' intelligence reports on German troop movements were incorrect. Nevertheless, they served as the basis for the Czechoslovak president's decision to order partial mobilization in his country. This move resulted in an acute exacerbation of the war of nerves in central Europe (Benes never admitted his mistake). The Czechoslovak troops thus mobilized were not only concentrated along the frontier with Germany, but also along the Hungarian and Polish borders.

The unfolding May Crisis of 1938 had a negative effect on Hungarian–Czechoslovak relations. It checked the progress of the still inchoate state of contacts aimed at eventual reconciliation. The Czechoslovak high command installed heavy artillery and machine gun emplacements along the whole length of the Hungarian border.[20] In response to these measures the Hungarian government called up five year-classes of reservists. This in turn invited strong protests from both the Czechoslovak and British governments.

During the crisis, the Hungarian government decided to bide its time. It wondered if war would break out. Would such a war be confined to the region or spread to engulf the whole of Europe? The government of Bela Imredy, in contrast to that of Kalman Daranyi, wished to keep Hungary out of any war, whatever the cost. According to the operational plans, in the event of the outbreak of a localized conflict, the Hungarian army would have marched across the Czechoslovak border to occupy Slovakia and Sub-Carpathian Ruthenia. The conditions of this plan, however, were that Czechoslovakia be incapacitated as a result of the German attack, and that Yugoslavia and Romania remain neutral. In other words, Hungary wished to repossess its former territories without having to fight for them. Imredy adhered to this concept. He would not renounce the principle even when, due to Berlin's insistence, he accepted the theory behind Hitler's concept of German–Hungarian cooperation in future military operations.

In the immediate aftermath of the May crisis, the German military leadership, seeking as it was to prevent the escalation of a future conflict, altered the plans for Hungary's participation in the war. In order to secure the neutrality of Yugoslavia and Romania, it was thought more appropriate if Hungary did not take part in military operations, but only allowed its territory to be used by the Germans for troop deployment and as a base of operations. To discuss these matters Field-Marshal Wilhelm Keitel, chief of the German Supreme Command, visited Hungary and held talks with various political and military leaders. He inspected the terrain and the troop deployments in Komarom. He examined the strategic options for an offensive to be launched from the territory of Hungary.[21] Budapest readily accepted the role of neutrality allotted to Hungary by the Germans. Nevertheless, Keitel's wish that Hungary make its territory available for the deployment of German troops was not accepted by the Hungarian leaders. They argued that even though the treaties establishing the Little Entente only referred to a direct attack by Hungary, they had received intelligence that Yugoslavia, and Romania especially, would construe the manoeuvre suggested by Keitel as a *casus belli*.

It is certainly evident that the Hungarian government could not ignore the existence of the Little Entente. But it is also beyond dispute that, until the Munich agreement was actually signed, the Hungarian government used the continued standoff between itself and the Little Entente as a means of evading the demands made by the German military leadership. At the same time, Imredy's government deemed it important to prepare Hungary for all eventualities. Such eventualities included the option of being forced to yield to German pressure to allow the territory of Hungary to be used as a base of operations against Czechoslovakia, or even to participate in military action. Therefore it is understandable that obtaining the neutrality of Yugoslavia was important for Budapest, especially because in June 1938 Mussolini had reminded Imredy that the construction of a horizontal axis required an agreement between Budapest and Belgrade.

On 18 July 1938 Imredy and his foreign secretary travelled to Rome, where they met Mussolini and Ciano and discussed the whole Czechoslovak problem. He informed the Italian leaders that Hungary wished to harmonize its conduct with Italy in every respect. However, it would not take unilateral action against Czechoslovakia. Nonetheless, it would not remain idle in case of an armed conflict between Germany and Czechoslovakia. But in that case it would only intervene if it was fully convinced of the neutrality of Yugoslavia. Imredy pointed out the duplicity of Belgrade's foreign policy: while it promised neutrality to the Axis powers, it also vowed solidarity with Prague, London and Paris. Imredy requested Mussolini and Ciano to restrain Yugoslavia from attacking Hungary. Should that prove impossible, Italy must participate in the defence of Hungary. In other words, he sought an Italian guarantee against Yugoslavia.[22] That request was roundly rejected by Rome.

The Hungarian–Little Entente agreement turned out just as Imredy had desired: mixed in character, open-ended and capable of being interpreted in many different ways. The Hungarian government managed to agree with Yugoslavia on all three outstanding questions, including nonaggression. These agreements were initialled by the parties. The agreement between Hungary and Czechoslovakia was not initialled because in one of the main items on the agenda, the question of the minorities, no understanding could be reached.[23] Thus, in relation to Czechoslovakia, the initialling of the agreement was postponed until the Czechoslovak party satisfied the demands of the Hungarian government regarding the Hungarian minorities.

The significance of the Bled agreement was overestimated both by the West and by Germany. It was given an unequivocal welcome by the British and French press, as well as by the journals of the Little Entente countries.[24] The reception in Berlin was the exact opposite. The news acted like a bombshell. Hitler angrily argued that the renunciation of the use of force would not bring the desired political results. To the contrary, Hungary blocked the path of intervention against Czechoslovakia, and made it much more difficult for Yugoslavia, in a moral sense, to abandon its ally. The impartial observer would judge that Hungary distanced itself from Germany's policy towards Czechoslovakia. The Italians, who understood the precise meaning of the agreement, reacted differently. Count Ciano remarked in his diary: 'In any case, the Bled meeting has marked a new phase in the crumbling of the Little Entente. Czechoslovakia is isolated. The French system of friendships is completely upset.'[25]

The Bled agreement cast a long shadow over Hungarian–German relations. The distrust of the German leaders was only increased by the demeanour evinced by the Hungarians at the negotiations at Kiel. When asked by Ribbentrop how the Hungarians would act if Germany responded with arms to a Czechoslovak provocation, the Hungarian prime minister and his foreign secretary did not deem Hungary's participation possible in such a venture.[26] Hitler was outraged by such a rejection of his offer of a military alliance. He told Imredy that he now expected nothing from Hungary. According to the notes taken by Ernst Freiherr von Weiszäcker, state secretary in the German foreign ministry, Imredy became noticeably relieved after hearing these words. His relief did not last long, however, as Hitler soon added: 'Those who want to take part in the feast must not exempt themselves from cooking.'[27] Hitler warned that if the Hungarians continued to sit on the fence they would be left out of the division of the spoils. However, if they took part in the invasion of Czechoslovakia, Slovakia as well as Sub-Carpathian Ruthenia would be theirs.

Imredy and Kanya, strongly influenced by the regent, finally gave up their objections. On 25 August 1938 Foreign Minister Kanya sought an audience with Hitler, during which he revised his earlier statement on the level of preparedness of the Hungarian army. He told the Führer that 'Hungary's situation was much better than I had previously thought. Rearmament will reach the stage by 1 October this year that would allow the country to participate in the envisaged armed conflict'.[28] In the end Hitler obtained an undertaking from the Hungarian delegation that Budapest would participate in the planned operations against Czechoslovakia. Despite this undertaking, it did everything to evade actual involvement. It hoped that the Wehrmacht would make decisive inroads into Czechoslovak territory during the first few days of the operations and that the Hungarians would only have to march in and occupy Slovakia and Sub-Carpathian Ruthenia without a shot being fired. After the return of the Hungarian delegation from Germany, the Hungarian government adopted a series of measures to accommodate the German demands and increased Hungary's preparedness for a possible conflict with Czechoslovakia. Ultimately, Budapest abrogated the Bled agreement with Czechoslovakia.

Following Neville Chamberlain's first visit to Germany, the United Hungarian Party's views regarding Czechoslovakia became more radical. Any discrimination between German and Hungarian interests was seen as intolerable. On 17 September the party advocated a plebiscite to be held in order to highlight the right to self-determination of the Hungarian minority in Czechoslovakia. At this time, the Hungarian government established channels of military cooperation with Germany and Poland. This was the purpose of the visits paid by the Hungarian military leaders to these two countries. On 6 September 1938 the chief of the general staff, Lajos Keresztes-Fischer, held talks in Berlin with General Franz Halder. The negotiators could not arrive at any specific agreement. Keresztes-Fischer insisted that Hungary could only join in an attack after some delay. On Hitler's orders, Halder disclosed no details of the military plan to the Hungarians, and the German–Hungarian staff talks yielded no concrete results.

The Hungarians also held talks with the chief of the Polish general staff, General Waclaw Stachiewicz. Based on their impressions gained in Germany they told the Polish military leaders that the Germans had consented to the Polish occupation of Tesin, and to the reattachment of Slovakia and Sub-Carpathian Ruthenia to Hungary. It turned out that the Polish military and the political leadership disagreed regarding the future of Czechoslovakia. The military leaders believed that the retention of an ethnically pure, Czech and Slovak, Czechoslovakia would best serve the national interests of Poland. But the political leadership, and especially Foreign Minister Jozef Beck, were strongly of the opinion that Slovakia, apart from a narrow strip in the north, which should be attached to Poland, ought to be annexed to Hungary. In the second half of September Budapest and Warsaw agreed to harmonize Hungarian and Polish foreign policy regarding Czechoslovakia.[29] The fear that the great powers would forget about the Hungarian and Polish demands during their transactions with Germany compelled the two states to join forces.

The news about Chamberlain's visit to Berchtesgaden was received with astonishment in Budapest. Those who believed that Imredy had overestimated the willingness of the West to get involved in a conflict in central Europe felt themselves vindicated. When the forthcoming visit was first announced on 14 September 1938 the Hungarian government launched an immediate diplomatic campaign aimed at the prevention of the feared selective treatment of the territorial disputes connected with the Czechoslovak crisis. The Germans learned that Hungary could not accept any settlement that did not embrace the interests of the Hungarian minority to the same degree as those of the Sudeten Germans. Ferenc Marosy, Hungarian counsellor of mission in London, delivered a note to the Foreign Office declaring that grave consequences would follow if any concessions made towards the Sudeten Germans were not also granted to the Hungarian minority. In the end, Chamberlain and Hitler discussed only the problem of ethnic Germans. The Hungarian minority was barely mentioned.[30] Budapest was disappointed.

The Hungarian government redoubled its campaign against such discrimination. Hermann Göring told the Hungarian minister in Berlin that Hungarian misfortunes were due to the fact that they did not fight hard enough for the satisfaction of their demands with regard to Czechoslovakia. Shortly thereafter Göring dispatched a message to Budapest declaring that the fateful moment had arrived for the Hungarians to join the operations against Czechoslovakia. It was very important for the German leadership that both Hungary and Poland embark on a strong course of anti-Czechoslovak policy. At Berchtesgaden Hitler and Chamberlain made mutual pledges that they would use all means available to them to prevent the escalation of the situation. To some extent, therefore, Berlin had limited options. Hence the vehement appeal issued by Göring to the Hungarians: (1) the Hungarian government must announce an official demand that the Hungarian minority in Czechoslovakia be allowed to exercise its right to self-determination; (2) the Hungarian government must provoke armed incidents and skirmishes in Czechoslovakia. Strikes should be fomented among the Hungarian minority. Hungarians should be incited not to respond to military call-ups. Only such strong and spectacular incidents could draw the attention of Western leaders and public opinion.[31] Göring told Döme Sztojay, the Hungarian minister, that it was necessary for all the minorities living in Czechoslovakia, the governments of the adjoining countries, as well as public opinion to form a big choir announcing the untenable nature of the Czechoslovak state.

The Hungarian government continued its campaign for equal consideration to be given to the minorities of Czechoslovakia at international talks. These diplomatic efforts were mainly concentrated on winning British support. On 16 September 1938 Imredy and Kanya summoned Sir Geoffrey Knox, the British minister to Hungary, and reminded him that the Hungarian minority in Czechoslovakia had to be treated on an equal basis with the Sudeten Germans. Autonomy, as a way of solving the problems of the Hungarians, was not acceptable if any part of the Sudeten German territory were annexed to the Reich.[32] On 18 September 1938 György Barcza, the Hungarian minister to Britain, repeated the Hungarian demand for equal treatment.[33] The next day he forwarded a similar memorandum to Prime Minister Chamberlain. On the same day Chamberlain sent a message to Budapest assuring the Hungarians of his sympathies. He assured them that he would remember their situation. He urged Budapest to continue the peaceful and calm demeanour that had characterized its conduct so far.[34] On 20 September Barcza visited Lord Halifax and requested the support of the British government. The British foreign secretary handed him a note admonishing Budapest to show patience. The Hungarian diplomatic activities in London were matched by steps taken in Paris. Unlike the British, French officials showed no sympathy towards the Hungarian position. When protests were delivered against differential treatment and French assistance was requested in search of a just solution by the Hungarian minister in Paris, Sandor Khuen-Hedervary, at the Quai d'Orsay and by Kalman Kanya at the French mission in Budapest, the answer they received was that the Hungarians should try to resolve their problem by contacting Prague.[35]

Simultaneously to these diplomatic manoeuvres the Hungarian government also took military measures. On 16 September 1938 two further year-classes were called up for service (another 100,000 men entered active service). The units were deployed along the Czechoslovak border. Numerous instances of unrest and skirmishes occurred within Slovak territory. While the Hungarians increased the intensity of their subversive activity in Czechoslovakia, their actions lagged behind those of the Germans in the Sudetenland and of the Poles in Tesin. Imredy disregarded further German calls for more decisive action, and also rejected proposals to the same effect arriving from Warsaw. Andras Hory, the Hungarian minister in Warsaw, made it clear to the Polish government that Budapest found the idea of simultaneous action with the Germans unacceptable.[36] To a great extent the Hungarian reserve was due to the pacifying effect of messages from Chamberlain and Lord Halifax.

While high-ranking British politicians promised support for the Hungarian position, tangible steps were taken to remedy only the German grievances. Budapest therefore decided to negotiate with Berlin before the planned meeting between Chamberlain and Hitler at Godesberg. The opportunity came with Horthy's visit to Göring on 18 September, planned well in advance. Given the fact that the purpose of the visit was game shooting, no official records of any political conversations survived. We may, however, surmise from other references that Horthy contacted Hitler through Göring, and that he also negotiated with Polish representatives.[37]

It is quite conceivable that Horthy's visit contributed to Hitler's readiness to receive the Hungarian prime minister, foreign secretary and chief of staff on 20 September 1938. The meeting took place in Obersalzberg, near Berchtesgaden. According to the minutes taken during the discussions: 'First the Führer rebuked the Hungarian dignitaries for the indecisive manner in which Hungary conducted itself in the present crisis.'[38] The moment had arrived for Hungary to join the campaign against Czechoslovakia, said Hitler. He then asked

Imredy and Kanya to demand an immediate plebiscite. The often
unclear notes imply that the German dictator urged that Hungary
before, or perhaps during, the talks at Godesberg begin military
operations against Czechoslovakia, 'because there is a real danger
that the Czechs will accept everything and then, for the time being,
we would have to do without the complete liquidation of
Czechoslovakia'.[39] Imredy, however, rejected the German idea
concerning a Hungarian attack. An attack on Czechoslovakia would
have meant immediate *casus belli* for Yugoslavia and Romania, and
would also have antagonized the Western powers. In addition,
Hungary could not be certain that Germany would come to its aid,
as the possibility remained for Hitler and Chamberlain to come to an
agreement after all. Such an eventuality would have left Hungary
completely isolated. The rejection of Hitler's latest demands brought
about renewed tension between Germany and Hungary.

At the end of the talks in Obersalzberg, Imredy, at Hitler's request,
drew up a memorandum containing Hungary's demands with regard
to Czechoslovakia. Hitler promised that he would represent these
demands at his forthcoming meeting with the British prime minister.
He made a similar pledge to Jozef Lipski, the Polish ambassador at
Berlin, with whom he also had intensive talks on the same day. It is
evident, however, that the Führer had no intention to keep these
promises. During the talks held on 23 September 1938 he only
mentioned German demands.[40] When it was revealed that the
Hungarian question was not discussed at Godesberg, the Hungarian
government resolved to take decisive steps. On 22 September it
dispatched an abrasive note to Prague, demanding that the territories
with a Hungarian majority be separated from Czechoslovakia and
that the Slovaks and Ruthenes be given the opportunity to exercise
their right to self-determination.[41] More reservists were called up and
troop concentrations were carried out alongside the Czechoslovak
border. Notes were delivered simultaneously in Berlin and London,
protesting against the differential treatment. In reply the Germans
called for even more aggressive diplomatic and military manoeuvres,
while the British urged caution. The Hungarian minister in London
delivered yet another note on 22 September 1938 to Sir Orme
Sargent, deputy undersecretary at the foreign office, against the
proceedings at Godesberg. In his reply Sargent expressed his

concerns about the Hungarian demands conveyed to Prague and the Hungarian troop movements along the Czechoslovak border. When Barcza said that the latter were normal measures of precaution, the deputy under-secretary answered that it was unthinkable that the Czechs would attack Hungary; therefore, he was not satisfied with the Hungarian answer.[42] Two days later Lord Halifax sent a letter to the Hungarian minister in which he assured him that the British government followed the Hungarian question with close attention, and that it would address the issues involved at the appropriate moment.[43] This was received in Budapest with relief and it further restrained the government in its actions regarding the Czechoslovak problem. More news was received that France was also getting ready to support Hungary's demands.[44] It only requested that Hungary continue to keep calm and preserve its neutrality.

In the light of these developments, the Budapest government tried to prevaricate amidst the constant German demands for military cooperation. This was the case on 26 September 1938 when Ribbentrop asked Budapest what it would do if Germany entered Czechoslovakia. Imredy's vague reply was: 'If at all possible, we would stay committed.'[45] It did not alleviate German uncertainty regarding Hungary. Ribbentrop and Göring warned the Hungarians that if they evaded military action (in which Poland was bound to participate), they would be left out of any spoils of the conflict. The Poles were given as an example to the much criticized Hungarians.[46] Dissatisfaction with the devious Hungarians reached its peak when confidential reports arriving in Berlin suggested that Grögy Barcza had assured Lord Halifax that Hungary would stay put in the event of German aggression against Czechoslovakia. Göring summoned Sztojay and demanded an explanation.[47] He was not convinced by the Hungarian minister's denial. The Germans' distrust was justified by Hungary's behaviour during the last days of September. Although the intensity of its diplomatic activity increased, it took great pains to keep out of a possible armed conflict.

Historians have made the point that Hungary's faltering attitude to the planned German aggression against Czechoslovakia may have become a factor in German strategy – a factor that may have been critical in persuading Hitler, who wanted the full dismantling of the Czechoslovak state and not a Munich-type deal, to accept the compromise of Munich.[48] It is true that in the aftermath of Munich Hitler criticized Imredy and Kanya (especially the former) for their behaviour during the crisis. He said that it was their insufficient commitment that forced him to grant concessions to the West. However, these statements were made at the time when Hitler wished to justify his opposition to the Hungarian demands regarding Slovakia and Sub-Carpathian Ruthenia, demands he had supported earlier. It is undeniable that the Hungarian military leadership wanted to evade participation in any German aggression in Hitler's plans against Czechoslovakia, especially if it meant marching simultaneously. This, however, did not influence Hitler's plans for Czechoslovakia. The preparation of the Hungarian army for a major conflict was inadequate. The absence of such a force could not have been decisive in Hitler's decision to abandon his plans for aggression. He was not deflected a year later by the direct refusal of Count Teleki's government to participate in the attack against Poland, even though by that time Hungary's military potential had significantly improved. In neither case did Hungary's attitude play a part in Hitler's decisions. It was the attitude of the Western powers and great power relations in general that influenced his judgement. The most important among these was British policy. Hitler was assured by Chamberlain that Germany could get whatever it wanted in Czechoslovakia without any war. At the time of Munich, Germany was not prepared for a full-scale war.[49]

Hitler's decision not to embark on the complete dismemberment of Czechoslovakia in the autumn of 1938 was based on his fear that if war had broken out it could have escalated into a war on two fronts. This danger was only eliminated a year later by the Molotov–Ribbentrop Pact. Hitler's alternatives were the following: he could risk war against Czechoslovakia, and thus topple Chamberlain and help bring to power a radical government in Britain, which could have declared war on Germany. In such a case France would also have fulfilled its obligations under the Franco-Czechoslovak treaty and that would have automatically activated the relevant provisions of the Czechoslovak–Soviet treaty, thus entailing a Soviet declaration of war. Hitler could not risk the two-front conflict that would have been the logical conclusion of this train of events. By temporarily accepting the compromise offered by

Chamberlain he retained the goodwill of the British for the time being, avoided the consequences of his aggressiveness, and occupied a part of Czechoslovakia. Such was the harsh logic behind Hitler's policy at Munich. Numerous secondary factors also contributed to this solution. Mussolini, for instance, objected to the complete liquidation of Czechoslovakia. The German high command, appalled at the thought of having to fight a European war of potentially catastrophic consequences, was of similar opinion. Hungary's reluctance to commit itself only played a very minor role in the European equation.

The government in Budapest was pleased to hear the news of the convening of the Munich conference. All the participating powers promised help for the settlement of the Hungarian question. Budapest stepped up its campaign once again. On 28 September 1938 its minister in Berlin interviewed Göring for a whole hour, asking whether the Hungarian question would be on the agenda of the conference. Göring assured him of the strongest possible German backing, even though he knew there was no plan to discuss the issue.[50] In London, Barcza could only forward his government's requests to Chamberlain on the day of the conference, just before the prime minister's departure for Munich.[51] Count Istvan Csaky, the cabinet secretary of the Hungarian foreign minister, had flown to Munich, where he talked to Hitler and Mussolini immediately before the conference commenced. Hungary's standpoint was that territories with a Hungarian majority, as established on the basis of the 1910 census, had to be returned to Hungary, and that plebiscites had to be held in Slovakia and Sub-Carpathian Ruthenia. Both Hitler and Mussolini received these proposals with sympathy.[52] However, Hitler was not interested in putting the Hungarian and Polish questions before the four power conference. He was particularly not interested in seeing Great Britain and France have a direct say in the solution of the problem. He was glad to hear the Western proposal for direct bilateral talks between Czechoslovakia and Hungary, on the one hand, and Czechoslovakia and Poland, on the other. Hitler knew that these talks could not be arranged without his involvement and that he would have the final word.

The Munich conference offered no solution for the Hungarian and Polish questions. All that happened was that the representatives of the four powers appended an annex to the Munich agreement, stating: 'The heads of Governments of the four Powers declare that the problems of the Polish and Hungarian minorities in Czechoslovakia, if not settled within three months by agreement between the respective Governments, shall form the subject of another meeting of the heads of Governments of the four Powers here present.'[53]

While the agreement at Munich created the conditions necessary for meeting the Hungarian claims with regard to Czechoslovakia, Budapest was not satisfied. This was as true for the government as for the various political parties and the press. Practically all sections of Hungarian society desired the revision of the Treaty of Trianon. They only differed in terms of strategy through which revision could best be achieved. An influential group, the conservative-liberal wing of the governing party (the group around Count Istvan Bethlen), the Social Democratic Party and the Civic Liberal Party, hoped to accomplish treaty revision by cooperating with the West, without the help of the nazi leadership in Berlin.[54] Only one political party, the Communist Party, opposed revisionism; however, the party was banned and operated underground.

The Imredy government had severe reservations about the Munich decision. Nonetheless, in a radio speech delivered on 1 October 1938, the prime minister pointed out that the Munich agreement held out a promise for Hungary. After all, the four great powers had signed a document in which a solution was demanded for the Hungarian question. However, the Hungarian government could not be content until this question had been settled on the same basis as the question of the Sudeten Germans. Imredy asserted: 'Everyone must realize that we shall not flinch from any hurdle on our path to the satisfactory conclusion of this matter.'[55]

While the Imredy government stepped up its campaign against Czechoslovakia in the aftermath of the Munich agreement, it stopped short, in spite of Polish encouragement to this effect, of emulating the Polish government by openly demanding the handing over of territories. The Polish government, in their deep indignation at not having been invited to the conference at Munich, decided to proceed without consideration of the great powers. On 30 September, that is on the day the Munich Agreement concluded, the Polish government issued an ultimatum demanding the immediate surrender of the Tesin territory by Prague. Simultaneously with the delivery of the ultimatum the Polish army was put on alert. In their rejoinder, dated 1 October 1938, the Czechoslovak government signalled their readiness to start negotiations on the details of the handing over of the territory demanded by the Poles.

The reasons why Imredy did not follow the Polish example were many. Hungary's geographic, political and military situation *vis-à-vis* Czechoslovakia differed greatly from that of the Poles. While Poland claimed a territory with a population of 250,000, the inhabitants of the lands demanded by Hungary amounted to over 1,030,000. Poland itself had a population of 34 million, and also had a large army. Hungary's population was nine million, and it had almost no armed forces. In such circumstances, Hungary could well expect that an ultimatum delivered in the manner of the Polish government would simply be rejected by the Czechoslovak government. The Czechoslovaks were under no obligation to comply with any such demands. In the case of the rejection of the ultimatum, Hungary would have found itself in an invidious position. It would either have had to launch an attack on Czechoslovakia, in which case it would have faced the mobilized and well-equipped Czechoslovak troops along the border (by the end of September 18 year-classes of reservists had been called up in Czechoslovakia), and would also have exposed Hungary to a possible attack by Romania. Alternatively, they could withdraw, suffering an unmitigated diplomatic defeat, resulting in a long-lasting negative effect on any future Czechoslovak–Hungarian negotiations. Therefore, the Hungarians chose a different path. On 1 October 1938 they sent a note to Prague requesting the Czechoslovak government to commence direct talks with Hungary in accordance with the provisions of the Munich agreement.[56] At the same time, they asked the governments in Berlin, London, Paris and Rome to exert all their influence to make Prague seek a settlement with Hungary. All four interceded in Prague urging early talks. Nonetheless, the Czechoslovak government asked for a one to two week deferment of the negotiations with Hungary in consequence of their serious difficulties concerning the Sudeten German and the Polish problems.[57] The Hungarian government began to fear that the Czechs were dragging their feet. They were suspected of trying to gain time while settling the German and Polish questions so that afterwards they could turn their full attention to opposing the Hungarian demands. This fear prompted Hungarian politicians to intensify their diplomatic and military activities. They requested the German, Italian and Polish governments not to guarantee the borders of Czechoslovakia until the latter met the demands submitted by Hungary. In accordance with the ethnographic principles on which the Munich agreement was based, official Hungarian claims could only refer to those territories of Czechoslovakia where Hungarians formed a majority. Therefore, in relation to the other territories of Slovakia and Sub-Carpathia, the Hungarian government requested the holding of plebiscites, hoping that they would turn out in their favour.

From 1935 onwards Hitler had been making promises to prime ministers Gyula Gömbös, Kalman Daranyi and Bela Imredy that he would back the annexation of Slovakia and Sub-Carpathia to Hungary. Now he was completely opposed to annexation. Why did the Führer change his mind? The *volte-face* has at least five reasons. First, in the immediate aftermath of Munich Hitler was still careful not to discredit the ethnic principles on which Munich was based and with the help of which he managed to enlist the support of the Western powers as well as to hijack part of the Western public's sympathy. Second, the undecided, vacillating behaviour of Hungarian politicians during the Munich crisis raised questions about their reliability for the purposes of German foreign policy. Third, as a result of the previous consideration, more store was set in Berlin by an independent Slovak state. Fourth, diplomatic and economic ties with Romania had in the meantime increased in importance for Germany. The Bucharest government only acquiesced in the reassignment of territories with a Hungarian majority to Hungary if they could be assured that the rest would not go to Hungary. In return for an advantageous economic treaty with Romania, with special emphasis on oil production and trade, Germany was willing to be a spokesman for Romanian interests in the region. Finally, Germany regarded a common Hungarian–Polish border, the consequence of the satisfaction of Hungary's territorial demands, to be contrary to its strategic interests. It was no secret that the quest for a common border, pursued by Poland, Hungary and Italy, was meant to counterbalance Germany's predominance in east-central Europe. Therefore, Hitler desired to resolve the problem of the rest of Slovakia on the basis of autonomy to be granted within the new Czechoslovakia that had become Germany's satellite. According to a memorandum prepared on 7 October 1938 at Wilhelmstrasse it was not in the interest of Germany to attach Slovakia to Hungary. The best solution would be to grant autonomy to Slovakia within a federal Czechoslovak state, as that state was totally under Germany's economic and political control. This solution left the door open for the creation of an independent Slovakia.[58] On the question of Sub-Carpathian Ruthenia the memorandum asserts:

> There is no disagreement on the question that we must by all means press for autonomy for Sub-Carpathia under the pretext of demanding the right to self-determination. The annexation of an autonomous Ukraine to Hungary must be avoided at all costs. This solution is desired by both Hungary and Poland. In that way a Polish-Hungarian border would be created, which would make it easier for an anti-German bloc to come into being. The high command of the Wehrmacht also opposes a Polish-Hungarian border from a military point of view.[59]

There is no doubt that one of the main reasons for the Hungarian government to desire a common border with Poland was that it would have improved Hungary's position by reducing its vulnerability *vis-à-vis* Germany.

While the Hungarian government surrendered to the resistance of Berlin and Bratislava on the question of Slovak sovereignty, it concentrated all its strength on acquiring the Sub-Carpathian region. The plan was to achieve this objective through Polish–Hungarian cooperation. Count Istvan Csaky, the cabinet secretary of the foreign minister, travelled to Warsaw on October 1938 to negotiate with Jozef Beck. Warsaw was glad to note that Budapest seemed to have abandoned its claim to Slovakia and concentrated its energy on the Sub-Carpathian region. However, Beck told Count Csaky that because of the threat from Russia (Russian troop concentrations had been reported from the Minsk area), Poland could only help Hungary through political and diplomatic channels.[60] Undaunted, the Hungarian government did not give up the idea of achieving a common border with Poland. From the beginning of October 1938 volunteer irregulars were given the order to infiltrate the Czechoslovak border, increasing the tension in the area. This operation was intended to coerce the Czechoslovak government into carrying out those provisions of the Munich agreement which dealt with the Hungarian question.

Changes occurring within Czechoslovakia also explained the increase in Hungarian nationalist activity. On 6 October 1938 an autonomous Slovak government was formed in the town of Zilina headed by the Catholic priest and political leader, Jozef Tiso. Czechoslovakia was transformed into a dualist state, resembling in structure the former Austro-Hungarian monarchy; Hungary's negotiating partners were no longer the representatives of a democratic Czechoslovakia but of Tiso's government, a puppet of Hitler's. Feeling the enormous strength of Germany behind them the Slovaks displayed unyielding resistance against Hungarian territorial claims.

These developments caused alarm in Budapest. Three emergency sessions of the council of ministers were held on 6–8 October 1938. A decision was made concerning troop concentrations along the border, and another note was sent to Prague.[61] The note was delivered by the United Hungarian Party, which had in the meantime been transformed into the Hungarian National Council. This council assumed the responsibility of representing the interests of the Hungarian minority of Slovakia while the border dispute remained unresolved. Disturbances in the region, including operations initiated by the Hungarian volunteer corps, intensified. In this atmosphere the Czechoslovak government decided to end its procrastination and tackle the Hungarian question. As a result, talks began in Komarno on 9 October 1938. The Hungarian demands presented at Komarno were a replica of Hitler's memorandum submitted in Godesberg. Budapest claimed those territories where, according to the data of the 1910 census, the percentage of the Hungarian population exceeded 50 per cent. Thus it asked for the surrender of 12,940 square kilometres of territory. At the same time it demanded the right of self-determination for the Slovaks and the Ruthenians. The latter demand was rejected by the Czechoslovak delegation outright as not falling within the scope of the negotiations. They argued that the

Munich agreement contained no provisions for this. They also found the territorial demands unacceptable. In fact they were not prepared to concede any territory, only a high degree of autonomy within the boundaries of the Czechoslovak state. Kanya was astonished to hear these statements. 'We were not even prepared to hear this kind of proposal from the Czechoslovak delegation', said the Hungarian foreign minister later. It was categorically rejected. Without territorial concessions, he declared, the talks served no purpose. Following this, Tiso offered the handing over of Zitny Ostrov (Csallóköz, Grosse Schütt) without Bratislava (Pozsony, Pressburg) and its environs, as well as the town of Komarno (the other half of Komarom north of the Danube) as a free port. This proposal would have resulted in the transfer of 1,838 square kilometres and a little over 105,000 inhabitants. This was a tenth of what the Hungarians demanded. After Kanya had rejected this offer, the Czechoslovak delegation appeared ready to hand over 5,200 square kilometres to Hungary with 345,000 inhabitants on the basis of the 1930 census. Kalman Kanya considered this also inadequate. The meeting was adjourned. Kanya and Count Teleki travelled immediately to Budapest, where they discussed the situation with Prime Minister Imredy. At the same time, Tiso sent Minister of the Interior Ferdinand Durcansky to Germany to obtain Hitler's views.

The final session of the Komarno talks took place on 13 October 1938. Kanya declared that the gap between the Hungarian and Czechoslovak standpoints was too wide. He regarded the negotiations concluded. He would submit Hungary's claims on Czechoslovakia to the signatories of the Munich agreement, asking for an early settlement of the problem. The Czechoslovak delegation acknowledged the statement, and hoped that the outcome would not be disadvantageous for them, as they felt Hitler's support behind the Czechoslovak position. Thus the talks at Komarno ended without solving the crisis.

There was anxiety in Hungarian government circles. On 13 October 1938 a meeting of the council of ministers was convened. A debate developed on whether they should order general mobilization or only a partial one. In the end they resolved to call up five more year-classes from the reserves. They also decided to submit Hungary's claim to the four signatories of the Munich agreement.

'Hungary cannot abandon the four power basis', emphasized Kanya, defying those who recommended military action.[62] The council of ministers decided that Kalman Daranyi, the speaker of parliament, be sent to Germany, while Count Csaky, head of the cabinet office at the foreign ministry, be dispatched to Italy for talks.

In the wake of the Munich crisis an increasing number of Hungarian government officials blamed Imredy and Kanya for the unsatisfactory state of affairs. In their analysis, it was because Imredy and Kanya had been reluctant to accept a military alliance with Hitler in August and September 1938 that Hungary proved unable to restore its historic frontiers. A situation was allowed to arise in which the ethnic principle that had been granted to Germany and Poland was denied to Hungary.

The remedy was thought to be in Hitler's hands. During those days, Czech, Slovak and Hungarian politicians followed on each other's heels to Hitler's residence. Frantisek Chvalkovsky, the Czechoslovak foreign minister, arrived in Germany. Before Daranyi's visit, Döme Sztojay held discussions with Ribbentrop, denying that Hungary was now seeking the creation of some kind of bloc that would be hostile to Germany. The same subject was taken up by Daranyi in his talks with the Führer. Daranyi told Hitler that Hungary wished to move closer to the Berlin–Rome Axis. Therefore it was ready to join the Anti-Comintern Pact and withdraw from the League of Nations. Daranyi also made suggestions for the improvement of German–Hungarian economic cooperation. With regard to Hungary's ethnic dispute, he told the Führer that, since Czechoslovakia had refused to hand over the territories, the Hungarian government had decided to take military action, and they were seeking German support for their policy.[63]

Hitler was glad to hear this. However, he tried to pour cold water on their sabre rattling. He turned unequivocally against their military plan. 'You should have fought when I asked you to!' he shouted animatedly. In his view, Hungary had missed the right moment. If war broke out in Czechoslovakia now, he said, Hungary would stand alone. Hitler rejected the proposals both for the convening of the four powers and for holding plebiscites in Slovakia and Ruthenia. He explained the refusal of the first idea by arguing that Britain and France would take the side of Czechoslovakia. With regard to the plebiscite he said that neither the Slovaks nor the Ruthenians wanted to be transferred to Hungary. He advised the Hungarians to come to a direct agreement with Czechoslovakia.

Hitler knew that, as a result of the conflict between them, the representatives of the small states would continue to seek his favour, outbidding each other in their offers of economic and political concessions. The German leader appointed Ribbentrop to act as intermediary in the Hungarian–Czechoslovak conflict. Ribbentrop's judgement in the matter differed substantially from that of the Hungarian government: he believed that Bratislava (Pozsony, Pressburg) and Kosice (Kassa, Kaschau) in Slovakia, as well as Uzgorod (Ungvar) and Mukacevo (Munkacs) in Ruthenia should remain part of the Czechoslovak state. Daranyi's visit to Germany was much less successful than the Hungarians had hoped. All he achieved was that the Germans started to give more pronounced support in the press and through diplomatic channels to the Hungarian claims than before.

Csaky's visit to Rome bore more fruit. Apart from the idea of plebiscites in Slovakia and Ruthenia, Mussolini was ready to back the Hungarian proposals. He accepted the plans for a four power summit and for limited mobilization in Hungary. He promised unqualified diplomatic and military assistance to Hungary. The Duce was glad to get a chance to be in the international spotlight again and proceeded to convene the four power conference, which he thought could be held in Italy during the following week.[64] Immediately following his conversation with Csaky, Ciano telegraphed to London, Paris, Berlin and Belgrade announcing that he was ready to deliver notes to the governments concerned giving full backing to Hungary's desire to discuss its claims at a four power conference.

On receipt of this communication in Berlin, Ribbentrop made a telephone call to Count Ciano. He warned that the idea of a four power conference was inexpedient, and could even be detrimental to Hungarian interests. All preparations for convening a conference must be stopped. Ciano listened to this very reluctantly because the Italian diplomatic machinery was in full swing by that time. To his complete surprise, Count Csaky paid another visit to him a day later and asked him to discontinue all activities because of the Führer's opposition. The Italians were now in an extremely invidious position.

Thereupon, Ciano recommended direct talks between the Hungarians and the Czechoslovak government. If the talks failed Hungary should request arbitration by Germany and Italy.

Simultaneously with these diplomatic manoeuvres the Hungarian government also took military measures. It now deployed the newly called five year-classes along the Czechoslovak border. The force was ready for action. However, the Hungarian high command warned the government again that the army was not equal to the task of fighting a war on two fronts which might result from a hostile Romanian response to an attack on Czechoslovakia. Therefore, after lengthy deliberations, Imredy decided to try to obtain Romanian neutrality in the conflict. In return for Romanian acquiescence in a Hungarian–Polish common border, he was ready to hand over to Romania an area from the territories to be conquered. Polish Foreign Minister Jozef Beck undertook to mediate between Hungary and Romania. He held talks on this question with King Carol II of Romania and Romanian Foreign Minister Nicolae Petrescu-Comnen. Beck later declared that the negotiations were successful. Other sources suggest that the Romanian leaders did not accept the Hungarian and Polish proposals. We tend to give more credit to the latter view.[65]

In the meantime, Ribbentrop prepared his own proposals for the settlement of the Czechoslovak–Hungarian territorial dispute. He sent his plan, compiled with the assistance of the Slovak leaders, including Tiso himself, to the Hungarian government, commenting that they represented the maximum that any German mediation could offer. According to the proposal, Bratislava (Pozsony, Pressburg), Nitra (Nyitra), Kosice (Kassa, Kaschau), Uzgorod (Ungvar) and Mukacevo (Munkacs) could not be returned to Hungary. The Hungarian government, quite predictably, rejected the proposal, and applied for German and Italian arbitration.[66] However, it was not ready to take up arms against the wishes of Germany.

How did the Western powers react to the Hungarian–Czechoslovak negotiations and the envisaged German–Italian arbitration? While the talks between Hungary and Czechoslovakia were followed in both Britain and France, Western politicians did not wish to be drawn into the process as active participants. Influential politicians in London, including Winston Churchill, acknowledged that Hungary had valid claims to make concerning Czechoslovakia.[67] Sir Alexander Cadogan, permanent under-secretary at the foreign office, accepted the view that the first proposal of the Czechoslovak delegation, offering autonomy for the Hungarian minority living in Slovakia, is nothing but a mockery of the ethnic principle.[68] The attitude in Paris was different. The French government laid most of the blame for the failure of the talks on the Hungarian negotiators and suggested that Hungary's territorial demands exceeded the mandate contained in the Munich agreement. Paris thought that Hungary ought to reduce its demands.[69] However, both the British and French governments endorsed the proposal for arbitration by the Axis powers. Later, in March 1939, when Sub-Carpathian Ruthenia was reattached to Hungary, their attitude was more equivocal.

Towards the end of October 1938, an unexpected change affected the Czechoslovak–Hungarian dispute. The Germans decided to grant full support to the Hungarian claims. What made them change their mind? The Hungarian question began to undermine the good relations between Berlin and Rome. The Germans could not afford any further deterioration of their ties with Italy. On 27 October 1938, Ribbentrop travelled to Rome to discuss the *impasse* over Hungary with Mussolini and Ciano. After a long debate, the German foreign minister consented to the return of Kosice (Kassa, Kaschau), Uzgorod (Ungvar) and Mukacevo (Munkacs) to Hungary. The price of this concession was that the Italian government had to forgo their desire for a common border between Hungary and Poland. A decision was reached in Rome for convening a conference for the official settlement of the dispute for 2 November 1938 in Vienna. In accordance with an annex of the Munich agreement, the Czechoslovak–Hungarian dispute should have come before the signatories of the protocols of the Munich conference. But Hitler and Mussolini determined that they would decide this matter without involving either Britain or France in the process. The British and French governments did not object to this solution. The arbitration itself took place in Vienna on 2 November 1938. The German and Italian foreign ministers decided that 12,400 square kilometres with one million inhabitants would be returned to Hungary. Of the five disputed towns, Kosice (Kassa, Kaschau), Uzgorod (Ungvar) and Mukacevo (Munkacs) were awarded to Hungary, while Bratislava

(Pozsony, Pressburg) and Nitra (Nyitra) were retained by Czechoslovakia. This arbitration, the so-called first Vienna Award, was based on the ethnographic principle.

The Hungarians were not content with the result of the arbitration. They objected to the arbitrators' refusal to allow a plebiscite in Ruthenia. In the case of a positive outcome for Hungary, the plebiscite would have resulted in a common border with Poland. Such a border, Hungarian officials argued, would prevent Hungary's encirclement by the German empire. Henrik Werth, chief of the Hungarian general staff, a well-known advocate of the Hungarian–German alliance, declared that 'the question of Sub-Carpathia had to be decided by the Germans in their own favour, then the Reich, that has already surrounded Hungary on the west and the north, would cut Hungary off from any possibility of following any other foreign political line than what Germany dictated'.[70] The state of being at Germany's mercy to such an extent was not desired even by the pro-German elements in Hungary. Hungarian politicians wished to cooperate in the rearrangement of the European system with Germans, not as satellites, but as equal partners. Miklos Kozma, the former minister of the interior, expressed these sentiments in one of his diary entries:

> 9 million Hungarians live their lives locked up in the cage of the Hungary created at Trianon. They are surrounded on three sides by the Little Entente, and on the fourth, since the *Anschluss,* by Germany. If, in the future, which is not doubted by anybody, either peacefully or by blood, we recover the Hungarian territories, this, in itself, would only mean that a few more Hungarians would live in a slightly bigger cage. The recovery of Ruthenia, on the other hand, would mean that we broke the ring of the Little Entente between Czechoslovakia and Romania, and created our contiguous border with Poland. Even then we would undoubtedly have to continue our friendly policy towards Germany. But we would continue that policy in different circumstances, we would become a valuable country, The Warsaw–Budapest–Belgrade–Rome line would not be opposed to the Rome–Berlin Axis, but it would mean a relief for us.[71]

Shortly after the first Vienna Award was made, the Hungarian leadership decided to take action for the repossession of Sub-Carpathian Ruthenia. They wished to create a *fait accompli*. Their premise was that the Western powers would simply acknowledge their decision, that Yugoslavia would remain neutral, and that Poland and Italy would provide active assistance. They hoped that Germany would, in the end, accept such a *fait accompli*. On 9 November 1938, a week after the arbitration in Vienna, Kanya sent the following telegram to Warsaw: 'It is possible that, following the handing over of Ungvar and Munkacs, the present government of Ruthenia may request the entry of Hungarian troops into the remaining territories of Ruthenia for the purpose of keeping law and order. In this case we are ready to move in with regular *honved* [army] troops.'[72] This had, however, already become reality. On 6 November 1938, a meeting had taken place with the participation of the regent, Miklos Horthy, where the Ruthenian question was discussed. It was decided that the Hungarian army would occupy the whole of Sub-Carpathian region. Arrangements were made so that the move took place at the invitation of the Ruthenian National Council. In order to carry out the operation, Hungary requested military assistance from Poland in the form of four army divisions, This request was, however, rejected by Beck.[73] Before commencing the operations, the Hungarian government wished to ascertain once again what the attitude of the Axis powers would be. Count Ciano admonished the Hungarians. He told them that an occupation of Sub-Carpathia would be most unpleasant for the Duce, as the three towns (Kassa, Ungvar and Munkacs) were procured in return for Hungary's pledge not to occupy the rest of Ruthenia, and the Duce guaranteed this settlement. Italy, therefore, did not support the Hungarian plan.[74]

On 15 November 1938, Miklos Horthy held personal talks with Otto von Erdmannsdorff, the German minister in Budapest. The regent enumerated all the reasons why he and his government were resolved to take action to occupy the Sub-Carpathian region. On 18 November 1938, Dome Sztojay submitted a note of similar content at the Wilhelmstrasse in Berlin. Berlin did not reject the Hungarian plans; it merely emphasized that 'such a step is a cause for concern, because they [the Germans] are afraid that the Czech government will respond in kind, causing complications, and they cannot come to our help'.

By the evening of 18 November 1938 both the German and Italian replies were discussed by the council of ministers in Budapest at a late night session. They interpreted the German response as being apprehensive for the security of Hungary given the fact that Germany was not in a position to provide it with assistance at that time. It is quite evident that this interpretation was a conscious misconstruction of the German reply. The council of ministers adopted a resolution in favour of launching an immediate attack. The date of the offensive was set for the night of 19 November 1938. The die was cast. However, a few minutes before the attack, a sense of caution prevailed. Both the government and the military leadership began to fear lest the Germans reacted too adversely to the Hungarian move. At the last minute the attack was called off and postponed for 24 hours. As a consequence, the element of surprise and *fait accompli* was lost. It was too late to stop the publication of the communique in *Felvidiki Magyar Hirlap* (Hungarian News of the Highlands). Thus, on the morning of 20 November 1938, the paper published the news in large headlines that the Ruthenian National Council had called for the assistance of the Hungarian military. A furore ensued in diplomatic circles.

On 21 November 1938, the German and Italian governments sent identical notes to Budapest that summed up their positions in four sharply critical points.[75] The notes stressed that the German and Italian governments had recently delineated the boundary between Hungary and Sub-Carpathian Ruthenia in Vienna in the form of arbitration at the request of the Hungarian and Czechoslovak governments. By signing the documents confirming the Vienna Award, the Hungarian government openly acknowledged before the whole world that it accepted this boundary as the final frontier of Hungary. The protest notes issued by the Axis created a very difficult situation for Hungary. The resulting diplomatic isolation also led to a serious internal crisis. Both the far right and the conservative-liberal faction became dissatisfied with the policy of the government. The former held the government responsible for its indecision in the late summer and early autumn, for not having concluded a military alliance with Germany, and for experimenting with the Little Entente instead. In their analysis, this was the reason why Hungarian revisionism did not yield satisfactory results, and Hungary's relations with Germany deteriorated. The far right saw only one way out of this disgraceful situation: an unequivocal shift towards the German Nazi alliance.

The liberal wing of the National Party of Unity criticized Imrody's government for all the opposite reasons. They censured the government for its concessions to the extreme right and for the plan to make Hungary a full member of the Axis that would withdraw it from the League of Nations.[76] This faction had so far abstained from publicly criticizing the government for fear of endangering the national programme for repossessing Sub-Carpathia. Following the spectacular failure, however, the pent-up dissatisfaction and differences broke to the surface. A general sense of disillusionment with the government took over. 'The government lost direction, and proved unequal to the historic task', wrote Miklos Kozma in his diary.[77]

After the formation of his second cabinet, Imredy heightened the intensity of Hungarian contacts with Germany. Kalman Kanya was made the scapegoat for his own earlier hesitation and insufficiently pro-German foreign policy and was left out of the new cabinet. Imredy told Berlin that Kanya had been the initiator of the operations in November 1938 which ended in such a fiasco. This helped to clear his name and incriminate Kanya, whom Hitler himself disliked intensely. Kanya was an established authority on foreign affairs, and he often managed to carry out his policy even in the face of the Führer's opposition. The pro-German Count Istvan Csaky, his successor, was a man of little vision and limited diplomatic skills. Thus he was eminently suited to carry out his superior's instructions to follow a pro-Berlin foreign policy. The new line-up was highly appreciated by Hitler. At the beginning of December, Ribbentrop signalled his willingness to open a new chapter in German–Hungarian relations and suggested that they should meet for discussions.

The new foreign minister travelled to Germany on 16 November 1938 to negotiate with the Führer and other members of his government. The talks began in a tense atmosphere. Hitler enumerated the crimes of the Hungarians. He accused them of disloyalty. Germany, he said, 'made the first border revision possible'. The Hungarians did not seem to appreciate this. Some of them even appeared to suggest that Germany prevented them from obtaining their rightful possessions. While he negotiated with Horthy, Kanya, whom he always considered to be an enemy of Germany, concluded the agreement in Bled, thereby revitalizing the Little Entente to the detriment of Germany. When the events unfolded, said Hitler, the Poles understood that it was time to move, while the Hungarians slept through the period, only bothering to take few half-hearted steps.[78] Hitler attributed his autumn success to the Western powers, who laid Czechoslovakia at his feet. What happened then, he continued, could only happen once in history. The Führer concluded that Germany and its allies could only plan for the future based on the proposition that any further results could only be achieved through the mutual coordination of all actions.

The Hungarian foreign minister tried to defend the Hungarian government against the accusations. He explained the indecision and caution prevailing in Hungary because of its military weakness, he assured the Führer that most Hungarians felt great friendship towards Germany, and promised that the government would abide by the basic requirements set out by the German government. Count Csaky showed remorse for Hungary's earlier mistakes. In return, Hitler was willing to let bygones be bygones and start a new phase in German–Hungarian relations. Thereafter Hitler's anger subsided to such an extent that he began discussing ways of cooperation. He divulged his plan for the complete dismemberment of Czechoslovakia: 'If we must abandon the ethnographic principle and embrace the territorial principle instead we must do that together.' In a diplomatic tone, he also hinted at the possible date for action, which would be in March 1939.[79]

In the aftermath of the Munich agreement and of the first Vienna Award, it became evident that the Western powers would not try to protect Czechoslovakia. However, it was also understood that, if only from the point of view of the European balance, they were not uninterested in the outcome of the territorial dispute over the Sub-Carpathian region. They were ready to acknowledge the change of sovereignty and were not averse to the assignment of this territory to Hungary. This was in spite of the fact that during the last phase of Imredy's administration, the Hungarian prime minister totally embraced the German line and Hungary's ties with the West suffered a significant setback. Imredy lost the support of those British politicians who had welcomed his appointment earlier. By the end of 1938, London in fact contemplated the withdrawal of all British support from the Hungarian prime minister.[80] The conservative-liberals, especially those associated with the group around Count Istvan Bethlen, were engaged in an attempt to bring down Imredy's second government. They were also manoeuvring to promote their candidate into the prime ministerial chair of Hungary, someone who would be able to contain the inexorable swing in foreign policy towards Germany. Their choice for this purpose was Count Pal Teleki. The group managed to convince Horthy, and he appointed Teleki as the next prime minister on 16 February 1939. The prime minister's first measures were aimed at the strengthening of Hungary's ties with Italy and the Western powers, while retaining good relations with Germany. He was also adamant that he should maintain Hungary's freedom of action in foreign policy. Within a short time he encountered the same dilemma as his predecessors Daranyi and Imredy had: either play Germany's game or be removed from power. Teleki would not accept either of these choices. In April 1941 he committed suicide.

During the first days of March 1939 news arrived in Berlin regarding the Slovak question. The leaders of the Hlinka Slovak People's Party began to hesitate. On 7 March 1939 the Germans informed Jozef Tiso and Karol Sidor that they had decided to break up the Czechoslovak state. The Slovak leaders were told that this decision served as their best opportunity for declaring the independence of Slovakia. Simultaneously, the Germans transported a large shipment of weapons from Austria to Slovakia and armed the so-called German *Ordeners*. In this situation, the government in Prague decided to take military measures. They arrested most members of the government in Bratislava and took control of Slovakia. Berlin warned the Slovaks to take advantage of the Führer's goodwill or deal with Budapest.

On 11 March 1939, Hitler ordered that a free hand be given to the Hungarian government with respect to the future of the Sub-Carpathian region. The note in which the communication to this effect was sent to Hungary also contained provisions relating to Germany's economic and political interests in Sub-Carpathia that the Hungarian government would have to respect. Count Teleki accepted them, whereupon Hitler summoned Döme Sztojay and gave his consent for the offensive to go ahead. He told Sztojay that the breakup of Czechoslovakia was imminent and that his government had 24 hours to solve the Ruthenian question.'[81] Teleki reacted with mixed feelings to this turn of events. On the one hand he was glad that at last Hungary could acquire a common border with Poland. On the other hand, he could not ignore that all this was made possible through Germany's assistance.

What made Hitler change his position on Sub-Carpathia? The main reason was the situation in Slovakia. On 12 March 1939, Karol Sidor rejected the Germans' call for an independent Slovakia. Thereupon Hitler summoned Jozef Tiso to Berlin and told him that two German divisions stood ready to occupy Bratislava. During his negotiations with Tiso, Hitler repeatedly reminded the Slovak politician that he saved the independence of Slovakia against Hungarian ambitions. It was 'by chance' that a report conveying the news of Hungarian troop concentrations along the Slovak border happened to be delivered to Ribbentrop, who participated at the talks while the negotiations were in progress. Hitler handed over the report to Tiso and asked: 'would Slovakia want to secede from the Czech lands, and become an independent state?'[82] The following day the Slovak parliament gave the answer: it proclaimed a Slovak state and Tiso asked for it to be put under the protection of the German Reich. Hitler granted protected status to the new German satellite.

The Hungarian occupation of Slovakia was complicated by the fact that, coinciding with the German entry into Prague on 15 March 1939, the Ruthenian nationalist leader Avgustin Voloshin carried out a *coup d'état*, declared the independence of Sub-Carpathian Ruthenia and asked for German protection. When Hitler left his plea unanswered, he fled to Romania where he proclaimed Ruthenia's union with Romania. The Romanian leaders were aware of the fact that the Hungarian occupation of Ruthenia took place with German approval, and therefore did not respond to Voloshin's request. Instead, they embarked on a peaceful attempt to acquire those parts of the Sub-Carpathian territory that they had claimed for themselves at the end of the First World War. The Polish government supported their bid, but Hungary rejected this claim in the most definite terms. On 17 March 1939, after a minor struggle with the so-called Sich

Guard, the Hungarian army took control of Ruthenia, putting an end to the one-day republic there.

These events were the logical consequences of the Munich Agreement. They shattered the state of Czechoslovakia and proved to be the precursor to the destruction of the whole central European system as conceived at Versailles at the end of the First World War.

Institute of History, MTA

NOTES

1. An exception to this is *Diplomáciai iratok Magyarország Külpolitikájához 1936–1938 (DIMK)*. Vol.2 is titled: *A Müncheni egyezmény létrejötte és Magyarország külpolitikája 1936–1938* (Budapest, 1965); Vol.3 is *Magyorország külpolitikája 1938–1939* (Budapest, 1970). Both edited by Magda Ádám. See also *München 1938* (Budapest, 1988); this offers much new information on the attitude of various central and eastern European political parties.

2. During these talks, held on 14 and 15 March 1921, the Hungarian ministers appealed for border revision on the basis of the so-called Millerand letter. Benes refused their request. He did not consider the letter to be binding on Czechoslovakia. The Archives of the Foreign Ministry of Czechoslovakia (AMFA). Political correspondence, PZ. Budapest, 1920–1929. Memorandum by the Czechoslovak Ministry of Foreign Affairs for Lejhanec, 18 March 1921.

3. The Little Entente was, in fact, established against a nonexistent danger. No one could have thought seriously that Hungary alone would attack any one of its members. None of them was, however, afforded protection by the bloc against the real threats, that is, Czechoslovakia against Germany, Romania against the Soviet Union, and Yugoslavia against Italy.

4. Lajos Kerekes (ed.), *DIMK, vol 1, A Berlin-Róma tengely kialakulása is Ausztria annexiója 1936-1938* (Budapest, 1962), Doc.313, p.502.

5. Ibid.

6. The minutes taken during the negotiations do not contain references to this detail. It is revealed, however, in a document produced at a later date. Országos Levéltár (National Archives [of Hungary], OL) Küm. res. pol. 1939-7/a-247.

7. During his visit to Budapest in April 1936, Marjan Koscialkowski, the Polish prime minister, assured the Hugarian government that Poland had no territorial demands in Slovakia or Sub-Carpathia. These territories should be annexed to Hugary. Other signs, however, indicated that mainly military circles in Poland began to deviate from this attitude.

8. *DIMK*, Vol.2, Doc.403, pp.665–66. In May 1938, Foreign Minister Kanya conducted lengthy negotiations with Tiso, who arrived for the Eucharistic Congress on the subject of Slovakia's annexation to Hungary. These secret conversations continued until the end of September 1938. Tiso deemed it important to inform the Hungarian government at the time of his meeting with Benes on 23 September 1938. He reiterated his intention to join Hungary. *DIMK*, Vol.2, Doc.388, pp.645–6.

9. *DIMK*, Vol.2, Doc.122, p.288.

10. Gratz had always been an advocate of finding a *modus vivendi* between Hungary and

Czechoslovakia. As foreign minister in 1921 he made an attempt at obtaining such an agreement. It has not been possible to establish whether his mission in 1938 was officially sanctioned. In any event, on his return from Prague, at Kanya's request, he prepared a report for the foreign minister. *DIMK,* Vol.1, Doc.407, pp.635–8.
11. Ibid.
12. Ibid.
13. OL. Küm. pol. 1938-21/7-1120.
14. AMFA, PZ, Budapest, 1938, 16539.
15. Pesti Naplo, 17 April 1938.
16. OL. Küm. pol. 1938-7/25-897.
17. Imredy accepted the Italian view that Italy and the countries sharing its perspective should form a so-called horizontal axis, which would lead from Rome through Belgrade and Budapest to Warsaw.
18. Országgyűlési Napló (Parliamentary Reports), 1935–40, Vol.8, 15 May 1938.
19. Igor Lukes, *Czechoslovakia between Stalin and Hitler: The Diplomacy of Edvard Benes* (New York, 1996), pp.143–57.
20. Simultaneously with taking these military measures, the Czechoslovak government dispatched a note to Budapest, assuring the Hungarians that the measures were not aimed against Hungary their purpose was the maintenance of internal order.
21. OL. Küm. res. pol. 1938-47-824.
22. OL. Küm. res. pol. 1938-23, without file number.
23. In the question of minorities, the Hungarian government set higher requirements for the Czechoslovaks than for the Yugoslavs and the Romanians.
24. The British *Daily Herald* praised the agreement, giving special credit to the flexibility evinced by the Hungarian statesmen. *The Daily Herald,* 24 Aug. 1938.
25. *Ciano's Diary 1937–1938,* trans. and notes by Andreas Mayor, intro. by Malcolm Muggeridge (London, 1952), p.146.
26. ADAP, Serie D, Bd.2, Doc.383, pp.486–7.
27. Ibid.
28. Ibid.
29. ADAP, Serie D, Bd.2, Doc.383, pp.486–7.
30. Hitler told Chamberlain that 'the Hungarians, the Poles and the Ukrainians also had demands. However, he did not wish to be their spokesman'. *Weltgeschichte der Gegenwart* Bd.1 (Munich, 1953), Doc.67, p.136.
31. *DIMK,* Vol.2, Doc.347, pp.605–7.
32. *DIMK,* Vol.2, Doc.346, p.605.
33. *DIMK,* Vol.2, Doc.363, pp.621–2.
34. *DIMK,* Vol.2, Doc.365, p.624.
35. *DIMK,* Vol.2, Doc.362, p.620.
36. *DIMK,* Vol.2, Doc.354, pp.611–13.
37. Miklós Szinai and László Szács (eds.), *Horthy Miklós titkav iratai* (Budapest, 1962), p.183.
38. ADAP, Serie D, Bd. 2, Doc. 5 54, pp.689–90.
39. Ibid. On further details of this subject, see György Ránki, 'Adatok a magyar külpolitikához a Csehszlovákiai agresszió idejé, *Szádok* 1–2 (1959), and Magda Ádám, 'La Hongrie et Munich', *Revue d'Histoire de la Deuxième Guerre Mondiale et des Confits Contamporains* 132 (Oct. 1983).
40. *ADAP,* Serie D, Bd.2, Doc.554, pp.689–90.
41. *DIMK,* Vol.2, Doc.378, pp.635–6.
42. *DIMK,* Vol.2, Doc.384, pp.640–41.
43. *DIMK,* Vol.2, Doc.392, pp.652–3.
44. *DIMK,* Vol.2, Doc.394, p.654.
45. *DIMK,* Vol.2, Doc.401, p.663.
46. *DIMK,* Vol.2, Doc.401, p.662.

47. Ibid.
48. Pál Pritz, 'A kieli találkozó' *Századok,* No.3 (1974), p.563. A similar view is put forward by Jorg Hoensch: 'Hungary's reluctance may have contributed to the fact that war was averted in September, and that the Munich agreement was concluded.' Jorg K. Hoensch, *Der ungarische Revisionismus und die Zerschlagung der Tschekoslowakei* (Tübingen, 1967), p.80.
49. Winston S. Churchill, *The Second World War,* Vol.1, *The Gathering Storm* (London, 1948), p.250, quoting Paul Reynauld, *La France a sauvé l'Europe,* Vol.I, p.561.
50. *DIMK,* Vol.2, Doc.415, pp.673–4.
51. *DIMK,* Vol.2, Doc.428, pp.684–85.
52. *DIMK,* Vol.2, Doc.423, pp.680–81.
53. *DBFP,* 3rd series, Vol.11, Doc.1124.
54. On this subject, *see* further László Szarka, 'Versuchung und Irrwege der Revision. Die tschekoslowakische Frage in der ungarische politischen Öffentlichkeit 1938', in Peter Glotz *et al.* (eds.), *München, 1938: Ende des alten Europas* (Essen, 1990), pp.321–44; and *München 1938: Diplomáciai es politikai* (Budapest, 1988).
55. *Pester Lloyd,* 2 Oct. 1938.
56. *DIMK,* Vol.2, Docs.432, 442, 449, pp.689, 696, 707.
57. *DIMK,* Vol.2, Doc.443, pp.696–7.
58. *ADAP,* Serie, Bd. 4, Doc.45, pp.45–7.
59. Ibid.
60. *DIMK,* Vol.2, Doc.463, p.721.
61. OL, Minutes of the Council of Ministers, 6 Oct. 1938.
62. Ibid.
63. *ADAP,* Serie D, Bd.4, Doc.63, pp.72–3.
64. *DIMK,* Vol.2, Docs.529, 530, 533, pp.796–8, 799–801.
65. On this subject, see Henryk Batowsky, 'Beck's Romanian Journey in October 1938', *Kwartalnik Historyczny,* No.2 (1958), pp.423–39.
66. *DIMK,* Vol.2, Doc.563, p.829.
67. *DIMK,* Vol.3, Doc.146, pp.257–60.
68. *DIMK,* Vol.2, Doc.548, pp.814–16.
69. *DIMK,* Vol.2, Doc.509, pp.780–81.
70. OL. Küm. res. pol. 1939-33/a-235–6.
71. OL. The papers of Miklós Kozma, folder 27, diary entries, 28 Sept. 1938.
72. *DIMK,* Vol.3, Doc.12, pp.97–8.
73. *DIMK,* Vol.3, Docs.28, 29, pp.118–19. There was a plan to support the Hungarian action by Polish irregulars. The Poles also undertook to secure Romanian neutrality. *DIMK,* Vol.3, Doc.40, pp.128–9.
74. *DIMK,* Vol.3, Doc.41, pp.129–30.
75. *DIMK,* Vol.3, Docs.58, 59, pp.143–5.
76. On 22 November 1938, a day after the receipt of the German and Italian protest notes, the Hungarian government sent a message to the German and Italian governments whereby they stated their readiness to join the Anti-Comintern Pact and withdraw from the League of Nations.
77. OL, the papers of Miklós Kozma, folder 27, Diary entries, 21 Nov. 1938.
78. Ignác Romsics, *Helyünk és sorsunk a Duna-medencében* (Budapest, 1996), pp.102–5.
79. C.A. Macartney, *October Fifteenth: The History of Modern Hungary, 1929–1945* (New York, 1956), p.361.
80. On this subject, also see Gyula Juhdsz, *A Teleki-kormciny külpolitikája 1939–1941* (Budapest, 1969), and Lóránt Tilkovszky, *Teleki Pál. Legenda és valóság* (Budapest, 1969).
81. *ADAP,* Serie D, Bd.4, Doc.84, pp.200–201.
82. *ADAP,* Serie D, Bd.4, Doc.202, p.214.

France and the Czechoslovak Crisis

MARTIN THOMAS

From April 1938 French premier Edouard Daladier wielded an executive power in excess of the classic *primus inter pares* of much Western cabinet government. This basic point rests uneasily with the image of the gruff, almost crest-fallen politician whose demeanour upon his return from the Munich Conference contrasted so strongly with the misguided triumphalism of Neville Chamberlain.[1] The fact remains that in 1938 Daladier cut a formidable figure in the council of ministers. His government was expected to restore financial confidence and curb the social division made manifest during the interlude of Popular Front administration in 1936–37. But, as will be shown, a volatile economic position and incipient financial breakdown in September 1938 are factors which deserve greater emphasis in assessments of French behaviour at the height of the Czech crisis. During 1937, French gold reserves declined by some 12,872 million francs and, following Léon Blum's brief return to office on 13 March 1938, this outflow accelerated once more. Overall, the gold reserve dwindled by a further 7,143 million francs in the first three months of the new year. In this setting of deepening financial crisis in pre-Munich France, as René Rémond emphasized some 20 years ago, Daladier was widely considered a strong man and a unifier.[2] Thanks to a diffuse and sometimes venal press susceptible to government manipulation, Daladier was also well placed to shape public opinion as the Czech crisis developed. Within his Radical-Socialist Party, Daladier was arbiter between a liberal left wing for whom participation in the Popular Front coalition with the socialists and communists remained defensible, and a growing 'neo-radical' right eager to reassert the party's defence of property and free-market capitalism.[3] Much like their principal centre-right rival in parliament – Pierre-Etienne Flandin's Alliance Démocratique – during 1938 neo-radicals such as Foreign Minister Georges Bonnet stressed France's material weakness and lack of national cohesion in order to denigrate popular frontism and communist endorsement of a collective security strategy. Ironically, Bonnet's influential presence in the cabinet helped Daladier to contain the conservative radicals, senators and industrialists whose interests the foreign minister generally advanced.[4]

If France was a nation still profoundly divided by the Popular Front experience, then the Radical Party represented that division in microcosm. On 8 November 1937 British Ambassador Sir Eric Phipps discussed the condition of France with Joseph Caillaux, one of the Radicals' elder statesman who had orchestrated senate opposition to Blum's first government five months earlier (and who would do so again in the spring of 1938). Caillaux poured scorn on popular frontism, he bemoaned the weakness of the French economy and he despaired of air force rearmament – all themes that would become familiar as the crisis over Czechoslovakia mounted. But Daladier escaped Caillaux's vitriol.[5] More than usual, the Radical Party's abiding strength resided in a leader who commanded popular confidence, regardless of the factional squabbles of his party colleagues. Once Daladier assumed the premiership in April 1938, his politics were sufficiently multi-faceted to keep his party intact. For the left, he remained a Jacobin republican respected for steering through the Popular Front's initial rearmament programme; for the right, he had broken with the Popular Front's social programme and set about restoring sound finance. Admittedly, this process remained incomplete. Not until Daladier and Paul Reynaud's decisive confrontation with organized trade unionism following the CGT's call for a general strike on 30 November 1938 did the political balance shift decisively towards employer interests, finally reversing the worker ascendancy of the early Popular Front era.[6]

Over recent years, several historians have questioned the assumption of weakness said to underpin the French loss of nerve in 1938. Similarly, the notion of French foreign policy as a mere appendage of British appeasement has been put under scrutiny, producing a more subtle appreciation of civil–military relations, France's financial position, the demise of its Eastern alliance system, the influence of public opinion and the actions of the Popular Front.[7] In spite of this work, the tendency persists to dismiss France during the Czech crisis as petrified, standing ostrich-like in the face of Germany's advance. This article examines certain aspects of this image. Was Daladier's government a weak and divided administration unwilling to face up to France's international obligations? What was the tenor and accuracy of the incoming information from key European ambassadors and attachés? Did diplomatic reportage and intelligence assessments shape the government's evaluation of its foreign policy options as the crisis over Czechoslovakia intensified? Or were minds made up in the wake of Hitler's success in Austria in March 1938? Did France's military leaders merely state harsh truths, and to what extent did their pessimism find a receptive audience within Daladier's cabinet as the nation's banking system neared collapse?

The administrative roots of Daladier's power are easily traced. He consolidated his prime ministerial authority within government through his executive control of the defence establishment and his shrewd, centrist leadership of the Radical-Socialist Party. After the disintegration of Popular Frontism in 1937, the Radicals reemerged as the dominant force within French parliamentary politics in the 1938–39 period. From its investiture on 10 April 1938, Daladier's third administration stood out from its interwar predecessors in being virtually a single-party affair. It was confirmed in office by an almost unanimous parliamentary vote (576 to 5).[8] Experienced Radical ministers took the senior portfolios of finance, interior and foreign affairs, and non-radicals, such as the Socialists Paul Ramadier and Ludovic-Oscar Frossard, and the liberal deputy, Louis de Chappedelaine, were confined to a handful of junior cabinet posts.[9] Much like its Soviet mentor, the one solidly anti-*Munichois* party, the Parti Communiste Français (PCF), was marginalized by the French government in September 1938.[10] In addition to his duties as premier, Daladier maintained his previous ministerial role as both head of the war ministry and executive minister in charge of national defence. His ministerial remit thus extended beyond the supervision of the French army as he coordinated the rearmament and strategic planning of all three armed forces. From mid-1936 Daladier was the civilian face of the French defence effort. Although it ended in defeat and personal humiliation for them both, between 1936 and 1940 Daladier and the chief of national defence staff, General Maurice Gamelin, formed a unique civil–military partnership which commanded a general respect within the 1938 administration.[11] Their expanding role in directing rearmament as well as strategic planning added to the influence of both men.

By contrast, the Quai d'Orsay lacked a comparable partnership between Foreign Minister Bonnet and his senior official, Secretary-General Alexis Léger. According to Léger's own secretary, Etienne de Crouy-Chanel, on the eve of the Munich conference in September (during which Léger served as aide to Daladier), the secretary-general steered clear of Bonnet in an effort to avoid receiving unpalatable instructions. Bonnet was anyway reluctant to spell out clear instructions to Léger lest he be saddled with principal responsibility should the conference fail. Political Director René Massigli was, in turn, ostracized and ultimately demoted by Bonnet, who disparaged Massigli's continuing firmness towards Germany.[12] Unsure of the loyalty of his senior advisers, during September Bonnet exploited copious embassy dispatches from Ambassador André François-Poncet in Berlin, which stressed Hitler's readiness to use force in Czechoslovakia. This merely confirmed Bonnet's view – starkly related to Czech Ambassador Stefan Osusky on 20 July – that France could not march without British military support. Conversely, Bonnet dismissed reports from Ambassador Robert Coulondre in Moscow suggesting that the Soviet Union might march in support of a Franco-Czechoslovakian coalition.[13]

The power of the Daladier–Gamelin combination was underlined in the immediate aftermath of the *Anschluss* when, at a famous session of the permanent committee of national defence (Comité Permanent de la Défense Nationale – CPDN) on 15 March, they stifled a call from premier Blum and his foreign minister, Joseph Paul-Boncour, to reconsider a concerted Franco-Soviet defence of Czechoslovakia.[14] In preparation for this meeting, Gamelin assessed the wider strategic impact of Germany's absorption of Austria. Almost encircled, Czechoslovakia's defensive planning and the security of its frontier fortifications were now undermined by the prospect of a secondary German thrust launched from Austrian territory. More importantly, the only two states that Gamelin identified as essential bulwarks to French-led operations in support of Czechoslovakia were Britain and Poland – perhaps the two nonrevisionist powers least likely to fight for Prague.[15] This set the tenor for French policy as the Czech crisis developed over subsequent months.

In early April, the London ambassador, Charles Corbin, sent the outgoing foreign minister, Paul-Boncour, a detailed intelligence report derived from Rome. This indicated that Hitler intended to press Mussolini to adopt a more stridently anti-French policy when he visited the Italian capital in early May. In return for firm German support of Italy's irredentist claims against France in the Mediterranean, Hitler expected Mussolini to acquiesce in Germany's expansion into central and eastern Europe. The two Axis states would meanwhile coordinate their efforts to foment political instability in France in an effort to slow the pace of French rearmament.[16] Corbin's report added fuel to a well-stoked fire. Paul-Boncour's outspoken opposition to the *Anschluss*, Blum's contempt for Mussolini, and the readiness of both ministers to stand by the Czechs, caused much alarm in London. On 21 March Paul-Boncour instructed Corbin to make every effort to sustain British interest in eastern Europe. Two days later, the foreign minister returned to this theme. Ignoring the conclusions of the 15 March CPDN, Paul-Boncour insisted that German rearmament was poorly matched to the requirements of a long war. If France mobilized with full British support, this action alone would force the Wehrmacht to concentrate its primary strength along the patchy fortifications of the Westwall. The endorsement of a two-front strategy of coalition warfare would, in other words, deter German aggression in the east.[17] Although Winston Churchill returned from a visit to Paris at the end of March proclaiming the benefits of closer Anglo-French strategic coordination, Paul-Boncour's entreaties fell on deaf ears in Chamberlain's cabinet. Relief at Paul Boncour's departure was a cornerstone of British governmental sympathy for Daladier's new administration, Ambassador Phipps having been instructed to lobby against the foreign minister's re-appointment. British pressure duplicated that applied by the chairs of the parliamentary foreign affairs commissions, Jean Mistler and Henry Bérenger, in support of Bonnet's selection to the Quai d'Orsay.[18]

Gamelin, too, was surely glad to see Paul-Boncour depart. At the end of March, and again a month later, the general took Paul-Boncour to task, insisting that the short-term strategic balance lay firmly in Germany's favour. Unable to assist Czechoslovakia directly, the effectiveness of French diversionary operations in the Rhineland, beyond Germany's still incomplete Siegfried Line fortifications, would depend in turn upon the extent of Romanian, Yugoslav and, possibly, Soviet assistance to the Czechs. In this respect, the terminal decline of the Czechoslovakian–Romanian–Yugoslav Little Entente underscored French military doubts about the effectiveness of Soviet intervention via Romanian soil or air space.[19] Gamelin further estimated that revisionist Hungary could easily cut any land corridor opened between Slovakia and Romania.[20] Daladier accepted Gamelin's conclusions during the 15 March CPDN. Cracks in the accord between the two men over the prospects for French military action only began to show during the final weeks before Munich. With a compliant fellow-Radical, Camille Chautemps, as deputy premier, and two like-minded party colleagues – César Campinchi and Guy La Chambre – at the naval and air ministries, in matters of defence policy Daladier's authority was little challenged before September. By contrast, financial policy and, above all, foreign affairs generated considerable division within the French government at various points during the Czech crisis.

Granted special powers for the purpose, the new government devalued the franc on 4 May 1938 (the third devaluation since October 1936), fixing its minimum rate at 176ff. to £1. The reestablished connection between franc parity and the London financial market underscored the new government's attachment to cooperation with Britain. By once more linking the franc to sterling, and so curbing the currency fluctuation characteristic of the free-floating 'Bonnet franc', Daladier's administration enjoyed a brief financial respite over the next three weeks.[21] But pressure on the currency – sparked off by the war scare of 20–22 May – increased during the tense international atmosphere of the summer months. Between January and September, Finance Minister Paul Marchandeau's senior monetary adviser, Jacques Rueff, head of the direction générale du mouvement des fonds, insisted that the government must either curb its immediate defence expenditure or find additional sources of short-term borrowing. Marchandeau estimated that ordinary charges upon treasury spending for 1938 would exceed 42 billion francs. This was more than double the comparable figure for 1935, the last complete financial year prior to the commencement of a long-term rearmament programme. Rueff warned of treasury bankruptcy once existing legal limits upon permissible short-term borrowing from the Bank of France were reached.[22] Questioned by the Senate Finance Commission about the condition of treasury reserves in the week Daladier took office, Marchandeau conceded that the treasury had scarcely 30 million francs on account, plus an additional 230 million in stop-gap funding from the Bank of France. With 4,500 million in estimated expenditure for May alone, Daladier's government was utterly reliant upon the success of its devaluation.[23] In practice, two further measures were critical to sustained rearmament expenditure and broader financial recovery. Strongly pressed by Rueff, Marchandeau established an autonomous national defence fund to meet the rising costs of rearmament. This was, in turn, dependent upon successful issues of short-term government bonds, deemed the most promising means by which to attract private investment capital in the still volatile French money market.[24] On 15 July 1938, the treasury reached the upper limit of 14.1 billion francs set for these bond issues. While this capital underpinned additions to army and air force defence spending and signified a welcome repatriation of private investors' money to France, it necessarily meant that, as the Czech crisis intensified in August and September, the finance ministry concluded that no further domestic loan funding could be raised.[25]

In mid-August, Daladier tried to calm worsening jitters on the Paris bourse with the promise that there would be no further franc devaluation and no resort to exchange controls. Since the franc was now exclusively tied to sterling, British reluctance to release additional loan funding to France left the French government with its hands tied. Denied the assurance of additional US or British financial support during the final month of the Czech crisis, the French government faced severe monetary problems whose origin could, in part, be traced to a war scare apparently manufactured by the Prague government in May. During August, financial confidence was further dented by the bitter dispute between the government, the employers' federation and the CGT over the relaxation of the statutory 40-hour week. This was still unresolved as the Czech crisis entered its final phase. Only with the replacement of Marchandeau by the fiercely independent Paul Reynaud in November 1938 did Daladier's cabinet finally turn its back on the lingering aftermath of Popular Front economic policy. Amidst mounting evidence that Munich had not altered the course of German foreign policy, Daladier's rightward shift in financial policy was driven by the requirements of the French rearmament effort and the urgent need to expand the provision of defence bonds.[26]

Paul Reynaud's appointment met the wishes of the Radical Party's 1938 congress at Marseille. A free market liberal, he had resigned in protest from the Alliance Démocratique at Flandin's fawning submission to Hitler immediately after Munich. As finance minister, Reynaud quickly reversed many key industrial reforms and restrictive practices enacted by Léon Blum's coalition.[27] Minister of justice until November 1938, Reynaud was perhaps the exception which proved the rule. He was the only 'maverick' politician promoted within the cabinet in 1938. Other ministers seen as potentially loose cannons during the Czech crisis did not have the clout to reorient foreign policy. Although Minister of Colonies Georges Mandel was a frequent foreign policy dissenter, not least over the fulfilment of France's alliance obligations to Czechoslovakia, he was still too junior a figure to rock the administration.[28] The same could be said of Jean Zay, a talented minister for education and a rising star of the Radical Party's reformist left-wing. Both Mandel and Zay opposed the abandonment of Czechoslovakia, but neither felt that the gesture of resignation would affect the direction of government policy. Outside the council of ministers, prominent anti-*Munichois* never coalesced into a united opposition. From disparate political backgrounds, their motives for supporting the Czech cause were many and varied. The right-wing deputy and editor of *L'Epoque*, Henri de Kérillis, agreed with his old friend Mandel that surrender to Germany would only increase Hitler's appetite. Progressive Catholic democrats, such as Francisque Gay, Georges Bidault and Edmond Michelet, considered nazism an evil which demanded unconditional resistance. And, like the PCF leadership, Gabriel Péri, the political editor of the communist daily, *L'Humanité*, followed Moscow's line that France should contribute to a collective security front in defence of Czechoslovakia.[29]

With outstanding financial difficulties, long-term rearmament problems, unpromising strategic alternatives and scant public enthusiasm for a confrontation with Germany, it is tempting to suggest that, whatever the ministerial arguments between Daladier's colleagues, the French were naturally predisposed to abandon the Czechs. British appeasers provided the shield to conceal French pusillanimity. This well-worn interpretation is central to the contention that France abdicated responsibility to Britain as the Czech crisis developed from June 1938 onwards. As a result, historians have rightly attached tremendous importance to the manner in which France's power was perceived by the country's civil and military leadership and its principal political parties in the 1938–40 period.[30] These discussions of national self-image emphasize the extent to which actual French capacity could be rendered irrelevant by prevalent estimates that the country's strategic position would only improve from 1939 as defence expenditure produced greater returns in the serial production of mechanized land forces and modern-design aircraft. Other historians have reversed the lens to illustrate how appreciations of Germany's capacity for war by the French air and military intelligence services further affected French resolve.[31] Similarly, evaluation of the role played by French service attachés in gauging the potential of France's eastern European clients indicates that, despite the high quality of incoming information, the French government sometimes ignored positive advice – most notably from General Louis-Eugène Faucher, military attaché in Prague – which did not conform to the prevailing assumption that war had to be avoided in the short term. With good reason, both war ministry intelligence and its secret intelligence-gathering arm, the Service de Renseignements, rejected Faucher's opinions as over-optimistic and strategically naive. In general, during 1937–38 the military attachés posted to Warsaw, Belgrade and Bucharest confirmed that their host governments would certainly not assist the Czechs. From 1936 Polish, Yugoslav and Romanian leaders gradually lost what residual faith in French power they had sustained until the Rhineland remilitarization. The Prague government was, in turn, resented for its refusal to submit meekly to German demands.[32] Beyond the decisionmakers, Yvon Lacaze's study of French public opinion during the Czech crisis describes a country profoundly unsure of its underlying strength. Opinion was volatile, but never confident. Right-wing and Radical voters recognized that without British support a firm stand made little sense. For the non-communist left, bolder talk rested on the wavering hope that Hitler's bluff could be called. This uncertainty permeated the senior ranks of the Radical Party and was mirrored in the radical press, particularly within the two newspapers closest to the party leadership: *L'Oeuvre* and *L'Ere nouvelle*. Although under the impulsion of its influential editorialist, Geneviève Tabouis, *L'Oeuvre* was initially hostile towards concessions to Berlin, ultimately the paper bent before the overwhelming public support for a diplomatic solution.[33] The output of the French film industry in 1938–39 echoes this erosion of confidence. In the 18 months before the war, French cinema goers were frequently offered a diet of nostalgic, insular films which tended to lampoon rather than revere French military prowess. Although the government sponsored a number of documentaries, such as *Sommes-nous défendus?* and *Le monde en armes*, intended to convince the nation of the benefits of French rearmament, these failed to dispel public unease. Only the vogue for colonial films celebrating past imperial conquest and France's civilizing mission presented an image of a formidable nation.[34]

French governmental preoccupation with the country's relative strength is obviously fundamental to the assessment of the French cabinet's response to the Czech crisis. Previous Franco-Czech alliance planning and extensive diplomatic dispatches and military intelligence assessments gave Daladier's ministers both the pretext and the means to mull over French strategic alternatives. But at no point was Daladier's administration receptive to the proposition that Czechoslovakia had to be defended and that such a defence would be better mounted in 1938 than at some later stage. Five days before Daladier took office, on 5 April, Paul-Boncour and Alexis Léger quizzed French ambassadors – specially recalled from eastern European capitals to Paris – regarding the political and strategic outlook among the Eastern allies. Prague Ambassador Victor de Lacroix confirmed that the Czech authorities were willing to negotiate over the Sudetenland. Only Bucharest representative, Adrien Thierry, reported that Romania might yet follow a French lead. In response, Moscow Ambassador Coulondre suggested a renewed diplomatic effort to secure a definitive Romanian–Soviet settlement over the disputed territory of Bessarabia.[35] This attempt to salvage some basis for an Eastern collective security strategy was nullified by Bonnet's arrival at the Quai d'Orsay in the following week. But Warsaw Ambassador Léon Noël appears to have spoken for his colleagues in arguing that France's credibility as a strong ally was already lost.[36]

Immediately after the *Anschluss*, General Faucher reported that the Czechoslovak general staff was determined to resist any German incursion stimulated by disorder within the Sudeten region. The military attaché further commented that the Prague government expected its military intelligence service to provide accurate information about any buildup of German forces on or near the Czech frontier.[37] On 7 April, General Ludvik Krejci, chief of the Czechoslovak army staff, pressed the French war ministry to agree a protocol specifying the terms by which either party could order a general mobilization without any requirement for last-minute consultations. This was essential if the Czech army was to occupy Sudetenland fortifications in the sure knowledge of France's support as soon as intelligence were received of an imminent German attack.[38] But, by emphasizing the Czechs' readiness to fight, Faucher glossed over Czechoslovakia's worsened strategic position following Germany's occupation of Austria. This undermined the force of his argument.[39] Evidence that the Czechs planned to act unilaterally in response to their own military intelligence on Germany was disquieting. Czechoslovakia might react to any German menace before France could restrain it. This knowledge of Prague's firm resolve, despite Czechoslovakia's greater exposure to a multi-pronged German attack, compounded French reluctance to assist their ally. Furthermore, it seems probable that the German intelligence service knew this to be the case. Hitler was by this point privy to intercepts of cable traffic between Paris and Prague, a tremendous political advantage the implications of which were not entirely appreciated by ministers in Paris even though this intelligence leak was revealed in April. As Coulondre noted when recalling discussions with Bonnet over Franco-Czech–Russian military talks, the eruption of the May crisis pushed French foreign policy still closer to the British position.[40]

Anxious to avoid conflict but as yet unwilling to abandon the Czechoslovakian alliance outright, the contradictions of French policy were laid bare by the May war scare. During the afternoon of

21 May, Faucher sent a sequence of telegrams indicating that the Czech government had firm proof of German military preparations intended to exert political pressure upon President Edvard Benes and his ministers. Although there was little German activity along the Austrian or Silesian frontiers – two obvious points from which a Wehrmacht offensive might be launched – the Prague government approved a partial mobilization and deployed an additional ten regiments to their frontier fortifications.[41] The May crisis underlined the potential for a swift escalation of a local conflict into a general war. Working in conjunction with their British and Belgian counterparts, exhaustive inquiries by the French military and air attachés to Berlin, General Georges Renondeau and Colonel de Geffrier, quickly revealed that Czech allegations of hostile German troop and aircraft movements in Silesia, Saxony and Lower Bavaria were false.[42] While the war scare was a mirage, its effects were lasting. Since Hitler ordered the destruction of Czechoslovakia in direct response to the affront he suffered in May, Renondeau's warning to Daladier on 22 May that war might now break out within days rather than weeks was scarcely alarmist.[43] Although the immediate threat receded, from late May onwards French foreign and defence policy was utterly consumed by the Czechoslovakian situation.

Close economic ties also demanded a careful evaluation of French options. France remained a major external investor in the Czechoslovakian economy, ranking third below Germany and Britain. Although stringent tariff and quota arrangements impeded the reduction of Czechoslovakia's trade deficit with France, the French armaments conglomerate, Schneider-Creusot, retained a majority holding in the Skoda armaments works. Other French banking and industrial consortia remained major capital holders in Czechoslovakia's mining industry and transport infrastructure.[44] As a key creditor to the Czech government, with whom a 698 million franc state loan was finalized in March 1937, France had much to lose if Czechoslovakia were attacked.[45] It was only after six months of bruising negotiations that the Prague authorities agreed higher import quotas for French automobiles and low-grade coal in 1937. Nonetheless, this was regarded by both sides as a new departure in Franco-Czechoslovakian trade.[46] But, as René Massigli emphasized in late March 1938, urgent French action was required to avert the 'economic strangulation' of Czechoslovakia consequent upon the *Anschluss* and Germany's growing economic penetration of Yugoslavia, Hungary and Romania. Gamelin, too, warned Daladier that the nazis' economic dominion in central Europe might undermine an Anglo-French war strategy of blockade against Germany.[47]

Armed with such warnings, the French cabinet was more thoroughly informed about Czechoslovakia's military potential and the economic ramifications of a German invasion than were some British ministers in early September 1938.[48] But this raises additional questions. France could only assist Czechoslovakia militarily by launching a direct attack on Germany. Hence, the government's dominant concern was less with the immediate prospects for a concerted two-front campaign than with France's capacity to withstand a long war against a profoundly unpredictable enemy. French policymakers could assume that the Czech government would do all possible to safeguard their national interest. But, as Robert Young has pointed out, logical deductions about German and Italian behaviour were far harder to make. At one extreme, Hitler might leave reason aside in his pursuit of glory. Equally, the economic pressures generated by rearmament and autarcky might drive him into territorial conquest, a fear compounded by the generally poor quality of French industrial intelligence.[49] French politicians relied upon specialist military opinion. But with regard to the nazi regime, it was almost impossible to be conclusive. The gulf between image and reality – between an awesome frontline military capacity and a chaotic economic organization, and between a persuasive defence of Germany's right to ethnic unity and the violence of Hitlerian methods – sowed confusion, particularly as Hitler's personal grip upon military and foreign policy planning increased during 1938.[50] The Berlin military attaché, General Renondeau, explained the problem in a telegram to the war ministry cryptographic unit on 20 July: 'My personal impression is that the [*Wehrmacht*] command cannot estimate itself any more ready than on 21 May and must request delays: but here Hitler's will can break all opposition and while there are a number of logical arguments to reckon against a coup against Czechoslovakia [at the] end of July, Hitler's mentality will not permit such a withdrawal.'[51]

To make matters worse, contradictory reports from Moscow and from Soviet diplomats regarding Stalin's readiness to assist Czechoslovakia, either with or without France's support, encouraged the Prague government to contemplate resistance. This added to French alarm.[52] The pro-collective security line espoused by Commissar for Foreign Affairs Maxim Litvinov was counterbalanced by the deliberate obfuscation of other Soviet figures, including Deputy Commissar V.P. Potemkin and the Prague representative, S. Alexandrovsky. Yet Stalin did not silence Litvinov in September, and Comintern instructions sustained French Communist Party agitation in support of the Czechs.[53] When in mid-July the Czech general staff proposed conversations over the coordination of French and Soviet military action in support of Czechoslovakia, Gamelin responded carefully, warning of the dangers of disclosing detailed plans to Moscow without an absolute assurance of Soviet intervention.[54] Daladier immediately sought Bonnet's opinion. The foreign minister's 12 August reply was equally meticulous. Having warned the Czech government in July to expect no aid from France, not surprisingly Bonnet advised against the introduction of three-year military service in Czechoslovakia for fear of provoking Berlin. In his view, Germany's bitter reaction to the May crisis also precluded tripartite French–Czechoslovak–Soviet talks. But, aware of the need to clarify the scale of Soviet support and the route that Soviet forces might take, Bonnet recommended informal dialogue with the Soviet government via the French and Czechoslovak military and air attachés in Moscow. This would be easier to conceal – and to deny. He was even willing to exert diplomatic pressure on the Poles and Romanians if required. Bonnet's sting in the tail was that London should be kept fully informed of these plans. A reasonable point, this nonetheless provided the foreign minister with an escape route, since the British were expected to object to even informal Franco-Soviet staff exchanges.[55]

Nine months prior to Munich, Gamelin made plain that the prospect of a French offensive in the West ought to give Germany pause for thought. But would Hitler react accordingly? Recognizing the possibility that French deterrence would not work, the general staff insisted that full mobilization was an essential prerequisite to any military intervention. There could be no distinction in practice between a limited Western strike in support of Czechoslovakia and a commitment to war against Germany.[56] With no demilitarized Rhineland bridgeheads to be easily occupied, the idea of 'limited invasion' had become meaningless. Belgian neutrality and probable Italian hostility further complicated offensive planning. Although covert Franco-Belgian staff contacts subsisted, since Belgium's declaration of neutrality in October 1936 French preparations for a swift deployment of forces within or across Belgian territory were inevitably curtailed.[57] Furthermore, as international tension mounted during 1938, the Belgian government, pressed by Flemish neutralists, again distanced itself from France. Having ended formal staff contacts in 1936, the Belgians constructed symbolic frontier defences along the French frontier at the direct expense of expenditure on anti-aircraft defence. Limited Belgian army manoeuvres against a theoretical French 'invasion' were staged in June and July.[58] As the Munich Conference convened on 29 September, the French military attaché in Brussels, Colonel Edmond Laurent, confirmed that Belgium's Maginot-style forts near the Belgian–German border were in a poor state of repair. Insufficient ventilation made for damp conditions in which sophisticated weaponry, such as mechanically rotating turrets, no longer worked.[59]

Anxious to avoid advanced mobilization measures liable to encourage a more spirited Czech resistance, most French ministers chose not to question strategic information which justified their preference for appeasement. But since the Czechoslovakian alliance could not be openly repudiated without compromising French power in Europe, Daladier's government recognized that France might have to march in September 1938. A critical question is thus how far the French government wanted to hear bad news from its general staff in the final three weeks of the crisis over Czechoslovakia, since this could justify a political decision to evade France's alliance obligation which, hitherto, the French government was unable to take. The Radical Party congress held in the month following the Munich settlement provides a partial answer to this. During the congress foreign affairs debate, a split emerged. On the one hand, speakers suggested that the abandonment of Czechoslovakia was the inevitable consequence of a rational calculation that France was strategically overextended. Just as the British had always done, France was now judging its alliance commitments against a minimal interpretation of the country's vital overseas interests. On the other hand, Daladier led those who insisted that France should correct the weaknesses exposed by the Czech crisis by redoubling its rearmament effort. The one point of agreement was that the picture of French military and economic frailty presented in September 1938 was real enough.[60]

On the basis of this common ground, in a vital cabinet session on 13 September Daladier brokered an agreement over the partial recall of reservists. Minister of Justice Paul Reynaud, Minister of Colonies Georges Mandel, Minister of Marine César Campinchi and Pensions Minister Jean Champetier de Ribes all favoured a more thorough mobilization in response to Hitler's inflammatory speech to the Nuremberg rally on the previous day. Ranged against these ministers, Georges Bonnet and deputy premier Camille Chautemps led a more senior group which trod the familiar ground of France's demographic weakness, the insufficiency of its air force and the people's reluctance to fight unless absolutely necessary.[61] What divided the cabinet was not whether these deficiencies were imagined or not, but rather to what extent they would or would not improve in forthcoming years. This was the same argument rehearsed at the Radical congress a month later.

Within the composite image of French unpreparedness for war presented to the cabinet in September 1938, four elements stand out. First, the army staff insisted that a straightforward comparison of frontline divisional capacity between France and Germany would distort the true picture of relative land strengths. Germany's larger manpower reserves and its greater offensive potential, as represented by armoured divisions, had to be considered. General Maurice Gauché, head of French military intelligence, recalled that the most striking aspects of Wehrmacht superiority lay in frontline divisional strength, speed of mobilization and concentration, the availability of well-trained reservist and Landwehr cadres, and the recent establishment of five armoured divisions backed by expanded light mechanized forces. Although incomplete, Germany's Siegfried Line fortifications were also inflated in Gauché's estimates into a powerful obstacle to the rapid advance of French armoured units into western Germany. Echoing Gauché's line, on 4 September Bonnet notified the British government that recent reinforcement of the Rhineland was intended to consolidate Germany's fixed defences.[62] Anthony Adamthwaite and Williamson Murray have stressed the importance of Gauché's overestimate of the Siegfried Line – plus his subsequent assertion on 27 September that the Wehrmacht could mobilize 120 divisions – because Gamelin exploited these exaggerated estimates to argue against French military action.[63] Theoretically required to mount an offensive against Germany in defence of a Czechoslovak state whose resistance might crumble in a matter of weeks, French ground forces would ultimately be faced with a single-handed war against Germany. Even if Britain joined the conflict, in the first six months of hostilities it could offer little meaningful military assistance beyond the two-division field force.

Six months earlier, on 9 April, Bonnet both endorsed Britain's support of German–Czech negotiations and accepted Britain's desire to reserve its position should talks break down. The foreign ministry suggested that, even though Czechoslovakia might be indefensible, Franco-British staff contacts would be a sensible measure.[64] This was typical of the balancing act that Bonnet was performing. His inclination was to support the British diplomatic offensive without reservation. But his endorsement of staff conversations satisfied Daladier and undermined Bonnet's domestic critics. More important, the British would use any such military dialogue to impress upon the French government the need for a diplomatic solution to the Sudeten problem. With difficulty, during Anglo-French ministerial discussions in London on 28 April preparatory to limited staff talks, Daladier forced British negotiators to concede low-level staff exchanges regarding the eventual deployment of its field force divisions. But the British government flatly refused to discuss joint operations attendant upon war breaking out in eastern Europe.[65] Britain's unimpressive military strength, its hostility to detailed strategic cooperation and the entire thrust of British diplomacy in Prague, Paris and Berlin justified French decisionmaking which placed minimal reliance upon Britain's eventual military support.

Closely linked to military potential, a second consideration for the French cabinet was the relative strength of the national economy. Lacking the decisive land force superiority to achieve rapid victory, France's long-term financial reserves and industrial potential were clearly vital. On both counts, the detail of France's economic capacity was perhaps less significant than the prevailing mood within a government seeking to rectify the Popular Front's economic 'mistakes' through measured devaluation, an end to restrictive industrial practices and the restoration of financial confidence. By definition, an economy in the process of recovery would become stronger over time. To do so, Marchandeau and Rueff agreed that peace was imperative, especially after the recourse to short-term defence bonds discussed earlier was exhausted in mid-July. During September, Marchandeau repeatedly made this point in daily reports on France's deteriorating financial position submitted to the premier's office.[66]

At two distinct points in September, information from the finance ministry was probably critical to policy formulation. At the start of the month, the treasury division estimated its loans requirement for the four weeks ahead at 4,225 million francs, a sum which it was confident of obtaining through a combination of Bank of France advances and a weekly turnover of some 200 million through the national defence fund.[67] But, following Hitler's violent Nuremberg speech on 12 September, frightened investors rushed to invoke the state repayment guarantees on outstanding short-term defence bonds. This brief financial panic quickly subsided, thanks largely to the apparent success of Chamberlain's visit to Berchtesgaden on 15 September. The message, however, was clear. If private investors deemed war likely, their inclination to hoard their money might precipitate a funding crisis and French financial collapse. This was brought home far more sharply two weeks later. Already reeling from the evident failure of the Godesberg talks on 22 September, the introduction of partial mobilization on 24 September caused wholesale upheaval in the French banking system. In the five days before the announcement of the Munich Conference on 29 September, cancelled subscriptions to defence bonds totalled 448 million francs. Partly in reaction to this, between 26 and 29 September daily treasury spending on the initial costs of mobilization exceeded earlier forecast predictions by some 1,200 million francs. The situation within the retail banking sector confirmed that Daladier's administration could not hope to maintain the flow of money market funding essential to rearmament. In the same five-day period, the major savings banks reported net losses of up to 50 per cent in their overall deposit holdings. According to finance ministry figures compiled on 3 October 1938, French savers withdrew 2,521 million francs between 24 and 29 September.[68]

As mobilization began on 24 September, Draconian legislation appeared necessary to prevent further cash withdrawals and so avert collapse in the banking system. This at a time when the call-up had itself generated additional pressures upon the economy. Even if financial breakdown were averted, a crisis in rearmament funding seemed bound to occur if France went to war. Voting with their withdrawal slips, French bank account holders had made their aversion to conflict over Czechoslovakia very plain. Already dependent upon emergency advances from the Bank of France, this dreadful financial picture surely made the abandonment of Czechoslovakia easier for Daladier's cabinet to stomach.[69]

A third aspect to the consideration of French options in September 1938 was the state of the air force. General Joseph Vuillemin, chief of the French air staff, returned chastened from an inspection tour of Germany between 16 and 21 August. Understandably anxious about France's relative air strength, he now became the chief apostle of doom. This has rightly attracted much historical attention.[70] Nowhere was French inferiority more clearly exposed than in the poverty of its frontline squadron strength and the sluggish expansion of its monthly aircraft output. As the Radical senator Edouard Herriot confirmed, air force weakness played very heavily upon ministers' minds in the weeks before Munich.[71] During 1938, as before it, Pierre Cot – the former Popular Front air minister who uniquely combined ardent pro-Sovietism with a Radical Party membership card – could not convince either his party or his erstwhile ministerial colleagues that French air strength should be calculated within the wider framework of coalition warfare. The air staff refused to include Soviet frontline aircraft within its estimates of an air war against Germany even though, before Vuillemin took charge in February, the air intelligence bureau calculated Soviet air strength at 4,660 aircraft (of which 1,250 were judged obsolete).[72] But Cot's estimates assumed that the French army would be able to hold back German forces whilst the combined French and British bomber fleets mounted a joint offensive – something to which the British had not even agreed.[73] When in October 1938 the French and

British air staffs began detailed planning of joint offensive operations against Germany, it became apparent that the French army staff still clung to the idea that French bombers would provide close air support to French ground attacks. This suggested that the very idea of a French aerial strike force with an independent strategic role remained open to question.[74]

To Cot's successor, Guy La Chambre, and the increasingly desperate Vuillemin, several points were clear by September 1938. The French air force could not withstand a sustained Luftwaffe offensive. A French aerial riposte would not deter German bombardments. And a further 18 months of peace were vital if the benefits of the French air rearmament scheme (Plan V) were eventually to make good France's pressing air force weakness. La Chambre warned the Senate Air Commission in February that approved 'modernization' measures for the French air force were already obsolete. Across the spectrum of fighters to medium bombers, German first-line aircraft were between 100 to 120kmph faster than their French equivalents.[75] In a series of four meetings held between 7 and 15 March 1938 against the background of the *Anschluss*, the supreme air council finalized the details of Plan V. Intended to increase first-line air force strength from 1,437 to 2,617 aircraft, the plan was to be accomplished over two 12-month stages between April 1938 and April 1940. But the French air staff planners acknowledged that inadequate productive capacity, poor infrastructure, insufficient repair and maintenance facilities and recruitment shortages were all likely to affect the proposed production targets. These were difficulties that could not be solved overnight by increased investment and the abrogation of Popular Front industrial legislation.[76] On 15 March La Chambre advised the CPDN that he expected monthly aircraft output to increase rapidly from 40 to 60 – but this was hardly a statistic to inspire confidence. Within a fortnight, General Vuillemin proposed cuts to the initial Plan V targets in an effort to maximize bomber production in the short term.[77] In a hangover from the Cot era, throughout 1938, the air staff too readily assumed that the Luftwaffe would pursue an independent strategic offensive which the French air force could not match. While German bombers certainly outclassed and outnumbered their French rivals, Luftwaffe preparations were still geared to close air support of ground operations rather than the city bombing campaign that the French dreaded.[78]

During sessions of the air ministry's principal rearmament committee, the comité du matériel, between March and September 1938, La Chambre attempted to clear the bottlenecks in French aircraft production. This was inevitably a long-term process which demanded a structural overhaul of industrial practices and skilled labour allocation. For instance, by April 1938, thanks to serialized production, the aircraft makers Bloch were reportedly in a position to produce 300 aircraft per year. But the producers of the more sought-after Morane 406 fighter could only produce 65 such aircraft in the same period, since each Morane 406 took 20,000 man hours to produce. Not surprisingly, La Chambre immediately ordered a feasibility study regarding the incorporation of US-purchased Pratt and Whitney aero-engines and Bristol Aeroplane Company motors into French-manufactured airframes. The first Bloch 150 aircraft mounted with a Pratt and Whitney engine were scheduled to roll off the production line at the end of September.[79]

By August 1938, French first-line air force strength had climbed to 1,120 aircraft. But the largest component within this was 570 multipurpose aircraft intended for both reconnaissance and light bombing roles. In fact, these models were poorly suited to either task. While there were a further 714 aircraft in nominal reserve, the air staff informed their British counterparts that these planes would only be available four months after hostilities began. There were other variables involved. Vuillemin's staff remained unsure how far output from airframe and aero-engine manufacturers could be improved over the coming winter, and French fighters (of which there were 340 in front-line service) were largely untested against a first-class power. In August 1938 the air staff stated that, in calculating additions to air rearmament, its key aim was to ensure that the offensive potential of the Armée de l'Air was at least equivalent to the Luftwaffe force likely to be deployed on the western front. This goal was far from realization.[80]

Vuillemin's later apocalyptic predictions to Daladier made sense. The air force offered no offensive options and scant protection in September 1938. Although the French and Czechoslovakian air intelligence bureaux intensified their exchange of information regarding Luftwaffe deployments following the May crisis, in September the French air ministry only contemplated a token transfer of French aircraft to operate in combination with the Czech air force.[81] Following Franco-Czechoslovakian air staff exchanges in the week following Chamberlain's first encounter with Hitler at Berchtesgaden, on 22 September Vuillemin noted that the Armée de l'Air's principal tasks would be to disrupt German troop movements towards Austria, Bohemia and Moravia by attacking the rail network in Bavaria. In addition, raids against German bomber bases in eastern Bavaria and western Saxony were planned in order to disrupt Luftwaffe strikes against Czech targets. French air intelligence advised Vuillemin on 17 September of the planned Czech air response to a German attack, and suggested that French frontline squadrons be placed on a war footing even though the Czechs did not expect immediate French air assistance to coincide with their own initial defensive actions. But Vuillemin noted that the bulk of French sorties could only take place at night, whilst German troop concentrations for an initial attack were a *fait accompli*.[82]

Although the air ministry had approved plans for four French bomber groups to operate from Bohemian bases in December 1935, the air staff's refusal to contemplate a tripartite air assistance pact with the Soviet Union stultified Franco-Czech air cooperation from 1936 onwards. By March 1938 Vuillemin's staff were in full retreat from their earlier ambitious schemes for joint air operations. During Franco-Czech air exchanges in July, French negotiators indicated that a French air offensive against south German and Austrian targets could be considered only after Czechoslovakia were attacked. Furthermore, the Czechs were warned that such support should not be considered automatic.[83] By the time the British air staff suggested a joint assessment of combined operations against Ruhr industrial targets in response to a German attack on Czechoslovakia, Vuillemin had already ruled out any such action. During air staff exchanges in May, the British had stipulated that it would take two months to prepare advanced bases for RAF units on French soil.[84] These were far from ready in late September. When questioned by La Chambre and Daladier about possible Armée de l'Air deployments, Vuillemin's meagre proposals put one in mind of an aerial charge of the Light Brigade into a hail of German fire. Such was the general's distress

that, prior to departing for Munich, Daladier decided not to press him any further.[85]

The final element to the French position in September 1938 was the potential contribution of likely allies. In this respect, too, Daladier's government accepted military advice with a political edge. Among France's eastern clients, Poland was the one state actively hostile to Prague. French efforts to diffuse Polish–Czechoslovak tension – spearheaded after the March 1936 Rhineland crisis by General Gamelin – met little positive response in Warsaw.[86] In a conversation with General Faucher on Christmas Day 1936, President Benes admitted that Polish hostility was *la raison déterminante* for Czechoslovakia's conclusion of a military pact with the Soviet Union in the previous year. The agreement was intended to preempt a possible Soviet–German *rapprochement* while giving Poland pause for thought.[87] This policy failed. Throughout 1938 Foreign Minister Josef Beck defended Poland's 1934 Non-Aggression Pact with Germany, even when over the summer months the Polish general staff pressed the French war ministry to meet Poland's most urgent supply requirements for medium tanks.[88] On 20 September the Warsaw government informed Paris that it intended to press its claims to Teschen during any international negotiations over the Sudetenland.[89] By this point the French general staff anticipated that Polish and Romanian intransigence would nullify any Soviet assistance to the Czechs, since adequate rights of transit from Russian territory were an essential prerequisite to the construction of a stable Czech front. Within the Quai d'Orsay, Secretary-General Léger accepted Bonnet's view that a military combination in defence of Czechoslovakia was impractical, though Léger worked hard to defend the integrity of the Czechoslovakian state both prior to and during the Munich Conference.[90] The underlying point is that in 1938 the French government accepted military advice that a Soviet alliance would not work and the planning of the Munich Conference proceeded on that premise.

To accept the primordial requirement for Soviet military support implied the loss of Polish and, perhaps, Romanian good will, fierce British opposition and an end to the appeasement of Hitler. On 16 March, in a response to British enquiries regarding French plans to assist Czechoslovakia, Gamelin omitted information about France's dismal air defences, stating only that France would draw what German forces it could westwards. If Poland and Czechoslovakia's Little Entente partners also fought against Germany, the prospects for victory were good. Since the construction of such an eastern coalition was manifestly improbable, the implication was that France would face a single-handed war against Germany. The Soviet Union was not even mentioned. Ostensibly encouraging, Gamelin's 16 March note actually captured his view of France's dilemma in a nutshell: there was no working alliance system with which to oppose German expansionism effectively.[91] Yet even a conservative estimate of Soviet air force potential, prepared by French air intelligence on 25 May, acknowledged the availability of 960 modern fighters and 2,260 light bombers, with adequate short-term reserves, along the European frontier of the Soviet Union.[92] On 12 July Coulondre reported the progress of a Czech military mission to the Soviet Union led by specialist engineers from the Skoda armament works and the Skoda company president, M. Hromadko. Prior to their return home, on 29 June the Czech representatives discussed plans to re-fit Soviet artillery. Foreign Minister Litvinov used the mission as a pretext to probe the French government on its readiness to assist Czechoslovakia. Coulondre concluded that Litvinov's approach must have been sanctioned by Stalin, indicating a genuine Soviet willingness to back the Czechs militarily. Since Benes had assured General Faucher on 12 July that Czechoslovak policy towards the Soviets would be 'subordinated' to French requirements, Litvinov's probing made sense.[93] Meanwhile, unverified information from the Polish embassy in Moscow suggested that the Soviets had pledged to support Czechoslovakia with a force of 900 bombers in the event of a combined German–Polish attack.[94]

Uncertainty about Soviet intentions reinforced the French military practice of denigrating Soviet military capacity and political reliability, a problem compounded by deuxième bureau disregard for more favourable reports received from Moscow military attaché, Colonel (later, General) Palasse.[95] On 17 August General Faucher warned that Czech intelligence had conclusive proof that the German Abwehr was colluding with Konrad Henlein in the preparation of a Sudeten uprising. Following talks between Benes and Faucher in Prague, three days later Daladier instructed Gamelin to begin

Franco-Czech staff exchanges over the details of Soviet aid to Czechoslovakia. Vuillemin was also instructed to report on the potential usefulness of Soviet air support and the likelihood that Romania would permit Soviet use of its air space. By the end of August, it seemed likely that the Romanian authorities would – at minimum – turn a blind eye to Soviet aircraft overflying their territory, whether or not the planes involved bore Soviet insignia.[96] But Vuillemin's preliminary reply on 1 September suggested that the Soviet air force could contribute little to the Czechs. Czechoslovakia lacked the infrastructure to support a large force of bombers, and Soviet aircraft operating from Russian bases would be confined to relatively minor operations against targets in East Prussia. A fortnight later, with the impressive evidence of Soviet frontline strength and the rising possibility of a favourable Romanian attitude boxing him into a corner, Vuillemin changed tack. This time he stressed the insufficiency of Romanian air bases in Transylvania and the deficiencies of the Soviet air command to prove his case.[97]

Meanwhile, the war ministry remained adamant that Czechoslovakia had little prospect of Romanian or Yugoslav assistance, the French eastern alliance system having broken down with the definitive failure of the scheme for a France–Little Entente pact in 1937. This analysis was true for Yugoslavia, but less so for Romania. Although, on 15 September, the Yugoslav government ordered the mobilization of infantry reservists to bring the three divisions guarding the Yugoslavia–Hungary border up to strength, Belgrade offered no direct assistance to the Czechs.[98] The Romanians shared Yugoslavia's dread of war, and, as both countries grew more authoritarian and trade-dependent upon Germany, so neutralism became increasingly dominant in Belgrade and Bucharest. Much as in Belgrade, between 15 and 17 September the Romanian government recalled reservists, placed armaments production under state control and issued legislation mobilizing women for work in the munitions industry.[99] But there was no Romanian expeditionary force for Czechoslovakia, nor was one expected. In January 1938, Bucharest military attaché, Lieutenant-Colonel Jules Delmas, noted that the Romanian government considered Czechoslovakia indefensible. Romania's King Carol II hoped that the Czechs would make generous concessions to their Sudeten minority.[100] The Little Entente powers still held regular conferences, although their discussions were increasingly confined to the discussion of common action against Hungarian revisionism. Such discussions were largely a face-saving exercise to conceal the collapse in meaningful Little Entente cooperation. After one such meeting held at Sinaia in Romania in early May, Delmas concluded that common action against Germany was out of the question.[101]

For all this disappointment, the Romanian government reacted surprisingly favourably to Czechoslovakia's mobilization on 20–21 May. At a subsequent Little Entente conference in Bled, Yugoslavia, the Romanian delegation left Czech Foreign Minister Dr Kamil Krofta optimistic that Soviet aircraft could overfly Romanian territory.[102] This was significant because French military intelligence attached greater importance to the use of Romanian air space than to Soviet access to Romania's overland communications. In September 1935 General Lucien Loizeau had caused uproar within the war ministry with a notoriously favourable report on Soviet military manoeuvres. Although Loizeau's conclusions were challenged, he convinced the army staff that, such was the inadequacy of the railway network through Bukovina, no more than one division of Soviet troops could be transported to Czechoslovakia within the first month of hostilities.[103] Understandably, as the summer of 1938 wore on, the Prague foreign ministry explored proposals for a new British-financed rail link between Czechoslovakia and Romania's Black Sea coast.[104] But this made no difference to the immediate problem of Soviet troop transports. On 11 September 1938 Romanian Foreign Minister Petrescu Comnène confirmed that his country's poor road and rail communications would limit the transfer of Soviet land forces to one division every 20 days at best.[105]

To Soviet embarrassment, on 24 September Romania apparently conceded transit rights for the passage of Red Army troops and equipment to Czechoslovakia. But in his summation of Czechoslovakia's strategic position to British ministers in London two days later, Gamelin suggested that Romania had not – and would not – agree to such a thing, the Romanians sticking to tacit acceptance of Soviet over-flights only.[106] During the afternoon of the 24th, Coulondre advised Bonnet that, despite the Czech government's submission to Anglo-French pressure for the cession of

Sudeten territory, the Soviet government had reaffirmed its commitment to the Czech–Soviet alliance. Deputy Commissar Potemkin informed the Prague government of his 'surprise and regret' that the Czechs had not requested the implementation of the Czech–Soviet mutual assistance clauses, independent of the prior operation of the Franco-Czech alliance. Potemkin further stated that the Soviets had reinforced their military deployments along the Soviet–Polish frontier in order to deter the Warsaw government from exploiting Czechoslovakian weakness.[107] By this stage a major Soviet mobilization west of the Urals was well under way. The Soviet mobilization measures in the Ukraine and Belorussia between 21 and 28 September – whether primarily intended as a show of strength, as a warning against Polish irredentism or as a serious preparation for war – appear to have been on a massive scale. The likelihood is, however, that these military preparations were indeed meant to restrain the Poles above all. As Jean-Baptiste Duroselle put it, there remained the contradiction between the clarity of Soviet support in principle and the vagueness over how that support could be rendered to Czechoslovakia in meaningful quantity.[108] If offered and seriously meant, Romania's belated offer of transit rights was surely unwelcome in Moscow. It was anyway unlikely to affect French military estimates of the limited usefulness of a land corridor for Soviet forces. By contrast, the prospect of Soviet air support being delivered via Romania was deliberately underplayed in French military assessments. While Soviet offers of air support to the Czechs never came to anything in practice, the French chose not to press the Soviets strongly to make good their promises.[109]

Instead, French diplomacy in Moscow during September 1938 sought to clarify Soviet intentions without in the process revealing France's disinclination to act in defence of Czechoslovakia. Not surprisingly, this attempt to shift the burden of responsibility added to the fog surrounding Soviet policy. This reached a climax on 21 September. After three weeks of fruitless speculation about Soviet intentions, Coulondre informed Bonnet that the Soviet government had promised Benes unconditional air support on 20 September. But, to Coulondre's knowledge, Moscow had done nothing to give effect to this, and showed little sign of doing so. Litvinov indicated to Coulondre and Bonnet that Soviet intervention might be conditional upon League of Nations Council approval. This was tantamount to inaction.[110] Although Coulondre played up the likelihood of Soviet intervention, the doubt which crept into his later reports was sufficient to enable Bonnet to discount the Soviets in the advice he tendered to Daladier in the week before the Munich Conference convened.

In the West, the course of British appeasement, the limited Franco-British defensive coordination yet accomplished, and the dismal scale of Britain's continental field force commitment offered ample reason to enter the Munich talks. On 24 April 1938 the general secretariat of the supreme council of national defence noted that, until Britain enacted conscription and could promise a fully mechanized field force, the basic military equation in western Europe remained a France of 40 million confronted by 75 million Germans and 40 million Italians.[111] The resultant calculation was very simple. Unconditional British support demanded French good behaviour. In practice, this meant cooperation in appeasement until the policy succeeded or until the British themselves woke up to its futility. To Bonnet, such a one-sided relationship was positively desirable. To Daladier, it was simply inescapable. Bonnet constructed his policy on the rock of British opinion. In his view, if France offered less than enthusiastic support to Chamberlain's shuttle diplomacy in September 1938, the British would sooner blame the French for the failure of appeasement than accept that the policy should be abandoned. As with the ultimate collapse of the Disarmament Conference in April 1934, Britain would cry foul loudest in Paris, not Berlin. For Bonnet, this offered the fail-safe justification for the abandonment of the Franco-Czechoslovakian alliance which, despite his best efforts to prove otherwise, remained juridically binding.[112] When confronted with intelligence from André François-Poncet in Berlin indicating that Hitler was determined to employ force against Czechoslovakia, Bonnet suggested that France's capacity for diplomatic intervention was compromised by the Führer's conviction that Paris would defer to London.[113] Meanwhile, in Daladier's eyes, the Franco-British war planning that alone would enable him to take a firmer line over Czechoslovakia was conditionally postponed in September 1938. Franco-Soviet war planning remained politically unacceptable. And Franco-Polish war planning in defence of Czechoslovakia was impossible.

In the resultant French military assessment, all that remained was the prospect of a highly prepared Czech army with at least 32 infantry divisions and four motorized divisions performing well enough to allow an Eastern coalition to coalesce around it. The 55 front-line squadrons of the Czech air force evaluated by French air intelligence in June 1938 were largely discounted in September.[114] Gamelin correctly identified the vital strategic points which the Czech army had to hold around Moravská Ostrava in Moravia, further west between Zamberk and Trutnov, and in northern Bohemia west of the Elbe valley. But he also warned that the occupation of these sensitive frontier areas in readiness for a German attack might be enough to provoke further Sudeten protest and the very German intervention that the Czechs were trying to prevent.[115] Hence, the alarm within the war ministry at Czechoslovakia's partial mobilization on 13–14 September.[116] Within the Quai d'Orsay, René Massigli, one of the keenest minds within French policymaking in September 1938, arrived at much the same conclusion as Gamelin. With the exception of its Slovak population, Czechoslovakia's ethnic minorities were concentrated in areas close to the frontiers of their various mother countries. The Prague government could not risk a plebiscite to determine the allegiance of the Sudeten areas without sparking off a series of territorial demands from ethnic Poles, Hungarians and even Slovaks. Massigli conceded that it was preferable to negotiate a surrender of Sudeten territory than to base a strategy of defence upon the very frontier regions that were least loyal to the Czech state. Crucially, however, Massigli failed to appreciate what Gamelin had understood; namely, that Hitler would demand the Sudetenland in its entirety, leaving the Czechoslovakian state with precious little fortifications or armaments capacity.[117] Thus, where Massigli saw some hope for Czechoslovakia's future as an independent nation, Gamelin saw little at all.

On 21 September, the day before the second Hitler–Chamberlain meeting at Godesberg, Gamelin advised Daladier that France should consider preliminary mobilization to counter the growing concentration of Wehrmacht forces along Czechoslovakia's northern and western frontier. But he presented this measure – which would necessitate a much broader reservist call-up and the evacuation of civilians close to the Maginot fortifications – as a diplomatic lever intended to strengthen Chamberlain's hand in talks. Gamelin still accepted that the Czechs could not themselves order a full mobilization without in the process destroying the prospects for a peaceful settlement.[118]

By the time the French government had firm proof of Soviet mobilization measures on 25 September, the Anglo-French diplomatic pressure of 20–21 September had already forced the Prague government to accept the concessions that were further codified during the Munich Conference itself.[119] Bonnet remained terrified that Litvinov might yet be instructed to offer fresh assurances to Prague. This was confirmed by his deliberate distortion of both the substance and the tenor of exchanges between Litvinov and Moscow Chargé Payart, and his own discussion with the Soviet foreign minister at Geneva on 11 September.[120] But the trend of Moscow policy indicated otherwise and, after the key decisions of 20–21 September, it was unlikely that Benes could have vested everything in any such Soviet offer. Bonnet's panic is easily explained. While the French government was anxious to avoid its military obligations to Czechoslovakia, it bears emphasis that the diplomatic pretext to do so was only assured within 48 hours of the Munich Conference. Lacking an absolute assurance of Soviet backing on 20–21 September, Benes was unable to force a reconsideration of French policy. Since the underlying thrust of Soviet diplomacy was always to ensure that France acted first in support of Czechoslovakia, Benes had hit a brick wall. During Franco-British staff talks in London on 26 September, Gamelin discounted Soviet assistance in the short term. Yet he still suggested that French military intervention might prove decisive, particularly if Poland and Hungary remained neutral, thus allowing Czech forces to hold the line in Moravia.[121] While the British chief of air staff, Sir Cyril Newall, took fright at Gamelin's methodical evaluation of the prospects for military intervention, in Paris, Vuillemin's devastating report on the weakness of the Armée de l'Air had just reached La Chambre's desk. Vuillemin's prediction of utter defeat – 40 per cent of initial French air force effectives destroyed within a month, 64 per cent within two months – bolstered Bonnet's case for a diplomatic settlement at all costs during the cabinet session on 27 September. Bonnet was first to grasp the nettle, but Daladier endorsed his foreign minister's line at

a further meeting between the two men later that afternoon.[122] With
François-Poncet and Sir Eric Phipps united in their final attempts to
coax Hitler towards a peaceful occupation of the Sudetenland, the
way was open for Mussolini's proposal for a conference settlement
on 28 September.[123]

Daladier's government at last had a means of escape. Hitherto
unable to repudiate the Czech alliance without irrevocably damaging
France's international standing, once mobilization began there was a
real threat of conflict escalation. The absence of British support,
distrust of the Soviets and an appalling air force position might seem
reason enough not to march. The threat of a near immediate financial
breakdown and the keen public anxiety to avoid war still more so.
Even so, the government remained trapped by its alliance
commitment. Trapped rather than committed: even the most resolute
of Daladier's ministers could have had no illusions that war over
Czechoslovakia would be, at best, an heroic gamble and, at worst, an
historic calamity. The general staff, their British partners, Bonnet and
the other cabinet appeasers had repeatedly told them so. Daladier's
government had to consider going to war and the preparations were
in hand to do so. But war in September 1938 was never seen as the
most viable course of action. In an improvised solution born of
desperation, the French leadership grabbed the lifeline of Munich in
the knowledge that the alternative was too grim to face.

University of the West of England

NOTES

The author wishes to thank Dr Zara Steiner and Dr Peter Jackson for their comments upon
earlier versions of this article. He is grateful to the British Academy for an overseas research
grant.

1. Regarding Daladier's return from Munich, see Robert J. Young, *In Command of
   France: French Foreign Policy and Military Planning, 1933–1940* (Cambridge, MA:
   Harvard University Press, 1978), p.215; Elisabeth du Réau, *Edouard Daladier
   1884–1970* (Paris: Fayard, 1993), pp.285–6.
2. Centre des Archives Economiques et Financières, Savigny-le-Temple (Finance
   Ministry archive – hereafter CAEF), Direction du Trésor, Carton B33.196, Jacques
   Rueff memo, 'Avances Banque de France et sorties d'or en 1937', 21 Nov. 1938; René
   Rémond and Janine Bourdin (eds.), *Edouard Daladier. Chef du Gouvernement (avril
   1938 – septembre 1939)* (Paris: Presses de la FNSP, 1977), pp.15–16.

3. Anthony Adamthwaite, *Grandeur and Misery: France's Bid for Power in Europe, 1914–1940* (London: Arnold, 1995), pp.175–6; Yvon Lacaze, *L'opinion publique française et la crise de Munich* (Berne: Peter Lang, 1991), pp.370–74.
4. Rosemonde Sanson, 'La perception de la puissance par l'Alliance Démocratique', *Revue d'Histoire Moderne et Contemporaine*, Vol.31 (1984), pp.660–61; Yvon Lacaze, 'Daladier, Bonnet and the Decision-Making Process during the Munich Crisis, 1938', in Robert Boyce (ed.), *French Foreign and Defence Policy, 1918–1940* (London: Routledge, 1998), pp.223–6.
5. University of Cambridge, Churchill College Archive, Sir Eric Phipps papers, Vol.1/19, Phipps to Anthony Eden, 9 Nov. 1937; Williamson Murray has stressed that Phipps deliberately took soundings from the most defeatist of French politicians, such as Caillaux and Bonnet, see his *The Change in the European Balance of Power, 1938–1939* (Princeton, NJ: Princeton University Press, 1984), p.167.
6. Serge Berstein, 'La perception de la puissance par le Parti Radical-Socialiste', *Revue d'Histoire Moderne et Contemporaine*, Vol.31 (1984), pp.619–20; René Girault, 'The Impact of the Economic Situation on the Foreign Policy of France, 1936–9', in Wolfgang J. Mommsen and Lothar I. Kettenacker (eds.), *The Fascist Challenge and the Policy of Appeasement* (London: George Allen and Unwin, 1983), p.221; William D. Irvine, 'Domestic Politics and the Fall of France', in Joel Blatt (ed.), *The French Defeat of 1940: Reassessments* (Oxford: Berghahn, 1998), pp.88–9.
7. Anthony Adamthwaite, *France and the Coming of the Second World War* (London: Frank Cass, 1977); Robert J. Young, *In Command of France: French Foreign Policy and Military Planning, 1933–1940* (Cambridge, MA: Harvard UP, 1978); Lieutenant-Colonel Henry Dutailly, *Les Problèmes de l'Armée de Terre Française (1935–1939)* (Paris: Imprimerie nationale, 1980); Jean Doise and Maurice Vaïsse, *Diplomatie et outil militaire, 1871–1991* (Paris: Imprimerie nationale, 1987); Colonel Pierre le Goyet, *Munich, 'un traquenard'* (Paris: Editions France-Empire, 1988); Yvon Lacaze, *L'opinion publique française et la crise de Munich* (Berne: Peter Lang, 1991); Martin S. Alexander, *The Republic in Danger: General Maurice Gamelin and the Politics of French Defence, 1933–1940* (Cambridge: CUP, 1992); Nicole Jordan, *The Popular Front and Central Europe: The Dilemmas of French Impotence, 1918–1940* (Cambridge: CUP, 1992); Robert Frank, *La hantise du déclin. Le rang de la France en Europe, 1920–1960. Finances, défense et identité nationale* (Paris: Belin, 1994).
8. Gilles Le Béguec, 'L'évolution de la politique gouvernementale et les problèmes institutionnels', in Rémond and Bourdin (eds.), *Edouard Daladier*, pp.55–7; du Réau, *Edouard Daladier*, pp.218–20; Lacaze, *L'opinion publique*, p.359.
9. Paul Marchandeau was finance minister until November 1938; Albert Sarraut held the interior ministry post; Georges Bonnet was foreign minister until his replacement by Daladier himself on 13 September 1939. Ramadier was minister of labour until his resignation on 23 August 1938. Minister of Public Works Frossard resigned alongside him. Louis de Chappedelaine, an acknowledged naval specialist, was minister responsible for the merchant marine.
10. Jean-Baptiste Duroselle, *Politique étrangère de la France. La décadence 1932–1939* (Paris: Imprimerie nationale, 1979), pp.361–2; Maurice Vaïsse, 'Against Appeasement: French Advocates of Firmness, 1933–8', in Mommsen and Kettenacker (eds.), *Fascist Challenge*, p.232.
11. Alexander, *The Republic in Danger*, pp.106–9, 385–90.
12. Elisabeth du Réau, 'L'information du "décideur" et l'élaboration de la décision diplomatique française dans les dernières années de la IIIe République', *Relations internationales*, Vol.32 (1982), pp.530–34; Lacaze, 'Daladier, Donnet and the Decision-Making Process', p.222.
13. Duroselle, *La décadence*, p.340; Ministère des Affaires Etrangères, *Documents Diplomatiques Français 1932–1939* (hereafter *DDF*) (Paris: Imprimerie nationale,

1974 *et seq.*), 2e Série, Vol.X, Nos.222, 237; Vol.XI, Nos.12, 95, 116, 266, 267, 291, 292, 426; Murray, *Change in the European Balance*, p.197.

14. Nicole Jordan, 'Léon Blum and Czechoslovakia, 1936–1938', *French History*, Vol.5, No.1 (1991), pp.67–8. The 15 March meeting is recounted in Adamthwaite, *France and the Coming of the Second World War*, pp.87–8; Young, *In Command of France*, pp.200–201; Duroselle, *La décadence*, pp.329–31; Alexander, *Republic in Danger*, pp.163–4.

15. Ministère des Affaires Etrangères archive (hereafter MAE), Papiers 1940, Fonds Daladier, Vol.I, No.1082, Gamelin memo, 'Note sur les conséquences de la réalisation de l'Anschluss', 14 March 1938.

16. Centre des Archives Diplomatiques, Nantes (hereafter CADN), Série Z, Vol.308, Italie – Politique Extérieure, Corbin letter to Paul-Boncour, 7 April 1938.

17. Jordan, 'Léon Blum and Czechoslovakia', pp.48–73; DDF, 2e Sér, Vol.IX, No.3, Paul-Boncour to Corbin, 21 March 1938; CADN, Grande-Bretagne, Vol.264, tel.953, Paul-Boncour to Corbin, 23 March 1938; regarding the state of Germany's western fortifications, see Murray, *Change in the European Balance*, pp.239–41.

18. R.A.C. Parker, *Chamberlain and Appeasement: British Policy and the Coming of the Second World War* (London: Macmillan, 1993), pp.140–41; Phipps papers, Vol.2/10, Orme Sargent tel. to Phipps, 17 March 1938. Sargent conveyed the foreign office central department view that 'it must be our sincere wish to see him [Paul-Boncour] out of office at the earliest possible moment'. Lacaze, 'Daladier, Bonnet and the Decision-Making Process', p.226.

19. DDF, 2e Sér, Vol.IX, No.73, Note du Vice-Président du Conseil Supérieur de la Guerre (Gamelin), 29 March 1938; No.251, Note du Chef d'Etat-Major de la Défense Nationale (prepared for Daladier), 27 April 1938.

20. MAE, Papiers 1940, Fonds Daladier, Vol.I, No.1082, Gamelin memo, 'Note sur les conséquences de la réalisation de l'Anschluss', 14 March 1938.

21. Robert Frank, *La hantise du déclin*, pp.182–3, and *Le prix du réarmement français (1935–1939)* (Paris: Publications de la Sorbonne, 1982), pp.190–91; Girault, 'The Impact of the Economic Situation', pp.220–42.

22. CAEF, B33.196, No.415/CD, Rueff, 'Note – Prévisions de Trésorerie, 2ème semestre 1937', 23 June 1937; No.549/CD, Rueff, 'Note sur la situation de la Trésorerie en 1937 et en 1938', 31 March 1938.

23. CAEF, B33.196, Commission des Finances du Sénat – projet de pleins pouvoirs Daladier-Marchandeau, 13 April 1938.

24. CAEF, B33.196, No.539/CD, Marchandeau to Chautemps, 2 March 1938; No.9547/CD, Marchandeau to M. le Président du Conseil d'administration de la Caisse autonome de la défense nationale, 28 June 1938.

25. CAEF, B33.196, No.599/CD, Marchandeau to Daladier, 3 Oct. 1938.

26. CAEF, B12.620/D2, No.68,109, Félix Le Norcy, London financial attaché, to Direction générale du mouvement des fonds, 20 Aug. 1938; Frank[enstein], *Le prix du réarmement*, pp.279–81.

27. Julian Jackson, *The Popular Front in France: Defending democracy, 1934–38* (Cambridge: CUP, 1988), pp.186–7.

28. Bertrand Favreau, *Georges Mandel ou la passion de la République 1885–1944* (Paris: Fayard, 1996), pp.341–2, 351–3.

29. Favreau, *Georges Mandel*, pp.340, 345; Duroselle, *La décadence*, pp.357–63; Vaïsse, 'Against Appeasement', p.233.

30. René Girault, 'Les décideurs français et la puissance française en 1938–1939'; Général Jean Delmas, 'La perception de la puissance militaire française'; Jean Bouvier and Robert Frank, 'Sur la perception de la "puissance" économique en France pendant les années 1930'; and Serge Berstein, 'La perception de la puissance par les partis politiques français en 1938–1939': all in René Girault and Robert Frank (eds.),

La Puissance en Europe, 1938–1940 (Paris: Publications de la Sorbonne, 1984); du Réau, 'L'information du "décideur"', pp.525–41, and idem, 'Edouard Daladier et l'image de la puissance française en 1938', *Revue Historique des Armées*, No.3 (1983), pp.27–39. On the radical and communist parties, see Serge Berstein, 'La perception de la puissance par le parti Radical–Socialiste', and Danièle Zeraffa, 'La perception de la puissance par le Parti Communiste', both in *Revue d'Histoire Moderne et Contemporaine*, Vol.31 (1984), pp.619–35 and 636–57.

31. Patrice Buffotot, 'La perception du réarmement allemand par les organismes de renseignement français de 1936 à 1939', *Revue Historique des Armées*, No.3 (1979), pp.173–84, and idem, 'Le réarmement aérien allemand et l'approche de la guerre vus par le IIe bureau air français (1936–1939)', in K. Hildebrand and K.F. Werner (eds.), *Deutschland und Frankreich 1936–1939* (Munich: Artemis, 1981), pp.249–89; Robert J. Young 'French Military Intelligence and Nazi Germany, 1938–1939', in Ernest R. May, *Knowing One's Enemies: Intelligence Assessment Before the Two World Wars* (Princeton, NJ: Princeton University Press, 1986), pp.271–301; Martin S. Alexander, 'Did the Deuxième Bureau Work? The Role of Intelligence in French Defence Policy and Strategy, 1919–1939', *Intelligence and National Security*, Vol.6, No.2 (1991), pp.293–333; Peter Jackson, 'La perception de la puissance aérienne allemande et son influence sur la politique extérieure française pendant les crises internationales de 1938 à 1939', *Revue Historique des Armées*, No.4 (1994), pp.76–87.

32. Peter Jackson, 'French Military Intelligence and Czechoslovakia, 1938', *Diplomacy & Statecraft*, Vol.5, No.1 (1994), pp.81–106; Général Maurice Gauché, *Le Deuxième Bureau au Travail (1935–1940)* (Paris: Amiot Dumont, 1953), p.55. Less convincing than Jackson, a different treatment of Faucher's mission is Antoine Marès, 'La faillite des relations franco-tchécoslovaques: la mission militaire française à Prague, 1926–1938', *Revue d'Histoire de la Deuxième Guerre Mondiale*, Vol.28, No.111 (1978), pp.45–71, and idem, 'Les attachés militaires en Europe centrale et la notion de la puissance en 1938', *Revue Historique des Armées*, No.1 (1983), pp.60–72.

33. Lacaze, *L'opinion publique*, pp.360–74, 591–5.

34. Rémy Pithon, 'Opinions publiques et représentations culturelles face aux problèmes de la puissance. Le témoignage du cinéma français (1938–1939)', *Relations internationales*, Vol.33 (1983), pp.98–100.

35. MAE, Papiers d'agents 217, René Massigli papers, Vol.15, record of meeting, Quai d'Orsay, 5 April 1938.

36. Elizabeth R. Cameron, 'Alexis Saint Léger', in G.A. Craig and F. Gilbert (eds.), *The Diplomats, 1919–1939* (Princeton, NJ: Princeton University Press, reprint 1981), pp.392–3; Adamthwaite, *France and the Coming of the Second World War*, p.154.

37. Service Historique de l'Armée de Terre, Paris (hereafter SHAT), 7N3097/MMF Prague, Faucher report, 'La Tchécoslovaquie et l'Anschluss', 22 March 1938.

38. *DDF*, 2e Sér, Vol.IX, No.128, General Krejci to General Gamelin, 7 April 1938.

39. Jackson, 'French Military Intelligence', p.93.

40. The information on intercepts of Paris–Prague cable traffic came from France's foremost spy, Hans-Thilo Schmidt: see Anthony Adamthwaite, 'French Military Intelligence and the Coming of War, 1935–1939', in Christopher Andrew and Jeremy Noakes (eds.), *Intelligence and International Relations, 1900–1945* (Exeter: Exeter University Press, 1987), p.201; Franklin L. Lord and Carl E. Schorske, 'The Voice in the Wilderness: Robert Coulondre', in Craig and Gilbert, *The Diplomats*, pp.566–7.

41. SHAT, 7N3037/MMF Prague, tels.5, 7, 8, Faucher to EMA–2, 21 May 1938.

42. *DDF*, 2e Sér, Vol.IX, No.442 annex, General Renondeau to Daladier, No.443, Colonel de Geffrier to Guy La Chambre, both 24 May 1938.

43. *DDF*, 2e Sér, Vol.IX, No.412, Renondeau to Daladier, 22 May 1938.

44. CAEF, B32.947, Ministère du Commerce, 4e Bureau, 'Note sur les capitaux français en Tchécoslovaquie', 20 Jan. 1939.
45. CAEF, B32.057, Direction du Trésor/Tchécoslovaquie, No.2193, Bonnet tel. to François-Poncet, 13 Oct. 1938.
46. CAEF, B32.947, No.749, M. Tarbé de Saint-Hardouin to Direction générale du mouvement des fonds, 24 March 1937.
47. DDF, 2e Sér, Vol.IX, No.74, annex, Note du Directeur Politique, 29 March 1938. Nicole Jordan points out that French financial investment in Czechoslovakia was not matched by a concomitant development of Franco-Czech commerce, see The Popular Front, pp.112–14, 129–35. For a detailed analysis of commerical penetration in Czechoslovakia, see Alice Teichova and P.L. Cottrell, International Business and Central Europe, 1918–1939 (Leicester: Leicester University Press, 1983).
48. Milan Hauner, 'Czechoslovakia as a Military Factor in British Considerations of 1938', Journal of Strategic Studies, Vol.2 (1978), pp.195–9.
49. Robert J. Young, 'Reason and Madness: France, the Axis Powers and the Politics of Economic Disorder', Canadian Journal of History, Vol.20 (1985), pp.72–9; on the gulf between French military and industrial intelligence, see Peter Jackson, France and the German Menace, 1933–1939 (Oxford: Oxford University Press, forthcoming), ch.8.
50. Young, 'Reason and Madness', pp.73–4.
51. SHAT, 7N3097, Renondeau to Section du Chiffre, 20 July 1938.
52. Igor Lukes, 'Did Stalin Desire War in 1938? A New Look at Soviet Behaviour during the May and September Crises', Diplomacy & Statecraft, Vol.2, No.1 (1991), pp.20–42.
53. Jonathan Haslam, 'The Soviet Union and the Czechoslovakian Crisis of 1938', Journal of Contemporary History, Vol.14, No.4 (1979), pp.443–4, 452–5.
54. SHAT, 5N579/D6, No.559/DN/S, Gamelin to Daladier, 18 July 1938.
55. SHAT, 5N579/D6, No.2430, Bonnet to Daladier, 12 Aug. 1938.
56. SHAT, 2N24, CPDN, procès verbal, 8 Dec. 1937; 2N25/D2, CPDN, procès verbal, 15 March 1938.
57. Martin S. Alexander, 'In Lieu of Alliance: The French General Staff's Secret Co–operation with Neutral Belgium, 1936–1940', Journal of Strategic Studies, Vol.14, No.4 (1991), pp.413–27; Alexander, The Republic in Danger, pp.202–6.
58. SHAT, 7N2731/EMA–2, Nos.72 and 96, AM, Colonel Edmond Laurent, rapports, 17 and 31 March 1938; Resumé des rapports, 22 Sept. 1938.
59. SHAT, 7N2731/Resumés, Resumé des rapports, 29 Sept. 1938.
60. Berstein, 'La perception de la puissance par le Parti Radical-Socialiste', p.624; Lacaze, L'opinion publique, pp.375–8.
61. DDF, 2e Sér, Vol.XI, No.150, n.3.
62. Gauché, Deuxième Bureau au Travail, pp.135–41; DDF, 2e Sér, Vol.XI, No.7, Bonnet to Corbin, 4 Sept. 1938.
63. Adamthwaite, France and the Coming of the Second World War, p.238, and 'French Military Intelligence and the Coming of War', p.192; Murray, Change in the European Balance, pp.241–3.
64. DDF, 2e Sér, Vol.IX, No.151, Aide-mémoire, 9 April 1938.
65. DDF, 2e Sér, Vol.IX, No.290, Bonnet to Daladier, 6 May 1938.
66. CAEF, B33.196, No.599/CD, Marchandeau summary to Daladier, 3 Oct. 1938.
67. CAEF, B33.196, Jacques Rueff, 'Note de Trésorerie', 21 Nov. 1938.
68. CAEF, B33.196, No.599/CD, Marchandeau summary to Daladier, 3 Oct. 1938.
69. CAEF, B50.977, Direction du Trésor – opérations exceptionelles, 'Recours à l'Institut d'émission, années 1935–1938', 12 Jan. 1939; Frank[enstein], Le prix du réarmement, p.194.
70. Patrick Facon, 'La visite du général Vuillemin en Allemagne (16–21 août 1938)',

Recueil d'articles et études (1981–1983) (Vincennes, Service Historique de l'Armée de l'Air, 1987), pp.223–62; Duroselle, *La décadence*, pp.341–2, 347–8; Adamthwaite, *France and the Coming of the Second World War*, p.202; Young, *In Command of France*, pp.197–8; Alexander, *The Republic in Danger*, pp.167, 234.

71. Berstein, 'La perception de la puissance par le Parti Radical-Socialiste', p.629.
72. Service Historique de l'Armée de l'Air, Paris (hereafter SHAA), 2B58/D1, EMAA–2, 'Bulletin de renseignements sur les aéronautiques étrangères', 2e trimestre 1937; SHAT, 2N235/D1, No.1994, Vuillemin report, 'Valeur de la puissance aérienne soviétique', 16 Sept. 1938.
73. SHAA, Carton 1B2, file 66, 'Note concernant l'Armée de l'Air Française. Son importance Européenne, la nécessité de son accroissement', n.d. Jan. 1938.
74. SHAT, 2N227/CSDN–3, No.2535, Vuillemin letter to Gamelin, 4 Nov. 1938.
75. SHAA, Archive Guy La Chambre, Z12930, memo. 'Le Plan V', n.d.; La Chambre note, 21 March 1938.
76. SHAA, 2B1, Doc.B132, EMAA–1, 'Note sur la réalisation du plan d'accroissement de l'Armée de l'Air, CSA séances 7, 8, 9, 15 Mars 1938', 18 March 1938; SHAA, Archive Guy La Chambre, Z12940, No.662, La Chambre to Daladier, 17 Sept. 1938.
77. SHAT, 2N25/D2, CPDN, procès verbal, 15 March 1938; SHAA, 2B8, Doc.121, EMAA–2, Vuillemin letter to Gamelin, 5 April 1938.
78. R.J. Young, 'The Strategic Dream: French Air Doctrine in the Inter-War Period', *Journal of Contemporary History*, Vol.9, No.4 (1974), pp.65–7; Alexander, *The Republic in Danger*, pp.159–60; Jackson, 'French Intelligence and Nazi Germany', pp.216–17.
79. SHAA, 1B6/D1, No.274, Comité du matériel, procès verbal, 25 March 1938 and 6 May 1938; 1B6/D1, Comité du Matériel, 19e séance, procès verbal, 2 Sept. 1938.
80. Public Record Office, London (hereafter PRO), Air Ministry Directorate of Operations and Intelligence files, AIR 9/95, EMAA reply to British Air Ministry enquiries, 13 Aug. 1938.
81. SHAA, 2B97/Tchécoslovaquie, No.2029, EMAA–2 note for Vuillemin, 11 Sept. 1938. A single squadron – the 32nd – was designated to operate from Czech territory.
82. SHAA, 2B97/Tchécoslovaquie, No.2122, EMAA–2 note for Vuillemin, 17 Sept. 1938; *DDF*, 2e Sér, XI, No.296, Vuillemin to General Mouchard, 22 Sept. 1938.
83. Thierry Vivier, 'La Cooperation aéronautique franco–tchécoslovaque, janvier 1933–septembre 1938', *Revue Historique des Armées*, No.1 (1993), pp.74–8.
84. SHAT, 2N224/D2, No.775/DN–3, Daladier letter to Bonnet, 26 Sept. 1938.
85. PRO, AIR 9/78, Points for discussion with Vuillemin, 24 Sept. 1938; Young, *In Command of France*, p.210; Alexander, *The Republic in Danger*, p.167.
86. Immediately after the Rhineland reoccupation, Gamelin urged the Polish and Czech army staffs to construct a common defensive front, see: SHAT, 7N3096/télégrammes, No.342/EMA–2, Gamelin to Faucher, Prague, 13 March 1936. Regarding Polish–Czech relations in general, see Piotr Wandycz, *The Twilight of French Eastern Alliances, 1926–1936: French–Czechoslovak–Polish Relations from Locarno to the Remilitarization of the Rhineland* (Princeton, NJ: Princeton University Press, 1988), pp.395–409; Jordan, *Popular Front*, pp.162–70, 274–5.
87. SHAT, 7N3096/MMF, Faucher record of conversation with Benes, 25 Dec. 1936.
88. SHAT, 7N3012/EMA–2 départs, EMA–2, note for Gamelin, 22 Aug. 1938. The Poles were trying to purchase large consignments of SOMUA, D2 and Hotchkiss tanks, but the war ministry refused to denude French mechanized division rearmament.
89. *DDF*, 2e Sér, Vol.XI, No.242, Entretien entre M. Georges Bonnet et M. Lukasiewicz, 20 Sept. 1938.
90. Cameron, 'Alexis Saint-Léger Léger', pp.394–5.
91. SHAT, 2N25/D2, No.1777/S, Gamelin note, 16 March 1938.
92. *DDF*, 2e Sér, Vol.IX, No.450, Note du 2e Bureau de l'EMAA, 25 May 1938.

93. SHAT, 5N579/D6, Faucher, 'Résumé d'un entretien avec le Président Beneš', 12 July 1938.
94. CADN, Tchécoslovaquie, Vol.140, tel.193, Coulondre to Bonnet, 12 July 1938.
95. SHAT, 7N3097, No.55, Faucher to EMA-2, 17 Aug. 1938; Patrice Buffotot, 'The French High Command and the Franco-Soviet Alliance, 1933–1939', *Journal of Strategic Studies*, Vol.5, No.4 (1982), pp.552–3; Maurice Vaïsse, 'La perception de la puissance soviétique par les militaires français en 1938', *Revue Historique des Armées*, No.3 (1983), pp.20–21.
96. G. Jukes, 'The Red Army and the Munich Crisis', *Journal of Contemporary History*, Vol.26, No.2 (1991), p.199.
97. *DDF*, 2e Sér, Vol.XI, No.295, Note de l'Etat-Major de l'Armée sur la suite donnée aux entretiens Beneš-Faucher, 22 Sept. 1938.
98. SHAT, 7N3203, No.57/S, Colonel Merson, Belgrade military attaché, to EMA-2, 14 Sept. 1938.
99. SHAT, 7N3052/D3, No.86, Delmas, Bucharest, to EMA-2, 18 Sept. 1938.
100. SHAT, 7N3052/D1, No.8/S, Delmas, Bucharest, to EMA-2, 23 Jan. 1938; 7N3052/D2, No.43/S, Delmas to EMA-2, 1 June 1938.
101. SHAT, 7N3052/D2, No.31/S, Delmas to EMA-2, 8 May 1938; MAE, Tchécoslovaquie, No.1223, Bonnet to Corbin, relay of Bucharest tel., 6 May 1938.
102. *DDF*, 2e Sér, Vol.IX, No.451, EMA-2 Compte rendu, 25 May 1938.
103. *DDF*, 2e Sér, Vol.XI, No.29, Note de la Direction Politique, 6 Sept. 1938; Adamthwaite, *France and the Coming of the Second World War*, p.238. Regarding Loizeau's 1935 report, see Alexander, *The Republic in Danger*, pp.293–4.
104. MAE, Roumanie, Vol.167, tel.1330, De Lacroix, Prague, to Foreign Ministry, 12 July 1938.
105. *DDF*, 2e Sér, Vol.XI, No.96, Note du Ministre, 11 Sept. 1938.
106. Lukes, 'Did Stalin Desire War in 1938?', p.36; Duroselle, *La décadence*, pp.353–4; *DDF*, 2e, Vol.XI, No.376, Compte rendu, 26 Sept. 1938.
107. CADN, Tchécoslovaquie, Vol.140, tel.3057, Bonnet to Corbin, 24 Sept. 1938.
108. G. Jukes suggests that up to 90 divisions, including three tanks corps, were mobilized: see his 'The Red Army', pp.197–202. Jonathan Haslam has also concluded that the Soviets were ready to act, although their initial mobilization measures may have been intended primarily to coerce the Poles: see his 'The Soviet Union and the Czechoslovakian Crisis', pp.452–7; Duroselle, *La décadence*, p.355.
109. Lukes, 'Did Stalin Desire War in 1938?', pp.31–2, 38–9.
110. *DDF*, 2e Sér, Vol.XI, No.12, Payart, Chargé, Moscow, to Bonnet, 5 Sept. 1938; No.29, Note de la Direction Politique, 6 Sept. 1938; Note du Ministre, 11 Sept. 1938; No.266 and 267, both Robert Coulondre to Bonnet, 21 Sept. 1938; Jiri Hochman, *The Soviet Union and the Failure of Collective Security, 1934–1938* (Ithaca, NY: Cornell University Press, 1984), pp.158–9.
111. SHAT, 2N224/D2, No.286/DN–3, CSDN, Secrétariat Général, 'Note sur la collaboration Franco-Britannique', 24 April 1938.
112. *DDF*, 2e Sér, Vol.XI, No.44, Bonnet to Victor de Lacroix, Prague, 8 Sept. 1938; No.196, Note juridique, 17 Sept. 1938. This document is an unsigned memorandum drawn from Bonnet's papers. It suggested three possible legal pretexts for abandoning the 1925 Franco-Czechoslovakian alliance: that, because the *Anschluss* altered Czechoslovakia's international frontiers, it rendered the original terms of the 1925 treaty invalid; that conflict over the Sudetenland was an internal matter which would not warrant French support; and that the 1928 Kellogg–Briand Pact disbarred France from recourse to war to settle international disputes.
113. *DDF*, 2e Sér, Vol.XI, No.55, Bonnet to Corbin, 9 Sept. 1938.
114. SHAA, 2B58/D2, EMAA-2, 'Notices sur les forces aériennes étrangères, tome II: Tchécoslovaquie', n.d. June 1938.

115. *DDF*, 2e Sér, Vol.XI, No.65, Gamelin note, 9 Sept. 1938.
116. SHAT, 7N3097, No.38, Faucher to EMA-2, 15 Sept. 1938.
117. *DDF*, 2e Sér, Vol.XI, No.195, Note du Directeur Politique, 17 Sept. 1938.
118. *DDF*, 2 Sér, Vol.XI, No.273, Gamelin to Daladier, 21 Sept. 1938. By contrast, Faucher agreed with Benes that full mobilization was fully justified, see SHAT, 7N3097, No.32, Faucher to EMA-2, 18 Sept. 1938.
119. Jukes, 'The Red Army', p.201.
120. Hochman, *The Soviet Union*, pp.156–9; Georges Bonnet, *Défense de la paix, I: De Washington au Quai d'Orsay* (Geneva: Editions du Cheval, 1946), pp.197–8.
121. *DDF*, 2e Sér, Vol.XI, No.376, Compte-rendu des conversations techniques de Général Gamelin, 26 Sept. 1938.
122. *DDF*, 2e Sér, Vol.XI, No.377, Vuillemin report to La Chambre, 26 Sept. 1938; No.400, note 1, Note du Ministre, 27 Sept. 1938.
123. *DDF*, 2e Sér, Vol.XI, No.385, François-Poncet to Bonnet, 27 Sept. 1938; Franklin L. Ford, 'Three Observers in Berlin: Rumbold, Dodd and François-Poncet', in Craig and Gilbert, *The Diplomats*, pp.466–7.

War and Peace:
Mussolini's Road to Munich

G. BRUCE STRANG

The Munich crisis holds a compelling interest for historians, even 60 years after the event. Despite this interest, however, few writers have paid much attention to the Italian role in the crisis. Telford Taylor's mammoth work on Munich, for example, cast Mussolini in only a minor, subservient role, primarily as a participant at the conference itself.[1] Similarly, two relatively recent scholarly collections, much less than having full-length articles on Italian policy, contain only fleeting references to Mussolini and his part at Munich.[2] Studies devoted to Italian foreign policy do not necessarily carry much more coverage of Munich. Denis Mack Smith, the acerbic British writer, disparaged the possibility of Italian participation in war over Czechoslovakia; in his view, the *opéra bouffé* character of the fascist regime's war preparations and matériel production precluded any serious Italian involvement.[3] Italian-language historians writing on Italian policy have tended to minimize Italy's role. Rosaria Quartararo, in her several hundred-page work on Italian foreign policy during the 1930s, *Roma tra Londra e Berlino*, devoted only a handful of pages to the Czech crisis. She argued that 'war in Europe failed to break out only because fascist Italy did not *want* to go to war and *never intended* to involve itself'.[4] The doyen of Italian historians, Renzo De Felice, in his multi-volume, magisterial biography of Mussolini, also devoted relatively brief coverage to Munich. He suggested that Italian activity was almost nonexistent until the middle of September 1938, when Mussolini finally had to consider the real possibility of war. As war appeared increasingly imminent, il Duce decided to go to war only if Great Britain did so first, making the conflict one of an 'ideological character'. De Felice argued that Mussolini acted throughout the Czech crisis as if he wanted 'to avoid any commitment'.[5] One writer, however, has suggested that Italian policy was more aggressive than this minimal commitment. In a necessarily brief reference to the crisis in the first chapter of *Mussolini Unleashed*, MacGregor Knox wrote that Italian war planning was rather more advanced. Mussolini had assured the German government that Italy would fight, and had instituted some basic preparations.[6] This limited survey shows that there is a serious shortage of detailed inquiry into Italian policy and the Czech crisis and, at the same time, wide differences of opinion in the recent historical debate.[7]

The paucity of coverage on Italian policy has occurred in part owing to the comparative difficulty of researching Italian subjects. Italian historians are still editing and publishing the series *I Documenti Diplomatici Italiani*; the crucial volumes covering the Munich crisis are not yet in print. Further, until much later than for the other major powers, the Italian foreign ministry archive limited access to its files. Compared to the well-organized and indexed files at the Public Record Office at Kew, for example, filing is rather haphazard at the foreign ministry in Rome, and working conditions are more difficult there. Not surprisingly, therefore, most of the writing on Italian policy to this date relies heavily on memoirs, the limited published primary material, or on the problematic diaries of Dino Grandi, the Italian ambassador in London.[8]

With the increasing openness of Italian records, we now have more detailed information on fascist policy, and the documentation allows us a deeper understanding. We can now address several important questions. First, what policy and actions did Mussolini and Galeazzo Ciano, his foreign minister, carry out in the events leading to Munich? Second, why did Mussolini support Germany's attempts to shatter Czechoslovakia, even to the point of general war? Third, why did Mussolini pull back at the last moment, forwarding Chamberlain's vitally important *démarche* that led to the Munich Conference? Mussolini's foreign policy carried a heavy ideological cast, but his plans for Czechoslovakia, Albania, Spain, Japan and the Western democracies carried internal contradictions. Some observers saw the resulting foreign policy as opportunistic, but it actually careered between reckless aggression and almost timid caution. Mussolini's policy and actions during the Czechoslovak crisis, therefore, were more important, purposeful and aggressive than historians have generally allowed.

Italy's early role in the destruction of Czechoslovakia was entirely unwitting. In April, as Hitler contemplated his future action against Czechoslovakia, he thought that it was essential to have Italian support. If recent Italian conquests in Africa and the potential victory in Spain sated Mussolini, then the lack of an Italian ally meant that the German strategic position would not favour a successful campaign against the Czechs. If, however, Mussolini hoped to create an African empire, then he could do so only with German help. The resulting ties and presumed Italian loyalty would most likely deter France from intervening militarily in a German–Czechoslovak war. Even if the French government did declare war, Hitler mused, then Italian pressure against the French alpine frontier and against Anglo-French interests in Africa would allow the Wehrmacht the time necessary to regroup after its victory over Czechoslovakia. Accordingly, Hitler believed that an alliance with Italy was an essential element of Germany's political and military strategy. Hitler returned from his visit to Rome in early May 1938 convinced that Mussolini's aggressive nature would lead him to fall in line with Hitler's script.[9]

Mussolini was not unwilling to fill the role in which Hitler had cast him. In the last half of May, as rumours of German aggression abounded and the Czechoslovak army subsequently mobilized, Mussolini offered his unqualified support. Though Italy had no direct interest in the issue, Galeazzo Ciano, the Italian foreign minister and Mussolini's son-in-law, said that Italy would support its Axis partner. He offered to issue a communiqué to that effect. Mussolini declared solemnly to Ciano that Italy would 'immediately enter the struggle by the side of the Germans'.[10] The following day, in order to issue this official 'Informazione Diplomatica', Ciano inquired whether Hitler planned to destroy Czechoslovakia or simply to achieve regional autonomy for the Sudeten Germans. Mussolini did not care which policy Hitler intended to pursue; il Duce wanted only to concert Italian aims with those of Germany to avoid working at cross-purposes. The crisis died down without further incident and the German government declined the Italian offer of an official statement. The German ambassador, Hans von Mackensen, entirely misinformed Ciano about the aggressive nature of German policy, suggesting that Hitler sought only negotiations regarding autonomy for Sudeten Germans. The Italians temporarily ceased their quest to determine Hitler's intentions. The display of Italian support, however, encouraged Hitler's belief about Mussolini's loyalty.[11] At the end of July, Mussolini further encouraged this view. In the context of anxious international concern over German demands against Czechoslovakia, Bernardo Attolico, the Italian ambassador in Berlin, informed German Foreign Minister von Ribbentrop of il Duce's policy. Mussolini promised to 'support German policy to the full'. If France were to mobilize, then so would Italy. If France attacked Germany, then Italy would attack France. In effect, 'Germany and Italy were so closely linked together that their relationship was tantamount to an alliance'. Mussolini hinted at the possible conclusion of a formal agreement, containing the usual soporifics of eternal friendship, but, more importantly, staff conversations and mutual declarations of diplomatic and military support in the case of outside interference.[12]

As European tension simmered over the early summer, Ciano worked to secure Germany's southern flank in the event of a confrontation with Czechoslovakia. During the May crisis, Ciano had promised to protect Italy's Hungarian client if Yugoslavia were to attack that country in honouring its obligations as a member of the Little Entente. This support would not be available, however, if Hungary joined in a German invasion of Czechoslovakia immediately. In that case, Mussolini would dissociate himself.[13] In June, Ciano's March 1937 pact with Yugoslavia and the resulting warmer relations with Prime Minister Milan Stoyadinovic bore fruit. At a meeting with Ciano, Stoyadinovic clarified Yugoslavia's policy. He had no intention of getting involved in a war with Germany despite his obligations under the Little Entente. He asked Ciano only that Italy intercede with Hungarian leaders to prevent them from taking the initiative. A Hungarian invasion would oblige Yugoslavia to honour its commitments. As long as Hungary restrained itself and sought only to benefit from a German-provoked crisis, then Yugoslavia would not intervene.[14]

When a Hungarian delegation arrived in Rome a month later, Mussolini did not hesitate to share this information. Kalman de Kanya, the Hungarian foreign minister, expressed concern that Yugoslavia would intercede to prevent Hungary from supporting

German action in the approaching crisis. Although de Kánya ruled out any Hungarian initiation of action, he distrusted any assurances from Stoyadinovic. He asked, therefore, for an Italian military guarantee against a possible attack from Yugoslavia. Mussolini reassured de Kánya, repeating the pledge from the prior meeting with the Yugoslav prime minister; as long as Hungary intervened only after a German attack, then it would not risk an attack from Belgrade. Mussolini urged the Hungarians to press their claims. 'The surest solution to the Czech problem lay in rapidity of action'. In addition, il Duce shared his belief that the crisis would be localized, but that Italy would support its Axis partner whatever that entailed.[15] A week later, a joint Italo-Hungarian military session considered possible cooperation in the event of war and Italian arms shipments to Hungary.[16] In short, despite Mussolini's contempt for the Hungarian leaders and Ciano's opinion that they were 'arrogant and petulant', Mussolini had strongly encouraged Hungary to intensify the impending confrontation.[17]

In August, a Czechoslovak crisis appeared increasingly likely. Italian intelligence sources produced a large number of reports that Hitler planned to invade Czechoslovakia at the end of September 1938. General Efisio Marras, the military attaché in Berlin, reported that Admiral Canaris, the German intelligence head, was convinced that Hitler was determined to attack Czechoslovakia despite the opposition of his senior military advisers. Canaris hoped that Mussolini could intercede to convince the Führer that Britain and France would intervene to protect the Czechoslovak democracy. The assistant military attaché echoed this prediction. Based on several reports from contacts in the high command, Colonel Badini wrote that Hitler had settled on action at the end of September. Again, the cardinal point was Hitler's assumption that Britain and France would not intercede.[18] The lack of official confirmation of these plans from Berlin worried Ciano. Accordingly, he gave Ambassador Attolico written instructions to determine Germany's precise intentions in order to allow the Italian military to act on its western Alpine frontier. Ciano noted that this *démarche* would 'have a considerable effect on the Germans as it demonstrates just how far we are prepared to go'. Mussolini had resolved himself to the need for action. If France were to stand by its Czech ally, Italy would have no choice but to support its German partner militarily. Far from discouraging their German partner as Canaris had hoped, Mussolini and Ciano encouraged Hitler through their as yet unqualified support.[19] Attolico, however, was unable to fulfil his orders. He met with von Ribbentrop on 26 August, but the German foreign minister avoided the Italian ambassador's probing.[20] Mussolini and Ciano repeated their orders. Attolico met once more with von Ribbentrop, insisting he needed to know Hitler's plans, as 'we must take measures of a military nature'. This time, von Ribbentrop was slightly more forthcoming. Hitler planned to liquidate Czechoslovakia, von Ribbentrop repeated several times, but he would not unleash the Wehrmacht for at least a month.[21] Even though Attolico's assessment of Hitler's intentions was highly accurate, Ciano distrusted his ambassador's reports, as he questioned Attolico's commitment to Mussolini's Axis policy. Mussolini directed Ciano to sound out the Prince of Hesse, who had acted as an important liaison in the past. Upon his return to Rome several days later, Hesse misled the Italian foreign minister, stating that Hitler had set no firm programme, and would attack Czechoslovakia only if provoked by the Czechs.[22]

At the end of August, Attolico questioned Mussolini's policy. He thought that il Duce was running the risk of dragging Italy into a re-run of the Great War. One could not simply assume that the Chamberlain government would stand aside in the event of war. Sir Nevile Henderson, the British ambassador in Berlin, had warned that if Germany attacked Czechoslovakia then Britain would intervene, and would fight to win. According to Efisio Marras, the military attaché, the German fleet would be entirely unable to contain a substantial element of the Royal Navy; accordingly, the weight of British naval power would fall *'practically entirely on Italy'*. In these circumstances, Attolico thought that it was imperative to find out both German intentions and Hitler's expectations of fascist Italy.[23] The next day, he reiterated and amplified these points. He wrote that Mussolini had given Hitler an 'illusory' picture of Italian support for German aggression. He wanted to clear the air in order to correct this impression.[24]

Mussolini had other plans, however, and he ploughed ahead with his reckless support for German revisionism. In the space of six days, il Duce issued three important official statements. In 'Informazione

Diplomatica #19', published on 9 September, Mussolini supported
Sudeten German leader Konrad Henlein's eight points of the
Karlsbad programme, and denounced the Czech state as tainted by
the French left and Moscow's communism. Five days later, Mussolini
went further, traducing Czechoslovakia as a 'paradoxical creature of
Versailles diplomacy', where ethnic Czechs subjugated a mosaic of
nations. In his view, there were only two solutions: giving Sudeten
Germans the right to determine their own destiny, or war. In his
'Letter to Runciman', published in the semi-official *Popolo d'Italia* on
15 September, Mussolini called for a plebiscite not only for the
Sudeten Germans, but also for all subject races. At that point,
Mussolini's demands outpaced those from Hitler.[25]

As il Duce fired this last public salvo, Ciano confirmed once more
to Hans von Mackensen, the German ambassador in Rome, that Italy
would remain by Germany's side in any eventuality. In Ciano's view,
British Prime Minister Neville Chamberlain's visit to meet with
Hitler in Germany showed that Great Britain was 'hollow and well
past its prime'. This weakness meant that Mussolini was spoiling for
a showdown with a France that apparently lacked a strong ally. Still,
Ciano returned to a familiar theme. Only if the Italians were fully
informed about Hitler's plans could Italy act in Germany's best
interests. Ciano, therefore, asked the ambassador once more for
fuller cooperation between the two Axis partners.[26] In particular,
Ciano said that Mussolini planned to make a major speech at Trieste
on 18 September during his tour of the northeastern provinces;
Ciano inquired as to what the German government would like him to
say. Hitler responded that the solution would have to be quick and
would have to free all of Czechoslovakia's minorities from Czech
rule. Mussolini believed that this solution would require military
action, including the possibility of general war. He declared to Ciano,
who had met Mussolini's train, that, 'If war breaks out in Germany,
Prague, Paris, and Moscow, I shall remain neutral. If Great Britain
intervenes, generalizing the struggle and giving it an ideological
character, then we shall throw ourselves into the flames. Italy and
Fascism could not be neutral'.[27]

Mussolini's speech the next day further inflamed the situation. He
fulminated that Italians would not shirk their responsibility to their
Axis partner, but would shoulder it in full. Axis solidarity included

the friendship of both Poland and Hungary, and Mussolini pressed forward their territorial claims against Czechoslovakia. He thunderously denounced his French enemy. Italy and the decadent France were ranged across the barricades in Spain, and fascism could not tolerate French interference. The only peaceful solution to the Czech crisis was for President Benes to concede a plebiscite for all national groups. If he did not, Mussolini suggested that Britain would not march in support of the obdurate Czechs, and without British leadership, no other nation would move in support of Czech resistance. Any further delay could spark a war, but il Duce still hoped for a peaceful solution. If war came, however, he expected it to be limited to southeast Europe.[28] Mussolini followed this speech with a week long series of speeches and articles trumpeting Italian martial preparedness. Italian fascists were committed to battle, and the current *status quo* was not acceptable: 'Italy today is a people on the fiery march.' Mussolini's wars in Africa and Spain had created a population of 'tempered steel', ready for war. He condemned his French foes, who were wed to a dead pluto-democratic ideology, and were 'too stupid to be dangerous'. Mussolini's propaganda barrage served to heighten the tension of the crisis even further, helping to create an atmosphere of imminent war.[29]

While Mussolini heightened the tension in public, Ciano worked through diplomatic means to support German aims. At the end of August, Miklos Horthy, the Hungarian regent, had visited Berlin for high-level talks with Adolf Hitler. Hungarian diplomats had negotiated the Bled agreement, culminating on 23 August. This arrangement, concluded with members of the Little Entente, exchanged concessions allowing Hungarian rearmament and minority rights in Little Entente countries for a Hungarian renunciation of the use of force. This last compromise ran directly cross-current to Hitler's expectations of the role that Hungary would play in his plans to liquidate Czechoslovakia. In a meeting with the Führer, Jeno Ratz, the Hungarian defence minister, stated in clear terms that his military was in no shape to carry out offensive operations, and could not play an aggressive role. The Hungarian delegation further insisted that a German attack would certainly provoke a general war that would have potentially catastrophic results for Hungary.[30] Prime Minister Bela Imredy and de Kanya shared these sentiments with Attolico, adding that Hungary would take no action until absolutely certain of Yugoslav neutrality.[31] As the crisis escalated at the end of September, Ciano sought to keep Hungarian and even Polish claims to the forefront. In order to ensure Yugoslav neutrality, Mussolini supported Hungary's plans only to follow in the German wake. He insisted, however, that Hungarian claims form a central part of any settlement, and that the Hungarian government should provoke ethnic confrontations to keep its claims at the forefront. Ciano made the need for an integral solution for all of the subject minorities clear in a meeting with the British ambassador.[32] Potentially more seriously, in light of rumours of potential Soviet air support for Czechoslovakia, Mussolini agreed to dispatch Italian fighters to Hungarian airfields near Miskolo. Italian airmen wearing Hungarian uniforms would pilot these planes. This action could potentially have led to direct Italo-Soviet confrontation in the skies above Budapest.[33] Mussolini and Ciano once again had taken actions that could seriously inflame the imminent crisis.

As Chamberlain met Hitler at Bad Godesberg on 22 September, Attolico informed the foreign ministry that the Prince of Hesse would carry an important message from Hitler to Mussolini. In the meantime, Chamberlain failed to dissuade Hitler, Czechoslovak, French and British forces began to mobilize, and Ciano learned officially that Hitler demanded cession of territory to begin on 1 October.[34] Mussolini, convinced that Hitler would not invade before that date, decided to continue his tour of the northeast. Ciano flew overnight on 24 September to meet Hesse, and the next day Ciano and Hesse drove to meet Mussolini in Schio, where il Duce would make a short stopover. Hesse carried only vague instructions. Hitler thanked Mussolini for his support, confirmed the 1 October deadline, and promised that the Wehrmacht would support Italy if necessary. In Hitler's view, Great Britain and France would not fight, but if they did, then Germany was prepared for that eventuality, as the balance of forces clearly favoured the Axis. The time was ripe for fighting the inevitable conflict with the Western democracies. In his discussion with Hesse, Mussolini generally concurred with this assessment. If the war became general, he promised Hesse that Italy would enter the war immediately after Great Britain, waiting only to avoid giving the British government a pretext for declaring war.

Mussolini wanted Ciano and von Ribbentrop to meet to consider precise terms for Italy's entry into the war.[35]

Given their knowledge of Hitler's determination to crush Czechoslovakia and the British, French and Czechoslovak mobilizations, Mussolini had to consider a general war a possible occurrence. Accordingly, on 26 and 27 September, Ciano and the Italian general staff planned Italy's initial preparations for war. Conditions could hardly be worse. The Wehrmacht, obviously, would engage Czechoslovakia, leaving only token forces in the West. The Regio Esercito could only fight a defensive battle on its Alpine frontier, and would be unable to carry out any offensive action in Europe. Years of intraservice infighting, combined with Mussolini's mania for counting battalions rather than assessing their effectiveness, had saddled the army with enormous numbers of poorly trained and equipped troops. Given the battles that Mussolini intended to fight in the desert, rational planners would have prepared a highly modern mechanized ground force, not hundreds of battalions of slow-moving infantry. In this context, the chiefs of staff could do little more than to mobilize ten divisions to protect Italy's northwest frontier against French action there.[36] The situation for the Regia Marina was little better. Mussolini's construction plans were far from complete, and he had only two modern battleships to send to battle. The Regia Marina faced the potential coalition of Anglo-French navies, and could take no major initiative in the face of superior enemy forces. It could only carry reinforcements and supplies to Libya and the Dodecanese, and naval commanders prepared fast convoys to do so.[37]

There was one small bright spot. On 27 September, Attolico reported from Berlin that the German government could not expect to support the Condor Legion in Spain if it went to war with either France or Britain; it offered to turn over the Condor Legion to the Italian forces on Majorca. If Mussolini accepted, then German planes and supporting technicians would be available to operate from Italian bases and under Italian command to interdict French communications with North Africa or for use against French naval and air forces.[38] With war seemingly imminent, Mussolini determined the need for a meeting between foreign ministers and senior military officials to coordinate broader German and Italian policy and to create 'organs of military co-operation'. Hitler concurred, and scheduled the meeting for noon, 29 September, at Munich. With Hitler's ultimatum due to expire at 2.00 pm on 28 September, both Mussolini and Ciano thought war inevitable as night fell on 27 September.[39]

On 28 September, as is well known, Mussolini received official *démarches* from both the British and American governments asking him to intercede with Hitler to postpone his ultimatum.[40] The British ambassador, Lord Perth, met Ciano at 10.00 that morning, and presented an official request for Mussolini's intercession. Ciano hurriedly travelled from the Palazzo Chigi to meet il Duce at the Palazzo Venezia. At 11.00, Mussolini seized this opportunity to prevent an immediate war, and telephoned Attolico in Berlin. His instructions were to 'go immediately to the Führer, and, on the premise that in any case I will be at his side, tell him that I suggest a postponement of twenty-four hours in the initiation of hostilities'. Having thus once more committed Italy to war at Hitler's discretion, Mussolini hoped that Hitler would accept Chamberlain's proposal for a four-power conference to arrange the cession of Czech territory. Hitler accepted Mussolini's proposal, provided il Duce would attend the meeting personally.[41] On their way to Munich, Ciano and Mussolini met Hitler at the frontier. The discussion centred on Hitler's desire to dismantle Czechoslovakia in order to free up divisions for a future campaign against France. The Führer told Ciano that 'the time will come in which together we will have to battle against the Western Powers. Better that this occur while at the head of our two countries will be il Duce and I, young and full of energy and that we represent the more powerful armies'. Mussolini supported Hitler's demand that the Czechs be prohibited from attending the conference.[42] Senior German foreign office officials had prepared a draft text of an agreement, which Hitler had approved. Attolico obtained a copy of the draft through unusual channels, and gave it to Mussolini. Il Duce presented it at the conference as if it were an Italian proposal and it formed the basis for the Munich Conference.[43]

The conference itself has received extensive coverage elsewhere; there is little need to discuss in detail already familiar terrain. It is important, however, to consider two important questions: first, why did Mussolini so recklessly push the Axis towards a confrontation over the disposition of ethnic Germans in Czechoslovakia; and, second, why did he intercede with Hitler to prevent the immediate outbreak of war? The answer to the first of these larger questions lies in two primary areas: Mussolini's disdain for the Czech democracy and his expansionist aims that would require German support.

Mussolini detested Czechoslovakia. In his view, this 'mongrel state', a creation of Versailles diplomacy, represented the worst elements of multi-ethnic bourgeois democracy and French international diplomacy. As a charter member of the Little Entente, Czechoslovakia resisted Hungarian revisionism, a goal that Mussolini had long supported. Czechoslovakia's relations with Rumania and Yugoslavia also extended French influence into the Balkans, and interfered with Italian efforts to develop its competing interests there. President Benes supported precisely the kind of internationalism that Mussolini despised. More directly, Czechoslovakia had supported the League in its sanctions policy against Italy.[44] Recently, Czechoslovakia had also aroused Mussolini's ire by supporting Ethiopian rebels. Italian intelligence reported that a French ship under Greek flags carried Czech arms to French Somalia. From there, the arms shipment travelled across the Djibouti frontier and into rebel hands.[45] Ciano had protested in the strongest terms, suggesting to his minister in Prague that the Czechs should keep their rifles there, as 'it could be that they will need them shortly!'[46] Though Italy had no direct interest at stake in German claims, il Duce had little love for Czechoslovakia and would take pleasure from its destruction. In addition, the absence of Czechoslovakia would allow Italy some greater freedom in extending its Balkan influence, though at the cost of increased German competition in the Danube basin.

Mussolini's own dreams, however, were more important. In his adult life, Mussolini had developed contempt for liberal democracy. In his view, that bankrupt ideology, derived from social conditions existing in the nineteenth century, was doomed. It emphasized class conflict, personal corruption and ambition. Democratic regimes operated on a level beneath public view; typically, cabals of Jews or Freemasons controlled the real levers of power.[47] Even worse, the odious stench of pacifism clung to democratic regimes after the Great

War. Mussolini believed that events such as the Oxford Union debate, where undergraduates refused to fight for king and country, defined a culture. He thought pacifism 'an absurdity or better a dangerous deformation'. This view underlay in part both his disdain for the Western democracies and his initial belief that they would not fight over Czechoslovakia.[48] Mussolini also placed great store in population demographics. He believed that demographic expansion was necessary lest Italy be reduced to the status of a colony. Italy needed to increase its population from the 40 million of the mid-1920s to 60 million by 1960. This growth was the prerequisite for Italy to face the challenge of an expected 90 million Germans and 200 million Slavs, plus 40 million Frenchmen supported by 90 million colonials and 56 million Englishmen supported by 450 million colonial subjects. He believed that demographic strength underpinned the economic and moral virility of nations.[49] He condemned Malthus's 'idiotic' reasoning. He simplistically equated demographic strength with military power; more population meant more soldiers.[50] He thought French demographic weakness in the wake of the Great War 'absolutely horrifying'. Both French and British demographics were so poor that Mussolini thought that the great imperial countries had had their 'life blood sapped'.[51]

The course of events in the 1930s confirmed this belief in Mussolini's mind. By 1938, il Duce's fascination for population demographics led him to believe that both Britain and France were in a perpetual state of decline. In Britain, for example, almost one-quarter of the population was over the age of 50, Mussolini argued, and that lack of vitality meant that Britain's imperial splendour would inevitably fade.[52] In August, Mussolini read a report from the London embassy citing a British peer's comments on British birth and death rates. Il Duce heavily underlined the section where the writer forecast a population decline from 40,000,000 to 4,000,000 in 100 years if then current trends continued.[53] Against this weakness, he trumpeted Italian demographic strength that would allow him to create great armies. In his view, military motorization could only succeed to a certain point. Infantry was still the queen of battle, and Mussolini not only had large numbers of infantry, his wars had tempered them like steel.[54] Eventually, his expansionistic impulses were bound to lead to confrontation with both of these great

Mediterranean empires, and Mussolini believed that the demographic power would allow him to win those wars.

Still, despite this demographic power, Mussolini needed to support his German partner in order to maintain the strength of the Axis. Only with German help could Mussolini hope to defeat two imperial powers. Accordingly, Italy's association with nazi Germany formed the centrepiece of Mussolini's foreign policy in the aftermath of the Ethiopian war. Mussolini began his early, halting steps to end his diplomatic isolation during the height of tension of that campaign. In January 1936, il Duce signalled his desire to end the hostility remaining in the wake of the 1934 Dollfuss affair, when Italy had stationed troops on the Brenner frontier to avert an Austrian nazi *putsch*. Mussolini astonished German Ambassador von Hassell by suggesting an Austro-German agreement 'which would in practice bring Austria into Germany's wake, so that she could pursue no other foreign policy than one parallel with Germany. If Austria, as a formally quite independent state, were thus in practice to become a German satellite, he would have no objection'.[55] German officials treated this *démarche* with extreme scepticism, but after repeatedly sounding Mussolini on the point, eventually accepted this sea change in Italian policy. In response to German probing, Mussolini also confirmed that he considered the Stresa front 'dead', and that he would take no part in action by Britain and France in the possible event of a German breach of the Locarno Treaty.[56] Hitler eventually sent Hans Frank, a minister without portfolio, to carry a personal message to Mussolini, assuring il Duce of Hitler's sympathy regarding the Ethiopian war and the Italian struggle against both bolshevism and the democracies.[57] Mussolini fulfilled his promise to place pressure on the Austrian government to come to an agreement with Germany. In essence, Mussolini implied that if Chancellor von Schuschnigg resisted German advances, then Austria would find itself isolated from all outside support.[58] Mussolini greeted the resulting accord, signed on 11 July 1936, with great pleasure, as it removed 'the only point of friction between Italy and Germany'.[59] By the middle of July, therefore, Mussolini had carried out a substantive *rapprochement* with Germany.[60]

Over the following two years, Mussolini and Hitler tightened their association. Mussolini's initially reluctant and low-level intervention in the Spanish Civil War escalated from sporadic shipments of arms to a full-scale military intervention. By early August 1936, with Mussolini's approval, General Roatta, head of the Italian intelligence organization Servizio Informazione Militari, had begun arrangements for Italo-German cooperation in supplying Franco with fuel. In addition, Mussolini allowed German transport planes to stage through Italian airfields in order to reach Spain.[61] These arrangements intensified into fuller cooperation during the remainder of August.[62] Mussolini's official proclamation of the Axis followed on 1 November 1936, during a bellicose speech denouncing democracy as the antithesis of fascism.[63] As Mussolini drew nearer to Germany, a massive Soviet commitment in Spain, including enormous shipments of arms and the financing and recruiting of the international brigades, saved Madrid from imminent nationalist occupation and threatened to prevent a nationalist victory.[64] Mussolini responded with an enormous escalation of Italy's intervention, including ever closer ties and cooperation with German officials to coordinate their respective policies.[65]

During 1937, Mussolini sought to develop closer economic relations with Germany, especially in the realm of war production and raw materials exchange. He thought that war with the Western democracies was likely in the future and that the Axis powers would need those instruments of economic development.[66] In London, where the largely futile workings of the nonintervention committee tried to limit foreign intervention in Spain, Italy and Germany worked in lockstep. They effectively preserved virtual freedom of action for Mussolini's massive intervention there.[67] Ciano attempted to arrange an alliance with Japan, including military and technical cooperation, but decided in the summer of 1937 that that policy would foreclose his attempts to isolate France through an Anglo-Italian accord.[68] Eventually, Italy joined the anti-Comintern Pact, which, despite its nominal foe, was in Mussolini's eyes entirely anti-British in nature.[69] In May 1938, Mussolini refused von Ribbentrop's offer of an open alliance. He still hoped for an eventual British implementation of the Anglo-Italian Easter Accord, signed on 16 April 1938, in which the British cabinet had conditionally conceded *de jure* recognition of Italy's Abyssinian conquest. Mussolini knew that an open alliance with Germany would end the possibility of formal British recognition. Accordingly, il Duce preferred Ciano's draft of a much looser formal arrangement, though he continued display a high degree of support for German revisionism.[70] Over the summer, as we have seen, Mussolini gave virtually unqualified encouragement to Hitler's threats and invasion plans for Czechoslovakia.

By the time of Munich, therefore, Mussolini had created ties to both Germany and Japan in order to place pressure on the Western democracies. Mussolini's long-term foreign policy aims required German and Japanese support to meet several objectives, particularly the annexation of Albania and the separation of France and Great Britain. This latter aim would allow Italy to acquire concessions and further conquests in the Mediterranean basin. Italy simply was not powerful enough, however, to achieve these goals without German and Japanese help, necessitating reciprocal Italian support for German goals. That Hitler's target for his revisionist policy was a French-allied democracy merely served to whet Mussolini's appetite for destruction. Paradoxically, these same issues, plus Italy's war in Spain, led Mussolini to determine that war over Hitler's demands against Czechoslovakia would be inopportune, perhaps even disastrous for Italy and for Mussolini's foreign policy.

Mussolini's territorial ambitions included the eventual annexation of Albania. Ciano had instituted some basic plans for increasing Italian penetration of Albanian economic, cultural and political life.[71] After Ciano's tour of Albania in May 1938, Mussolini and Ciano agreed that Italy should begin determined planning for the annexation of the Italian protectorate. This move would serve several purposes. Following the Anschluss, Mussolini feared possible German interest in the pre-war Austrian sphere of influence. Annexation of Albania could decisively prevent further German economic or political moves there, and could help to restore the balance of Italo-German influence in the Balkan region. Strategically, Italian occupation of Albania would turn the Adriatic Sea into a *Mare Italiano*, and release Italian naval resources for use against Anglo-French forces in the Mediterranean basin. Finally, Ciano also noted that Albania had extensive deposits of coal and potential reserves of other minerals to exploit for Italian production.[72] Mussolini, however, assumed that Britain, France and Yugoslavia would oppose

Italian annexation, so he needed time to prepare the diplomatic terrain. He would need first to conclude a pact with Germany to intimidate Yugoslavia and to secure German support against the Western democracies. For tactical reasons, the German pact itself was contingent on prior British ratification of the Easter Accords. Given these conditions, Mussolini tentatively scheduled the invasion for May 1939. In the meantime, Francesco Jacomoni, the Italian minister to Albania, would institute public works, land reclamation and other economic projects and sponsor charitable and sporting events to raise the Italian profile, while at the same time increasing Italian military presence in Albania.[73] Though these plans proceeded more quickly than initial estimates, they were not complete by the time of Munich. War over Czechoslovakia threatened to complicate or to prevent Italian annexation of Albania, potentially frustrating one of Mussolini's major policy goals.

Mussolini's commitment to the war in Spain was a further consideration for avoiding war in 1938. By the end of the summer of 1938, Mussolini had once again despaired of imminent victory. Nationalist leader Francisco Franco had established a clear superiority of numbers and quality of troops and equipment. Despite this advantage, however, his troops had been unable to finish off republican resistance. Mussolini, frustrated by the delays, flirted with the possibility of removing all Italian infantry from Spain.[74] This proposal would force the British cabinet to decide either to implement the 16 April 1938 Easter Accord or to let it lapse. If the cabinet decided on the latter course, then Mussolini would be free to sign a military alliance with Germany.[75] Mussolini eventually determined that this move would look as if he were abandoning his ally, so he decided to continue his commitment, though relations with Franco remained strained.[76] As the threat of war over Czechoslovakia loomed, Franco faced a difficult choice. The Spanish republican government staked its last chance for survival on a general war over Czechoslovakia. If France and Britain went to war, then it planned to declare war immediately on Germany and Italy. In theory, Britain and France both would be obliged to accept republican Spain as an ally. Franco feared that such a scenario could lead to a French occupation of Spanish Morocco, the Balearics, and even Catalonia. Franco's intelligence sources informed him, however, that if he remained neutral, then both Britain and France would not intervene.[77] Further, nationalist Spain could count on significant support from neither Germany nor Italy. Not surprisingly, therefore, Franco declared to the representatives of the Western democracies that he would remain neutral in the imminent conflict.[78] This decision disgusted Ciano. He wrote that the Italian war dead would 'turn in their graves'. In a fit of pique, he briefly considered ordering the evacuation of Italian troops and specialists. After Mussolini and Ciano discussed the situation, however, they decided on 26 September that Franco's neutrality was inevitable and sensible, and that they would leave the Corpo Truppe Voluntarie in place.[79]

The situation in Spain, therefore, strongly argued against going to war in 1938. Despite Mussolini's pessimism regarding Franco's chances for victory, the balance of forces in Spain suggested that Franco would win in the near future. Franco's troops outnumbered the republic's by nearly a two to one margin, and Italian and German support gave the nationalist army a clear technical advantage. At the time of Munich, Italy still had more than 40,000 men in Spain, plus roughly 100 light tanks, 600 artillery pieces and 250 planes. Italy had spent almost six billion lire (over 60 million pounds sterling at the official exchange rate). Over the course of the war, Italy had sent more than 700 aircraft.[80] Mussolini could expect to recoup this extraordinary commitment in money, men and arms only when Franco achieved final victory. A premature Italian war with France would jeopardize that victory. France could potentially take a series of steps, from reopening the frontier to volunteers and supplies to an outright invasion of Spain to defeat Franco and his Axis allies. It made little sense to risk defeat given Italy's bloody, expensive and lengthy intervention. A peaceful settlement of the Czechoslovak question doomed the republican government and ensured an eventual nationalist victory. Mussolini's last-minute intercession with Hitler offered the hope that Italy could save its army in Spain, could recoup its investment, and could eventually establish a strong ally hostile to France on the Pyrenees frontier.

Mussolini's attempt to create a tripartite alliance with Germany and Japan represented another reason for delaying war with the West. Since the latter half of 1936, Mussolini and Ciano had begun to lessen their formerly tight relations with Chiang Kai-Shek's nationalist Kuomintang government. Chiang Kai-Shek's support for the League of Nations and for sanctions during the Abyssinian campaign had annoyed Mussolini, while Japan's 'intrepid resistance' to international opposition over its wars in China had pleased him. Still, Italy maintained important commercial and military missions in China, and did not want to lose these investments entirely. Ciano hoped to be able to direct both Kuomintang and Japanese efforts primarily to fighting Chinese communists in order to continue to establish a position of equilibrium between the two enemies.[81] Accordingly, Ciano worked primarily in the diplomatic realm; he arranged a mutual *de jure* recognition of Japan's Manchukuo and Italy's Abyssinian conquests.[82] Most importantly, though, Mussolini believed that a virile, expansionistic Japan would tie up British and Soviet resources in the Far East, which would '*diminish their power and liberty of action in Europe*'. A three-power association between Italy, Germany and Japan would represent a severe challenge to British power in the Mediterranean, and would allow Italy much greater freedom of action in its growing confrontation with the Western democracies.[83] This inchoate *rapprochement* represented the first steps toward the signing of the Anti-Comintern Pact in 1937.

Mussolini and Ciano strengthened their ties to Japan in 1937. After sporadic attempts to improve Italo-Japanese economic and cultural ties, Hirota Koki, the foreign minister in a new and more aggressive cabinet, spoke to Giacinto Auriti, the Italian ambassador in Tokyo, about strengthening political and diplomatic ties to Italy.[84] Simultaneously, the leader of the Italian air mission in China suggested that it would be more profitable to close the mission and to send one to Japan instead. Recent massive Soviet shipments of modern aircraft had allowed Chinese nationalists to establish air superiority over Japan. In that circumstance, Italy could receive greater political rewards from technical assistance to Japan.[85] After the Marco Polo Bridge incident on 7 July 1937 sparked dramatically intensified fighting, Ciano could no longer try to maintain a middle ground.[86] Mussolini decided to close the mission in China and to try to arrange an alliance with Japan. He found Japan's regard for Italian military prowess flattering, and the economic implications of potential Japanese arms purchases were promising. More importantly, however, the opportunity to intimidate Britain was too promising to forego. At the same time, however, Mussolini's attempts to receive British *de jure* recognition of the Abyssinian conquest and to drive a wedge between Britain and France required him to proceed carefully; he could not alienate the British government entirely.[87] Ever-shifting Japanese political alignments led the Japanese government to draw back from a formal alliance, but this reticence did not deter Ciano. He essentially broke relations with the Chinese nationalist government, and he continued to pursue a tighter association with Japan.[88] Mussolini's and Ciano's goal reached fruition later that year, as Italy joined the Anti-Comintern Pact, making the pact a tripartite association.[89] Despite the nominal enemy, Mussolini aimed the anti-Comintern arrangement entirely against the British empire.[90] Ciano believed that the new pact created the 'most formidable political and military combination that has ever existed', and was 'anti-Communist in theory but in practice unmistakenly anti-British'. He expected that the strength of the three revisionist powers would force Britain 'to reconsider her position everywhere' and would allow fascist Italy to 'break through the crust which is stifling the energy and aspirations of the young nations'. The ultimate enemy of all three powers was, in both Mussolini's and Ciano's eyes, the decadent British empire.[91]

Japanese reticence, combined with the continuing need to account for British sensibilities, prevented Mussolini and Ciano from securing a more definitive agreement during the first half of 1938. Still, in March 1938, Mussolini had continued to try to tighten the relationship between the two anti-Comintern signatories. He had dispatched a letter to Prime Minister Konoe Fumimaro, citing the common aspirations of the two countries that had bound them in a pact against 'the dissolute ideologies that infect the sacred patrimony of humanity'.[92] A May 1938 shuffle brought a new foreign minister and war minister to power in Konoe's cabinet. Lieutenant-General Itagaki Seishiro, the war minister, hoped to use Germany and Italy to try to intimidate the Western powers and the Soviet Union to limit their interference in Japan's escalating aggression against China.[93] Accordingly, the Japanese military attaché in Rome approached Ciano at the end of May with an offer of a secret pact. Ciano, naturally, concurred, and dispatched a senior admiral to Japan to begin discussions of a parallel military accord. He also instructed

Auriti to negotiate a pact including articles on benevolent neutrality if either party went to war, political consultations, and military and technical cooperation. Opposition from the Gaimusho, the Japanese foreign minister, and from within the navy, however, stalled this initiative for some four months.[94] As the Munich crisis reached its height at the end of September, Mussolini learned that the Japanese government had decided to proceed with a tripartite alliance. Within a few weeks, Italy could expect to sign a formal military alliance with Germany and Japan.[95] Despite the prospects of achieving this foreign policy coup, Mussolini could count on no meaningful Japanese military support against the British empire in the event of war over Czechoslovakia. Only if he were able to avoid a general European conflict could he secure Japan as an ally in the eventual campaign against the Western democracies. For Mussolini, it made little sense to risk this major diplomatic and strategic advantage in order to fight a war in 1938 in which Italy held no direct interest.

Mussolini's remaining concern was the apparent failure to have separated France from Great Britain. Mussolini had worked for more than two years to try to accomplish this goal. While he tried to reach an accord with Great Britain through the so-called 'gentlemen's agreement' and the 16 April 1938 Easter Accord, Mussolini explicitly excluded any French involvement in these discussions. As his troops conquered Addis Ababa and he prepared the ground for his *rapprochement* with Germany, il Duce began his programme of separating his potential French and British enemies. Italy's closer relations with Germany would worry British policymakers and increase their desire to reach some kind of Mediterranean accord with Italy. Accordingly, Mussolini directed Dino Grandi, his ambassador in London, to reorient British thinking away from a multilateral Mediterranean pact and toward a bilateral Anglo-Italian accord. Grandi should belittle the idea that France, 'nailed to the cross of the Soviets', would make an effective British partner in Mediterranean affairs. As France was too concerned about the German threat, Britain should jettison its association with the French in favour of a *modus vivendi* with Italy. Mussolini aimed to drive a wedge between the Western democracies in an attempt to isolate France.[96] The result of this policy, the gentlemen's agreement of 2 January 1937, excluded any meaningful French diplomatic participation.

Similarly, as Ciano began in the summer of 1937 the lengthy series of steps and retreats towards the Easter Accords, he rejected the proffered hand of French friendship. The new Camille Chautemps cabinet was not as ideologically opposed to fascism as had been the prior Blum administrations. Still, Ciano refused Vittorio Cerruti, his ambassador in Paris, the freedom to try to lessen Franco-Italian tension.[97] Ciano thought it better that 'Paris understands only that our intransigence is absolute'.[98] By maintaining this hostile attitude toward France, Ciano hoped that negotiations with Great Britain could create Mussolini's hoped-for wedge between the two Western democracies, perhaps even leading to a permanent split. To that end, he was willing to make concessions to secure an agreement with Britain.[99] Mussolini maintained his attitude of the year before; he wanted an attitude of 'strict severity in his confrontation with France'. To signal his disdain, he eventually withdrew Cerruti from Paris at the end of October.[100] As he neared the completion of the Easter Accord negotiations in Rome, Ciano emphasized once more the anti-French nature of that agreement. 'An accord between Italy and Great Britain is destined to accentuate French isolation', he wrote, 'the consequence will be to weaken the system or systems of a collective nature on which France pinned its hopes'. Italy accordingly had vetoed every British attempt to bring in other Mediterranean powers.[101]

One can see the result of this policy most clearly in the failed Franco-Italian discussions at the end of April and beginning of May 1938. Mussolini and Ciano briefly flirted with the possibility of a Franco-Italian accord to parallel the one recently signed with Britain. The French request for conversations occurred during the aftermath of the *Anschluss*, which had temporarily soured Mussolini's view of the Axis. Primarily, ethnic Germans in the Sud Tyrol, former Austrian territory then controlled by Italy, created demonstrations akin to those seen in Czechoslovakia by the Sudeten Germans. In the light of Hitler's imminent arrival in early May, Mussolini used these inchoate Franco-Italian negotiations as a possible alternative to the Axis should Hitler prove truculent in supporting German irredentism. Despite the optimism of French diplomats and statesmen, there was little chance of any substantial agreement. Mussolini refused to consider three of the French proposals: French association with the

Anglo-Italian agreement in the Red Sea area; negotiation of the status of Tunisia on the basis of the 1935 Rome Accord; and, more importantly, a declaration of Italian disinterest in territorial acquisition and the eventual withdrawal of Italian troops from Spain.[102] Mussolini rudely rejected this French *démarche* after Hitler's visit had smoothed over the cracks in the Axis; Hitler had guaranteed the integrity of the common Italo-German border and promised to reign in any German irredentists in the Sud Tyrol.[103] Mussolini needed German support to enable the annexation of Albania, which both Britain and France would certainly oppose. After taking this decision, Mussolini made a thunderously bellicose anti-French speech on 14 May at Genoa, and slammed shut the door on French hopes for a *rapprochement*. In a fit of pique, he denounced France as 'a nation ruined by alcohol, syphilis and journalism'.[104] Even at the nadir of Axis solidarity, Mussolini could scarcely stomach an association with France, and he was entirely unwilling to grant France status equivalent to that negotiated by the British in the Easter Accord. During the summer, Mussolini returned to his attempts to drive a wedge between France and Britain, deliberately fomenting virulently anti-French propaganda and 'a wave of Gallophobia'.[105]

At the time of Munich, though, his long-term policy to separate the Western democracies had not yet reached fruition. The Chamberlain cabinet had not implemented the Easter Accord, and, worse, seemed to have drawn closer to France. With both Britain and France mobilizing, Mussolini faced the very combination of hostile forces that he sought to avoid. Still worse, his Axis partner, whom Mussolini hoped would contain the French army, was preparing to fight in eastern Europe, and had stationed only a modest holding force in the West. If Britain supported a French declaration of war, as appeared possible, then Italy would likely face defeat in the ensuing war. Given the array of potential problems, it is not surprising that Mussolini seized the lifeline thrown by Chamberlain on 28 September. Bluntly put, conditions were not yet ripe for the war that Mussolini contemplated.

Mussolini's role in the Munich crisis, therefore, is an equivocal one, as was so often the case with il Duce. Acclaimed as a peacemaker for his last-minute intercession with Hitler, he also did what he could to escalate the Czech crisis to breaking point. Hitler would not and could not have proceeded with his plans to eliminate Czechoslovakia without Italian support, and Mussolini was pleased to encourage those plans. On several occasions, Mussolini gave his virtually unqualified approval and promised to stand by his Axis partner whatever occurred. In the last week before Munich, he slightly amended his stance; Italy would only fight if Great Britain entered the war first. Even this slight change was calculated primarily to avoid giving the British government a pretext to declare war, thus giving the Chamberlain government a greater incentive to abandon its potential French ally. Only at the last minute did Mussolini pull back from the brink. In forwarding Chamberlain's peace proposal to Hitler, Mussolini committed Italy to fight if the Führer chose to ignore the request, but at the same time, Hitler understood that il Duce's ardour for war had temporarily cooled. Still, throughout most of the Czechoslovakian crisis Mussolini had played the role of provocateur and brinksman, and it is somewhat ironic that he earned a reputation as the more reasonable of the two fascist dictators in the aftermath of Munich.

Mussolini pushed forward Hitler's expansionist aims because he detested the Czechoslovak state. In Mussolini's view, it represented French interests in southeast Europe, collective security through Benes' support of the League of Nations generally and sanctions against Italy in particular, and had about it the taint of liberal internationalism that Mussolini despised. Italy had no direct interest in Czechoslovakia's destruction, but Mussolini, far from lifting a finger to stop it, was pleased to participate in its dismemberment. More importantly, Mussolini supported Germany because the Axis represented the heart of Italian foreign policy. Only through fidelity to its German partner could Mussolini hope to carry forward his plans for expansion in the Mediterranean. On 28 September, when war appeared almost certain, Mussolini belatedly realized that he had committed Italy to fight a war in which it had virtually nothing to gain and an enormous amount to lose. Germany would provide little military might in the West to defend Italy against a potential Anglo-French coalition. France would have nearly a free hand in Spain, possibly eliminating the prospect of recouping any of Mussolini's vast commitment of men, money and matériel during the civil war. Japanese forces would remain on the sidelines, freeing substantial elements of the Royal Navy for action against Italy. Most seriously, war over Czechoslovakia could forge an Anglo-French alliance, when Mussolini had spent two years trying to convince the British government to jettison its association with France. War in September 1938 most likely would have been a disaster for Mussolini's Italy.

This description and explanation of Mussolini's policy during the Czech crisis suggests some serious failings in the historiography. Italy's admittedly limited war preparations belies Mack Smith's dismissal of Italian military power, and his belief that Mussolini was nothing more than a propagandist does not account for Mussolini's nature as an ideological thinker. De Felice did not give appropriate coverage and weight to Mussolini's extensive commitment of diplomatic and military support during the months leading to the Munich conference. Similarly, Quartararo did not fully explain Mussolini's policy. There is ample evidence to suggest that Mussolini considered going to war; even his *démarche* to Hitler on 28 September committed Italy to battle at Hitler's discretion. Her argument that Italy '*never intended* to involve itself' lacks supporting evidence.[106] Only MacGregor Knox has indicated the seriousness of Mussolini's policy and planning. Mussolini's decisions during the Czech crisis, however, do highlight some of the difficulties in studying Italian history during the fascist era. He was no mere opportunist, nor was he a strictly rational thinker; his ideological predispositions obviously coloured his decisionmaking. It is impossible, therefore, to put forward entirely structuralist arguments about the complex of influences, whether concerning military, economic, political or strategic considerations, or dealing with public opinion. At times, Mussolini paid attention to these elements of decisionmaking; at times he ignored them. Still, any ideologue, no matter how irrational, has to act in an environment over which he has only partial control. Events sometimes conspire to present or to prevent opportunities. Mussolini sometimes acted as a clever opportunist, and sometimes made appallingly irrational and fatally stupid decisions. In the end, of course, his foreign policy carried him to a desperate end, and his 'peace-making' at Munich only postponed temporarily the terrible price that Europe would pay during the Second World War in order to stop fascist expansionism.

McMaster University

NOTES

1. Telford Taylor, *Munich: The Price of Peace* (London: Hodder and Stoughton), 1979.
2. Maya Lytinski (ed.), *Reappraising the Munich Pact: Continental Perspectives* (Washington, DC: Woodrow Wilson Center Press, 1992); Melvin Small and Otto Feinstein (eds.), *Appeasing Fascism: Articles from the Wayne State University Conference on Munich after Fifty Years* (Lanham, MD: University Press of America, 1991). Similarly, a recent journal reflection virtually ignored Italy. Gerhard L. Weinberg with William R. Rock and Anna M. Cienciala, 'Essay and Reflection: The Munich Crisis Revisited', *International History Review*, Vol.11, No.4 (Nov. 1989), pp.668–88.
3. Denis Mack Smith, *Mussolini's Roman Empire* (New York: Penguin Books, 1976), pp.130–31.
4. Rosaria Quartararo, *Roma tra Londra e Berlino: La politica estera fascista dal 1930 a 1940* (Roma: Editore Bonacci, 1980), p.399, emphasis in original.
5. Renzo De Felice, *Mussolini il duce: II. Lo Stato totalitario, 1936–1940* (Torino: Giulio Einaudi, 1981), pp.509–17.
6. MacGregor Knox, *Mussolini Unleashed 1939–1941: Politics and Strategy in Fascist Italy's Last War* (Cambridge: Cambridge University Press), pp.37–8.
7. For more thorough discussion of the historiography of Italian foreign policy, see Stephano Corrado Azzi, 'The Historiography of Italian Foreign Policy', *The Historical Journal*, Vol.36, No.1 (1993), pp.187–203. This article is more useful as an informational survey. Its analytical focus, dividing historians into groups of traditionalists and revisionists, is rather blunt and links otherwise disparate arguments. One can find a more cogent discussion of recent Italian historical writing in MacGregor Knox, 'The Fascist Regime, its Foreign Policy and its Wars: An 'Anti-Anti-Fascist' Orthodoxy?' *Contemporary European History*, Vol.4, No.3 (1995), pp.357–65. Rather than the somewhat awkward term 'anti-anti-fascist orthodoxy', I personally use the phrase 'the De Felice school' to indicate these revisionists. That term has its own problems, however, as De Felice actually borrowed some of his argument from Quartararo. See the excellent historiographical chapter in R.J.B. Bosworth, *The Italian Dictatorship: Problems and Perspectives in the Interpretation of Mussolini and Fascism* (London: Arnold, 1998), pp.82–105, especially pp.94–6.
8. For example, a recent monograph on Italian foreign policy between the wars uses only a very small number of files from Italian archives, and none from the Munich period. H. James Burgwyn, *Italian Foreign Policy in the Interwar Period, 1918–1940* (Greenwood, CT: Praeger, 1997). Both Quartararo and De Felice have made use of Grandi's diaries. These documents, while important, tend to skew interpretation. Though Grandi believed in a genuine Anglo-Italian *rapprochement*, he did not create Italian foreign policy. There is no compelling evidence to suggest that Mussolini's ultimate aim was merely to achieve a British recognition of Italian parity in the Mediterranean, as Quartararo, and to some extent, De Felice have argued. See MacGregor Knox, 'The Fascist Regime', for a useful description of De Felice's and Quartararo's views.
9. *Documents on German Foreign Policy* [hereafter DGFP], *D, II* (London: His Majesty's Stationery Office, 1950) No.32, date unknown, Notes made by the Führer's Adjutant (Schmundt) on Observations made by the Führer on the Contemporary Strategic Situation, 238–9. Schmundt probably made this note sometime in April. For more on the likely date and the context in which Schmundt wrote this document, see Gerhard L. Weinberg, *The Foreign Policy of Hitler's Germany: Starting World War II, 1937–1939* (Chicago, IL: The University of Chicago Press, 1980), pp.337–40. British intelligence information suggests that, during the meetings at the beginning of May, Mussolini had given Hitler a virtual *carte blanche*

in dealing with Czechoslovakia, provided that Hitler handled the matter without a general European war. Public Record Office, London [hereafter PRO], Foreign Office [hereafter FO] 371, R5700/43/22, Perth to Jebb, 16 June 1938, entire.

10. Malcolm Muggeridge (ed.), *Ciano's Hidden Diaries, 1937–1938* (tr. Andreas Mayor) [hereafter CHD] (New York: E.P. Dutton, 1953), 26 May 1938, p.121.

11. *DGFP, D, II*, #220, von Mackensen to von Ribbentrop, 29 May 1938, pp.356–7; #229, 1 June 1938, p.373. *CHD*, 27, 28, 31 May 1938, pp.121–3.

12. *DGFP, D, II*, #334, von Ribbentrop Memorandum, 4 Aug. 1938, pp.533–4.

13. *CHD*, 20 May 1938, p.118.

14. Archivio Storico del Ministero degli Affari Esteri, Rome [hereafter ASMAE], Ufficio di Coordinamento, [hereafter UC] 49, Appunto per il Duce, 18 June 1938. For the published translation in English, see Malcolm Muggeridge (ed.), *Ciano's Diplomatic Papers* (tr. Stuart Hood) [hereafter CDP] (London: Odhams, 1948), pp.212–6.

15. ASMAE, UC 49, Colloquio a palazzo venezia tra il Duce, Ciano, Imrédy and de Kánya, 18 July 1938.

16. ASMAE, UC 58, Conversazioni militari italo–ungherese, 25, 26 July 1938. The document was dated 30 July 1938.

17. *CHD*, 18 July 1938, p.138.

18. ASMAE, UC 5, Attolico to Ciano, 9 Aug. 1938. Ufficio Spagna [hereafter US] 225, Commando Truppo Voluntarie to Pietromarchi, 11 Aug. 1938; Attolico to Ciano, 18 Aug. 1938; *CHD*, 19 Aug. 1938, pp.144–5.

19. *CHD*, 20 Aug. 1938, 145.

20. *DGFP, D, II*, #401, von Ribbentrop Memorandum, 27 Aug. 1938, p.651. *CHD*, 26 Aug. 1938, pp.147–8.

21. ASMAE, UC 5, Attolico to Ciano, 1 Sept. 1938. Mussolini heavily underlined the section of this document where Attolico noted the timing of Hitler's plans.

22. *CHD*, 2, 5, 6, 7, Sept. 1938, pp.148–9, 151–3.

23. ASMAE, UC 5, Attolico to Ciano, 30 Aug. 1938. Emphasis by Mussolini, who heavily marked the passages on the potential threat of British seapower.

24. Ibid., Attolico to Ciano 31 Aug. 1938.

25. Eduardo and Duilio Susmel (eds.), *Opera Omnia di Benito Mussolini* [hereafter OO], Volume XXIX. (Florence: La Fenice, 1959), Informazione Diplomatica #19, 9 Sept. 1938, pp.488–9, Informazione Diplomatica #20, 14 Sept. 1938, pp.499–500, Lettera a Runciman, *Popolo d'Italia*, 15 Sept. 1938, pp.141–3.

26. *DGFP, D, II*, #494, von Mackensen to von Ribbentrop, 15 Sept. 1938, pp.804–5.

27. *CHD*, 17 Sept. 1938, 157. De Felice argued that Britain's resort to war would have permanently foreclosed any option of an agreement with Italy, and would have frustrated Mussolini's goal of reaching equidistance between Berlin and London. *Lo Stato Totalitario*, p.517. More accurately, Britain's abstention from a major French war would have meant that Mussolini had succeeded in his two-year campaign to separate France from its potential British ally. Further, Italian entry into such an arrangement of forces would almost certainly provoke a British declaration of war and campaign directed in the first instance against Italy. See note 35.

28. *OO, XXIX*, Discorso di Trieste, 18 Sept. 1938, pp.144–7.

29. Ibid., Al Popolo di Udine, 20 Sept. 1938, pp.152–3; Discorso di Treviso, 22 Sept. 1938, pp.155–6; Al Popolo di Belluno, 24 Sept. 1938, pp.159–60.

30. For detailed coverage on this state visit, see Thomas L. Sakmyster, 'The Hungarian State Visit to Germany of August 1938: Some new Evidence on Hungary's Pre-Munich Policy', *Canadian Slavic Studies*, Vol.3, No.4 (Winter 1969), pp.677–91.

31. ASMAE, UC 58, Attolico to Ciano, 27 Aug. 1938.

32. ASMAE, UC 5, Appunto per il Duce, 22 Sept. 1938. See also, *CDP*, 22 Sept. 1938, pp.234–5.

33. ASMAE, UC 58, Reparti dell'Aeronautica Italiana in Ungheria, 24 Sept. 1938.

34. ASMAE, UC 89, Attolico to Ciano, 23 Sept. 1938.
35. *CHD*, 22 Sept. 1938, pp.159–60; 25 Sept. 1938, pp.161–2. Ciano noted that neither he nor Mussolini had done anything to incite Germany. It is difficult to see how their further confirmation of Italian support for Germany's potential war could have done anything other than to encourage Hitler's intransigence.
36. Brian R. Sullivan, 'The Italian Armed Forces, 1918–1940', in Alan R. Millet and Williamson Murray (eds.), *Military Effectiveness: Volume II, The Interwar Period* (Boston, MA: Unwin Hyman, 1988), pp.169–70, 182–3.
37. *CHD*, 26 Sept. 1938, pp.162–3, 27 Sept. 1938, p.163. Knox, *Mussolini Unleashed*, pp.37, 309 n.102. For planning of troop shipments to Libya, see Sullivan, 'The Italian Armed Forces, 1918–1940', pp.189–90.
38. ASMAE, US 226, Attolico to Ciano, 26 Sept. 1936.
39. *CHD*, 27 Sept. 1938, p.163. Events overtook the meeting, and neither it nor the Condor Legion's redeployment ultimately occurred. Attolico wrote in the immediate aftermath of Munich that Hitler had approved this meeting. ASMAE, UC 5, Attolico to Ciano, 4 Oct. 1938.
40. For more on these parallel proposals, see Weinberg, *Starting World War II*, pp.444–5, especially notes 308 and 311. Quartararo argues that Grandi was entirely responsible for Chamberlain's initiative, but her evidence is thin. According to British records, it is *possible* that Grandi spoke to Chamberlain at an 'opportune time'. If Grandi did so, no compelling evidence apparently exists of that *démarche*. Rosario Quartararo, 'Inghilterra e Italia. Dal Patto di Pasqua a Monaco', *Storia Contemporanea*, Vol.7, No..4 (Dec. 1976), p.640; *Roma tra Londra e Berlino*, p.399. The first British dispatch to Perth to ask for Mussolini's intercession left London on the evening of 27 September.
41. ASMAE, UC 89, Cronica della giornate 28, 29, 30 settembre 1938. See also, *OO*, XXIX Prima telefonata ad Attolico, 28 Sept. 1938, p.165, Seconda telefonata ad Attolico, s.d., p.165. *CHD*, 28 Sept. 1938, pp.165–6.
42. ASMAE, UC 89, Cronica della giornate, 28, 29, 30 Sept. 1938; *CHD*, 29–30 Sept. 1938, pp.166–8. Ciano's diary contains a slightly shorter and different version of Hitler's words than the original record.
43. For more on this process, see *DGFP*, D, II, No.670, p.1005 n.10.
44. For more detail on Mussolini's relations with Czechoslovakia, see Francesco Leoncini, 'Italia e Cecoslovakia, 1919–1939', *Rivista di Studi Politici Internazionali*, Vol.45 (1979), pp.357–72.
45. National Archives, Washington [hereafter NA], T586, roll 412: f004932, Addis Abeba to Ministero dell'Africa Italiana, 9 April 1938; f004932, Lt. Col. Valfrè di Bonzo (Prague) to Servizio Informazione Militare, 4 Feb. 1938.
46. ASMAE, Gabinetto [hereafter GAB] 29, Ciano to Prague, 10 April 1938.
47. See, for example, *OO*, XXII (1957), *Intervista con* Associated Press, 1 Aug. 1926; *Il Popolo d'Italia*, 6 Aug. 1926, pp.187–8; *OO*, XLIV (1980), Appendix VIII, *Intervista con* Henry Massis, 26 Sept. 1933.
48. Quoted in Pier Giorgio Zunino, *L'ideologia del fascismo: Miti, credenze e valori nella stabilizazione del regime* (Bologna: Il Mulino, 1985), p.345; Mack Smith, *Mussolini* (London: Weidenfeld and Nicolson, 1981), pp.194–5.
49. *OO*, XXII, *Discorso alla Camera dei Deputati*, 1 June 1927, pp.360–90.
50. *OO*, XLIV, Appendix VIII, *Discorso al Consiglio Nazionale del Partito nazionale fascista*, 26 Oct. 1933, pp.70–76.
51. *OO*, XXIII (1957), Mussolini's preface to Ricardo Korherr, *Regresso delle nascite: morte dei popoli*, also published in *La Gerarchia*, 9 Sept. 1928, pp.209–16.
52. *OO*, XXIX, *Popolo d'Italia*, 30 Jan. 1938, pp.51–2.
53. ASMAE, Serie Affari Politici [hereafter SAP] – Gran Bretagna, B. 24, Crolla to Ciano, 17 Aug. 1938.

54. *OO, XXIX*, Discorso al Senato, 30 March 1938, pp.74–82.
55. *DGFP, C, IV* (1962), # 485, von Hassell to the foreign ministry, 7 Jan. 1936, 974–7.
56. *Ibid.*, # 579, von Hassell to the foreign ministry, 22 Feb. 1936, p.1170. This declaration was especially important owing to Hitler's imminent remilitarization of the Rhineland. See also Renzo De Felice, 'Alle Origini del Patto d'Acciaio: L'icontro e gli accordi tra Bocchini e Himmler del Marzo–Aprile 1936', *La Cultura*, Vol.1 (Sept. 1963), pp.524–38.
57. Gerhard L. Weinberg, *The Foreign Policy of Hitler's Germany: Diplomatic Revolution in Europe 1933–36* (Chicago, IL: The University of Chicago Press, 1970), pp.266–7.
58. *I Documenti Diplomatici Italiani*. [hereafter *DDI*], *Ottava Serie, IV* (Roma: Istituto Poligrafica e Zecca dello Stato, 1993) #192, Colloquio del Mussolini con Schuschnigg, 5 June 1936, pp.240–43.
59. ASMAE, GAB 22, Aloisi appunto sul colloquio di Mussolini con von Hassell, 11 July 1936. For more detail on Austro-German–Italian relations leading to this agreement, see Pietro Pastorelli, 'L'Italia e l'accordo austro-tedesco dell'11 luglio 1936', *Annali dell'Istituto storico italo–germanico di Trento*, Vol.15 (1989), pp.395–410.
60. ASMAE, UC 84, Colloquio con l'ambasciatore di Germania, 29 June 1936. See also GAB 25, Apppunto per il Duce, 18 and 29 June 1936.
61. *DDI, 8, IV*, #685, Roatta to the Gabinetto, 5 Aug. 1936, pp.751–2, 752 n.1. For the standard account of Italy's role in this conflict, see John Coverdale, *Italian Intervention in the Spanish Civil War* (Princeton, NJ: Princeton University Press, 1975).
62. ASMAE, UC 44, US 1, Proposte e richieste recate da admiriglio Canaris il 28 agosto 1936 a nome del governo tedesco, 28 Aug. 1936. *DDI, 8, IV*, No.819, Colloquio tra Ciano e Canaris, 28 Aug. 1936, pp.892–6.
63. *OO, XXVIII* (1959), 1 Nov. 1936, pp.67–72
64. R. Dan Richardson, *Comintern Army: The Internatinal Brigades and the Spanish Civil War* (Lexington, KY: The University Press of Kentucky, 1982), p.176. ASMAE, SAP – Spagna, B. 10, Ciano to Grandi, 3 Nov. 1936, US 30, Ministero di Guerra, Commando del Corpo di Stato Maggiore, Promemoria per il Sig. Capo Ufficio S del Ministero degli Esteri, 15 Nov. 1937. Public Record Office, FO 371 20586, W16391/9549/41, Major Napier (War Office) to St.C. Roberts, 23 Nov. 1936.
65. ASMAE, UC 44, US 1, Verbale della riunione a Palazzo Venezia del 6 Dicembre 1936, 6 Dec. 1936. For more information on the development of Italo-German cooperation in Spain, see Coverdale, *Italian Intervention in the Spanish Civil War*, pp.156–75, and Weinberg, *Starting World War II*, pp.142–6, and his earlier volume, *Diplomatic Revolution in Europe*, among others.
66. *DGFP, C, VI*, (1983), #247, von Hassel to von Neurath, 5 March 1937, p.503. *DGFP, D, III*, (1950) #236, von Hassel to von Neurath, 25 March 1937, pp.258–60. *DGFP, C, VI*, #368, Secret Protocol between the German and Italian Governments, 14 May 1937, pp.752–5. See also No.536, Foreign Ministry to von Plessen, 28 Aug. 1937, pp.1041–2, and 1042 n.2.
67. ASMAE, UC 6, Grandi to Ciano, 7 July 1937.
68. ASMAE, UC 53, Ciano to Grandi, 2 Aug. 1937, Grandi to Ciano, 5 Aug. 1937.
69. *CHD*, 22 Oct. 1937, pp.23–4; ASMAE, UC 53, Appunto per il Duce, 20 Oct. 1937; Colloquoi con l'ambasciatore di Giappone, 23 Oct. 1937; *OO, XLII* (1979), Mussolini to Vittorio Emmanuele, 4 Oct. 1937, pp.194–5; *CHD*, 1, 2 Nov. 1937, p.27; 6 Nov. 1937, pp.28–9.
70. *CHD*, 1 May 1938, p.111; 5 May 1938, p.112. For more on von Ribbentrop's failed proposal, see D.C. Watt, 'An Earlier Model for the Pact of Steel: The Draft Treaties Exchanged between Germany and Italy during Hitler's Visit to Rome in May 1938', *International Affairs*, Vol.33, No.2 (April 1957), pp.185–97. For a different view of Hitler's goals for this visit, see Weinberg, *Starting World War II*, p.340, especially p.340 n.99. For the best published English-language description of Italy's relations

with Germany and Japan before Munich, see Mario Toscano, *The Origins of the Pact of Steel* (Baltimore, MD: The Johns Hopkins University Press, 2nd edn 1967), pp.3–44.

71. *CHD*, 26 April 1938, p.94.
72. ASMAE, UC 55, Appunto per il Duce, 2 May 1938.
73. *CHD*, 10 May 1938, p.114; ASMAE, UC 55, Jacomoni to Ciano, 6 June 1938; Appunto del M. Jacomoni, n.d. (internal evidence suggests June 1938); Appunto del M. Jacomoni, 13 June 1938.
74. ASMAE, UC 46, Berti to Mussolini, Mussolini to Berti, 20 Aug. 1938.
75. Ibid. See also *CHD*, 21 Aug. 1938, p.145. For the most cogent account of British strategic policy and Italy during this period, see Lawrence Pratt, *East of Malta, West of Suez: Britain's Mediterranean Crisis, 1936–1939* (Cambridge: Cambridge Univesity Press, 1975).
76. ASMAE, UC 46, Berti to Ciano, 6 Sept. 1938; Mussolini to Berti, 7, 8 and 9 Sept. 1938; *CHD*, 11 Sept. 1938, p.154.
77. ASMAE, US 229, Viola to Ciano, 17 Sept. 1938. This telegram reported an official communiqué from the Spanish minister for foreign affairs, noting that the French government would occupy Catalonia and Spanish Morocco in the event of war.
78. ASMAE, US 226, Attolico to Ciano, 26 Sept. 1938. See also *DGFP, D, III*: No.665, Johannes Bernhardt Memorandum, 26 Sept. 1938, p.748; No.666, von Stohrer to the foreign ministry, 28 Sept. 1938, pp.749–50.
79. *CHD*, 26 Sept. 1938, pp.162–3.
80. ASMAE, US 1, Final Report of the Ufficio Spagna, 1939, no date. See also Coverdale, *Italian Intervention in the Spanish Civil War* pp.367–8, 392–3.
81. NA, T586, roll 1289, Ufficio V, Cina 1936, f#107185, Ufficio V, Giappone 1936, f#107386. See also Valdo Ferretti, *Il Giappone e la politica estera Italiana, 1935–41* (Roma: Giuffrè Editore, 1983), pp.115–19.
82. ASMAE, SAP – Giappone, B.13, 7, 18, 20 Nov. 1936, Auriti to Ciano.
83. Mussolini added the emphasis. *DDI, 8, IV*, No.428, Auriti to Ciano, 2 July 1936, pp.487–91.
84. ASMAE, SAP – Giappone, B.18, Auriti to Ciano, 5, 25 May 1937.
85. ASMAE, SAP – Giappone, B.18, Chiapparo to Ministero dell' Aeronautica and Ministero degli Affari Esteri, 6 June 1937.
86. ASMAE, GAB 26, Appunto per il Duce, UC 84, Colloquio con l'ambasciatore di Giappone, 19 July 1936. For more detail, see Michael R. Godley, 'Fascismo e nazionalismo cinese, 1931–1938. Note preliminari allo studio dei rapporti italo-cinese durante il periodo fascista', *Storia Contemporanea*, Vol.4, No.4 (Dec. 1973), pp.772–3.
87. ASMAE, UC 53, Ciano to Grandi, 2 Aug. 1937; Grandi to Ciano, 5 Aug. 1937.
88. ASMAE, SAP – Giappone, B.18, Il Capitano di Vascello to Ciano, 30 Sept. 1937. For Auriti's perceptions of the complicated relationship between the Japanese parliament, the Gaimushó, and the various factions of the military, see ASMAE, SAP – Giappone, B.18, Auriti to Ciano, 3 July 1937; ASMAE, SAP – Cina, B.61, Ciano to Consulato Shanghai, 26 Aug. 1937; *CHD*, 23 Aug. 1937, p.3; 27 Aug. 1937, p.5.
89. ASMAE, GAB 28, Ciano to Ausiti, 3 Oct. 1937; ASMAE, UC 53, Appunto per il Duce, 20 Oct. 1937; Colloqui con l'ambasciatore di Giappone, 23 Oct. 1937. CHD, 22 Oct. 1937.
90. *OO, XLII*, Mussolini to Vittorio Emmanuele, 4 Oct. 1937.
91. *CHD*, 1, 2 Nov. 1937, p.27; 6 Nov. 1937, pp.28–9.
92. *OO, XXIX*, Mussolini to Prince Fumimaro Konoe, 19 March 1938, p.410.
93. For a brief description of internal Japanese political machinations, see Akira Iriye, *The Origins of the Second World War in Asia and the Pacific* (London: Longman, 1987), pp.59–61. See also Ferretti, pp.213–18.

 94. ASMAE, UC 53, Ciano to Auriti, 6 June 1936; Auriti to Ciano, 24 June 1938; *CHD*, 31 May 1938, 1, 6, 21 June 1938, pp.123, 124, 125–6, 129.
 95. ASMAE, UC 53, Auriti to Ciano, 15, 26, 29 Sept. 1938. See also Toscano, *The Origins of the Pact of Steel*, pp.41–2.
 96. ASMAE, GAB 25, 17 June 1936, Mussolini to Grandi.
 97. ASMAE, SAP – Francia, B.36, Cerruti to Ciano, 23 June 1937; US 229, Cerruti to Ciano, 26 June 1937.
 98. ASMAE, US 229, Cerruti to Ciano, 5 July 1937; Ciano to Cerruti, 6 July 1937.
 99. ASMAE, US 227, Ciano to Grandi, 3 July 1937; GAB 28, Ciano to Grandi, 5 July 1937.
100. ASMAE, GAB 28, Ciano to Grandi, 17 Oct. 1937; *CHD*, 11 Oct. 1937, p.19; 12 Oct. 1937, pp.19–20; 31 Oct. 1937, p.27; 17 Nov. 1937, p.34.
101. ASMAE, UC 4, Ciano to Attolico, 17 March 1938.
102. For the decision to undertake discussions, see *CHD*, 16 April 1938, pp.101–2. The French proposals appear in ASMAE, UC 61, Promemoria consegnato da Blondel il 16 aprile 1938, and Promemoria consegnato da Blondel il 22 aprile 1938. In a later document, Mussolini heavily scrawled 'no' in the margins of the articles on the Red Sea and withdrawal of volunteers. ASMAE, UC 61, Promemoria consegnato da Blondel il 2 maggio 1938. Ciano confirmed this attitude in a diary entry, *CHD*, 12 May 1938, p.115.
103. For more on the confrontation of competing nationalisms, see Mario Toscano, *Alto Adige–South Tyrol: Italy's Frontier with the German World* (Baltimore, MD: The Johns Hopkins University Press, 1975), pp.35–41.
104. *CHD*, 10–14 May 1938, pp.114–16. Quartararo blamed clumsy French diplomacy for the failure of these discussions. Quartararo, *Roma tra Londra e Berlino*, pp.395–7. In her view, these approaches actually initiated in Rome. Mussolini, she argued, intended to create 'a solid Anglo-French–Italian front against Germany'. This move would restore Italy's 'decisive weight'. Only the extensive and extreme list of French desiderata prevented any progress and provoked Mussolini's backlash. Ciano directly contradicted this view in the preceding diary entries. Significantly, Quartararo cited only French sources indicating their hopes for a possible *rapprochement* as evidence that Mussolini wanted any genuine *rapprochement*. In short, she provided no compelling evidence to bolster her strained conclusion. William Shorrock also overemphasized the possibility of a genuine Franco-Italian *rapprochement*. He blamed Alexis Léger-Saint-Léger, the French secretary-general at the foreign ministry, who distrusted any of Mussolini's promises, for almost deliberately sabotaging any discussions. William I. Shorrock, *From Ally to Enemy: The Enigma of Fascist Italy in French Diplomacy, 1920–1940* (Kent, OH: Kent State University Press, 1988), p.227. In Shorrock's view, Léger deliberately saddled the negotiations with a long and complex list in order to ensure the difficulty of any discussions. Actually, Italian documentation shows that Mussolini rejected out of hand the cardinal French point – an Italian declaration analogue to that in the Easter Accord regarding disinterest in acquiring Spanish territory and the eventual withdrawal of volunteers. ASMAE, UC 61, Promemoria consegnato da Blondel il 22 aprile 1938, and Promemoria consegnato da Blondel il 2 maggio 1938, plus Mussolini's handwritten markings on both.
105. See *CHD*, 3–6 May 1938, pp.124–6, for example.
106. Quartararo, *Roma tra Londra e Berlino*, p.399, emphasis in original.

Germany and the Munich Crisis: A Mutilated Victory?

RICHARD OVERY

On 21 February 1945 Hitler explained to his deputy and personal record keeper, Martin Bormann, what had gone wrong in 1938 at the time of the Munich settlement: 'We ought to have attacked in 1938. It was the last chance we had of localizing the war.' Hitler scolded himself for not holding his nerve over the invasion of Czechoslovakia, which would have been a 'short war' only. Britain and France would have remained passive, their political stock in ruins. Above all, mused Hitler, 'we should thus have gained the time required to enable us to consolidate our position, and we would have postponed world war for several years to come'. The chief culprit in Hitler's view was Neville Chamberlain, whose intention it had been all along to blind Hitler with promises in September 1938 while buying time for England to prepare a ruthless war.[1]

Though Hitler gained much of what he wanted at Munich, it is clear that the recollection of the negotiated settlement, in place of the short, sharp military campaign he had intended, still rankled almost seven years later. He did not discuss it once in his so-called 'Table Talk' during the war, but in the face of imminent defeat in 1945 he began to reflect more candidly on past errors. He did recall Munich, however, in the days leading to the outbreak of the Second World War, when he told his commanders on 22 August that his only fear in the coming conflict with Poland was 'that at the last minute some *Schweinhund* will make a proposal for mediation'. The Polish crisis was in many respects a re-run of the one the year before. Hitler was determined to have the short victorious war he had been denied in 1938, but this time he would not back away. Britain and France, he believed with an obstinate consistency, would make gestures but not actually fight. 'Our enemies are little worms', he added, 'I saw them at Munich.'[2]

The details of the confrontation between Germany and Czechoslovakia in 1938 are too well known to need repetition here.[3]

Yet important questions remain to which there have not been entirely satisfactory answers. The first is the question raised some years ago by Gottfried Niedhart: why resort to *war* in 1938?[4] The answer is by no means as simple as it might seem. Even in German history, the deliberate, premeditated decision to wage a war of aggression against a neighbouring state is the exception, not the rule. Niedhart's conclusion, that war was seen as a necessary and unavoidable instrument of policy by the military and political elite in Germany fits with the continuities suggested by the Fischer thesis, but as an explanation it operates at a level of generality that fails to account for the specific decision taken in 1938. The decision for war, as Niedhart also points out, ran on this occasion entirely counter to the aspirations of the military leadership and of most politicians, bar Hitler and Ribbentrop. It is true that for Hitler war was an overweening element of his world view,[5] but this knowledge alone does not explain the timing or nature of the decision for war in 1938. Indeed, it fits ill with Hitler's fear of conflict with the West over the public declaration of rearmament in 1935 and the occupation of the Rhineland in 1936, and his fear of Italian military action if Germany acted precipitously over the issue of an Austrian *Anschluss*.[6]

The second question derives from the first. Why, having resolved on war in 1938, did Hitler accept a negotiated settlement at Munich? The straightforward answer has always been that Hitler no longer had a pretext for war once the Western powers caved in on the issue of the transfer of the Sudeten German areas. This is the core of the argument for seeing Munich as an unalloyed victory for German aggression. Yet the answer is again not so simple. Right up to 28 September, when the Western powers and the Czechs had already made all the concessions that were necessary for a clear German diplomatic triumph, Hitler strained at the leash to use force in some way. The day following, a general mobilization was to be ordered. If this was a gamble in order to extract more concessions, there is scant evidence for it. Hitler's agitated and ill-tempered state in the days before the Munich Conference are testimony to his extreme reluctance to abandon publicly the stand he had taken in May, in the presence of Germany's senior military leaders, to smash Czechoslovakia by force. A week after Munich he again threatened to unleash the German army in Czechoslovakia in a fit of pique at the slow process of occupation under the gaze of an international commission.[7] A year later he played out the same charade of negotiation with the Western powers and Poland, but nothing this time deflected him from his 'iron decision' for war.

Both questions, the decision for war in the first place, and the decision to abandon war four months later, have major bearing on Hitler's later actions during the Polish crisis. In 1938 he ran a great risk over Czechoslovakia and was deterred; in 1939 he ran a great risk over Poland and was not. The purpose of this paper is to explore some possible answers to the questions surrounding the issue of war in 1938. Much, of course, must remain speculative. Hitler left almost no intimate record of the factors that influenced his key decisions at the time they were taken; after Munich he rationalized his policy in order to save face, so that the climb-down from war came to be seen as a mark of statesmenlike cunning, a view echoed in Ribbentrop's dimly recollected memoirs. The limitations of the surviving source material must be borne in mind when ascribing motives. On one question there is, however, no doubt: Hitler alone took the decisions for war and peace in 1938. They were decisions shaped by circumstances, influenced by others perhaps, certainly endorsed by some, but neither was a collective decision. The nature of Hitler's personal dictatorship precluded such an eventuality by 1938.

The Decision for War

Explanations for Hitler's decision to wage a war in 1938 have been found both in the external circumstances confronting Hitler over the Czech issue, and in the domestic political and economic situation. These two approaches are by no means mutually exclusive, as Bernd-Jürgen Wendt has demonstrated in his study of German foreign policy and economic expansion in the second half of the 1930s.[8] Indeed, Hitler's well-known foreign policy conception – the necessity of 'living space' as a precondition for the establishment of a healthy German polity – bound domestic and foreign policy together *a priori*. The distinction often (and occasionally misleadingly) drawn between the 'primacy of foreign policy' and the 'primacy of domestic policy' is irrelevant in Hitler's case: the long-term development of the

German race was, in Hitler's view, predicated on the necessity of
violent economic imperialism.[9]

Nonetheless, many of the explanations for Hitler's decision in
1938 to destroy Czechoslovakia have relied on the pressure of
external circumstances. One example is the influence allegedly
exerted by the Sudeten Germans themselves. Organized in the
Sudetendeutsche Partei by Konrad Henlein, they developed
unappeasable irredentist appetites in the 1930s that could not be
satisfied by Czech concessions. The violent confrontation between
Czech and German, so the argument goes, reached a crescendo in
1938, forcing Hitler, good pan-German that he was, to act in their
defence. It is significant to recall here Hitler's Habsburg background.
The Sudeten Germans were not former citizens of imperial Germany
but were Germans living in Habsburg Bohemia. The issue of
autonomy for the Sudeten Germans went back to the inter-racial
squabbles of the 1890s. The Austrian pre-1914 pan-German
movement recruited the Sudetendeutsche to its cause.[10] Hitler could
not have been unaware of the pre-war struggles, and it might
plausibly be suggested that he brought to the crisis in 1938 an
Austrian's prejudice against Czech ascendancy.

Such a connection might also explain the particular violence of
Hitler's reaction to the so-called Weekend Crisis of 20–21 May 1938
when the Czech government ordered partial mobilization in response
to what they saw as an imminent threat of German attack. The crisis
brought warnings to Hitler from both the British and French
governments not to act unilaterally and violently in the Czech issue,
and, so it is claimed, occasioned the meeting a week later, on 28 May,
at which Hitler, infuriated at the humiliation heaped on by the
Czechs, finally told an assembly of generals, ministers and party
chiefs at the Reich chancellery, in words recorded by his Wehrmacht
adjutant, 'I am utterly determined that Czechoslovakia should
disappear from the map'.[11] On 30 May the armed forces were
presented with a directive, *Fall 'Grün'*, for a war against
Czechoslovakia to be waged by 1 October 1938, and to be won in a
lightning campaign of four days.[12]

Though Hitler no doubt was affected by the terms of the older
German–Czech confrontation, and reacted with characteristic spleen
over the Weekend Crisis, neither explanation can account for the fact

that Hitler had already indicated, well before the crisis in the spring of 1938, his intention of destroying Czechoslovakia as an independent state. At the meeting in the chancellery on 5 November 1937 Hitler made public to his military leaders and to the foreign ministry his intention to annex Austria and Czechoslovakia when circumstances made an attack possible. No mention was made of the Sudetendeutsche; no hint can be found that Hitler was reacting to external pressures. The announcement that Austria and Czechoslovakia were to be absorbed into the German orbit was made matter of factly, almost obliquely. A month later the armed forces produced the outlines of a contingency plan for the invasion of Czechoslovakia.[13]

This was perhaps unsurprising, for leading party circles had never made much secret of their ambitions for Greater Germany. In February 1937 Göring told a British acquaintance, Group Captain Christie, that Czechoslovakia was to become part of the Reich and the 'Czechs to be almost destroyed'.[14] He elaborated his view of German territorial ambitions in July the same year: 'Austria will come into the Reich of its own free will, but if the Czechs remain unyielding we shall have to take Bohemia and Moravia.'[15] General Bodenschatz, Göring's adjutant, recalled in his postwar interrogation that Hitler could often be heard expressing the (geopolitically unsophisticated) view that 'whoever is in possession of Czechoslovakia has power in Central Europe'.[16]

A more satisfactory explanation for the timing of Hitler's decisions in the Czech crisis in 1938 might be derived from simple diplomatic opportunism. In the November 1937 meeting Hitler indicated that action over Austria and Czechoslovakia would be dictated by the opportunities presented by the wider diplomatic and military picture. By the time Hitler told Henlein in late March 1938 that it was time to solve the Czech question much had changed from the previous November. The successful *Anschluss* of Austria on 12 March was made possible by Mussolini's decision not to obstruct the German move, and the failure of the Western states to intercede. Italy was now regarded by German leaders as an important factor in holding France and Britain in check while the German position in central Europe was consolidated. On 20 May Hitler published a new draft of the Operation 'Green' directive in which he announced that with Italy firmly in the German camp 'France fears, or at the very lest hesitates, to unleash a European war through her intervention against Germany'.[17] Without France, Britain was not expected to act. On 28 May, war was formally announced by Hitler in the meeting at the chancellery. One of the foreign office officials present reported Hitler's words to a colleague: 'We will only have to deal with Czechoslovakia alone since the Western powers are not in the position to come to the aid of the Czechs.'[18] The recollections of the meeting penned by General Beck, chief-of-staff of the army, showed a Hitler willing to place the most optimistic gloss he could on the present international situation: 'Russia: will not take part, not geared up for a war of aggression. Poland and Romania: Fear of Russian aid, will not act against Germany. East Asia: Reason for England's caution.' According to Beck, Hitler drew the conclusion that the 'favourable moment must be seized. ... Lightning march into Czechoslovakia'.[19]

Yet this kind of opportunism still begs the question of why Hitler was so determined to smash Czechoslovakia by force rather than compel her through diplomatic isolation and economic necessity to be drawn into the German orbit. 'There is no question', Hitler was reported as saying on 28 May, 'that we can avoid the real thing', a war against the Czechs. There were, of course, many other options open to Germany over the Sudeten question. The choice of war was not dictated by necessity, but by Hitler's wilful pursuit of violence. [The German foreign office official Erich Kordt, who watched German leaders at close quarters, drew the unavoidable conclusion that Hitler simply wanted war for its own sake: 'For Hitler [the Sudeten question] concerned a question of pure power politics ... I won the impression that it mattered much less to Hitler to draw Czechoslovakia into the German power bloc, and much more to overcome Czechoslovakia by force ... Now the dictator finally wanted to win real glory in war.'[20] Kordt believed that Hitler had wanted a war over Austria too, and vented his frustration over the failure to 'reconquer' his homeland on the unfortunate Czechs.]

Kordt's argument is certainly consistent with Hitler's well-known view of war as a product of historical necessity in the struggle of peoples for existence, and as an instrument for moulding a tough and martial race.[21] Eberhard Jaeckel has argued that Hitler did not just see war as an extension of politics in the traditional Clausewitzian formulation, but that Hitler's driving force was the pursuit of war for its own sake, unlimited and essential: 'there must be war under any circumstances.'[22] Even the most casual reading of *Mein Kampf* or, more usefully, of Hitler's so-called second, or secret, book from 1928, shows an unyielding belief in a vulgar Darwinian view of world affairs: struggle and violence between human races was for Hitler a *natural* phenomenon, not a product of political calculation. In this sense it is surely correct to see Hitler as someone for whom the question 'why war?' was superfluous.

Nevertheless, the timing of Hitler's pursuit of 'real war' in 1938, as opposed to the metaphors of conflict with which his world view was utterly permeated, might be open to other explanations. In the first place, Hitler was as aware as anyone that in the space of only two years war had moved to the centre of the international stage. Mussolini's invasion of Ethiopia in October 1935 was followed by the Spanish Civil War, and great power intervention, which began in July 1936 and was still not within sight of ending when the Hossbach Conference assembled in November 1937. In July 1937 Japan became embroiled in large-scale war with China. Whether Hitler liked it or not, war had overtaken him, and it was largely prosecuted by the two states, Italy and Japan, with whom Germany had begun to establish close political ties from the autumn of 1936. Hitler was deeply affected by the Spanish Civil War, to which limited numbers of German soldiers and airmen were committed on the nationalist side. In the weeks following the outbreak of civil war there were wild rumours circulating in Berlin about the possibility of a European war.[23] In this context, Hitler's decision to announce a policy of war is more understandable. It is not unlikely that for Hitler the sight of the 'senior' fascist, Mussolini, exploiting the martial achievements of his people in Ethiopia and Spain was not entirely welcome, whatever public expressions of dictatorial solidarity Hitler might have indulged in.

The immanence of armed conflict was father to a profound war psychosis which manifested itself in different ways among the powers of Europe. In Germany, however, Hitler appropriated it for his own purposes. The strategical memorandum he drafted at Berchtesgaden in August 1936 (usually referred to as the four-year plan memorandum), immediately following the onset of the Spanish crisis,

contained two central arguments: first, that the conflict with
Bolshevism was unavoidable and historically necessary for Germany;
second, that Germany should embark on a massive programme of
military and economic rearmament to be completed within four years
(a number determined not by any war timetable, but by the fact that
there had been a 'first four-year plan' begun in 1933).[24] References in
the memorandum to Italy and Japan as fighting states in the war
against 'Bolshevism' reinforce the impression that Hitler used the
memorandum to justify to himself, and the tiny handful of his
colleagues who were shown its contents, the move from diplomacy
to war as the central instrument of foreign policy.

The immediate and direct threat posed by 'Bolshevism' was
central to the shift in policy. Constantin von Neurath, German
foreign minister until February 1938, later recalled that from the
summer of 1936 Hitler's language became noticeably more violent
when discussing foreign relations ('If they won't see it, I will force
them', and so on),[25] and particularly so in reference to Russia. Hitler
was clearly worried by the possibility that Spain might descend into
communism. In a later war-crimes affidavit, the four-year plan
official, Kurt Lange, talked of the threat of 'Bolshevist encirclement'
felt from 1936.[26] Although Hitler came to discount Soviet
intervention in 1938, it was a simple matter to cast Czechoslovakia
as the Bolshevik Trojan horse – even more so given the large number
of German socialists and communists still conducting anti-fascist
politics in Prague. In this sense action against the Czechs and German
intervention in Spain were more of a piece than might be
immediately obvious. Both were components of what Donald Watt
has called a 'European civil war'. In both Hitler had a vested interest
in the destruction of popular democracy.

The memorandum of 1936, however, was much more than a
declaration of war against European communism. It summarized
Hitler's arguments, developed extensively in the secret book of 1928,
that war and economic power were inseparable. The contest with
Bolshevism as a world force required the mobilization of German
domestic economic resources, but could only ultimately be solved by
aquiring more. It was Hitler's conviction that further resources could
only be gained by war. In 1928 he wrote: 'The acquisition of soil is
always linked with the employment of force.'[27] The popular

connection made in Germany between economic health and wars of conquest has its roots, it has recently been suggested, in an obsession with 'territoriality' engendered by the pattern of German unification and the partition imposed in 1919.[28] In Hitler's case the link derived very precisely from his arguments about the large-scale mobilization of economic resources for war. And in the case of Czechoslovakia, and later of Poland, it was the desire to engross additional resources to fuel German military build-up that was a major consideration in German policy.

The link is clear from the evidence not only of the strategic memorandum of 1936, but from the major documents surrounding the Czech crisis. In the Hossbach conference of November 1937, for example, the main part of the discussion was not of plans for war, as is often suggested, but about the economic necessity of extending economic empire, by force if necessary, over the neighbouring states of central Europe: 'areas producing raw materials can be more usefully sought in Europe, in immediate proximity to the Reich.'[29] Austria and Czechoslovakia were, Hitler continued, necessary to supply food and manpower (he might have added foreign exchange, gold and substantial heavy industry). The final directive for Case 'Green', published at the end of May 1938, contained a concluding set of instructions that enterprises in Czechoslovakia should be occupied as soon as possible and integrated with German war preparations, and that German forces must at all costs avoid damaging economic installations.[30] When the Sudetenland was occupied in October 1938, and rump Bohemia and Moravia in March 1939, German economic authorities seized the major industrial and raw material assets immediately and took them under direct German control.[31] Wilhelm Keppler, one of the Nazi Party's leading economic experts, recalled under interrogation in 1945 a meeting with Hitler on 8 March 1939 in which he argued that the raw material position in Czechoslovakia was endangered by political instability and that the rump state would have to be occupied by German forces to secure its economic supplies.[32] The threat to foreign supplies of raw materials vital to German military build-up was perceived to be a pressing issue from 1936. In Spain strenuous efforts were made to safeguard supplies which would have been difficult to guarantee in a war with the West. In Austria and Czechoslovakia resources were available but by no means secure. War was, for Hitler, the only way to be sure of making them so.[33]

It is in this respect that Hitler's motives for war form a bridge between external and internal circumstances. The formal establishment of the Four-Year Plan in October 1936 ushered in a period of accelerated rearmament and the establishment of gigantic capital projects – the Reichswerke iron and steel complex, the synthetic fuel programme, the chemical and aluminium programmes – whose demands could not be fully met by a policy of import substitution and industrial rationalization. Hossbach's report of the meeting in November 1937 has Hitler's claim that 'autarky, in regard to food and to the economy as a whole, could not be maintained'.[34] The economic exploitation of central and eastern Europe was seen as one avenue out of the *impasse*, and not only by Hitler. What the German leader brought to the discussion was the view that only war and occupation would make such exploitation possible, rather than a strategy of economic penetration or political pressure. In the 'secret book' he had argued that violence was a necessary and hence legitimate way to secure economic resources: 'If a really vigorous people believes that it cannot conquer another with peaceful economic means ... the vapours of economic phraseology will be suddenly torn asunder and war, that is the continuation of politics with other means, steps into its place.'[35]

In the strategic memorandum of 1936 he returned to the idea that additional economic resources to secure German strength could only be acquired by what he had called 'breaking in' to neighbouring countries and seizing them. Hitler despised what he regarded as 'bourgeois' strategies for economic development. In his mind there was a seamless connection between the revival of German domestic power and the pursuit of economic imperialism. This is not to suggest that Hitler regarded war in 1938 as a sudden necessity because of economic contradictions exposed by rearmament (though it has recently been pointed out that there might have been greater economic justification for such a decision in 1938 rather than 1939).[36] He simply saw war instrumentally, as the Japanese had done in Manchuria, as a way to expand the German resource base and to secure it against other powers.

Nonetheless, such a view, though clearly significant in Hitler's own mind, does not do full justice to the domestic influences on Hitler's decision for war in 1938 rather than later. The conferences of April and May in which Hitler conveyed his decision for war took place only a matter of weeks after the revolution in domestic politics occasioned by the resignation of the war minister, Werner von Blomberg, and the sacking of the army commander-in-chief, Werner von Fritsch and foreign minister, von Neurath. This crisis offered a climax to a period of almost two years in which the German conservatives, who had collaborated with Hitler since 1933, had struggled against the influence of more radical or ambitious NSDAP leaders on economic, military and foreign policy. The details of the crisis are not of concern here,[37] but it produced two consequences which are important in understanding the shift to a war policy. First, it propelled two prominent nazis, Göring and Joachim vom Ribbentrop, into key positions in the state, the first as a virtual economic dictator following the resignation of Hjalmar Schacht in November 1937, the second as Neurath's replacement at the foreign office.

It has been tempting to see Ribbentrop as the evil genius behind the radical diplomacy of the Czech crisis.[38] He was evidently not that, since the initiative in the Czech affair stayed with Hitler, but he tied himself resolutely to Hitler's policy and urged him to risk everything in order to wage a war of some kind. No one who came into official contact with Ribbentrop during the spring and summer of 1938 was left in ignorance for long of Ribbentrop's desire for a fight somewhere. Mussolini was scathing: '[Ribbentrop] belongs to the category of Germans who are a disaster for their country. He talks about making war right and left, without naming an enemy or defining an objective.'[39] During the Weekend Crisis of 20–21 May, Ribbentrop informed the British ambassador that Germany would happily annihilate the Czechs ('there would not be a living soul left in that state') and wage war to the death against Britain and France.[40] Few people took him seriously, though his ability to make mischief was obvious. For Hitler, however, Ribbentrop had one big advantage: he was not an old-school diplomat. He knew from Neurath's unenthusiastic reaction to the meeting on 5 November 1937 that the foreign office would be a brake on more radical diplomacy. Under Ribbentrop restraint was abandoned, but the key decisions in foreign policy could be made by Hitler, whom Ribbentrop could not, in the end, challenge,

The second consequence of the February crisis was unarguably the more important, but has never occasioned the same historical interest: on 4 February 1938 Hitler assumed supreme command of the armed forces and abolished the war ministry. This was an extraordinary move on Hitler's part, and there is a dearth of evidence as to why he made it. The obvious explanation is his unwillingness, once he had reflected on the situation, to allow anyone else to exercise the kind of influence on military and foreign policy issues that von Blomberg had tried to exert. Goering's deputy in the air ministry, Erhard Milch, suggested to his interrogators in 1945 that Blomberg 'might have stood up to Hitler in 1938', and his loss certainly left the armed forced bereft of an obvious replacement.[41] Hitler knew that much of the army leadership was anxious about the risks evident in his foreign policy and rearmament plans. The only person Hilter could rely upon was himself.

The assumption of supreme command placed the armed forces in a difficult position. For the first time it gave Hitler what his chief-of-staff, General (later Field Marshal) Wilhelm Keitel, called 'an immediate power of authority', distinct from the more abstract authority that stemmed from being Führer. The commanders-in-chief of the three services were 'subordinated to him directly'. Hitler disapproved, Keitel wrote after the war, of the implicit tensions contained in the Prussian dualist tradition of minister of war and chief of the general staff.[42] He was an active supreme commander, and surrounded himself quickly with the trappings of command, 12 major departments, and a central operations staff, where the key decisions about strategy and combat could be taken only through Hitler. The appointment of Keitel, Blomberg's former deputy, as Hitler's chief-of-staff was, according to Albert Speer, deliberate, since Hitler knew that Keitel was a character he could easily dominate: 'at that time Hitler wanted to take over personally the direction of military affairs. He often used to say that it was convenient to have Keitel in this position … who was "as true as a dog".'[43] The power relationship between Hitler and the military shifted seismically in the spring of 1938, and gave him an even greater freedom of manoeuvre than he enjoyed in the sphere of foreign policy, which remained nominally in Ribbentrop's hands until 1945.

It is at least plausible to suggest that Hitler was keen to demonstrate to his more timid generals that he was going to be an active supreme commander. The *Anschluss* passed off without war. The Czech crisis was an opportunity to challenge and test the officer elite, as well as the surviving conservatives in the government. It may well be – the evidence is insufficient to assert with confidence – that the decision to fight the Czechs was taken almost spontaneously, in reaction to the unaccustomed responsibilities of high military office, and was not the fruit of careful deliberation. If the decision was taken partly to signal the change in the balance of domestic political forces, it explains why it was taken despite the lack of support for war evident throughout the wider German elite, and under what were perceived to be increasingly disadvantageous international conditions. For Hitler the warlord, the months after February 1938 represented a period of self-indulgent role playing.

Such an argument is not intended to suggest that the Czechs were victims on a mere whim. But it does suggest that the changing domestic situation, and the transformation of the German economy to large-scale militarization, made it more likely that Hitler would choose to resolve the Czech crisis by war. In an international arena in which war had become once again an instrument of policy for states with revisionist agenda, Hitler's preexisting belief in the inexorability of conflict and in the necessity for economic imperialism became magnified and legitimized. In this sense there were evident links between the foreign policy conjuncture Hitler faced (and his interpretation of it) and the particular set of domestic circumstances that affected his foreign policy choices. The unfortunate coincidence of these several factors transformed Czechoslovakia into the first object of calculated German aggression.

The Abandonment of War

The decision to launch war on the Czechs was, in reality, ill-judged, for it locked Hitler into a confrontation with other major powers that a more skilful diplomatist could well have avoided. In the end he did not get his first experience as warlord. Nor did he achieve the destruction of the Czech state which he had sworn to carry out in 1938. Though he was granted the areas inhabited by predominantly

German populations, there remained a strong sense that he had had to collaborate with states which, as he put it in 1939, 'talked the language of Versailles'.[44] Yet he did go to the brink in 1938. On 27 September he was within hours of ordering general mobilization and the unilateral invasion of the German-speaking areas of Czechoslovakia. Military preparations were in their final stages. The explanation could hardly have been mere brinkmanship, since all the substantive gains had been made. The other powers did not grant him additional concessions, but succeeded in forcing him to act with restraint. They did so, of course, at the price of Czech sovereignty; but that fact in itself does not sufficiently explain why Hitler came back from the brink.

One obvious answer is that the international situation, which had apparently seemed so favourable after the *Anschluss*, gradually worsened to the point where war with Czechoslovakia carried too many risks. There had always been an element of realism in Hitler's calculation. His operations chief, Colonel Alfred Jodl, later suggested that Hitler's reasoning ran as follows: 'One solution cannot be taken into consideration, that I should attack Czechoslovakia out of a clear sky. I cannot do such a thing or else I would get on my neck the whole world. I would have to wage war against England, against France, which I could not wage.'[45] The Weekend Crisis exposed just such risks, for it alerted Britain and France to the threat to Czechoslovakia, and brought a British intervention that might otherwise have been delayed or perhaps averted entirely. Although Hitler subsequently ordered preparations for war against Czechoslovakia, he realized that he would have to undertake the attack at the point where he could be confident of British and French abstention. Yet the more involved the two powers became in the Czech crisis, the more difficult it became to localize the conflict or to undertake any form of unilateral action. The British insistence on an international commission under Lord Runciman in August threatened to tie Hitler into a solution short of war which he could defy only at the risk of flouting world opinion. The advantage enjoyed by both the Japanese in Manchuria and the Italians in Ethiopia is that they acted first before the international community could intervene.

Yet although the intervention of Britain was perceived in Berlin to be the critical factor, Hitler remained confident that in the event of conflict with the Czechs Britain would still abstain. 'What will England do?' Goebbels asked himself in his diary on 1 September, 'will she put up with a conflict with the Czechs or not? The question on which everything else depends. The Führer himself is in good shape. He does not believe that London will intervene and is firmly resolved on action.' For most of the period between May and September 1938 Hitler did not allow himself to be deflected by the less favourable international situation. 'He knows what he wants', Goebbels added to his diary entry, 'and goes straight for it.'[46]

On 2 September in Berlin Hitler met with Admiral Horthy, the regent of Hungary, to take the opportunity to explain German policy and to invite Hungarian participation in the dismemberment of Czechoslovakia. Here again he reiterated his intention to wage war in late September/early October, and the argument that 'England and France according to the German view will not intervene'.[47] The same Hossbach who took down notes at the meeting in November 1937 told a colleague at the end of August 1938 that 28 September was openly talked about in Berlin as the 'day of attack against the Czechoslovak Republic'. The international situation, however, continued to deteriorate in September. Italy made clear its unwillingness to support a war policy. Hungary and Poland, while keen to take advantage of German policy, would not be pushed out in front. At the League of Nations the Soviet foreign minister, Maxim Litvinov, made public his government's pledge to honour the Soviet–Czech pact. The nightmare of a second July crisis began to take shape. Yet at the party congress in mid-September Hitler was reported to be adamant: 'He *wants* war.'[48]

A second explanation might be derived from the hostility Hitler encountered at home to his plans for conquest. This was first exposed in the lukewarm reception accorded Hitler's strategic confidences in November 1937, the first time, according to von Blomberg, who was present, that Hitler had spoken openly about his strategic plans. Blomberg recalled after the war that the military leadership had already made it clear to Hitler, prior to the meeting, 'that it would be impossible to have a warlike conflict before the years 1943 to 1945' for the reason that German military preparations 'had been entirely insufficient'. Hitler's observations about the prospects for war 'did not at any rate convince us at all'.[49]

German soldiers were not shy of telling Hitler their views, and many were pensioned off early in 1938. General Ludwig Beck, army chief-of-staff, survived longer, and in July 1938 felt sufficiently strongly about the unacceptable risks that Hitler appeared to be running to pen a critical memorandum that cost him his job. The gist of the memorandum, written on 16 July, was that the Czech crisis could not be localized, and would turn into a war 'of life and death with Germany', like the crisis 24 years before.[50] Beck did not by any means rule out future action against Czechoslovakia, but only when the military conditions were more favourable. The same day he wrote more candidly to his fellow officer, the army commander Walther Brauchitsch: 'All upright and serious German men in public office must feel duty bound to exploit every imaginable means and ways whatever the consequence in order to turn away from a war with the Czechs, whose results must lead to a world war that will mean the end of Germany.'[51] Hitler was told the contents of Beck's objections in August, and Beck was compelled to resign.[52]

There was also protest from within the foreign office. At the end of August 1938, Ernst von Weizsäcker, the state secretary, who survived the purging of Neurath in February, wrote a memorandum for Ribbentrop on 'The Political Situation at the End of 1938' in which he echoed Beck's view that a Czech war would become a European war: 'in my opinion the German political leadership must revise their plans. ... Either short or long, this war would end with German capitulation.'[53] Weizsäcker kept his job, but Ribbentrop made every effort to keep from Hitler the unfavourable views of German diplomats and officials. The ineffectiveness of the efforts of the conservatives to dissuade Hitler was evident right down to the final crisis in late September, and surely owes much to the fact that Hitler's choice of war was seen as a deliberate challenge to the more timid conservative elites. On 27 September Weizsäcker noted tersely in his diary: 'Peace can now only be protected through a miracle.'[54] The following day the Polish ambassador in Berlin wrote to the Polish foreign minister that the majority of diplomats in the capital believed that the pace was quickening 'in the march towards a European war'.[55] Neither the changing diplomatic circumstances, nor the hesitancy of the German military and diplomatic leadership was sufficient to stifle Hitler's will to war. Indeed, it seems likely that the more Hitler was obstructed by enemies abroad and doubters at home, the more determined he became.[56]

Hitler's decision to accept a negotiated settlement instead of war was taken at the very last moment sometime between the evening of 27 September and mid-morning on the following day because, against all apparent odds, he was deterred from going to war by the military threat posed by Britain and France. Whatever role in Hitler's thinking was played by his knowledge of domestic hostility to war, the final decision to accept a settlement short of war was prompted by a debilitating uncertainty over the question of whether Britain and France would intervene militarily on Czechoslovakia's behalf if he simply invaded. The military balance was itself unpredictable. Hitler told Horthy early in September that the operation against the Czechs was 'assured', not least because of Germany's overwhelming superiority in the air.[57] Yet throughout 1938 Hitler had made it plain in his discussions that he did not want a war with Britain and France at the same time. Historians have since demonstrated that the military gap between the two sides was much less than conventional wisdom has assumed.[58] The rearmament programmes and the build-up of the necessary strategic industries were far from complete. The major reorientation of the economy to war purposes announced by Göring as head of the Four-Year Plan organization in June 1938 was predicated on several more years of peace.[59] In the wake of Munich, Hitler ordered a colossal increase in armaments – a five-fold increase in air strength, a trebling of munitions output – which no doubt reflected his own frustration with the military stalemate in September.[60]

Hitler's loss of confidence emerged piecemeal during the crisis days of September, when Chamberlain flew to meet him twice to broker a peaceful solution. On 25 September, two days after the stormy meeting at Bad Godesberg, it was rumoured in Berlin that Hitler was 'backing away from Chamberlain's determined stance and does not want to occupy the Czech areas'.[61] This is, of course, a different Chamberlain from the popular image of the guilty man. The perception of British intentions in Berlin suggests a more robust approach to the Czech crisis than is usually allowed, and it is this perception – whatever the reality in London, or Paris – that is significant in understanding Hitler's behaviour. On 16 September,

Weizsäcker told Ulrich von Hassell that Chamberlain had made it clear that Britain 'would go to war if Germany used force'.[62] Sir Nevile Henderson, who had seen his position as British ambassador in Berlin as a mission to secure peace, told von Hassell a few days later: 'if Germany resorts to force, and France finds it necessary to act, the English will march with France.'[63] The British ambassador in Rome told the Italian foreign minister on 22 September that 'if Germany intends to push its ambitions beyond the bounds laid down by justice, it would be necessary to settle the affair by arms'.[64] The head of German counterintelligence, Admiral Canaris, later claimed that Britain would have fought in September 1938 if Czech blood had been spilt.[65]

The situation by 27 September appeared in Berlin to be more clearcut than it actually was. Hitler was determined to invade Czechoslovakia on a timetable of his own choosing; both Britain and France had stated that they would engage in war if Hitler violated Czech sovereignty by force. To allay any further doubt, Chamberlain dispatched a personal emissary to confront Hitler face to face on the issue. Sir Horace Wilson met with the Führer and delivered the message in a confrontation that was, according to the version recorded by Hitler's interpreter, remarkably frank. Wilson told Hitler twice that if Germany attacked Czechoslovakia, France was committed to honour her treaty obligations and fight Germany, and if that happened 'then England would feel honour bound, to offer France assistance'.[66] According to Weizsäcker's account of the meeting given to Lipski the same day – but missing from the official record – Wilson insisted to Hitler 'that he was quoting Chamberlain's ideas correctly'.[67] Hitler, for his part, told Wilson that if the Czechs refused his timetable for occupation he would destroy them and that, if Wilson's view of British and French intentions were true, a European war would break out within the week.

This situation had never been Hitler's intention. Though Ribbentrop continued during the evening of 27 September and the following day to insist on war with the Czechs in the belief that the Western powers were bluffing, Hitler at some point recognized the stark choice he was faced with. The details of his change of heart are well known. During an interview in the morning of 28 September with the French ambassador, André François-Poncet (during which he repeated the French intention to oppose invasion), came the telephone call from the Italian ambassador with Mussolini's suggestion, at British prompting, for an international conference.[68] After François-Poncet's departure he received a delegation led by Göring and Neurath which arrived at the chancellery in mid-morning determined to warn Hitler not to risk general war. To Neurath's reported question, 'My Führer, do you actually want to wage a war whatever the case', Hitler replied: 'What do you mean? whatever the case? Obviously not!'[69] Hitler accepted Mussolini's suggestion and Munich, already the site of an agreed meeting between Ribbentrop and Ciano for the following day, was chosen for the venue. His army adjutant recorded in his diary that day: 'F.[ührer] wants no war' and 'F.[ührer] above all things does not think of war with England'.[70] From the perspective of those in Berlin who feared the coming of war, Hitler's climbdown was obvious and public. 'Führer has finally given in, and thoroughly' wrote one observer in a diary the same day; and two days later '*Strong* concessions from the Führer!' [italics in original].[71]

The question whether Britain, France or even the Soviet Union would have fought Germany in 1938 remains open, though military preparations were more extensive, the deterrence posture more declaratory and the war psychosis more pronounced than was consistent with the crude image of appeasement usually ascribed to them.[72] From the point of view of explaining Hitler's decision not to launch war, it was his perception of the possibility of intervention, with all the military complications and domestic political difficulties that might have flowed from it that forced him to abandon war. Characteristically, Hitler blamed others for his own loss of nerve. The unenthusiastic behaviour of the Berlin population during the crisis was used by Hitler as an excuse for holding back,[73] but was surely an insufficient explanation in itself. Hitler was the only one responsible for taking the crisis to the brink, and it was his own political ineptitude that forced him to climb down from war in front of all those to whom he had asserted again and again the necessity for real conflict. Erich Kordt, a German foreign office official, described in his memoirs the effect on the Führer:

> Hitler … had seized the chance offered at the last moment to seek a diplomatic solution instead of the military one so greatly

desired. But as a result the forceful destruction of Czechoslovakia was rendered impossible. He did his utmost to give the peaceful ordering of the Sudeten German question the character of a humiliation for the Western powers. Nevertheless he did not see Munich as a victory after his own heart. Hitler became a hero of peace against his will.[74]

The Aftermath

The failure to wage war in 1938 had profound implications for the future. Hitler almost immediately ordered military planning for the destruction of Czech independence at some future date. A few days after Munich found Hitler already discussing the question of Poland in violent terms. In the ten days following his decision to abandon war he wavered on several occasions in favour of some show of violence in the occupation of the areas ceded to him at Munich.[75] When in 1939 the whole drama repeated itself over the issue of Danzig, Hitler could not afford a second time to take Germany to the brink and step back. The intention of Britain and France to obstruct a unilateral and violent assault on Polish sovereignty was made as clear, if not clearer, than had been the case over Czechoslovakia. Domestic fears of general war were voiced as they had been in 1938. The difference lay with the lessons Hitler drew from Munich.

In the first place, Hitler consciously chose to ignore the advice of experts in order to avoid a repetition of the chorus of dissenting voices expressed during the Czech crisis. On 1 September 1939, following the invasion of Poland, Hitler was warned by one of the foreign office French experts that France would fight. His reported response to his foreign minister is revealing: 'You must understand, Ribbentrop, that I have at last decided to do without the opinions of people who have misinformed me on a dozen occasions, or even lied to me, and I shall rely on my own judgement, which has in all these cases [from the Rhineland to the occupation of Prague] given me better counsel than the competent experts.'[76] His intuition told him that he should have held out over Czechoslovakia; his intuition in the Polish crisis told him he should hold out regardless.

The second lesson he drew was scarcely supported by the evidence of the final crisis on 28 September, but was nonetheless fateful for the issue of peace or war the following year. He maintained against all objections that the Western powers would abandon the Poles as they had abandoned the Czechs. When he found himself in the last week of August 1939 assailed by the same doubts and second-thoughts that had afflicted him a year before – and by the same doubters around him – he overcame his inner inhibitions and remained, as his army adjutant recalled on the eve of the Polish invasion, 'exceptionally irritable, bitter and sharp' with all those around him who counselled caution.[77] The source of this psychological turmoil lies, beyond reasonable doubt, in the unbearable recollection of the previous year, where he had taken himself to the limit and, in his own terms, been found wanting. A year later the desire to act the warlord was so overwhelming that it consumed all rational judgement: 'He simply could not understand a soldier who feared war.'[78] Given such a disposition, the Western powers' hope that deterrence would work a second time was groundless. Many of those around Hitler in August 1939 *were* deterred, but the success of deterrence in September 1938 was its undoing. Hitler hovered on the brink a second time, but this time could do nothing other but safeguard his credentials as Germany's supreme commander and leap over.

King's College, London

NOTES

1. *Hitlers politisches Testament: die Bormann Diktate vom Februar und April 1945* (Hamburg, 1981), pp.99–100.
2. Hitler's speech to the commanders-in-chief, 22 Aug. 1939 in International Miltary Tribunal, *Nazi Conspiracy and Aggression* (Washington, 1947), Vol.3, p.582.
3. There is a vast literature on Munich. See particularly G. Weinberg, *Hitler's Foreign Policy, 1937–9* (Chicago, 1980); T. Taylor, *Munich: The Price of Peace* (London, 1979); R. Smelser, *The Sudeten Problem 1933–38: Volkstumspolitik and the Formation of German foreign policy* (Folkestone, 1975); P. Glotz *et al.* (eds.), *München 1938: Das Ende des alten Europas* (Essen, 1990).
4. G. Niedhart, 'The Problem of War in German Politics in 1938', *War & Society*, 2 (1984), pp.55–63.
5. See the discussion in E. Jaeckel, *Das deutsche Jahrhundert: eine historische Bilanz* (Stuttgart, 1990) pp.185ff.
6. Most recently on Hitler's role in these crises see I. Kershaw, *Hitler. Volume 1, Hubris 1889–1936* (London, 1998), pp.580–90.
7. *Documents diplomatiques français 1932–1939* (DDF) 2nd series, Vol.xii, pp.43–4, François-Poncet to Bonnet, 5 Oct. 1938.

8. B.-J. Wendt, *Grossdeutschland: Aussenpolitik und Kriegsvorbereitung des Hitler-Regimes* (Munich, 1987).
9. *Hitler's Secret Book*, intr. T. Taylor (New York, 1961), esp. chs. 1, 2, 9.
10. Smelser, *Sudeten Problem*, pp.42–50.
11. F. Wiedemann, *Der Mann der Feldherr werden wollte* (Kettwig,1964), p.128.
12. *Akten zur Deutschen auswärtigen Politik, 1918–1945 (ADAP)*, Series D, Vol.2 (Baden-Baden, 1950), Doc.221, pp.281–5, Weisung für Plan 'Grün', 30 May 1938.
13. *ADAP*, Series D, Vol.1, pp.25–32 Doc.19, minutes of the meeting in the Reich chancellery, 5 Nov. 1937. For a discussion of its authenticity and significance see J. Wright and P. Stafford, 'Hitler, Britain and the Hossbach Memorandum', *Militärgeschichtliche Mitteilungen*, 42 (1987), pp.78–84; Wendt, *Grossdeutschland*, pp.11–37. On the details of military planning for an invasion of Czechoslovakia see W. Deist, *The Wehrmacht and German Rearmament* (London, 1981), pp.96–8.
14. Christie Papers, Churchill College, Cambridge, ChP 180/1 5, notes of a conversation with Goering, 3 Feb. 1937, pp.51, 54.
15. Christie Papers, 180/1 5, Report of a meeting with Goering, 28 July 1937.
16. Imperial War Museum, London, FO 646/ Box 155, Bodenschatz interrogation, 6 Nov. 1945, pp.5–6.
17. *ADAP*, Series D, Vol.2, Doc.175, p.238, draft of a new directive 'Green', 20 May 1938.
18. Cited in E. Kordt, *Nicht aus den Akten: die Wilhelmstrasse in Frieden und Krieg* (Stuttgart, 1950), p.228.
19. This translation from J. Noakes and G. Pridham, *Nazism 1919–1945: Vol.3, Foreign Policy, War and Extermination* (Exeter, 1988), p.712.
20. Kordt, *Nicht aus den Akten*, p.229.
21. *Hitler's Secret Book*, ch.1 passim. In an almost Hobbesian passage [p.6] Hitler asserts that 'Self-preservation and continuance are the great urges underlying all action'.
22. Jaeckel, *Das deutsche Jahrhundert*, pp.185–6.
23. L.E. Hill (ed.), *Die Weizsäcker-Papiere 1933–1950* (Frankfurt am Main, 1974) p.100, diary entry for 25.10.36: 'Here too [in Berlin] much is talked of course about war and alarms about war.
24. Memorandum in W. Treue, 'Der Denkschrift Hitlers über die Aufgaben eines Vierjahresplans', *Vierteljahreshefte für Zeitgeschichte* 3 (1954), pp.205–10. The tasks of the first four-year plan, announced in 1933, are discussed in P. Schmidt, *Deutsche Wirtschaftsfreiheit durch den Vierjahresplan* (Breslau, n.d. [1937?]) [Wiener Library, London].
25. IWM, FO 646/ Box 159, interrogation of von Neurath, 2 Oct. 1945, p.9.
26. IWM, Trial of the War Criminals, background documents, Case XI, Koerner Document Book 1b, p.11. On the role of anti-Bolshevism see K. Patzold, 'Antikommunismus und Antibolschewismus als Instrumente der Kriegsvorbereitung und Kriegspolitik', in N. Frei and H. Kling (eds.), *Der nationalsozialistische Krieg* (Frankfurt am Main, 1990), pp.122–36.
27. *Hitler's Secret Book*, p.24.
28. See A.A. Kallis, 'Expansionism in Italy and Germany between Unification and the First World War: On the Ideological and Political Origins of Fascist Expansionism', *European History Quarterly*, 28 (1998), pp.435–60; G.H. Herb, *Under the Map of Germany: Nationalism and Propaganda 1918–1945* (London, 1997), esp. ch 8.
29. *ADAP*, Series D, Vol.1, p.27
30. *ADAP*, Series D, Vol.2, Doc.221, p.285, Directive for Plan 'Green', 30 May 1938.
31. Details in R.J. Overy, 'Goering's Multi-National Empire', in A. Teichova and M. Levy-Leboyer (eds), *International Business and Central Europe 1918–1939* (Leicester, 1983), pp.272–5.
32. IWM, FO 645/ Box 158, Interrogation of Wilhelm Keppler, 6 Nov. 1945, p.6. See, too, D. Eichholtz *et al.* (eds.), *Anatomie des Krieges* (Berlin, 1969), Doc.88, p.204, Bericht

von Wilhelm Keppler über die Rede Adolf Hitlers, 8 März 1939.
33. See recently C. Leitz, *Economic Relations between Nazi Germany and Franco's Spain 1936–1945* (Oxford, 1996), esp. ch.1. On German economic diplomacy see D. Kaiser, *Economic Diplomacy and the Origins of the Second World War* (Princeton, 1980), esp. chs.6, 10; Wendt, *Grossdeutschland*, pp.139–48.
34. *ADAP*, Series D, Vol.1, p.27
35. *Hitler's Secret Book*, p.24.
36. See A. Ritschl, 'Die deutsche Zahlungsbilanz 1936–41 und das Problem des Devisenmangels vor Kriegsbeginn', *Vierteljahreshefte für Zeitgeschichte*, 39 (1991), pp.103–22.
37. See, for example, H. Deutsch, *Hitler and his Generals: The Hidden Crisis, January–June 1938* (Minnesota, 1974), esp. pp.80–87, 98–104; A. Simpson, 'The Struggle for Control of the German Economy 1936/7', *Journal of Modern History*, 21 (1959), pp.37–45; J.L. Heinemann, *Hitler's First Foreign Minister* (Berkeley, 1979), esp. pp.167–70.
38. Much of the recent literature on Ribbentrop has suggested that he exerted considerable influence on Hitler's foreign policy outlook in 1938 and 1939. See, for example, W. Michalka, *Ribbentrop und die deutsche Weltpolitik 1933–1940* (Munich, 1980); J. Weiss, *Hitler's Diplomat* (London, 1992). For a more critical assessment see S. Kley, *Hitler, Ribbentrop und die Entfesselung des Zweiten Weltkrieges* (Paderborn, 1996); M. Bloch, *Ribbentrop* (London, 1992). On Ribbentrop's foreign policy outlook see also G. Waddington, 'Hitler, Ribbentrop, die NSDAP und der Niedergang des Britischen Empire 1935–1938', *Vierteljahreshefte für Zeitgeschichte*, 41 (1992).
39. Bloch, *Ribbentrop*, p.182.
40. Ibid., p.185.
41. IWM, FO 645/ Box 159, interrogation of Erhard Milch, 27 Oct. 1945. Milch believed that Blomberg 'was the only soldier who was clever enough to reconcile military and political questions'.
42. IWM, FO 645/ Box 158, memorandum by Wilhelm Keitel, 'The Position and the Powers of the Chief of the OKW', 9 Oct. 1945, pp.1–2. On the establishment of OKW see R. O'Neill, *The German Army and the Nazi Party, 1933–1939* (London, 1966), pp.198–210; W. Deist et al., *Das Deutsche Reich und der Zweite Weltkrieg. I: Ursachen und Voraussetzungen der deutschen Politik* (Stuttgart, 1979), pp.506–12.
43. IWM, Speer Collection, Box S369, US Group Control Council, Intelligence Report no EF/Min/2, 'Nazi Foreign Policy and Military Leadership', p.10.
44. *Nazi Conspiracy and Aggression*, Vol.3, p.583.
45. IWM, FO 645/ Box 157, interrogation of Alfred Jodl, 7 Sept. 1945, p.3.
46. E. Fröhlich (ed.), *Die Tagebücher von Joseph Goebbels: sämtliche Fragmente* (4 vols., Munich, 1987), Vol.3, p.525.
47. H. Groscurth, *Tagebuch eines Abwehroffiziers* (Stuttgart, 1970), p.108.
48. Ibid., p.107.
49. IWM, FO 645/ Box 155, interrogation of Werner von Blomberg, 17 Nov. 1945, pp.4–5; see too Box 159, Milch interrogation, 27 Oct. 1945: 'A long time ago I had talked to Field Marshal von Blomberg in 1937 about the danger of war on account of the careless policy of our politicians, and we feared at that time that England and France wouldn't tolerate that policy in the long run. The 1st November 1937 I had a long discussion with von Blomberg about this matter, and he was of the same opinion, and all the others.' See too O'Neill, *German Army*, pp.193–4.
50. H. Michaelis and E. Schraepler (eds.), *Ursachen und Folgen vom deutschen Zusammenbruch 1918 bis 1945. Vol. 12, Das sudetendeutsche Problem* (Berlin, n.d.), pp.205–6, Doc.2682 (a), Denkschrift des Generalstabschefs des Heeres, 16 Juli 1938.
51. *Ursachen und Folgen*, Vol.12, p.207, Doc.2682 (b), Notiz des Generalstabschefs Beck für den Vortrag beim Oberbefehlshaber des Heeres, 16 Juli 1938.

52. K.-J. Müller, *The Army, Politics and Society in Germany, 1933–1945* (New York, 1987), pp.88–90.
53. Hill (ed.), *Die Weizsäcker-Papiere 1933–1950*, p.139, Weizsäcker to Ribbentrop, 30 Aug. 1938, 'Die politische Lage Ende August 1939'.
54. *Weizsäcker-Papiere*, p.139, diary entry for 27 Sept. 1938.
55. J. Lipski, *Diplomat in Berlin 1933–1939* (Columbia UP, 1968), pp.431–2, Doc.113, Lipski to Beck [Polish foreign minister], 28 Sept. 1938.
56. See Speer's comments on Hitler's conduct of foreign policy in IWM, Speer Collection Box S369, 'Nazi Foreign Policy', pp.7–9, who claimed that in the spring of 1938 Hitler deliberately set out to establish a group of men around him who were 'active, aggressive and obedient to him', in contrast to the old Wehrmacht leadership.
57. Groscurth, *Tagebuch*, p.108.
58. See, for example, W. Murray, 'German Air Power and the Munich Crisis' *War and Society*, 2 (1975); M. Messerschmidt, 'The Political and Strategic Siginficance of Advances in Armament Technology. Developments in Germany and the Strategy of "Blitzkrieg"', in R. Ahmann *et al.* (eds.), *The Quest for Stability* (London, 1993); R.J. Overy, 'German Air Strength 1933–1939: A Note', *The Historical Journal*, 27 (1984), pp.465–71.
59. National Archives, Washington, T77, Roll 71, frames 791892–7, Goering to all ministers on issue of Reich defence, 18 June 1938; frame 791891, OKW circular, 'Ausbau der Reichsverteidigung', 27 June 1938.
60. Details in International Military Tribunal, *Trial of the Major War Criminals* (42 vols., Nuremberg, 1947), Vol.32, p.413, note on the meeting of the Reich Defence Council, 18 Nov. 1938.
61. Groscurth, *Tagebuch*, p.124.
62. U. von Hassell, *The von Hassell Diaries 1938–1944* (London, 1948), p.12.
63. *von Hassell Diaries*, p.10. For a reassessment of Henderson's role in Berlin see P. Neville, 'The Appointment of Sir Nevile Henderson, 1937 – Design or Blunder?', *Journal of Contemporary History*, 33 (1998), pp.609–20.
64. M. Muggeridge (ed.), *Ciano's Diplomatic Papers* (London, 1948), p.235, conversation with the British ambassador, 22 Sept. 1938.
65. *Nazi Conspiracy and Aggression*, Vol.3, p.581, Doc.795–PS, conversation with General Keitel, 17 Aug. 1939.
66. *ADAP*, Series D, Vol.2, p.772, Doc.634, minutes of meeting between Hitler and Horace Wilson, 27 Sept. 1938.
67. Lipski, *Diplomat in Berlin*, p.425, Doc.109, Lipski to Beck, 27 Sept. 1938.
68. *DDF*, 2nd Series, Vol.11, pp.646–7, Doc.426, François-Poncet to Bonnet, 28 Sept. 1938; Heinemann, *Hitler's First Foreign Minister*, pp.181–2.
69. *Ursachen und Folgen*, Vol.12, pp.438–40, Doc.2722, Fritz Wiedemann über seine Eindrücke am 28 Sept. 1938.
70. G. Engel, *Heeresadjutant bei Hitler 1938–1943* (ed H. von Kotze, Stuttgart, 1974), p.39, diary entry for 28 Sept. 1938.
71. Groscurth, *Tagebuch*, p.128, diary entries for 28, 30 Sept. 1938.
72. On Soviet intentions see G. Jukes, 'The Red Army and the Munich Crisis', *Journal of Contemporary History*, 26 (1991), pp.196–8; I. Lukes, 'Stalin and Benes in the Final Days of September 1938', *Slavic Review*, 52 (1993), pp.28–48. On French policy see E. De Réau, *Edouard Daladier, 1884–1970* (Paris, 1993), pp.265–70; Y. Lacaze, 'Daladier and the Munich Crisis', in R. Boyce (ed.), *French Foreign and Defence Policy, 1918–1940: The Decline and Fall of a Great Power* (London, 1998), pp.215–30; P. Le Goyet, *Munich: pouvait-on et devait-on faire la guerre en 1938?* (Paris, 1988). On Britain, see D. Reynolds, *Britannia Overruled: British Policy and World Power in the 20th Century* (London, 1991), pp.134–6. For a general assessment see D.C. Watt, *How War Came* (London, 1989).

73. See the version in Kordt, *Nicht aus den Akten*, pp.271–2 or *DDF*, Series 2, Vol.12, pp.35–6, Doc.19, François-Poncet to Bonnet, 4 Oct. 1938 who reported the view that the lack of popular enthusiasm for war was a shock for Hitler, 'which had rendered him more accessible to the offensive from the Marshal [Goering] and the former Minister of Foreign Affairs'.
74. Kordt, *Nicht aus den Akten*, p.272.
75. See, for example, Engel, *Heeresadjutant*, pp.40–41.
76. J. Toland, *Adolf Hitler* (London, 1976), p.571.
77. Engel, *Heeresadjutant*, p.60.
78. Ibid., p.59.

The Munich Crisis and British Propaganda Policy in the United States

NICHOLAS J. CULL

What in history has been more shameful than England and France conferring with Benes at midnight in Prague while they played Judas to Czechoslovakia? Let England go into the wilderness and perish with her sins. They are all guilty; Germany, France and England. Guilty as dogs![1]

This ringing declaration of the isolationist Senator William E. Borah in 1940 typified responses to Munich in the United States. British perfidy seemed an issue on which all Americans, left and right, east and west could agree. Any British bid to woo the United States into the benevolent neutrality essential for Britain's survival in a protracted war seemed doomed. Yet the Munich crisis was more than an obstacle in Britain's struggle to secure American sympathy. The crisis was also an essential learning experience for British propagandists. The lessons of 1938 were the foundations for the successes of 1940 and 1941. The key insight derived from the Munich crisis was that the best way of reaching American opinion was to cultivate the American journalists and broadcasters based in London. Yet British officials did not create their links with the American news channels out of thin air. The good relations came as people who already enjoyed such links were promoted into positions of power within the British propaganda bureaucracy and the British government as a whole.[2]

Britain's Problem: The Crisis in American Information Policy.

By the mid-1930s, the British faced the alarming prospect of a war with both Germany and Japan without the support of the United States. As the tightening of American neutrality laws became an annual congressional ritual, the British government found itself caught in a vicious circle. Prudence dictated a peace overture to Mussolini, but this reinforced old American stereotypes of Perfidious Albion. The sympathetic President Roosevelt found little room to manoeuvre. As Prime Minister Neville Chamberlain himself noted in January 1938: 'The USA has drawn closer to us, but the isolationists there are so strong and so vocal that she cannot be depended on for help if we should get into trouble.'[3] The foreign secretary, Anthony Eden, however, still believed that 'Everything must give way to the primary importance of good relations with Roosevelt and America'.[4] When Chamberlain chose appeasement over any fresh approach to America, Eden resigned from the cabinet. American sympathy left with him. By the early summer of 1938, the columnist Dorothy Thompson declared bitterly that appeasement had 'brought British stock to an all time low' in the minds of the American public.[5]

Adverse public opinion was not an uncommon problem for the British in this era, and indeed the government had developed a standard series of propaganda initiatives for exactly such circumstances. In London the news department of the foreign office, under Great War propaganda veteran Rex Leeper, managed the press relations aspects of British foreign policy. The British applied a vigorous programme of national projection establishing such organs as the Travel Association for tourist publicity in 1929, the British Council for cultural propaganda in 1934 and foreign language services of the BBC in 1937. Unfortunately, it was a *sine qua non* of British publicity policy that such organizations could not operate in the United States. Memories of the British campaign to draw the United States into the First World War were simply too raw. Hence, the British limited their public relations activity in the United States to the British Library of Information in New York (BLI), a small office left over from the Great War. The BLI provided information only on request, which generally concerned tax law or the Royal Family. The library's only venture into propaganda was to maintain a list of all Americans who submitted requests for information regarding India.[6] The BLI was simply not equipped to slay the dragon of American isolation even if Whitehall had favoured such a course.

In 1935 Britain began to rearm for war. To address the need for wartime propaganda machinery the Committee of Imperial Defence established a shadow ministry of information, but its planners soon became preoccupied with internal feuds and the question of domestic propaganda.[7] They had little time for the question of overseas publicity, let alone planning propaganda in the United States. 1937 brought a cabinet committee under Sir Kingsley Wood to report on the presentation of British news to the world. More was needed. In February 1938, at Eden's behest, parliament established a special committee under the former undersecretary of state for foreign affairs, Robert Vansittart, to investigate overseas publicity. Rex Leeper was duly assigned to carry out the committee's wishes with the rank of assistant undersecretary of state. Vansittart's report begged for preparedness in the field of propaganda. He stressed the strength of Britain's potential enemies in that field and called for such basic advances as the appointment of press secretaries in British embassies beyond those already assigned to Paris, Rome and Berlin.[8] But even Vansittart could not send an attaché to Washington DC; his deliberations coincided with a major initiative on Capitol Hill to stamp out all foreign propaganda, including the British variety.

In June 1938 congress passed House Resolution 1591: the Foreign Agents Registration Act. The act required all foreign agents to be registered with the state department and all propaganda literature to be labelled so that the American public would thereby be aware of any foreign attempts to subvert their neutrality.[9] Two months later Representative Martin Dies launched the Committee for the Investigation of Un-American Activities, pledging to dig out communist, nazi and British propaganda.[10] The British ambassador in Washington, Ronald Lindsay, realized that such initiatives threatened even such limited British operations as the library in New York. He drew a measure of comfort from a state department pledge that the criteria of registration would be lenient. The library survived the indignity of being listed as a propaganda agency in the *New York Times*.[11]

As the European situation worsened, those Britons convinced of the need to stand against Hitler and build an Anglo-American future became even more desperate to get their message across. Such legitimate opportunities for British activities as the forthcoming New York World's Fair of 1939 became major enterprises, while key figures in British cultural diplomacy continued to press for a more active approach to the United States. In June, Lord Lloyd, chairman of the British Council, proposed sending British lecturers to visit American universities forthwith. Vansittart and the news department agreed.[12] Ronald Lindsay did not. In a curt letter to Leeper of 10 July 1938 he pointed to the new anti-propaganda laws in the United States and bluntly asked the foreign office 'what they were at'.[13] Lindsay's response reinforced the 'No Propaganda' policy at a crucial moment. It was not seriously questioned again until after the fall of France in the summer of 1940. Those interested in promoting Anglo-American relations looked for an alternative route.

The British had long believed that the best way to win American sympathy was to appeal to the makers of American public opinion, rather than to address the American public directly. This had been the principle behind the list of top Americans who, during the Great War, had received pointed personal letters explaining the British point of view from the leading lights of the empire.[14] During the course of the 1930s, those Britons who believed that the destinies of the American republic and their own nation should be intertwined for mutual benefit kept this approach alive by cultivating top American visitors to Britain. Advocates of such work included the American-born MP, Ronald Tree, whose home had long been open to visiting American dignitaries. Such ideas also figured in the thinking of Sir George Schuster, president of Lipton's Tea, who discussed plans for reforming British publicity in America with Vansittart and the foreign secretary, Lord Halifax. Schuster proposed an integrated approach, cultivating the American press in both London and the United States. He called for a press office in the Washington embassy, a syndicated radio commentary on British life for United States stations, and a nationwide British press operation in the United States to monitor and counter American misunderstandings of British policy and 'feed out' helpful stories. Schuster also recommended a policy of making Britain's leaders accessible to American journalists, who he argued, were now Britain's hope: the American journalists in London

Leeper already had such matters in hand. On the evening of 26 July 1938, a small group of foreign office officials and advocates of closer Anglo-American relations met over dinner at the House of Commons. Those present included Leeper, the secretary of the Rhodes Trust, Lord Lothian, Angus Fletcher of the BLI, the Atlantic-minded Labour MP Josiah Wedgewood, and Frank Darvall, director of research and discussion at the English Speaking Union. Darvall presented the classic pedigree of an Anglo-American, having both studied American politics at Columbia University as a Commonwealth Fund Fellow and married an American.[15] This group decided that American opinion had to be treated as 'a case absolutely apart' and that to this end Vansittart ought to form a special subcommittee of his committee to coordinate British publicity abroad, devoted to the question of American public opinion.[16] They hoped that this body might monitor Britons travelling to the United States, assemble lists of Americans travelling to Britain 'in order that suitable attention should be paid them', and encourage professional and industrial bodies to invite Americans to visit Britain for conferences and conventions.[17] Colonel Wedgewood suggested that the committee commission an Anglo-American anthology 'of prose and verse to celebrate the virtues, struggles and triumphs of democracy and freedom as they are understood in England and America'. Wedgewood, working with the American historian Allan Nevins, compiled just such a collection under the title *Forever Freedom*. It appeared just in time to help in the battle for American sympathy in 1940.[18] Leeper was in no hurry to bring his proposed American subcommittee into existence. He concluded his report on the evening: 'this sub-committee might be formed after the holidays, towards the end of September.'[19] The committee's views moved further to the centre of Anglo-American relations in August 1938, when Halifax named Lord Lothian as Lindsay's successor in the Washington embassy.

Of the American visitors to Britain none had such significance for the propaganda planners as the American press corps and broadcasters. Although the American public clearly desired to remain aloof from the affairs of Europe, they nevertheless wished to know exactly what they were missing. Throughout the 1930s, American news chains and regional papers had strengthened their representation in Europe. By 1937 the press had been joined by a new and untried breed of journalist, the radio correspondents. Both linguistic and technical convenience dictated that London be the centre for American broadcast operations in Europe. The radio correspondents arrived accordingly. The most significant arrival came in 1937: he was Edward R. Murrow, the first European director of the Columbia broadcasting system.[20]

The American journalists in London initially held as wide a variety of political views as the American people as a whole, yet years spent contemplating the nazis forged a marked orthodoxy that Hitler had to be stopped and that appeasement was not the way to do it.[21] This led to an informal alliance between the journalists and similarly inclined members of the British elite. The American journalists knew that the crop of rogue British journalists, thinkers and politicians accumulating around such figures as Eden and the writer Robert Bruce Lockhart could provide them with stories and introductions to the 'right people', while the members of the emerging anti-appeasement bloc realized that American sympathy was the key to the future, and in any case relished the opportunity to exchange ideas with like-minded people over cocktails at Whites Club or dinner at the home of the passionate anti-appeaser Victor Gordon Lennox, diplomatic correspondent with the *Daily Telegraph*.[22]

During the summer of 1938 the foreign office news department formally cultivated the Americans only by gathering them in the foreign office briefing room for a daily audience with the deputy director of the news department, Charles Peake. In the afternoon things relaxed a little as Leeper met individual correspondents. In the evenings, as a member of the anti-appeasement set, he courted them socially.[23] Valuable work also happened under the auspices of internationalist bodies like the Royal Institute of International Affairs (Chatham House). Some correspondents had a longstanding connection to the cause of internationalism. Murrow first visited London in 1935 as an officer of the International Institute of Education, and retained many internationalist links. Within months of his arrival in 1937 he had addressed the RIIA. Murrow also found eager hosts among pro-American British politicians and soon became an intimate of the emerging anti-Chamberlain circle.[24]

By September 1938 Britain's information policy towards the United States had stabilized. On 6 September 1938 Leeper gave the Washington embassy formal notice of the foreign office decision to maintain 'in full force' the 'old principle' of avoiding propaganda in United States. Yet he also made it clear that he intended to continue to investigate plans for recruiting American students to British university summer schools and to cultivate the American press corps in London. To this end the news department would be 'overhauling' its facilities in the immediate future.[25] Before Leeper could accomplish his 'overhaul', the storm struck. On 12 September 1938 Hitler assured a Nuremberg rally that he would never abandon the Germans of Czechoslovakia. Within hours the Germans of the Sudetenland were rioting in the streets. The Munich crisis had begun.

The Crisis

The Munich crisis unfolded swiftly enough to keep both the foreign office news department and the American broadcasters off balance; however, the result was compulsive listening for American radio audiences. By 28 September, when Hitler finally agreed to a meeting at Munich, American radio audiences had lived through over two weeks of rumours, initiatives, punditry and programmes interrupted with bulletins from both sides of the Atlantic.[26] Now, for the first time, the mechanisms of foreign broadcast news that had been established during the 1930s worked to capacity. Its impact was not lost on the planners of British propaganda policy.

Initially, most Americans favoured Chamberlain's bid to solve the Czech crisis by negotiating with Hitler. The German ambassador to Washington conceded that 'the vast majority of the American people' were 'glad that a grave conflict has been avoided'.[27] The BLI reported that any adverse American had been superseded by positive responses to Chamberlain's moving speech of 27 September, although they warned London that: 'the dangerous time so far as British prestige is concerned will be when the results of the conference emerge.'[28] Any return to the crisis of the early autumn promised to produce an Anglophobic backlash. By January 1939, returning English Speaking Union lecturers reported that 'anti-Chamberlain feeling' was 'intense'.[29] Dismayed, the foreign office noted America's failure to comprehend the necessity of the British move and found isolationism to be resurgent.[30] Such had not been the intention of Chamberlain when he formulated his policy in September.

During the crisis, Chamberlain finally attempted to fuse his European appeasement policies with a concern for American public opinion. At Munich he replaced the old frontiers of Germany – dictated at Versailles and hence long discredited in the United States – with new boundaries. These borders would be tied to solid principles of self-determination by plebiscite and clothed in a mantle of international agreement. An abrogation of such an agreement would provide the clear-cut *casus belli* hitherto absent from the European scene. Thus, Chamberlain took particular care to ensure that his efforts were well presented in the United States. To this end he contrived what became the most famous news image of the build-up to war. Before leaving the Munich Conference, Chamberlain prevailed on Hitler to sign a supplementary declaration that Britain and Germany regarded the Munich Agreement as 'symbolic of the desire' of their two peoples 'never to go to war with one another again'. According to his private secretary, Viscount Dunglass (later Prime Minister Sir Alec Douglas-Home), Chamberlain explained his plan to his staff thus: 'If Hitler signed it and kept the bargain, well and good … if he broke it, he would demonstrate to all the world that he was totally cynical and untrustworthy … this would have its value mobilising public opinion against him, particularly in America.'[31] Chamberlain's behaviour fits with his secretary's account. On his return to Britain, he gave particular emphasis to the supplementary agreement, holding the piece of paper aloft at Heston airport. The scene was immortalized by the newsreel cameras and a primitive television unit, but British audiences saw the drama from a skewed perspective, for the best camera positions had, apparently on the orders of 10 Downing Street, been given to the American newsreel cameras.[32] But dramatic pictures and ringing phrases could not compensate for the wave of revulsion that swept America following the cession of the Sudetenland. Events transformed the image of the 'piece of paper' contrived to woo American opinion into an enduring icon of political folly.

Of course the prime minister was not alone in attempting to manipulate the media during the crisis. Just as he moved the British fleet onto a war footing, so he activated the country's as yet incomplete propaganda machinery, including a 'black' propaganda campaign against nazi Germany using the facilities of Radio Luxembourg.[33] Whatever the achievements of Britain's clandestine warriors, the shortcomings of overt publicity were many and public. The ministry of information did not open for business until 28 September 1938. It proved so disorganized as to require the dismissal of Sir Stephen Tallents as director-general designate.[34] American correspondents had difficulty covering the House of Commons: only one American press agency had access.[35] Chamberlain's staff added to the problems. In an angry series of articles appearing in the American journal *Editor and Publisher* in October 1938, Walter Harrison of the *Oklahoma City Daily Oklahoman and Times* reported all manner of injustices from 'unofficial censorship' to American journalists being rudely abandoned to the elements outside 10 Downing Street.[36]

Such support as the Americans received came from the usual quarters. At the foreign office news department Rex Leeper pressed on valiantly. In an apparent attempt to press the government into making a stand he released a communiqué assuring the world that if Germany attacked Czechoslovakia both Britain and the Soviet Union would 'certainly stand by France' and fight. His enemies used this gambit as an excuse to kick him upstairs to planning duties, leaving the more pliable Charles Peake in charge of press relations. Yet Leeper's personal campaign had at least awakened key members of the cabinet to the need to cultivate the press. The home secretary, Samuel Hoare, promptly began daily briefings.[37]

In New York, the BLI served as a source of official documents and, to the surprise of the staff, the point of contact for British ex-service volunteers and young Americans eager to join the RAF. The library reported that the peak of demand for BLI material on British policy was immediately before and after the crisis. Americans clearly understood that the BLI was not a source for 'spot news' of 'hour by hour developments'.[38] For the duration of the crisis, the library arranged a special free news wire service for small American papers based on BBC news (as furnished by Reuters).[39] But hour-by-hour coverage came only from the radio, and here the key British performers were not civil servants, but members of the broader Anglo-American set.

During the abdication crisis the American press and broadcasters had learned to make use of the director of the English Speaking Union in London, Sir Frederick Whyte. Whyte had worked in propaganda during the Great War, and later served in positions as varied as MP for Perth, president of the Indian Legislative Assembly and political adviser to Chiang Kai Shek, but by the late 1930s he had found his niche at the helm of the ESU.[40] Whyte was particularly well used by CBS. On 16 September Whyte made the first of many appearances during the crisis, joining Edward R. Murrow on the air to provide what CBS termed 'word pictures of the present European crisis'.[41] Whyte, and his research director Frank Darvall, who also worked with Murrow on the air, clearly represented a valuable resource for the future development of Britain's approach to the United States.

While the Americans had excellent reason to be proud of their performance during the crisis, the BBC had less cause for complacency. Some elements of the BBC's performance during the crisis seemed absurd. Were addresses for obtaining gas-proof kennels for dogs and pamphlets on the protection of domestic animals really a priority? Even so, the foreign office sent formal thanks for the contribution of the home service news department. The BBC's programme policy board felt that a successful balance had been achieved in the extent of government control of the BBC. The controller of programmes noted: 'there was a clear distinction between interference with broadcasting by the Government on its own behalf, of which there was none during the crisis, and advice by the Foreign Office on matters affecting national interests, which would have been sought by the BBC if not first offered.' The only cloud on the horizon was an unfortunate technical error. On 29 September, the corporation launched an investigation into the speeding up of the recording of Chamberlain's remarks on returning from Godesburg, 'which was said to have altered the pitch and thus the general impression of his voice', or, in lay terms, made the prime minister sound squeaky. The BBC eventually blamed 'extraneous circumstances'.[42] The Munich crisis did, however, raise one major issue for future broadcast policy: live coverage of air raids. As the crisis reached its climax, the BBC's man in New York, Felix Green, wrote to the ministry of information regarding the possibility of relaying air raids. It was the perfect radio response to Chamberlain's grim musings on the impact of German airpower as he flew home to London. On 29 September 1938, Sir Stephen Tallents, then acting head of the ministry of information, replied: 'I can see no hope of such programmes being permitted; that would be contrary to standing censorship instructions applicable to press telegrams etc.'[43] This question was not resolved until the summer of 1940.

Britain's Approach to the United States after Munich

The months following Munich brought fresh attempts to consolidate Anglo-American relations. A flurry of treasury concessions delivered the hitherto elusive Anglo-American Trade Agreement on 17 November 1938, thereby removing a long-standing source of friction.[44] The foreign office and its associated committees gave renewed attention to both the planned British pavilion at the New York World's Fair of 1939 and FDR's invitation for the king and queen to visit the United States that summer.[45] Less well known are the contrasting 'post-Munich' approaches to American opinion mounted by the two contenders for the anti-Chamberlain succession – Winston Churchill and Anthony Eden.

Eden and Churchill both had excellent connections to the Anglo-American lobby in Britain. Both men believed in the importance of cultivating American friendship and believed that they knew how to handle American audiences. In the event, both men proceeded to demonstrate the difficulties of approaching the United States. On 16 October, Churchill broadcast a 'Reply to Hitler' over NBC. Castigating Hitler and Mussolini in the words of Byron's ode to Napoleon as 'pagod things of sabre sway, with fronts of brass and feet of clay', Churchill urged the United States to accept its duty to stand with 'the English-speaking peoples'.[46] Opinion divided over the merits of the speech. Although 'rather horrified' by such a 'direct form of propaganda', Ambassador Ronald Lindsay joined the bulk of the American press in conceding that the speech was 'rather good stuff'. William Randolph Hearst, however, demanded a right of reply, and took to the airwaves to condemn British propaganda and schemes 'to dominate Europe, absorb Africa, and control the Orient'. President Roosevelt let it be known that he, too, regarded Churchill's broadcast as 'unfortunate'.[47]

Eden's approach was more subtle. In December 1938 he accepted an invitation to address the National Association of Manufacturers in New York and set out to visit the United States for the first time. His itinerary included meetings with leading American journalists, bankers and politicians, including President Roosevelt. He sailed with Ronald Tree and, by good fortune, the actor Douglas Fairbanks Jr, a regular of the Bruce Lockhart set. Fairbanks revised the drafts of

Eden's speeches and warned the politician not to take American sympathy for granted.[48] Eden's arrival attracted the attention of an American press. The *New York Times* devoted a front page column and the whole of its third page to his arrival and first speech. In his address – delivered on 9 December to one of the largest dinners ever held at the Waldorf-Astoria and broadcast by over 300 CBS affiliates nationwide – Eden declared that Britain was 'neither decadent or faint hearted' in the face of the nazi threat. Avoiding the pit into which Churchill had tumbled, he stressed that Britain did not seek to 'lure others to pull our chestnuts from the fire' and would stand on the principles of its democratic heritage.[49] Moreover, Eden pointedly addressed his message to British listeners. The technique of reaching Americans by allowing them to eavesdrop on stirring words apparently meant for a domestic audience would serve Britain well during the war. In May and June of 1940, Churchill proved that he had learned his lesson.

Eden left the United States profoundly troubled by the scale of the anti-reaction against Munich and Chamberlain. His concern proved infectious.[50] By early 1939 even Roosevelt was tired of Chamberlain's procrastination. When Lord Lothian urged the president to accept the responsibilities of global power in Britain's place, Roosevelt angrily suggested that the British take a 'good stiff grog' and get on with the job themselves.[51] The American journalists in Europe displayed similar concerns. In March 1939, the BLI noted that Vincent Sheean of the *New York Herald Tribune* had both attacked Chamberlain and argued that fascism could not be checked without war. The library concluded that 'this bellicose spirit seems to be gaining ground'.[52]

Worry over American public opinion haunted British policy making during the spring and summer of 1939. When Hitler invaded Czechoslovakia on 15 March 1939, such concern figured largely in the British response.[53] Despite Chamberlain's hope in September 1938 that a German violation of the Munich agreement might rally international opposition to Hitler, he proved slow to respond to the Czech coup. The American press left the foreign office news department in no doubt that Britain's inactivity did little for its standing in America. Despairing, Vansittart wrote: 'if we cannot show more resolution and reprobation than this, we shall certainly lose any possibility of effective cooperation from the United States when our hour comes.' On 17 March, Chamberlain rose to the challenge. In a speech heard over a radio hook-up across the United States, he denounced Hitler's coup and gave the first indication that, from this point on, Britain would take a firm stand against Hitler. His resolve brought Britain one step closer to war and thus gave a new imperative to planning of the country's wartime propaganda machine.[54]

The only parties to emerge victorious from the Munich crisis were the American radio networks. The correspondents who covered the crisis – Ed Murrow, William Shirer and their colleagues – became household names across the United States. The American public was sufficiently unnerved by the experience to be ready to believe the worst when a month after the end of the crisis Orson Welles presented his radio version of the *War of the Worlds*.[55] No one now doubted the power of the radio, least of all at the British Library of Information in New York. The twin phenomena of the persistence of the United States' fear of propaganda and the success of the American radio networks during the Munich crisis conditioned their policy recommendations. Writing on 21 September 1938, Angus Fletcher urged the foreign office not to consider repeating the propaganda methods of the Great War, but advised: 'The principle on which we should proceed is to leave to existing agencies, especially commercial agencies, the work of supplying American needs, and concentrate upon improving facilities for those agencies.'[56] Developing his argument in November, Fletcher noted that unless the British government cultivated the American correspondents in London, the lure of 'spicy news' would draw them to 'find their friends among those who are discontented with the government of the day'. Fletcher continued: 'If, however, someone would take the trouble to cultivate a man like Edward R. Murrow ... it is expected that he would respond.'[57]

In London, Leeper was thinking along similar lines. However, rather than appointing someone to seek out Murrow and his colleagues, he selected a wartime director for British propaganda in the United States who already knew the American broadcasters well. He chose the principal British commentator on CBS during the Munich Crisis, Sir Frederick Whyte.[58] When responsibility for planning propaganda in the United States passed from the foreign office to the ministry of information and a secret enquiry commissioned under the auspices of the Royal Institute of International Affairs, Whyte remained the designated director of its American division and coordinator of American planning.[59] Whyte retained close links to American broadcasters and journalists throughout the planning process. On 1 February and 17 May 1939, he convened closed meetings to discuss both broadcasting and British foreign policy followed at the ESU's Dartmouth House. Whyte acted as chairman, with the contributors drawn from a cross-section of the Atlanticist circle. The meetings represented a confluence of all the developing streams of interest in Britain's cultivation of the United States. American contributors included William Stoneman of the *Chicago Daily News*, Clifford Stark, London bureau chief of the Associated Press, and Harold Callender of the *New York Times*, who was also a member of the ESU's public affairs committee. All the principal speakers had recently visited the United States, and included Ronald Tree, Sir Arthur Willert and Marcel Wallenstein (London correspondent of the *Kansas City Star*). Ed Murrow himself provided a keynote address on the subject of 'The USA and the Post-Munich Situation'.[60]

The minutes of these post-Munich discussions circulated within Whitehall. They established an authoritative picture confirming that American opinion was, with remarkable regional and cross-party consistency, anti-dictator. Yet equally, the speakers reported American opinion to be solidly opposed to propaganda, the war debt and Neville Chamberlain. Thus the discussions served as a powerful endorsement of the view expressed by Willert that 'the people who should explain the English point of view to America were Americans who knew something about England', and specifically the American broadcasters in London. Murrow left his audience in no doubt as to the power of the broadcast word, noting that: 'Americans listened to an average of about 20 broadcasts a day from Europe' and adding, in the words of farmer in Montana: 'You can't have these fellows [Hitler and Mussolini] coming into your dining room without disliking them.'[61]

Interest in transatlantic broadcasting increased with the fall of Czechoslovakia. The British Council called for transatlantic radio exchanges.[62] Ambassador Lindsay, for his part, recalled Munich coverage and appealed for a liberal broadcasting policy in wartime.[63] 'If America ever comes into a European war', he wrote, 'it will be some violent emotional impulse which will provide the last and decisive thrust. Nothing would be so effective as the bombing of London, translated by air into the homes of America.'[64] Unfortunately, the committee of imperial defence remained in the era of the newspaper, requiring that all radio scripts be precensored and transmitted under a cut-out button.[65] American journalists were at least kept fully briefed throughout the summer, and they knew that key officials like Sir Frederick Whyte supported a liberal policy.[66] One war office representative even breached security to ensure that Murrow knew what to expect from British censors if war should come.[67] Both the ministry of information American division and the BBC wartime plans now included sections dedicated to supporting the American networks. Murrow and his colleagues knew that they would not fight for free broadcasting alone.[68]

The early summer of 1939 brought the success of the royal visit and British pavilion at the New York World's Fair, but the failure of attempts to revise the Neutrality Act in the senate. On 20 July 1939 the ministry of information publicity division planners submitted their report. There were few surprises in Sir Frederick Whyte's recommendations for British policy in America. Building on the lessons of Munich he resolved to trust most of their effort to 'American agencies' – commercial newsreel, press and radio. The system threw a burden of supply onto the ministry of information. Whyte thus began the battle to assist their coverage by asking that the Americans be given special access to the press galleries of the House of Commons. The Munich crisis had also shown the value of the BLI. Now, the planners recommended an immediate expansion of the BLI to cope with the anticipated increase in demand for its services. While maintaining the policy of providing information only on request, the planners remained adamant that American public opinion should not be taken for granted. They joined the news department in suggesting library branches in the south, on the west coast, and in the isolationist heartland of Chicago, though fear of the anti-propaganda feeling ensured that this was not done until 1941.[69] Unfortunately, all was not well at the helm of the ministry of information. Neville Chamberlain installed his own men in its higher reaches. His choice of the allegedly pro-fascist Lord Perth as director-general caused particular consternation among American journalists.[70]

Beyond such negative themes, the propaganda planning in the wake of Munich underscored the importance of cooperation with like-minded Americans. The sympathetic Americans had helped with the planning and the British propagandists knew that success in wartime would turn on their continued sympathy. The system that emerged blurred the line between British propaganda and American news reporting. In some instances, the two became interchangeable. For the internationally minded participants of either nationality, it was a single effort for a single cause. As the last hope of peace in Europe withered and died, an Anglo-American 'special relationship of the mind' was born. When war came in September 1939 it found American correspondents ready to cover its events and special departments within the British bureaucracy ready to help.

In one respect, the news lesson of Munich misled the British. They assumed that the war would unfold in the same way as the crisis, with desperate speeches and 'we interrupt this programme …' announcements. Britain designed its propaganda structure for a war of action, news and bombs falling on London. The phoney war would not be so easy to report. The spring of 1940 changed that. The crisis of 1940 combined with the lessons of 1938 to produce a winning combination. It was not so much that the British government unanimously resolved to develop links with the American broadcasters, but rather those members of the elite who already had close links to Murrow and his fellow American journalists were incorporated into the government. The only limitation on their insight, and application of the lessons learned during the broadcasting of the Munich crisis, was the degree to which hardline Chamberlainites remained in key positions. By the summer of 1940, the entire government structure from press officer to minister of information was drawn from the Anglo-American elite and Britain's media approach to the United States really took off. With Churchill at the helm, Eden in the war office, A.V. Alexander at the admiralty and Duff Cooper at the ministry of information, the key members of the war cabinet all knew the need to impress the United States. It was possible to work closely with the American media at home and in the

United States and to begin the job of dispelling the memories of appeasement and begin the slow task of building a new Britain in American minds: a Britain to worthy in due course of American aid. By the autumn of 1941 that task was all but complete.

The story of Britain's war effort has always been a story of a race against time. Historians have often pointed out that had war broken out in 1938 the RAF would have been without its Spitfires. It should also be noted that had war come in 1938 the British would also have lacked the lightness of touch in matters of public relations that later enabled them to do such a good job of telling America about those Spitfires. It was fortunate for British propaganda that policymakers were able to start their learning process in the autumn of 1938; any later and American opinion might have swung towards Britain too late do any more than weep over the ashes.

University of Leicester

NOTES

1. Borah, quoted in Harold Lavine and James Weschler, *War Propaganda in the United States* (New Haven, 1940), p.118. For elaboration, see *Propaganda Analysis*, Vol.2, No.2 (1 Nov. 1938), pp.1–5.
2. These successes are the subject of the author's monograph: Nicholas J. Cull, *Selling War: British Propaganda Against American Neutrality in the Second World War* (New York, 1995), and articles developing specific elements within this story, including: 'Broadcasting and the Art of Understatement: British Radio Propaganda and American Neutrality, 1939–1941', *Historical Journal of Film, Radio and Television*, Vol.13, No.4 (1993), pp.403–31; 'Selling Peace: The Origins, Promotion and Fate of the Anglo-American New Order during the Second World War', *Diplomacy & Statecraft*, Vol.7, No.1 (1996), pp.1–28; 'Overture to an Alliance: British Propaganda and the New York World's Fair of 1939', *Journal of British Studies*, Vol.16, No.3 (1997), pp.325–54; and 'Faked Boundaries: Latin America, "Nazi Maps" and Britain's Secret War Against United States Neutrality', *LABSA Journal (Latin American British Studies Association)*, Vol.1, No.2 (1997), pp.9–20.
3. Neville Chamberlain Diary, 19 Feb. 1938. Chamberlain Papers, Birmingham University: NC 2/24 A, 19 Feb. 1938.
4. John Harvey (ed.), *The Diplomatic Diary of Oliver Harvey 1937–1940* (London, 1970), p.73, 18 Jan. 1938.
5. Christopher Thorne, *Border Crossings* (New York, 1988), p.69.
6. Cull, *Selling War*, pp.10–11; Philip M. Taylor, *The Projection of Britain* (Cambridge, 1981); and on the BLI's India list, see PRO FO 395/612, P2484/643/150, Fletcher (BLI) to Ridsdale (News Dept.), 9 Aug. 1938.
7. Philip M. Taylor, 'If War Should Come: Preparing the Fifth Arm for Total War 1935–1939', *Journal of Contemporary History*, Vol.16 (1981), pp.27–51; Robert

Cole, 'The Conflict Within: Stephen Tallents and Planning Propaganda Overseas before the Second World War', *Albion*, Vol.12 (1982), pp.50–71.

8. PRO PREM 1/272, Report submitted 28 May 1938.
9. On the FARA see Manfred Jonas, *Isolationism in America, 1935–41* (Ithaca, 1969), p.138.
10. PRO FO 115/3418/224, Mallet (Embassy) to Halifax, 20 Jan. 1939; Raymond Clapper, 'Dies on Trial', *Washington Daily News*, 24 Aug. 1938; 'Mr. Dies Goes to Town', *Propaganda Analysis*, Vol.3 No.4 (15 Jan. 1940), pp.43–52.
11. PRO FO 395/611, P2089/643/150, Lindsay to FO, 14 June 1938; PRO FO 395/612, P2340/643/150, Lindsay to Halifax, No.666, 15 July 1938.
12. PRO FO 395/611, P2205/643/150 and PRO FO 395/616, P2345/1157/150, Leeper (News Dept.) to Bridge (British Council), 27 July 1938.
13. PRO FO 395/616, P2345/1157/150, Lindsay to Leeper, 10 July 1938.
14. Michael Sanders and Philip M. Taylor, *British Propaganda during the First World War, 1914–1918* (London, 1982), pp.167–207.
15. PRO FO/395/616, P2345/1157/150, minute of meeting of 26 July 1938, Leeper to Vansittart, 27 July 1938. Present: Lothian, Leeper, Fletcher, Darvall, Col. Josiah Wedgewood MP (1872–1943, later 1st Baron Wedgewood), Lord de la Warr (1900–1976: former parliamentary under-secretary of state for colonial affairs and at this time Lord Privy Seal), A.P. Herbert (1880–1971: writer and independent MP for Oxford University), Sir Geoffrey Fry (1881–1965: private Secretary to Lord Baldwin) and A.C.B. Bossom, 1881–1965, a British architect who had worked extensively in the United States, married an American and founded 'The Co-operative Government Movement'. Biographical information *Who's Who* (London: various).
16. PRO FO 395/616, P2345/1157/150, Leeper to Bridge (British Council), 27 July 1938.
17. PRO FO 395/616, P2345/1157/150, memo Leeper to Vansittart, 27 July 1938.
18. PRO 395/616, P2367/1157/150, memo by Angus Fletcher, 2 Aug. 1938; Josiah Wedgewood and Allan Nevins, *Forever Freedom* (Harmondsworth, 1940).
19. PRO FO 395/616, P2345/1157/150, Leeper to Vansittart, 27 July 1938.
20. John Gunther, *The Story of the Inside Books: A Fragment of Autobiography* (London, 1962), p.5. For general background, see Robert W. Desmond, *Crisis and Conflict: World News Reporting between Two 1920–1940* (Iowa, 1982), Ch.14; David H. Hosely, *As Good As Any: Foreign Correspondence on American Radio, 1930–1940* (Westport, CT, 1984); David Culbert, *News for Everyman: Radio and Foreign Affairs in Thirties America* (Westport, CT, 1976).
21. The key anti-nazi books published by American journalists during this period included Dorothy Thompson, *I Saw Hitler* (New York, 1932), and Edgar Mowrer, *Germany Puts the Clock Back* (New York, 1933); both of them earned expulsion from Germany on the strength of their work; John Gunther, *Inside Europe* (New York, 1935) and Vincent Sheean's, *Personal History* (New York, 1935).
22. Interviews: Graham Hutton and Helen Kirkpatrick. Vincent Sheehan came to know Churchill while on holiday in the South of France: Vincent Sheehan, *Between the Thunder and the Sun* (New York, 1943), pp.30–33; Ronald Tree recalled particularly his friendship with Knickerbocker and Gunther: Tree, *When the Moon was High* (London, 1975), pp.93–4.
23. Interviews: James Reston (30 March 1989) and Wallace Carroll (16 July 1993).
24. Interviews: Janet Murrow (14 Nov. 1988), Drew Middleton (2 Feb. 1989), Eric Sevareid (30 March 1989); A.M. Sperber, *Murrow: His Life and Times* (London, 1986) Ch.3; R. Franklin Smith, *Edward R. Murrow: The War Years* (Kalamazoo, MI, 1978), pp.7–12; Joseph E. Persico, *Edward R. Murrow: An American Original* (New York, 1988), p.148.
25. FO 395/616, P2345/1157/150, Leeper to Lindsay, 6 Sept. 1938.
26. For transcriptions of the CBS broadcasts during the crisis see State Historical Society

234

of Wisconsin: NBC papers, Box 61/42, CBS, Crisis, Sept. 1938. A narrative of broadcasting during the crisis may be found in Robert J. Brown, *Manipulating the Ether: The Power of Broadcast Radio in Thirties America* (Jefferson, NC, 1998), pp.160–72.

27. *Documents on German Foreign Policy, 1918–1945* (Washington, DC, 1951), Series D, (1937–1945), Vol.4, Dieckhoff to Ribbentrop, 30 Sept. 1938, p.633.

28. PRO FO 395/622, P/2755/2645/150, Fletcher to Leeper, 28 Sept. 1938.

29. PRO FO 395/656, P/151/151/150, Wrench to Leeper, 6 Jan. 1939.

30. PRO FO 395/656, minute by Beith (American Department), 24 Jan. 1939.

31. Alec Douglas-Home, *The Way the Wind Blows: An Autobiography* (New York, 1976), p.66.

32. Philip M. Taylor, 'Film as Evidence', presentation to Summer School of Institute of Contemporary British History, London School of Economics, July 1989. For a still from the American cameras, see Raymond Fielding, *The American Newsreel, 1911–1967* (Norman, OK, 1972), p.262. On the TV unit, see BBC/WAC: R.34/325.

33. Nicholas Pronay and Philip M. Taylor, 'An Improper Use of Broadcasting', *Journal of Contemporary History*, Vol.18 (1983), pp.357–84.

34. On the MoI in September 1938, see PRO INF 1/15 and INF 1/17, also Taylor, *The Projection of Britain*, p.275; Taylor, 'If War Should Come...', pp.42–5.

35. PRO FO 395/616, P3423/1157/150, Sir Owen Chalkey to Scott (FO American department), 12 Dec. 1938; Minute by Warner, 23 Dec. 1938.

36. *Editor and Publisher*, 1 Oct. 1938 and 8 Oct. 1938; PRO FO 395/623, P3147/2646/150, Wilberforce to Leeper, 22 Oct. 1938.

37. Taylor, *The Projection of Britain*, pp.36–37; Viscount Templewood, *Nine Troubled Years* (London, 1954), p.318; Richard Cockett, *Twilight of Truth* (London, 1989), pp.82–5.

38. PRO FO 395/640, P/340/36/150, Fletcher and Wilberforce (Directors), BLI: Annual Report 1938, Jan. 1939, p.2. PRO FO 395/656, P368/151/150. Fletcher to FO, 25 Nov. 1939.

39. PRO FO 395/656, P/368/151/150, Fletcher to News Department, 25 Nov. 1938.

40. Interview: Ann Thoms (née Whyte), 5 July 1988.

41. For transcriptions the Murrow/Whyte's CBS broadcast of 16 September 1938 see SHSW: NBC papers, Box: 61/42, 'CBS Crisis September 1938' (transcription of all CBS Munich coverage compiled in November 1938).

42. BBC/WAC: R.34/325 and BBC/WAC R.34/600/10, PPB minutes, 6 Oct. 1938.

43. PRO INF 1/183, Graves (BBC) to Woodburn (MoI), 12 April 1939.

44. David Reynolds, *The Creation of the Anglo-American Alliance* (London, 1981), pp.52–3.

45. Cull, 'Overture to an Alliance' *British Studies*, Vol.36, No.3 (1997), pp.325–45; and David Reynolds, 'FDR's Foreign Policy and the British Royal Visit to the USA, 1939', *The Historian*, Vol.45 (1983), pp.461–72.

46. New York Times, 17 Oct. 1938.

47. *New York Journal and American*, 22 Oct. 1938; PRO FO 395/623, P3147/2646/150, Wilberforce (BLI) to Leeper, 27 Oct. 1938 and P3030/2645/150, Leeper to Lindsay, 18 Oct. 1938 and Minute by Halifax, 5 Nov. 1938; For text of Hearst's speech see State Historical Society of Wisconsin, Madison: NBC papers, Box 61/43.

48. Tree, *When the Moon was High,* pp.79–81. Interview: Douglas Fairbanks Jr (9 March 1990).

49. *New York Times*, 10 and 14 Dec. 1938.

50. Harold Nicolson, *A Diary with Letters*, Vol.1 (London, 1967), p.383.

51. Reynolds, *The Creation of the Anglo-American Alliance*, pp.43–4.

52. PRO FO 395/657, P976/151/150, Alan Dudley to News Dept., 10 March 1939; *New York Herald Tribune*, 5 March 1939.

53. Sidney Aster, *1939* (New York, 1973), pp.34, 75.
54. PRO FO 371/22993, C3313/19/18 and FO 371/22966, C3102/15/18.
55. For analysis, see Robert J. Brown, *Manipulating the Ether: The Power of Broadcasting in Thirties America* (Jefferson, NC, 1997), pp.195–254.
56. PRO FO 395/616, P2769/1157/150, memo on British propaganda in the United States during the Great War, 21 Sept. 1938.
57. PRO FO 395/656, P368/151/150, Fletcher to News Department, 25 Nov. 1938, 'Memorandum on British propaganda in the United States'.
58. PRO FO 395/624, P2853/2853/150, minute by Warner, 6 Oct. 1938; Whyte to Leeper, 28 Sept. 1938; P2960/2853/G, Leeper to Whyte, 1 Nov. 1938.
59. PRO INF 1/20, subfiles A and B; PRO INF 1/755.
60. BLPES: Charles Webster papers, 7/7, minutes of ESU private group discussion, 'The USA and the Post-Munich Situation', 1 Feb. 1939; also PRO FO 395/657, P2474/151/150, minutes of ESU private group discussion, 'The USA and the European Situation', held 17 May 1939, forwarded to the FO by Frank Darvall (ESU), 16 June 1939, and circulated widely within FO including foreign publicity department (FPD) to BLI and embassy, 11 July 1939. On American use of BBC studio facilities, see BBC/WAC: E.1/110, correspondence circa April 1939.
61. Webster Papers, 7/7.
62. PRO FO 395/640, P1254/37/150, Col. Bridge (British Council) to Warner (news dept), 29 March 1939.
63. PRO FO 395/656, P368/151/150, Lindsay to Warner (news dept), 3 Feb. 1939.
64. PRO FO 395/648, P1120/6/150, Lindsay to Leeper, 17 March 1939.
65. PRO INF 1/183, Leeper to Sir Ernest Fass (MoI director general designate), 5 April 1939; PRO FO 395/647, P2078/105/150, CID subcommittee on MoI, 'Transmission by Radio Telephony of Programmes for Broadcasting Overseas', C.N. Ryan (joint secretary to the subcommittee), 25 May 1939.
66. BBC: WAC, R 61/2, 'Transatlantic Broadcasting: Report of a Private Discussion held at the English Speaking Union', 1 June 1939.
67. PRO INF 1/719, general meeting of enquiry of 'channels of publicity', meeting No.8, 4 April 1939, item 57; PRO FO 395/647, P2078/105/150, minutes by Dudley and Warner (news dept), 8 June 1939; Leeper to Lindsay, 13 June 1939.
68. See Cull, 'Broadcasting and the Art of Understatement' *HJFRT*, Vol.13, No.4 (1993), pp.403–31.
69. Planning section; memo No.271 'Report on the British Service of Information in the United States in Time of War', 20 July 1939.
70. PRO FO 395/640, P2715/105/150, BLI to news dept, 20 June 1939.

Searching for Peace in Munich, not Geneva: The British Government, the League of Nations and the Sudetenland Question

PETER J. BECK

At 1400 hours on 1 October 1938 German troops entered the first area of the Czech Sudetenland to be occupied in accordance with the recently concluded four power Munich agreement.[1] Their entry, signalling yet another German success in revising borders defined by the 1919 Versailles treaties, prompted the exodus of an ever growing number of Czechs, whose plight was among agenda items discussed at the next session of the League of Nations council held in January 1939. Significantly, the council was dealing already with the Austrian refugee problem consequent upon a previous phase of German expansionism, that is, the *Anschluss* of March 1938.[2]

In many respects, the council's concentration on nonpolitical developments, though giving it a meaningful role in Czech affairs, highlighted the manner in which the League of Nations, another creation of the discredited peace treaties, had failed in its fundamental peacekeeping role. Despite being in scheduled session for most of September 1938 and including Czechoslovakia among its membership, the league was bypassed by events. Berchtesgaden, Godesberg, and then Munich, alongside Berlin, London, Paris, Prague and Rome, proved the principal focus of attention and, during the month's closing days, the eyes of the world were fixed on Munich, not Geneva, to see whether the Czech crisis could be resolved without recourse to war.[3] From this perspective, the resulting Munich agreement reaffirmed the resolve of Britain and France, the league's leading members, to deal with the German question through more direct diplomatic channels. In turn, it became even easier to dismiss the league as a political irrelevance located in a Swiss backwater cut off from the diplomatic mainstream. And yet, paradoxically, its invaluable refugee work – in December 1938, the Nansen International office won the 1938 Nobel peace prize – illustrated the manner in which this role was continuing to grow in the wake of political problems kept away from Geneva.[4]

From Manchuria to Munich via Ethiopia

Looking back from the league's final session held at Geneva in 1946, Philip Noel Baker, minister of state at the foreign office, observed: 'We know the World War began in Manchuria 15 years ago ... Manchuria, Abyssinia, Munich have killed another great illusion, the belief that appeasement, seeking the national interest at the expense of others, ... could bring us peace.'[5] The League of Nations, albeit viewed as a product of the nineteenth-century 'Concert of Europe', proved a novel feature of post-1919 international affairs, and particularly a new factor to be considered by governments during the formulation and conduct of foreign policy. In the event, the 'new diplomacy', defined to mean arbitration, disarmament, and collective security through the league, failed in the face of the more enduring 'old diplomacy', rearmament and force.

The Manchurian (1931–33) and Ethiopian (1935–36) crises, like the failure of the disarmament conference, figure prominently as major stages in what many interpret as the downward spiral culminating in the league's eventual demise and replacement by the UN. Noel-Baker's assertion reminds us that, in many respects, the 1938 Czech crisis, though rarely considered as part of this sequence, represented perhaps the most serious setback to the league's peacekeeping role throughout its brief period of life. After all, as Earl de la Warr, the British delegate, told the assembly on 16 September 1938, 'the League was created in consequence of a war which came near to destroying the foundations on which our civilization had been built', and, for many people, the events of September 1938 offered perhaps the closest resemblance hitherto to the events preceding the First World War.[6] In Britain, immediately prior to the Munich Conference, vivid images of a country preparing for war were conveyed by the media, which reported, say, trenches being dug in London parks, queues at gas mask fitting stations, the mobilization of the fleet, and the plans for the evacuation of children upon the outbreak of war. Neville Chamberlain, the prime minister, emphasized the danger in a parliamentary statement delivered on 28 September: 'Today, we are faced with a situation which has had no parallel since 1914'.[7] But August 1914 was not repeated in September 1938, for a note from Hitler enabled Chamberlain to interrupt his address to announce the Munich Conference, thereby allowing MPs to disperse 'in an atmosphere tingling with relief and with hope'.[8]

League Appearances and Realities

A year or so earlier, the opening of the *Palais des Nations*, the league's grandiose headquarters building located on the shores of Lake Geneva, gave the impression of business as usual in spite of the fact that there existed a widening gulf between appearances and realities; thus, the league was being pushed increasingly to the sidelines of international affairs, even if those threatened or invaded were members of the league.

Despite occasional supranational visions, as reflected in the abortive Geneva Protocol (1924), the league remained an intergovernmental organization operating in a world of sovereign nation states: 'it existed merely to help states do together what they could not so easily do alone. The watch-word was voluntarism through and through.'[9] This principle defined the framework within which the league performed what both contemporaries and historians have viewed as its central function, that is, the preservation of peace, and particularly the prevention of another 1914-type war. Individual members were allowed to do what seemed appropriate and desirable, which, of course, might just as easily be nothing as a lot. By 1938, the league seemed to have failed the test as far as peacekeeping was concerned, even if it soldiered on, held regular council and assembly sessions, and the covenant was 'reformed' to accommodate changed conditions. But the league, though often supported in this period's ministerial rhetoric, rarely figured as a priority in the minds of policymakers working for the great powers, as evidenced by not only the relative lack of meaningful league references in the archives but also the way in which international histories covering the late 1930s concentrate upon the great powers. This was, of course, a serious weakness for an intergovernmental organization, and was reflected in the declining status of league delegations, diminishing media coverage of its proceedings, and withdrawals from membership. Even worse, in some countries the league aroused strong hostility; in particular, the German, Italian and Japanese governments, having departed from its ranks, refused subsequently to recognize its jurisdiction in matters appertaining to their respective interests.[10] Unsurprisingly, their escalating threats to the territorial integrity and political independence of league members, like Albania, Austria, China or Czechoslovakia, were treated as unsuitable cases for reference to Geneva.

Chamberlain's Dismissal of the League Option

During the late 1930s, Anglo-French influence over the league's evolution was accentuated by the departure of Germany, Italy and Japan alongside the continued absence of the USA. The Soviet Union's belated accession in 1934 failed to alter the fact that, during this crucial period, a majority of the seven major powers were non-members. Obviously, insiders, like Britain and France, exerted considerable influence, but the league's peacekeeping role was not unaffected by the attitude of powerful outsiders, given a natural Anglo-French reluctance to push for action in a direction likely to be opposed by them.

Like their French counterparts, British governments approached the league in a pragmatic and instrumental manner; thus, they sought to ensure that it evolved according to an assessment of present-day *national* policy interests rather than doctrinaire internationalism. Despite being reelected in 1935 on a pro-league platform, the national government in Britain was not distinguished by practical support for the league's political work. This trend became more pronounced once Neville Chamberlain, who shared the basic antipathy towards the league displayed by many members of the Conservative Party, succeeded Baldwin as prime minister in May 1937. Significantly, in June 1936 Chamberlain had been to the fore through his 'midsummer of madness' speech at the 1900 Club in calling for the end of league sanctions against Italy.[11]

Chamberlain's preference to retain direct control over decisionmaking, in conjunction with the adoption of a proactive approach towards the dictators, contributed to British predominance in determining what became the league's virtual non-role in the German problem and other major international issues: 'It is perfectly evident, surely, now that force is the only argument Germany understands, and that "collective security" cannot offer any prospect of preventing such events until it can show a visible force of overwhelming strength backed by determination to use it.'[12] He inclined to methods 'which don't require meetings at Geneva and resolutions by dozens of small nations who have no responsibilities'. In any case, the German government, dismissing the bankrupt and 'worthless' nature of collective security, refused to accept league jurisdiction in any matter affecting its interests.[13] After all, Hitler, declaring that 'we shall not return to Geneva', had walked out of the disarmament conference, and then the league.[14] Subsequently, the British embassy in Berlin reaffirmed that Hitler's attitude towards the league still 'remains hostile as before', even if for a time he employed a possible return to Geneva as a bargaining counter, as happened in the wake of the 1936 Rhineland crisis.[15] But by 1938 Hitler had stopped doing this, given his fundamental hostility to a body viewed as synonymous with the 1919 *status quo*. Clearly, the German government would neither accept nor recognize any league intervention in the Sudeten question.[16] Indeed, such interference was deemed likely to render any peaceful solution more difficult, while doing little for the league's battered reputation.

Against this background, by the early months of 1938, Chamberlain was prepared to risk the opprobrium of the electorate and the opposition parties by making his reservations public, especially as Anthony Eden's resignation as foreign secretary removed one of the government's more visible league supporters:

> At the last Election it was still possible to hope that the League might afford collective security. *I believed it myself.* I do not believe it now ... The League as constituted today is unable to provide collective security for anybody ... we must not try to delude ourselves, and still more, we must not try to delude small weak nations, into thinking that they will be protected by the League against aggression and acting accordingly, when we know that nothing of the kind can be expected.[17]

Within days, Germany's takeover of Austria gave substance to this parliamentary assertion, which prompted alarm on the part of league supporters both at home and abroad.[18] Moreover, as Chamberlain informed his cabinet colleagues, 'the present weakness [of the league] becomes greater after each failure'.[19] The dominion high commissioners agreed, and, coming together in March 1938 with representatives of the dominions office, seconded the British government's view that resort to the league for the Austrian question 'would only expose its impotence'.[20]

By contrast, a large part of public opinion retained faith in the league's peacekeeping role, even in Britain, where a league-based foreign policy was pressed strongly by the League of Nations Union (LNU). Admittedly, membership, having peaked at *circa* 407,000 in 1931, declined throughout the 1930s (1939: 193,000), but the LNU, presenting itself as 'an all-party organization pledged to support the principles of the Covenant of the League of Nations, and their application by any Government, whatever its political complexion may be', remained an active force in British politics.[21] League supporters, whose 'uncritical loyalty' and 'messianic zeal' for collective security was undeterred by the Manchurian and Ethiopian setbacks, blamed such failures on Britain and other leading members, not the league itself, while believing that collective security could work next time, even against Germany.[22]

In reality, the *Anschluss*, suggesting also that Czechoslovakia was next on Hitler's shopping list, highlighted the league's political irrelevance. Thus, inaction proved a function of the view of leading members that, by this time, the league's peacekeeping role was largely redundant, especially as its proven inability to contain great power aggression was compounded by the covenant's close identification with the much criticized peace treaties. The *Anschluss* also raised serious questions for small states, which were left to draw their own conclusions about the strength of the protective umbrella still provided through the league. Few drew reassuring answers. Despite strong indignation expressed by certain delegates about the 'serious infringement' of the covenant arising from the annexation of one of its members, the league council merely took note of the German communication announcing Austria's incorporation in the Reich and the consequent termination of its league membership.[23] As a result, by

April 1938, to quote *The Times,* 'the League of Nations has dropped further into the background, and the well-tried method of the old diplomacy is being taken up again'.[24] The league existed, but the Chamberlain government believed that its key foreign policy objectives were best pursued through other channels.

Calls for a League-Based Policy towards the Sudetenland Question

During September 1938, the spectre of Armageddon brought the Czech crisis to the forefront of world attention. *The Times*, welcoming Chamberlain's return from his 'peace mission' to Berchtesgaden (15–16 September), observed that it was basically a 'question of method' of resolving the Sudeten question.[25] Demands for a league-based policy from the TUC congress, meeting at Blackpool (7–8 September 1938), the LNU, as well as from both the Labour and Liberal parties, among others, failed to deflect the Chamberlain government from its basic line, as emphasized on 16 September by de la Warr's statement at the league assembly.[26] Pointing to its lack of universality and the growing problem of rearmament, de la Warr argued that the league was faced now with a situation never contemplated by its founders. The British government wished to preserve the institution – 'if the League did not exist today, statesmen would be seeking means of constructing a league' – but took a realistic view of its capabilities and limitations, particularly given its apparent role in preserving the 1919 *status quo* rather than facilitating peaceful change.[27] In this vein, the sixth committee's discussions about league reform were employed to announce the British government's opt-out from article 16 of the covenant, the sanctions article.

The Labour Party, attacking the government' rejection of the league option for the Sudeten problem, employed these developments to launch an attack on the government's priorities. Speaking at St Austell on 23 September, Herbert Morrison asserted:

> We are paying the price not only for the evil and short-sighted peace treaties of 1918 [*sic*], but still more for the steady drift from the League of Nations and from the collective organisation which has characterised British policy since 1931.

If we go on as we are the world will fall to pieces. How long will it be before the nations understand that the way out is by the strong and confident collective organisation of the peaceful nations?[28]

On the same date, the LNU executive committee, pointing to Britain's 'progressive abandonment' of the league, regretted the government's choice of 'a different procedure' in defiance of both the alleged will of the people and its general election pledges.[29]

But, for the British government, the Sudeten crisis was not interpreted as a suitable case for league treatment. Indeed, addressing the House of Commons on 28 September, Chamberlain moved on from a critique of the peace treaties to express regrets about the repeated failure to employ article XIX of the covenant for peaceful change: 'For that omission all members of the League must bear the responsibility.'[30] In turn, his interruption of this parliamentary statement to announce acceptance of Hitler's invitation for the Munich Conference reinforced the government's rejection of the 'new diplomacy'. Nor did the French government press a league strategy. Butler, who often stressed the need to make the Geneva atmosphere 'more real', summarized his reading of the French position: 'As the French have so rightly pointed out to me in conversations which I have had with them, supposing that Czechoslovakia were to invoke the use of article 17 [dealing with non-members] it would be rather difficult to use it against Germany and thereby help to gain herself allies for a fight.'[31]

The League Soldiers on, September 1938

Anglo-French rejection of the league-based 'new diplomacy' was illustrated most graphically in September 1938 when the German threat to Czechoslovakia came to a head. The Sudetenland problem was resolved, at least in the short term, principally through direct great power exchanges conducted at Berchtesgaden (15–16 September) and Godesberg (22–23 September) followed by the Munich Conference (29–30 September). Although both the council (9–17, 26–30 September) and assembly (12–30 September) were in scheduled session at Geneva throughout the crisis – 49 governments, including the Czech government, were represented – the league was not seized of the Czech problem. The league's role was confined to debate, not action, but even then 'debate' was restricted to little more than the occasional brief reference.

British and French priorities were indicated by the presence at Munich of Neville Chamberlain and Eduard Daladier, their respective prime ministers. The simultaneous league session, where the British delegation was led by de la Warr (Lord Privy Seal) and Richard Butler (parliamentary undersecretary of state at the foreign office), received a lesser ministerial presence. Admittedly, Lord Halifax, upholding the tradition of attendance by British foreign ministers, had been scheduled to leave for Geneva on 9 September, but the escalating Czech crisis led him to remain in London ready for consultations and emergency cabinet meetings.[32] Georges Bonnet, his French counterpart, made a flying visit to Geneva on 11 September, when he used his brief stay principally for informal conversations with Butler and Litvinov, the Soviet delegate, among others; indeed, the opportunity to meet Litvinov proved a prime reason for his trip.[33] His absence from the assembly itself meant that Britain's second team was paralleled by a French delegation composed of yesterday's men, that is, former ministers like Paul-Boncour or Paul Elbel.[34] Of course, the German and Italian governments, the other two participants at Munich, were no longer represented at Geneva.[35] Significantly, Hitler employed his speech delivered at Nuremberg on 12 September 1938 – this happened also to be the assembly's opening day – to make his usual anti-league jibe; thus, he argued that the 1935 Anglo-German naval agreement 'meant for European peace more than all the talk made in Geneva's League of Nations'.[36] Admittedly, Czechoslovakia, the victim faced with dismemberment or force, was represented at Geneva, but its delegation, lacking Kamil Krofta, the foreign minister, proved invisible, as highlighted by its failure to deliver an assembly statement. Another significant absentee was the Polish foreign minister, Józef Beck, whose disillusionment with the league – he told the British ambassador even before the *Anschluss* that the league was 'finished' – was reflected also in his government's decision not to seek reelection to the council.[37]

Throughout its session, held between 12 and 30 September, the assembly was 'overshadowed' by events elsewhere.[38] The agenda, noteworthy for the absence of the Sudeten question, implied the league's powerlessness in current conditions, particularly respecting what contemporaries saw as the most serious international crisis since the First World War. Admittedly, the league remained seized of the Sino-Japanese dispute, but hitherto China had received little more than moral support. More importantly, the nonrepresentation of Austria, reports about the plight of Austrian refugees, and Emperor Haile Selassie's complaints about the exclusion of the Ethiopian problem, offered delegates a vivid reminder of the league's recent failings. Furthermore, recent notices of withdrawal from Salvador (August 1937), Italy (December 1937), Chile (June 1938) and Venezuela (July 1938) highlighted the league's increasing lack of universality. For delegates, the growing sense of crisis was emphasized by the fact that even neutral Switzerland was making special defence arrangements, as evidenced by plans for the reinforcement of frontier forces and a trial blackout of the whole country.[39] Symbolically, the *Palais des Nations* was not unaffected by the blackout, which took place on 27 September.

Jordan (New Zealand), opening the assembly, observed that it was 20 years since governments, shaken by the First World War, adopted 'a new code of international behavior'.[40] He noted continued 'confusion' about the institution's fundamental predicament: had the league failed its members or had the nations failed the league? Whatever the reason, Jordan pointed to the need to regain the road that had been lost, but conceded the league's non-role in the Czech crisis: 'I'm sure you would not have me say one word that might add to the perplexities of those who today bear such heavy responsibility We hope that peace will be preserved.'[41] Meanwhile, Eamon de Valera (Eire), who was elected president, continued this theme: 'the League had been acclaimed some 20 years ago as providing the alternative that reason suggested to the madness of force. Let us cling to it and seek to make it effective by using it as an instrument for the righting of international wrong wherever it exists.' In effect, Jordan and de Valera, though articulating members' hopes for a peaceful outcome, admitted international realities, most notably, the fact that there was no prospect of 'using it as an instrument' for the solution of the Czech problem. Nor was the league adjudged likely to do more in the Sino-Japanese dispute. In fact, what is striking about newspapers published in September 1938 is the juxtaposition of the Sudetenland and Sino-Japanese disputes. Like Czechoslovakia, China was subjected to escalating pressure from a predatory power, as demonstrated by the fact that the week or so preceding the Munich Conference saw press reports about the Japanese advance on Hankow and 47,000 Chinese deaths in one battle sector over a four-week period.[42] But the league, faced by China's appeal and Japan's refusal to accept the obligations of the covenant for the purpose of the dispute, was not expected to do much beyond offering moral support to the victim. There was no prospect of military sanctions.[43]

Unsurprisingly, several delegates criticized the league's agenda, or rather what was not listed thereupon.[44] On 19 September, Alvarez del Vayo, speaking for Spain, complained that members, standing aside from events in, say, Austria, China and Czechoslovakia, were playing the game of the totalitarian states. Two days later, his views were echoed by Maxim Litvinov, who not only disclaimed any Soviet responsibility for the current crisis but also argued that the league was still strong enough to take collective action: 'Four nations have already been sacrificed, and a fifth is next on the list.'[45] And yet, he lamented, these disputes 'passed unnoticed by the League of Nations'.

Nor did the Czech government seek to disturb the situation. President Eduard Benes, though not an uncritical league supporter, had been closely associated with the 'new diplomacy', as evidenced by his involvement with proposals for the Geneva Protocol in the mid-1920s and one-time speculation about his candidature for the secretary-general's post.[46] At the same time, recent events – significantly, he acted as president of the assembly dealing with the Ethiopian dispute in 1935 – led Benes to acknowledge international realities, including the difficulty of getting key actors to accept recourse to Geneva.[47]

> At the time of the Austrian crisis I was waiting to see what the Great Powers, France and Great Britain, were going to do, and whether Austria or some other country would turn to the League of Nations But in 1938 all Europe was already so far gone that Geneva as an instrument of European democracy was already dead. This was proved on several other occasions before the League itself closed down during the war.[48]

Following the *Anschluss*, the Czech government continued to watch 'what the Great Powers, France and Great Britain, were going to do'; indeed, the league proved a significant omission from Benes' broadcast on the Sudeten crisis to the Czech people on 10 September.[49] On 19 September, Benes, shocked by Anglo-French proposals for the cession of Sudetenland, touched briefly on the league dimension during a lengthy exchange with Alexandrovsky, the Soviet ambassador in Prague. The Czech president, complaining that the league moved too slowly for the country's needs, proved sceptical about the prospects for Geneva-based collective action.[50] Nor did the uncertainties about Soviet intentions help. Despite Litvinov's pro-league pronouncements, Benes was not alone in suspecting a mismatch between appearances and realities; thus, Robert Coulondre, the French ambassador in Moscow, accused the Soviet government of 'taking shelter behind the League of Nations' at a time when even Litvinov conceded the league's impotence.[51]

As a result, the league remained outside the international mainstream, thereby forcing those at Geneva to look on as events unfolded elsewhere. On 25 September, de Valera, broadcasting from Geneva to the USA, told listeners that assembly delegates were following closely and anxiously diplomatic efforts to resolve the Czech crisis.[52] Two days later, he sent Chamberlain a message supporting his peace mission: 'let nothing daunt you or deflect you in your efforts to secure peace' and save people from 'terrible doom'.[53] Subsequently, on 29 September, the assembly, still avoiding any meaningful intervention, reaffirmed its virtual non-role in the Czech crisis when adopting a resolution expressing grave anxiety at the European situation and advocating reliance on peaceful methods.

> Representatives of 49 states meeting as delegates to the Assembly of the League of Nations have watched with deep and growing anxiety, the development of the present grave situation in Europe. The Assembly is convinced that the existing differences are capable of being solved by peaceful means. It knows that recourse to war, whatever be its outcome, is no guarantee of a just settlement, and that it must inevitably bring untold suffering to millions of individuals and imperil the whole structure of civilisation in Europe. The Assembly therefore, voicing the

prayers of the people of all countries, expresses the earnest hope that no government will attempt to impose a settlement by force.[54]

In this manner, league members gave the appearance of doing something, but did nothing of substance, as evidenced by the lack of any meaningful discussion of the Czech question.

Naturally, news of the Munich agreement was greeted with relief and satisfaction in Geneva, where de Valera employed the assembly's closing session, held as scheduled on 30 September, to review the rapid pace of events paralleling the assembly's session. Rejoicing at news of the Munich agreement, he drew a picture of a world brought back from the edge of a precipice: 'One thing at least is certain. The public opinion of the world stood out against the making of war on a question it believed capable of a peaceful solution.'[55] The conflict potential of minority problems led him to urge members to continue the process of reform of the covenant in spite of fears, fuelled by the way in which several members, including Britain, had already declared their freedom of action under article XVI, that the league would be reformed out of existence, at least as a peacekeeping body. Paradoxically, the September 1938 assembly agreed to remove one of Germany's key complaints by formally separating the covenant from the peace treaties, but this concession, undertaken as part of the 'reform' process, came too late to exert any impact upon events in general or German attitudes in particular. In the event, the sense of ongoing crisis meant that the assembly was adjourned, not closed, even if recent history suggested that the league was unlikely to be called upon to play a major part in dealing with the escalating German threat. Within a year, the German occupation of Prague and the Polish problem proved the point.

Munich's British Parliamentary Postscript

The general sense of relief consequent upon the Munich agreement did not prevent the articulation of critiques regarding both the contents and the mode of its conclusion. One early pro-league view was articulated by Sir Archibald Sinclair, the Liberal Party leader, who issued a statement regretting that 'the destinies of Europe now rest in the hands, not of the League of Nations, but of the four powers, Germany, Italy, France, and Britain'.[56] Of course, the continent's destinies had never been in the league's hands, but this failed to prevent the use of mythologies to make a point.

In Britain, four days of parliamentary debate, yielding varying perspectives, encouraged several speakers, particularly those in the House of Lords, to reappraise the league's position in international affairs. Predictably, speakers from the Liberal and Labour parties gave greater prominence to the league dimension. Indeed, the Commons amendment moved by the Labour opposition critical of government policy towards Czechoslovakia included demands for 'active support of the method of collective security through the League of Nations'.[57] Predictably, given the national government's large majority, on 6 October the government's motion was passed by a substantial majority (366–144) with the opposition amendment being rejected equally decisively (150–369). Winston Churchill and Anthony Eden were prominent among Conservative abstainers, but, despite the former's 'Arms and the Covenant' campaign and Eden's pro-league reputation, neither pushed the league dimension in their contributions to the debate.[58] Nor did Duff Cooper, whose resignation speech immediately preceded the House of Commons Munich debate on 3 October.

Predictably, Clement Attlee, the Labour leader, launched a strong attack on Chamberlain's 'cold-shouldering' of Geneva: 'The League of Nations has been sitting and I understand that Lord de la Warr and the Under-Secretary of State for Foreign Affairs have been in attendance, and I am not aware that at any time any attempt has been made to bring the matter before the League.'[59] Chamberlain flew to Germany, not Switzerland, for talks. Both Herbert Morrison and Philip Noel-Baker, presenting Munich as a triumph for force, echoed their leader's views when identifying the way in which the government's retreat from the league had brought Britain to the edge of war.[60] In the upper house, perhaps the government's most outspoken league critic was the Earl of Lytton, whose LNU loyalties led him to argue that the government, departing from its election pledges, had failed to make the league the sheet-anchor of British policy, let alone an instrument of appeasement.[61] In this vein, the Archbishop of Canterbury pressed for a 'revived and reconstituted' league, as did Lord Cecil, a long-time league supporter critical of members for persistently failing the league.[62]

One of the more revealing features concerned the relative lack of reference to the league dimension on the part of ministers, except in terms of making the occasional negative comment. On 6 October, Chamberlain, having ignored it completely in his opening statement, referred only briefly to the league when closing the debate; in particular, he stressed both its lack of universality and the failure of collective security: 'it certainly is not collective in any sense'.[63] Similarly, Sir John Simon, the chancellor of the exchequer, attacked the weak and flimsy nature of the covenant, as exemplified by the inadequacy of the peaceful change provisions of article XIX.[64] One of the more robust ministerial contributions emanated from Leslie Burgin, the minister of transport, who responded to Morrison's attack: 'He has talked of the League of Nations and of collective security, and he has given no indication of anything that the League of Nations could have done. He has not, when he talked of collective security, given us the slightest idea whom he would collect or what security could be guaranteed.'[65] Reportedly, his riposte was greeted by 'ministerial cheers'.[66] Then, Butler, reminding members that he had been in Geneva throughout the September crisis, articulated the fundamental problem: 'in constructing a peace system, we have to decide whether we are going to ignore the forces which are outside the League or not, and we emphatically do not accept the position that we should leave the dictator countries outside in our consideration of the construction of a peace system.'[67] Meanwhile, 'the more I examine it [the league], the more I find it is not easy of application at the present time'. The league was ignored by most peers, but some speakers in the House of Lords talked about scrapping it – for example, Lord Ponsonby argued that league jargon 'must be dropped' – and starting again with a 'more restricted' approach (for example, Marquess of Crewe, Lord Kenilworth, Viscount Samuel).[68]

Conclusion: 'An Overshadowed Assembly'

Reviewing the course of events at Geneva during September, *The Times* referred to the 'overshadowed Assembly': 'The mighty events of the last few weeks had swept out of the public's ken the meeting of the Assembly of the League of Nations.'[69] In this vein, two months later, Lord Halifax, speaking in a House of Lords debate on 'the League and International Relations' reaffirmed the British government's dismissal of the league option for recent events. What was feasible for the league in the 1920s, he observed, had not proved possible during the 1938 Austrian and Czech crises.[70] By implication, in future, the league's prime focus should be directed towards its increasingly useful nonpolitical work, not peacekeeping. Subsequently, in May 1939, Lord Halifax joined Bonnet – together, they represented the league's most powerful members – at Geneva to perform a double act at the scheduled council session. On the surface, their presence gave an impression of normality, but in reality it was employed to remind members that key international problems continued to be dealt with *by other means*, as emphasized by Halifax's review of recent events, including the German occupation of Prague: 'The particular action which His Majesty's Government has taken has not been carried out through the League. This was, in the circumstances, impossible.'[71] In the meantime, he sought to disarm critics by pointing out that the league still met regularly, attracted strong British support, and undertook invaluable nonpolitical work. Bonnet offered a similar message: 'In the presence of these successive upheavals, the League has not shown itself to be in a position to supply the necessary remedies.'[72]

Respecting the Czech problem during 1938–39, the league's role was confined to nonpolitical matters, as demonstrated by the fact that, for both the assembly and council sessions held in September 1938, the only index reference to Czechoslovakia in league minutes referred to a committee report on drugs and traffic in opium![73] Despite being compared frequently to the events culminating in the 1914 war, the Sudeten crisis itself was kept off the agenda, even if the league was in session and readily available on the very days when key negotiations were taking place at Berchtesgaden, Godesberg and Munich. Instead, the decision of the major powers to manage the Czech problem outside the league meant that the assembly and council confined themselves to general expressions of support for diplomatic efforts taking place well away from Geneva; for instance, García-Calderón (Peru), the council chairman, specifically acknowledged that key decisions were being taken elsewhere, when praising Chamberlain's role as a 'knight of peace'.[74] It was also apparent that several small states, particularly those represented on the council (for example, Belgium Latvia, Sweden), had no desire to expose themselves to German animosity through the league's intervention in the Sudeten question.[75]

Whereas the eyes of the world were fixed on Munich, Geneva attracted minimal attention from governments, the media and public opinion.[76] The general indifference to its work seemed a true measure of the league's lack of influence in international affairs, for its peacekeeping work was, to quote *The Times*, 'carried through *by other men in other ways*'. Butler, like others attending the assembly and council, complained about being 'off-stage discussing minor issues like signs at level crossings', not matters affecting world peace.[77] Writing home from Geneva, he conceded that 'it really has been extraordinarily interesting here, although I'm sure we haven't appreciated the intense drama that has been going on in England; and your anxiety'.[78] Subsequently, he informed parliament of the 'strange experience' of being in Geneva, where he missed the anxiety and tension felt by those back in Britain.[79] His feelings, including complaints about the perpetual meetings, were echoed by Sir Henry Channon, his parliamentary private secretary, who resented 'unsitthroughable' meetings of 'that absurd Assembly'.[80] Perhaps equally revealing, given the Soviet government's exclusion from the Munich conference, was the presence of the Soviet foreign minister in Geneva at the height of the Czech crisis.

In January 1939, Butler accompanied Halifax to Geneva for the scheduled council session. Butler had frequently expressed admiration of the new *Palais des Nations* – he described it as a 'quite beautiful and spacious and comfortable' 'palace of the democracies' – but shared the reservations articulated by the foreign secretary, who 'discoursed on the sad tendency of men to build great palaces like the League building at a time when the ideas they represent incline downward'.[81] Some two decades later, C. Northcote Parkinson's well-known book, entitled *Parkinson's Law*, articulated similar sentiments:

> Perfection of planned layout is achieved only by institutions on the point of collapse ... Just such a sequence can be found in the

history of the League of Nations ... Its physical embodiment,
however, the Palace of the Nations, was not opened until 1937.
It was a structure no doubt justly admired. Deep thought had
gone into the design ... Everything was there which ingenuity
could devise – except, indeed, the League itself. By the year
when its Palace was formally opened the League had practically
ceased to exist.[82]

Even worse, the closing years of the decade witnessed the outbreak
of the Second World War, that is, the very conflict that the League of
Nations had been created to prevent. In turn, war led to the
emergence of the United Nations, a new edifice of international
solidarity, in place of the discredited league. As a result, historians
feel duty-bound to assume its almost inevitable failure when writing
about the league, even if such an approach fosters a somewhat
partial, even distorted, history of an institution deserving to be
presented rather as an episode in the history of international
organization. The league died, but the idea, alongside the legacy of
its invaluable nonpolitical work, lived on.[83]

Speaking at Hanley on 8 October 1938, Attlee presented Munich
as a terrible blow to the League of Nations.[84] Subsequently, in 1939
Gilbert Murray, formerly president of the LNU, asserted that, if only
Britain had consistently supported the league system, 'the whole
course of history would have been different'.[85] We shall never know,
but Britain, and especially Chamberlain, received, and continues to
receive, a large share of the blame for the league's failure as a
peacekeeping body. Frank Walters, a Briton who worked for the league
secretariat, was extremely critical of the manner in which 'the
proceedings of the Council were made to alternate with conversations'
between the great powers 'in which the Covenant was often forgotten
and the interests of the League were treated as of small account': 'The
process whereby ... the League's authority was undermined had been
going on for some years. It was a general degeneration, marked by a
few outstanding events ... but moving continuously forward under the
ceaseless activity of nationalist diplomacy.'[86]

More recently, R.A.C. Parker's *Chamberlain and Appeasement*
(1993), a counter-revisionist study favouring a partial return to the
'guilty men' view, argued that the 1938 Austrian and Czech crises

furnished conditions enabling the formation of a combination of states, 'more or less shrouded under the League Covenant', intended 'to build a barrier to Hitler's expansion'.[87] From this perspective, the league option, having been dismissed as unrealistic by Chamberlain as well as by the revisionist studies published during and after the 1960s, merits reappraisal as an alternative to appeasement, even if the 1938 Sudeten crisis raises serious doubts about its feasibility, given the apparent superiority of the 'old diplomacy' over the 'new diplomacy' in securing peaceful change. To a large extent, league action was dependent upon 'the measure of agreement among its members to take forceful action in a particular dispute', and, as Lord Halifax observed prior to the Sudeten crisis, 'reduced membership and the divided counsels among its remaining members' imposed severe imitations on League action.[88] The league's non-role in the Sudeten crisis was also foreshadowed by Butler:

> The operation of the system [collective security] depends on the willingness of Governments to make it work. Most states today are not in fact prepared to participate unreservedly in the collective action to restrain an aggressor for which the Covenant provides. Further some of the most important states are not only not prepared to participate but are hostile to the system itself and actively desire its destruction.[89]

This line, though unpopular with league supporters, seemed realistic in the light of contemporary circumstances, given the fact that the 1938 Czech crisis represented a major failure for the league-based 'new diplomacy'. Within this context, an interesting postscript concerns Lord Ponsonby's presentation of Chamberlain's actions in September 1938 – 'he took an aeroplane; he went to see Hitler, face to face' – as the real 'new' diplomacy, that is, a 'new fangled' type of summit diplomacy.[90]

Kingston University

NOTES

1. *The Times*, 3 Oct. 1938.
2. Council, 17 Jan. 1939, *League of Nations Official Journal (LNOJ)* 20 (1939), pp.72–3.
3. 'The City of Munich', *The Times*, 30 Sept.1938.
4. During 1938–39 the refugee work was restructured; thus, a league high commissioner

for refugees took over the work of both the Nansen International office and the high commissioner for refugees from Germany.

5. League Assembly, 18 April 1946, *League of Nations Special Supplement 194, 20th and 21st Assembly*, p.65.

6. De La Warr, 16 Sept. 1938, *League of Nations Records of Assembly 19th Session 1938 Special Supplement*, p.44. For example, see Baldwin's maiden speech in Lords: *Hansard Parliamentary Debates (Lords)*, 5th Series, Vol.110, col.1393, 4 Oct. 1938.

7. *Hansard Parliamentary Debates (Commons)*, 5th Series, Vol.339, col.5, 28 Sept. 1938.

8. *The Times*, 29 Sept. 1938.

9. F.S. Northedge, *The League of Nations: Its Life and Times, 1920–1946* (Leicester: Leicester University Press, 1986), p.52; Peter J. Beck, 'From the Geneva Protocol to the Greco-Bulgarian Crisis: The Development of the Baldwin Government's Policy towards the Peacekeeping Role of the League of Nations, 1924–25', *British Journal of International Studies*, Vol.6, No.1 (1980), pp.67–8.

10. See F. Walters to Foreign Office, 12 Jan. 1938, FO371/22507, W473/3/98. Cabinet (CAB) and foreign office (FO) papers are located at the Public Record Office, Kew, London.

11. *The Times*, 11 June 1936; Chamberlain to Hilda Chamberlain, 14 June 1936, NC18/1/965. The Neville Chamberlain Papers (NC) are located at the Manuscripts Library, University of Birmingham, and are quoted by kind permissions of the librarian.

12. Chamberlain to Hilda Chamberlain, 13 March 1938, NC 18/1/1041.

13. Neurath's speech, October 1937, encl. Sir Nevile Henderson to A. Eden, 2 Nov. 1937, in Peter Beck, *British Documents on Foreign Affairs, Reports and Papers from the Foreign Office Confidential Print: Part II, Series J, the League of Nations 1918–1941* (University Publications of America, Maryland, 1992), Vol.2, p.332.

14. Quoted, Northedge, *League of Nations*, p.133.

15. Sir Eric Phipps, 22 Jan. 1936, Berlin Diary: September 1935–April 1937, PHPP 10/2, Phipps Papers, Churchill Archives Centre, Churchill College, University of Cambridge. Extracts from the Phipps Papers are quoted by kind permission of the master and fellows of Churchill College; Christoph M. Kimmich, *Germany and the League of Nations* (Chicago: University of Chicago Press, 1976), pp.190–93.

16. Minutes, F. Roberts, 11 June 1938, H. Malkin, 13 June 1938, FO371/22547, W7921/383/98.

17. Chamberlain, *Hansard (Commons)*, Vol.332, col.227, 22 Feb.1938; col.1565, 7 March 1938; Peter Beck, 'Britain and Appeasement in the Late 1930s: Was There a League of Nations' Alternative', in D. Richardson and G. Stone (eds.), *Decisions and Diplomacy: Essays in Twentieth Century International History* (London: Routledge/LSE, 1995), pp.153–68.

18. See Lord Cecil to Lord Halifax, 8 March 1938, FO371/22509, W341/3/98.

19. Cabinet Minutes, 2 Feb. 1938, Cab.3 (38), CAB23/92.

20. Note, H. Batterbee, 13 March 1938, RAB F79/4–6. The Lord Butler of Saffron Walden Papers (RAB) are located at the library, Trinity College, University of Cambridge, and are quoted by kind permission of the master and fellows of Trinity College, Cambridge.

21. For an indication of its perceived political influence, see Neville Chamberlain to Stanley Baldwin, 7 Dec. 1938, Vol.174, fo.19, Lord Baldwin Papers, Cambridge University Library; Earl of Lytton to Sir Douglas Hacking, 12 June 1939, Chartwell 2/378, Winston Churchill papers, Churchill Archives Centre, Churchill College, Cambridge University.

22. Geoffrey Goodwin, 'The Political Role of the United Nations: Some British Views', *International Organization*, Vol.15 (1961), p.581; Donald S. Birn, *The League of Nations Union* (Oxford: Oxford University Press, 1981), pp.142–54.

23. *LNOJ 19* (1938), p.237.

24. *The Times*, 4 April 1938.

25. *The Times*, 17 Sept. 1938.

26. *The Times*, 6, 8, 9, 23 Sept. 1938; David M. Roberts, 'Hugh Dalton and the Labour

Party in the 1930s' (unpubl. Ph.D. dissertation, Kingston Polytechnic (now Kingston University), 1978), p.130.

27. *Records of Assembly 19th Session 1938 Special Supplement*, p.45.
28. *The Times*, 24 Sept. 1938.
29. Ibid.
30. *Hansard (Commons)*, Vol.339, col.26, 28 Sept.1938.
31. R. Butler, Geneva, to Lady Butler, 16 Sept. 1938, RAB D11/2 82 ii.
32. Lord Halifax to Norton, 8 Sept. 1938, FO371/22568, W11828/3991/98.
33. Jiri Hochman, *The Soviet Union and the Failure of Collective Security, 1934–1938* (Ithaca, NY: Cornell University Press, 1984), pp.157–9.
34. *Records of Assembly 19th Session 1938 Special Supplement*, p.70.
35. Italy, having given notice of withdrawal in December 1937, no longer attended league meetings.
36. *The Times*, 13 Sept. 1938.
37. H. Kennard to Orme Sargent, 9 Feb. 1938, FO371/22508, W2022/3/98.
38. *The Times*, 12 Sept. 1938.
39. *The Times*, 15 Sept. 1938.
40. *The Times*, 13 Sept. 1938.
41. Ibid.
42. *The Times*, 24 Sept. 1938.
43. *LNOJ* 19 (1938), pp.880–881.
44. For a British view of the agenda, see memorandum, R. Skrine Stevenson, 19 July 1938, *British Documents on Foreign Affairs*, Vol.1, pp.276–9.
45. *Records of Assembly 19th Session 1938 Special Supplement*, p.76.
46. Zbynek Zeman with Antonin Klimek, *The Life of Edvard Benes, 1884–1948: Czechoslovakia in Peace and War* (Oxford: Clarendon Press, 1997), pp.92–94; Godfrey Lias (trans.), *Memoirs of Dr Eduard Benes: From Munich to New War and New Victory* (London: George Allen and Unwin, 1954), p.8.
47. Lias, *Memoirs of Dr Eduard Benes*, pp.12, 24, 28.
48. Ibid., p.37.
49. *The Times*, 12 Sept. 1938.
50. Zeman with Klimek, *The Life of Edvard Benes*, p.125; Hochman, *The Soviet Union*, pp.161–2.
51. Hochman, *The Soviet Union*, pp.158–9; Jane Degras (ed.), *Soviet Documents on Foreign Policy, vol.3* (London: Oxford University Press, 1954), pp.285–286; Viscount Chilston, Moscow, to Foreign Office, 8 Sept. 1938, encl. RAB F84/278.
52. *The Times*, 26 Sept. 1938.
53. *The Times*, 28 Sept. 1938.
54. *Records of Assembly 19th Session 1938 Special Supplement*, pp.94–5.
55. *Records of Assembly 19th Session 1938 Special Supplement*, p.100.
56. *The Times*, 1 Oct. 1938.
57. *The Times*, 6 Oct. 1938; *Hansard (Commons)*, Vol.339, col.500, 6 Oct. 1938.
58. *Hansard (Commons)*, Vol.339, cols.359–73, 5 Oct. 1938. Nor did, say, Jim Thomas, a close associate of Eden, when justifying abstention to his constituents: Speech at Ledbury, 14 Oct. 1938, Acc. 5605, Cilc.Coll.55, Viscount Cilcennin Papers, Carmarthenshire Records Office, Carmarthen; *Hereford Times*, 15 Oct. 1938.
59. *Hansard (Commons)*, Vol.339, cols.56–9, 66 (Attlee), 3 Oct. 1938; cols.172–3 (Morrison) 4 Oct. 1938; Roberts, *Hugh Dalton and the Labour Party*, pp.133–4.
60. *Hansard (Commons)*, Vol.339, cols.172–3 (Morrison), 4 Oct. 1938; cols.500–510, 6 Oct. 1938.
61. *Hansard (Lords)*, Vol.110, cols.1451–2, 5 Oct. 1938. See his complaints to Conservative Central Office: Earl of Lytton to Sir Douglas Hacking, 12 June 1939, Chartwell 2/378, Churchill Papers.
62. *Hansard (Lords)*, Vol.110, cols.1323–24 (Canterbury), col.1335 (Cecil), 3 Oct. 1938.
63. *Hansard (Commons)*, Vol.339, cols.40–50, 3 Oct. 1938; col.549, 6 Oct. 1938.

64. *Hansard (Commons)*, Vol.339, col.344, 5 Oct. 1938.
65. *Hansard (Commons)*, Vol.339, col.183; 4 Oct. 1938.
66. *The Times*, 5 Oct. 1938.
67. *Hansard (Commons)*, Vol.339, cols.452–3, 5 Oct. 1938.
68. *Hansard (Lords)*, Vol.110, cols.1317, 1389, 1395–7, 1477, 4 Oct. 1938.
69. *The Times*, 3 Oct. 1938.
70. *Hansard (Lords)*, Vol.111, col.286, 30 Nov. 1938.
71. *LNOJ* 20 (1939), 23 May 1939, pp.264–5. Following the German occupation of Prague, Benes, who was now working at an American university, sent a protest note, dated 13 May 1939, to the league secretariat. However, the latter, pointing out that it did not emanate from a recognized state, refused to act upon his protest: Lias, *Memoirs of Dr Eduard Benes*, pp.64–5; *Report on the Work of the League 1938/39* (Geneva: League of Nations, 1939), pp.16–17.
72. *LNOJ* 20 (1939), p.265.
73. Work of Advisory Committee on Traffic in Opium and Drugs, 17 Sept. 1938, *LNOJ* 19 (1938), pp.1005, 1041.
74. *LNOJ* 19 (1938), 30 Sept. 1938, p.877.
75. British delegation, Geneva, to Lord Halifax, 28 Sept. 1938, *Documents on British Foreign Policy 1919–1939 Third Series, Vol.2*, ed. E.L. Woodward and R. Butler (London: HMSO, 1949), p.594.
76. 'The City of Munich', *The Times*, 30 Sept. 1938.
77. Author's interview with Lord Butler, April 1980; R. Butler, Geneva, to Mrs. Butler, 16 Sept. 1938, RAB D11/2/81; Lord Butler, *The Art of the Possible* (London: Hamish Hamilton, 1971), p.66; Report of Committee for Communications and Transit, *LNOJ* 19 (1938), pp.1109–10.
78. Quoted, Anthony Howard, *The Life of R.A. Butler* (London: Cape, 1987), pp.76–7; R. Butler to Mrs. Butler, 16 Sept. 1938, RAB D11/281.
79. *Hansard (Commons)*, Vol.339, cols.452–3, 5 Oct. 1938.
80. R. Rhodes James (ed.), *Chips. The Diaries of Sir Henry Channon* (London: Weidenfeld and Nicolson, 1967), pp.164–8; Beck, *British Documents on Foreign Affairs, Vol.1*, pp.276–84.
81. R. Butler, Geneva, to Lady Butler, 29 Sept. 1938, RAB F79/63; R. Butler, Geneva, to Mrs. Butler, 9 Sept. 1938, RAB D11/2/77 i–ii, 17 Jan. 1939, RAB D11/2/90; R. Butler, Geneva, to Lady Butler, 18 Jan. 1939, RAB D48/1106–1108.
82. C. Northcote Parkinson, *Parkinson's Law; or the Pursuit of Progress* (London: John Murray, 1958), pp.84–6.
83. David Armstrong, Lorna Lloyd and John Redmond, *From Versailles to Maastricht: International Organisation in the Twentieth Century* (London: Macmillan, 1996), p.33.
84. *The Times*, 10 Oct. 1938.
85. Gilbert Murray, *From the League to U.N.* (London: Oxford University Press, 1948), pp.71–6.
86. F.P. Walters, *A History of the League of Nations* (London: Oxford University Press, 1960 edn.), pp.628, 782.
87. R.A.C. Parker, *Chamberlain and Appeasement: British Policy and the Coming of the Second World War* (London: Macmillan, 1993), p.347.
88. Lord Halifax to Lord Cecil, 21 March 1938, FO371/22509, W3561/3/98; R. Butler to Capt. Crookshank, 17 June 1938, FO371/22542, W8261/140/98; Lord Halifax to R. Campbell, Paris, 29 Aug. 1938, *British Documents on Foreign Affairs, Vol.4*, p.175. See also Lord Halifax's speech to LNU, Southampton, 24 Feb. 1937, A4.410.1/175, Lord Halifax Papers, Borthwick Institute of Historical Research, University of York.
89. R. Butler to Crookshank, 17 June 1938, FO371/22542, W8261/140/98.
90. *Hansard (Lords)*, Vol.110, cols.1395–7, 4 Oct. 1938.

Nevile Henderson and Basil Newton
Two British Envoys in the
Czech Crisis 1938

PETER NEVILLE

In the period between the *Anschluss* and the Munich Conference in 1938, the strategy of the British government and the foreign office was to keep Germany guessing about any likely British response to aggression on Hitler's part against Czechoslovakia. The primary agents of this policy in the diplomatic service were Sir Nevile Henderson in Berlin and Basil Newton in Prague, although a significant subsidiary role was played by Sir Eric Phipps in Paris. Henderson's role was to convince the Germans that the British government might well side with France, if it had to honour its 1935 treaty commitment to the Czechs, while Newton's was to put pressure on the Prague government to make concessions to the Sudeten German minority in Czechoslovakia and thus avoid war.

Of the two representatives, Henderson has been given a much higher profile by historians (although some still virtually ignore him), while Newton has been largely ignored.[1] Henderson has been castigated as the man who 'misrepresented Britain to Hitler and Hitler to Britain'[2] and the 'Beau Brummel'[3] of diplomacy, while Newton, too, has had his detractors. One contemporary journalist mentions a description of him as 'bone from the collar-stud upward'[4] while President Benes dismissed Newton as just being 'dumb'. A seminal anti-appeasement study in the 1960s, commenting on his period at the Prague legation, highlighted Newton's 'hostility to Czechs and Germans living together'. Very few analysts however, have accepted this study's view that in the Czech crisis of 1938 'the views and actions of Newton became all-important'.[5]

A good deal has been written about Henderson's anti-Slav prejudices, but much less attention has been paid to Newton's attitude to the Czechs and its evolution. Here the role played by his predecessor, Sir Joseph Addison, seems to have been crucial. Addison was the British minister in Prague from 1930 to 1936 who made virtually no attempt to conceal either his contempt for his hosts or his belief that Czechoslovakia was a bizarre mongrel state in central Europe. When asked by a visitor whether he had any Czech friends (and he had a seven-year posting to make some) Addison reportedly replied: 'Friends! ... They eat in their kitchens.' Such friends as the minister did have were Bohemian German nobles whose natural allegiance was to the defunct Hapsburg dynasty, and not to the governments of Masaryk and Benes.[6] Addison, like his successor Newton, had a long diplomatic stint in Berlin, which predisposed both of them to be sympathetic to the Sudeten German minority. Observers noticed that when the British mediator Lord Runciman arrived in Prague on 3 August 1938, Newton brought two Sudeten German leaders to the railway station to meet him.

Addison has been accused of being 'very much responsible for cultivating a negative view of the Czechs and their country in British official circles', and the charge is substantiated by the documentary evidence available in Foreign Office files.[7] Addison came to believe that the Czech state was an unviable consequence of the postwar peace settlement, which was in itself unfair to Germany. Newton agreed with him. In this revisionist perspective he had much in common with Henderson, but little with Henderson's predecessor in Berlin, Eric Phipps. Addison also shared Henderson's prejudices about Slavs, writing to the foreign office that 'order, method, punctuality, honesty in dealing with one's fellow human beings are as alien to the Slav character as water to a cat'. And the then journalist and later distinguished diplomatic historian Elizabeth Wiskemann wrote on meeting Addison in 1935 that he 'seemed obsessed with the traditional German view that Germans were gentlemen and Czechs were not'.[8] The counsellor in Prague, R.H. Hadow ('Shadow Hadow' as he was known in the diplomatic service), was also sympathetic to the Germans rather than the Czechs, and helped Addison influence the foreign office.[9]

In February 1937 Hadow reported his view after an interview with Benes that 'proper and friendly British pressure would facilitate a solution of this [the Sudeten] problem'. He also believed that Benes knew that 'Soviet Russia is a doubtful reed to lean upon in case of war, and his people are all too conscious of the shorn locks of the French Samson. Great Britain is therefore that only hope and for Great Britain's support President Benes is fighting for dear life'. In melodramatic fashion Hadow claimed that if Britain did not bring Germany and the Czechs together in bilateral talks, there might be 'a second Thirty Years War'.[10] This bizarre analysis overlooked the fact that he and Addison had little reputation for being friendly to the Czechs, who certainly did not look to London in 1937 for guidance about the Sudeten problem. Benes was not liked in Whitehall, so that even a supporter of collective security like Vansittart commented that he 'was a blind little bat, who has done a lot of flapping in his night'.[11] But an alternative viewpoint in the foreign office was that Czechoslovakia was a Bolshevik outpost because of its 1935 defence pact with the USSR. Its champion was Orme Sargent, the assistant secretary of state, who strongly opposed that alliance, and the parallel Franco-Soviet alliance which was signed in the same year. In Sargent's view, Czechoslovakia was 'Practically ... the aircraft mother-ship' of Moscow, and it was this bolshevization of Czechoslovakia and not the Sudetenland which had sparked off the anti-Czech German press campaign which started after Hitler's speech at the Nuremberg Rally in September 1936. Sargent suspected that Czechoslovakia was offering facilities to the Comintern, and thought that when Newton took up his post in Prague on 3 March 1937 it would be useful for him to investigate and report back on this question (Vansittart minuted, 'I agree', but he did not agree with Sargent's suggestion that France and Czechoslovakia should be urged 'to cut adrift from Soviet Russia').[12]

Thus prejudice against Czechoslovakia operated at two levels. First of all the Czechs were accused of mistreating the German minority, with whom successive British ambassadors sided. And, secondly, the Czechs were regarded as Bolshevik stooges who offered offence to Germany because of their alliance with the USSR. The two views were not complementary, for, as indicated above, Sargent believed that the link with Moscow, rather than the Sudeten problem, was the basic cause of the Czech–German tensions. He also raised the issue of morality over the Sudeten issue. It should be addressed not because it would make agreement with Germany possible, but because 'it would put Czechoslovakia right in the eyes of he world, and at the same time strengthen her internally, in case of trouble ahead'.[13]

Anthony Eden also disagreed with Hadow's analysis in a telegram sent to Prague on 23 February, informing him that information available to the foreign office tended 'to show that the German government's policy is directed towards the disintegration and domination of Czechoslovakia'. He also instructed Newton when he had taken up his appointment that the British government would not make 'any definite statement in regard to whatever negotiations with Germany the Czechoslovak government may have it in mind to undertake'. It would be wrong, Eden went on, to discourage Benes from talking to the Germans lest he later blame Britain for letting slip an opportunity for Czech–German *rapprochement*. Nevertheless, the government would not be 'ready to attempt any sort of mediation in such conditions either in Berlin or Prague to bringing about a settlement of difficulties between Germany and Czechoslovakia'.[14] This policy of nonintervention had clearly been abandoned by the summer of 1938, when the Addison–Hadow line of pro-Sudeten German mediation was taken up, culminating in the personal intervention of Neville Chamberlain in September.

Nevertheless, steering between a policy of encouragement of bilateral Czech–German talks, while avoiding one of direct mediation over the Sudeten question was a difficult task for the incoming minister in Prague. And it must be open to question whether 'Newton was or could be really impartial when dealing with the Sudeten problem. He was plunged into an environment where most of his colleagues in Prague and London had already convinced themselves that the Czechs were morally in the wrong'. Newton had also 'read and accepted much of what Addison had written about Czechoslovakia's German minority'.[15] Henderson, in particular, once posted to Berlin in April 1937, was to become obsessed with the need for the British position over Czechoslovakia to be 'morally copper bottomed'.[16] But Henderson, like his colleagues, had been influenced by Joseph Addison's prejudices over a number of years via the diplomatic bag, while Newton must have been both influenced by his predecessor's perception of Czechoslovakia and weakened by the knowledge that Addison's anti-Czech prejudice had largely destroyed any influence which the British might have had in Prague.[17] He soon destroyed any remaining credit he might have had with Benes and his colleagues by appearing to be both arrogant and stupid. Benes soon came to regard him as a 'thick-headed ignoramus'. Influence, it can be argued, therefore, was to be replaced by *'force majeure'* in the summer of 1938 as Prague effectively became 'a victim embassy' and the Czechs were pressurized by Britain and France into abandoning a truly independent foreign policy.[18]

The main difficulty in assessing Newton's role during the Czech crisis is the absence of any personal papers. Whereas Henderson was a prolific correspondent, Newton was not, and we are therefore dependent on the published documents in the *Documents on British Foreign Policy* series and the references to Newton in collections of personal papers (like Henderson's) at the Public Record Office and elsewhere. The information on what colleagues and superiors thought about Newton's performance in Prague is sketchy, although there is some evidence that Newton was criticized by the anti-appeasement Vansittart group in the foreign office. Hadow, for example, referred in 1938 to the fact that Henderson's telegrams had been 'castigated by Van'. This was not surprising, as Henderson and Vansittart (sidelined at the beginning of 1938 to the post of chief diplomatic adviser) were at daggers drawn over German policy. But Newton was also included in the criticism, although Hadow told Henderson that both diplomats' work had been 'endorsed by Butler and S of S'.[19]

Attention can perhaps be directed more profitably at the extent of Newton's influence on policymaking in Whitehall, and the degree to which Newton's views complemented or contrasted with those of Henderson in Berlin. For, although Henderson wrote in his memoirs that 'The negotiations in Prague were not my concern',[20] he had plenty to say about the conduct of the Czech government in the months after the *Anschluss*, and a contrary view in Prague might have provided the cabinet and the foreign office with a counterweight to Henderson's complete endorsement of the appeasement policy.

Such a counterweight was not forthcoming on the evidence available in the documents. Newton's sympathies were made clear on the day after the German occupation of Austria in March 1938 when he opined that 'if I am right in thinking that Czechoslovakia's present political position is not permanently tenable, it will be no kindness in the long run to try and maintain her in it'.[21] This was exactly in line with Henderson's own thinking, for he telegraphed to the foreign secretary, Lord Halifax, on 16 March stating his view that 'British interests and the standard of morality can only be combined if we insist upon the fullest possible equality for the Sudeten minority of Czechoslovakia'.[22]

It is clear that Halifax was influenced by Newton's comments on 15 March, for he referred to them at the meeting on 18 March of the cabinet's foreign policy committee saying that Great Britain should not be put at risk of war 'to shore up a present situation which seems to us untenable'.[23] In fact Halifax went even further. When Newton argued for a discreet application of pressure in Prague about the Sudetenland, Halifax rejected this approach. He demanded instead that more pressure should be applied to the Czechs. After all, Benes might find himself dealing with more extreme Sudeten German leaders, if he would not do business with the 'moderate' Konrad Henlein (ironically Vansittart, the arch-critic of Chamberlain and Halifax's policy was responsible for creating the fiction that Henlein was a moderate).[24] Nevertheless Newton's view that the Czech state was not viable in the long run was obviously of crucial importance. It was also what Halifax and Neville Chamberlain wanted to hear, anxious as they were to keep Britain out of any war to preserve Czechoslovakia's existing frontiers. Their problem was that, however reluctant Britain might be to defend the Czechs, Britain was committed to defend France, and France had a treaty commitment to Czechoslovakia.[25] Conversely, Halifax did not want the Germans to know of Britain's unwillingness to assist France in the event of war over the Sudetenland in 1938. He shared Newton's view that if war broke out 'nothing that we or France could do would save Czechoslovakia from being overrun'.[26] This was always Henderson's view as well.

The paradoxical feature of the triangular relationship between Halifax, Henderson and Newton is that it was Newton, who would have been expected to want to defend the Czechs, who appeared willing to concede most to Germany. When, in fact, Henderson saw the Czech minister in Berlin, Mastny, on 17 March, he telegraphed to Halifax that he had told Mastny that in his own opinion Hitler would not risk all his gains in the *Anschluss* for 'a secondary objective like the Sudetenland.[27] By contrast, Newton in Prague was stepping up the pressure on President Benes. When he saw the Czech president on 20 March, Benes told him that it was his belief that as many as 25 per cent of the German Sudeten minority would not support Henlein's Sudeten German party's demand for more autonomy. Newton did not believe this assurance, telling Halifax that: 'In this as indeed in attitude which he continues to maintain to the minority questions, I fear that the President may be cherishing illusions.'[28] This was language that was very much in the Addison tradition, which saw the Czechs rather than the Germans as being responsible for ethnic tensions in the Sudetenland. Newton's conduct ceases to be a surprise if his diplomacy is viewed in the longer context of British policy towards Prague going back to Addison's arrival there in 1930. In Prague, therefore, there was continuity in British policy, whereas in Berlin, Henderson was clearly more sympathetic to German grievances than his predecessors Eric Phipps and Horace Rumbold had been.[29] Henderson also supported the Addison–Newton line in Prague, praising Newton's 'sage counsel' in his memoirs.[30]

The primacy of the Addison line in British thinking about Czechoslovakia was evident three days later on 23 March when Halifax wrote to Newton. Halifax told his minister that he should reassure the Czechs about British responsibilities under the League of Nations charter, but that it was 'with the greatest regret that His Majesty's Government have been forced to the conclusion that they are unable to take any further direct and definite commitment in respect of Czechoslovakia'. Newton was to add, however, with what has been described as 'a touch of Gilbert and Sullivan', that the British government would 'do everything to assist the Czechoslovak Government, who can be assured of their sympathy and goodwill towards a solution of their difficulties'. The exact nature of this goodwill remained unspecified. This statement by Halifax was endorsed by Neville Chamberlain in a statement in the House of Commons on 24 March, which underlined the British view that any further commitment to the Czechs would destroy the autonomy of British foreign policy.[31]

At this stage Henderson remained unconvinced that the Germans were ready to intervene in Czechoslovakia. On 1 April he reported to Halifax that if such an intervention did take place it would 'not be for a year or so. All other things being equal there should still remain therefore a period during which either preparation can be made at home for another world war or for the negotiation of a peaceful settlement as regards the Sudeten'.[32] This, on the face of it, surprising statement by an arch critic of the Czechoslovak state (allowing for a wider timescale than he later envisaged to solve the Sudeten Question) was supported at the time by Newton's own military attaché in Prague, Lieutenant-Colonel Stronge. He also believed that the German army was not ready for a war, and that in a year's time the Czech forces would be in a much better position to resist.[33]

Newton did not seem to be much interested in shoring up the position of his hosts. He shared Henderson's antagonism towards the USSR, which, as has been noted, was commonplace in the foreign office, and therefore his hostility to the Czech–Soviet pact of 1935 negotiated by Benes.[34] Indeed, he went further. While Henderson merely made unsympathetic references to the alliance between Prague and Moscow, Newton went so far as to question whether 'a permanent solution can be expected unless Czechoslovakia is, if not to give up her existing alliance with France, at least to challenge its character'. Even Henderson, the most fervent disciple of appeasement, never went this far. In this dispatch, Newton also showed the same anti-Czech prejudices for which his predecessor had been notorious. The Czechs, he told Halifax, suffered from 'temperamental obstinacy' which made them uncompromising and liable to make their state 'more untenable every day'. And no reprimand from Lord Halifax appears in the published documents for this lapse into racial prejudice, in contrast to the several well-known ones which Henderson received.[35] This strengthens the writer's view that the complaint put forward in 1971 by T. Desmond Williams about Henderson's treatment in the *Documents on British Foreign Policy*, is largely justified.

In the same dispatch Newton suggested that Czechoslovakia be given a neutral Swiss-style status which would make it into a 'kind of sanctuary or reserved area immunized against aggression'. There was nothing, in any case, that Britain could send in the event of German aggression, and the country was vulnerable to economic strangulation by Germany.[36] There could scarcely have been a bleaker analysis of Czechoslovakia's position, coming as it did barely a month after the

Anschluss, from the man on the spot. It was endorsed by Newton's line in an interview with the Czech Foreign Minister Krofta on 9 May when he stated in blunt terms the British view that it 'would be very difficult to defend Czechoslovakia', and that in the event of a wider European conflict it 'would still have to be decided whether the Czechoslovak State could be re-established in its present form'. To take a stronger line with the Germans, Newton had told Krofta, was impossible because British public opinion would not gamble on war over the Sudeten issue. Newton had taken it upon himself to stress the fact that Britain would not indulge in such a 'bluff' because 'it is not uncommon for Czechs to take the line that Germany would never venture on war if she knew in advance that France, Great Britain and Russia would come to the aid of Czechoslovakia'.[37]

Newton was prepared to go even further in his attempts to pressurize Benes, and was doubtful in a telegram sent to Halifax on 16 May (received by him on the eve of the so-called 'May Scare') whether there was 'any permanent halfway house between a Czechoslovakia within her present frontiers ... and the abandonment to Germany of the whole area covered by the Historic Provinces (save perhaps such parts as might be snatched by the Poles)'.[38] This was extraordinary language indeed, which apparently conceded the loss of Bohemia and Moravia to Germany, and the coalmining area of Teschen, taken by the Czechs in 1920, to Poland. What sort of ramshackle Czech state would survive such territorial surgery Newton did not say, but his observations might have made Benes feel, had he known, that with friends like these, Czechoslovakia had no need of enemies. Shiela Grant Duff, the then *Observer* correspondent in Prague was to write later that she had been 'terribly depressed by the cynical and uncaring attitude of my fellow countrymen' and told of how an attaché at the embassy had told her as far back as July 1936: 'The Czechs know they are doomed and will be fools to resist. The French will not help them and neither will we.'[39]

In the light of Newton's comments above, Henderson's behaviour seems almost circumspect, although it has not saved him from castigation.[40] While his colleague in Prague was advocating the break-up of the Czechoslovak state, Henderson had been considering, he told Halifax, 'how to secure, if we can, the integrity of Czechoslovakia'. On 30 March he saw Mastny, his Czech counterpart in Berlin, and agreed that the Czech government extended more rights to national minorities than perhaps any other. Henderson believed nonetheless that a 'Federal State' was Czechoslovakia's best hope which was what he thought the founder of the republic, Tomas Masaryk, had originally intended. He concluded the interview with Mastny by advising his colleague to rely on a Prague–Berlin–Paris axis rather than the existing Prague–Paris–Moscow one.[41] This contrasted sharply with what Newton was to telegraph to Halifax on 16 May, and was a more moderate position than the one being advocated by the British legation in Prague. The documentary evidence between the *Anschluss* and the 'May Scare' suggests, in fact, contrary to his reputation, that Henderson did make some effort to accede to his instructions about Czechoslovakia and that he personally believed that a solution was possible over a timescale of a year or more.[42]

All this changed over the weekend of 20–21 May 1938. Henderson was badly shaken by the events of that weekend when false rumours about a German mobilization precipitated a partial Czech mobilization. His dispatches between the May Scare and the Munich Conference were littered with warnings about how this crisis must never be allowed to recur, and his anxieties were sharpened by a widespread misunderstanding of the British legation's role in that crisis.[43] It was 'more and more brought home to me', Henderson wrote to the permanent undersecretary at the foreign office, Sir Alec Cadogan, on 4 September, 'how unfortunate was the public interpretation of our action here on 21 May'. The British warning to Germany (on the false assumption that it was about to march) had, Henderson told Cadogan, been 'resented especially by Hitler'.[44]

As the Czech crisis sharpened in intensity in the summer of 1938 and reached its zenith in the month of September, Newton fell into the background, and Henderson became more and more prominent a player in the crucial events.[45] Henderson was brought over to attend the important cabinet meeting on 30 August, and he, along with Sir Horace Wilson and Halifax, was the first to learn of Plan Z, Chamberlain's plan to go to Germany and meet Hitler in person. Henderson was also able to prevent a repetition of the 21 May warning at the party rally at Nuremberg in early September, which he felt would be provocative.

Henderson and Newton were mutually supportive. When Henderson wrote an encouraging note to Newton on 19 May, he replied in flattering terms. He hoped that Henderson would 'be awarded the Nobel Peace Prize and when that is done, I hope I may receive honourable mention. You have much the hardest job'.[46] This generous assessment of Henderson's work was not shared by others in the foreign office, and Newton's ultimate fate was to be ignored by historians apart from the odd reference. He was packed off to be minister in Iraq when Czechoslovakia disappeared from the map, before a final spell in the foreign office before retirement.

More curiously, Henderson felt obliged to draw to Halifax's attention a campaign by the Germans to suggest that Newton was pro-Czech. They were alleging, Henderson reported, 'that Newton has become very pro-Czech and anti-German and that this contributes to stiffen the Czech opposition to concessions and is likely to indispose Lord Runciman also' [Runciman had been sent to mediate between the Czechs and Sudetens in early August].[47] This was just German mischief-making, for Newton was still playing his part in 'persuading' Benes to make further concessions. And Runciman already had such a pronounced pro-Sudeten German bias that nothing Newton said to him was likely to affect him, had he been pro-Czech. Runciman's wife was prone to declaim about alleged 'Bolshevik influence' in Czechoslovakia.

On 4 September he chided Benes for a failure to make real changes. 'Evidences of progress were in my opinion scanty and unconvincing', Newton told the beleaguered Czech leader, and Benes' failure to honour promises made in 1937 about the appointment of German-speaking officials in the Sudetenland 'had made a very bad impression' in London.[48] Newton remained the enthusiastic agent of a policy of pressure in Prague, as Henderson remained one of conciliation in Berlin.

Only on the eve of the disintegration of the country to which he was accredited, did Newton have some real sympathy for Czechoslovakia in its agony. Just before the meeting between Hitler and Chamberlain at Godesberg, Newton sent a dispatch to Halifax commenting on the 'far-sighted patriotism, moral courage and wisdom of the Czech government and people. I think it is very important not only to sweeten the pill for M. Benes and his

Government personally but also to help them in every possible way to convince their public that decision is in the best interests of the country'.[49] Newton's pangs of conscience were in any case not sufficient to prevent him from suggesting that 'a kind of ultimatum' should be presented to the Czechs if they, as they did on 20 September, rejected Anglo-French proposals to settle the Sudeten imbroglio. The ultimatum should state, advised Newton, that if the Czechs refused to concede 'His Majesty's Government will take no further interest in the fate of the country'. When the Czechs threatened to invoke their 1936 Arbitration Treaty with Germany, Newton had tartly pointed out that 'an appeal to arbitration would be folly and would mean war'. Newton was to telegraph again on 22 September, the very day of the Godesberg conference, about his 'experience of the National Socialist German methods as applied both in Germany and here and I am gravely apprehensive that those in control of the Reich may now allege that conditions have so gone to pieces in Czechoslovakia that a new situation has arisen entitling them almost as a duty to intervene after all'.[50] He had predicted with uncanny accuracy the very excuses used by Hitler to destroy what was left of the Czech state in March 1939, but the pill was not to be sweetened for Dr Benes and his people either in 1938 or for seven bitter years to come. The leading contemporary Czech poet, Frantisek Halas, expressed his people's feeling at the time when he wrote:

> The bell of treason is tolling
> Whose hand made it swing
> Sweet France
> Proud Albion
> And we loved them.

Newton and Henderson were both enthusiastic agents of British foreign policy in their respective postings. Both thought that there was no alternative to the policy of concessions which the Anglo-French were imposing on the Czechs in 1938, which offered appropriate redress for German grievances. Newton may have been influenced by the inbuilt prejudices of his predecessor which had poisoned the Anglo-Czech relationship, but it is strange that only in his dispatch of 22 September 1938 did he bring his own experiences of nazi Germany to bear on the situation. Henderson was certainly influenced by the views of Joseph Addison like many of his foreign office contemporaries, and never showed much sympathy for the Czech position.[51] They in their turn felt that they were not liked in London as Jan Masaryk, their colourful minister there put it: 'The English dislike us intensely. We are a dead-weight for them and they curse the day on which we were founded.'[52]

Yet there is a paradox here about Newton's behaviour. When R. Bruce Lockhart, who knew his Czechoslovakia, visited Prague during a Vansittart-inspired lecture tour in the spring of 1938, he was impressed by Newton. According to Bruce Lockhart, Newton 'knew both the Czech and the German points of view. A descendent of Cochrane he has much of that great admiral's phlegm'.[53] Bruce Lockhart had briefly worked with Newton just after the war and found him to be calm and patient.

> Shrewd in judgement [Bruce Lockhart wrote shortly after his visit] and tactful in manner, he possesses an almost judicial impartiality, a quality valuable in a diplomatist, essential in a country like Czechoslovakia and, unfortunately, not possessed by all previous British ministers in Prague [a side-swipe at Addison?]. Basil Newton, I felt, was a sound man for a delicate and most difficult situation.[54]

Newton may not have been the boor that Benes presented him as (Bruce Lockhart commented on the way the Prague legation was 'exotically furnished'[55] with Chinese treasures Newton had brought back from previous service in Peking), but his quality of impartiality was not evident in 1938. The Czechs plainly regarded him as an insensitive bully (by contrast, the French minister, Laçroix, was frequently reduced to tears by the unpleasantness of his task).[56] Bruce Lockhart admired and liked the Slav peoples, and his opinion about Newton, who spoke Czech, is significant even if it was published before the tensions of the spring turned into the tragedy of Munich. By then Newton had become one of the harbingers of Czechoslovak destruction.

Newton was by no means the only diplomat or statesman to be duped by nazi Germany, but he had the experience behind him in Germany to know better. And Henderson's desire to preserve the peace was obsessive and questionable when he too could write of 'Hitler and his gangster crowd' in a dispatch to the foreign office.[57] What began with the blinkered chauvinism of Joseph Addison ended with the insensitivity of Newton, and the desperate, optimistic revisionism of Henderson.[58]

A final caveat needs to be entered about the performance of Henderson and Newton in the Czech crisis. There was, and is, a danger that the influence of individual ambassadors or ministers in such a crisis can be exaggerated and overstated. In the last analysis, British policy in 1938 and subsequently was made in London and not in the Berlin or Prague embassies. This fact was fully recognized by Halifax's private secretary, Oliver Harvey, a consistent critic of Henderson's, who wrote in 1939: 'No ambassador is going to swing Hitler or German opinion. German policy is governed by British policy in London.'[59] Newton was able to apply pressure on Benes in Prague, but ultimately he too was merely the agent of British foreign policy with its flawed perception of what was practicable in dealing with Hitler. As a former British ambassador in Rome, Lord Bertie, once complained: 'In Downing Street one can at least pull the wires whereas an Ambassador is only a d...d marionette.'[60]

University of Wolverhampton

NOTES

1. For specialist studies of Nevile Henderson, see Donald Cameron Watt, 'Chamberlain's Ambassadors', in M. Dockrill and B. McKercher (eds.), *Diplomacy and World Power: Studies in British Foreign Policy 1890–1950* (Cambridge, 1996); Felix Gilbert, 'Two British Ambassadors: Perth and Henderson' in G. Craig and F. Gilbert (eds.), *The Diplomats* (New York, 1968); Bruce Strang, 'Two Unequal Tempers: Sir George Ogilvie-Forbes, Sir Nevile Henderson, and British Foreign Policy 1938–39', *Diplomacy & Statecraft*, Vol.5, No.1 (March 1994); Vaughan B. Baker, 'Nevile Henderson in Berlin: A Re-evaluation', *Red River Valley Historical Journal*, No.4 (Winter 1977); Peter Neville, 'The Appointment of Sir Nevile Henderson 1937: Design or Blunder?', *Journal of Contemporary History* (October 1998).
2. Donald Cameron Watt, *How War Came* (London, 1989), p.614.
3. Lewis Namier, *Diplomatic Prelude* (London, 1948), p.218.
4. Shiela Grant Duff, *The Parting of Ways: A Personal Account of the Thirties* (London, 1982), p.96. Grant Duff met Newton for the first time in 1935 when he was Counsellor at the Berlin embassy. She could not recall whether it was Bernstorff or Wheeler Bennett (both Newton and Wheeler Bennett were fellow guests at Bernstorff's house at Stintenburg) who used this phrase about Newton; Igor Lukes,

Czechoslovakia. Between Stalin and Hitler (Oxford, 1996), p.179. Professor Lukes uses the Czech word *tupy*.

5. Martin Gilbert and Richard Gott, *The Appeasers* (London, 1963), pp.113–14; see also Keith Middlemass, *Diplomacy of Illusion* (London, 1972), p.245.

6. Duff, *The Parting of Ways*, p.127.

7. Mark Cornwall, 'The Rise and Fall of a "Special Relationship": Britain and Czechoslovakia 1930–1948', in B. Brivati and H. Jones (eds.), *What Difference Did the War Make?* (London, 1993), p.132; Addison to the Foreign Office 25 Aug. 1936, R5216/32/12 (FO 371/20375); also 7 Oct. 1936, R6487/32/12 (FO 371/20375). But when Addison criticized the Czechs, Eden, the then foreign secretary, replied: 'Whatever the faults of the Czechs they are tough and have a good fighting record.' *The Eden Memoirs: Facing the Dictators*, p.503. Minuting about the August memo, Cheetham of the central department told his FO superiors: 'This monumental despatch amounts to a ruthless condemnation in Sir Joseph Addison's best style of all that Czechoslovakia stands for.' Vansittart agreed that it was 'very caustic'. Both minutes 5 Sept.1936 in FO 371/20375.

8. Cornwall, 'The Rise and Fall of a "Special Relationship"', p.133; E. Wiskemann, *The Europe I Saw* (London, 1968), p.77.

9. Hadow wrote secretly to Nevile Henderson in 1938 to support the line he was taking in Berlin and attacking the clique who 'would not allow of any right on the German side', Hadow to Henderson 11 May 1938, Henderson Papers, PRO 800 1269. By then Hadow was a first secretary in the northern department.

10. Hadow to Foreign Office 16/2/37, DBFP, 2nd Series, Vol.XVIII, No.185; Hadow to Eden 2/2/37, ibid., No.141.

11. Vansittart minute 23 Feb. 1937, ibid., No.185, note 5.

12. Sargent memorandum on Czech–German talks 9 Feb. 1937, ibid., No.160; Vansittart minute 9 Feb. 1937. For a detailed analysis of Sargent's hostility to the USSR, see Michael J. Carley, 'A Fearful Concatenation of Circumstances: The Anglo-German Rapprochement 1934–6', *Contemporary European History*, Vol.5, No.I (1996), pp.29–69.

13. Sargent memo 9 Feb. 1937, DBFP, 2, XVIII, No.160.

14. Eden to Hadow, 23 Feb. 1936, ibid., No.200; *The Eden Memoirs*: *Facing the Dictators* (London, 1962), pp.502–3. Eden also tells of his disagreement with Addison's view of Czechoslovakia in the autumn of 1936. 'I did not believe he realized the European dangers of the problem.' Eden minute 15 Sept. 1936 in R 5216/32/12, FO 371/20375.

15. Cornwall, 'The Rise and Fall of a "Special Relationship"', p.136.

16. Nevile Henderson, *Failure of A Mission* (London, 1940), p.130; Henderson to Halifax 12 Aug. 1938, No.849, DBFP, 3rd Series, No.2.

17. Cornwall, 'The Rise and Fall of a "Special Relationship"', p.136.

18. Interview with Sir Frank Roberts 10/10/96. Sir Frank worked as a desk officer in the central European department during 1938–39.

19. Hadow to Henderson, 11 May 1938, Henderson Papers PRO. Hadow's letter, covering a memo he had drawn up for Halifax on Anglo-Russian relations, which, as he himself observed, he had no authority to send on to Henderson, also contained an unpleasant anti-semitic reference to the secretary of state for war, Leslie Hore-Belisha. He shared this prejudice with his former boss Joseph Addison. Cornwall, 'The Rise and Fall of a "Special Relationship"', pp.131–50.

20. Henderson, *Failure of A Mission*, p.133.

21. Newton to Halifax 15 March 1938, DBFP, 3, I, No.86.

22. Henderson to Halifax 16 March 1938, Henderson Papers, PRO 800/269, Henderson also telegraphed on 17 March that 'I share unreservedly and in all respects views expressed by Mr Newton in this telegram' (that is No.86 above), DBFP, 3, I, p.56, n.2.

23. Cabinet Committee on Foreign Policy 18/3/38, CAB 27/623, FP (36) 26.

24. Newton to Halifax, 2 June 1938; Henderson to Halifax, 6 June 1938; Halifax to Newton, 8 June 1938, Nos.368, 378,384, DBFP, 3, I. Halifax accepted what Henderson had suggested in his telegram of 6 June, namely that pressure be applied 'relentlessly' on Benes and his government.

25. It has been suggested that it was France, not Britain, which really made the running in the policy of appeasement during the Czech crisis; H. Aulach, *Britain and the Sudeten Issue 1938*, JCH (18) No.2, 1983.

26. Newton to Halifax, 15 March 1938, No.86.

27. Henderson to Halifax, 17 March 1938, No.93.

28. Newton to Halifax, 20 March 1938, No.100. Benes had made clear to the German minister in Prague, Eisenlöhr, in 1937 his scepticism about Anglo-French involvement in the Sudeten question, telling him that they were 'too far away to understand things'. Eisenlöhr to Wilhelmstrasse, 21 Dec. 1937, Documents on German Foreign Policy, Series D, Vol.II, No.38. Benes had also told Addison that 'Wars on a large scale are not started by the small powers, but by the interference of great powers', *The Eden Memoirs*, p.113.

29. Although Mark Cornwall points out that before Addison's arrival in Prague British attitudes towards Czechoslovakia were far more benign. Henderson could be seen in the d'Abernon tradition.

30. Henderson, *Failure of a Mission*, p.129; Sir Nevile Henderson also wrote a more general memoir on his diplomatic career since 1905, called *Water Under the Bridges*. This was published posthumously in 1945.

31. In 1939 critics of the guarantee given to Poland on 31 March were to make precisely this point; House of Commons Debates, 24 March 1938, 5th Series, Vol.333, Cols.1403–7; Halifax to Newton, 23 March 1938, DBFP, 3, II, No.110.

32. Henderson to Halifax, 1 April 1938, DBFP, 3rd Series, Vol.I, No.121. Characteristically, Henderson added a comment that Benes could 'save his face' by yielding to Anglo-French advice.

33. Newton to Halifax, covering Stronge's report on the readiness of the Czech army, 3 April 1938, No.129. See also Lukes, *Czechoslovakia: Between Stalin and Hitler*, pp.119–20.

34. As has been indicated, Orme Sargent, then undersecretary of state, was a ferocious opponent of better relations with the USSR, although often portrayed as a critic of appeasement. Vansittart and Laurence Collier, the head of the northern department, battled vainly to improve Anglo-Soviet relations; see Carley, *A Fearful Concatenation of Circumstances*.

35. Henderson to Halifax, 1 April 1938; Newton to Halifax, 12 April 1938, No.140; Shiela Grant Duff quotes Newton's reference to the Czechs as 'an obstinate people with whom fear may more easily breed hatred than readiness to yield' dating the comment in October 1937. A search of the relevant volume of DBFP by the writer could not trace the reference however. Grant Duff, *The Parting of the Ways*, p.159.

36. Ibid., No.140.

37. Newton to Halifax, 9 May 1938, DBFP, 3, I, No.195. In Gerard Weinberg's *The Foreign Policy of Hitler's Germany: Starting World War Two 1937–9* (Chicago, IL, and London, 1980) the author points out that Krofta's version of the interview with Newton is in T-120, 1039/1809/412188-94 (being German translations of Czech documents seized by the Germans in 1939 and then captured by the Allies in 1945 and microfilmed), p.360, n.187 refers.

38. Newton to Halifax, 16 May 1938, No.221.

39. Grant Duff also asked Addison at the time about British policy towards eastern Europe. The minister replied: 'British policy! You flatter them.' *The Parting of the Ways*, p.129.

40. For a particularly savage attack on Henderson's diplomacy during the Czech crisis, see P. Meehan, *The Unnecessary War* (London, 1992), pp.160–68. It is symptomatic of

Newton's invisibility that, as usual, he does not receive a mention at all.

41. Henderson to Halifax, 16 March 1938, Henderson Papers PRO 800/269; Henderson to Halifax, 30 March 1938, ibid. Henderson was correct in this assumption. His son Jan Masaryk, the Czech ambassador in London, told Sir Samuel Hoare, the then home secretary (and former foreign secretary), on 25 March 1938 that 'his father had originally supported the idea of a Federation on the lines of Switzerland, and that he himself had not excluded the possibility of a confederation of Germans, Slovaks and Czechs'. As cited in Lord Templewood, *Nine Troubled Years* (London, 1954), p.295.

42. Henderson had in fact warned Goering on 16 April that any German aggression against the Czechs 'was likely to have far more serious consequences than in the case of Austria'. Henderson to Halifax, 20 April 1938, 3, II, No.152.

43. The fact that some embassy staff were taking normal leave that weekend was responsible for a rumour that the British were evacuating their embassy prior to the outbreak of war. A recent article which analyses the background of the May crisis comes to no definite conclusion about who was responsible for the rumours that caused the 'scare'. Igor Lukes, 'The Czech Partial Mobilisation 1938', *JCH*, 314 (Oct. 1996).

44. Henderson to Cadogan, 4 Sept. 1938, DBFP, 3rd Series, Vol.11, No.772. See also Henderson to Halifax, 10 Sept. 1938 (two references in the same telegram), No.823; Henderson to Halifax, 12 Sept. 1938, No.839. In a private letter to Halifax on 13 September Henderson also quoted the opinion of former German Foreign Minister von Neurath that a repetition of 21 May would be the 'straw that broke the camel's back as far as the Führer was concerned', Henderson to Halifax 13 Sept. 1938, Henderson Papers, PRO 800/269.

45. This is shown by the weight of telegrams emanating from Berlin in the relevant volume of the DBFP series. In one sense, of course, this demonstrated the primacy of Berlin over Prague as a decisionmaking centre.

46. Newton to Henderson, 27 May 1938, Henderson Papers, PRO 800/269.

47. Henderson to Halifax, 12 Aug. 1938, Halifax Papers, PRO 800/314.

48. Newton to Halifax, 4 Sept. 1938, DBFP, 3, II, No.760.

49. Newton to Halifax, 21 Sept. 1938, No.994.

50. ibid., 22 Sept. 1938, No.1021; 20/9/38, No.979; 20 Sept. 1938, No.981.

51. Henderson to Vansittart, 24 June 1935, Henderson Papers, PRO 800/268. Henderson questioned in this letter the viability of the Czech state which he thought uncertain, adding: 'I fancy Joseph Addison would give you a definite expression of opinion.' Addison's influence was still evident in May 1938 when Eric Phipps forwarded a memorandum by him (Addison was visiting Paris) on the Sudeten question. It contained his usual anti-Czech diatribe, saying that Anglo-French assistance to Prague would 'merely be attempting to bolster up an injustice' and that HMG 'do not ... intend to move one single man or ship in defence of Czechoslovakia, but only in defence of our own vital interests'. He also dismissed Newton's suggestion that Czechoslovakia be neutralized. Memorandum by Sir J. Addison, 21 April 1938, C3745/1941/18, FO 371/21717. Henderson had suggested that Addison might be a member of Lord Runciman's delegation. Wisely, the foreign office declined.

52. Cited in Cornwall, 'The Rise and Fall of a "Special Relationship"', p.138.

53. R. Bruce Lockhart, *Guns or Butter?* (London, 1938), pp.263–4.

54. Ibid.

55. Ibid., p.294.

56. Lukes, 'The Czech Partial Mobilisation 1938', p.226.

57. Henderson to Foreign Office, 14 May 1937, C 3557/270/18 (FO 371/20735), PRO.

58. Grant Duff attacks the diplomacy that led to Munich as 'the final fruits of ... the appointment of Nevile Henderson to Berlin and Basil Newton to Prague': *Parting of the Ways*, p.178. Henderson died in 1942. His offer to return to Belgrade, where he

had been minister from 1929 to 1935, was refused by the FO on the outbreak of war (this was hardly surprising as he was an extremely sick man, the cancer which eventually killed him having forced him to take extensive sick leave in 1938–39). Basil Newton was posted to Iraq after the collapse of the Czech state in 1939. He remained there until 1941, before returning to duty at the FO; he retired in 1946. Interestingly, Newton had been involved in the monitoring by the FO of the Nuremberg Trials in 1945–6 thus seeing at first hand the consequences of nazi genocide and aggrandisement, 24 June 1946, FO 371/55693. Newton thought 'we were not being very successful in using the trials to educate German public opinion'.

59. J. Harvey (ed.), *The Diaries of Oliver Harvey* (London, 1970), 27 May 1939, p.292.
60. Cited in Chirol to Hardinge, 10 Aug. 1904, Hardinge Papers 7, Cambridge University Library.

Neville Chamberlain, the British Official Mind and the Munich Crisis

ERIK GOLDSTEIN

The name of Neville Chamberlain has become inextricably linked with the events of the Munich crisis, his performance during it resonating through succeeding decades as a parable of diplomatic failure. Any consideration of the British official mind and the Munich crisis must begin with the prime minister. The facts supporting the conclusion that Chamberlain's policy was an abysmal failure are overwhelming, but how did the leader of the world's largest empire come to go so badly wrong? The crisis was not of Chamberlain's making, but was the result of the German confrontation with Czechoslovakia, and analyses of Chamberlain's actions start from the point of the inadequacy of his *reaction* to the German menace. Chamberlain, though, did not see himself as reacting, but as acting. He was performing with the political courage which had characterized so much of his political career, such as his resolute action in 1931 when, as chancellor of the exchequer, he stopped the flight from the pound. There is nothing to suggest that Chamberlain ever saw Britain, and therefore himself, as being in anything but the lead position throughout the crisis, acting not as the cause of a crisis but as the only source of essential preventive medicine. On becoming prime minister he had embarked on an active foreign policy, seeking through diplomacy to restore Europe to equilibrium.

Chamberlain came to office in 1937 not only with well-defined domestic plans but also with a vision of foreign policy. His years in government dealing with health and financial issues had convinced him of the inherent wastefulness of armaments races. For Chamberlain, the idea of arms control and reduction that had been produced by the Washington Conference of 1921–22 provided an attractive model of an effective approach in this area, which in turn would benefit national economies. He confided to his sisters in October 1937: 'the far reaching plans which I have in mind for the appeasement of Europe & Asia and for the ultimate check to the mad armaments race, which if allowed to continue must involve us all in ruin.'[1] This is a Chamberlain who saw himself as the motive force in international affairs, the leader of the one power with a truly global role. Appeasement is now a word loaded with negative meanings, but as it was used by Chamberlain it was a label defining the diplomatic tactics he hoped to use to achieve his strategic objectives. As Chamberlain would explain to the Archbishop of Canterbury in the wake of the Munich Conference: 'I am sure that some day the Czechs will see that what we did was to save them for a happier future. And I sincerely believe that we have at last opened the way to that general appeasement which alone can save the world from chaos.'[2] His tragic misreading of the future is all too evident in this statement, but it succinctly sums up the conclusions Chamberlain sincerely had reached, and which run through his thinking, as reflected in his letters and comments during this period.

Chamberlain's failures in the years leading up to the Second World War are often explained by his lack of experience of foreign affairs. In fact he had been exposed to the realities of world politics and *Machtpolitik* from the earliest age. A member of a close-knit political family, Neville Chamberlain had been surrounded by discussions of high policy from an early age and enjoyed access to the country's leaders. He was the son of Joseph Chamberlain, the leading exponent of empire at the turn of the century and the architect of Britain's seizure of the resource-wealthy southern African Boer republics. Neville's Nobel Peace Prize winning brother, Austen, had been foreign secretary during the 1920s and had overseen the reorientation of Britain's policy towards Europe that culminated in the Locarno Pact, which sought to restore equilibrium to western Europe.[3] The family legacy is an important component of Chamberlain's world view.

Chamberlain's view of Britain's role in the world was not unique, but was consistent with that of most of the officials working in foreign policy circles. The concept of 'exceptionalism' is one often used by historians to denote certain strands in American diplomatic thinking. The same concept applies equally well to Britain in this period. There is a distinct sense of mission in much of the thinking about Britain's international role that is particularly evident in the aftermath of the armageddon of the First World War. At the 1921 Imperial Conference Lord Curzon, then foreign secretary, had expressed the belief that 'The British Empire is a saving fact in a very distracted world'.[4] Austen Chamberlain, while foreign secretary, wrote in March 1925:

> I am not without hope that the influence of Great Britain may still be made the decisive factor in restoring the comity of nations. With America withdrawn, or taking part only where her interests are directly concerned in the collection of money, Great Britain is the one possible influence for peace and stabilisation. Without our help things will go from bad to worse.[5]

Britain was seen as having a special role, and therefore an obligation, to maintain order. Chamberlain was acutely aware of the special position Britain held in the firmament of world politics as the only global power. As the 1938 *Anschluss* crisis evolved, Chamberlain commented: 'France, as usual has been caught bathing, and the world looks to us.'[6]

Chamberlain revelled in the authority inherent in his post as leader of the British empire. In the summer of 1937, not long in office, he observed a lessening of European tension and was flattered that the Italian ambassador, Count Dino Grandi, attributed this to him. Chamberlain basked in his newfound role, stating: 'it gives one a sense of the wonderful power that the Premiership gives you. As Ch[ancellor] of [the] Ex[chequer] I could hardly have moved a pebble: now I have only to raise a finger & the whole face of Europe is changed!'[7] When his former colleague from the Lloyd George government, the noted historian H.A.L. Fisher, sent a copy of his newly published and highly acclaimed *History of Europe* in March 1938, Chamberlain responded: 'At the present moment I am too busy trying to make the history of Europe to read about it.'[8] Unlike his predecessor, Stanley Baldwin, who expended as little effort as possible in exercising power, Chamberlain preferred a proactive role. His aim was to keep ahead of events and guide them, rather than to be the victim of events and have to struggle to recover lost ground. This difference in approach is one of the fundamental consequences of the change of administration in Britain between Baldwin and

Chamberlain and provides the background to the shift in foreign policy that begins to occur in 1937.

Chamberlain's world map, like that of his predecessors, was global, alive with imperial concerns and therefore not Eurocentric. These concerns found a mirror image in his analysis of the objectives of Hitler's foreign policy. After Lord Halifax's visit to Germany in 1937 there was much discussion in British policymaking circles of the possibility of Germany demanding some restitution of its colonial empire lost after the First World War. Chamberlain made up his mind 'that the Colonial question was the most difficult part of any agreement with the Germans'.[9] In retrospect, it is clear that colonial aspirations were not of importance to Hitler, but Britain's own preoccupation with imperial issues led to an assumption that there was a similar fascination in Berlin, resulting in a serious diversion of attention and energy away from what proved to be the main arena.

In Europe, the cornerstone of British policy had, since the early years of the century, been its alliance with France. France, though, was viewed by many officials in the interwar period as a nervous, highly strung country, whose succession of shaky governments provided little opportunity for sound action. As 1938 began, Chamberlain wrote to his sisters: 'it is a great nuisance that the French Government has disintegrated just at the moment when strength & continuity in that quarter would have been particularly useful.'[10] A month later he observed: 'France though very deeply attached to her understanding with us has been in a terribly weak condition being continually subject to attacks on the franc & flights of capital together with industrial troubles & discontent.'[11] His confidence in the French Popular Front government, not strong at the best of times, diminished further during the course of 1938, leading him to the view that in Paris there was 'a French Government in which one can cannot have the slightest confidence and which I suspect to be in the closest touch with our opposition'.[12] Chamberlain's deep concern about his own domestic political front is reflected in this opinion. Matters were not improved when a new government was formed in April 1938. Chamberlain had known the new French foreign minister, Georges Bonnet, since 1932 and considered him to be an ambitious schemer,[13] an ironic conclusion, given Bonnet's subsequent sympathy for Chamberlain's foreign policy. Neville Chamberlain shared the view of many officials that France was an undesirable ally, and one which had further weakened its credibility through its relationship with the Soviet Union. Lord Tyrrell, a former permanent undersecretary at the foreign office and ambassador to France, and normally one of the leading francophiles, commented during the Czechoslovak May Crisis that, 'I think the moment is approaching when the French must choose between us & the Russians.'[14] Given this pervasive lack of faith in France, were there other options open to Britain?

Chamberlain's map of world power dismissed the United States as a factor in the solution of the problems Britain faced. The United States in theory might now be the world's greatest state given its economic edge, but Chamberlain saw that in applied power Britain was still the dominant force. Chamberlain, who had an American stepmother through whom he had enjoyed contact with many members of the American establishment, felt that it would be quite wrong to go on attempting to involve the United States in British plans. He believed that the British empire was sufficiently strong, if need be, to go it alone in foreign policy. In 1934 Chamberlain had advised: 'As for the U.S.A. don't let us be brow beaten by her. She will never repay us for sacrificing our interests in order to conciliate her and if we maintain at once a bold & a frank attitude towards her I am not afraid of the result.'[15] His view of America was well summed up in the summer of 1937, when he commented: 'But the Americans have a long way to go before they become helpful partners in world affairs. I tried to get them to come in on China & Japan but they were too frightened of their own people though I believe if they had been willing to play there was an off chance of stopping hostilities.'[16] After the events in East Asia which had resulted in Roosevelt's famous 'quarantine' speech, Chamberlain concluded that, 'after a lot of ballyhoo the Americans will somehow fade out and leave us to carry all the blame and the odium'.[17] When an American ship was attacked by Japan, Chamberlain suspected the United States still would do nothing, though he hoped they might, as he confided to his sister: 'It is always best and safest to count on nothing from the Americans except words.'[18] As Chamberlain came to deal with foreign affairs more and more, and to enjoy what he saw as his success, so his view of any role for the United States diminished. He made no attempt to establish personal relations with Franklin Roosevelt and the discussions around a new appointment to the Washington embassy elicited the view that 'the Americans are so rotten it does not matter who we send there'.[19] Chamberlain was the first prime minister since Asquith for whom there was no American factor in his policy calculations. His attitude may well have been due to a mix of frustration stemming from his negotiations with the United States over wartime debt questions, the legacy of America's failure to implement its commitments after the First World War when Woodrow Wilson's plans were defeated in the senate, and a jealousy of its inherent power which threatened his own predominant position.

This left Chamberlain with the option of either a *rapprochement* with Germany or Italy. He noted in his diary in early 1938: 'From the first I have been trying to improve relations with the 2 storm centres Berlin & Rome. It seemed to me that we were drifting into worse & worse positions with both with the prospect of having ultimately to face 2 enemies at once.'[20] His aim was to separate these two possible adversaries if at all possible. His views varied over time as to which of the two countries he would prefer to have better relations with. Early in his premiership he observed: 'If only we could get on terms with the Germans I wouldn't care a rap for Musso.'[21]

Chamberlain was facing a difficult set of decisions as to what policy to follow. The interwar period saw two classic studies of British foreign secretaries, C.K. Webster's *Castlereagh* and H.W.V. Temperley's *Canning*. Whereas the former was read by Austen Chamberlain on the eve of his Locarno initiative, Neville was reading the latter at the time of the September crisis. Whereas Austen had extrapolated lessons about the nature of the European equilibrium, Neville drew the lesson: 'Again and again Canning lays it down that you should never menace unless you are in a position to carry out your threats and although if we have to fight I should hope we should be able to give a good account of ourselves we are certainly not in a position in which the military advisers would feel happy in undertaking to begin hostilities if we were not forced to do so.'[22] This aptly sums up the concerns confronting Chamberlain and reflects the advice he was receiving from his preferred advisers. Chamberlain met Hitler without senior or technical advisers, but he had received much advice from them in the weeks and months preceding the crisis that had helped shape his understanding of the options available to him. He sought to build equilibrium, but was reluctant to follow any policy that might require the use of force.

Chamberlain was not alone in shaping foreign policy, and his views were informed by those of the wider foreign policy community. Many thought that the new political architecture of eastern Europe was either inherently unstable, and therefore contrary to British interests, or simply unimportant. The former Labour Party foreign secretary, Arthur Henderson, had had scant time for 'All these snuffling little countries',[23] as he called these post-First World War creations, complaining of having to deal with 'all these wretched little places. Many of them must only be about half the size of Yorkshire!'[24] A less than positive view pervaded much of the official *mentalité* towards eastern Europe. The young diplomat Renell Rodd, who by 1938 was an influential financier, wrote in 1921 to Harold Nicolson: 'From one point of view Bulgaria is of course entirely unimportant, except in so far as peace or war is concerned, in the same way as Czecho-Slovakia or Switzerland. They do not matter to the British Empire as a whole. Yet each of these funny little people might matter as much as Greece is conceived to matter.'[25] Paul Gore-Booth recorded in his diary in 1936 his impression 'that whereas the Czechs look totally bourgeois the Poles can give a more aristocratic appearance'.[26] Joseph Addison wrote from the Prague legation in 1933 his view that 'The Czech is not celebrated either for his (or her) beauty or for his (or her) charm. The Jewish population justifies the worst excesses of Hitler while the Austrian Germans, or whatever they call themselves, have acquired local colour.'[27] Nevile Henderson, while ambassador at Berlin, wrote to Halifax: 'The Teuton and the Slav are irreconcilable – just as are the Briton and the Slav. Mackenzie King told me last year after the Imperial Conference that the Slavs in Canada never assimilated with the people and never became good citizens.'[28] Czechoslovakia's strategic importance might be appreciated by many officials, but there was little or no empathy for the peoples caught up in the maelstrom.

Chamberlain's decision on how to handle the crisis had as much to do with domestic as foreign events. Chamberlain had proved to be a tremendous popular success as prime minister, an unlikely experience for a man who only reached the highest office as he approached his seventieth birthday and who had hitherto spent his life in the political shadow of others. His sudden popularity was as unexpected as that enjoyed by Calvin Coolidge in the United States. He was, in retrospect, a consummately skilled politician and a manipulator of the media, understanding the need to grasp the popular imagination. This is one of the factors that influenced the development of his Plan Z, the secret scheme that he evolved for a surprise meeting with Hitler. He saw the scheme as both 'unconventional and daring.'[29] Today, in an age when summit meetings occur between leaders almost weekly at some place on the globe, it is important to recall how rare these were in Chamberlain's period. His decision to fly to any such meeting was also important. The first two political leaders to use airplanes had been Hitler and Roosevelt, in their respective presidential bids, both utilizing the new technology to add a sense of dynamism. In Britain, the return of Edward VIII to London by air to assume throne in January 1936 had provided a powerful image. The private secretary's office at the foreign office commented on the scheme: 'It would seem that the spectacular effect on public opinion everywhere of making the journey *by air* is likely to be considerable.'[30] When it was announced, even such sceptics as the former diplomat and now member of parliament Harold Nicolson were delighted, noting in his diary: 'My first feeling is one of enormous relief.'[31] Chamberlain was all too aware that, while he had succeeded to the leadership of his party and therefore the premiership, he had yet to win a general election. Many of his actions during 1938 must have been calculated with one eye on the looming inevitability of a general election in a period of economic depression and the consequent need to find successes for his government. Any consideration of foreign policy has to take account of Chamberlain's home front.

In terms of public diplomacy, Chamberlain's tactics were brilliant, though in terms of applied diplomatic experience and the realities of statecraft his planning was lamentable. In Chamberlain's decision to meet Hitler there is a critical divergence from British diplomatic practice – there were no advance preparations and Chamberlain travelled without expert advisers. Britain's extensive planning ahead of the 1919 Paris Peace Conference, together with the presence of well briefed technical advisers, had proved critical to Britain's success in those negotiations.[32] Extensive preparations had also preceded all other interwar conferences, but no such planning preceded Chamberlain's meetings with Hitler. As a result Chamberlain entered into the most critical negotiations of his career without the benefit of either expert advice or of advisers who could provide him with cross-bearings for what emerged in his discussions with the German leader. He went to his first meeting with Hitler, at Berchtesgaden, with, as he told George VI, 'a "hunch" ... that we shall get through this time without the use of force'.[33]

One reason for the lack of contingency planning was Chamberlain's mistrust of the foreign office. That the British official mind was not entirely of one mind caused Chamberlain dissatisfaction. After only a few months in office he told his sister: 'I am not too happy with the F.O. who seem to me to have no imagination & no courage.'[34] He particularly did not care for the warnings of the permanent undersecretary, Sir Robert Vansittart, about the growing menace from Germany. Chamberlain considered it a great achievement when he succeeded in shifting Vansittart to a sinecure where he would have little influence, delightedly noting: 'he will be removed from active direction of F.O. policy & I suspect that in Rome & Berlin the rejoicings will be loud & deep.'[35] When Eden resigned as foreign secretary a few weeks later, enabling Chamberlain to complete his changes at the top of the foreign office, the prime minister hoped that he would now have a compliant instrument for the conduct of his grand strategy. Chamberlain's aim was to be able to more boldly direct foreign policy. The changes at the top, though, did not alter the office entirely to his liking. Even after the Munich Conference, but before that settlement began to unravel, Chamberlain summed up his bafflement of the foreign office, observing that it was 'tempted to follow the old Eden lines and chortle at the prospect of "defeating fascist aims." I simply cannot keep their minds fixed on our real purpose; the dislike they have of totalitarian states is so strong that it will keep bursting out'.[36]

Chamberlain was right to suspect that there was resistance to his policy from some career diplomats. Sir Horace Rumbold, recently retired but still influential, who had served as ambassador to Berlin at the time of Hitler's rise to power, considered that Chamberlain did

not know 'the technique of dealing with Dictators who are
necessarily bullies. The more you truckle to them the more arrogant
they become'.[37] The events which were unfolding in central Europe
did not come as a surprise to many officials. In April 1938 Vansittart
warned: 'We now have considerable grounds ... for believing that
Hitler does intend not only to disrupt Czechoslovakia by the eventual
annexation of the Sudetendeutsch districts, but also by the
distribution of other parts of the corpse to Poland and Hungary.'[38]
Those who saw the danger in Chamberlain's policy, though, were
forced simply to observe as the prime minister seized control of
foreign policy. Frank Roberts, one of the members of the foreign
office central department who dealt with the Czech crisis, and whose
later career gave ample evidence of a robust attitude towards
threatening regimes, recalled:

> The differences between us and the Prime Minister were over
> the right steps to avoid war, not only then but later, and over
> the Prime Minister's refusal to accept that Hitler's ambitions
> went far beyond bringing Germans from Austria,
> Czechoslovakia and Poland into the Reich. We shared the
> general sense of relief that war had been averted. But there was
> also a strong sense of shame over our treatment of
> Czechoslovakia and of regret that we and the French were
> mainly responsible.[39]

This failure would be a painful memory in the British diplomatic
mind in the postwar years.

In the mounting crisis in Europe, of which Chamberlain was well
aware, what role did he see for Czechoslovakia, or indeed east-
central Europe? Chamberlain was in many ways the heir of his
brother's foreign policy. Austen Chamberlain had desired to return to
Britain's traditional concept of the European balance of power that
sought to prevent any one power from dominating western Europe
and thus posing an invasion threat. Britain was far less concerned
about balance in the east, where stability was the key, its part being
to remain stable and thereby avoid causing consequential
disturbances to the western European balance. Austen Chamberlain's
own view of eastern Europe's role and its importance to Britain
remained consistent throughout his period at the foreign office. He

saw Britain as having very different interests in Europe, observing 'that in Western Europe we are a partner ... in Eastern Europe our rôle should be that of a disinterested *amicus curiæ*'.[40] He famously informed Lord Crewe that 'no British Government ever will or ever can risk the bones of a British grenadier' for the Polish corridor.[41] Lord Simon, a former foreign secretary and the leading Liberal Party coalition member in the cabinet, advised after the assassination of Dolfuss: 'Our own policy is quite clear. We must keep out of trouble in Central Europe at all costs.'[42] James Headlam-Morley, the foreign office historian, in studying the history of British policy had advised that 'in the past our diplomacy has always failed when it was confronted by problems arising in the east of Europe'.[43] The inability to see continental issues as a whole remained part of the official mind and it is not surprising to find Neville Chamberlain speaking during the Czech crisis of 'a quarrel in a faraway country between people of whom we know nothing'.[44] Even in the aftermath of the Munich Conference, Lord Halifax commented: 'It is one thing to allow German expansion in Central Europe, which to my mind is a normal & natural thing, but we must be able to resist German expansion in Western Europe or else our whole position is undermined.'[45] As the crisis escalated in April 1939, the influential Maurice Hankey wrote: 'The whole point is that *we* cannot save these eastern nations.'[46]

These views informed Chamberlain's perception of the strategic importance of central Europe. Chamberlain shared the general assessment that there was little or nothing Britain could do about events concerning Czechoslovakia. Lord Simon noted in his diary after an emergency Sunday cabinet meeting during the May 1938 Czechoslovak mobilization crisis:

> We are endeavouring, at one & the same time, to restrain Germany by warning her that she must not assume that we could remain neutral if she crossed the frontier; to stimulate Prague to make concessions; and to make sure that France will not take some rash action such as mobilisation (when has mobilisation been anything but a prelude to war?) under the delusion that we would join her in defence of Czechoslovakia. We won't and can't – but an open declaration to this effect would only give encouragement to Germany's *intransigence*.[47]

This view was the product of earlier conclusions reached during previous Hitler-inspired crises. At the time of the *Anschluss* Chamberlain concluded: 'You have only to look at the map to see that nothing that France or we could do could possibly save Czecho-Slovakia from being over-run by the Germans if they wanted to do it.'[48] It was at this stage that he decided against any guarantee backing France's obligations to Prague. The natural consequence of conceding Britain's inability to act in central Europe was to accept it as part of Germany's natural sphere of influence. Already in November 1937 Chamberlain had commented on German ambitions: 'Of course they want to dominate Eastern Europe; they want as close a union with Austria as they can get without incorporating her in the Reich and they want much the same things for the Sudetendeutsche as we did for the Uitlanders in the Transvaal.'[49] This, incidentally, is the earliest mention of the Sudetenland in his papers.

The reference to one of the critical events of his father's career, and the role of memory, is an element in his attempt to rationalize Hitler's objectives. In the same letter he notes that what he wanted 'was to convince Hitler of our sincerity & to ascertain what objectives he had in mind and I think both of these objects have been achieved'. Again, this is an effort to see Hitler's policy as part of a rational universe. Chamberlain was reluctant to see the situation in Berlin as anything other than the normal give and take of statecraft. At the beginning of 1938, while reading *The House that Hitler Built*, he observed that it was 'an extremely clever & well informed but very pessimistic book. If I accepted the author's conclusions I should despair but I don't & won't'.[50] As the Czech crisis unfolded, Chamberlain admitted to his sister, with unusual despondency, 'Is it not positively horrible to think that the fate of hundreds of millions of people depends on one man and he is half mad'.[51] After his first meeting with Hitler, however, he reassuringly reported that he did not see any trace of insanity in the German leader.[52]

The first evidence of Plan Z appears in Chamberlain's papers on 3 September, when he reveals it to Halifax. As the crisis mounted in the early days of September it was decided to implement it, with Chamberlain flying to meet Hitler at Berchtesgaden on 15 September. There Chamberlain seemed to revel in his role of appearing with the military strongman of Europe, and came away with the belief that he could negotiate a solution. The image he had built of the tough British politician aided the initial popular expectations of what he might achieve. Nicolson observed that 'at the time we all assumed it was a gesture of strength'.[53] At that first meeting, though, Chamberlain made a critical concession by accepting the idea of plebiscites, which would inevitably cost Czechoslovakia strategically important territory. Clearly this gain by Germany was meant to appease Hitler. Britain, after applying pressure on France, arranged an Anglo-French warning to Benes that his country would be expected to turn over all districts which were considered over 50 per cent German. At his second meeting with Hitler at Bad Godesberg on 22 September, the settlement looked as if it would come unstuck when Hitler presented new demands. Chamberlain, desperate to salvage his status as peacemaker, flew back to London, and at a cabinet meeting on 24 September advised his colleagues that Britain should acquiesce to Hitler's insistence on German control of the disputed districts by 1 October. Chamberlain's dominance of the cabinet held, but his heretofore compliant foreign secretary, Lord Halifax, began to waver.

The origin of Halifax's change of view lies with his permanent undersecretary, Alec Cadogan. Chosen to replace Vansittart in the hope that he would be less vocal, he proved an adroit diplomatist during the Second World War, and was kept in post by Churchill and Eden. In his diary on 24 September he wrote: 'A week ago we moved (or were pushed) from "autonomy" to cession, many of us found great difficulty in the idea of ceding people to Nazi Germany.'[54] Cadogan now launched an effort to get the foreign secretary to reconsider, noting in his diary that he 'gave him a bit of my mind'. Cadogan was concerned, as were many others, that Britain and France were not militarily prepared, but, as he recorded, 'I'd rather be beat than dishonoured'. After a sleepless night, Halifax had a change of mind, which came as a rude shock to Chamberlain in cabinet, who now must have feared that he was about to lose control of his colleagues. This minor ministerial revolt had the effect of forcing Chamberlain to modify his plans to push through a settlement on the lines demanded by Hitler.[55] The officials who had been unhappy with the direction of policy had now found an opportunity to push for a change of policy.

Chamberlain, in a last desperate effort to rescue his mediation efforts before any potential growing pressure from within the cabinet forced a change of policy, now effectively gave way to Hitler, responding to a note from the German leader: 'After reading your letter, I feel certain that you can get all essentials without war, without delay.'[56] So it proved. When the same afternoon Hitler proposed a meeting at Munich, Chamberlain did not even convene the cabinet again before he left, no doubt to avoid any further pressure on him. He was determined to return with a settlement that prevented any immediate war, knowing that the popular relief would legitimize his actions and reestablish his predominance. Chamberlain did indeed leave the Munich Conference seemingly having averted war in Europe. He returned to Britain to a hero's welcome, and was accorded the rare honour of appearing on the balcony at Buckingham Palace.[57] Plan Z had been a brilliant public relations triumph for Chamberlain, sending his reputation soaring. It was this issue which was on his mind during his triumphal drive into London, commenting to Halifax that 'All this will be over in three months' – referring not to the longevity of the Munich accord but to his concern over the fickleness of the British electorate.[58]

Why, though, did he engage in three journeys to meet Hitler, conceding more ground on each? Lord Lloyd was led to comment sardonically: 'If at first you don't concede, fly, fly again.'[59] While great hopes had hung on his first visit, it was thought that the leader of the British empire had gone to speak from a position of strength. Once the fruits of his visit were known, despondency set in in many quarters. Nicolson observed that Chamberlain's '"gallant actions" had declined into a mere senile visit to Canosa'.[60] Chamberlain had invested so much in producing a diplomatic triumph to bolster his political standing in Britain that, by the time of the Munich meeting, he was willing to accept any settlement which could be portrayed positively at home. The efficacy of summit meetings has often been debated and perhaps Chamberlain should have heeded the advice of Philip de Commenyes that great rulers who wished to enjoy good relations should never meet, but rather it was better 'that they accommodated their differences by the mediation of wise and faithful ministers'.[61] Chamberlain's experiences are a set-piece example of the dangers of summitry, where the meeting acquires a momentum and necessities of its own, where little time is provided to resolve the finer points at issue, and where a result is demanded to create a public relations success. Hitler was operating to a different agenda.

At the beginning of the crisis, Chamberlain had been determined to grasp the nettle of foreign affairs and drive events; by the end of the September 1938 crisis he was no more than a passive actor. Perhaps Chamberlain became caught up in the excitement which surrounded seeing himself as the arbiter of Europe. His immense popularity after his accession to the premiership had come as something of a surprise. Although now 70 years of age, he still considered himself the least of the Chamberlains, in the shadow of his colossus of a father and his Nobel Prize winning brother. Neville Chamberlain was not without political skills and had in some ways shown something of a flair for international relations. He could be credited, in attempting to find a way to seize the initiative from Hitler, of inventing shuttle diplomacy. The speed at which events evolved and the focus of Chamberlain's seemingly vigorous efforts to deal with the crisis not only influenced domestic popular opinion but must have also had some effect on the prime minister. His supercharged state is evident in his famous declaration, upon his return from Munich, of having achieved peace in our time, a statement which he regretted on calmer reflection. Somewhere, though, between the initial crisis and the first meeting with Hitler, show had become a substitute for substance. The pressures of the domestic audience, the only one that would resonate with a political leader sensitive to his electoral laws of survival, had come to obscure the original object of standing firm against Hitler's confrontational diplomacy. The realities of diplomacy and the requirements of statecraft had subtly but surely shifted during the days of the September crisis until, by its end, Neville Chamberlain's initial ideal of action and courage had become pretence, then timidity and finally façade.

Boston University

NOTES

1. N. Chamberlain to Ida Chamberlain, 30 Oct. 1937. NC 18/1/1026. Neville Chamberlain Papers, University of Birmingham Library.
2. N. Chamberlain to Archbishop Lang, 2 Oct. 1938. NC 7/11/31/163.
3. Erik Goldstein, 'British Diplomatic Strategy and the Locarno Conference', in M. Dockrill and B.J.C. McKercher, *Diplomacy and World Power: Studies in British Foreign Policy, 1890–1951* (Cambridge, 1996).
4. CAB 32/2, Imperial Conference, 1st Meeting, 20 June 1921. Cabinet Papers, Public Record Office, London.
5. *Documents on British Foreign Policy, 1919-1939* [hereafter DBFP], 1st series, Vol.27 (London, 1986), Doc.256, Chamberlain to Howard (Washington), 18 March 1925.
6. N. Chamberlain to Hilda Chamberlain, 13 March 1938. NC 18/1/1041.
7. N. Chamberlain to Ida Chamberlain, 8 Aug. 1937. NC 18/1/1015.
8. N. Chamberlain to HAL Fisher, 21 March 1938. HAL Fisher 77. Fisher Papers, Bodleian Library, Oxford.
9. N. Chamberlain diary, 19 Feb. 1938. NC/2/24a.
10. N. Chamberlain to Ida Chamberlain, 16 Jan. 1938. NC 18/1/1035.
11. N. Chamberlain diary, 19 Feb. 1938. NC/2/24a.
12. N. Chamberlain to Ida Chamberlain, 20 March 1938. NC 18/1/1042.
13. N. Chamberlain to Hilda Chamberlain, 24 April 1938. NC 18/1/1048.
14. Tyrrell to Phipps, 20 May 1938. PHPP 2/15. Phipps Papers, Churchill College, Cambridge.
15. N. Chamberlain to Simon, 1 Sept. 1934. Simon 79. Simon Papers, Bodleain Library, Oxford.
16. N. Chamberlain (Balmoral Castle) to Hilda Chamberlain, 29 Aug. 1937. NC 18/1/1018.
17. N. to Hilda Chamberlain, 9 Oct. 1937. NC 18/1/1026.
18. N. to Hilda Chamberlain, 17 Dec. 1937. NC 18/1/1032.
19. Cited in Telford Taylor, *Munich: The Price of Peace* (New York, 1980), p.660.
20. N. Chamberlain, 19 Feb. 1938. NC/2/24a.
21. N. Chamberlain to Ida Chamberlain, 4 July 1937. NC 18/1/1010.
22. N. Chamberlain to Ida Chamberlain, 11 Sept. 1938. NC 18/1/1068.
23. Quoted in Dalton diary 13, 27 March 1930. Dalton Papers, British Library of Political and Economic Science, London.
24. Dalton diary 10, 17 June 1929.
25. Francis Rodd (Sofia) to Harold Nicholson (*sic*), 25 Aug. 1921. 2nd Lord Rennell of Rodd Papers. Bodleian Library, Oxford.
26. Diary fragment of trip from Vienna to Poland, 15 Sept. 1936. Gore-Booth MS.Eng.c.4547. Bodleian Library, Oxford.
27. Joseph A. (Addison) (Prague) to Bland, 8 Aug. 1933. BLND 9/13. Bland Papers, Churchill College, Cambridge.
28. Nevile Henderson to Halifax, 22 Aug. 1938. FO 371/21743/C11048/1941/18. Foreign Office Papers, Public Record Office, London.
29. N. Chamberlain to Ida Chamberlain, 3 Sept. 1938. NC 18/1/1066.
30. Memorandum, Sept. 1938. FO 371/21731/C9708/1941/18.
31. Harold Nicolson, *Diaries and Letters, 1930–1939*, ed. Nigel Nicolson (New York, 1966), p.360, entry for 14 Sept. 1938.
32. Erik Goldstein. *Winning the Peace: British Diplomatic Strategy, Peace Planning, and the Paris Peace Conference, 1916–1920* (Oxford, 1991).
33. N. Chamberlain to George VI, 6 Sept. 1938. NC 7/3/27 [copy from Royal Archives].
34. N. Chamberlain to Hilda Chamberlain, 12 Sept. 1937. NC 18/1/1020.
35. N. Chamberlain to Ida Chamberlain, 12 Dec. 1937. NC 18/1/1031.

36. N. Chamberlain to Ida Chamberlain, 12 Feb. 1939. NC 18/1/1085.
37. Sir Horace Rumbold to Anthony Rumbold, 2 March 1938. Rumbold additional V/5. Rumbold Papers, Bodleian Library, Oxford.
38. Minute by Vansittart, 8 April 1938. FO 371/21715/C3065/1941/18.
39. Frank Roberts, *Dealing with Dictators: The Destruction and Revival of Europe, 1930–70* (London, 1991), p.31.
40. FO 371/11064/W1252/9/98, minute by A. Chamberlain, 21 Feb. 1925.
41. *DBFP*, 1st series, Vol.27 (London, 1986), Doc.200, Chamberlain to Crewe, 16 Feb. 1925.
42. Simon to prime minister, 27 July 1934. Simon 79.
43. FO 371/11064/W1252/9/98.
44. *Documents on International Affairs, 1938*, Vol.II, ed. Monica Curtis (London, 1943), pp.270–71.
45. Halifax to Phipps, 1 Nov. 1938. PHPP 1/21.
46. Hankey to Phipps, 4 April 1939. PHPP 3/3.
47. Simon diary, 22 May 1938. Simon 7.
48. Neville Chamberlain to Ida Chamberlain, 20 March 1938. NC 18/1/1042
49. Neville Chamberlain to Ida Chamberlain, 26 Nov. 1937. NC 18/1/1030
50. Stephen Roberts, *The House that Hitler Built* (London, 1937). N. Chamberlain to Hilda Chamberlain, 30 Jan. 1938. NC 18/1/1037.
51. N. Chamberlain to Ida Chamberlain, 3 Sept. 1938 NC 18/1/1066.
52. N. Chamberlain to Ida Chamberlain, 19 Sept. 1938 NC 18/1/1069.
53. Nicolson, *Diaries and Letters*, p.365, entry for 22 Sept. 1938.
54. David Dilkes (ed.), *The Diaries of Sir Alexander Cadogan, 1938–1945* (London, 1971), p.103.
55. Andrew Roberts. 'The Holy Fox': A Biography of Lord Halifax (London: Nicolson, 1991).
56. *DBFP*, 3rd series, Vol.II, Doc.1158, 28 Sept. 1938.
57. This has only occurred once since, on VE day when Churchill appeared, possibly to erase the memory of this earlier event.
58. Discussed in R.A.C. Parker, *Chamberlain and Appeasement: British Policy and the Coming of the Second World War* (New York, 1993), p.181.
59. Lloyd to Loraine, 20 Oct. 1938. GLLD 19/8. Lord Lloyd Papers, Churchill College, Cambridge.
60. Nicolson, *Diaries and Letters*, p.362, entry for 20 Sept. 1938.
61. Andrew R. Scoble (ed.), *The Memoirs of Philip de Commines*, 2 vols. (London, 1855), Vol.I, p.121.

Agents and Structures:
The Dominions and the Czechoslovak
Crisis, September 1938

MICHAEL GRAHAM FRY

Elevated effortlessly and rightfully in the course of an imperial conference, Neville Chamberlain became prime minister on 28 May 1937. Within a year Britain and the commonwealth faced the possibility of involvement in a European war over Czechoslovakia. With every confidence in Chamberlain, and just as much in the validity of their own convictions, the elites of the three major dominions – Australia, Canada and South Africa – had roles to play in the September crisis. Three historians, Nicholas Mansergh, Ritchie Ovendale and Donald Watt, carried an enquiry into those roles and the broader question of the dominions and appeasement that began in the Second World War.[1] They and others who challenged the Eurocentricity of the literature and made active appeasement a matter of rational choice by setting out the global balances of power and vulnerability, turned to the significance of structural constraints on statesmen, elites and governments. Paul Kennedy and Reinhardt Meyers took the same approach.[2] That is the point of departure here, making unprecedented use of the South African archives.[3]

Structures

In January 1938 Chamberlain set out the predicament and the paradox which governed the debate on grand strategy: 'We are a very rich and very vulnerable Empire, and there are plenty of poor adventurers not very far away who look on as with hungry eyes.'[4] The empire was Britain's joy and its cross. It could neither carry it nor lay it down, nor easily arrange for the United States to share the burden. The dominions for their part were grappling with economic and strategic realities, functioning in an experimental commonwealth, and judging Europe through the lens of a maturing belief system.

Economic Imperatives

The interwar years, and especially the 1930s, was the second period in British imperial history when the empire was crucial to Britain's economic wellbeing. Britain turned inward to the empire, to the system of imperial preference and the sterling area. Its economic security depended substantially on intra-imperial trading and financial arrangements. The dominions in turn enjoyed certain access to British markets and capital.[5] The political consequences were clear. Peace, the indispensable friend of trade and investment, the certain source of prosperity, was the highest value to be served, its preservation the goal of high policy. The unity of the empire must be maintained for all the economic benefits it brought in peace and would bring to Britain in a general, protracted war. Yet, as part of the inescapable paradox, the very system of imperial trade and finance provoked Germany, Italy and Japan, and alienated the United States. Neither economic nor colonial appeasement materially altered German policy. South Africa nevertheless regarded Germany as a reliable partner for Britain in Africa. It should be allowed to regain some of its former colonies. It would, hopefully, accept monetary compensation for not recovering south-west Africa. Australia remained as resolutely opposed to surrendering its Pacific mandates as it was to admitting Asian immigrants. Both dominions found merit, therefore, in cooperating with Germany in Europe. Australia and New Zealand led the opposition to opening British and empire markets to United States exports, so as to protect their agricultural exports. Only Canada had a trade agreement with the United States. The engagement of the United States remained, with that exception, largely neglected.[6]

Strategic Realities

The global distribution of military power; the threats from Germany, Italy and Japan; the flawed assumption that a regional conflict would become a global war; the possibility that their fate could be settled in far-off places;[7] and Britain's decision to create an essentially defensive air deterrent against Germany which was not credible in September 1938 led Australia and South Africa, if not Canada, to the following conclusions – that the Royal Navy, the engine of imperial security, was receiving insufficient funds; that the Singapore strategy for countering Japan was in jeopardy; that Mussolini had his thumb on the windpipe of empire; and that Italy presented the greatest threat to the empire's vital lines of communication.[8] South Africa, moreover, judged Italy and France – the 'Latins', raising black armies and undermining white communities – to be a threat to its mission of leading a white power bloc in sub-Saharan Africa and thus to white civilization in Africa.[9]

The remedies the dominions preferred were diplomatic rather than military; active appeasement rather than deterrence. Deterrence was at best given a secondary role in the primary strategy of mediation and conciliation. That preference followed from three conclusions. First, Britain was not likely to give the Mediterranean priority over the North Sea in its strategic planning. Second, dominion rearmament, begun in 1936–37, had provided only those increments of security that economic recovery, solvency and politics permitted, and status demanded. Individually and collectively the defence capabilities of the dominions by September 1938 ranged from the puny to the paltry. It would have been as preposterous as it was politically impossible for the dominions to have declared in 1938 that they would throw their armed forces into a European war.[10] Third, while British rearmament had deterrent value, as the May 1938 crisis had demonstrated, and would help liberate Britain from France's menacing policies, it was not free of danger. It could strengthen the case for sanctions, for collective security through the League of Nations, and might bring about a replay of the pre-1914 arms race with Germany. Deterrence, expressed in Britain's determination to stand with France in the event of war, strengthened ties with France that would be even more dangerous if France misread the signals in a crisis. In such a crisis, as the air deterrent was not in place, Chamberlain would be gratifyingly less but Hitler more risk acceptant.[11]

Far better, therefore, to rely in 1938 on diplomacy. Britain should actively pursue an agreement with Germany principally over central and eastern Europe. Anglo-German cooperation would help bring Italy to heel and prevent Mussolini from poisoning Hitler's mind against Britain. Chamberlain needed to consummate the Anglo-Italian agreement; recognize Italy's annexation of Abyssinia but put an end to further Italian territorial ambitions in East Africa; end intervention in the Spanish civil war; and prevent Spain from becoming an Italo-German province.[12] In Asia, Britain needed to induce Japan to exhaust itself in China, and let China suffer. The Sino-Japanese war enabled Australia to live, albeit uneasily to the point of disbelief, with British assurances that the empire in Asia-Pacific was secure; that Britain would implement the Singapore strategy should Japan threaten the Pacific dominions; and that Japan could not invade Australia in a Pacific war. Australia had no alternatives.[13]

The consequence that was clear was deplorable. Threat reduction would come at the expense of others. Czechoslovakia, like Abyssinia and China, was a prime candidate. The consequence that brought uncertainty put sovereignty to the ultimate test. Would the dominions join in a war in which Britain was a belligerent? Jan Smuts, deputy minister and minister of justice in South Africa, judged Canada as hopeless, Australia as uncertain and South Africa as, at best, cautious. Each would join in a European war to the extent that it found the idea of Britain's defeat at the hands of its enemies intolerable, and what Britain stood for, and its enemies threatened, indispensable. As a group, the dominions were 'thoroughly pacific and also remote from Central Europe'. They would not fight to uphold the 1919 treaties. Smuts even doubted whether they would fight once again for Belgium and France. Could Britain therefore count on them? Only in two cases, Smuts suggested – if Britain was in danger of being attacked, and if a member of the commonwealth was actually attacked.[14] Britain would then reap the inestimable economic and strategic benefits of commonwealth unity in the long haul of a protracted war. That expectation, in turn, gave the dominions leverage to constrain British policy, to ensure that Britain made peace the highest value.

Praxis

In matters of foreign policy the dominions functioned oligocratically. A small oligarchy, political leaders around and more or less loyal to a prime minister, determined policy, dominating cabinets and answering to parliaments. Prime ministers were very powerful. They were advised by officials in infant departments who were sufficiently small in number, if not always cohesive, to be personal staffs. In Australia J.A. Lyons, leader of the United Australia Party, had been prime minister since 1931. W.M. Hughes, minister for external affairs, R.G. Menzies, attorney general and minister for industry, Sir Earle Page, leader of the Country Party and minister for commerce, and R.G. Casey, treasurer and minister for development, made up an inner group. Lyons and the inner group, able largely to ignore the full cabinet on matters of foreign policy, were served by the prime minister's personal staff and the department of external affairs, headed by W.R. Hodgson. P. Liesching, Britain's acting high commissioner, saw the consequences. While the cabinet was in touch with public opinion, Lyons was often out of touch with all but the inner group. The cabinet suffered from a lack of sustained exposure to foreign affairs.[15]

In Canada, W.L. MacKenzie King headed a Liberal government, its most prominent members being Ernest Lapointe, minister of justice, and in Geneva in September 1938, Ian MacKenzie, minister of defence and Charles Dunning, minister of finance, King was also secretary of state for external affairs, served principally by O.D. Shelton, the nationalist and experienced undersecretary of state, and the even more experienced Loring Christie, counsellor in the department. The fusionist, United Party government in South Africa rested uneasily on the shoulders of two gentlemanly autocrats: J.B.M. Hertzog, the prime minister and minster for external affairs, a pro-German but not pro-nazi Afrikaner, and Smuts. The latter, difficult to digest, then and now, was a statesman of international reputation, an Atlanticist well-connected in Britain and the United States, loyal to Britain, but as suspect in certain circles there as he was in South Africa. Oswald Pirow, minister of defence and minister of railways and harbours, and sympathetic toward nazi Germany, N.C. Havenga, minister of finance, and P.G.W. Grobler, minister of native affairs, joined them in an inner group. All three were loyal to Hertzog, not Smuts. Hertzog consulted the full cabinet only intermittently and did not keep it fully informed. He was more likely to make a statement of his preferences when it met and expect its approval than to consult it.[16]

H.D.J. Bodenstein, able and clever, a nationalist and a republican, opposed both to British influence in South African affairs and to imperial cooperation, stood resolutely for South African sovereignty, status and an independent foreign policy. He distrusted Smuts. As state secretary he dominated the ministry of external affairs. As intellectual *eminence grise*, he had no equal in his influence on Hertzog. The prime minister saw him as indispensable. Sir William Clark, the British high commissioner, regarded him with a distaste bordering on loathing, and feared his influence. Bodenstein, a friend of the German consul general in Cape Town, Emile Wiehle, hand-in-glove and improperly so with the nationalist newspaper *Die Burger*, was difficult, duplicitous, secretive and blundering, and incurably suspicious of Britain. He wrote Hertzog's policy statements, and, having Hertzog in the palm of his hand, enjoyed complete freedom from cabinet scrutiny. Indeed, Clark reported, Bodenstein, on constitutional and imperial issues, 'is the government'. One should weigh carefully Clark's sniffing condescension and personal animus, but Malcolm MacDonald, when dominions secretary, actually wrote that being rid of 'Body', 'is one of the most important changes required in the British Commonwealth'.[17]

The imperial policy community, which Lloyd George had created in 1917 and which functioned through the Washington Conference of 1921–22, had long since ceased to exist. Instead, there were plural channels of information and consultation flowing from London, well and routinely used, giving the dominions opportunities to influence British policy. Prime ministers corresponded, governors general, British except for Sir Patrick Duncan in South Africa, and British high commissioners played their constitutional and political roles in the dominion capitals. They reported formally to the dominions office in London. Dominion high commissioners in London – Stanley Bruce for Australia, Vincent Massey for Canada and Charles te Water for South Africa[18] – helped channel information between the dominions and external affairs officials and their respective prime ministers. They were well-connected if not always well regarded in London, and also represented their governments at the League of Nations,[19] Bruce and te Water were held in higher esteem at home than the embarrassed but energetic Massey. They had begun to meet in May 1936, at Massey's suggestion, as an informal consultative group, occasionally in routine times, frequently in crisis, sometimes with the foreign secretary or another British cabinet minister present.[20]

Britain, however, in 1938 was still the window on the world for the dominions, its diplomatic and intelligence networks dominating the supply and analysis of information, its diplomatic and consular services acting as agents for the whole empire. The dominions had invested only modestly in diplomatic and intelligence capabilities. Australia was represented in Washington and Tokyo, at low levels; Canada in Washington, Tokyo and Paris; and South Africa in Washington, Paris, Berlin and Stockholm, Rome, the Hague and Copenhagen, and Lisbon. Stefanus Gie, the Germanophile minister in Berlin, saw Jewish conspiracies aimed at Germany everywhere and was contemptuous of Smuts' concern for Zionism. Australia claimed a special insight into the Japanese threat and Lyons a personal intimacy with Mussolini, Canada a unique knowledge of United States policy and South Africa a particular understanding of Nazi Germany, but it was still very much a case of dependence on Britain.

Beliefs

Dominion elites shared, by 1938, a set of beliefs about the international system in general and Europe in particular. This belief system constituted a set of first principles. When information, especially in crises, challenged them, the governing principles prevailed. One might see it as the triumph of *ideés fixes* over evidence, of the deductive over the inductive. 1938 was a time for action out of conviction, not questioning beliefs. Dominion oligarchies held beliefs not necessarily equally or uniformly, not always with the same level of commitment, intensity and passion, not without inner reservations, but sufficiently in common to constitute an intellectual and psychological structure. It was the foundation of their confidence and trust in, and admiration for, Chamberlain. That was why Chamberlain could anticipate what the dominions preferred and expected of him. The issue is less that the belief system was deeply flawed, and it was, and more that dominion elites shared it, flaws and all. That was clear by, and in part because of, the Imperial Conference of May–June 1937. The New Zealand critique was inconsequential.

Peace, the condition of order, was the highest value to be served. Peaceful change, the peaceful resolution of disputes and crises, was the optimal means of managing the international system. Reason, ethics, moderation, justice, fairness in adjudication and optimism demanded its adoption. All interstate relations were positive sum.

These assumptions fed into a contempt, a distrust bordering on despair, for and with Europe as a system, and underpinned expectations of Britain that outpaced admiration for it. Europe, with France rampant, could not manage its affairs morally and sensibly. Only Britain could orchestrate peaceful change through active, evenhanded mediation in and resolution of disputes. Chamberlain, dedicated to active appeasement, decisive, able to control the cabinet and carry public opinion, well rid of Eden, supported loyally by Lord Halifax and thus free of foreign office pusillanimity would do just that. And time seemed short in 1938; indeed, it was the enemy of peace. 'Immediacy, impartiality and sincerity' were the principles Herzog expected to guide British policy.[21]

These beliefs about peace and peaceful change gave appeasement its definition, one that dominion elites saw as succumbing neither to blackmail nor bad bargaining. Appeasement was not haggling by adversaries over mutually reciprocal concessions. Rather, it was a dramatic, proactive process, granting concessions that were morally justified and transferring resources peacefully, in this case to Germany, even at the expense of others. It would build confidence, facilitate a general settlement and, crucially, serve the highest value – peace.

King, reviewing the evidence of the Spanish civil war, was not alone among dominion leaders in seeing the world apocalyptically. He spoke of violent clashes, on a global scale, between classes and social systems, of a struggle between Louis Pasteur's forces of blood, destruction and death and those of peace, work and health. That was his conceptualization of the predicament of liberalism, as it faced the challenge from the collectivisms of the left and right. Yet King and his colleagues at the Imperial Conference of 1937 insisted that ideological differences should not be allowed to stand in the way of international appeasement. The Labour Party seemed prone to that error. This dominion preference, however, was decidedly one-sided. Communism, not fascism, presented the principal threat to order and peace, within each democratic society and globally. Pirow, no friend of democracy, put combating the communist menace within South Africa and to the world as the first principle of Hertzog's foreign policy. Encouraging Germany to act as a bulwark against communism in Europe was the second principle.[22] National Socialism in action, in the *Anschluss* for example, was repugnant to all but the most dedicated apologist for nazi Germany, Gie among them. Smuts, the gentile Zionist, denounced the brutal methods and resulting nazification of Austria as rape. Nazi Germany was 'Prussianism plus paganism', a combatant in a war of religion against Christianity, a war it would lose.[23] Lyons, a Roman Catholic, denounced, in private, the nazi treatment of both his co-religionists and the Jews. These moral judgements were not allowed, however, given the realities of the multipolar world, to cloud the issue.

Te Water, Lyons and Smuts, for very different reasons, found merit in Soviet policies and potential, countering Japan and Germany, for example. Speculation on all sides, rife since 1919, about the threat of a Russo-German alliance, which Japan might join, had evaporated. Yet, dominion elites concluded, no good could come of collaboration with the Soviet Union, no benefits would flow from an alliance. Duncan opposed an Anglo-Russian alliance even in July 1939. The Soviet Union was not a normal state; its elite drew legitimacy only from terror and subversion. It did not conform to established norms of civilized conduct. It was, in any case, divided internally and weak economically and militarily. The Soviet commitments to Czechoslovakia and France were forged to impress the league, ensnare the West and benefit from a capitalist war. Intelligence reports and rumours from Paris in early September 1938 confirmed this judgement.[24]

Germany lay at the heart of the belief system, particularly in South African official circles, in quite extraordinary ways. In contrast to the Soviet Union, Germany was a normal state, run by an ideologically radical and difficult but legitimate elite. Hitler, volatile and unstable, could be made to see reason. He was personally friendly towards Britain and, preferring an Anglo-German *rapprochement*, would not repeat the pre-1914 error of challenging the empire. His outstretched hand was one of friendship. The nazi government, populated by hawks and doves, moderated by office and success, was risk acceptant only because it must correct intolerable injustices and throw off unacceptable burdens. Unlike the mischievously unreliable Italian government, it would honour to the letter obligations freely entered into, as it had the Anglo-German naval agreement of 1935.[25]

Germany was entirely justified in challenging the moral validity of the Versailles settlement and seeking to amend it in its own favour. It was correct to question the economic, political and strategic viability of its territorial provisions, especially those applied to central and eastern Europe. It was both immoral and pointless to defend the 1919 treaty. Nazi Germany was, therefore, little different in this regard from Weimar Germany. Hertzog was prepared to see Hitler use arbitrary means, and force, to revise the peace settlement. The lesson to be drawn was that Britain must not repeat the failure of the 1920s; it must seize the opportunity to accommodate Germany. In that way, justice for Germany was a 'cause', not just for guilt-ridden liberals but for all fair-minded people. Pirow installed it as the third principle of Hertzog's foreign policy.

This reasoning seemed particularly apposite because Germany's goals were judged to be limited, driven by economic necessity and consistent with the principle of national self-determination. Smuts, for example, felt that Hitler, faithful to *Mein Kampf,* was bent on economic expansion into central and eastern Europe. His determination in 1938 to challenge and even destroy Czechoslovakia was put in that context. One might even welcome Germany's economic mastery of central and eastern Europe. It might eliminate what slim appetite Hitler had for recouping Germany's colonies. In Europe he was set on uniting all Germans in a greater Germany, but not incorporating non-Germans. Racialism as a basis of policy was thus moderation. The brutal nazification of the reclaimed *volk* was as regrettable as it was loathsome, but it was now Germany's internal affair. With Austria incorporated, Hitler had unlocked the door to southeastern Europe. Germany's domination of the region, economically, perhaps strategically, accomplished peacefully, might extend to the Bosphorus. But, in the absence of the Russian counterforce, there was something inevitable about all that; history was unfolding as it should. In any case, the certain prospect of a German hegemony made negotiations with Germany more, not less, necessary. In contrast to Japan, Germany was not seen as an aggressive, cruelly racist, expansionist state. It was not likely actually to attack Czechoslovakia, except under extreme provocation, Gie was sure, let alone the Low Countries, France and England. There was honour in Germany; the future lay with it. The principle of national self-determination was one of the keys to the peaceful management of Europe. It would not be a lethal weapon in Hitler's hands.[26]

As the 'trustee of world peace' and honest broker, Britain must engage Germany, cooperate with it to bring about peaceful revision in German's favour, and settle all its just grievances. Such a policy was not regarded as radical. It simply meant treating Germany with absolute sincerity and as an equal with France. It was, in the final analysis, a matter of fairness, restoring Germany to its rightful, inevitable place. Germany would not see that as weakness but as a genuine attempt to permit it to share the responsibility for maintaining the peace of Europe. That was the sixth principle of Hertzog's policy. It led, logically, to Hertzog's reaffirmation to Chamberlain from March to June 1938 that South Africa would not join Britain in wars lacking cause or justification, that is, to prevent Germany either achieving justice from Czechoslovakia or securing hegemony in central and east Europe. Prophetically, the third of Hertzog's given names was Munnik. Bruce, at the high commissioners' meeting with Halifax and Lord Stanley, the dominions secretary, on 25 May 1938, argued that as Germany could secure its economic and ideological goods by peaceful means or war, why let war occur? It was 'an ugly picture from the point of view of democracy' and smacked of defeatism, Smuts conceded, but no other posture was possible.[27]

The payoff for Britain would be an Anglo-German *rapprochement* and removal of both the Italian threat and French mischief. Britain and Germany would manage Europe; France and Italy would have no alternative but to follow their lead. Peace in Europe would help bring about a more orderly world. Japan would be robbed of its opportunity, the Soviet Union condemned to isolation, and the United States would be at least more cooperative and, if not, less dominant. Britain, with the colonial problem solved, would rest secure in and with its empire: a 25-year peace would come to pass. The stakes were that high; there was more to it than mere coexistence, Germany in Europe and Britain overseas.[28]

The logical consequence of these extraordinary beliefs about Germany was that France was cast as the principal threat to European peace and order. France, in its intransigence, its irrational fear, its devotion to the 1919 treaty system and the balance of power, in its determination to encircle Germany, prevent its hegemony and perpetuate its subjugation, was planning to win the next war, not prevent it. Obsessed with its own security, caring nothing for Europe, France was capable of the insanity of preventive war. That was why France protected Czechoslovakia, saw the Czech–German dispute as an excuse for war, and allied with the Soviet Union. That was why it was attempting to reconstitute the Stresa Front. Hitler, understandably, would not join a Western security pact that countenanced the Franco-Soviet alliance. France's diabolical anti-German schemes perpetuated the errors of the past rather than solved the problems of the present. Europe must be protected from them. French commitments in eastern Europe spelled war. Hertzog's faith in France was exhausted. Chamberlain must avoid giving a prior commitment of British support to France in the event of war. France must be told that the commonwealth would be dragged into war neither to prevent German hegemony nor because of France's commitment to Czechoslovakia. Hertzog and other dominion leaders welcomed Britain's warning to France of 22 May 1938, and the reassurances they received from Halifax and Stanley on those counts. The latter were, however, not entirely satisfactory; perhaps they kept alive the lingering suspicion in South Africa that Britain, joining in a war alongside a France unduly susceptible to Jewish influence, was bent on destroying an industrial competitor, not nazism. Smuts saw it differently but agreed that France, must, in effect, be protected from itself.[29]

The indictment of France, more in anger than regret, spilled over to Czechoslovakia before and during 1938. The Czech state stood in defiance of the principle of national self-determination: its president, Eduard Benes, was the epitome of irresponsibility and intransigence. Loring Christie, in November 1937, described Benes as 'a clever intriguer and blackmailer, incessantly at it and missing few tricks'. How far Benes had compromised and entrapped Britain through the Franco-Soviet alliance were the questions for 1938. Hertzog instructed te Water, on 22 March, to inform Halifax that South Africa was utterly uninterested in the political affairs of Czechoslovakia and the states of eastern Europe.[30] The dominions applauded Chamberlain's speech of 24 March severely circumscribing Britain's commitment to Czechoslovakia while reasserting its enduring interest in resolving the situation.

The May crisis convinced Massey and, more emphatically, King that the danger, and thus the clue to peace, lay more in Prague than

Berlin. King was perturbed by the Czech mobilization against what he concluded were purely imaginary German military moves. Both saw Britain being dragged into war by Czech intransigence in the face of British advice and France's alliance. Bruce, Menzies and Page, at a meeting with Halifax on 25 May, were brutally frank – Benes must compromise and surrender the Sudetenland to Germany. Te Water reported in July that Halifax had returned from Paris with a promise that France would follow Britain's lead in asserting pressure on Benes and take no action to defend Czechoslovakia without consulting Britain. That was encouraging news to both the South African and Australian governments, reinforced as it was in the last week of August. Indeed, it seemed crucial because Germany, making military plans and withdrawing forces from Spain, would strike if Benes proved obdurate. As Smuts did not expect Lord Runciman's mediation to succeed, unless he was 'an instrument of the Lord', it seemed wise, as Sir John Simon said at Lanark in 27 August, to continue to avoid more specific commitments to Czechoslovakia.[31]

Menzies informed Lyons early in August that he found the German foreign office understandably gloomy. Germany, not seeking immediate annexation, would be satisfied at that point with Sudeten autonomy within a federal Czechoslovakia. Its officials, impressed with Britain's rearmament, looked to Britain to prevent France from behaving foolishly. Benes egged on by France, bluffing in disregard of more vital considerations, remained the problem. Gie reported in similar fashion in mid-August. Germany, willing to accept a compromise, could afford to be patient; the Sudetenland would be its soon enough. Gie felt that Hitler – the 'Olympian Jove' – and his entourage probably shared that view. 'They will, however, not stand for overmuch Czech intransigence. If the Czechs want a war they'll get it.'[32]

On 30 August the dominions office informed the dominions that a critical moment had arrived. Hitler, determined to force a solution on the Sudetenland and unchecked by the army, was prepared to use force if necessary in the second half of September. The Australian cabinet met on 1 September. Lyons and Casey, against Hughes, argued that Britain, its vital interests not at stake, must avoid involvement in war, a war in which Australia would ultimately participate. In view of that sobering, tragic possibility, the cabinet indicted Benes for the lack of progress, this time for refusing to fulfil immediately and unreservedly his seven-point liberal package of proposals, the 'Third Plan', as the basis for further negotiations. The Lyons government welcomed the prospect of further British pressure on Benes to make the concessions 'which alone will enable a peaceful solution'. If Benes refused, Britain would have to decide whether it should terminate its involvement entirely. Bruce reported that the Australian initiative had been 'most useful and helpful', reinforcing the sense in London that additional pressure on Benes must be asserted. Runciman, would do so publicly. If Hitler had advised Konrad Henlein to continue to negotiate – surely he had – and if Hitler's Nuremberg speech was conciliatory, as winter approached, the prospect of war would diminish. Te Water came to the same conclusion. Italy and Poland were supportive, Chamberlain had offered Hitler an arms limitation agreement and a trade treaty, and there was an universal public desire to avoid war. Both the Australian and South African governments remained convinced, however, that the French and Benes were the principal obstacles to peace.[33]

There remained, for the belief system, the question of institutionalizing methods and practices to effect peaceful, orderly change. Only if the League of Nations were reformed could it be part of the answer; only if it were made a moral force where consultation was mandatory and coercion optional, a hybrid league, would it serve these purposes. That was the position of the Lyons and Hertzog governments, but not that of Canada; all three governments agreed that the Covenant must be detached from the 1919 treaty so as to restore its moral authority.[34]

The League Assembly convened on 12 September 1938 only for its agenda to be made seemingly irrelevant by the threat of war over Czechoslovakia. The British case for reform made on 16 September was not well received. The dominions concluded, as did Eamon DeValera for Ireland, that the prospects for peaceful change remained in the right hands – Chamberlain's – and in the appeasement of Germany. Hitler, presumably, read the signal.[35]

Dominion elites saw this belief system as abandoning neither their idealism nor their realism, but exorcising the pre-1914 practices that had been so flawed and so disastrous in their consequences.

Appeasement in action was an ingenious blend of realism and idealism. The belief system was morally sound, and logically consistent. Dominion elites acted in accordance with it, with conviction, in September 1938. The constraints on their actions were thus largely self-imposed.

The Crisis – September 1938

On 14 September the dominion governments acknowledged that Britain, and therefore the commonwealth, faced a crisis which, if mishandled, could result minimally in a German attack on Czechoslovakia and possibly in a European war. The ambiguity and uncertainty of 12 and 13 September all but evaporated.[36] Optimism and a sense of relief flourished, however, from 15 to 21 September.[37] What followed, therefore, from 22 to 28 September, was all the more emotionally wrenching – seven days of high tension; 24 September was the most difficult day for the dominion high commissioners to assess, 26 and 27 September the most nerve wracking. Te Water reported on 26 September: 'Zero hour is very nearly reached, issue hanging on Hitler's acceptance or rejection.' 28 September proved decisive. The afternoon ended with Chamberlain's dramatic announcement to the House of Commons that he would fly to Germany the next morning. 'The drift to war has been arrested', te Water reported, 'I believe the situation has been saved.' The high commissioners congratulated Chamberlain and thanked him; he was 'deeply moved'. Massey and te Water were at Heston airport to see Chamberlain off on 29 September. Throughout, te Water's reports to Hertzog captured the public drama in London – anxiety, tension, uncertainty; throngs of people in the streets; the indignity and black humour of being fitted with gas-masks; carpenters boarding up South Africa House on 27 September in case of air raids; the stupefaction of newly arrived visitors; the flood of 'stop the war' pamphlets on 28 September.[38]

Apart from King's futile letter to Ribbentrop of 14 September and Lyons's appeals to Roosevelt and Mussolini on 28 September,[39] the dominions, logically, monitored the crisis largely through the unfolding of British policy. That was both their point of reference and what they might influence directly; any marginal effect they could have on French and Czech behaviour would come through Britain. They depended almost exclusively on the flow of information, hourly, day and night, from the foreign and dominion offices and the processes of consultation. Arrangements were agreed upon on 12 September.[40] They were held to and were augmented by informal representations. The high commissioners accepted MacDonald's proposition at the outset, on 12 September, that time for consultation before decisions were made and action taken by the British government might at times be unavoidably short, and, on occasion, so short as to preempt consultation. In such extreme cases, the dominions office would cable the dominion governments, inform the high commissioners, give an explanation of the decision and ask for an immediate response, which, it was hoped, would be supportive.

Consultation, more routinely, seemed ample. MacDonald presided over the meetings of the 'trade union' of high commissioners almost daily from 12 September. Chamberlain and Halifax, with MacDonald and Leo Amery present, met with them once, on the evening of 26 September. Chamberlain stayed in touch with the dominion prime ministers, and, on occasion, met high commissioners individually. Bruce attended the inner cabinet meeting in the afternoon of 27 September. The high commissioners agreed that MacDonald kept Chamberlain and the cabinet adequately informed of dominion views and that formal, direct representation to them, on 26 and 27 September for example, were not necessary. They accepted his version of what transpired in the cabinet and inner cabinet and his advice as to what would be helpful to Chamberlain. That was why, perhaps, they never seemed to be aware of Halifax's revolt, attributing Chamberlain's problems to every source other than the 'Holy Fox'. They took seriously, from 22 September, the threat that Chamberlain's government could collapse. At the end of the day the high commissioners were content, lavishing praise on MacDonald and the dominions office.[41] They had been, they concluded, fully advised of the unfolding situation; their governments had been perhaps better informed than the full cabinet. The dominion governments acquiesced in decisions made and actions taken without consultation, such as Chamberlain agreeing to join in an international guarantee of the rump of Czechoslovakia on 18 September, settling for MacDonald's explanation to the high commissioners. Secrecy was maintained, on Plan Z for example, of which the dominions learned on 14 September.[42] The dominion governments and high commissioners did not use the information they were fed in ways unhelpful to Chamberlain. Parliamentary statements were timed in deference to British concerns. The dominion oligarchs remained in control of policy at home and acted oligocratically. King kept his distance from parliament, the acting British high commissioner, Stephen Holmes, and Massey. Lyons' inner group, unswayed by Hughes' dissent and public opinion, kept a firm hand on policy. Hertzog went his own way, following his conscience, leaving Smuts to follow his.[43] Bruce, until 24 September, was the most independently minded of the high commissioners, Massey, his memoirs notwithstanding, no more effective in informal diplomacy than te Water and Bruce.

Yet the crisis, as an exercise in commonwealth diplomacy, had been disturbing. No one endorsed and most ridiculed Hughes' call in August for the closing of the dominions office and the recreation of a centralized, imperial policy community. But te Water, for example, since Canada did not want influence and Australia was too indolent to reach for it in a sustained way, felt that danger lurked in the present system of consultation. 'The Powerful Party shows the way', public opinion 'like a flock of sheep' follows blindly, and the dominions were caught up in the process with no way out. There resulted a loss of 'our national discretion' before the event; neutrality was not a safe harbour. Te Water looked, therefore, for a way for the dominions to assert direct influence in crises, so as to enable them to be a collective, corrective check on Britain in the cause of peace.[44] There was merit in te Water's diagnosis, but the problems were essentially structural, and, where not, stemmed as much from dominion as British behaviour.

Dominion preoccupation with British policy reflected in part their dismissive assessment of the role the USSR, the United States and even Italy could play in the crisis. At their meeting on 19 September the high commissioners did query the decision not to involve the Soviet Union in helping secure Czech acceptance of the Anglo-French plan. No one baulked, however, at MacDonald's explanation – the Soviet Union would not be particularly helpful as French influence on the Czech government was far more potent and likely to produce acceptance.[45] Dominion acquiescence followed logically from the assumption, reinforced in September by intelligence reports from Paris and Moscow, that Stalin, ultra-cautious, persistently noncommittal, deplored Chamberlain's mediation attempts and looked to an Anglo-French–German war to eliminate the German threat to the Soviet Union.[46] With the Munich Conference behind them, the wisdom of avoiding Soviet involvement seemed uncontestable. Skelton and Christie were blunt, the latter vitriolic in his contempt. Ivan Maisky, the Soviet ambassador in London, came in for sharp criticism from Christie and te Water. Te Water reported on Maisky's 'unutterable disgust with the Chamberlain policy', and his fear that the Munich accord would spawn a four power pact which would institutionalize Russia's isolation. The Labour Party, te Water was sure, shared Maisky's fears.[47]

Roosevelt, in comparison, said and did the right things in September 1938, publicly and privately, if tardily, but, with public approval, kept his distance. The dominions welcomed every United States initiative. Roosevelt's diplomatic intervention on 26 September, for example, urged all parties to continue to negotiate. It might have an impact on world opinion even if it failed to influence Hitler. Massey wanted US mediation; Chamberlain and MacDonald were sceptical; Halifax slightly more encouraging. Lyons took up the call for US mediation on 28 September, asking Roosevelt to use his moral authority in the cause of peace. None of the high commissioners judged Roosevelt's appeal to Mussolini on 27 September and his message to Hitler the next day as instrumental in the arranging of the Munich Conference. The conference rendered US mediation irrelevant. No high commissioner expressed regret. Yet to te Water at least, the United States, free of 'political entanglements' and Europe's 'mesh of hatreds' was an exemplar for the whole commonwealth.[48]

Intermittently in September, the dominions examined Mussolini's influence on Hitler and on the choice between negotiation and force. The high commissioners judged Mussolini's speech of 21 September to have been made after consulting Hitler, and not useful. Hertzog felt later in the crisis that Mussolini might be helpful. On 27 September, te Water delivered two messages personally to

Chamberlain, suggesting that he involve Mussolini, who was 'itching to play a part'. The idea, he reported to Hertzog, was already in Chamberlain's mind. Lyons, parading his being on 'good personal terms' with Mussolini, followed Hertzog, knowingly or not. Early in the morning of 28 September Lyons instructed Bruce to suggest to Chamberlain that he, Bruce, be used as a messenger to make a direct appeal to Mussolini to intercede with Hitler to renew the negotiations and seek a peaceful settlement. Bruce found that Chamberlain had already appealed to Hitler and Mussolini and did not question the content of those final initiatives, those capitulations. If anything, Mussolini's response on 28 September confirmed for the dominions that Italy must be a partner in the proposed four power pact, and party to the attempts to restrain Poland in early October.[49]

The commitment to peace, the principle of national self-determination and peaceful, orderly change led dominion elites to what they considered to be the moral high ground in the September crisis. Their reasoning was sequentially rational and ultimately reprehensible. Peace and war were made, morally, binary opposites; any course of action, any alternative outcome, was preferable to war. For Massey it was a question of saving civilization. Specifically, Britain should fight neither to preserve the political and territorial integrity of Czechoslovakia nor because of France's obligation to Czechoslovakia and any British commitment to France on that score. Such wars, te Water argued, were exclusively the concern of France and Russia. They should be insulated from outside intervention as had been the Boer War. The dominions found merit neither in a war to uphold the 1919 treaty system nor to maintain the prevailing European balance of power. A war to prevent Germany hegemony in central and eastern Europe would be, Lyons warned on 26 September, 'ruinous and perhaps inconclusive'. Te Water, on 27 September, insisted that such a war would 'decide nothing'. If Britain made such considerations a matter of vital national interest it would test commonwealth unity.[50]

The dominion elites made the implementation of the principle of national self-determination – the redrawing of state boundaries on racial not strategic grounds – synonymous with the preservation of peace. They cast the September crisis in those terms. Te Water and Massey agreed on 14 September that risking war over the Czech 'incident' – this 'astonishing episode' – rather than implementing the principle was inconceivable. They held to that view no matter how dubious the method and the consequences of implementation. It had become, in te Water's words, 'acknowledged as a sound ethical basis for a fair and proper settlement of the dispute'. More than that, te Water insisted, a war could not be legitimated as a counter to German aggression against Czechoslovakia. That would occur only if Britain, France and the Czechs refused to implement the principle. In that situation, they, not Germany, would be in the wrong. When such reasoning opened the door to the claims of the Polish and Hungarian minorities in Czechoslovakia, the principle became divisible. The dominion elites found it mandatory for the Sudeten Germans, but inappropriate for the Polish and Hungarian minorities. Te Water disagreed with the policy of granting German claims a higher moral and political validity only because he thought it best 'to administer the whole dose of caster oil'.

In all this there was a certain contempt for the Poles and Hungarians; they were jackals, threatening a settlement. Yet the dominion high commissioners, te Water particularly, knew that the Polish and Hungarian governments were not acting alone and, indeed, would threaten Czechoslovakia only with German support. They had evidence of meetings between German, Polish and Hungarian representatives. The principle of national self-determination was acknowledged to be, from 21 September, a weapon in Hitler's hands which he used both to reinforce his claims against Czechoslovakia and evade a commitment to preserve the rump of Czechoslovakia, and also to demonstrate his restraint as he held the jackals in check. Predictably, the dominion high commissioners judged Polish demands of 27 September, and its ultimatum of 30 September, to Czechoslovakia to be the principal, immediate threat to the Munich settlement.[51]

With the principle of self-determination conceded, in their view, by 18 September – the 'great and generous gesture' of the Anglo-French plan – the dominions turned resolutely to the question of implementation. That was the case even as the German proposals, tabled at Godesburg on 23 September, pushed aside the Anglo-French plan. With MacDonald's assurance on 24 September that the Czech frontier would be drawn on racial not strategic grounds, the high commissioners on 24 and 26 September, Lyons in a morning phone call to Chamberlain on 26 September, and Hertzog in a telegram of the same day judged the difference between the Anglo-French and German proposals to be 'mainly one of method'. The dominions then established the connection between method and war. Lyons urged Chamberlain to weigh not the value of what was already conceded but the poverty of the details still at issue. The 'Berlin proposals should be accepted'. Hertzog agreed: 'As the issue was one of no material substance but merely involves a matter of procedure for arriving at a result to which it is common cause between disputants Germany is entitled', war was out of the question, certainly for South Africa. The high commissioners, on 24 September, agreed that Chamberlain must continue to mediate and, as te Water put it at the 26 September meeting, 'find a way out'. He must, to be sure, secure the best terms possible for Czechoslovakia and lighten the burden of the Godesburg demands where possible. If Hitler held firm, however, the German terms, already modified at the margin and by far a lesser evil than war, must be accepted. Massey, Bruce, F.T. Sandford for New Zealand and J.W. Dulanty for Eire agreed.

Each successive method, the progression of concessions to Germany – granting the Sudeten Germans immediate local autonomy; plebiscites in specified areas, at times and under supervision that were appropriate; and 'direct cession', that is, the transfer of defined territory from Czechoslovakia to Germany, in equally appropriate circumstances – were put to the test and found preferable to war. Only Bruce of the high commissioners protested against an immediate plebiscite as an 'absolute outrage'. 'Direct cession' of territory replaced the plebiscites as marginally more palatable to Czechoslovakia and France, though still being 'a great deal to swallow', as MacDonald acknowledged at the 19 September meeting. It seemed initially to have the singular merit, however, of being a way to evade Polish and Hungarian claims.

The timing and terms of the transfer of territory thus became the issue. The point of departure for the dominions was that those areas where the German population was in a simple majority, that is, more than 50 per cent, should be incorporated in Germany. Bruce felt able to join the consensus on 24 September because the German memorandum – 'a great advance in tone and substance' – was preferable to war. The details demonstrated the wisdom of that judgement – the areas to be transferred to Germany were only 'slightly greater' than under the Anglo-French plan; plebiscites would rectify errors and allow areas that voted to rejoin Czechoslovakia to do so; acceptance of the German memorandum merely anticipated what would happen in six weeks or two months; Germany was not contemplating the destruction of Czechoslovakia; and displaced Czechs would be compensated for lost assets. German demands as to who could vote in the plebiscites, that is, only those living in the contested areas in October 1918, were not unreasonable, providing exceptions were made for areas of subsequent heavy Czech settlement. An international commission should supervise the adjusting of the Czech–German frontiers.

A difference of opinion between the dominions and a segment of Chamberlain's cabinet, which did not include Halifax, emerged by 24 September. Massey suggested it reflected 'geographic distance', not a conflicting sense of honour. As the high commissioners waited on MacDonald's assessment of Chamberlain's report to the cabinet, 'the atmosphere for the moment', Bruce reported, was 'distinctly more hopeful'. Te Water seemed sure that South African opinion, though divided, would support acceptance of the Godesburg proposals. Chamberlain's prestige was that high. Surely he would carry the cabinet on 25 September, and the country, for it seemed clear that, if the German memorandum was rejected, Hitler, undeterred by an Anglo-French declaration of support for Czechoslovakia, would attack.[52]

When Hitler demanded that German troops be allowed to occupy the Sudetenland immediately, the dominions confronted a further principle – that the threat of force must not triumph over negotiation and force itself must not oust peaceful change. Bruce argued, at the 23 September meeting, that Chamberlain must make a stand on this principle in order to earn not only public support at home and in the dominions but also the respect of neutral states. Failure to do so meant that Britain would not have and would not deserve support in the future. It was a matter of reputation. Massey, te Water and Dulanty concluded that the occupation of the Sudetenland by German troops was not an issue of principle but merely, yet again, one of method. Chamberlain, MacDonald reported, shared Bruce's view. But a compromise solution could surely be worked out. What te Water described as 'a liberal interpretation of principle' seemed attractive – an international force to keep order would follow the German occupying troops into the Sudetenland.

The more menacing question was the threat of preemptive German military action, averted initially by Chamberlain's sortie to Berchtesgaden, and thus Czechoslovakia's right to mobilize and prepare to defend itself. Bruce insisted, on 23 September, that a settlement based on the direct transfer to Czech territory to Germany must not be, and must not be regarded as, an abject surrender to Hilter's ultimata and threats of force. Yet Hertzog, after what had transpired at Godesburg and after reading Hilter's Sportspalast speech of 26 September, informed te Water that he felt 'very deeply that if after this an European war was still to take place the responsibility for that will not be placed upon the shoulders of Germany'. The dominions, however, could never dismiss entirely the evidence to the contrary.[53]

There remained two issues, each of them significant in themselves and because they were further, psychologically comforting, steps to more of the moral high ground. Bruce demanded, at the 23 September meeting, that a settlement based on the German proposals be an honourable one, leading to a secure future. The settlement must be defensible and permanent, the end of all further claims on Czechoslovakia. It must be the preface to a wider settlement, to full appeasement, eliminating the possibility of future German aggression in Europe. His fellow high commissioners agreed, unanimously.[54] On 19 September, MacDonald had informed the high commissioners that Chamberlain had agreed, as a necessary concession to France and to secure Czech acceptance of the Anglo-French plan, that Britain would join in an international guarantee of the restructured Czech state. As he had not had time to consult them he had not committed the dominions. The Anglo-French plan, MacDonald assured the high commissioners, protected Czechoslovakia's vital interests and left it defensible, its line of fortifications intact. Bruce, on political and moral grounds, applauded the step. It was necessary to make Czechoslovakia secure, and to put an end to German expansion across east and southeast Europe, which would result in war with the

USSR. Indeed, the guarantee would provide the justification for asking the Czechs to make the sacrifice of territory so as to avoid war. Bruce asked Lyons to support Chamberlain's actions, publicly as well as privately, and alarmed his colleagues in London by suggesting that the dominions join in the guarantee.

Massey offered no opinion, but reported to King that the other dominions insisted on the guarantee. Te Water, on 19 September, was initially categorical – South Africa would not join in the guarantee. He met with Bruce after the meeting and reported to Hertzog that 'he will be more cautious in future'. Te Water then hedged – South Africa might just participate if the guarantee were brought under a revised League of Nations and if Germany either participated or signed a nonaggression pact with Czechoslovakia. He was not sanguine. A guarantee embracing Britain, France, Germany, Russia and the neighbouring states was not likely to be efficacious. Germany could nullify it at will, and, in any case, would not participate if the Soviet Union were included. As te Water understood it, the guarantee would be against 'unprovoked aggression and not of the new boundaries'. He judged a unilateral declaration of intent by Germany better than nothing; Britain, he concluded, preferred a Czech–German nonaggression pact accompanied by an international guarantee treaty that excluded Germany. Yet British policy demonstrated that Chamberlain's government had 'rather a queer mind, as always thoroughly illogical but in a more volatile state than I have ever known it'. Britain rejected Polish and Hungarian claims on the grounds that they constituted the dismemberment of Czechoslovakia, accepted the Sudeten German claims and compounded the error by joining in an international guarantee. The fact that Britain was following a French lead, and, on the face of it, dramatically extending its obligations in Europe and thus potentially involving the dominions was doubtless at the root of te Water's discontent.

When Lyons, on 26 September, urged a further bout of mediation by Chamberlain to secure acceptance of the German proposals, he returned to the issue. Public opinion would demand adequate assurances of Czechoslovakia's future. If Germany unilaterally guaranteed the new Czech frontiers as it should, and then violated them, it 'would involve a definite moral issue'. An international guarantee would be a 'moral front'. In that way the dominions convinced themselves that not only were they not participating in the dismembering of Czechoslovakia but actually protecting a reconstituted, legitimate state.[55]

The dominions concluded that both British and German involvement in what they regarded as a question of minority rights was entirely legitimate and, indeed, unavoidable. That was particularly the case because article 19 of the League Covenant was inoperative. Czech sovereignty was already at bay. By its failure to honour its obligations, its oppressive treatment of racial minorities and its ignoring of British representations the Czech government had brought the crisis on itself. The Czechs and Sudeten Germans simply could not live together any longer. The principle of national self-determination, the dominions insisted, made the preservation of the territorial integrity of the polyglot, arbitrarily created Czech state indefensible – a lost cause to be written off. Initially, they made Czech acceptance of the Anglo-French plan the central issue. Benes' preference notwithstanding, it was a gesture to the Czech fear of plebiscites and, the dominions concluded, a just solution. It left a stable, defensible Czechoslovakia intact. Benes' reluctance to accept the direct transfer of territories where the German population exceeded 50 per cent complicated Chamberlain's mediation efforts. A Czech rejection of the Anglo-French plan invited more incidents in the Sudetenland, Czech mobilization and a German attack. Czech not German policy was thus the problem or, as Massey put it, the Czechs were just as likely as the Germans to make a peaceful solution impossible. Benes' slippery intransigence as much as Hitler's appetite threatened a resolution of the crisis. Hitler's distrust of Benes was entirely understandable even though his insulting public comments were deplorable. The Australian government agreed with Nevile Henderson; there was every reason to assert 'extreme final pressure' on Benes.[56]

Benes accepted the Anglo-French plan and Hitler behaved as he did at Godesburg, but neither development exonerated Benes or made Czechoslovakia a cause. The German proposals of 24 September, the dominion high commissioners agreed, were weighted against the Czechs. The Czech population of the transferred areas would be treated inhumanely, given no opportunity to relocate. International commissions would have the opportunity neither to supervise population transfers nor the adjustment of frontiers.

However, te Water found far more than was justified in the three concessions made by Germany. He and Bruce, on 24 September, balked at Britain's refusal to press the Czech government to accept the German proposals, but they did not expect to alter the decision to allow the Czechs to mobilize.

At their morning meeting on 26 September the high commissioners learned that Czechoslovakia, with French support, had rejected unconditionally the German terms 'in their present form'. Their response, and that of their governments, in the next two days was that Chamberlain, directly or through Horace Wilson, must continue to mediate. He must secure the best terms possible for Czechoslovakia but he must not allow the crisis to result in war. They supported Chamberlain's final representation to Benes and monitored closely the British government's exchanges with Prague and Berlin on 26 and 27 September, and particularly Hitler's reply to Chamberlain of 27 September. The dominions found every reason to welcome Chamberlain's appeals to Hitler and Mussolini on 28 September. Hitler could have 'all the essentials without war and without delay'; Britain and France guaranteed that the Benes government would carry out its promises 'fairly and fully and forthwith'.

The dominion high commissioners, informed by MacDonald on 28 September that Benes was less than enthusiastic about Chamberlain's initiative and, on the evening of 29 September, that Benes had protested against the British position at Munich, were incensed. It was not enough, Bruce insisted, that Britain had warned the Czechs that they must not attempt to tie Chamberlain's hand. That was far too encouraging. The dominions expected a far firmer line, a 'very stiff' telegram to Basil Newton, the British minister to Prague, instructing him to warn the Czechs 'that the obstructive tactics of the Czech Government were unwelcome to the British and Dominion Governments'. Te Water and Massey agreed. To appeal to Benes not to tie Chamberlain's hands was an error. It suggested that 'Benes had the right to do so'; he did not. Benes, te Water suggested, still did not quite understand – the Munich Conference would probably have to 'whittle down' somewhat Chamberlain's most recent proposals, not expand them in Czechoslovakia's favour.[57]

Only Canadian officials found merit and nuance in French policy during the crisis, and even then Skelton concluded that France had, in the final analysis, ignored its treaty obligations and thrown an ally to the wolves. For the most part, contempt was the only sentiment that diluted dominion dislike of French policy. They deplored French support of Czech intransigence and France's failure to bring the Czechs to heel. France's endorsement of Czechoslovakia's rejection of the German proposals and its declaration, on 26 September, that it would honour its obligations to Czechoslovakia seemed particularly regrettable and dangerous. Te Water, at the high commissioner's meeting with MacDonald on 26 September, wanted France informed that the dominions would not join in a war brought about by the rejection of the German proposals. Lyons thought it necessary to support Chamberlain against France as well as his domestic critics. Both might stiffen British resolve to take a stand against the German proposals, the French role in such a ploy being evident in the Anglo-French conversations on 25 September. The French had already led Britain down the path of the international guarantee of Czechoslovakia; they might still, as a consequence of their pact with Czechoslovakia, which te Water denounced as 'a menace to peace', embroil Britain in war. He told Chamberlain in their private meeting on 27 September that 'It seemed intolerable that French commitments should be the cause of the British Commonwealth of Nations being drawn into war'; with peace and war in the balance, why is it 'thought wrong to insist that the French should contribute to his peace efforts by another approach to their allies the Czechs'. The dominion high commissioners greeted with relief the news on 28 September that France had agreed to take no offensive action without first consulting Britain. Massey interpreted that to mean that Chamberlain had regained control of the crisis.

That seeming capitulation, the dominions concluded, was, after all, not surprising. Te Water had felt all along that France really wanted to find a way out of its obligations to Czechoslovakia. Even France's stated determination, on 26 September, to honour its obligations to Czechoslovakia seemed vague. Chamberlain told the high commissioners that evening that he was not sure that France would in fact honour its obligation to Czechoslovakia. What, the dominions asked, did France mean; why did France not specify what military steps it would take if Germany attacked? And what had happened to French influence in eastern Europe, beyond

Czechoslovakia; why were Poland and Hungary running with Germany? Such developments merely confirmed that French attempts to prevent a German hegemony were a futile exercise in self-delusion.[58]

The contrast with dominion views of Hitler and nazi policy in the crisis could not have been more marked. Te Water, feeding no doubt off Gie, pictured the Führer as volatile, oratorically violent, risk acceptant, fanatically determined and difficult to predict. The Czech crisis had brought him to the point where he was 'patently in an overwrought state of mind possibly verging on abnormality'. Hitler must be handled with care; it would be dangerous, 'psychologically wrong', te Water warned at the 28 September high commissioners' meeting, to blame Hitler publicly for the desperate situation. Bruce and Massey agreed; some way must be found to prevent members of parliament from making bellicose statements that might prejudice the negotiations.[59]

Not a single recorded word of criticism of Hitler's policies and conduct passed dominion lips before 24 September. Dominion elites never questioned the assumption that the Czech crisis must be settled immediately and in Germany's favour. They held true to dogma; Germany's aims were limited and racial, not territorial. Once Hitler had completed the entirely justifiable task of returning the ten million Germans in Austria and Czechoslovakia to Germany, he harboured 'no further Continental designs jeopardizing Europe'. He coveted nothing in Lithuania and was silent on Poland. Hitler spoke of justice or war, but if Germany received justice from the Czechs and the democracies he would join them in a general settlement, in the appeasement of Europe.

The dominion elites gave Hitler the benefit of every doubt before 24 September. His benchmark Nuremberg speech of 12 September was brutal and bombastic, but he insisted neither on a plebiscite nor self-determination, and, preferring a peaceful outcome, did not threaten war. His 'violent anger' at Britain's apparent opposition to the national self-determination principle was 'understandable'. On 19 September, te Water, awaiting the German response to the Anglo-French plan, speculated that 'the incalculable Hitler might yet astonish everyone by playing his part'. Though undeterred by the prospect of war, Hitler would work with Chamberlain at Godesburg to craft a solution. Hitler's support for Polish and Hungarian claims would not be flagrantly irresponsible. Clearly, Chamberlain's assessment of Hitler after the Berchtesgaden meetings, passed on by Stanley and MacDonald, influenced these judgements. Bruce, however, corrected Stanley's report to Lyons. Hitler had not issued an ultimatum to Chamberlain. The conversations at Berchtesgaden, while frank, had been friendly and useful. If Chamberlain assured him, next week, that Britain, France and the Czechs accepted the national self-determination principle, Hitler would agree 'to some reasonable conditions for its application', and peace would be maintained. If, however, the Czechs were allowed to haggle, if they attempted to settle the terms for implementing self-determination before and as a condition of accepting the principle itself, Hitler would act preemptively. Everything hung, therefore, on prior acceptance of the principle. Hitler had assured Chamberlain, in any case, that he would not use force before their next meeting, unless events forced his hand.[60] Dominion determination to discount troubling information was already apparent.

Godesburg provided the test. It drained morality from the German case, violated the Anglo-French plan, and demonstrated both that German aims were most likely not limited and that Hitler was prepared to threaten and use force to effect change. Yet the dominion grasped at all the evidence to the contrary, emanating from Chamberlain, via MacDonald. In his report to the cabinet on 24 September, MacDonald told the high commissioners, Chamberlain had recounted how Hitler would neither join in an international guarantee of, nor sign a nonaggression pact with, Czechoslovakia unless Polish and Hungarian demands were met. Hitler had reiterated his claim that, but for the Berchtesgaden meetings, he would have invaded Czechoslovakia and set frontiers on strategic not racial grounds. Yet, Chamberlain claimed, Hitler was concerned only with 'nationality questions'. His objectives were limited in that he had no plan to dominate Europe. He wanted Britain's friendship, the colonial question was no reason for war, and a settlement of the Czech crisis would herald a general European settlement. Chamberlain, te Water reported, was pleasantly surprise by Hitler's moderation at Godesburg. If they could turn the corner, 'it may be the beginning of an Anglo-German understanding'. Hitler had become 'dramatic when Czech mobilisation, of which he was obviously aware, was announced during conversations, threatening to interrupt negotiations. Chamberlain laughed him out of his mood and at same time roundly accused him of not attempting to make a contribution'. Hitler's retort was that his contribution had been made – he had not marched into Czechoslovakia and drawn military boundaries favourable to Germany. At the evening meeting with the high commissioners on 26 September, Chamberlain had noted that Hitler was prepared to accept some amendments to the German proposal and had 'actually accepted' some improvements.[61]

Nevertheless, te Water concluded: 'Chamberlain found it difficult to understand the type of mind and methods of the Chancellor, while … Hitler appeared to be at a loss to understand Mr. Chamberlain's astonishment at the tone of the Hitler ultimatum which latter described as merely a memorandum.' Te Water met privately with Chamberlain on 27 September and chided him, gently:

> I was a little uncertain of his reading of Hitler's character and motives which I felt could only be truly judged by a people and its leaders who had actually experienced the bitterness of defeat in war. We would not for instance read as readily deep-laid and sinister motives into Hitler's words and actions which he [Chamberlain] confessed he did. I implored him not to allow his suspicions in this regard to govern his judgment of the Hitler plan. I gave Hitler's constant reiteration of the phrase, "I am no coward." "History cannot judge me a coward" as the more simple and safer key to his insistence on immediate occupation of the ceded territories by a certain date. That and his lack of faith in allied undertakings and their inaction in the past and in Benes's character.[62]

But the source of dominion anxiety went deeper than that. The dominions had entered the September crisis with their confidence in Chamberlain substantially intact. The high commissioners led the dominions along a path of trust in and admiration for Chamberlain that did not begin to deviate until 23 September. Te Water reported that day that Britain's 'Dictator' had behaved superbly. That judgement rested on five foundations. First, Chamberlain, loyal to his 24 March and Simon's 27 August speeches, had championed self-determination, authored the Anglo-French plan, handled all parties to the controversy effectively and, as Pirow said on 21 September, 'brought Europe back to realities'. Chamberlain's impeccable policies would preserve peace.[63]

His conduct seemed truly remarkable. Plan Z, the visit to Berchtesgaden, dazzled the dominions. It was inspired and dynamic, the product of vision, daring and courage, and, as te Water reported, had completely changed the atmosphere. King called it a 'striking and noble action', Bruce 'unprecedented and courageous', and Lyons described how it 'excites our immediate admiration and will completely consolidate British opinion over the whole world'.[64] Third, the dominions expected Britain to maintain a position of detachment from which it could play its vital role as mediator and conciliator. Te Water was adamant – Britain, unlike the continental powers, was not a party to the dispute. Its reputation, its 'impregnable position', came from its impartiality; it was, therefore, the only state that could act decisively. Chamberlain met every expectation on that count. He was even-handed, flexible and creative, never writing off or supporting the Czechs even though he admitted to te Water that Benes was 'an unreliable and unsatisfactory character'. Chamberlain fulfilled Hertzog's expectations that he would act with 'sincerity, impartiality and immediacy'. His skill as a negotiator seemed patent.[65]

That led to the fourth consideration – Chamberlain's handling of Hitler. At Berchtesgaden, Chamberlain had been open, fair, frank and firm, even tough, as he had promised to be. He had spine; he would 'not crawl on his hands and knees'. He had not left Hitler guessing and, quite appropriately, had warned him strongly, te Water reported, so as to deter him. If German forces occupied more than the Sudetenland and if atrocities occurred an outraged British public would demand that Britain assist Czechoslovakia. Britain would face its responsibilities and join in a war brought on by irresponsible German conduct. In planning for the Godesburg meetings, Chamberlain balanced skilfully between Czech and German expectations, deciding to propose not what Benes wanted and Hitler would reject. The strategy would work because the Berchtesgaden meeting, after Chamberlain had threatened to leave if Hitler were not cooperative, had, Stanley assured Lyons, 'ended on a note of manifest friendliness'.[66] Finally, and crucial to the dominions, Chamberlain had asserted British leadership, brought France to heel, and thereby, surely, would bring realism to Czech policy.[67] In sum, the commonwealth, before 23 September, was united behind Chamberlain.

By 26 September, as a result of the Godesburg confrontation, the dominions were forced to face the fact that they were out of step with significant sections of British opinion, the press and the House of Commons. It became even more apparent that critics of Chamberlain's policy had surfaced in the cabinet, but Halifax's loyalty was never questioned. Te Water saw the drift of things – public opinion was hardening; the 'first flush of relief' with and approval of Chamberlain's diplomacy was wearing thin; unflattering comparisons were being made with the Hoare–Laval fiasco; feelings of shame were creeping in. Indeed, if Chamberlain capitulated to Hitler, the government, in the face of public outrage, would fall. Chamberlain had made two errors – relinquishing in part the leadership to France – an error not corrected until 28 September – and, at Godesburg, losing his touch with Hitler. There had been more than a failure of communication, te Water felt, 'the document might have been reshaped and the tragic possibilities now threatening avoided'.

But beyond that how far had Chamberlain's own views changed; was he likely to succumb to his critics; would he stay the course of appeasement? Three pieces of evidence were especially troubling. First, Chamberlain, through Horace Wilson, seemed bent more on threatening than accommodating Hitler. Principle, not method, was now at issue. Britain and France must make a stand or be 'swallowed by the Prussian machine'. The toughness the dominions had earlier applauded now seemed dangerous. Second, at his evening meeting with the high commissioners on 26 September and in his private meeting with te Water on 27 September Chamberlain seemed to have lost faith in Hitler. He was not sincere:

> something more lies behind the Hitler conditions than is manifest on their face ... he still could explain Hitler's insistence on settlement by October 1st as that he must and could only be activated by the belief that the only way to

achieve his ends is by force and not by peaceful methods. His army organisation, mobilisation, will reach peak on that date and will inevitably deteriorate thereafter while the weather factor would also jeopardise his plans.

Hitler's refusal to compromise meant that he had larger, unspecified, designs.

Finally, in his radio address of 27 September, the prime minister, while describing armed conflict as a 'nightmare' and promising to continue to work for peace, had asserted that 'if I were convinced that any nation had made up its mind to dominate the world by fear of its force, I should feel that it must be resisted'. Chamberlain seemed poised, therefore, to elevate the principle of negotiation over force above that of self-determination. He had joined, however reluctantly, a cabinet consensus which threatened everything the dominions preferred. MacDonald confirmed, on 27 September, that the cabinet had concluded that if a Czech refusal to accept the German proposals resulted in German aggression and the invoking of the Franco-Russian pact, Britain must stand by France, even if that resulted in world war. Its vital interests were at stake. German hegemony, achieved by force, was unacceptable; the balance of power had reemerged as the foundation of statecraft.[68]

Chamberlain, then, was wavering and, understandably, growing weary, but the dominions maintained that the answer lay with him. That judgement also reflected the fact that they preferred Chamberlain, infinitely so, to any of his contemptible critics – the Labour Party, Sir Archibald Sinclair for the Liberals, renegade Tories outside the cabinet, that is, Eden, 'his paper', the *Yorkshire Post*, and Churchill, 'fishing as always in troubled waters', and disloyal foreign office officials accusing Chamberlain of leading Benes 'up the garden path'.[69]

Dissent within the cabinet, emerging by 24–25 September, had centred, te Water reported on 7 October, on Duff Cooper, first lord of the admiralty, Oliver Stanley, president of the board of trade, William Morrison, agriculture minister, and Walter Elliot, minister of health. They, and perhaps others, argued, as the high commissioner's understood it, that the Anglo-French plan, sound morally and politically, met all legitimate German expectations, left a viable

Czechoslovakia, and both protected and compensated the displaced Czechs of the Sudetenland. To yield to Hitler's demands at Godesburg, to modify the Anglo-French plan under the threat of force, would, therefore, be intolerable. If he refused he would unite the country and the empire. Furthermore, as Bruce reported, Chamberlain's critics suggested that taking a stand now and facing a war was preferable to fighting a war in the future to protect the rump of Czechoslovakia. Britain and the empire would be divided, international support would have dwindled and a dejected and weaker Czechoslovakia would not fight in its own defence. The dominion high commissioners preferred the counterarguments. As Britain and France had already conceded the outcome, they would be risking war over method and procedure, not principle. As plebiscites would follow the territorial transfer, Germany could be relied on to return territories that voted to remain in Czechoslovakia. As Britain, so vulnerable to air attacks, was not prepared for war it required a 'breathing space'.

The cabinet, meeting three times on 25 September, Bruce reported, agreed that, as Germany could not be deterred, the stark options were capitulation to the German demands, war, or a further diplomatic initiative, crafted by Chamberlain. The time had come for the dominions to step up their efforts to convince Chamberlain to hold firm, and stay the course of appeasement. They must do what they could to help him overcome his critics within the cabinet, manage parliament, lead public opinion and combat French intransigence. In that way they would influence British policy and help avert a catastrophic war. That was what the dominions understood was at stake; there lay their allotted role.[70]

Beyond providing Chamberlain with ammunition, the high commissioners made sure that he understood fully dominion expectations, and realized that the dominions would support him unreservedly in a final effort to preserve peace. Te Water explained to Bodenstein on 26 September that something must be done to bolster Chamberlain, who 'must be suffering from fatigue' and because 'the resistance of a tired man might be broken down', psychologically and emotionally. He and Bruce arranged for Hertzog and Lyons to contact Chamberlain, on 26 September, to reaffirm their admiration for him and their support for the appeasement policy. Dominion preferences were set out, directly through MacDonald and through informal channels, giving Massey his moment in the shade, and unequivocally – the German proposals must, in the final analysis, be accepted so as to avert war; British mediation remained crucial; dominion opinion would endorse the peace strategy; war would invoke the issue of commonwealth unity.[71]

The high commissioners met on the morning of 26 September, before the cabinet acquiesced in the Horace Wilson mission to Berlin. They were willing, on MacDonald's advice, to await the outcome of the cabinet meeting, and the impact of Roosevelt's initiative, before making further direct representations to Chamberlain. MacDonald, they understood, had briefed him and the cabinet. The prime minister knew their views and, in any case, they were scheduled to, and did, meet with him and Halifax that evening. They agreed, on 27 September, while awaiting the outcome of the Horace Wilson mission, that, given MacDonald's effectiveness, they need not meet Chamberlain again to assist him in introducing dominion views in his statement to parliament the next day. But Bruce met with the inner cabinet that afternoon to confirm that the German terms were not sufficient reason to risk war. No one perhaps was more skilfully eloquent than te Water in his personal meeting with Chamberlain on 27 September, where he delivered Hertzog's cables of the previous day. He appealed to him 'to set aside pride, prejudice and even those feelings of false honor which in the face of the ultimate calamity would be ashes in other men's mouths. I told him that we and millions of men and women gave him our admiration and confidence and looked to him to stand firm against the influences of disruption'. Chamberlain, visibly moved, promised to 'go on under almost intolerable strain struggling for peace'.[72]

Te Water emphasized to Chamberlain that 'it was surely not the part of the intermediary to become involved in the dispute itself'. He then sought out MacDonald to urge him, the youngest and least tired member of the cabinet, to promote yet another mediation attempt, the Horace Wilson mission having failed. Te Water reported that 'he [presumably MacDonald] has proposed a plan which entails another approach to the Czechs', which was receiving consideration. When the high commissioners learned at their meeting late on 27 September that Chamberlain, supported by 'overwhelming opinion' in the cabinet, would, in his statement to parliament the next day, confirm that he would act as mediator until the last possible moment unless either Hitler or Benes rejected his 'reasonable offer', they were greatly relieved, if not excessively sanguine. Bruce, Massey and te Water agreed that to adopt any other course would be disastrous, costing Chamberlain his 'great position and prestige'.[73]

The issue of the international guarantee of a rump Czech state had the potential to threaten commonwealth unity. It could be a recipe to involve Britain and, therefore, the dominions in war. In the September crisis, however, the international guarantee was never made a test of commonwealth unity.[74] Involvement in war because of the failure to resolve the crisis did invoke, however, the question of unity, but not as portrayed in the literature. The issue went on the Anglo-dominion agenda on 26 September. The most starkly dramatic outcome would be dominion declarations of neutrality as Britain found itself locked in war. Yet paradox ruled, as it so often does. The stakes of the deepening crisis made dominion neutrality less, not more, likely.

That was true even for South Africa. By 15 September, when the Czech crisis seemed resolvable, the inner cabinet had adopted Hertzog's declaration of policy, that is, a statement of neutrality tilted in Britain's favour, in the event of war resulting from a central or east European crisis. It was scarcely a model of clarity and was subject to a parliamentary vote, where Smuts' wing of the party, opposed to neutrality, held a majority.[75] In Ottawa, King, primed by Christie, with his eye on domestic politics, stated on 17 September that he endorsed Chamberlain's peace efforts. If they failed, an unlikely outcome it seemed, he would summon parliament and submit the government's recommendations to it.[76]

In London, by 26 September, the British characterization of the crisis, of what was at issue, what the stakes were, placed the high commissioners, and especially te Water, in the eye of the paradox. At their meeting that day with MacDonald, they agreed that in the event of war the dominions, 'however reluctantly would be in sooner or later on the side of the United Kingdom'. At the meeting with Chamberlain and Halifax that evening, however, te Water was true to his brief: it was 'unthinkable' that South Africa would be drawn into a war over Czechoslovakia and the invoking of the Franco-Soviet pact.[77] The next day, 27 September, the hand-wringing continued. The high commissioners agreed that the dominions would join in a war that seemed unavoidable, but for which there was no justification, albeit reluctantly, 'most unwillingly' in te Water's phrase, and without conviction. Bruce and te Water, seemingly resigned to participation in war, warned, however, that such involvement would 'endanger the future unity and cohesion of the Commonwealth'. Te Water saw it as strengthening the nationalists in South Africa who were opposed to the link with Britain. Massey and Dulanty saw similar scenarios unfolding in Canada and Ireland. Te Water reported to Hertzog: 'Bruce, Massey, Dulunty and I left nothing unsaid in explaining again the dangers to the commonwealth system of Great Britain involving dominions in a war with which they were out of sympathy and on grounds which in their opinion – did not constitute direct threat to its security.'[78]

Chamberlain and MacDonald, however, were casting the crisis in terms of negotiation and fair dealing prevailing over the threat of force, British honour and vital interests, and the preservation of a balance of power. Smuts' first of two cases bringing the dominions into war, articulated in March – Britain in peril and likely to be attacked, in this case by German air power – was in the logic of their argument. Smuts' second case was irrelevant. Te Water still insisted, on 29 September, that 'If the States of the Commonwealth are to be used to preserve the balance of power in Europe the system must inevitably break ... collective action for the preservation of peace', would work. 'Collective action for the making of war will break it.'[79] But the crisis had overtaken the dominions, and left them where they had always been – bound to Chamberlain, and praying at the eleventh hour that he would find a way out.

King, alone of the dominion prime ministers, issued a statement endorsing, in its entirety, Chamberlain's radio address on the evening of 27 September. His statement was significant politically, not diplomatically or militarily. Unsure of parliamentary sentiment and public opinion, he reported that preparatory security measures were being taken. In the event of a breakdown he would report to parliament and let it determine policy.[80] On 28 September, Hertzog steered his declaration of policy through the full cabinet, but in restrained fashion. Parliament would determine policy if Germany attacked Britain. Smuts had no reason to dissent; Chamberlain, by late afternoon, no cause for undue concern. The message te Water gave Chamberlain at Heston airport the next morning was one of support and praise. The neutrality policy could not have been implemented without cost both to South Africa's reputation and national unity. Te Water told Pirow in late November that he had denied to the British press that South Africa had made a declaration of neutrality in September. South Africa, like all the dominions, had vested interests, economic, political, strategic and diplomatic, in commonwealth unity.[81]

Beyond that, Canadian officials asked that if when Britain was at war Canada was at war, in what sense, the rhetoric of parliament deciding notwithstanding, was Canada self-governing? If the Munich agreement did not lead to an era of general appeasement, and as loyalty to the crown and commonwealth, concern for Britain's welfare, commitment to democratic values and economic self-interest meant that isolationism was not a viable option, something must be done, but what? As there could be no common commonwealth policy, no 'one-voice system', as te Water put it, especially in crises, the future lay in breaking the dependence diplomatically on Britain, and attempting to ensure that all vital decisions were made in Ottawa. Until that was achieved, Christie concluded, 'There could be no separate Canadian foreign policy in matters of peace or war'. Canada was one of a 'new species of the dependent state known as the part sovereign state, for which the metropolitan state, Britain, exercised the full-sovereign function'.[82]

Conclusion

The dominions made no immediate effort to assess carefully the various factors and influences that had brought about the Munich Conference. Instead, the relief – the sense of release – poured out in a flow of admiration, appreciation and gratitude to Chamberlain for his courage, indefatigability and statesmanship. He would enjoy, King wrote, an 'abiding and illustrious place among great conciliators'. The dominion oligarchs had, throughout the crisis, remained true to their belief system, supporting Chamberlain's policy and urging him to remain faithful to appeasement when it seemed he might not stay the course. Smuts, wont to dream of a pacifism born not of defeatism and capitulation 'but of inner conviction, humanity and wisdom', justified their dedication to appeasement in brutally simple fashion. He was sorry for and strongly supportive of the Czechs, 'but world peace ranks above all territorial issues ... I do not think a world war was justified over Czechoslovakia'.[83]

The dominions were confident, not of the magnitude of their influence on British policy, but of the correctness, morally and politically, of whatever influence they had wielded. MacDonald had assured the high commissioners on the evening of 27 September that the cabinet, fully informed of their views, 'was pursuing its policy in light of the appreciation'. Te Water was cautiously sanguine. 'It is difficult to say how far our governments opinions will influence cabinet policy but we believe our united efforts went far towards production of new plan which is now being offered to Germany and Czechoslovakia.' Perhaps they had also helped Chamberlain bring France to heel. MacDonald was to have spoken on the role of the dominions in the parliamentary debate from 3 to 6 October. He had not done so, explaining to a sceptical te Water that he was now preoccupied with Palestine. Te Water felt that MacDonald's silence was deliberate so as to avoid confirming what the press had uncovered – that on 26–27 September 'a clear-cut difference of opinion between the Dominion Governments and this government was manifest'. Chamberlain had been guarded and brief in his reference to dominion support.[84]

The dominions remained loyal to Chamberlain and in sharp disagreement with his critics, within and outside the cabinet, who had been instrumental in steering him dangerously astray. Their criticisms were as tired as they were unfounded – and dangerous. *The Times*, in te Water's view, had it right; the policy of Chamberlain and Halifax was 'coherent, consistent and positive'; it 'saved the peace last week and offers the hope of saving it hereafter. If it fails its failure will be the work of others and it will involve this country neither in weakness nor disgrace'.[85]

The high commissioners, on MacDonald's prompting, found the Munich settlement to be an improvement on the Godesburg demands. Te Water called it a 'considerable advance'. The territories to be transferred were smaller than under the German plan. The

German military occupation would occur in stages, and thus be delayed slightly, benefiting the Czech population. International commissions would decide on additional plebiscite areas, supervise the plebiscites, and rule on the areas to be occupied by German forces and on the final Czech–German frontiers. It seemed likely that they would be 'substantially approximating' the areas designated in the Anglo-French proposals. Most of the Czech fortifications remained, it seemed, in the rump Czech state which would be protected by an international guarantee. Beyond the detail, the high commissioners saw the agreement as a triumph of negotiation over force and for the principle of self-determination.

They were uncertain, but mildly positive, as they looked ahead. Hitler had not raised the issue of colonies; it would have to be resolved but surely without war. The high commissioners were particularly gratified to learn that Chamberlain came home feeling 'that Herr Hitler was a man with whom it would be possible to negotiate a general settlement'. That was what the dominions wanted; Munich was merely one step, however important, towards that goal. That was why they agreed with MacDonald that perhaps the most important result of Munich was the fact that the dictators and the democratic leaders have 'got to know each other'. Mutual confidence had been strengthened; suspicion had begun to evaporate. Hertzog, applauding Chamberlain's 'great and beneficial services', welcomed his plan for an international conference to settle all outstanding issues with Germany. That was the way, Hertzog agreed, to secure 'a more general and fundamental appeasement of Europe'. South Africa would play its part, offering monetary compensation but not southwest Africa to Germany. Te Water agreed: 'It would be sheer lust if Europe went to war now.'

But he and Gie could not be sure. Britain, te Water felt, was at a crossroads. Would it take the high road of cooperation with Germany or the low road of distrust, resorting to balance of power strategies? Chamberlain remained the answer. As dynamic as ever, he preferred the high road, but he was a rearmer and not immune to the virus of power politics. His critics were as vocal as ever, making it difficult to reach a colonial settlement with Germany. Hitler was equally problematic. He might be restrained, cooperative on armaments and reasonable about the colonies. Te Water found comfort in re-reading

Mein Kampf. Hitler had always regarded Britain as the natural ally of Germany; surely Chamberlain's conduct at Munich had reaffirmed that belief. Gie warned of dangerous forces in Britain and Germany – one of them being 'The Hitler of Godesburg and his Sportspalast speech'. But, as there was nothing left justifying a war 'for two years at least', the opportunity existed to establish a real and lasting peace. Germany and Britain, with Hitler and Chamberlain in the lead, would dominate the four power pact that would regulate Europe, hold communism at bay and the Soviet Union at arms length, and bring 'peace in our time'.[86]

Skelton, reasoning differently, arrived at similar conclusions.[87] Chamberlain had, in fact, engineered a deeply flawed settlement of which one could not be proud. It had modified marginally the Godesburg demands but retreated significantly from the Anglo-French plan. Czechoslovakia, its industrial base ruined, its security dangerously compromised, had paid the price. The rump state was not viable. Hitler, strengthened at home, his megalomania reinforced, had achieved more by the threat of force than he would have by war. The road to the Danube lay open; only his 'brittle promises' barred the way. Europe without champions, idealism and a sense of the common good, was in a deplorable condition, prey to predators both minor and major. The League of Nations had 'adjourned' and the neutrals had taken to the 'storm cellars'. The reputations of Britain and France were gravely damaged.

Yet, Skelton concluded, the bad peace was infinitely preferable to a horrific and unpredictable preventive war and might yet provide the path to a better future. A breathing space had been earned and people, in their relief, recoiled from the prospect of war. Chamberlain, the brilliant mediator, would renew his efforts for peace. Hitler, isolated, might escape his inferiority complex and 'revenge obsession' and act cooperatively. Mussolini, equally isolated, might realize that the axis ground only for Germany's benefit.

Smuts, rejecting both Lothian's flabby and Sir Maurice Hankey's misguided optimism, was less confident that Europe could save itself. Germany, Italy and Japan were not satisfied powers. Hitler 'the lion' had 'tasted blood and his appetite may continue'. Chamberlain, to be sure, must act quickly to achieve a general settlement with Germany and thus eliminate a major source of war. But permanent peace,

Smuts felt, meant rebuilding the League of Nations, uniting the democracies, animating the commonwealth to provide selfless leadership, and bringing the United States into the fold and world affairs. By December 1938, te Water and Pirow, planning South African rearmament, were decidedly pessimistic.[88] But to the self-delusion, the sheer wrongheadedess of dominion beliefs had been added, however briefly, utterly futile expectations of appeasement and the Munich agreement.

University of Southern California

NOTES

1. Nicholas Mansergh, *Survey of British Commonwealth Affairs: Problems of External Policy, 1931–1939* (London, 1952); idem, *The Commonwealth Experience* (London, 1969); Ritchie Ovendale, *Appeasement and the English Speaking World* (Cardiff, 1975); idem, 'Britain, the Dominions and the Coming of the Second World War 1933–9', in W.J. Mommsen and L. Kettenacker (eds.), *The Fascist Challenge and the Policy of Appeasement* (London, 1983), pp.323–38; idem, 'Appeasement in Europe and the Far East' 1931–9' (unpublished paper, Conference on Australian Diplomacy and Defense, 1901–39, London 1995); idem, 'Canada, Britain and the United States and the Policy of Appeasement', in C.C. Eldgridge (ed.), *Kith and Kin: Canada, Britain and the United States from the Revolution to the Cold War* (Cardiff, 1997), pp.177–203; D.C. Watt, 'Imperial Defence Policy and Imperial Foreign Policy, 1911–1939: The Substance and the Shadow', and 'The Influence of the Commonwealth on British Foreign Policy: The Case of the Munich Crisis', in *Personalities and Policies* (London, 1965) pp.139–74; idem, 'South African Attempts to Mediate Between Britain and Germay, 1935–1938', in K. Bourne and D.C. Watt, *Studies in International History* (London, 1967), pp.402–22. Watt's mature assessment of Chamberlain and his colleagues is his *Personalities and Appeasement* (Austin, TX, 1991).
2. Reinhardt Meyers, 'Britain, Europe and the Dominions in the 1930s', *Australian Journal of Politics and History*, 22 (1976), pp.36–50; idem, *Britische Sicherheits Politik, 1934–1938* (Dusseldorf, 1976); idem, 'British Imperial Interests and the Policy of Appeasement', in Mommsen and Kettenacker, *The Fascist Challenge*, pp.339–51; Paul Kennedy, 'The Tradition of Appeasement in British Foreign Policy 1865–1939', *British Journal of International Studies*, 2 (1976), pp.195–215; idem, 'Appeasement and British Defence Policy in the Inter-War Years', *British Journal of International Studies*, 4 (1978), pp.161–77.
3. The National Archives in Pretoria hold the Ministry of External Affairs files, the J.B.M. Hertzog papers, the Prime Minister's Office files, the Governors-General Office files, and the papers of Jan Smuts and Charles te Water. I could not consult the files of the defence ministry, which may include the papers of Oswald Pirow. The archives of the University of Cape Town house the papers of Sir Patrick Duncan and Sir William Clark.
4. K. Feiling, *The Life of Neville Chamberlain* (London, 1946), p.336.
5. Michael Graham Fry, 'The Development of Canada's Relations with Japan, 1919–1947, in K.A.J. Hay (ed.), *Canadian Perspectives on Economic Relations with*

Japan (Montreal, 1980), pp.7–67; idem, 'Decolonisation: Britain, France and the Cold War', in Karen Dawisha and Bruce Parrott (eds.), *The End of the Empire: The Transformation of the USSR in Comparative Perspective* (New York, 1997), pp.121–54.

6. Gie, the South African minister in Berlin, put the failure to stimulate German exports to South Africa down to a Jewish boycott, British exploitation of the boycott and a South African prejudice against non-British goods (Gie to te Water, 6 Feb. 1935 and 17 June 1936, te Water papers, A-78, vol.13). See also te Water to Hertzog, 1 Feb. and 13 March, and Hertzog to te Water, 2 March 1938, te Water Papers vol.13; Smuts to S.G. Millen, 22 March 1938, in Jean van der Poel, *Selections from the Smuts Papers*, VI, Dec. 1936–Aug. 1945 (Cambridge, 1973), pp.122–3, Smuts to D.W.F. Ballard, 15 Nov. 1938, ibid., pp.142–3; Smuts to Amery, 9 Dec. 1937, ibid., pp.110–13, and 1 Nov. 1938, Smuts papers, Vol.243; Smuts to F. Lamont, 13 March, and Smuts to Millen, 22 March 1938, Poel, *Smuts Papers*, VI, pp.116–20 and 122–3.

7. Lawrence R. Pratt, *East of Malta, West of Suez Britain's Mediterranean Crisis 1936–1939* (New York, 1975), p.xi; Michael Howard, *The Continental Commitment* (London, 1972); and Michael Graham Fry, 'The Pacific Dominions and the Washington Conference 1921–1922', in Erik Goldstein and John Maurer (eds.), *The Washington Conference 1921–22* (London, 1994), pp.60–101.

8. Report by chiefs of staff subcommittee of CID on questions raised by Australia delegation to Imperial Conference, 9 June 1937, Lyons to Page, 6 July and reply 8 July, and H. Thornby (minister of defence) to Lyons, 20 July 1938, R.G. Neale (ed.), *Documents on Australia Foreign Policy, 1937–1949* (hereafter DAFP) (Canberra, 1975)), I, pp.144–56, 338–9, and 390–92. Between seven and nine capital ships, the Mediterranean fleet in effect, would redeploy to Singapore, taking a maximum 70 days to do so. Te Water to Hertzog, 1 Feb. and 13 March, Hertzog to te Water, 2 March and Hertzog to Chamberlain, 2 Feb. 1938, te Water papers, Vol.13; Smuts to E.F.C. Lane, 11 July 1938, Poel, *Smuts Papers* VI, pp.130–32; Smuts regretted Eden's departure, roundly criticized Chamberlain's errors of policy, but welcomed Halifax's appointment as the right man to reach an agreement with Germany. Smuts to M.C. Gillett, 6 Dec. 1937 and 25 Feb. 1938, Smuts to Amery, 9 Dec. 1937, Smuts to F. Lamont, 13 March 1938, and Smuts to Lane, 11 July 1938, Poel, *Smuts Papers*, VI, pp.107–10, 114–16; 110–13, 116–20 and 130–32.

9. Oswald Pirow, *James, Barry, Munnik Hertzog* (Cape Town, 1957), pp.221–41.

10. King Speeches, 10 March 1936, 19 Feb. and 25 March 1937, 24 May and 20 Aug. 1938, and report on Imperial Conference of May 1937, in Walter A. Riddell (ed.), *Documents on Canadian Foreign Policy*, 1917–1939 (Toronto, 1962), pp.211–22, 222–30, 230–31, 231–3 and 234–35; Smuts to Gillett, 10 June and 15 July 1938, Smuts papers, Vol.243; te Water to Hertzog, 22 Nov. 1938, and Gie to te Water, 20 May and 4 June 1936, te Water papers, Vols 13, and 14, defence ministry memorandum, 9 Nov. 1938, ibid., Vol.41, Pirow, *Hertzog*, pp.221–241; and n.8. South Africa stood midway between Canada, which feared challenges to its domestic unity more that external threats to its security, and Australia which took the opposite view. Australia made the highest per capita investment in defence of any dominion. Only its navy could claim to be a respectable force in 1938. Hitler may have laughed at the news of South Africa's declaration of war in September 1939.

11. Te Water to Hertzog, 15 March and 13 Dec 1938, te Water papers, vol.14. Te Water forecast that the European arms race would, if left unchecked, result in war by 1940–41; Smuts to Lane, 11 July 1938, Poel, *Smuts Papers*, VI, pp.130–32; Massey to King, 26 May 1938, J.A. Munro (ed.), *Documents on Canadian External Relations* (hereafter DCER), (Ottawa, 1972), VI, pp.1081–9.

12. See n.8.

13. Memorandum for W.M. Hughes, 1 Sept. 1938, Neale, *DAFP*, I, pp.412–15. Smuts was

convinced that Japan could not win in China (Smuts to Lane, 11 July 1938, Poel, *Smuts Papers*, VI, pp.130–32).

14. Smuts to Amery, 28 March, to Lothian, 20 May and to Gillett, 10 June 1938, Smuts papers, vol.243.

15. Liesching to Stanley, 2 Sept. 1938, Neale, *DAFP*, I, pp.417–18.

16. Robert Citino, *Germany and the Union of South Africa in the Nazi Period* (New York, 1991) is a valuable addition to the literature on South African foreign and defence policies.

17. Clark to Sir Edward Hasting (dominions office) 8, 10 and 11 March 1937, and MacDonald to Clark, 22 Feb. 1937, Sir William Clark papers BC 81.

18. Te Water was a friend of Pirow and 'second author' of Pirow's biography of Hertzog (te Water – Pirow correspondence on the biography of Hertzog, te Water papers, Vol.27).

19. All three dominions had small permanent delegations in Geneva. A.T. Stirling represented the Australian department of external affairs in London. Financial, legal and trade officials maintained necessary intergovernmental, departmental contacts alongside those of the armed forces.

20. Te Water to Gie, 27 May 1936, te Water papers, Vol.13. See also Vincent Massey, *What's Past is Prologue* (London, 1962).

21. Citino, *Germany and the Union*, pp.170–71; te Water to Hertzog, 1, 22 and 26 Feb. and Hertzog reply, 18 Feb., te Water, to Hertzog, 15 and 17 March and 2 and 24 June 1938, and te Water to H.T. Andrews (South African delegate to the league) 13 April 1938, te Water papers, Vol.13; and M. Norman (Bank of England) to Smuts, 31 Aug. 1938, Smuts papers, file 243. Hertzog, Smuts, Pirow and te Water, and Bruce, shared this view of Chamberlain. Their confidence in him spread to Neville Henderson, a remarkably effective and perceptive ambassador.

22. King speech, 19 Feb. 1937, Riddell, *Documents*, pp.222–30; Pirow, *Hertzog*, p.221; te Water to Hertzog, 17 March, and reply, 24 March 1938, te Water papers, Vol.13. Gie looked to Germany to defeat the Soviet Union in war and destroy communism.

23. Smuts to Amery, 28 March 1938. Smuts papers, Vol.243, and Smuts to Lane, 11 July 1938, Poel, *Smuts Papers*, VI pp.131–2.

24. Smuts to Amery, 28 March and 1 Nov, Smuts to Lothian, 20 and 28 March, Smuts to Gillett, 16 June and 22 July, 1938, Smuts papers, Vols.243–4; Duncan to Lothian, 16 June and 21 July 1939, Sir Patrick Duncan papers, BC 294, d. 1, 12.1 to 23.9. Massey to King, 26 May, and reply 28 June 1938, Munro, *DCER* VI, pp.1081–7 and 1087–9; department of external affairs, memorandum, 1 Sept., and Stirling to Hughes, 9 Sept. 1938, Neale, *DAFP*, 1, pp.412–15 and 428–9. Maxim Litvinov had said that Russia would wait to see what France did to fulfil its obligations to Czechoslovakia and then refer the crisis to the League of Nations!

25. Te Water to Hertzog, 1, 22 and 26 Feb. and 24 June, and Hertzog to te Water, 22 March 1938, Gie to te Water, 4 Feb. 1937, and Gie to Hertzog, 7 Feb. and 8 and 13 March 1938, te Water papers, Vol.13; and Smuts to Amery, 9 Dec. 1937, Poel, *Smuts Papers*, VI, pp.110–13. Gie, enjoying the Berlin social scene, was full of admiration for Hitler and his entourage, although Ribbentrop had turned against England in March 1938. King left his meeting with Hitler in June 1937 convinced that it would be wise to appease Germany rather than fight a war Hitler did not want and Britain could not win. (W. Blair Neathy, *William Lyon Mackenzie King, III* (Toronto, 1962), pp.222–4.

26. Smuts to Amery, 9 Dec. 1937, Poel, *Smuts Papers*, VI, pp.110–13; Smuts to Lothian, 20 May 1938, Smuts papers, Vol.243; Gie to te Water, 4 Feb. 1937 and 15 Aug. 1938, and Hertzog to te Water, 22 and 24 March and 5 May 1938, te Water papers, Vol.13.

27. Gie to te Water, 20 May and 4 June, and te Water to Gie, 27 May 1936, te Water to Hertzog, 1 Feb., 13, 15 and 17 March, 29 April, 28 May and 16 June, Hertzog to te Water, 10, 22 and 24 March, 5 and 27 May and 15 and 21 June 1938, and te Water

to Stanley, 23 June and reply, 28 June 1938, te Water papers, Vol.13; Smuts to Amery, 28 March 1938, Smuts papers, Vol.243 and Lothian to Smuts, 2 June 1938, ibid., Vol.242.

28. Smuts to Lothian, 20 May 1938, Smuts papers, Vol.242, and Lothian memorandum, 4 June 1936, te Water papers, Vol.41.

29. Gie to te Water, 20 May and 6 June 1936, 4 Feb. 1937 and 15 Aug. 1938; te Water to Hertzog, 1 Feb., 15 March, 29 April and 9 and 28 May, and Hertzog to te Water, 22 and 24 March, 5 and 27 May, and 15 June 1938, te Water papers, Vol.13; Smuts to Gillett, 16 June 1938, Smuts papers, Vol.243. MacDonald and Halifax denied the existence of any prior military commitment to France. Te Water reported on 28 May, however, that Halifax had said that if France assisted the Czechs against German aggression Britain must 'rescue' France. Stanley then assured te Water that Britain, under the Locarno treaties, would assist France only if it was the victim of unprovoked aggression. There would be no joint Anglo-French military response to assist Czechoslovakia against German aggression (Stanley to te Water, 3 June 1938, te Water papers, Vol.13.) Duncan assured R.H. Brand in August that if Britain joined France in a war over Czechoslovakia more than one dominion would be 'hard put' to follow her (Duncan to Brand, 25 Aug. 1938, Duncan papers, BC 294, A 16.1 – 3. and 14).

30. Hertoz to te Water, 22 March 1938, te Water papers, Vol.13; Christie to Skelton, and reply, 30 Nov. 1937, Munro, DCER, VI, pp.1080–81. Skelton was more generous, but agreed that Benes was an 'accomplished wirepuller'.

31. Massey to King, 26 May, and King to Massey, 28 June 1938, ibid., pp.1081–7 and 1087–9; Ovendale, 'Appeasement in Europe and the Far East', pp.13–14; te Water to Hertzog, 21 July, te Water papers, Vol.13, Smuts to Gillett, 28 July, and Amery to Smuts, 2 Aug., Smuts papers, Vols.242 and 243. The dominions found merit, however, in keeping Hitler guessing about the consequences of aggression, even though it seemed likely that Britain would restrain France, let Czechoslovakia be overrun and avoid involvement in war.

32. Menzies to Lyons, 6 Aug., Neale, DAFP, 1, pp.400–401, and Gie to te Water, 14 Aug. 1938, te Water papers, Vol.13; Duncan to Brand, 25 Aug. 1938 and Duncan to Lothian, 16 June 1939, Duncan papers, BC 294. A 16.1 – 3 and 14.

33. Liesching to Stanley, 31 Aug.and 2 Sept., DEA memorandum, 1 Sept., Cabinet minutes, 1 Sept., Lyons to Chamberlain, 2 Sept. and reply, 3 Sept. and Bruce to Lyons, 4 Sept. 1938, Neale, DAFP, l, pp.410–11, 412–20; te Water to Hertzog, 2 Sept. 1938, te Water papers, Vol.14. He had met with R.A. Butler.

34. Minutes of the imperial conference, 22 May 1937, Hume Wrong (Geneva) to King, 28 Feb. and 5 March and Stanley to King, 30 July 1938, Munro, DCER V!, 917–19, 924–34; te Water to Hertzog, 1 and 23 Feb. 1938, te Water papers, Vol.13; Stanley to Lyons, 29 July 1938, Neale, DAFP, I, pp.394–97; Bruce to Lyons, 4 and 18 Aug. and reply 23 Aug., Hughes memorandum, 17 Aug., cabinet minutes, 18 Aug., and Lyons to Bruce, 19 Aug., ibid., pp.397, 408–40910; King to Stanley, 18 Aug. and reply, 23 Aug., and King to MacDonald, 31 Aug. 1938. Munro, DCER, VI, pp.935–41; Bodenstein to Gie and te Water, 27 Aug. 1938, Ministry of External Affairs files, 2/1/15, LNI/47; and Duncan to Brand, 25 Aug. 1938, Duncan papers, BC 294, A 1.8.

35. Wrong to King, 15, 16 and 20 Sept. 1938, Munro, DCER, VI, pp.941–42, 943–4; Stirling to Hughes, 16 Sept. 1938, Neale, DAFP, I, pp.436–7, and H.T. Andrews (Geneva) to Hertzog, 6 Oct. 1938, Ministry of External Affairs files, 2/1/15, LNI/47

36. Te Water to Hertzog, 12, 13 and 14 Sept., te Water papers, Vol.14; Massey to King, 14 Sept., Munro, DCER, VI, pp.1089–90; Bruce to Lyons, 12 and 15 Sept., Hodgson to Stirling, 14 Sept. and Stanley to Liesching, 14 Sept. 1938, Neale, DAFP, I, pp.429–430, 431–2, 434–5. Goering's most recent speech seemed more menacing than Hitler's Nuremburg speech. Bruce judged the incidents in the Sudetanland to be spontaneous and not inspired from Berlin.

37. Te Water to Hertzog, 17, 19, 21 and 23 Sept., te Water papers, Vol.14; MacDonald–Bruce conversation, 15 Sept., Bruce to Lyons, 15 Sept., Neale, *DAFP*, I, pp.433, 434–5; and high commissioners' meeting, 21 Sept. 1938, ibid., p.450.
38. Te Water to Hertzog, 19, 23, 24, 26, 27, 28 and 29 Sept. and te Water to Bodenstein, 26 Sept., te Water papers, Vol.14; high commissioners' meetings, 23, 24, 26, 27 and 28 Sept., Neale, *DAFP*, I, pp.451–2, 455–6, 460–62, 465–6, 467–8 and 470–71; Stanley to Lieshing, 28 Sept., ibid., p.473, and Stanley to Lyons, 28 Sept. 1938, ibid., p.475: MacDonald informed the high commissioners very late on 22 September that the news from Godesburg was bad.
39. King to Neville Henderson, 14 Sept. and reply 15 Sept., and Ribbentrop to King, 18 Sept., Munro, *DCER*, VI, pp.1090–91, 1094, and Lyons to Chamberlain, 28 Sept. 1938, Neale, *DAFP*, I, p.469. Hertzog, through Gie, may have approached Hitler. Te Water claimed to be in daily contact with Henderson and in total agreement with him. (Te Water to Hertzog, 14 Sept. 1938, te Water papers, Vol.14.)
40. Te Water to Hertzog, 12 and 14 Sept., ibid.; Bruce to Lyons 12 Sept. 1938, Neale, *DAFP*, I, pp.429–30.
41. Te Water to Hertzog, 13 and 30 Sept., te Waters papers, Vol.14; Bruce to Lyons, 24 Sept., Neale, *DAFP*, I, pp.453–5; high commissioners' meetings, 26, 29 and 30 Sept. 1938, ibid., pp.460–2, 473–5, 476–8; King speech, 30 March 1939, Riddell, *Documents*, pp.162–5.
42. Stanley to Liesching, 14 Sept., and Hodgson to F.K. Officer (Australian counsellor, British embassy, Washington), 27 Sept. 1938, Neale, *DAFP*, I, pp.431–2, 464–5.
43. Liesching to Stirling, 14, 21 and 27 Sept., Hodgson to Stanley, 14 Sept., Hodgson to Officer, 27 Sept., and Lyons to Chamberlain, 26 Sept., ibid., pp.430–31, 449, 459, 462–3, 464–5; high commissioners' meeting, 26 Sept. 1938, ibid., pp.460–62.
44. Te Water to Hertzog, 19 and 28 Sept., te Water papers Vol.14; Hughes speech, 8 Aug. 1938, Neale, *DAFP*, I, p.478 n.5.
45. High commissioners' meeting, 19 Sept., ibid., pp.442–4; te Water to Hertzog, 19 Sept. 1938, te Water papers, Vol.14.
46. Hodgson to Stirling, 21 Sept. and reply, 21 Sept., Neale, DAFP, I, pp.447, 448.
47. Te Water to Hertzog, 7 Oct., te Water papers, Vol.14; and Skelton memorandum, 3 Oct., and Christie memorandum, 10 Dec. 1938, Munro, *DCER*, VI, pp.1100–1103, 1110–11.
48. Massey to King, 26 Sept., ibid., pp.1096–7; te Water to Hertzog, 27 Sept., te Water papers, Vol.14; high commissioners' meetings, 26 and 28 Sept., Lyons to Roosevelt; 28 Sept. and Officer to depart. of external affairs, 28 Sept. 1938, Neale, *DAFP*, I, pp.460–62, 468, 469, 470–71.
49. High commissioners' meetings, 21 and 28 Sept. and 1 Oct.; Lyons to Chamberlain, 28 Sept., ibid., pp.409, 450, 470–71, 478–9; and te Water to Hertzog, 26 and 27 Sept. 1938, te Water papers, Vol.14.
50. Te Water to Hertzog, 26, 27 and 29 Sept., ibid.; Massey to King, 26 Sept., Munro, *DCER*, VI, pp.1096–7, and Lyons to Chamberlain, 26 Sept. 1938, Neale, *DAFP*, I, p.459.
51. High commissioners' meetings, 21 and 23 Sept. and 1 Oct., ibid., pp.450, 451–2, 478–9; te Water to Hetzog, 14, 19, 21, 23, and 26 Sept. and 1 Oct., te Water papers, Vol.14; and Smuts to Millen, 14 Sept. 1938, Smuts papers, Vol.243.
52. te Water to Hertzog, 19, 24 and 26 Sept., Gie to Hertzog, 26 Sept., Hertzog to te Water 26 Sept. and Hertzog to Chamberlain, 26 Sept., te Water papers, Vol.14. Te Water described Australian opinion as uncertain. High commissioners' meetings, 19, 24 and 26 Sept., Bruce to Lyons, 15, 19, 24 and 26 Sept., and Bruce–MacDonald conversations, 14 and 25 Sept. 1938, Neale, *DAFP*, I, pp.433, 434–5, 442–4, 446–7, 455–6, 457, 458, 460–62. After each cabinet meeting on 25 September, Bruce pressed MacDonald emphatically on the need to accept the German proposals.

53. High commissioners' meetings, 23, 24 and 26 Sept., ibid., pp.451–52, 453–6, 460–62; Massey to King, 26 Sept., Munro, *DCER*, VI, pp.1096–7; Massey, *What's Past*, pp.259–61; Hertzog to te Water, 27 Sept. and te Water to Hertzog, 23, 26 and 29 Sept. 1938, te Water papers, Vol.14.
54. Te Water to Hertzog, 21, 23, 24 and 26 Sept., ibid., high commissioners' meetings, 15 Sept., ibid., and 17, 21, 23, and 24 Sept. 1938, Neale, *DAFP*, I, pp.441, 450, 451–2 and 455–6.
55. High commissioners' meetings, 17, 19 and 26 Sept., Bruce to Lyons, 19 Sept., Bruce–MacDonald conversation, 19 Sept., and Lyons to Chamberlain, 26 Sept., ibid., pp.441, 442–4, 445–6, 446–7, 459, 460–62; te Water to Hertzog, 19, 22, 23, and 26 Sept., te Water papers, Vol.14; and Stanley to King, 19 Sept. 1938, Munro, *DCER*, VI, pp.1094–5. Te Water found former Canadian prime minister, R.B. Bennett, utterly opposed to a guarantee of 'a ramshackle State' which would bind the dominions as well as Britain.
56. Massey to King, 14 Sept., ibid., pp.1089–90, te Water to Hertzog, 17 Sept., te Water papers, Vol.14; Bruce to Lyons, 12, 15, 17, and 19 Sept., Liesching to Stanley, 14 Sept., and high commissioners' meeting, 19 Sept. 1938, Neale, *DAFP*, I, pp.429–30, 430–31, 434–5, 437–8, 442–4, 446–7.
57. High commissioners' meetings, 23, 24, 26, 27, 28 and 29 Sept., Stanley to Lyons, 17 Sept., and Bruce to Lyons, 28 Sept., ibid., pp.439–40, 451–2, 455–6, 460–62, 465–6, 472–3; and te Water to Hertzog, 23, 24, 26 and 27 Sept. 1938, te Water papers, Vol.14.
58. Te Water to Hertzog, 19 and 26 Sept., and te Water to Bodenstein, 26 Sept., ibid., Canadian minister (Paris) to King, 9 Sept., Massey to King, 14 and 26 Sept., and Skelton memorandum, 3 Oct., Munro, *DCER*, VI, pp.1089, 1096–7, 1100–103; Bruce to Lyons, 19 Sept., and high commissioners' meetings, 19, 26, 27 and 28 Sept. 1938, Neale *DAFP*, I, pp.442–4, 446–7, 460–62, 465–6, 470–71. Massey reported that the French were not giving unswerving support to the Czechs, were considering the plebiscite option and preferred that a four power conference resolve the crisis.
59. High commissioners' meeting, 28 Sept., ibid., pp.470–71; te Water to Hertzog, 13, 14, and 17 Sept., te Water papers, Vol.14; The Canadian minister in Paris saw Hitler as too intelligent to jeopardize his 'wonderful achievements' in Germany by war. (Report to King, 9 Sept. 1938, Munro, *DCER*, VI, pp.1089.)
60. Te Water to Hertzog, 13, 14, 17 and 19 Sept., te Water papers, Vol.14; Bruce to Lyons and Stanley to Lyons, 17 Sept. 1938, Neale, *DAFP*, VI, pp.437–8, 439–40.
61. High commissioners' meetings, 23 and 24 Sept. and Bruce to Lyons, 24 and 26 Sept., ibid., pp.451–2, 453–5, 455–6, 458; te Water to Hertzog, 24, 26 and 27 Sept. and Hertzog to te Water, 27 and 29 Sept., te Water papers, Vol.14, and Massey to King, 26 Sept. 1938, Munro, *DCER*, VI, pp.1096–7.
62. Massey to King, 26 Sept., ibid.; te Water to Hertzog, 26 and 27 Sept., te Water papers Vol.14; and high commissioners' meeting, 27 Sept. 1938, Neale *DAFP*, VI, pp.467–8.
63. Liesching to Stanley, and Bruce to Lyons, 15 Sept., ibid., pp.432–3, 434–5; Pirow to te Water, 21 Sept. and te Water to Hertzog, 23 Sept. 1938, te Water papers, Vol.14.
64. Hertzog to Chamberlain, 17 Sept., ibid.; King to Chamberlain, 14 Sept. and King statement, 17 Sept., Munro, *DCER*, VI, pp.1090, 1093–4; Smuts to Norman, 15 Sept., Smuts papers, Vol.243 and Smuts to J. Power, 15 Sept., Poel, *Smuts Papers*, VI, pp.139–40; and Liesching to Stanley, 15 Sept. and Bruce to Lyons, 17 Sept. 1938, Neale, *DAFP*, I, pp.432–3, 437–8.
65. Te Water to Hertzog, 14 Sept. 1938, te Water papers, Vol.14.
66. Te Water to Hertzog, 15 and 17 Sept., and high commissioners' meeting, 15 Sept., ibid.; high commissioners' meeting, 19 Sept., and Stanley to Lyons, 17 Sept., Neale, *DAFP*, I, pp.442–4, 439–40.
67. Bruce to Lyons, 17 Sept. 1938, ibid., pp.437–8.

68. High commissioners' meetings, 23, 24, 26, 27, and 28 Sept., ibid., pp.451-2, 455-6, 460-62, 465-8, 470-71; high commissioners' meeting with Chamberlain and Halifax, 26 Sept., Munro, *DCER*, VI, pp.1090-97; and te Water to Hertzog, 23, 24, 26, 27 and 29 Sept. 1938, te Water papers, Vol.14.

69. Te Water to Hertzog, 23 Sept. 1938, ibid. Foreign office officials were snubbing *The Times* for supporting Chamberlain's pro-German policy. Hitler's dislike of Eden and Churchill would te Water concluded, strengthen Chamberlain's hand.

70. Te Water to Hertzog, 23, 24, and 26 Sept., and te Water to Bodenstein, 26 Sept., ibid.; Bruce to Lyons, 24 and 26 Sept. and high commissioners' meeting, 26 Sept. 1938, Neale, *DAFP*, I, pp.453-5, 458, 460-62.

71. Lyons to Chamberlain, 26 Sept., Liesching to Stanley, 27 Sept. and high commissioners' meetings 24, 26, and 27 Sept., ibid., pp.455-6, 459, 460-62, 462-3, 465-8; high commissioners' meeting with Chamberlain and Halifax, Munro *DCER*, VI, pp.1096-7; and te Water to Hertzog, 26 and 27 Sept. and te Water to Bodenstein, 26 Sept. 1938, te Water papers, Vol.14. MacDonald met twice with Bruce on 25 September and with te Water on 27 September. What Chamberlain made of the information he received from and about the dominions, and how he used it is left to other essayists.

72. Te Water to Hertzog, 27, 28 and 29 Sept., ibid., Bruce to Lyons, 26 Sept., and high commissioners' meetings, 26 and 27 Sept., Neale, *DAFP*, I, pp.458, 460-462 and 465-468. The second meeting on 27 September went on until 2.0 am on 28 September.

73. High commissioners' meeting, 27 Sept., ibid., pp.465-8; te Water to Hertzog, 26, 27 and 28 Sept. 1938, te Water papers, Vol.14.

74. Skelton memorandum, 3 Oct., Munro, *DCER*, VI, pp.1100-103; MacDonald-Bruce conversation, 19 Sept., 1938, Neale, *DAFP*, I, pp.445-6. See also King speech, 30 March 939, Riddell, *Documents*, pp.160-65.

75. Pirow, *Hertzog*, pp.226-7; Citino, *Germany and the Union*, pp.153, 180-83. Citino cites the German ambassador's reports to Berlin of 15 September and 9 October 1938. He did not expect South Africa to opt for neutrality. See also Smuts to Duncan, 12 Sept. 1938, Duncan papers, D1., 35.1-67. Smuts insisted on limiting the declaration to the central and east european case.

76. Christie memorandum, 15 Sept. and King statement, 17 Sept. 1938, Munro, *DCER*, VI, pp.1091-4; Christie assumed that Canada would be bound constitutionally by a British decision for war.

77. High commissioners' meeting, 26 Sept., Neale, *DAFP*, I, pp.460-62; te Water to Hertzog, 26 Sept. 1938, te Water papers, Vol.14.

78. Te Water to Hertzog, 28 Sept.; ibid.; and high commissioners' meeting, 27 Sept. 1938, Neale, *DAFP*, I, pp.465-8. MacDonald reported the sense of the meeting to the cabinet that evening.

79. Te Water to Hertzog, 19 and 29 Sept. 1938, te Water papers, Vol.14.

80. King statement, 27 Sept., Munro, *DCER*, VI, p.1097. He had Lapointe's support from Geneva, but rumours of possible clashes between ardent, pro-British and French Canadians were circulating (Officer to Hodgson, 26 Sept. 1938, Neale, *DAFP*, I, p.464.) King did not refer to Chamberlain's press release that morning, which was decidedly conciliatory.

81. Pirow, *Hertzog*, p.227; Citino, *Germany and the Union*, pp.180-81; te Water to Hertzog, 29 Sept. and te Water to Pirow, 22 Nov. 1938, te Water papers, Vol.14.

82. Te Water to Hertzog, 28 Sept., te Water papers, Vol.14, Wrong memorandum, 7 Dec., and Christie memorandum, n.d. (after Munich), Munro, *DCER*, VI, pp.1104-10 and XI.

83. Hertzog to Chamberlain, 28 Sept., te Water papers, Vol.14; Smuts to Gillett, 1 and 10 Oct. 1938, Smuts papers, Vol.243; King to Chamberlain, 29 Sept., Munro, *DCER*, VI, pp.1099; and Lyons to Chamberlain, 30 Sept. 1938, Neale, *DAFP*, I, p.476.

84. Te Water to Hertzog, 28 Sept. and 7 Oct. 1938, te Water papers, Vol.14.
85. Te Water to Hertzog, 7 Oct., ibid.; high commissioners' meeting, 30 Sept. 1938, Neale, *DAFP*, I, pp.476–8. Te Water advised Hertzog, to praise all the Munich participants.
86. High commissioners' meeting, 1 Oct. 1938, Neale, *DAFP*, I, pp.476–8; te Water to Hertzog, 30 Sept., 1 and 7 Oct., 22 Nov. and 13 Dec., Hertzog to Chamberlain, 10 Oct., Gie to te Water, 17 Oct. and te Water to Gie, 19 Oct., te Water papers, Vols.13 and 14. Bodenstein, reportedly, saw Munich as a German triumph.
87. Skelton memo, 3 Oct. 1938, Munro, *DCER*, VI, pp.1100–103. King's considered and public judgement of Chamberlain's performance in September 1938 was remarkable, concluding, approvingly, that Chamberlain's commitments to France and Czechoslovakia were last-minute and conditional, and that Chamberlain did everything to ensure that they would not have to be met (King statement, 30 March 1939, Riddell, *Documents*, pp.160–65).
88. Lothian to Duncan, 27 Oct. and Smuts to Duncan, 7 Nov. 1938, Duncan papers, D1. 12.1–23.9, and D1. 35.1–67; Hankey to Smuts, 29 Dec. 1938, Poel, *Smuts Papers*, VI, pp.147–8.

China, the Sino-Japanese Conflict and the Munich Crisis

HSI-HUEY LIANG

The following essay pretends to be no more than a footnote to the tragic history of Munich, a somewhat elaborate accounting for a historical might-have-been. It concerns the chance for a solution to the central European crisis of the 1930s other than by capitulation to German expansionism, and that was by synchronizing it with the ongoing revolutionary changes in the Far East. This alternative was strongly advocated by some two dozen men in the German foreign office, the ministry of economics, the war ministry and by some leading industrialists. It was ultimately rejected by Hitler, though not before the Führer had given the Chinese option a moment of consideration.

Ironically, the two countries that would most have benefited from such an alternative development – Czechoslovakia and China – were not consulted. Worse, neither seems to have been aware that the great dangers they each faced in 1937 and 1938 were linked by their common dependency on Germany's choice of strategic partner in the far-flung Eurasian balance of power. A recent inquiry with the director of Asian affairs at the Czech foreign ministry, Dr Milos Pojar, whether his department had records suggesting that the German commitments in China since 1928 might have postponed if not cancelled 'Fall Grün' altogether, produced no result.[1] Twenty years earlier I had asked Mr Yeh Kung-chao a similar question. Mr Yeh had directed the European department in the Chinese foreign ministry at the time of Munich. Did he remember any Chinese contacts to German politicians and intelligence agents with ties to the anti-Hitler resistance between 1937 and 1940? After a silence, he said: 'Well, nothing ever came of any of this, did it?'[2]

Dr Kurt Jahnke was one of the most successful German operatives in the secret game of powerbroking in the twentieth century, a kind of *eminence grise* in the German intelligence world. Born in 1882, a well-to-do estate owner from Saxony, he served the Wilhelmine empire as a sabotage agent in the USA and in Mexico during the First World War. He was the confidant of chancellors Wilhelm Cuno (1920–23), Gustav Stresemann (1923) and Heinrich Brüning (1930–32) during the Weimar Republic, and in the Third Reich he served in the intelligence office of Hitler's deputy, Rudolf Hess. In addition to all this he had his own 'Büro J' at the German foreign office, a department entrusted with clandestine contacts to foreign powers. His name appeared only in a few publications during his lifetime, the last time as '*Vortragender Legationsrat Jahnke*' in a British *Who's Who in Nazi Germany and Austria* for use by the British occupation forces.[3] Most of my knowledge about him comes from lengthy interviews with his two closest former aides: Police Captain Walther Stennes, who worked under his orders from 1925 to 1930, and Dr Carl Marcus, his right-hand man from 1930 to about 1943.[4] Marcus in particular sought to portray Jahnke as a master puppeteer or as a second Baron von Holstein. If we are to believe him, it was Jahnke who thought up the Russo-German agreement of Rapallo (1922) and engineered the subsequent technical collaboration between Reichswehr and Red Army. His most important and nearly successful enterprise, however, had an immediate if indirect bearing on the Munich crisis of 1938. This was Janhke's idea of overcoming Germany's strategic encirclement by France and its east European allies by means of a Eurasian partnership with China. The project was set in motion in 1927 and faced its decisive test ten years later. For by 1937 the German investments in China had produced results so impressive as to provoke a Japanese preemptive strike against China. At this critical point the question was whether the Hitler regime would hold the course and gamble its future on the emergence of a truly strong China in another ten to 15 years, or else trade in China's friendship for a Japanese alliance so as to have a free hand for immediate military action against Austria and Czechoslovakia.[5]

Not one of Jahnke's ideas, and in fact a project he had rejected out of hand, was the Kapp *putsch* of 1920. Jahnke was asked by Wolfgang Kapp to be minister of interior in his rebel government, but after meeting Hitler and Trebitsch-Lincoln, whose personalities he found distasteful, he declined.[6] According to Marcus, Hitler never forgave Jahnke his refusal to work with him in 1920, and his rancour may ultimately have doomed Jahnke's China plan in 1937.

Jahnke's search for a strategic breakthrough on the supra-European level had begun by sounding out Bolshevik Russia in 1920 with General Hans von Seeckt personally contacting Karl Radek, Lenin's emissary in Berlin. But the Russians soon proved to be far too suspicious of the Germans to be counted on for a partnership over many years.[7] Jahnke's next choice was Latin America. This may explain a mysterious six-months trip by General Alexander von Falkenhausen to Cuba and Mexico in 1928/29. Falkenhausen was then commander of the Infantry School in Dresden and there was never an official explanation why this important man should have been given a leave of half a year ostensibly 'to study the flora and fauna of Mexico'.[8] In his posthumous legacy we find a cryptic note written on the eve of his departure for Mexico in which he records a visit he had to make to a certain Jahnke in Münster. (Another note, written in a peremptory note and signed 'Vogt', ordered Falkenhausen to go to an address in Berlin just before he left for China in 1934. When asked about these consultations, Marcus assured me that they all involved last-minute instructions from 'our Jahnke'.)[9]

Most important was the trip made by Colonel Max Bauer (1869–1929) to China in December 1927. Bauer had served as Field Marshal Erich von Ludendorff's right-hand man in the First World War and had been implicated in the abortive Kapp *putsch* of 1920. He arrived in south China just as Stalin's emissaries, Heinz Neumann and Gerhard Eisler, organized communist uprisings in Canton and Shanghai in pursuit of a Eurasian strategy directed against Britain and Japan, not unlike Jahnke's conception for the recovery of Germany. These insurrections quickly failed and ushered in ten years of Kuomintang ascendancy under Chiang Kai-shek.[10] Bauer's travel diaries from these years are a goldmine for the historian of Sino-German relations in the late 1920s.[11] A chance meeting shortly after Christmas 1927 between him and the rising star of the Kuomintang in a Shanghai hotel resulted in a very productive if short-lived collaboration between these two men (Bauer died unexpectedly of smallpox in 1929).[12] Bauer became Chiang Kai-shek's principal European military adviser. In March of the following year he was asked to escort a Chinese mission to Berlin, charged with recruiting German military experts for service in China and to purchase German weapons and machinery so as to expand and modernize China's primitive war industry.[13]

While it is true that since 1918 hundreds of Chinese students had on their own chosen to study in Germany, the particular relationship established between the German military-industrial complex and the Nanking government after 1928 produced stupendous results. Through the Chinese legation's new 'trade department' various new organizations were founded, notably the HAPRO (Handels-gesellschaft zur Verwertung industrieller Produkte), which was to supervise all China's importation of German munitions, technicians and weapons instructors. A German military advisory team was established in Nanking with a liaison office in the German war ministry to help screen suitable officers for service in China. The German advisory team was under the command, successively, of four high-ranking German generals: Hermann Kriebel (1929–30), Georg Wetzell (1930–34), Hans von Seeckt (1934), and Alexander von Falkenhausen (1934–38), whose mission to Mexico had ended so inconclusively. But in China he was to make an enormous contribution, if not to German interests then to those of his host country. If, in addition, we count the Chinese officers who arrived for general staff training in Germany and the number of important German firms engaged in the China trade – Otto Wolff, Siemens, Carlowitz, Melcher, Kunst & Albers, Reuter-Bröckelmann – we can only conclude that if all this was part of a 'Jahnke plan' then his initiative succeeded in a very short time in mobilizing hundreds of people on two continents and committing many millions of Reichsmark and Mexican dollars in financial investments.[14]

It surely would be appropriate for the reader to ask at this point what evidence we have that all the developments described above were Jahnke's work? Could he have controlled men with such high public reputation and political experience as Hans von Seeckt and Alexander von Falkenhausen, who in the war had helped the Turks run their military operations against the British and in the Weimar Republic had rebuilt Germany's armed forces? Could he even be sure of someone like Max Bauer, considering that Bauer's devotion to Chiang Kai-shek before long became well nigh absolute?[15]

Above all, Jahnke did not control the Chinese politicians. Chiang Kai-shek liked Bauer as a friend and Jahnke may have assumed that as long as Chiang remained China's dictator Bauer's position close to the marshal would be sufficient guarantee of Chinese cooperation. But Bauer died after two years. His successor, General Kriebel, did not get along with Chiang, and the next chief adviser, Wetzell, did not do much better. At this point, there were rumours that the Chinese were considering dropping the German advisory team for a French team under Marshal Philippe Pétain.[16] This obviously would have utterly ruined Jahnke's plan for the restoration of Germany's international standing with China's help. On his first visit to China in 1933 Seeckt was very careful to manage Chinese sensibilities in order, so he told the German officers in Nanking, to save the German military mission from being closed down. The Chinese were already turning to Italy rather than Germany for help to build an air force, if only because the Italians treated the Chinese with greater courtesy.[17] At this point, to safeguard his investment, fortune would have it that Jahnke's former assistant, Captain Stennes, was obliged to leave nazi Germany *persona non grata* because of an earlier dispute with Hitler, whereupon he asked to go to China. He did not join the military mission in Nanking, but became head of Chiang Kai-shek's personal bodyguard, which placed this Jahnke agent in the household of China's generalissimo. But Stennes, who in 1931 had defied Hitler's authority, was nobody's easy subordinate. Another 'insurance' was Ernst Bauer, the son of Max Bauer, for whom a clerical position was found in the Chinese legation in Berlin. However, Ernst Bauer soon joined the Nazi Party and became an informer for the NSDAP on Chinese affairs.[18]

II

This brings me to the diplomat who most directly linked the Sino-German relationship to the Czechoslovak crisis in 1938, Dr Lone Liang (1894–1967). In the 1920s he was dean of the Canton Law School, then professor of constitutional law at Peking University, president of the College of Law and Political Science, and judge on the supreme court and on the provisional court of the international settlement of Shanghai, Liang was a seasoned lawyer by training. At

34 he had entered the Chinese diplomatic service and in his first post in Berlin, from 1928 to 1933, he was largely responsible for organizing the project of inviting German experts for service in China. As counsellor and chargé d'affaires, he was the legation's chief executive officer, while his superiors, General Tsiang Tso-ping (Chinese minister to Germany from January 1929 to March 1931) and Liu Wen-tao (Tsiang's successor from December 1930 to September 1933) held their positions only for relatively short periods.[19] If that made Liang the tool of a vaster Jahnke plan in the service of Germany, then that was only because Jahnke's initiative happened to agree with many earlier Chinese endeavours to elicit help for the newly created Sun Yat-sen republic from defeated Germany.[20] Besides, Minister Tsiang Tso-pin and Counsellor Lone Liang on their own also pursued the idea of a German–Chinese alliance, though with the inclusion of Russia. Their chief contact for this undertaking was not Jahnke but Maxim Litvinov, who headed the Soviet Russian delegation to the preparatory conference on disarmament in Geneva.[21] In time, Tsiang and Liang submitted a proposal for a Russo-Chinese nonaggression treaty to Nanking, apparently with Litvinoff's approval, but it came too late to forestall a futile Chinese attempt to wrestle the Chinese Eastern Railway in Manchuria from Russian control by force (July 1929). The Red Army quickly put down the Chinese troops and restored the *status quo ante*.[22] But since it was the German foreign ministry which next offered its good services to settle this dispute, the opportunity was given to continue exploring the chance for a future collaboration between 'the three dissatisfied great land powers of Eurasia'. In the summer of 1932 the Chinese delegates in Geneva, Liang and Minister Liu Wen-tao, offered the Russians yet another nonaggression pact.[23]

I hasten to explain that my knowledge on this particular point is influenced by childhood memories of stories told to me by Lone Liang on long walks in the Stromovka park in Prague when I was a small boy. For Lone Liang was my father. By the time I was old enough to pick up anecdotes from his political life he was Chinese minister to Czechoslovakia. I even remember asking him innocently one day why he and Minister Tsiang had wanted China, Germany and Russia to become allies, and being awestruck when he answered me with a straight face, seemingly perplexed at my naïveté: 'We wanted to dominate the world, of course!' He may only have sought to amuse his seven-year-old offspring, but it convinces me personally that he could never have been a mere instrument in the hands of a foreign government servant like Jahnke. As a member – albeit one of the younger ones – of an emerging élite of well-educated and sophisticated Chinese diplomats such as China was finally producing after the First World War, he was too strongly committed to the goal of a united and independent China to serve any other cause but that of his country.

Liang remained in the Berlin legation for five years. But the arms-buying project which Max Bauer had urged on Chiang Kai-shek served the Chinese government not only to modernize its defences. After over two decades of warlordism, banditry and regional threats of secession, the Kuomintang regime decided to use the trade department in Berlin to put an end to years of domestic strife by undercutting all arms imports not authorized by Chiang Kai-shek himself. After all, China in the 1930s was, in the words of John F. Fairbank, still a 'fragmented, premodern society'.[24] Kwangtung and Kwangsi, under Generals Pai Chung-hsi and Li Tsung-jen, constituted a *de facto* autonomous south Chinese republic, Sinkiang was under heavy Russian influence, and until the Japanese assassinated its strongman, Marshal Chang Tso-lin, in 1928, Manchuria even had its own representative at the League of Nations.[25] Above all, there was the Chinese Communist Party with its renowned Eight Route army, perhaps the strongest communist movement in the world outside Russia. The south Chinese, the Manchurians and the Communists all had their own people roaming Europe in search of political support and, more often than not, in search of surplus weapons. True, in the face of Japan's growing aggressiveness, notably after its seizure of Manchuria (1931) and its assault on Shanghai (1932), most of these political agents and military men began to accept nominal subordination to the Chiang Kai-shek government. But the drive to stop all competitive arms buying by different Chinese factions continued, difficult though this was from the one trade department office in the Berlin legation. In 1934 Counsellor Tann Beue in Berlin was asked to take over the Stockholm legation to stop Swedish arms shipments to Kwangtung and Kwangsi. And in 1933 Lone Liang was sent to Prague to deal with a case of corruption involving the Chinese minister to Warsaw.[26]

China had recognized the Czechoslovak republic as early as 1919,[27] but though legations were opened in the two countries, China appointed no resident minister to Prague. Instead, China's minister to Poland was also accredited to Czechoslovakia, though only nominally, and he seldom left Warsaw to visit Prague. Chinese interests in Czechoslovakia were dealt with by a local chargé d'affaires. Then, in 1933, the current minister to Poland came under suspicion of accepting bribes in return for signing fake Chinese purchasing orders for Czechoslovak arms that were actually destined for Spanish Morocco.[28] Lone Liang arrived in Prague with rank of chargé d'affaires to clear up this corruption scandal. By 1936 he had gathered enough evidence against Minister Chang Hsin-hai in Warsaw to force his resignation from the Chinese diplomatic service. Thereupon, Liang was promoted in rank to minister extraordinary and plenipotentiary, with the result that Prague finally had its own Chinese minister in residence and that Sino-Czechoslovak relations significantly improved – a development surely of no interest to Jahnke.

My father's transfer to Prague in 1933 was therefore not motivated by the change in regime in Germany but came about because of a Chinese internal disciplinary affair. But, in retrospect, his reassignment acquired political importance, for it facilitated a reorientation in Chinese foreign policy, when, in the course of the next five years, Sino-German relations became increasingly strained. As Germany under the nazis began feverishly to prepare for a war in Europe, the Chinese were now better positioned to consider Czech armament production as one of a number of alternative sources of modern ordnance. There had been earlier economic transactions between China and Czechoslovakia. In 1928 China bought an electric power plant from Skoda and in 1933 a sugar processing plant. A treaty of amity and commerce between China and Czechoslovakia was signed in 1930.[29] In 1932, Kung Hsiang-hsi (H.H. Kung) as minister of finance had already visited Brno and Pilsen on a general tour of European armaments works.[30] By 1937, according to a Reuters report, China tried (though unsuccessfully) to raise a loan in the United States with which to purchase the majority interest in the Czecho-Moravian Armament Works in Brno, then the property of the Czechoslovak government.[31]

Far be it from me to exaggerate the importance of Chinese–Czechslovak relations in the years before the crisis of 1937–38. Mutual knowledge between the two countries was still very scant, and often no better than anecdotal. Intriguing, but never explained, is a letter to the Czech politician Milan Hodza from Lou Heng-tsiang of the Chinese delegation to the Paris Peace Conference on 10 September 1919, in which the Chinese diplomat suggests that a theatrical play set in ancient China by Georges Clemenceau, 'La voile du Bonheur', be translated into the Czech language: 'Je crois qu'elle pourra aussi intéresser les lecteurs de votre pays.'[32] (And yet, was not Albrecht Haushofer, a member of the German resistance, moved to try his hand as a playwright on a similar theme when, shortly before his arrest by the Gestapo, he wrote 'Chinesische Legende'?)[33] If anyone, it was Czech rather than Chinese scholars who tried to make up for this scantiness through literary and philological studies.[34] Due to the mounting interest in arms purchases from Czechoslovakia, however, various Chinese military officers visited Prague after Lone Liang's arrival. On these occasions my father would invite high-ranking Czech officers to meet them at our legation. Among the photographs I found in my father's papers after his death are pictures showing the former Chinese minister of interior, Huang Fu, a veteran of the Sun Yat-sen revolution and the author of numerous books on European lessons for the future of China, sitting together with General Silvestr Blaha, who headed the military cabinet of President Masaryk, General Ludvik Krejci, who was chief of the general staff, and General Karel Husarek, director of fortifications. In another picture the Chinese visitor is General Yang Chieh, commander of the Military College in Nanking and vice-chief of the Chinese general staff. His meeting with Czechoslovak military men in 1933 is interesting since Georg Wetzell at that time still headed the German military mission in Nanking, and General Yang was known to be very critical of Wetzell.[35]

In the late 1930s China had 17 diplomatic mission in Europe. The largest missions with embassy status were in London, Paris, Moscow, Berlin and Rome.[36] By contrast, Warsaw, Lisbon, Vienna and Prague counted only as secondary posts, but maintaining good relations with these smaller 'non-treaty powers' (countries that had no extraterritorial rights in China) was still important to bolster China's claim to equal status in the international community. Besides, China also needed as much support as it could get from friendly governments at international conferences. The high prestige of the Czechoslovak republic between the two wars, and the important role of President Benes at the League of Nations were duly noted by the Chinese.

And still, almost inevitably, the relations between these two countries were negatively affected by the growing war fever in the Far East and in central Europe. The Czech and the Chinese situations being so different discouraged any thought of mutual consultation and cooperation. Compared to China, Czechoslovakia was a very tightly structured, centralized political entity, and because of its small territory it was highly vulnerable to single acts of subversion and terrorism (the assassination of Theodor Lessing and Rudolf Formis by nazi agents readily come to mind). Because Czechoslovakia was liable to succumb to any sudden attack by one of its neighbours it was indeed in a situation where 'domestic discord was a luxury we simply cannot afford'.[37] Visions of a cataclysmic war over Czechoslovakia, in which squadrons of bombers and motorized troops would force a decision in a matter of days, belonged to the popular fantasy of the day.[38] Czechoslovakia's defences depended on elaborate and costly underground fortifications along the German and Hungarian frontiers and on the national discipline of its people, who in an emergency would have to be called up in a matter of hours. China, on the other hand, had over the past 100 years surrendered piece after piece of its territorial sovereignty and still continued to exist. Its people were held together by traditions of loyalty to family and clan rather than through legal obligations to the state, and their social structure was so diffuse as to preclude any thought of introducing a national service system. China had no contingencies for rapid mobilization; it was simpler to keep its numerous though ill trained and poorly equipped soldiers on a permanent war footing.

Ideologically, therefore, Czechoslovakia belonged to a postnationalist age, whereas China still stood at the beginning of its transformation into a political nation. In Europe the continued existence of a political system based on perpetual war readiness and competition for power had in the twentieth century become self-destructive. No one was more aware of that than Czechoslovak politicians like Thomas G. Masaryk, Edvard Benes, Kamil Krofta and Milan Hodza. While acutely aware of the need to defend their country against aggressive neighbours, they were also persuaded that Czechoslovakia's future depended on the emergence of a new European order founded on international cooperation.[39] China, as Alexander von Falkenhausen so rightly observed, was politically where Germany had been in the eighteenth and nineteenth centuries: in need of establishing firm political order based on military hegemony as the precondition for social, economic and cultural progress.[40] To be sure, China and Czechoslovakia shared the recency of their latest political overhaul – the founding of their respective republics in 1911 and 1918 – and both needed immediate foreign help to assure their national defences. But while the Czechs soon could afford to dispense with French military advice, the Chinese became increasingly – indeeed, desperately – dependent on their German military advisers.[41]

   Not surprisingly, the two countries took very different positions towards Germany and towards the League of Nations; towards the immediate problem how to deal with the rise of Hitler and towards the long-range political problem of what kind of better new world to strive for. One way to describe their different outlook is to compare their different sense of time. The Chinese based their view of Germany on impressions (largely favourable) going back to the German colonial administration in Shantung in the 1890s. Their search for closer collaboration with Germany dated from the Weimar Republic, when, to quote Yü Ta-wei, 'there were scientists of the calibre of Albert Einstein, Max Planck, and Ulrich von Willamowitz-Möllendorf teaching at German universities – what other country could boast intellectual resources of that calibre?'[42] Many Chinese misinterpreted nazism as no more than a particularly efficient version of the same boyscout patriotism that China also sought to instill among its youth. Here Chinese military men on short visits to the Third Reich often showed keener perception than the Chinese diplomats in Berlin. While the latter strained to keep up the good relations to German government circles dating from the time of the Weimar Republic, regardless of the new uniforms and new slogans, prominent generals like Chang Fa-kuei, Wu Yat-chi, Huang Cheng-ch'iu, and Tsai T'ing-k'ai more or less openly expressed disgust with the nazi witch-hunt on Jews and other 'social undesirables'.[43] To be sure, German foreign policy began to shift from sympathy for China to interest in an alignment with the much stronger and much more modern Japan. The shift in sympathy from China to Japan in German newspapers editorials was duly noted by the Chinese foreign ministry in Nanking.[44] But to many Chinese this was a recent and possibly only a passing aberration. Until the very eve of the crisis of July 1937 – the beginning of the full-scale Sino-Japanese conflict – the nazis time and again appeased the Chinese diplomats in Berlin with little gestures that kept them hoping for continued German assistance: there was Walther Funk's friendly assurance to Minister Liu Wen-tao that certain offensive remarks about the Chinese race would be removed from Hitler's *Mein Kampf*,[45] Hitler's rejection of Japanese demands for an immediate withdrawal of the German advisers in China, and Germany's very extensive barter agreement (German arms for Chinese tungsten) in 1936. On that occasion, General Reichenau (considered the one truly loyal nazi on the German general staff) attended the signing in Nanking and presented Chiang Kai-shek with a Mercedes-Benz automobile as a personal gift from war minister, Werner von Blomberg.[46] The Chinese efforts to maintain good relations with Germany continued even after the military mission was withdrawn from Nanking in July 1938 and did not end until Germany recognized the Japanese puppet government under Wang Ching-wei in July 1941.

What the Chinese largely failed to perceive was the growing split inside the German ruling establishment, where a latent opposition to Hitler developed the closer Hitler came to triggering another war in Europe. With only a few exceptions (notably General Kwei Yung-chin and Professor Lin Tsiu-sen, who will be mentioned shortly) it also escaped their notice that many of these opponents of Hitler's war policy happened to be partisans of China for a mixture of reasons: fondness for Chinese art and literature, sympathy for an ancient country seeking to free itself from foreign exploitation, and strong opposition to Hitler's warlike policies in Europe.

Benes had far less time to play with than the Chinese. The endurance of the Czech nation in the long history of German–Slav rivalry offered little comfort in the age of air power, chemical warfare and clandestine Gestapo assassins from across the frontier. Benes knew that if a new system of collective security was to develop in time to save Czechoslovakia it had to come fast. This meant limiting new experimental forms of international cooperation to the European members of the family of nations and not squandering them on conflicts in the Orient (as in the Manchurian crisis of 1931) where the conditions for developing a postnational order did not exist.

One factor, I believe, saved the Chinese presence in Czechoslovakia from insignificance. That was the fact that in Prague Liang and his three to four attachés and secretaries did not man a lone Chinese outpost in central Europe. Liang belonged to a close team of Chinese diplomats abroad, all of them well trained in foreign languages and international law, most of them former fellow students at the best universities of Europe and America and life-long friends. They were also brought together by their need to discuss common problems and to share experiences and advice. Following their initial posting abroad most of them never saw China again until their diplomatic careers were over. All political news from their homeland was at least two to three weeks out of date because Chinese newspapers came by boat or by trans-Siberian railway and government instructions were, more often than not, too vague or based on too little knowledge of conditions in Europe. The Chinese diplomats dealt with this situation by consulting with one another frequently. My father often travelled to Berlin, Paris and London to talk with his colleagues and he appreciated the yearly sessions at the League of Nations in April as an opportunity for foreign policy discussions with his friends. In addition, there were the Chinese notables who regularly toured European capitals to collect information and to bring the local Chinese heads of mission up to date on developments at home. Madame Sun Fo, the daughter-in-law of Sun Yat-sen, H.H. Kung and Wang Ching-wei (before becoming a collaborator with the Japanese in 1938 still one of the most popular and influenial members in the Kuomintang Party) all came to Prague to consult the renowned physician, Professor Wilhelm Nonnenbruch, and at the same time to become acquainted with Czechoslovakia. I remember Wang Ching-wei as so powerful an orator that, after a patriotic speech he gave in our house over dinner, even our Czech servants in the kitchen felt moved, though they had not understood one word. In 1936 the Chinese Olympic team accompanied by Prime

Minister T'ai Chi-t'ao stopped in Prague on their way to the Berlin games. China's relationship to the Czechoslovak republic was in other words part of an integral foreign political stance collectively shaped by the heads of China's missions abroad. In the mid-1930s they included such notables as Quo T'ai-chi in London, Wellington Koo in Paris, Tsiang T'ing-fu in Moscow and – in the smaller countries – Tsien T'ai in Brussels and Lone Liang in Prague.

The one weak link in this impressive chain was Chen T'ien-fong, in 1936 China's first envoy to Germany with ambassadorial rank. While China's diplomats in all the other countries began to endorse the idea of resistance to fascist aggression, in the critical moment when the survival of China in Asia and of Czechoslovakia in Europe depended on Hitler, China's representatives in Berlin happened to be a Kuomintang party favourite with no experience in foreign affairs and very little knowledge of Germany. His attempt to score success with the nazi government through obsequious flattery for Hitler greatly diminished China's influence in one of the most important power centres in Europe at the very moment when it was most needed.[47] By contrast, at the time when Chen began to court Hitler, the Chinese newspaper *Ta Kung Pao* came out with a sober warning about nazi Germany:

> If Hitler wants to fight Bolshevism and world Jewry, he may find Germany not strong enough. We hope [antisemitism] is no more than propaganda.

> If Hitler wants to make Germany economically self-sufficient with four-year plans, he will need more technical innovations.

> If Hitler wants to recover Germany's lost territories he should reconsider, for that would mean war.[48]

Cheng resigned his post and returned to China in August 1938, thereby leaving the post of Chinese envoy to Germany vacant on the eve of the Munich crisis. After the Austrian *Anschluss* he had warned about the possibility of a war in Europe over Czechoslovakia, but it is difficult to see in his message more than a repetition of the editorials in countless newspapers of the day.[49]

Nanking was actually aware that Cheng was not the right man to represent China in nazi Germany. He lacked the *savoir-faire* and the forcefulness of someone like the Japanese military attaché in Berlin, General Oshima. Rumour had it that Foreign Minister Wang Ching-wei had offered Chen the Berlin post only as a courtesy, never expecting that he would accept. In 1936 all this was the more cause for concern as the Chinese knew that the moment for the final showdown with Japan was drawing near. In Nanking Falkenhausen was already advising Chiang not to give in to any more Japanese demands, and to begin planning counterattacks against the Japanese in north China.[50] Consequently, China proceeded quickly to dispatch more representatives and agents to Germany. The powerful chief of the Kuomintang's investigation division, Chen Li-fu, accompanied the new ambassador to his post in 1936, albeit in the strictest *incognito*.[51] In the same year, State Secretary Hwang You and three other Chinese police officials went to Germany for 'police training'. They presumably were all in touch with Chinese intelligence.[52] Last but not least, the military commission in Nanking sent Professor Lin Tsiu-sen to establish a propaganda service in Europe. Lin founded a weekly bulletin, the *China Post*, and also lectured on Chinese art and literature at the Sinological Institute of Berlin University. As a member of the Chinese Supreme National Defense Council Lin was in confidential contact with Sun Fo and Chiang Kai-shek throughout his four years in Germany.[53]

In the spring of 1937 China's finance minister, H.H. Kung, went to attend the coronation of King George VI in England. His retinue included Lieutenant-General Kwei Yung-chin (1900–1954), one of the most capable political negotiators the Chinese possessed at that time.[54] Kwei was the kind of military figure that Ernst von Weizsäcker and Erich Kordt of the German foreign ministry had hoped the British would send to Berlin in 1938 to read Hitler the riot act.[55] After talks with British military leaders Kwei proceeded to Germany, where he was personally received by Hitler and Goering and invited by Keitel to attend two weeks of manoeuvres by a German armoured division. In his memoirs he records that he put China's case to Goering in such strong words that Chiang Kai-shek wired him with instructions to moderate his tone. Kwei wired back to Nanking: 'I know these people. If you speak to them softly they lose interest in you.' Kwei also debated Germany's prospects in a future war with Keitel, Rommel and Guderian, and warned them not to underestimate the British empire. When the Sino-Japanese conflict erupted at Lukuochiao on 7 July 1937, he immediately cut short his sojourn in Europe and hastened home to take part in the fighting.[56]

Kwei did not return to Berlin until the autumn of 1940, long after Lukuochiao had escalated into a fullscale Japanese invasion and the whole China coast line was in Japanese hands, long also after the Munich conference, the establishment of the Protectorate of Bohemia and Moravia, and the outbreak of war over Poland. As China's new military attaché in Berlin, Kwei continued to meet with Goering for exploratory talks and made the acquaintance of 'Yang-K'e and Ma-K'oo-Sze of the German intelligence'. Through the autumn of 1940 Jahnke visited Kwei in his apartment once or twice a week, usually late at night.[57]

In the context of the different world situation after the fall of France, Jahnke no doubt had long abandoned what projects he once nourished for Germany's recovery under the Weimar Republic. Now he predicted a German war against Russia in the near future and sounded Kwei out about the chances for a Sino-German–British pact following the destruction of the Soviet Union. And yet in the summer of 1937 he still made one last attempt at preventing the outbreak of war in Europe, for the outbreak of fighting in China gave him the chance to propose joint mediation in the Far East by Germany and Great Britain, to be followed by a settlement of all outstanding differences between England and Germany in Europe. In Jahnke's estimation the opportunity was too good to be missed, because the crisis in Asia made it necessary for Hitler to decide finally for or against the military tie to China that Germany had cultivated since the days of Max Bauer. According to Marcus, the text for a general agreement with Britain was drawn up and ready for signing by around September 1937, and the British were interested enough to dispatch a secret emissary to Berlin. Who that emissary was Marcus would not tell me and whether or not he had cabinet clearance to commit the British government to an agreement with Germany was unknown to him.[58] But Marcus believed the chances of Hitler endorsing the Jahnke proposal were reasonably good, considering that it had the recommendation of Reichenau and Goering, of General Georg Thomas of the Wehrwirtschaftsamt, of War Minister Werner von Blomberg, and of bank president Hjalmar Schacht, plus many more partisans of China in the foreign office and in German industry. Only a few weeks earlier Thomas, Schacht and Blomberg had told H.H. Kung on his visit to Berlin how much they personally hoped Hitler would allow German help for China to continue as before.[59]

The main obstacle in September 1937 was the vigorous opposition to this agreement by Ribbentrop as chief of the Nazi Party's foreign bureau and by Himmler as Reichsführer SS and chief of German police.[60] As Marcus described that fateful day in September:

> We had our pens ready for Hitler to affix his signature when Ribbentrop managed to gain Hitler's ear one more time. He somehow succeeded to change the Führer's mind in the last minute. After that there was nothing more we could do. Reichenau was disgraced. He soon left Berlin for a new post in Munich. Jahnke and I took great care that the British agent made it safely back to England. But the good man was shaken and as he bade us farewell, he uttered the grim words: 'This means war!'

The tragic sequel to this episode was that a few weeks later, at a conference with the chiefs of Germany's armed forces on 5 November 1937, Hitler gave orders to prepare for an imminent attack on Czechoslovakia. The Chinese embassy in Berlin, meanwhile, struggled to prevent a final break with Germany. In a report to the Waichiaopu in February 1938, it presented Hitler's attitude as pessimistic but still not entirely unfriendly towards China:

> Hitler said in a recent speech that he does not think China spiritually and materially strong enough to resist a Bolshevik onslaught. A Japanese victory would be a lesser danger for the world than a Bolshevik victory. But Germany has always had good relations with China and wishes to remain neutral in the present Sino-Japanese conflict.[61]

The connection between the war in China and Czechoslovakia's security did not end abruptly with the failure of Jahnke's proposal for a British–German agreement in 1937. The German military advisers in China obstinately stayed at their post for another 12 months, fighting side by side with their Chinese protégés. They only gave up and returned to Germany in July 1938 when Ribbentrop, by then German foreign minister, threatened their families at home with *Sippenhaft*. Falkenhausen arrived in Berlin on 9 August 1938, and almost immediately went into conference with Chinese diplomats he knew in Paris and also joined the circle of anti-nazi conspirators around Ludwig Beck and Carl Goerdeler. There was talk of plots to remove Hitler from power. Two of these should be mentioned here because they affected Czechoslovak interests directly:

The first plot was prepared at the height of the Sudeten crisis, in September 1938, and involved some Wehrmacht officers and some civil servants. Its aim was to overthrow Hitler as soon as war broke out with Czechoslovakia and its Western allies. The man assigned to seize and possibly to kill Hitler was Captain Wilhelm Friedrich Heinz, commander of a special armed unit of the German Abwehr in Berlin. Heinz and his wife Hedwig were close friends of Professor Lin Tsiu-sen, who often was in a room upstairs when the conspirators met in Heinz's villa in Berlin-Dahlem. Heinz kept Lin informed of all the particulars of this conspiracy and Lin in turn conveyed this information to Nanking. In Heinz's own postwar affidavit (he was for a short while West Germany's intelligence chief under Konrad Adenauer) he testifies to the close collaboration between the German resistance in 1938 and Chinese intelligence.[62] As is generally known, the conspiracy was aborted when the four-power agreement was signed in Munich.

The second plot rested on the personal relationship between Falkenhausen and Adam von Trott zu Solz, a young official at the German foreign ministry. Falkenhausen himself was less given to political scheming than Trott, but the two men were drawn together by their common fascination with Chinese culture. In 1937, at the time when Falkenhausen was fighting with Chinese troops against Japan, the young Trott had gone on a private trip to Peking to study Confucian philosophy with a Chinese teacher. His hope was to find in China's ancient wisdom a solution to the political troubles of Western civilization – a venture reminiscent of Clemenceau's and Albrecht Haushofer's attempts to introduce Chinese thought to their countrymen with 'La voile du Bonheur' and 'Chinesische Legende'. Fearing war in Europe, Trott returned to Germany at the same time as Falkenhausen. After the German occupation of the Sudetenland he suggested to Falkenhausen that he might simply shoot Hitler as he walked behind the Führer through an underground passage during the inspection tour of Czech underground bunkers planned for October 1938. Falkenhausen, however, refused, calling it an act incompatible with soldierly honour.[63]

It should be noted that Trott was not known as a friend of Czechoslovakia.[64] But then nor were the other people in the German resistance who, like Friedrich Wilhelm Heinz, Alexander von Falkenhausen and Albrecht Haushofer, were willing to take some political risks to help the Chinese but did nothing on behalf of their Czech neighbours. Could they have felt a latent solidarity with the ethnic Germans of Czechoslovakia, that 'artifical new republic, created by the same politicians who drew up the Versailles Treaty in 1919'? The question that comes to mind today is: might they have acted more decisively against Hitler in 1938 had they taken to heart not only the surival of Chinese civilization and the need for peace in Europe, but also the welfare of the smaller nations of eastern Europe?

If personal sympathy for a country and its people plays a role in political behaviour, I like to think that the six happy years that Lone Liang – and indeed our whole family – spent in Prague between 1933 and 1939 made for a *rapprochement* between China and Czechoslovakia that was good for both countries. I cannot speak for Czechoslovakia, but I think I can speak of a growing appreciation for the democratic ideas of President Masaryk and President Benes on the Chinese side. My father respected Benes, and ten years later, when I was already a student and Benes had just died, he spoke to me with affection of his meetings with Czechoslovakia's long-time foreign minister and its second president.

The two men were, no doubt, different in a very fundamental way. My father, for one, was never deeply concerned about Europe's cultural and moral crisis in the twentieth century. Born into a family of imperial officials and raised on Confucian classics, but drawn as a student into the mealstrom of China's revolutionary movement, he belonged to that first generation of educated Chinese whose entry into Western culture never progressed far beyond a grasp of political and economic realities. Y.C. Wang, in his study *Chinese Intellectuals and the West* (1966), very aptly concluded that their attempt to blend the ethics of the Chinese and Western worlds generally ended in failure, leaving most of them for the rest of their lives stranded in a moral vacuum.[65] In a moral vacuum – or should I say a state of moral perplexity? – whenever they were drawn into disputes among Europeans involving ethical choices. Though he denounced the process of '*Gleichschaltung*' through persecution and suppression of dissidents 'such as we see being done in certain undemocratic countries',[66] I do not believe my father shared quite the same abhorrence that Thomas Masaryk and Edvard Benes felt for nazi Germany. Like so many Kuomintang politicians of his generation, Liang was still a Confucian at heart, a believer in China's ancient culture, always more inclined to compromise with a Chinese warlord than to become involved with a foreign government. Benes, by contrast, gave high priority to good relations with neighbouring countries, hoping that peace would give the minorities in his small republic the time and the confidence to join together in one national community.

Given this difference in political outlook, not to mention the formal restrictions imposed by diplomatic protocol, I wonder whether there ever was much likelihood of Lone Liang discussing with Czech government officials China's political problems in Germany and their possible repercussions for Czechoslovakia. I do not know whether my father knew about Jahnke and his activities in the world of intelligence and secret diplomacy, but he did travel to Berlin often and knew most of the people involved in Germany's political relations to China: Yü Ta-wei and Tann Beue, Falkenhausen and other military men who had gone to China, and above all Kwei Yung-chin and Professor Lin Tsiu-sen, for whom he arranged the distribution of a Czech edition of *China Post* in Prague. However, just as Jahnke could only initiate political consultations on the highest level after the Lukuochiao incident in China, so my father in Prague may have waited for a suitable opportunity for an exchange of political confidences with a high-ranking Czech official – an opportunity that apparently never came.

According to records on relations to China in the Benes papers, the Chinese minister Lone Liang called on the Czechoslovak foreign minister Kamil Krofta one week after the incident at Lukuochiao to inform him of China's determination to resist Japan.[67] He called a second time on 19 November 1937, after the dramatic confrontation between Goering and Ribbentrop in Berlin and after Hitler's order to prepare the attack on Czechoslovakia had already gone out. This time my father did mention to Krofta that China had the support in Berlin of Foreign Minister von Neurath, War Minister von Blomberg, and Reichbank president Schacht, but whether he actually described them as a 'China lobby' trying to steer German foreign policy away from a war in Europe, as Marcus did when he talked to me 30 years later, is not clear. There certainly is no indication that either Liang or Krofta thought the fighting in China had any direct bearing on Czechoslovak national security.[68] Presumably the Czechoslovak government relied more on its own representatives in the Far East for information on the Sino-Japanese conflict than on Lone Liang and his Japanese counterpart, Keinosuke Fukii, in Prague. A report sent to Prague from Shanghai by Minister Jan Seba on 27 December 1937 recognized the great efforts made by German military advisers and engineers in China, but questioned the effectiveness of their teaching in improving China's fighting capacity. In the battle for Shanghai, he wrote, Chinese artillery tried for six weeks to hit the Japanese cruiser 'Idzumo' and never succeeded, even though the distance was no more than from the beer brewery in Prague-Smichov to the National Theatre in Narodni trida.[69] In May 1938, Seba wrote that German newspapers in Shanghai had begun accusing the Czechs of oppressing the Sudeten Germans, but that the public showed little interest in the subject.[70] Finally, in a report that Seba filed on 13 September 1938 – when in Europe the German menace to Czechoslovakia was reaching its peak – he submitted no more than a sober assessment of the military situation in China which, in his view, was beginning to stabilize itself.[71]

Had the first Czechoslovak republic not been that model democracy so often praised in the West, but an authoritarian state with secret police and powerful intelligence organizations, things might have developed differently. There apparently was no Czechoslovak equivalent of a 'Büro J' to take in hand unofficial negotiations with foreign powers, and no Czech Jahnke who called on foreign representatives in the middle of the night.[72] Lost among the many documents in the Czechoslovak military archive in Prague-Invalidovna is the file on Lieutenant Li Ban, the son of the Chinese minister of interior, Li Han-hun, who in 1938 applied for training in the Czechoslovak army and so became the one and only Chinese soldier in the Czech armed forces at the time of Munich. Li Ban had applied for transfer from the Wehrmacht to the Czechoslovak army because of his growing unhappiness over nazi Germany's pro-Japanese sympathies. But the consequence which this one young Chinese drew from Hitler's Asian policy, namely that as long as he was in Europe he would rather stand on the side of Czechoslovakia than that of Germany, however astonishing, drew no public attention.[73]

III

Much of the above report is based on information provided by Dr Carl Marcus (1911–89), a sophisticated intellectual with degrees in law and philosophy, an avid student of medieval history and an admirer of that brilliant but politically elusive legal theoretician, Carl Schmitt. It is possible that he belonged to the SS – when the question came up in one of our conversations all he would say was that 'some of Germany's most intelligent people also belonged to it'. Marcus talked to me on three separate occasions in France (14 September 1973), and in Germany (4 June 1974 and 30 June 1977), each time for six to seven hours without a break. While he occasionally referred to documents in his cupboard, he never allowed me to have more than a brief glance at the signatures on the letters and reports in his files – to show that they carried genuine authority. He gave as his reason for talking to me at such length his gratitude to the Chinese (Kwei and Lin) who on returning to Germany in 1945 had saved his mother from starvation. He did astonish me by his very detailed knowledge of many Chinese personalities that I had also known through my parents, among them Yü Ta-wei, Chiang Wego, Lin Tsiu-sen and Tann Beue.

I have known only two other scholars who were interested in Jahnke and Marcus: the German historian Reinhard Doerries and the late Adrian Liddell Hart in England. I owe to Liddel Hart a few particulars about Marcus: that he left Jahnke around 1943 and was drafted into the Wehrmacht after Jahnke had made an unsuccessful attempt to dismantle the nazi regime following Stalingrad; that he deserted in 1944 during the allied invasion of northern France and offered his services to allied intelligence; and that after the war, for a short time, the British occupation forces installed Marcus as mayor of Rheydt.[74]

Marcus was an accomplished *raconteur*, but though 40 years had passed since he had taken his oath of secrecy under a regime long since defunct and discredited, he still withheld many details from me (names, dates, or the content of certain messages), even after I told him that I had to cross-check his story against outside sources. At the end of our second meeting I told him that the least I could do was find the name of the British agent who, he had said, had come to Berlin when Hitler nearly signed the Jahnke agreement in 1937.

I travelled to London, and a colonel who once served in the Chinese nationalist military attaché's office introduced me to two retired British secret service men who were in China during the 1930s: Charles Boxer and Charles Drage. Boxer knew Falkenhausen in Nanking; his name is mentioned in Falkenhausen's memoirs as someone who bade him goodbye when he returned to Germany.[75] Drage, however, particularly interested me because, though he denied having gone to Germany in 1937, he did say he was an old friend of Walther Stennes and that he had heard of Jahnke.[76]

On my return to the continent I telephoned Marcus long distance from Switzerland to tell him that I had met a man in London called Drage. Marcus became very excited and shouted to me: 'Herr Professor! No names over the telephone, please!' then he asked me to meet him at a certain address in Krefeld, West Germany, the following evening at seven o'clock. The address turned out to be that of a popular Italian restaurant in a lower class district of Krefeld. I found Marcus inside, sitting at a table surrounded by a noisy crowd of fellow diners. While we waited to be served, he raised his glass to me and said, with a big smile: 'So, I do believe you have found the man who has caused you so much puzzling in the past!' But when I asked him to confirm to me that Drage was the British agent who had come to Berlin in 1937, he waved a hand: 'Later. We shall go to my home later to talk business.'

Two hours later in the privacy of Marcus' living room in Rheydt he shook his head sadly when I reminded him that he had not answered my question. 'There is a provision in our service rules to cover my situation', he said, 'A secret agent is sometimes excused if he makes a slip of the tongue during a joyous occasion, for example a surprise encounter with a long lost friend. But it is absolutely intolerable for him to commit such an indiscretion during a quiet tête-à-tête such as we are having now.'

Shortly before he died in August 1989, Marcus sent me a letter to America saying that because of some unspecified events he was now free to tell me more from his secret store of knowledge on China and central Europe. As a token of his new freedom he sent me a faded passport photo of Kurt Jahnke. Alas, when I arrived in Europe for more studies the following year he was no longer among the living.

Vassar College

NOTES

All Chinese names are spelled the way their bearers preferred that they be written out (Tann Beue, not T'an Po-yü) to facilitate identification.

1. Interview, Dr Milos Pojar, Prague, 25 July 1995.
2. Interview with former Foreign Minister Yeh Kung-chao (George Yeh), in Taipei, 2 Aug. 1972.
3. HMSO, *Who's Who in Nazi Germany and Austria* (London, 1945), p.16; Henry Landau, *The Enemy Within* (New York, 1937); and Walter Schellenberg, *Memoiren* (Cologne, 1959) describe Jahnke's activities in the First and Second World Wars, respectively, though the second work is not very reliable. Harold J. Gordon Jr. mentions him as 'Mahnke' in his *The Reichswehr and the German Republic, 1919–1926* (Princeton, NJ, 1957), p.348; and Jean-François Favez in *Le Reich devant l'occupation franco-belge de la Ruhr en 1923* (Geneva, 1969). He also appears in the unpublished memoirs of Heinrich von Eckardt, 'Erinnerungen des Herren Gesandten von Eckardt' (typescript, probably 1942), courtesy of his grandson Oliver von Mühlen; and in the unpublished memoirs of General Kwei Yung-chin (in Chinese, no title, no date), courtesy of his son Professor George Kwei.
4. Interviews Stennes, Lüdenscheidt, 8 Sept. 1973; and Marcus, Cleebourg (France) 14 Sept. 1973, and Rheydt (West Germany) 4 June 1974 and 30 June 1977.
5. Marcus also credits Jahnke for suggesting peace feelers to England in 1941, which Hess than bungled with his solo flight to Scotland; and with trying to overthrow Himmler and Ribbentrop in 1942. After the war Jahnke was supposed to have served the German Democratic Republic. Marcus: 'The Guillaume affair of 1974 had all the hallmarks of a Jahnke operation!'
6. See 'Lincoln Trebitsch als Verbindungsoffizier?', *Berliner Tageblatt*, 20 Nov. 1920.
7. Helm Speidel, 'Reichswehr und Rote Armee', *Vierteljahrshefte für Zeitgeschichte*, Vol.1, No.1 (1953), pp.9–45.
8. Falkenhausen's *vita*, written when he was a prisoner of the Americans in 1947, refers to this trip only as a 'Ferienreise'. See pencilled notes, in Nachlass Falkenhausen, BA/MA (Freiburg i.B).

9. The first meeting is mentioned in Falkenhausen, 'Spiel der Wellen' (handwritten draft for an autobiography). The second note, dated 3 April 1934, is in folder 'Appointment in China'. Both are in Nachlass Falkenhausen. Unfortunately, Falkenhausen's published memoirs, *Mémoires d'outre-guerre* (Brussels, 1974), edited by Jo Gerard, completely leave out the crucial years from 1897 to 1934 when Falkenhausen must have been in contact with Jahnke.
10. Margarete Buber-Neumann, *Von Potsdam nach Moskau. Stationen eines Irrweges* (Stuttgart, 1957), pp.174–94; and Jürgen Domes, *Vertagte Revolution. Die Politik der Kuomintang in China, 1923–1937* (Berlin, 1969), pp.226–7.
11. 'Berichte Bauers über seine Reisen nach China', in Nachlass Max Bauer, No.39, Bundesarchiv Koblenz.
12. We stress Bauer's historical importance however much his philosophical diatribes, as revealed in his travel diaries, inspire distrust. See the characterization of Bauer in Ernst-Otto Schüddekopf, *Linke Leute von rechts* (Stuttgart, 1960), pp.251, 453 n.9; and Bauer's dream of a holocaust to rekindle Germany's spirit of defiance in F.W. Heinz, *Sprengstoff* (Berlin, 1930), p.117. The author of this novel played a role in the plot to kill Hitler in 1938.
13. Letter of appointment, Chiang Kai-shek to Max Bauer (in German), Nanking, 1 March 1928, Nachlass Bauer.
14. Bernd Martin (ed.), *Die deutsche Beraterschaft in China 1927–1938* (Düsseldorf, 1981) is the best general source. See also William C. Kirby, *Germany and Republican China* (Stanford, 1984); and Hsi-Huey Liang, *The Sino-German Connection* (Assen/Amsterdam, 1978).
15. See Bauer's abject farewell letter to Chiang Kai-shek when he was on his deathbed in 1929, as quoted in Fritz Lindemann, *Im Dienste Chinas* (Peking, 1940), pp.126–30.
16. E.G. Mohr, 'Sino-German Relations in the Period of Chiang Kai-shek', in *Conference on Chiang Kai-shek and Modern China* (Taipei, 1986), p.11.
17. Interview, General Sun T'ung-kan, commander of Chinese bomber wing during the war, Taipei, 6 July 1972.
18. See correspondence of Ernst Bauer, in Nachlass Bauer, op. cit.
19. Prior to his arrival in Berlin, the German firm of Carlowitz & Co in Shanghai sent the Berlin AA a positive assessment of Liang: 'Tsiang Tso-pin's executive chief, Lone Liang, is a very pleasant Chinese, well brought up, educated in Cambridge. He speaks German and English. He has recently held the post of judge in the International Settlement in Shanghai.' Letter, Dr March to Dr Mota at the AA, Hamburg, 28 Dec. 1928, in P.A. (Bonn), Abt. IV, Po.11, Nr. 3, 'Personalien der Staatsmänner in China'.
20. On Sun Yat-sen's contacts to Germany in 1922, ibid., Po. 5 A, 'Die südchinesische Republik (Sitz Kanton).'
21. This plan is also mentioned under 'Chiang Tso-pin [Tsiang Tso-pin]' in *Dictionary of Republican China* (New York, 1967), Vol.I, pp.358–63; and was confirmed to me by Yang Shu-jen in an interview in Taipei, 25 and 29 July 1972. In 1929 Yang was a young attaché at the Chinese legation in Berlin who had just been transferred to Germany from an earlier assignment to Moscow.
22. Khabarovsk Protocol of 22 Dec. 1929.
23. P.A. (Bonn), Abt. IV, Po.3.adh, 'Politische Beziehungen zwischen China und Russland'; and David J. Dallin, *Soviet Russia and the Far East* (New Haven, CT, 1948), p.63.
24. Introduction to Graham Peck, *Two Kinds of Time* (Boston, MA, 1967), p.3.
25. Hui-lan Koo (Mrs Wellington Koo), *An Autobiography* (New York, 1943), p.273.
26. Interview, Tann Beue, in Washington DC, 23 Jan. 1973. Dr Tann is my main source of information on the circumstances of my father's transfer from Berlin to Prague in 1933.
27. Antoine Marès, 'Formation et développement du ministère des Affaires étrangères tchécoslovaque (1918–1932)', *Relations internationales*, No.31 (automne 1982), p.306.

28. Already on 5 Oct. 1931, the French police in Lyon had reported Czechoslovak rifles and ammunitions intended for China arriving in Spanish Morocco. See Archives National (Paris), Série Europe, sous-série Tchécoslovaquie, Vol.173, 'Tchécoslovaques en France'.
29. Chinese Ministry of Foreign Affairs, *Treaties between the Republic of China and Foreign States, 1927–1957* (Taipei, 1958), p.71.
30. 'H.H. Kung', in BDRC, Vol.II, pp.263–9. According to a German police report, the Japanese also were buying Czechoslovak arms. Polizeipräsidium Berlin, Abt. I, to AA, Berlin, 16 June 1932, in P.A. (Bonn) Abt. IV, Po.3.adh. 'Waffenlieferungen aus Anlass des chinesisch-japanischen Konflikts'.
31. Reuters Agency news clipping, in the files of the Waichiaopu, Taipei.
32. Archiv narodniho muzea (Prague) papers of Milan Hodza, karton 2.
33. Albrecht Haushofer, *Chinesische Legende* (Berlin, 1949).
34. In the 1930s Jaroslav Prusek was one of the latest Czech sinologues about to attain international recognition. See the tribute by his student Augustin Palat, 'Jaroslav Prusek', *Archiv orientalni*, 34 (1966), pp.481–93.
35. *Who's Who in China. Biographies of Chinese Leaders* (Shanghai, 1932), pp.111, 268. On Yang's dislike of Wetzell: German legation to AA, Nanking, 31 Oct. 1933, in P.A. (Bonn), Abt. IV, Po 11, Nr. 3, 'Personalien der Staatsmänner in China.'
36. Waichiaopu, *Register of Chinese Ambassadors and Ministers Abroad* (Taipei, 1969).
37. Foreign minister Benes to the French journalist H.J. Duteile, as quoted in *Prager Abendblatt*, 4 May 1934, p.1.
38. Movies like 'The Mysterious Mr. Moto' (1938) about the theft of a secret steel making process from a Czech industrialist, or Graham Greene's novel *A Gun for Sale* (1936) portray the Czechs as the easy victims of war mongers. Sydney Fowler Wright's *Prelude in Prague. A Story of the War of 1938* (London, 1935) paints a devastating picture of Czechoslovakia's vulnerability to attack. Wright's book was used by Slovak separatists to denounce the weakness of the Benes Republic. Conseil slovaque, *Prague aux abois. Lettre ouverte à la Nation Tchèque* (Paris, 1938), p.3. For an earlier German novel depicting the future conquest of Czechoslovakia, see Max René Hesse, *Partenau* (Munich, 1929).
39. On Benes's disposition to move in the right direction even if there was little he could do to bring about such change, see, for example, his talk with the Austrian Chancellor Seipel in Prague, 13–14 Feb. 1928, in HHStA (Vienna), Neues Politisches Archiv, Karton 415, Liasse Tschechoslowakei I/III Geheim, folder 1-417.
40. Alexander von Falkenhausen, 'Spiel der Wellen', (n.p.) op. cit.
41. On the French military mission, see 'Francouska vojenska mise v Praze' in the Czech military archive (Prague-Invalidovna); and the reports in Service Historique de l'Armée de Terre (Paris-Vincennes), S.C. Série N, Attachés Militaires 1920–1940. Also Erhard Preissig, *Die französische Kulturpropaganda in der ehemaligen Tschechoslowakei* (Stuttgart, 1943).
42. Interview Yü Ta-wei, Taipei, 19 July 1972. Another Chinese scholar who understood Europe well, Minister of Education Chu Chia-hwa, was one of the few German-educated Chinese politicians openly to denounce nazism. BDRC, Vol.I, pp.437–40.
43. Interviews with Generals Chang Fa-kuei and Huang Cheng-chiu, and Mrs Wu Yat-chi, Taipei and Hong Kong, July 1972. On Tsai T'ing-k'ai, the famous defender of Shanghai in 1932, J.W. Philipps, 'A Close look at General Tsai T'ing-k'ai', *China Today*, Vol.I, No.1 (Oct. 1934), pp.8–9.
44. Analysis of German newspaper articles on China before and after 1933, in Waichiaopu report 349/127 (1937), Taipei.
45. Waichiaopu report 349/127: 'Reports from the Embassy to Germany' (1937). Liu's démarche was also reported in the *Neue Zürcher Zeitung*, 19 Dec. 1935.
46. Reichskriegsministerium to AA, Nr. 3630/36, Berlin, 7 Aug. 1936, in P.A. (Bonn), Abt.

VIII, Po 2, 'Politische Beziehungen Chinas zu Deutschland, 1936–1937'. On the importance of this barter agreement, Pardee Lowe, 'Hitler straddles the Oriental Fence', *Amerasia*, Vol.II, No.4 (June, 1938), pp.199–202. At the same time, it must be understood that Germany sought similar agreements also with agrarian countries in south-eastern Europe. Nicole Jordan, *The Popular Front and Central Europe* (London, 1992), p.11.

47. At Hitler's New Year's reception for the diplomatic corps in 1937, Cheng said to the Führer: 'Chiang Kai-shek is for China what you are for Germany. Marshal Chiang admires you!' Reported in *Wai-pu Chou-kan* [The Foreign Ministry Weekly], No.153 (1937), pp.7–8. In his memoirs, *Chao-nien hui-i-lu* [Memoirs of my Early Years] (Taipei, 1968) Chen Tien-fong as much as admits his inadequacy for the difficult task he undertook in Berlin.

48. *Ta Kung Pao*, Tientsin, 16 Sept. 1936.

49. Telegram, Chen Tien-fong to Waichiaopu, 12 March 1938, in WCP 77/29.

50. Falkenhausen's recommendations to the Chinese Military Affairs Commission, 'Beurteilung der möglichen kriegerischen Massnahmen Japans gegen China', Nanking, 1 April 1936, in Falkenhausen Nachlass, CH 6. According to Lee, after the outbreak of the Sino-Japanese conflict in 1937 the British were inclined to blame Chinese bellicosity for the fighting. Had not Foreign Minister Wang Ch'ung-hui in a recent speech predicted China would soon retake Manchuria, if necessary by force? Bradford A. Lee, *Britain and the Sino-Japanese War, 1937–1939* (London, 1973), p.25.

51. 'Ch'en Li-fu', in BDRC, Vol.I, p.208.

52. Interview Hwang You, Taipei, 1972. Hwang and his colleagues attended the higher police school in Eiche and met RSHA chief Reinhard Heydrich, Orpo chief Kurt Daluege, Reichskriminaldirektor Arthur Nebe and other high police officials. Interestingly, Nebe asked them to find him a job in China.

53. Interview Lin Tsiu-sen, Taipei, 1972; and 'Lin Tsiu-sen', *China Yearbook 1975* (Taipei, 1975), p.558. At his home Lin still kept several notebooks full of coded telegrams he had sent to Sun Fo from Berlin in 1938, but he no longer possessed the key to the code.

54. Kwei Yung-chin was among the first graduates of the Whampoa Military Academy. He then attended the Potsdam Infanterieschule and the Generalstabsschule in Dresden. He headed Chinese intelligence in Europe during the Second World War and was chief of a military mission to Germany, 1945–46. Kwei Yung-chin's unpublished memoirs, in Chinese, written in Taipei in 1952–54 were put at my disposal by his son, Professor George Kwei.

55. Ernst von Weizsäcker, *Erinnerungen* (Munich, 1950), p.179; and Dieter Ehlers, *Technik und Moral einer Verschwörung. 20. Juli 1944* (Frankfurt, 1964), pp.111–12. Hjalmar Schacht had a similar idea when he told the British in June 1939 to send a negotiator to Berlin 'who was strongly anti-German and likely to drive a hard bargain'. See Undersecretary of State for the Colonies, 'Report on a visit by H. Schacht to Ceylon, June 1939', in PRO (London), FO 371 23089.

56. Goering's friendliness to the Chinese goes back to the 1920s when he met Chinese student flyers at the German civil aviation school in Braunschweig. One of them, Sun T'ung-kan, flew him and Hitler to speaking engagements in the course of his training. Interview, Sun T'ung-kan, op. cit., and Kurt Raabke, retired flying instructor, Braunschweig, 17 Aug. 1973.

57. Kwei Yung-chin, memoirs.

58. On the many individuals with official, semi-official, or self-assumed 'official' powers who tried to bring about a deal between England and Germany in 1937, see Josef Henke, *England in Hitlers politischem Kalkül 1937–1939* (Boppard a.R., 1972), pp.67–85; and Andreas Hillgruber, 'England's Place in Hitler's Plans for World Dominion', in *Jour. of Cont. Hist.*, Vol.9, No.1 (Jan. 1974), pp.5–22.

59. Unsigned note, 13 Aug. 1937 reporting on a conversation between Thomas, Schacht,

and H.H. Kung; and notes taken by Ernst von Weizsäcker at a meeting of Blomberg, Schacht, and Kung in Schacht's country home outside Berlin, in PA (Bonn), Abt. VIII, China, Po 3 A: 'Der chinesisch-japanische Konflikt im Jahre 1937', Vol.I, IX.

60. Marcus believed that Ribbentrop and Himmler acted as they did not only because they counted on the SS and on Sudeten German Freikorps to undermine Czechoslovak defences through terror and subversion, but also because they were in Japanese pay.

61. 'German Recognition of Manchukuo', in WCP, 82/15.

62. 'Es gab ... zwischen der chinesischen Gruppe Lin Tsiu Seng ... und dem gewissermassen offiziellen Führer der deutschen Widerstandsbewegung kaum ein Geheimnis' F.W. Heinz, 'Von Wilhelm Canaris zur NKWD' (typescript), p.64, in Institut für Zeitgeschichte, Munich. Also Interview Lin Tsiu-sen in Taipei and Hedwig Heinz, widow of F.W. Heinz, Wiesbaden, 7 Feb. 1974. The plot is also described in Gert Buchheit, *Der deutsche Geheimdienst* (Munich, 1966), pp.148–9; Peter Hoffmann, *Widerstand-Staatsstreich – Attentat. Der Kampf der Opposition gegen Hitler* (Munich, 1969), p.123; and Ehlers, *Technik und Moral einer Verschwörung*, p.116.

63. This story is told in Harold C. Deutsch, *Verschwörung gegen den Krieg. Der Widerstand in den Jahren 1939–1940* (Munich, 1969), pp.337–8. An examination of Trott's papers involving China, and a bundle of letters exchanged between Falkenhausen and Trott, courtesy Mrs Claritta von Trott, Berlin, make no mention of this affair, but then both men were very careful not to commit their clandestine work to paper.

64. Czechoslovakia was the chief point of dispute between Trott and the British woman journalist Shiela Grant Duff during their friendship in England in the 1930s. See Shiela Grant Duff, *The Parting of Ways: A Personal Account of the Thirties* (London, 1982); and Tim Mason and David Astor, 'The Terrible Failure of Two Dedicated Loners', *The Guardian*, 11 March 1982.

65. Y.C. Wang, *Chinese Intellectuals and the West, 1872–1949* (Chapel Hill, NC, 1966), preface.

66. Lone Liang, *China muss siegen. Drei Vorträge* (Prague, 1938), p.96.

67. 'Rozmluva pana ministra dra K. Krofty s cinskym vyslancem drem Liangem', 15 July 1937, Benes Papers, Archiv Ustavu TGM (Prague).

68. 'Rozhovor pana ministra Dra K. Krofty s cinskym vyslancem Dr. Liangem', 24 Nov. 1937, in ibid.

69. Jan Seba to C.S. foreign ministry, 'Pomer cinske-nemecky', 27 Dec. 1937, in ibid.

70. Jan Seba to C.S. foreign ministry, 'Zprava o Nemecke proticeskoslovenske tiskove ofensive na Dalnem Vychode' Shanghai, 27 May 1938, in ibid.

71. Jan Seba to C.S. foreign ministry, 'Vojenska situace uprostred zari 1938', 13 Sept 1938, in ibid.

72. On Czechoslovak intelligence, see Igor Lukes, 'The GPU and GRU in Pre-World War II Czechoslovakia', *International Journal of Intelligence and Counterintelligence*, Vol.8, No.1 (Spring 1995).

73. Letter on behalf of Li Ban, Lone Liang to Czech foreign ministry, Prague, 7 July 1938, Vojensky historicky archiv (Prague-Invalidovna). Also Interview, Li Ban, Hong Kong, 5 Aug. 1972.

74. 'Dr. Carl Marcus, Rheydts erster Nachkriegs-OB, wurde 70', in *Stadtpanorama* (Rheydt), 19 Nov. 1981.

75. Interview Charles Boxer, London, 25 June 1977; and Falkenhausen, *Memoires d'outre-guerre*, p.82. Falkenhausen erroneously writes that Boxer died in a Japanese POW camp in 1942.

76. Interview, Charles Drage, London, 25 June 1977. Drage has written a biography of Stennes, *The Amiable Prussian* (London, 1958), but Jahnke's name appears only briefly in connection with Stennes' work for him in the Ruhr, 1923.

Notes on Contributors

Magda Ádám is Professor of History, the Institute of History of the Hungarian Academy of Sciences. She has been Visiting Professor at Oxford University (St Hilda's College) and a Visiting Fellow at the Woodrow Wilson Center, Washington, DC. Her main field of research concerns central and eastern Europe between World War I and World War II. She has published 14 books in Hungarian, French, English, and German as well as some 200 papers in different languages.

Peter Beck is Professor of International History, Kingston University, Kingston upon Thames. His publications include *British Documents on Foreign Affairs. Reports and Papers From the Foreign Office Confidential Prints: The League of Nations 1918–1941, vols. 1–10* (1992–95), and *The Falkland Islands as an International Problem* (1988). Forthcoming publications include *Scoring for Britain: International Football and International Politics, 1900–1939* (1998–99) and 'Politicians versus Historians: Lord Avon's "Appeasement Battle" against "Lamentably Appeasement-Minded" Historians', *Twentieth Century British History* (1999).

Anna Cienciala is Professor of History, University of Kansas. Her publications include, *Poland and the Western Powers 1938–39: A Study in the Interdependence of Eastern and Western Europe* (1968), *From Versailles to Locarno. Keys to Polish Foreign Policy, 1919–1925* (1984); editor, *Polska Polityka Zagraniczna 1926–1939* (1992) and over 40 articles and chapters in books.

Nicholas J. Cull is Professor of American Studies, University of Leicester. He trained at the University of Leeds and studied at Princeton as a Harkness Fellow. He has published widely in the field of film and propaganda. He is the author of *Selling War: British Propaganda and American Neutrality in World War Two* (1995) and he is currently writing a history of the United States Information Agency.

Michael Graham Fry is Professor of International Relations, University of Southern California. His most recent publication in international history is on British Revisionism in 1919 and after. He is the author of *Lloyd George and Foreign Policy* (1977), and *The North Pacific Triangle: The United States, Japan and Canada at Century's End* (1998).

Erik Goldstein is Professor of International Relations, Boston University. He is the author of *Winning the Peace: British Diplomatic Strategy, Peace Planning, and the Paris Peace Conference, 1916–1920* (1991), *Wars and Peace Treaties* (1992), co-editor of *The End of the Cold War* (1990) and *The Washington Conference, 1921–22: Naval Rivalry, East Asian Stability, and the Road to Pearl Harbor* (1993). He is co-director of the Diplomatic Studies Program and founder-editor of *Diplomacy & Statecraft*.

Hsi-Huey Liang is Professor Emeritus, Vassar College. He has been an Alexander-von-Humboldt Fellow and a Guggenheim Fellow, and is the author of *The Berlin Police Force in the Weimar Republic* (1970, in German 1977), *The Sino-German Connection* (1977), and *Berlin and the European State System* (1992).

Igor Lukes is Associate Professor of International Relations and History, Boston University. His main publications are focused on the crisis in central Europe on the eve of World War II and in the early stages of the Cold War. He is the author of the award-winning *Czechoslovakia Between Stalin and Hitler: The Diplomacy of Edvard Benes in the 1930s* (1996); co-author of *Inside the Apparat* (1990); and *co-editor of Gorbachev's USSR* (1990).

Peter Neville is Senior Lecturer in Twentieth-Century European History, University of Wolverhampton. He is the author of a forthcoming book on Nevile Henderson.

Richard Overy is Professor of Modern History at Kings College in London. His principal publications are *The Air War, 1939–45* (1980), *Goering: The 'Iron Man'* (1984), *Origins of the Second World War* (1987), *War and Economy in the Third Reich* (1994), and *Why the Allies Won* (1996).

Bruce Strang is currently completing his thesis, 'In Dubious Battle: Mussolini, Ideology, and Foreign Policy, 1936–1939', at McMaster University. He has also written articles on foreign policy, and teaches European history at McMaster University.

Martin Thomas is Reader in International History at the University of the West of England. He is the author of *Britain, France and Appeasement: Anglo-French Relations in the Popular Front Era* (1996) and *The French Empire at War, 1940–45* (1998). He is currently working on French imperial defence policy in the interwar period.

Gerhard Weinberg is William Rand Kenan, Jr., Professor of History, University of North Carolina at Chapel Hill. His current research project studies the views of eight major World War II leaders on the postwar world – assuming their country won – and whether and how that vision changed during the war and in what ways. His recent books dealing with this general area are: *The Foreign Policy of Hitler's Germany, 1933–1939* (2 vols.); *World in the Balance: Behind the Scenes of World War II; A World at Arms: A Global History of World War II;* and *Germany, Hitler, and World War II.* His broader interests deal with diplomatic, political, and military history of Europe, 1871–1945 and international security issues since 1945.

Bibliography

ARCHIVAL SOURCES

Austria
Haus-, Hof- und Staatsarchiv, Vienna
  Neues Politisches Archiv

China
Archives of the Chinese Foreign Ministry [Waichiaopu], Taipei

Czech Republic
Archives of the Central Committee of the Communist Party of Czechoslovakia, Prague
Archives of the Ministry of Foreign Affairs, Prague
Archives of the Ministry of Interior, Prague
Institute of Tomas G. Masaryk, Prague
  Archives of Edvard Benes
Military Office of the President of the Republic, Prague
Office of the President of the Republic, Prague
State Central Archives, Prague
Archives of the National Museum, Prague
  Zdenek Fierlinger Papers
  Milan Hodza Papers

France
Archives National, Paris
  Série Europe, sous-série Tchécoslovaquie
Centre des Archives Diplomatiques, Nantes
Centre des Archives Economiques et Financières, Savigny-le-Temple
  Direction du Trésor
Ministère des Affaires Etrangères archive
  Papiers 1940, Fonds Daladier
  Papiers d'agents 217, René Massigli papers
Service Historique de l'Armée de l'Air, Paris
  Archive Guy La Chambre
Service Historique de l'Armée de Terre, Paris-Vincennes
  Attachés Militaires, 1920–1940

Germany
Bundesarchiv, Koblenz
  Max Bauer Papers
Bundesarchiv – Militärarchiv, Freiburg-im-Breisgau
  Alexander von Falkenhausen Papers
Politisches Archiv des Auswärtigen Amts, Bonn

Hungary
National Archives of Hungary, Budapest
  Miklós Kozma Papers
  Minutes of the Council of Ministers

Italy
Archivio Storico del Ministero degli Affari Esteri, Rome
Gabinetto
   Serie Affari Politici
   Ufficio di Coordinamento
   Ufficio Spagna

South Africa
National Archives, Pretoria
   Governors-General Office files
   Prime Minister's Office files
   Ministry of External Affairs files
   J.B.M. Hertzog Papers
   Jan Smuts papers
   Charles te Water Papers
University of Cape Town Archives
   Sir William Clark Papers
   Sir Patrick Duncan Papers

United Kingdom
Bodleian Library, Oxford
   HAL Fisher Papers
   Lord Gore-Booth Papers
   2nd Lord Rennell of Rodd Papers
   Sir Horace Rumbold Papers
   Lord Simon Papers
Borthwick Institute of Historical Research, University of York
   Lord Halifax Papers
British Library of Political and Economic Science, London
   Hugh Dalton Papers
   Sir Charles Webster Papers
Carmarthenshire Records Office, Carmarthen
   Viscount Cilcennin Papers,
Churchill College Archive Centre, Churchill College, Cambridge
   Sir Neville Bland Papers
   Sir Winston Churchill Papers
   Malcolm Christie Papers
   Lord Lloyd Papers
   Sir Eric Phipps Papers
Imperial War Museum, London
   Albert Speer Collection
   Records Relating to War Crimes Trials (FO 645)
Public Record Office, Kew, London
   Air Ministry Papers
   Cabinet Papers
   Foreign Office Papers
   Sir Nevile Henderson Papers (FO 800)
   Ministry of Information Papers
   Prime Minister's Office Papers
Trinity College, Cambridge
   Lord Butler of Saffron Walden Papers
University Library, Cambridge
   Lord Baldwin Papers

Lord Hardinge Papers
University of Birmingham
Neville Chamberlain Papers

United States
Columbia University, New York, NY
Archives of Jaromir Smutny
National Archives, Washington

PUBLISHED DOCUMENTS

Akten zur deutschen Auswärtigen Politik 1918–1945, Serie D (Baden-Baden, 1950).
Anatomie des Krieges, ed. D. Eichholtz *et al.* (Berlin, 1969).
British Documents on Foreign Affairs, Reports and Papers from the Foreign Office Confidential Print: Part II, Series J, *The League of Nations 1918–1941,* ed. Peter Beck (Maryland, 1992).
Ceskoslovensko-polska jednani o konfederaci a spojenectvi, 1939–1944. Ceskoslovenske diplomaticke dokumenty [Czechoslovak-Polish Negotiations on the Establishment of an Alliance and Confederation, 1939–1944 . Czechoslovak documents], ed. Ivan Stovicek and Jaroslav Valenta (Prague, 1995).
Das Abkommen von München 1938: Tschechoslowakische diplomatische Dokumente 1937–1939, ed. Vaclav Kral (Prague, 1968).
Diplomáciai iratok Magyarország külpolitikájához 1936–1945 [Diplomatic Papers Relating to the Foreign Policy of Hungary 1936–1945]: vol 1, *A Berlin-Róma tengely kialakulása és Ausztria annexiója 1936–1938* [The Formation of the Berlin-Rome Axis, and the Annexation of Austria 1936–1938], ed. Lajos Kerekes (Budapest, 1962); vol. II, *A Müncheni egyezmény létrejötte és Magyarország külpolitikája 1936–1938* [The Munich Agreement and Hungarian Foreign Policy 1936–1938], ed. Magda Adam (Budapest, 1965); vol. III, *Magyarország külpolitikája 1938–1939* [The Foreign Policy of Hungary 1938–1939], ed. Magda Adam (Budapest, 1970).
Documenti Diplomatici Italiani, 8th ser., vol. IV (Roma, 1993).
Documents Diplomatiques Français 1932–1939 (Paris, 1974 *et seq.*).
Documents on Australian Foreign Policy, 1937–1949, vol. I., ed. R.G. Neale (Canberra, 1975) .
Documents on British Foreign Policy, 3rd ser. (London, 1947–61)
Documents on Canadian External Relations, vol. VI, ed. J.A. Munro (Ottawa, 1972).
Documents on Canadian Foreign Policy, 1917–1939, ed. Walter A. Riddell (Toronto, 1962).
Documents on German Foreign Policy, 1918–1945, Series D (1937–1945) (Washington, DC, 1949–64).
Documents on International Affairs
Dokumenty i materiali po istorii sovietsko-chekhoslovatskikh otnoshenii, ed. P.N. Pospelov *et al.* (Moscow, 1973–78).
Dokumenty i materialy do historii stosunkow polsko-radzieckich [Documents and Materials on the History of Polish-Soviet Relations], vol. VI, *1933–1938,* eds. Euzebiusz Basinski *et al.* (Warsaw, 1967).
Dokumenty z dziejów polskiej polityki zagranicznej 1918–1939. Tom I., 1918–1932 [Documents on the History of Polish Foreign Policy, 1918–1939, vol. I., 1918–1932], ed. Tadeusz Jedruszczak and Maria Nowak-Kielbikowa (Warsaw, 1989).
Foreign Relations of the United States, 1938, vol. I (Washington, 1955).
God krizisa, 1938–1939: dokumenty i materialy (Moscow, 1990).
International Miltary Tribunal, *Nazi Conspiracy and Aggression,* vol. 3 (Washington, 1947).

International Military Tribunal, *Trial of the Major War Criminals*, 42 vols. (Nuremberg, 1947).
Mnichov v dokumentech [Munich in Documents], vols. I–II (Prague, 1958).
Monachium 1938. Polskie dokumenty dyplomatyczne [Munich 1938. Polish Diplomatic Documents], no.1, ed. Z. Landau and J. Tomaszewski (Warsaw, 1985).
München 1938. Diplomáciai és politikai dokumentumok [Munich 1938. Diplomatic and political documents] (Budapest, 1988).
Powstanie II Rzeczypospolitej. Wybor dokumentow 1866–1925 [The Rise of the Second Republic. Selected documents 1866–1925], ed. Halina Janowska and Tadeusz Jedruszczak (Warsaw, 1981).
'Powstanie' na Zaolziu w 1938 r: Polska akcja specjalna w swietle dokumentów Oddzialu II Sztabu Glównego WP, ['Uprising' in Trans-Olza in 1938. Polish special action in light of documents of the 2nd Section, General Staff, Polish Army], Kazimierz Badziak and Pawel Samus, Gennady Matviejew, eds. (Warsaw, 1997).
Register of Chinese Ambassadors and Ministers Abroad, comp. Waichiaopu (Taipei, 1969).
Soviet Documents on Foreign Policy, vol. 3, ed. Jane Degras (London, 1954).
Treaties between the Republic of China and Foreign States, 1927–1957, comp. Chinese Ministry of Foreign Affairs (Taipei, 1958).
Ursachen und Folgen vom deutschen Zusammenbruch 1918 bis 1945, vol. 12, *Das Sudetendeutsche Problem*, ed. H. Michaelis and E. Schraepler (Berlin, n.d.).
Weltgeschichte der Gegenwart in Dokumenten, Bd. 1 (Munich, 1953).
Who's Who in Nazi Germany and Austria, comp. HM Stationery's Office (London, 1945).

OFFICIAL PUBLICATIONS

Hansard Parliamentary Debates
League of Nations Official Journal
League of Nations Records of Assembly, 19th Session, 1938, Special Supplement
League of Nations Special Supplement 194, 20th and 21st Assembly
Országgyálési Napló [Parliamentary Reports, Hungary]
Report on the Work of the League 1938/39 (Geneva, 1939)
Wai-pu Chou-kan [The Foreign Ministry Weekly]

NEWSPAPERS

Berliner Tageblatt
Daily Herald
Editor and Publisher
The Guardian
Hereford Times
Neue Zürcher Zeitung
New York Herald Tribune
New York Journal and American
New York Times
Pester Lloyd
Pesti Napló
Popolo d'Italia
Prager Abendblatt
The Times
Washington Daily News

MEMOIRS and PUBLISHED DIARIES and PAPERS

Beck, Józef. *Dernier rapport, Politique polonaise 1926–1939* (Neuchâtel /Paris, 1951/1952). [English ed. *Final Report* (New York, 1957)].
Benes, Edvard. *Mnichovske dny* [Munich days] (Praha, 1968).
Benes, Edvard. *Memoirs of Dr Eduard Benes: From Munich to New War and New Victory*, trans. Godfrey Lias (London, 1954).
Biddle, A.J. Drexel. *Poland and the Coming of the Second World War. The Diplomatic Papers of A. J. Drexel Biddle, Jr., United States Ambassador to Poland 1937–1939*, ed. Philip V. Cannistraro, Edward D. Wynot, Jr., and Theodore P. Kovaloff (Columbus, OH, 1976).
Borman, Martin. *Hitlers politisches Testament: die Bormann Diktate vom Februar und April 1945* (Hamburg, 1981).
Cadogan, Sir Alexander. *The Diaries of Sir Alexander Cadogan, 1938–1945*, ed. David Dilks (London, 1971).
Channon, Henry James. *Chips. The Diaries of Sir Henry Channon*, ed. R. Rhodes (London, 1967).
Ciano, Count. *Ciano's Diplomatic Papers*, ed. Malcolm Muggeridge (London: Odhams, 1948).
Ciano, Count. *Ciano's Hidden Diaries, 1937–1938*, ed. Malcolm Muggeridge (London, 1952/ New York, 1953).
Douglas-Home, Alec. *The Way The Wind Blows: An Autobiography* (New York, 1976).
Eckardt, Heinrich von 'Erinnerungen des Herren Gesandten von Eckardt' (unpublished ts., circa 1942), courtesy of his grandson, Oliver von Mühlen.
Eden, Anthony. *The Eden Memoirs: Facing the Dictators* (London, 1962).
Engel, G. *Heeresadjutant bei Hitler 1938–1943*, ed. H. von Kotze (Stuttgart, 1974).
Falkenhausen, Alexander von. *Mémoires d'outre-guerre*, ed. Jo Gerard (Brussels, 1974).
Goebbels, Joseph. *Die Tagebuecher von Joseph Goebbels*, ed. E. Froehlich (4 vols., Munich, 1987).
Harvey, Oliver. *The Diplomatic Diary of Oliver Harvey 1937–1940*, ed. John Harvey (London, 1970).
Hassell, Ulrich von. *The von Hassell Diaries 1938–1944* (London, 1948).
Henderson, Nevile. *Failure of a Mission* (London, 1940).
Henderson, Nevile. *Water Under the Bridges* (London, 1945).
Hitler, Adolf. *Hitler's Secret Book* (New York, 1961).
Horthy, Miklós. *Horthy Miklós titkos iratai* [The Secret Papers of Miklós Horthy], ed. Miklós Szinai and László Szács (Budapest, 1962).
Hui-lan Koo (Mrs Wellington Koo). *An Autobiography* (New York, 1943).
Kwei Yung-chin. Unpublished memoirs, courtesy of his son, Prof. George Kwei.
Laroche, Jules. *La Pologne de Pilsudski: souvenirs d'une ambassade* [Pilsudski's Poland: Memories of an Embassy] (Paris, 1953).
Lipski, Józef. *Diplomat in Berlin 1933–1939: Papers and Memoirs of Jozef Lipski, Ambassador of Poland*, ed. Waclaw Jerzejewicz (New York, 1968).
Lukasiewicz, Juliusz. *Diplomat in Paris. Papers and Memoirs of Juliusz Lukasiewicz Ambassador of Poland*, ed. Waclaw Jerzejewicz (New York/London, 1970) .
Nicolson, Harold. *Diaries and Letters, 1930–1939*, ed. Nigel Nicolson (New York, 1966).
Nicolson, Harold. *A Diary With Letters*, vol.1 (London, 1967).
Roberts, Frank. *Dealing with Dictators: The Destruction and Revival of Europe, 1930–70* (London, 1991).
Rose, William John. *The Polish Memoirs of William John Rose*, ed. Daniel Stone (Toronto, 1975).
Smuts, Jan. *Selections from the Smuts Papers*, vol. VI, *December 1936–August 1945*, ed. Jean van der Poel (Cambridge, 1973).

Susmel, Eduardo and Duilio, eds. *Opera Omnia di Benito Mussolini*, vol. 29 (Florence, 1959).
Szembek, Jan. *Diariusz i Teki Jana Szembeka 1935-1939* [Diary and Files of Jan Szembek, 1935–39]; vol. IV, ed. Józef Zaranski (London, 1972).
Templewood, Viscount. *Nine Troubled Years* (London, 1954).
Weizsäcker, Ernst von. *Erinnerungen* (Munich, 1950).
Weizsäcker, Ernst von. *Die Weizsaecker-Papiere 1933–1950*, ed. L.E. Hill (Frankfurt am Main, 1974).

INTERVIEWS

Tann Beue (23 Jan. 1973), by Hsi-Huey Liang.
Charles Boxer (25 June 1977), by Hsi-Huey Liang.
Lord Butler (April 1980), by Peter Beck.
Wallace Carroll (16 July 1993), by Nicholas Cull.
Chang Fa-kuei (July 1972), by Hsi-Huey Liang.
Charles Drage (25 June 1977), by Hsi-Huey Liang.
Douglas Fairbanks Jr. (9 March 1990), by Nicholas Cull.
Hedwig Heinz (7 Feb. 1974), by Hsi-Huey Liang.
Gen. Huang Cheng-chiu (July 1972), by Hsi-Huey Liang.
Graham Hutton (June–July 1988), by Nicholas Cull.
Helen Kirkpatrick (Aug. 1993), by Nicholas Cull.
Li Ban (5 Aug. 1972), by Hsi-Huey Liang.
Lin Tsiu-sen (1972), by Hsi-Huey Liang.
Carl Marcus (14 Sept. 1973), by Hsi-Huey Liang.
Drew Middleton (2 Feb. 1989), by Nicholas Cull.
Janet Murrow (14 Nov. 1988), by Nicholas Cull.
Milos Pojar (25 July 1995) by Hsi-Huey Liang.
James Reston (30 March 1989) by Nicholas Cull.
Sir Frank Roberts (10 Oct. 1996) by Peter Neville.
Yeh Kung-chao (George Yeh) (2 Aug. 1972), by Hsi-Huey Liang.
Eric Sevareid (30 March 1989), by Nicholas Cull.
Walther Stennes (8 Sept. 1973), by Hsi-Huey Liang.
Gen. Sun T'ung-kan (6 July 1972), by Hsi-Huey Liang.
Ann Thoms (née Whyte) (5 July 1988), by Nicholas Cull.
Mrs. Wu Yet-chi (July 1972), by Hsi-Huey Liang.
Yang Shu-jen (25, 29 July 1972), by Hsi-Huey Liang.
Yü Ta-wei (19 July 1972), by Hsi-Huey Liang.

SECONDARY SOURCES

Ádám, Magda. 'La Hongrie et Munich', *Revue d'Histoire de la Deuxième Guerre Mondiale et des Conflits Contemporains* 132 (Oct. 1983).
Adamthwaite, Anthony. *France and the Coming of the Second World War* (London, 1977).
Adamthwaite, Anthony. *Grandeur and Misery. France's Bid for Power in Europe, 1914–1940* (London, 1995).
Adamthwaite, Anthony. 'French Military Intelligence and the Coming of War, 1935–1939', in Christopher Andrew and Jeremy Noakes, eds., *Intelligence and International Relations, 1900–1945* (Exeter, 1987).
Alexander, Martin S. 'Did the Deuxième Bureau Work? The Role of Intelligence in French Defence Policy and Strategy, 1919–1939', *Intelligence and National Security*, 6:2 (1991).

Alexander, Martin S. 'In Lieu of Alliance: The French General Staff's Secret Co-operation with Neutral Belgium, 1936–1940', *Journal of Strategic Studies* 14:4 (1991).

Alexander, Martin S. *The Republic in Danger. General Maurice Gamelin and the Politics of French Defence, 1933-1940* (Cambridge, 1992).

Amort, Cestmir *et al.*, eds. *Dokumenty a materialy k dejinam ceskoslovensko-sovetskych vztahu* (Prague, 1975–1984).

Armstrong, David, Lorna Lloyd and John Redmond. *From Versailles to Maastricht: International Organisation in the Twentieth Century* (London, 1996).

Aster, Sidney. *1939* (New York, 1973).

Aulach, H. 'Britain and the Sudeten Issue 1938', *Journal of Contemporary History* 18:2 (1983).

Azzi, Stephano Corrado. 'The Historiography of Italian Foreign Policy', *The Historical Journal* 36:1 (1993).

Baker, Vaughan B. 'Nevile Henderson in Berlin: A Re-evaluation', *Red River Valley Historical Journal* 4 (1977).

Balcerak, Wieslaw. 'Legenda bez pokrycia', *Studia z Dziejów ZSRR i Europy Srodkowej* 9 (1973).

Balcerak, Wieslaw. 'Sprawa polsko-czechoslowackiego sojuszu wojskowego w latach 1921–1927', *Studia z Dziejów ZSRR i Europy Srodkowej* 3 (1967).

Batowski, Henryk. *Rok 1938. Dwie agresje hitlerowskie* (Poznan, 1985).

Batowski, Henryk. *Zdrada Monachijska* (Poznan, 1973).

Beck, Peter. 'Britain and Appeasement in the Late 1930s: Was There a League of Nations' Alternative', in D. Richardson and G. Stone, eds., *Decisions and Diplomacy: Essays in Twentieth Century International History* (London, 1995).

Beck, Peter. 'From the Geneva Protocol to the Greco-Bulgarian Crisis: The Development of the Baldwin Government's Policy towards the Peacekeeping Role of the League of Nations, 1924–25', *British Journal of International Studies* 6:1 (1980).

Benes, Edvard. *Memoirs: From Munich to New War and New Victory* (Boston, 1954).

Benes, Edvard. *Mnichovske dny* (Prague, 1968).

Berstein, Serge. 'La perception de la puissance par le Parti Radical-Socialiste', *Revue d'Histoire Moderne et Contemporaine* 31 (1984).

Berstein, Serge. 'La perception de la puissance par les partis politiques français en 1938–1939', in René Girault and Robert Frank, eds., *La Puissance en Europe, 1938–1940* (Paris, 1984).

Birn, Donald S. *The League of Nations Union* (Oxford, 1981).

Bittenfeld, Hans Herwarth von. *Against Two Evils* (New York, 1981).

Bloch, M. *Ribbentrop* (London, 1992).

Bonnet, Georges. *Défense de la paix, I: De Washington au Quai d'Orsay* (Geneva, 1946).

Boorman, H.L. *Biographical Dictionary of Republican China* (New York, 1967).

Bosworth, R.J.B. *The Italian Dictatorship: Problems and Perspectives in the Interpretation of Mussolini and Fascism* (London, 1998).

Bouvier, Jean and Robert Frank. 'Sur la perception de la "puissance" économique en France pendant les années 1930', in René Girault and Robert Frank, eds., *La Puissance en Europe, 1938–1940* (Paris, 1984).

Brown, Robert J. *Manipulating the Ether: The Power of Broadcast Radio in Thirties America* (Jefferson, NC, 1998).

Bruegel, J.W. 'Dr. Benes on the Soviet 'Offer of Help' in 1938', *East Central Europe* 4:1 (1977).

Buber-Neumann, Margarete. *Von Potsdam nach Moskau* (Stuttgart, 1957).

Buchheit, Gert. *Der deutsche Geheimdienst* (Munich, 1966).

Buffotot, Patrice. 'La perception du réarmement allemand par les organismes de renseignement français de 1936 à 1939', *Revue Historique des Armées* 3 (1979).

Buffotot, Patrice. 'Le réarmement aérien allemand et l'approche de la guerre vus par le IIe

bureau air français, 1936–1939', in K. Hildebrand and K.F. Werner, eds., *Deutschland und Frankreich 1936–1939* (Munich, 1981).

Buffotot, Patrice. 'The French High Command and the Franco-Soviet Alliance, 1933–1939', *Journal of Strategic Studies* 5:4 (1982).

Burgwyn, H. James. *Italian Foreign Policy in the Interwar Period, 1918–1940* (Westport, CT, 1997).

Butler, Lord. *The Art of the Possible* (London, 1971).

Cameron, Elizabeth R. 'Alexis Saint Léger', in G.A. Craig and F. Gilbert, eds., *The Diplomats, 1919–1939* (Princeton, NJ, 1981).

Campbell, F. Gregory. *Confrontation in Central Europe: Weimar Germany and Czechoslovakia* (Chicago, 1975).

Carley, Michael J. '"A Fearful Concatenation of Circumstances": The Anglo-German Rapprochement 1934–6', *Contemporary European History* 5:1 (1996).

Cerny, Vaclav. *Vyvoj a zlociny panslavismu* (Prague, 1995).

Champinnois, Suzanne. 'Le colonel Beck at la diplomatie française', in Michal Pulaski *et al.*, eds., *Z dziejów Europy srodkowej w XX wieku. Studia ofiarowane Henrykowi Batowskiemu w 90. rocznice urodzin* (Cracow, 1997).

Chen Tien-fong. *Chao-nien hui-i-lu* (Taipei, 1968).

Churchill, Winston S. *The Second World War*, vol. 1, *The Gathering Storm* (London, 1948, reprinted 1983).

Cienciala, Anna. 'German Propaganda for the Revision of the Polish-German Frontier and the Corridor: Its Effects on British Opinion and the British Foreign Policy-Making Elite in the Years 1919–1933', *Antemurale* 20 (1976).

Cienciala, Anna. 'Marxism and History. Some Recent Polish and Soviet Interpretations of Polish Foreign Policy in the Era of Appeasement: An Evaluation', *East European Quarterly* 6:1 (1972).

Cienciala, Anna. 'Nastawienie Austena Chamberlaina do Polski w latach 1924–1933', in Antoni Czubinski, ed., *Polska-Niemcy-Europa* (Poznan, 1977).

Cienciala, Anna. *Poland and the Western Powers, 1938–1939: A Study in the Interdependence of Eastern and Western Europe* (London/Toronto, 1968).

Cienciala, Anna. 'Poland in British and French Policy in 1939: Determination to Fight or Avoid War?' *Polish Review* 34:3 (1989).

Cienciala, Anna. 'Polish Foreign Policy, 1926–1939: "Equilibrium", Stereotype and Reality', *Polish Review* 30:1 (1975).

Cienciala, Anna. 'The Significance of the Declaration of Non-Aggression of January 24, 1934, in Polish-German and International Relations', *East European Quarterly* 1:1(1967).

Cienciala, Anna and Titus Komarnicki. *From Versailles to Locarno. Keys to Polish Foreign Policy 1919–1925* (Lawrence, KS, 1984).

Cienciala, Anna and Piotr Wandycz. 'Polona Restituta – czyli Noël redivivius', *Zeszyty Historyczne* 72 (Paris, 1985).

Citino, Robert. *Germany and the Union of South Africa in the Nazi Period* (New York, 1991).

Cockett, Richard. *Twilight of Truth: Chamberlain, Appeasement, and the Manipulation of the Press* (London, 1989).

Cohen, Barry Mendel. 'Moscow at Munich', *East Central European Quarterly* 12:3 (1978).

Cole, Robert. 'The Conflict Within: Stephen Tallents and Planning Propaganda Overseas Before The Second World War', *Albion* 12 (1982).

Conseil slovaque. *Prague aux abois. Lettre ouverte à la Nation Tchèque* (Paris, 1938).

Cornwall, Mark. 'The Rise and Fall of a "special relationship": Britain and Czechoslovakia 1930–1948' in *What Difference Did the War Make?*, B. Brivati and H. Jones, eds. (London, 1993).

Coverdale, John. *Italian Intervention in the Spanish Civil War* (Princeton, 1975).

Craig, Gordon and Felix Gilbert, *The Diplomats* (New York, 1968).

Culbert, David. *News For Everyman: Radio and Foreign Affairs in Thirties America* (Westport, CT, 1976).

Cull, Nicholas J. 'Broadcasting and the Art of Understatement: British Radio Propaganda and American Neutrality, 1939–1941', *Historical Journal of Film, Radio and Television* 13:4 (1993).

Cull, Nicholas J. 'Faked Boundaries: Latin America, 'Nazi Maps' and Britain's Secret War Against US Neutrality', *Latin American British Studies Association Journal* 1:2 (1997).

Cull, Nicholas J. 'Overture to an Alliance: British Propaganda and the New York World's Fair of 1939', *Journal of British Studies*, 16:3 (1997).

Cull, Nicholas J. 'Selling Peace: The Origins, Promotion and Fate of the Anglo-American New Order during the Second World War', *Diplomacy & Statecraft*, 7:1 (1996).

Cull, Nicholas J. *Selling War: British Propaganda Against American Neutrality in the Second World War* (New York, 1995).

Dallin, David J. *Soviet Russia and the Far East* (New Haven, CT, 1948).

Davies, Norman. *White Eagle, Red Star: The Polish-Soviet War, 1919–1920* (London, 1972).

De Felice, Renzo. 'Alle Origini del Patto d'Acciaio: L'icontro e gli accordi tra Bocchini e Himmler del Marzo-Aprile 1936', *La Cultura* 1 (1963).

De Felice, Renzo. *Mussolini il duce*. vol II, *Lo Stato totalitario, 1936–1940* (Torino, 1981).

Deist, W. *et al. Das Deutsche Reich und der Zweite Weltkrieg*. I: *Ursachen und Voraussetzungen der Deutschen Politik* (Stuttgart, 1979).

Deist, W. *The Wehrmacht and German Rearmament* (London, 1981).

Delmas, Général Jean.'La perception de la puissance militaire française', in René Girault and Robert Frank, eds., *La Puissance en Europe, 1938–1940* (Paris, 1984).

Desmond, Robert W. *Crisis and Conflict: World News Reporting Between Two 1920–1940* (Iowa City, 1982).

Deutsch, Harold C. *Hitler and his Generals: The Hidden Crisis, January–June 1938* (Minneapolis, 1974).

Deutsch, Harold C. *Verschwörung gegen den Krieg. Der Widerstand in den Jahren 1939–1940* (Munich, 1969).

Dlugajczyk, Edward. 'Polska dywersja wojskowa na Zaolziu w latach 1935–1938', *Slezsky Sborník* 94:1 (Opava, 1996).

Dlugajczyk, Edward. *Tajny Front na granicy cieszynskiej. Wywiad i dywersja w latach 1919–1939* (Katowice, 1993).

Doise, Jean and Maurice Vaïsse. *Diplomatie et outil militaire, 1871–1991* (Paris, 1987).

Domes, Jürgen. *Vertagte Revolution. Die Politik der Kuomintang in China, 1923–1937* (Berlin, 1969).

Drage, Charles. *The Amiable Prussian* (London, 1958).

Drtina, Prokop. *Ceskoslovensko muj osud* (Toronto, 1982).

Du Réau, Elisabeth. *Edouard Daladier, 1884–1970* (Paris, 1993).

Du Réau, Elisabeth. 'Edouard Daladier et l'image de la puissance française en 1938', *Revue Historique des Armées* 3 (1983).

Du Réau, Elisabeth. 'L'information du "décideur" et l'élaboration de la décision diplomatique française dans les dernières années de la IIIe République', *Relations internationales* 32 (1982).

Duff, Shiela Grant. *The Parting of Ways. A Personal Account of the Thirties* (London, 1982).

Duroselle, Jean-Baptiste. *La Décadence. 1932–1939* (Paris, 1979).

Duroselle, Jean-Baptiste. *Politique étrangère de la France. La décadence 1932–1939* (Paris, 1979).

Dutailly, Henry. *Les Problèmes de l'Armée de Terre Française, 1935–1939* (Paris, 1980).

Ehlers, Dieter. *Technik und Moral einer Verschwörung. 20. Juli 1944* (Frankfurt, 1964).

Facon, Patrick. 'La visite du général Vuillemin en Allemagne, 16–21 août 1938', *Recueil d'articles et études (1981–1983)* (Vincennes, 1987).

Favez, Jean-François Favez. *Le Reich devant l'occupation franco-belge de la Ruhr en 1923* (Geneva, 1969).

Favreau, Bertrand. *Georges Mandel ou la passion de la République 1885–1944* (Paris, 1996).

Feierabend, Ladislav Karel. *Politicke vzpominky*, vol. III (Prague, 1996).

Feiling, K. *The Life of Neville Chamberlain* (London, 1946).

Fierlinger, Zdenek. *Ve sluzbach CSR: pameti z druheho odboje* (Prague, 1947).

Fierlinger, Zdenek. *Zrada ceskoslovenske burzoazie a jejich spojencu* (Prague, 1951).

Finney, Patrick ed. *The Origins of the Second World War* (London, 1997).

Ford, Franklin L. 'Three Observers in Berlin: Rumbold, Dodd and François-Poncet', in G. Craig and F. Gilbert (eds.), *The Diplomats* (New York, 1968).

Frank, Robert. *Le prix du réarmement français (1935–1939)* (Paris, 1982).

Frank, Robert. *La hantise du déclin. Le rang de la France en Europe, 1920–1960. Finances, défense et identité nationale* (Paris, 1994).

Fry, Michael Graham. 'Decolonisation: Britain, France and the Cold War', in Karen Dawisha and Bruce Parrott, eds., *The End of the Empire. The Transformation of the USSR in Comparative Perspective* (New York, 1997).

Fry, Michael Graham. 'The Development of Canada's Relations with Japan, 1919–1947', in K.A.J. Hay, ed., *Canadian Perspectives on Economic Relations with Japan* (Montreal, 1980).

Fry, Michael Graham. 'The Pacific Dominions and the Washington Conference 1921–1922', in Erik Goldstein and John Maurer, eds., *The Washington Conference 1921–22* (London, 1994).

Gannon, Franklin Reid. *The British Press and Germany, 1936–1939* (Oxford, 1971).

Gauché, Maurice. *Le Deuxième Bureau au Travail (1935–1940)* (Paris, 1953).

Gilbert, Felix. 'Two British Ambassadors: Perth and Henderson', in G. Craig and F. Gilbert, eds., *The Diplomats* (New York, 1968).

Gilbert, Martin and Richard Gott. *The Appeasers* (London, 1963).

Girault, René. 'Les décideurs français et la puissance française en 1938–1939', in René Girault and Robert Frank, eds., *La Puissance en Europe, 1938–1940* (Paris, 1984).

Girault, René. 'The Impact of the Economic Situation on the Foreign Policy of France, 1936–9', in Wolfgang J. Mommsen and Lothar I. Kettenacker, eds., *The Fascist Challenge and the Policy of Appeasement* (London, 1983).

Glotz, P. and K.H. Pollak *et al.*, eds. *München 1938: Das Ende des alten Europas* (Essen, 1990).

Godley, Michael R. 'Fascismo e nazionalismo cinese, 1931–1938. Note preliminari allo studio dei rapporti italo-cinese durante il periodo fascista', *Storia Contemporanea* 4:4 (1973).

Goldstein, Erik. 'British Diplomatic Strategy and the Locarno Conference', in M. Dockrill and B.J.C. McKercher, eds., *Diplomacy and World Power: Studies in British Foreign Policy, 1890–1951* (Cambridge, 1996).

Goldstein, Erik. *Winning the Peace: British Diplomatic Strategy, Peace Planning, and the Paris Peace Conference, 1916–1920* (Oxford, 1991).

Goldstein, Erik and John Maurer, eds. *The Washington Conference 1921–22* (London, 1994).

Goodwin, Geoffrey. 'The Political Role of the United Nations: Some British Views', *International Organization* 15 (1961).

Gordon Jr., Harold J. *The Reichswehr and the German Republic, 1919–1926* (Princeton, NJ, 1957).

Gottwald, Klement. 'J.V. Stalin i chekhoslovatskii narod', *Za prochnyi mir, za narodnuyu demokratsiu* 32:59 (1949).

Goyet, Pierre le. *Munich, "un traquenard"* (Paris, 1988).
Greene, Graham. *A Gun for Sale* (London, 1936).
Gromyko, Andrei. *Memoirs* (New York, 1989).
Groscurth, H. *Tagebuch eines Abwehroffiziers* (Stuttgart, 1970).
Grzelonski, Bogdan. *Dyplomacja Stanów Zjednoczonych wobec zagrozenia Czechoslowacji i Polski* (Warsaw, 1995).
Gunther, John. *Inside Europe* (New York, 1935).
Gunther, John. *The Story of the Inside Books: A Fragment of Autobiography* (London, 1962).
Hajek, Jiri. *Mnichov* (Prague, 1958).
Haslam, Jonathan. 'The Soviet Union and the Czechoslovakian Crisis of 1938', *Journal of Contemporary History* 14:3 (1979).
Hauner, Milan. 'Czechoslovakia as a Military Factor in British Considerations of 1938', *Journal of Strategic Studies* 2 (1978).
Hauner, Milan. 'Zari 1938: Kapitulovat ci bojovat?' *Svedectvi* 49 (1975).
Haushofer, Albrecht. *Chinesische Legende* (Berlin, 1949).
Heidrich, Arnost. 'International Political Causes of the Czechoslovak Tragedies' (Washington, 1962).
Heinemann, J.L. *Hitler's First Foreign Minister* (Berkeley, 1979).
Heinz, F.W. *Sprengstoff* (Berlin, 1930).
Henke, Josef. *England in Hitlers politischem Kalkül 1937–1939* (Boppard a.R., 1972).
Herb, G.H. *Under the Map of Germany: Nationalism and Propaganda 1918–1945* (London, 1997).
Herben, Ivan. 'Benes o sve navsteve u Roosevelta a o Mnichovu', Ladislav Karel Feierabend, *Politicke vzpominky*, vol. III (Prague, 1996).
Hesse, Max René. *Partenau* (Munich, 1929).
Hiller von Gaertringen, Friedrich Freiherr, ed. *Die Hassell-Tagebücher 1938–1944: Ulrich von Hassell, Aufzeichnungen vom Andern Deutschland* (Berlin, 1988).
Hillgruber, Andreas. 'England's Place in Hitler's Plans for World Dominion', *Journal of Contemporary History* 9:1 (1974).
Hochman, Jiri. *The Soviet Union and the Failure of Collective Security, 1934–1938* (Ithaca, NY, 1984).
Hoensch, Jorg K. *Der ungarische Revisionismus und die Zerschlagung der Tschekoslowakei* (Tubingen, 1967).
Hoffmann, Peter. *Widerstand-Staatsstreich – Attentat. Der Kampf der Opposition gegen Hitler* (Munich, 1969).
Hosely, David H. *As Good As Any: Foreign Correspondence on American Radio, 1930–1940* (Westport, CT, 1984).
Howard, Anthony. *The Life of R.A. Butler* (London, 1987).
Howard, Michael. *The Continental Commitment* (London, 1972).
Iriye, Akira. *The Origins of the Second World War in Asia and the Pacific* (London, 1987).
Irvine, William D. 'Domestic Politics and the Fall of France', in Joel Blatt, ed., *The French Defeat of 1940: Reassessments* (Oxford, 1998).
Jackson, Julian. *The Popular Front in France. Defending Democracy, 1934–38* (Cambridge, 1988).
Jackson, Peter. 'French Military Intelligence and Czechoslovakia, 1938', *Diplomacy & Statecraft* 5:1 (1994).
Jackson, Peter. 'La perception de la puissance aérienne allemande et son influence sur la politique extérieure française pendant les crises internationales de 1938 à 1939', *Revue Historique des Armées* 4 (1994).
Jaeckel, E. *Das deutsche Jahrhundert: eine historische Bilanz* (Stuttgart, 1990).
Janka, Otto. *General Stanovsky: letec a gentleman* (Prague, 1997).
John, Miloslav. *Ceskoslovenske letectvo v roce 1938* (Beroun, 1996).

John, Miloslav. *Zari 1938* (Brno, 1997).

Jonas, Manfred. *Isolationism in America, 1935–41* (Ithaca, 1969).

Jordan, Nicole. 'Léon Blum and Czechoslovakia, 1936–1938', *French History* 5:1 (1991).

Jordan, Nicole. *The Popular Front and Central Europe. The Dilemmas of French Impotence, 1918–1940* (Cambridge, 1992).;

Juhász, Gyula. *A Teleki-kormány külpolitikája 1939–1941* (Budapest, 1964).

Jukes, G. 'The Red Army and the Munich Crisis', *Journal of Contemporary History* 26:2 (1991).

Kaiser, David. *Economic Diplomacy and the Origins of the Second World War* (Princeton, NJ, 1980).

Kallis, A. 'Expansionism in Italy and Germany between Unification and the First World War: On the Ideological and Political Origins of Fascist Expansionism', *European History Quarterly* 28 (1998).

Kaplan, Karel. *Mocni a bezmocni* (Toronto, 1989).

Kennedy, Paul. 'Appeasement and British Defence Policy in The Inter-War Years', *British Journal of International Studies* 4 (1978).

Kennedy, Paul. 'The Tradition of Appeasement in British Foreign Policy 1865–1939', *British Journal of International Studies* 2 (1976).

Kershaw, Ian. *Hitler.* Vol. 1, *Hubris 1889–1936* (London, 1998).

Kiesling, Eugenia C. *Arming against Hitler: France and the Limits of Military Planning* (Lawrence, KS, 1996).

Kimmich, Christoph M. *Germany and the League of Nations* (Chicago, IL, 1976).

Kirby, William C. *Germany and Republican China* (Stanford, CA, 1984).

Kisielewski, Tadeusz. 'Wodpowiedzi historykowi czeskiemu. Polemika z Jaroslavem Valenta w sprawie stosunków polsko-czeskich w latach 1938–1945', *Dzieje Najnowsze* 25:2 (1993).

Kley, S. *Hitler, Ribbentrop und die Entfesselung des Zweiten Weltkrieges* (Paderborn, 1996).

Klimek, Antonin. *Boj o hrad (1). Hrad a petka. Vnitropoliticky vyvoj Ceskoslovenska 1918–1926 na pudorysu zapasu o prezidentske nastupnictvi* (Prague, 1996).

Klochko, V.F. *et al.*, eds. *New Documents on the History of Munich* (Prague, 1958).

Knox, MacGregor. 'The Fascist Regime, its Foreign Policy and its Wars: An 'Anti-Anti-Fascist' Orthodoxy?' *Contemporary European History* 4:3 (1995).

Knox, MacGregor. *Mussolini Unleashed 1939–1941: Politics and Strategy in Fascist Italy's Last War* (Cambridge, 1982).

Komisja Historyczna (Historical Commission) eds. *Polskie sily zbrojne w drugiej wojnie swiatowej.* Tom I. *Kampania wrzesniowa 1939.* Czesc pierwsza (London, 1951).

Kordt, Erich. *Nicht aus den Akten: die Wilhelmstrasse in Frieden und Krieg* (Stuttgart, 1950).

Kovács, Mária M. 'Nemzeti önrendelkezés és politikai szabadság', *Világosság* 2 (1998).

Kozenski, Jerzy. *Czechoslowacja w polskiej polityce zagranicznej w latach 1932–1938* (Poznan, 1964).

Kwiatkowski, Eugeniusz. 'Jozef Beck', *Arka* 12 (Cracow, 1985) and *Zeszyty Historyczne* 76 (Paris, 1986).

Lacaze, Yvon. 'Daladier, Bonnet and the Decision-Making Process during the Munich Crisis, 1938', in Robert Boyce, ed., *French Foreign and Defence Policy, 1918–1940* (London, 1998).

Lacaze, Yvon. *L'opinion publique française et la crise de Munich* (Berne,1991).

Landau, Henry. *The Enemy Within* (New York, 1937).

Landau, Z. and J. Tomaszewski. *Gospodarka Polski miedzywojennej. Tom IV. 1936–1939* (Warsaw, 1989).

Lavine, Harold and James Weschler. *War Propaganda in the United States* (New Haven, CT, 1940).

Le Béguec, Gilles. 'L'évolution de la politique gouvernementale et les problèmes

institutionnels', in René Rémond and Janine Bourdin, eds., *Edouard Daladier. Chef du Gouvernement (avril 1938 – septembre 1939)* (Paris, 1977).
Le Goyet, P. *Munich: pouvait-on et devait-on faire la guerre en 1938?* (Paris, 1988).
Lee, Bradford A. *Britain and the Sino-Japanese War, 1937–1939* (London, 1973).
Leitz, Christian. *Economic Relations between Nazi Germany and Franco's Spain 1936–1945* (Oxford, 1996).
Leoncini, Francesco. 'Italia e Cecoslovakia, 1919–1939', *Rivista di Studi Politici Internazionali* 45 (1979).
Liang, Lone. *China muss siegen. Drei Vorträge* (Prague, 1938).
Liang, Hsi-Huey. *The Sino-German Connection* (Assen/Amsterdam, 1978).
Lindemann, Fritz. *Im Dienste Chinas* (Peking, 1940).
Lockhart, R.H. Bruce. *Guns or Butter?* (London, 1938).
Lowe, Pardee. 'Hitler Straddles the Oriental Fence', *Amerasia* 2:4 (1938).
Lucaze, Y. 'Daladier, Munich Crisis', in R. Boyce, ed., *French Foreign and Defence Policy, 1918–1940: The Decline and Fall of a Great Power* (London, 1998).
Lukes, Frantisek. 'Benes a SSSR', *Sesity pro mladou literaturu* 21 (1968).
Lukes, Frantisek. 'Poznamky k cs.-sovetskym stykum v zari 1938', *Ceskoslovensky casopis historicky* 16:5 (1968).
Lukes, Igor. 'Benesch, Stalin und die Komintern: Vom Münchner Abkommen zum Molotow-Ribbetrop Pakt', *Vierteljahrshefte für Zeitgeschichte* 3 (1993).
Lukes, Igor. *Czechoslovakia Between Stalin and Hitler: The Diplomacy of Edvard Benes in the 1930a* (New York, 1996).
Lukes, Igor. 'Did Stalin Desire War in 1938? A New Look at Soviet Behaviour During the May and September Crises', *Diplomacy & Statecraft* 2:1 (1991).
Lukes, Igor. 'Stalin and Benes at the End of September 1938: New Evidence from the Prague Archives', *Slavic Review* 52:1 (1993).
Lukes, Igor. 'The Czechoslovak Partial Mobilization in May 1938: A Mystery (Almost) Solved', *Journal of Contemporary History* 31:4 (1996).
Lukes, Igor, 'The GPU and GRU in Pre-World War II Czechoslovakia', *International Journal of Intelligence and Counterintelligence* 8:1 (1995).
Macartney, C.A. *October Fifteenth, the History of Modern Hungary, 1929–1945* (New York, 1956).
Maiski, Ivan Mikhailovich. *Vospominania sovetskogo diplomata, 1925–1945* (Moscow, 1987).
Mal'tsev, V.F., ed. *Dokumenty po istorii miunkhenskogo sgovora, 1937–1939* (Moscow, 1979).
Mansergh, Nicholas. *Survey of British Commonwealth Affairs: Problems of External Policy, 1931–1939* (London, 1952).
Mansergh, Nicholas. *The Commonwealth Experience* (London, 1969).
Manusevich, A.Ia. 'Sanatsiia bez Pilsudskogo', in F.G. Zuev, V.A. Svetalov and S.M. Falkovich, eds., *Kratkaia Istoriia Pol'shi* (Moscow, 1993).
Marès, Antoine. 'Formation et développement du ministère des Affaires étrangères tchécoslovaque (1918–1932)', *Relations internationales* 31 (1982).
Marès, Antoine. 'La faillite des relations franco-tchécoslovaques: la mission militaire française à Prague, 1926–1938', *Revue d'Histoire de la Deuxième Guerre Mondiale*, 28:111 (1978).
Marès, Antoine. 'Les attachés militaires en Europe centrale et la notion de la puissance en 1938', *Revue Historique des Armées* 1 (1983).
Martin, Bernd, ed. *Die deutsche Beraterschaft in China 1927–1938* (Düsseldorf, 1981).
Massey, Vincent. *What's Past is Prologue* (London 1962).
Maya Lytinski, ed. *Reappraising the Munich Pact: Continental Perspectives* (Washington, DC, 1992).
Mazurowa, Kazimiera. 'Przymierze polsko-francuskie z roku 1921', *Najnowsze Dzieje Polski* 11 (1967).
Meehan, P. *The Unnecessary War* (London, 1992).

Messerschmidt, M. 'The Political and Strategic Significance of Advances in Armament Technology: Developments in Germany and the Strategy of "Blitzkrieg"', in R. Ahmann et al., eds., *The Quest for Stability* (London, 1993).

Meyers, Reinhardt. 'Britain, Europe and the Dominions in the 1930s', *Australian Journal of Politics and History* 22 (1976).

Meyers, Reinhardt. *Britische Sicherheits Politik, 1934–1938* (Dusseldorf, 1976).

Meyers, Reinhardt. 'British Imperial Interests and the Policy of Appeasement', in Wolfgang Mommsen and Lothar Kettenacker, eds., *The Fascist Challenge and the Policy of Appeasement* (London, 1983).

Michalka, W. *Ribbentrop und die deutsche Weltpolitik 1933–1940* (Munich, 1980).

Middlemass, Keith. *Diplomacy of Illusion* (London, 1972).

Mikhailov, V.I. *Prolog k voine* (Moscow, 1964).

Mohr, E.G. 'Sino-German Relations in the Period of Chiang Kai-shek', *Conference on Chiang Kai-shek and Modern China* (Taipei, 1986).

Mowrer, Edgar. *Germany Puts the Clock Back* (New York, 1933).

Mueller, K.-J. *The Army, Politics and Society in Germany, 1933–1945* (New York, 1987).

Murray, Gilbert. *From the League to U.N.* (London, 1948).

Murray, Williamson. 'German Air Power and the Munich Crisis', *War and Society* 2 (1975).

Murray, Williamson, ed. *Military Effectiveness*, vol. II (London, 1988).

Murray, Williamson. *The Change in the European Balance of Power, 1938–1939* (Princeton, NJ, 1984).

Namier, Lewis. *Diplomatic Prelude* (London, 1948).

Neathy, W. Blair. *William Lyon Mackenzie King*, vol. III (Toronto 1962).

Neville, Peter, 'The Appointment of Sir Nevile Henderson 1937: Design or Blunder?', *Journal of Contemporary History* 33:1 (1998).

Niedhart, G. 'The Problem of War in German Politics in 1938', *War & Society* 2 (1984).

Noakes, J. and G. Pridham. *Nazism 1919–1945*, vol. 3, *Foreign Policy, War and Extermination* (Exeter, 1988).

Northedge, F.S. *The League of Nations: Its Life and Times, 1920–1946* (Leicester, 1986).

Olivova, Vera. 'Ceskoslovensko-sovetske vztahy mezi obema valkami', *50. vyroci Ceskoslovenske republiky: Materialy z vedecke konference* (Prague, 1968).

O'Neill, R. *The German Army and the Nazi Party, 1933–1939* (London, 1966).

Orlof, Ewa. *Dyplomacja polska wobec sprawy slowackiej w latach 1938–1939* (Cracow, 1980).

Ovendale, Ritchie. *Appeasement and the English Speaking World* (Cardiff, 1975).

Ovendale, Ritchie. 'Appeasement in Europe and the Far East, 1931–9', unpublished paper, Conference on Australian Diplomacy and Defence, 1901–39 (London, 1995).

Ovendale, Ritchie. 'Britain, the Dominions and the Coming of the Second World War 1933–9', in W.J. Mommsen and L. Kettenacker, eds., *The Fascist Challenge and the Policy of Appeasement* (London, 1983).

Ovendale, Ritchie. 'Canada, Britain and the United States and the Policy of Appeasement', in C.C. Eldgridge, ed., *Kith and Kin: Canada, Britain and the United States from the Revolution to the Cold War* (Cardiff, 1997).

Overy, R.J. 'Goering's Multi-National Empire', in A. Teichova and M. Levy-Leboyer, eds., *International Business and Central Europe 1918–1939* (Leicester, 1983).

Overy, R.J. 'German Air Strength 1933–1939: A Note', *The Historical Journal* 27 (1984).

Palat, Augustin. 'Jaroslav Prusek', *Archiv orientalni* 34 (1966).

Parker, R.A.C. *Chamberlain and Appeasement. British Policy and the Coming of the Second World War* (London/New York, 1993).

Parkinson, C. Northcote. *Parkinson's Law; or The Pursuit of Progress* (London, 1958).

Patzold, K. 'Antikommunismus und Antibolschewismus als Instrumente der Kriegsvorbereitung und Kriegspolitik', in N. Frei and H. Kling, eds., *Der nationalsozialistische Krieg* (Frankfurt am Main, 1990).

Peck, Graham. *Two Kinds of Time* (Boston, MA, 1967).

Persico, Joseph E. *Edward R. Murrow: An American Original* (New York, 1988).

Pfaff, Ivan. *Die Sowjetunion und die Verteidigung der Tschechoslowakei, 1934–1938: Versuch der Revision einer Legende* (Köln, 1996).

Pfaff, Ivan. 'Jak tomu opravdu bylo se sovetskou pomoci v mnichovske krizi?' *Svedectvi* 56 (1978) and 57 (1979).

Philipps, J.W. 'A Close Look at General Tsai T'ing-k'ai', *China Today* 1:1 (1934).

Pirow, Oswald. *James Barry Munnik Hertzog* (Cape Town, 1957).

Pithon, Rémy. 'Opinions publiques et représentations culturelles face aux problèmes de la puissance. Le témoignage du cinéma français (1938–1939)', *Relations internationales* 33 (1983).

Prasolov, S.I. 'Sovietskii soyuz i Chekhoslovakia v 1938 g.', in V.K. Volkov, ed., *Myunkhen: preddverie voiny* (Moscow, 1988).

Pratt, Lawrence R. *East Malta, West of Suez Britain's Mediterranean Crisis 1936–1939* (Cambridge/New York, 1975).

Preissig, Erhard. *Die französische Kulturpropaganda in der ehemaligen Tschechoslowakei* (Stuttgart, 1943).

Pritz, Pál. 'A kieli találkozó', *Századok* 3 (1974).

Prochazka, Zdenek. *Vojenske dejiny Ceskoslovenska* (Prague, 1987).

Pronay, Nicholas and Philip M. Taylor, 'An Improper Use of Broadcasting', *Journal of Contemporary History* 18 (1983).

Quartararo, Rosaria. *Roma tra Londra e Berlino: La politica estera fascista dal 1930 to 1940* (Roma, 1980).

Quartararo, Rosario. 'Inghiltera e Italia. Dal Patto di Pasqua a Monaco', *Storia Contemporanea* 7:4 (1976).

Ránki, György. 'Adatok a magyar külpolitikához a Csehszlovákiai agresszió idején', *Századok* (1959).

Rémond, René and Janine Bourdin, eds. *Edouard Daladier: Chef du Gouvernement (avril 1938–septembre 1939)* (Paris, 1977).

Reynolds, David. *Britannia Overruled: British Policy and World Power in the 20th Century* (London, 1991).

Reynolds, David. 'FDR's Foreign Policy and the British Royal Visit to the USA, 1939', *The Historian* 45 (1983).

Reynolds, David. *The Creation of the Anglo-American Alliance* (London, 1981).

Richardson, D. and G. Stone, eds. *Decisions and Diplomacy: Essays in Twentieth Century International History* (London: 1995).

Richardson, R. Dan. *Comintern Army: The International Brigades and the Spanish Civil War* (Lexington, 1982).

Ripka, Hubert. *Unorova tragedie* (Prague, 1995).

Ritschl, A. 'Die deutsche Zahlungsbilanz 1936–41 und das Problem des Devisenmangels vor Kriegsbeginn', *Vierteljahreshefte für Zeitgeschichte* 39 (1991).

Roberts, Andrew. *'The Holy Fox': A Biography of Lord Halifax* (London, 1991).

Roberts, Cynthia A. 'Planning for War: The Red Army and the Catastrophe of 1941', *Europe–Asia Studies* 47:8 (1995).

Roberts, David M. 'Hugh Dalton and the Labour Party in the 1930s', unpubl. Ph.D. dissertation, Kingston Polytechnic (now Kingston University), 1978.

Roberts, Henry L. 'The Diplomacy of Colonel Beck', in Gordon A. Craig and Felix Gilbert, eds., *The Diplomats 1919–1939* (Princeton, NJ, 1960).

Romsics, Ignác. *Helyünk és sorsunk a Duna-medencében* (Budapest, 1996).

Rzheshevskii, Oleg A. *Europe 1939: Was War Inevitable?* (Moscow, 1989).

Sakmyster, Thomas L. 'The Hungarian State Visit to Germany of August 1938: Some new Evidence on Hungary's Pre-Munich Policy', *Canadian Slavic Studies* 3:4 (1969).

Sanders, Michael and Philip M. Taylor. *British Propaganda During the First World War, 1914–1918* (London, 1982).

Sanson, Rosemonde. 'La perception de la puissance par l'Alliance Démocratique', *Revue d'Histoire Moderne et Contemporaine* 31 (1984).

Schellenberg, Walter. *Memoiren* (Cologne, 1959).

Schmidt, P. *Deutsche Wirtschaftsfreiheit durch den Vierjahresplan* (Breslau, n.d.).

Schüddekopf, Ernst-Otto. *Linke Leute von rechts* (Stuttgart, 1960).

Scoble, Andrew R., ed. *The Memoirs of Philip de Commines*, 2 vols. (London, 1855).

Seton-Watson, Hugh. *Eastern Europe Between the Wars, 1918–1941* (3rd ed., Hamden, CT, 1962).

Shaposhnikov, Boris Mikhailovich. *Vospominania: voenno-nauchnye trudy* (Moscow, 1974).

Sheean, Vincent. *Personal History* (New York, 1935).

Sheehan, Vincent. *Between the Thunder and the Sun* (New York, 1943).

Shorrock, William I. *From Ally to Enemy: The Enigma of Fascist Italy in French Diplomacy, 1920–1940* (Kent, OH, 1988).

Sierpowski, Stanislaw. *Stosunki polsko-wloskie w latach 1918–1940* (Warsaw, 1975).

Simpson, A. 'The Struggle for Control of the German Economy 1936/7', *Journal of Modern History* 21 (1959).

Small, Melvin and Otto Feinstein, eds. *Appeasing Fascism: Articles from the Wayne State University Conference on Munich after Fifty Years* (Lanham, MD, 1991).

Smelser, R. *The Sudeten Problem 1933–38: Volkstumspolitik and the Formation of German Foreign Policy* (Folkestone, 1975).

Smith, Denis Mack. *Mussolini's Roman Empire* (New York, 1976).

Smith, Denis Mack. *Mussolini* (London, 1981).

Smith, R. Franklin. *Edward R. Murrow: The War Years* (Kalamazoo, MI, 1978).

Spacil, Dusan *et al.*, eds. *Dokumenty k historii mnichovskeho diktatu, 1937–1939* (Prague, 1979).

Speidel, Helm. 'Reichswehr und Rote Armee', *Vierteljahrshefte für Zeitgeschichte* 1:1 (1953).

Sperber, A.M. *Murrow:His Life and Times* (London, 1986).

Stanislawska, Stefania. *Wielka i mala polityka Józefa Becka* (Warsaw, 1962).

Starzenski, Pawel. *Trzy Lata z Beckiem*, ed. Bogdan Grzelonski (Warsaw, 1991).

Stepanov, S. 'Pered Myunkhenom', *Voyenno-istoricheskii zhurnal* 4–5 (1992).

Strang, Bruce. 'Two Unequal Tempers: Sir George Ogilvie-Forbes, Sir Nevile Henderson, and British Foreign Policy 1938–39', *Diplomacy & Statecraft* 5:1 (1994).

Sullivan, Brian R. 'The Italian Armed Forces, 1918–1940', in Alan R. Millet and Williamson Murray, eds., *Military Effectiveness*, Vol. II, *The Interwar Period* (Boston, MA, 1988).

Szarka, László. 'Versuchung und Irrwege der Revision. Die tschekoslowakische Frage in der ungarische politischen Öffentlichkeit 1938', in Peter Glotz *et al.*, eds., *München, 1938. Das Ende des alten Europa* (Berlin, 1990).

Szklarska-Lohmannowa, Alina. *Polsko-Czechoslowackie stosunki dyplomatyczne w latach 1918–1925* (Wroclaw, 1967).

Taborsky, Edward. 'Benes and the Soviets', *Foreign Affairs* 27:2 (1949).

Taylor, Philip M. 'If War Should Come: Preparing the Fifth Arm for Total War 1935–1939', *Journal of Contemporary History* 16 (1981).

Taylor, Philip M. *The Projection of Britain* (Cambridge, 1981).

Taylor, Telford. *Munich: The Price of Peace* (London/New York, 1979/1980).

Teichova, Alice and P.L. Cottrell. *International Business and Central Europe, 1918–1939* (Leicester, 1983).

Terry, Sarah Meiklejohn. *Poland's Place in Europe: General Sikorski and the Origin of the Oder-Neisse Line, 1939–1943* (Princeton, NJ, 1983).

Thompson, Dorothy. *I Saw Hitler* (New York, 1932).

Thorne, Christopher. *Border Crossings* (New York, 1988).

Tilkovszky, Lóránt. *Teleki Pál. Legenda és valóság* (Budapest, 1969).
Toepfer, Marcia Lynn. 'The Soviet Role in the Munich Crisis: An Historiographical Debate', *Diplomatic History* 1:4 (1977).
Toland, John. *Adolf Hitler* (London, 1976).
Toscano, Mario. *Alto Adige–South Tyrol: Italy's Frontier with the German World* (Baltimore, MD,1975).
Toscano, Mario. *The Origins of the Pact of Steel*, 2nd ed. (Baltimore, MD, 1967).
Tree, Ronald. *When the Moon Was High* (London, 1975).
Treue, Wilhelm. 'Der Denkschrift Hitlers über die Aufgaben eines Vierjahresplans', *Vierteljahreshefte für Zeitgeschichte* 3 (1954).
Treue, Wilhelm, ed., 'Rede Hitlers vor der deutschen Presse (10. November 1938)', *Vierteljahrshefte für Zeitgeschichte* 6:2 (April 1958).
Vaïsse, Maurice. 'Against Appeasement: French Advocates of Firmness, 1933–8', in Wolfgang J. Mommsen and Lothar I. Kettenacker, eds., *The Fascist Challenge and the Policy of Appeasement* (London, 1983).
Vaïsse, Maurice. 'La perception de la puissance soviétique par les militaires français en 1938', *Revue Historique des Armées* 3 (1983).
Vivier, Thierry. 'La Cooperation aéronautique franco-tchécoslovaque, janvier 1933–septembre 1938', *Revue Historique des Armées* 1 (1993).
Volkoganov, D.A. 'Drama reshenii 1939 goda', *Novaia i noveisheia istoria* 4 (1989).
Volkoganov, Dmitri. *Stalin: Triumph and Tragedy* (New York, 1991).
Volkov, V.K, ed. *Myunkhen: preddverie voiny* (Moscow, 1988).
Volkov, V.K. *et al. 1939 god: uroki istorii* (Moscow, 1990).
Waddington, G. 'Hitler, Ribbentrop, die NSDAP und der Niedergang des Britischen Empire 1935–1938', *Vierteljahreshefte für Zeitgeschichte* 41 (1992).
Wallace, William V. 'New Documents on the History of Munich: A Selection from the Soviet and Czechoslovak Archives', *International Affairs* 35:4 (1959).
Walters, F.P. *A History of the League of Nations* (London, 1960).
Wandycz, Damian S. 'Zapomniany List Pilsudskiego do Masaryka', *Orzel Bialy* 32 (580) – 35 (583) (1953); reprint, New York, n.d; English translation: 'A Forgotten Letter of Pilsudski to Masaryk', *Polish Review* 9:4 (1964).
Wandycz, Piotr S. *Czechoslovak–Polish Confederation* (Bloomington, IN, 1956).
Wandycz, Piotr S. *France and Her Eastern Allies 1919–1925: French-Czechoslovak-Polish Relations from the Paris Peace Conference to Locarno* (Minneapolis, MN, 1962).
Wandycz, Piotr S. *Soviet–Polish Relations, 1917–1921* (Cambridge, MA, 1969).
Wandycz, Piotr S. *The Price of Freedom. A History of East Central Europe from the Middle Ages to the Present* (London/New York, 1992).
Wandycz, Piotr S. *The Twilight of French Eastern Alliances 1926–1936: French–Czechoslovak–Polish Relations from Locarno to the Remilitarization of the Rhineland* (Princeton, NJ, 1988).
Wang, Y.C. *Chinese Intellectuals and the West, 1872–1949* (Chapel Hill, NC, 1966).
Watt, D.C. 'An Earlier Model for the Pact of Steel: The Draft Treaties Exchanged between Germany and Italy during Hitler's Visit to Rome in May 1938', *International Affairs* 33:2 (1957).
Watt, D.C. 'Chamberlain's Ambassadors', in M. Dockrill and B. McKercher, eds., *Diplomacy and World Power: Studies in British Foreign Policy 1890–1950* (Cambridge, 1996).
Watt, D.C. *How War Came: The Immediate Origins of the Second World War, 1938–1939* (London/New York, 1989).
Watt, D.C. *Personalities and Appeasement* (Austin, TX, 1991).
Watt, D.C. *Personalities and Policies: Studies in the Formulation of British Foreign Policy in the Twentieth Century* (London/South Bend, IN, 1965).
Watt, D.C. 'South African Attempts to Mediate Between Britain and Germay, 1935–1938', in K. Bourne and D.C. Watt, eds., *Studies in International History* (London, 1967).

Wedgewood, Josiah and Allan Nevins, *Forever Freedom* (Harmondsworth, 1940).

Weinberg, Gerhard L. *The Foreign Policy of Hitler's Germany: Diplomatic Revolution in Europe 1933–36* (Chicago, IL, 1970).

Weinberg, Gerhard L. *The Foreign Policy of Hitler's Germany. Starting World War II, 1937–1939* (Chicago, IL, 1980, and Atlantic Highlands, NJ, 1993).

Weiss, John *Hitler's Diplomat* (London, 1992).

Wendt, B.-J. *Grossdeutschland: Aussenpolitik und Kriegsvorbereitung des Hitler-Regimes* (Munich, 1987).

Werth, Alexander. *Twilight of France, 1933–1940* (New York, 1942).

Wheeler-Bennett, Sir John. *Knaves, Fools and Heroes: In Europe Between the Wars* (New York, 1974).

Who's Who in China. Biographies of Chinese Leaders (Shanghai, 1932).

Wiedemann, F. *Der Mann der Feldherr werden wollte* (Kettwig, 1964).

Wiskemann, E. *The Europe I Saw* (London, 1968).

Wright, J. and P. Stafford. 'Hitler, Britain and the Hossbach Memorandum', *Militärgeschichtliche Mitteilungen*, 42 (1987).

Wright, Sydney Fowler. *Prelude in Prague. A Story of the War of 1938* (London, 1935).

Young, R.J. 'The Strategic Dream: French Air Doctrine in the Inter-War Period', *Journal of Contemporary History* 9:4 (1974).

Young, Robert J. 'French Military Intelligence and Nazi Germany, 1938–1939', in Ernest R. May, ed., *Knowing One's Enemies: Intelligence Assessment Before the Two World Wars* (Princeton, NJ, 1986).

Young, Robert J. 'Reason and Madness: France, the Axis Power and the Politics of Economic Disorder', *Canadian Journal of History* 20 (1985).

Young, Robert J. *In Command of France. French Foreign Policy and Military Planning, 1933–1940* (Cambridge, MA, 1978).

Zakharov, Matvei Visil'evich. *General'nyi shtab v predvoyennye gody* (Moscow, 1989).

Zeman, Zbynek with Antonin Klimek. *The Life of Edvard Benes, 1884–1948: Czechoslovakia in Peace and War* (Oxford, 1997).

Zeraffa, Danièle. 'La perception de la puissance par le Parti Communiste', *Revue d'Histoire Moderne et Contemporaine* 31 (1984).

Zgorniak, Marian. *Sytuacja militarna Europy w okresie kryzysu politycznego 1938 r* (Warsaw, 1979).

Zunino, Pier Giorgio. *L'ideologia del fascismo: Miti, credenze e valori nella stabilizazione del regime* (Bologna, 1985).

Index

Note: The following terms appear on so high a proportion of pages that it would have been meaningless to include them in the index: Czechoslovakia, Germany (during the Third Reich), Hitler, Munich conference.

Books of Related Interest

Whitehall Officials and the Suez Crisis

Anthony Gorst and **Saul Kelly** (Eds)

Whitehall Officials and the Suez Crisis is an entirely original piece of research which casts new light on Suez, not least through the novelty of the angle of its approach – a chapter each on such players as, among others, General Sir Gerald Templer (Chief of the Imperial General Staff); Sir Norman Brook (Secretary to the Cabinet), Patrick Dean (head of the Permanent Under Secretary's Department of the Foreign Office).

The book reflects on the past ten years of scholarship, incorporating the releases of 1956 documents at the Public Record Office under the Open Government Initiative. The on-going historical debate on the role of British officials and their departments in the formulation of British foreign policy in general.

192 pages 1999
0 7146 5018 8 cloth
0 7146 8077 X paper

Imperial Defence, 1868–1887

A Study in the Decisive Impulses behind the Change from 'Colonial' to 'Imperial' Defence

Donald M Schurman, *Royal Military College, Canada*
Edited by **John Beeler**, *University of Alabama*

Professor Schurman's classic study reveals how British statesmen, military and naval professionals, and administrators came to grips with the radically transformed strategic situation, evolved a suitable response based on the creation of a comprehensive system of defended coaling stations, determined priorities for such stations, and took the initial steps toward implementing this new policy. However, Schurman also places the creation of this steam-age imperial defence policy firmly in the context of political ideology and partisanship, surveying the divide between Liberals and Conservatives on matters of imperialism, differences of opinion within both parties' leadership, the wrangling between Admiralty, War Office, Colonial Office and Treasury and the diverging views of politicians, soldiers and sailors wrestling with imperial defence policy. Based on extensive archival research, Schurman's work is the definitive examination of this important subject.

224 pages 2000
0 7146 5006 4 cloth
Naval Policy and History Series No. 12

FRANK CASS PUBLISHERS
Newbury House, 900 Eastern Avenue, Ilford, Essex, IG2 7HH
Tel: +44 (0)181 599 8866 Fax: +44 (0)181 599 0984 E-mail: info@frankcass.com
NORTH AMERICA
5804 NE Hassalo Street, Portland, OR 97213 3644, USA
Tel: 800 944 6190 Fax: 503 280 8832 E-mail: cass@isbs.com
Website: www.frankcass.com

The Washington Conference, 1921–22

Naval Rivalry, East Asian Stability and the Road to Pearl Harbor

Erik Goldstein, *University of Birmingham* and
John Maurer, *United States Naval War College* (Eds)
With a Foreword by *Ernest R May*

> *'The Washington Conference provides both a model and a cautionary tale on the limits of cooperation. In providing this instructive model for our time, Erik Goldstein and John Maurer have used the best standards of international history.'*
> **John B. Hattendorf, The International History Review**

320 pages 1994
0 7146 4559 1 cloth
0 7146 4136 7 paper
A special issue of the journal Diplomacy and Statecraft

Personalities, War and Diplomacy

Essays on International History

T G Otte, *University of Buckingham* and
C Pagedas, *University of Birmingham* (Eds)
With a Preface by **Roy Jenkins**

History is an old, yet constantly changing discipline. Traditionally, the interpretation of the past oscillated between two opposed poles; on the one hand, there were those who believed that events were determined not by individuals but by an impersonal process (though, of course, there were contending views of what that process is, or how it unravels), and on the other hand, there were those who stressed the contingent aspects of politics and history, and hence the impact of personalities. Neither of these two concepts of history is new.

Combining essays on the 'personality dimension' in 19th and 20th century international history, this book places in a proper historical perspective the impact of individual diplomats, politicians and military strategists on foreign policy-making as well as the role of perception in the policy-making

process.

Contributors: Roy Jenkins, T G Otte, John H Maurer, Erik Goldstein, Jonathan Wright, Tadashi Kuramatsu, Glyn Stone, W Scott Lucas, Paul-Henri Spaak, Pierre-Henri Lauren, Sergei Khrushchev, Kendrick Oliver.

316 pages 1997
0 7146 4818 3 cloth

FRANK CASS PUBLISHERS
Newbury House, 900 Eastern Avenue, Ilford, Essex, IG2 7HH
Tel: +44 (0)181 599 8866 Fax: +44 (0)181 599 0984 E-mail: info@frankcass.com
NORTH AMERICA
5804 NE Hassalo Street, Portland, OR 97213 3644, USA
Tel: 800 944 6190 Fax: 503 280 8832 E-mail: cass@isbs.com
Website: www.frankcass.com

THE PENGUIN CLASSICS
EDITED BY E. V. RIEU
L10

THE
ADVENTURES OF
DON QUIXOTE

BY

Miguel de Cervantes Saavedra

TRANSLATED BY
J. M. COHEN

PENGUIN BOOKS

Penguin Books Ltd, Harmondsworth, Middlesex

U.S.A.: Penguin Books Inc., 3300 Clipper Mill Road, Baltimore 11, Md

CANADA: Penguin Books (Canada) Ltd, 178 Norseman Street,
Toronto 18, Ontario

AUSTRALIA: Penguin Books Pty Ltd, 762 Whitehorse Road,
Mitcham, Victoria

SOUTH AFRICA: Penguin Books (S.A.) Pty Ltd, Gibraltar House,
Regent Road, Sea Point, Cape Town

—

First published 1950
Reprinted 1952, 1954, 1956

Made and printed in Great Britain
by Richard Clay & Company, Ltd,
Bungay, Suffolk

CONTENTS

THE SECOND PART

TRANSLATOR'S INTRODUCTION

SOME excuse seems necessary for reintroducing in a fresh translation a book which has been one of the world's best sellers for three centuries, and which already exists in seven or eight English versions. But, for all that, the modern reader would be hard put to it to choose a good Don Quixote. The best and raciest version, Shelton's, being almost contemporary with the original, is the nearest to Cervantes in spirit. It suffers, however, like other seventeenth-century work, from a lack of familiarity with the idiom; many of Shelton's most picturesque touches bear little resemblance to Cervantes' phrases which they purport to translate. The eighteenth-century versions, available in cheap editions, are all of them readable, but none of them appreciably closer to the Spanish than Shelton's, and all prone to omit the passages they do not understand; and what the nineteenth-century translators gained in accuracy they lost in style. So when Mr Rieu offered me an opportunity of producing another version to go before a large public at a reasonable price, I felt that the field was still open, and set about the same task as each of my predecessors, the task of reconciling faithfulness to Cervantes with the writing of contemporary English: with what success it is for the reader to judge.

Don Quixote enjoys a peculiar place among the world's books, as the only well-known representative of a considerable literature; for from the fourteenth to the seventeenth centuries the Spanish was among the great literatures of the world. But although there are other books which deserve to be known, it is in the untranslatable field of poetry and verse drama that Spanish is strongest, and particularly in that most untranslatable of all, the traditional ballad, in which the Spaniards are as rich as ourselves.

It was as a skit on this universally popular poetry that Don Quixote began; and the first seven chapters, which seem to have been modelled on an obscure playlet of the day, are devoted to a crazy gentleman, who sets out to imitate the deeds recorded in the ballads, and ends up by convincing himself that he is the Knight Baldwin; in which character he addresses his neighbour, who is bringing him home on his ass from the first of his misadventures. If the book had gone no further than this *variation on a theme already several times attempted, Don Quixote would have been little more striking than that other madman of Cervantes' invention, the student in one of the* Exemplary Novels *who imagined that he was made of glass, and took precautions accordingly. But, like Fielding's Joseph Andrews, Don Quixote came alive in his author's hands; and if we search for the actual passage in which this miracle happened, it is surely when he turns on this neighbour of his, who protests that he is neither Baldwin nor the Moor Abindarraez, but plain Señor Quixana – Master Lantern-jaws. 'I know who I am,' replies the knight, 'and I know that I am capable of being not only the characters I have named, but all the Twelve Peers of France and all the Nine Worthies as well, for my exploits are far greater than all the deeds they have done, all together and each by himself.' It is with his historic attempt to make good this boast in despite of all the powers of reality that the rest of the book is concerned. While in the process the crazy gentleman is transformed from the victim of other people's horse-play into a dreamer who sometimes succeeds in imposing his vision on those he meets, and even in his most preposterous battles with the sordid forces of here-and-now has always our loving sympathy; though only too often we may have to hold our thumbs for him, as we might for some reckless child who has strayed on to an unrailed roof with a sheer drop to the street. But for all our fears, when he does fall, which he invariably does, he picks himself up, and is only a little the worse for each shaking.*

Cervantes, however, does not come out baldly on the side of the ideal and imaginary against the workaday world. Don Quixote does not live only in his own fantasies, like a Kafka hero. After that first expedition, he is seldom separated from his squire, Sancho Panza, whose peasant common-sense is often near to bringing his master to earth. The adventures of these two are the core of the book; and several modern writers have reminded us that the two of them stand for opposing forces that have been active in Spain ever since the book was written: the spirit of Quixote, living in the mind, oblivious of the successive defeats his country has sustained, master of the huge ramshackle Spanish Empire, whose riches invariably drained into foreign hands, a poor gentleman concerned more with his title to nobility than with the bareness of his larder; and the spirit of Sancho, the shrewd peasant whose simplicity was forever exploited, and whose poverty has never diminished.

Now, once the book got under way with Don Quixote's second ex-

*pedition and the introduction of Sancho, Cervantes' irony was turned
away from the ballads, which he always quotes with evident pleasure,
and on to the romances of chivalry, extravagant adventure stories most
popular in Spain at that time, a sort of mannered imitation of the old
epics of chivalry which have come down to us in prose in Malory's
Morte d'Arthur. Here Cervantes was on firmer ground than in mocking
at the ballads, for just how ridiculous were the many imitations of
'Amadis of Gaul' can be seen in the Clavileño episode in the second
part of our story. But the book is not just a satire on an exaggerated
literary fashion: the romances of chivalry would long ago have been
forgotten if Cervantes had not attacked them, and Don Quixote
would have less readers to-day if his author had not done more than
attack Amadis and his brood. For the book is what Don Quixote would
have wished it to be, an adventure story. But, unlike most adventure
stories it is rich in characters, not only in its principal characters, but in
all the many minor personages, some of whom make only a single appearance: the stout innkeeper with his fondness for the stories the
reapers used to read in his inn; his wife, kindly enough until any of her
property is in danger; their ladylike daughter; the slut Maritornes; the
monks on their hired mules; the braggart convict Gines with his half-
finished autobiography, and all the rest of them, as lively a bunch as
ever Chaucer rode to Canterbury with. And then there are the rather
more detailed figures: the priest, the barber, Sampson Carrasco, and
that most imaginary of all characters, Don Quixote's version of the
brawny Aldonza Lorenzo with the loud voice and the slight moustache,
his mistress Dulcinea del Toboso.*

*Character and incident come together, then, against the back-
ground of the Spain of that day, and Cervantes' eye for detail gives us
a shrewd insight into the class structure of the country. On one side we
see the Duke and Duchess living in feudal luxury in one of their country houses, and Don Ferdinand's father, a rich landowner, sending for
the son of a smaller gentleman, who sees in this unexpected condescension the prospect of a brilliant career for the young man. We see, too,
the awe in which these people are held by such prosperous farmers and
stock-breeders as Dorothea's father. Yet the middle class contribute not
only well-to-do farmers, but such worthies as the Captive's brother, the
judge who has picked up a good job in the colonies; and the lady travelling with the Basque squire to join her husband at Seville may well be of*

the same origin; while the Captive himself shows us another means of livelihood resorted to by the sons of the impoverished gentry, a military career under one of the great captains, the career which Cervantes took up himself as a young man with no conspicuous success. Inset in the first part of the book we have a long account of this captain's captivity in Algiers, culminating in an exciting escape, and describing by the way the battle of Lepanto and other actions at which the author has himself been present. In this digression we get a detailed picture of life in Barbary; while in the second part we get its counterpart, an account of the expulsion of the prosperous Moorish population of Spain, the Moriscos, by Philip III. Then, as for artisans and craftsmen, we are shown the making and printing of books at Barcelona, and the small town administration of that 'isle' in which Sancho enjoyed his brief governorship. Lastly, we get a cross-section of the underworld in the accounts the convicts in the chain gang give of themselves. And every minor figure, from the gentleman whom Sancho observed at court walking with his equerry behind him, to the barber who served two villages and was so unlucky as to put his new brass basin on his head to protect his new hat from the rain, stands out clearly. Only the goatherds and shepherds are sentimentalised; for Cervantes was deeply affected by a convention of his own time, which is as tiresome to us as the extravagancies he himself parodies – I mean the pastoral convention, which involved the pretence that only simple folk had deep and genuine sentiments, and sent the fashionable gentry for a century out into their carefully tended parks in the fancy dress of shepherds and shepherdesses, as Don Quixote found them that day when he and Sancho got entangled in the nets they had stretched among the trees to snare the birds.

These too-eloquent shepherds and goatherds, carving their mistresses' names on the bark of the cork trees and composing poems in their honour, are certainly to our present-day taste the weak spot of the book. And while with Sancho we appreciate the goatherds' good fare, their full wine-skins and their fresh cheese, we find their habit of dying of love neither credible nor poetic, and remain unmoved by the sugar-candy perfection of their shepherdesses, and the artificiality of their sentiments and language. How far Cervantes subscribed to this pastoral convention, or how much he wrote in it to please his readers, is anyone's guess. We know that his first, unsuccessful, book, La Galatea, was in this manner, and that he did not choose to write the promised second part.

Another feature of our book which takes the contemporary reader aback is what we may broadly call its sexual morality. This is based on a crude scale of values by which honour is preserved so long as any seduction, however sordid, is covered up by marriage. This very masculine point of view is by no means confined to Cervantes, but is assumed throughout the Spanish literature of the time. But it is difficult for a present-day reader to accept Don Ferdinand's inclusion among the happy bridal couples at the end of the first part. For after seducing Dorothea under promise of marriage, he attempts to steal Lucinda from his best friend, and only after failing is he content to yield himself magnanimously to the loving Dorothea. This highly dubious behaviour, however, in the rich man's son is accepted, and even applauded, by all, including the genial priest; and here we can only assume that Cervantes accepted the conventions of his age without much question. About the 'Tale of Foolish Curiosity' we can hardly be so charitable; for neither its morality nor its psychology bears a moment's examination, and except perhaps for a mild interest in the turn of events, it is difficult to see what amusement the average reader can find in it. My advice to anyone who has found his patience wearing thin, say during Marcela's speech in praise of freedom, is to skip it. Yet we are assured that everyone who heard it thought it a most delightful story, and even the priest approved of it, though with certain reservations.

Nor, despite his frequent shafts of satire against officials and ecclesiastics, can we think of Cervantes as a social critic. If the travelling monks on their sleek mules or the mumbling priests escorting the dead body are figures of fun, the village priest and the canon are both intelligent, charming and broad-minded men. The same rule applies to such public officials as we meet, and as for the Inquisition, which seems to have so far interfered with our author as to make him change Don Quixote's shirt-tail rosary for one of oak-galls, we can discover no protest against its ubiquitous activities, and even find a rather fulsome apology for the combined activities of Church and State in the expulsion of the Moriscos put into the mouth of the Morisco Ricote. It is unnecessary to take this justification for Cervantes' own point of view. But there can be no reason to suppose that he saw the action in the light of history, as an act of arbitrary cruelty which robbed Spain of an industrious and valuable population. The age of the Counter Reformation was not one of social protest, and Cervantes was by no means peculiar in confining himself to satire against individual corruptions rather than against a system which had once and for all suppressed such protestant and bourgeois criticism as had arisen. If we are to deduce Cervantes' ideals from any one character, it must be from the Man in the Green Overcoat, one of those quiet country gentlemen who remained the most enlightened and civilised figures in Europe until well on into the eighteenth century.

But however much we may be delighted and entertained by the rich detail of the social background, it is in the twin figures in the foreground that the true magic lies. It is impossible to lay our fingers on the qualities in the Knight of the Sad Countenance which make him a more and more lovable figure as the book progresses, even though he never becomes any less ridiculous than when he first stood vigil over his arms in the inn yard. How little we should have regretted his violent disillusionment then! Yet by the time of his final overthrow by the Knight of the White Moon we are on his side against all the forces of reason and sanity. For his madness is something we all share, a fantastic protest against the limitations of worldly existence, which makes us lend instant sympathy to the subtlest of all its critics, the comics who take its knocks; to Falstaff, or Charlie Chaplin, or to a more resilient mocker like Groucho Marx.

But if Don Quixote increasingly gains our sympathy as the book progresses, and the sadistic slapstick of the first chapters gives way to the inventive richness of the knight's disquisitions on chivalry, his conversations with his squire, and his magnificently staged penance, Sancho wins our affection by leaps and bounds. A genius seems to develop in the man whose first preoccupations were his belly and his comfort. We watch the coward of the adventure of the fulling mills pull off his first exercise in fiction, the report of his interview with Dulcinea. We see him go from strength to strength, and note the ebb and flow of his credulity, until we have to applaud his consummate skill in passing a peasant girl off on his master as Dulcinea herself, under enchantment. From there to his successful spell as governor of his 'isle' we see his wonder and amazement at his own ingenuity. But we are hardly distressed at his return to the humdrum life of his village. For however much his master's insanity may have drawn him after it into exalted spheres of action, his credulity was never complete and his feet were in reality always well planted on the ground.

There is no doubt at all that the book improves as it progresses; the second part, published some ten years after the first, is by far and away the richer and subtler. It is also more of a unity. For such digressions as there are do not take the form of separate tales, but are incorporated in the main body of the story. These digressions certainly offer an obstacle to the present-day reader; and my advice to anyone who finds himself bogged down by the goatherd's tale in the twelfth chapter is to skip it judiciously, without missing any of Don Quixote's observations, then to read on from the fifteenth chapter, to skip the Cardenio–Lucindo–Dorothea episodes in the twenty-fourth and twenty-eighth, and to cut out the 'Tale of Foolish Curiosity', but to read the Captive's story – which is interesting, though it does not bear on the main theme of the book – and so right on to the end of the first part, leaving out the goatherd's story in chapter fifty-one. For it would be a sad thing indeed if any reader of Don Quixote were to miss the enchantment of Dulcinea, the knight's descent into Montesinos' cave, Master Peter's puppet-show, the adventure of the enchanted bark, or Sancho's spell of government, all in the second part, merely through getting stuck by the pastoral stories in the first. Of the parts devoted to the knight and his squire no one will have any cause to complain, even though Cervantes sometimes drowses – in the rather too sadistic fight with the goatherd at the end of the first part, for instance – and is frequently careless and inconsistent about his detail: the reappearance of the stolen Dapple or the disappearance of the second guard with a firelock in the adventure of the galley-slaves are flagrant examples. The story is leisurely and episodic, being designed no doubt for reading aloud, as the innkeeper tells us the reapers read their stories, in the midday heat; and Cervantes seems never to have made a thorough revision of his book with a view to removing these inconsistencies, which no doubt arose through his making changes in the story as he wrote it.

The author's own life is typical of the all-round activity of the men of his day. Our own Edmund Spenser, Walter Raleigh and Philip Sidney were respectively an administrator, a courtier and adventurer, and a soldier, yet for all that the finest poets of their day. He was born in 1547, the son of a poor doctor, got some education from a schoolmaster who was permeated by the new critical spirit, and at twenty-one took service in Italy. Then, as a regular soldier, he was present at the naval battle of Lepanto (1571), described in the Captive's story and, though ill of fever, insisted on taking his place on the deck, where he received three wounds, one of which permanently maimed his left hand. After taking part in other engagements also recorded in the Captive's story, the action at Navarino and the failure to relieve the Goletta, he was captured with his brother by pirates on his voyage back to Spain in 1575, and taken to Algiers, where he became the slave of a renegade Greek, made three unsuccessful attempts to escape, and was finally ransomed in 1580. For the rest of his life he was preoccupied with the difficulties of making a living and with unsuccessful attempts to get a good position under the Crown in reward for his services as a soldier. In the early eighties he was writing plays, two of which survive, and a pastoral novel, La Galatea, which was a self-confessed failure. In 1587 he was employed in the provisioning of the 'Invincible Armada', and incurred excommunication for laying hands on some corn which proved to be ecclesiastical property. This, however, was a less uncommon penalty than it might seem, and he was soon released from the Church's ban. A petition for an important post in America failed in 1590; and in the nineties Cervantes was in great poverty and several times in prison, once for failing to produce vouchers for official moneys spent. In 1592 he offered to write six plays at fifty ducats apiece, each to be one of the best ever produced in Spain, but no success came to him till the publication of the first part of Don Quixote in 1604, which brought him instant popularity. Such was the book's success that three pirated editions were produced within a few weeks. How much profit he made by it is not clear; he appeared still to be poor, and in 1610 was again hoping for preferment. But his daughter seems to have had some property, which she would not have got from any other source but her father. So his extreme poverty is by no means established. In 1613 he published a collection of short stories, The Exemplary Novels, an uneven book in which the tales of low life and the satires are as entertaining as the conventional tales of the type of our 'Tale of Foolish Curiosity' are dull. In the preface to the novels he promised a continuation of Quixote, and this was hurried on by the publication of Avellaneda's attempt at a sequel, which, from internal evidence, seems to have found Cervantes engaged on his fifty-ninth chapter. It was published in 1614, and in the next year Cervantes died, 'old, a soldier, a gentleman and poor', as a French visitor found him. But the book was already famous, and the first part translated into English and French.

And now for a few words to the reader who has no Spanish and wonders how much he is missing. There are of course puns and turns of phrase that are untranslatable; there are allusions that a Spaniard would see more readily than an Englishman; but the majority of these are topical and are the subject of long notes in the more ponderous editions of the book. For in this respect Cervantes is as heavily annotated as Shakespeare. The whole of the story is here — or if it is not, the fault is in the translation. The characters' names are best pronounced in the English way. We have grown used to giving Don Quixote our English 'x'; and the guttural Castilian sound was new-fangled in Cervantes' own day, when the x would have been commonly pronounced 'sh', as it is in the French 'Quichotte'. The 'ʒ' in Panʒa and the 'c' in Rocinante sound right in our ears as the English 'ʒ'; in South American Spanish they are pronounced as 's' and in Castilian as 'th'. The rest of the names I have anglicised where possible — Sampson Carrasco, Dorothea, Lucinda, etc. — and the reader is best advised to pronounce them all in the English way, all the more so because the pronunciation of Spanish has changed since Cervantes' time. My only doubt has been in the case of Roland. For the Roland of our story is often not the paladin of Charlemagne, but the Italian hero of Ariosto's poem 'Orlando Furioso'. I have preferred, however, to give him his English name throughout.

And finally, a word on the translation itself. I have taken as few liberties with the text as possible, and tried to adhere to a modern vocabulary and modern word order, except in those passages where the original language is deliberately archaic. I have had to translate most of Sancho's proverbs, though occasionally I have found an English saying sufficiently close to be able to substitute it. My chief difficulties have been in the pastoral narratives, where the language of the original is frequently stilted, and no amount of adaptation can make the story flow very freely. Some of the oaths and expletives have had to be toned down, as in this respect the richness of our vocabulary has been considerably depleted since the seventeenth century, and such a literal rendering as 'By God's hand!', or 'Woe is me!' is now merely funny. We have no doubt lost something by reducing our stock of epithets, but the translator must make do with what remain. As to the interpolated poems I cannot pretend to be happy. One or two of the sonnets have distinction, but most of the pieces are not very good. But, since they are put into the mouths of various characters, we must think of them as incidental only to the story, and not as a serious endeavour at poetry-writing by Cervantes. I have generally taken versions from the older translators, often adapting them, particularly when they are Shelton's: for I do not feel any confidence that my own attempts would be better. But the prefatory verses I have left out, and generally produced my own renderings of the ballads, as I feel that the versions in full rhymes usually quoted make them appear more akin to 'The Inchcape Rock', than to 'King Estmere' or 'Chevy Chase', with which they belong. I have put hardly any notes at the bottom of the page. For I feel that the obscurities are few, and no attempts to explain them do much more than pile up indigestible historical references, that prevent the reader from getting along with the book; which is one of the best adventure stories in the world, and contains two of the greatest characters in all fiction.

January 1947.   J. M. C.

THE ADVENTURES OF
DON QUIXOTE

THE FIRST PART

To the Duke of Bejar

Marquis of Gibraleon, Count of Benalcazar and Bañares, Viscount
of the Town of Alcocer, and Lord of the Towns of Capilla,
Curiel and Burguillos

TRUSTING *in the favourable reception and honour your Excellency accords to all kinds of books, as a Prince so well disposed to welcome the liberal arts, more especially those which, out of nobility, are not abased to the service and profit of the vulgar, I have decided to publish the* Ingenious Gentleman Don Quixote de la Mancha *under the shelter of your Excellency's most illustrious name, begging you with the respect I owe to such greatness to receive him graciously under your protection; so that, although naked of that precious adornment of elegance and erudition in which works composed in the houses of the learned usually go clothed, in your shadow he may safely venture to appear before the judgment of some who, undeterred by their own ignorance, are in the habit of condemning the works of others with more rigour than justice. For when your excellency's wisdom takes account of my good intentions, I trust that you will not disdain the poverty of so humble an offering.*

MIGUEL DE CERVANTES SAAVEDRA

The Adventures of Don Quixote

THE FIRST PART

PROLOGUE

IDLE reader, you can believe without any oath of mine that I would wish this book, as the child of my brain, to be the most beautiful, the liveliest and the cleverest imaginable. But I have been unable to transgress the order of nature, by which like gives birth to like. And so, what could my sterile and ill-cultivated genius beget but the story of a lean, shrivelled, whimsical child, full of varied fancies that no one else has ever imagined – much like one engendered in prison, where every discomfort has its seat and every dismal sound its habitation? Calm, a quiet place, the pleasantness of the fields, the serenity of the skies, the murmuring of streams and the tranquility of the spirit, play a great part in making the most barren muses bear fruit and offer to the world a progeny to fill it with wonder and delight. It may happen that a father has an ugly and ill-favoured child, and that his love for it so blinds his eyes that he cannot see its faults, but takes them rather for talents and beauties, and describes them to his friends as wit and elegance. But I, though in appearance Don Quixote's father, am really his step-father, and so will not drift with the current of custom, nor implore you, almost with tears in my eyes, as others do, dearest reader, to pardon or ignore the faults you see in this child of mine. For you are no relation or friend of his. Your soul is in your own body, and you have free will with the best of them, and are as much a lord in your own house as the King is over his taxes. For you know the old saying: under my cloak a fig for the king – all of which exempts and frees you from every respect and obligation; and so you can say anything you think fit about this story, without fear of being abused for a bad opinion, or rewarded for a good one.

I would have wished to present it to you naked and unadorned, without the ornament of a prologue or the countless train of customary sonnets, epigrams and eulogies it is the fashion to place at the beginnings of books. For I can tell you that, much toil though it cost me to compose, I found none greater than the making of this preface you are reading. Many times I took up my pen to write it, and many times I put it down, not knowing what to say. And once when I was in this quandary, with the paper before me, my pen in my ear, my elbow on the desk and my hand on my cheek, thinking what to write, a lively and very intelligent friend of mine came in unexpectedly and, seeing me so deep in thought, asked me the reason. I did not conceal it, but said that I was thinking about the prologue I had to make for the history of Don Quixote, and that it so troubled me that I was inclined not to write one, and even not to publish the exploits of that noble knight; 'For how could you expect me not to be worried,' I went on, 'at what that ancient lawgiver they call the public will say when it sees me now, after all these years I have been sleeping in the silence of oblivion, come out with all my years on my back, with a tale as dry as a rush, barren of invention, devoid of style, poor in wit and lacking in all learning and instruction, without quotations in the margins or notes at the end of the book; whereas I see other works, never mind how fabulous and profane, so full of sentences from Aristotle, Plato and the whole herd of philosophers, as to impress their readers and get their authors a reputation for wide reading, erudition and eloquence? And when they quote Holy Scripture! You will be bound to say that they are so many St. Thomases or other doctors of the church, observing such an ingenious solemnity in it all that in one line they will depict a distracted lover and in the next preach a little Christian homily, that is a treat and a pleasure to hear or read. My book will lack all this; for I have nothing to quote in the margin or to note at the end. Nor do I even know what authors I am following in it; and so I cannot set their names at the beginning in alphabetical order, as they all do, starting with Aristotle and ending with Xenophon – and Zoilus or Zeuxis, although one of them was a libeller and the other a painter. My book must go without introductory sonnets as well – or at least sonnets, by dukes, marquises, counts, bishops, great ladies or famous poets; although were I to ask two or three friends in the trade, I know that they would give me them; and such good ones as would be unequalled by the productions of the most highly renowned poets in this Spain of ours. In fact, my dear friend,' I continued, 'I have decided that Don Quixote shall stay buried in the archives of La Mancha till Heaven provides someone to adorn him with all the jewels he lacks; for I find myself incapable of supplying them because of my inadequacy and scanty learning, and because I am too spiritless and lazy by nature to go about looking for authors to say for me what I can say myself without them. That is the cause of the perplexity and abstraction you found me in, for there is reason enough for my mood in what I have just told you.'

When my friend had heard me to the end he slapped his forehead and broke into a loud laugh, saying: 'Good Lord, brother, you have just relieved my mind of an error I have been in ever since I have known you, for I have always thought you were sensible and judicious in all your actions. But I see now that you are as far from being so as the sky is from the earth. How is it possible for matters of so little importance and so easily put right to have the power to perplex and preoccupy as ripe an intelligence as yours, so fitted to break down even greater difficulties and trample them underfoot? This does not spring from any lack of ability, I promise you, but from excess of laziness and poverty of resource. Would you like to be convinced that what I say is true? Then listen to me and you will see me confute all your difficulties in the twinkling of an eye, and set right all the defects which, you say, perplex and frighten you into giving up the publication of the history of your famous Don Quixote, light and mirror of all knight errantry.'

'Tell me,' I replied. 'By what means do you propose to fill the void of my fear and reduce the chaos of my confusion to clarity?'

'Your first stumbling block,' he replied, 'the sonnets, epigrams and eulogies which you lack for your introduction, and which should be by important and titled persons, can be got over by your taking a little trouble and writing them yourself. Afterwards you can baptise them and give them any names you like, fathering them on Prester John of the Indies or the Emperor of Trebizond; who, I have heard it rumoured, were famous poets: and even if they were not, and some pedants and graduates turned up to snap and growl

at you behind your back in the name of truth, you need not bother
about them a bit; for even if they convict you of a falsehood, they
cannot cut off the hand you wrote it with.

'As to quoting in the margins the books and authors from whom
you gathered the sentences and sayings you have put in your history, all you have to do is to work in some pat phrases or bits of
Latin that you know by heart, or at least that cost you small pains
to look out. For example, on the subject of liberty and captivity
you might bring in:

'"Non bene pro toto libertas venditur auro."

'And in the margin cite Horace, or whoever said it. Then if you
are writing of the power of death, you might make use of:

'"Pallida mors aequo pulsat pede pauperum tabernas
Regumque turres."

'If you are dealing with friendship and the love God bids you
bear to your enemy, come to the point at once with Holy Scripture, which you can do with a little bit of research by quoting the
words of no less an authority than God himself: "Ego autem dico
vobis: diligite inimicos vestros." If you are on the subject of evil
thoughts, make use of the Gospel: "De corde exeunt cogitationes
malae."

'On the instability of friendship there is Cato, who will give you
his couplet:

'"Donec eris felix, multos numerabis amicos,
Tempora si fuerint nubila, solus eris."

'With these little bits of Latin and such like, they may even take
you for a scholar; and it is no small honour and profit to be one
nowadays. As to putting notes at the end of the book, you may safely
follow this method: if you mention a giant in the text, see that it is
the giant Goliath. And by that alone, which will cost you almost
nothing, you have a grand note, since you can write: *The giant
Goliath or Golias was a Philistine, whom the shepherd David killed
with a sling-shot in the Vale of Terebinth, as is recounted in the Book
of Kings*—in whatever chapter you find it is. After that, to show that
you are learned in the humanities and in cosmography, contrive to
work some mention of the river Tagus into your story, and you
will find yourself at once with another famous note: *The river
Tagus was so called by a king of Spain; it has its source in such a place*

and flows into the Ocean, kissing the walls of the famous city of Lisbon. It is reported to have sands of gold, etc.' If you are writing of thieves I will give you the story of Cacus, which I know by heart; if of prostitutes, there is the Bishop of Mondoñedo, who will assist you with Lamia, Laïs and Flora, and that note will gain you great credit; if of cruel women, Ovid will produce Medea for you; if of witches and sorceresses, Homer has Calypso and Virgil Circe; if of brave commanders, Julius Caesar will lend himself to you in his *Commentaries*, and Plutarch will give you a thousand Alexanders. If you are on the subject of love and have two pennyworth of Italian, you will come across Leon Hebreo, who will give you full measure. But if you do not want to travel into foreign parts, at home you have Fonseca *On the love of God*, which contains everything that you or the cleverest of them could want on the subject. In fact you have nothing more to do but to cite these names in your tale, or touch on the stories I have mentioned, and leave the task of putting in the notes and quotations to me; for I swear I will fill your margins and use up four pages at the end of the book.

'Let us come now to references to authors, which other books contain and yours lacks. The remedy for that is very simple; for you have nothing else to do but look for a book which quotes them all from A to Z, as you say. Then you put this same alphabet into yours. For, granted that the very small need you have to employ them will make your deception transparent, it does not matter a bit; and perhaps there will even be someone silly enough to believe that you have made use of them all in your simple and straightforward story. And if it serves for no other purpose, at least that long catalogue of authors will be useful to lend authority to your book at the outset. Besides, nobody will take the trouble to examine whether you follow your authorities or not, having nothing to gain by it. What is more, if I understand you rightly, this book has no need of any of the things that you say it lacks, for the whole of it is an invective against books of chivalry, which Aristotle never dreamed of, Saint Basil never mentioned, and Cicero never ran across. Nor do the niceties of truth or the calculations of astrology come within the scope of its fabulous narrative; nor is it concerned with geometrical measurements; nor with arguments which can be confuted by rhetoric; nor does it set out to preach to anyone, mingling the human with the divine; which is a kind of motley in which no Christian understanding should be dressed. In what you are writing you have only to make use of imitation, and the more perfect the imitation the better your writing will be. And since this book of yours aims at no more than destroying the authority and influence which books of chivalry have in the world and among the common people, you have no reason to go begging sentences from philosophers, counsel from Holy Writ, fables from poets, speeches from orators, or miracles from saints. You have only to see that your sentences shall come out plain, in expressive, sober and well-ordered language, harmonious and gay, expressing your purpose to the best of your ability, and setting out your ideas without intricacies and obscurities. Be careful too that the reading of your story makes the melancholy laugh and the merry laugh louder; that the simpleton is not confused; that the intelligent admire your invention, the serious do not despise it, nor the prudent withhold their praise. In short, keep your aim steadily fixed on overthrowing the ill-based fabric of these books of chivalry, abhorred by so many yet praised by so many more; for if you achieve that, you will have achieved no small thing.'

I listened in complete silence to my friend's words, and his arguments so impressed themselves on my mind that I accepted them as good without question, and out of them set about framing my prologue. By which, kind reader, you will see his wisdom, and my own good fortune in finding such a counsellor in a time of such need; and yourself be relieved at the straightforward and uncomplicated nature of the history of the famous Don Quixote de la Mancha; who, in the opinion of all the inhabitants of the district around the plain of Montiel, was the chastest lover and the most valiant knight seen in those parts for many a year. I do not want to exaggerate the service I am doing you by introducing to you so notable and honoured a knight. But I do want your thanks for making you acquainted with the famous Sancho Panza, his squire, in whom I think I present to you an epitome of all those squirely humours scattered through the swarm of vain books of chivalry.

And so, God give you health, and may He not forget me.

Farewell.

Chapter 1. Which treats of the quality and way of life of the famous knight Don Quixote de la Mancha.

IN a certain village in La Mancha, which I do not wish to name, there lived not long ago a gentleman – one of those who have always a lance in the rack, an ancient shield, a lean hack and a greyhound for coursing. His habitual diet consisted of a stew, more beef than mutton, of hash most nights, boiled bones on Saturdays, lentils on Fridays, and a young pigeon as a Sunday treat; and on this he spent three-quarters of his income. The rest of it went on a fine cloth doublet, velvet breeches and slippers for holidays, and a homespun suit of the best in which he decked himself on weekdays. His household consisted of a housekeeper of rather more than forty, a niece not yet twenty, and a lad for the field and market, who saddled his horse and wielded the pruning-hook.

Our gentleman was verging on fifty, of tough constitution, lean-bodied, thin-faced, a great early riser and a lover of hunting. They say that his surname was Quixada or Quesada – for there is some difference of opinion amongst authors on this point. However, by very reasonable conjecture we may take it that he was called Quexana. But this does not much concern our story; enough that we do not depart by so much as an inch from the truth in the telling of it.

The reader must know, then, that this gentleman, in the times when he had nothing to do – as was the case for most of the year – gave himself up to the reading of books of knight errantry; which he loved and enjoyed so much that he almost entirely forgot his hunting, and even the care of his estate. So odd and foolish, indeed, did he grow on this subject that he sold many acres of corn-land to buy these books of chivalry to read, and in this way brought home every one he could get. And of them all he considered none so good as the works of the famous Feliciano de Silva. For his brilliant style and those complicated sentences seemed to him very pearls, especially when he came upon those love-passages and challenges frequently written in the manner of: 'The reason for the unreason with which you treat my reason, so weakens my reason

31

that with reason I complain of your beauty'; and also when he read: 'The high heavens that with their stars divinely fortify you in your divinity and make you deserving of the desert that your greatness deserves.'

These writings drove the poor knight out of his wits; and he passed sleepless nights trying to understand them and disentangle their meaning, though Aristotle himself would never have unravelled or understood them, even if he had been resurrected for that sole purpose. He did not much like the wounds that Sir Belianis gave and received, for he imagined that his face and his whole body must have been covered with scars and marks, however skilful the surgeons who tended him. But, for all that, he admired the author for ending his book with the promise to continue with that interminable adventure, and often the desire seized him to take up the pen himself, and write the promised sequel for him. No doubt he would have done so, and perhaps successfully, if other greater and more persistent preoccupations had not prevented him.

Often he had arguments with the priest of his village, who was a scholar and a graduate of Siguenza, as to which was the better knight – Palmerin of England or Amadis of Gaul. But Master Nicholas, the barber of that village, said that no one could compare with the Knight of the Sun. Though if anyone could, it was Sir Galaor, brother of Amadis of Gaul. For he had a very accommodating nature, and was not so affected nor such a sniveller as his brother, though he was not a bit behind him in the matter of bravery.

In short, he so buried himself in his books that he spent the nights reading from twilight till daybreak and the days from dawn till dark; and so from little sleep and much reading, his brain dried up and he lost his wits. He filled his mind with all that he read in them, with enchantments, quarrels, battles, challenges, wounds, wooings, loves, torments and other impossible nonsense; and so deeply did he steep his imagination in the belief that all the fanciful stuff he read was true, that to his mind no history in the world was more authentic. He used to say that the Cid Ruy Diaz must have been a very good knight, but that he could not be compared to the Knight of the Burning Sword, who with a single backstroke had cleft a pair of fierce and monstrous giants in two. And he had an even better opinion of Bernardo del Carpio for slaying the enchanted Roland at Roncesvalles, by making use of Hercules' trick when he throttled the Titan Antaeus in his arms.

He spoke very well of the giant Morgante; for, though one of that giant brood who are all proud and insolent, he alone was affable and well-mannered. But he admired most of all Reynald of Montalban, particularly when he saw him sally forth from his castle and rob everyone he met, and when in heathen lands overseas he stole that idol of Mahomet, which history says was of pure gold. But he would have given his housekeeper and his niece into the bargain, to deal the traitor Galaon a good kicking.

In fact, now that he had utterly wrecked his reason he fell into the strangest fancy that ever a madman had in the whole world. He thought it fit and proper, both in order to increase his renown and to serve the state, to turn knight errant and travel through the world with horse and armour in search of adventures, following in every way the practice of the knights errant he had read of, redressing all manner of wrongs, and exposing himself to chances and dangers, by the overcoming of which he might win eternal honour and renown. Already the poor man fancied himself crowned by the valour of his arm, at least with the empire of Trebizond; and so, carried away by the strange pleasure he derived from these agreeable thoughts, he hastened to translate his desires into action.

The first thing that he did was to clean some armour which had belonged to his ancestors, and had lain for ages forgotten in a corner, eaten with rust and covered with mould. But when he had cleaned and repaired it as best he could, he found that there was one great defect: the helmet was a simple head-piece without a visor. So he ingeniously made good this deficiency by fashioning out of pieces of pasteboard a kind of half-visor which, fitted to the helmet, gave the appearance of a complete head-piece. However, to see if it was strong enough to stand up to the risk of a sword-cut, he took out his sword and gave it two strokes, the first of which demolished in a moment what had taken him a week to make. He was not too pleased at the ease with which he had destroyed it, and to safeguard himself against this danger, reconstructed the visor, putting some strips of iron inside, in such a way as to satisfy himself of his protection; and, not caring to make another trial of it, he

B

accepted it as a fine jointed headpiece and put it into commission.

Next he went to inspect his hack, but though, through leanness, he had more quarters than there are pence in a groat, and more blemishes than Gonella's horse, which was nothing but skin and bone, he appeared to our knight more than the equal of Alexander's Bucephalus and the Cid's Babieca. He spent four days pondering what name to give him; for, he reflected, it would be wrong for the horse of so famous a knight, a horse so good in himself, to be without a famous name. Therefore he tried to fit him with one that would signify what he had been before his master turned knight errant, and what he now was; for it was only right that as his master changed his profession, the horse should change his name for a sublime and high-sounding one, befitting the new order and the new calling he professed. So, after many names invented, struck out and rejected, amended, cancelled and remade in his fanciful mind, he finally decided to call him Rocinante, a name which seemed to him grand and sonorous, and to express the common horse he had been before arriving at his present state : the first and foremost of all hacks in the world.

Having found so pleasing a name for his horse, he next decided to do the same for himself, and spent another eight days thinking about it. Finally he resolved to call himself Don Quixote. And that is no doubt why the authors of this true history, as we have said, assumed that his name must have been Quixada and not Quesada, as other authorities would have it. Yet he remembered that the valorous Amadis had not been content with his bare name, but had added the name of his kingdom and native country in order to make it famous, and styled himself Amadis of Gaul. So, like a good knight, he decided to add the name of his country to his own and call himself Don Quixote de la Mancha. Thus, he thought, he very clearly proclaimed his parentage and native land and honoured it by taking his surname from it.

Now that his armour was clean, his helmet made into a complete head-piece, a name found for his horse, and he confirmed in his new title, it struck him that there was only one more thing to do: to find a lady to be enamoured of. For a knight errant without a lady is like a tree without leaves or fruit and a body without a soul. He said to himself again and again: 'If I for my sins or by good luck were to meet with some giant hereabouts, as generally happens to knights errant, and if I were to overthrow him in the encounter, or cut him down the middle or, in short, conquer him and make him surrender, would it not be well to have someone to whom I could send him as a present, so that he could enter and kneel down before my sweet lady and say in tones of humble submission: "Lady, I am the giant Caraculiambro, lord of the island of Malindrania, whom the never-sufficiently-to-be-praised knight, Don Quixote de la Mancha, conquered in single combat and ordered to appear before your Grace, so that your Highness might dispose of me according to your will"?' Oh, how pleased our knight was when he had made up this speech, and even gladder when he found someone whom he could call his lady. It happened, it is believed, in this way: in a village near his there was a very good-looking farm girl, whom he had been taken with at one time, although she is supposed not to have known it or had proof of it. Her name was Aldonza Lorenzo, and she it was he thought fit to call the lady of his fancies; and, casting around for a name which should not be too far away from her own, yet suggest and imply a princess and great lady, he resolved to call her Dulcinea del Toboso — for she was a native of El Toboso —, a name which seemed to him as musical, strange and significant as those others that he had devised for himself and his possessions.

Chapter II. Which treats of the First Expedition which the ingenious Don Quixote made from his village.

ONCE these preparations were completed, he was anxious to wait no longer before putting his ideas into effect, impelled to this by the thought of the loss the world suffered by his delay, seeing the grievances there were to redress, the wrongs to right, the injuries to amend, the abuses to correct, and the debts to discharge. So, telling nobody of his intention, and quite unobserved, one morning before dawn — it was on one of those sweltering July days — he armed himself completely, mounted Rocinante, put on his badly-mended headpiece, slung on his shield, seized his lance and went out into the plain through the back gate of his yard, pleased and delighted to see with what ease he had started on his fair design. But scarcely was he in open country when he was assailed by a thought so terrible that it almost made him abandon the enterprise he had just begun. For he suddenly remembered that he had never received the honour of knighthood, and so, according to the laws of chivalry, he neither could nor should take arms against any knight, and even if he had been knighted he was bound, as a novice, to wear plain armour without a device on his shield until he should gain one by his prowess. These reflections made him waver in his resolve, but as his madness outweighed any other argument, he made up his mind to have himself knighted by the first man he met, in imitation of many who had done the same, as he had read in the books which had so influenced him. As to plain armour, he decided to clean his own, when he had time, till it was whiter than ermine. With this he quieted his mind and went on his way, taking whatever road his horse chose, in the belief that in this lay the essence of adventure.

As our brand-new adventurer journeyed along, he talked to himself, saying: 'Who can doubt that in ages to come, when the authentic story of my famous deeds comes to light, the sage who writes of them will say, when he comes to tell of my first expedition so early in the morning: "Scarce had the ruddy Apollo spread the golden threads of his lovely hair over the broad and spacious face of the earth, and scarcely had the forked tongues of the little painted birds greeted with mellifluous harmony the coming of the rosy Aurora who, leaving the soft bed of her jealous husband, showed herself at the doors and balconies of the Manchegan horizon, when the famous knight, Don Quixote de la Mancha, quitting the slothful down, mounted his famous steed Rocinante and began to journey across the ancient and celebrated plain of Montiel"?' That was, in fact, the road that our knight actually took, as he went on: 'Fortunate the age and fortunate the times in which my famous deeds shall come to light, deeds worthy to be engraved in bronze, carved in marble and painted on wood, as a memorial for posterity. And you, sage enchanter, whoever you may be, to whose lot it falls to be the chronicler of this strange history, I beg you not to forget my good Rocinante, my constant companion on all my rides and journeys!' And presently he cried again, as if he had really been in love: 'O Princess Dulcinea, mistress of this captive heart! You did me great injury in dismissing me and inflicting on me the cruel rigour of your command not to appear in your beauteous presence. Deign, lady, to be mindful of your captive heart, which suffers such griefs for love of you.'

He went on stringing other nonsense on to this, all after the fashion he had learnt in his reading, and imitating the language of his books at best he could. And all the while he rode so slowly and the sun's heat increased so fast that it would have been enough to turn his brain, if he had had any. Almost all that day he rode without encountering anything of note, which reduced him to despair, for he longed to meet straightway someone against whom he could try the strength of his strong arm.

There are authors who say that the first adventure he met was that of the pass of Lapice. Others say it was the windmills. But what I have been able to discover of the matter and what I have found written in the annals of La Mancha, is that he rode all that day, and that at nightfall his horse and he were weary and dying of hunger. Looking in all directions to see if he could discover any castle or shepherd's hut where he could take shelter and supply his urgent needs, he saw, not far from the road he was travelling on, an inn, which seemed to him like a star to guide him to the gates, if not to the palace, of his redemption. So he hurried on, and reached it just as night was falling. Now there chanced to be standing at the inn door two young women *of easy virtue*, as they are called, who were on the way to Seville with some carriers who happened to have taken up their quarters at the inn that evening. As everything that our adventurer thought, saw or imagined seemed to follow the fashion of his reading, as soon as he saw the inn he convinced himself that it was a fortress with its four towers and pinnacles of shining silver, complete with a drawbridge, a deep moat and all those appurtenances with which such castles are painted. So he approached the inn, which to his mind was a castle, and when still a short distance away reined Rocinante in, expecting some dwarf to mount the battlements and sound a trumpet to announce that a knight was approaching the fortress. But when he saw that there was some delay, and that Rocinante was in a hurry to get to the stable, he went up to the inn door and, seeing the two young women standing there, took them for two beauteous maidens or graceful ladies taking the air at the castle gate. Now at that very moment, as chance would have it, a swineherd was collecting from the stubble a drove of hogs – pardon me for naming them – and blew his horn to call them together. But Don Quixote immediately interpreted this in his own way, as some dwarf giving notice of his approach. So with rare pleasure he rode up, whereupon those ladies, thoroughly frightened at seeing a man come towards them dressed in armour with lance and shield, turned to go back into the inn. But Don Quixote, gathering from their flight that they were afraid, raised his pasteboard visor, partly revealing his lean and dusty face, and addressed them with a charming expression and in a calm voice: 'I beg you, ladies, not to fly, nor to fear any outrage; for it ill fits or suits the order of chivalry which I profess to injure anyone, least of all maidens of such rank as your appearance proclaims you to be.'

The girls stared at him, trying to get a look at his face, which was almost covered by the badly made visor. But when they heard themselves called maidens – a title ill-suited to their profession – they could not help laughing, which stung Don Quixote into re-plying: 'Civility befits the fair; and laughter arising from trivial causes is, moreover, great folly. I do not say this to offend you nor to incur your displeasure, for I have no other wish than to serve you.'

His language, which was unintelligible to them, and the uncouth figure our knight cut, made the ladies laugh the more. Whereat he flew into a rage, and things would have gone much farther, had not the innkeeper, a very fat man and therefore very peaceable, emerged at this moment. Now when he saw this grotesque figure in his equipment of lance, shield and coat of armour, which sorted so ill with his manner of riding, he was on the point of joining the young women in their demonstrations of amusement. But, fearing such a collection of armaments, he decided to speak politely, and addressed him thus: 'If your worship is looking for lodging, Sir Knight, except for a bed – we have none in this inn – you will find plenty of everything.'

And Don Quixote replied, seeing the humility of the warden of the fortress – for such he took the innkeeper to be: 'For me, Sir Castellan, whatever you have is enough. My ornaments are arms, my rest the bloody fray.'

The host thought that he had called him castellan because he took him for a safe man from Castile, though he was an Andalusian from the Strand of San Lucar, as thievish as Cacus and as tricky as a student or a page. So he replied: 'At that rate, your bed shall be the cruel rock, your sleep to watch till day, and that being so, you can safely dismount here in the certainty that you will find in this house ample reason for lying awake not only for one night but for a whole year.'

As he spoke he went to take Don Quixote's stirrup, and our knight dismounted with great labour and difficulty, as he had fasted all day. He then bade the host take good care of his steed, saying that no better piece of horseflesh munched oats in all the world. The innkeeper stared at the beast, which did not seem as good as Don Quixote said, not by a half. However, he put him up in the stable and, when he came back for his guest's orders, he found that the maidens had made it up with him and were taking off his armour. But although they had got off his breast-plate and back-piece, they had no idea how to get him out of his gorget, nor how to take off his counterfeit head-piece, which was tied with green ribbons that would have to be cut, as they could not undo the knot. But to this he would on no account agree, and so he stayed all that night with his helmet on, cutting the strangest and most ridiculous figure imaginable. And whilst he was being disarmed, imagining that these draggled and loose creatures were illustrious ladies and the mistresses of that castle, he addressed them most gracefully:

> 'Never was there knight
> By ladies so attended
> As was Don Quixote
> When he left his village.
> Maidens waited on him,
> On his horse, princesses –

or Rocinante, which, dear ladies, is the name of my horse, and Don Quixote de la Mancha is mine. For, although I did not wish to reveal myself till deeds done in your service and for your benefit do so for me, the need to adapt this old ballad of Lancelot to the present occasion has betrayed my name to you before the due season. But the time will come when your ladyships may command me and I shall obey; and the valour of my arms will then disclose the desire I have to serve you.'

The girls, who were not used to hearing such high-flown language, did not say a word in reply, but only asked whether he would like anything to eat.

'I would gladly take some food,' replied Don Quixote, 'for I think there is nothing that would come more opportunely.'

That day happened to be a Friday, and there was no food in the inn except some portions of a fish that is called pollack in Castile and cod in Andalusia, in some parts ling and in other troutlet. They asked whether his worship would like some troutlet, as there was no other fish to eat.

'So long as there are plenty of troutlet they may serve me for one trout,' replied Don Quixote, 'for I had just as soon be paid eight separate *reals* as an eight *real* piece. What is more, these troutlet may be like veal, which is better than beef, or kid, which is better than goats' meat. But, however that may be, let me have it now, for the toil and weight of arms cannot be borne without due care for the belly.'

They set the table for him at the inn door for coolness' sake, and the host brought him a portion of badly soaked and worse cooked salt cod with some bread as black and grimy as his armour. It made them laugh a great deal to see him eat because, as he kept his helmet on and his visor up, he could get nothing into his mouth with his own hands, and required someone's assistance to put it in; and so one of those ladies performed this task for him. But to give him anything to drink would have been impossible if the innkeeper had not bored a reed, put one end into his mouth and poured the wine into the other. All this he bore with patience rather than break the ribbons of his helmet.

While they were thus occupied there happened to come to the inn a hog-gelder, and as he arrived he blew his reed whistle four or five times; which finally convinced Don Quixote that he was at some famous castle, that they were entertaining him with music, that the pollack was trout, the black bread of the whitest flour, the whores ladies and the innkeeper warden of the castle. This made him feel that his resolution and his expedition had been to good purpose, but what distressed him most deeply was that he was not yet knighted, for he believed that he could not rightfully embark on any adventure without first receiving the order of knighthood.

Chapter III. *Which tells of the pleasant method by which Don Quixote chose to be knighted.*

So, troubled by these thoughts, he cut short his scanty pothouse supper, and when he was done called the host. Then, shutting the stable door on them both, he fell on his knees before him and said: 'Never will I arise from where I am, valiant knight, till you grant me of your courtesy the boon I am going to beg of you; it is one which will redound to your praise and to the benefit of the human race.'

Seeing his guest at his feet and hearing such language, the innkeeper stared in confusion, not knowing what to do or say, and pressed him to get up; but in vain, for the knight refused to rise until his host had promised to grant him the boon he begged.

'I expected no less from your great magnificence, dear sir,' replied Don Quixote. 'So I will tell you that the boon I begged of you, and you in your generosity granted, is that you will knight me on the morning of to-morrow. This night I will watch my arms in the chapel of this castle of yours, and to-morrow, as I said, my dearest wish will be fulfilled, and I shall have the right to ride through all quarters of the world in search of adventures, for the benefit of the distressed, according to the obligations of knight-hood and of knights errant like myself, whose minds are given to such exploits.'

The innkeeper, who, as we have said, was pretty crafty and had already a suspicion that his guest was wrong in the head, was confirmed in his belief when he heard this speech, and, to make some sport for that night, decided to fall in with his humour. So he told him that he was doing a very proper thing in craving the boon he did, and that such a proposal was right and natural in a knight as illustrious as he seemed and his gallant demeanour showed him to be. He added that he, too, in the day of his youth had devoted himself to that honourable profession and travelled in divers parts of the world in search of adventures, not omitting to visit the Fish Market of Malaga, the Isles of Riaran, the Compass of Seville, the Little Market Place at Segovia, the Olive Grove at Valencia, the Circle of Granada, the Strand of San Lucar, the Colt-fountain of Cordova, the Taverns of Toledo and sundry other places, where he had exercised the agility of his heels and the lightness of his fingers, doing many wrongs, wooing many widows, ruining sundry maidens and cheating a few minors – in fact, making himself well-known in almost all the police-courts and law-courts in Spain. Finally he had retired to this castle, where he lived on his own estate and other people's, welcoming all knights errant of whatever quality and condition, only for the great love he bore them – and to take a share of their possessions in payment for his kindness.

He added that there was no chapel in the castle where he could watch his arms, for it had been pulled down to be rebuilt. But he knew that a vigil might be kept in any place whatever in case of need. So that night he might watch his arms in a courtyard of the castle, and in the morning, God willing, the due ceremonies might be performed, and he emerge a full knight, as much a knight as any in the whole world. He asked him if he had any money with him, and Don Quixote replied that he had not a penny, since he had never read in histories concerning knights errant of any knight that had. At this the innkeeper said that he was wrong: for, granted that it was not mentioned in the histories, because their authors could see no need of mentioning anything so obvious and necessary to take with one as money and clean shirts, that was no reason for supposing that knights did not carry them. In fact, he might take it for an established fact that all knights errant, of whom so many histories were stuffed full, carried purses well lined against all eventualities, and also took with them clean shirts and a little box full of ointments to cure the wounds they got. For on the plains and deserts where they fought and got their wounds they had not always someone at hand to cure them, unless of course they had some magician for a friend. A sorcerer, of course, might relieve them at once by bearing through the air on a cloud some maiden or dwarf with a flask of water of such virtue that after tasting a single drop they were immediately cured of their sores and wounds, and it was as if they had never had any injuries. However, in default of this, the knights of old made certain that their squires were provided with money and other necessaries, such as lint and ointment, to dress their wounds. But when such knights chanced to have no squires – there were only a few rare instances – they carried it all themselves on the cruppers of their horses in bags so very thin that they hardly showed, as though they contained something of even more importance. For, except for such purposes, the carrying of bags was not tolerated among knights errant. So he advised Don Quixote – though as his godson, which he was so soon to be, he might even command him – not to travel in future without money and the other requisites he had mentioned, and he would see how useful they would prove when he least expected it.

Don Quixote promised to do exactly as he recommended, and promptly received his instructions as to keeping watch over his armour in a great yard which lay on one side of the inn. He gathered all the pieces together and laid them on a stone trough, which stood beside a well. Then, buckling on his shield, he seized his lance and began to pace jauntily up and down before the trough. And just as he began his watch, night began to fall.

The innkeeper told everyone staying in the inn of his guest's craziness, of the watching of the armour, and of the knighting he was expecting; and, wondering at this strange form of madness, they came out to observe him from a distance, and watched him, sometimes pacing up and down with a peaceful look and sometimes leaning on his lance and gazing on his armour, without taking his eyes off it for a considerable time. Night had now fallen, but the moon was so bright that she might have rivalled the orb that lent her his light; so that whatever the novice knight did was clearly visible to all. Just then it occurred to one of the carriers who was staying at the inn to go and water his mules, and to do this he found it necessary to remove Don Quixote's armour, which lay on the trough. But the knight, seeing him draw near, addressed him in a loud voice: 'You, whoever you are, rash knight, who come to touch the armour of the most valorous errant that ever girt on a sword, take heed what you do. Do not touch it unless you wish to lose your life in payment for your temerity.'

The carrier paid no attention to this speech – it would have been better if he had regarded it, for he would have been regarding his own safety – but, laying hold of the straps, threw the armour some distance from him. At this sight Don Quixote raised his eyes to heaven, and addressing his thoughts, as it seemed, to his lady Dulcinea, cried: 'Assist me, lady, in the first affront offered to this enraptured heart! Let not your favour and protection fail me in this first trial!'

And, uttering these words and others like them, he loosened his shield and, raising his lance in both hands, dealt his adversary a mighty blow on the head with it, which threw him to the ground so injured that, if it had been followed by a second, the carrier would have had no use for a surgeon to cure him. This done, Don Quixote gathered his arms together again and paced up and down once more with the same composure as before.

A little later a second carrier, not knowing what had happened since the first man still lay stunned, came out with the same intention of watering his mules. But, just as he was going to clear the armour from the trough, Don Quixote, without uttering a word or begging anyone's favour, loosened his shield again, once more raised his lance and made more than three pieces of the second carrier's head – for he opened it in four places – without damage to his weapon. At the noise all the people in the inn rushed out, among them the innkeeper. Whereupon Don Quixote buckled on his shield and, putting his hand to his sword, cried: 'O beauteous lady, strength and vigour of this enfeebled heart! Now is the time to turn your illustrious eyes on this your captive knight, who is awaiting so great an adventure.'

With this it seemed to him that he gained so much courage that if all the carriers in the world had attacked him he would not have yielded a foot. When the fellows of the wounded men saw them in that plight they began to shower stones on Don Quixote from some way off. He protected himself from them as best he could with his shield, but dared not leave the trough, for fear of abandoning his armour. And the innkeeper shouted to them to leave him alone, for he had already told them that he was a madman and, being mad, would go scot-free, even though he killed them all.

Don Quixote shouted also, even louder, calling them cowards and traitors, and swearing that the lord of the castle must be a despicable and base-born knight for allowing knights errant to be so treated, and that if he had received the order of knighthood he would have made him sensible of his perfidy.

'But of you, base and vile rabble, I take no account,' he cried. 'Throw stones! Come on, attack! Assail me as hard as you can, and you will see what penalty you have to pay for your insolent folly!'

He spoke with such spirit and boldness that he struck a lively terror into all who heard him; and for that reason, as much as for the innkeeper's persuasions, they stopped pelting him. Then Don Quixote allowed them to remove the wounded, and returned to watch his arms with the same quiet assurance as before.

Now the innkeeper had begun to dislike his guest's pranks, and decided to cut the matter short and give him his wretched order of knighthood immediately, before anything else could go wrong. So he apologized for the insolence with which those low fellows had behaved without his knowledge, adding, however, that they had been soundly punished for their audacity. And seeing, as he had said before, that there was no chapel in that castle, there was no need, he declared, for the rest of the ceremony; for, according to his knowledge of the ceremonial of the order, the whole point of conferring knighthood lay in the blow on the neck and the stroke on the shoulder, and that could be performed in the middle of a field. And Don Quixote had already more than fulfilled the duty of the watching of arms, for he had been more than four hours on vigil, whereas all that was required was a two hours' watch.

Don Quixote believed all this, and said he was ready to obey him. He begged him to conclude the matter as briefly as possible; for if he were again attacked, once knighted, he was resolved to leave no one alive in the castle, except such as he might spare at the castellan's bidding, and out of regard for him.

Forewarned and apprehensive, the castellan then brought out the book in which he used to enter the carriers' accounts for straw and barley. Then, followed by a boy carrying a candle-end and by the two maidens already mentioned, he went up to Don Quixote and ordered him to kneel. Next, reading out of his manual, as if he were reciting some devout prayer, in the middle of his reading he raised his hand and dealt the knight a sound blow on the neck, followed by a handsome stroke on the back with the Don's own sword, all the while muttering in his teeth as if in prayer. When this was over he bade one of the ladies gird on Don Quixote's sword, which she did with great agility and some discretion, no small amount of which was necessary to avoid bursting with laughter at each stage of the ceremony. But what they had already seen of the new knight's prowess kept their mirth within bounds. And as she girt on his sword the good lady said: 'God make your worship a fortunate knight and give you good luck in your battles.'

Don Quixote asked her to tell him her name, as he wished to know in future days to whom he owed the favour received, for he meant to confer on her some part of the honour he was to win by the strength of his arm. She replied very humbly that her name was La Tolosa, and that she was the daughter of a cobbler in Toledo who lived among the stalls of Sancho Bienaya, adding that, where-ever she might be, she was at his service and he should be her master. Don Quixote begged her, in reply, as a favour to him, henceforth to take the title of lady and call herself Doña Tolosa, which she promised to do. The other lady then put on his spurs, and his conversation with her was almost the same as with the lady of the sword. He asked her her name, and she replied that she was called La Molinera, and that she was the daughter of an honest miller in Antequera. The Don requested her also to take the title of lady and call herself Doña Molinera, renewing his offers of service and favours.

Now that these unprecedented ceremonies had been hurried through post-haste and at top speed, Don Quixote was impatient to be on horseback and to ride out in search of adventures. So, saddling Rocinante at once, he mounted; then, embracing his host, he thanked him for the favour of knighting him in such extrava-gant terms that it is impossible to write them down faithfully. The innkeeper, once he saw him safely out of the inn, replied to his speech rather more briefly but in no less high-flown terms and, without even asking him to pay the cost of his lodging, was heartily glad to see him go.

Chapter IV. *What happened to our Knight when he left the Inn.*

IT must have been daybreak when Don Quixote left the inn, so pleased, so gay, so enraptured at being now a knight that his joy seemed likely to burst his horse's girths. But, calling to mind his host's advice about the essential provisions he must carry, especially money and clean shirts, he decided to go home and provide himself with them all, and with a squire as well. He reckoned to take into his service a neighbour of his, a poor labourer who had a large family, but was very suitable for the part of squire in chivalry. With this in mind he turned Rocinante for home, and the horse, as if he smelled his home pastures, began to trot with such zest that his feet seemed not to touch the ground.

He had not gone far when from a thicket on the right he heard a faint voice, raised, so it seemed to him, in complaint; and no sooner did he hear this than he cried: 'I thank Heaven for granting this favour and giving me so prompt an opportunity to perform the duty I owe to my order, and whereby I may be able to gather the fruit of my honourable desires. These cries come no doubt from some man or woman in distress, and in need of my protection and assistance.'

Then, turning his reins, he guided Rocinante towards the place from which the voice seemed to come; and, when he had ridden a little way into the wood, he saw a mare tied to an oak, and tied to another a lad of about fifteen, naked to the waist. It was he who was shouting, and with good reason, for a well-built countryman was flogging him soundly with a belt, and accompanying each blow with mingled scolding and advice, crying: 'Keep your tongue still and your eyes open.'

To which the boy replied: 'I won't do it again, sir. I swear to God I won't do it again. I promise I'll take better care of your sheep in future.'

When Don Quixote saw what was happening he exclaimed in an angry voice: 'Discourteous knight, it is unseemly to attack a defenceless person. Mount your steed, and take your lance' – for the other also had a lance leaning against the oak to which his mare was tied – 'and I will teach you that you are acting like a coward.'

When the countryman saw this figure in full armour come at him brandishing his lance over his head, he gave himself up for dead and answered mildly: 'Sir Knight, this lad I am punishing is my servant. His job is to watch a herd of sheep that I keep around here. But he is so careless that every day I lose one. And because I'm punishing him for his carelessness or his roguery he says I'm doing it through meanness, so as not to have to pay him his due wages. But I swear to God and on my life he's lying.'

'Lying, you say, and in my presence, you wretched boor?' said

Don Quixote. 'By the sun that shines on us, I have a good mind to run you through with this lance. Pay him now and without another word. If you do not, by God who rules us, I will despatch you and annihilate you this very minute. Untie him immediately!'

The farmer bowed his head, and without replying untied his lad, whom Don Quixote asked how much his master owed him. He answered, for nine months at seven *reals* a month. Don Quixote calculated, and found that it came to sixty-three *reals*, whereupon he told the countryman to disburse them immediately, unless he wished to pay with his life. The farmer, in a fright, swore by his present plight and the oath he had taken – though he had not taken any oath – that it did not come to so much, because they must deduct from the reckoning three pairs of shoes he had given him, and a *real* paid for two blood-lettings, when he was sick.

'That is quite right,' Don Quixote answered. 'But set the shoes and the blood-lettings against the undeserved flogging you have given him. For, if he broke the leather of the shoes you gave him, you have broken the skin of his body and, if the barber let his blood when he was sick, you have done the same now, when he is well. So on that score he owes you nothing.'

'The trouble is, Sir Knight, that I have no money here. If Andrew will come home with me I will pay him every *real*.'

'I go home with him?' said the lad. 'Oh Lord, no, sir! Not on your life! Because if I went alone he would flay me like St. Bartholomew.'

'He will do no such thing,' replied Don Quixote. 'I have only to lay my command on him, and he will respect it; and on condition that he gives me his oath on the order of knighthood which he has received, I shall let him go free and will guarantee the payment.'

'Think what you are saying, your worship,' said the lad. 'This master of mine isn't a knight, and hasn't received any order of chivalry. He is the rich John Haludo, and lives at Quintanar.'

'That is no matter,' replied Don Quixote, 'for there may be knights in the Haludo family. It is very probable, for every man is the child of his own works.'

'That's quite right,' said Andrew, 'but this master of mine, what works is he the child of, when he refuses me wages for my sweat and labour?'

'I don't refuse them, Andrew my friend,' replied the farmer. 'Do me the favour of coming with me, and I swear by all the orders of chivalry in the world to pay you every single *real*, and perfumed into the bargain.'

'The perfuming I excuse you,' said Don Quixote, 'Give it him in *reals* and I shall be satisfied. But take care that you do what you have sworn, or else, by the same oath, I swear I will come back and look for you and punish you; and I shall find you, even if you hide better than a lizard. And if you wish to know who lays this command on you, so that you may feel the more strictly bound to obey it, know that I am the valorous Don Quixote de la Mancha, the redresser of wrongs and injuries. God be with you, and do not be unmindful of what you have promised under oath, on pain of the penalty pronounced.'

As he spoke he spurred Rocinante, and in a short while had left them. The farmer followed him with his eyes; and when he saw that he had left the wood and was out of sight, returned to his servant and said: 'Come here, my lad. I want to pay you what I owe you, as that redresser of wrongs ordered me to.'

'I swear you will,' said Andrew. 'Indeed you had better comply with that good knight's commands, God bless him! For he is such a brave man and such a fair judge that, by my life, if you don't pay me, he will come back and do what he said.'

'I swear I will, too,' said the countryman, 'but to show you how much I love you, I want to increase the debt, so that I can increase the payment.'

Then, grasping him by the arm, he tied him up once more to the tree and flogged him so soundly that he left him for dead.

'Now, Master Andrew,' said he, 'call on that redresser of wrongs, and he won't redress this one, you'll see. Though I have not finished yet, I think, for I have a mind to flay you alive, as you feared.'

But at last he untied him and gave him leave to go and look for his judge to execute the sentence he had pronounced. Andrew set off in a fury, swearing to go and find the valorous Don Quixote de la Mancha and tell him exactly what had happened. Then his master would have to pay him sevenfold. But for all that, he wept as he went, and his master remained behind laughing; and thus did the valorous Don Quixote redress that wrong.

He rode on, however, highly delighted at what had passed, for it seemed to him that he had made a most happy and glorious beginning in his knight errantry; and, very pleased with himself, he repeated half aloud as he he made his way towards his village: 'Well may you call yourself fortunate above all women living on earth to-day, O Dulcinea del Toboso, more beautiful than all beauties, since it has fallen to your lot to hold as a humble subject to your least desire and pleasure so valiant and famous a knight as is and shall be Don Quixote de la Mancha, who yesterday, as all the world knows, received the order of knighthood and to-day has righted the greatest injury and wrong that injustice could invent or cruelty perpetrate. To-day he wrested the scourge from the hand of the pitiless enemy who was so undeservedly whipping that delicate infant.'

He now came to a place where the road divided into four, and there immediately leapt into his mind those crossways where knights errant used to stop to consider which of the roads they should take. So, following their example, he halted a moment, and after deep thought let go the reins, submitting his will to Rocinante, who followed his first instinct, which was to take the road towards his stable. When he had gone about two miles Don Quixote sighted a large crowd of people who, as he afterwards learnt, were merchants from Toledo going to buy silks in Murcia. There were six of them, riding beneath their sunshades, with four servants, all on horseback, and three muleteers on foot. As soon as Don Quixote saw them in the distance he imagined this to be matter for some new adventure, and it seemed to him that here was just the right opportunity to make the closest possible imitation of the encounters he had read of in his books. So with a gallant and resolute air he steadied himself in his stirrups, grasped his lance, covered his breast with his shield and, taking up his position in the middle of the road, awaited the arrival of those knights errant; for such he had already decided they were. So when they arrived within sight and earshot Don Quixote raised his voice, and called out in an arrogant tone: 'Let the whole world stand, if the whole world does not confess that there is not in the whole world a more beauteous maiden than the Empress of la Mancha, the peerless Dulcinea del Toboso.'

The merchants stopped when they heard this speech, and saw the strange figure who made it; and both from his appearance and his words they divined that the speaker was mad. But wanting to know more fully what this confession that he required of them really meant, one of them, who was a bit of a joker and very sharp-witted, said: 'Sir Knight, we do not know who this good lady is that you speak of. Show her to us and, if she is as beauteous as you say, we will most willingly and without any pressure acknowledge the truth demanded of us by you.'

'If I were to show her to you,' replied Don Quixote, 'what merit would there be in your confessing so obvious a truth? The essence of the matter is that you must believe, confess, affirm, swear and maintain it without seeing her. If you will not, you must do battle with me, monstrous and proud crew. Now come on! One by one, as the law of chivalry requires, or all together, as is the custom and evil practice of men of your breed. Here I stand and await you, confident in the right which I have on my side.'

'Sir Knight,' replied the merchant, 'I beg your worship in the name of all these princes here present that you will kindly show us a portrait of this lady, even one no bigger than a grain of wheat; because we would not burden our consciences by testifying to something that we have never seen or heard and, what is more, something so detrimental to the Empresses and Queens of Alcarria and Estremadura. For the skein can be judged by the thread, and we shall rest assured and satisfied with this, and your worship will be pleased and content. I even think that we are so far inclined to her side already that supposing your portrait shows us that she squints in one eye and drips vermilion and sulphur from the other, even then, to please you, we will say all that you ask in her favour.'

'Her eyes do not drip, vile scoundrels!' replied Don Quixote in great fury. 'Her eyes do not drip what you say, but ambergris and civet. She is not squinting or humpbacked, but straighter than a spindle of Guadarrama. And you shall pay for the blasphemy you have spoken against such transcendent beauty as my lady's.'

With these words he couched his lance and ran at the man who

had spoken with such rage and fury that, if Rocinante had not fortunately stumbled and fallen in the road, things would have gone
badly for the rash merchant. Rocinante fell, and his master went
rolling some distance over the plain; but when he tried to get up
it was in vain, so encumbered was he by his lance, shield, spurs and
helmet, together with the weight of his ancient armour. And, whilst
he was struggling to get up and could not, he kept shouting: 'Fly
not, you coward brood! Stay, you slavish crew! It is not my fault,
but my horse's, that I lie here.'

One of their muleteers who was not very good-natured, hearing
the arrogant language of the poor man on the ground, could not
refrain from dealing him an answer in the ribs; and going up to
him, snatched his lance, and broke it in pieces. Then he began to
give our Don Quixote such a beating with one of the bits that, in
spite of his armour, he pounded him like wheat in a mill. The lad's
masters shouted to him not to beat the knight so hard and to let
him alone; but he was irritated, and would not give up the game
till he had completely vented his rage. So, picking up the other bits
of the lance, he broke them all over the poor prostrate knight, who,
beneath all that storm of blows which rained on him, never once
closed his mouth, but howled continuous threats to heaven and
earth against those brigands, as he took them to be. At last the lad
tired himself out, and the merchants went on their way with enough
to talk about for the rest of the journey on the subject of that poor
belaboured gentleman. Now, when Don Quixote found himself
alone, he tried once more to see if he could rise. But if he could not
do so when he was hale and well, how could he now that he was so
pounded and almost destroyed? Yet, for all this, he reckoned himself fortunate. For it seemed to him that this was a disaster peculiar
to knights errant, and he attributed it entirely to the fault of his
horse. But it was impossible for him to get up, his whole body was
so battered.

Chapter v. Continuing the story of our Knight's Disaster.

SEEING then that he was in fact unable to stir, it occurred to him
to resort to his usual remedy, which was to think of some passage
in his books. Whereupon his madness called into his mind that part

of the story of the Marquis of Mantua, when Carloto left Baldwin wounded on the mountain, a tale familiar to children, not unknown to youth, and enjoyed and even believed by old men, though for all that no truer than the miracles of Mahomet. It seemed to him to fit his present plight to a T; and so he began to roll about on the ground with every sign of intense pain and to repeat in a languishing voice those words which are attributed to the wounded Knight of the Wood:

> Oh, where are you, my lady,
> That you grieve not for my plight?
> Either you know not of it
> Or else you are faithless and light.

He went on with the ballad in this way till he came to the lines which go:

> O noble Marquis of Mantua,
> My uncle and natural lord!

As chance would have it, when he came to this verse a labourer of his own village, a neighbour of his, passed on his way to take a load of wheat to the mill and, seeing a man lying on the ground, went up and asked him who he was and what it was that made him groan so sadly. Now Don Quixote firmly believed that this was the Marquis of Mantua, his uncle, and so made him no answer, but went on with his quotation, giving an account of his misfortune and of his wife's intrigue with the Emperor's son, all in the words of the ballad. The labourer was astonished at hearing this nonsense and, taking off the knight's visor, which was now battered to pieces from the beating, wiped his dust-covered face and immediately recognized him.

'Master Quixada,' he cried – this must have been his name before he lost his senses and changed himself from a quiet gentleman into a knight errant – 'who has put your worship in this plight?'

But he answered every question by going on with his ballad. Therefore the good man took off his back- and breast-plates, as best he could, to see if he had any wounds. But he saw no blood nor sign of any hurt. Then he tried to get him up from the ground, and with a great effort heaved him on to his own ass, which seemed to him the quieter mount. And gathering up his arms, even to the splinters of his lance, he tied them on Rocinante and, leading him by the bridle and his ass by the halter, took the road for the village,

much concerned to hear the nonsense that Don Quixote was talking. Our knight was no less concerned, being too bruised and
battered to stay on the ass, and from time to time he breathed
groans deep enough to reach heaven, so that his neighbour was
compelled to ask him again what pain he felt. Now it must have
been the Devil himself who put into his mind stories applicable to
his plight; for at that instant he forgot Baldwin and remembered
the Moor Abindarraez, when the governor of Antequera, Rodrigo
de Narvaez, captured him and held him prisoner in his castle. So
that when the labourer asked him once more how he was, and how
he felt, he replied in the very words and phrases in which the
captive Abencerrage answered Rodrigo de Narvaez, as he had read
the story in Jorge Montemayor's *Diana*, applying it so appositely
that the labourer wished himself to the Devil for having to listen
to such a pack of rubbish. Realizing now that his neighbour was
mad, he made haste to the village, to be quit of the nuisance of
listening to Don Quixote's harangue; at the close of which the
knight exclaimed: 'Be it known to your worship, Don Rodrigo de
Narvaez, that this beauteous Xarifa I mentioned is now the fair
Dulcinea del Toboso, for whom I have done, am doing and shall
do the most famous deeds of chivalry that the world has ever seen,
can see or will see.'

To which the labourer replied: 'Look you, your worship, as I am
a sinner, I am not Don Rodrigo de Narvaez, nor the Marquis of
Mantua, but your neighbour Pedro Alonzo. And your worship is
not Baldwin or Abindarraez, but that worthy gentleman Master
Quixada.'

'I know who I am,' replied Don Quixote, 'and I know, too,
that I am capable of being not only the characters I have named,
but all the Twelve Peers of France and all the Nine Worthies as
well, for my exploits are far greater than all the deeds they have
done, all together and each by himself.'

They were deep in such conversation when they reached the
village at nightfall. But the labourer waited till it was rather darker,
so that no one should see the battered gentleman on so shameful a
mount. When he thought it was the proper time he entered the
village, and went to Don Quixote's house, which he found in a
great uproar. The priest was there and the village barber, great

friends of Don Quixote's, and his housekeeper was addressing them at the top of her voice: 'What do you think, Doctor Pero Perez' – for that was the priest's name – 'of my master's misfortune? It is three days now he has not been seen, nor his horse, nor his shield, nor his lance, nor his armour either! Oh dear! Oh dear! What can I think? It is the truth, as sure as I was born to die, that these cursed books of knight errantry of his, that he is always reading, have turned his brain. For now I come to think of it, I have often heard him talking to himself about turning knight errant and going about in those worlds in search of adventures. Satan and Barabbas take all such books for ruining the finest understanding there was in all La Mancha.'

The niece said much the same and something more: 'You know, Master Nicholas,' – for that was the barber's name – 'it has very often happened that dear uncle has gone on reading those soulless books of misadventures for two days and nights on end. Then, when he has finished, he will fling his book down, draw his sword and go slashing the walls; and when he is exhausted he will say that he has killed four giants as tall as towers, and that the sweat that is pouring from him out of exhaustion is blood from the wounds he has got in the battle. Then he will drink a great jug of cold water and lie quiet and easy, saying that the water is a most precious draught which the sage Esquife has brought him, a great magician and a friend of his. But I am to blame for all this, because I did not tell your worships of my dear uncle's follies, so that you could have cured him before he got so far, and burnt all those cursed books. For he has a great many which well deserve to be burnt, just as much as if they were heretics.'

'I agree with that,' said the priest, 'and I swear that to-morrow shall not pass without a public inquisition being held over them. And let them be condemned to the flames, so that they shall not cause others who read them to imitate our good friend.'

The labourer, who with Don Quixote overheard all this, was confirmed in his belief that his neighbour was deranged, and so began to shout: 'Open, your worships, to Sir Baldwin and to the Lord Marquis of Mantua, who comes sore wounded, and to Master Moor Abindarraez, whom the valorous Rodrigo de Narvaez, governor of Antequera, brings captive.'

At this noise they all went out and, recognizing their friend, master and uncle, ran to embrace him, though he had not yet dismounted from his ass, because he could not. But he cried: 'Stop, all of you, for I come sorely wounded through the fault of my steed. Carry me to my bed and, if it is possible, call the wise Urganda to examine and cure my wounds.'

'See, in the name of mischief,' the housekeeper broke in at this point, 'if my heart didn't tell me truly on which leg my master was lame! Come up, your worship. I'm right glad to see you. We'll know how to cure you here, without sending for your Urganda. Oh, confound, confound, confound those books of chivalry which have brought your worship to this pass!'

They took him straight to his bed, but on searching for his wounds could find none. He said that he was bruised all over from taking a grievous fall with his horse Rocinante in a fight with ten of the most monstrous and audacious giants to be found anywhere on earth.

'So ho!' cried the priest. 'So there are giants in the dance? Well, I swear I'll burn them to-morrow before nightfall.'

They asked Don Quixote a great number of questions, but the only reply he would make was to ask them to give him something to eat and to let him sleep; for that was his most urgent need. They did so, and the priest inquired of the labourer at some length how he had found their friend. The peasant told him everything and repeated the nonsense the knight had talked when he discovered him, and as he brought him home. This made the priest more eager to do what he did the next day, which was to call on his friend, master Nicholas the barber, and to go with him to Don Quixote's house.

Chapter VI. *Of the great and pleasant Inquisition held by the Priest and the Barber over our ingenious gentleman's Library.*

THE knight was still asleep when the priest asked the niece for the keys of the room where he kept his books, the authors of the mischief. She was delighted to give them to him. Then they all went in, the housekeeper with them, and found more than a hundred large volumes, very well bound, and some small ones as well. As soon as the housekeeper saw them, she ran out of the room in great haste, and returned presently with a bowl of holy water and a bunch of hyssop. 'Take this, your worship,' she said, 'and sprinkle this room, in case there is some enchanter about, out of all the lot there are in these books, for fear he might put a spell on us, to punish us for the bad turn we're going to deal him by banishing them all out of the world.'

The priest laughed at the housekeeper's simplicity, and bade the barber hand him the books one by one, so that he could see what they were about; for he might find some of them that did not deserve punishment by fire.

'No,' said the niece, 'there is no reason to pardon any of them, for they have all of them caused the trouble. Better throw them out of the windows into the courtyard, and make a pile of them, and set them on fire; or else take them out into the back-yard and have the bonfire there, where the smoke won't be a nuisance.'

The housekeeper agreed, so anxious were they both for the massacre of those innocents; but the priest would not consent without at least reading the titles first. And the first that Master Nicholas handed him was *The Four Books of Amadis of Gaul*. 'This is very curious,' said the priest, 'for, as I have heard tell, this was the first book of chivalries printed in Spain, and all the others took their origin and beginning from it. So it seems to me that, as the first preacher of so pernicious a sect, we must condemn it to the flames without any mercy.'

'No, sir,' said the barber, 'for I have heard that it is the best of all the books of this kind ever written. So, as it is unequalled in its accomplishment, it ought to be pardoned.'

'That is true,' said the priest, 'and therefore let its life be granted for the present. Let us have a look at that other one beside it.'

'That,' said the barber, 'is *The Exploits of Esplandian*, the legitimate son of Amadis of Gaul.'

'In truth,' said the priest, 'the father's goodness shall not help the son. Take him, Mistress Housekeeper. Open that window and throw him into the yard. He shall be the foundation for the bonfire we shall have to make.'

The housekeeper obeyed with great pleasure, and the good Esplandian went flying out into the yard to wait in all patience for the threatened conflagration.

'Let us get on,' said the priest.

'The next,' said the barber, 'is *Amadis of Greece*. In fact, as far as I can see, all these on this side are of the same lineage as *Amadis*.'

'Then into the yard with all of them,' cried the priest, 'for rather than not burn queen Pintiquinestra and the shepherd Darinel with their eclogues and their author's devilish contorted sentences, I would burn the father that begot me as well, if he went about in the shape of a knight errant.'

'I am of the same opinion,' said the barber.

'And I too,' added the niece.

'Since that is so,' said the housekeeper, 'come, into the yard with them!'

They handed them to her and, as there were a great number, to spare herself the stairs she flung them down out of the window.

'What is that huge thing?' asked the priest.

'It is *Don Olivante de Laura*,' answered the barber.

'The author of that book also wrote *The Flower Garden*,' said the priest, 'and to be frank with you, I cannot make out which of the two is the more truthful, or rather the less mendacious. I can only say that for its arrogant nonsense it shall go into the yard.'

'This next is *Florismarte of Hyrcania*,' said the barber.

'What, is Master Florismarte here?' replied the priest. 'Well, he is for a quick end in the yard, I promise you, despite his extraordinary birth and his fantastic adventures. His style is so harsh and dry he deserves nothing better. Into the yard with him and with that other one too, Mistress Housekeeper.'

'With the greatest of pleasure,' she replied, and with much joy she did his bidding.

'Here is *The Knight Platir*,' said the barber.

'That is an old book,' said the priest. 'I can find nothing in it that deserves mercy. Let him join the others without more ado.' And so he did. Then they opened another book, and found its title to be *The Knight of the Cross*.

'For a title as holy as this book has, its ignorance might be pardoned. But they always say "the devil lurks behind the cross". So, to the fire with it.' Then, taking up another book, the barber observed: 'This is *The Mirror of Chivalries*.'

'I know the book well,' said the priest. 'Therein are Lord

Reynald of Montalban with his friends and companions, worse thieves than Cacus; and the Twelve Peers, and that faithful historian Turpin. But I am for condemning them to nothing worse than perpetual banishment, if only because they had a share in inspiring the famous Mateo Boiardo, from whom the Christian poet Ludovico Ariosto also spun his web. If I find him here speaking any language but his own I shall show him no respect. But if he speaks his own tongue, I will wear him next my heart.'

'I have him in Italian,' said the barber, 'but I don't understand him.'

'It would not do you any good if you did,' replied the priest. 'We could have done without the good captain bringing him to Spain and making him a Castilian, for he has robbed him of much of his native value. That is what happens with all authors who translate poetry into other languages. However much care they take, and however much skill they show, they can never make their translations as good as the original. In short, I say that this book and every one we find that deals with these affairs of France, shall be thrown out and deposited in a dry well till we see, after further deliberation, what is to be done with them; excepting one, *Bernardo de Carpio*, which is here somewhere, and another called *Roncesvalles*. For they shall pass straight from my hands into the housekeeper's, and from there into the flames without remission.'

The barber concurred in all this, holding it very fit and proper; for he knew the priest to be too good a Christian and too great a lover of the truth to tell a lie for anything in the world. Opening another book, they saw that it was *Palmerin de Oliva*, and beside it was another called *Palmerin of England*, at the sight of which the priest exclaimed: 'Let that olive be cut to splinters and burnt, so that not so much as the ash remains. But that palm of England, let it be kept and treasured as a rarity, and a casket be made for it, like the one Alexander found among the spoils of Darius and dedicated to the preservation of the works of Homer. This book, my friend, deserves respect for two reasons: one, because it is very good in itself, and the other because it is said to have been written by a wise King of Portugal. All the adventures in the castle of Miraguarda are excellent and very well contrived, and the speeches polished and clear, for they observe and bring out the character of

each speaker with great truth and understanding. I say, then, subject
to your judgment, Master Nicholas, that this and *Amadis of Gaul*
shall be spared the fire, and all the rest perish without any further
trial or enquiry.'

'No, my good friend,' replied the barber, 'for the one I have here
is the renowned *Sir Belianis*.'

'He too,' said the priest, 'and his second, third and fourth parts,
need a little rhubarb to purge their excess of bile. We shall have to
cut out all that part too about the Castle of Fame and other nonsense more serious still. So we will allow them time to put in their
defence, and as they show signs of amendment, mercy or justice
shall be accorded them. Meanwhile, friend, keep them in your house,
but let no one read them.'

'With pleasure,' replied the barber. And the priest, not being inclined to tire himself by reading any more books of chivalry, bade
the housekeeper take all the big ones and throw them into the yard.
His request did not fall on deaf ears, for she would rather have burnt
those books than woven the broadest and finest cloth in the world.
So, seizing them about eight at a time, she flung them out of the
window. And as she took so many together, one fell at the barber's
feet; and he, curious to see what it was, found that its title was *History of the Famous Knight Tirante the White*.

'Good heavens!' exclaimed the priest in a loud voice. 'Is *Tirante
the White* here? Give it to me, friend, for to my mind that book is
a rare treasure of delight and a mine of entertainment. Here is
Lord-have-mercy-on-us of Montalban, a valiant knight, and his
brother Thomas of Montalban and the knight Fonseca, and the
fight the valiant Tirante had with the great mastiff, and the witti-
cisms of the maiden Joy-of-my-life, with the amours and tricks of
widow Quiet, and the lady Empress in love with her squire Hip-
polito. Really, my friend, for its style it is the best book in the
world. Here the knights eat and sleep and die in their beds, and
make their wills before they die, and other things as well that are
left out of all other books of the kind. On that account, the author
is a deserving fellow. For he did not commit all those follies
deliberately, which might have sent him to the galleys for the rest
of his life. Take him home and read him, and you will see that all
I have said of him is true.'

'So be it,' replied the barber. 'But what shall we do with these little books that are left?'

'Those,' said the priest, 'are probably not books of chivalry but of poetry.'

He opened one, and saw that it was Jorge de Montemayor's *Diana*, and supposing that all the rest were of the same kind, said: 'These do not deserve burning with the rest, because they do not and will not do the mischief those books of chivalry have done. They are books of entertainment and can do no one any harm.'

'Oh, sir,' cried the niece, 'your worship should have them burnt like the rest. For once my uncle is cured of his disease of chivalry, he might very likely read those books and take it into his head to turn shepherd and roam about the woods and fields, singing and piping and, even worse, turn poet, for that disease is incurable and catching, so they say.'

'The girl is right,' said the priest, 'It would be well to rid our friend of this stumbling-block and danger for the future. And since we are beginning with Montemayor's *Diana*, I am of the opinion that it should not be burnt, but all the part dealing with the witch Felicia and the enchanted water should be taken out, and almost all the longer poems too, but we will gladly leave it the prose and the honour of being the first book of its kind.'

'The next one,' said the barber, 'is the *Diana*, called the second, by the Salmantine; and here is another of the same name by Gil Polo.'

'Let the one by the Salmantine join and increase the company of those condemned to the yard. But Gil Polo's we will preserve as if it were by Apollo himself. But get on, friend; let us hurry, for it is getting late.'

'This volume,' said the barber, opening another, 'is *The Ten Books of the Fortune of Love*, by Antonio de Lofraso, poet of Sardinia.'

'As true as I am in orders,' cried the priest, 'there has never been such a humorous, whimsical book written since Apollo was Apollo, the Muses Muses and the poets poets. In its way it is the best and most singular book of that kind that ever saw the light of day, and anyone who has not read it can reckon he has never read anything really delightful. Give it to me, friend, for I had rather have found this than have the present of a Florentine serge cassock.'

He put it aside with the greatest delight, and the barber went on, saying: 'The next are *The Shepherd of Iberia, The Nymphs of Henares,* and *The Unveiling of Jealousy.*'

'Well, there is nothing else to do with them,' said the priest, 'but to deliver them over to the secular arm of the housekeeper. Don't ask me why, or we shall never have done.'

'The next is *Filida's Shepherd.*'

'He is no shepherd,' said the priest, 'but a very ingenious courtier. Let him be kept as a precious jewel.'

'This big one here is called *The Treasury of Divers Poems,*' said the barber.

'If there were not so many of them,' said the priest, 'they would have been better thought of. This book ought to be weeded and cleansed of some poor verses it has among its fine things. Take care of it, because its author is a friend of mine, and out of respect for other more heroic and exalted works he has written.'

'This,' the barber went on, 'is Lopez Maldonado's song-book.'

'The author of that book is also a great friend of mine,' replied the priest. 'Everyone admires his verses that hears them from his own mouth; his voice is so sweet he enchants when he chants them. His eclogues are rather long, though you can never have too much of a good thing. Let him be preserved with the elect. But what is that book beside him?'

'The *Galatea* of Miguel de Cervantes,' said the barber.

'That Cervantes has been a great friend of mine for many years, and I know that he is more versed in misfortunes than in verse. His book has some clever ideas; but it sets out to do something and concludes nothing. We must wait for the second part he promises, and perhaps with amendment he will win our clemency now denied him. In the meantime, neighbour, until we see, keep him as a recluse in your room.'

'With pleasure, my good friend. Now here come three together: *The Araucana* of Don Alonso de Ercilla, *The Austriada* of Juan Rufo, magistrate of Cordova, and *The Monserrat* of Christoval de Virues, the Valencian poet.'

'These three books,' said the priest, 'are the best in heroic verse

DON QUIXOTE, PART I, CH. VI—VII   63

ever written in Castilian. They can compare with the most famous in Italy. Let them be preserved as the richest treasures of poetry Spain possesses.'

The priest was too tired to look at any more books, and therefore proposed that the rest should be burnt, contents unknown. But the barber had already opened one called *The Tears of Angelica*.

'I would have shed them myself,' said the priest on hearing the title, 'if I had ordered a book like that to be consigned to the flames. For its author was one of the most famous poets not only in Spain but in the world, and was most happy in translating some of Ovid's fables.'

Chapter VII. *Of the Second Expedition of our good Knight Don Quixote de la Mancha.*

AT this point Don Quixote began to shout at the top of his voice: 'Here, here, valorous knights! Here there is need to show the strength of your valorous arms, for the courtiers are getting the better of the tourney!'

At this frightful noise all rushed upstairs, and the examination of the remaining books proceeded no further. And that is why, so it is believed, *The Carolea* and *The Lion of Spain*, with the *Feats of the Emperor*, compiled by Don Luis de Avila, went on the flames unseen and unheard. For no doubt they must have been among the remaining books, and perhaps if the priest had seen them they would not have suffered so severe a sentence. When they got into Don Quixote's room he was already out of bed, and repeating his shouting and raving, laying about him with his sword in all directions with slashes and back-strokes, as wide awake as if he had never been asleep. They grappled with him, and put him back to bed by main force; and when he had rested quietly a little he started to address the priest, saying:

'Certainly, my Lord Archbishop Turpin, it is a great default in us, who call ourselves the Twelve Peers, to give these courtier knights the victory in this tournament without more ado, seeing that we, the Adventurers, have gained the prize on the three preceding days.'

'Peace, dear comrade,' replied the priest, 'for God may yet grant

us a change of fortune, and what is lost to-day may be won back
to-morrow. But for the present you must mind your health; for
you seem to me to be over-wearied, if not severely wounded.'

'Not wounded,' said Don Quixote, 'but bruised and battered.
There is no doubt of that, for that bastard Roland has pounded me
with the trunk of an oak, and all out of envy, since he knows I am
his only rival in prowess. But let me never be called Reynald of
Montalban again if, when I rise from this bed, I do not pay him
for it despite all his enchantments. But for the present let me be
brought food, for I believe that is what I am in most need of; and
leave me to take care of my revenge.'

They did as he asked, and gave him some food, after which he
went to sleep again, leaving them wondering at his madness.

That same night the housekeeper set light to all the books in the
yard and all those in the whole house as well, and burnt them. Some
that were burnt deserved to be treasured up among the eternal archives, but fate and the laziness of the inquisitor forbade it. And
so in them was fulfilled the saying that the saint sometimes pays for
the sinner.

One of the remedies that the priest and the barber then resorted
to for their friend's complaint was to wall up and close the room
where he had kept his books, so that he should not find them when
he got up. For perhaps if the cause were removed, the effect might
cease; and they might say that an enchanter had carried them off,
room and all.

This was quickly done, and when two days later Don Quixote
got up, the first thing he did was to go and look for his books; and
when he failed to find the room where he had left them he went all
over the house searching for it. Finally he went to the place where
the door used to be, and felt for it with his hands, and ran his eyes
over everything again and again, without saying a word. Then
after a good while he asked his housekeeper whereabouts his book-
closet was, and she, being well primed in her answers, replied:
'What room? Or rather what on earth is your worship looking for?
There is no room and no books in this house now, for the Devil
himself has carried everything off.'

'That was no devil,' put in his niece, 'but an enchanter who
came one night on a cloud, after you went away, and getting down

from the dragon he was riding on, went into the room. I don't
know what he did inside, but after a little while he went flying out
through the roof, and left the house full of smoke. And when we
decided to look and see what he had done, there was no room
and not a book to be seen. Only we remember very well, both of
us, that as he left, the wicked old man shouted out that we would
see later what havoc he had wrought in the house, out of a secret
grudge he bore the owner of those books. What's more, he said
he was called the sage Muñaton.'

'Freston he must have said,' put in Don Quixote.

'I don't know,' replied the housekeeper, 'whether he was called
Freston or Friton. I only know that his name ended in *ton*.'

'That is right,' said Don Quixote. 'He is a learned enchanter,
and a great enemy of mine. He bears me malice, for through his
arts and spells he knows that in the fullness of time I shall engage
a favourite knight of his in single combat, and that I shall conquer
him, and he will not be able to prevent it. That is why he tries
to serve me every ill-turn he can. But I tell him that he cannot
gainsay or avert what Heaven has decreed.'

'Who doubts that?' cried his niece. 'But what concern of yours
are these quarrels, my dear uncle? Wouldn't it be better to stay
peacefully at home, and not roam about the world seeking better
bread than is made of wheat, never considering that many go for
wool and come back shorn?'

'Dear niece,' replied Don Quixote, 'you are a long way out in
your reckoning! Before they shear me I will pluck out and tear off
the beards of all who think to touch so much as the tip of one hair
of mine.' And neither of the women cared to make further reply,
for they saw that he was getting into a rage.

As it turned out, he stayed fifteen days at home very quietly,
showing no sign of any desire to repeat his former strange behaviour; and during that time he had some most pleasant arguments
with his two friends, the priest and the barber, on the subject of his
statement that the world's greatest need was of knights errant, and
that knight errantry should be revived in his person. The priest
sometimes contradicted him, and sometimes gave in to him, for if
he had not resorted to this trick, he would not have stood a chance
of bringing him to reason.

C

All this while Don Quixote was plying a labourer, a neighbour of his and an honest man – if a poor man may be called honest – but without much salt in his brain-pan. In the end, he talked to him so much, persuaded him so hard and gave him such promises that the poor yokel made up his mind to go out with him and serve him as squire. Don Quixote told him, amongst other things, that he ought to feel well disposed to come with him, for some time or another an adventure might occur that would win him in the twinkling of an eye some isle, of which he would leave him governor. These promises and others like them made Sancho Panza – for this was the labourer's name – leave his wife and children and take service as his neighbour's squire. Then Don Quixote set about raising money, and by selling one thing, pawning another, and making a bad bargain each time, he raised a reasonable sum. He also fixed himself up with a shield, which he borrowed from a friend, and patching up his broken helmet as best he could, he gave his squire Sancho notice of the day and the hour on which he proposed to set out, so that he should provide himself with all that was most needful; and he particularly told his squire to bring saddle-bags. Sancho said that he would, and that he was also thinking of bringing a very fine ass he had, for he was not too good at much travelling on foot. At the mention of the ass Don Quixote hesitated a little, racking his brains to remember whether any knight errant ever had a squire mounted on ass-back; but no case came to his memory. But, for all that, he decided to let him take it, intending to provide him with a more proper mount at the earliest opportunity by unhorsing the first discourteous knight he should meet. He provided himself also with shirts and everything else he could, following the advice which the innkeeper had given him. And when all this was arranged and done, without Panza saying goodbye to his wife and children, or Don Quixote taking leave of his house-keeper and niece, they departed from the village one evening, quite unobserved, and rode so far that night that at daybreak they thought they were safe, and that even if anyone came out to search for them they would not be found.

Sancho Panza rode on his ass like a patriarch, with his saddle-bags and his leather bottle, and a great desire to see himself governor of the isle his master had promised him. It chanced that Don

Quixote took the same route and struck the same track across the plain of Montiel as on his first expedition; but he travelled with less discomfort than before, as it was the hour of dawn, and the sun's rays, striking them obliquely, did not annoy them. Then presently Sancho Panza said to his master:

'Mind, your worship, good Sir Knight Errant, that you don't forget about the isle you promised me; for I shall know how to govern it, never mind how big it is.'

To which Don Quixote replied: 'You must know, friend Sancho Panza, that it was a custom much in use among knights errant of old to make their squires governors of the isles or kingdoms they won; and I am determined that, for my part, so beneficial a custom shall not lapse. On the contrary, I intend to improve on it: for they often, perhaps most often, waited till their squires were grown old; and when they were worn out in their service, from bad days and worse nights, they gave them some title of count, or perhaps marquis, of some valley or province of more or less importance. But if you live and I live, it may well be that before six days are gone by I may win some kingdom with others depending upon it, and one of them may prove just right for you to rule. Do not think this any great matter, for adventures befall knights errant in such unheard and unthought-of ways that I might easily be able to bestow on you even more than I promise.'

'At that rate,' said Sancho Panza, 'if by any of those miracles your worship speaks of I were to become king, Juana Gutierrez, my poppet, would be a queen, no less, and my children princes.'

'Well, who doubts it?' answered Don Quixote.

'I doubt it,' replied Sancho Panza, 'for I'm pretty sure that even if God rained kingdoms on the earth, none of them would sit well on Mary Gutierrez' head. As a queen she would not be worth a half-penny, sir. Countess might suit her better, with God's help.'

'Put the matter in God's hands, Sancho,' replied Don Quixote. 'He will give her what is best for her. But do not humble your heart so low as to be content with anything less than to be Captain General.'

'I won't, dear sir,' replied Sancho Panza, 'especially with a master as grand as your worship, who will know how to give me all that will be good for me and that I can bear.'

Chapter VIII. *Of the valorous Don Quixote's success in the dreadful and never before imagined Adventure of the Windmills, with other events worthy of happy record.*

AT that moment they caught sight of some thirty or forty windmills, which stand on that plain, and as soon as Don Quixote saw them he said to his squire: 'Fortune is guiding our affairs better than we could have wished. Look over there, friend Sancho Panza, where more than thirty monstrous giants appear. I intend to do battle with them and take all their lives. With their spoils we will begin to get rich, for this is a fair war, and it is a great service to God to wipe such a wicked brood from the face of the earth.'

'What giants?' asked Sancho Panza.

'Those you see there,' replied his master, 'with their long arms. Some giants have them about six miles long.'

'Take care, your worship,' said Sancho; 'those things over there are not giants but windmills, and what seem to be their arms are the sails, which are whirled round in the wind and make the millstone turn.'

'It is quite clear,' replied Don Quixote, 'that you are not experienced in this matter of adventures. They are giants, and if you are afraid, go away and say your prayers, whilst I advance and engage them in fierce and unequal battle.'

As he spoke, he dug his spurs into his steed Rocinante, paying no attention to his squire's shouted warning that beyond all doubt they were windmills and no giants he was advancing to attack. But he went on, so positive that they were giants that he neither listened to Sancho's cries nor noticed what they were, even when he got near them. Instead he went on shouting in a loud voice: 'Do not fly, cowards, vile creatures, for it is one knight alone who assails you.'

At that moment a slight wind arose, and the great sails began to move. At the sight of which Don Quixote shouted: 'Though you wield more arms than the giant Briareus, you shall pay for it!' Saying this, he commended himself with all his soul to his Lady Dulcinea, beseeching her aid in his great peril. Then, covering himself with his shield and putting his lance in the rest, he urged Rocinante forward at a full gallop and attacked the nearest windmill, thrusting his lance into the sail. But the wind turned it with such violence that it shivered his weapon in pieces, dragging the horse and his rider with it, and sent the knight rolling badly injured across the plain. Sancho Panza rushed to his assistance as fast as his ass could trot, but when he came up he found that the knight could not stir. Such a shock had Rocinante given him in their fall.

'O my goodness!' cried Sancho. 'Didn't I tell your worship to look what you were doing, for they were only windmills? Nobody could mistake them, unless he had windmills on the brain.'

'Silence, friend Sancho,' replied Don Quixote. 'Matters of war are more subject than most to continual change. What is more, I think – and that is the truth – that the same sage Friston who robbed me of my room and my books has turned those giants into windmills, to cheat me of the glory of conquering them. Such is the enmity he bears me; but in the very end his black arts shall avail him little against the goodness of my sword.'

'God send it as He will,' replied Sancho Panza, helping the knight to get up and remount Rocinante, whose shoulders were half dislocated.

As they discussed this last adventure they followed the road to the pass of Lapice where, Don Quixote said, they could not fail to find many and various adventures, as many travellers passed that way. He was much concerned, however, at the loss of his lance, and, speaking of it to his squire, remarked: 'I remember reading that a certain Spanish knight called Diego Perez de Vargas, having broken his sword in battle, tore a great bough or limb from an oak, and performed such deeds with it that day, and pounded so many Moors, that he earned the surname of the Pounder, and thus he and his descendants from that day onwards have been called Vargas y Machuca. I mention this because I propose to tear down just such a limb from the first oak we meet, as big and as good as his; and I intend to do such deeds with it that you may consider yourself most fortunate to have won the right to see them. For you will witness things which will scarcely be credited.'

'With God's help,' replied Sancho, 'and I believe it all as your worship says. But sit a bit more upright, sir, for you seem to be riding lop-sided. It must be from the bruises you got when you fell.'

'That is the truth,' replied Don Quixote. 'And if I do not complain of the pain, it is because a knight errant is not allowed to complain of any wounds, even though his entrails may be dropping out through them.'

'If that's so, I have nothing more to say,' said Sancho, 'but God knows I should be glad if your worship would complain if anything hurt you. I must say, for my part, that I have to cry out at the slightest twinge, unless this business of not complaining extends to knights errants' squires as well.'

Don Quixote could not help smiling at his squire's simplicity, and told him that he could certainly complain how and when he pleased, whether he had any cause or no, for up to that time he had never read anything to the contrary in the law of chivalry.

Sancho reminded him that it was time for dinner, but his master replied that he had need of none, but that his squire might eat whenever he pleased. With this permission Sancho settled himself as comfortably as he could on his ass and, taking out what he had put into the saddle-bags, jogged very leisurely along behind his master, eating all the while; and from time to time he raised the bottle with such relish that the best-fed publican in Malaga might have envied him. Now, as he went along like this, taking repeated gulps, he entirely forgot the promise his master had made him, and reckoned that going in search of adventures, however dangerous, was more like pleasure than hard work.

They passed that night under some trees, from one of which our knight tore down a dead branch to serve him as some sort of lance, and stuck into it the iron head of the one that had been broken. And all night Don Quixote did not sleep but thought about his Lady Dulcinea, to conform to what he had read in his books about knights errant spending many sleepless nights in woodland and desert dwelling on the memory of their ladies. Not so Sancho Panza; for, as his stomach was full, and not of chicory water, he slept right through till morning. And, if his master had not called him, neither the sunbeams, which struck him full on the face, nor the song of the birds, who in great number and very joyfully greeted the dawn of the new day, would have been enough to wake him. As he got up he made a trial of his bottle, and found it rather limper than the night before; whereat his heart sank, for he did not think they were taking the right road to remedy this defect very quickly. Don Quixote wanted no breakfast for, as we have said, he was determined to subsist on savoury memories. Then they turned back on to the road they had been on before, towards the pass of Lapice, which they sighted about three in the afternoon.

'Here,' exclaimed Don Quixote on seeing it, 'here, brother Sancho Panza, we can steep our arms to the elbows in what they call adventures. But take note that though you see me in the greatest danger in the world, you must not put your hand to your sword to defend me, unless you know that my assailants are rabble and common folk; in which case you may come to my aid. But should they be knights, on no account will it be legal or permissible, by the laws of chivalry, for you to assist me until you are yourself knighted.'

'You may be sure, sir,' replied Sancho, 'that I shall obey your worship perfectly there. Especially as I am very peaceable by nature and all against shoving myself into brawls and quarrels. But as to defending myself, sir, I shan't take much notice of those rules, because divine law and human law allow everyone to defend himself against anyone who tries to harm him.'

'I never said otherwise,' replied Don Quixote, 'but in the matter of aiding me against knights, you must restrain your natural impulses.'

'I promise you I will,' replied Sancho, 'and I will observe this rule as strictly as the Sabbath.'

In the middle of this conversation two monks of the order of St. Benedict appeared on the road, mounted on what looked like dromedaries; for the two mules they were riding were quite as big. They were wearing riding-masks against the dust and carrying sunshades. And behind them came a coach, with four or five horsemen escorting it, and two muleteers on foot.

In the coach, as it afterwards turned out, was a Basque lady travelling to Seville to join her husband, who was going out to take up a very important post in the Indies. The monks were not of her company, but merely journeying on the same road.

Now no sooner did Don Quixote see them in the distance than he said to his squire: 'Either I am much mistaken, or this will prove the most famous adventure ever seen. For those dark shapes looming over there must, beyond all doubt, be enchanters bearing off in that coach some princess they have stolen; and it is my duty to redress this wrong with all my might.'

'This will be a worse job than the windmills,' said Sancho. 'Look, sir, those are Benedictine monks, and the coach must belong to some travellers. Listen to me, sir. Be careful what you do, and don't let the Devil deceive you.'

'I have told you,' replied Don Quixote, 'that you know very little of this subject of adventures. What I say is true, and now you will see it.'

So saying, he rode forward and took up his position in the middle of the road along which the monks were coming; and when they got so near that he thought they could hear him, he called out in a loud voice: 'Monstrous and diabolical crew! Release immediately the noble princesses whom you are forcibly carrying off in that coach, or prepare to receive instant death as the just punishment for your misdeeds.'

The monks reined in their mules, and stopped in astonishment at Don Quixote's appearance and at his speech.

'Sir Knight,' they replied, 'we are neither monstrous nor diabolical, but two monks of St Benedict travelling about our business, nor do we know whether there are any princesses being carried off in that coach or not.'

'No fair speeches for me, for I know you, perfidious scoundrels!' cried Don Quixote. Then, without waiting for their reply, he spurred Rocinante and, with his lance lowered, charged at the foremost monk with such vigour and fury that, if he had not slid from his mule, he would have been thrown to the ground and badly hurt, if not killed outright. The second monk, on seeing his companion so treated, struck his heels into his stout mule's flanks and set her galloping over the plain fleeter than the wind itself. When Sancho Panza saw the monk on the ground, he got down lightly from his ass, ran up and started to strip him of his clothes. Upon this, two servants of the monks arrived and asked him why he was stripping their master. Sancho replied that the clothes fell rightly to his share as spoils of the battle which his master, Don Quixote, had won. The lads, who did not get the joke nor understand this talk of spoils and battles, saw that Don Quixote had gone off and was talking with the ladies in the coach, and so fell upon Sancho and knocked him down. And, pulling every hair from his beard, they kicked him mercilessly, and left him stretched on the ground, breathless and stunned. Then, without a moment's hesitation, the monk remounted his mule, trembling, terrified and as white as a sheet; and as soon as he was up he spurred after his comrade, who was waiting for him some distance off, watching to see the upshot of this sudden attack. But without caring to wait for the end of the adventure, they went on their way, crossing themselves more often than if they had had the Devil himself at their backs.

Don Quixote, as we have said, was talking with the lady in the coach: 'Your fair ladyship may now dispose of yourself as you desire, for now the pride of your ravishers lies in the dust, overthrown by this strong arm of mine. And lest you be racked with doubt as to the name of your deliverer, know that I am Don Quixote de la Mancha, knight errant, adventurer and captive to the peerless and beautiful lady, Dulcinea del Toboso. And in requital of the benefit you have received from me, I would ask no more of you than to go to El Toboso and present yourself on my behalf before that lady, telling her what I have done for your deliverance.'

All that Don Quixote said was overheard by one of the squires accompanying the coach, a Basque. And when he saw that the knight would not let them pass, but was talking of their turning back at once to El Toboso, he went up to Don Quixote and, grasping his lance, addressed him in bad Castilian and worse Basque.

'Get along, you ill-gotten knight. By God who made me, if you do not leave coach I kill you, sure as I be Basque.'

Don Quixote understood him very well, and replied with great calm: 'If you were a knight, as you are not, I should have punished your rash insolence by now, you slavish creature.'

'I not gentleman? I swear you liar, as I am a Christian. You throw down lance and draw sword, and you will see you are carrying the water to the cat. Basque on land, gentleman at sea. A gentleman, by the devil, and you lie if you say otherwise!'

' "Now you shall see," said Agrages,' quoted Don Quixote, and threw his lance down on the ground. Then, drawing his sword and grasping his shield, he rushed at his antagonist, determined to take his life. When the Basque saw him coming he would have liked to get down from his mule, as it was a poor sort of hired beast and not to be trusted, but there was nothing for it but to draw his sword. He was, however, lucky enough to be near the coach, from which he was able to snatch a cushion to serve as a shield; whereupon they immediately fell to, as if they had been two mortal enemies. The rest of the party tried to pacify them, but could not; for the Basque swore in his uncouth language that if they did not let him finish the battle, he would himself kill his mistress and all who hindered him.

The lady in the coach, amazed and terrified at the sight, made the coachman drive off a little way, and sat watching the deadly struggle from a distance. In the course of the fight the Basque dealt Don Quixote a mighty blow on one shoulder, thrusting above his shield, and had our knight been without defence he would have been cleft to the waist. When Don Quixote felt the weight of that tremendous stroke he cried out aloud: 'O lady of my soul, Dulcinea, flower of beauty, come to the aid of this your knight, who for the sake of your great goodness is now in this dire peril!'

To speak, to raise his sword, to cover himself with his shield and attack the Basque: all this was the work of a moment. For he had resolved to risk everything upon a single stroke. The Basque, seeing him come on, judged Don Quixote's courage by his daring, and decided to do the same as he. So he covered himself well with his cushion and waited, unable to turn his mule in either direction, for the beast was now dead weary, and not being made for such games, could not budge a step.

Don Quixote, as we have said, rushed at the wary Basque with sword aloft, determined to cleave him to the waist; and the Basque watched, with his sword also raised and well guarded by his cushion; while all the by-standers trembled in terrified suspense, hanging upon the issue of the dreadful blows with which they threatened one another. And the lady of the coach and her waiting-women offered a thousand vows and prayers to all the images and places of devotion in Spain, that God might deliver their squire and them from the great peril they were in.

But the unfortunate thing is that the author of this history left the battle in suspense at this critical point, with the excuse that he could find no more records of Don Quixote's exploits than those related here. It is true that the second author of this work would not believe that such a curious history could have been consigned to oblivion, or that the learned of La Mancha could have been so incurious as not to have in their archives or in their registries some documents relating to this famous knight. So, strong in this opinion, he did not despair of finding the conclusion of this delightful story and, by the favour of Heaven, found it, as shall be told in our second part.

Chapter IX. Of the conclusion of the stupendous Battle between the gallant Basque and the valiant Manchegan.

IN the first part of this history we left the valiant Basque and the famous Don Quixote with naked swords aloft, on the point of dealing two such furious downward strokes as, had they struck true, would have cleft both knights asunder from head to foot, and split them like pomegranates. At this critical point our delightful history stopped short and remained mutilated, our author failing to inform us where to find the missing part. This caused me great annoyance, for my pleasure from the little I had read turned to displeasure at the thought of the small chance there was of finding the rest of this delightful story. For it seemed to me that the greater part was missing. It appeared to my mind impossible, and contrary to all sound custom, that so good a knight should have lacked a sage to undertake the writing of his unparalleled achievements, since there never was one of those knights errant who – as the people say – go out on their adventures, that ever lacked one. For every one of them had one or two sages ready at hand, not only to record their deeds, but to describe their minutest thoughts and most trivial actions, however much concealed; and so good a knight could not have been so unfortunate as to lack what Platir and the like had in such abundance. I really could not bring myself to believe that such a gallant history could have been left maimed and mutilated, and laid the blame on the malice of time, the devourer and consumer of all things, for either concealing or destroying the sequel. On the other hand, I thought that, as there had been found among Don Quixote's books some as modern as *The Unveiling of Jealousy* and *Nymphs and Shepherds of Henares*, his history must be modern too, and that, though it might not be written down, it would be remembered by the people of his village and of the neighbourhood. This thought made me anxious and eager for real and authentic knowledge of the whole life and marvels of our famous Spaniard, Don Quixote de la Man-

cha, the light and mirror of Manchegan chivalry, and the first man
of our times, of these calamitous times of ours, to devote himself to
the toils and exercise of knight errantry; to redress wrongs, aid
widows and protect maidens, such as roam up-hill and down-dale
with their whips and palfreys and their whole virginities about
them. For there were virgins in the olden days who, unless ravished
by some rogue or by a boor with his steel cap and axe or by some
monstrous giant, never slept a night under a roof all their lives, and
at the age of eighty went to their graves as spotless virgins as the
mothers that bore them. Now I say that for this, and for many other
reasons our gallant Quixote deserves continuous and immemorial
praise; and even I should have my share, for my toil and pains in
searching for the end of this delightful history. Though well I know
that if Heaven, chance, and good fortune had not aided me, the
world would have remained without the amusement and pleasure
which an attentive reader may now enjoy for as much as two hours
on end.

This is how the discovery occurred: – One day I was in the Al-
cana at Toledo, when a lad came to sell some parchments and old
papers to a silk merchant. Now as I have a taste for reading even
torn papers lying in the streets, I was impelled by my natural inclination to take up one of the parchment books the lad was selling,
and saw in it characters which I recognized as Arabic. But though I
could recognize them I could not read them, and looked around to
see if there was not some Spanish-speaking Moor about, to read
them to me; and it was not difficult to find such an interpreter there.
For, even if I had wanted one for a better and older language, I
should have found one. In short, chance offered me one, to whom I
explained what I wanted, placing the book in his hands. He opened
it in the middle, and after reading a little began to laugh. I asked him
what he was laughing at, and he answered that it was at something
written in the margin of the book by way of a note. I asked him to
tell me what it was and, still laughing, he answered: 'This is what
is written in the margin: "They say that Dulcinea del Toboso, so
often mentioned in this history, was the best hand at salting pork of
any woman in all La Mancha."'

When I heard the name of Dulcinea del Toboso I was surprised
and astonished, for I immediately surmised that these books must

contain the story of Don Quixote. With this idea I pressed him to read the beginning, and when he did so, making an extempore translation from the Arabic into Castilian, he said that the heading was: History of Don Quixote de la Mancha, written by Cide Hamete Benengeli, Arabic historian. I needed great caution to conceal the joy I felt when the title of the book reached my ears. Running to the silk merchant, I bought all the lad's parchments and papers for half a *real*, but if he had had any sense and known how much I wanted them, he might very well have demanded and got more than six *reals* from the sale. I then went off with the Moor into the cloister of the cathedral, and asked him to translate for me into Castilian everything in those books that dealt with Don Quixote, adding nothing and omitting nothing; and I offered to pay him whatever he asked. He was satisfied with fifty pounds of raisins and three bushels of wheat, and promised to translate them well, faithfully, and very quickly. But, to make the business easier and not to let such a prize out of my hands, I took him to my house; and there in little more than six weeks he translated it all just as it is set down here.

On the first sheet was a very life-like picture of Don Quixote's fight with the Basque. Both were shown in the very postures the story describes, with swords aloft, the one covered by his shield, the other by his cushion, and the Basque's mule so life-like that you could tell from a mile off that it was a hired one.

At the feet of the Basque was a scroll that read: '*Don Sancho de Azpeitia*', which no doubt was his name: and at Rocinante's was another which read: '*Don Quixote*'. Rocinante was marvellously painted, so long and lank, so hollow and lean, with such a sharp backbone, and so far wasted in consumption that it was quite clear at a glance how wisely and rightly he had been called Rocinante. Beside him stood Sancho Panza, holding his ass by the halter, and at his feet was another label which read: '*Sancho Zancas*'; and according to the picture he must have had a big belly, a short body, and long shanks; which must be what gave him the names of Panza and Zancas, for he is called by both these names at different times in the history. There were some other details to be seen, but they are none of them of great importance, and have no concern with the faithful telling of this story; – and no story is bad if it is truthful.

Now, if any objection can be made against the truth of this history, it can only be that its narrator was an Arab – men of that nation being ready liars, though as they are so much our enemies he might be thought rather to have fallen short of the truth than to have exaggerated. So it seems to me; for when he could and should have let himself go in praise of so worthy a knight he seems deliberately to have passed on in silence; an ill deed and malicious, since historians are bound by right to be exact, truthful, and absolutely unprejudiced, so that neither interest nor fear, dislike nor affection, should make them turn from the path of truth, whose mother is history, rival of time, storehouse of great deeds, witness of the past, example and lesson to the present, warning to the future. In this history I know that you will find all the entertainment you can desire; and if any good quality is missing, I am certain that it is the fault of its dog of an author rather than any default in the subject. To conclude, the second part, according to the translator, began thus:

The trenchant swords of the two valorous and furious combatants, brandished aloft, seemed to threaten the heavens, the earth, and the pit of hell, such was their courageous aspect. The first to strike his blow was the choleric Basque; and he struck with such force and fury that if the edge of his sword had not turned in its descent, that one blow would have been enough to finish the dire conflict and all our knight's adventures. But good fortune was preserving him for greater things, and twisted his enemy's sword, so that, although it struck him on his left shoulder, it did him no other injury than to disarm all that side, taking with it a great piece of his helmet with half an ear, all of which fell to the ground in hideous ruin, leaving our knight in a very evil plight.

God help me, but who is there could worthily describe the rage which now entered the heart of our Manchegan on finding himself thus treated? All that can be said is that he rose once more in his stirrups and, grasping his sword tighter in both his hands, brought it down with such fury full on the Basque's cushion and on his head, that despite that protection he began to spout blood out of his nostrils, his mouth, and his ears, as if a mountain had fallen on him. He looked as if he was going to tumble off his mule, which he would no doubt have done if he had not clung round her neck. But even so he lost his stirrups and then let go with his arms; while the beast, terrified by the weight of the blow, began to gallop about the field, and with a plunge or two threw her master on to the ground.

Don Quixote was looking on most composedly. But, when he saw the squire fall, he jumped down from his horse and, running very nimbly up to him, put the point of his sword between his enemy's eyes, bidding him surrender or he would cut off his head. The Basque was so stunned that he could not answer a word, and things would have gone badly with him, so blind with rage was Don Quixote, if the ladies in the coach, who till then had been watching the fight in dire dismay, had not run to the spot, and begged him very earnestly to do them the great kindness and favour of sparing their squire's life. To which request Don Quixote replied very haughtily and gravely:

'Certainly, fair ladies; I am most willing to do what you ask. But there must be one condition agreed, which is that this knight shall promise me to go to the town of El Toboso, and present himself from me before the peerless Lady Dulcinea, so that she may deal with him according to her pleasure.'

The terrified and distressed ladies did not consider what Don Quixote required nor ask who Dulcinea was, but promised him that the squire should carry out the knight's command.

'Then, upon your word,' said Don Quixote, 'I will do him no other hurt, though he richly deserves it at my hands.'

Chapter x. *Of the Pleasant Conversation between Don Quixote and his Squire Sancho Panza.*

IN the meantime Sancho Panza had got up again after his rough handling by the monks' servants, and had stood watching the battle Don Quixote was fighting, praying to God in his heart to be pleased to grant his master the victory, and that out of it he might gain an isle of which he could be governor, as he had been promised. Then, when he saw that the contest was over and his master about to remount Rocinante, he ran up to hold his stirrup, and, before Don Quixote was up, fell down on his knees before him, seized his hand, kissed it, and said:

'Be so kind, my dear lord Don Quixote, as to make me governor

of the isle you have won in this dreadful fight; for however big it
is, I feel strong enough to govern it as well as any man who ever
governed isles in all the world.'

To this Don Quixote replied: 'Observe, brother Sancho, that
this adventure and others of this kind are not adventures of isles but
of cross-roads, from which nothing is to be gained but a broken
head and the loss of an ear. Be patient, for adventures will occur
whereby I shall not only be able to make you governor, but something greater still.'

Sancho thanked him warmly and, once more kissing his hand and
the hem of his coat, helped him to mount Rocinante. Then he got
on to his ass and began to follow his master, who went off at a brisk
trot without taking leave of the ladies in the coach or saying a word
more to them, and rode into a near-by wood. Sancho followed him
as fast as his ass could go, but Rocinante moved so swiftly that he
found himself left behind, and had to shout after his master to wait
for him. This Don Quixote did, reining Rocinante in until his weary
squire came up, to say as he overtook him:

'I think, sir, that it would be wise for us to retire to some church.
For, seeing in what a bad way you left that man you fought with, I
shouldn't wonder if they were to report the matter to the Holy
Brotherhood and have us arrested; and, my goodness, if they do
that, we shall sweat blood before we get out of gaol.'

'Silence!' said Don Quixote. 'Where have you ever heard or read
of a knight errant being brought before a judge, however many
homicides he may have committed?'

'I don't know anything about your *omecides*,' replied Sancho. 'I
have never tried one in my life. I only know that the Holy Brotherhood has something to say to people who fight in the fields, and the
other matter's no concern of mine.'

'Do not worry, my friend,' said Don Quixote. 'I will deliver you
from the hands of the Chaldeans, let alone the Holy Brotherhood.
But tell me, on your oath, have you ever seen a more valorous
knight than I am on the whole face of the earth? Have you ever read
in histories of one who has or had more spirit in the attack, more
wind in the holding out, more art in the wounding, or more skill
in the overthrowing?'

'To tell you the truth,' replied Sancho, 'I've never read any histories at all, because I can't read or write. But I'll stake my oath I've never served a braver master than your worship in all the days of my life. Pray God these brave deeds won't be paid for where I just said! But, I beg you, your worship, let me attend to you, for you are losing a lot of blood from that ear, and I've lint here and a little white ointment in the saddle-bag.'

'All that would have been quite needless,' replied Don Quixote, 'if I had remembered to make a flask of the Balsam of Fierabras. One single drop of that would save us both time and medicine.'

'What flask and what balsam is that?' asked Sancho Panza.

'It is a balsam,' replied Don Quixote, 'the recipe for which lies in my memory. With it there is no need to fear death nor so much as to think of dying of any wound. So, when I have made some and given it to you, if ever you see me cut through the middle in some battle – as very often happens – you have only to take the part of my body that has fallen to the ground and place it neatly and cunningly, before the blood congeals, on to the half that is still in the saddle, taking especial care to make them fit exactly. Then you must give me just two drops of this balsam to drink and, you will see, I shall be as sound as an apple.'

'If that's so,' said Panza, 'from now on I renounce the governorship of the promised isle, and all I want in payment for all my good services is for your worship to give me the recipe for that marvellous liquor. For I think it would be worth more than two *reals* an ounce, and I need no more than that to spend the rest of my life in honour and comfort. But I should like to know now whether it costs much to make.'

'For less than three *reals* you can make half a gallon or more,' answered Don Quixote.

'Good Lord!' replied Sancho. 'What's preventing you from making it, sir, and teaching me as well?'

'Hush, friend,' replied Don Quixote. 'I mean to teach you even greater secrets and do you even greater favours. But for the moment let us dress our wounds, for my ear hurts me more than I like.'

Sancho got some lint and ointment out of the saddle-bag. But when Don Quixote saw his helmet he almost went out of his mind. Putting his hand to his sword and raising his eyes to Heaven, he cried, 'I swear on oath, by the Creator of all things, and by the four

Holy Gospels in which they are amply recorded, to lead the life that the great Marquis of Mantua led when he swore to avenge the death of his nephew Baldwin, vowing not to eat bread at table, nor lie with his wife – and some other things, which, though I cannot remember them, I will take as here spoken – until I have exacted entire vengeance on the man who has done me this outrage.'

On hearing which Sancho exclaimed: 'Consider, Don Quixote, that if the knight has complied with your orders and presented himself before my lady Dulcinea del Toboso, he will already have done his duty, and deserves no other punishment unless he commits a new crime.'

'You have spoken well and justly,' replied Don Quixote; 'and so I annul my oath so far as it concerns wreaking fresh vengeance on him. But I swear and confirm anew, that I will lead the life I have vowed to until by force of arms I win from some knight another helmet as good. Do not imagine, Sancho, that I take this oath as a mere bubble. For I know very well what precedent I am following, since exactly similar events occurred in the case of Mambrino's helmet, which cost Sacripante so dear.'

'I wish your worship would send these oaths to the devil, dear master,' replied Sancho, 'for they're very bad for the health and very harmful to the conscience. Besides, tell me now – if perhaps we don't meet a man armed with a helmet for a long time, what shall we do then? Have we got to keep the vow, and put up with all the inconvenience and discomfort of lying in our clothes, and never sleeping in a village, and all those hundreds of penances in that mad old Marquis of Mantua's oath, that your worship's set on reviving? Consider carefully, sir. There aren't any men in armour travelling on any of these roads, but only carriers and carters, who not only don't wear helmets, but have probably never heard of them in all the days of their life.'

'You are wrong about that,' said Don Quixote, 'for we shall not be two hours at these cross-roads before we see more armed men than came to the siege of Albraca to carry off the fair Angelica.'

'Then I agree!' said Sancho. 'And please God we come well out of it, and the time arrives when you win that isle which is costing me so dear – And then let me die!'

'I have told you already, Sancho, not to worry on that account.

For if there is no isle to be had, there is always the Kingdom of Denmark or of Sobradisa, that will fit you like a ring on your finger. What is more, you should like them better, as they are on dry land. But let us leave this to time, and see if you have anything for us to eat in those saddle-bags, because soon we are going in search of a castle where we can lodge to-night and make for ourselves the balsam I spoke of; for I swear to God this ear of mine hurts me exceedingly.'

'I have an onion here and a bit of cheese,' said Sancho, 'and a few hunks of bread. But they are not the victuals for a valiant knight like your worship.'

'How little you understand,' replied Don Quixote. 'I would have you know, Sancho, that it is a point of honour with knights errant not to eat once in a month; and when they do eat to take what they find nearest to hand. You would have realized this if you had read as many histories as I have. For in all the many I have read I have never found more than a passing mention of what knight errants ate, except at those sumptuous banquets they used to be given; for the rest of their days they lived on the flowers of the field. But although it is to be understood that they could not live without eating and satisfying all the other needs of nature – for of course they were men like ourselves – it must be presumed that, as they spent the greater part of their lives roaming through woods and wastes, and without a cook, their most ordinary food would be country fare, like that you are offering me now. So, Sancho, my friend, do not worry about what pleases me, nor seek to build the world anew, nor wrench knight errantry off its hinges.'

'Pardon me, your worship,' said Sancho, 'but since, as I told you before, I can't read or write, I don't know or understand the rules of the profession of knighthood. Still from now on I will fill the saddle-bags with all kinds of dried fruit for your worship, because you are a knight. But for myself, as I am not, I'll provide something more substantial in the way of poultry.'

'I do not say,' replied Don Quixote, 'that knights errant are obliged to eat nothing but the fruit you mention, only that it and certain herbs they used to find in the fields were their ordinary fare.'

'It's a good thing,' replied Sancho, 'to know those herbs, for I'm inclined to think that we may need to make use of that knowledge one day.'

Then he took the good things he had mentioned out of the bag, and the two of them ate their dinner peacefully and companionably. Though, as they were anxious to look for somewhere to lodge that night, they cut their poor dry meal rather short and, mounting at once, made haste to reach some inhabited place before nightfall. But both the sun and their hopes of doing so failed them together near some goatherds' huts; and so they decided to spend the night there. And if it caused Sancho distress not to reach a village, it was a source of satisfaction to his master to sleep beneath the open sky. For it seemed to him that each time he did so he was confirming his title to knighthood by a new act of possession.

Chapter XI. *What passed between Don Quixote and some Goatherds.*

THE knight was very warmly welcomed by the goatherds, and Sancho did what he could for Rocinante and his ass before following the odour given off by certain pieces of goat's meat, which were boiling in a pot over the fire. He would have liked at that very moment to see if they were ready to be transferred from the pot to the stomach, but refrained, as the goatherds themselves took them off the fire and, spreading some sheepskins on the ground, hurriedly set out their rustic table. Then, with a great show of goodwill, they invited knight and squire to share what they had. Six of them who belonged to that fold begged Don Quixote with rough compliments to sit on a trough which they had set upside down for him, and then seated themselves round on the skins. The knight took this seat, but Sancho remained standing to fill his master's cup, which was a horn one. But when he saw his squire in this posture, Don Quixote said:

'So that you may see, Sancho, the virtue there is in knight errantry, and how speedily those who perform any function in it may attain the honour and estimation of the world, I wish you to sit here beside me in these good people's company, and to be on terms of equality with me, who am your master and natural lord. Eat from my plate and drink from the vessel I drink from; for it can be said of knight errantry as of love: that it puts all things on the same level.'

'I thank you,' said Sancho, 'but I must confess to your worship that so long as I have plenty to eat, I can eat it as well, and better, standing by myself, as seated beside an Emperor. And, to tell you the truth, even if it's only bread and onion that I eat in my corner without bothering about table manners and ceremonies, it tastes to me a great deal better than turkey at other tables where I have to chew slowly, drink little, and wipe my mouth often, and where I can't sneeze and cough when I want to, nor do any of those other things which solitude and freedom allow of. So, dear master, let the honours your worship means to confer on me for being a servant and follower of knight errantry – which being your squire, I am – be exchanged for something of more use and profit to me. For though I acknowledge these honours as received in full, I renounce them from now on and until the end of the world.'

'You must sit down all the same, for whosoever humbleth himself, God doth exalt.' And, seizing him by the arm, Don Quixote compelled Sancho to sit beside him.

The goatherds did not understand this gibberish about squires and knights errant, but just ate in silence and watched their guests, who with a good grace and appetite crammed down lumps as big as their fists. When the meat course was finished they spread a great quantity of shrivelled acorns on the skins, and set beside them half a cheese, which could not have been harder if it had been made of mortar. All this while the horn cup was not idle, for it went the rounds so often, first full and then empty like the bucket at the well, that they easily exhausted one of the two wineskins which hung in sight.

After Don Quixote had sufficiently satisfied his hunger, he took up a handful of acorns and, looking at them intently, gave utterance in the following strain: 'Happy the age and happy the times on which the ancients bestowed the name of golden, not because gold, which in this iron age of ours is rated so highly, was attainable without labour in those fortunate times, but rather because the people of those days did not know those two words *thine* and *mine*. In that blessed age all things were held in common. No man, to gain his common sustenance, needed to make any greater effort than to reach up his hand and pluck it from the strong oaks, which literally invited him to taste their sweet and savoury fruit. Clear springs and running rivers offered him their sweet and limpid water in glorious abundance. In clefts of the rock and hollow trees the careful and provident bees formed their commonwealth, offering to every hand without interest the fertile produce of their fragrant toil. Spontaneously, out of sheer courtesy, the sturdy cork-trees shed their light and broad bark, with which men first covered their houses, supported on rough poles only as a defence against the inclemencies of the heavens. All was peace then, all amity, all concord. The crooked plough had not yet dared to force open and search the kindly bowels of our first mother with its heavy coulter; for without compulsion she yielded from every part of her fertile and broad bosom everything to satisfy, sustain, and delight the children who then possessed her. Then did the simple and lovely shepherdesses go from valley to valley and from hill to hill, with their tresses loose, and without more clothes than were needed to cover modestly what modesty requires, and has always required, to be concealed. Nor were there such ornaments as are in fashion to-day, all trumped up with Tyrian purple and silk in so many contorted shapes. Yet, with only a few green leaves of dock and ivy plaited together, they must have looked as splendid and elegant as our court ladies with the rare and outlandish inventions which idle curiosity has taught them. In those days the soul's amorous fancies were clothed simply and plainly, exactly as they were conceived, without any search for artificial elaborations to enhance them. Nor had fraud, deceit, or malice mingled with truth and sincerity. Justice pursued her own proper purposes, undisturbed and unassailed by favour and interest, which so impair, restrain, and pervert her to-day. The law did not then depend on the judge's nice interpretations, for there were none to judge or to be judged. Maiden modesty roamed, as I have said, wherever she would, single and solitary, without fear of harm from strangers' licence or lascivious assault; and if she was undone it was of her own will and desire.

'But now, in this detestable age of ours, no maiden is safe even though she be hidden in the centre of another Cretan labyrinth; for even there, through some chink or through the air, by dint of its accursed persistence, the plague of love gets in and brings them to ruin despite their seclusion. Therefore, as times rolled on and wickedness increased, the order of knights errant was founded for their protection, to defend maidens, relieve widows, and succour the orphans and the needy. Of this order am I, brother goatherds, whom I thank for the welcome and entertainment which you have given to me and my squire; for although by the law of nature all men are bound to befriend knights errant, yet, as you received and entertained me without knowing of this obligation, I should rightly acknowledge your goodwill with the utmost gratitude.'

Our knight delivered all this harangue, which might well have been spared, only because the acorns they served him reminded him of the golden age. That is why it came into his head to deliver this purposeless discourse to the goatherds, who listened to him in fascination and bewilderment, without answering a word. Sancho was silent too, for he was busy devouring the acorns and making frequent visits to the second wineskin, which they had hung up on a cork-tree to keep the wine cool. Don Quixote devoted more time to talking than to finishing his supper, but finally the meal was over and one of the goatherds said: 'So that you can truly say, Sir Knight Errant, that we have been ready and glad to entertain you, we should like to offer you the pleasure of a song by one of our mates, who will soon be here. He is a clever lad and very much in love; and, what is more, he can read and write, and plays the fiddle as beautifully as can be.'

Scarcely had the goatherd finished speaking when the sound of a fiddle reached their ears, and very soon afterwards the musician came in, a very handsome lad of about twenty-two. His companions asked him if he had had supper, and on his answering Yes, the goatherd who had asked the question said: 'In that case, Antonio, you might do us the favour of a song or two. We want to show this gentleman, our guest, that even in the mountains and woods there are people who know something about music. We have told him of your accomplishments, and we should like you to prove to him that we spoke the truth. So sit down, please, and sing the song about your love, which your uncle the priest composed for you, the one they liked so much in our village.'

'I shall be glad to,' replied the lad; and without waiting to be asked twice, he sat down on the trunk of a fallen oak and tuned his fiddle. Then presently he began to sing most charmingly:

'I know, Olalla, thou dost me adore,
    Though yet to me the same thou hast not said;
Nor shown it once, by one poor glance or more,
    Since love is soonest by such tongues betrayed.

'But as I ever held thee to be wise,
    I am assured thou bearest me good will,
For he is not unfortunate who sees
    That his affections are not taken ill.

'Yet, for all this, Olalla, it is true
    I, by observance, gather to my woe
That thy mind's framed of brass, by art undue
    And flint thy bosom is, though it seems snow.

'And yet amidst thy rigour's winter face
    And other shifts thou usest to delay me,
Sometimes hope, peeping through, doth promise grace;
    But, woe is me! I fear 'tis to betray me.

'Sweetest, once in the balance of thy mind
    Poise with just weights my faith, which never yet
Diminished, though disfavour it did find;
    Nor can increase more, though thou favouredst it.

'If love be courtesy, as some men say,
    I can expect of your humanity
That my hopes shall, howe'er thou dost delay,
    Reap their reward truly and finally.

'If many services be of esteem
    Or power to render a hard heart benign,
Such things I did for thee as make me deem
    I've gained the match, and that thou shalt be mine.

'For if at any time thou'st taken heed,
    Thou more than once might'st view how I was gay
To honour thee, on Mondays, in the weed
    Which got me credit on God's holiday.

'For love and finery ever must consort
    Together, since they travel the same ways,
Which made me, when I did to thee resort,
    Come always neat and fine beneath thy gaze.

'Here I omit the dances I have done,
    And music I have at thy window given;
When at cock-crow thou listenedst alone,
    And seem'dst, hearing my voice, to be in heaven

'Neither will I the praises here recount
    Which of thy beauty I've so often sung,
Which, though they all were true, were ever wont
    To cause the envious to judge me wrong.

'When I spoke to the maid of Berocal,
    Teresa, of thy worth and of thy shape,
"You think," she said, "you're in an angel's thrall,
    And yet, for idol, you adore an ape.

'"She to her trinkets thanks may give, and chains,
    False hair and other shifts that she doth use
To mend her beauty, with a thousand pains
    And tricks, which might love's very self abuse."

'Stung by her words, I gave her straight the lie,
    Which did her and her cousin so offend,
He challenged me to fight him presently,
    And well thou knowest how that affair did end.

'I do not seek to buy thy favours cheap,
    And when I court and woo thee to be mine
I swear thy virtue need not fear a trap.
    For purer far than that is my design.

'The church has bonds which do so surely hold
    As no silk cord for strength comes to them near;
To thrust thy neck now in the yoke be bold
    And see if I, to follow thee, will fear.

'If thou wilt not, here solemnly I vow,
    By holiest saint enwrapt in precious shrine,
Never to leave those hills where I dwell now,
    Unless it be to become a Capuchin.'

Here the goatherd ended his song and, although Don Quixote asked him to give them some more, Sancho did not agree. He was more inclined for sleep than for music, and so he said to his master: 'Your worship had better arrange now where you are going to rest to-night. These men work too hard all day long to be able to spend their nights in singing.'

'I understand you, Sancho,' replied Don Quixote. 'It is indeed clear to me that your visits to the wineskin require payment in sleep rather than in music.'

'God be praised, but we all enjoyed the drink,' replied Sancho.

'I do not deny that,' replied Don Quixote. 'So settle where you will; but watching befits men of my profession better than sleep. However, it would be as well if you would dress this ear of mine again, for it is hurting me more than it need.'

Sancho obeyed. But one of the goatherds looked at the wound and told him not to worry, for he would apply a remedy that would easily heal it. Then, taking some leaves of rosemary, which grew plentifully thereabouts, he chewed them and, mixing them with a little salt, applied them to the ear, which he bandaged tightly, assuring the knight that he would need no other remedy; which proved true.

Chapter XII. *Of What a Goatherd told Don Quixote and his Companions.*

MEANWHILE another lad arrived – one of those whose job it was to bring the provisions up from the village.

'Do you know what is happening in our place, fellows?' said he.

'How should we know?' answered one of them.

'Then I'll tell you,' the lad went on. 'The famous shepherd-student Chrysostom died this morning, and the rumour is that he died of love for that devilish Marcela, rich William's daughter, the girl who is always roaming about these parts dressed as a shepherdess.'

'For Marcela, you say?' asked one.

'Yes, I do,' replied the lad; 'and the strange thing is that he has directed in his will that he's to be buried in the fields like a Moor, at the foot of that rock where the spring is, beside the cork-tree, because, the rumour goes – and they say they had it from his own lips – that it was at that spot he saw her for the first time. He has left some other requests as well, such odd ones that the clergy say they mustn't be carried out; and quite right too, because they have a heathenish smack about them. But his great friend Ambrosio the student, who used to go about with him dressed as a shepherd too, answers that everything is to be done exactly as Chrysostom direct-ed. The whole village is in an uproar about it. But, from all they say, they'll end up by doing just as Ambrosio and his friends the shepherds want; and to-morrow they're coming to bring him with great ceremony to the place I spoke of. It will be a sight worth seeing I can tell you, and I shan't miss it, even if it means I can't get back to the village to-morrow.'

'We will all see it too,' answered the goatherds, 'and cast lots which of us is to stay and mind the goats.'

'I agree, Peter,' said one of them, 'though you needn't trouble about casting lots, for I will stay behind for everybody. And don't put it down to generosity on my part or think that I don't want to see what's going on. It's only because of the splinter which stuck into my foot the other day, so that I can't walk.'

'We thank you all the same,' replied Peter.

Don Quixote requested Peter to tell him who the dead man was, and who was the shepherdess. Peter replied that all he knew was that the dead man was a rich gentleman from a village in those mountains, who had been studying for many years at Salamanca and had finally returned home with the reputation of being very learned and well-read. He was especially famous for knowing the science of the stars, and what the sun and the moon were doing up in the skies, for he could always give accurate notice of the *clipse* of the sun and moon.

'*Eclipse* it is called, friend, not *clipse* – the obscuration of those two great luminaries,' put in Don Quixote.

But Peter took no notice of this trifle, and went on with his story, saying: 'Also he used to foretell whether the year would be fruitful or stale.'

'*Sterile* you mean, friend,' put in Don Quixote.

'*Sterile* or *stale*,' replied Peter, 'it comes to the same thing. So from what he told them, his father and his friends got very rich, because they believed him and did what he advised. He used to say: This year sow barley and not wheat, or: Now you can sow chick-peas and not barley, or: Next year there will be a full crop of olive-oil, and the three years following there won't be a drop.'

'That science is called Astrology,' said Don Quixote.

'I don't know its name,' replied Peter, 'but I know that he knew all that and more too. But to come to the point: one day not many months after he came from Salamanca, he threw away the long scholar's gown he used to wear, and appeared all of a sudden dressed like a shepherd with his crook and sheepskin jacket; and at the same time his great friend Ambrosio, who had been his fellow-student, dressed himself as a shepherd too. I had forgotten to say that poor Chrysostom, the dead man, was a great one at making verses, and was so good at them that he used to write the carols for Christmas Eve and the plays for Corpus Christi, which the boys of our village used to act; and everyone said that they were first-class. When the villagers saw the two students unexpectedly dressed as shepherds they were astonished, and could not guess what had in-duced them to make such an extraordinary transformation. By this time Chrysostom's father had died, and he inherited considerable property, goods as well as land, and quite large flocks and herds, and a great deal of money. He was left in desolate possession of all this, and indeed he deserved it too, for he was a very good fellow and charitable, and a friend to all good men. And he had a face like a blessing. Afterwards it came out that he had changed his dress only to wander about these wild places after that shepherdess Marcela, whom our lad spoke of a while ago, for poor dead Chrysostom had fallen in love with her. And now I must tell you, for your informa-tion, who this young baggage is; for perhaps – no, there is no per-haps about it – you won't hear anything like this in all the days of your life, even if you live longer than Sarna.'

'Say *Sarah*,' replied Don Quixote; who could not bear the goat-herd's blunders.

'*Sarna* (the itch) lives long enough too,' replied Peter. 'If you make me correct my words at every turn, sir, we shan't be done in a twelvemonth.'

'Pardon me, friend,' said Don Quixote, 'but there is such a differ-ence between Sarna and Sarah that I had to tell you. However, you answered very rightly, for the itch lives longer than Sarah. So go on with your story, and I will not interrupt you again.'

'I was saying, then, my beloved sir,' said the goatherd, 'that there was a farmer in our village even richer than Chrysostom's father. His name was William and, over and above his many great riches, God gave him a daughter, whose mother, the most respected wo-man in all these parts, died in giving her birth. I can just see her now, with that face of hers, the sun on one side, as you might say, and the moon on the other. And what a good housewife she was, and such a friend to the poor, and I'm sure that for that alone her soul is this very moment enjoying of God in the other world. Her husband William died of grief at the death of his good wife, leaving his daughter Marcela, young and rich, in the care of one of her uncles, a priest and the parson of our village. The child grew up so beautiful that she used to put us in mind of her mother, who was a great beauty herself, though people thought that the daughter would be even lovelier. So when she was fourteen or fifteen everyone who saw her praised God for giving her such beauty, and most of them fell desperately in love with her. Her uncle kept her very carefully and seldom let her go out. But, all the same, the fame of her great loveliness spread far and wide, and for that reason as much as for her great wealth not only our villagers, but some of the best men for many miles around as well, were begging, persuading and pestering her uncle to give them her hand in marriage. However, he was a really good Christian and, though he would have liked to marry her off soon, since she was of age, would not do so without her consent. Not that he had an eye to the advantage or profit that he would get from managing the girl's estate and putting off her marriage — and that has been remarked in the good priest's favour by more than one circle of village gossips, I can promise you. For I should like you to know, Sir Errant, that in these little places they poke their noses into everything and gossip about everything. You can take my word for it, a parson has to be extraordinarily good to have his parishioners speaking well of him, especially in a village.'

'That is true,' said Don Quixote; 'but go on. It is a very good story, and you, my good Peter, are telling it with a fine grace.'

'May the Lord's grace never fail me: that is the chief thing. To continue, I must tell you that, although her uncle set out and described to his niece the qualities of each one of her many suitors separately, begging her to choose and marry whom she liked, her only answer was that she didn't want to for the present, because, being so young, she did not feel able to bear the responsibilities of matrimony. And as these excuses seemed reasonable to her uncle, he ceased to press her, and waited till she should be somewhat older and know how to choose a companion to her taste. For, he said, and said rightly, parents ought not to settle their children against their will. But, lo and behold, when we least expected it, the modest Marcela suddenly appeared dressed like a shepherdess and, in spite of her uncle and everyone in the village who tried to dissuade her, off she went into the fields with the other village shepherdesses and started to tend her own flock. And once she had appeared in public and her beauty was exposed to all eyes, I couldn't truthfully tell you how many rich youths, gentlemen, and farmers put on the same dress as Chrysostom, and wandered about these fields, courting her. One of them, as I have told you, was our dead man who, they said, no longer loved her, but adored her. Now you mustn't think that because Marcela adopted this free and unconstrained way of life, with little or no privacy, her modesty or her virtue has fallen under any shadow of suspicion. Far from it; she guards her honour so well that not one of her many suitors has boasted — nor has the right to boast — that she has given him the slightest hope of obtaining his desire. For, although she does not avoid the shepherds' company and conversation, but treats them in a friendly and courteous way, if anyone comes to her to reveal his intentions even by a proper and holy proposal of marriage, she flings him off, like a stone from a catapult. And by this kind of behaviour she does more damage in these parts than if the plague had got in, for her easy manner and her beauty win the hearts of all who have to do with her. They court and love her, but her disdain and her plain speaking drive them to the verge of despair. So it is that they don't know what to say to her, but loudly call her cruel and unkind, and by other such names which clearly show her character. If you were to stay here awhile, sir, one day you would hear the hills and valleys echo with the lament of her rejected suitors. Not far from here is a place where there are about two dozen great beeches, and every one of them has Marcela's name cut on its smooth bark. Above it, too, on some of them, there is a crown carved, as if her lover meant to declare in the clearest terms that Marcela wears and deserves the crown of all human beauty. Here one shepherd sighs; there another moans; from the distance you can hear songs of love; from near at hand dirges of despair. There will be one spending all the hours of the night seated at the foot of an oak or of a crag, never closing his tear-dimmed eyes till the sun finds him there next morning, sunken and lost in his thoughts; and there will be another giving no rest or truce to his sighs, but lying stretched on the burning sand in the most sultry heat of a summer afternoon, and sending his complaints up to the merciful heavens; and over every one of them the beautiful Marcela triumphs, free and unconcerned. And all of us who know her are waiting to see how her haughtiness will end, and who will be the lucky man to come and conquer so intractable a nature and enjoy a beauty so perfect. As all that I have told you is well-known fact, I can easily understand that what our lad has said about the cause of Chrysostom's death is the truth as well. So I advise you, sir, to be sure to join us to-morrow at his burial. It will be very well worth seeing, for Chrysostom has many friends; and it's not more than a mile and a half from here to the place where he directed them to bury him.'

'I will certainly be there,' said Don Quixote, 'and I thank you for the pleasure you have given me by telling me such a delightful story.'

'Oh,' replied the goatherd, 'I don't know even half the things that have happened to Marcela's lovers. But maybe to-morrow we shall fall in with some shepherd on the way who may tell us more. But it would be as well for now if you were to go to sleep under cover, for the night dew might hurt your wound, though the ointment they put on it is so good that there's no fear of trouble.'

Sancho Panza also, who already wished the goatherd to the devil with his endless story, begged his master to go and sleep in Peter's hut. This he did and, in imitation of Marcela's lovers, he spent the rest of the night in thoughts of his lady Dulcinea; while Sancho Panza's sleep, as he settled down between Rocinante and his ass, was not that of a rejected lover, but of a soundly kicked human being.

Chapter XIII. *The conclusion of the Tale of Marcela the Shepherdess and Other Matters.*

SCARCELY had day begun to show itself on the balconies of the East when five of the six goatherds got up, and went to wake Don Quixote and to inquire if he still intended to go and see the famous burial of Chrysostom, for if he did they would keep him company. Nothing delighted the knight more, and so he got up and ordered Sancho to saddle the horse and the ass at once. This was quickly done, and with the same despatch they all set off on their way. They had gone less than a mile when they came to a cross road, where they saw approaching them along another track some six shepherds dressed in black skins, with their heads crowned with garlands of cypress and bitter bay. Each of them had a stout holly-stick in his hand, and with them came also two gentlemen on horseback, handsomely equipped for travelling, accompanied by three servants on foot. When the two parties met they exchanged courteous greetings, and on each one asking where the other was going, discovered that they were all bound for the burial-place. So they travelled together.

As they rode on, one of the horsemen observed to his companion: 'I think, Señor Vivaldo, that we can count the hours passed in attending this remarkable funeral time well spent. For, if we are to trust the strange accounts these herdsmen have given us of the dead shepherd and the merciless shepherdess, it cannot fail to be a remarkable event.'

'I agree with you,' replied Vivaldo, 'and I would waste not one day but four rather than miss the sight.'

Don Quixote asked them what they had heard about Marcela and Chrysostom. And the traveller answered that early that morning they had met the shepherds and, seeing them in such mournful attire, had asked them why they were so dressed. Then one of them had explained, and related the strange behaviour and beauty of a shepherdess called Marcela, the loves of her many suitors, and the death of that Chrysostom to whose burial they were going. In short, he had told them all that Peter had told Don Quixote. Here this conversation ceased and another began, the one called Vivaldo asking Don Quixote what made him travel thus armed in so peaceful a country. To which the knight replied: 'The exercise of my profession does not allow or permit me to ride in any other fashion. Ease, luxury, and repose were invented for soft courtiers; but labour, unease, and arms alone were designed and made for those whom the world calls knights errant, of whose number, though unworthy, I am the very least.'

On hearing this, they concluded that he was a madman. But, to make sure of it and to discover what kind of madness his was, Vivaldo went on to ask him what exactly he meant by knights errant.

'Have you not read, sirs,' replied Don Quixote, 'the annals and histories of England, treating of the famous deeds of King Arthur, whom in our Castilian tongue we commonly call King Artus. There is an ancient and widespread tradition concerning him throughout that kingdom of Great Britain, that he did not die, but by magic art was turned into a crow; and they say that in course of time he will come back to reign, and recover his kingdom and sceptre. For which reason no Englishman can be proved ever to have killed a crow, from that day to this. Now in this good king's reign there was instituted that famous order of chivalry, the Knights of the Round Table, and there took place, exactly as they are recorded, the loves of Sir Lancelot of the Lake and Queen Guenevere, in which that honourable Lady Quintañona acted as intermediary and confidante. Whence arose that ballad so widely known and so often sung in modern Spain:

> Never was there knight
> By ladies so attended
> As was Lancelot,
> When he came from Britain.

– with its sweet and charming story of his deeds of love and his bravery. Now, from that time on, this order of chivalry has been gradually growing and spreading through many and various parts of the world. Famous and renowned for their exploits in that order, were the valiant Amadis of Gaul with all his sons and grandsons to the fifth generation, the valorous Felixmarte of Hyrcania, the never sufficiently praised Tirante the White, and that knight whom we have seen and heard and spoken with almost in our own times, the invincible and valorous Sir Belianis of Greece. That, gentlemen, is what it is to be a knight errant, and what I have described to you is the order of chivalry, in which, as I have already said, though a sinner, I have made my profession. What the knights I have told you of professed I profess too; and that is why I am travelling through these wastes and deserts in quest of adventures, with mind resolved to oppose my arms and my person to the greatest perils which fortune may present, in aid of the weak and those in need.'

From these arguments the travellers finally decided that Don Quixote was out of his wits, and realized what form of madness it

D

was that possessed him. And they were as astonished as everyone else had been on first making that discovery. Now Vivaldo was a shrewd and cheerful fellow and, to relieve the boredom of the short journey they had still to take before arriving at the place of burial, he tried to give Don Quixote an opportunity of continuing his wild talk, and consequently observed: 'It seems to me, Sir Knight Errant, that you have adopted one of the strictest professions on earth; and it is my opinion that even the Carthusian monks' is not so severe a calling.'

'The monks' profession may well be as strict,' replied Don Quixote, 'but whether it is as necessary in the world I am within a hair's breadth of doubting. For, truly, the soldier who carries out his captain's orders does no less than the captain who gives the orders. I mean that the religious, in all peace and quiet, pray Heaven for the well-being of the world; but we soldiers and knights carry out what they pray for, defending it with the strength of our arms and the edge of our swords, beneath no roof but the open sky, exposed to the intolerable beams of the sun in summer and the biting frosts in winter. We, therefore, are God's ministers on earth, and the arms by which His justice is executed here. And whereas matters of war and things of that kind cannot be performed without sweat, toil, and labour, it follows that men whose profession is war must, unquestionably, endure more than those who in assured peace and repose are for ever praying God to help the powerless. Far be it from me to say, or even to think, that the state of a knight errant is as good as a cloistered monk's. I only want to argue from my own sufferings that it is most certainly a more painful and belaboured one, hungrier and thirstier, more miserable, ragged and lousy; for there is no doubt that knights errant of old suffered much ill-usage in the course of their lives. And if some of them rose by the valour of their arms to be Emperors, they assuredly paid dearly for it in blood and sweat; and if those who did rise so high had had no enchanters or sages to help them, they would have been defrauded of their desires and cheated of their hopes.'

'I agree with you,' replied the traveller, 'but there is one thing in particular about knights errant that seems wrong to me. That is that when they are on the point of embarking on a great and perilous adventure in which there is manifest danger to their lives, never at the moment of attack do they think of entrusting their souls to God, as every Christian in such peril is bound to do. Instead they commend themselves to their mistresses, with as much fervour and devotion as if these were their God, a practice which seems to me to smack somewhat of paganism.'

'Sir,' replied Don Quixote, 'on no account can it be otherwise, and it would go badly with the knight errant who should act differently. For it is the use and custom of chivalry for the knight errant, in embarking on any great feat of arms, to have his lady before him, and to turn his eyes softly and lovingly upon her, as if thereby begging her favour and protection in the hazardous enterprise that faces him. And even if no one hears him, he is obliged to breathe certain words between his teeth, commending himself to her with all his heart; and of this practice we have innumerable examples in the histories. But it is not to be inferred that they neglect to commend themselves to God; for they have time and opportunity to do so in the course of their task.'

'All the same,' replied the traveller, 'I am still uncertain on one point. I have often read of two knights beginning by bandying words. Then, little by little, their anger begins to kindle, and they turn their horses, make a wide circle in the field, and next, without more ado, charge one another at full speed, commending themselves to their ladies in the midst of the charge; and the usual result of their encounter is that one falls over the cruppers of his horse, speared right through by his opponent's lance; and his opponent too has to cling on to his horse's mane to avoid falling to the ground. Now, I cannot see how the dead man could have had the time to commend himself to God in the course of so very rapid an action. It would have been better if the words spent on commending himself to his lady as he charged had been employed in his duties and obligations as a Christian. What is more, I believe that not all knights errant have ladies to commend themselves to, for they are not all in love.'

'That is impossible,' replied Don Quixote. 'I say that it is impossible that there could be any knight errant without a lady. For it is as right and proper for them to be in love as for the sky to have stars; and I can vouch for it that there has never been a knight errant without a lady in any history whatever. For the very fact of his having no lady would show him to be no legitimate knight, but a bastard who has entered the fortress of chivalry not through the gate but over the fence, like a thief and a robber.'

'Nevertheless,' said the traveller, 'if I remember rightly, I have read that Sir Galaor, brother of the famous Amadis of Gaul, never had a definite lady to commend himself to, and yet was none the worse thought of for that, and was a very valiant and famous knight.'

To which Don Quixote replied: 'Sir, one swallow does not make a summer. Besides, I know that Sir Galaor was secretly very much in love. Indeed, his habit of paying court to any ladies who attracted him was a trait in his nature which he was unable to control. But, to be brief, it is very well authenticated that he had only one lady whom he had made mistress of his heart, and that he commended himself to her very often and secretly, for he prided himself on being a very secretive knight.'

'Then, if it is essential for every knight errant to be in love,' said the traveller, 'it may be fairly presumed that you, your worship, being a professed knight, have also a lady. If, then, you do not pride yourself on your secrecy like Sir Galaor, I beg you most earnestly, on behalf of all this company and of myself, to inform us of the name, the country, the degree, and the beauty of your lady. For she would count herself fortunate to have all the world know that she is loved and served by such a knight as your worship appears to be.'

Here Don Quixote heaved a deep sigh and said: 'I cannot affirm whether my sweet enemy is pleased or not at the whole world's knowing that I serve her. I can only say, in reply to your very polite question, that her name is Dulcinea; her country El Toboso, a village in La Mancha; her degree at least that of Princess, for she is my Queen and mistress; her beauty superhuman, for in her are realized all the impossible and chimerical attributes of beauty which poets give to their ladies; that her hair is gold; her forehead the Elysian fields; her eyebrows rainbows; her eyes suns; her cheeks roses; her lips coral; her teeth pearls; her neck alabaster; her breast marble; her hands ivory; she is white as snow; and those parts which modesty has veiled from human sight are such, I think and believe, that discreet reflection can extol them, but make no comparison.'

'We should like to know her lineage, race, and family,' said Vivaldo.

And Don Quixote replied: 'She is not of the ancient Curtii, Caii, or Scipios of Rome; nor of the modern Colonnas and Orsinis; nor of the Moncadas and Requesenes of Catalonia; nor yet of the Rebellas and Villanovas of Valencia; of the Palafoxes, Nuzas, Rocabertis, Corellas, Lunas, Alagones, Urreas, Fozes, and Gurreas of Aragon; of the Cerdas, Manriques, Mendozas, and Guzmans of Castile; nor of the Alencastres, Pallas, and Meneses of Portugal; but of El Toboso of La Mancha, a lineage which, though modern, may yet give noble birth to the most illustrious families of future ages. Let no one contradict me in this except under the conditions which Cervino put beneath the trophy of Roland's arms:

> Let no one move them
> But one who dares his prowess against Roland.'

'Although I am descended from the Cachopines of Laredo,' replied the traveller, 'I shall not dare to compare my family with the El Tobosos of La Mancha; though, to tell you the truth, such a surname has never reached my ears till now.'

'How not reached you!' exclaimed Don Quixote.

The whole party was listening most attentively to this conversation, and everyone, even the goatherds and shepherds, realized how very much out of his wits Don Quixote was. Only Sancho Panza took all that his master said for truth, knowing who he was and having known him from his birth. But where he rather hesitated was in believing all that about the fair Dulcinea del Toboso, for he had never heard of such a name or such a princess, although he lived near El Toboso. Now, as they went along deep in this talk, they saw coming down through a gap between two high mountains some twenty shepherds, all in skins of black wool and crowned with garlands which, as they made out later, were, some of them, of yew and some of cypress. Six of their number were carrying a bier covered with a great variety of flowers and branches, and at this sight one of the goatherds remarked: 'These men must be bearing Chrysostom's body. The foot of that mountain is the place where he directed them to bury him.'

So they hurried forward, and reached the place just as the newcomers had placed the bier on the ground, and as four of them were beginning to hollow the grave beside a hard rock with their pick-

axes. The parties exchanged courteous greetings, and then Don
Quixote and his companions immediately went to look at the bier,
on which they saw a dead body, dressed like a shepherd and apparently about thirty years old, covered with flowers; and, dead though
he was, it was clear that in life he had been a handsome and courtly
young man. Around him on the bier were several books and a great
number of papers, some open and some sealed; and everyone there,
spectators, grave-diggers and the rest, kept a strange silence, till
one of the dead man's bearers said to another: 'Look carefully, Ambrosio, and see if this really is the place which Chrysostom meant,
since you wish all the directions in his will to be punctiliously
observed.'

'This is it, I know,' replied Ambrosio, 'for here my luckless
friend often told me the tale of his misfortune. Here, he said, he first
saw that mortal enemy of the human race; here it was too that he
first declared to her his passion, which was as honourable as it
was ardent; here it was that Marcela finally rejected and scorned
him, which caused him to put an end to the tragedy of his miserable
life; and here in remembrance of so much misfortune he wished to
be consigned to the bowels of eternal oblivion.'

Then, turning to Don Quixote and the travellers, he went on:
'This body, gentlemen, which you are gazing on with eyes of pity,
was the dwelling-place of a soul in which Heaven had placed an
infinite portion of its riches. This is the body of Chrysostom, a man
of unique genius, singular courtesy and extreme gentleness, a
phoenix in friendship, magnificent beyond measure, grave without
arrogance, gay without coarseness; and, in short, first in all the art
of goodness, and second to none in all the ways of misfortune. He
loved and was hated; adored and was disdained; he courted a
savage; he strove to soften marble; he pursued the wind; he cried
to the desert; he served ingratitude, whose only reward was to make
him the prey of death in the midst of his life's course. For he was
brought to his end by a shepherdess whom he strove to render immortal in the memory of mankind, as those papers you are gazing at
could well prove, if he had not ordered me to commit them to the
flames as we are committing his body to the earth.'

'Then you would be more rigorous and cruel to them than their
owner himself,' broke in Vivaldo; 'for it is neither just nor proper

to carry out a man's bequests when what he orders exceeds all reason. It would not have been right in Augustus Caesar himself if he had consented to carry out all that the divine Mantuan ordered in his will. Therefore, Ambrosio, although you commit your friend's body to the earth, you should not commit his writings to oblivion; for if he was so wronged as to ask it, you should not be so unwise as to comply, but rather, by granting life to these papers, let Marcela's cruelty live forever and serve as an example to men in times to come, so that they may shun and avoid such pitfalls. For we all know the story of your enamoured and ill-fated friend; and we know of your friendship and the reason for his death, and of the instructions he left in his last hours. From this lamentable tale can be judged the greatness of Marcela's cruelty and of Chrysostom's love, and the sincerity of your friendship. We can learn from it, too, the fate of those who rush recklessly down the path which headlong love opens before their eyes. Last night we heard of Chrysostom's death, and that he was to be buried in this place; and so from curiosity and pity we have turned out of our direct way, and agreed to come and see with our own eyes what moved us to such pity when we heard of it. In return for our compassion and our desire, if it were possible to find a remedy, we pray you, wise Ambrosio – at least I do for my part – that instead of burning these papers you will let me take some of them away.'

Then, without waiting for the shepherd's reply, he stretched out his hand and took some of them that lay nearest him. Seeing which, Ambrosio said: 'Out of courtesy, sir, I will consent to your keeping those you have taken: but it would be vain to think that I shall not burn the rest.'

Vivaldo, who longed to know what was in the papers, opened one immediately, and saw that its title was *A Song of Despair*. On hearing which Ambrosio said: 'That is the last piece the unhappy man wrote; and so that you may see, sir, to what a pass his misfortune brought him, read it aloud. For you will have time enough for that while they are digging his grave.'

'I will do so most gladly,' said Vivaldo; and, as all the bystanders were equally curious, they gathered round him in a circle, as he read in a clear voice the poem which follows.

Chapter XIV. *The Despairing Verses of the Dead Shepherd and other Unexpected Matters.*

'Since you would have me publish, cruel maid,
From tongue to tongue, from one to the other pole
The efficacy of thy rigour sharp
I'll constrain hell my grieving soul to aid,
And in my breast infuse a ton of dole,
Whereon my voice, as it is wont, may harp
And labour, as I wish, at once to carp
And tell my sorrows and thy murdering deed.
The dreadful voice and accents shall agree,
And, with them mixed, for greater torture be
Lumps of my wretched bowels, which still bleed.
Then listen, and lend thy attentive ear,
Not well-consorted tunes but howling to hear,
That from my bitter bosom's depth takes flight,
And, by constrainèd raving borne away
Issues forth for mine ease and thy despite.

'The lion's roaring, and the dreadful cries
Of ravening wolf, and hissing terrible
Of scaly serpent; and the fearful yell
Of some grim monster; and the ominous crow's
Foreboding, sinister caw; the horrible
Sound on the tossing sea of the blustering gale;
The implacable bellow of the new-conquered bull;
The lonely widowed turtle's sobbing moan,
Most mournful, and the dreary night descant
Of the envious owl, commingled with the plaint
Of all the infernal black battalion;
Let all together cry from my aching soul
United in one sound of such sad dole
That all the senses may confounded be,
For my fierce torment needs a manner new
Wherein I may recount my misery.

'The doleful echoes of such great confusion
Shall not resound o'er father Tagus' sands
Nor touch the olive-watering Betis' ears.
Of my dire pangs I'll only make effusion
'Midst these steep rocks and in the hollow lands,
With my tongue dead, yet with a living cry;
Or in some hidden vale, or on the shy
Shores that no feet of human kind defile,
Or where the sun has never shown his beam,

Or 'midst the venomous crew of beasts unclean
That draw their being from the teeming Nile.
For though amongst those lofty table-lands
The hollow echo indistinctly sounds
Thy matchless rigour and my cruel pain,
Yet, by the privilege of my niggard fates,
It will their force throughout the world proclaim.

Disdain doth kill; and, whether false or sound
Suspicions will all patience overthrow;
But jealousy with greater rigour slays;
A lengthy absence doth our life confound;
Against fear of oblivion to ensue
Firm hope of best success gives little ease.
Inevitable death lurks in all these.
But I – amazing miracle! – still live,
Jealous, absent, disdained, and certain too
Of the suspicions that my life undo.
Drowned in oblivion, I my fire revive,
And amongst all those pains have never scope
Once to behold the shadow of a hope,
Nor, thus despairing, will I hope allow;
But rather, to exacerbate my wrong,
To live for ever hopeless here I vow.

'At one same time can hope and fear exist?
Or is it reason that they should do so,
Seeing how much more cause there is for fears?
If before me dire jealousy persist,
Shall I then shut my eyes, since it will show
In my soul through a thousand bleeding scars?
Or who will not the gates unto despair
Fling open wide the moment that he spies
Murdering disdain, and notes each sad suspicion
Confirmed as truth – O bitter transformation! –
Whilst limpid truth is turned to a pack of lies?
O tyrant of love's state, fierce jealousy!
With cruel chains these hands together tie,
With twisted rope couple them, rough disdain!
But, woe is me, with bloody victory
Your memory is by my suffering slain!

'And now I die; and since all hope I've lost
Ever in life or death, to prosper now,
I obstinate will rest in fantasy,
And say he does the best who loves the most,

And that the soul most liberty doth know
When most enslaved by Love's old tyranny.
I will swear that my constant enemy
In her fair body a fair soul contains,
That her unkindness by my fault arose,
And only by the grievous hurt he does
Can Love his empire in just peace maintain.
And in this fancy, and with this hard knot
I'll hasten my appearance in that court
Where by her bitter scorn I'm forced to come,
And offering to the winds body and soul,
Forfeit the future's laurel wreath and palm.

' Thou that by multiplying wrongs dost show
The reason forcing me to violence
Against this weary life, that's now grown hateful,
Since now by signs notorious thou dost know
From my heart's deepest wound how gladly sense
Doth sacrifice me to thy scorns ungrateful,
Shouldst thou, perchance, my merits find so fruitful
As to dim the clear heaven of your eyes,
And cloud them with my death, yet weep not so.
For I'll yield you no tribute by my woe,
Nor give you my soul's booty as your prize.
But rather, laughing at my funeral sad,
Show how my end begins to make thee glad.
But 'tis a folly to advise thee this,
For I know that in hurrying on my death
Consists my glory and thy chiefest bliss.

' Let Tantalus from the profoundest deeps
Come, for it is high time now, with his thirst;
And Sisyphus with his oppressive stone;
Let Tityus bring his vulture that ne'er sleeps,
Nor Ixion delay with wheel accursed;
Nor the three sisters, ever labouring on;
And let them all at once their mortal pain
Translate into my breast, and scarce aloud
(If funeral rites are granted my despair)
Chant their sad obsequies with doleful air
Over a corpse even denied a shroud.
And the three-faced infernal porter grim,
With thousand monsters and chimaeras come
And swell the mournful descant of despair;
No greater pomp than this, I fear, is due
To any constant lover on his bier.

Despairing song, I beg thee not to grieve
When my sad company thou com'st to leave;
But rather since the course whence thou didst spring
By my misfortune grows more fortunate,
Even in the grave thou must shun sorrowing.'

Chrysostom's song pleased its hearers, though Vivaldo said that
it did not seem to him to conform to the account he had heard of
Marcela's modesty and goodness. For in it Chrysostom complained
of jealousy, suspicions, and neglect, all to the prejudice of Marcela's
good name and fame. But Ambrosio answered him out of the knowledge of his friend's most private thoughts: 'To satisfy your doubt,
sir, I must tell you that when the unfortunate man wrote this song
he had voluntarily banished himself from Marcela to see if absence
would have its customary effect upon him. And as there is nothing
that does not vex the absent lover, and no fear that does not pursue
him, so Chrysostom was tormented by imaginary jealousies and
suspicions, as fearful as if they were real. Marcela's goodness, therefore, is as true as fame proclaimed it; for, except for cruelty, some
haughtiness, and much scorn, there is no fault that envy itself can
rightly find in her.'

'That is true,' replied Vivaldo. And he was going to read another
of the papers which he had saved from the fire when he was prevented by a miraculous vision – for such it seemed   which suddenly
appeared before their eyes. For on the top of the rock in which they
were digging the grave appeared the shepherdess Marcela, looking
even more beautiful than she had been described. Those of them
who knew her well were just as amazed. But no sooner did Ambrosio catch sight of her than he cried with some show of anger:

'Have you come here, perhaps, fiery basilisk of these mountains, to
see if the wounds of this wretch, whom your cruelty killed, will bleed
afresh at the sight of you? Or have you come to triumph at your
nature's cruel work? Or to gaze from that height, like another pitiless Nero, upon the flames of burning Rome? Or, in your pride, to
trample this miserable corpse, as Tarquin's ungrateful daughter did
her father's? Tell us quickly why you have come, or what you desire. For, as I know that Chrysostom never failed to be obedient to
you during his life, I will take care that even in his death all who
call themselves his friends obey you.'

'I have come, Ambrosio, for none of the reasons you give,' replied Marcela, 'but rather to defend myself, and to prove how wrong are those who blame me for their own sufferings and for Chrysostom's death. So I ask all of you here to give me your attention, for it will not take me much time or waste many words to persuade all sensible men of the truth. Heaven made me, you say, so lovely that my beauty makes you love me despite yourselves; and in return for the love you show me, you claim, and even demand, that I should be bound to love you. I know by the natural sense which God has given me that whatever is beautiful is lovable; but I do not understand why, merely because she inspires love, a woman who is loved for her beauty is obliged to love the man who loves her. Besides, it may chance that the man who loves what is beautiful is himself ugly; and, as ugliness is loathsome, it would be absurd for him to say: "I love you for your beauty; love me although I am ugly." But, even supposing that both are equally beautiful, the attraction need not therefore be equal on both sides. For not all beauties inspire love; some only please the eye, but do not subdue the heart. Now if all beauty inspired love and made conquests, the hearts of men would wander confused and astray, not knowing where to alight; for as beauties are infinite, the feelings they inspire must be infinite too. Besides, as I have heard, true love cannot be divided, but must be free and unconstrained. If this is so, as I believe it is, why do you ask me to do violence to my heart, merely because you say you love me? Tell me, if the Heavens had made me ugly instead of beautiful, should I have had the right to complain of your not loving me? What is more, you must consider that I did not choose to be beautiful. My beauty, such as it is, the Heavens gave me freely, without my choice or asking; and just as the viper deserves no blame for the poison which nature gave her, even though she kills with it, I cannot be blamed for being beautiful. For beauty in a modest woman is like distant fire or a sharp sword; the one does not burn nor the other cut the man who does not come near it. Modesty and the virtues are the adornments of the soul, and without them, even if the body is beautiful, it ought not to appear so. Now if modesty is one of the virtues and the fairest adornment of the body and the soul, why must the woman who is loved for her beauty lose it to gratify the desires of a man who, for his pleasure alone, tries with all his strength and ingenuity to rob her of it? I was born free, and to live free I chose the solitude of the fields. The trees on these mountains are my companions; the clear waters of these streams my mirrors; to the trees and the waters I disclose my thoughts and my beauty. I am the distant fire and the far-off sword. Those whom I have attracted with my eyes I have undeceived with my words. If desires are nourished on hope, as I never gave any to Chrysostom or to any other, it may not justly be said that any man's end was my doing, since it was his persistence rather than my cruelties that killed him. And if it is objected that his intentions were honest, and that therefore I was obliged to reciprocate them, my answer is that when he revealed to me the honesty of his intentions on this same spot where now you are digging his grave, I told him that my will was to live in perpetual solitude, and that only the earth would enjoy the fruit of my chastity and the spoils of my beauty. If, despite all this discouragement, he chose to persist against hope and to sail against the wind, is it surprising that he should have drowned in the gulf of his own folly? If I had encouraged him in hope, I should have been false; if I had gratified him, I should have acted against my better feelings and resolutions. He persisted despite discouragement, despaired although not hated. Judge then whether it is right that I should pay the penalty for his sufferings! If I have deceived anyone, let him complain; if I have broken my promise to anyone, let him despair; if I lure anyone on, let him declare it; if I encourage anyone, let him boast of it. But let me not be called cruel or murderous by those whom I have never promised, deceived, lured on, or encouraged. Heaven has not yet fated me to love; and it is folly to think that I shall love out of choice. May this general warning serve for the particular benefit of every man who woos me; and henceforth be it understood that if anyone dies on my account, he will not die out of jealousy or from rejection; for she who loves no man can make no man jealous, and discouragement must not be taken for disdain. If anyone calls me a wild beast and a basilisk, let him shun me as a mischievous and evil thing; if he calls me ungrateful, let him serve me no more; if he calls me strange, know me no more; if cruel, follow me no more; for this wild beast, this basilisk, this ungrateful, strange, and cruel creature will in no way seek, serve, know, or follow him. If Chrysostom's impatience and headstrong passion killed him, why should my modesty and reserve be blamed? If I preserve my purity in the company of the trees, why should he who would have me keep the company of men desire me to lose it? I, as you know, have riches of my own, and covet no one else's. I have a taste for freedom and no wish for subjection. I neither love nor hate any man. I do not deceive one man and encourage another. I do not trifle with one nor keep another in hope. I enjoy the modest company of the village shepherdesses and the care of my goats. My desires are bounded by these mountains; and if they extend beyond them, it is to contemplate the beauty of the sky, a step by which the soul travels to its first abode.'

When she had finished, she turned round without waiting for a reply and plunged into the densest part of the nearby woods, leaving everyone as amazed at her good sense as at her beauty. Some whom the mighty arrow of her fair eyes' gaze had wounded made as if to follow her, heedless of the plain words of discouragement they had just heard. But here Don Quixote, thinking that this was an occasion to exercise his chivalry by the succouring of a maiden in distress, put his hand on his sword-hilt, and loudly and clearly exclaimed:

'Let no man, of whatsoever estate or condition, dare to follow the fair Marcela, under pain of incurring my most furious indignation! She has shown with clear and sufficient argument that she bears little or no blame for Chrysostom's death, and how far she is from yielding to any of her lovers' desires. Wherefore it is right that, instead of being pursued and persecuted, she should be honoured and esteemed by all good men in the world, for she has proved that she is the only woman living with such pure intentions.'

Now whether because of Don Quixote's threats or of Ambrosio's request that they should fulfil the debt they owed to his friend, not one of the shepherds stirred or moved from the place until the grave had been dug, Chrysostom's papers burnt, and his body buried amidst the tears of the spectators.

They sealed the grave with a heavy stone until such time as they should have a tombstone ready, which Ambrosio informed them he intended to have made, and inscribed with the following epitaph:

Here a poor loving swain's
Frozen corpse lies.
He was a shepherd and
Died of disdain.

Died of the cruelty
Of a coy, thankless, fair
Maid, by whom Love's empire
Widens its tyranny.

Then they spread flowers and branches in plenty over the grave, and each of the shepherds, after condoling with his friend Ambrosio, bade him good-bye. Vivaldo and his companions did the same, and Don Quixote said farewell to his hosts and to the travellers, who pressed him to come with them to Seville, which was just the place to strike adventures in, they said, for there are more to be found there, in every street and round every corner, than can be met with in any other place. Don Quixote thanked them for their advice and their evident desire to do him a service, but said that for the present he neither could nor should go to Seville until he had cleared all those mountains of the thieves and robbers who were said to infest them.

In view of this honest purpose, the travellers did not care to press him further. But once more bidding him farewell, they left him and pursued their journey, in the course of which they did not fail to discuss the story of Marcela and Chrysostom as well as the follies of Don Quixote. As for him, he decided to go in search of the shepherdess Marcela and offer her all the service in his power. But things did not turn out as he expected, as will be told in the course of this true story, of which the second part ends here.

Chapter XV. *Of the unfortunate Adventure which befel Don Quixote on his Encounter with some Merciless Yanguesans.*

THE sage Cide Hamete Benengeli relates that as soon as Don Quixote had bidden farewell to his hosts and to everyone who had been present at the shepherd Chrysostom's burial, he and his squire entered that same wood into which they had seen the shepherdess Marcela disappear. And when they had travelled through it for more than two hours, looking for her in vain in all directions, they halted in a meadow, rich in fresh grass, beside which ran a pleasant and refreshing brook, which invited them, or rather induced them, to spend the sultry hours of midday there; for the heat had already become oppressive. Don Quixote and Sancho dismounted and, leaving the ass and Rocinante at large to feed on the abundant grass, they ransacked their saddle-bags. Then, without ceremony, master and man ate the contents in peace and good fellowship. Now Sancho had not troubled to fetter Rocinante, secure in his belief that he was so mild and so little lustful a beast that all the mares in the pastures of Cordova would not provoke him to any impropriety. But as Fate, or the Devil – who is not always sleeping – would have it, there was a herd of Galician mares grazing in that valley. They belonged to some carriers from Yanguas whose habit it is to spend midday with their droves where there is grass and water; and the place where Don Quixote happened to be suited the Yanguesans very well. So it came about that Rocinante was taken with the desire to disport himself with the lady mares and, abandoning his natural pace and habits the moment he smelt them, asked no permission of his master, but set off at a brisk trot to acquaint them of his needs. But they, apparently, preferred the pastures, and gave him such a welcome with their hooves and teeth that in a very short while they had broken his girths and left him stripped of his saddle and naked. But what must have hurt him more was that the carriers, seeing the violence he was offering to their mares, ran up with pack-staves, and laid into him so hard that he was soon on the ground in a very sorry state. At this point Don Quixote and Sancho, who had witnessed Rocinante's beating, ran up panting, the knight saying to his squire:

'From what I can see, friend Sancho, these are no knights, but vile and low-bred men. I say this so that you may freely help me to take due vengeance for the outrage which they have done to Rocinante before our very eyes.'

'How the devil can we take revenge,' replied Sancho, 'when there are more than twenty of them, and we are only two – or perhaps no more than one and a half?'

'I am equal to a hundred,' answered Don Quixote. Then without further discussion he drew his sword and attacked the Yanguesans; and Sancho Panza was spurred on by his master's example to do the same. At the first blow Don Quixote gave one of them a slash, which slit the leather coat he was wearing and cut a great gash in his shoulder. But the Yanguesans, seeing so many of themselves so roughly treated by a mere two men, seized their pack-staves and, surrounding the pair, began to lay into them with might and main. In fact, they stretched Sancho on the ground at their second blow, and the same fate soon befell Don Quixote, his skill and courage availing him nothing; and, as Fate would have it, he fell at the feet of the still prostrate Rocinante. All of which goes to show what hard bruises pack-staves will deal in the hands of angry rustics. Then, seeing the damage they had done, the Yanguesans loaded their beasts as fast as they could and went on their way, leaving the two adventurers in an evil plight and a worse humour.

The first to regain his senses was Sancho Panza who, finding himself beside his master, cried in a weak and piteous voice: 'Don Quixote! Ah, Don Quixote!'

'What is the matter, brother Sancho?' answered Don Quixote in the same faint and plaintive tones.

'Well, sir,' said Sancho Panza, 'I should be glad if your worship could let me have two gulps of that drink of Fair Bras's, if you've got it handy. Perhaps it might be as good for broken bones as it is for wounds.'

'Why,' replied Don Quixote, 'if I had some here, wretch that I am, what more could I want? But I swear to you, Sancho Panza, on my word as a knight errant that, unless fortune ordains otherwise, I will have some in my possession before two days have passed, or it will be no fault of mine.'

'How long does your worship suppose it will be before we shall be able to use our feet?' asked Sancho Panza.

'For myself,' replied the bruised knight Don Quixote, 'I must say that I can see no end to our present plight. But I take the blame for everything upon myself, for I should not have drawn my sword against men who were not dubbed knights, as I am. That is why I believe that the God of battles has permitted me to be so chastised – for breaking the laws of chivalry. So, Sancho Panza, you must be warned by what I am going to say, for it greatly concerns the welfare of us both. It is, that when you see us insulted by such rabble you must not wait for me to draw my sword on them, for I shall on no account do so. But you must draw your own and chastise them at your pleasure. Should any knights come to their aid or defence, I shall know how to protect you and shall attack them with all my strength; and you have already had a thousand signs and proofs of the height to which the valour of this strong arm of mine can reach.' So arrogant was the poor gentleman at his victory over the brave Basque.

But Sancho Panza did not find his master's instructions so good that he could refrain from replying, 'Sir, I am a peaceable, mild, quiet man, and I can overlook any kind of injury, for I have a wife to keep and children to bring up. So let me tell your worship by way of a hint – for it's not my place to give orders – that I shall on no account draw my sword against peasant or against knight, and that from now on, before God, I pardon whatever insults have been, or shall be, done me, whether by person high or low, rich or poor, by gentleman or by commoner, without exception of rank or quality.'

On hearing this, his master replied: 'I wish that I had breath enough to say a few words at my ease, and that the pain I feel in this rib would die down even slightly, so that I could convince you, Sancho Panza, of your error. Listen, wretch! Suppose that the winds of fortune, now so contrary, should turn in our favour, swelling the sails of our desires, and we should reach harbour, safely and unhurt, in one of those isles I promised you – what would become of you if I won it and made you its master? You would ruin everything by not being a knight, nor desiring to be one, having neither the courage nor the resolution to avenge insults and defend your dominions. For you must know that in newly conquered kingdoms and provinces the minds of the natives are never so quiet, or so well disposed to their new lords there, as to leave no fear of their planning some revolt, so as to reverse the state of things once more and, as they say, try their luck again. So the new master must needs have the intelligence to know how to rule, and the courage to take offensive and defensive measures in every emergency.'

'I wish I had had the intelligence and courage you speak of,' replied Sancho, 'when this last thing happened to us; but you must take a poor man's word for it that I'm in greater need of plasters than of sermons. Try, sir, if you can't get up; and we'll see if we can help Rocinante, although he doesn't deserve it, for he was the chief cause of all the knocking about we got. I never thought it of him; for I imagined he was as chaste and peaceable a fellow as I am myself. It is a good saying, after all, that it takes a long time to get to know people, and that there's nothing certain in this life. Who would have said that after all those great sword-thrusts you dealt that wretched knight errant, this great storm of blows would have followed up so fast and burst on our shoulders?'

'Yours,' replied Don Quixote, 'must have been made for such a storm, but as mine were nurtured between cambrics and fine linen, clearly they are more sensitive to the pain of this mishap. If it were not that I imagine – why do I say imagine? – that I most certainly know that all these discomforts are inseparable from the profession of arms, I would be ready to die here of pure vexation.'

To which the squire replied: 'Sir, if these misfortunes are the fruit of chivalry, will your worship tell me if they happen very often, or if they only occur at set times? For it seems to me that after two such crops we should be useless for the third, unless God, of His infinite pity, were to come to our aid.'

'You must know, friend Sancho,' replied Don Quixote, 'that a knight errant's life is subject to countless perils and mischances. Yet he has none the less the potentiality of rising at any moment to become King or Emperor, as experience has demonstrated in the case of many and divers knights whose histories I know in detail. If my pain would let me I could tell you now of some who have climbed, by the valour of their arms alone, to the high degree I mentioned; yet those very knights, both beforehand and afterwards, sustained various calamities and misfortunes. For the valorous Amadis of Gaul was once in the power of his mortal enemy, Arcalaus the enchanter, who, it is well attested, when he held him prisoner, tied him to a pillar in a courtyard and gave him more than two hundred lashes with the reins of his own horse. There is a little-known author too of no small reputation, who says that the Knight of the Sun, being caught in a certain castle by means of a trap-door which gave way beneath his feet, found himself after his fall bound hand and foot in a subterranean cavern; and there they administered to him what is called an enema, of snow-water and sand, which nearly killed him; and if a certain sage who was a great friend of his had not succoured him in his dreadful plight, things would have gone very badly with the poor knight. So I can well afford to suffer in such good company, since they sustained greater affronts than we are suffering now. For I would have you know, Sancho, that wounds dealt with instruments which are accidentally in the hand do not disgrace a man; that is expressly laid down in the law of the duel. So if a shoemaker strikes a man with the last he is holding, even though it is of wood, it shall not therefore be said that the man whom he struck was cudgelled. I say this in case you may suppose that, because we have come out of this struggle soundly bruised, we are disgraced; since the arms which those men carried and pounded us with were no other than their pack-staves; and not one of them, so far as I can remember, carried a rapier, sword, or dagger.'

'They did not give me a chance,' replied Sancho, 'to observe them so closely. For I had no sooner put my hand to my blade than they made so many crosses on my shoulders with their sticks, that they knocked the sight out of my eyes and the strength out of my feet, and laid me out where I'm lying now. I don't care a hang, down here, whether the beating was a disgrace or not, but I do mind a lot about the pain I got from it, and that's likely to stay as deeply in my memory as it bit into my back.'

'For all that, brother Panza,' replied Don Quixote, 'let me tell you that there is no memory which time does not efface, nor any pain that death does not destroy.'

'But what misfortune could be worse,' replied Sancho, 'than one that waits for time to efface it and death to destroy it? If ours were the sort of misfortune that could be cured with a couple of poultices it wouldn't be so bad. But I'm beginning to think that all the plasters in a hospital wouldn't be enough to give it a turn for the better.'

'No more of that, Sancho,' replied Don Quixote, 'but make the best of a bad business, and I shall do the same. Let us see how Rocinante is, for it seems to me that the poor creature got by no means the smallest share of the disaster.'

'There's nothing marvellous about that,' replied Sancho, 'since he's a knight errant too. What does astonish me is that my ass has got off scot-free, while we've got our ribs broken.'

'Fortune always leaves one door open in disasters, to admit a remedy,' said Don Quixote. 'I say this because your little beast will now serve instead of Rocinante to carry me from here to some castle where my wound may be cured. What is more, I shall not consider such a mount a disgrace, for I remember reading how good old Silenus, tutor and guide to the merry god of laughter, rode most gladly on a very handsome ass when he entered the city of the hundred gates.'

'It's very likely he rode as your worship says,' replied Sancho; 'but there's a great deal of difference between riding astride and being laid across like a sack of dung.'

'Wounds received in battle,' answered Don Quixote, 'rather confer honour than take it away. So, friend Panza, give me no more answers, but do as I have told you. Get up as best you can and place me on your ass in any way you like. Then let us depart, before night comes and overtakes us in this wilderness.'

'Yet I have heard your worship say,' said Panza, 'that it is quite the thing for knights errant to sleep in moorland and deserts for the greater part of the year, and to think themselves very fortunate to do so.'

'That is when they cannot help it,' said Don Quixote, 'or when they are in love. In fact there have been knights who have stayed on a rock exposed to sun and shade and all the inclemencies of Heaven for two years, unknown to their ladies; and one of these was Amadis, when he assumed the name of Beltenebros and took up his lodging on the Bare Rock, for eight years, or perhaps eight months – for I am not sure of my reckoning. Suffice it that he was doing penance there for some displeasure the lady Oriana had caused him. But let us leave the matter, before some misfortune like Rocinante's befalls the ass.'

'That would be the devil and all,' observed Sancho. And then, uttering thirty groans, sixty sighs, and a hundred and twenty damns and curses on whoever it was that had got him there, he raised himself, but stopped half-way, bent like a Turkish bow, unable to straighten himself up. However, despite his pain, he harnessed his ass, who had also taken advantage of that day's excess of liberty to stray a little. He then got Rocinante up; and he, if he had had a tongue to complain with, would certainly not have been outdone by squire or master. In the end, Sancho settled Don Quixote on the ass and, tying Rocinante to his tail, led his beast by the halter, making as best he could for the direction in which he thought the highway lay.

And he had not gone more than two miles when Fortune, who was guiding their affairs from good to better, brought him to the road, on which he sighted an inn, which, to his grief and Don Quixote's pleasure, must needs be a castle. Sancho swore that it was an inn, and his master that it was no inn but a castle; and the argument lasted so long that it was not finished when they arrived there, and Sancho entered without further enquiry, followed by his string of beasts.

Chapter XVI. *What happened to the ingenious knight in the Inn that he took for a Castle.*

THE innkeeper, who saw Don Quixote lying across the ass, asked Sancho what was wrong with him. Sancho replied that it was nothing, that he had fallen off a rock and bruised his ribs slightly. Now the innkeeper's wife was a woman of a different sort from the generality of hostesses, for she was kindly by nature and felt for her neighbours' misfortunes. So she immediately set about the cure of Don Quixote and made her young daughter, a very good-looking girl, help her to tend him.

There was an Asturian maid at the inn, broad-faced, flat-nosed, and with a head that seemed to have no back to it; she was blind of one eye and not too sound in the other. But she made up for her other shortcomings by her bodily allurements; she was not more than three feet high from head to toe, and her shoulders, which were rather on the heavy side, made her look down on the ground more than she liked. This charming maid, then, helped her young mistress, and the two of them made a very poor bed for Don Quixote in an attic which had evidently served once, for a long time, as a straw-loft.

There was a carrier lodging in this garret as well. His bed stood a little farther from the door than our knight's; and, although it consisted only of his mule's saddles and blankets, it was a good deal better than Don Quixote's, which was made up of four badly planed boards resting on a pair of not too even trestles; a mattress thin as a quilt and full of lumps, which were as hard as stones to the touch but appeared through various rents in the cover to be wool; two sheets, made of the leather used for shields, and a coverlet whose every thread anyone who wished could have counted without missing a single one.

On this execrable bed Don Quixote lay down, whereupon the hostess and her daughter poulticed him from head to foot, while Maritornes – for this was the Asturian maid's name – held a light.

The hostess, as she plastered him, seeing that parts of his body were covered with weals, remarked that he must have had a beating, not a fall.

'It wasn't a beating,' said Sancho, 'but the rock had a lot of jags and knobs, and each one must have made its mark. And, by the way, if you could be so very kind as to leave a little of that wadding, it might come in handy for someone, for my back's giving me a bit of trouble too.'

'Oh, I see,' replied the hostess; 'you must have had a fall as well.'

'I didn't fall,' said Sancho, 'but I got such a shock from seeing my master tumble that my body aches all over, as if I had been beaten black and blue.'

'That may well be,' said the innkeeper's daughter, 'for very often I've dreamt I fell off a tower and never reached the ground. And when I've woken up I've found myself as bruised and bumped as if I had really tumbled.'

'But here's the point, lady,' replied Sancho Panza. 'I wasn't dreaming. I was more wide awake than I am now, and there I was, almost as bruised as my master Don Quixote.'

'What's the gentleman's name?' asked the Asturian maid.

'Don Quixote de la Mancha,' replied Sancho Panza. 'He's a knight errant. One of the best and bravest the world has seen for a very long time.'

'What's a knight errant?' asked the maid.

'Are you so green that you don't know that?' replied Sancho. 'Then I'll tell you, my girl, that a knight errant – to cut a long story short – is beaten up one day and made Emperor the next. To-day he's the most unfortunate and poverty-stricken creature in the world; to-morrow he'll have two or three kingdoms to give to his squire.'

'Well, seeing that you have such a fine master,' said the hostess, 'how is it you aren't at least a count?'

'There's plenty of time yet,' replied Sancho. 'We've only been out seeking adventures for a month, and up to now we haven't come across anything worth calling one; and sometimes when you're looking for one thing you find another. But I promise you that, if my master Don Quixote recovers from his wound or fall, and I'm not crippled by mine, I won't swap my chances for the noblest title in Spain.'

Here Don Quixote, who had listened very attentively to all this chatter, sat up in bed as best he could and, taking the hostess's hand, addressed her:

'Believe me, beauteous lady, you may count yourself fortunate to have lodging in your castle a person whom I must refrain from praising only because self-praise is said to be a practice unworthy of a gentleman. But my squire will tell you who I am. I will only say that I shall bear the services you have done me eternally inscribed in my memory, so that I may remain grateful to you all the days of my life. Had it not pleased Heaven to keep me in such abject servitude to love's laws and to the eyes of that ungrateful beauty whose name I dare hardly breathe, then the eyes of your beauteous daughter would hold my freedom captive.'

The hostess, her daughter, and the worthy Maritornes were bewildered by the knight errant's words, which might have been Greek so little could they understand them, though they realized that they were all intended as thanks and compliments. But, as they were not used to such language, they stared at him in amazement; for he seemed so very different from the sort of men they were accustomed to. So, thanking him in their innkeepers' language, they left him, and the Asturian maid tended Sancho, who was in no less need of attention than his master.

Now the carrier had arranged with her that they should spend the night together in healthy sport; and she had promised that once the guests were quiet and her master and mistress asleep she would come to him and give him all the pleasure he could desire. And it is told to the credit of this good girl that she never made such promises without fulfilling them, even if she made them far away in the mountains and without any witness at all. For she prided herself on being a maiden of breeding, and did not feel degraded by serving in an inn, because only misfortune and ill-chance, as she said, had brought her to that pass.

Don Quixote's hard, narrow, miserable apology for a bed was the first in this starlit barn; and next beside him Sancho had made his, which consisted only of a rush mat and a horse-blanket, which seemed to be of threadbare canvas rather than of wool. Beyond these two came the carrier's bed, made, as we have said, of the saddles and all the trappings of the two best mules he had. He had twelve glossy, well-covered, splendid beasts, for he was one of the richest muleteers in Arevalo, as the author of this history tells us; and he makes a special mention of this carrier, because he knew him very well, and it is even suggested that he was some relation of his. But, however that may be, Cide Hamete Benengeli was a very exact historian and very precise in all his details, as can be seen by his not passing over these various points, trivial and petty though they may be. He should be an example to those grave historians who give us so short and skimped an account of events that we scarcely taste them, and so the most substantial part of their work, out of carelessness, malice, or ignorance, remains in their ink-horns. A thousand blessings then on the author of *Tablante de Ricamonte* and the writer of that other book which tells us of the deeds of Count Tomillas, for the exhaustiveness with which they describe everything.

But to return to the story. After the carrier had visited his mules and given them their second feed, he stretched himself on his pack-saddles and awaited his most punctual Maritornes. By now Sancho was poulticed and had lain down; but, though he tried to sleep, the pain in his sides would not allow him. Don Quixote, too, with the pain of his ribs was no more able to close his eyes than a hare. The whole inn was in silence, and there was no other light in it but that of a hanging lamp which burnt in the centre of the doorway.

This phenomenal quiet and his habitual preoccupation with the adventures that are related on every page of those books that had been his undoing wrought one of the strangest possible fancies in our knight's imagination. He thought that he had arrived at a famous castle – for, as we have said, every inn where he stayed seemed to him a castle – , and that the innkeeper's daughter was really the

daughter of the warden. Overwhelmed by his nobility, she had
fallen in love with him and, what is more, she had promised that
very night, when her parents were asleep, to come and lie with him
awhile. And taking all this fantasy which he had invented for the
sober truth, he began to be disturbed and to think of the critical
danger to which his honour was exposed, deciding in his heart to
commit no treason against the lady Dulcinea del Toboso, even
though Queen Guinevere and her lady Quintañona should appear
before him.

Whilst he was brooding on this nonsense, unfortunately for him
the time arrived for the Asturian maid's visit. She came in her shift,
with bare feet and hair done up in a fustian kerchief. With soft and
noiseless steps she entered the garret in which the three men were
lodged, in search of the carrier. But scarcely had she reached the
door when Don Quixote heard her; and, sitting up in bed, despite his
plasters and his aching ribs, he stretched out his arms to receive his
beauteous maiden. She was gliding modestly and silently, groping
with outstretched hands for her lover, when she stumbled into the
arms of Don Quixote, who seized her tightly by one wrist and,
drawing her to him, she not daring to say a word, forced her to sit
on his bed.

Then he felt her shift and, although it was of sackcloth, it seemed
to him of the finest, most delicate satin. The glass beads that she
wore on her wrist had for him the sheen of rare orient pearls. Her
hair, which was coarse as a horse's mane, seemed to him strands of
the most glistening gold of Arabia, whose splendour eclipsed the
very sun. And her mouth, which, no doubt, reeked of the stale salad
of the night before, seemed to him to breathe out a sweet and
aromatic odour. In short, he bestowed on her each several feature
of that famous princess who came, in the books that he had read, to
visit the sore-wounded knight whom she loved so well. In every detail of dress and bearing his imagination copied her exactly. And so
blind was the poor knight that neither her touch nor her breath nor
anything else about the good maiden revealed his mistake to him,
though she would have turned the stomach of anyone but a carrier.
Far from it, he imagined that he held in his arms the goddess of
beauty and, gripping her tight, in soft, amorous tones he began:

'Would that I could find means, most lovely and high-born lady, with which I could repay the singular favour you have done me in displaying your great beauty. But Fortune, which is never weary of persecuting good men, has laid me on this bed, so bruised and battered that even if I wished to satisfy your desires I could not. And besides that impediment there is another and greater, the pledge of faith I have given to the peerless Dulcinea del Toboso, sole mistress of my most secret thoughts. But were I not prevented in this way, I should not be so simple a knight as to let pass the happy chance you have deigned to offer me.'

Maritornes was bathed in a sweat of anguish at finding herself grasped by Don Quixote and, without understanding or paying the least attention to his protestations, tried silently to break loose. As for the good carrier, whose lusts kept him awake, he had heard his wench from the moment she came in, and had been listening attentively to the knight's every word. Suspecting that the Asturian maid had broken her promise to him in favour of another, he edged nearer and nearer to Don Quixote's bed, silently waiting to see what his incomprehensible speech might lead to. But, when he saw the maid struggling to break loose and Don Quixote trying to hold her, the jest seemed to him to have gone too far. Whereupon he raised his arm and dealt the amorous knight so terrible a blow on his lean jaws that his mouth was filled with blood; and, not content with this, he trod on his ribs and trampled him up and down at a lively rate.

The bed was rather weak and supported on no firm foundations. So, unable to bear the additional weight of the carrier, it gave way with a great crash. This woke the innkeeper, who called for Maritornes and, getting no reply, suspected that she must be the cause of the noise. With this in his mind he got up and, lighting a lamp, made his way towards the scene of the disturbance. The maid, hearing her master coming in and knowing his very bad temper, in fear and alarm climbed into the bed of the still-sleeping Sancho and huddled up in a ball.

At this point the innkeeper entered shouting: 'Where are you, you whore? This is all your doing; I'm sure of it.'

Whereat Sancho, feeling this weight almost on top of him, thought it was a nightmare and began to strike out right and left. A good number of his blows fell on Maritornes, who with the pain of them forgot her modesty and gave him as many in return. This dispelled his dream and, finding himself thus treated and not knowing by whom, he clinched with Maritornes, and the two of them started the most stubborn and comical scuffle in the world. Whereupon the carrier, seeing by the light of the innkeeper's lamp how ill his mistress was faring, left Don Quixote and joined in to give her all necessary help. So did the innkeeper, but with a different purpose: to beat the maid, under the impression that she was the sole cause of all that harmony. And then, as the saying goes, the cat chased the rat, the rat chased the rope, the rope chased the stick. The carrier beat Sancho, Sancho beat the maid, the maid beat him, the innkeeper beat the maid, and they all laid it on so fast that they never took a moment's rest. While, to improve the joke, the innkeeper's lamp went out and left them all in a heap in the dark, lamming out unmercifully and dealing great execution wherever they hit.

It happened that there was staying in the inn that night an officer of the Ancient and Holy Brotherhood of Toledo, who also heard the extraordinary din of the fight and, seizing his wand of office and the tin box with his warrants in it, went into the room in the dark, crying: 'Stop in the name of justice! Stop in the name of the Holy Brotherhood!'

Now the first person he collided with was the poor, trampled knight, lying on his back unconscious amidst the ruins of his bed. And his hand touching the knight's beard as he groped, the officer repeated: 'Help the officers of the Law!' But, seeing that the man he had seized neither struggled nor stirred, he took him for dead and the people in the garret for his murderers; which made him shout even louder: 'Shut the inn door! Let no one go out. There's been a man murdered here!'

This cry alarmed them all, and as soon as they heard it they stopped the brawl. The innkeeper slipped back to his room, the carrier to his pack-saddles, the maid to her corner. Only the unfortunate Don and Sancho were unable to stir from where they lay. At this the officer let go Don Quixote's beard and went out to find a light, with the intention of seeking and arresting the criminals. But he could not find one, because the innkeeper had purposely put out the lamp when he retired to his quarters. So the officer had to go across to the hearth, where, after much time and trouble, he lit another.

Chapter XVII. *Concerning countless more hardships which the brave Don Quixote and his good squire Sancho Panza endured in the Inn which he unfortunately mistook for a Castle.*

BY this time Don Quixote had recovered from his swoon and, in the same tones in which he had called his squire the day before, when he was lying in the Valley of the Stakes, began to cry: 'Sancho, my friend, are you asleep? Are you asleep, friend Sancho?'

'Sleep, confound it,' replied Sancho in gloom and despair. 'How can I sleep when all the devils in hell must have been at me to-night?'

'You are right about that, for certain,' replied Don Quixote. 'For, if I know anything, this castle is enchanted. You should know ... But what I am going to tell you now you must swear to keep secret till the day of my death.'

'I swear,' replied Sancho.

'You must swear, because I hate to take away anyone's reputation,' continued Don Quixote.

'I do swear, I tell you,' repeated Sancho, 'that I will keep silent to the very last days of your honour's life. And please God I may be free to speak to-morrow.'

'Have I done you such harm, Sancho,' replied Don Quixote, 'that you would have me die so soon?'

'It's not that,' answered Sancho, 'but I hate to keep things long in case they go mouldy from over-keeping.'

'Be that as it may,' said Don Quixote, 'I would trust even greater matters to your love and courtesy. I would have you know that to-night I have encountered one of the strangest adventures imaginable. In short, just now there came to me the daughter of the warden of this castle, the most graceful and beauteous damsel that could be found over the greater part of the world. What could I not tell you of the loveliness of her body? Of her sprightly intelligence? And of those other hidden things that, to keep the faith I owe to my lady Dulcinea del Toboso, I will let pass untouched and unspoken? I will only tell you that, whether because Heaven was envious of the great boon that this adventure had brought me, or perhaps – more probably – because, as I have said, this castle is enchanted, just as I was in sweet and amorous colloquy with her, there came a hand and an arm of some monstrous giant. Where it came from I did not see, nor could I imagine, but it gave me such a blow on the jaws that I was bathed in blood. And after that it pounded me so that I am in worse plight than yesterday, when the carriers did us the injury you know of on account of Rocinante's excess of spirits. From which I conclude that the treasure of that damsel's beauty must be guarded by some Moorish enchanter and is not for me.'

'Nor for me either,' replied Sancho, 'for more than four hundred Moors have mauled me, so that the carriers' beating was tarts and gingerbread in comparison. But tell me, sir, what sort of a fine and rare adventure do you call it that leaves us in this plight? Indeed your worship came off best, for you had in your arms that incomparable beauty you spoke of. But what did I get but the worst beating I ever expect to get in all my life? I wish I had never been born! I am no knight errant and I don't ever expect to be one; but I get the greater share of the misfortunes for all that.'

'Then you got beaten as well?' asked Don Quixote.

'Didn't I say so, devil take it?' Sancho replied.

'Do not worry about that,' said Don Quixote. 'For now I will make up the precious balsam, which will heal us in the twinkling of an eye.'

By then the officer had lit his lamp and come in to view the supposed corpse, and Sancho, seeing an ugly-faced man in his shirt and night-cap with his lamp in his hand, asked his master: 'Will this perhaps be the Moorish enchanter come to give us another hiding, in case there's anywhere he forgot to hit us last time?'

'It cannot be the Moor,' replied Don Quixote, 'for magicians never allow themselves to be seen by anyone.'

'If you can't see them you can certainly feel them,' said Sancho; 'my shoulders can vouch for that.'

'So might mine,' replied Don Quixote; 'but that is not enough to prove that that man is the Moorish enchanter.'

The officer approached. But, seeing them conversing so calmly, he stopped in surprise. Don Quixote, indeed, was still lying on his back, unable to move because of his thrashing and the plasters, when the officer came up to him and said: 'Well, how goes it, my man?'

'I should speak more politely if I were you,' replied Don

Quixote. 'Is it the custom in this country to address knights errant in that way, lout?'

The officer could not suffer this treatment from a wretch of the sorry appearance of Don Quixote and, raising the lamp, which was full of oil, brought it down on the knight's head, leaving him with a fine bruise on his scalp. Then, under cover of darkness, he hurriedly left the room.

'No doubt,' said Sancho Panza, 'that is the Moorish enchanter. He must be keeping the treasure for someone else, and only reserving his beatings and bashings for us.'

'You are right,' replied Don Quixote, 'but there's no point in taking any notice of matters of enchantment, nor in getting angry and enraged about them. For, as these magicians are invisible and supernatural, we shall find no one to take vengeance on, however hard we try. Get up, Sancho, if you can, and call the governor of this fortress, and try to get him to give me a little oil, some wine, some salt, and some rosemary, so that I can make the healing balsam. Indeed, I think that now I am in much need of it, for I am losing a great deal of blood from the wound that apparition gave me.'

Sancho got up with sadly aching bones and went in the dark to find the innkeeper. Running, however, into the officer, who was listening to find out how things were with his enemy, he said:

'Sir, whoever you are, be so very kind as to give us a little rosemary, some oil, some salt, and some wine, for they are needed to heal one of the best knights errant in the world, who is lying on that bed, sorely wounded at the hands of the Moorish enchanter who is in this inn.'

When the officer heard this he thought that Sancho was out of his wits. But, as dawn was breaking by now, he opened the inn door and shouted out to the innkeeper what the poor fellow wanted. The host provided it all, and Sancho took it to Don Quixote, whom he found with his head clasped in his hands, groaning from the pain of his lamp-bashing, which, however, had done him no more harm than to raise a couple of largish bumps; what he took for blood being no more than the sweat which had poured from him in the anguish of the last storm.

In short, he took his ingredients, mixed them and cooked them for some time, till they appeared to be ready. Then he asked for a

flask to put them in. But, as there was none in the inn, he decided to
use a tin oil-can which the innkeeper gave him for nothing. After
that he said eighty Paternosters and as many Ave Marias, Salves, and
Credos over it, and at each word crossed himself by way of benediction. At which ceremony Sancho, the innkeeper, and the officer
were present, but the carrier had by now gone peacefully off and
was looking to his mules.

When this was done Don Quixote was anxious to make an immediate test of the virtue of this precious balsam, as he imagined it to
be, upon himself; and so he drank off more than a pint, which would
not go into the can and was still in the pot he had cooked it in. Now
no sooner had he drunk it than he began to vomit, bringing up
everything that was in his stomach; and with the pain and distress
of his sickness he broke into so copious a sweat that he asked to be
covered up and left alone. This was done, and he slept for more than
three hours; at the end of which time he awoke feeling very much
soothed in his body and so much better from his beating that he
thought himself cured and, verily believing that he had hit upon
the Balsam of Fierabras, he felt that thenceforth, with such a remedy,
he could undertake without fear any assaults, battles, or fights,
however perilous.

Sancho Panza, who also took his master's recovery for a miracle,
begged him for what remained in the pot – and there was a good
deal of it. Don Quixote granted his request; and he, taking the pot
in both hands, with a strong faith and better will, gulped it down,
swallowing almost as much as his master. The fact is, though, that
poor Sancho's stomach was not as delicate as Don Quixote's; and
so, before he was sick, he suffered so many twinges and pangs, so
many sweats and swoons, that he thought his last hour had come in
good earnest; and in his affliction and dismay he cursed the ointment and the scoundrel who had given it to him.

When Don Quixote saw him in such anguish, he observed: 'I
think, Sancho, that all this pain comes from your not being a knight;
for it is my opinion that this liquor cannot be of service to any that
are not.'

'If your worship knew that,' replied Sancho, 'the devil take me
and all my family, why did you let me taste it?'

At this the potion began to work and the poor man to empty

himself at both ends, so violently that soon the rush mat on which
he had thrown himself and the coarse blanket that covered him were
of no more use. His sweats, his paroxysms, and spasms were such
that he, and everyone else as well, thought that he was at the point
of death. And this tornado of misery lasted almost two hours, at the
end of which time, unlike his master, he was left so battered and
broken that he could not stand.

But Don Quixote, as we have said, felt recovered and well, and
was anxious to set out immediately in search of adventures. For it
seemed to him that every moment he delayed he was depriving the
world, and everyone in distress in it, of his favour and protection.
And he was encouraged in this feeling by his security and confidence
in his balsam. So, urged on by this desire, he saddled Rocinante
himself and bridled his squire's ass, helping Sancho to dress himself
and climb on his back. Then he mounted his steed and, seeing a
javelin in a corner of the inn, seized it to serve as a lance. Everyone
in the inn was watching him, and there were more than twenty
there. The innkeeper's daughter watched him too, and he did not
take his eyes from her, but from time to time heaved a sigh which
seemed to be torn from the depths of his bowels, and which everyone thought must be from the pain in his ribs; or so at least thought
those who had seen him poulticed the night before.

When the two of them were on horse Don Quixote stopped at
the inn door, called the host, and addressed him in very calm and
grave tones: 'Many and great are the favours, my lord governor,
that I have received in your castle, and I shall remain deeply obliged
for them all the days of my life. If I can repay you by taking vengeance for you on any proud man who may have done you wrong,
know that my office is to protect the helpless, to avenge wrongs and
to punish treachery. Search your memory and, if you have anything of this kind to entrust to me, you have only to say so, and I
promise you, by my order of knighthood, to give you reparation
and amends to your full satisfaction.'

The innkeeper replied in the same grave tones: 'Sir Knight, I do
not need your worship to avenge any injuries, for I know how to
take fitting vengeance for all wrongs done me. I only want your
worship to pay the score you have run up this night in my inn, for
straw and fodder for your two beasts, and for your supper and beds.'

E

'Then this is an inn?' asked Don Quixote.

'Yes, and a very respectable one,' replied the host.

'Then I have been in error till this moment,' answered Don Quixote, 'for I truly thought that it was a castle, and a considerable one too. But, since it is no castle but an inn, there is nothing for it now but for you to excuse my paying, for I cannot contravene the knight errant's rule. I am most certain – and I have never yet read of any case to the contrary – that they never paid for lodging or for anything else at any inn at which they stayed. For they deserve, by privilege and right, whatever hospitality they receive, in repayment for the intolerable hardships they undergo in seeking adventures by night and day, in winter and summer, on foot and horse, in thirst and hunger, in heat and cold, subject to all the inclemencies of the skies and all the discomforts of the earth.'

'That is nothing to do with me,' replied the innkeeper. 'Settle your reckoning, and spare us your tales and your knighthoods. I'm only concerned with getting my money.'

'You are a fool and a vile hosteller,' answered Don Quixote. Then, putting spur to Rocinante and brandishing his javelin, he left the inn without anyone stopping him; and without looking back to see if his squire was following, he rode for some way. When the innkeeper saw him go without paying, he ran to Sancho Panza for his money. But Sancho answered that, as his master had not been willing to pay, he would not either. For, as he was squire to a knight errant, the same rule held for him as for his master, to pay nothing in inns or hostelries. This put the host in a great temper, and he threatened, if he did not pay, to get the money out of him in a way he would not like. But Sancho persisted that by the law of knighthood, which his master had received, he would not pay a single farthing, even if it cost him his life. For he would not be the man to break the good old custom of knights errant, nor should the squires of future knights have to complain and reproach him for violating a privilege so well deserved.

But, as ill fate would have it, among the people in the inn were four wool-combers from Segovia, three needle-makers from the Colt Square in Cordova, and a couple from the Market of Seville, cheerful, well-meaning, playful rogues who, almost of one accord, ran up to Sancho and pulled him from his ass. Then one of them went in for the blanket from the host's bed and threw him on to it. But when they looked up they saw that the roof was rather too low for their purpose, and decided to go out into the back-yard, whose ceiling was the sky; and there, placing Sancho in the centre of the blanket, they began to toss him up and amuse themselves at his expense, as they do with dogs at Shrovetide.

The poor wretch's shouts at his blanket-tossing were loud enough to reach his master's ears, and Don Quixote, stopping to listen carefully, thought that some new adventure was on the way, until he realized that it was only his squire shouting. Whereupon he turned towards the inn at a painful gallop and, finding the door shut, rode round to find somewhere to get in. But no sooner did he get to the walls of the back-yard, which were not very high, than he saw the trick they were playing on his squire. He saw him fall and rise in the air so gracefully and so nimbly that, had it not been for his rage, he would certainly have burst out laughing. He tried to get from his horse on to the thatched wall, but he was so bruised and battered that he could not even dismount. And so from his horse he began to hurl insults and abuse at Sancho's tormentors, so many that it is impossible to record them. But this did not make them stop their tossing and laughter, nor did the flying Sancho cease his lamentations, which were mixed with threats alternating with pleas, though it was all of no use, and they did not give up until they were quite exhausted. Then they brought him his ass, put him on, and threw his greatcoat over his shoulders; and the tender-hearted Maritornes, seeing that he was worn out, thought it right to restore him with a jug of water and, so that it should be really cold, went to the well to draw it. Sancho took it, but just as he was going to put it to his lips he was stopped by his master's shouts.

'My good Sancho,' he cried, 'don't drink it. It will kill you. Look, I have the most holy balsam here' – and he held up the can of liquor. 'Drink two drops of this and you will most certainly be cured.'

At these words Sancho gave his master a sidelong glance and called even louder: 'Has your worship forgotten, by any chance, that I am not a knight, or would you have me bring up such guts as I've still got? Keep your liquor in the devil's name and leave me alone.'

No sooner had he spoken than he began to drink. But, finding at the first draught that it was only water, he would swallow no more, and begged Maritornes to bring him wine, which out of her good nature she did, and paid for it with her own money. For it is said of her that though she was of that trade, there was some shadow and vestige of a Christian about her.

So as soon as he had finished the wine, Sancho dug his heels into his ass's sides and, the inn door being opened for him, went out, very pleased that he had had his way and not paid a penny, though it had been at the cost of his shoulders, which usually went bail for him.

The innkeeper, it is true, remained in possession of his saddle-bags in payment for the reckoning, for Sancho went out in such confusion that he did not miss them. As soon as he was outside, the host wanted to bar the door after him, but the tossers would not agree, for they were the sort of men who would not have cared two straws even if Don Quixote had really been one of the Knights of the Round Table.

Chapter XVIII. *In which are recorded the conversation between Sancho Panza and his master Don Quixote, and other noteworthy adventures.*

SANCHO was so faint and dispirited when he caught his master up, that he could not drive his ass. And, seeing him in that state, Don Quixote said: 'Now I am quite certain, my good Sancho, that that castle or inn is enchanted. For what could those creatures who made such villainous sport with you be but phantoms and creatures of the other world? What makes me positive of it is that, when I was watching the acts of your sad tragedy over the thatched wall of the yard, I could not climb on to it, nor even dismount from Rocinante, for they must have had me under a spell. Because I swear to you on my faith as a Christian that, if I could have climbed on or dismounted, I would have so avenged you that those cowardly scoundrels would have remembered the joke as long as they lived, even if by so doing I had broken the laws of chivalry; which, as I have often told you, do not permit of a knight's striking one who is not a knight except in a case of urgent and extreme necessity, in defence of his own life and person.'

'I would have avenged myself, too, if I could, knight or no knight,' replied Sancho, 'but I couldn't, though it's my opinion that the creatures who amused themselves at my expense were not phantoms or enchanted, as your worship says, but flesh-and-blood men like ourselves. And they had all got names, for I heard them when they were tossing me: one of them was called Pedro Martinez, another Tenorio Hernandez, and I heard them call the innkeeper Juan Palomeque, the left-handed. So it was something different from enchantment that stopped your getting over the yard wall or dismounting from Rocinante. And what I gather from all this is that these adventures which we are always seeking will lead us in the long run to such misadventures that we shan't know our right foot from our left. It would be a good deal better and more proper, my little understanding tells me, for us to go home, now that it's harvest-time, and look after our own affairs, and stop wandering from pillar to post, out of the frying-pan into the fire, as they say.'

'How little you understand matters of chivalry, Sancho,' replied Don Quixote. 'Be silent and patient, for the day will come when you will see with your own eyes how honourable it is to follow this profession. Tell me now, what greater pleasure can there be in the world, what joy equal to that of winning a battle and triumphing over an enemy? There can be no doubt of it. None.'

'That may well be,' replied Sancho, 'for all I know. But I do know that since we have been knights errant – or your worship has, for I cannot count myself of that honourable number – we have never won a battle except that one over the Basque, and even from that one your worship came off with the loss of half an ear and half a helmet. But since then it has been nothing but beatings and still more beatings, punches and still more punches, – and I got my tossing into the bargain, and that from persons enchanted, on whom I can't take revenge, and so learn for myself what pleasure there is in conquering an enemy, as your worship says.'

'That is an affliction which I bear and you must bear, Sancho,' replied Don Quixote. 'But from now on I will try to have at hand a sword of such craftsmanship that no kind of enchantment can be worked against its bearer. It is even possible that my fortune may procure me the sword Amadis wore when he was called the *Knight of the Burning Sword*. It was one of the best ever worn by any knight in all the world. For it not only had the virtue I mentioned,. but also cut like a razor, and there was no armour, however strong and enchanted, which could stand up to it.'

'Such is my luck.' said Sancho, 'that when this comes about and your worship finds such a sword, it will only be of use and profit to knights, like that balsam. As for squires, they may sup on sorrow.'

'Never fear that,' said Don Quixote, 'for Heaven will deal more kindly with you.'

While Don Quixote and his squire rode on, deep in conversation, our knight saw a great thick cloud of dust approaching them along the road they were taking; and, on seeing it, he turned to Sancho and said: 'This is the day, Sancho, on which shall be seen the good fortune which fate has in store for me. It is on this day, I say, as much as on any other, that the valour of my arm shall be displayed. To-day I shall perform deeds that will remain written in the book of fame for all future ages. Do you see that dust-cloud rising over there, Sancho? It is all churned up by a prodigious army of various and innumerable nations that is marching this way.'

'In that case there must be two armies,' said Sancho, 'for in the opposite direction there is a similar cloud of dust rising as well.'

Don Quixote turned to look and, seeing that Sancho was right, rejoiced exceedingly, being quite certain that there were two armies advancing to the attack, and that they would meet in the middle of that wide plain. For every hour and every minute his mind was always full of those battles, enchantments, adventures, miracles, loves, and challenges which are related in books of chivalry; and everything that he said, thought or did was influenced by his fantasies. As for the dust-cloud he had seen, it was caused by two great flocks of sheep, which were being driven along that road in opposite directions, but owing to the dust they were not visible until they drew near. So emphatically, however, did Don Quixote affirm that they were armies, that Sancho came to believe him and asked: 'Sir, what must we do now?'

'What?' cried Don Quixote. 'Favour and aid those in need and distress. I must tell you, Sancho, that the army which is coming towards us is led and commanded by the great Emperor Alifanfaron, lord of the great island of Taprobana; the other which is marching behind us is the army of his enemy, the King of the Garamantas,

Pentapolin of the Naked Arm, so called because he always rides into battle with his right arm bare.'

'Why do these two lords hate one another, then?' asked Sancho.

'They hate one another,' replied Don Quixote, 'because this Alifanfaron is a furious pagan, and is in love with Pentapolin's daughter, a very lovely and, what is more, a very gracious lady, and a Christian, whose father will not give her to the pagan king unless he first foreswears the faith of his false prophet, Mahomet, and is converted to his own.'

'By my beard,' said Sancho, 'but that Pentapolin is right, and I'll help him all I can.'

'In that you will be doing your duty, Sancho,' said Don Quixote, 'for you do not need to be a knight to take part in battles like this.'

'I can well understand that,' replied Sancho. 'But where shall we put this ass so as to be certain of finding him when the skirmish is over? For I don't think it has ever been the custom to ride into battle on a beast like this.'

'That is true,' said Don Quixote. 'The only thing that you can do is to leave it to chance whether he is lost or not, for we shall have so many horses when we emerge victorious that even Rocinante will be in danger of being exchanged for another. But listen to me and look, for I want to point out the chief knights in these two armies. And so that you may see and note them better, let us retire up that slope, from which we should be able to make out both hosts.'

So they did, and took up their positions on a hillock from which they would have clearly seen both the flocks which Don Quixote had transformed into armies but for the clouds of dust they raised, which obscured and blinded their vision. This, however, did not prevent Don Quixote from imagining what was neither visible nor existing and, raising his voice to say: 'That knight over there in bright yellow armour, with a crowned lion couchant at a damsel's feet on his shield, is the valorous Laurcalco, Lord of the Silver Bridge. The other in the armour flowered with gold, and with three crowns argent on a field azure on his shield, is the redoubtable Micocolembo, Grand Duke of Quirocia. The other, on his right, with gigantic limbs, is the undaunted Brandabarbaran of Boliche, Lord of the three Arabias; he wears a serpent's skin for armour, and has for shield a gate which, report has it, is one of the gates of the temple that Samson pulled down when with his death he avenged himself on his enemies.

'But look in the other direction, and you will see in front, and leading the other army, the ever-victorious, never-vanquished Timonel of Carcajona, Prince of New Biscay; his armour is quartered azure, vert, argent and gold, and on his shield he bears a cat or on a field gules with a scroll inscribed *Miau* – which is the initial of his lady; who, so they say, is the peerless Miaulina, daughter of Duke Alfeñiquen of Algarbe. The other who burdens and oppresses the back of that powerful and spirited war-horse, with armour as white as snow and a white shield without a device, is a new knight of the French nation, called Pierre Papin, Lord of the Baronies of Utrique. That other, pricking with iron heel the flanks of his piebald courser, and bearing for arms the azure cups, is the powerful Duke of Nerbia, Espartafilardo of the Wood, who bears on his shield the device of an asparagus plant, with a motto in Castilian which runs: *Thus trails my fortune.*'

So he went on, naming many imaginary knights in each squadron; for each of whom he improvised armour, colours, devices, and mottoes, carried away by his strangely deluded imagination, and continuing without a pause:

'That squadron in the front is made up of men of various nations: here are drinkers of the sweet waters of the famous Xanthus; mountaineers who tread the Massilian fields; sifters of the pure and fine gold of Arabia Felix; dwellers on the famous cool shores of clear Thermodon; men who in various ways drain golden Pactolus for its precious sand; faithless Numidians; Persians famous for their bows and arrows; Parthians; Medes who fight as they fly; Arabs with no fixed abode; Scythians as cruel as they are fair; Ethiopians with their lips bored; and countless more nations whose visages I see and recognize but whose names I do not remember.'

'In that other squadron come drinkers of the crystal waters of olive-bearing Betis; men who burnish and polish their faces with the liquor of the ever-rich and golden Tagus; men who enjoy the health-giving waters of the divine Genil; dwellers in the Tartesian plains with their abundant pastures; men who enjoy the Elysian fields of Jerez; men of La Mancha, rich and crowned with golden corn; men clad in iron, survivors of the ancient Gothic race; bathers in the Pisuerga, famous for its mild current; men who graze their flocks on the broad pastures of the winding Guadiana, famous for its secret bed; men who shiver with the cold of the wooded Pyrenees and among the white snows of the lofty Apennines – in short, all whom Europe contains within its boundaries.'

Good Lord! how many provinces he reeled off, how many nations he enumerated, giving to each one with marvellous readiness its proper attributes, being completely soaked and immersed in all that he had read in his lying books! Sancho Panza hung on his words and said nothing. But from time to time he turned to see if he could distinguish the knights and giants whom his master named. But, as he could not make out one of them, he said: 'Sir, devil a man or a giant, or a knight your worship mentions is to be seen, for all that. At least, I can't see them. Perhaps it's all enchantment, like the apparitions last night.'

'How can you say that?' replied Don Quixote. 'Cannot you hear the horses neighing and the trumpets blaring and the beating of the drums?'

'The only thing that I can hear,' replied Sancho, 'is a great bleating of rams and ewes.' And that was the truth, for the two flocks were getting near.

'It is your fear,' said Don Quixote, 'which prevents your seeing or hearing aright, for one of the effects of fright is to disturb the senses and make things appear as they are not. If you are so afraid, go aside a little and leave me alone, for I am sufficient on my own to ensure victory to the party to which I lend my aid.'

And so saying, he spurred Rocinante, put his lance in its rest and rushed down the little slope like a thunderbolt, with Sancho shouting after him:

'Turn back, Don Quixote, for I swear to God, sir, they are rams and ewes you are going to attack. Turn back! Oh, I wish I had never been born! What madness is it this time? Look, there is not a giant or a knight at all, nor cats, nor arms, nor shields quartered or entire, nor cups azure or bedevilled. What are you doing? Poor sinner that I am!'

But this did not make Don Quixote turn. Instead he went on,

shouting loudly: 'Ho, knights who follow and fight beneath the banner of the valorous Emperor Pentapolin of the Naked Arm, follow me, all of you, and you shall see how easily I will give him his revenge on his enemy Alifanfaron of Taprobana!' With which words he charged into the middle of the squadron of ewes and began to spear them with as much courage and daring as if he were in very truth spearing his mortal enemies. The shepherds and herdsmen who were with the flock shouted to him to stop. But, seeing that this had no effect, they unbuckled their slings and began to salute his ears with stones the size of fists.

Don Quixote took no heed of stones, but galloped all over the place, shouting: 'Where are you, proud Alifanfaron? Come to me. I am a single knight, and desire to prove your valour hand to hand, and to take your life for the wrong you have done the valorous Pentapolin the Garamantan.'

At that moment came a pebble from the brook and, hitting him on the side, buried two of his ribs in his body. Finding himself so battered, he thought that he was certainly killed or badly wounded. So, remembering his balsam, he took out his can, and, putting it to his mouth, began to toss the liquor into his stomach. But before he had managed to swallow what seemed to him sufficient, another sugared almond hit him on the hand and struck the can so fairly that it smashed it in pieces, taking three or four of his teeth out of his mouth on the way and badly bruising two fingers of his hand. So hard was the first blow and so hard the second that the poor knight was knocked from his horse on to the ground. The shepherds then came up to him and, concluding that they had killed him, hurriedly rounded up their flocks, took up the dead sheep, which were about seven in number, and made off without further enquiry.

All this time Sancho stood on the hill and watched his master's strange performance, tearing his beard and cursing the hour and the moment that Fortune had brought them together. But when he saw him lying on the ground and the shepherds gone, he went down the hill to him and found him not stunned but in a very bad way.

'Didn't I tell you, Don Quixote, sir,' he said, 'to turn back, for they were not armies you were going to attack, but flocks of sheep?'

'What a way that scoundrel of an enchanter, my enemy, has of transforming things and making them invisible! You must know, Sancho, that it is a very easy thing for enchanters to give things whatever appearance they please. For this wicked sorcerer, my persecutor, being envious of the glory he saw I was sure to gain from this battle, has turned the hostile squadrons into flocks of sheep. If you do not believe me, Sancho, do one thing, I beg of you, and you will discover that you are mistaken and that I am speaking the truth. Get on your ass, and follow them stealthily. Then you will see that as soon as they get a little way from here they will turn back to their original shapes, and will not be sheep any more but well-built proper men, as I first described them to you. But do not go now, for I have need of your help and service. Come near to me and look how many of my teeth are missing, for I do not think they have left me any in my head.'

Sancho came so near as almost to thrust his eyes into his master's mouth; and that was the very moment when the balsam began to work in Don Quixote's stomach; so that just as Sancho drew close to peer into his mouth the knight threw up what was in him more violently than a shot from a gun, and sent it all over the beard of his compassionate squire.

'Holy Mary!' cried Sancho. 'What has happened to me? Sure, this poor sinner is mortally wounded, since he is vomiting blood.'

But on examining things a little more closely, he realized, from its colour, taste, and smell, that it was not blood but the balsam from the can, which he had seen him drinking; and this so turned his stomach that he threw up his very guts over his master; and the pair of them were then in the same pickle. Sancho ran to his ass to get out of his saddle-bags something with which to clean himself and cure his master, and when he found the bags missing almost went out of his mind. He cursed himself once more, and decided in his heart to leave Don Quixote and return home, even if he were to lose the payment for his services and his hopes of the governorship of the promised isle.

At this the knight got up and, with his left hand to his mouth to prevent the rest of his teeth from falling out, took in the other the reins of the faithful Rocinante, whose disposition was so good and loyal that he had never stirred from his master's side. Then he went over to his squire, who was leaning against his ass with his hand on his cheek, a position expressing great dejection and, seeing his melancholy mood, said to him: 'I tell you, Sancho, that no man is worthier than another unless he does more than another. All these squalls which greet us are signs that the weather will soon clear and things go well with us; for neither good nor evil can last for ever; and so it follows that as evil has lasted a long time, good must now be close at hand. You must not grieve, therefore, at the disasters which befall me, for surely no share of them fell to you.'

'How not?' replied Sancho. 'Wasn't it my father's son who got tossed in the blanket yesterday? And the saddle-bags that I've lost to-day with all my valuables in them, whose were they but mine?'

'What, are your saddle-bags missing, Sancho?' asked Don Quixote.

'Yes, they are,' replied Sancho.

'In that case we have nothing to eat to-day,' said Don Quixote.

'That would be so,' replied Sancho, 'if there were not any of those herbs in the fields, which your worship says you know, and which unfortunate knights errant like yourself use to supply their needs in cases like this.'

'All the same,' replied Don Quixote, 'I would rather have a hunk of bread or a loaf, and a couple of pilchards' heads, than all the herbs in Dioscorides' herbal with all Doctor Laguna's illustrations thrown in. But, anyhow, get on your ass, good Sancho, and follow me. For God, the provider of all things, cannot let us want, especially as we are engaged in His service, since He does not fail the gnats of the air, the worms in the ground, nor the tadpoles in the water, and He is so merciful that He makes the sun rise on the good and the bad, and rains on the just and the unjust.'

'Your worship,' said Sancho, 'would make a better preacher than a knight errant.'

'Knights errant, Sancho, knew – and have to know – about everything,' said Don Quixote; 'for in the olden times a knight errant would be as ready to deliver a sermon or make a speech in the middle of the royal camp as if he were a graduate of the university of Paris; whence it can be inferred that the lance has never blunted the pen, nor the pen the lance.'

'Well, I'll take your worship's word for it,' replied Sancho. 'Let's go on now and try to find somewhere to lodge tonight, and pray God it may be a place where there are no blankets or blanket-tossers, or apparitions, or Moorish enchanters; for if there are, I'll fling meat and hook to the Devil.'

'Ask that of God, son,' said Don Quixote, 'and lead me where you like, for this time I am going to leave the choice of lodging to you. But lend me your hand, and feel with your finger how many teeth are missing from the top jaw on my right side, for that is where I feel the pain. '

Sancho put his fingers in and, as he felt around, asked: 'How many molars used your worship to have on that side?'

'Four,' replied Don Quixote, 'and a wisdom tooth, all sound and whole.'

'Think well what you say, sir,' replied Sancho.

'I say four, or perhaps five,' replied Don Quixote, 'for in all my days I have never had a tooth drawn, nor one fall out, nor destroyed by decay.'

'Well, in this lower jaw,' said Sancho, 'your worship has only two teeth and a half, and on the top not so much as a half, for it is all as smooth as the palm of my hand.'

'Oh, what a misfortune!' exclaimed Don Quixote on hearing his squire's sad news. 'I had rather have lost an arm, provided it were not my sword arm. For I would have you know, Sancho, that a mouth without molars is like a mill without a stone, and a tooth is more precious than a diamond. But we who profess the strict order of chivalry are subject to all such misfortunes. Mount, my friend, and lead on. I will follow at your pace.'

Sancho obeyed, and took the direction in which he thought he might be likely to find lodging, keeping to the highway, which was well beaten in those parts. And as they went along slowly, because the pain in Don Quixote's jaws gave him no rest nor any disposition to hurry, Sancho tried to entertain him and divert his mind by talk. And some of the things he said will be found in the next chapter.

Chapter XIX. *Of the sensible conversation between Sancho Panza and his master, of the Adventure with a Corpse, and other famous happenings.*

'IN my opinion, sir, there isn't a shadow of doubt that all these misfortunes which have happened to us lately have been a punishment for your worship's sinning against the law of chivalry by not fulfiling the oath you took, not to eat bread off a table-cloth nor lie with the queen, and all the rest of the things you swore, until you had got that helmet from Malandrino, or whatever they call the Moor – I can't remember.'

'You are quite right, Sancho,' said Don Quixote, 'but, to tell you the truth, it had slipped my memory. And you can be just as certain that it was for not reminding me of it in time that the affair of the blanket happened to you. But I will make amends; for in the law of chivalry there are ways of compounding for everything.'

'Did I swear something then, by any chance?' asked Sancho.

'It is no matter that you did not swear,' said Don Quixote; 'it is enough that I consider you not very clear of complicity. But whichever way it is, there will be no harm in providing a remedy.'

'If that's so then,' said Sancho, 'take good care, your worship, not to forget that too, like the oath; or perhaps the phantoms may take it into their heads to have their fun with me again, and even with your worship, if they find you so wilful.'

When darkness fell they were still on the high road deep in their conversation, and had not found any place to shelter that night; what was worse, they were dying of hunger, for with their saddle-bags they had lost their whole larder and store. And, to complete their misfortunes, there followed an adventure that did not require any contrivance actually to look like one.

The night set in dark, but still they rode on, Sancho thinking that, as they were on the highway, they should by rights find a good inn within six or eight miles. As they continued, then, on their way, the night being dark, the squire hungry and his master more than a little disposed to eat, they saw coming towards them on their road a great number of lights, which looked more like stars in motion than anything else.

Sancho was alarmed at the sight of them, and his master did not altogether like them either. The squire checked his ass, and Don Quixote his horse, and they stopped still, peering attentively to make out what it could be. They saw that the lights were coming near, and the nearer they got the bigger they seemed. At this Sancho began to tremble as if he had taken quicksilver, and the hair of Don Quixote's head stood on end. But the knight gained a little courage and said: 'This, Sancho, beyond a doubt, must be a very great and most perilous adventure, and I shall need to show all my valour and courage.'

'Oh dear me!' replied Sancho. 'If this is an adventure with phantoms, as it seems, where shall I find ribs to endure it?'

'Never mind if they are phantoms,' said Don Quixote. 'I will not let them touch a thread of your garment. If they played the fool with you last time it was because I could not get over the yard wall. But now we are on open ground where I can wield my sword as I please.'

'What if they put a spell on you and cramp you as they did before?' cried Sancho. 'What will it matter if you are on the open ground or not?'

'Nevertheless,' replied Don Quixote, 'I beg you, Sancho, to have courage, for experience will give you proof of mine.'

'I will, if it please God,' replied Sancho. And the pair of them stood a little back from the road, and once more watched carefully to see what those travelling lights might be. Then after a while they made out a number of forms in white surplices, at which frightful vision Sancho Panza's courage absolutely vanished, and his teeth began to chatter as if he had the quartan ague. And his trembling and chattering grew even worse when they distinctly made out what it was; for they saw some twenty horsemen with blazing torches in their hands, and behind them a litter covered in black, followed by six more horsemen swathed in mourning down to their mules' feet – it was evident from their slow pace that they were not horses. The figures in white were muttering to themselves as they came, in low and mournful tones.

This extraordinary spectacle at such an hour and in such a lonely place was quite enough to strike terror into Sancho's heart and even into his master's. The squire's courage was long since exhausted, but it was otherwise with Don Quixote, for by this time his vivid imagination had suggested that this was one of the adventures out of his books. It seemed to him that the litter was a bier on which they were carrying some dead or badly wounded knight, and that the task of avenging him was reserved for himself. So without more ado he couched his lance, steadied himself in the saddle, and with exquisite bearing and courage took up his position in the middle of the road along which the white figures would have to pass. Then, when he saw them approaching, he cried:

'Stop, knights, or whoever you may be, and inform me who you are, where you come from, where you are going, and what it is you are carrying on that bier. For, by all appearances, either you have done or suffered some injustice, and it is proper and needful that I should know it, either to punish you for the wrong you have done, or to avenge the outrage done upon you.'

'We are in a hurry,' replied one of the men in white, 'for the inn is some distance away. We can't stop to answer all your questions.'

Then he spurred his mule and pressed on. But Don Quixote, very indignant at this reply, laid hold of his bridle and said: 'Stop, and be rather more civil. Give me the information that I asked for, or else do battle with me, all of you.'

The mule was timid, and was so frightened at being seized by the bridle that she rose on her hind legs and threw her rider to the ground. A servant who was on foot saw the white-robed figure fall and began to abuse the now furious Don Quixote, who without more ado couched his lance and attacked one of the mourners, throwing him to the ground too, with a severe wound. He then turned on the others, and the speed with which he attacked and routed them was a wonder to see, for Rocinante seemed in that moment to have sprouted wings, so swiftly and proudly did he move. The men in white, a cowardly and unarmed crew, fled from the battle most promptly, and were off in one moment, running across the plain with their flaming torches, looking like nothing so much as masked figures flitting about on a carnival or festival night. As for the mourners, they were so swathed and muffled in their long skirts and gowns that they could not stir, and Don Quixote thrashed them all without the least danger to himself, forcing them to quit the field, much against their will; for they all thought that he was no man, but a devil from Hell come to bear off the corpse which they were carrying on the litter. Sancho looked on at all this, admiring his master's dauntless courage and saying to himself, 'There's no doubt that my master is as valiant and mighty as he says.'

There was a torch burning on the ground beside the first man who had been thrown by his mule, and as soon as Don Quixote saw him by its light he went up to him and poked his lance-point in his face, calling on him to surrender on pain of death. To which the fallen man replied: 'I am surrendered enough already, since I can't move. One of my legs is broken. I beg your worship, if you are a Christian gentleman, not to kill me. You would be committing a great sacrilege, for I am a Master of Arts and have taken my first orders.'

'Then, what the devil brought you here?' cried Don Quixote, 'if you are a churchman?'

'What, sir?' replied the fallen man. 'My bad luck.'

'A still worse fate threatens you,' said Don Quixote, 'if you do not answer satisfactorily all the questions I asked of you in the first place.'

'Your worship shall soon be satisfied,' replied the Master of Arts; 'and I must tell you that although I said before that I was a Master of Arts, I am only a Bachelor. My name is Alonso Lopez, native of Alcobendas. I am on my way from Baeza with eleven other priests – the men with the torches who have run away. We are going to the city of Segovia, escorting a corpse which is lying on that litter. The dead man was a gentleman who died at Baeza, where he was laid, and now, as I say, we are taking his bones to his tomb, which is in Segovia, his native town.'

'And who killed him?' asked Don Quixote.

'God, by means of a pestilent fever which took him,' replied the Bachelor.

'In that case,' said Don Quixote, 'our Lord has relieved me of the task of avenging his death, which I should have taken upon myself, had he fallen by any other hand. But seeing Who it was that killed him, there is nothing for it but to be silent and shrug my shoulders. For I should do the same were He to slay me. But I would have your Reverence know that I am a knight of La Mancha, Don Quixote by name, and that it is my office and profession to roam about the world, righting wrongs and relieving injuries.'

'I don't know what this righting of wrongs may be about,' said the Bachelor; 'for I was all right, and by leaving me with a broken leg which will not be right for all the days of my life you have made me all wrong. The injury you have relieved in me has left me so injured that I shall remain injured for life; and it has been sufficient misadventure to have met on your quest for adventure.'

'You can never tell how things will turn out,' replied Don Quixote. 'The trouble, Sir Bachelor Alonso Lopez, arose from your coming in the night as you did, dressed in those surplices, with your flaming torches, muttering your prayers and swathed in mourning, for you truly looked like some evil things from the other world. I could not therefore refrain from fulfilling my duty by attacking you; and I should have attacked you even if I had known for certain that you were the very devils from Hell which I judged and took you to be.'

'Since my fate would have it so,' said the Bachelor, 'I entreat your worship, Sir Knight Errant, who have done me such arrant mischief, to help me from under this mule, which has caught one of my legs between the stirrup and the saddle.'

'I might have gone on talking till to-morrow,' said Don Quixote. 'How long would you have waited to tell me of your plight?'

Then he shouted for Sancho Panza. But his squire did not choose to come, because he was busy unloading one of the good gentlemen's mules, which carried the stores and was well laden with good things. Sancho made a bag from his overcoat and, cramming all that he could into it, loaded his ass. Which done, he turned to his master's call and helped to get the Bachelor from under the weight of his mule. Then he helped him on and gave him his torch, while Don Quixote bade the poor fellow follow his companions and beg their pardon on his behalf for the injury which he had been unable to avoid doing them. And said Sancho as he departed: 'If by chance these gentlemen wish to know who the valorous knight was that did them such mischief, tell them, your worship, that it was the famous Don Quixote de la Mancha, who also bears the name of The Knight of the Sad Countenance.'

With that the Bachelor rode off, and Don Quixote asked Sancho what had made him call him the Knight of the Sad Countenance at that particular moment.

'I'll tell you,' answered Sancho. 'It's because I was watching you for a while by the light of the torch that poor wretch was carrying, and really your worship has lately got the most dismal face I've ever seen. It must be either from weariness after the battle or from your worship's losing his teeth.'

'It is from neither,' replied Don Quixote, 'but because the sage whose task it is to write the history of my deeds must have thought it right for me to take some title, as all knights did in the olden days. One called himself *The Knight of the Burning Sword*; another *of the Unicorn*; one *of the Damsels*; another *of the Phoenix*; another *The Knight of the Griffin*; and yet another *of Death*; and by these names and devices were they known all round the world. That is why I say that the sage I mentioned has put it into your thoughts and into your mouth to call me now *The Knight of the Sad Countenance*, a name which I intend to use from this day on; and to make it fit me better, I intend to have a very sad countenance painted on my shield when I have an opportunity.'

'There's no need to waste time and money on painting a face,' said Sancho. 'Your worship has only to uncover your own and show it to anyone who looks at you, and they'll call you *The Knight of the Sad Countenance* all right, without any picture or shield, and that's the truth. Believe me, sir – though I'm speaking in fun – hunger and loss of teeth have given you such a dismal face that you can easily do without the sad painting.'

Don Quixote laughed at Sancho's joke; nevertheless he decided to take that name as soon as he could have it painted on his shield or buckler, as he had proposed.

'I fear, Sancho,' he said, 'that I have incurred excommunication for laying violent hands on holy things – *Juxta illud, si quis suadente diabolo*, &c, although I know that I did not lay my hands on them, but this lance; and, what is more, I did not suspect that I was injuring priests or Church property, which, good Catholic and faithful Christian that I am, I respect and adore, for I thought that they were phantoms and spectres from the other world. But if it comes to the worst I remember what happened to the Cid Ruy Diaz, when he broke the chair of that King's Ambassador in the presence of his

Holiness the Pope, who excommunicated him for it; notwithstanding which the good Rodrigo de Vivar bore himself like a very honourable and valiant knight that day.'

By this time the Bachelor had gone, as has been said, without making Don Quixote any reply, and the knight was anxious to see if the body on the litter was a skeleton or not; but Sancho would not agree, saying: 'Sir, your worship has concluded this perilous adventure at less cost to yourself than any that I have seen. But although these people are conquered and defeated, it may occur to them that they were beaten by one man alone; and that may so abash them and shame them that they will pluck up some courage and come back after us; and then we shall have work enough on our hands. The ass is all right; the mountain's near; hunger presses; and we have nothing to do but to beat a graceful retreat and, as the saying is, to the grave with the dead and the living to their bread.' So, driving his ass before him, he begged his master to follow; and Don Quixote, feeling that Sancho was right, did so without another word.

They took their way between two hills, and had not gone far when they found themselves in a wide, secluded valley, where they alighted and Sancho unloaded the ass; and, stretched on the green grass, with hunger for sauce, they took their breakfast, lunch, dinner, and supper all in one, appeasing their hunger from more than one hamper which the dead man's noble clerics – who seldom fail to look after themselves – had brought on their baggage-mule. But another misfortune befell them, and to Sancho this was the worst of all: they had no wine, nor even water, to drink, and were parched with thirst. Sancho, however, saw that the meadow they were in was thick with fresh green grass, and said – what shall be recorded in the following chapter.

Chapter XX. *Of the unparalleled Adventure achieved by the valorous Don Quixote de la Mancha with less peril than any ever achieved by any famous knight in the whole world.*

'To judge from this grass, sir, there must certainly be a spring or a brook about here to keep it moist. So it would be a good idea if we were to go on a little farther, for we might find somewhere to quench this terribly annoying thirst, which is a great deal more distressing than hunger itself.'

This suggestion seemed reasonable to Don Quixote. So he took Rocinante by the rein, and Sancho took his ass by the halter, though not till he had loaded him with what remained from their supper. Then they began to move forward through the meadow, feeling their way, for the night was so dark that they could not see anything. But before they had gone two hundred yards a great noise came to their ears, like the roar of a waterfall tumbling from some huge, high cliff. This sound cheered them enormously. But as they stopped to listen from what direction it came, they heard another loud noise, which drowned the pleasure they got from the sound of the water, especially Sancho's, for he was timid by nature and not at all courageous. What they heard was the sound of regular blows and a sort of clanking of iron and chains which, combined with the furious roaring of the water, would have struck terror into any other heart but Don Quixote's. The night, as has been said, was dark, and they had happened to stray beneath some tall trees, the movements of whose leaves in the soft wind made a gentle but alarming sound; so that, taken all together, the solitude, the locality, the darkness, the roaring of the water and the rustling of the leaves produced a horror and dread, which increased when they found that the blows did not cease, nor the wind die down, nor morning dawn. And to make matters worse, they had no idea where they were. Don Quixote, however, his courage never failing, leapt upon Rocinante, braced his shield, brandished his lance, and cried:

'Sancho, my friend, you must know that, by the will of Heaven, I was born in this iron age of ours to revive the age of gold or, as it is generally called, the golden age. It is for me that are reserved perils, mighty feats, and valorous exploits. It is I, I say once more, who must revive the order of the Round Table, the Twelve Peers of France, and the Nine Worthies, and consign to oblivion the Platirs, Tablantes, Olivantes and Tirantes, the Knights of the Sun and the Belianises, and all that herd of famous knights errant of olden times, by performing in this age in which I live such prodigies, such wonders, and such feats of arms as to eclipse the most famous deeds they ever performed. Observe, loyal and faithful squire, the darkness of this night, its strange silence, the dull, confused sound of these trees, the fearful noise of the water which we came to seek, and which seems to be hurled headlong from the high mountains of the moon, and that ceaseless thumping which wounds and afflicts our ears; which things, taken all together and each by itself, are sufficient to infuse fear, terror, and dread into the breast of Mars himself; and how much more so into one who is unaccustomed to such events and adventures. Yet all that I am describing to you serves only to spur and rouse my courage, and makes my heart bound in my breast with desire to embark on this adventure, however arduous it may prove. Therefore tighten Rocinante's girths a little, and God be with you! Wait for me here three days and no more; at the end of which time, if I should not come back, you may return to our village, and from there, as a favour and service to me, you will go to El Toboso and tell my incomparable lady Dulcinea that her captive knight died attempting deeds which might make him worthy to call himself hers.'

When Sancho heard this speech of his master's, he began to weep most piteously, saying: 'I don't know why your worship wants to start on this frightful adventure. It is night now, and no one can see us here. We can easily turn off the road and get out of danger, even if it means not drinking for three days. And, as there's nobody to see us, no one can call us cowards. What is more, I have heard the priest of our village, whom your worship knows very well, preach that the man who seeks danger perishes in it. So it isn't right to tempt Providence by taking on such a tremendous feat, from which we could only escape by a miracle. Be satisfied with the miracles Heaven has worked for your worship in saving you from the blanket-tossing I got, and bringing you off victorious, safe and sound, from all those enemies there were with that dead man. And, if all this isn't enough to soften that hard heart of yours, perhaps it will be moved by the thought that the very moment your worship has gone from here I'll be sure to give up my soul out of pure fear to anyone who may wish to bear it off. I left my country and forsook my wife and children to come and serve your worship, believing that I should do better and not worse; but as greed burst the bag, so it has rent my hopes; for just as I was most hopefully expecting to get that accursed and unlucky isle your worship has so often promised me, I see that instead you mean to leave me now in this place, far from all human company. In God's name, sir, do me not this wrong. Even if your worship will not altogether give up this exploit, put it off at least till morning. For by the science I learned when I was a shepherd, it can't be more than three hours till dawn, since the muzzle of the Bear is at the top of his head, and at midnight it is in line with the left paw.'

'How can you see, Sancho, where the line is, or the muzzle, or the top of the head you speak of? The night is so dark that there is not a star to be seen in the whole sky.'

'That's true,' said Sancho, 'but fear has many eyes, and can see things underground. So it'll easily see things up above in the sky. Besides, it's reasonable to suppose that it won't be long till dawn.'

'Long or not,' replied Don Quixote, 'it shall never be said of me, now or at any time, that tears and prayers deflected me from my duty as a knight. Therefore, Sancho, pray be silent. For God, who has put it into my heart to embark on this unparalleled adventure, will take care to watch over my safety and to console your grief. All that you have to do is to tighten Rocinante's girths well and wait here, for I will return soon, alive or dead.'

Sancho saw that his master was finally resolved, and that his tears, advice, and prayers had little effect on him. So he decided to use his ingenuity and, if he could, compel his master to wait till day. So, while he was tightening the horse's girths, slyly and unnoticed he tied Rocinante's fore-legs together with the halter of his ass, so that when Don Quixote wanted to start he could not, for his horse could move only by leaps. And when Sancho saw that his trick was successful he exclaimed: 'See, sir, the Heavens are moved by my tears and prayers. They have ordained that Rocinante shall be unable to stir. If you persist in urging, spurring, and striking him, it will be provoking Fortune and, as the saying goes, kicking against the pricks.'

At this Don Quixote grew exceedingly vexed, for the more he spurred his horse the less could he make him go. Therefore, without suspecting the reason, he thought it best to be calm and wait till dawn, or till Rocinante could move, no doubt ascribing the trouble to some cause other than Sancho's ingenuity. And so he said to him: 'Since it is a fact, Sancho, that Rocinante cannot move, I am content to wait here until dawn smiles, although I weep at her delay.'

'There's no need to weep,' replied Sancho, 'for I will entertain your worship and tell you stories from now till daylight, unless you would like to dismount and snatch a little sleep on this green grass, as knights errant do, so that you may be less weary when day comes and it's time to embark on this incomparable adventure that awaits you.'

'Who is it you ask to dismount or to sleep?' asked Don Quixote. 'Am I by chance one of those knights who take their rest amidst dangers? Sleep yourself, for you were born to sleep, or do what you will. I will do what best suits my profession.'

'Don't be annoyed, good master,' replied Sancho. 'I didn't mean to make you angry.' Then he went closer to Don Quixote and put one hand on the pommel of his saddle and the other on the cantle, so that he stood clasping his master's left thigh without daring to stir an inch from him, so frightened was he of the blows which still continued to sound in regular succession. Don Quixote then bade him tell a tale for his entertainment, as he had promised; and Sancho replied that he would, if his dread of the noise would allow him. 'But, for all that,' he said, 'I will endeavour to tell you a story and, if I manage to tell it without interruption, it'll be the best story in the world. Pay good attention, your worship, for I'm going to begin. – Once upon a time; may good befall us all and evil strike the man who seeks it. Notice, your worship, that the ancients didn't begin their stories just as they pleased, but with a sentence by Cato, the Roman censor, who says – "Evil strike the man who seeks it"; and that fits in here like a ring on a finger, meaning that your worship must stay quiet and not go anywhere seeking harm, but that we must turn up some other road, since nobody is making us follow this one, where there are so many terrors to frighten us.'

'Go on with your story, Sancho,' said Don Quixote, 'and leave the road we are to follow to me.'

'I tell you, then,' Sancho resumed, 'that in a village in Estremadura there was once a shepherd – a goatherd I should say, for he kept goats – and this shepherd or goatherd, as my story tells, was called Lope Ruiz. Now this Lope Ruiz fell in love with a shepherdess called Torralba, which shepherdess called Torralba was the daughter of a rich herdsman; and this rich herdsman ...'

'If you tell your story that way, Sancho,' said Don Quixote, 'and repeat everything you have to say twice over, you will not be done in two days. Tell it consequentially, like an intelligent man, or else be quiet.'

'The way I'm telling it,' replied Sancho, 'is the way all stories are told in my country, and I don't know any other way of telling it. It isn't fair for your worship to ask me to get new habits.'

'Tell it as you like,' replied Don Quixote, 'and since it is the will of Fate that I cannot help listening, go on.'

'And so, my dear master,' Sancho went on, 'as I said, this shepherd fell in love with the shepherdess Torralba, who was a plump, high-spirited girl, and rather mannish, for she had a slight moustache – I can almost see her now.'

'Really, did you know her, then?' asked Don Quixote.

'I didn't know her,' replied Sancho, 'but the man who told me this story said that it was so true and authentic that when I told it to anyone else I could swear on my oath that I had seen it all. So, as the days came and the days went, the Devil, who never sleeps and tangles everything up, brought it about that the love which the shepherd had for the shepherdess turned to hatred and ill-will; and the reason was, as evil tongues told, that she caused him a number of little jealousies, such as exceeded the bounds and trespassed on the forbidden; and thenceforth the shepherd loathed her so much that, to avoid her, he decided to leave that country and go where his eyes should never see her again. But when Torralba found that Lope scorned her, she immediately fell to loving him more than she had ever loved him before.'

'That is natural in women,' said Don Quixote, 'to scorn those who love them, and love those who loathe them. Go on, Sancho.'

'It came about that the shepherd put his resolution into effect,' said Sancho, 'and set out driving his goats across the plains of Estremadura to cross into the kingdom of Portugal. Torralba heard of his plan, and followed him at a distance, on foot and bare-legged, with a pilgrim's staff in her hand and a satchel round her neck, which contained, the story goes, a bit of mirror and a broken comb, and some little bottle or other of washes for her face. But whatever it was she carried, I don't mean to set about inquiring now. I'll only say that the story tells how the shepherd came with his flock to cross the Guadiana river, which at that season was swollen and almost overflowing; and at the place he struck it there wasn't a boat of any kind, nor anyone to ferry him or his flock to the other side. This put him very much out, because he saw Torralba coming near, and she was sure to bother him a great deal with her entreaties and tears. He went on looking about him, however, until he saw a fisherman close beside a boat, which was so small that it could only hold one man and one goat. But, all the same, he hailed him and arranged for him to take himself and his three hundred goats across. The fisherman got into the boat and took one goat over, came back and fetched another, and came back once more and took another. Keep an account of the goats which the fisherman is taking over, your worship, for if you lose count of one the story will end, and it won't be possible for me to tell you another word of it. I'll continue now and mention that the landing-place on the other side was very muddy and slippery, which delayed the fisherman a good deal in his journeys backwards and forwards. But, all the same, he came back for another goat, and another, and another.'

'Take it that they are all across,' said Don Quixote, 'and do not go on coming and going like that, or you will never get them all over in a year.'

'How many have got over so far?' asked Sancho.

'How the devil should I know?' replied Don Quixote.

'There now, didn't I tell you to keep a good count? Well, there's an end of the story. God knows there's no going on with it now.'

'How can that be?' replied Don Quixote. 'Is it so essential to the tale to know exactly how many goats have crossed that if you are one out in the number you cannot go on?'

'No, sir, not at all,' answered Sancho. 'But, when I asked your worship to tell me how many goats had got across and you replied that you didn't know, at that very moment everything I had left to say went clean out of my head, though there were some good and amusing things coming, I promise you.'

'So,' said Don Quixote, 'the story is finished, then?'

'As sure as my mother is,' said Sancho.

'Really,' replied Don Quixote, 'you have told me one of the strangest tales — true or false — that anyone could imagine in the whole world; and never in a lifetime was there such a way of telling it or stopping it, although I expected no less from your excellent intelligence. But I am not surprised, for this ceaseless thumping must have disturbed your brains.'

'That may well be,' replied Sancho, 'but I know that so far as my story goes there is nothing more to say, for it just ends where the error begins in counting the goats that cross over.'

'All right, let it end where it will,' said Don Quixote. 'And now let us see if Rocinante can move.' He dug in his spurs once more, and the horse gave a few more leaps. Then he stood stock still, so fast was he tied.

At this point, it seems, either the cold of morning, which was just breaking, or something laxative he had eaten for supper or, as seems more likely, the natural course of things, gave Sancho the inclination and desire to do what no one else could do for him; but so much fear had entered into his heart that he dared not stir a hair's breadth from his master. Yet it was quite impossible even to think of not fulfilling his needs. So what he did was to take a middle course. Very gently he moved his right hand from the crupper of the saddle, and with it neatly and noiselessly loosened the running knot, which was all that kept his breeches up, so that when it was undone they fell down and held him like fetters. After which he hitched up his shirt as best he could, and bared a pair of ample buttocks to the air. This done, which he thought was all he needed to relieve himself of his terrible griping pains, another greater problem confronted him: he was afraid that he could not relieve himself without making some report or noise. So he began to grind his teeth and contract his shoulders, holding his breath as much as he could. But despite all these precautions he was so unfortunate as in the end to make a little noise very different from the din which was causing him so much terror. And when Don Quixote heard it he asked: 'What is that noise, Sancho?'

'I don't know, sir,' he replied. 'It must be something fresh, for these adventures and misadventures never begin for nothing.'

He tried his luck again, and with such success that he relieved himself, without any more noise or disturbance, of the burden which had caused him such discomfort. As Don Quixote's sense of smell, however, was as keen as his hearing, and as Sancho was clinging so closely to him, it was impossible for some of the odour, which ascended almost perpendicularly, not to reach his nose; and no

sooner did it get there than he went to the rescue and, holding his
nostrils between two fingers, observed in rather snuffling tones:
'You seem to be very frightened, Sancho.'

'Yes, I am,' replied Sancho, 'but how is it that your worship particularly notices it now?'

'Because you smell more now, and not of ambergris,' replied
Don Quixote.

'That may be,' said Sancho, 'though it isn't my fault, but your
worship's for dragging me out at such unearthly hours into such
extraordinary places.'

'Go two or three paces off, friend,' said Don Quixote, without
taking his fingers from his nose, 'and pay more attention in future
to your person and to the respect that you owe me; for it is my
great familiarity with you that has engendered this contempt.'

'I'll bet,' replied Sancho, 'your worship thinks that I have done
... something that I shouldn't with my person.'

'The less said about it the better, friend Sancho,' replied Don
Quixote.

Master and servant spent the night in conversation of this sort,
and when Sancho saw that morning was fast approaching, he very
cautiously unfettered Rocinante and tied up his breeches. And as
soon as the horse found himself free, although never very mettle-
some by nature, he seemed to revive, and began to paw the ground,
for prancing – begging his pardon – was beyond him. Don Quixote
took Rocinante's movements as a good omen and a sign for him to
attempt that perilous adventure.

Dawn having broken by now and made objects distinctly visible,
the knight saw that they were standing beneath some tall chestnut
trees, which cast a very deep shadow. He also noticed that the blows
had not ceased, though he could not see what the cause of them was.
So without more delay he put spur to Rocinante and, turning to
take leave of Sancho, told him to wait for him there for three days
at most, as he had already bidden him, and if he had not returned
by that time, to take it as certain that, by God's will, he had ended
his days on that perilous adventure. He once more spoke of Sancho's errand and of the message which he was to take on his behalf
to his lady Dulcinea. As for payment for his services, said the
knight, his squire need not worry. For, by the will which he had

made before leaving home, Sancho would find himself completely satisfied in the matter of his wages, which would be duly proportionate to the time he had served. Should God, however, bring him through this peril safe, sound, and unharmed, his squire might reckon himself more than certain, he said, of the promised isle. Sancho burst into fresh tears at again hearing his good master's pitiful words, and determined not to leave him until the final issue and end of the business.

From these tears and this very honourable resolution the author of this history concludes that Sancho Panza must have been well born and at least an *Old Christian*. His master was rather touched by his feelings, but not sufficiently to show any weakness. On the contrary, concealing it as best he could, he began to ride in the direction from which the sounds of the water and the blows seemed to come. Sancho followed him on foot, as usual, leading by the bridle his ass, his constant companion in good and evil fortune; and when they had gone some way under those shady chestnut trees, they came out into a little meadow at the foot of a high cliff, from which fell a great head of water. Beneath the cliff were a few tumble-down houses, which looked more like ruins than dwellings, and from them, they discovered, came the hideous and still unceasing din of the hammering. Rocinante started at the noise of the water and of the thumping, but Don Quixote pacified him, and gradually advanced towards the houses, commending himself to his lady meanwhile with all his heart, and imploring her to favour him in his formidable task and enterprise; and on his way he also commended himself to God that He might not forget him. Sancho did not leave his side, but craned his neck as far as he could to peer between Rocinante's legs and to make out the cause of his fears and alarms. They must have gone another hundred paces when, on their turning a corner, there appeared, clear and visible, the indubitable cause of that horrific and, to them, most dreadful sound, which had kept them all that night in such a state of terror and suspense. It was – do not take it amiss, good reader! – six fulling-hammers whose regular strokes made all that din.

Don Quixote was dumbfounded and utterly abashed at this sight and, when Sancho looked at him, his head hung down on his breast in confusion. But when Don Quixote looked at Sancho and clearly saw from his swollen cheeks and his laughing mouth that he was on the point of exploding, despite his own gloom he could not help laughing at the look of him. And as soon as Sancho saw that his master had begun, he let himself go with such violence that he had to hold his sides for fear of bursting. Four times he calmed down, and four times he broke into fresh laughter as violently as before. At this Don Quixote wished him to the devil, especially when he heard him say in mockery: 'You must know, friend Sancho, that I was born by the will of Heaven in this our iron age to revive the age of gold, or the golden age. It is for me that are reserved perils, great exploits, and valorous deeds.' And so he went on, repeating all or most of what his master had said when they first heard that frightful hammering.

When Don Quixote realized that Sancho was making fun of him, he got so furiously angry that he lifted his lance and dealt him two blows which would have relieved the master of the duty of paying his squire's wages, unless perhaps to his heirs, had they caught him on the head instead of on the shoulders. But when Sancho found himself so poorly rewarded for his joke, he was afraid that his master might carry the matter farther, and said to him with great humility: 'Gently, your worship; I was only joking, I swear.'

'You may be joking, but I am not,' replied Don Quixote. 'Come here, master joker. Do you think that if these fulling-hammers had really been some perilous adventure I should not have shown the courage necessary to undertake it and carry it through? Am I, by chance, obliged, being as I am a knight, to recognize and distinguish sounds, and know whether they are fulling-hammers or not? For the case might be – as indeed it is – that I have never seen such things in my life, though you have seen them, wretched peasant that you are, and were born and brought up among them. But turn those six hammers into six giants, and let them beard me one by one or all together, and if I do not lay them all on their backs, make as much fun of me as you will.'

'No more, dear master,' replied Sancho. 'I confess I laughed a little too much. But tell me, your worship, now that we are at peace – and may God bring you as safe and sound through all adventures that befall you as through this one – isn't the awful fright we were in rather a joke, and doesn't it make a good story? At least the fright that I was in, for your worship, I know very well, doesn't so much as know what fear or fright is.'

'I do not deny,' replied Don Quixote, 'that what happened to us is a thing worth laughing at. But it is not worth telling, for not everyone is sufficiently intelligent to be able to see things from the right point of view.'

'At least your worship knew how to point your lance all right when you pointed it at my head but hit my shoulders, thanks to Providence and my prompt ducking. But let that pass. It will all come out in the wash, and I have heard it said, if he makes you weep it is a sure sign he loves you. Besides, when men of quality scold their servants they generally give them a pair of breeches afterwards, though I don't know what they generally give them after a beating, unless perhaps in the case of knights errant it's isles, or kingdoms on dry land.'

'The dice may so fall,' said Don Quixote, 'that every word you say will prove true. Forgive what is past, for you are sensible enough to know that first impulses are outside man's control. But take heed of one thing: you must abstain and refrain from overmuch speech with me in future, for never in any of the countless books of chivalry which I have read have I found a squire who talked to his master as much as you do to yours. In fact I look upon it as a great fault in you and in me: in you for showing me so little respect, and in me for not making myself more respected. We read of Gandalin, the squire of Amadis of Gaul, that though he was Count of the Firm Isle he always spoke to his lord cap in hand, with bowed head and body bent in the Turkish fashion. Then what shall we say of Gasabal, Sir Galaor's squire, who was so quiet that, to inform us of the perfection of his marvellous silence, once only is his name mentioned in the whole of that great and authentic history? From all that I have said, Sancho, you must infer that a distinction must be kept between master and man, between lord and servant, and between knight and squire. So from to-day we must behave with more respect, and not give ourselves rope; since, for whatever reason I may be annoyed with you, it will always be the pitcher that comes off worst. The favours and benefits which I promised you will arrive in due course; and if they do not arrive, your wages at least will not be lost, as I have told you already.'

'What your worship says is all very well,' said Sancho, 'but I should like to know, in case the time for favours never comes and we have to fall back on wages, how much a knight errant's squire earned in those days, and if they contracted by the month, or by the day like builders' labourers.'

'I do not believe that squires ever worked for wages,' replied Don Quixote, 'only for favours; and I have assigned you some now in the sealed will which I have left at home, to provide against accidents; since I do not yet know how chivalry will fare in these calamitous times of ours, and I should not wish my soul to suffer for trifles in the other world. For I would have you know, Sancho, that there is no state more perilous than a knight errant's.'

'That is true,' said Sancho, 'since the mere sound of the hammers of a fulling-mill was enough to alarm and disturb the heart of so valiant a knight errant as your worship. But you may rest assured that henceforth I shall not open my lips to make fun of your worship's business, but shall honour you as my master and natural lord.'

'In that case,' replied Don Quixote, 'your days will be long on the face of the earth, for next to our parents we are bound to honour our masters as we would our fathers.'

Chapter XXI. *Of the high Adventure and rich prize of Mambrino's Helmet with other things which befell our invincible Knight.*

ABOUT this time it began to rain a little, and Sancho wanted to go into the fulling-mills; but Don Quixote had conceived such a loathing of them, on account of the wretched joke, that he would on no account agree. So, turning to the right, they struck another road, like the one they had ridden on the day before, and had not gone far before Don Quixote caught sight of a man on a horse carrying something on his head which shone like gold; on seeing which he turned to Sancho and said: 'It seems to me, Sancho, that there is no proverb which is not true, for they are all drawn from experience itself, which is the mother of all sciences. This is especially true of the saying: When one door shuts another opens. This I say because if last night Fortune shut the door which we were looking for, and deceived us with the fulling-mills, it is now opening wide to us another, better, and more certain adventure. And if I do not succeed in passing through this one, the fault will be mine, and cannot be attributed to my scanty knowledge of fulling-mills or to the darkness of the night. This I say because, if I am not mistaken, there is someone approaching us bearing on his head that helmet of Mambrino, about which I swore the oath you know of.'

'Take good care what you say, your worship,' said Sancho, 'and even greater care what you do, for I shouldn't like some other fulling-mills to end up by milling and mashing your brains out.'

'The devil take you, fellow,' replied Don Quixote. 'What has a helmet to do with fulling-mills?'

'I've no idea,' replied Sancho, 'but I swear that if I might talk as I used to, I could probably give you some reasons that would make your worship see that you are mistaken.'

'How can I be mistaken, unbelieving traitor?' asked Don Quixote. 'Tell me, can you not see that knight coming towards us on a dapple-grey steed with a gold helmet on his head?'

'What I see and perceive,' replied Sancho, 'is nothing but a man on a grey ass like mine with something glittering on his head.'

'Why, that is Mambrino's helmet,' said Don Quixote. 'Stand aside and leave me to deal with him. You will see how, so as to save time, I shall complete this adventure without uttering a word, and the helmet I have so much desired will be mine.'

'I shall take good care to stand aside,' replied Sancho, 'but pray God it is sweet marjoram, and not fulling-mills.'

'I have told you already, brother, not to remind me again, even by so much as a thought, of those fulling-mills,' said Don Quixote, 'or I swear – and I will say no more – that I will mill your very soul.'

Sancho fell silent, fearing that his master would fulfil the oath he had flung at him so roundly.

Now the truth of this matter of the helmet, the horse, and the horseman that Don Quixote saw is this. There were in that district two villages, one so small that it had neither an apothecary's shop nor a barber, while the other, near-by, had both. So the barber of the bigger place served the smaller, in which there was a sick man who needed bleeding and another fellow who wanted to be shaved; which was why the barber was now on the road carrying a brass

F

basin. Now fate would have it that, as he came along, it began to rain. So, fearing that his hat, which was no doubt a new one, might get spoiled, he put the basin on his head; and, as it was clean, it shone from more than a mile away. He rode, as Sancho said, on a grey ass, and that is the reason why Don Quixote took them for a dapple-grey steed, a knight, and a golden helmet. For everything which he saw he adapted with great facility to his wild, chivalrous and errant fancies. So, when he saw the luckless horseman draw near, without entering into any parley with him, he urged Rocinante into a canter and attacked him with lance couched, intending to run him through and through; and as he got up to him without checking the fury of his career, he cried out: 'Defend yourself, base caitiff creature, or surrender of your own free will what is so rightfully mine.'

The barber, seeing this apparition descending on him so unexpectedly and without warning, had no other means of avoiding his lance but by sliding down from his ass. But, once on the ground, he leapt up lighter than a deer, and began to run across the plain faster than the wind. The basin he left on the ground, and the delighted Don Quixote observed that the pagan had acted most prudently in imitation of the beaver, who, when hard pressed by the hunters, with his own teeth bites off what he knows by his natural instinct to be the object of the chase. So he bade Sancho pick up the helmet. And when he had it in his hands, the squire exclaimed: 'By God, it's a good basin, and worth a *real* if it's worth a farthing.'

He then gave it to his master, who placed it on his head, turning it round and round to find the vizor. But, unable to discover it, he remarked: 'Certainly the pagan to whose measure this famous headpiece was first shaped must have had an enormous head; and the worst of it is that one half of it is missing.'

When Sancho heard the basin called a head-piece he could not restrain his laughter; but suddenly he remembered his master's anger, and stopped short.

'What are you laughing at?' asked Don Quixote.

'It makes me laugh,' he replied, 'to think what a big head that pagan must have had, who owned that head-piece. It's like nothing so much as a barber's basin. Just like it, it is.'

'Do you know what I think, Sancho? This famous piece, this

enchanted helmet, must have fallen by some strange accident into the hands of someone who did not esteem it at its true value. So, not knowing what he was doing, and seeing that it was pure gold, he must have melted down the other half for the sake of the metal, and made from this half what looks like a barber's basin, as you say. But, however that may be, its metamorphosis is of no consequence to me, who know what it really is. For I will have it set right in the first village where there is a smith, and so well that it will not be surpassed or even equalled by the helmet which the god of smithies forged and made for the god of battles. In the meantime, however, I will wear it as best I can, for something is better than nothing; and, besides, it will do very well to defend me from a stoning.'

'So long as they don't shoot with slings,' said Sancho, 'the way they did in that battle between the two armies, when they knocked out your worship's teeth and broke the can which held that most blessed liquor that made me vomit up my guts.'

'Its loss does not trouble me much,' said Don Quixote, 'for, as you know, I have the recipe by heart.'

'So have I,' replied Sancho, 'but if I ever make it up or try it again in all my life, may this be my last hour. What's more, I don't mean to put myself in the way of requiring it, for I intend to use all my five senses to avoid being wounded or wounding anyone. I say nothing about another blanket-tossing, for such misfortunes are difficult to prevent, and if they come there's nothing for it but to hunch your shoulders, hold your breath, close your eyes, and let yourself go where fate and the blanket send you.'

'You are a bad Christian, Sancho,' said Don Quixote; 'you never forget an injury once done you, though you should know that a noble and generous heart sets no store by such trifles. Did you come out with a lame foot or a broken rib or a cracked skull, that you cannot forget that jest? For, when you look at it carefully, it was only a jest and a sport; and if I had not taken it as such, I should long ago have returned there and done more execution to avenge you than the Greeks did for the rape of Helen who, if she had lived in our times, or my Dulcinea in hers, would most certainly not have had such a reputation for beauty as she had.' And here he heaved a sigh that echoed to the clouds.

'Let it pass for a jest, then,' said Sancho, 'since it can't be

avenged in earnest. But I know the quality of those jests and earn-
ests, and I know, too, that they won't slip from my memory any
more than the feel of them will from my shoulders. But to leave the
subject, tell me, your worship, what shall we do with this dapple-
grey steed that looks like a grey ass, which that fellow your worship
knocked down has left abandoned? For to judge by the dust he
kicked up and the way he skipped off he doesn't look as if he will
ever come back for it. And I'll be blowed if the dapple is not a good
ass.'

'It is not my custom,' said Don Quixote, 'to plunder those whom
I conquer, nor is it the usage of chivalry to take their horses and
leave them to go on foot, unless the victor has lost his own mount
in the fight, in which case it is lawful for him to take the beaten
knight's as won in fair combat. Therefore, Sancho, leave the horse,
or ass, or whatever you would have it be, for as soon as its master
sees that we have gone away he will come back for it.'

'God knows I should like to take it,' replied Sancho, 'or at least
to swap it for my own, for it seems a better beast. Really the laws
of chivalry are very strict, if they don't even stretch to letting one
ass be swapped for another. But I should like to know if I couldn't
at least swap the trappings.'

'I am not very certain on that point,' replied Don Quixote; 'but,
as it is a doubtful case, until I am better informed I should say that
you might make the exchange, if you are in extreme need.'

'So extreme,' replied Sancho, 'that if it were for my own person
I couldn't need them more.' So, with this permission, he made an
immediate *mutatio capparum*, and put all the finery on his ass, which
came off very much the better for the exchange. When this was done
they breakfasted off the remains of the provender which they had
plundered from the baggage-mule, and drank from the stream which
turned the fulling-mills, though without once glancing in their
direction, so heartily did they loathe them for the fright they had
put them in.

Then, with their anger and even their gloom abated, they
mounted, and without deciding what road to take – the custom of
knights errant being to leave this matter to chance – they set out
in the direction chosen by Rocinante. For his will acted as guide to
his masters and to the ass as well, who always followed him in love

and good fellowship, wherever he led. But all the same they came back to the highway and followed it at random without any definite plan.

As they were going along Sancho said to his master: 'Sir, will your worship give me permission to say a few words? For since you laid that harsh command of silence upon me several things have been rotting in my stomach, and there's one that I have on the tip of my tongue at the moment and that I shouldn't like to go bad.'

'Tell me,' said Don Quixote, 'and be brief in your arguments, for nothing long is ever pleasing.'

'Well, sir,' replied Sancho, 'for several days lately I've been thinking how little profit is gained from wandering after the adventures which your worship seeks in these wastes and at these cross-roads. For even when the most perilous of them are victoriously concluded, there's no one to see or hear of them; and so they must remain in perpetual oblivion despite your worship's good intentions and their own deserts. So it seems to me that it would be better – with due deference to your worship's better judgment – for us to go and serve an Emperor or some other great Prince who is engaged in some war. In his service your worship might show the valour of your person, your great strength, and greater wisdom. Then, when this lord whom we should serve came to see your worship's quali-ties, he would be bound to reward us, each according to our deserts; and in that case there couldn't fail to be someone to set down your worship's exploits in writing for everlasting remembrance. About my own I say nothing, because they must not be greater than a squire's should be, although I can say that, if it is customary in chivalry to record the deeds of squires, I don't think that mine will be left out.'

'There is something in what you say, Sancho,' replied Don Quixote, 'but before he gets to that stage a knight must wander through the world, on probation as it were, in pursuit of adven-tures; so as to gain such a name and reputation, by achieving a few, that, if he goes to the court of some great monarch, he will already be well known by his deeds. Then as soon as the boys see him ride through the city gates, they will all follow him and surround him and shout: "Here is the Knight of the Sun!" – or of the Serpent, or of any other device under which he may have performed his great deeds. "Here," they will cry, "is that knight who in single battle conquered the great giant Brocabruno of mighty strength, the knight who freed the Great Mameluke of Persia from the long enchantment which had held him for almost nine hundred years." Thus from mouth to mouth they will go on proclaiming his deeds, till suddenly, hearing the cries of the boys and the rest of the people, the King of that kingdom will appear at the windows of his royal palace. As soon as he sees the knight, he will recognize him by his armour or by the device on his shield, and then of course he will cry: — "Ho, there, let all the knights of my court ride out to receive the flower of chivalry, who is approaching." All will ride out at his command, and the King himself will come half-way down his staircase, embrace him most warmly, greet him, kiss him on the cheek, and lead him to the chamber of his lady Queen. There the knight will find her with the Princess, her daughter, who is sure to be one of the loveliest and most perfect damsels to be found anywhere, however hard you may search the greater part of the known world. Then immediately afterwards, she will gaze into the knight's eyes, and he into hers, and each will seem to the other rather divine than human; and without knowing how or why, they will be enmeshed and captured in the intricate net of love, and be in great anguish of heart, not knowing in what words to reveal their feelings and desires. From there he will no doubt be taken to some richly furnished room in the palace, where they will strip off his armour and bring him a rich scarlet cloak to wear; and if he is handsome in his armour, he will look still better in the quilted jacket he wears under it. When night falls he will sup with the King, the Queen, and the Princess, never taking his eyes from her, but gazing on her stealthily; and she will do the same with the same caution. For, as I have said, she is a very discreet damsel. The tables will be removed, and suddenly there will enter through the hall door an ugly little dwarf with a beautiful lady following behind him, escorted by two giants, to introduce a certain adventure, so contrived by a most ancient sage that the knight who brings it to a successful conclusion shall be accounted the best in the world.

'Then the King will immediately order all the knights present to attempt it, but none of them will bring it to a victorious conclusion except the stranger knight, to the great enhancement of his fame. At this the Princess will be much delighted, and think herself well rewarded into the bargain, in having firmly set her desires in so exalted a quarter.

'Now it happens, most fortunately, that this King, or Prince, or whatever he is, is engaged in a most stubborn war with another as powerful as himself, and the stranger knight, after some days spent at court, begs for permission to go and serve him in the said war. The King will grant his request with great pleasure, and the knight will kiss his hands most courteously for the favour. Then that night he will take leave of his lady the Princess through the railings of a garden which adjoins her sleeping-chamber; and there it will be that he has spoken with her many times before by the help of a damsel much trusted by the Princess and privy to the whole matter. He will sigh; she will swoon; the damsel will bring water and be much distressed. For it will be nearly morning, and she will fear for her lady's honour that they may be discovered. Finally the Princess will come to herself and put her white hands through the railings for the knight, who will kiss them a thousand, thousand times and bathe them in tears. They will agree how to let one another know their news, good or bad, and the Princess will implore the knight to stay away as short a time as possible, which he will promise with many oaths. Once more he kisses her hands, and bids her farewell with such grief as will come near to ending his life. From there he goes to his chamber, throws himself on the bed, but cannot sleep for the grief of parting. He gets up early in the morning, and goes to take his leave of the King, the Queen, and the Princess. When he has bidden farewell to the royal pair they tell him that the lady Princess is indisposed and cannot receive a visit; the knight concludes that it is from grief at his departure; his heart is pierced and he very nearly betrays his sorrow. The Princess's confidante is present; must observe everything; goes to inform her lady, who receives her with tears, and tells her that one of her greatest griefs is her ignorance of her knight's name, and of whether he is of royal descent or no. The damsel assures her that such courtesy, gentleness, and valour as he displays cannot exist in any but a royal and illustrious person. This consoles the Princess; she endeavours to be calm, so as not to call her parents' attention to herself; and at the end of two days appears in public.

'The knight has already gone off; he fights in the war; conquers the King's enemies; captures many cities; triumphs in many battles; comes back to court, and sees his lady in the place where he had seen her before. They agree that in reward for his services he shall ask her father for her hand in marriage, but the King will not consent, since he does not know who the knight is. Yet, however that may be, either by carrying her off or in some other way, he marries the Princess, and her father in the end considers it a most fortunate affair, for it is revealed that the said knight is the son of a valorous king – of what kingdom I do not know, for I do not think it can be on the map. The father dies; the Princess succeeds him; in fact the knight becomes king. Now comes the time for bestowing favours on his squire, and on all who have helped him to climb to his high estate. He marries his squire to one of the Princess's damsels, no doubt the one who was privy to his love, the daughter of a very important duke.'

'That's what I want, a fair field and no favour,' said Sancho, 'and that is what I expect, for it's all literally bound to turn out like that, since your worship has taken the name of *The Knight of the Sad Countenance.*'

'Most certainly, Sancho,' replied Don Quixote, 'for in that very way, and by the very steps I have described to you, knights errant rise and have risen to be Kings and Emperors. All that we need now is to look out and find some king, Christian or pagan, who is at war and has a beautiful daughter. Though there will be plenty of time to think about that. For, as I have said, we have first to win fame elsewhere before we go to court. And there is something else lacking besides, for even supposing that I find a king at war and with a beautiful daughter, and that I have won incredible fame throughout the whole universe, I do not know how it can be proved that I am of royal blood, or even second cousin to an Emperor; and the King will not want to give me his daughter for a wife until he is perfectly assured on this point, whatever the merits of my famous deeds. So I am afraid that without this proof I shall lose the rich reward of my valour. True it is that I am a gentleman of known family, of possessions, and property, and that my life is worth five hundred pounds fine by the old law; and it may be that the sage who comes to write my history will so establish my parentage and descent that I shall find I am fifth or sixth in descent from a King. For I would have you know, Sancho, that there are two kinds of lineages in the world: those which trace their descent from princes and monarchs, and which little by little time has diminished and reduced to a point, like a pyramid upside down; and others which derive their origin from common folk, and climb step by step till they achieve the dignity of great lords. So that the difference is between those who were and are no longer, and those who are but once were not. It is possible that I may prove to be one of the former, and that, on enquiry, my descent may prove great and noble, which should content the King, my father-in-law to be; but if it does not, the Princess will have to love me so much that, despite her father, she will take me for her lord and husband, even though she clearly knows that I am the son of a water-carrier. And, if she does not, it is a case of stealing her and carrying her off wherever I wish, for time or death must put an end to her parents' displeasure.'

'Yes,' said Sancho, 'it is a case too of Never ask as a favour for what you can take by force, as some good-for-nothings say; although it would suit the situation better to say: A leap over the hedge is better than good men's prayers. This I say because, if the lord King, your worship's father-in-law, shouldn't deign to yield you my lady the Princess, there's nothing for it, as your worship says, but to steal her and hide her. But the trouble is that until peace is made and you can enjoy the kingdom quietly, the poor squire may go whistle for this reward of his, unless the go-between maiden, who is to be his wife, comes away with the Princess, and he shares his misfortunes with her until Heaven ordains otherwise. For it would be quite possible, I think, for his master to give her to him straight off in lawful marriage.'

'There is no one to stop that,' said Don Quixote.

'Well, since that's the case,' replied Sancho, 'we have only to commend ourselves to God and let fortune take what course it will.'

'May God grant it,' replied Don Quixote, 'as I desire and you require and let the man who thinks he is be wretched.'

'So be it, in God's name,' said Sancho, 'for I'm an old Christian, and that is enough ancestry for a count.'

'And more than enough,' said Don Quixote. 'But even if you were not it would not matter, for if I am King I can easily make you noble without either purchase or service on your part; and, if I make you a count, there you are, a gentleman, let them say what they will; for they will have to call you your Lordship, whether they want to or no.'

'You can take it from me that I shall know how to bear my indignity,' said Sancho.

'*Dignity* you should say, not indignity,' put in his master.

'As you will,' replied Sancho Panza, 'I say that I shall know how to carry it off well. For I was once beadle to a brotherhood, and the beadle's gown suited me so nicely that they all said I looked important enough to be the steward of the brotherhood. So what will it be like when I wear a duke's robe on my shoulders, or dress all in gold and pearls, after the fashion of a foreign count? They'll come from hundreds of miles off to see me, I'll be bound.'

'You will look fine,' said Don Quixote, 'but you will need to trim your beard rather often, for you wear it so thick and matted and bushy, that unless you take a razor to it every day at least they will see what you are a gun-shot away.'

'Why,' said Sancho, 'what more have I to do than to get a barber and keep him in the house on wages? And I'll even make him follow me round at a pinch like a grandee's groom.'

'But how do you know,' asked Don Quixote, 'that grandees have their grooms following them?'

'I'll tell you,' replied Sancho. 'Some years ago I spent a month about the court, and there I saw a very little gentleman taking a walk, and they said he was a great grandee. Now wherever he went he had a man following him on horseback, turning everywhere he turned, more like his tail than anything else. I asked why that fellow never caught the other man up but always rode behind him. They told me that he was his groom, and that it was the fashion for grandees to have men like that riding after them. And I've known it ever since, and it's so stuck in my head that I've never forgotten it.'

'You are quite right, I admit,' said Don Quixote, 'and you can take your barber round like that. For customs did not all arise together, nor were they all invented at once, and you may well be the first count to carry your barber round after you. Indeed, trimming a beard is a more intimate duty than saddling a horse.'

'Leave this matter of the barber to me,' said Sancho, 'and let your worship's job be to try and become a King and make me a count.'

'So it shall be,' replied Don Quixote. And, raising his eyes, he saw what shall be told in the next chapter.

Chapter XXII. How Don Quixote set at liberty many unfortunate Creatures who were being borne, much against their will, where they had no wish to go.

CIDE HAMETE BENENGELI, the Arabian and Manchegan author, relates in his most grave, eloquent, meticulous, delightful, and ingenious history that after that conversation between the famous Don Quixote de la Mancha and Sancho Panza, his squire, which is set down at the end of the twenty-first chapter, Don Quixote raised his eyes and saw on the road which he was taking some dozen men on foot, strung by the neck like beads on a great iron chain, and all manacled. With them were two horsemen and two men on foot, the horsemen carrying firelocks,* the footmen javelins and swords. And as soon as Sancho Panza saw them he said: — 'Here's a chain of galley-slaves, men forced by the King, going to serve in the galleys.'

'What! Men forced?' asked Don Quixote. 'Is it possible that the King uses force on anyone?'

'I don't say that,' answered Sancho; 'but they are men condemned for their crimes to serve the King in the galleys, and they go perforce.'

'In fact,' replied Don Quixote, 'however you put it, these men are taken, and go by force and not of their own free will.'

'That is so,' said Sancho.

'Then,' said his master, 'this is a case for the exercise of my profession, for the redressing of outrages and the succouring and relieving of the wretched.'

'Consider, your worship,' said Sancho, 'that justice — that is the King himself — is doing no wrong or outrage to such people, but only punishing them for their crimes.'

At this moment the chain of galley-slaves came up, and in most courteous terms Don Quixote begged the guards to be so kind as

* N.B. Only one firelock is accounted for in the subsequent events. The second Cervantes seems to have forgotten.

to inform him of the cause or causes why they were bearing those people off in that fashion. One of the horsemen replied that they were galley-slaves belonging to His Majesty on the way to the galleys, such was the truth of the matter and there was no more to say.

'Nevertheless,' replied Don Quixote, 'I should like to learn from each one of them separately the cause of his misfortune.' He went on in such very polite language to persuade them to give him the information he desired, that the other mounted guard replied: 'Although we have with us here the copies and certificates of the sentences on each of these wretches, there is no time to take them out and read them. But your worship may come and ask them themselves, and they may tell you, if they please – and they will, for they are the sort who not only enjoy acting the villain but boasting of it afterwards too.'

With this permission, which Don Quixote would have taken if it had not been granted, the knight went up to the chain, and asked the first man for what sins he was in that evil plight. He replied that it was for falling in love.

'For no more than that?' cried Don Quixote. 'But if they send men to the galleys for falling in love, I should long since have been rowing there myself.'

'It isn't the kind of love your worship imagines,' said the galley-slave. 'Mine was an over-great affection for a basketful of white linen, which I clasped to me so tight that if the law hadn't wrested it from me by force I shouldn't have let it go of my own free will even to this day. I was taken red-handed; there was no need of the torture; the trial was short; they accommodated my shoulders with a hundred lashes, and three years in the *gurapas* thrown in, and the job was done.'

'What are the *gurapas*?' asked Don Quixote.

'*Gurapas* are galleys,' replied the galley-slave, who was a lad of about twenty-four, and came, as he said, from Piedrahita.

Don Quixote asked the same question of the second man, who was too melancholy and dejected to answer a word. But the first man replied for him: 'This man is here for being a canary – I mean a musician and singer.'

'How is that?' asked Don Quixote. 'Do men go to the galleys for being musicians and singers?'

'Yes, sir,' replied the galley-slave: 'for there is nothing worse than singing in anguish.'

'I have always heard the opposite,' said Don Quixote. 'Sing away sorrow, cast away care.'

'Here it's the reverse,' said the galley-slave. 'If you sing once you weep for a lifetime.'

'I do not understand,' said Don Quixote. But one of the guards put in: 'Sir, singing in anguish with these ungodly people means confessing on the rack. They put this sinner to the torture, and he confessed his crime, which was cattle-thieving; and on his confession they sentenced him to six years in the galleys, besides two hundred lashes on the back; and the reason why he is dejected and melancholy is that the rest of the thieves back there, and these marching here, abuse him and bully him, and mock him and despise him, because he confessed and hadn't the courage to say no. For, as they say, *no* takes no longer to say than *yes*, and a crook is in luck if his life depends on his own tongue and not on witnesses and proofs; and I think that they are not far wrong.'

'I agree,' replied Don Quixote. Then, passing to the third man, he asked him the same question as the others, and the man answered very readily and calmly:

'I am going to their ladyships the *gurapas* for five years because I was short of ten ducats.'

'I will give you twenty with pleasure,' said Don Quixote, 'to free you from this distress.'

'That,' replied the galley-slave, 'looks to me like having money when you're in mid-ocean and dying of hunger, and there's nowhere to buy what you need. Because if I had had those twenty ducats your worship now offers me at the right time, I should have greased the clerk's pen with them and livened up my lawyer's wits to such effect that I should have been in the Zocodover square in Toledo to-day, and not dragging along this road like a greyhound on a leash. But God is great. Patience — that's enough.'

Don Quixote went on to the fourth, a man of venerable appearance with a white beard reaching below his chest who, when asked why he was there, began to weep and answered not a word. But the fifth convict lent him a tongue and said: 'This honest fellow is going to the galleys for four years after parading the town in state and on horseback.'

'I suppose you mean that he was exposed to public shame,' said Sancho Panza.

'That's right,' replied the galley-slave, 'and the offence for which he got his sentence was trafficking in ears, in fact in whole bodies. What I mean is that this gentleman is here for procuring, and also for having a touch of the wizard about him.'

'If it had not been for that touch,' said Don Quixote, 'and if it were merely for procuring, he would not deserve to go and row in the galleys, but to be their general and command them. For the office of procurer is no easy one. It requires persons of discretion and is a most essential office in a well-ordered state. Only men of good birth should exercise it. Indeed, there ought to be an overseer and controller of these procurers, as there are of other professions, and only a certain number should be appointed and recognized, like brokers on the Exchange. In that way a great many troubles would be avoided, which are caused through this office getting into the hands of idiots and people of little intelligence, such as half-witted servant-maids and little pages and buffoons, raw and inexperienced folk. Then, at the critical moment, when they have a really important affair to manage, they let the morsel freeze between their fingers and their mouth, and do not know their right hand from their left. I should like to go on and explain why it is necessary to select those who are to hold so necessary a position in the State; but this is no proper place. But some day I will put the matter before those who can furnish a remedy. Now I can only say that the grief caused me by the sight of these white hairs and this venerable countenance in such distress for procuring has been entirely removed by the mention of witchcraft, though I know very well that there are no wizards in the world capable of affecting or compelling the affections, as some simple people believe; for our will is free and there is no drug or spell that can control it. What such simple servant-maids and lying rogues generally do is to make up mixtures and poisons which drive a man crazy, under the pretence that they have the power to excite love; whereas, as I have said, it is impossible to compel the affections.'

'That is so,' said the old fellow, 'and really, sir, as to being a wizard, I was not guilty, though I can't deny the procuring. But I never thought that I was doing any harm. All I wanted was for everyone to have a good time and live in peace and quiet, without quarrels or troubles. But the best intentions didn't serve to keep me from going to a place I don't expect to come back from, being stricken in years and having a bladder complaint which never gives me a moment's rest.' Here he burst into tears once more, and Sancho was so sorry for him that he took a *real* from under his shirt and gave it to him out of charity.

Don Quixote passed on and asked another his crime, and this one replied with rather more freedom than the last:

'I am here for having a bit too much fun with two girl cousins of mine, and two other cousins who were not mine. In fact, I had such fun with them all that the result of the joke was an intricate tangle of relationships that is more than any devil of a clerk can make out. It was all proved against me; I had no friends; I had no money; I was within an inch of having my gullet squeezed; they sentenced me to six years on the galleys; I submitted; it's the punishment for my crime. I'm young; if only my life holds out, all may yet come right. But, sir, should your worship have anything about you to give us poor wretches, God will repay you in Heaven, and here on earth we'll be sure to beseech him in our prayers that your worship's life and health may be as long and as prosperous as your good looks deserve.'

The fellow who spoke wore the dress of a student, and one of the guards said that he was a great talker and a very good Latin scholar. Behind the rest came a man of about thirty, of very good appearance except that he squinted when he looked at you. He was fettered in a different way from the others. For he had a chain on his leg so long that it was wound right round his body, and two collars about his neck, one secured to the chain and the other of the kind called a *keep friend* or *friend's foot*. From this two iron bars reached down to his waist, with two manacles attached in which his wrists were secured by a heavy padlock, so that he could neither lift his hands to his mouth nor bend his head down to his hands. Don Quixote asked why this man had so many more fetters than the rest, and the guard replied that it was because he had committed more crimes than all the others put together, and that he was so bold and desperate a criminal that even though he was chained in that way they were not sure of him, but feared he might escape.

'What crimes, then, can he have committed?' asked Don Quixote, 'if they have not earned him a heavier penalty than the galleys?'

'He is going for ten years,' replied the guard, 'which is a sort of civil death. I need tell you no more than that this fellow is the famous Gines de Pasamonte, alias Ginesillo de Parapilla.'

'Not so rough, sergeant,' put in the galley-slave. 'Don't let us be settling names and surnames now. I am called Gines, not Ginesillo, and Pasamonte is my surname, not Parapilla as you say. Let everyone have a good look in his own cupboard, and he'll not be doing too badly.'

'A little less insolence,' replied the sergeant, 'you double-dyed thief, or I may have to shut you up, and then you'll be sorry.'

'You may see,' replied the galley-slave, 'that man proposes and God disposes; but one day somebody may learn whether my name is Ginesillo de Parapilla or not.'

'Isn't that what they call you, then, rogue?' asked the guard.

'Yes, they do,' replied Gines, 'but I'll stop them calling me that or I'll pluck them – but no matter where. If, sir, you have anything to give us, give it us now, and go in God's name; for you weary me with your prying into other men's lives. But if you want to know about mine, I am Gines de Pasamonte, and I have written my life with these very fingers.'

'He is speaking the truth,' put in the sergeant. 'He has written his own story, as fine as you please, and left the book behind at the prison pawned for two hundred *reals*.'

'And I mean to redeem it,' said Gines, 'even if it were pledged for two hundred ducats.'

'Is it as good as that?' said Don Quixote.

'It's so good,' replied Gines, 'that Lazarillo de Tormes will have to look out, and so will everything in that style that has ever been written or ever will be. One thing I can promise you is that it is all the truth, and such well-written, entertaining truth that there is no fiction that can compare with it.'

'And what is the title of the book?' asked Don Quixote.

'*The Life of Gines de Pasamonte*,' replied that hero.

'Is it finished?' asked Don Quixote.

'How can it be finished,' replied the other, 'if my life isn't? What is written begins with my birth and goes down to the point when I was sent to the galleys this last time.'

'Then you have been there before?' said Don Quixote.

'Four years I was there before,' replied Gines, 'in the service of God and the King, and I know the taste of the biscuit and the lash already. I am not greatly grieved at going, for I shall have a chance there to finish my book. I have a lot more to say, and in the Spanish galleys there is more leisure than I shall require, though I shan't need much for what I have to write, because I know it by heart.'

'You seem a clever fellow,' said Don Quixote.

'And an unfortunate one,' replied Gines, 'for misfortunes always pursue men of talent.'

'They pursue rogues,' replied the sergeant.

'I have already requested you to use better language, sergeant,' replied Pasamonte, 'for your superiors did not give you that staff to maltreat us poor devils, but to guide and lead us where his Majesty commands. If you do not, by God – but enough! – perhaps one day the stains that were made at the inn will come out in the wash. And let everyone hold his tongue, live virtuously and speak better. Now let us get along, for this is a bit too much of a joke.'

The sergeant raised his staff to strike Pasamonte in return for his threats. But Don Quixote interposed and begged him not to ill-treat him, for it was no great matter if a man who had his hands tied let his tongue free a little. Then, addressing the whole chain-gang, the knight said:

'From all that you have told me, dearest brethren, I clearly gather that, although it is for your faults they have punished you, the penalties which you are to suffer give you little pleasure. You are going to them, it seems, very reluctantly and much against your wills; and possibly it is only lack of courage under torture in one, shortage of money in another, lack of friends in another – in short, the unfair decisions of the judge – that have been the cause of your undoing and of your failure to receive the justice which was your due. All of which is now so clear in my mind that it bids me, persuades me, and even compels me, to demonstrate on you the purpose for which Heaven has sent me into the world and made me profess therein the order of chivalry which I follow, and the vow I made to succour the needy and those who are oppressed by the strong. Conscious, however, that it is the part of prudence not to do by foul means what can be done by fair, I would beg the gentlemen of the guard and the sergeant to be so good as to release you and let you go in peace, since there will be no lack of men to serve the King out of better motives; for it seems to me a hard case to make slaves of those whom God and nature made free. Furthermore, gentlemen of the guard,' added Don Quixote, 'these poor men have committed no wrong against you. Let everyone answer for his sins in the other world. There is a God in Heaven, who does not neglect to punish the wicked nor to reward the good, and it is not right that honourable men should be executioners of others, having themselves no concern in the matter. I make this request in a calm and gentle manner, so that I may have cause to thank you if you comply; but if you do not do so willingly, then this lance and this sword, together with the valour of my arm, will force you to do so under compulsion.'

'This is fine foolishness,' replied the sergeant. 'It is a good joke he has taken all this time hatching! He would like us to let the King's convicts go, as if we had authority to free them, or he had it to order us to! Get along with you, sir, and good luck to you! Put that basin straight on your head, and don't go about looking for a cat with three legs.'

'You are the cat, the rat, and the rascal!' replied Don Quixote. Then, matching deeds to his words, he attacked him so swiftly that he had dealt him a serious wound with his lance and brought him to the ground before he had a chance to defend himself; and, luckily for Don Quixote, this was the man with the firelock. The rest of the guards were dumbfounded by this unexpected turn of events. They recovered themselves, however, and the horsemen drew their swords, while the men on foot seized their javelins and rushed at Don Quixote, who awaited them in complete calm. And no doubt things would have gone badly for him if the galley-slaves had not seen their chance of gaining their liberty and taken advantage of it to break the chain which linked them together. Such was the confusion, in fact, that the guards ran first to the galley-slaves, who were struggling loose, and then to deal with Don Quixote, who was attacking, and so achieved no good purpose. Sancho, for his part, helped in releasing Gines de Pasamonte, who was the first to leap free and unfettered into the open, where he attacked the fallen sergeant and seized his sword and his firelock. Then, first levelling the gun at one man and then picking on another, without ever firing it he cleared the field of all the guards, who fled from Pasamonte's gun and from the showers of stones, as well, flung by the now liberated galley-slaves.

Sancho was much grieved at this business, for he guessed that the guards who had fled would report the matter to the Holy Brotherhood, who would sound the alarm and come out in pursuit of the criminals. This thought he communicated to his master, begging him that they might clear out immediately and hide in the nearby mountains.

'That is all very well,' said Don Quixote, 'but I know what is right for us to do now.' Then he called all the galley-slaves, who were running about excitedly and had stripped the sergeant to the skin; and when they had gathered around him to hear what his orders might be, he addressed them thus:

'It is a mark of well-born men to show gratitude for benefits received, and ingratitude is one of the sins which most offend God. I say this, gentlemen, because you have already had good experience of benefits received at my hands; as payment for which it is my will that you bear this chain which I have taken from your necks and immediately take the road to the city of El Toboso, there to present yourselves before the Lady Dulcinea del Toboso and tell her that her knight, the Knight of the Sad Countenance, presents his service to her. Then you are to tell her, point by point, every detail of this famous adventure up to the restoration of your long-coveted liberty; and when you have done so you may go wherever you will, and good luck go with you.'

Gino de Pasamonte answered for them all, and said: 'What your worship commands, lord and liberator, is of all impossibilities the most impossible for us to perform, since we cannot appear on the roads together, but must go singly and separately, each one on his own. And we must try to hide in the bowels of the earth for fear of being found by the Holy Brotherhood, for there is no doubt that they will come out in search of us. What your worship can do, and what you should do, is to substitute for this service and tribute to the lady Dulcinea del Toboso some number of Ave Marias and Credos, which we will say for your worship's benefit, this being a thing which can be performed by night and by day, on the run or resting, in peace or in war. But to think of our returning now to the flesh-pots of Egypt, I mean of our taking up our chain and setting out on the road for El Toboso, is to imagine that it is already night when it is not yet ten in the morning, and you can no more ask us for that than you can ask pears from an elm-tree.'

'Then I swear by Heaven,' cried Don Quixote in fury, 'sir son of a whore, Don Ginesillo de Parapillo, or whatever you are called, – that you shall go yourself alone, with your tail between your legs and the whole chain on your back!'

Pasamonte was quite certain from Don Quixote's crazy action in giving them their liberty that he was not right in the head; and being far from long-suffering, when he found himself treated in this way he tipped his companions the wink. They then drew back and began to rain such a shower of stones upon Don Quixote that he could not contrive to cover himself with his shield, and poor Rocinante took no more notice of the spur than if he had been made of brass. Sancho got behind his ass and used him as a defence against the cloud and hailstorm of stones which descended on the pair of them. But Don Quixote could not shield himself well enough, and was hurt by some of the pebbles, which struck him on the body with such force that they knocked him to the ground. The moment he was down the student leapt on him, and seizing the basin from his head, brought it down three or four times on his shoulders, and as many more on the ground, till it was almost smashed to pieces. They also stripped him of a jacket which he wore over his armour, and would have taken off his stockings too if his leg armour had not prevented them. While from Sancho they took his overcoat, and left him in his shirt. Then, dividing the rest of the spoils of battle, they fled, each in a separate direction, more intent on escaping from the dreaded Brotherhood than on loading themselves with the chain and going to present themselves to the lady Dulcinea del Toboso.

All that remained were the ass and Rocinante, Sancho and Don Quixote; the ass pensively hanging his head and shaking his ears

now and then, imagining that the storm of stones which had whizz-
ed by his head had not yet ceased; Rocinante prostrate beside his
master, for he had also been brought down by a stone; Sancho in
his shirt and terrified of the Holy Brotherhood; and Don Quixote
much distressed at finding himself so vilely treated by the very men
for whom he had done so much.

Chapter XXIII. *Of what happened to the famous Don Quixote in
the Sierra Morena, one of the rarest Adventures in the course
of this true History.*

FINDING himself in so bad a way, Don Quixote said to his squire:
'I have always heard, Sancho, that doing good to base fellows is like
throwing water into the sea. If I had believed what you said to me I
should have avoided this trouble. But now that it is done, patience;
and let this be a warning for the future.'

'Your worship will take as much warning,' replied Sancho, 'as
I'm a Turk. But, as you say that you would have avoided this
disaster if you had trusted me, trust me now and you'll avoid even
worse. For there's no trying chivalry on the Holy Brotherhood, let
me tell you. They don't care a row of pins for all the knights errant
in the world; and, believe me, I can hear their arrows whizzing past
my ears already.'

'You are a coward by nature, Sancho,' said Don Quixote, 'but I
do not want you to say that I am obstinate and never do what you
suggest. So this time I am going to take your advice, and retire before the fury which you so much dread. But on one condition:
never, in life or death, are you to tell anyone that I retreated and
withdrew from this peril out of fear. I do it only to humour your
entreaties, and if you say otherwise it will be a lie. Yes, from now till
then and from then till now I give you the lie, and say that you lie
and will lie every time that you either say it or think it. Do not
answer me with another word; for at the mere thought that I am
retreating and withdrawing from any peril, particularly from this,
which seems to have some faint shadow of danger about it, I am
inclined to stay here and await alone, not only the Holy Brotherhood, whose name you speak in terror, but the Brethren of the
twelve tribes of Israel, and the seven Maccabees, and Castor and

Pollux, and all the brothers and brotherhoods in the world as well.'

'Sir,' replied Sancho, 'withdrawing is not flight, nor is it prudent to stay when danger outweighs hope. It is a wise man's duty to save himself for to-morrow, and not risk everything on one day. Let me tell you that I've still got some idea of what they call good conduct, although I may be an ignorant peasant. So don't be sorry that you've taken my advice, but climb upon Rocinante if you can – or if you can't I'll help you – and follow me; for my thinking-cap tells me that we've more need of our feet just now than of our hands.'

Don Quixote mounted without another word; and with Sancho leading the way on his ass, they rode into a nearby part of the Sierra Morena, it being Sancho's intention to cross the whole range and come out at Viso or Almodovar del Campo, and to hide for a few days in that rough country, so as not to be found if the Holy Brotherhood came after them. He was encouraged in this plan by finding that the provisions he carried on the ass's back had escaped from the skirmish with the galley-slaves, which he took as a miracle, considering how much they had taken and how closely they had searched everything.

Now by nightfall they had got into the heart of the Sierra Morena; where Sancho thought it would be well to spend that night, if not some days, or at least as long as the provisions they had with them should last. And so they camped between two crags among a number of cork-trees. But fatal destiny which, according to those who lack the light of true faith, guides, shapes, and disposes everything in its own way, decreed that Gines de Pasamonte, the famous cheat and robber, whom by his valour and madness Don Quixote had delivered from the chain, had decided to hide in those mountains, out of fear of the Holy Brotherhood, which he had good reason to dread. And his luck and fear took him to the spot to which the same motives had brought Don Quixote and Sancho Panza, while it was still light enough for him to recognize them and just as they were falling asleep. Now as the wicked are always ungrateful and necessity drives them to evil deeds, and as present needs outweigh any thought for the future, Gines, who was neither grateful nor well-disposed, decided to steal Sancho Panza's ass, not caring for Rocinante, a security neither pawnable nor saleable. Sancho

Panza slept; Gines stole his ass;* and before morning he was too far off to be found.

Dawn came forth, bringing joy to the earth but grief to Sancho Panza, who missed his Dapple and, when he found himself without him, burst into the saddest and most doleful lament in all the world. So loud was his grief that Don Quixote woke up to hear him cry: 'O child of my bowels, born in my very house, my children's play-mate, my wife's delight, envy of my neighbours, ease of my burdens, and half my means of livelihood besides, for the sixpence halfpenny a day you earned me was the half of my living!'

On seeing his tears and learning the cause Don Quixote consoled his squire with the best reasoning he could, begging him to be patient and promising to give him a bill of exchange entitling him to three of the five ass-foals he had left at home. This comforted Sancho, who dried his tears, controlled his sobs and thanked Don Quixote for this favour. As for the knight, his heart grew glad as they cut into the mountains, for they seemed to him a most suitable scene for the adventures he was seeking. They recalled to his memory the marvellous things which had happened to knights errant in similar wastes and fastnesses; and he rode on with his mind dwelling on such things, and so absorbed and rapt by them that he remembered nothing else. And Sancho's only thought, now that he supposed them out of danger, was of satisfying his stomach with the relics of the clerical booty; so he walked on behind his master, loaded with all that the ass should have carried, taking morsels out of the bag and cramming them into his belly; and while thus employ-ed he would not have given a halfpenny for any other adventure.

While thus engaged, however, he looked up and saw that his master had stopped and with the point of his lance was trying to lift up some bundle lying on the ground. So he hurried on, to catch him up, and help him if necessary; and overtook his master just as he was raising on his lance-point a saddle-cushion with a leather bag at-tached, partly rotten, or rather entirely so and falling to pieces. But it was so heavy that Sancho had to get down and pick it up for him. His master then bade him look what was in the bag. And this he very quickly did. For, although it was secured by a chain and pad-

---

* The stealing of the ass is another of Cervantes' oversights. Four pages later Sancho is riding him again, and a little later once more without him.

lock, he could see what was inside through the rents and rotten places. There were four shirts of fine cambric, some other fine and fashionable linen, and a considerable pile of gold coins in a hand-kerchief, at the sight of which Sancho cried out: 'Blessed be Heaven for affording us one profitable adventure!' And on a further search he found a little note-book, richly decorated. This Don Quixote asked for, but he told Sancho to take the money for himself and keep it. The squire acknowledged this favour by kissing his master's hands and, rifling the linen, stowed it in their provision bag.

Now when Don Quixote had taken all this in, he observed: 'There seems to me, Sancho, to be no doubt whatever that some traveller must have lost his way in these mountains, and have been attacked by robbers, who must have killed him and brought him to this remote spot to bury him.'

'That can't be so,' replied Sancho, 'for if they had been thieves they wouldn't have left this money here.'

'You are right,' said Don Quixote. 'So I cannot divine or guess what it can be. But wait; let us see if there is not something written in this note-book which will give us a clue.'

He opened it, and the first thing that he saw in it was a beauti-fully written copy of a sonnet, which he read aloud for Sancho to hear. It ran like this:

> Know'st thou, O love, the pangs which I sustain,
> Or, cruel, dost thou view those pangs unmoved?
> Or has some hidden cause its influence proved,
> By all this sad variety of pain?
>
> If Love's a god, then surely he must know,
> And knowing, pity wretchedness like mine.
> From other hands proceeds the fatal blow.
> Is then the deed, unpitying Chloe, thine?
>
> Ah no, a body formed so perfectly
> A soul so merciless can ne'er enclose.
> Nor can it be from Heaven my ruin flows.
> But it's most certain that I soon shall die,
> For when the cause of the complaint's unsure
> 'Twould be a miracle to find a cure.

'We can learn nothing from that poem,' said Sancho, 'unless from that clue we can come to the thread of the matter.'

'What clue do you mean?' asked Don Quixote.

'I thought your worship mentioned a clue?'

'I did not say clue, but Chloe,' replied Don Quixote, 'and that, no doubt, is the name of the lady the author of this sonnet is complaining about. He is a pretty good poet, I am sure, or I am a poor judge of the art!'

'Your worship knows about poetry-writing too, then?' observed Sancho.

'Yes, and better than you think,' replied Don Quixote, 'as you will know when you take a letter written in verse from beginning to end to my lady Dulcinea del Toboso. For I would inform you, Sancho, that all or most knights errant in the olden times were great troubadours and great musicians as well. For these two accomplishments, or rather graces as I should say, belong with love errantry; though it is true that the poems of the knights of old have more spirit than elegance about them.'

'Read some more, your worship,' said Sancho, 'for we may yet find something to satisfy our curiosity.'

Don Quixote turned the page and said, 'This is prose, and looks like a letter.'

'An ordinary letter, sir?' asked Sancho.

'From its opening it looks more like a love-letter,' replied Don Quixote.

'Then read it aloud, your worship,' said Sancho. 'I very much enjoy this love business.'

'With pleasure,' said Don Quixote and, reading it aloud as Sancho had asked him, he found what follows:

'Your false promise and my certain misfortune bear me to a place from which you will sooner hear the news of my death than the sound of my complaining. You have cast me off, ungrateful that you are, for one with more possessions but no more worth than I have. Yet if virtue were esteemed as wealth is, I should envy no man his fortune, nor bewail my own misfortune. What your beauty raised up your deeds have destroyed; from your form I thought you were an angel; from your acts I know you are a woman. Peace be with you, though you cause war in me; and may Heaven grant that your husband's deceptions remain concealed for ever, so that you may not eternally regret what you have done, nor I take a vengeance which I do not desire.'

When he had finished reading the letter Don Quixote observed:
'We can gather less about the writer from this than from the verses,
except that he was some scorned lover.' And fingering through the
greater part of the little book, he found more verses and letters,
some of which he could read and others not. But the contents of all
alike were complaints, laments, misgivings, longings and pains,
favours and slights – celebrated or deplored. While Don Quixote
examined the book, Sancho went through the bag, not leaving a
corner of it, or of the saddle-cushion, that he did not search, pry
into and explore, nor a seam which he did not rip, nor a tuft of wool
that he did not pick, in case anything might be lost out of carelessness or want of diligence; such was the greed aroused in him by the
discovery of the money, which amounted to more than a hundred
crowns. And although he found no more, still he thought himself
well compensated for the blanket-tossing, the vomiting of the balsam,
the benedictions of the pack-staves, the blows of the carrier, the
loss of the saddle-bags, the stealing of his coat, and all the hunger,
thirst, and weariness which he had undergone in his worthy master's
service. In fact he counted himself amply repaid for everything by
Don Quixote's favour in handing over to him the treasure trove.

Now the Knight of the Sad Countenance had a great desire to
know who was the possessor of the bag, guessing from the sonnet
and the letter, from the gold coins and the fine quality of the shirts,
that he must be a lover of some consequence, whom his lady's scorn
and ill-treatment had brought to some desperate end. But as there
was likely to be no one in this uninhabited and rugged country who
could inform him, he found nothing for it but to ride on, leaving the
choice of road to Rocinante – who chose the most passable – labouring under the perpetual illusion that he could not fail to find some
extraordinary adventure among those thickets. As he rode on then,
with this idea in mind, he saw on the top of a knoll, which showed
up straight ahead, a man leaping from rock to rock and from bush
to bush with extraordinary agility. He made out that he was half-
naked, with a matted black beard, his hair long and tangled, and his
legs and feet bare; while his thighs were clad in a pair of breeches,
which seemed to be of brown velvet but were so tattered that in
many places his skin showed through. His head too was bare; and
although he moved swiftly, as has been said, still the Knight of the

Sad Countenance saw and noted all these details. But try as he might, he could not follow him, for it was not given to Rocinante in his weakness to travel over such rough places, he being, besides, slow and sluggish by nature. Then, presently, Don Quixote came to the conclusion that this was the owner of the saddle-cushion and the bag, and he made up his mind to seek him, even though it might mean spending a year among those mountains before he found him. And so he ordered Sancho to dismount from his ass and to cut over one side of the mountains, while he went across the other; as by such measures they might come upon the man who had run away from them so fast.

'I couldn't do that,' replied Sancho, 'for when I leave your worship's side fear springs upon me at once and visits me with all kinds of alarms and visions; and let these words of mine serve as a warning that I won't stir a finger's breadth from your worship's presence from now on.'

'Very well,' said he of the Sad Countenance. 'I am glad that you rely on my courage, which shall never fail you though your soul shall desert your body. Follow me, therefore, slowly or however you can, and use your eyes for lanterns. We will go round this spur, and then perhaps we shall meet the man whom we saw. There can be no doubt that he is none other than the owner of the things we have found.'

To which Sancho replied: 'It would be much better not to look for him. Because if we find him and he happens to be the owner of the money, it is plain that I must give it back; and so it would be better not to take this unnecessary trouble, but for us to keep it faithfully until its real owner turns up in some less strange and laborious way. Perhaps by then I shall have spent it, and then the King's law will acquit me of responsibility.'

'You are wrong on that score,' replied Don Quixote, 'for now that we have a suspicion of who the owner is, and have him almost before our eyes, we are obliged to seek him and restore these things to him; and if we do not seek him, the strong presumption we have of his identity makes us as guilty as if he were really the owner. So, Sancho my friend, you must not let this search grieve you, seeing how much it will relieve my mind to find him.'

Then he pricked Rocinante on, and Sancho followed on foot and loaded, thanks to Ginesillo de Pasamonte. And when they had gone round part of the mountain, they found in a stream bed a dead mule saddled and bridled, half eaten by dogs and picked by crows; all of which confirmed their suspicion that the man who had run away from them was the owner of the mule and of the saddle-cushion.

As they were gazing at it they heard a whistle like that of a shepherd guarding his flock. Then suddenly on their left appeared a great number of goats, and behind them on the mountain top their goatherd, a very old man. Don Quixote shouted to him to come down to them. And he called back to ask who had brought them into that place, which was hardly ever visited except by goats or wolves and other wild beasts which haunted the neighbourhood. Sancho replied that they would explain everything if he would come down, and so he descended, and coming to where Don Quixote was standing, said:

'I'll bet that you are looking at the hired mule, lying dead in that hollow. It has been in that place a good six months, I can tell you. But tell me, have you come across its owner about here?'

'We have met nobody,' replied Don Quixote, 'and seen nothing except a saddle-cushion and a little leather bag, which we found lying not far from here.'

'I found it too,' replied the goatherd, 'but I never liked to pick it up or come near it, for fear of some mishap, or of being charged with stealing it. For the devil's a sly one, and things start up under a man's feet which make him trip and fall, without his knowing how or why.'

'That's just what I say,' replied Sancho. 'I found it too, but wouldn't go within a stone's throw of it. There I left it, and there it is just as it was, for I don't want a dog with a bell.'

'Tell me, my good fellow,' said Don Quixote, 'do you know who is the owner of these articles?'

'All that I can say,' replied the goatherd, 'is that six months ago, more or less, there arrived at a certain shepherd's hut, which will be about nine miles from this spot, a good-looking, well-mannered youth on that same mule that is lying there dead, and with that same saddle-cushion and bag which you say you found and didn't touch. He asked us what part of this range was the roughest and most remote; and we told him that it was where we are now – and that's the

truth. For if you were to go on a mile or two more you would possibly never find your way out again; and I am wondering how you
were able to reach here, because there's no road or track leading to
this place. Well, I tell you, when the youth heard our reply he
turned and rode towards the spot we pointed out to him, leaving us
all delighted at his handsome appearance, and astonished at his questions and at seeing him ride off so fast in the direction of the mountains. From that time on we did not see him again, until some days
ago he appeared on the path in front of one of our goatherds, went
up to him without a word and dealt him several punches and kicks.
Then he went to our baggage-donkey and took all the bread and the
cheese he carried; after which he ran back again into the mountains
at an amazing speed. When we heard about this, several of our
herdsmen spent almost two days looking for him in the roughest
part of this mountain, and finally found him hiding in the hollow
of a huge cork-tree. He came out to us, very mild, with his clothes
torn and his face disfigured and scorched by the sun, so that we
scarcely knew him again. But his clothes, torn as they were, were
sufficiently recognizable to convince us that he was the man we were
looking for. He greeted us courteously, and in a few polite words
begged us not to be surprised to see him wandering about in that
state; for he had to do so to fulfil a certain penance which had been
laid on him for his many sins. We asked him to tell us who he
was, but could not get that out of him. We also begged him to tell
us where we could find him, so that we could bring him food when
he stood in need of it, for without it he could not exist; and if this
was not to his liking, we asked him at least to come and ask for it,
and not take it from the herdsmen by force. He thanked us for our
offer, asked our pardon for past assaults, and promised for the future
to beg for food in God's name, and not do violence to anyone. As
to his dwelling-place, he said that he had none but such as chance
offered when night overtook him; and he ended his speech with
such touching tears that we must have been made of stone if we had
not wept too to hear him, considering the change in his appearance
since the first time we had seen him. For, as I have said, he was a
very charming and handsome young man and, to judge from his
courteous and nicely chosen speech, obviously a well-born and very
gentlemanly person. For though we that listened to him were country

men, even our simple minds could tell from his good manners what
sort of man he was. But he suddenly fell silent in the middle of his
speech and fixed his eyes on the ground for quite a while. We waited
quietly and expectantly, though in some alarm to see how this fit
would end. He opened his eyes wide and stared fixedly at the ground
for a long while without so much as stirring an eyelid. Then he
closed his eyes, pressed his lips together, and scowled. From all this
we could easily tell that some fit of madness had come upon him.
And he quickly showed us that we were right. For in a great fury he
got up from the ground, where he had thrown himself, and attacked
the man nearest to him with such reckless rage that he would have
punched and bitten him to death, if we hadn't pulled him off. And
all the while he shouted: "Ferdinand, you traitor! You shall pay
here, here, for the wrong you have done me! These hands shall tear
out your heart, which harbours every crime at once, and the greatest
of them all, fraud and deceit!" He went on to abuse that Ferdinand
a great deal more and accused him of treachery and perjury.

'Well, we got our fellow away from him at last with no little
trouble, and he left us without a word and ran off to hide in those
briars and thickets, so that it was impossible for us to follow him.

'So we suppose that he gets fits of madness at times, and that
someone called Ferdinand must have injured him very grievously,
to reduce him to the wretched condition he is in. All this has been
confirmed since, for he will very often come out on to the path,
sometimes to beg the herdsmen for some of their food, and sometimes to take it by force. For when the fit of madness is on him he
will not accept it, even though they offer it gladly, but prefers to
attack them and snatch it from them. Yet when he is in his senses he
asks for it courteously and politely for the love of God, and accepts
it with thanks and sometimes with tears. And, to tell you the truth,
sirs,' the goatherd went on, 'yesterday we decided, I and four herdsmen – two of our fellows and two friends of mine – to search for
him till we find him, and then to take him, willy-nilly, to the town of
Almodovar, which is about twenty-four miles away. There we'll get
him cured, if his disease is curable, or find out who he is when he is
in his senses, and whether he has any relations whom we can inform
of his misfortune. That, gentlemen, is all the answer that I can give
to your questions; and you may be sure that the owner of the

articles which you found is this same man whom you saw run by so naked and so nimble' – for Don Quixote had already told him that they had seen a man leaping among the rocks.

Our knight was amazed at the goatherd's tale, and more anxious than ever to know who the unfortunate madman was. So he decided to carry out a plan which he had already been considering, and to search the whole range for him, leaving no cranny or cave unexplored till he found him. But chance contrived for him better than he hoped or expected. For at that very instant there appeared from a cleft in the mountains, which opened on the place where they were standing, the very youth he was seeking, muttering to himself some words that were unintelligible near-to, let alone at a distance. His clothes were as the goatherd had described them: only when he drew near Don Quixote noticed that the torn leather coat which he wore still smelt of ambergris, from which he concluded that the wearer of such clothes could not be of a very low class. When the youth came up he greeted them in a rough and toneless voice, but very courteously. Don Quixote returned his greetings no less politely and, charmingly and graciously dismounting from Rocinante, advanced to embrace him, and held him for some time clasped in his arms, as if he had known him for a long while. The other, whom we may call the Ragged Knight of the Sorry – as Don Quixote was of the Sad – Countenance, after allowing himself to be embraced drew back a little and, placing his hands on Don Quixote's shoulders, stood gazing at him, as if to see whether he knew him, being no less surprised, perhaps, to see Don Quixote's face, figure, and armour than Don Quixote was to see him. In the end, the first to speak after the embrace was the Ragged Knight, and what he said will be told in the next chapter.

Chapter XXIV. *The Adventure in the Sierra Morena continued.*

THE history tells that Don Quixote listened with the very greatest attention to the ill-starred Knight of the Mountains, who made him the following address:

'Most certainly, sir, whoever you may be – for I do not know you – I thank you for the demonstrations of courtesy you have shown me, and I wish I were in the position to repay you for your gracious reception with more than my good-will. But my luck gives me nothing to offer in return for the kindness you have done me except the desire to respond.'

'My only wish,' replied Don Quixote, 'is to serve you; so much so that I was determined not to leave these mountains till I had discovered you, and learnt from you if there is any sort of remedy to be found for the affliction which your strange way of life shows you to suffer under; and if so, to make every possible effort to find it. But should your misfortune be such as to close all doors to every kind of consolation, it was my intention to join you, as best I could, in your grief and lamentations; for it is still some consolation in sorrows to find someone to grieve for them. If my good intentions, then, deserve to be met by any kind of courtesy, I entreat you, sir, by the great courtesy that is clearly in your nature, and by the person whom in this life you have loved or love best, to tell me who you are, and the cause which has brought you to live and die in these wastes like a brute beast, for your dress and your person show that this is far from being your proper abode. I swear,' added Don Quixote, 'by the order of knighthood which I have received, although an unworthy sinner, and by the profession of knight errant, that if you will oblige me, sir, in this, I will serve you with all the endeavour which it is my duty to exert, either by relieving your misfortune, if any relief is possible, or by joining you in bewailing it, as I have promised.'

When the Knight of the Wood heard the Knight of the Sad Countenance speak in this style, he stared at him in silence, gazing at him again and again, and viewing him from head to foot. Then, when he had gazed his fill, he said: 'If you have anything to give me to eat, for the love of God give it to me; and when I have had some food I will do all that you ask to acknowledge the kind offer you have just made me.'

Then Sancho took from his saddle-bag, and the goatherd from his pouch, enough to satisfy the Ragged Knight's hunger; and he ate what they gave him like a man in a daze, so hurriedly that he did not leave a moment between one mouthful and the next, rather gobbling his meal than eating it; and all the while he ate neither he nor the bystanders said a word. When he had finished he made signs to them to follow him, which they did; and he led them to a little green meadow that lay behind some crags a short way away. When he got there he lay down on the grass, and the others did the same, all in utter silence until the Ragged Knight had made himself comfortable, and began:

'If you wish me to explain to you, gentlemen, the immensity of my misfortunes in a few words, you must promise not to interrupt the thread of my sad tale with any question or remark; for the moment you do so, my narrative will end.'

These words recalled to Don Quixote's mind that tale of his squire's which had been broken off because he had not kept count of the number of goats which had crossed the river. But to return to the Ragged Knight, he went on: 'This warning I give you because I should like to pass briefly over the story of my misfortunes. For to recall them to mind is only to add to them; and the less questions you ask me the quicker I shall come to the end of my tale. Yet I will not leave out anything of importance, as it is my wish to satisfy your curiosity completely.'

Don Quixote promised in the name of the rest not to interrupt him, and with this assurance the Ragged One began: 'My name is Cardenio; my birthplace one of the finest cities here in Andalusia; my family noble; my parents rich; my misfortunes so great that my parents were forced to weep and my relations to grieve for them, being unable to relieve them for all their wealth. For fortune's goods can do little to remedy misfortunes willed by Heaven. There dwelt in this same land a heaven in which Love had placed all the glory I could desire; such is the beauty of Lucinda, a maiden as noble and rich as I but more fortunate, and less firm in her faith than love so honest as mine deserved. This Lucinda I loved, desired, and adored from my tenderest and earliest years, and she loved me with the innocence and seriousness of her youth. Our parents knew of our feelings, and were not disturbed by them, for they clearly saw that their development could lead only to marriage, which the equality of our blood and fortune seemed almost to demand. As we grew older our love grew also, till Lucinda's father thought himself obliged, for prudence' sake, to deny me the house, in this closely imitating the parents of that Thisbe so much sung of by poets. Now this denial added flame to fire and love to love; for although they silenced our tongues, they could not stop our pens, which are

G

more freely used than tongues to express the heart's secrets to the
beloved; since often the presence of the loved one confuses and
silences the most resolute heart and the boldest tongue. Heavens,
how many letters I wrote her! What delicate and modest replies I
received! How many songs and love-poems I penned, in which my
soul declared and revealed its feelings, painted its warm desires,
went over its memories and refreshed its passion! In the end, my
patience exhausted and my heart consumed with desire to see her, I
determined to put into effect what seemed to me the most suitable
plan for gaining my desired and deserved prize. This was to ask her
father for her hand in lawful marriage, which I did.

'He replied by thanking me for the honour I intended him, and
for wishing to honour myself with his beloved treasure; but that
as my father was alive, it was properly his duty to make this request,
for Lucinda was no woman to be taken or given in an underhand
way without his wish and approval. I thanked him for his kindness,
thinking that he was right in what he said, and that my father would
consent to my proposal as soon as I told him of it. Therefore I immediately went to inform him of my desires. But when I entered the
room where he was, I found him with an open letter in his hand,
which he passed to me before I had uttered a word, saying: "You
will see from this latter, Cardenio, that Duke Richard wishes to do
you a service."

'This Duke Richard, you must know, gentlemen, is a grandee of
Spain, whose estate lies in the richest part of Andalusia. I took and
read the letter, which was so complimentary that even I thought my
father would be wrong not to accept his request that I should be
sent to him immediately. He wanted me as a companion – not
as a servant – for his eldest son, and promised to put me in a
position corresponding to his high opinion of me. I read the letter
and was dumbfounded as I read. But I was even more astonished to
hear my father say: "You will set out the day after to-morrow,
Cardenio, and do as the Duke wishes. Give thanks to God for
opening you a way to the fortune I know you deserve." And he
added some fatherly advice.

'The day came for my departure. I talked one night with Lucinda; I told her all that had happened, and told her father too.
I begged him to wait for a few days and postpone the settling of her

marriage until I saw what Duke Richard wanted of me. He made me a promise, and she confirmed it with innumerable vows, made between fits of fainting. Then at last I reached Duke Richard's, and was so well received and treated that envy soon began to do its work. His old servants considered every sign of favour the Duke made me as prejudicial to themselves. But one person was most delighted at my coming, the Duke's second son Ferdinand, a gay lad with a charming, liberal and amorous disposition. In a very short time he was so eager for my friendship that everyone noticed it; but although his elder brother liked me and was kind to me, he did not show me the same extreme affection and attention as did Ferdinand.

'Now as there are no secrets between friends, and the favour which Ferdinand showed me soon ceased to be favour and turned to friendship, he told me all that was in his mind, and particularly of a love affair which was causing him some little anxiety. He was in love with the daughter of a farmer, a tenant of his father's. Her parents were rich, and she was so beautiful, so modest, discreet, and virtuous that no one of her acquaintance could decide in which of these qualities she was richest. The charms of the fair farmer's daughter reduced Ferdinand to such straits that he decided to gratify his desires and overcome her virtue by a promise of marriage, knowing that it would be impossible to succeed by any other means. Prompted by friendship, I employed the best arguments I knew and warned him as strongly as I could in an endeavour to dissuade him from his purpose. But, finding it was all in vain, I decided to inform his father, the Duke, of the matter. Now Ferdinand was astute and intelligent enough to suspect and fear that; for it was obvious to him that, as a faithful servant, I could not conceal from my Lord the Duke a matter so prejudicial to his honour. So, to put me off the scent, he told me that the only means he could find of getting the beauty who so enthralled him out of his mind was to go away for a few months; and he proposed that we should spend this time together at my father's, and that he should tell the Duke by way of excuse that his journey to my city was to purchase horses, for the best in the world are bred there.

'No sooner had he made this suggestion than my own love prompted me to welcome it as the best imaginable solution, though I should have done so if it had been less good, for I saw what a rare opportunity it gave me of seeing my Lucinda again. So in this frame of mind I approved his scheme and encouraged his plan, advising him to put it into execution at the very earliest opportunity, for absence would certainly have its effect, however strong his affections.

'Now, at the time when he told me this plan, as it came out afterwards, he had already enjoyed the farmer's daughter under promise of marriage, and was waiting for an opportunity of safely divulging the matter. For he was afraid of what the Duke, his father, might do when he came to know of his infatuation. Now, as a lad's love is for the most part not love but lust and, aiming only at gratification, dies when it attains its purpose, what appears to be love then weakening, since it cannot persist beyond its natural limits, which limits do not exist in true love – I mean to say that as soon as Don Ferdinand had enjoyed the farmer's daughter his desires grew calm and his ardour cooled, so that if at first he had pretended that he wanted to go away in order to relieve his passion, now he was really anxious to go to avoid fulfilling his promise.

'The Duke gave him permission and bade me go with him. We came to my city, and my father gave him the reception due to his rank. Presently I visited Lucinda; my passion came to life, although in fact it had been neither dead nor dull and, to my undoing, I spoke of it to Don Ferdinand, for I thought that his great friendship for me forbade my keeping any secrets from him. I praised Lucinda's beauty, her grace and wit, so much so that my praise roused a desire in him to see a maiden endowed with such virtues. To my own misfortune I yielded to him, and let him see her one night by the light of a candle at a window through which it was our habit to talk.

'She was dressed in a loose wrap, looking so beautiful that he forgot all the beauties he had ever seen. He was struck dumb; he lost his senses; he was spellbound; and, in short, fell deeply in love, as you will see in the course of the tale of my misfortunes. And the more to inflame his passions, which he concealed from me but revealed to God in solitude, he chanced one day upon a letter of hers, begging me to ask her father for her hand in marriage, a letter so sensible, so modest, and so full of love, that on reading it he said that in Lucinda alone were united all the charms of beauty and understanding which were the portions of all the other women in the world. It is true, as I confess now, that though I acknowledged the justice of Ferdinand's praise, it vexed me to hear this eulogy from his mouth, and I began to grow fearful and jealous of him; for there was not a moment when he did not want to talk of Lucinda, and he would start the conversation himself, even if he had to drag her in by the hair. This awoke a vague jealousy in me; not that I had any reason to fear a change in Lucinda's faith and virtue, yet, for all that, my fate made me dread the very danger against which she seemed to secure me. Don Ferdinand always tried to read the letters I sent her and her replies. He pretended to derive great pleasure from our turns of phrase. Now Lucinda happened to ask me for a book of chivalry to read, one which she was very fond of. It was *Amadis of Gaul* ...'

No sooner did Don Quixote hear mention of a book of chivalry than he exclaimed: 'If you had told me, sir, at the beginning of your story that the lady Lucinda was fond of books of chivalry, you would have needed no further amplification to convince me of the sublimity of her understanding. For it would not have been as excellent as you, sir, have described it, if she had lacked a taste for such delightful reading. So that there is no need to waste more words in declaring to me her beauty, worth and understanding; for at the mere mention of this passion of hers I pronounce her the loveliest and most intelligent woman in the world. But I could have wished, sir, that you had sent her with *Amadis of Gaul* the good *Sir Rugel of Greece*, for I know that the lady Lucinda would be delighted with Daraida and Garaya, and with the wit of the shepherd Darinel, and with those admirable lines in his bucolics, sung and performed by him with such charm, wit and freedom. But a time may come for remedying this omission. It can be amended whenever you care to come with me to my village, sir. For there I can show you more than three hundred books, which are the treasure of my heart and the delight of my life: – though now it occurs to me that I have none, thanks to the malice of evil and envious enchanters. Pardon me, sir, for having broken our promise not to interrupt your story; but when I hear of matters of chivalry and of knights errant, I can no more prevent myself from talking of them than the sun's rays can help giving heat, or the moon's moisture. So excuse me, and go on, for that is the important thing now.'

Whilst Don Quixote was saying all this, Cardenio let his head fall on his breast, seemingly plunged in deep thought; and although the knight twice asked him to go on with his story, he neither raised his head nor answered a word. But at the end of a good while he looked up and said: 'One thing I cannot get out of my mind, and no one in the world can persuade me or convince me otherwise – indeed, anyone holding the contrary opinion would be an idiot. That arch-scoundrel Master Elisabat was Queen Madasima's lover.'

'That is false, I swear,' replied Don Quixote in great wrath, bursting out in his usual fashion, 'and a most malicious, or rather villainous calumny. Queen Madasima was a very noble lady, and it is not to be supposed that so great a princess would take a quack for a lover. Whoever says otherwise lies like an arrant scoundrel, and I will make him acknowledge it, on foot or horse, armed or unarmed, by night or day, or however he will.'

Cardenio sat staring at him very attentively. For a fit of madness had come on him and he was in no state to continue his tale; nor would Don Quixote have listened if he had, so disgusted was he by what he had heard concerning Madasima. It was extraordinary to see him take her part as though she were in fact his real and natural mistress; such was the power his unholy books had over him.

But, as I said, Cardenio was now mad, and when he heard himself called a liar and a scoundrel and other such names, he took the joke in bad part. In fact he picked up a stone from beside him, and hit Don Quixote so hard on the chest that he knocked him backwards. When Sancho Panza saw his master thus treated, he attacked the madman with clenched fists. But the Ragged Knight gave him such a reception that he had him stretched at his feet at the first blow, after which he got on top of him and trampled his ribs to his heart's content. The goatherd, who tried to defend him, met with the same fate, and after Cardenio had threshed and bruised them all, he left them and retired quietly to his mountain ambush.

Sancho got up and, furious at his undeserved beating, ran to take vengeance on the goatherd, saying that it was all his fault for not having advised them that the man was subject to fits of madness; for had they known it, they would have been prepared to defend themselves. The goatherd replied that he had told them, and it was not his fault if Sancho had not heard. Sancho argued; the goatherd replied; and the dispute ended in their grasping each other's beards and punching each other so hard that they would have thrashed one another to pulp if Don Quixote had not interposed. But Sancho still kept a tight hold on the goatherd as he exclaimed:

'Leave me alone, Sir Knight of the Sad Countenance; for he's a peasant like me and no knight, and I can safely avenge the injury he has done me by fighting him hand to hand, like a man of honour.'

'That is true,' said Don Quixote. 'But I know that he is not to blame for what happened.'

With this he pacified them, and again asked the goatherd if it would be possible to find Cardenio, for he was most anxious to hear the end of his story. The herdsman repeated, as he had done before, that there was no knowing for certain where Cardenio had his lair; but if Don Quixote were to wander much about the district he would not fail to find him, sane or mad.

Chapter XXV. Of the Strange Things which happened to the valorous Knight of La Mancha in the Sierra Morena, and of his Imitation of the Penance of Beltenebros.

DON QUIXOTE took leave of the goatherd and, remounting Rocinante bade Sancho follow him, which he did on his ass,* most unwillingly. They then went slowly on into the most desolate part of the mountains. Sancho all the while was dying to talk to his master, but not wishing to disobey his orders, waited for him to start the conversation. At last, however, unable to bear the long silence, he said:

'Don Quixote, please give me your blessing and my liberty, for I want to go back home now to my wife and my children. I shall at least be able to talk to them as much as I like. For your worship's wanting me to ride through these lonely parts day and night and never to speak to you when I've a mind to, is like burying me alive. If nature allowed animals to talk, as they did in Aesop's days, it wouldn't be so bad. Then I could talk to my ass about anything I like, and forget my bad luck that way. For it's hard, and more than patience can bear, to spend all one's life looking for adventures and finding nothing but kicks and blanket-tossings, brick-battings and

* The ass is now Sancho's again, and Cervantes has forgotten its theft by Gines.

beatings, and still to have to keep one's mouth tight shut and not dare to say what's in one's heart, just as if one were dumb.'

'I understand you, Sancho,' replied Don Quixote. 'You are dying for me to raise the prohibition I have imposed on your tongue. Consider it raised and say what you will, on condition this licence lasts only so long as we are travelling in these mountains.'

'Very well,' said Sancho. 'Let me talk now, for God knows what will come afterwards; and now, to begin to take advantage of your permission, I should like to ask what made your worship stand up so warmly for that Queen Magimasa, or whatever she's called. What did it matter if that abbot was her friend or not? For if your worship had let it pass, since you were not her judge, I really think that the madman would have gone on with his story, and we should have been spared the stone and the kicks, and more than half a dozen back-handers in the face.'

'I swear, Sancho,' replied Don Quixote, 'that if you knew, as I know, what a great and honourable lady Queen Madasima was, you would certainly say that I showed great patience in not smashing the face that mouthed such blasphemies. For it is great blasphemy to say or to think that a Queen could take a barber-surgeon for a lover. The truth of the story is that this Master Elisabat the madman spoke of was a very wise man and a very good counsellor, and served the Queen as tutor and physician; but to think that she was his lover is a folly deserving the severest punishment. Yet you must see that Cardenio did not know what he was saying; for you must remember that he was already out of his mind when he said it.'

'That's what I say,' answered Sancho, 'and you oughtn't to have taken any notice of what a madman said. What's more, if good luck had not come to your worship's aid, and the stone had struck your head instead of your chest, we should have been in a fine way for standing up for that great lady, God damn her. And just think, Cardenio would have got off scot-free as a madman.'

'Against all men, sane or mad,' said Don Quixote, 'it is every knight errant's duty to defend the honour of all women of whatever rank; particularly of queens as exalted and virtuous as Queen Madasima was. I have a particular regard for her on account of her good qualities; for not only was she very beautiful but prudent too, and very patient in her countless misfortunes; and the advice and company of Master Elisabat were of great advantage and comfort to her, and enabled her to bear her trials with prudence and patience. That is what made the ignorant and malicious rabble say and think that she was his mistress; and they lie, I say again, and two hundred times more I repeat that every one of them who thinks so or says so lies.'

'I don't say so, nor think so,' replied Sancho. 'There let it rest. Let them eat the lie and swallow it with their bread. Whether the two were lovers or no, they'll have accounted to God for it by now. I have my own fish to fry. I know nothing. I'm not one to pry into other people's lives. It's no good lying about the price; your purse always knows better. What's more, I was born naked and naked I am now; I neither lose nor win. Suppose they were lovers, what's that to me? Plenty of people expect to find bacon where there's not so much as a hook to hang it on. Who can hedge in the cuckoo? Especially as God Himself is not spared.'

'Good Lord!' cried Don Quixote, 'what a string of nonsense, Sancho! What have all these proverbs to do with the matter we were discussing? For Heaven's sake be quiet, and in future see you spur your ass and do not interfere with what does not concern you. And get it into your five senses that all my actions, past, present and future, are very well based in reason and conform in every way to the rules of chivalry. For I know these rules better than any knights who have ever professed them in the world.'

'Sir,' replied Sancho, 'is it a good rule of chivalry for us to get lost looking for a madman in these mountains, where there isn't a road or a track? And when we find him, perhaps he'll choose to finish the job he has begun, – not his story, but breaking your head and my ribs till there isn't a whole bone left in our bodies.'

'Once more, Sancho, be quiet,' exclaimed Don Quixote, 'for I would have you know that it is not only my wish to find the madman that draws me to these parts, but my intention of performing a deed here which will gain me perpetual renown and glory throughout all the known world. It shall be such a deed that by it I shall attain the utmost perfection and renown of which a knight errant is capable.'

'And is this deed very perilous?' asked Sancho Panza.

'No,' replied the Knight of the Sad Countenance, 'although the dice may so fall that we throw a blank instead of a double. But everything depends on your diligence.'

'On my diligence?' repeated Sancho.

'Yes,' said Don Quixote, 'because if you come back quickly from the place I mean to send you to, my penance will be soon over and my glory will speedily begin. But it is not right to keep you longer in suspense, hanging on the purport of my words. So I would have you know, Sancho, that the famous Amadis of Gaul was one of the most perfect of knights errant. I was wrong to say *one*; he was the sole, the first, the unique, the prince of all there were in the world in his day. A fig for Sir Belianis and for all who claimed to be in any respect his equal! For I swear they are mistaken. What is more I say that when any painter wishes to win fame in his art, he endeavours to copy the pictures of the most excellent painters he knows; and the same rule obtains for all professions and pursuits of importance that serve to adorn the commonwealth. So what any man who wants a reputation for prudence and patience must do, and does, is to imitate Ulysses, in whose person and labours Homer paints for us a lively picture of prudence and patience; just as Virgil shows us in the person of Aeneas the virtue of a dutiful son and the sagacity of a brave and skilful captain. They do not paint them or describe them as they were, but as they should have been, to serve as examples of their virtues for future generations. In the same way Amadis was the pole-star, the morning star, the sun of all valiant knights and lovers, and all of us who ride beneath the banner of love and chivalry should imitate him. This being the case, Sancho my friend, I conclude that the knight errant who best copies him will attain most nearly to the perfection of chivalry. Now one of the ways in which this knight most clearly showed his wisdom, virtue, valour, patience, steadfastness and love was when, scorned by his lady Oriana, he retired to do penance on the Bare Rock, changing his name to Beltenebros, a name most certainly significant and suitable to the life which he had voluntarily chosen. Therefore, as it is easier for me to imitate him in this way than in cleaving giants, beheading serpents, killing dragons, routing armies, shattering fleets, and breaking spells; and since this place is so fitting for such a purpose, there is no reason for me to let this opportunity pass now that it so conveniently offers me the forelock.'

'What is it then that your worship really means to do in this out-of-the-way place?' asked Sancho.

'Have I not told you,' replied Don Quixote, 'that I intend to imitate Amadis, and to act here the desperate, raving, furious lover; at the same time following the example of the valiant Sir Roland when he found by a spring evidence that the fair Angelica had dishonoured herself with Medoro, for grief at which he turned mad, tore up trees, muddied the waters of the clear springs, killed shepherds, destroyed flocks, fired cottages, pulled down houses, dragged off mares, and performed a hundred thousand extravagant feats, which deserve eternal fame and remembrance? Now although I do not intend to imitate Roland, or Orlando, or Rotolando – for he bore all those names – exactly in all the mad things he did, said and thought, I will sketch them in as best I can, in what appear to me to be their essentials. But perhaps I shall come to be content to imitate Amadis alone, for he attained unrivalled fame by a madness that lay not in wild deeds but in tears and grief.'

'It seems to me,' said Sancho, 'that the knights who did things like that were provoked and had a reason for their follies and penances. But what reason has your worship for going mad? What lady has scorned you, or what evidence have you found that the lady Dulcinea del Toboso has done anything she shouldn't with Moor or Christian?'

'That is the point,' replied Don Quixote, 'and in that lies the beauty of my plan. A knight errant who turns mad for a reason deserves neither merit nor thanks. The thing is to do it without cause; and then my lady can guess what I would do in the wet if I do all this in the dry. What is more, I have sufficient reason in my long absence from my ever supreme mistress Dulcinea del Toboso. For, as you heard that shepherd Ambrosio say the other day, the absent feel and fear every ill. So, friend Sancho, do not waste time advising me to give up so rare, so happy, and so unprecedented an imitation. I am mad, and mad I must be till you come back with the reply to a letter which I intend to send by you to my lady Dulcinea. If it proves such as my fidelity deserves, my raving and my penance will be ended; but if it be unfavourable I shall be mad in earnest, and when I am I shall feel nothing. So, whichever way she replies, I shall be done with the conflict and distress in which you will leave me. For if it is good tidings you bring me, I shall enjoy them in my right mind; and if it is evil, I shall not feel them, being mad. But tell me, Sancho, have you taken good care of Mambrino's helmet? For I saw you pick it up from the ground when that ungrateful wretch tried to destroy it, though he could not do so – and that shows how finely it was tempered.'

To which Sancho replied: 'In God's name, Sir Knight of the Sad Countenance, I cannot endure or bear with patience some of the things your worship says. They make me think that all you tell me about chivalries and winning kingdoms and empires, and giving isles and doing other favours and mighty deeds, as knights errant do, must be just wind and lies, and all friction or fiction or whatever you call it. For to hear your worship say that a barber's basin is Mambrino's helmet, and persist in that error for more than four days, what can one think? Only that a man who persists in saying a thing like that must be cracked in the brain. I have the basin in the bag, all dented, and I'm taking it home to mend it and to use it for shaving, if God is so gracious as to let me live with my wife and children one day.'

'Look you, Sancho, by the same oath as you swore just now, I swear,' said Don Quixote, 'that you have less brains than any squire has or ever had in the whole world. Is it possible that all this while you have been with me you have not discovered that everything to do with knights errant appears to be chimaera, folly and nonsense, and to go all contrariwise? This is not really the case, but there is a crew of enchanters always amongst us who change and alter all our deeds, and transform them according to their pleasure and their desire either to favour us or injure us. So what seems to you to be a barber's basin appears to me to be Mambrino's helmet, and to another as something else. It shows a rare foresight in the sage who is on my side to make what is really and truly Mambrino's helmet seem to everyone a basin. For, as it is of such great value, the whole world would persecute me in order to get it from me. However, as they see that it is nothing more than a barber's basin, they do not trouble about it, as was evident in the case of the wretch who tried to destroy it and left it behind him on the ground; for I promise you that if he had recognized it he would never have left it there. Take care of it, my friend. I do not need it for the present. On the contrary, I must strip off all my armour and be naked as I was born; that is, if I decide to imitate Roland in my penance rather than Amadis.'

Deep in this conversation they came to the foot of a high mountain which stood alone, almost as though it had been cut off from the many which surrounded it. At its foot ran a gentle stream, encircling a meadow so green and luxuriant that it pleased the eyes of all who saw it. There were many woodland trees there, and some shrubs and flowers that made the place pleasant. This site the Knight of the Sad Countenance chose for the performance of his penance, and at the sight of it he began to speak aloud, as if he were out of his wits:

'This is the place, Heavens, where I select and choose to bewail the misfortune into which you yourselves have plunged me. This is the spot where the moisture from my eyes will swell the waters of this little stream, and my deep and incessant sighs perpetually stir the leaves of these mountain trees, in testimony and sign of the grief my tortured heart endures. On you, whoever you may be, rustic deities who have your abode in this inhospitable spot, hear the plaints of this ill-starred lover, whom long absence and some fancied jealousy have brought to mourn among these rugged wastes, and to complain of the cruel nature of that ungrateful beauty, the sum and perfection of all human loveliness! O you, wood-nymphs and dryads, whose custom it is to haunt the mountain thickets, may the swift and sensual satyrs, who love you in vain, never disturb your sweet quiet, that you may aid me to lament my ill fortune, or at least not grow weary of hearing it! O Dulcinea del Toboso, day of my night, glory of my grief, pole-star of my journeys, star of my fate, may Heaven grant you all that you pray for in full measure. Consider now the place and the condition to which your absence has brought me, and grant me in return such reward as my fidelity deserves! O solitary trees, which henceforth must be the companions of my solitude, give me some sign, by the gentle stirring of your branches, that my presence does not offend you! And you, my squire, pleasing companion of my prosperous and adverse fortunes, impress on your memory what you will see me do here, so that you may tell and recite it to the sole cause of it all!'

As he spoke, he dismounted from Rocinante and, stripping him in an instant of bridle and saddle, gave him a slap on the haunches, saying: 'He who lacks liberty bestows it on you, O steed as excellent in your performance as you are unfortunate in your fate! Go where you will; for on your forehead it is written that not Astolfo's Hippogriff, nor yet the famous Frontino which cost Bradamante so dear, was your equal in speed.'

At this Sancho put in: – 'God bless the man who has saved us the trouble of unharnessing Dapple.* He wouldn't have gone short of smacks or speeches in his praise. Though if he were here I would let nobody take off his harness. There would be no reason for it, seeing that the general rules about people in love and in despair were no concern of his, since his master was not one of them. For when it pleased God I was his master. Truly, Sir Knight of the Sad Countenance, if my journey and your worship's madness are going to be in real earnest, it would be a good thing to saddle Rocinante again to serve instead of the ass, for that'll save me time on my double journey. If I do it on foot I don't know when I shall get there or when I shall get back, for I am a very poor walker indeed.'

'Very well, Sancho,' replied Don Quixote, 'it shall be as you wish. Yours does not seem a bad plan to me. And you shall leave in three days' time, for I want you in the interval to observe all that I do and say for her sake. Then you will be able to report everything to her.'

'Well, what more have I to see than I've seen already?' asked Sancho.

'A great deal you know about the story!' replied Don Quixote. 'There still remains the tearing of my garments, the scattering of my arms, the running of my head against the rocks, and other things of the kind which will astonish you.'

'For God's sake,' cried Sancho, 'take care, your worship, how you go hitting your head, for you might strike a rock in such a place that you would put paid to the whole business of this penance with the first blow. But since your worship thinks that these knocks on the head are necessary, and this job can't be done without them, it's my opinion that you ought to be content, since this is all a pretence and a counterfeit and a joke, – you ought to be content, I say, with hitting your head on the water, or on something soft like cot-

* Who is apparently lost again, and remains so until recovered.

ton, and leave the rest to me. For I'll tell my lady that your worship dashed your head against a pointed rock harder than a diamond.'

'I thank you for your kind intentions, friend Sancho,' replied Don Quixote; 'but I would have you know that all these things which I am doing are not in jest, but very much in earnest. Otherwise I should be infringing the laws of chivalry, which bid us tell no lie on pain of degradation; and to do one thing instead of another is the same as a lie. Therefore the blows on the head must be real, hard and efficacious, without any sophistry or deception; and you will have to leave me some lint to heal me since, as ill-luck would have it, we have lost our balsam.'

'Losing the ass was worse,' replied Sancho, 'for with him we lost the lint and all. But please, your worship, don't remind me of that accursed drink, for not only my stomach but my very soul turns over at the mere mention of it. As for the three days allowed me for seeing your mad pranks, please reckon them as already passed. For I take everything you've said for granted and I'll tell wonders to my lady. So write the letter and send me off immediately, for I'm dearly longing to come back and rescue your worship from this purgatory I'm leaving you in.'

'Do you call it purgatory, Sancho?' asked Don Quixote. 'You would do better to call it hell, or even worse, if there is anything worse.'

'For him that's in hell,' replied Sancho, '*nulla est retentio*, as I've heard say.'

'I do not understand what you mean by *retentio*,' said Don Quixote.

'*Retentio*,' answered Sancho, 'means that once a man is in hell he never gets out, and can't. But it'll be the reverse with your worship, or I'll wear out my heels – that is, if I take spurs to liven up Rocinante. Let me once get to El Toboso and into the presence of my lady Dulcinea, and I'll tell her such stories of the follies and mad pranks – for they're all the same – which you have done and are still doing that I'll make her suppler than a glove, even if I find her harder than a cork-tree. Then I'll come back with her sweet and honeyed answer, riding the air like a wizard, and get your worship out of this purgatory, which looks like hell and isn't. For you have a hope of getting out, and that, as I said, people who are in hell haven't got. I don't think your worship will contradict me.'

'That is the truth,' said the Knight of the Sad Countenance, 'but how shall we manage to write the letter?'

'And the bills of asses as well,' added Sancho.

'It will all be included,' said Don Quixote; 'and since there is no paper, it will be as well to write it as the ancients did, on the leaves of trees or on wax tablets; although they would be as difficult to find now as paper. But I have just thought of a good – no, of an excellent – place to write it, and that is in the little note-book which was Cardenio's. Then you can see that it is copied on to paper in a good hand, at the first village you come to in which there is a school-master; or, failing that, a parish clerk will transcribe it for you. But do not give it to a lawyer's clerk to write, for they use a legal hand that Satan himself will not understand.'

'But what's to be done about the signature?' asked Sancho.

'Amadis' letters were never signed,' replied Don Quixote.

'That's all very well,' replied Sancho, 'but the order for the asses must have a signature, or if it is copied they will say that the signature is false, and I shall be left without the ass-colts.'

'The order will be signed in the little note-book itself, so that when my niece sees it she will make no difficulty about complying with it. As for the love-letter, you will put by way of signature: "*Yours till death, The Knight of the Sad Countenance*". It will make no great difference that it is in a strange hand since, as far as I remember, Dulcinea cannot write or read, and she has never seen a letter or writing of mine in all her life. For our love has always been platonic, and never gone farther than a modest glance. And even that so occasionally that I can truly swear that in all the twelve years I have loved her more than the light of these eyes which the earth will one day devour, I have not seen her four times. And perhaps on those four occasions she did not even once notice that I was looking at her; such is the reserve and seclusion in which her father, Lorenzo Corchuelo, and her mother, Aldonza Nogales, have brought her up.'

'Well, well!' exclaimed Sancho. 'So Lorenzo Corchuelo's daughter is the lady Dulcinea del Toboso, otherwise called Aldonza Lorenzo?'

'She is,' said Don Quixote, 'and she it is who deserves to be mistress of all the world.'

'I know her well,' said Sancho, 'and I can tell you that she pitches a bar as well as the strongest lad in the whole village. Praise be to God! She's a brawny girl, well built and tall and sturdy, and she will know how to keep her chin out of the mud with any knight errant who ever has her for his mistress. O the wench, what muscles she's got, and what a pair of lungs! I remember one day she went up the village belfry to call in some of their lads who were working in a fallow field of her father's, and they could hear her as plainly as if they had been at the foot of the tower, although they were nearly two miles away. And the great thing about her is that she's not a bit shy. There's a good deal of the court-lady about her too, for she has a crack with everybody, and makes a joke and a mock of them all. I tell you, Sir Knight of the Sad Countenance, that you're not only quite right to play your mad pranks for her, but you've good reason to despair and hang yourself for her as well. Indeed any one who knows will say you acted better then well, even though the Devil himself should carry you off afterwards. Oh, I wish I were on the road only for the joy of seeing her. I haven't set eyes on her for ever so long. She must be changed, too, for always trudging about the fields in sun and wind greatly spoils a woman's looks. But I must confess to you, Don Quixote, that I have been very much mistaken on one point up to now. I really and truly thought that the lady Dulcinea must be some princess your worship was in love with, or at least a person of quality, to deserve the rich presents you sent her, the Basque and the galley-slaves, for instance, and all the other things you must have won in all the victories your worship must have had before I was your squire. But when you come to think of it, what good is it to the lady Aldonza Lorenzo, I mean the lady Dulcinea del Toboso, to have all the knights you have conquered and sent to her, or all that you ever will send, going down on their knees before her? Just when they arrive she'll very likely be dressing flax or threshing in the barn. Then they'll be confused at seeing her, and she'll burst out laughing and not think much of your present.'

'I have told you very often before now, Sancho,' said Don Quixote, 'that you are a very great babbler. Yet although your wits are

blunt your remarks sometimes sting. But just to prove your foolishness and my wisdom, I want you to listen to a little story.

'Once upon a time there was a beautiful widow, young, gay, rich
and not a bit prudish, who fell in love with a stout and lusty young
lay-brother. His superior heard of it and addressed the good widow
one day by way of brotherly reproof: "I am astonished, madam," he
said, "and with good reason, that a woman of your quality, beautiful and rich as you are, should have fallen in love with such a coarse,
low, ignorant fellow as So-and-So, seeing that we have so many
graduates, divinity students, and theologians in this house, and you
could pick and choose any of them like pears, and say: I like this
one, and not that one." But she answered most gaily and impu-
dently: "You are much mistaken, my dear sir, and very old-
fashioned in your ideas, if you think that I have made a bad choice
in that fellow, idiot though he may seem, seeing that for all I want
of him he knows as much philosophy as Aristotle, and more." So,
Sancho, for what I want of Dulcinea del Toboso she is as good as
the greatest princess in the land. For not all those poets who praise
ladies under names which they choose so freely, really have such
mistresses. Do you think that the Amaryllises, the Phyllises,
Sylvias, Dianas, Galateas, Phyllidas, and all the rest that books and
ballads and barbers' shops and theatres are so full of, were really
flesh-and-blood ladies, and the mistresses of the writers who wrote
about them? Not a bit of it. Most of them were invented to serve
as subjects for verses, and so that the poets might be taken for
lovers, or men capable of being so. I am quite satisfied, therefore, to
imagine and believe that the good Aldonza Lorenzo is lovely and
virtuous; her family does not matter a bit, for no one will inquire
into that for the purpose of investing her with any order and, for
my part, I think of her as the greatest princess in the world. For you
must know, Sancho, if you do not know it already, that two things
arouse love more than all others. They are great beauty and a good
name; and these two qualities are present in Dulcinea to a surpassing degree; for in beauty she has no rival, and few can equal her in
good name. To make an end of the matter, I imagine all I say to be
true, neither more nor less, and in my imagination I draw her as I
would have her be, both as to her beauty and her rank; unequalled
by Helen, unrivalled by Lucretia, or any other famous woman of

antiquity, Greek, Barbarian, or Roman. Let anyone say what he likes, for though the ignorant may reproach me for it, men of judgement will not condemn me.'

'What I say is that your worship's always right,' replied Sancho, 'and I'm an ass. But I don't know how that word ass comes to my lips, for one shouldn't talk of halters in the hanged man's house. But give me the letter and good-bye, for I'm off.'

Don Quixote took out the note-book and, drawing a little aside, very calmly set about writing the letter. And when he had finished it he called Sancho, saying that he wanted to read it to him so that he might commit it to memory in case he were to lose it on the way; for with his bad luck anything might happen.

To which Sancho replied: 'Write it two or three times there in the book, your worship, and give it to me. I will carry it very carefully. But it would be mad to think of my learning it by heart, for my memory's so bad that I often forget my own name. Yet read it to me all the same, your worship. I shall enjoy hearing it. It must be as good as a bit of print.'

'Listen; it goes like this,' said Don Quixote:

Don Quixote's letter to Dulcinea del Toboso.

Sovereign and sublime lady,

One stabbed by the dart of absence and pierced to the heart's core wishes you, sweetest Dulcinea del Toboso, the health which he does not himself enjoy. If your beauty scorns me, if your merit acts to my disadvantage, if you disdain my anguish, although inured to suffering I shall be ill able to bear an affliction which is not only severe but of very long duration. My good squire Sancho will give you a full account, O ungrateful beauty and beloved enemy, of the state to which I am reduced for your sake. If it be your pleasure to relieve me, I am yours. If not, do as you will; for by my death I shall have satisfied your cruelty and my passion.

Yours till death,
The Knight of the Sad Countenance.

'God bless my father!' cried Sancho on hearing the letter. 'It's the finest thing I've ever heard! I'll be blowed if your worship doesn't say just what you want to! And how well the *Knight of the*

Sad Countenance fits into the signature. Your worship's the Devil himself, I swear, and there's nothing you don't know.'

'You have to know everything,' replied Don Quixote, 'in the profession I follow.'

'Well, then,' said Sancho, 'put the order for the three colts on the other side of the leaf, sir, and sign it very clearly so that they'll know your hand when they see it.'

'So I will,' answered Don Quixote. And when he had written it, he read it aloud as follows:

'At sight of this my first bill of asses, dear niece, give order that three out of the five which I left at home in your charge be given to Sancho Panza, my squire. Which three colts I order to be delivered in payment for the like amount counted and received of him here; and this with his receipt shall be your discharge. Given in the heart of the Sierra Morena, on the twenty-second of August of the current year.'

'That's right,' said Sancho. 'Please sign it, your worship.'

'There is no need to sign it,' said Don Quixote. 'I need only put my flourish, for that is the same as a signature and will be good enough for three asses, or even for three hundred.'

'I trust your worship,' replied Sancho. 'Now let me go and saddle Rocinante. And get ready, sir, to give me your blessing, for I'm going now. I shan't wait to see the pranks your worship's going to perform, but I'll tell her I saw you do so many that she'll be satisfied.'

'At least I want you to see me naked, Sancho, and performing a dozen wild pranks or so. I will run through them in less than half an hour; and when you have seen them with your own eyes you can safely swear to any others that you may care to add. You will not tell her of as many as I mean to perform, I promise you.'

'For God's sake, dear master, don't make me see you naked. It'll grieve me so that I shan't be able to stop crying, and my head is so bad from the tears I shed last night for Dapple that I'm in no condition for fresh weeping. If your worship wants me to see some of your mad pranks, do some in your clothes – but short ones, and only the most important. Though really I've no need of anything of the sort. For, as I said before, if I go now it'll hasten my return with the news your worship desires and deserves. That I will bring.

Otherwise let the lady Dulcinea look out. For if she doesn't reply as she should, I take my solemn oath that I'll kick and punch a kind answer out of her guts. Wouldn't it be a shame, indeed, for a famous knight errant like your worship to go mad without the least reason in the world, for a –. The lady had better not give me cause to say it or, by God, I'll blurt it out and let her have it wholesale, even though it spoils the market. I'm pretty good at that. She doesn't know me. If she did, I swear she would treat me with proper respect.'

'Really, Sancho,' said Don Quixote, 'as far as I can see, you are no saner than I am.'

'I'm not so mad as you,' replied Sancho, 'but I've a worse temper. But never mind that. What is your worship going to eat till I return? Are you going out on to the road to steal your food from the shepherds like Cardenio?'

'Do not be troubled on that score,' replied Don Quixote, 'for I should not eat anything but the herbs and the fruit which this meadow and these trees provide, even if I had it. The point of this business of mine lies in my fasting and in enduring all such hardships. Farewell, then.'

'But, your worship,' replied Sancho, 'do you know what I'm afraid of? Perhaps I mayn't be able to find my way back to the place I'm leaving you in. It's so out of the way.'

'Observe the landmarks, and I will try to remain near this spot,' said Don Quixote. 'And I will even take the precaution of climbing the highest of these crags to look out for you on your return. But your surest way of not missing me, and not getting lost yourself, will be for you to cut some of the broom that is so plentiful around here. Scatter it at intervals as you go till you get out to open country. The sprigs will serve as landmarks and signs for you to find me by when you come back, just like the thread in Theseus' labyrinth.'

'That's what I'll do,' replied Sancho Panza; and cutting some broom, he asked for his master's blessing and, not without many tears on both sides, took his leave. Then he mounted Rocinante, after receiving an especial charge from Don Quixote to take as good care of him as of his own person, and set out for the plain, scattering the broom sprigs at intervals, as his master had advised. So he rode off, despite Don Quixote's repeated requests that he should stay and watch him perform at least a couple of his wild pranks. But he had not gone above a hundred yards before he turned round and said:

'I think that you were quite right, your worship. It would be as well for me to watch, say, one of your mad pranks, so that I can swear I've seen you doing them with a safe conscience. Though I've seen you doing one very mad thing already, by staying here I mean.'

'Did not I tell you so?' said Don Quixote. 'Wait, Sancho, I will perform several as quickly as you can say a Credo.'

And hurriedly stripping off his breeches, he stood in his skin and his shirt. And then, without more ado, he took two leaps into the air, and twice turned head over heels, revealing such parts of his person as caused Sancho to turn Rocinante's head for fear he might see them a second time. So he departed fully satisfied that he could swear to his master's madness. And so we will leave him pursuing his journey till his return, which was speedy.

Chapter XXVI. *A Continuation of the Refinements practised by Don Quixote to express his love in the Sierra Morena.*

To continue the account of the actions of the Knight of the Sad Countenance once he was alone, our history tells that, after the falls or somersaults performed with his upper parts clothed and his lower parts naked, and after he had seen Sancho depart, unwilling to wait and see any more of his antics, Don Quixote climbed to the top of a high rock, and there turned his thoughts once more to a problem on which he had already pondered many times without reaching any conclusion. This was to decide which was the better and would stand him in the greater stead: to imitate Roland's downright madness or Amadis' melancholy moods. So, communing with himself, he argued: 'If Roland was as good a knight and as valiant as they all say, where is the wonder? since, after all, he was enchanted, and no one could kill him except by stabbing a long pin into the sole of his foot, which was the reason why he always wore shoes with seven iron soles. But these contrivances were of no avail against Bernardo del Carpio, who understood them, and throttled him with his bare hands at Roncesvalles. But, setting his bravery on one side, let us consider his madness, which certainly arose from the evidence he found beside the spring and the news which the shepherd gave him that Angelica had slept more than two afternoons with Medoro, a little curly-haired Moor and page to Agramante. Now if he believed that this was true, and that his lady had done him this foul wrong, it is not surprising that he went mad. But how can I imitate him in his madness without a similar cause? For I dare swear that my Dulcinea del Toboso has never seen a real Moor in his real Moorish dress in all her life, and that she is to-day as her mother bore her; and I should do her a grave injury were I to imagine otherwise and go mad, after the fashion of Roland the Furious.

'On the other hand, I know that Amadis of Gaul achieved an unrivalled reputation as a lover without ever losing his wits or having raving fits. For, as the history tells, on finding himself scorned by his lady Oriana, who had commanded him to appear no more in her presence until it was her pleasure, what he did was merely to retire to the Bare Rock in the company of a hermit; and there he wept his fill and commended himself to God so earnestly that Heaven succoured him in the midst of his greatest tribulation. Now if this is true – and it is – why do I now take pains to strip myself stark naked and give pain to these trees which have done me no harm, and disturb the clear water of these streams, which must give me drink when I am thirsty? All honour then to the memory of Amadis, and let him be the model, so far as it is possible, for Don Quixote de la Mancha, of whom it shall be said, as it was said of that other, that if he did not achieve great things he died attempting them. If I am not cast off and despised by Dulcinea del Toboso, let it suffice, as I have said, that I am absent from her. So now to work! Come into my mind, deeds of Amadis, and teach me where to begin to imitate you. I remember now that most of the time he prayed and commended his soul to God. But what shall I do for a rosary, for I have none?'

At this there came into his head a way of making one. He tore a great strip from the tail of his shirt, which was hanging down, and made eleven knots in it, one fatter than the rest; and this served him for a rosary all the time he was there, during which time he recited a million Ave Marias. But one thing did trouble him a great deal; there was no hermit in the district to hear his confession and administer consolation. He amused himself, however, by pacing about the little meadow, writing and carving in the bark of the trees and tracing on the fine sand a great number of verses, all suited to his sad state, and some of them in praise of Dulcinea. But the only ones which were found complete and could be deciphered afterwards were the following:

> Ye plants, ye herbs, and ye trees,
>   That flourish in this pleasant site
> In lofty and verdant degrees,
>   If my harms do you no delight,
> Hear my holy plaints, which are these.
> And let not my grief you molest,
>   Though it ever so feelingly went,
> Since here for to pay your rest,
> Don Quixote his tears hath addressed,
>   Dulcinea's lack to lament
>   del Toboso.
>
> In this very place doth abide
>   The loyallest lover and true,
> Who himself from his lady did hide,
>   But yet felt his sorrows anew,
> Not knowing whence they might proceed.
> Love doth him cruelly wrest
>   With a passion of evil descent,
> Which robbed Don Quixote of his rest,
> Till a keg with his tears was full pressed,
>   Dulcinea's lack to lament
>   del Toboso.
>
> In search of adventures he pined
>   Among these rough woods and rocks,
> Still cursing his pitiless mind;
>   For a wretch amidst bushes and brakes
> And crags will misfortunes find.
> And Love's whip gave it him hot,
>   Nor did his lashes relent
> Till he'd touched his tenderest spot,
> And drawn tears from poor Don Quixote,
>   Dulcinea's lack to lament
>   del Toboso.

His tacking of *del Toboso* on to Dulcinea's name made the discoverers of the poem laugh heartily. For they supposed Don Quixote must have imagined that the verse would not be understood unless he added del Toboso when he named Dulcinea; and they were right, as he afterwards confessed. He wrote a great number more. But, as has been said, only these three stanzas could be deciphered and were found complete. He passed the time in this writing, and in sighing and calling on the fauns and satyrs of those woods, on the nymphs of the streams and on mournful humid Echo, to listen, reply, and console him. He also searched for herbs to serve as food till Sancho's return. But if he had been away three weeks instead of three days, the Knight of the Sad Countenance would have been so wasted away that he would have been unrecognizable even by the mother who bore him.

But here it will be well to leave him, deep in his sighs and verses, to tell what happened to Sancho Panza on his mission. When he had emerged on to the highway, he set out to find the El Toboso road, and the following day reached the inn where he had suffered his misadventure with the blanket. Now no sooner did he catch sight of it than he felt himself once more sailing through the air; and he had no desire to enter, even though he had come at an hour when he properly should have gone in. For it was dinner-time and he was longing for something hot to eat, since it was a long time since he had eaten anything but cold fare. His inclinations brought him close to the inn, but he was still doubtful whether to enter or not at the moment when two persons came out and presently recognized him.

'Tell me, Master Licentiate,' one of them asked the other, 'isn't that man on the horse Sancho Panza who, so our adventurer's housekeeper told us, went off with her master as his squire?'

'Yes, it is,' replied the Licentiate, 'and that is our Don Quixote's horse.'

They knew him very well, for they were the priest and the barber of his own village, the same men who had performed the trial and general holocaust of the books. And once they were quite certain of Sancho Panza and Rocinante, being anxious for news of Don Quixote, the pair of them went up to him, and the priest called him by name and asked: 'Friend Sancho Panza, where did you leave your master?'

Sancho Panza recognized them at once, and decided not to tell them where his master was, nor to describe the state he had left him in. So he replied that Don Quixote was occupied in a certain place with a certain matter of great importance to him, which he could not reveal for all the eyes in his head.

'No, no, Sancho Panza,' said the barber; 'if you don't tell us where he is, we shall imagine – in fact we already do – that you've killed and robbed him, for here you come riding on his horse. Yes, you'll certainly have to produce the owner of that mount, or it'll be the worse for you.'

'You have no cause to use threats on me. I'm not the man to rob or murder anyone. Let every man die when fate decrees, or when God his Maker calls him. My master's in the heart of these mountains, doing a penance and very much in his element.'

Then he told them right off without stopping of the state he had left his master in, of the adventures which had befallen him, and all about the letter he was taking to the lady Dulcinea del Toboso, the daughter of Lorenzo Corchuelo, and how the knight was up to his ears in love with her. The pair of them were amazed at Sancho's tale. For, although they already knew the nature of Don Quixote's madness, they were astonished afresh every time they had news of him. They then asked Sancho Panza to show them the letter he was taking to the lady Dulcinea del Toboso. He replied that it was written in a note-book, and that his master's orders were that he must have it copied down on paper in the first village he came to. Here the priest asked to see it, and promised to write it out himself in a very good hand. Sancho Panza then felt beneath his shirt for the little book, but could not find it; and he would not have found it if he had searched till this day, because it was still in Don Quixote's possession and had never been given to him. In fact he had not remembered to ask for it.

When Sancho saw that the book was not to be found, he turned pale as death, and felt once more very hurriedly all over his body, only to realize afresh that he could not find it. Without more ado he plunged both hands into his beard and tore half of it out. Then he rapidly dealt himself a dozen blows without stopping, on the face and on the nose, until both were bathed in blood. At this sight the priest and the barber asked him what had happened to make him treat himself so roughly.

'What do you think?' replied Sancho. 'Only that in a single instant I've let three ass-colts slip through my fingers, three ass-colts, each one of them as strong as a castle.'

'How is that?' asked the barber.

'I've lost the note-book,' answered Sancho, 'which had the letter for Dulcinea in it, and a bill signed by my master, ordering his niece to give me three of the four or five ass-colts he has at home.'

Then he told them about the loss of Dapple, and the priest consoled him by promising that when he found his master he would make him renew the order and draw up the bill of exchange in the usual and customary form; for orders drawn in note-books were never honoured or accepted. Sancho was comforted by this, saying that in that case he did not much care about the loss of Dulcinea's letter, for he knew it almost by heart, and so they could take it down where and when they pleased.

'Repeat it to us, then, Sancho,' said the barber, 'and we'll write it down afterwards.'

Sancho Panza stopped and scratched his head to drag the letter up into his memory, standing first on one foot and then on the other. Sometimes he looked down at the ground and sometimes up at the sky. Then, when he had gnawed away half the top of one finger, keeping everyone who was waiting for him to speak in suspense, he burst out after a very long pause: 'God's Truth, Master Licentiate, the devil take all I remember of the letter; though at the beginning it said, *Sublime and suppressed lady*.'

'It wouldn't be suppressed,' said the barber, 'but superhuman or sovereign.'

'That's right,' said Sancho. 'Then, if I remember rightly, it went on ... *He that is oppressed with sleep and wakeful and wounded kisses your hands, ungrateful and most thankless beauty*. Then it said something about the health and sickness which he sent her, and so he went running on till he ended: *Yours till death, the Knight of the Sad Countenance*.'

The pair of them were not a little amused at Sancho's excellent memory and congratulated him warmly upon it. They asked him to recite the letter twice more so that they too might learn it by heart, and write it down when the time came. Sancho said it through three times more, and three times he repeated three thousand comical mistakes. After that he told them more about his master, but he did not say a word about the blanket tossing he had got at the inn, and still refused to enter. He also told them that once he had brought him a favourable despatch from the lady Dulcinea del

Toboso his master was going to set out and try to become Emperor, or at least Monarch, for so they had agreed between them. It was a thing that could be managed very easily, considering the valour of the knight's person and the strength of his arm. And once he had done this, his master was going to find a wife for his squire. For by that time he could not possibly fail to be a widower, and would marry one of the Empress's waiting-women, the heiress to a rich and large estate on dry land – and none of your isles or wiles, for he had no use for them.

Sancho brought all this out with such gravity, wiping his nose from time to time, and so crazily, that the pair of them were aston-ished afresh at the strength of Don Quixote's madness, since it had carried this poor man's wits along after it. They did not fancy the trouble of dispelling the squire's illusion. In fact it seemed to them better to leave him in it, since it did no harm to his conscience, and particularly as they found it most amusing to listen to his nonsense. So they bade him pray God for his master's health, it being both possible and feasible that he might in the course of time become an Emperor, as he had suggested, or at the least an Archbishop, or something of equal dignity. To which Sancho replied:

'Gentlemen, supposing that by a stroke of fate my master should take it into his head not to be an Emperor but to be an Archbishop, I should like to know here and now what Archbishops are accus-tomed to give to their squires?'

'Generally,' replied the priest, 'they give them a benefice, or a simple parish, or a sextonship, which brings them in a good tithe besides the altar-gifts, which are usually reckoned at as much again.'

'But for that,' replied Sancho, 'the squire would have to be un-married, and at the very least know how to assist at the Mass. Now if that's so I'm out of luck, because I'm married and don't know the first letter of the A.B.C. What will happen to me if my master gets the idea of being an Archbishop, and not an Emperor as is the use and practice of knights errant?'

'Don't worry, friend Sancho,' said the barber. 'We'll entreat your master and advise him, and even put it to him as a matter of conscience, that he shall be an Emperor and not an Archbishop. It'll be much the easier for him, besides, since he is more of a soldier than a scholar.'

'It has always seemed like that to me,' replied Sancho, 'although I must say that he's clever enough for anything. What I shall do is to pray Our Lord to put him wherever it's best for him, and where he can do me the greatest benefits.'

'You speak like a wise man,' said the priest, 'and you will be acting like a good Christian. But what we have got to do now is to contrive a way of releasing your master from that fruitless penance you say you left him doing. And if we are to think out a means of doing so and get something to eat as well – for it is time – it would be a good idea if we were to go into this inn.'

Sancho answered that they might go in, but that he would wait outside, and tell them afterwards the reason why he was unwilling to enter. But he begged them to bring him out something warm to eat, and some barley too for Rocinante. So they went in and left him outside, and a little later the barber brought him out some food. And afterwards, when they had thoroughly discussed the course to be pursued if they were to achieve their purpose, the priest struck an idea very applicable to Don Quixote's humour, and to the end they had in mind. This was, as he explained to the barber, for him to dress himself up as a damsel errant, and for the barber to make the best show he could of being her squire. Then they would go in that disguise and find Don Quixote – he pretending to be an afflicted damsel in distress – and beg a boon of him. This, as a valorous knight errant, he could not refuse to grant; and the boon which the damsel would ask of him would be to come with her wherever she might lead him, to redress an injury which a wicked knight had done her. She would also beg him not to require her to remove her mask, nor to make any enquiries about her rank, until he had wreaked vengeance for her upon the wicked knight. The priest was quite certain that Don Quixote would consent to anything they might ask him on these terms, and that they could get him away in this way, and take him home to his village, where they would try to find some cure for his strange madness.

Chapter XXVII. *How the Priest and the Barber carried out their plan, and other matters worthy of mention in this great history.*

THE priest's plan did not seem a bad one to the barber – quite the opposite, in fact – and so they set about its immediate execution. They borrowed a dress and a head-dress from the landlady, and left the priest's new cassock for security. Then the barber made himself a long beard from a sorrel and grey ox tail, which the innkeeper kept to hang his comb in. And when the landlady asked them why they wanted all this, the priest told her something about Don Quixote's madness, and said that they needed this disguise to entice him away from the mountains, where he then was. The innkeeper and his wife at once realized that the madman was their guest of the balsam and the master of the blanket-tossed squire, and told the priest the whole story, not omitting the part which Sancho had been so anxious to conceal. In the end the landlady equipped the priest to perfection. She gave him a cloth dress, stiff with black velvet stripes a good eight inches wide, all slashed, and a bodice of green velvet bordered with white satin trimmings, both of which must have been made in the time of King Wamba. The priest would not agree to have his head dressed like a woman's, but put on the little quilted linen cap he generally used for a nightcap, tied one of his black taffeta garters across his forehead, and made a mask with the other, which covered his beard and his face very well. He then put on his broad hat, large enough to serve as a sunshade and, wrapping his cloak around him, mounted his mule side-saddle like a woman, while the barber got up upon his, with his beard reaching to his waist, part sorrel and part white. For, as we have said, it was made from the tail of a pied ox.

They said good-bye to everyone, including the good Maritornes, who promised to recite a whole rosary, sinner though she was, that God might give them success in the very arduous and Christian task they had undertaken. But no sooner were they out of the inn than it struck the priest that he was doing wrong in dressing up in that fashion; for it was indecent for a churchman to appear in such a garb, however deeply he was concerned in the business. This he told the barber, and asked him to change clothes. It would be more fitting, he said, if his friend were to play the distressed maiden and himself be the squire, which part would be less prejudicial to his dignity. And if the barber would not agree he refused to go a step further, even though the devil should run away with Don Quixote. At this point Sancho joined them, and could not help laughing when he saw them in their disguise. In the end the barber gave in to the priest, and they changed their plan. The priest then began to instruct the barber how to act, and what to say to Don Quixote, so as to compel him to come away and cease haunting the place which he had chosen for his fruitless penance. The barber replied that he could carry it off to perfection, without any tuition. But he refused to put on the clothes until they should reach the place where Don Quixote was; and so he folded them up. The priest then stowed away his beard, and they went on their way under the guidance of Sancho Panza, who told them as they went along the story of the madman whom they had found in the mountains. But he kept quiet about the discovery of the leather bag and about its contents; for with all his simplicity he was rather a greedy rascal.

The next day they reached the place where Sancho had strewn the sprigs to guide him to the spot where he had left his master. And when he recognized the place, he told them that this was the way in; and that they had better dress up, if that was necessary for the rescue of his master. For they had already told him that it was of the utmost importance to go thus clothed and disguised, if they were to save Don Quixote from the miserable life that he had chosen; and they had impressed on him that he must not tell his master who they were, or that he knew them. And if Don Quixote were to ask him, as he was bound to, whether he had given Dulcinea the letter, he must reply that he had, but that as she could not read, she had replied by word of mouth, commanding him to come and see her immediately on pain of her displeasure. This, they assured Sancho, was most essential; for in this way, and by means of certain things they intended to say to Don Quixote themselves, they felt certain that they could bring him to a better life, and so contrive it as to put him immediately on the road to becoming an Emperor or a Monarch, for as to his being an Archbishop there was nothing to fear.

Sancho listened to all this and treasured it up in his memory.

He thanked them warmly for their intention of advising his master
to be an Emperor and not an Archbishop, being certain in his own
mind that, so far as bestowing favours on their squires went, Emperors could do more than Archbishops-errant. He also said that
it would be better if he were to go ahead to look for his master and
give him his lady's reply; for that alone might be sufficient to get
him away from the place, without their putting themselves to all
that trouble. They approved Sancho Panza's idea, and so decided to
wait for him to return with the news that he had found his master.
The squire then struck into the mountain clefts, leaving the two of
them in a ravine, which was watered by a little gentle stream and
pleasantly cool from the shade of the rocks and trees surrounding it.
It was a hot day in August, the month when the heat is usually most
intense in those parts; and the time was three o'clock in the afternoon, which made the place even more pleasing. In fact it invited
them to wait there for Sancho's return, which they did. But as the
two of them were lying at their ease in the shade, there came to their
ears a voice singing sweetly and melodiously, though unaccom-
panied by any instrument. Which surprised them not a little, for
this seemed a most unlikely place in which to find so good a singer.
For although report has it that shepherds with excellent voices are to
be found in woods and fields, that is rather poetic exaggeration than
sober truth. They were even more astonished when they heard the
words of his song. For they were not rough shepherd's verses, but
well-turned and courtly, as will be clear from the following lines:

What turns my happiness to pain?
Disdain.
And greater makes my woe for me?
Jealousy.
What sorest tries my patience?
Absence.
If that be so, then for my wrong
No remedy may I obtain,
Since my best hopes I find are slain
By disdain, jealousy, and absence long.

Who through my breast this anguish drove?
Love.
Who doth my happiness abate?
Fate.

Who consents to this my pain?
        Heaven.
If that be so, I fear 'twill prove
That I must die in this sad plight,
Since for my overthrow unite
The heavens, fate, and love.

Who can better hope bequeath?
        Death.
What are the means to make me free?
        Inconstancy.
And wherein lies the cure for sadness?
        Madness.
If that be so, it's merely silly
To seek my passion's cure,
For there's no remedy that's sure
But death and change and folly.

The time, the season, the solitude, the voice and skill of the singer, all astonished and delighted the two listeners, who waited quietly in the hope of hearing more. But when the silence had continued for rather a long while, they decided to go out and look for this musician with so fine a voice. Just as they were going to do so, however, the same voice came once more to their ears, and kept them motionless throughout the singing of this sonnet:

O sacred friendship that with nimble wing,
Thy phantom leaving here on earth below,
With blessed souls in heaven communing
Up through the empyrean halls dost go.
Thence, at thy pleasure, to us is assigned
Just peace, her features covered with a hood,
But oft, instead of her, Deceit we find
Clad in the garb of virtue and of good.
Leave heaven, friendship, and do not permit
Foul fraud thus openly thy robes to wear
And so all honest purposes defeat.
For if you leave him in your semblance fair
Dark chaos will once more engulf the world
And all to primal anarchy be hurled.

The song ended with a deep sigh, and the pair of them waited attentively to see if he would sing again; but when they heard the music turn to sobs and groans of sorrow, they agreed to go and find out who the unhappy person was who had so excellent a voice and

H

so sorrowing a heart. And they had not gone far when, on coming round the corner of a rock, they saw a man in form and figure resembling Sancho Panza's description of Cardenio. The man did not start at the sight of them, but stayed still, with his head on his breast in a pensive attitude, and did not raise his eyes to look at them again after their first sudden appearance. Now the priest had recognized him from Sancho's account, and consequently knew the cause of his misfortunes; and being a man of ready speech, he went up to him and implored him most persuasively in a few well-chosen words to give up his wretched way of life, and not risk dying in that desolate place, which would be the greatest of all misfortunes. At that time Cardenio was sane, and free from the wild fits which so often drove him out of his mind. Seeing, therefore, the two of them dressed so unlike the usual frequenters of those lonely parts, he could not help being surprised, and was even more so when he heard them speak of his own affairs as if they were common knowledge – for that was the impression he got from the priest's speech. And so he replied:

'I see, gentlemen, whoever you may be, that Heaven, which takes care to succour the good, and often the bad as well, has sent to me, unworthy as I am, even in this remote and desolate spot so far from the traffic of human kind, some persons to show me, by forcible and lively argument, the unreasonable nature of the life I lead, and to endeavour to tempt me away from here to a better place. But not knowing, as I do, that were I to fly from this misery I should fall into a worse, they must take me for a fool, or even worse for a madman. And that would not be surprising. For I am myself aware that the strength of my misery is so intense, and drives me to such distraction, that I am powerless to resist it and am turning to stone, void of all knowledge and feeling. This I realize when I am shown the evidence of the deeds I have done under the mastery of these terrible fits. Then I can only vainly lament and fruitlessly curse my fate, and to excuse my madness tell any who will hear it the story of its cause. For when sensible men learn its cause they will not be surprised at its effects. Though they will be unable to offer me any relief, at least they will not blame me, and their anger at my violence will turn to pity for my misfortunes. If you, sirs, have come with the same intention as the others, I beg you to listen to the story of my misfortunes before you continue with your sensible arguments. For when you have heard it, you will perhaps spare yourselves the trouble of trying to offer consolation for an inconsolable sorrow.'

The pair of them wanted nothing better than to hear the cause of his grief from his own mouth, and begged him to tell them his story, promising to take no measures without his consent either for his relief or for his consolation. Then the unhappy gentleman began his piteous tale, in almost the same words and phrases as he had used in telling it to Don Quixote and the goatherd a few days before, when the story had remained unfinished on account of Master Elisabat and Don Quixote's punctiliousness in defending the dignity of knight errantry. But fortunately this time Cardenio had no fit of madness and was able to tell it to the end. So, when he reached the subject of the letter which Don Ferdinand had found between the leaves of *Amadis of Gaul*, he said that he remembered it perfectly, and that it read as follows:

' "*Lucinda to Cardenio:*

'"*Each day I find in you virtues which oblige and compel me to think more highly of you; and, therefore, if you would relieve me of this debt without prejudice to my honour, you may easily do so. My father knows you and loves me; he will never force me, but he will comply with your just demands, if you value me as you say, and as I believe you do.*"

'This letter moved me, as I have already told you, to ask for Lucinda's hand, and proved her in Don Ferdinand's opinion one of the most discreet and sensible women of her time. And it was this letter which made him determine to ruin me before my design could be put into effect. I told Ferdinand of her father's insistence that mine should make the request, and that I dared not mention the matter to my father for fear that he would not consent. Not that he was ignorant of Lucinda's rank, goodness, virtue and beauty – for he knew that she had virtues enough to ennoble any family in Spain – but because, as I understood, he did not wish me to marry before we knew what Duke Richard might do for me. To be brief, I told him that I dared not ask my father, not only because of this obstacle, but because of other vague apprehensions which made me fear that my desires would never be realized. Ferdinand's reply was that he would speak to my father for me, and make him speak to Lucinda's. O greedy Marius! Cruel Catiline! Criminal Sulla! Crafty Galalon! Treacherous Vellido! Vindictive Julian! Covetous Judas! Cruel, vindictive, crafty traitor! What harm had this poor wretch done you, who so frankly revealed to you the secrets and joys of his heart? How had I offended you? Did I ever say a word, or give you advice, which was not intended for your benefit and honour? But why do I complain, miserable wretch that I am. For it is certain that when the stars in their courses bring disaster, rushing down with fury and violence, no power on earth can stop them, no human ingenuity avert them. Who could have thought that Don Ferdinand, a noble and intelligent gentleman, indebted to me for my services and absolutely certain of success wherever his amorous fancy led him, would be bitten – as they say – with the desire to take from me my one ewe-lamb, who was not even yet mine? But these thoughts are vain and fruitless. Let them rest, and we will take up the broken thread of my unfortunate story.

'Don Ferdinand, then, finding that my presence hindered him from putting his false, wicked plan into practice, decided to send me to his elder brother, on the pretext of borrowing some money from him to pay for six horses, which he had bought on the very day he offered to speak to my father, purposely to provide himself with an excuse for getting me out of the way, the better to carry out his wicked plan. Could I have foreseen this treachery? Could I even have imagined it? No, certainly not. On the contrary, I offered to go immediately with the greatest of pleasure, and was delighted at the good bargain he had made. That night I spoke to Lucinda, told her of my arrangement with Don Ferdinand, and said that we had good reason to hope for a favourable result. She was as unsuspecting as I of Don Ferdinand's treachery, and bade me hurry back, for she was certain that the fulfilment of our desires would be delayed no longer than it would take for my father to speak to hers. I do not know how it was, but as she spoke her eyes filled with tears, and a sudden choking in her throat prevented her speaking another word, though she seemed to have much more to say. This excess of emotion, which I had never seen in her before, surprised me; because on such occasions as my good fortune and my diligence provided, we always talked happily and merrily enough, without mingling tears, sighs,

jealousies, suspicions, or fears with our conversation. I would ex-
patiate on my good fortune, thanking Heaven for giving her to me
for my mistress, praising her beauty, and extolling her virtue and
good sense. She in reply would praise the qualities in me that seemed
to her, as my lover, worthy of praise. During these conversations
we amused ourselves with a hundred thousand trifles, and gossiped
about our neighbours and friends; and the greatest freedom I allowed myself was to take, almost by force, one of her lovely white
hands and press it to my lips, as well as the narrowness of the bars
between us would allow. But on the night before the sad day of my
parting she wept, moaned, and sighed, and then fled, leaving me
full of confusion and dread at these new and unusual signs of sorrow and tenderness in Lucinda. But, not to destroy my hopes, I
attributed all this to the strength of her love for me, and to the grief
which absence always causes true lovers. In short I departed, sad
and thoughtful, my mind full of fancies and suspicions, but uncertain what it was I suspected or imagined – all of which clearly pre-
saged the miserable and dark fate which awaited me.

'I came to the town I was sent to, and delivered the letters to Don
Ferdinand's brother. I was well received, but not quickly dismissed.
For, to my disgust, he bade me wait eight days in a place out of sight
of the Duke, his father, since his brother had asked for a certain sum
of money to be sent him without his father's knowledge. But all
this was a stratagem of the false Don Ferdinand. For his brother was
not short of money and might have sent me back with it immediately. I felt much inclined to disobey this order, for it seemed quite
impossible to live so long away from Lucinda, especially as I had
left her in such a state of distress. But, for all that, like a good servant I obeyed, although I knew it to be to my own detriment. On
the fourth day after my arrival, however, a man came after me with
a letter which by the address I knew was from Lucinda, for the writing was hers. I opened it in fear and trembling, convinced that it
must be something extraordinary which had moved her to write to
me in my absence, seeing how seldom she did so when I was near.
Before I read it I asked the man who had given it to him, and how
long he had been on the road. He told me that as he had happened
to be going down one of the city streets about midday, a very
beautiful lady had called him from a window, her eyes full of tears,

and had said to him very earnestly: 'Brother, if you are a Christian, as you seem to be, I beg you, for the love of God, to carry this letter quickly to the place and the person to whom it is directed – for they are well known. In this you will be performing an act of charity, and that you may not lack the means to do it, take what is wrapped in this handkerchief.' "As she said this," he pursued, "she threw me a handkerchief out of the window ; and in it were a hundred *reals*, this gold ring here, and the letter I have given you. Then, without waiting for my reply, she left the window; though first she had seen me take up the letter and the handkerchief, and give her a sign that I would do what she asked. So, seeing how well I was paid for my trouble, and learning from the envelope that the letter was for you, sir, whom I know very well – and moved too by that beautiful lady's tears – I decided not to trust anyone else, but to come myself to deliver it to you; and in the sixteen hours since she gave it to me I have done the journey, which as you know is fifty-four miles." While the kind impromptu messenger was speaking I hung on his words, my legs trembling so that I could scarcely stand. At length I opened the letter and read these words:

'Don Ferdinand has fulfilled his promise to persuade your father to speak to mine, more to his own satisfaction than to your advantage. I must tell you that he has asked for my hand in marriage, and that, carried away by the advantages he thinks Don Ferdinand has over you, my father has agreed with such eagerness that the betrothal is to take place two days hence, so secretly and privately that the only witnesses will be Heaven, and some of our own household. You can imagine how I feel. Consider whether you should not return. The outcome of the matter will show you whether I love you or not. God grant this may reach your hands before mine are joined to those of a man who keeps his pledged word so ill.

'These, then, were the contents of the letter, which caused me to set out without waiting for the answer or the money. For now I saw clearly that it was not the purchase of the horses, but the indulgence of his own desires, that had caused Don Ferdinand to send me to his brother. Rage against him and fear of losing the treasure which I had earned by so many years of love and devotion lent wings to my feet, and the next day I reached our town at the most favourable moment for going to speak to Lucinda. I rode in secretly and, leaving my mule at the house of the good man who had brought me the letter, by good luck I found Lucinda posted at the grating which had been the constant witness of our loves. She recognized me immediately, and I her; yet not with our usual joy. But who in the world can boast that he has fathomed and understood the confused mind and changeable nature of a woman? No one, of course. For as soon as Lucinda saw me, she said: "Cardenio, I am dressed for the betrothal. The traitor Don Ferdinand and my greedy father are now waiting for me with the other witnesses in the hall, but they shall rather be witnesses of my death than of my betrothal. Do not be disturbed, my friend, but contrive to be present at this sacrifice. If I cannot prevent it by words, I carry a dagger about me which can oppose the most determined violence by putting an end to my life, and proving the love I bear and have always borne for you."

'I answered her hurriedly and distractedly, for I was afraid that I might lose my opportunity of replying:

' "May your actions, lady, confirm your words. If you have a dagger to secure your honour, I have a sword here to defend you with, or to kill myself with if fortune proves adverse."

'I do not think that she could have listened to all that I said, since I heard them hurriedly call her away. For the bridegroom was waiting. Here the night of my sadness fell; the sun of my happiness set; the light went out of my eyes, the sense from my brain. I could not go into her house nor move in any direction. But when I thought how important my presence was, whatever events might arise, I took better heart and entered. As I knew all the ways in and out, and as the whole household was in a secret bustle, no one noticed me, and I was able to take up my position in the recess formed by a window of the hall itself. This hiding-place was masked by the edges and folds of two pieces of tapestry, between which I could observe everything that happened there without myself being seen. How can I tell you with what alarm my heart beat while I stood there, what thoughts came into my head, what reflections passed through my mind? So many were they, and of such a nature, that they cannot and should not be told. Enough that Don Ferdinand came into the hall, not dressed as a bridegroom but in his usual clothes. His groomsman was a first cousin of Lucinda's, and there was no other person in the whole hall, except the servants. Shortly afterwards Lucinda came out of a dressing-room, accompanied by her mother and two of her maids, adorned as her rank and beauty deserved, and looking the very perfection of fashion and courtly splendour. My distraction and anxiety gave me no opportunity of noting in detail what she wore. I could only mark the colours, which were crimson and white, and the flashing of the jewels and precious stones on her head-dress and all over her clothes. But most beautiful of all was her lovely golden hair, which rivalled her jewels and the light of the great torches which lit the hall, and brought her beauty even more brilliantly before my eyes. O memory, mortal enemy of my peace! To what purpose do you recall to me the incomparable beauty of my beloved enemy? Would it not be better, cruel memory, to picture to me what she did next; so that, under the stress of so flagrant an injury, I may strive, if not to avenge it, at least to lose my life? Do not grow weary, gentlemen, of hearing these digressions of mine; for my grief cannot be told succinctly and methodically, since every circumstance of it seems to me to deserve a long discourse.'

To which the priest replied that not only were they not weary of his tale, but that they were glad to hear the details; since they were not of the sort to be passed over in silence, and deserved the same attention as the main thread of the story.

'Then,' continued Cardenio, 'when they were all in the hall the parish priest came in, and took them each by the hand to perform the ceremony. When he said: "Will you, lady Lucinda, take the lord Don Ferdinand, here present, for your lawful husband, as Holy Mother Church commands?", I stuck my whole head and neck out between the tapestries and listened with straining ears and distracted mind for Lucinda's reply, awaiting from it sentence of death or a fresh lease of life. If only I had then dared to come out and cry: "Lucinda, Lucinda, beware what you do! Consider what you owe me! Remember you are mine, and cannot be another's! Be warned that to say Yes is instantly to end my life. O treacherous Don Ferdinand, thief of my glory, death of my life! What do you want? What claim can you make? Consider that, as a Christian, you cannot achieve your desire, because Lucinda is my wife and I am her husband!" What a madman I am! Now that I am far away from the danger I say what I should have done, but did not do. Now that I have let my dear treasure be stolen I curse the robber, on whom I might have taken vengeance if I had been as prompt to act then as I now am to complain! Then I was a coward and a fool; no wonder that I am dying now, ashamed, repentant, and mad.

'The priest stood waiting for Lucinda's reply, and she did not answer for some time. But when I thought that she was going to draw her dagger in defence of her honour, or raise her voice to utter the truth, or make a protest which might redound to my advantage, I heard her say in weak and fainting tones: "I will". Don Ferdinand pronounced the same words and gave her the ring, and they were tied by an indissoluble bond. But as the bridegroom turned to kiss his bride she put her hand to her heart and fell fainting into her mother's arms.

'It only remains for me to describe my state of mind when I saw in that one Yes my hopes deceived, Lucinda's word and promise broken, and myself for ever powerless to recover all that I had lost in that one instant. I was resourceless. Heaven, it seemed, had abandoned me; sustaining earth had become my enemy; air denied me breath for my sighs, and water moisture for my tears; only fire grew so strong that I seemed to burn all over with rage and jealousy.

'Everyone was thrown into confusion by Lucinda's fainting, and when her mother unlaced her dress to give her air a folded paper was discovered there, which Don Ferdinand immediately snatched and started to read by the light of one of the torches. When he had finished it, he sat down on a chair and put his hand to his cheek, apparently deep in thought, and paying no attention to the attempts which were being made to bring his bride round from her swoon.

'When I saw the whole household in commotion I ventured out, not caring whether I were seen or not, and determined, if I were, to do so desperate a deed that everyone would learn from my punishment of the treacherous Don Ferdinand and from the fickleness of the swooning traitress what just indignation I harboured in my breast. My fate, however, which must be preserving me for worse disasters – if there can possibly be worse – ordained that at that moment I had full use of my reason, which since then I have lacked. So, instead of taking vengeance on my greatest enemies, which would have been easy, since they had no suspicions of my presence,

I resolved to inflict on myself, and with my own hand, the punishment which they deserved – a punishment perhaps more severe than I should have inflicted on them by instant execution. For sudden death swiftly ends all pain, but death which is protracted by torture for ever kills but never puts an end to life.

'At last I left the house, and returned to the place where I had left my mule. I had it saddled, and without saying good-bye to my host I left the city, like another Lot, not daring to look back. When I found myself alone in the fields, concealed by the darkness of the night, its silence invited me to complain without fear of being heard or recognized. I then gave vent to violent curses on Lucinda and Don Ferdinand, as if that were a means of taking vengeance for the wrong they had done me. I called her cruel, faithless, false, ungrateful, but most of all mercenary, since my enemy's riches had blinded the eyes of her love, and made her take her affections from me and transfer them to a man of greater wealth. But in the middle of this storm of reproaches and abuse I found excuses for her. It was not surprising, I cried, that a maiden immured in her parents' house, and always accustomed to obey them, should willingly submit, on their proposing so noble, so rich, and so well-bred a gentleman as her husband. For if she had not accepted him, she would either have been thought senseless or have incurred the suspicion of having engaged her affections elsewhere, which would have seriously prejudiced her honour and good name. Then I thought that, if she had said that I was her husband, they would have realized that she had not made a bad choice and must have excused her. For before Don Ferdinand made his offer they could not themselves reasonably have desired a better match for their daughter than myself. She might easily have declared, I thought, before being finally compelled to give her hand to Don Ferdinand, that I had already given her mine; and I should then have come forward and confirmed any story she might have invented. In fact, I concluded that lack of love, foolishness, ambition and the desire for greatness had made her forget her promise, which had deceived, encouraged, and sustained me in my fervent hopes and honest love.

'With these reflections and in this disquietude I travelled for the rest of the night, and at dawn struck a pass into these mountains, over which I wandered for three days, far from any road or track, until I stopped in some meadows, on which side of the range I do not know. There I asked some herdsmen where the wildest parts of the mountains lay, and they pointed in this direction. Here I came at once, intending to end my life; and when I reached these crags my mule fell dead of weariness and hunger, or as I believe, to rid herself of so useless a burden as myself. So I was left on foot, exhausted and hungry, without so much as a thought of looking for help. I do not know how long I lay on the ground in this state, but at length I got up without the feeling of hunger, and found some goatherds beside me. It must have been they who had satisfied my needs, for they told me how they had discovered me talking so wildly that I must clearly have gone out of my mind. And since then I have been conscious that I am not always well, but sometimes so weak and deranged that I behave like a madman, tearing my clothes, shouting in these wastes, cursing my fortune, and vainly repeating the dear name of my enemy. My only wish and purpose at these times is to wear out my life in lamentations. And when I recover my senses, I am so exhausted and bruised that I can hardly move.

'My usual dwelling is a hollow cork-tree large enough to shelter this wretched body. The cowherds and goatherds who frequent these parts feed me out of charity. They leave me food by the tracks and on the rocks, where they expect I may pass and find it. So, even when my senses are disordered, Nature makes me know my food, and rouses the instinct in me to take it and eat it. At other times, they tell me when they find me in my senses, I rush out on to the tracks and take the food the shepherds bring up from the village to the sheepcotes. I snatch it by force, they say, even though they would give it me willingly. So I spend what remains of my miserable life till Heaven shall please to bring it to an end, or to blot Lucinda's beauty and treachery from my memory, and obliterate Don Ferdinand's perfidy as well. If Heaven should do so and not end my life, I will turn my thoughts to some better course. If not I can only implore God's infinite mercy for my soul. For I feel no strength or virtue in myself to fetch my body out of this pass into which I have elected to bring it of my own accord.

'That, sirs, is the bitter story of my misfortunes. Tell me if it deserves to be told with less emotion than I have shown. Do not trouble to persuade me or advise me to take some remedy which your reason may suggest to you. For it will be of no more use to me than a famous doctor's prescription to a patient who will not take it. Without Lucinda I do not desire health; and since it has pleased her to be another's, when she is or should be mine, let me give myself up to misery, since I might have been given up to happiness. She elected by her fickleness to make my perdition permanent, and I choose to comply with her wishes and achieve my final destruction. And it shall be an example to future generations that I alone have lacked what other wretches have in abundance. There is comfort for them in the impossibility of consolation. But for me this is the cause of greater afflictions and evils, which I truly think will not end even with my death.'

Here Cardenio concluded the long recital of his sad love story. But, just as the priest was preparing to offer him some words of consolation, he was prevented by a voice, which came to his ears, uttering in mournful tones what will be related in the fourth part of this narrative. For at this point the wise and judicious historian, Cide Hamete Benengeli, brought his third part to an end.

Chapter XXVIII. *Of a Novel and Pleasing Adventure which befell the Priest and the Barber in the same Mountains.*

How happy and fortunate was that age in which the boldest of knights, Don Quixote de la Mancha, was born into the world. Since, thanks to his honourable resolution of reviving and restoring to the earth the lost and almost defunct order of knight errantry, we enjoy to-day in our present age, which lacks all pleasant entertainment, not only the delights of his authentic history, but also the tales and episodes set in it. For in some ways these are no less agreeable, ingenious and authentic than the history itself, the thread of which, being carded, twisted, and reeled, may now be resumed. It relates that just as the priest was about to console Cardenio, he was prevented by a voice speaking in mournful tones to this effect:

'O God, is it possible that I have found a spot which will afford a secret grave to the weary burden of my body, which I so unwillingly bear? This will be the place, if the solitude these hills promise does not deceive me. Miserable creature that I am, what company can I have more welcome than these crags and thickets, which will allow me to tell my misery to Heaven, since there is no one on earth from whom I can expect counsel in my perplexities, comfort in my grief, or remedy in my troubles!'

The priest and his companions heard the words distinctly, and got up to look for the speaker, who could not be far away. They had not gone twenty yards, in fact, when from behind a rock they saw a youth dressed like a peasant, who was sitting at the foot of an ash. They could not at first see his face, because his head was bent over a running stream in which he was washing his feet. And so silently did they come up that he did not hear them. For he was busily engaged in washing his feet, which looked like nothing so much as two pieces of pure crystal, lying among the other pebbles of the brook. Their whiteness and beauty astonished the gazers. For they did not seem to be made for breaking clods, nor for following oxen and the plough, as the dress of their owner suggested. So, seeing that they were unobserved, the priest, who was ahead, signed to the other two to crouch behind some near-by fragments of rock; which they did, and watched all that youth's movements attentively.

He was dressed in a short grey double cape, tied round his waist with a white cloth. He wore breeches and leggings of grey cloth and a grey cap on his head. And he had hitched his leggings half-way up his legs, which were as white as alabaster. After washing his lovely feet, he wiped them with a kerchief, which he took from under his cap. And, as he did so, he raised his face, in which the watchers saw such peerless beauty that Cardenio whispered to the priest: 'Since this is not Lucinda it is no human creature. It must be divine.'

The youth took off his cap; and as he shook his head from side to side, there began to fall about his shoulders hair which the sun itself might have envied. By this they realized that here was no peasant lad but a delicate woman, and the most beautiful that two of them had ever seen till then. And Cardenio would have known none lovelier, had he not gazed on Lucinda. For, as he afterwards declared, only Lucinda's beauty could compare with hers. Her long golden hair not only covered her shoulders but fell all round her, hiding her entire body except for her feet. Then she combed it with hands which in contrast to the crystal of her feet seemed to be made of driven snow. All of which increased the astonishment of the three watchers and their desire to know who she was; and so they decided to reveal themselves. But as they moved to get up, the lovely maiden raised her head and, parting her hair from before her eyes with both hands, looked to see who had made the noise. And no sooner did she see them than she got up and, without waiting to put on her shoes or tie up her hair, hurriedly seized a bundle lying beside her, which might have contained clothes, and started to run away in surprise and alarm. But she had not gone six paces when her tender feet were so hurt by the sharp stones that she fell down. At this point the three of them came out, the priest being the first to speak:

'Stop, lady, whoever you are. We only desire to serve you. You have no reason to run away. Besides, it would be of no use. Your feet would not allow it, and we should not permit it.'

She was so astonished and bewildered that she could make no reply. So they went up to her, and the priest, taking her by the hand, continued: 'What your dress, lady, denies, your hair reveals. Clearly you must have had no trivial reason for disguising your beauty in so unsuitable a dress, and coming to so wild a spot, where it has been our good fortune to find you. If we cannot relieve your distress, we can at least advise you. For no evil short of death can be so dire that the sufferer may absolutely refuse to listen to comfort gladly offered. So, dear lady, or dear sir – whichever you prefer – dismiss the fears which our appearance cause you, and tell us of your fortune, good or bad. For in all of us together or each of us separately you will find sympathizers in your distress.'

While the priest was talking, the disguised maiden stood stupefied, gazing at them without moving her lips or saying a single word, like some peasant suddenly confronted with rare treasures never seen before. But when the priest said more to the same effect, she gave a deep sigh and broke her silence:

'Since these lonely mountains cannot hide me, and my hair will not permit my tongue to lie, it would be vain to make a further pretence; which you could accept only out of politeness, and for no other reason. Therefore, gentlemen, I thank you for the offer you have made me, and feel obliged to comply with your request, though I am afraid that the tale of my misfortunes will cause you grief as well as pity. For you can find no remedy nor any consolation to allay them. Nevertheless, so that you may be in no doubt as to my honour, now that you have discovered that I am a woman and seen me, young, alone, and in these clothes – circumstances which singly or all together are enough to destroy any honest reputation – I must tell you what I would rather conceal if I could.'

As she said all this without hesitation, she seemed not only beautiful but eloquent and sweet-voiced as well, which made them admire her good sense no less than her beauty. They once more offered her their help, and begged her to fulfil her promise. Then, after modestly putting on her shoes and tying up her hair, she sat down on a stone without more ado; and the other three sat round her, choking back the tears which sprang to their eyes, as in a calm and clear voice she began the story of her life:

'Here in Andalusia there is a town from which a Duke takes his title, by virtue of which he is a Grandee of Spain. He has two sons, the elder the heir to his estate and, apparently, to his virtues, and the younger, heir to I do not know what, unless it be Vellido's treachery and Galalon's deceit. My parents are tenants of this lord, people of humble birth, but so rich that if their rank were equal to their fortune they could have nothing more to desire. Nor, if that had been so, need I have feared to find myself in my present misfortune; for perhaps my troubles arose only because they were not noble. Not that their rank is shamefully low, but it is not high enough to make me certain that my disaster was not caused by the humbleness of their station. In short they are farmers, simple people without any taint of ignoble blood, and what is generally called "rusty old Christians"; people whose wealth and fine way of life are gradually earning them the name of gentlefolk, or even nobles. But their greatest wealth and nobility in their own eyes lay in having me for their daughter. And, as they had no other heir, and as they were most loving parents, I was the most pampered of children. I was the light of their eyes, the staff of their old age and, save for Heaven, the sole object of their affections – and my wishes never differed from theirs by a jot, such good parents they were. Now just as I was mistress of their affections, I was also mistress of their household. It was I who engaged and dismissed the servants, and the accounts of sowings and crops passed through my hands. The oil-mills, the wine-presses, the stock list and the beehives were under my control. In fact, I kept the complete accounts of a rich farm – for rich my

father's was. I was the stewardess and controller, and fulfilled my
duties to their absolute satisfaction. Such part of my day as remained after dealing with the overseers, the foremen, and the day-
labourers, I spent in occupations proper to young ladies, sewing,
lace-making, and often spinning. And if I left these tasks at times to
refresh my mind, I turned to some book of devotion or to playing
the harp. For experience taught me that music composes disordered
thoughts and eases the troubles which are born of the spirit. This,
then, is how I lived in my parents' house, and if I have described it
in some detail, it has not been out of ostentation, nor to show that
I am rich, but to prove how little I am to blame for falling from that
happy state into my present misery.

'So it was that I spent my life, busy and in almost monastic seclusion, seen by nobody, as I supposed, but the household servants.
For when I went to Mass it was so early in the morning, my mother
and I were so surrounded by our servants, and I was so closely
veiled and guarded, that my eyes scarcely saw more of the earth than
my feet trod. But for all this the eyes of love, or more correctly of
idleness, which are keener than a lynx's, discovered me, the eyes of
the importunate Don Ferdinand. For that is the name of the Duke's
younger son, whom I spoke of.'

No sooner did she mention Don Ferdinand's name than Cardenio's face changed colour, and he began to sweat and to show so
much emotion that the priest and the barber looked at him in apprehension, fearing one of those attacks of madness which they had
heard he was subject to. But he merely sweated and stayed still,
staring hard at the farmer's daughter and reflecting who she might
be. She, however, did not notice Cardenio's disturbance, but went
on with her story, saying:

'And he had no sooner seen me, as he afterwards declared, than
he fell violently in love with me, as his actions soon showed. But, to
conclude the tale of my misfortunes quickly, I will pass in silence
over the devices Don Ferdinand employed to declare his passion to
me. He bribed all the house servants, and offered and gave presents
to my relations. Every day was a festival and a holiday in our street;
and at night music kept everyone awake. The love-letters which
came into my hands – I do not know how – were countless, full of
declarations and protestations of passion, and containing more pro-

mises and oaths than syllables. All of which did not soften me. On the contrary, they made me harder, as if he were my mortal enemy; and everything that he did to bend me to his will had quite the opposite effect. This was not because I disliked Don Ferdinand's gallantry, or found his wooing excessive. Not at all. I was quite pleased to be desired and admired by so great a nobleman, and not at all displeased to read my praises in his letters; for however plain we women are I think we are always pleased to hear ourselves called beautiful.

'My modesty, however, resisted, and was backed by the repeated advice of my parents, who were well aware of Don Ferdinand's feelings by now, since he did not care if the whole world knew of them. They told me that they relied on my virtue and goodness alone, and trusted me with their honour and good name. They bade me reflect on the difference between Don Ferdinand's rank and mine, and realize that his plans were directed to his own pleasure rather than to my advantage, whatever he might say to the contrary. If I wished to put an end to his wicked suit, they were willing to marry me then and there to anyone I might choose. I could have the best man in our own town or in the whole district; for with their great wealth and my good name anything was possible. With these promises and the assurance they gave me I strengthened my resistance, and never gave Don Ferdinand so much as a word of reply which might offer him even a distant hope of achieving his purpose.

'All my precautions, which he no doubt took for scorn, must have whetted his lascivious appetite. For that is all I can call his passion for me, since if it had been what it should have been, you would never have heard of it: I should have had no occasion to describe it to you. At length Don Ferdinand learned that my parents were going to make a match for me, so as to put an end to his hopes of possessing me, or at least so that I should have better guards to look after me; and this intelligence, or suspicion, was the cause of his doing what I shall now tell you. One night I was sitting in my room, attended by only one serving-maid, with the doors well bolted for fear that my virtue might be carelessly exposed to any peril, when suddenly – I could not imagine how – despite all my precautions I found him standing in front of me in the solitude of my silent retreat. The sight of him so disturbed me that my eyes went blind and I was struck dumb. I had no strength to shout; nor do I believe that he would have let me do so. For he came up to me immediately and took me in his arms. I was so confused, as I said, that I had not the strength to defend myself. Then he began to make violent protestations. I do not know how it is possible for the most skilful lying to make such falseness seem true.

'The traitor reinforced his words with tears and his desires with sighs. And I, poor creature, alone in the midst of my own family, and inexperienced in these matters, began – I do not know how – to believe his falsehoods, though his sighs and tears were far from moving me beyond a virtuous compassion. And so, when I had recovered from my first surprise, I began to regain my lost spirits a little, and said with more courage than I had credited myself with: "Sir, if I were in the grasp of a fierce lion, instead of being, as I am, in your arms, and if I could only get free from them by doing or saying something to the prejudice of my honour, it would be no more possible for me to do or say such a thing than it is to alter the past. For, though you hold my body in your arms, my soul is secured by the purity of my thoughts; and how different they are from your evil ones you will see if you violently persist in your plans. I am your tenant, not your slave. Your noble blood can have no right to dishonour and insult my humility. For, peasant and farmer's daughter though I am, I count myself as good as a gentleman and a noble like yourself. Your violence will have no effect on me, nor will your riches. Your words will not deceive me, nor your sighs and tears move me. If I were to find any of your qualities in a man chosen by my parents for my husband, I should bow to his will, and have no other wishes but his. Were it not for my honour, in fact, I would freely yield to you, sir – though without pleasure – what you are trying to gain by force. This I say so that you may not think for a moment that anyone but a lawful husband can gain anything from me.

'"If you are reluctant only on that account, most lovely Dorothea" – for that is this unfortunate woman's name – exclaimed the treacherous gentleman, "here I give you my hand to be yours. May the Heavens, from whom nothing is hidden, be my witness, and this image of Our Lady, that you have here."'

When Cardenio heard her say that her name was Dorothea his agitation returned, and he was confirmed in his first suspicions. He did not choose to interrupt the story, however, being anxious to hear the ending, which he had almost guessed already. And so he only said:

'Then Dorothea is your name, lady? I have heard of another Dorothea whose misfortunes are perhaps similar to yours. Go on, and later I may tell you something which will both astonish you and arouse your pity.'

Struck by Cardenio's words and by his strange and ragged dress, Dorothea asked him to tell her straight away if he knew anything about her affairs. For if misfortune had left her one virtue, it was courage to suffer any possible disaster in the certainty that nothing could worsen her present lot.

'I should not omit to tell you my thoughts, dear lady,' replied Cardenio, 'if what I imagine were true. But so far there has been no occasion to, and it would not profit you to know what is in my mind.'

'Very well,' replied Dorothea. 'To continue my story: Don Ferdinand then took up an image which stood in the room, and called on it to witness our betrothal. He pledged himself with most binding oaths and solemn vows to marry me, even though before he had finished speaking I begged him to think what he was doing, and consider how angry his father would be at finding him married to a peasant girl, one of his own tenants. I implored him not to let my beauty, such as it was, blind him; for it was not sufficient to excuse his error. If he wished to express the love he bore me by doing me a kindness, I begged him to let my fortune take a course befitting my rank, since such unequal marriages are never happy, and do not preserve for long such joy as they begin with. All these arguments I used on him and many more which I do not remember; but they did not deflect him from his purpose. For he was like a man who finds no difficulty in concluding a bargain because he does not intend to pay.

'I thought the matter over briefly at this juncture, saying to myself: "I shall certainly not be the first to rise from low to high estate by marriage, nor will Don Ferdinand be the first whom beauty or blind love – the second is the more likely – have impelled to take a humble bride. Since, therefore, I am doing nothing that has not been done before, it would be as well to accept this honour which fortune offers. For even though his desire may last only until he has had his way, I shall be his wife in the eyes of God all the same. But if I reject him with scorn, I see that he will wickedly force me in the end, and I shall be dishonoured and universally blamed. For who could know how innocently I have come into this predicament? What reasoning could be strong enough to persuade my parents and others that this gentleman has entered my room without my consent?"

'All these reflections I turned over in my mind in a single moment. What is more, Don Ferdinand's oaths, the witnesses he invoked, the tears he shed and, finally, his charm and good looks began to incline me forcibly to a course which proved to be my undoing. For all this together with the many signs of true love he gave me were enough to conquer any heart, even one as independent and modest as mine.

'I called my maid to add her earthly witness to Heaven's. Don Ferdinand repeated and confirmed his oaths, calling on yet more saints, and invoking innumerable curses on himself should he break his promise. The tears came once more to his eyes, and he sighed deeply. He clasped me more firmly in his arms, which had never let me go. Whereafter, when my maid had left the room, I ceased to be a maid and he became a perfidious traitor.

'Day followed on the night of my undoing, but not so fast, I think, as Don Ferdinand desired. For once the appetite is satisfied man's greatest desire is to escape. This I say because Don Ferdinand hurriedly departed with the aid of my maid – it was she who had brought him in – even before it was light in the street. As he took his leave he promised me, though with less ardour than when he came in, that I could rely on his faith and on his oaths; and as further confirmation of his words he took a fine ring from his finger and put it on mine. Finally he left, and I remained, whether sad or glad I do not know. But of one thing I am certain: I was troubled and anxious, and almost beside myself at this strange event. And either I had not the heart, or I forgot, to scold my maid for her treachery in hiding Don Ferdinand in my room; for I had not yet made up my mind if the events of the night had been good or bad.

I told Don Ferdinand, however, as he departed, that he could come to me on other nights in the same way, until such time as he wished the marriage to be made public, for I was now his. He came on the following night, but never again; and for more than a month I tried in vain to see him in the street or at church, till I grew tired of fruitless waiting; for I knew that he was in the town and on most days went hunting. He was very fond of the sport.

'Indeed, these were sad, melancholy days for me, and I began to doubt, even to deny, his fidelity. I remember that I gave my maid the scolding for her presumption which she had escaped before. I had to control my tears and compose my looks for fear my parents might ask me what was making me unhappy, and I be obliged to invent a lie. But a moment arrived when my caution and delicacy came to an end, when I lost patience and my secret thoughts escaped me. This was when I heard in the town some days later that Don Ferdinand had married in the near-by city a young lady of extreme beauty and very noble family, though not so rich that her dowry could justify so great a match. Her name was said to be Lucinda, and various astonishing details were told about the wedding.'

On hearing Lucinda's name Cardenio only shrugged his shoulders, bowed his head, bit his lips and frowned. But soon a flood of tears burst from his eyes. Dorothea did not pause in her story, however, but continued:

'When I heard this sad news, so far was my heart from freezing that in my burning rage I could scarcely prevent myself from rushing into the streets and proclaiming the treacherous wrong he had done me. But my fury was assuaged for a while by a plan which I put into effect that very night. I borrowed the dress I am now wearing from a shepherd in my father's service. I told him my troubles, and asked him to come with me to the city where I heard that my enemy was. He first took me to task for my rashness and decried my plan. But when he saw that I was resolved, he offered to accompany me, as he said, to the end of the world. Then I packed some of my own clothes, some jewels and some money, in a pillow-case – against any eventuality; and in the silence of the night, without telling my treacherous maid, I left my home with my servant, my mind full of anxiety, and set out for the city on foot. For, though I could not prevent what had been done, I was determined at least to demand of Don Ferdinand how his conscience had allowed him to do it.

'I was two and a half days on the way, and when I got to the city I asked for the house of Lucinda's parents. The first man whom I questioned told me more than I wanted to hear. He pointed out the house and informed me of all that had happened at their daughter's betrothal. It was such common knowledge in the city that all the gossips were discussing it. He told me that on the night of the betrothal, after the bride had given her consent, she had fallen into a deep faint, and that when the bridegroom had loosened her dress to give her air, he had found in her breast a letter written in her own hand. It declared that she could not be Don Ferdinand's wife, for she was already married to Cardenio; who, this person told me, was a noble gentleman of that city. If she had said Yes to Don Ferdinand, it continued, it was only so as not to disobey her parents. And the letter concluded by saying that she intended to kill herself at the end of the ceremony, and gave her reasons for ending her life. All this, they say, was confirmed when they found a dagger somewhere in her clothing. Don Ferdinand was so enraged at finding himself deluded, mocked, and slighted that he attacked her before she came out of her faint, trying to stab her with the dagger which they had just found on her; and he would have succeeded if her parents and the witnesses had not prevented him. It was said that Don Ferdinand fled instantly, and that Lucinda did not recover from her faint till the next day, when she told her parents that she was in truth the wife of that Cardenio I spoke of. I learnt too that this Cardenio was said to have been present at the ceremony, and that when he saw her married, which he had never supposed she could be, he had rushed from the city in despair, leaving a letter declaring the wrong Lucinda had done him and his resolution to fly from mankind for ever.

'All this was a matter of public discussions throughout the city. Everyone was talking about it, and they gossiped even more when they heard that Lucinda was missing from her parents' house; that she could not be discovered in the town; that her parents had almost gone out of their minds and did not know what to do to find her. This news gave me some hope. For I was gladder not to have found

Don Ferdinand than to have found him married, since it seemed that all possibility of redress was not yet closed to me. I thought that Heaven might have prevented this second marriage in order to show him his duty to the first and to make him realize that, as a Christian, he was more firmly bound by his conscience than by worldly considerations. I turned all these thoughts over in my mind and got some consolation, though no comfort, from inventing wan and distant hopes to sustain my life, which is now abhorrent to me.

'I was still in the city, and did not know what to do since I could not find Don Ferdinand. Then one day I heard a public crier announcing that a large reward would be paid to anyone finding me, and describing my person and the very clothes I was wearing. I even heard a rumour that I had eloped with the shepherd who had escorted me from home. It stung me to the quick to find my reputation fallen so low. For I had not only lost it by coming away, but, even worse, by my choice of so low and unworthy a companion. The instant I heard the crier I left the city with my servant, who was already showing signs of wavering in his promised fidelity; and that night through fear of being discovered we took refuge in the remotest part of these mountains.

'But one evil calls down another, as they say, and the end of one disaster is often the beginning of a worse. So it was in my case. For, once we were alone in these wilds, my good servant, till then faithful and reliable, tried to take advantage of the opportunity which that wild spot appeared to offer him and, prompted by brutishness rather than by my beauty, lost all respect and made shameless love to me. Then, when I answered him with just contempt, he ceased the entreaties by which he had at first thought to gain his will, and tried to use force. But just Heaven, which seldom or never fails to favour virtue, so favoured mine, that despite my feeble strength I was easily able to force him back over the edge of a precipice. Whether I left him dead or alive I do not know. Then I fled with more speed than might have been expected from my fright and exhaustion, and made my way into these mountains, with no other thought or plan than to hide from my father and anyone he might send to seek me.

'I do not know how many months I had been here when I found

a herdsman who took me as his servant to a village in the heart of this range. I have worked for him as a shepherd all this time, trying always to keep out in the fields so as to conceal this hair of mine, which you have now so unexpectedly discovered. All my anxieties and precautions, however, were in vain, for my master got to know that I was not a man, and conceived the same wicked idea as my servant. But as fate does not always find an immediate remedy for every ill, I found no precipice or cliff to throw my master down, as I had my servant. And so I thought it would be less unpleasant to leave him and hide in these wilds again, than to try my strength or my protests against him. So, as I said, I took to the mountains once more, to seek a place where I can implore Heaven undisturbed with sighs and tears to take pity on my plight, and to give me grace and strength to escape from it; or else to die among these wastes and leave no memory of this miserable creature, who has so innocently given men cause to speak ill of her, in her own district and abroad.'

Chapter XXIX. *Of the ingenious plan contrived to extricate our enamoured Knight from the very severe Penance he had set himself.*

'THIS, gentlemen, is the true story of my tragedy. Judge for yourselves whether my sighs, my protests and my tears were not more than justified. Now that you know the nature of my misfortune you will see that all consolation is vain, since there is no possible cure. I only beg of you one favour, which you may easily grant: to advise me where I can live in safety, free from my present fears and from the dread of being discovered. For although I know that my parents love me so much that they would give me a kind welcome, I am so overwhelmed by shame at the mere thought of appearing in their presence, so different from the daughter they had supposed me, that I think it would be the lesser evil to banish myself for ever from their sight. Rather that than look them in the face, and know their thoughts. For they will consider that I have lost the honour they had the right to expect of me.'

She fell silent, her blushes clearly showing her grief and shame, and her hearers' minds were filled with pity and wonder at her misfortunes. Then, just as the priest was about to offer her consolation and advice, Cardenio forestalled him by saying:

'Then, lady, you are the fair Dorothea, the only daughter of the rich Clenardo?'

Dorothea was startled to hear her father's name spoken by such a miserable-looking creature – for, as we have already said, Cardenio was in rags.

'Who are you, my friend,' she asked, 'that know my father's name? For I have not mentioned it till now, if I remember rightly, in the whole story of my misfortune.'

'I am that unfortunate Cardenio,' he answered, 'whom, as you said, lady, Lucinda declared to be her husband. I am the hapless Cardenio, reduced to my present state by that same man who brought you to the condition you are in. Ragged, naked, comfortless and, what is worse, out of my mind. For I am sane only in the brief intervals that Heaven grants me. I, Dorothea, was witness of Ferdinand's crime and waited to hear that Yes with which Lucinda declared herself his wife. I had not the courage to see what would come of her fainting, or what became of the letter which was found in her breast. For my heart could not bear to witness so many disasters all together. So I rushed headlong from the house, only leaving a letter with my host to be put into Lucinda's hands. Here I came to these wastes with the intention of bringing my days to an end, for from that moment I loathed life as a mortal enemy. But fate has refused to end my existence and deprived me only of reason, perhaps to preserve me for my good fortune in meeting you. If your story is true, however – as I believe it is – Heaven, perhaps, has in store for us both a better ending to our misfortunes than we suppose. For, since Lucinda is mine and therefore unable to marry Don Ferdinand, as she has so publicly declared, and as he is yours and so also unable to marry, we may yet hope that Heaven will restore to us our own partners; for nothing is irretrievably lost. Since we have this comfort, then, which springs from no very distant hopes or wild imaginings, I beg you, lady, to take fresh courage, as I intend to. Let us adapt ourselves to the expectation of better fortune. For I swear to you, as a Christian gentleman, that I will not forsake you till I see you Don Ferdinand's wife; and if argument cannot bring him to acknowledge his duty to you, I will use my gentleman's privilege and duly challenge him for the wrong he has done you. I will take no account of the injuries he has done me, but leave Heaven to avenge them, whilst I revenge yours here on earth.'

Dorothea was dumbfounded by Cardenio's speech. She did not know how to thank him, and tried to kiss his feet; but Cardenio would not allow her. The priest replied for himself and for her by approving Cardenio's generous determination. But he most earnestly begged, advised and urged them to come to his village, and there provide themselves with all the things they needed. And there too, he said, they could decide on their best course of action : either to search for Don Ferdinand, or to take Dorothea to her parents, or to do anything else which might seem proper. Cardenio and Dorothea thanked him and accepted his offer.

The barber, who had listened in silent amazement to all this, then made a courteous speech, offering no less generously than the priest to do them any service he could. At the same time he told them briefly what had brought the priest and himself there, described Don Quixote's strange madness, and informed them that they were waiting for his squire, who had gone to look for him. Then, like a dream, Cardenio's quarrel with Don Quixote came back into his memory, and he described it to the others, although he could not tell them the cause of the dispute.

At that moment they heard shouts, which they recognized as Sancho Panza's. For he had not found them where he had left them, and was calling out after them at the top of his voice. They went to meet him, and asked him after Don Quixote. He answered that he had found him naked except for his shirt, lean, sallow and half dead with hunger, sighing for his lady Dulcinea. He had told him of her commands that he should leave that place and come to El Toboso, where she was waiting for him. But he had replied that he was determined not to appear in her beauteous presence until he had done deeds worthy of her favour. If that went on much longer, said Sancho, there was a danger that he might never become an Emperor, as he was in honour bound to do, nor even an Archbishop, which was the least he could be. Therefore they must think out a means of getting him away. The priest replied that he had no need to worry, for they would bring him with them, willy-nilly. Then he told Cardenio and Dorothea of the plan they had thought out for curing

Don Quixote, or at least for getting him home. Dorothea then observed that she could play the damsel in distress better than the barber and, what was more, she had a dress with her in which she could do it to the life. They could rely on her to act the part and do all that was necessary. For she had read many books of chivalry, and knew the style in which afflicted maidens were accustomed to beg their boons of knights errant.

'There there is nothing more we need,' said the priest. 'Let us get to work at once. For there is no doubt that luck is in our favour. It has unexpectedly begun to offer you, my friends, a little hope of better things, and made this job of ours easier as well.'

Then Dorothea took a handsome woollen dress and a cloak of fine green cloth out of her bundle, and out of a jewel-box a necklace and other jewels. These she put on, and was instantly transformed into a rich and grand lady. All these things and more, as has already been said, she had brought from home in case she should need them, but had had no use for them till then. Her gracefulness, her elegance, and her loveliness charmed them all, and showed up Don Ferdinand's lack of taste in deserting such a beauty. But most admiring of all was Sancho Panza, who thought that he had never seen so lovely a creature in all the days of his life – and indeed he had not. He asked the priest most insistently to tell him who this beautiful lady was, and what she was looking for in those wild parts.

'This beautiful lady, brother Sancho,' replied the priest, 'is, to be very brief, heiress in the direct male line of the great Kingdom of Micomicon. She has come to seek your master to beg of him a boon, which is to redress a wrong or injury which a wicked giant has done her. For, thanks to your master's reputation as a brave knight throughout all the known world, this princess has come from Guinea in quest of him.'

'She's been lucky to find him,' exclaimed Sancho Panza. 'And she'll be even luckier if my master is so fortunate as to undo that injury, and redress that wrong, and kill that son of a whore – I mean that giant you mentioned, sir. And he'll kill him if he finds him, unless he's a phantom; for my master has no power at all against phantoms. But there's one thing I particularly beg of you, Master Priest. Advise my master to marry this princess right off, sir, so that he doesn't take it into his head to be an Archbishop, as I very much fear he may. Then he'll be incapable of taking Archbishop's orders, and he'll easily come to his Empire, and I shall get everything I want. For I've thought the matter over, and I've figured it out that it won't suit me for my master to be an Archbishop. For I'm no good for the Church, you see, being a married man; and going about getting dispensations to let me hold a church living, seeing that I have a wife and children, would be an endless job. So it all depends on my master marrying this lady straight away, sir – I don't know her name yet, so I can't call her by it.'

'Her name,' replied the priest, 'is Princess Micomicona, as obviously it would be since her kingdom is called Micomicon.'

'Of course,' replied Sancho. 'I've known plenty of men take their titles and surnames from the places they live in – people like Pedro de Alcala, Juan de Ubeda, and Diego de Valladolid. The custom must be the same over there in Guinea, and the queens there take their names from their kingdoms.'

'Yes, you must be right,' said the priest, 'and in this matter of your master's marrying, I will do everything in my power.'

Sancho was content with his assurance; and the priest was amazed at his simplicity, and at the hold these absurdities of his master's had on his imagination. For he seemed seriously to believe that Don Quixote would become an Emperor.

By this time Dorothea had mounted the priest's mule, and the barber had fixed his ox tail beard to his chin. So they told Sancho to guide them to Don Quixote, warning him not to say that he knew the priest or the barber, because the whole matter of his master's becoming an Emperor hung on their not being recognized. Neither Cardenio nor the priest would go with them. For Cardenio was afraid that the sight of him might remind Don Quixote of their quarrel, and the priest did not consider his own presence necessary for the moment. So they let the others ride ahead, and followed slowly on foot. The priest, however, could not forbear instructing Dorothea in the part she had to play. But she said that there was no need for him to worry, for she would conform in every way to the details prescribed in books of chivalry. They had gone little more than two miles when they caught sight of Don Quixote among a maze of rocks, dressed now, but without his armour. Sancho pointed him out to Dorothea, who immediately whipped on her palfrey, followed by the well-bearded barber. When they reached the knight, the squire leapt from his mule to take Dorothea in his arms; and she dismounted with great sprightliness and fell on her knees at Don Quixote's feet. From which position, despite his efforts to raise her, she addressed him in this fashion:

'I will not arise from here, valorous and courageous knight, until your goodness and courtesy grant me a boon, which will redound to the honour and glory of your person and to the advantage of the most disconsolate and wronged damsel beneath the sun. For if the valour of your mighty arm corresponds to the report of your immortal fame, you are obliged to protect this luckless wight who comes from a far country, attracted by the odour of your fame, to seek from you a remedy for her misfortunes.'

'I will not give you a word in answer, beauteous lady,' replied Don Quixote, 'nor hear anything more of your plight till you rise from the ground.'

'I will not rise, sir,' replied the afflicted damsel, 'ere of your courtesy you have granted me the boon I crave.'

'I grant it freely,' replied Don Quixote, 'provided my compliance be not to the disservice or prejudice of my King, my country, or of that lady who holds the key of my heart and liberty.'

'It is not to the disservice or prejudice of any of these, my dear sir,' replied the sorrowing damsel.

At this point Sancho Panza put his lips to his master's ear, and whispered very softly: 'Your worship can easily grant her the boon she begs. It's only a trifle – just to kill a great giant. And the lady herself is the high and mighty princess Micomicona, Queen of the great Kingdom of Micomicon in Ethiopia.'

'Whoever she may be,' replied Don Quixote, 'I shall act as my duty and my conscience dictate, and in obedience to the rules of my profession.' And turning once more to the maiden, he said: 'Fairest lady, arise, for I grant you whatever boon you would ask of me.'

'What I ask,' said the damsel, 'is that, of your magnanimity, you shall come with me instantly where I shall lead you; and that you promise me to engage in no other adventure or enterprise till you have avenged me on a traitor who has usurped my kingdom in despite of all law, human or divine.'

'I repeat that I grant your request,' replied Don Quixote; 'and so, lady, from henceforth you may cast off the melancholy which oppresses you, and allow your fainting hopes to recover new strength and courage. For, with the help of God and my right arm, you shall soon see yourself restored to your kingdom, and seated on the throne of your ancient and high estate, in despite and defiance of all rogues who would oppose it. Now, hands to the wheel! For in delay, it is said, lies danger.'

The distressed damsel struggled persistently to kiss his hands; but Don Quixote, who was in every respect a civil and courteous knight, refused to allow her. On the contrary, he forced her to rise, and embraced her most civilly and courteously. Then he bade Sancho look to Rocinante's girths, and arm him with all speed. The squire took down his armour, which was hanging from a tree like a trophy, looked to the girths and speedily armed his master, who cried as soon as he saw himself in armour: 'Let us go from hence, in God's name, to succour this great lady.'

The barber was still on his knees, taking great care to hide his laughter and to keep his beard from falling off. For their fine plan might miscarry if it fell. But seeing the boon already granted and Don Quixote diligently preparing to fulfil his promise, he got up and took his lady by the other hand, the two of them helping her on to her mule. Then Don Quixote mounted Rocinante, and the barber settled on his mount, leaving Sancho on foot; which made him grieve afresh for the loss of Dapple, whom he now missed. But he bore it all cheerfully, since now his master seemed to be on the way, and just on the very point of becoming Emperor. For Sancho had not the slightest doubt that he would marry the Princess and become at least King of Micomicon. One thought alone distressed him: that this kingdom was in Negro country, and that the people he would have for subjects would all be black. But he at once invented a good remedy for this, saying to himself: 'What do I care if my vassals are black? I've only to put them on board ship and bring them to Spain, where I shall be able to sell them, and be paid in cash. Then with the money I can buy a title or a post on which I can live at my ease for all the days of my life. I've got eyes in my head, and I'm fly enough to sell ten thousand subjects in the winking of an eye – or thirty thousand even. I'll shift 'em, the little ones with big ones, or any other way I can. Never mind how black they start,

I'll turn them into whites or yellows. I think I know how to lick my own fingers.' With these thoughts he trudged on in such good spirits that he forgot the fatigue of going on foot.

Cardenio and the priest had watched all that passed from behind some brambles, and could think of no pretext for joining the company. But the priest, who was a great schemer, presently invented one. With a pair of scissors, which he carried in a case, he hastily cut off Cardenio's beard and dressed him in his own grey jacket and black cape, himself remaining in his breeches and doublet. This so transformed Cardenio's appearance that he would not have known himself if he had looked in a mirror. This done, although the others had gone ahead while they were changing clothes, they had no difficulty in gaining the main road before them. For the thickets and broken paths thereabouts did not allow horsemen to go as quickly as men on foot. In fact they took up their position on the plain, where the pass comes down from the mountains. When Don Quixote and his comrades emerged, the priest stared at the knight for some time, pretending that he was trying to recognize him. Then, after standing for some time gazing at him, he ran up to him with open arms, crying:

'Welcome, mirror of chivalry, my good compatriot Don Quixote de la Mancha, flower and cream of gallantry, protector and aid of the needy, quintessence of knight errantry.'

And as he spoke he clasped Don Quixote's left knee. The knight was alarmed at the man's appearance and at his language, and surveyed him carefully. When he finally recognized him too, he was still amazed to see him, but made a great effort to dismount. The priest, however, would not allow him to, which caused Don Quixote to exclaim:

'Permit me, Master Priest. It is not right that I should be mounted, and so reverend a person as your worship should be on foot.'

'On no account will I allow you,' said the priest. 'Remain mounted, since on horseback it was that your Mightiness performed deeds and exploits unparalleled in our age. I am but an unworthy priest, and it shall be enough for me to ride muleback behind one of those gentlemen of your company, if they are agreeable. And truly I shall count myself mounted on the steed Pegasus, or on the zebra or courser of the famous Moor Muzaraque, who lies to this day beneath a spell on the great hill of Zulema, not far from the grand Compluto ...'

'I did not think of that, my dear Master Priest,' replied Don Quixote; 'but I know that my lady the Princess will be delighted, as a favour to me, to order her squire to give you the saddle of his mule. For he can ride on the crupper if the beast will stand it.'

'Yes, the beast will stand it, I think,' replied the Princess; 'and I am sure that there will be no need to command my squire, for he is too courteous and well-bred to suffer an ecclesiastic to go on foot when he may ride.'

'That's right,' replied the barber. And quickly getting down, he offered the priest the saddle, which he took without much pressing. But unfortunately as the barber was getting up behind, the mule, which was a hired one – and that is as much as to say that it was a bad beast – reared its hind quarters and gave two such kicks, that if they had caught Master Nicholas on the chest or on the head, he would have cursed the day he started rambling after Don Quixote. As it was he fell down in a fright, with so little care for his beard that it came off. Now when he found that he had lost it he could not think what to do except to clasp both hands hurriedly to his face, and cry out that his jaw was broken. Then, seeing all that mass of beard lying without jaws or blood some distance away from the fallen squire's face, Don Quixote exclaimed: 'Good Heavens! This is a great miracle! His beard has been torn as clean from his face as if he had been shaved.'

The priest saw the danger of his plot being discovered. So he instantly ran to the beard and to Master Nicholas, who was still moaning. He quickly clasped the barber's head to his chest, and stuck the beard on in a twinkling, mumbling some words over him, which he said were an infallible charm for refixing beards, as they should see. Then, when it was fixed, he moved away, leaving the squire as well bearded and as sound as before. Don Quixote was vastly amazed at this, and begged the priest to teach him the charm when he had the time. For he was convinced that its efficacy must extend beyond the mere refixing of beards, since clearly the flesh must have been all lacerated and bloody when the beard was torn out. So, as the spell had effected a complete cure it must be good for more than just beards.

'It is,' said the priest, and promised to teach it him at the first opportunity.

They agreed that the priest should ride first, and after him the three of them take turns till they came to the inn, which must have been six miles off. So three of them being now mounted – Don Quixote, the Princess, and the priest – and three on foot – Cardenio, the barber and Sancho Panza – Don Quixote addressed the damsel: 'Lead on, your Highness, in whatever direction you will.'

But before she could reply, the priest put in: 'To what kingdom will your ladyship guide us? Is it perhaps to Micomicon? It must be so surely, or I know very little about kingdoms.'

And Dorothea was quick-witted enough to know that she had to agree, which she did.

'Yes, sir, towards that land my way lies.'

'If that is so,' said the priest, 'we have to pass through my village. From there your worship will take the route for Cartagena, where, if you are fortunate, you may find a ship. Then, if you have a favourable wind, a calm sea and no storms, in less than nine years you will be in sight of the great Meona lake, I mean the Meotis – from which it is little more than a hundred days' journey to your Highness's kingdom.'

'You are mistaken, my good sir,' said she. 'For I left less than two years ago, and have had bad weather all the way. But for all that I am here and have seen the person I so ardently desired to see – that is my lord Don Quixote de la Mancha. His renown came to my ears the moment I set foot in Spain, and impelled me to seek him in order to commend myself to his courtesy and entrust my just cause to the strength of his invincible arm.'

'No more. Cease your praises!' cried Don Quixote at this juncture. 'I hate any kind of flattery and, although this may not be flattery, still such compliments offend my chaste ears. All that I can say, my lady, is that, whether I have valour or no, such as I have or have not shall be employed in your service, even to the death. But leaving this matter till its due time, I beg you to tell me, Master Priest, what has brought you into these parts, alone like this, without attendants, and so thinly clad that you alarm me?'

'I will reply briefly,' answered the priest. 'I must tell you, sir, that I was travelling to Seville with Master Nicholas, our barber and

I

friend, to collect some money sent me by a relative of mine, who settled in the Indies long ago. And it was no small sum either, but more than sixty thousand silver dollars, which is a tidy bit. Now as we were travelling in these parts yesterday we were attacked by four highwaymen, who stripped us to our very beards, so that the barber thought it wise to put on a false one. And as for this young man here' – pointing to Cardenio – 'he was quite transformed. The strange thing is that it is well known about here that the men who robbed us are galley-slaves. They are said to have been set free almost at this very spot, by a man so very valiant that he released them despite the sergeant and the guards. He must either be out of his senses or as great a rogue as they. He can have no soul or conscience to have let the wolf out amongst the sheep, the fox amongst the hens, the fly amidst the honey. For he has deliberately defrauded justice, and rebelled against his King and natural lord, for he acted against his legal authority. He deliberately robbed the galleys of their hands, I tell you, and alarmed the Holy Brotherhood, who have been undisturbed for many years. In short, he has done a deed by which his body will gain nothing and his soul may be lost.'

Sancho had told the priest and the barber the adventure of the galley-slaves, which his master had concluded with so much glory; and the priest laid it on so thick in telling his story to see what Don Quixote would do or say. The knight changed colour at every word, and dared not confess that he had been those good people's liberator.

'Well,' said the priest, 'those were the men who robbed us. May God, in his mercy, pardon the man who prevented their going to the punishment they deserved.'

Chapter XXX. *Of the fair Dorothea's cleverness and other pleasant and amusing matters.*

SCARCELY had the priest finished when Sancho cried out: 'It was my master, Sir Priest, who did that deed. I swear it was. And not for want of my telling him beforehand. I warned him to look out what he was doing. I said it was a sin to set them at liberty. For they were all going to the galleys because they were very great villains.'

'Blockhead!' broke in Don Quixote. 'It is no concern or duty of knights errant to investigate whether the distressed, chained, and oppressed persons they meet on the roads are brought to that pass, or suffer that anguish, for their crimes or for their whims. Their only task is to succour them because they are in distress, taking account of their sufferings and not of their villainies. I met some mournful, miserable wretches strung together like beads on a rosary, and did for them what my duty requires. The rest is no affair of mine. If anyone objects, saving Master Priest's holy dignity and his reverend person, I say that he knows very little of the matter of chivalry, and that he lies like the son of a whore and a bastard. And I will prove it on him with my sword, which shall answer him at greater length.'

As he said this he steadied himself in his stirrups and pulled down his head-piece. For he carried the barber's basin, which was Mambrino's helmet in his estimation, hanging at his saddle-bow, till such time as the damage which the galley-slaves had done to it could be repaired.

Dorothea was too quick and intelligent not to understand Don Quixote's crazy humour. She saw that everyone except Sancho Panza was making fun of him, and was anxious not to be left out. So, seeing him in such a rage, she said to him:

'Remember, Sir Knight, the boon your worship granted me, and that you are bound by it not to interpose in any other adventure, however urgent it may be. Calm your spirit, therefore. For if the worthy priest had known that it was by that unconquered arm that the galley-slaves were freed, he would have put three stitches through his lips, or even bitten his tongue three times, rather than have uttered a word which might redound to your worship's disparagement.'

'I swear I would,' said the priest. 'I would even have pulled out one of my moustaches.'

'I will be silent, my dear lady,' said Don Quixote, 'and restrain the just anger which has risen in my breast. I will remain quiet and peaceful till I have accomplished the promised boon for you. But, to reward this resolution of mine, I beg you to tell me – if it does not cause you too much pain – the nature of your distress, and the number, names and qualities of the persons on whom I have to take dire, satisfactory and complete revenge.'

'I will do so with all my heart,' replied Dorothea, 'if it will not weary you to hear of griefs and misfortunes.'

'It will not weary me, my lady,' replied Don Quixote.

To which Dorothea replied: 'Since that is so, then give me your attention, your worships.'

With that Cardenio and the barber caught up with her, wishing to hear what sort of story the ingenious Dorothea would invent; and Sancho, who was as much taken in by her as was his master, did the same. Then, settling comfortably into her saddle, after a preliminary cough and other preparatory gestures, she began her story with considerable dash:

'First, gentlemen, you must know that my name is ...' And here she stopped a moment because she had forgotten the name the priest had given her. But he saw what had happened and rushed to her aid, saying:

'It is no wonder, my lady, that your Highness is confused and embarrassed at telling your misfortunes. For affliction often impairs the memory to such an extent that miserable sufferers cannot even remember their own names, as has happened in the case of your exalted Ladyship, who has forgotten that she is the princess Micomicona, lawful heiress to the great Kingdom of Micomicon. Now with this reminder your Highness will be able to call to your distracted memory all that you wish to tell us.'

'You are right,' replied the damsel. 'From now on I think I shall be in no need of prompting, and I shall bring my true story to its proper conclusion. To continue then: My father, King Tinacrio the Sage, was very skilled in what are called the magic arts, and foresaw by his science that my mother, Queen Jaramilla, would die before him, and that very soon afterwards he too would die, and I be left an orphan. But this, he would say, disturbed him less than the certain knowledge that a monstrous giant, ruler of a large island almost bordering on our kingdom, would attack me. This giant bears the name of Pandafilando of the Frowning Eye – for it is a well-known fact that, although his eyes are straight and set in the proper place, he always squints as if he were cross-eyed. This he does out of ill-nature and to strike fear and dread into all on whom he looks. Well, as I told you, my father knew that once this giant heard that I was left an orphan he would invade my kingdom with a powerful army, and take it all from me, not leaving me so much as a little village to retire to. And though he knew that I could avert all this ruin and misfortune by marrying the giant, my father thought it very unlikely that I should ever consent to such an ill-assorted match. He was quite right, for I have never so much as thought of marrying that giant, or any other, however huge and monstrous. My father's counsel was: not to stay after his death nor put up any defence against Pandafilando's invasion of my kingdom, for that would be my ruin; but to leave the kingdom voluntarily to him, if I wished to avoid the death and total destruction of my good and loyal subjects, since I should be unable to defend myself against the giant's hellish power. He bade me instantly set out with some of my subjects for Spain, where I should find a relief for my troubles by meeting a knight errant, whose renown at that time would extend throughout the whole kingdom, and whose name, if I remember rightly, was to be Don Azote or Don Gigote.'

'Don Quixote he must have said,' put in Sancho Panza, 'otherwise called the Knight of the Sad Countenance.'

'You are right,' said Dorothea. 'He also said that he would be a tall, thin-faced man, and that he would have a dark brown mole with hair on it like bristles on his right side under his left shoulder, or somewhere thereabouts.'

Here Don Quixote said to his squire: 'Come, Sancho, help me to strip. I want to see if I am the knight this sage king spoke of in his prophecy.'

'Why should your worship want to take off your clothes?' asked Dorothea.

'To see if I have that mole your father spoke of,' replied Don Quixote.

'There's no reason to strip,' said Sancho. 'I know your worship has a mole just like that in the middle of your spine. It's a sign of strength.'

'That is enough,' said Dorothea; 'for there is no need to look into such trifles among friends, and whether it is on your shoulder or your spine scarcely matters. Enough that you have a mole; wherever it is, it is all the same flesh. No doubt my father was right in all respects. And I am right in commending myself to Don Quixote, for he it is my father meant. That is proved by his features and by the renown he bears not only in Spain but throughout La Mancha. For as soon as we landed at Osuna I heard so many tales of his exploits that my heart told me at once he was the knight I had come to seek.'

'But how, dear lady, did you come to land at Osuna,' asked Don Quixote, 'since it is not a seaport?'

But before Dorothea could reply, the priest put in: 'The lady princess surely means that after she landed at Malaga, the first place where she had news of your worship was Osuna.'

'That is what I meant,' said Dorothea.

'That clears things up,' said the priest. 'Will your Majesty continue?'

'There is no more to say,' replied Dorothea, 'except that finally I have had the good fortune to find the noble Don Quixote, and reckon myself now as good as Queen and Mistress of my whole Kingdom. For, of his courtesy and generosity, he has granted me my boon, and will follow me wherever I conduct him; which shall be into the presence of that Pandafilando of the Frowning Eye, that he may slay him and restore to me what this giant has so wrongfully usurped. All this will come to pass to the letter, for that is the prophecy of my good father, Tinacrio the Sage. He left it recorded too in Chaldean or Greek writing — I cannot read it — that if after beheading the giant this knight of the prophecy should wish to marry me, I should give myself to him without demur as his lawful wife, and grant him possession of my kingdom and my person.'

'What do you think, friend Sancho?' cried Don Quixote at this point. 'Do you hear that? Did I not tell you? See if we have not a kingdom to rule already, and a Queen to marry.'

'I swear you have,' said Sancho. 'Devil take the bastard who wouldn't marry as soon as Sir Pandafilando's windpipe's split! And she isn't a bad bit of goods, the Queen! I wish all the fleas in my bed were as good.'

At that he leapt into the air twice in sign of extreme delight. Then he ran to seize the bridle of Dorothea's mule and, making her stop, fell on his knees before her, beseeching her to give him her hands to kiss, in token that he took her for his Queen and Mistress. And not one of the party could help laughing at the master's madness and the man's simplicity. Dorothea held out her hands to him, and promised to make him a great lord in her kingdom, as soon as she should by the grace of Heaven recover it and enjoy it again. And Sancho thanked her in such language that they all burst out laughing afresh.

'That, gentlemen,' Dorothea went on, 'is my story. It only remains to tell you that of the attendants I brought with me out of my kingdom none but this well-bearded squire survives. All the rest were drowned in a great storm which struck us within sight of harbour. By a miracle he and I got ashore on a couple of planks; and indeed the whole course of my life has been one long miracle and mystery, as you will have noted. And if I have exaggerated in any way, or have not been as exact as I should be, remember what the reverend gentleman said at the beginning of my story. For perpetual and extreme hardships deprive the sufferer even of memory.'

'They will not rob me of mine, exalted and courageous lady,' said Don Quixote, 'however many I may endure in your service, and however great and unprecedented they may be. So once more I confirm the boon I have granted you, and swear to go with you to the end of the world, till I confront your fierce enemy; whose proud head, by the help of God and my strong arm, I mean to cut off with the edge of this ... I will not say good sword, thanks to Gines de Pasamonte, who carried mine off.' These last words he muttered under his breath, and then went on: 'When I have cut off his head and restored to you the peaceful possession of your kingdom, it shall rest with your own choice to dispose of your person in whatever manner you please. For, so long as my memory is engrossed, my heart captive and my mind enthralled by that ... I say no more; it is impossible that I could so much as think of marriage, even with the Phoenix.'

Sancho was so taken aback at his master's last words on the subject of not wishing to marry that he exclaimed in great fury:

'Good God, your worship! You must be out of your mind, I swear! How could there possibly be any doubt about marrying a grand princess like this one? Do you think fortune will offer you a stroke of luck like this round every corner? Can my lady Dulcinea possibly be more beautiful? Of course she isn't, not by half. I should say she isn't good enough to tie this lady's shoes. A poor chance I have of getting my countship if your worship goes fishing for dainties at the bottom of the sea. Marry her! Marry her at once, for the devil's sake, and lay hold of this kingdom, that's falling into your hands like a ripe cherry. And when you're a king, make me a marquis or a viceroy, and then to hell with the rest!'

When Don Quixote heard these blasphemies against his lady Dulcinea he could bear no more. So he raised his lance and, without word or warning, he dealt Sancho two such blows that he knocked him down. And if Dorothea had not called out to the knight to stop he would no doubt have taken his squire's life on the spot.

'Do you think, miserable villain,' asked Don Quixote after a while, 'that I must always let you pull me by the nose, and that there is to be nothing but sinning on your side and pardoning on mine? Do not think that, excommunicate rogue! For that you certainly are, for defaming the peerless Dulcinea. Do not you know, you clod, you ignominious vagabond, that but for the power she infuses into my arm I should not have the strength to kill a flea? Tell me, you viper-tongued villain, who do you think has conquered this kingdom and cut this giant's head off, and made you a marquis — for I take all this as an accomplished fact — if it is not the might of Dulcinea, employing my arm as the instrument of her exploits? She fights and conquers through me, and I live and breathe and have my life and being in her. You villain, you son of a whore! What ingratitude you show, seeing yourself raised up out of the dust of the earth to be a titled lord, and your only thanks for such a benefit is to malign the lady that bestowed it on you!'

Sancho was not too badly hurt to hear his master's reproaches. He got up rather hurriedly, ran behind Dorothea's palfrey, and addressed his master from there:

'Now think, sir, if your worship's determined not to marry this great princess, it's plain that the kingdom will not be yours. Now in that case what favours can you do me? That's what I'm complaining about. Marry this Queen, sir, once for all, now that we have her here, dropped down from heaven as it were. You can go back to my lady Dulcinea afterwards; for there have been plenty of kings in the world who have kept mistresses. As for the matter of beauty, it's no affair of mine. To tell you the truth, they both seem handsome to me, though I've never seen the lady Dulcinea.'

'What! You have never seen her, blasphemous traitor?' cried

Don Quixote. 'But have not you just brought me a message from her?'

'I mean that I didn't have time to observe the beauty of her fair features one by one,' said Sancho, 'but she looked all right to me on the whole.'

'Well, I pardon you now,' said Don Quixote, 'and you must forgive me the injury I have done you. For primary impulses are not within man's power to check.'

'So I see,' replied Sancho, 'and in me the need to talk is a primary impulse, and I can't help saying right off what comes to my tongue.'

'All the same,' said Don Quixote, 'watch what you say, Sancho, for the pitcher can go too often to the well ... I say no more.'

'Well, well,' replied Sancho, 'God's in heaven and sees all man's tricks. He'll judge which of us is wickeder, I for my bad words or your worship for your bad actions.'

'No more of that,' said Dorothea. 'Run, Sancho, kiss your master's hand, and beg his pardon. And from now on be more careful with your praises and slanders, and say nothing against this lady Tobosa, of whom all I know is that I am her humble servant. And put your trust in God that he will not fail to bring you to an estate where you can live like a prince.'

Sancho hung his head and begged his master for his hand, which Don Quixote gave him in all gravity. Then, when he had kissed it, the knight gave him his blessing, and bade him come ahead a little, for he had something to ask him and matters of great importance to discuss with him. Sancho obeyed, and once they were slightly in advance of the others Don Quixote said:

'Since your return I have had neither the time nor the opportunity to ask you for many details about the message you took and the answer you brought back. But now that chance has given us both time and opportunity, do not deny me the pleasure that your good news will give me.'

'Ask any questions you like, your worship,' replied Sancho, 'I'll get out of all of them as easily as I got in. But I beseech your worship not to be so vindictive in future.'

'Why do you say that, Sancho?' asked Don Quixote.

'The beating you gave me just now, you know,' replied Sancho, 'was because of the quarrel the Devil raised between us the other night, and not for what I said against my lady Dulcinea, whom I reverence like a holy relic. – Of course she's nothing of the sort – but I love her just because she belongs to your worship.'

'No more of this talk, Sancho, at your peril,' said Don Quixote, 'for it offends me. I pardoned you then, and you know the saying very well: Fresh sin, fresh penance!'

As they were talking they saw a man on an ass coming down the road, and when he got nearer they made him out to be a gipsy. But whenever Sancho Panza saw a donkey he followed it with his eyes and with his heart, and no sooner did he catch sight of the man than he knew that he was Gines de Pasamonte. Now this clue of the gipsy led him to recognize his ass; for it was his own Dapple which Pasamonte was riding. He had put on gipsy dress so as to be able to sell the ass unrecognized, speaking, as he did, the gipsy language and many others like a native. But Sancho knew him as soon as he saw him, and instantly shouted out:

'Gines, you thief! Let go my jewel! Let go my life! Don't rob me of my comfort! Let go my ass! Let go my treasure! Get out, you bastard! Get away, you thief! Give up what isn't yours!'

There was no need of all those words or curses, for Gines jumped down at the first, and took to his heels at a lively trot. In one second, in fact, he had disappeared from before their eyes. Sancho meanwhile ran up to his Dapple and embraced him, crying:

'How have you been, my dear, my darling Dapple, my darling companion?'

And all the time he kissed him as if he had been a human being. The ass stayed quiet and let Sancho caress him without answering a word. Then the others came up and congratulated the squire on recovering his beast, most of all Don Quixote, who said that he would not annul the draft for the three colts all the same. Sancho returned him thanks for this.

Whilst the pair of them were engaged in their conversation, the priest congratulated Dorothea on her ingenuity in telling her story, on its brevity and its close resemblance to the tales of knight errantry. She owned that she had often amused herself by reading them, but that she did not know where provinces and seaports lay, and so had said at a venture that she had landed at Osuna.

'I realized that,' said the priest. 'That was why I interrupted as I did, and put everything right. But is it not marvellous to see how easily this poor gentleman believes all these inventions and lies, simply because they are in the same style as the nonsense in his books?'

'It is,' said Cardenio. 'It is so strange and rare that I do not know whether anyone trying to invent such a character in fiction would have the genius to succeed.'

'There is another strange thing about it,' said the priest. 'If you talk to the good gentleman about anything that does not touch on his madness, far from talking nonsense, he speaks very rationally and shows a completely clear and calm understanding. In fact nobody would think him anything but a man of very sound judgement, unless he were to strike him on the subject of chivalries.'

While they were engaged in this conversation Don Quixote continued with his, saying to Sancho: 'Let us let bygones be bygones, friend Panza, and tell me now, forgetting all anger and rancour, where, how, and when did you find Dulcinea? What was she doing? What did you say to her? What did she answer? How did she look when she read my letter? Who copied it for you? Tell me every detail you think I should wish to know about the matter. Do not add or invent anything to please me, and please do not cut the tale short, for that will spoil my pleasure.'

'To tell you the truth, sir,' replied Sancho, 'no one copied the letter for me, because I had no letter with me.'

'Yes, it is just as you say,' replied Don Quixote. 'For I found I had the little note-book I wrote it in still in my possession two days after you had gone. It grieved me deeply, since I did not know what you would do when you found that you had not got the letter. I always thought that you would come back as soon as you missed it.'

'So I should have done,' replied Sancho, 'if I hadn't learnt it by heart when your worship read it to me. So that I repeated it to a parish clerk, who wrote it down exactly from my memory. He said he had never read as nice a letter in all the days of his life, although he had seen and read plenty of letters of excommunication.'

'Do you still remember it now, Sancho?' asked Don Quixote.

'No, sir,' replied Sancho. 'For as soon as I had said it to him, I saw it wouldn't be any more use, and let it out of my mind. If I remember anything at all it's that "*Suppressed*" – I mean "*sovereign-*

lady", and the ending: "*Yours till death, the Knight of the Sad Countenance*". And in between I put more than three hundred "*souls*", "*lives*" and "*dear eyes*".'

Chapter XXXI. *Of the delectable Conversation which passed between Don Quixote and Sancho Panza his squire, and other incidents.*

'ALL this does not displease me at all. Go on,' said Don Quixote. 'You got there; and what was that queen of beauty doing? I am sure that you found her stringing pearls, or embroidering a device with thread of gold for this, her captive knight.'

'No, she wasn't doing that,' replied Sancho, 'but winnowing a couple of bushels of wheat in her back yard.'

'Then you can be certain,' said Don Quixote, 'that the grains of that wheat turned to pearls at the touch of her hand. Did you observe, my friend, whether it was of the white or brown sort?'

'It was neither, but red,' replied Sancho.

'Then I promise you,' said Don Quixote, 'that, winnowed by her hands, it made the finest white bread. There can be no doubt of that. But go on. When you gave her my letter, did she kiss it? Did she put it on her head? Did she perform any ceremony worthy of such a letter? Or what did she do?'

'When I went up to give it to her,' said Sancho, 'she was in the middle of the job with a good lot of wheat in her sieve, and she said: "Put the letter down, friend, on that sack. I can't read it till I've finished sifting what I have here."'

'A wise lady,' said Don Quixote. 'That must have been so that she could read and enjoy it at her leisure. Go on, Sancho. And whilst she was about her task, what speech did she hold with you? What questions did she ask concerning me? And what did you reply? Come, tell me everything. Do not leave a drop in the inkhorn.'

'She didn't ask me anything,' said Sancho. 'But I told her how your worship was here doing your penance for her service, naked from the waist up, buried in all these mountains like a savage, sleeping on the ground, never eating bread off a table-cloth, nor combing your beard, and weeping and cursing your fate.'

'You spoke wrong in saying that I was cursing my fate,' said Don Quixote. 'On the contrary, I bless it, and shall bless it all the days of my life, for making me worthy of loving so high a lady as Dulcinea del Toboso.'

'So high,' answered Sancho, 'that I swear she's a good hand's breadth taller than I am.'

'How do you know that, Sancho?' asked Don Quixote. 'Did you measure yourself against her?'

'I did,' replied Sancho. 'Like this. I went to help her load a sack of corn on to an ass, and so got we very close together. That's how I noticed she was a good hand's breadth taller than I am.'

'But is it not true,' replied Don Quixote, 'that her great height is accompanied and adorned by a thousand million intellectual graces? One thing you cannot deny me, Sancho. When you stood close to her, did you not smell a spicy odour, an aromatic fragrance, something unutterably sweet to which I cannot give a name? I mean an essence or aroma, as if you were in some rare glover's shop?'

'All that I can say,' answered Sancho, 'is that I got a sniff of something rather mannish. It must have been because she was running with sweat from the hard work.'

'It would not be that,' replied Don Quixote. 'You must have had a cold or have smelt yourself. For well I know the scent of that rose among thorns, that lily of the field, that liquid ambergris.'

'It's quite possible,' replied Sancho, 'for very often there's that same smell about me that seemed to be coming from the lady Dulcinea. But it's not surprising, for one devil is like another.'

'Well, then,' continued Don Quixote, 'she has finished winnowing her corn and sent it to the mill. What did she do when she had read my letter?'

'She didn't read the letter,' said Sancho, 'for she said she couldn't read or write. She tore it up instead, and told me she wouldn't give it to anyone to read, so that her secrets shouldn't be known all over the village. She said it was quite enough that I had told her by word of mouth about your worship's love for her and about the extra-ordinary penance you had stayed behind to do for her sake. She ended up by telling me to tell your worship that she kissed your hands, and that she had far rather see you than write to you. So she begged and commanded you, at sight hereof, to leave these bushes and briars and stop doing these mad antics, and set out at once on the road for El Toboso, if more important business didn't prevent you; for she was most anxious to see your worship. She laughed a lot when I told her how you were called *the Knight of the Sad Countenance*. I asked her if that Basque of yours had been there. She said that he had, and that he was a very decent sort of man. I asked her about the galley-slaves too, but she said that she hadn't seen any of them yet.'

'So far so good,' said Don Quixote. 'But tell me, what jewel did she give you on your departure, in thanks for the news you brought her of me? For it is an ancient and time-worn custom among knights errant and their ladies to reward squires, damsels, or dwarfs who bring them news of their ladies or knights with some rich jewel in gratitude for their welcome news.'

'That's very likely, and I think it's a good custom. But they must have done that in the olden times, for nowadays the habit seems to be just to give them a bit of bread and cheese. That's what my lady Dulcinea gave me, anyhow, over the top of the yard wall when she said good-bye to me. And what's more, it was a sheep's-milk cheese.'

'She is generous in the extreme,' said Don Quixote; 'and, if she did not give you a gold jewel, it was no doubt only because she had not one there at hand to give you. But it is never too late. Gifts are still good after Easter. I will see her, and all shall be put right. But do you know what does astonish me, Sancho? You must have gone and returned through the air. For you have only taken three days travelling to El Toboso and back, and it is a good ninety miles. From which I conclude that the sage necromancer, who is my friend and looks after my affairs – for I certainly have such a friend, or I should not be a true knight errant – I say that this necromancer must have assisted you on your journey without your knowing it. For there are enchanters who have picked up a knight errant asleep in his bed, and next day, he will not know how or why, but he will wake up more than a thousand miles from the place where he went to sleep. If it were not for that, it would be impossible for knights errant to come to one another's aid in their perils, as they do at every turn. One of them, perhaps, is fighting in the Armenian mountains with some dragon or fierce monster, or with another knight. He is getting the worst of the battle, and is just at the point

of death. Then, when you least expect it, there appears another
knight, on a cloud or in a chariot of fire. This friend, who was the
moment before in England, comes to his assistance, saves his life,
and is back that night in his own lodging, enjoying his supper.
Very often the distance from the one place to the other is six or
seven thousand miles. Now all this is effected by the skill and wisdom of these sage enchanters who watch over valorous knights.
So, friend Sancho, I do not find it difficult to believe that you made
the journey to and from El Toboso in so short a time; since, as I
have said, some friendly sage must have carried you through the
air without your knowing it.'

'That may be so,' said Sancho, 'for certainly Rocinante went like
a gipsy's ass with quicksilver in its ears.'

'Quicksilver!' exclaimed Don Quixote. 'And a legion of devils
besides, for they are the sort of gentry who travel – and make others
travel – tirelessly, as much as they please. But, to leave the subject,
what do you think I ought to do about my lady's command to go
and see her? For, although I am clearly obliged to fulfil her behests,
I find myself prevented by the boon I have granted to the Princess
in whose company we are, and the law of chivalry compels me to
put my oath before my pleasure. On the one hand I am perplexed
and harassed by the desire to see my lady; on the other incited and
summoned by my pledged faith and the glory I shall gain in this
enterprise. What I propose to do is to press on and get quickly to
the place where this giant is. Then, when I get there, I will cut off
his head, restore the Princess peacefully to her throne, and instantly
return to behold the light which illumines my senses. I will offer her
such excuses that she will come to approve my delay. For she will
see that it all redounds to her greater glory and fame, since everything which I have achieved, am achieving, and shall achieve by
force of arms in this life proceeds wholly from her favour and from
my being her knight.'

'Oh dear!' cried Sancho. 'Your worship must be downright
crazy! Tell me, sir, do you mean to take the journey for nothing,
and let a rich and princely marriage, with a kingdom for dowry, slip
through your fingers? They say that her country's more than sixty
thousand miles round, and full of everything you want to support
human life. I've heard that it's bigger than Portugal and Castile put

together. Don't talk any more, for Heaven's sake. You ought to be ashamed of what you've said. Take my advice, please, and marry her straight away, in the first village where there's a priest. Or else there is our own priest here, who'll do the job a treat. I'm old enough, mind you, to offer advice, and what I advise you now fits the case like a glove. For a bird in the hand is worth two in the bush, and he who had good and chose bad must not be vexed for the ill he had.'

'Look you, Sancho,' replied Don Quixote, 'if you are advising me to marry, so that I may be king when I have killed the giant, and have the means of doing you favours and fulfilling my promise to you, I would inform you that I can very easily gratify your wishes without marrying. For I will make it a condition before I go into the battle that when I come off victorious, they shall give me part of the kingdom which I can bestow on anyone I will, even though I do not marry her. And when I get it, whom do you think I shall give it to but you?'

'That's fair enough,' replied Sancho. 'But take good care, your worship, to choose a piece on the coast, so that if I don't like the life I can put my black subjects on board ship, and do what I said with them. Don't trouble to go and see my lady Dulcinea for the time being, but go and kill the giant, and let's settle that business. For I swear to God I think it'll bring us great honour and profit.'

'Yes, Sancho,' said Don Quixote, 'you are in the right, and I will take your advice about going with the Princess before I visit Dulcinea. But I warn you to say nothing to anyone about what we have been discussing and arranging, not even to our companions. For since Dulcinea is so shy that she does not want her feelings known, it would not be right for me, or for anyone acting for me, to reveal them.'

'But if that's the case,' said Sancho, 'why, your worship, do you make everyone you conquer by your mighty arm present himself to my lady Dulcinea? For that says you love her and that she's your sweetheart, as clearly as if you'd put your signature to the fact. And seeing that you force them to go down on their knees in her presence, and to say that they come from your worship to offer her their obedience, how can the feelings of the pair of you stay hidden?'

'Oh, how stupid and simple you are!' exclaimed Don Quixote. 'Do you not see, Sancho, that this all redounds to her greater glory? You must know that in this our state of chivalry it is a great honour for a lady to have many knights errant serving her, with no greater ambition than of serving her for what she is, and without hope of any other reward for their zeal than that she shall be pleased to accept them as her knights.'

'That's the kind of love,' said Sancho, 'I've heard them preach about. They say we ought to love our Lord for Himself alone, without being moved to it by hope of glory or fear of punishment. Though as for me, I'm inclined to love and serve Him for what He can do for me.'

'The devil take you!' said Don Quixote. 'What a peasant you are, and yet what apt things you say at times! One would almost think you had been to school.'

'But I swear I can't read,' replied Sancho.

At this point Master Nicholas called out to them to wait a bit, for the company wanted to stop and drink at a small spring by the road-side. Don Quixote halted, much to Sancho's satisfaction, since by this time he was tired of telling all those lies, and afraid that his master might catch him out. For although he knew that Dulcinea was a peasant girl from El Toboso, he had never seen her in his life. In the meantime Cardenio had put on the clothes which Dorothea was wearing when they met her, and although they were not very good they were a great improvement on his own. They all dismounted at the spring, and with the provisions which the priest had brought from the inn did something to satisfy their great hunger.

And whilst they were thus occupied a lad, who chanced to be passing along the road, stopped and stared at the party, and then, after a moment, rushed up to Don Quixote and clasped him round the legs, most opportunely bursting into tears:

'Oh, my lord,' he cried, 'don't you know me? Take a good look at me. I'm the boy Andrew whom your worship untied from the oak I was bound to.'

Don Quixote recognized him and, taking him by the hand, turned to say to the others: 'To convince you of the importance of having knights errant in the world to redress the outrages and wrongs which are committed here by insolent and wicked men, I would have your worships know that some days ago, as I was passing by a wood, I heard most piteous shouts and cries, as of someone afflicted and in distress. Immediately, as was my duty, I hastened in the direction from which the sad cries seemed to come, and there I found this lad who is now before you bound to an oak. And now my soul rejoices at the sight of him, for he shall be my witness and will not let me stray from the truth in any way. He was tied to a tree, I tell you, naked to the waist; and a country fellow, who I learnt afterwards was his master, was lashing him with the reins of his horse. As soon as I saw him I demanded the reason for this atrocious flagellation, and the brute replied that he was beating him because he was his servant and for certain negligences of his which seemed to spring rather from roguery than from foolishness. At this the child cried: "Sir, he is only whipping me because I asked him for my wages." The master answered with some sort of talk and excuses, which I of course heard but did not admit. To be brief, I made the peasant untie the boy, and made him swear to take him and pay him *real* for *real* – and perfumed at that. Now, is not this all true, Andrew my lad? Did you not note with what authority I gave my orders, and with what humility he promised to do all that I commanded and specified and required? Answer; do not be confused or hesitant. Tell these good gentlemen what happened, so that they may see and reflect how useful it is, as I say, to have knights errant on the roads.'

'All that your worship has said is quite true,' replied the boy, 'but the end of the business was very much the opposite of what you suppose.'

'How the opposite?' demanded Don Quixote. 'Did not the peasant pay you, then?'

'Not only didn't he pay me,' replied the boy, 'but as soon as your worship was out of the wood and we were alone, he tied me up again to the same oak and beat me again so hard that I was left flayed like St. Bartholomew. And at every stroke he gave me, he mocked and jibed at your worship. So that, if it hadn't been for the pain, I should have burst out laughing. In fact, he gave me such a welting that I've been in a hospital ever since, getting cured of the injuries the wicked wretch did me. And your worship's to blame for it all. For if you'd gone on your way and not come when you weren't called, and not interfered with other people's business, my master would have been content to given me a dozen or two lashes. Then he would have let me go and paid me what he owed me. But as your worship abused him so needlessly and called him so many names, he got into a temper, and seeing that he couldn't vent it on you he let fly such a rain of blows on me, once we were alone, that I shall never be a whole man again for the rest of my life.'

'The trouble was,' said Don Quixote, 'that I went away. I should not have gone till I had seen you paid. For, as I ought to have known from long experience, there is never a peasant who keeps his word if he finds it does not suit him. But you remember, Andrew, that I swore I would go and look for him if he did not pay you, and find him too, even if he hid in the whale's belly.'

'That's right,' said Andrew, 'but it wasn't any good.'

'Now you will see if it is any good or not,' exclaimed Don Quixote, getting up very quickly and bidding Sancho bridle Rocinante, who had been browsing during their meal.

Dorothea asked him what what it was he intended to do. He answered that he was going to look for the villain, punish him for his wicked conduct, and see that Andrew was paid to the last farthing, in despite of and in the teeth of every peasant in the world. But she replied by reminding him that he could not. For by the boon he had granted her, he must not engage in any enterprise until hers was accomplished. And as he knew this better than anyone else, he must restrain his anger until his return from her kingdom.

'That is true,' replied Don Quixote, 'and Andrew must be patient till my return, as you say, my lady. But I swear again, and renew my promise, not to rest until I have seen him avenged and paid.'

'I don't believe in these vows,' said Andrew. 'I'd rather have something now to get me on to Seville, than all the vengeance in the world. Give me something to eat and take with me, if you have anything here. Then God bless your worship and all knights errant, and may they be as good errants for themselves as they've been for me.'

Sancho took a piece of bread and some cheese out of his bag and gave it to the lad, saying: 'Take this, brother Andrew, for each of us has a share in your misfortune.'

'Well, what's your share, then?' asked Andrew.

'This share of bread and cheese that I'm giving you,' replied Sancho. 'God knows whether I mayn't need it myself. For I must tell you, my friend, that we squires of knights errant are subject to great hunger and bad luck, and to other things too, which are better felt than told.'

Andrew seized his bread and cheese and, when he saw that no one was going to give him anything more, made his bow and took to the road; though, as he turned to go, he said to Don Quixote:

'For God's sake, Sir Knight Errant, don't come to my help if you meet me again, even though you see me being cut to pieces. But leave me to my troubles, for they can't be so bad that the results of your worship's help won't be worse. And God blast you and every knight errant ever born on the face of the earth!'

Don Quixote started up to punish him; but he ran off so fast that nobody attempted to follow. Our knight was very much abashed at Andrew's story, and the others had much trouble in not completing his discomfiture by laughing outright.

Chapter XXXII. *Of what befell Don Quixote and all his company at the inn.*

As soon as their excellent meal was over they saddled at once, and arrived next day without any noteworthy incident at that inn which was the dread and terror of Sancho Panza. But although he would rather not have gone in, this time he could not avoid it. And when they saw Don Quixote and Sancho coming, the innkeeper, his wife, their daughter and Maritornes came out to receive them with a great show of pleasure. The knight accepted their welcome with gravity and approbation, and bade them put him up a better bed than they had given him the time before. To which the landlady replied that she would give him one fit for a prince, if he would pay them better than the last time. Don Quixote answered that he would, and so they provided him with a tolerable one in the same loft as before. And there he lay down immediately, for he was severely shaken in body and mind. But no sooner had he shut himself in than the landlady attacked the barber, seizing him by the beard and crying:

'Bless my soul! You shan't use my ox tail for a beard any more.

Give me back my tail, for my husband's what-d'ye-call-it's so kicked about on the floor that it's a shame. I mean his comb that he used to stick into my tail.'

But the barber would not part with it for all her tugging, until the priest told him to give it to her, since they had no more need of disguise. For he could reveal himself in his own shape now, and tell Don Quixote he had fled to that inn after he had been robbed by the galley-slaves. Then, if the knight were to ask after the Princess's squire, they could tell him that she had sent him ahead to inform her subjects that she was on her way, and was bringing their common liberator with her. At this the barber cheerfully returned the landlady her tail, and they gave her back all her property too that she had lent them for Don Quixote's deliverance.

Everyone in the place was struck by Dorothea's beauty, and by the handsomeness of the shepherd Cardenio. The priest ordered them to prepare such food as the inn could provide, and the landlord, in hope of better payment, quickly served them with a tolerable meal. All this while Don Quixote slept, and they agreed not to wake him, since he was in greater need of sleep than of food. The landlord, his wife, his daughter, Maritornes and all the travellers were at the table, and they discussed Don Quixote's strange madness and the state in which they had found him. The landlady told them of his adventures with the carrier. Then she looked to see if Sancho was present and, finding that he was not, told them the tale of his tossing in the blanket, which amused them quite a bit. But when the priest said that it was the books of chivalry which he had read that had turned Don Quixote's brain, the landlord remarked:

'I don't know how that can be, because really I think there's no better reading in the world. I have two or three of them here and some other writings. They've truly put life into me, and not only into me but into plenty of others. For at harvest time a lot of the reapers come in here in the mid-day heat. There's always one of them who can read, and he takes up one of those books. Then as many as thirty of us sit round him, and we enjoy listening so much that it saves us countless grey hairs. At least I can say for myself that when I hear about those furious, terrible blows the knights deal one another, I get the fancy to strike a few myself. And I could go on listening night and day.'

'I agree absolutely,' said the landlady, 'for I never get any peace in my house except when you're listening to the reading. You're so fascinated then that you forget to scold for once.'

'That's right,' said Maritornes. 'I tell you I enjoy hearing them all too. They're very pretty, particularly the parts when some lady or other is lying in her knight's embraces under some orange-trees, and there's a damsel keeping watch for them, dying of envy and frightened to death. It's all as sweet as honey, I say.'

'And you, what do you think about it, young lady?' the priest asked the innkeeper's daughter.

'I don't know, sir, truly I don't,' she answered. 'I listen too, and really, though I don't understand it, I do enjoy it. But I don't like the fighting that pleases my father so much. I prefer the complaints the knights make when they're away from their ladies. Sometimes they actually make me cry, I pity them so much.'

'Then you would give them some relief, young lady,' asked Dorothea, 'if they were weeping for you?'

'I don't know what I'd do,' replied the girl. 'Only I know that some of those ladies are so cruel that their knights call them tigers and lions and lots of other nasty names. And, Jesus, I can't imagine what sort of heartless, conscienceless folk they can be to leave a decent man to die or go mad, rather than look at him. I don't know what's the good of all their coyness – if it's for the sake of their virtue, let 'em marry them, for that's what the gentlemen are after.'

'Be quiet, girl,' said the landlady. 'You seem to know rather much of these matters, and it's not right for young ladies to know or talk so much.'

'But as this gentleman asked me,' she answered, 'I couldn't help answering him.'

'Well, well,' said the priest, 'bring in those books, Master Landlord. I should like to see them.'

'With pleasure,' he replied; and going into his room, brought out a little old trunk, fastened with a small chain, which he undid, revealing three big books and some manuscript papers written in a very fine hand. The first book he opened was *Don Cirongilio of Thrace*, the others *Felixmarte of Hyrcania* and *The History of the Great Captain Gonzalo Hernandez of Cordova* together with the *Life of Diego Garcia de Paredes*.

On reading the titles of the two first, the priest observed to the barber: 'We need our friend's housekeeper here now, and his niece.'

'No, we don't,' replied the barber, 'for I'm just as capable of carrying them to the yard or to the fireplace; and there's a very good fire there now.'

'What,' said the innkeeper, 'does your worship want to burn my books?'

'Only these two,' replied the priest. 'This Don Cirongilio and this Felixmarte.'

'Are my books heretical or phlegmatic, by any chance,' asked the innkeeper, 'that you want to burn them?'

'Schismatic, you mean, my friend,' said the barber, 'not phlegmatic.'

'Yes, yes,' said the innkeeper. 'But if you've a mind to burn any, let it be this one about the Great Captain and Diego Garcia, for I'd rather have one of my children burnt than either of the others.'

'My friend,' pronounced the priest, 'these two books are full of lies and foolishness and vanity. But the one about the Great Captain is true history, and relates the deeds of Gonzalo Hernandez of Cordova, whom the whole world deservedly called The Great Captain, on account of his many great exploits. It is a famous and illustrious name which was earned by none but him. And that Diego Garcia de Paredes too was a noble gentleman, born in the city of Truxillo in Estremadura, a very brave soldier, and of such natural strength that with one finger he stopped a mill-wheel turning at full speed. Once too when he was posted with a two-handed sword at the approaches of a bridge, he prevented a whole vast army from crossing. He did so many other things of that sort too that if instead of his writing them down himself with the modesty of a gentleman who is his own chronicler, a stranger had written a free and dispassionate account of them, his deeds would have cast the exploits of all your Hectors, Achilleses, and Rolands into oblivion.'

'Tell that to my father!' said the innkeeper. 'So that's what astonished you. Just stopping a millwheel! I swear you ought to see what I've read about Felixmarte of Hyrcania. He cut five giants in half with one back-stroke, just as if they'd been so many beans that children make their mannikins of. And another time he attacked a huge and most powerful army of more than one million six hundred thousand soldiers, all in armour from head to foot, and routed them all as if they had been flocks of sheep. I wonder what would you say about the worthy Don Cirongilio of Thrace. He was a valiant and courageous knight, as you may read in the book, where it tells you how once, a fiery serpent came out of the water as he was sailing on a river. As soon as he saw it he rushed at it, got astride its scaly shoulders, and pressed its throat so hard with both his hands that it had no other way of saving itself from being throttled than by diving to the bottom of the river, dragging the knight, who would not leave go, after it. And when they got there, he found himself among such marvellously beautiful palaces and gardens! Then the serpent turned into an old man, and told him such things as were never heard before. Say no more, sir, for if you were to listen to that book you would go mad with pleasure. A fig each for your Great Captain and your Diego Garcia!'

At this Dorothea whispered to Cardenio: 'Our host is not far short of being a second Don Quixote.'

'I agree,' replied Cardenio. 'To judge by what he says, he takes everything in those books for gospel truth, and the barefoot friars themselves wouldn't make him believe otherwise.'

'See here, brother,' began the priest, 'there never were such people in the world as Felixmarte of Hyrcania, or Don Cirongilio of Thrace, or any of the other knights in those books of chivalry. They are all fictions, invented by idle brains who composed them for the very purpose you spoke of, to pass the time as your reapers do in reading them. For I swear to you that really such knights never existed in the world, and all these feats and follies never happened.'

'Try that bone on another dog!' replied the innkeeper. 'As if I didn't know how many beans make five, and where my own shoe pinches! Don't try to feed me with pap, your worship, for I wasn't born yesterday! It's a nice thing for you to try and persuade me that all these fine books say is only nonsense and lies, when they're printed by licence of the Lords of the Privy Council – as if they were people who would allow a pack of lies to be published, and enough battles and enchantments to drive you out of your wits!'

'I have told you already, my friend,' replied the priest, 'that it is done to divert our idle moments. Just as in all well-ruled states such games as chess, tennis, and billiards are permitted for the amusement of men who do not want to work, or do not have to, or cannot; so these books are allowed to be published, in the very reasonable belief that there can be no one so ignorant as to take any of them for true history. If I were permitted now, and my hearers desired it, I would say something about the qualities that books of chivalry require in order to be good. This might perhaps make them useful to some people, and enjoyable too. But I hope that a time will come when I can explain my ideas to those who can turn my criticism to account. In the meantime, Master Landlord, believe what I tell you. Take your books, and decide for yourself whether they are truth or lies, and much good may they do you! But I pray God you never limp on the same foot as your guest Don Quixote.'

'I shan't do that,' replied the innkeeper. 'I shall never be fool enough to turn knight errant. For I see quite well that it's not the fashion now to do as they did in the olden days when they say those famous knights roamed the world.'

Sancho had entered in the middle of this conversation and was much astonished and depressed to hear that knights errant were now out of fashion, and that all books of chivalry were nonsense and lies. And so he decided in his own mind to wait and see how this expedition of his master's turned out; and if the result was not up to his expectations, he resolved to leave Don Quixote and go back to his wife and children and to his usual occupation.

The innkeeper was just taking away the trunk and the books when the priest said to him: 'Wait. I should like to see what is in those papers that are written in such a good hand.' The landlord took them out, and handed them to the priest who found about eight sheets of manuscript, and at the beginning a title in large letters: *The Tale of Foolish Curiosity*. He then read some three or four lines to himself, and said: 'Really, the title of this tale rather takes my fancy, and I have a mind to read it through.'

At which the innkeeper replied: 'Your reverence might do well to read it. Let me tell you that some of my guests who've read it here have enjoyed it very much and have pressed me to give it to them. But I wouldn't let them have it, as I mean to return it to the man who left this trunk behind with all these books and papers. He must have forgotten them, but he may quite likely come this way again some time. Then I'll certainly return him the books, though I know I shall miss them. For I may be an innkeeper, but still I'm a Christian!'

'You are very right, my friend,' said the priest, 'but all the same, if I like the tale you must let me copy it.'

'With the greatest of pleasure,' replied the innkeeper.

Whilst the two of them were talking, Cardenio had picked up the tale and begun to read it. He formed the same opinion of it as the priest had done, and begged him to read it aloud so that they could all hear it.

'I would,' said the priest, 'if it were not better to spend our time in sleeping than in reading.'

'It will be sufficient rest for me,' said Dorothea, 'to pass an hour listening to a story, for my mind is not yet quiet enough to let me sleep.'

'Well, in that case,' said the priest, 'I will read it, if only out of curiosity. Perhaps there will be something pleasant in it.'

Master Nicholas urged him to do so, and Sancho as well. So seeing that it would give them all pleasure, and himself as well, the priest began:

'Well, well! Listen to me, all of you, for this is how the tale begins:

Chapter XXXIII. *The Tale of Foolish Curiosity.*

IN Florence, a wealthy and famous Italian city in the province called Tuscany, lived Anselmo and Lothario, two rich and noble gentlemen, and such close friends that everyone who knew them referred to them as *The Two Friends*. They were bachelors, lads of the same age and the same habits, which was sufficient reason for the affection that united them. It is true that Anselmo was rather more inclined to affairs of the heart than was Lothario, who was fonder of hunting. But when the occasion arose, Anselmo would give up his pleasures to take part in Lothario's, and Lothario his to follow Anselmo's. Their minds, in fact, worked in such unison that no clock could keep better time.

Anselmo fell deeply in love with a noble and beautiful damsel of that city. So good was her family and so good was she that he decided, with the approval of his friend Lothario, without which he did nothing, to ask her parents for her hand. And this he did. Lothario himself was the messenger; and it was he who concluded the business so much to his friend's satisfaction that in a short time Anselmo gained the object of his desires. Camilla too was so pleased to have got Anselmo for a husband that she never ceased to thank Heaven and Lothario, the joint agents of her good fortune. For the first few days – which as in all marriages, were spent in feasting – Lothario continued to visit his friend Anselmo's house as usual, striving to do him honour and to entertain and amuse him in every possible way. But once the wedding celebrations were over and the stream of visitors and congratulations had subsided, he began deliberately to visit Anselmo's less often; since it seemed to him, as it should to all reasonable men, that men should not continue to haunt the houses of their married friends as they did when they were bachelors. For though good and true friends should not be in any way suspicious, yet a married man's honour is so delicate that it can be injured even by his own brother. How much more so by his friend.

Anselmo noticed the falling off in Lothario's visits, and made it the subject of loud complaints. He said that he would never have married if he had known that his marriage was going to deprive him of his friend's company. He begged him not to let the charming title of *The Two Friends*, which they had earned by their bachelor harmony, lapse through exaggerated caution. He implored him, in fact, if such a word could rightly be used between them, to treat his house as his own again, and to come and go as before. He assured him that his wife Camilla had no pleasure or desire except such as he wished her to have, and that she was troubled to see Lothario turned so shy, knowing as she did the warmth of their friendship.

Lothario replied to this and to the many arguments Anselmo used to persuade him to come to the house again as he used to do, so prudently, discreetly and judiciously, that Anselmo was satisfied with his friend's decision, and they agreed that Lothario should dine with him twice a week and on feast-days. But although this was settled between the pair of them, Lothario decided to do no more than what seemed best to serve his friend's honour; for he prized Anselmo's good name more than his own. He used to say, and rightly, that a married man on whom Heaven has bestowed a lovely wife has to take as much care of what friends he brings to the house as of what women friends his wife consorts with. For what is not done or arranged in market-places and churches, or at public shows or church-goings – which a husband cannot always deny his wife – is often managed and facilitated at the house of that very woman friend or relative in whom he has most confidence. Lothario used to say too that every married man has need of a friend to warn him of the shortcomings in his behaviour. For it often happens that out of his great love for his wife, a husband does not warn her, for fear of annoying her, that some of her actions may redound either to his honour or to his shame. Though all this could easily be remedied if he had a friend to advise him. But where might a man find a friend as discreet, as loyal, and as faithful as Lothario postulated? Indeed I do not know. Lothario alone was the man, for he guarded his friend's honour with so much care and vigilance that he tried to reduce, shorten, and diminish the agreed times for his visits to the house, for fear that the idle crowd and straying malicious eyes might criticize the visits of a rich, noble, and high-born young man with the attractive qualities which he considered himself to have, to the house of so lovely a woman as Camilla. For even though her goodness and worth might be sufficient to bridle malicious tongues, he did not want to have her good name or his friend's called into question. Therefore he spent most of the days agreed upon in other business and amusements, and pretended that these were unavoidable. So it was that a great part of the hours they spent together passed in complaints on one side and excuses on the other.

Now it happened one day, as the two friends were taking a walk in the fields outside the city, that Anselmo addressed the following remarks to Lothario:

'You may think, friend Lothario, that I am incapable of responding with sufficient gratitude for the favours which God has bestowed on me in making me the son of such parents and in giving me with no mean hand both of nature's and of fortune's goods, and for the greatest blessing of all which He bestowed on me in giving me you for a friend and Camilla for a wife – two treasures which I value as much as I am able, if not as much as I should. Yet with all these blessings, which are commonly the sum with which men should and do live content, I am the most fretful and discontented man in all the world, since for some time now I have been vexed and bothered by a desire so strange and peculiar that I am astonished at myself. I blame and scold myself for it when I am alone, and try to stifle it and to conceal it from my own thoughts. But all this has been of so little use that my whole intention might have been to proclaim it to the world. And since it must come out in the end, I should like it to be kept in the secret archives of your breast. For I am confident that in that way, and through the efforts which you, as my faithful friend, will take to relieve me, I shall be quickly freed from the distress it causes me. Through your sympathy I expect to become as happy as by my own foolishness I am now unhappy.'

This speech of Anselmo's astonished Lothario, for he had no idea where its long preface or preamble was leading to. For although he tried to imagine what desire could possibly be tormenting his friend, he was always wide of the mark. So to rid himself quickly of the distress which this suspense caused him, he answered that Anselmo was doing a clear injustice to their great friendship by searching for round-about ways of telling him his most secret thoughts. For he could count on him either for advice or for help.

'That is true,' replied Anselmo. 'I am confident of that, and I will tell you, friend Lothario, what distresses me. It is the question whether my wife Camilla is as good and perfect as I think. I cannot be sure of the truth except by testing her by an ordeal which shall prove the purity of her virtue, as fire shows the purity of gold. For it is my opinion, my friend, that a woman is good only in proportion to her temptations, and that the only constant woman is one who does not yield to promises, gifts, tears, or the continuous importunities of persistent lovers. What reason has one to thank a woman for being good,' said he, 'if no one has tempted her to be bad? What merit is there in her being reserved and modest, if she has no opportunity of going astray and knows that she has a husband who will kill her if he catches her in her first slip? That is why I do not have the same regard for the woman who is good out of fear or lack of opportunity as for the woman who is wooed and pursued, yet comes off with the crown of victory. So, for these reasons and for many others that I could give you, I want support and confirmation for the opinion I hold. I want my wife Camilla to pass through the ordeal, and be purged and refined in the fire of temptation and solicitation by someone worthy of her. Then, if she comes out, as I believe she will, with the palm of victory, I shall account myself the most fortunate of men. I shall be able to say that the cup of my desires is full. I shall say that I have been fated to possess the virtuous woman of whom the wise man says: *Who shall find her?* And if things should turn out contrary to my expectations, with the satisfaction of having proved the truth I shall bear uncomplainingly the pain that so dearly bought an experiment will cause me. Now it being understood that nothing you say in opposition to my purpose will be of the slightest effect in dissuading me from it, I want you, my friend Lothario, to prepare to be the instrument for carrying this plan of mine into effect. I shall give you an opportunity of doing it, and I shall omit nothing that seems to me necessary, if you are to woo a woman who is chaste, honourable, reserved and in no way mercenary. What most urges me to entrust this arduous enterprise to you is the knowledge that if Camilla is conquered by you, you will not carry your victory to the ultimate extreme, but only do what is necessary by the terms of our agreement. And so I shall be wronged only in the intention, and my injury will remain buried in your virtuous silence; which, I know, will be as eternal as the silence of death, in any concern of mine. Therefore, if you want me to enjoy anything deserving the name of life you must now enter into this conflict of love, not half-heartedly or sluggishly, but with the earnestness and diligence which my plan requires, and with the loyalty our friendship assures me of.'

These were Anselmo's arguments, to which Lothario listened so attentively that he did not open his lips until his friend had finished, except to say the few words here recorded. And then he stared at him for some time as if he were gazing at some dreadful and amazing object, the like of which he had never seen before.

'I cannot persuade myself, friend Anselmo,' he said, 'that what you have just been saying is not a joke. For, if I had thought you were in earnest, I should not have let you go so far. I should not have listened, and that would have cut short your long speech. It is my belief that either you do not know me or I do not know you.

But no, I know very well that you are Anselmo, and you know that I am Lothario. The trouble is that I think you are not the Anselmo you used to be, and you seem to have imagined that I am not the Lothario I ought to be. For what you have just said to me is unworthy of my friend Anselmo, and you should not have made the demands you did of the Lothario you know. Good friends ought to use and prove their friends, as the poet says, *usque ad aras*: I mean that they must not use friendship for purposes offensive to God. And if such was the opinion of a heathen, how much more must a Christian hold to it, knowing as he does that the divine friendship must not be forfeited for a human one? When a friend goes so far as to set aside his duty to God to fulfil that of friendship, it must not be for trifles and trivialities, but for something on which his friend's life and honour depend. Now tell me, Anselmo, is it your life or your honour that is in such danger that I must risk myself to satisfy you, and do the detestable thing you are asking of me? Neither most certainly. On the contrary, as far as I understand, you are asking me to try hard to rob you, and to rob myself of life and honour. For if I take your honour it is clear that I take your life, since a man without honour is worse than dead. If I become the instrument of such an evil as you wish, should I not emerge dishonoured and, consequently, dead? Listen, Anselmo my friend, and have the patience not to answer till I have finished telling you all my thoughts on the subject of this request of yours. There will be time enough after that for you to reply and for me to listen.'

'Most willingly,' said Anselmo. 'Say what you like.'

Then Lothario went on to say: 'You seem to me, Anselmo, to be in the position of the Moors, who cannot be convinced in the error of their sect by quotations from Holy Scripture, nor by arguments drawn from intellectual speculation or based on the canons of faith, but have to have examples, palpable, simple, intelligible, demonstrable and indubitable, with irrefutable mathematical proof, like: *If equals be taken from equals the remainders are equal.* And when they do not understand this in words, as in fact they do not, then you have to show it to them with your hands and put it in front of their eyes. But even then no one can convince them of the truths of our holy faith. Now I shall have to use the same method with you. For this new desire of yours is so extravagant and so far from all

shadow of sense that it seems to me it would be waste of time to try
and convince you of your foolishness – for that is the only name I
can give it at present. Yes, I am even inclined to abandon you to your
folly as a punishment for your wickedness. But my friendship for
you will not let me treat you so cruelly as to leave you in such obvious danger of destruction. Now, to make the matter clear to you,
Anselmo, tell me: did you not ask me to solicit a modest woman?
To tempt a chaste one? To bribe an honest one? To woo a prudent
one? Yes, that is what you asked. But if you know that you have a
modest, chaste, honest, prudent wife, what are you searching to find
out? If you believe that she will emerge victorious from all my attacks – as no doubt she will – what titles do you intend to give her
afterwards better than those she already has? What more will she be
afterwards than she is at present? Either you do not take her for
what you say, or you do not know what you are asking. If you do
not take her for what you say, why do you want to test her instead
of treating her as a bad woman, and punishing her as you think she
deserves? But if she is as good as you think, it will be an impertin-
ence to experiment with truth itself, for when the trial is over it cannot have a higher value than it had before. So we must conclude
that to attempt things which are more likely to result in harm than
in good is the mark of unreasoning and rash minds. All the more so
if they attempt such things voluntarily, when it is clear from a mile
away that the attempt is sheer madness. Difficult works are attempted for the sake of Heaven, for the world's sake, or for both. The
first are tasks undertaken by the saints, who attempt to live the lives
of angels in human frames. The second are performed by men who
navigate the boundless ocean, and journey through distant countries and changing climates, to acquire what are called the goods of
fortune. And those who brave hazardous enterprises for the sake of
both God and man are stout soldiers, who no sooner see in the
enemy's rampart a breach made by a single cannon-ball than, regardless of all fear and danger, they are borne on the wings of ambition to fight for their faith, their nation, and their king, and rush
boldly into the midst of death which awaits them in a thousand
shapes.

　'Such are the hazards commonly undertaken, and it is honour,
glory, and gain to attempt them, however charged they may be with

difficulties and danger. But the project you suggest attempting will gain you glory neither from above, nor the goods of fortune, nor renown among men. For, supposing that the result is satisfactory, you will be no happier, no richer, and no more honoured than you are at present; and if you do not succeed, you will be in the greatest imaginable misery. It will do you no good then to think that no one knows your misfortune, for it will be enough to afflict and undo you that you know it yourself. As confirmation I will quote a stanza of the famous poet Luis Tansilo from the end of the first part of his *Tears of St. Peter*, which goes like this:

> In Peter's heart the shame and anguish grew
> As the day broke, and though no man was by
> To see his sin, he knew his own offence
> And blushed deep for his guilt. A noble heart
> Needs no observer to arouse his shame,
> But is abashed at sight of his own guilt,
> Though no one but the heavens and earth can see it.

'So you will not alleviate your grief by secrecy, but will have cause for incessant tears. For even though you may not weep openly, tears of blood will flow from your heart. So wept that simple doctor of whom our poet tells, who made the trial of the cup which the cautious Rinaldo, with greater discretion, declined. Even though that is a poetic fiction, it contains a hidden moral worth observing and following. Moreover, if you will listen to what I am now going to say, you will be finally convinced that it is a great error you now wish to commit. Tell me, Anselmo, if the Heavens or good fortune had made you the owner and lawful possessor of a very fine diamond, and every jewel merchant who saw it was satisfied of its goodness and quality; and if, all together and with one voice, they said that it attained the utmost possible perfection in every respect, and you believed them yourself and had not a suspicion to the contrary – supposing all this, would it be reasonable for you to take it into your head to pick up this stone and put it between the anvil and the hammer, and thus by mere weight of blows and brawn prove whether it was as hard and as fine as they said? Now would it be any more reasonable to put this plan of yours into effect? For supposing that the stone resisted such a stupid trial, would it have any greater value or reputation for that? And if it

K

broke – which well might happen – would not everything be lost?
Yes, and its owner would count in the general estimation as a fool.

'Now think of Camilla, Anselmo my friend, as a rare diamond,
both in your estimation and others', and consider whether there is
any reason for exposing her to the risk of destruction; for even if
she remains unbroken, she cannot rise to a greater value than she
now has. But, if she fails and does not stand up to the trial, reflect
on the state you would be in without her. Think what reason you
would have for self-reproach if you were to be the cause of her destruction and your own. For there is no jewel in the world so precious as a chaste and virtuous woman, and the whole honour of
women lies in their good reputation. Now, since your wife's virtue
is the very highest imaginable, as you know, why should you want
to call its truth into question? Look, my friend, woman is an imper-
fect creature, and you must not put stumbling-blocks in her path,
so that she may trip and fall; but rather clear her road of every obstacle, so that she may run free and unburdened to gain the perfection she lacks, which consists in a good life.

'Naturalists tell us that the ermine is a little animal with a fur of
extreme whiteness, and that when hunters wish to catch it they use
this trick: they find the places it usually passes and frequents, and
stop them up with mud; and then, starting their quarry, they drive
it that way. Now, when the ermine reaches the mud it stands still
and lets itself be seized and caught rather than pass through the dirt,
and soil and lose its whiteness, which it values more than its life and
liberty. The chaste and virtuous woman is an ermine, and the virtue
of chastity is whiter and purer than snow. If man does not wish her
to lose it, but to keep and preserve it instead, he must not treat her
like the ermine. He must not put mud in front of her – that is to
say the gifts and addresses of importunate lovers – for perhaps –
no, certainly – she has insufficient virtue and natural strength to
trample down and pass through those obstacles on her own. He
must remove them from her way, therefore, and set before her the
purity of virtue and the beauty which lies in a good name. For a
good woman is also like a mirror of clear and shining glass, which
is liable to be stained and dimmed by every breath which touches it.
A chaste woman must be treated like holy relics, which are to be
adored but not touched. A good woman must be guarded and

prized like a beautiful garden full of flowering roses, whose owner
does not allow anyone to walk in it or to touch them; enough that
they enjoy its fragrance and beauty from afar off through its iron
railings. Last of all I want to quote you some verses which have
come into my mind, and which I heard in a modern play; they seem
to me very much to our present point. A shrewd old man is advising
another, the father of a young lady, to look after her, guard her, and
keep her in the house, and among other reasons he adduces these:

> Truly woman's made of glass;
> Therefore no one ought to try her
> Whether she may break or no,
> Seeing all may come to pass.
>
> For the break's the likelier,
> And it's very foolish
> To risk a thing so brittle
> And, once smashed, beyond repair.
>
> So I would have all men dwell
> In this sound opinion;
> For if Danaës abound,
> There are golden showers as well.

'All that I have said to you so far, Anselmo, touches yourself, but
now you must hear something from my side. Forgive me if I am
long-winded, for the labyrinth you are in, and which you want me
to get you out of, makes me so. You count me your friend; yet you
wish to deprive me of that honour, which is against all friendship.
And not only that, but you want me to rob you of your own honour
as well. It is clear that you want to deprive me of mine. For when
Camilla sees me wooing her, as you wish, she is sure to take me for
a man without principles or honour, seeing me attempt something
so contrary to my duty to myself and my friendship to you. There
is no doubt that you wish me to rob you of your own honour. For
when Camilla sees me wooing her she will think that I have detected
some lightness in her, that has made me so bold as to reveal my
wicked desires to her; and when she considers herself dishonoured,
her disgrace will affect you as a part of her. From this arises a well-
known situation: although the husband of an adulterous woman
does not know her guilt, and has never given his wife an excuse for
being what she should not be, or ever had it in his power to prevent

his misfortune, which does not arise from his carelessness or lack of precaution, he is still called by a vile and opprobrious name, and to some extent regarded with eyes of contempt rather than of pity by those who know of his wife's guilt; even though it is not by his fault, but by his guilty partner's will that misfortune has struck him. But I could tell you the reason why the guilty woman's husband is dishonoured, although he does not know of her wickedness, and is not to blame, and has had no hand in it nor ever given her an excuse for her sin. Do not grow tired of listening; it will all serve for your advantage.

'When God created our first father in the earthly paradise, Holy Scripture tells us that He caused a deep sleep to fall on him, and in his sleep took one of the ribs of his left side and created our mother Eve; and when Adam awoke and looked on her, he said: *"This is now bone of my bones and flesh of my flesh."* And God said: *"Therefore shall a man leave his father and his mother, and they shall be one flesh."* Then was instituted the divine sacrament of marriage, whose bonds are soluble only by death. This miraculous sacrament has such strength and virtue that it makes two different persons one single flesh; and with happily married couples it does more, for though they have two souls they have only a single will. Hence it arises that, as the flesh of the wife is one with the flesh of the husband, the blemishes which fall on her or the defects she incurs recoil upon the flesh of the husband, although, as I have said, he may be in no respect the cause of the trouble. For, just as the whole body feels the pain of the foot or of any other limb, since they are all one flesh; and the head feels the ankle's pain, although it is not the cause of it; so the husband shares his wife's dishonour, being one with her. Now as all this world's honours and dishonours spring from flesh and blood, and the bad wife's are of this kind, part of them must inevitably fall on the husband; and he must be considered dishonoured, even though he does not know of it. Reflect, then, Anselmo, on the danger you expose yourself to in seeking to disturb your good wife's peace. Consider what vain and foolish curiosity it is that prompts you to stir the passions which now lie quiet in your chaste wife's breast. Be warned that you stand to gain little and to lose so unspeakably much that words fail me to express its value. But, if all that I have said is not enough to deflect you from your wicked plan, you must certainly look for someone else to effect your disgrace and misery. For I do not intend to play the part, even though I lose your friendship by refusing; and that is the greatest loss I can imagine.'

With these words the virtuous and wise Lothario concluded, and left Anselmo so troubled and thoughtful that he could not reply with so much as a word for some time. But at length he said:

'I have listened with attention to all that you have said, Lothario my friend; and your arguments, examples, and comparisons prove your great wisdom and perfect friendship. I see too – and I confess it – that if I do not follow your opinion but my own, I shall be abandoning the good and pursuing the evil. Yet, though I admit this, you must consider that I am now suffering from an illness common in women, which makes them long to eat earth, chalk, coal and other worse things, loathsome to the sight and much more loathsome to the palate. It is necessary, therefore, to find some art to cure me; and this can easily be done, if you will only begin to make up to Camilla, even weakly and hypocritically; for she cannot be so frail that her virtue will fall at the first encounter. I shall be content with just a beginning, and then you will have done what our friendship requires, for not only will you be restoring me my life but convincing me that I retain my honour. This you must do for one reason alone; and that is, that as I am determined to put this plan into practice, you cannot allow me to reveal my obsession to any other person, and so endanger my honour which you are so anxious to save. Even if your own does not stand as high as it should in Camilla's estimation, while you are wooing her, that hardly matters at all: for in a very short time, when we find the integrity in her which we expect, you will be able to tell her the simple truth about our plot; and then you will stand as high in her opinion as before. So since you can give me so much happiness at so little risk to yourself, do not refuse to do as I ask, whatever difficulties it may involve for you. For, as I have said, if you will make only a beginning, I will reckon the matter concluded.'

When Lothario saw Anselmo's resolution, he did not know what further instances to choose, or what fresh arguments to use, in order to dissuade him. Seeing, therefore, that he threatened to divulge his wicked plan to some one else, he resolved to give in to him, to pre-

vent greater mischief, and to do as he wanted; with the sole object
and intention of so managing the business that Anselmo should be
satisfied at no cost to Camilla's peace of mind. So he replied by asking his friend not to tell anyone else of his plan, and promised to
undertake the enterprise and to begin whenever he pleased. Anselmo embraced Lothario tenderly and affectionately, and thanked
him for his offer, as if his friend had done him some great favour.
Then the pair of them agreed that the work should begin on the
very next day. Anselmo would give Lothario time and opportunity
to speak to Camilla alone, and provide him too with money and
jewels to offer her as presents. He advised him to serenade her and to
write verses in her praise; and if he would not, offered to be at the
pains of composing them himself. All this Lothario undertook,
though not with the intention which Anselmo imagined; and with
this understanding they went back to Anselmo's house, where they
found Camilla worried and anxiously awaiting her husband, for he
was later than usual in coming back that day.

Lothario went home, leaving Anselmo contented, but very
puzzled himself as to what line he should take to get out of this
stupid business. But that night he thought of a way of deceiving
Anselmo without offending Camilla; and next day he came to dine
with his friend and was welcomed by Camilla, who always received
him very cordially, knowing how fond her husband was of him.
When they had finished dinner and the table-cloths were removed,
Anselmo asked Lothario to stay with Camilla while he went out on
some urgent business, from which he would be back within an hour
and a half. Camilla begged him not to go, and Lothario offered to
accompany him, but all to no purpose. For Anselmo pressed Lothario all the harder to stay till his return, as he had something of
great importance to discuss with him. Also he told Camilla not to
leave Lothario alone till he got back. In fact, the excuse for his absence was so well sustained that no one could tell it was false.

Anselmo departed, and Camilla remained alone at table with Lothario; for the rest of the household had gone off to dinner. So Lothario found himself engaged in the duel, as his friend desired,
facing an enemy capable of conquering a squadron of armed horsemen with her beauty alone. Indeed, Lothario had reason to fear her!
But all he did was to place his elbow on the arm of his chair and his

hand on his cheek. Then, begging Camilla's pardon for his bad manners, he said that he wanted to take a little rest, till Anselmo's return. Camilla replied that he would rest more comfortably on cushions than in a chair, and begged him therefore to go into the withdrawing room and sleep. But Lothario refused, and stayed there dozing till Anselmo's return. When his friend came back, and found Camilla gone to her room and Lothario sleeping, he concluded that he had been out long enough to give the pair of them time to talk and to sleep as well, and could hardly wait for Lothario to wake, so anxious was he to go out with him and learn what success he had had.

Everything fell out as he wished. Lothario woke up; the pair of them left the house. Then in answer to Anselmo's questions Lothario replied that he had not thought it advisable to reveal himself entirely the first time, and so had merely praised Camilla's beauty, saying that there was no other subject of conversation in the whole city but her loveliness and intelligence. 'This,' he said, 'seemed to me a good way of gaining her confidence and inclining her to listen to me with pleasure next time. It is the method the Devil uses when he wants to deceive the wary. Angel of darkness though he is, he transforms himself into an angel of light, and assumes a cloak of virtue before finally revealing his true character. It is a plan which usually succeeds, unless the deception is discovered at the outset.' This satisfied Anselmo, who said that he would give his friend the same opportunity every day. He would not leave the house, however, but would be so busy there that Camilla would not suspect his plot.

After that came many days on which Lothario never spoke a word to Camilla, but told Anselmo that he had talked to her yet never been able to draw from her the slightest sign of encouragement, or even so much as a shadow of hope. On the contrary, he said, she threatened him that she would have to tell her husband if he did not give up his wicked designs.

'That is good,' said Anselmo. 'Up to now Camilla has resisted words. Now we must see how she resists deeds. To-morrow I will give you two thousand crowns in gold to offer her – no, to give to her – and the same amount to buy jewels to tempt her. For women, particularly beautiful women, are very fond of being well dressed and looking handsome, however chaste they are. If she resists this temptation I shall be satisfied and trouble you no more.'

Lothario answered that, having begun it, he would see the plot through to the end, since he believed that he would come out of it weary and vanquished. The next day he accepted the four thousand crowns in great perplexity, for he did not know what new lie to invent. But, in the end, he made up his mind to tell Anselmo that Camilla was as impervious to gifts and promises as to words, and that there was no purpose in his troubling himself further, since he was wasting his time. But fate guided matters in another way. For when Anselmo had left Lothario and Camilla alone as before, he shut himself into a room and stood at the keyhole, to watch and to listen. And when he saw that Lothario did not throw a single word to Camilla in more than half an hour, and would not have done if he had waited a century, he realized that all his friend had told him about Camilla's replies was nothing but fiction and lies. To make certain of this he came out of the room and, calling Lothario aside, asked him what news he had, and what frame of mind Camilla was in. Lothario answered that he would not budge another step in the business, for she had answered him so sharply and rudely that he had not the courage to speak to her again.

'Oh, Lothario, Lothario,' cried Anselmo, 'how badly you fulfil your duty to me, and my great trust in you! I was watching you just now through the keyhole of that door, and I saw that you did not address a word to Camilla; from which I must infer that you have not said a word yet. If that is so, – and I have no doubt it is, – why are you deceiving me? Why are you trying to deprive me, by this trick of yours, of the only means I can find of obtaining my desire?'

Anselmo said no more, but this was enough to leave Lothario abashed and confused. Being caught in a lie Lothario took almost as a blemish on his honour; and he swore to Anselmo that from that moment he would undertake to satisfy him, and tell no more lies, as his friend would see if he watched carefully. But Anselmo need not put himself to any trouble, because what he now intended to do would satisfy him entirely and free him from all suspicions. His friend believed him and, to give him an opportunity free from interruption, decided to leave his house for a week and go to a friend who lived in a village not far from the city. He arranged with this same friend to send and summon him very urgently, so that he should have an excuse for his departure that would satisfy Camilla.

Unfortunate and ill advised Anselmo, what are you doing? What are you plotting and contriving? See, you are acting against yourself, plotting your own dishonour, and contriving your own undoing. Your wife Camilla is virtuous; in peace and security you possess her; no one interferes with your pleasures; her thoughts do not pass beyond the walls of her house; you are her Heaven upon earth; the goal of her desires; the fulfilment of her joys and the measure by which she rules her will, adapting it in every way to yours and to that of Heaven. Then, since the mine of her honour, beauty, modesty and virtue yields you without any toil all the riches it contains and that you can desire, why must you dig the earth and seek fresh veins of new and unseen treasure? You are taking the risk that everything may collapse, seeing that it is held up only by the feeble props of her frail nature. Remember that by seeking the impossible you may justly be denied the possible or, as a poet has expressed it better:

> In death I seek for life,
> Health in infirmity,
> In jail for liberty;
> I look for rest in strife,
> And faithfulness in treachery.
>
> But envious fate, which still
> Conspires to work my ill,
> With Heaven has decreed
> That easy things shall be denied,
> Since what I crave's the impossible.

Next day Anselmo went to the village, telling Camilla that Lothario would come to look after the house and dine with her while he was away, and that she was to take care to treat him as she would himself. Being a sensible and honest woman, Camilla was distressed at her husband's order, and asked him to consider how wrong it was for anyone to occupy his chair at table while he was away. If this, she said, was because he had no confidence that she could manage the house, let him try for once and learn by experience that she was capable of even greater responsibilities. Anselmo replied that such was his wish, and that she had nothing to do but to bow her

head and obey. Camilla acquiesced, though against her will, and
Anselmo departed. The next day Lothario came to his house and
Camilla gave him an affectionate and modest welcome. She never
sat in any room, however, where Lothario might find her alone, but
went about surrounded by her men-servants and maids, particularly
by her own maid, Leonela, of whom she was very fond. For they
had been brought up together from their girlhood in Camilla's
parents' house, and she had brought her to Anselmo's when she
married him.

For the first three days Lothario did not say a word, though he
had an opportunity when the cloth was removed and the household
went off to their dinner, which, by Camilla's instructions, was a
hurried one. Camilla gave her maid orders to dine before she did
and never to leave her side. But the girl had no thought except for
her own pleasure, and needed the time for her own affairs. So she
did not always comply with her mistresses's orders, but instead left
them alone together, as if by instruction. Camilla's modest behaviour and gravity of expression, however, were sufficient to curb
Lothario's tongue.

But whatever advantage they gained from Camilla's virtues
silencing Lothario's tongue led afterwards to harm for both of
them. For, if his tongue was silent, his thoughts ran on; and he had
time to contemplate, one by one, all Camilla's perfections of mind
and body – and they were enough to inspire love in a marble statue,
let alone in a heart of flesh. Lothario gazed at her all the time he
should have been speaking to her, thinking how worthy of his love
she was; and this reflection began little by little to impinge on his
respect for Anselmo. A thousand times he made up his mind to
leave the city and go where Anselmo would never see him again,
nor he Camilla; but his new-found delight in gazing at her prevented
him and kept him back. He struggled and fought with himself to
resist the pleasure he felt in looking at her. When he was alone he
blamed himself for his madness, calling himself a bad friend, and
even a bad Christian. He reasoned, and made comparisons between
himself and Anselmo; but he always concluded by saying that Anselmo's folly and over-confidence were greater than his own breach
of faith, and that, if he had as good an excuse before God as before
men, he would fear no punishment for his crime.

In fine, Camilla's beauty and goodness, combined with the opportunity which the ignorant husband had put in his way, completely overthrew Lothario's loyalty; and when Anselmo had been
away three days, during which time he had continuously battled to
resist his passion, he began to woo Camilla, without thought for
anything but his own gratification. He was so impetuous, in fact,
and so warm in his language that Camilla got up shocked, and could
think of nothing else to do but retire to her room, without answering
so much as a word. But Lothario's hopes were not discouraged by
her coldness, for hope is always born with love. On the contrary,
he valued Camilla even more highly. She, however, seeing this unexpected side of Lothario's character, did not know what to do.
But, as it seemed to her neither safe nor proper to give him an opportunity to speak to her again, she decided to send one of her servants to Anselmo that same night with a letter in which she wrote
as follows:

Chapter XXXIV. *The Tale of Foolish Curiosity, continued.*

'IT is generally said that an army looks ill without its general and a
castle without its warden, and I say that a young married woman
looks even worse without her husband, unless he is detained by the
most urgent business. I am so badly off without you, and so powerless to bear your absence, that if you do not come quickly I shall
have to go and stay at my parents' house, even though I leave yours
unguarded. For the guardian you have left me – if he is here in that
character – is more concerned with his own pleasures than with your
interest. As you are a wise man I need say no more, and it is as well
that I do not.'

When Anselmo received this letter, he realized that Lothario had
begun the enterprise, and that Camilla must have responded as he
himself would have wished. So, in extreme delight, he sent to
Camilla a message in reply, telling her on no account to move from
the house, for he would be back in a very short time. Camilla was
astonished at this reply, which threw her into greater confusion
than ever; she dared not stay at home, and was even more afraid to
go to her parents. For by remaining she would endanger her
honour, and in going disobey her husband's orders. Finally she re-

solved on what proved to be the wrong course: which was to stay, and not to avoid Lothario, for fear of giving her servants cause to talk. And now she was sorry that she had written as she had to her husband, and afraid that he might think that some frivolity in her conduct had encouraged Lothario to forget the respect he owed her. But, confident in her virtue, she trusted in God and in her own resolve to answer anything Lothario might say by silence, and to say no more to her husband about the matter; so as not to involve him in any quarrel or unpleasantness. She even thought out ways of excusing Lothario to Anselmo when he should ask her what had prompted her to write him that letter.

Firm in these resolutions, which did more credit to her honour than to her wisdom, Camilla stayed next day to listen to Lothario, and so pressing was he that her steadfastness began to waver; and her virtue had all it could do to guard her eyes, and prevent their showing signs of the compassion which Lothario's tears and arguments had stirred in her breast. All this Lothario observed, and his desire grew the warmer. In the end it seemed to him necessary to take full advantage of the opportunity which Anselmo's absence gave him, and to intensify the siege of the fortress. So he assailed her self-love with praise of her beauty; for there is nothing which reduces and levels the embattled towers of a beautiful woman's vanity so quickly as this same vanity posted upon the tongue of flattery. In fact, he most industriously mined the rock of her integrity with such charges that Camilla would have fallen even if she had been made of brass. Lothario wept, beseeched, promised, flattered and swore, with such ardour and with such signs of real feeling, that he overcame Camilla's chastity and achieved the triumph which he least expected and most desired.

Camilla gave in; she gave in. But what wonder, if Lothario's friendship could not stand its ground? A clear proof that the passion of love can only be conquered by flight, and that it is vain to struggle against so powerful an enemy. For divine force is needed to subdue the power of the flesh. Only Leonela knew of her mistress's failing, for this pair of treacherous lovers could not conceal it from her. Lothario did not tell Camilla of Anselmo's scheme, nor of his having purposely afforded him the chance of doing what he had done. For he was afraid that she might set less store by his love, and think that it was by chance that he had wooed her, and not by premeditation.

A few days later Anselmo returned, and did not see that the treasure he had held most lightly, yet valued most, was missing. He immediately went to see Lothario, found him at home and, when they had embraced, asked him for the fateful news.

'The news I have for you, friend Anselmo,' said Lothario, 'is that you have a wife worthy to be called the model and crown of all good women. The words I spoke to her were wasted on the air; my promises she scorned; my gifts she refused; my pretended tears she greeted with open mockery. In fact Camilla is not only the sum of all beauty, but the treasure-house where modesty resides and where dwell gentleness, prudence, and all the virtues which make an honest woman praiseworthy and happy. Take back your money, my friend. Here it is. I have had no need to touch it. For Camilla's integrity will not yield to such low things as gifts and promises. Be content, Anselmo, and make no more trials. You have passed dryshod over a sea of difficulties and dispelled those suspicions which men are bound to have on the subject of women. Do not return to the gulf of fresh disquietudes, nor test with another pilot the goodness and strength of the ship which Heaven has allotted to you, to bear you over the seas of this world. Consider yourself now safe in harbour, moor yourself with the anchors of happy thoughts, and stay until one comes to demand of you the debt which no privilege of nobility exempts you from paying.'

Anselmo was highly delighted at Lothario's speech, and believed in it as firmly as if it had been pronounced by an oracle. But he begged him all the same not to abandon the enterprise, even if it were for nothing more than curiosity and amusement. Although in future, he said, he would not use such urgent methods as he had hitherto. All that he wanted his friend to do was to write some verses in her praise under the name of Chloris. He would give Camilla to understand that his friend was in love with a lady to whom he had given that name, so that he might write of her without injuring her modesty. And, should Lothario not wish to take the trouble to write the verses, he would do so himself.

'There will be no need of that,' said Lothario. 'The muses are not so much my enemies that they do not visit me now and then during the year. Tell Camilla of this fictitious love affair of mine. I will write the verses; and if they are not as good as the subject deserves, at least they shall be the best I can compose.'

So the foolish husband and his treacherous friend agreed. And when Anselmo returned home he asked Camilla her reason for writing him that letter she had sent him. She was surprised he had not asked before, and replied that Lothario had seemed rather freer in his glances than when her husband was at home, but that she now knew she had been mistaken. It had been merely her imagination, for Lothario had avoided seeing her and being alone with her. Anselmo said that she might well dismiss that suspicion, because he knew that Lothario was in love with a noble maiden of the city, and wrote verses to her under the name of Chloris. But, even if he were not, she had no cause to doubt Lothario's loyalty and his great friendship for them both. Now, if Camilla had not been advised by Lothario that this love of his for Chloris was an invention and that he had himself told Anselmo about it so that he could now and then write poems in Camilla's own praise, she would no doubt have fallen into the desperate snare of jealousy; but as she was forewarned she survived this assault unharmed.

The next day, when the three of them were at table, Anselmo begged Lothario to recite some of the verses he had composed for his beloved Chloris. For, as Camilla did not know her, he could safely say what he pleased.

'Even though she did know her,' replied Lothario, 'I should conceal nothing. For when a lover praises his lady's beauty and taxes her with cruelty he does no harm to her good name. But, however that may be, I will tell you that I wrote a sonnet yesterday on the ingratitude of this Chloris. It runs like this:

'In the dead silence of the peaceful night,
    When others' cares are hushed in soft repose,
    The sad account of my neglected woes
To conscious Heaven and Chloris I recite.
And when the sun with his returning light
    Forth from the east his radiant journey goes,
    With accents such as sorrow only knows
My griefs to tell is all my poor delight.
And when bright Phoebus from his starry throne
    Sends rays direct upon the parched soil,

Still in the mournful tale I persevere;
  Returning night renews my sorrow's toil;
And though from morn to night I weep and moan,
Nor heaven nor Chloris my complainings hear.'

The sonnet pleased Camilla much, but Anselmo even more. He was loud in its praises, and said that the lady who did not respond to such patent truth was excessively cruel. And Camilla's comment was: 'So everything that these love poets say is true, then?'

'They do not say it as poets,' answered Lothario. 'But as lovers they are both slow to complain and truthful.'

'There is no doubt of that,' replied Anselmo, anxious to support Lothario's opinions before Camilla, who had no suspicion of Anselmo's trick, so deeply was she in love with Lothario.

And so, delighted as she was with anything of his and, moreover, taking it that his feelings and verses were addressed to herself and that she was the real Chloris, she begged him to recite another sonnet or poem, if he had one by heart.

'I have,' replied Lothario, 'but I do not think that it is as good as the first or, to put it better, any less bad. But you can judge, for here it is:

'Fair and ungrateful one, I feel the blow,
  And glory in the near approach of death;
  For when thou seest my corpse devoid of breath,
My constancy and truth thou sure willst know.
Welcome to me Oblivion's shade obscure!
  Welcome the loss of fortune, life, and fame!
  But thy loved features, and thy honoured name,
Deep graven on my heart, shall still endure.
And these, as sacred relics, will I keep
  Till that sad moment when to endless night
  My long-tormented soul shall take her flight.
Alas for him who on the darkened deep
  Floats idly, sport of the tempestuous tide,
  No port to shield him, and no star to guide!'

Anselmo praised this sonnet too, as he had the first; and so he went on adding link on link to the chain in which he was embroiling himself and binding up his own dishonour. For the more Lothario dishonoured him, the more he assured him of his unblemished honour. And so the lower Camilla sank into the abyss of infamy, the higher she rose, in her husband's opinion, towards the peak of virtue and renown. Now once, when Camilla was alone with her maid, she happened to say to her:

'I am ashamed, Leonela, my friend, to see how cheap I have made myself by not making Lothario spend some time purchasing the full possession of what I gave him so quickly and so willingly. I am afraid that he must despise my easiness and lightness, and not realize that he used such violence with me that I could not resist him.'

'Do not worry on that score, my lady,' replied Leonela, 'for it is not worth it. There is no reason why a thing should lose its value because it is easily given, if in fact the gift is a good one and valuable in itself. They even say that he who gives quickly gives twice over.'

'Yes,' said Camilla, 'but they say too that what costs little is little prized.'

'That saying does not apply to you,' replied Leonela, 'because love, I have heard it said, sometimes flies and sometimes walks. With one person it runs, with another creeps; some it cools and some it burns; some it wounds and others it kills; in a single instant it starts on the race of passion, and in the same instant concludes and ends it; in the morning it will besiege a fortress, and by evening it has subdued it, for there is no force that can resist it. That being so, what is it that alarms you and frightens you? For the very same thing must have happened to Lothario, when love took my master's absence as the instrument of your defeat. It was unavoidable that the plan love had determined on should be carried through in that time, and leave no chance of the work's being cut short by Anselmo's return. For love has no better minister to execute its desires than opportunity; it uses opportunity in all its enterprises, but especially in their beginnings. I know all this very well, more by experience than by hearsay, and one day I will tell you, my lady, for I am flesh and blood too, and young blood at that. What is more, lady Camilla, you would never have given yourself over or spoken so soon if you had not first seen Lothario's whole soul in his eyes, in his sighs, in his declarations, his promises, and his gifts; and learnt from its perfection how worthy he was of your love. So, since that is the case, do not let these scruples and prudish thoughts seize hold of your imagination, but be certain that Lothario values you as you value him. Be content and satisfied, since you have fallen into love's snare, that your captor is a worthy and honourable man, who not only possesses the four *S's*, which they say all good lovers should have, but a whole A.B.C. as well. Just listen to me, and you will see that I know it by heart. He is, as I see it, and as far as I can judge, *Amiable, Bountiful, Courteous, Discreet, Enamoured, Firm, Gallant, Honourable, Illustrious, Loyal, Mild, Noble, Open, Prudent, Quiet, Rich* – and the *S's*, according to the saying – and then, *True, Valorous. X* does not fit him because it is a harsh letter; *Y* – yes, I have said it, and *Z* – he is *zealous* of your honour.'

Camilla laughed at her maid's A.B.C., and concluded that she was more practised in matters of love than she said. In fact, she confessed as much by telling Camilla that she was having a love affair with a young gentleman of that city; which disturbed her mistress, who feared that this might endanger her own honour. Camilla pressed to know if their affair had gone farther than mere words, and Leonela quite shamelessly and brazenly replied that it had. For it is certain that the mistress's failings rob their maids of all shame. Since, when they see their ladies trip, girls think nothing of stumbling themselves, and do not care if it is known. Camilla could only beg Leonela not to say anything about her mistress's affairs to the young man she said was her lover, and to manage her own with secrecy, so that they should not come to the notice of Anselmo or Lothario. Leonela agreed, but her way of keeping her promise was enough to confirm Camilla's fears that she would lose her reputation through her maid. For the immoral and brazen Leonela, once she saw that her mistress's behaviour was not what it used to be, had the effrontery to bring her lover into the house and keep him there, confident that her mistress would not dare to expose him, even if she were to see him. This is one of the troubles that mistresses pile up for themselves by their sins. Thus they become the slaves of their own maids, and are obliged to conceal their dishonesties and vices, as happened in Camilla's case. For although she very often knew that Leonela was with her lover in one of the rooms of the house, she not only did not dare to scold her, but gave her the chance to hide him, and removed every obstacle from his path for fear that her husband might see him. But she could not prevent Lothario from observing

him come out on one occasion at daybreak. At first he did not recognize him, but thought that he must be a ghost. But when he saw
him walk away, carefully and cautiously wrapping and muffling
himself up, he abandoned this silly notion for another, which would
have been the ruin of them all if Camilla had not found a remedy.
Lothario did not think that the man whom he had seen leave Anselmo's house at such a strange hour could have gone in for Leonela's sake, for he did not even remember Leonela's existence. He
only thought that Camilla was being just as easy and light with
someone else as she had been with him. For these are the consequences a bad woman's wickedness brings with it: she loses her
reputation for honour with the very man to whose prayers and
entreaties she has yielded; and he believes that she gives herself even
more easily to others, and places implicit credence in any suspicion
that comes into his head.

All Lothario's common sense certainly failed him at this juncture, and all his wise reasonings went out of his mind. For without
so much as a single sound – or even a reasonable thought – impatient
and blind with the jealous rage which gnawed at his entrails, and
dying to take vengeance on Camilla, who had done him no sort of
wrong, he went without more ado to Anselmo, who had not yet got
up, and said:

'I must tell you, Anselmo, that I have been battling with myself for
a long time, and doing myself violence in not telling you something
that it is neither possible nor right for me to conceal any longer.
You must know that Camilla's fortress has now surrendered and is
at my absolute mercy. If I have delayed in revealing this fact to you,
it has only been to see if it was merely a light fancy in her, or if it
was to test me and see whether the love I addressed to her by your
permission was seriously meant. I believed too that, if she were
what she should be and what we both thought her to be she would
already have informed you of my wooing. Seeing, however, that she
has not yet done so, I realize that the promises which she has given
me are in earnest, and that the next time you are away from home
she will speak with me in the closet where you keep your valuables.'
– That in fact was the place where Camilla generally received him.
'I do not want you to rush wildly into taking some sort of vengeance. For the sin so far has been committed only in intention, and

it may be that, between now and the time for action, Camilla will change her mind and repentance will be born instead. So, since you have always followed my advice, either wholly or in part, take the advice I am going to give you now. Then you will be able to satisfy yourself, without any possibility of error, as to the best measures to take. Pretend to go away for two or three days, as you have done before, but contrive to hide in your closet instead. The tapestries there, and other possible coverings, will make this extremely easy. Then you and I will see with our own eyes what Camilla will do; and if she is guilty, which is possible but by no means certain, you may then silently, cautiously, and discreetly avenge your wrongs.'

Anselmo was astonished, amazed, stunned, by Lotario's statements, which caught him at a time when he least expected to hear them. For now he thought of Camilla as triumphant over Lotario's pretended assaults, and was beginning to enjoy the glory of her victory. He was silent for some time, gazing at the ground without so much as moving an eyelash. But finally he said:

'Lotario you have done all that I expected of your friendship. I must follow your advice in everything. Do what you please, and keep this matter secret. That is the only course in this incredible business.'

Lotario promised he would. But by the time he left he had completely repented of what he had said, and realized how stupidly he had acted, since he might have revenged himself on Camilla in a less cruel and dishonourable way. He cursed his stupidity and his feeble resolution. But he was at a loss for a means of undoing what he had done, and could think of no way out. Finally he decided to tell Camilla the whole story and, as there was no lack of opportunity, that same day he found her alone. But as soon as the chance offered it was she who spoke:

'Lotario, my friend, my hearts pains me so that I think it will burst in my breast. It will be a miracle if it does not. Leonela's shamelessness has gone so far that she lets her lover into this house every night, and stays with him till morning. It will greatly harm my reputation, for any one who sees him come out of my house at such an unusual hour will be perfectly free to condemn me. What troubles me is that I cannot punish her or scold her, because her knowledge of our affairs puts a bridle on my tongue, and I must be silent about her. I am afraid that some harm will come of this.'

At the beginning of this tale of Camilla's Lothario thought that it was a trick to make him believe that the young man whom he had seen come out of the house was Leonela's lover and not hers. But when he saw her tears and her distress, and when she asked for his help, he realized the truth, and in that moment was filled with confusion and remorse. But, for all that, he told Camilla not to worry, for he would contrive a means of stopping Leonela's insolence. He told her, too, what his furious rage of jealousy had driven him to say to Anselmo, and how it was agreed that her husband should hide in the closet and witness her faithlessness to him. He begged her to forgive him this folly, and to advise him how to remedy it and find a way out of the tortuous labyrinth his stupidity had put him into.

Camilla was alarmed at Lothario's story, and turned on him in a great fury with justifiable reproaches, cursing his wicked suspicions and the bad and foolish scheme he had contrived. But, as women have naturally a readier wit for good or for evil than men, although it fails them when they set about deliberate reasoning, Camilla instantly found a way of remedying this seemingly irremediable business. She told Lothario to try to get Anselmo to hide next day in the place he had spoken of, for she thought she could turn this hiding to good purpose. They might, in fact, be able to take their pleasure together in future without any fear of surprise. She did not tell him the whole of her plan, but warned him, once Anselmo was hidden, to be certain to come as soon as Leonela called him, and to answer any questions she might ask him just as he would if he did not know that Anselmo was listening. Lothario pressed her to tell him the whole of her scheme, so that he could do whatever might seem needful with more certainty and caution.

'I assure you,' said Camilla, 'that there are no more precautions to take. Only answer the questions I shall ask you.'

Camilla did not want to tell him her intentions beforehand because she was afraid that he would not follow this plan, which seemed so excellent to her, and might think out another which might not be so good.

At this Lothario went off; and next day Anselmo left the house, making the excuse of a visit to that friend of his in the country. He then came back to hide, which he conveniently could because Camilla and Leonela had deliberately given him the opportunity. Anselmo was now concealed, and his state of anxiety can be imagined; for he expected to see the very heart of his dishonour laid bare before his own eyes. He saw himself, in fact, on the point of losing the supreme treasure which he supposed that he possessed in his beloved Camilla. Then, once Camilla and Leonela were certain that Anselmo was hidden, they went into the closet; and Camilla was no sooner in than she heaved a deep sigh and said:

'Leonela, my friend, before I carry out my intention, which I do not wish you to know for fear you may try to prevent me, would it not be better if you were to take Anselmo's dagger, which I have asked you for, and plunge it into this wicked heart of mine? But do not do it; it would not be right for me to bear the burden of another's sin. First I must know what it is that Lothario's bold, licentious eyes saw in me to give him the courage to reveal his evil designs against his friend and against my honour. Stand at that window, Leonela, and call him; for he is certainly in the street, waiting to carry out his wicked purpose. But first I shall carry out mine, which shall be both cruel and honourable.'

'Oh, my lady,' answered the wily Leonela, who was in the plot, 'what are you going to do with that dagger? Do you perhaps mean to take your own life, or Lothario's? Whichever you do will involve the loss of your honour and good name. Better hide your injury, and not give that wicked man a chance to come into the house now and find us alone. Think, my lady, how weak we women are. He is a man, and resolute. And, being bent on such a villainous purpose, in his blind passion he may possibly do something to you that will be worse than murder, before you have a chance of carrying out your plan. I blame my master Anselmo for making that shameless scoundrel so free of his house. But if you kill him, my lady, as I think you mean to, what shall we do with him when he is dead?'

'What then, my friend?' replied Camilla. 'We will leave him for Anselmo to bury. For he should have the agreeable task of burying his own dishonour. Call him quickly; for every moment I delay in taking due vengeance for my wrong I seem to be failing in the loyalty I owe my husband.'

Anselmo was listening to all this, and at each word that Camilla spoke his mind changed. But when he heard that she was resolved to kill Lothario he decided to emerge and reveal himself, for fear she might do so. But he was restrained by his desire to see where this spirited and virtuous resolution would end. So he decided only to come out just in time to prevent the act.

At this point Camilla fell into a deep swoon; and Leonela, laying her on a bed which was there, began to weep more bitterly, crying: 'Oh, what a misfortune to have, dying here in my arms, the flower of the world's chastity, the crown of pure women, the pattern of virtue!'

And she said so much more in that style that anyone overhearing her would have thought she was the most piteous and faithful maid-servant in the world, and her mistress another persecuted Penelope. Camilla was not long, however, in coming round from her faint, and as she came to, she said:

'Why do you not go, Leonela, and call that most loyal of friends the sun ever saw or the night hid? Be quick, run, hurry, go, or the fire of my anger may be quenched by the delay and the rightful vengeance I desire pass off in threats and curses.'

'I am going to call him now, my lady,' said Leonela. 'But first you must give me that dagger, for fear you may do something with it while I am away, which would leave all of us who love you weeping for the rest of our lives.'

'Do not fear, friend Leonela, I shall not do it,' replied Camilla. 'For though in your eyes I may seem bold and rash for defending my honour, I shall not be as bold as Lucretia. They say she killed herself although she had committed no crime, and without first slaying the cause of her dishonour. I will die, if I must. But my vengeance must be satisfied on the man who has brought me to this pass, in which I weep for his insolence, though it sprang from no fault of mine.'

Leonela required some further entreaties before going out to call Lothario. But at last she went and, whilst awaiting her return, Camilla spoke, as if in soliloquy:

'Heaven help me! Would it not have been better to have sent Lothario away, as I have often done before, and not have allowed him, as I have done now, to think me dishonest and wicked, if only for the little time I must wait before undeceiving him. It would certainly have been better, but then I should not be revenged; nor would my husband's honour be satisfied if he were to escape so neatly and easily from the predicament his wickedness has brought him into. Let the traitor pay for his lecherous desires with his life. Let the world know – if it ever does – that Camilla not only kept faith with her husband, but avenged him on the man who dared to offend him. Yet perhaps it would be better to tell Anselmo of this. Though I have already hinted at it in the letter I sent to him to the country. Seeing that he did not hasten to remedy the trouble I wrote of, I can only imagine that pure goodness and trustfulness prevents his believing that so much as a thought of his dishonour can dwell in the breast of so staunch a friend. I did not believe it myself for a long while, and I should never have believed it if his insolence had not grown so great, and his open bribes, his grand promises, and continual tears had not made it clear to me. But, why all these speeches now? Can a brave resolution have need of any arguments? No, indeed no! Away with you, then, traitors! Now for vengeance! Let the false villain enter; let him come; let him draw near; let him die and be done with, come what may! Pure I came into the possession of the husband Heaven gave me; pure I must go from him, even though I go bathed in my own chaste blood, and in the impure blood of the falsest friend that ever was in all the world.'

As she talked, she paced about the room with the dagger unsheathed, taking such uneven and unsteady strides, and striking such gestures, that she seemed to be out of her wits. She was like no delicate woman, but a desperate ruffian.

All the while Anselmo looked on in utter amazement, concealed behind some tapestries. What he had seen and heard already seemed to him sufficient to refute even graver suspicions, and he would willingly have dispensed with the further proof upon Lothario's arrival; for he was afraid of some sudden disaster. But, as he was on the point of showing himself and emerging to embrace and reassure his wife, he stopped. For Leonela returned leading Lothario by the hand. And as soon as Camilla saw him she drew with the dagger a long line on the floor before her, and said:

'Listen to me, Lothario. If you dare by any chance to pass beyond this line here, or even to approach it, I will plunge this dagger I hold in my hand into my breast, the moment I see you are going to. Now, before you reply by so much as a word, I want you to hear me speak. Afterwards you may answer as you please. Tell me first, Lothario, if you know my husband Anselmo, and what opinion you hold of him. And next, I want to know whether you know me. Answer me. Do not be confused or hesitant in your replies, for these are not riddles that I am asking you.'

Lothario was not so stupid as not to have realized Camilla's plan when she told him to make Anselmo hide. So he fell in with her scheme most cleverly and aptly, and the pair of them made their imposture pass for truer than truth itself. Therefore he answered Camilla in this way, 'I did not think, beauteous Camilla, that you had summoned me to ask me questions so far from the purpose for which I have come. If your intention is to put off granting the favour you promised, you might have postponed it from a greater distance. For the nearer our hopes of possession the more we are tormented by our desires. But, so that you shall not accuse me of not replying to your questions, I will answer that I know your husband Anselmo, and that we have known one another since our tenderest years. Of our friendship I will say nothing. You know all about that, and I do not want to testify against myself. But the wrong I am doing, love – which excuses the greatest of faults – compels me to do. You too I know, and I value you as highly as he does. If that were not so, for lesser charms than yours, I should not have transgressed the holy laws of friendship, which I have now broken and violated at the instigation of that mighty enemy, love.'

'If you confess to that,' replied Camilla, 'mortal enemy of all true love, how can you have the effrontery to appear before the woman whom you know to be his very mirror and reflection? If you would look at yourself in her eyes you would see how little excuse you have for wronging him. But now, poor wretch that I am, I know what has made you break your faith. It must have been some lightness in me. I will not call it immodesty, for it did not spring from deliberate design. It was just one of those indiscretions into which women often carelessly fall when they think that reserve is unnecessary. But tell me, traitor, when did I answer your entreaties with so much as a word or sign that could awaken any shadow of hope in you of accomplishing your wicked desires? When were your words of love not sternly and bitterly and scornfully rejected? When did I accept your presents, or believe in your many promises? But I know that no one can persevere in his wooing unless sustained by some hope. So I will take the blame for your insolence, for no doubt it is my negligence that has made you persist in your suit so long. I will punish myself, therefore, and inflict the penalty of your guilt upon myself. I have brought you here to see that, being so cruel to myself, I could not be anything but cruel to you, and so that you may witness the sacrifice I intend to make to the wounded honour of my most honoured husband. You injured him with the greatest possible deliberation, and I by my lack of precaution in giving you an opportunity – if I did so – of furthering your wicked desires. What troubles me most, I repeat, is my suspicion that some carelessness of mine bred these rash thoughts in you. And that I most fervently desire to blot out with my own hands; for if I were to have any other executioner, my guilt would be more public.

'But before I die, I mean to satisfy my desire for vengeance, and take with me the man who has reduced me to this desperate plight. For when in that other place, wherever it may be, I see the punishment which impartial and unswerving justice will award him, I shall be completely satisfied.'

As she spoke she sprang upon Lothario with incredible strength and swiftness, flourishing the naked dagger; and so determined she appeared to bury it in his heart that even he was almost uncertain whether her demonstrations were false or true. For he had to use all his dexterity to prevent her stabbing him.

So convincingly did she perform her extraordinary act of deceit and fraud that she even shed her own blood to lend it colour. Finding that should could not wound Lothario – or pretending that she could not – she said: 'Though fate denies me complete satisfaction, at least it shall not be so strong as to prevent my attaining it in part.'

At this she wrenched her dagger-hand free from Lothario's grasp and, pointing the knife where it could not wound her deeply, she stabbed herself, burying the weapon above her breast under her left shoulder. She then let herself fall to the ground, as if in a faint.

Leonela and Lothario were speechless with astonishment at this unexpected act, and did not know what to think when they saw

Camilla stretched on the ground and bathed in her own blood. Breathless and shaken with fright, Lothario hurriedly ran to pull out the dagger. But when he saw how small the wound was his fears vanished, and he was amazed afresh at the fair Camilla's ingenuity, coolness, and ready wits. But, to play his part, he broke into a long and doleful lament over her body, just as if she were dead, calling down great curses upon himself and also on the man who had been the cause of the catastrophe. And, knowing that his friend Anselmo was listening, he spoke so that anyone hearing him would have pitied him even more than Camilla, even if he had supposed that she was dead. Leonela took her in her arms and placed her on the bed, begging Lothario to go and find someone to attend to her in secret. She asked him also to advise her what they should say to Anselmo about her mistress's wound, if he were to return before she was healed. He replied that they might say what they pleased, for he was no person to give useful advice. He only told her to try to staunch the blood, for he was going where no man should see him again. Then he left the house with a great show of grief and emotion. But, once he was alone and unobserved, he could not stop crossing himself in amazement at Camilla's ingenuity and Leonela's very apt acting. He reflected how positive Anselmo must be that his wife was a second Portia, and longed to meet him so that they might rejoice together at the most plausible imposture imaginable.

Leonela staunched her mistress's blood as she was told, though there was only just enough to make her performance convincing. Then she washed the wound with a little wine, and bound it up as best she could, making such an outcry as she did so that, even if nothing had been said before, that alone would have been enough to convince Anselmo that in Camilla he possessed the image of chastity. To Leonela's protestations Camilla added others of her own. She reproached herself for cowardice, and for lacking the courage to end her own days at that moment when it was most necessary; for life was abhorrent to her. She asked her maid's advice whether she should tell her beloved husband all that had happened or not, and Leonela advised her not to. For this would compel him to take vengeance on Lothario, which would involve him in great risk to himself. It was a good wife's duty, said the maid, to give her husband no occasion for quarrels. but rather to save him as many as she could. Camilla replied that this was good advice, and that she would follow it; but they would certainly have to find some explanation of her wound, for Anselmo would not fail to see it. Leonela's only reply to this was that she could not tell a lie, even in jest.

'Then how should I, my dear?' asked Camilla. 'I should not dare to invent or brazen out a lie if my whole life depended on it. If we cannot think how to get out of this fix, it would be better to tell him the naked truth than for him to catch us out in a lying tale.'

'Do not worry, my lady,' replied Leonela. 'Between now and tomorrow I will think out something to say. Perhaps you may be able to hide the wound, it being where it is, and he will not see it. Then Heaven may smile on the justice of our case. Be calm, my lady, and try to control your feelings, so that my master shall not find you upset. Leave the rest to me and to God, who always aids good intentions.'

Anselmo had stood listening and watching with rapt attention at this tragedy representing the death of his honour, and performed by the players with such strange and moving passion that they seemed transformed into the very characters they were acting. He longed for night, which would give him an opportunity of slipping out of the house and going to his friend Lothario, to rejoice with him over the pearl which he had found, in the unveiling of his wife's virtue. The pair of them took care to give him an opportunity of getting away; and he took advantage of it to go immediately in search of Lothario. It is impossible to recount how often he embraced him when he found him, what he said in his delight, and how much he praised Camilla. Lothario listened to all this without being able to show any signs of joy, for he could not get out of his mind the thought of how greatly his friend was deceived and how cruelly he had wronged him. But, although Anselmo noticed that Lothario did not show any joy, he supposed that it was because Camilla had been wounded and he had been responsible. So, in the course of their conversation, he told him not to worry about Camilla's accident, for the wound must certainly be a slight one, since they had agreed to hide it from him. Lothario, in fact, had nothing to fear, he said, but should rejoice and be gay with him, since it was through his friend's means and contriving that he had been raised to the highest attainable peak of happiness. What was more, he would have no other pastime from that day on but to write verses in Camilla's praise, to render her memory eternal for future ages. Lothario commended his resolution and promised to assist him in raising so noble an edifice.

From that time on Anselmo was the most deliciously deluded man in the whole world. He himself led home by the hand the man who had completely destroyed his good name, in the firm belief that he had brought him nothing but glory. Camilla received Lothario with seemingly averted glances but with a smiling heart; and this deception lasted for some time, until after many months Fortune turned her wheel, their cunningly concealed wickedness became public, and Anselmo's foolish curiosity cost him his life.

Chapter XXXV. *Of the fierce and monstrous Battle which Don Quixote fought with some Skins of Red Wine, with the conclusion of the Tale of Foolish Curiosity.*

VERY little more of the tale remained to be read when Sancho Panza rushed in alarm from the loft where Don Quixote was lying, shouting at the top of his voice: 'Come quickly, gentlemen, and help my master. I've never seen such a fierce and stubborn battle as he's got himself into. God in Heaven! He's dealt that giant, the lady Princess Micomicona's enemy, such a slash that he's sliced his head clean off like a turnip.'

'What's that you say, brother?' asked the priest, leaving the rest of the tale unread. 'Are you in your senses, Sancho? How the devil can all that be true, seeing that the giant is six thousand miles away?'

Here they heard a tremendous noise in the room and Don Quixote shouting: 'Hold, thief, scoundrel, braggart! Ah, I have you at last. Your scimitar will not help you now.'

And he seemed to be slashing at the walls.

Then Sancho said: 'You shouldn't stand there listening. You ought to go in and get between them, or go to my master's aid. Though there'll be no need now, for the giant's certainly dead by now, and giving an account to God of the wicked life he's led. I saw his blood on the floor, and his head cut off and fallen on one side. It's as big as a great wineskin.'

'Good God!' exclaimed the innkeeper at this point. 'If that

Don Quixote, or Don devil, hasn't been slashing at one of the skins of red wine at the head of his bed! Full they were, and what this fellow takes for blood must be the wine spilt on the floor.'

With that he ran into the room, and the others after him. They found Don Quixote in the strangest outfit in the world. He was in his shirt, which was not long enough in front to cover his thighs completely, and was six inches shorter behind. His legs were very long and thin, covered with hair, and not over-clean. On his head he wore a little greasy red cap which belonged to the innkeeper, and round his left arm he had wound the blanket of the bed—against which Sancho bore a grudge, and very well he knew why. In his right hand was his naked sword, with which he was lamming out in all directions, shouting all the time as if he were really fighting with a giant. The cream of the joke was that his eyes were not open, because he was asleep, and dreaming that he was battling with the giant. For his imagination was so bent on the adventure which he was going to achieve, that it made him dream he had got to the kingdom of Micomicon and was already at grips with his enemy.

What is more, he had slashed the wine-skins so many times, in the belief that he was getting at the giant, that the whole room was flooded with wine. At the sight of this the innkeeper flew into such a fury that he fell on Don Quixote, and began punching him repeatedly with his clenched fists. Indeed if Cardenio and the priest had not pulled him off he would soon have put an end to the war with the giant. But, despite all this, the wretched knight did not wake up until the barber brought a large pitcher of cold water from the well and threw it with a jerk all over his body. This awakened Don Quixote, but not sufficiently for him to realize the state he was in. Seeing how lightly and scantily he was dressed, Dorothea did not care to go in and see the battle between her champion and her adversary; and as for Sancho, he went about looking all over the floor for the giant's head and, not finding it, observed: 'Now I know that everything about this house is enchanted. The last time, right in this very spot where I'm standing, I got a regular punching and beating; yet I never knew who gave it me and never saw anybody at all. And this time the head isn't to be found, though I saw it cut off with my own eyes, and the blood pouring from the body like a fountain.'

'What blood and what fountain are you talking about, enemy of God and His saints?' cried the innkeeper. 'Can't you see, you great thief, that your blood and your fountain are nothing else but these skins here, which are slashed through, and the red wine which this room is swimming in? I should like to see the soul of the man who slashed them swimming in hell.'

'All I know,' replied Sancho, 'is that I'm going to be very unlucky. If I don't find that head, my countship will melt away like salt in water.' For Sancho awake was worse than his master asleep, so obsessed was he with the promises which his master had made him.

The innkeeper was in despair at the imperturbability of the squire and the damage which his master had done, and swore that this time he should not get away without paying, as he had done the time before; and that the privileges of knighthood should not save him from settling both reckonings, down to the very cost of the patches which would have to be stuck on to the torn wineskins.

The priest was holding Don Quixote down by the hands, when, thinking that he had finished the adventure and was now in the presence of Princess Micomicona, the knight dropped on his knees before him and said: 'Exalted and most famous lady, Your Highness may henceforth live secure from any ill this low-born creature may do you; and, from to-day too, I also am released from the pledge which I gave you. For, by the help of God on high and through the favour of her for whom I live and breathe, I have perfectly fulfilled it.'

'Wasn't that just what I said?' exclaimed Sancho, when he heard this. 'So I wasn't drunk then. It looks as if my master has pickled the giant sure enough. The bulls are all right; I'm sure of my countship.'

Could anyone have kept from laughing at the nonsense of these two, master and servant? Everyone did laugh except the innkeeper, who cursed his luck. At length the barber, Cardenio, and the priest managed, with no little labour, to get Don Quixote into the bed, where he dropped off to sleep in a state of great exhaustion. They left him sleeping and went out to the inn door to console Sancho Panza for not having found the giant's head, although they had more to do to pacify the innkeeper, who was in despair at the sudden death of his wine-skins. The landlady too was shouting and screaming:

'It was an ill wind which blew that knight errant into my house. I wish I'd never set eyes on him, so dear he's cost me! Last time he went off he owed us for the night. Supper and bed for him and his squire, and straw and barley for a horse and an ass. He said that he was a knight adventurer — God send a bad end to his adventures, and the like to all other adventurers in the world! — and that he wasn't supposed to pay anything, that it was written so in the knight errantry regulations. And now, because of him, there comes this other gentleman and takes away my tail, and gives it me back with a pretty pennyworth of damage, with the hair all off, so that it's no good any more for what my husband wants it for. And on top of all that, to burst my wine-skins for me and spill out the wine. I'll see his blood spilt, I will! He shan't get away with it. By my poor father's bones and my blessed mother's grey hairs, if they don't pay me every single penny I'm not called what I am, and I'm not my father's daughter!'

This and more like it the landlady poured out in a great fury, and her good maid Maritornes backed her up; but her daughter kept quiet and smiled from time to time. The priest quietened them down by promising to compensate them for their loss as far as he was able, both for the skins and for the wine, and especially for the damage to the tail, which they made so much of. Dorothea consoled Sancho Panza by promising that, as soon as ever it was certain that his master had cut off the giant's head and once she was in peaceful possession of her kingdom, she would give him the best countship in it. At this Sancho took comfort, vowing that she could be certain that he had seen the giant's head, and, as proof more positive, that the monster had had a beard down to his waist. But, if it did not turn up, it was because everything which happened in that house was bewitched, as he had found the last time he had stayed there. Dorothea said that she believed him, and that he had no need to worry, for all would go well and turn out to his heart's content.

When everyone was quiet the priest expressed a wish to finish reading the tale, for he saw that there was very little left. Cardenio, Dorothea, and all the others begged him to do so and, being

anxious to please them all, besides wanting to read it himself, he
went on with the story.

'So it came to pass that through the satisfaction which Anselmo
took in Camilla's virtue he led a happy and carefree life; and Camilla purposely looked sourly on Lothario, so that Anselmo should
take her feelings for him to be the opposite of what they were. And
to reinforce this pretence, Lothario asked leave not to come to the
house, saying that he could clearly see how much Camilla disliked
seeing him. But the deluded Anselmo replied that he would not
agree on any account; and thus in a thousand ways Anselmo was
the architect of his own dishonour, while he believed that he was
making happiness for himself. At this time Leonela's pleasure in
finding herself licensed in her love affair reached such a pitch that
she pursued it unrestrainedly without any other thought, confident
that her mistress would screen her, and even show her how to carry
it on without arousing more than slight suspicion. But finally, one
night, Anselmo heard steps in Leonela's room and, when he tried
to go in and see who it was, found the door barred against him;
which made him the more eager to force it. He pushed so hard, in
fact, as to prise it open, and broke in just in time to see a man leap
out of the window into the street. But when he ran quickly to catch
him or see who he was, he could do neither, because Leonela clung
to him, crying:

'Calm yourself, my lord, and don't make a disturbance. Don't
follow the man who jumped out there. It's my affair; in fact he's
my husband.'

Anselmo would not believe her; but blind with rage, drew his
dagger and tried to wound her, commanding her to tell him the
truth or he would kill her. Then, out of fear, and not knowing what
she was saying, she exclaimed: 'Do not kill me, sir, and I will tell
something more important than you can imagine.'

'Tell me, then, at once,' said Anselmo. 'If not, you are a dead
woman.'

'I can't just now,' said Leonela. 'I'm so upset. Give me till to-
morrow, and then I'll tell you something which will amaze you.
But I swear to you that the man who jumped out of this window is
a young man of this city, who has given me his word that he will
marry me.'

Anselmo was satisfied with this, and content to wait the time she asked, for he did not expect to hear anything against Camilla, so absolutely satisfied was he of her virtue. So he went out of the room and left Leonela locked up, saying that she would not be let out till she had told him all that she had promised to reveal.

Then he went straight to Camilla and told her all that had passed between him and her maid, and of her promise to tell him something great and important. There is no need to say whether Camilla was alarmed or not. For so great was her fright, believing as she did and had good reason to, that Leonela was going to tell Anselmo all that she knew about her unfaithfulness, that she had not the courage to wait and see whether her suspicions were justified or not. That same night, when she thought that Anselmo was asleep, collecting her finest jewels and some money, she left the house unobserved and went to Lothario's. Once there, she told him what had happened, and begged him to find a hiding-place for her, or to take her away somewhere where they would both be safe from Anselmo. Lothario was thrown into such confusion that he could not answer a single word, still less make up his mind what to do. In the end he decided to take Camilla to a nunnery of which one of his sisters was prioress. Camilla agreed to this, and with the swiftness which the situation demanded Lothario took her and left her at the nunnery, then himself immediately quitted the city, informing no one of his departure.

When the day broke, so eager was Anselmo to learn what Leonela was going to tell him that he did not notice Camilla's absence from his side, but got up and went to the room where he had left the maid locked up. He opened the door and went in, but could not see Leonela. All he found were some sheets knotted to the window-bars – evidence that she had climbed down and fled. Then he returned at once rather sorrowfully to tell Camilla, and was astounded not to find her in bed or anywhere in the house. He asked the servants where she was, but no one could answer his question. Then, by chance, as he was searching for her, he noticed that her boxes were open and most of her jewels missing. From this he began to realize his disaster, and that Leonela was not the cause of his trouble. So, just as he was, without troubling to finish dressing, he went sadly and dejectedly to tell his friend Lothario of his misfortune. But when he found him gone, and his servants told him that their

L

master had departed that night and had taken all the money he had with him, he thought he would go out of his mind. And on top of all this, when he got back to his house he found not one of the men or maid-servants there, and the house silent and deserted.

He did not know what to think or say or do, but little by little his wits seemed to be returning to him. He reflected; and saw himself at one blow wifeless, friendless, and servantless, seemingly abandoned by the Heavens above and, worst of all, robbed of his honour. For in Camilla's flight he saw his own damnation. Finally, after a long while, he resolved to go to his friend in the country, with whom he had stayed when he had given them their opportunity of contriving the whole disaster. He locked the doors of his house, mounted his horse, and with failing heart set out on the road. But he had gone no more than half-way when, harassed by his thoughts, he was compelled to dismount and tie his horse to a tree, at the foot of which he lay down, heaving piteous and sorrowful sighs. There he stayed almost till nightfall, when he saw a man coming on horseback from the city, of whom, after greeting him, he asked what news there was in Florence.

'The strangest news that we've heard there for many a long day,' replied the townsman. 'It's publicly reported that Lotharío, Anselmo's great friend, the rich man who used to live at San Giovanni, carried off Anselmo's wife Camilla last night, and that Anselmo himself is also missing. All this was revealed by a servant of Camilla's, whom the Governor found, last night also, letting herself down from the window of Anselmo's house by a sheet. I don't know, indeed, exactly what happened. I only know that the whole city is amazed at the business, for such a thing was most unexpected, considering the great and intimate friendship between these two. It was so remarkable that they're supposed to have been called *the Two Friends*.'

'Do you know by any chance,' asked Anselmo, 'what road Lotharío and Camilla have taken?'

'I've no idea,' replied the townsman, 'although the Governor has been very active in looking for them.'

'God be with you, sir,' said Anselmo.

'And with you,' replied the townsman and rode off.

At this disastrous news Anselmo was not merely on the point of going out of his mind, but on the verge of putting an end to his life. He got up as best he could, and reached the house of his friend, who had not yet heard of his misfortune. But when he saw him come in, pale, exhausted, and haggard, he realized that some serious misfortune had befallen him. Anselmo begged them at once to help him to bed and give him some writing materials, which they did, and left him alone in bed with the door locked, just as he asked. Once alone, he was so overwhelmed by the thought of his disaster that he clearly saw his life was drawing to a close. So he decided to leave an account of the cause of his strange death. He began to write. But before he had finished setting down all he wished his breath failed him, and he yielded up his life into the hands of that grief which his foolish curiosity had brought upon him. The master of the house, seeing that it was late and Anselmo had not called out, decided to go in and find out if he was any worse. He discovered him lying on his face, with half of his body on the bed and the other half on the desk, and with the paper he had written unsealed and the pen still in his hand. But, seeing that he did not respond and finding him cold, he realized that he was dead. Amazed and deeply grieved, he called his household to see the disastrous end that had befallen Anselmo and, later, read the paper on which he recognized Anselmo's hand. It said:

'*A foolish and ill-judged craving has cost me my life. If the news of my death should come to Camilla's ears, let her know that I pardon her. For she was not obliged to perform miracles nor did I need to ask her to. So, since I was the contriver of my own dishonour, there is no reason why ...*'

Anselmo had written only so far, and it was clear that his life had ended before he could finish his sentence. The next day his friends advised Anselmo's relations of his death. They already knew of his misfortune and of Camilla's retreat to the nunnery, where she was almost in a state to accompany her husband on his inevitable journey; not because of the news of his death, but from what she had heard of her absent lover. It was said that, although she was now a widow, she would not leave the nunnery, nor even less take nun's vows. But not many days later news reached her that Lothario had been killed in a battle, which took place just then between

Monsieur de Lautrec and the great Captain Gonzalo Hernandez de Cordoba, in the kingdom of Naples where Anselmo's friend had retired, repentant too late. When Camilla heard this news she made her profession as a nun, and not long afterwards yielded her life into the cruel hands of sorrow and melancholy. This then was the end of these three, arising from such foolish beginnings.'

'I like the tale,' said the priest, 'but there is something unconvincing about it. If the author invented it he did it badly, for it is impossible to believe that there could be a husband so stupid as to want to make the costly experiment Anselmo did. If it were a case of a lover and his mistress it might pass; but between husband and wife there is something impossible about it. Though as for the manner of its telling, that does not displease me at all.'

Chapter XXXVI. *Of other strange events at the Inn.*

JUST then the landlord, who was standing at the inn door, called out: 'Here's a fine troop of guests coming. If they stop here we can sing "Praise the Lord".'

'What sort of people?' asked Cardenio.

'Four men on horseback,' replied the innkeeper, 'riding with short stirrups, with lances and shields, and all in black travelling-masks. There's a woman dressed in white with them riding side-saddle, with her face covered too, and two others, servants, on foot.'

'Are they very near?' asked the priest.

'So near,' replied the landlord, 'that they are here already.'

Hearing this, Dorothea veiled her face, and Cardenio went into Don Quixote's room; but they had hardly had time to do this when the whole party the host had described came into the inn. The four horsemen, who had a very well-bred appearance and bearing, dismounted and helped the lady down from her side-saddle. Then one of them took her in his arms and seated her in a chair, which stood at the entrance of the room where Cardenio had hidden. All this time neither she nor they had taken off their masks, nor said a word. Only, as she sat down, the lady in the chair heaved a deep sigh, and let her arms fall, as if she were ill or in a faint. The servants then led the horses to the stable.

The priest looked on and, wishing to know who these people were, so strangely dressed and so silent, went over to the servants and asked one of them. His answer was: 'Indeed, sir, I can't tell you who they are. All I know is that they seem to be important people, especially the man you just saw take the lady in his arms. Why I think so is because all the others pay him respect, and do nothing but obey his orders and directions.'

'And who is the lady?' asked the priest.

'I couldn't say either,' answered the servant, 'for I haven't set eyes on her face the whole way. I have only heard her sigh very often and moan as if she were ready to give up the ghost. It's not surprising that we don't know more than we've told you, because my mate and I have only been with them for the last two days. We met them on the road, and they begged and persuaded us to come with them as far as Andalusia, and offered to pay us very well.'

'Have you heard the name of any of them?' asked the priest.

'No, I haven't,' answered the servant. 'They all ride in perfect silence. It's very queer. The only sound we hear from any of them is the poor lady's sighs and sobs, which make us feel sorry for her. It's our firm belief that she's being forced to go wherever it is she's going and, as far as we can gather from her dress, she's a nun, or is going to become one more likely. Perhaps it's because she isn't taking the veil of her own free choice that she looks so sad.'

'That is very possible,' said the priest, and left them, to join Dorothea, whose natural pity was so stirred by the sighs and groans of the lady in disguise, that she went up to her and asked:

'What is your trouble, dear lady? If it is anything that it is in a woman's power to relieve, I would most willingly help you.'

The sorrowful lady made no reply and, although Dorothea repeated her offer, she remained silent till the masked horseman – the one whom the servant had said the others obeyed – came up and said to Dorothea:

'Do not weary yourself, lady, by showing this woman any courtesy, for she is always most ungrateful for whatever is done for her; and do not press her to reply if you do not want to hear her tell you some lie.'

'I have never told one,' exclaimed the lady, breaking her silence at this point. 'It is because I have been so truthful and so guileless that I am in my present unhappy plight. I call you as a witness to that, since it is the pure truth in me which shows you up as a false liar.'

Cardenio heard these words clearly and distinctly, as he was extremely near the speaker, only the door of Don Quixote's room being between them; and directly they came to his ears he cried out: 'Good God! What is that I hear? What voice is that?'

The lady turned her head in alarm at these cries and, not seeing who it was that spoke, rose to her feet and made to go into the room. But the gentleman immediately held her back and would not let her move a step. In her disturbance and agitation, however, her mask fell off, revealing a face of marvellous and incomparable beauty, though pale and frightened. For her eyes searched every spot within sight in such distress that she seemed to be out of her mind; and Dorothea, and all who saw her, were filled with pity for her, though they did not understand the reason for her behaviour. The gentleman held her firmly by the shoulder, but was so busy keeping his grip that he could not manage to hold up his mask, which in the end fell off. So when Dorothea, who had caught the lady in her arms, looked up, she saw that the man who was also holding her was her husband, Don Ferdinand; and the moment she recognized him she fell back senseless, uttering a deep and heartfelt groan. In fact if the barber had not been close by and caught her in his arms, she would have fallen to the ground. The priest at once hastened to take off her veil and throw water in her face; and as soon as he uncovered it, Don Ferdinand – for he it was who was holding the other lady in his arms – recognized her and was almost struck dead at the sight. Nevertheless he did not let go of Lucinda – for she it was – who was struggling to get free from his arms, having recognized Cardenio by his cry, as he had recognized her. Cardenio also heard Dorothea's moan as she fell fainting and, thinking that it was Lucinda's, rushed terrified out of his room. The first person he saw, however, was Don Ferdinand, holding Lucinda in his arms; and as Don Ferdinand also recognized Cardenio at once, all three, Lucinda, Cardenio, and Dorothea, were struck dumb with amazement, hardly knowing what had happened to them.

They all gazed at one another in silence, Dorothea at Don Ferdinand, Don Ferdinand at Cardenio, Cardenio at Lucinda, Lucinda at Cardenio. But the first to break the silence was Lucinda, who addressed Don Ferdinand:

'Leave me, Don Ferdinand, out of regard for yourself if for no other reason. Let me cling to the wall of which I am the ivy, to the prop from which neither your persistence, your threats, your promises, nor your bribes have been able to part me. See how Heaven, by ways strange and mysterious to us, has brought me to my true husband; and well you know by a thousand costly proofs that only death can blot him from my memory. So let this plain declaration tell you – since you have no alternative – to turn your love to rage, your affection to hatred, and put an end to my life. Yet, as I shall die before the eyes of my dear husband, I shall account my life well lost. For it may be that he will be convinced by my death that I have kept faith with him to the last act of my life.'

During this time Dorothea had come to herself, and had been listening to the whole of Lucinda's speech, from which she had realized who she was. Then, seeing that Don Ferdinand still did not let her go or reply to her words, she summoned up all the strength she could, got up, and threw herself on her knees at his feet. Then, bursting into a flood of lovely and piteous tears, she began to speak:

'If, my dear lord, the rays of that sun which you are holding in eclipse within your arms have not dimmed and darkened the light of your eyes, you will have seen that she who kneels at your feet is, as long as you will have it so, the luckless and unhappy Dorothea. I am that humble country girl, whom you chose, out of your kindness or for your pleasure, to raise to the height where she could call herself yours. I lived a contented life, enclosed within the bounds of virtue until, at the voice of your persistent and seemingly genuine and loving affection, I opened the gates of my modesty and entrusted the keys of my liberty to you: a gift which you appreciated very little, as is clearly shown by my being forced to hide in the place where you find me now, and by my seeing you as I do now. But, for all that, I would not have you think for one moment that I have come here along the road of dishonour; grief alone has brought me here, and sorrow at seeing myself deserted by you. It was your wish that I should be yours; and you wished it to such effect that, although now you would not have it so, it will be impossible for you ever to cease to be mine. Think, my lord, that the matchless love I have for you may be a compensation for the beauty and nobility of her for whom you are deserting me. You cannot be the fair Lucinda's, because you are mine; nor can she be yours, because she is Cardenio's. It will be easier, if you will think a moment, to make your heart love the woman who loves you, than to force into loving you a woman who loathes you. You pursued my innocence; you wore down my integrity with your prayers; you were not ignorant of my rank; well you know how completely I gave myself up to your will; you have no ground or reason to plead deception. If that is the truth, as it is, and you are a Christian and a gentleman, why do you put off with all these evasions, making me as happy at the end as you did at the beginning? If you do not want me for what I am, your true and lawful wife, desire me at least and have me for your slave. For if I am in your possession I shall count myself happy and fortunate. Do not leave me and abandon me so that my shame becomes the subject of gossip, or cause my parents a miserable old age. For they have given your parents loyal tenant's service and do not deserve such treatment. If you think that your blood will be debased by mixing with mine, reflect that there is little or no nobility in the world which has not travelled the same road, and that descent on the woman's side is not what counts in the most distinguished lineage. Moreover true nobility lies in virtue and, if you forfeit that by denying me my just rights, I shall be left with higher claims to it than you. Finally, sir, my last word is that I am still your wife, whether you like it or not. Your own promise is a witness which must not and cannot speak falsely, if you pride yourself on possessing what you despise me for lacking. Let your own signature testify, and Heaven, which you invoked to bear testimony to your promise. Should all these fail, your own conscience cannot but whisper in the midst of your joys, repeating the truth I have just spoken to disturb your greatest pleasures and delights.'

The unhappy Dorothea said this, and more like it, with such feeling and tears that everyone present sympathized with her, including even the men who had come with Don Ferdinand. That gentleman himself listened without answering a word till she finished speaking, and broke into such sobbing and sighing that only a heart of bronze would not have been melted by signs of such distress. Lucinda stood gazing at her, pitying her grief and admiring her good sense and her beauty. But, although she wanted to go and say something to comfort Dorothea, Don Ferdinand still held her tight in his arms and prevented her. Though, after gazing fixedly at Dorothea for some time, he was overwhelmed with shame and horror, and opened his arms to let Lucinda go.

'You have conquered, fair Dorothea,' he said. 'You have conquered. I cannot possibly have the heart to deny a combination of so many truths.'

When Don Ferdinand released her, Lucinda almost fell down from the faintness that had seized her. But Cardenio was close by, having taken up his position behind Don Ferdinand so as not to be recognized – and, setting fear aside, he defied all danger, ran up to catch her, and clasped her in his arms.

'If merciful Heaven,' he cried, 'be pleased to grant you some rest at last, my loyal, steadfast and lovely lady, nowhere, I believe, will you find it more securely than in these arms which clasp you now as they clasped you once before, when Fortune was pleased to let me call you mine.'

At these words Lucinda, who had first begun to recognize him by his voice, fixed her gaze on Cardenio and, assuring herself with her eyes that it was he, almost beside herself and regardless of the proprieties, threw her arms round his neck. Then, putting her face close to his, she said: 'Yes, my dear lord, you are the true master of this slave of yours, however much adverse fortune may oppose us and threaten this life of mine, which depends on yours.'

This was a strange spectacle for Don Ferdinand, and for all the rest, who were astonished at such unforeseen happenings. Dorothea, however, seeing Don Ferdinand change colour and move his hand in the direction of his sword, imagined that he intended to take his revenge on Cardenio, and instantly, with extraordinary quickness, clasped him round the knees, kissing them and holding them so fast that he could not move. Then, without ceasing her tears, she said:

'What is it you mean to do, you who are my only refuge in this unexpected crisis? Here at your feet is your wife, and the woman you desire is in her husband's arms. Reflect whether it will be right or possible for you to undo what Heaven has done; or whether it will not be better to decide to raise to your level one who stands before you, steadfast in her faith and constancy despite all obstacles, and bathing her true husband's face and breast in loving tears. For God's sake, and your own, I beg you not to let this public exposure increase your anger, but rather to allay it; so that you may be able calmly and peacefully to suffer these two lovers to live all the days that Heaven allows them, without any hindrance from you. In that way you will show the generosity of your illustrious and noble soul, and the world will see that reason has more power over you than passion.'

While Dorothea was speaking Cardenio did not take his eyes from Don Ferdinand, even though he held Lucinda in his arms. For he was determined, if he saw him make any hostile movement, to defend himself, and to resist any attack to the uttermost, even at the cost of his life. But at this point Don Ferdinand's friends – with the priest and the barber, who had been present all the time, and even honest Sancho Panza – all surrounded Don Ferdinand, imploring him to be moved by Dorothea's tears and, if she was speaking the truth, as they believed she was, not to suffer her to be defrauded of her just expectations. They begged him to reflect that it was not by chance, as it appeared, but by a special providence of Heaven, that they had all come together in such an unexpected place. The priest warned him, too, that only death could part Lucinda and Cardenio, and that they would joyfully accept their death, even if they were sundered by the sword's edge. In these irremediable circumstances, he said, it would be wisdom to restrain and conquer himself, and to show a generous heart by allowing these two, of his own free will, to enjoy the good fortune which Heaven had granted them. If he would turn his gaze on Dorothea's beauty, he would see that few or none could equal her, much less excel her. And besides her beauty he should consider her humility, and her very great love for him. Above all, he must remember that, if he counted himself a gentleman and a Christian, he could not fail to honour his promises, and in doing so he would be doing his duty to God and be applauded by all men of good sense. For they know and recognize that it is the prerogative of beauty, even though in a humble subject, to rise equal to any dignity. For so long as it is united with virtue, it casts no shadow of reflection on the man who raises it to his own level. For where the strong laws of passion obtain, so long as there is no sin no man can be blamed for obeying them.

In short, he added so many compelling arguments that Don Ferdinand's valorous heart – which was, after all, nurtured by generous blood – softened, and allowed itself to be conquered by the truth, which he could not deny if he would. And the sign he gave of his surrender and acceptance of the priest's good advice, was to stoop down and embrace Dorothea, saying:

'Rise, my lady! The woman I hold in my heart must not kneel at my feet. If I have given no proof of what I say till now, perhaps it has been by Heaven's decree, that by seeing how faithfully you love me I might know how to value you as you deserve. What I beg of you is not to upbraid me for my misconduct and my neglect, for the same compelling reason which moved me to win you for mine drove me to struggle against being yours. For proof that this is true, turn and look into the eyes of the now happy Lucinda. There you will find an excuse for all my errors. Now, since she has obtained her desires, and I have found my fulfilment in you, I wish her a long and peaceful life, safe and happy with her Cardenio, and I pray Heaven to grant me the same happiness with my Dorothea.'

With these words he embraced her once more, pressing his face to hers with such tender feeling that it was all he could do not to burst into tears in true sign of his love and repentance. But Lucinda, Cardenio, and almost all the rest of the company as well, showed no such restraint, and began to shed so many tears, some for their own happiness and some for others', that it might have been thought some grievous disaster had befallen them all. Even Sancho Panza wept, though he said afterwards that he was only crying at finding that Dorothea was not, as he had believed, that Queen Micomicona from whom he had expected such benefits. It was some time before the general weeping and amazement calmed down; and then Cardenio and Lucinda went down on their knees before Don Ferdinand, and thanked him so courteously for the kindness he had shown them that he did not know how to reply. So he raised them up and embraced them with every mark of politeness and affection.

Then he asked Dorothea to tell him how she had come to that place so far from her home. She told him, briefly and sensibly, all that she had previously told Cardenio; and Don Ferdinand and his companions were so delighted with her story that they would have liked it to last longer, so charmingly did she tell the tale of her misfortunes. As soon as she had finished, Don Ferdinand related what had happened to him in the city, after he had found the paper in Lucinda's breast in which she had declared that she was Cardenio's wife and could not be his. He said that he had wanted to kill her, and would have done so if her parents had not prevented him. Then he had left the house angry and ashamed, and determined to take his revenge on a more convenient occasion. On the next day he had learnt that Lucinda had left her parents' house and that no one could say where she had gone; and finally, after some months, he had discovered that she was in a nunnery and intended to spend the rest of her life there, if she could not spend it with Cardenio. As soon as he had learnt of this he had chosen those three gentlemen for his companions and gone to the place where she was. But he would not speak with her for fear that, if they knew he was there, the convent would be better guarded. So he had waited for a day when the porter's lodge was open, and left two of his companions to secure the door, while he and the third had gone into the nunnery to look for Lucinda, whom they had found in the cloisters talking to a nun. Then they had snatched her up without giving her a chance to resist, and taken her to a place where they provided themselves with everything necessary for her abduction. All this they had been able to do in perfect safety as the nunnery was in the country, a good way outside the town. He said that when Lucinda found herself in his power she lost all consciousness, and when she came to herself did nothing but weep and moan, and never spoke a single word. So, to the accompaniment of silence and tears, they had reached the inn, which to him was like reaching Heaven, where all the ills of the earth are over and done with.

Chapter XXXVII. *A continuation of the History of the renowned Princess Micomicona, and other pleasant Adventures.*

To all this Sancho listened in no small distress of mind, seeing that his hopes of a title were disappearing and going up in smoke, since the lovely Princess Micomicona had turned into Dorothea, and the giant into Don Ferdinand; while there was his master sound asleep and quite oblivious of all that had happened. Dorothea could not feel certain that her happiness was not a dream. Cardenio was in the same state, and Lucinda's thoughts ran a similar course. Don Ferdinand gave thanks to Heaven for favours received, and for extricating him from the intricate labyrinth in which he had been within an ace of losing his honour and his soul. And everyone at the inn was pleased and delighted too, at the happy turn which this difficult and desperate situation had taken. The priest, like a man of sense, set everything in its true light, and congratulated everyone on what each had gained. But the most joyful and contented person in the inn was the landlady, because of the promise which Cardenio and the priest had made her to pay her all the cost and damage she had suffered on Don Quixote's account. Only Sancho, as we have said, felt wretched, disappointed, and sad; and so, with a melancholy expression, he went in to his master, who was just then waking up, and said:

'You can sleep soundly for as long as you like, Sir Sad Countenance, and not trouble about killing any giant or restoring the Princess to her kingdom. For it's all done and finished already.'

'I believe you,' replied Don Quixote, 'for I have fought the most monstrous and outrageous battle with that giant that I ever expect to fight in all the days of my life. With one back stroke – whack! – I slashed his head to the ground; and so much blood poured from him that it ran in streams along the earth, just like water.'

'More like red wine, you might say,' answered Sancho; 'for I would have your worship know, if you don't already, that the dead giant is a slashed wine-skin, and his blood the twelve gallons of red wine it had in its belly, and the head you cut off is ... my bitch of a mother – and the devil take the lot!'

'What is that you say?' retorted Don Quixote. 'You must be crazy, man!'

'If your worship will get up,' said Sancho, 'you'll see what a fine job you've done, and what we shall have to pay. And you'll see the Queen turned into an ordinary lady called Dorothea, and other things which will make you wonder, when you get the hang of them.'

'I should marvel at nothing of that sort,' replied Don Quixote.

'Last time we were here, if you remember rightly, I told you that everything which happened in this place was by way of enchantment. So it would not be surprising if it were the same this time.'

'I should believe it all,' answered Sancho, 'if my blanket-tossing had been that sort of thing. But it wasn't. It was real and true enough. I saw this innkeeper, who is here to-day, holding one end of the blanket, bouncing me up and down in fine trim, and laughing for all he was worth. I may be a simpleton and a sinner, yet it's my opinion that where you start recognizing people there's no enchantment about it, but plenty of bruising and bad luck.'

'Well, God will remedy that,' said Don Quixote. 'Give me my clothes and let me go out there. I want to see these changes and transformations you speak of.'

Sancho handed him his clothes; and while he was dressing, the priest told Don Ferdinand and the others of Don Quixote's madness, and of the trick they had played to get him away from the Bare Rock where, as he imagined, his lady's disdain had brought him. He told them too almost all the adventures which Sancho had described to him, at which they wondered and laughed quite a bit, thinking, like everyone else, that it was the strangest kind of madness that ever attacked a distraught mind. The priest said also that, since the lady Dorothea's good fortune would prevent their going on with their scheme, they would have to invent and work out another way of bringing him home to his village. Cardenio, however, offered to carry on with the original plan, and suggested that Lucinda should take over and play the part of Dorothea.

'No,' cried Don Ferdinand, 'that must not be. I wish Dorothea to carry on the scheme herself. This good knight's village cannot be very far away, and I shall be very glad to see him cured.'

'It is not more than two days' journey from here.'

'Even if it were more I should be glad to make the journey for such a good purpose.'

At this moment Don Quixote came out, armed with all his gear: with Mambrino's helmet, bashed in as it was, on his head; grasping his shield, and leaning on his tree-branch, or lance. Don Ferdinand and the others were astounded at his extraordinary appearance, and gazed upon his face, half a mile long, shrivelled and sallow, his miscellaneous weapons and his grave bearing in attentive silence until, staring very solemnly and intently on the fair Dorothea, the knight pronounced:

'I am informed, beauteous lady, by this squire of mine that your greatness has been cast down and your very being destroyed, since from the Queen and great lady that you were you have turned into a humble maiden. If this has been by command of the necromancer King, your father, out of his fear that I shall not give you due and necessary aid, I say that he has never known, and does not know, the half of his art, and that he has very little acquaintance with histories of chivalry. For, had he read them and studied them as attentively and as much at his leisure as I have, he would have found at every step how other knights, of less renown than I, have achieved things much more difficult. For it is no great matter to kill a paltry giant, however arrogant he may be. Not very long ago, in fact, I fought with him myself and ... I prefer to be silent, in case I may be accused of falsehood. But time, which unveils all mysteries, will reveal this one when we least expect it.'

'It wasn't a giant you fought, but two wine-skins,' put in the inn-keeper at this point. But Don Ferdinand told him to be quiet and on no account to interrupt Don Quixote's remarks. Then the knight went on:

'Indeed, as I say, exalted and disinherited lady, if for the reasons I have stated your father has performed this metamorphosis in your person, you should put no trust in him at all. For there is no peril on earth through which my sword cannot cleave a way, and in the shortest time I can cast your enemy's head to the earth and place the crown of your country upon yours.'

Don Quixote said no more, but waited for the Princess's reply; and she, knowing that Don Ferdinand intended to continue the deception until they had brought Don Quixote home, answered very gracefully and gravely: 'Whoever told you, valorous Knight of the Sad Countenance, that I have altered and transformed myself, did not tell you the truth, for I am the same to-day as I was yesterday. It is true that certain strokes of good fortune have worked some change in me, by giving me the desire nearest to my heart. But, for all that, I have not ceased to be the person I was before, nor to have the same intention as I have always had, of availing myself of the might of your valorous and invincible arm. Therefore, dear sir, of your grace, restore his honour to the father who begot me; and think of him as a man far-seeing and wise, in that he found by his science such an easy and certain way of remedying my misfortune. I believe, sir, that if it were not for you, I should never have succeeded in gaining the happiness I have; and in this I speak nothing but the truth, as most of these gentlemen here will bear witness. All that remains is for us to set out on our way to-morrow, for we shall not be able to travel far to-day. And the rest of the good fortune that I expect, I will leave to God and the valour of your heart.'

So spoke the subtle Dorothea and, when he had heard her, Don Quixote turned to Sancho, and said with signs of great indignation:

'Now I tell you, miserable Sancho, that you are the most despicable rogue in Spain. Tell me, you vagabond thief, did not you say just now that this Princess had turned into a damsel called Dorothea, and that the head, which, as I believe, I cut off a giant, was the bitch that bore you, and all sorts of other nonsense that put me into the greatest perplexity I have ever known in all the days of my life? I swear ...' – he looked up to Heaven and gritted his teeth – 'that I have a mind to work such havoc on you as will put salt into the brainpans of all the lying squires of knights errant in the whole world, from now till the end of time.'

'Please be calm, my dear master,' replied Sancho. 'It's very possible that I was mistaken in the matter of the lady Princess Micomicona's transformation. But as for the giant's head, or rather the piercing of the skins, and the blood being red wine, I swear to God I'm not mistaken. For there the skins lie slashed at the head of your worship's bed, and the red wine has turned the room into a lake. If you don't believe me, you'll see it when the eggs are fried – I mean when his honour the innkeeper here asks you to pay for all the damage. As for the rest, my heart rejoices that the lady Queen is the same as she always was, for I shall get my share and so will every neighbour's child.'

'Now really, Sancho,' said Don Quixote, 'you are a loon, forgive the expression. And now let us drop the subject.'

'Enough,' said Don Ferdinand. 'Let no more be said of the matter and, since the lady Princess says that we must ride on to-morrow because it is too late to-day, let us do so. We shall be able to spend the night in pleasant conversation till daybreak. Then we will all bear Don Quixote company, for we are anxious to witness the valorous and incredible exploits he is to perform in the course of this great enterprise which he has undertaken.'

'It is I who shall serve you and bear you company,' replied Don Quixote, 'and I am very grateful for the favour you have done me and the high opinion you have of me, which I shall try to justify, or it shall cost me my life – and even more, if that is possible.'

Many compliments and offers of service passed between Don Quixote and Don Ferdinand. But they were all cut short by a traveller who entered the inn at that moment, a man who by his dress seemed to be a Christian newly arrived from the land of the Moors. He wore a short blue cloth cape with half sleeves and no collar, his breeches were of linen and blue also, and he wore a cap of the same colour. He had long boots, date-brown, and a Moorish short sword slung on a strap across his breast. Behind him on an ass came a woman dressed in Moorish fashion, with her face covered and a veil on her head, wearing a little cap of gold brocade, and swathed in a cloak which enveloped her from her shoulders to her feet. The man was of a robust and pleasant appearance, a little more than forty, rather dark-skinned, with long moustaches and a very well-trimmed beard. It was obvious, in fact, from his appearance that if he had been well dressed he would have passed for a person of birth and quality.

On entering he asked for a room, and seemed annoyed when he heard that there was not one to be had in the inn; but going up to his companion, who seemed from her dress to be Moorish, he lifted her down. Lucinda, Dorothea, the landlady, her daughter, and Maritornes were attracted by the novelty of her dress, which was strange to them, and gathered round the Moorish lady; and Dorothea, who was always charming, courteous, and sensible, seeing that both she and her escort were troubled at there being no room, said to her:

'Do not be concerned, dear lady, at the lack of accommodation here, for it is the way of inns to have none. But, all the same, if you would care to lodge with us' – pointing to Lucinda – 'perhaps you would find your reception better than some you may have met with in the course of your journey.'

The veiled lady made no answer, but simply got up from her seat and, crossing her hands on her breast and bowing her head, inclined her body from the waist in token of thanks. From her silence they concluded that she must certainly be a Moor and not know the Christian tongue. Presently the gentleman who up to then had been busy with other things, drew near and, seeing that they were all grouped round his companion and that she did not reply to anything they said, remarked:

'Ladies, this young woman can hardly understand our language, and can only speak the tongue of her own country. She has not replied to your questions because she cannot.'

'The only thing we have asked her,' replied Lucinda, 'is whether she will accept our company for to-night and share our sleeping-room, where she shall have as much comfort as the accommodation will allow. We will do her every kindness, for we are bound to serve all strangers who are in need, and women most of all.'

'On her behalf and mine,' replied he, 'I kiss your hands, my lady, and value your offer as highly as it deserves. For on an occasion like this, and from such people as your appearance shows me you are, it is clearly a great favour.'

'Tell me, sir,' said Dorothea, 'is this lady a Christian or a Moor? For her dress and her silence make us think that she is what we hope she is not.'

'Moorish she is in body and dress; but in her soul she is a very good Christian, for she has the greatest desire to become one.'

'Then she is not baptised?' asked Lucinda.

'There has been no opportunity,' replied he, 'since we left Algiers, her country and her home; and up to now she has not been in such instant peril of death as to be obliged to receive baptism without first being instructed in all the ceremonies our Mother, the Holy Church, requires. But, please God, she will soon be baptised with the formalities due to her rank, which is greater than her dress or mine shows.'

This answer roused the curiosity of all the party to know who the Moorish lady and the gentleman were. But no one cared to ask just then, for at that time of night it was clearly better to help them get some rest than to ask them questions about their lives. Dorothea took the Moorish lady by the hand, made her sit down beside her, and asked her to take off her veil. But the stranger looked towards her escort, as if to ask him what they were saying and what she should do. He told her in Arabic that they were asking her to take off her veil; which she did, revealing a face so lovely that Dorothea thought her more beautiful than Lucinda, and Lucinda judged her lovelier than Dorothea, while the others were of the opinion that if any woman was the equal of those two in looks it was the Moorish lady; and some of them thought that in some ways she was the loveliest of the three. Now as it is the privilege of beauty to win over all hearts and attract all minds, everyone yielded instantly to the desire of waiting on the lovely Moor.

Don Ferdinand asked her escort for her name, and he replied that it was Lela Zoraida; but when she heard his answer, understanding what the Christian had asked, she broke in hastily and charmingly, though in some dismay:

'No, no, Zoraida: Maria, Maria' – giving them to understand that her name was not Zoraida but Maria.

Her words and the feeling with which she spoke drew tears from some of her hearers, especially from the women, who were naturally tender-hearted. Lucinda embraced her most warmly and said: 'Yes, yes, Maria, Maria.'

And the Moorish lady replied: 'Yes, yes, Maria – Zoraida "*macange*" ' – that is to say, not Zoraida at all.

Meanwhile night had fallen, and under the supervision of Don Ferdinand's companions the innkeeper had taken considerable pains to provide the best supper he could. So, when the time came, they all sat down together at a long refectory table, for there was not a round or a square one in the inn. They gave the most important seat at the head to Don Quixote, though he repeatedly declined it. And he asked the lady Micomicona to sit beside him, since he was her protector. Next Lucinda and Zoraida took their places, and opposite them Don Fernando and Cardenio; beside them the newcomer and the rest of the gentlemen, and next to the ladies the priest and the barber. So they ate their supper with great pleasure, which grew still greater when they saw Don Quixote leave off eating and, moved by the same spirit that had prompted his long speech when he supped with the goatherds, prepare to address them: –

'Most truly, gentlemen, if the matter be deeply considered, great and most extraordinary are the experiences of those who profess the order of knight errantry. For who is there of all men living upon earth who would judge us and know us for what we really are, if he were to come in now through the gate of this castle and see us as we appear at present? Who would be able to guess that this lady at my side is the great queen we all know her to be, and that I am that Knight of the Sad Countenance, so trumpeted by the mouth of Fame? Now there is no doubt that this art and exercise is greater than any discovered by man, and must be the more highly valued the more perils it is subject to. Away with those who say that Letters have the advantage over Arms. For I will tell them that they do not know what they are saying, whoever they are. The argument which such people generally use, and on which they most rely, is that the labours of the spirit are greater than those of the body, and that Arms is only an exercise of the body; as if the practice of it were mere labourer's work for which nothing is needed but sheer bodily strength; or as if the pursuit of what we, who follow it, call the profession of arms, did not entail acts of courage that require great intelligence to carry them through; or as if a warrior commanding an army or defending a besieged city does not labour with his mind as well as with his body. Let it be shown, then, how by mere bodily strength he can come to guess at and know the enemy's intentions, plans, stratagems, and traps, and how foresee what dangers are impending; for all these are activities of the mind, in which the body plays no part. Seeing, therefore, that Arms, like Letters, require intelligence, let us consider now which of the two performs the greater mental labour, the man of letters or the man of war; for this will be decided by the end and object at which each is aiming – since the purpose which has the noblest end in view must be the more highly valued. The end and object of learning – I am not speaking now of theology, whose goal is to aid souls on the way to Heaven; for no other aim can be compared to a purpose so infinite as that – I am speaking of the humanities, whose aim is to maintain impartial justice, to give every man his rights, to make good laws, and to see that they are kept. That is certainly a lofty and generous aim, and highly praiseworthy, though not so much so as the profession of Arms, whose aim and object is peace, the greatest good which men can desire in this life. For the first good news the world and mankind received was proclaimed by the angels on that night which was our day, when they sang in the sky: *"Glory to God in the highest and peace on earth to men of good will"*; and the greeting which the best Master on earth or in Heaven taught His favoured disciples to give when they entered a house was: *"Peace be to this house."* And many other times He would say: *"My peace I give unto you; my peace I leave with you; peace be with you"*; which, given and bequeathed by such a hand, was a jewel and a treasure; indeed such a jewel that there can be no happiness on earth or in Heaven without it. This peace is the true aim of war; for Arms and war are all one. Admitting then this truth, that the aims of war are peace, and that thereby it excels the art of Letters, let us come now to the bodily hardships of the scholar and of the man whose profession is Arms, and see which are the greater.'

Don Quixote pursued his discourse so rationally and in such well-chosen language that none of his hearers could possibly take him for a madman just then. On the contrary, as most of them were gentlemen connected with the profession of Arms, they listened with great pleasure, as he went on speaking:

'I say then that the hardships of the student are these: first of all, poverty — not because they are all poor, but to put the case as strongly as possible — and when I say that they suffer poverty I do not think that there is anything more to say about their misery; for the poor man lacks everything that is good. This poverty they suffer in various forms: sometimes hunger, sometimes cold, sometimes nakedness, sometimes all of them together. But, all the same, things are not so bad that they do not eat, although it may be a little later than they are used to, or from the leavings of the rich man's table; for what students call *"going on the soup"*, or begging for their supper, is their worst misery. And moreover they do share some-one's brazier or hearth, which may not warm them but at least takes the edge off the cold; and, last of all, they sleep under cover at night. I do not want to go into other details — lack of shirts, for instance, and shortage of shoes, or scanty and threadbare clothing — or to describe their way of stuffing themselves over-eagerly when Fortune sends them a feast. But by the rough and difficult path which I have indicated, stumbling at times and falling, getting up and falling once more, they do acquire the degree they desire. And when they have got it, I have seen many of them, once passed through those shoals, those Scyllas and Charybdises, as if borne on the wings of Fortune's favour; – I say that we have seen them command and govern the world from an armchair, their hunger exchanged for a full stomach, their cold for a pleasant coolness, their nakedness for fine clothes, and their sleep on a mat for comfortable rest on fine linen and damask: the justly merited rewards of their virtue. But if we set their hardships against those of the militant soldier and compare them, they are left far and away behind, as I shall now explain.'

Chapter XXXVIII. *Don Quixote's curious Discourse on Arms and Letters.*

DON QUIXOTE then went on: 'Since we began in the case of the student by dealing with his poverty and its circumstances, let us consider whether the soldier is any richer. We shall see that he is the poorest of the poor. For he is limited to his wretched pay, which comes either late or never, or to what he can loot with his own hands, at considerable risk to his life and his conscience. Sometimes too he is so naked that a slashed doublet serves him both for uniform and for shirt, and in the open field in the depth of winter he has nothing to warm him against the inclemencies of heaven but the breath of his mouth which, coming out of an empty place, must certainly come out cold, against all the laws of nature. But wait till night-fall; for then he can rest from his discomforts in the bed which awaits him, and which, except by his own fault, will not sin by being too narrow. For he can measure out as many feet as he likes on the earth, and roll about to his heart's content without fear of the sheets rumpling up. Then, at last, comes the day and the hour for him to receive his degree in his art: the day of battle dawns, when they will put on him a doctor's cap made of lint, to heal some bullet wound which may have pierced his temples or left him maimed in arm or leg. And if this does not happen, but merciful Heaven preserves him and keeps him whole and alive, he will very likely remain in the same poverty as before; and there must needs be one skirmish after another and one battle after another, and he must come out victorious from every one, before he has any success at all; but such miracles rarely occur. Now tell me, gentlemen, if you have ever considered it, how many more perish by war than profit by it? Unquestionably your reply will be that there is no comparison. For there is no counting the dead, and those who have benefited by war and survived can be reckoned in three figures.

'It is quite the reverse with scholars; for by their salaries – I will not say by their perquisites – they have all enough to make do, so that although a soldier's hardships are greater, his rewards are less. But you may reply that it is easier to reward two thousand scholars than thirty thousand soldiers; because scholars are rewarded by the gift of posts given to men of their profession, but soldiers cannot be recompensed except out of the very property of the lord they serve. This impossibility makes my argument even stronger.

'Leaving this on one side, however, for it is a very difficult labyrinth to find a way out of, let us come back to the pre-eminence of Arms over Letters, – a question which remains still to be resolved, since each side puts up so many arguments on its own behalf. Besides those which I have given, the scholars say that without them arms could not survive. For war too has its laws and is subject to them, and laws fall within the province of letters and learning. But to this Arms reply that laws could not survive without them; because by Arms states are defended, kingdoms preserved, cities guarded, the roads kept safe, and the seas swept free of pirates. In short, if it were not for them, states, kingdoms, monarchies, cities, and the highways on land and sea, would be subject to the savagery and confusion which war entails, so long as it lasts and is free to exercise its privileges and powers.

'What is more, it is a well-known truth that what costs most is, and should be, the most highly valued. Now to attain eminence in the learned professions costs a man time, nights of study, hunger, nakedness, headaches, indigestion, and other such things, some of which I have mentioned already. But to reach the point of being a good soldier, requires all that it requires to be a student, but to so much greater a degree that there is no comparison; for the soldier is in peril of losing his life at every step. What fear of poverty or want that can befall or afflict a student can compare with the fear a soldier knows when he is besieged in a fortress, on watch or guard in some redoubt or strongpoint, knowing that his enemies are mining towards the spot where he is, and that he may on no account leave his post, or run away from the danger which threatens him so closely? The only thing which he can do is to inform his captain of what is happening, in the hope that he will meet the situation with a counter-mine; and he must stand calmly, though in fear and expectation of suddenly rising to the clouds without wings and sinking again to the depths against his will. If this seems a small danger, let us see if it is equalled or surpassed in the head-on collision of two galleys in the midst of the high seas. For when ships are locked and grappled together, the soldier has no more space left him than two feet of plank on the beak-head. But though he sees in front of him countless pieces of artillery threatening from the enemy's side, each a minister of death, and no more than a spear's length from his body; and though he knows that at his first careless step he will go down to visit the deep bosom of Neptune, nevertheless with undaunted heart, sustained by the honour which spurs him on, he exposes himself as a mark for all their shot, and endeavours to pass along that narrow causeway into the enemy's ship. And, most amazing of all, no sooner does one man fall, never to rise again this side of Doomsday, than another takes his place; and if he, in his turn, falls into the sea, which lies in wait for him like an enemy, another, and yet another, takes his place, without a moment passing between their deaths: the greatest display of valour and daring to be found in all the hazards of war. Blessed were the times which lacked the dreadful fury of those diabolical engines, the artillery, whose inventor I firmly believe is now receiving the reward for his devilish invention in hell; an invention which allows a base and cowardly hand to take the life of a brave knight, in such a way that, without his knowing how or why, when his valiant heart is fullest of furious courage, there comes some random shot – discharged perhaps by a man who fled in terror from the flash the accursed machine made in firing – and puts an end in a moment to the consciousness of one who deserved to enjoy life for many an age. And when I think of that, I am tempted to say that it grieves me to the heart to have adopted this profession of knight errantry in such a detestable age as we now live in. For although no danger frightens me, still it causes me misgivings to think that powder and lead may deprive me of the chance of winning fame and renown by the strength of my arm and the edge of my sword, over all the known earth. But let Heaven do what it will. If I achieve my purpose, I shall be the more highly esteemed for having faced greater dangers than did the knights errant of past ages.'

All this long rigmarole Don Quixote spoke whilst the others were eating their supper, forgetting to put a mouthful into his mouth although Sancho Panza urged him several times to eat, with the remark that he would have time to say all he wanted to afterwards. His hearers were moved once more to pity at seeing a man, apparently of such sound intelligence and with such understanding of everything he spoke of, lose it so entirely on the subject of his foul and accursed chivalry. The priest said that there was much justice in all that he had said in favour of arms, and that he was of the very same opinion himself, although a scholar and a graduate.

Then, their supper finished, the table-cloths were removed, and whilst the landlady, her daughter, and Maritornes were clearing up Don Quixote de la Mancha's attic, where they had decided that the women should be lodged by themselves that night, Don Ferdinand asked the newcomer to tell them his life's story. For, from so much as they had gathered by his coming in Zoraida's company, it could not fail to be strange and enjoyable. He replied that he would most gladly comply, only he feared that his story would not give them as much pleasure as he would like. But he would tell it all the same, rather than appear disobliging. The priest and all the others thanked him and pressed him to begin; and when he found them all so urgent he assured them that there was no need of entreaties, for their mere request was enough.

'Listen then, gentlemen, and you will hear a true story, and I doubt whether you will find its equal in the most detailed and careful fiction ever written.'

At these words they all sat down in perfect silence; and when he saw them quiet and waiting for him to speak, he began in a smooth and pleasant voice:

Chapter XXXIX. *The Captive tells the story of his Life and Adventures.*

'My family had its origin in a village among the mountains of Leon; and nature was kinder and more generous to them than fortune was, although in those very poor villages my father had the reputation of being rich; and indeed he would have been if he had been as good at keeping his money as he was at spending it. This liberal and wasteful disposition of his came from his having been a soldier in the days of his youth. The soldier's trade is a school in which the mean man learns to be liberal and the liberal man prodigal; for if there are sometimes soldiers who are misers, they are, like monsters, rarely seen. My father passed the bounds of liberality and verged on those of prodigality, a quality which is no advantage to a married man, with children to inherit his name and station. My father had three, all sons and all of an age to choose their professions. So, seeing that he could not, as he said, bridle his nature, he decided to deprive himself of the cause and means which made him a prodigal and a spendthrift; in other words, to give up his estate, without which Alexander himself would have been reckoned a miser. So, calling us all three one day into a room alone, he addressed us in some such way as this:

'"My sons, to assure you that I love you, it is quite enough to say that you are my sons; and to convince you that I do not love you, it is enough to say that I do not control myself in order to preserve your fortune. But so that you may know in future that I love you like a father and do not want to ruin you like a stepfather, I intend to do something for you, which I have been thinking over for a long time, and have decided on after mature consideration. You are of an age to take up a calling, or at least to choose some profession that will bring you honour and profit when you are older. My plan is to divide my estate into four parts. Three of them I will give you, an absolutely equal portion for each, and I shall live on the fourth part for as long as Heaven is pleased to preserve my life. But I want each one of you, once you have received your share of the estate, to follow one of the paths which I shall indicate. There is a proverb in this Spain of ours – a very good one I think, as all of them are, for they are brief maxims collected from long and deep experience. The one I am thinking of is: *The Church, the Sea, or the King's Palace.* The meaning of that is: if you want to be powerful and rich, follow the Church, or go to sea and practise the merchant's calling, or take service with kings in their palaces. For it is said: *Better the King's crumb than the lord's favour.* I mean by all this that I wish one of you to pursue learning, another commerce, and the third to serve the King in his wars, as it is difficult to get a place in his household; for although war does not bring much riches, it generally brings great fame and renown. Within a week I will give you each your share in money, to the last farthing, as you will see. Tell me then if you are willing to follow my counsel and take the advice I have offered you."

'He called on me, as the eldest, to answer, and I entreated him not to part with his fortune, but to spend it as freely as he liked, for we were young enough to be able to win one ourselves. But in the end, I said that I would obey his wishes and that my choice would be to follow the profession of arms, thereby serving God and my King. My younger brother protested to the same effect, and then elected to go the Indies and invest his portion in merchandise. The youngest, and I think the wisest of us, said that he would follow the Church and go and complete his studies at Salamanca.

'So when the agreement was made and we had each chosen our profession, our father embraced us all, and carried out his promise just as quickly as he had said he would; giving us each, as I remember, three thousand ducats in money, an uncle of ours having bought the estate so that it should not go out of the family, and paid for it in cash. We all three bade our dear father good-bye on the same day. But it seemed to me inhuman to leave so old a man with so little means, and I made him take two thousand of my three thousand ducats, the rest being sufficient to provide me with all that a soldier needs. My two brothers followed my example, and each gave him a thousand ducats; so that he was left with four thousand ducats in money and three thousand more, the value of his share of the estate, which he was unwilling to sell but had kept in land. Well, as I said, we took our leave of him and of this uncle of ours, with great emotion and tears on all sides, they insisting that we should let them have news of us, good or bad, at any favourable opportunity. We promised to do so, embraced them, and received our father's blessing. Then one of us took the road for Salamanca, one for Seville, and I for Alicante, where I had heard that there was a Genoese ship loading with wool for Genoa.

'It is now twenty-two years since I left my father's house, and for all that time I have heard nothing of him or of my brothers, although I have written several letters; and what I have gone through in the interval I will tell you briefly. I went aboard at Alicante, arrived after a prosperous voyage at Genoa, went from there to Milan, where I bought arms and some military clothing, and from there decided to go and enlist in Piedmont. But as I was on the road to Alessandria I got news that the great Duke of Alva was marching into Flanders. So I changed my plans, went with him, and served him in all his campaigns, being present at the deaths of Counts Egmont and Horn. I rose to be an ensign under a famous captain from Guadalajara by the name of Diego de Urbina. After some time news came to Flanders of the alliance his Holiness Pope Pius V, of happy memory, had made with Venice and Spain against the common enemy, the Turk, whose fleet had just then taken the famous island of Cyprus, which had been under the rule of the Venetians: a lamentable and disastrous loss. It was known for certain that the commander of this alliance would be Don John of Austria, the natural brother of our good King Don Philip; and news was abroad of the great preparations which were being made for the war. All this aroused in me a great desire to take part in the expected campaign. So, although I had hopes and almost certain prospects of being promoted to a captaincy as soon as occasion offered, I decided to give it all up and go to Italy, which I did. As my luck would have it, Don John of Austria had just arrived at Genoa on his way to Naples to join up with the Venetian fleet, which he afterwards did at Messina. So, to be brief, I was present at that most glorious battle, being by that time a captain of infantry, to which honourable rank I was promoted rather by luck than merit. On that day, so fortunate for Christendom, since then the world and all the nations learnt how wrong they were in supposing that the Turks were invincible on the sea – on that day I say, when the insolent pride of the Ottomans was broken for ever, among all the fortunate men there – for the Christians who died there were more fortunate than those who survived victorious – I alone was unlucky. For in place of some naval crown, which I might have expected in the days of ancient Rome, I found myself on the night following that famous day with chains on my feet and handcuffs on my hands.

'This is how it happened: Aluch Ali, King of Algiers, a bold and successful pirate, had attacked and beaten the Maltese flagship; and only three knights were left alive in her, and those three badly wounded. Then Juan Andrea's flagship, aboard which I was with my company, came to the rescue, and, doing what was my duty in the circumstances, I jumped aboard the enemy's galley; which then disengaged from our ship, that had grappled her, and thus prevented my men from following me. So I found myself alone among my enemies, unable to resist as they were so many. In fact they took me prisoner, covered with wounds. Now, as you will have heard, gentlemen, Aluch Ali escaped with his whole squadron; and I remained a prisoner in his power, being the only sad man among so many that rejoiced, the only prisoner among all those set free. For there were fifteen thousand Christians rowing that Turkish fleet who that day gained their coveted liberty.

'They took me to Constantinople, where the Grand Turk Selim made my master Commander of the Sea – for doing his duty in that battle and bearing off the standard of the Knights of Malta, as a proof of his valour. The next year – that was 'seventy-two – I was at Navarino, rowing in the admiral's flagship, and witnessed the opportunity of catching the Turkish fleet in harbour which was then lost. For every Turkish sailor and janissary aboard was quite certain that they would be attacked in the port itself, and had his clothes and his "*passamaques*" – which are their shoes – ready, to escape at once by land without waiting to fight; such terror had our navy inspired in them. But Heaven ordained otherwise, through no fault or neglect of our commander but for the sins of Christendom, and because God ordains that there shall always be some scourge to chastise us. In the end Aluch Ali took refuge in Modon, an island close to Navarino and, putting his men ashore, fortified the entrance to the port and stayed there quietly till Don John had retired. In this expedition the galley called "The Prize" was taken. Her captain was a son of the famous pirate Barbarossa. The flagship of Naples, "The She-Wolf", took her, under the command of that thunderbolt of war and father to his soldiers, that fortunate and unbeaten captain, Don Alvaro de Bazan, Marquis of Santa Cruz.

'I do not want to leave out what happened at the capture of "The Prize". The son of Barbarossa was so cruel, and treated his slaves so badly, that as soon as the rowers saw the "She-Wolf" galley nearing them and about to board, they all dropped their oars at once and seized hold of him, where he stood at his station shouting at them to row hard. Then they tossed him from bench to bench, from stern to prow, biting him again and again, so that he had hardly gone farther than the mast before his soul had passed into hell; so cruelly did he treat them, as I said, and so bitterly did they hate him.

'We returned to Constantinople, and the next year – that was 'seventy-three – the news came that Don John had conquered Tunis, wresting that kingdom from the Turks and giving it to Muley Hamet; which deprived Muley Hamida, the cruellest and bravest Moor in the whole world, of his hopes of recovering the throne. The Grand Turk felt this loss very severely and, with the cunning natural to all his house, made peace with the Venetians, who wanted it much more than he. Then the following year, which was 'seventy-four, he attacked the Goletta, and the fort near Tunis which Don John had left half constructed. In all these actions I was at the oar, without any hope of liberty – at least I had no hope of getting it by ransom, for I was resolved not to send the news of my misfortunes to my father.

'In the end the Goletta was lost, and the fort as well. Attacking these places were seventy-five thousand Turkish regular soldiers, and more than four hundred thousand Moors and Arabs from all over Africa. This vast host was supplied with such a quantity of ammunition and material, and with so many sappers, that they could have buried the Goletta and the fortress deep in earth with their bare hands alone. The Goletta, which had been considered impregnable till then, was the first to fall. It was through no fault of its garrison, who defended it to the best of their power and ability, but because, as experience showed, earthworks could be thrown up very easily in that sandy desert; for though water used to be found about 16 inches down, the Turks did not strike it now at six foot. So with a great quantity of sandbags they raised their works high enough to command the walls of the fort and fired from above, so that no one could stay there to put up a defence.

'It was generally thought that our men should not have shut themselves up in the Goletta, but should have opposed the landing in open country. But the people who say that speak from a distance and with little experience of such matters. For as there were hardly seven thousand soldiers in the Goletta and the fort together, how

could so small a number, however resolute, have taken the field, as
well as held the forts against the enemy's great numbers? And how
is it possible not to lose a fort which is not relieved, particularly
when it is besieged by such a host of determined enemies and in their
own country? Many, however, were of the opinion – as I was myself –
that Heaven bestowed a special grace and mercy on Spain by permitting the demolition of that breeding-place and cloak of iniquities: that glutton, sponge, and sink of the infinite money which was
wasted there to no advantage, to serve no other purpose than to
preserve the memory of its conquest – the auspicious memory of the
most invincible Charles V – as if that tract of earth were needed to
make his name eternal, as it is and ever will be.

'The fort fell as well. But the Turks had to win it foot by foot.
For the soldiers defending it fought so bravely and fiercely that they
killed more than twenty-five thousand of the enemy in the twenty-
two general assaults they made. Not one of the three hundred survivors was taken unwounded, a clear and manifest proof of their
fierceness and bravery and of how well they defended and maintained their positions. A small fort or tower in the middle of the
lake, under the command of Don Juan Zanoguera, a Valencian
gentleman and a famous soldier, surrendered on terms. They captured Don Pedro Puertocarrero, the commander of the Goletta,
who had done everything he could to defend his post, and felt its
loss so much that he died of grief on the way to Constantinople,
where they were taking him as a prisoner. They also captured the
commander of the fort, Gabriel Cervellon by name, a Milanese
gentleman, a great engineer and a most courageous soldier. In those
two fortresses died many people of note, one of whom was Pagan
Doria, a Knight of the Order of St. John, a man of generous character, as was shown by his very liberal treatment of his brother, the
famous John Andrew Doria. What made his death even more deplorable was that he fell at the hands of some Arabs in whom he had
trusted when he saw that the fortress was lost. They had offered to
take him, disguised as a Moor, to Tabarca, a small seaport or station
on that coast held by the Genoese, who are engaged in coral-fishing.
These Arabs cut off his head and took it to the commander of the
Turkish fleet, who proved on them the the truth of our Spanish
proverb that though the treason pleases, we abhor the traitor. For

they say that the general ordered the men who brought him the present to be hanged for not bringing him alive.

'Among the Christians captured in the fort was one Don Pedro de Aguilar, who came from somewhere in Andalusia. He had been an ensign in the garrison, and was a soldier of great repute and rare intelligence; and he had a remarkable gift for what they call poetry. I mention him because it was his lot to come to my bench in my galley, and to be slave to my own master, and before we left that port this gentleman composed two sonnets by way of epitaphs, one on the Goletta and the other on the fort. And I must really repeat them, for I know them by heart and I think you will probably like them.'

The moment the Captive named Don Pedro de Aguilar Don Ferdinand glanced at his comrades, and all three smiled; then, at the mention of the sonnets, one of them said:

'Before you go any further, sir, please tell me what became of this Don Pedro de Aguilar you spoke of.'

'All I know,' answered the Captive, 'is that after he had been two years in Constantinople he escaped, disguised as an Albanian, with a Greek spy. I do not know whether he got his liberty, but I suppose he did, for I saw that Greek a year later in Constantinople, though I could not ask him whether the escape had been successful.'

'It was,' replied the gentleman. 'That Don Pedro is my brother, and he is at our home now, well and rich, and married with three children.'

'God be praised,' said the Captive, 'for all the mercies He did him; for there is no joy on earth in my opinion so good as regaining one's liberty.'

'What is more,' the gentleman went on, 'I know those sonnets my brother wrote.'

'Then recite them to us, sir,' said the Captive, 'for you will be able to do it better than I.'

'With pleasure,' replied the gentleman, 'the one on the Goletta went like this:

Chapter XL. *The Captive's Story continued.*

'Blest souls, discharged of life's oppressive weight,
    Whose virtue proved your passport to the skies,
You there procured a more propitious fate,
    When for your faith you bravely fell to rise.
When pious rage, diffused through every vein,
    On that ungrateful shore inflamed your blood,
Each drop you lost was bought with crowds of slain,
    Whose vital purple swelled the neighbouring flood.
Though crushed by ruins and by odds, you claim
That perfect glory, that immortal fame
    Which, like true heroes, nobly you pursued;
On these you seized, even when of life deprived,
For still your courage even your lives survived;
    And sure 'tis conquest thus to be subdued.'

'Yes, those are the words that I know,' said the Captive.

'And the one on the fort, if my memory is right,' said the gentle-man, 'goes like this:

'Amidst these barren fields and ruined towers,
    The bed of honour of the falling brave,
Three thousand champions of the Christian powers
    Found a new life and triumph in the grave.
Long did their arms their haughty foes repel,
    Yet strewed the fields with slaughtered hopes in vain;
O'ercome by toils the pious heroes fell,
    Or but survived more nobly to be slain.
This dismal soil, so famed in ills of old,
In every age was fatal to the bold,
    The seat of horror and the warrior's tomb!
Yet hence to Heaven more work was ne'er resigned
Than these displayed; nor has the earth combined
    Resumed more noble bodies in her womb.'

The sonnets were much appreciated, and the Captive went on with his tale, delighted with the news they had given him of his comrade:

'Then, when the Goletta and the fort surrendered, the Turks gave orders for the Goletta to be dismantled. But the fortress was in such a state that there was nothing left to demolish. And to save time and labour they mined it in three places. But none of the mines could blow up what appeared its weakest part; which was the old walls, although all that was still standing of the new fortifications,

M

built by El Fratin, came down most easily. Finally the fleet returned to Constantinople, triumphant and victorious, and several months later my master Aluch Ali died. They used to call him *Uchali Fartax*, which means in Turkish "the scabby renegade", which he was. For it is a custom among the Turks to name people by any defect, or by any good quality, they may have. That is because they have only four surnames among them, and those belong to families of Ottoman descent. The rest, as I have said, take their names and surnames either from their bodily defects or from their characters. This Scabby was at the oar as a slave of the Great Turk for fourteen years, and when he was over thirty-four turned renegade, in his fury at a Turk who had given him a slap on the face while he was rowing. In fact he renounced his faith to get his revenge. He had such character too that he came to be king of Algiers and, afterwards, Commander of the Sea – which is the third post in their empire – without resorting to the base methods by which most of the Great Turk's favourites rise. He was a Calabrian by birth, a good moral man, and treated his prisoners with great humanity. In the end he had three thousand of them, who were divided after his death, in accordance with his will, between the Grand Turk – who is reckoned a son and heir of all who die and takes his share with the rest of the dead man's sons – and his renegades. I fell to the share of a Venetian renegade, who had been a ship's cabin-boy when Aluch Ali captured him, for whom his master had such a liking that he was one of his most pampered favourites. He proved to be one of the cruellest renegades ever seen. He was called Hassan Aga and became very rich, eventually rising to be King of Algiers. With him I came from Constantinople, rather pleased to be so near to Spain; not because I thought of writing to tell anyone of my unhappy fate, but because I meant to see if Fortune would not be kinder to me in Algiers than in Constantinople, where I had attempted a thousand ways of escape, but had had no luck with any of them. I thought that in Algiers I would find other means of getting what I so much desired. For I never gave up hope of gaining my liberty, and when the result did not shape with my design in such plans as I contrived, worked out and put in practice, I never gave up, but immediately devised some new hope, never mind how slender and weak, to keep me going.

'So I passed my life, shut up in a prison-house, called by the Turks a *bagnio*, where they keep their Christian prisoners: those belonging to the King and those belonging to private people, and also those who are called the slaves of the *Almazen* – that is to say, of the township – who are employed in the public works of the city and in other communal employment. Slaves of this last kind have great difficulty in gaining their liberty because, as they belong to the community and have no master of their own, there is no one with whom to bargain for their ransom, even if they have the money. To these *bagnios*, as I have said, some private people of the city take their prisoners, particularly when they are waiting to be redeemed. For they are kept here in idleness and safety until their ransom comes. The King's captives, if they are to be ransomed, do not go out to work with the rest of the gang either, except if their ransom is delayed; in which case, to spur them to write more urgently for it, they make them work and fetch firewood with the others, which is no light job.

'I was one of those put on ransom. For as it was known that I was a captain, nothing could prevent their putting me on the list of gentlemen to be redeemed, although I pleaded that I had small means and no property. They put a chain on me, more as a sign that I was to be ransomed than for my safe keeping; and so I spent my life in that *bagnio* with many more gentlemen and men of quality chosen to be held for ransom. And although hunger and lack of clothes distressed us at times – in fact almost always – nothing disturbed us so much as to hear and witness, wherever we went, the unparalleled and incredible cruelty which my master practised on Christians. Every day he hanged someone, impaled another, and cut off the ears of a third; and this on the slightest excuse or on none at all, so that even the Turks acknowledged that he did it only for the sake of doing it, and because it was in his nature to be the murderer of the entire human race. The only one who held his own with him was a Spanish soldier, called something de Saavedra; for his master never so much as struck him, nor bade anyone else strike him, nor even spoke a rough word to him, though he did things which those people will remember for many years, all in efforts to recover his liberty; and the rest of us were afraid that his least actions would be punished by impaling, as he himself feared they

would be more than once. And if it were not for lack of time I
would tell you something about that soldier's deeds, which you
would find much more entertaining and surprising than this story
of mine.

'Now, overlooking the courtyard of our prison were the windows of the house of a rich and important Moor, which, as is usual
in Moorish houses, were more like loopholes than windows, and
even so were covered by thick and close lattices. And I happened
one day to be on a flat roof in our prison with three companions,
trying to wile away the time by seeing how far we could jump in
our chains. We were on our own because all the other Christians
had gone out to work. It was by the merest chance that I looked
up, and when I did I saw a cane with a handkerchief tied to the end
of it appear through one of those little closed windows I spoke of.
It was being waved and jerked up and down, as though it were
summoning us to go and take it. We stared at it; and one of my
companions went and placed himself just below it to see if it would
be dropped, or what else would happen; but no sooner did he get
there than the cane was raised and jerked from side to side, as if
someone were shaking his head to say no. The Christian came back,
and again the cane was let down, to make the same movements as
before. Another of my companions went up, but with the same result as the first. Last of all the third went, and was treated in the
same manner as the first and the second. At this I was tempted to
try my luck, and as soon as I got there and stood below the cane, it
was let fall, and dropped into the prison just at my feet. I ran up at
once to untie the handkerchief, in which I found a knot and in it ten
zianies, which are coins of gold alloy that the Moors use, each worth
ten of our *reals*. There is no need to tell you whether I was pleased
at this windfall; I was delighted and astonished, but I could not
think who could have directed this present, especially to me; since
the refusal to drop the cane to anyone else was a clear sign that it
was for me the favour was meant. I took my precious money; I
broke the cane; I returned to the little roof; I looked up at the window, and saw the whitest of hands emerge to open and shut it very
quickly. By this we learnt, or guessed, that it was a woman living
in that house who had done us this kindness and, to show our
thanks, we made *salaams* after the Moorish fashion, bowing our

heads, bending our bodies, and laying our hands on our breasts. Somewhat later a little cross made of cane was put out of the same window and immediately drawn in again. This signal convinced us that there must be a Christian woman slave in the house, and that it was she who had given us the present; but the whiteness of her hand and the bracelets we saw on it contradicted this idea. Then we imagined that she must be a renegade Christian; for often the Moors are glad to marry slaves of this sort, whom they value more highly than women of their own people.

'In all our surmises we were very far from the truth. Our sole occupation from that day on, however, was watching, and the window where our star had appeared was the pole by which we steered. But a good fortnight went by before we saw any further sign. And although in that time we made every effort to find out who lived in the house, and if there was any renegade Christian woman there, no one could tell us anything except that a rich and important Moor called Hadji Murad lived there, and that he had been the governor of Bata, which is one of their most important posts. But when we least expected it to rain more ¿ianies, we saw the cane suddenly appear with another handkerchief on the end, tied in another, bigger knot; and this, as before, was at a time when the prison was empty and deserted. We made the customary experiment, each one of the three going before me; but the cane was delivered to none but me, and was dropped as soon as I got there. When I undid the knot I found forty Spanish crowns in gold and a paper written in Arabic, and at the end of the writing there was drawn a large cross. I kissed the cross, took the crowns, and returned to the roof. Then we made our *salaams* and, the hand appearing again, I promised by signs to read the letter; at which the window was closed. We were all astonished and delighted at events. But, as none of us could understand Arabic, our curiosity to know what was in the paper was great and our difficulty in finding anyone to read it to us even greater. In the end I decided to confide in a Murcian renegade, who professed to be a good friend of mine and had exchanged pledges with me which bound him to keep any secret I might entrust him with. For there is a custom among some renegades, when they have a mind to return to Christian lands, to carry with them certificates from important prisoners, testifying, in such form as they can, that such and such a renegade is an honest man, has always behaved well to Christians, and proposes to escape at the first possible opportunity. Some of them procure these testimonials with honest intentions; others want them for an emergency, meaning to produce them should they happen to be shipwrecked or taken prisoner on a plundering expedition in Christian lands, and to use those certificates as evidence that their purpose in coming is to stay behind on Christian soil, and that this is their only reason for coming on a raid with the Turks. In that way they escape the first violence of their captors, and safely make their peace with the Church; and when they see their chance, they return to Barbary to be what they were before. There are others, though, who make proper use of these papers and get them with the honest intention of remaining in Christian lands. One such renegade was this friend of mine, who had testimonials from all our comrades in which we vouched for him in the highest possible terms; and if the Moors had found these papers on him they would have burnt him alive. I was aware that he knew Arabic very well, and could not only speak but write it; but before taking him completely into my confidence, I asked him to read me the paper, saying that I had found it by chance in a hole in my cell. He unfolded it, and spent some time examining it and spelling it over, muttering under his breath. I asked him if he understood it. Perfectly, he said, and if I would give him pen and ink, he would give me an exact translation. We instantly supplied him with what he asked, and he wrote down a literal translation, observing, when he had finished:

' "I have translated this Moorish letter into Spanish for you word for word, but you must note that where it says Lela Marien it means Our Lady the Virgin Mary."

'We read the paper, and this is how it ran: "When I was a girl my father had a woman slave, who taught me the Christian prayers in my own tongue, and spoke to me often about Lela Marien. This Christian died, and I know that she did not go to the fire but to Allah. For I saw her twice afterwards, and she told me to go to Christian lands and see Lela Marien, who loved me very much. I do not know how to go. I have seen many Christians out of this window, but none of them except you has seemed a gentleman. I am young and very beautiful, and have much money to take with me.

See if you cannot find a way for us to go; and you shall be my husband, if you will; and if you will not I do not mind, for Lela Marien will find me someone to marry. I wrote this; be careful to whom you give it to read. Do not trust any Moor; they are all deceitful. That worries me very much. I do not want you to take anyone into your confidence, because if my father finds out he will immediately throw me down a well and cover me with stones. On to the cane I will fasten a thread. Tie your reply to it. But if you have no one who can write Arabic for you, tell me your answer by signs; Lela Marien will help me to understand you. May she and Allah protect you – and this cross, which I often kiss as my slave told me to."

'Consider, sirs, whether we had not reason to be surprised and delighted at the contents of this letter. Indeed, our feelings were so great that the renegade realized we had not found the paper by chance, but that it was really written to one of us. So he implored us, if his suspicions were correct, to take him into our confidence and tell him the truth, for he would risk his life for our liberty. As he spoke, he took a metal crucifix from under his shirt, and swore with tears in his eyes by the God, whose image it was and in whom he, wicked sinner though he was, truly and faithfully believed, and promised to be loyal to us and to keep anything we might reveal to him secret. For he could almost foretell that he and all of us would gain our liberty with the help of the woman who had written that letter, and that he would gain what he so much desired, re-admission to the body of the Holy Mother Church, from whom he had been severed as a rotten limb, cut off by his ignorance and sin. The renegade spoke with such tears of repentance that we all agreed with one accord to tell him the truth of the matter; and so we told him the whole story, concealing nothing. We showed him the little window out of which the cane had appeared, and by that he noted the house, and promised to take great and special care to find out who lived there. We agreed at the same time that it would be as well to reply to the Moorish lady's letter, since we had someone there who could do it; and the renegade at once wrote, straight off, to my dictation. I can give you the exact words, for I have not forgotten a single material detail of that adventure; nor shall I forget one as long as I live. So this is what I replied to the Moorish lady:

'"The true Allah keep you, dear lady, and the blessed Marien,

who is the true Mother of God and who has put it into your heart
to go to a Christian land, for she loves you well. Pray to her to be
pleased to teach you how you can put her commands into practice;
for she is so kind that she will certainly do so. On behalf of myself
and all my Christian companions, I promise that we will do everything we can for you, even unto death. Do not fail to write and inform me of what you intend to do. I shall always reply; for the
great Allah has given us a Christian prisoner who can speak and
write your language well, as you can judge from this letter. So you
need have no fear, and can tell us anything you wish. As to your saying that you would be my wife if you were to reach Christian soil,
I promise you as a good Christian that this shall be so. And remember that Christians carry out their promises better than Moors.
Allah and Marien His mother protect you, dear lady."

'When this letter was written and sealed I waited two days till
the *bagnio* was deserted as usual, and then I went to the usual place
on the little flat roof to see if the cane would appear; which it did
not take long in doing. As soon as I saw it, although I could not see
who was holding it, I held up the paper as a signal for her to tie on
the thread; but I found that it was already on the cane, and attached
the letter to it. Then, a little while later, our star appeared once
more with the white flag of peace, the knotted handkerchief, tied
to it. It was dropped and, on picking it up, I found inside more
than fifty crowns in all kinds of silver and gold coins; which multi-
plied our joy fifty times more and strengthened our hopes of gaining
our liberty. That very night our renegade returned with the news
that he had found out that the Moor we had been told of before did
live in that house; that he was called Hadji Murad; that he was exceedingly rich, and had an only daughter, the heiress to all his fortune. It was the general opinion, he said, throughout the city that
she was the loveliest woman in all Barbary, and many of the Vice-
roys who came there had asked for her hand; but she would never
consent to marry. He had also found out that she had once a Christian slave, who was now dead – all of which agreed with the contents
of the letter.

'We then consulted the renegade as to any possible plan for
carrying off the Moorish lady and all of us escaping on to Christian
soil. But in the end we agreed to wait, for the time being, for a

second letter from Zoraida – for that was her name, though she now wishes to be called Maria – since it was quite clear to us that she, and she only, would be able to find a solution of all our difficulties. After we had agreed on that, the renegade told us not to worry; for he would either set us at liberty or lose his life in the attempt. The *bagnio* was full of people for the next four days, which meant that for four days the cane did not appear; at the end of that time, when the prison was once more empty as usual, it appeared with a big handkerchief which promised a happy delivery. The cane with its burden pointed to me, and I found in it another letter and a hundred crowns all in gold. The renegade was there, and when we had returned to our cell we gave him the paper to read. He translated it like this:

'"I do not know, dear sir, how to arrange for our going to Spain. Lela Marien has not told me, although I have asked her. What I can do is to pass you a great deal of money through this window. You can then ransom yourself and your friends; and one of you can go to a Christian country, buy a ship, and come back for the others. I can be found in my father's country house at the Babazoun gate, beside the seashore, where I shall be all this summer with my father and servants. You will be able to carry me off from there by night without risk, and take me to the ship. Remember that you must marry me, or I will pray to Marien to punish you. If there is no one you can trust to go for the ship, ransom yourself and go. For I know that you are more certain to return than anyone else, because you are a gentleman and a Christian. Try to find our country house, and when you come on to the roof I shall know that the *bagnio* is empty and give you large sums of money. Allah preserve you, dear sir."

'Those were the words of the second letter; and when we had all seen it, each one said he was willing to be the man ransomed, and promised to go and to return with all speed; and I offered myself as well. But the renegade was totally opposed to this plan, and said that he would on no account agree to anyone getting his liberty till we all did so together; because experience had shown him how badly men fulfil the promises which they have made as prisoners once they are free. For very often prisoners of consequence had tried the expedient of ransoming someone to go to Valencia or

Majorca with money to equip a boat and return for the men who had ransomed them; but they had never come back; for the fear of losing their new-found liberty had expunged every obligation in the world from their memories. To confirm the truth of this, he briefly told us a case which had happened very recently indeed to some Christian gentlemen, the most extraordinary affair that had ever occurred in those parts, where astonishing and marvellous things happen every day. He concluded by suggesting what should be done with the money intended for the ransom of one of us. We were to give it to him to buy a ship with, there in Algiers, on the pretence that he intended to set up as a merchant to trade with Tetuan and along the coast. Once he was owner of the boat, he would easily contrive a way of getting us out of the *bagnio* and of taking us all on board. Besides, if the Moorish lady were to give us enough money to ransom us all, as she promised, we should be free; and then it would be extremely easy to get us aboard, even in the middle of the day. Our greatest difficulty was the fact that the Moors do not allow a renegade to buy or own a ship, unless it is a large ship to go on a pirate expedition; for they are afraid that his only reason for buying a small ship, particularly if he is a Spaniard, is to escape on to Christian soil. Our renegade would get over this difficulty, however, by taking a Tagarine Moor as his partner in the purchase of the craft, and in the trading profits. By this subterfuge he would become master of the ship; and once he had got that, he reckoned that the rest would follow. Now, although both my companions and I thought it a better plan to send to Majorca for the ship, as the Moorish lady suggested, we dared not contradict him, for fear that he might betray us if we did not do what he said, and so put us in danger of execution; especially if he were to report the part played by Zoraida, for whose life we would all willingly have sacrificed our own. So we decided to put ourselves in the hands of God and the renegade and, at that juncture, replied to Zoraida that we would follow her suggestions, for she had advised us as well as if Lela Marien had instructed her; and that it rested with her alone whether the plan should be delayed or put into execution at once. I repeated my promise to marry her, and then the *bagnio* happening to be empty, at various times during the next day she gave us two thousand crowns in gold by means of the cane and handkerchief, together with a letter in which she said that she was going to her father's country house on the next *Juma*, – that is Friday, – and that she would give us some more money before she went. But if that was not enough, we were to let her know; and she would give us as much as we required, for her father had so much that he would not miss it, especially as she had the keys of everything.

'We immediately gave the renegade five hundred crowns to buy the ship, and with eight hundred I redeemed myself, giving the money to a Valencian merchant who was in Algiers at the time. He ransomed me from the King by giving his word that he would pay the money on the arrival of the first ship from Valencia. For if he had paid it down, it would have made the King suspicious that my ransom had been in Algiers for some time, and that the merchant had concealed it for his own profit. In fact, my master was so full of suspicion, he said, that I dared not on any account pay out the money at once. On the Thursday before the Friday on which the fair Zoraida was to go to the country house, she gave us another thousand crowns, and advised us of her departure; asking me, if I ransomed myself, to discover her father's estate at once, and at all costs to find some opportunity of going to see her there. I replied briefly that I would do so, and that she must be sure to commend us to Lela Marien by all the prayers which the slave woman had taught her. After this we set about getting our three companions ransomed, to make it easier for us to leave the *bagnio*; and in case, seeing me ransomed and themselves not – though we had the money – they might get alarmed, and the Devil might put it into their heads to do something which would endanger Zoraida. For although their characters might have relieved me of that fear, yet I did not wish to put the matter to any risk. So I had them ransomed in the same way as I had ransomed myself, delivering the whole sum into the hands of the merchant, so that he might the more confidently and safely go surety for us. But we never revealed our plan or our secret to him, for that would have been too dangerous.

Chapter XLI. *A further continuation of the Captive's story.*

'Before a fortnight had gone by our renegade had bought a very good ship, capable of taking more than thirty people; and to lend colour to his design and ensure its success, he proposed to make a trip to a place called Cherchel, which is seventy-two miles from Algiers in the direction of Oran, where there is a great trade in dried figs. This he did, and made two or three trips in the company of the Tagarine I mentioned. In Barbary they call the Moors of Aragon Tagarines, and those of Granada Mudejares; and in the Kingdom of Fez they call the Mudajares Elches – those are the people the King makes most use of in war. To proceed: each time he passed in his ship she anchored in a cove not two bow-shots from the country house where Zoraida was waiting; and there, very deliberately, the renegade would take up his position with the young Moors who rowed for him, sometimes to say his prayers and sometimes to rehearse his plan. So he would go to Zoraida's estate and beg for fruit, which her father would give him without recognizing him. But although he tried to speak with Zoraida, as he afterwards told me, and tell her she might be happy and confident, for he was the man who was to carry her away to the Christian country by my instructions, it was never possible; because Moorish ladies never let themselves be seen by any Moor or Turk, unless by the orders of their husbands or fathers, though they let Christian slaves be with them and converse to them, even more than is proper. Indeed, it would have displeased me if he had talked to her, since it might have alarmed her to find her affairs entrusted to the mouth of a renegade. But God decreed otherwise, and did not give this fellow a chance of carrying out his plan. He saw, however, how safely he could go backwards and forwards to Cherchel; that he could anchor when and how and where he chose; and that his Tagarine partner had no will of his own but obeyed him entirely. So seeing that I was ransomed and that all that was left to do was to find some Christians to row, he told me to look out for the men I intended to take with me, in addition to the ransomed men, and to arrange with them for next Friday, which he had fixed on for our start. Thereupon I spoke to a dozen Spaniards, all strong oarsmen and men who could readily leave the city. It was no small matter to find so many at that moment. For there were twenty ships out privateering, and they had taken all the oarsmen with them. These men would not have been available if it had not been that their master had stayed behind that summer to complete a small galley he had on the stocks. I gave them all the

same instructions, that the next Friday evening they should creep
out one by one, and make their way to Hadji Murad's estate and
wait for me there. I gave these directions to each one separately, and
told them all that, should they see other Christians there, they were
to say nothing except that I had told them to wait for me.

'This part of the business settled, I had still to do one more thing
of the greatest importance to me. That was to advise Zoraida how
the matter had progressed, so that she might be prepared and on the
watch, and not be alarmed if we rushed upon her suddenly before
she imagined the Christian's ship would be back. So I decided to
go to the garden, and see if I could speak to her; and I went there
one day before our departure on the pretence of gathering herbs.
The first person I met was her father, who spoke to me in the language that is spoken between slaves and Moors all over Barbary,
and even in Constantinople: it is neither Moorish nor Castilian, nor
the tongue of any other country, but a mixture of every language, in
which we can all understand one another. Well, as I say, he asked
me in this tongue what I was looking for in his garden and whose
man I was. I answered that I was a slave of Arnaut Mami – this, because I knew for certain that this man was a very great friend of his
– and that I was looking for herbs to make a salad. After that he
asked me if I was for ransom or not, and how much my master
wanted for me. Whilst we were engaged in this conversation the
fair Zoraida, who had not seen me now for a long time, came out of
the house; and since Moorish women, as I have said, are not at all
shy of showing themselves to Christians, and not in the least bashful
with them, she made nothing of coming to where her father stood
talking to me. Indeed, when he saw her approaching rather slowly,
he called to her to come right up.

'It would be too much to describe to you now Zoraida's great
beauty and grace, or the rich and gay dress in which she then
appeared. I will only say that more pearls hung from her lovely
neck, her ears, and her hair than she had hairs on her head. On her
ankles which, in the Moorish fashion, were bare, she had two *car-
cajes* – that is the Moorish word for rings and bracelets for the feet –
of purest gold, set with so many diamonds that she told me afterwards her father valued them at ten thousand dollars; and those she
wore on her wrists were worth as much. The pearls were in great

numbers and very good. For fine and seed pearls are the chief pride
and adornment of Moorish women – which is why there are more
pearls among the Moors than among all other nations – and Zoraida's
father was famous for having some of the best in Algiers, and also
for possessing more than two hundred thousand Spanish crowns, of
all of which she was mistress, who is now mine. Judge how lovely
she must have looked in all her finery from so much of her beauty
as remains after all her troubles.

' Women's beauty, as we know, has its days and times, and varies
according to accidents; and it is natural enough for the emotions to
increase it or diminish it, though most often they destroy it. But I
will be brief, and say that she was then so magnificently attired and
so surpassingly lovely that she seemed to me the most perfect
creature I had ever seen; and more than that, when I remembered
my indebtedness to her, she seemed to me a heavenly goddess come
down to earth to bring me happiness and relief.

'As soon as she approached, her father told her in their language
that I was a slave of his friend Arnaut Mami, and had come to pick
a salad. She broke in to ask me in that mixture of languages whether
I was a gentleman, and why I did not ransom myself. I replied that
I was already ransomed, and the price would show her how highly
my master valued me. For I had given fifteen hundred *sultanies* for
myself. To which she replied:

' "If you belonged to my father I would certainly see that he did
not part with you for twice as much, because you Christians always
lie and make yourselves out poor to cheat us Moors."

' "That may be so, lady," I answered, "but I assure you that I
have dealt honestly with my master, as I do with everyone in the
whole world, and always shall."

' "When do you go then?" asked Zoraida.

' "To-morrow, I think," said I, "for there is a ship here from
France which is sailing in the morning, and I intend to go in her."

' "Would it not be better," asked Zoraida, "to wait until one
comes from Spain, and go in that instead of with the French, for
they are not your friends?"

' "No," I replied, "although if it is true, as I hear, that there is a
ship coming from Spain, I might wait longer for her, but it is more
likely that I shall start to-morrow. For I am so eager to be home and

with the people I love that I cannot bear to wait even for a better opportunity, should it mean delay."

'"Then no doubt you are married in your own country," asked Zoraida, "and you want to go and see your wife."

'"No, I am not married," I replied, "but I have given my word to marry when I get home."

'"Is the lady whom you have promised to marry beautiful?" asked Zoraida.

'"She is so beautiful," I replied, "that, to tell you the truth about her beauty, she is much like you."

'At this her father laughed heartily and cried: "By Allah, Christian, she must be very beautiful if she is like my daughter, who is the most beautiful woman in the whole kingdom. Look at her well, and you will see I am telling you the truth."

'Zoraida's father, as the better linguist, acted as interpreter for the greater part of this conversation; for although she spoke the bastard language which, as I have said, is in use there, she expressed her meaning more by gestures than by words. Now whilst we were engaged in this conversation a Moor came running up and shouted out that four Turks had jumped over the fence, or the wall, of the garden and were picking the fruit, although it was not yet ripe. The old man got alarmed, and Zoraida too; for the Moors' fear of the Turks is widespread, and second nature to them: especially their terror of soldiers, who are so overbearing and so tyrannical towards the Moors, their subjects, that they treat them worse than slaves. Therefore it was that Zoraida's father said to her: "Go back to the house, daughter, and shut yourself in, while I go and speak to these dogs. And you, Christian, pick your herbs and go on your ways in peace. May Allah bear you safely to your own country."

'I bowed, and he went off to look for the Turks, leaving me alone with Zoraida, who began to make a show of going off as her father had bidden her. But no sooner had she got under the shade of the garden trees, than she turned to me with her eyes full of tears and said:

'"*Tameji*, Christian, *tameji?*" – which means: "Are you going away, Christian, are you going away?"

'"Yes, lady," I replied, "but on no account without you. Expect me next *Juma*, and do not be alarmed when you see us, for we shall most certainly go to Christian lands."

'I said this in such a way that she now perfectly understood all our previous conversation; and putting her arm round my neck, she began to walk towards the house with trembling steps. As Fortune would have it – and things might have gone very badly with us if Heaven had not decreed otherwise – whilst we two were walking in the manner I have described, with her arm round my neck, her father returned from packing the Turks off, and saw us in this compromising situation; and we saw that he had seen us. But Zoraida was resourceful and self-possessed, and did not take her arm from my neck; but drawing closer to me instead, leant her head on her breast, went limp at the knees, and made as if she were fainting, while I acted as if I were forced to hold her up. Then her father came running to us and, seeing his daughter in this condition, asked her what was the matter. But as she made no answer, he said:

'"No doubt she has fainted with fright at those dogs coming into the garden." And taking her from my breast, he rested her against his. Then she heaved a sigh, and with her eyes not yet dry from their tears, spoke again "*Ameji*, Christian, *Ameji*" – ("Go away, Christian, go away"). To which her father replied:

'"There is no need for the Christian to go. He has done you no harm, and the Turks are gone now. Do not be at all alarmed, for there is nothing to frighten you. The Turks, I tell you, went when I asked them to, by the same way as they came in."

'"It was they who alarmed her, sir, as you said," I observed to her father; "but seeing that she tells me to go I do not want to annoy her. Peace be with you, and with your permission I will come to this garden again for herbs, if they are needed; for my master says that nobody has better salad herbs than you."

'"Come as often as you like," answered Hadji Murad. "My daughter did not tell you to go out of annoyance with you or with any other Christian, but probably mistook you for the Turks, or thought it was time for you to pick your herbs."

'At this I took immediate leave of both of them, and she went off with her father, looking as if her heart were torn. Then I wandered all about the garden at my pleasure, pretending to gather herbs, and took a good look at all the ways in and out, at the defences of the house, and at everything we might make use of for the furtherance of our plan.

'When I had done, I returned and gave the renegade and my companions an account of all that had happened, saying how I longed for the moment when I could enjoy undisturbed the happiness which Fortune offered me in the fair and beautiful Zoraida. Now the time passed; at last the longed-for day arrived; and by following the plan which we had settled on after mature consideration and many long arguments, we achieved the success we had hoped for. On the Friday after the day when I had spoken to Zoraida in the garden, our renegade anchored at nightfall with his boat almost opposite the place where the fair Moor lived. The Christians who were to row were already warned, and hidden in different places in the neighbourhood. They were all anxiously and excitedly waiting for me, and longing to seize the ship, which lay before their eyes. For they did not know the renegade's plan, but thought that they would have to gain their liberty by force of arms and by killing all the Moors aboard. So as soon as my companions and I showed ourselves, all the rest came out of their hiding-places. It was already the time when the city gates are shut, and there was no one to be seen over that whole countryside. But once we were all together, we were uncertain whether it would be better first to go for Zoraida or to overpower the Bagarine Moorish oarsmen. While we were in this quandary our renegade came up to us and asked why we were waiting, for it was already time, and his Moors were off their guard and most of them asleep. We told him the reason for our delay, and he said that the most important thing was to get control of the ship first, which could be done most easily and at no risk at all. Then we could go for Zoraida afterwards. We all thought his advice good, and so went to the boat, under his guidance, without further delay. He was the first to jump in and, putting his hand on his cutlass, cried out in Moorish: "Do not move from where you are, not one of you, unless he wants to be killed." By this time almost all the Christians were aboard. The Moors were a poor-spirited lot, and terror-stricken at hearing such a threat from their captain. So without a single one of them drawing a weapon – few or hardly any of them had one – they let the Christians handcuff them without a word. This was very quickly done, the captain threatening the Moors that they would all be put to the sword immediately if they raised any sort of alarm.

'When this was done, half of our number stayed on guard, and the rest of us, still under the renegade's leadership, went to Hadji Murad's garden; and, as good luck would have it, when we came to open the door it gave as easily as if it had not been locked; and so, in absolute calm and silence, we reached the house unnoticed. The lovely Zoraida was watching for us at the window, and as soon as she heard people moving, asked in a whisper if we were "*Nizarani*" – that is to say, Christians. I replied Yes, and bade her come down. When she recognized me, she did not delay an instant, but without a word of reply came in a flash and opened the door, revealing herself to us in all her beauty, and so richly dressed that I cannot attempt to describe her. As soon as I saw her I took her hand and began to kiss it; the renegade and my two companions did the same; and the others, who did not understand the situation, imitated us, thinking that we were giving her thanks for our freedom. The renegade then asked her in Moorish if her father was in the house. She replied that he was, and asleep.

'"Then we shall have to wake him," said the renegade, "and take him with us, and everything of value in this lovely place."

'"No," she replied, "my father must on no account be touched. There is nothing in the house except what I am bringing with me. That will be quite enough to make you all rich and happy. Wait a moment and you shall see."

'With these words she went back into the house, saying that she would return in a moment, and that we must keep still and make no noise. I asked the renegade what conversation had passed between them; and when he told me I said that Zoraida's wishes must be obeyed in every way. She then came back, bringing a small box full of gold crowns, so heavy that she could hardly carry it. But as ill luck would have it, her father had woken up in the meantime, and heard the noise going on in the garden. He had looked out of the window and, seeing that all the men there were Christians, had started to shout loudly and wildly in Arabic: "Christians, Christians! Thieves, thieves!" These cries threw us all into the greatest confusion and alarm. But, seeing our danger and the importance of getting our plan through before we were detected, the renegade rushed up the steps to Hadji Murad's room, and some of our party with him. As for me, I dared not let go of Zoraida, who had fallen fainting into my arms. To be brief, the men who went into the house managed so well that the next moment they brought Hadji Murad down, with his hands tied and a handkerchief stuffed into his mouth, which prevented his uttering a word – and they threatened him that if he did cry out it would cost him his life. When she saw him, she covered her eyes to avoid the sight; while he was frightened to death, not knowing how very willingly she had put herself into our hands. But at that point all we needed was our legs, and we got aboard ship with all caution and speed. For those on board were already expecting us, and were afraid that we had met with disaster.

'Some two hours of the night must have passed before we were all on the ship, where we untied Zoraida's father's hands and took the gag out of his mouth, though the renegade repeated his threat to kill him if he uttered so much as a word. When he saw his daughter there, however, he began to sigh very deeply; and he groaned when he saw how tightly I was clasping her and that she made no attempt to resist or complain or fight shy, but stayed quiet. Yet, for all that, he remained silent out of fear that the renegade's fierce threats might be put into effect. Then, when Zoraida was on board and saw that we were going to start rowing, looking at her father there and the other Moors, all tied up, she bade the renegade ask me to do her the favour of releasing the Moors and granting her father his liberty. She pleaded that she would rather fling herself into the sea than see her father, who loved her so well, carried off before her eyes, a prisoner on her account. The renegade translated her request and I replied that I would gladly agree, but he objected that it was impossible. For, if we left them there, they would immediately raise the country and give the alarm in the city, which would bring the Unbelievers out after us in light frigates, to cut us off by sea and by land, so that we could not escape. What we could do was to set them free at the first Christian port we touched. We were all agreed on this, and Zoraida also was satisfied when she was told of our decision and of our reasons for not immediately complying with her request. Then, in joyful silence, happily and vigorously, every one of our valiant rowers took his oar and, commending ourselves to God with all our hearts, we began to steer towards the Balearic Islands, which are the nearest point of Christian land. But because a slight north wind began to blow and the sea got rather rough, it was impossible for us to hold our course for Majorca; and we were forced to keep along the shore in the direction of Oran, in considerable fear of being observed from the town of Cherchel, which is about seventy miles along the coast from Algiers. We were also afraid of meeting one of those small galleys which are engaged in bringing goods from Tetuan; though each one for himself, and all of us jointly, felt confident that if we were to meet a merchant galley, so long as it was not armed for piracy, we not only would not be taken, but would capture a ship in which we could finish our voyage in greater safety. And all the while we rowed, Zoraida lay with her head in my arms to avoid seeing her father. I felt that she was calling on Lela Marien to aid us.

'We must have rowed a good thirty miles when dawn found us about three gunshots from the shore, which we saw to be desert without any inhabitants to observe us. But, for all that, we rowed as hard as we could to get farther out to sea. It was now a little smoother; and when we had got about six miles off, the order was given that only every fourth man should row; so that we might have something to eat, for the ship was well provided with stores. But the rowers said that this was no time to rest, and that those who were not rowing could feed them, as they certainly did not mean to let the oars out of their hands. We did feed them. But at that time a stiff breeze began to blow, obliging us to hoist a sail and stop rowing, and to steer for Oran, for it was impossible to make any other course. All this was done with great speed; and so we sailed at more than eight knots, without any other fear than that of meeting some ship which might prove to be a pirate. We gave our Tagarine Moors food, and the renegade comforted them by saying that they were not prisoners, but would be given their freedom at the first opportunity. He gave the same assurance to Zoraida's father, who replied:

'"I could expect and believe anything else of your generosity and liberality, Christians, but do not think me so simple as to imagine that you will grant me my liberty. You did not put yourselves to the danger of robbing me of it, only to return it to me so freely, particularly since you know who I am and how much you stand to gain by a bargain. If you would name the sum, I offer you here and now as much as you want for myself and for this unhappy daughter of mine; or failing that, for her alone, who is the greater and better part of my soul."

'At these words he began to weep so bitterly that we were all moved to pity, and Zoraida was compelled to look in his direction; and she was so melted at the sight of the old man weeping that she got up from my feet and went over to embrace him. Then, as she put her face to his, they both burst into tears of such affection that many of us did the same. But when he saw that she was in her finest clothes and wearing all those jewels, he asked her in their tongue:

'"What is this, my daughter? Last night, before our present terrible misfortune overtook us, I saw you in your ordinary houseclothes; and now, though you have not had the time to dress yourself up, nor any good news to celebrate by adorning and beautifying yourself, I find you decked out in the best clothes I was able to give you when Fortune was kindest to us. Answer my question, for this is more surprising and alarming to me even than my present misfortune."

'The renegade translated to us all that the Moor said to his daughter, but she did not answer a word. However, when he saw on one side of the ship the little box in which she kept her jewels, and which he was certain he had left at Algiers and not taken to their country house, he was even more disturbed, and asked her how the box had come into our hands, and what was inside it. To which the renegade answered, without waiting for Zoraida to reply:

'"Do not trouble yourself, sir, to ask your daughter Zoraida so many questions, for I can reply to all of them in one word. Let me tell you that she is a Christian; it is she who has been the file to our chains and the key to our captivity. She is with us of her own free will; as glad, I imagine, to be where she is, as a man coming out of darkness into light, out of death into life, out of pain into glory."

'"Is it true, what he says, daughter?" asked the Moor.

'"It is," replied Zoraida.

'"That, in fact, you are a Christian," asked the old man, "and it is you who has put your father into his enemies' power?"

'To which Zoraida replied: "I am a Christian, but it is not I that brought you to this pass, for it was never my wish to leave you or to do you any harm. I only wished to do myself a benefit."

'"And what benefit have you done yourself, daughter?"

' "That," she replied, "you must ask Lela Marien, for she will be able to tell you better than I."

'No sooner did the Moor hear this than he threw himself with incredible agility head foremost into the sea, and no doubt would have drowned if the long and cumbrous clothes he wore had not kept him just above water. Zoraida cried out for us to rescue him; whereat we all instantly went to his aid and, grasping him by his long robes, pulled him out, half drowned and unconscious. And so distressed was Zoraida that she burst into a tender and sorrowful lament over him, as if he were really dead. We turned him face downwards, at which he brought up a great deal of water, and after two hours came to. During this time the wind changed and drove us back towards the land, and we had to row hard to avoid running aground. But by good luck we made a little cove beside a small promontory or cape, which is called by the Moors the Cape of the "*Cava Rumia*"; which means in our language the wicked Christian woman. For there is a tradition among the Moors that it is the place where that "*Cava*" lies buried, through whom Spain was lost; for "*cava*" in their tongue means wicked woman and "*rumia*" Christian. They even look on it as a bad omen to have to anchor there, if necessity drives them to – and otherwise they never do so. But for us it was no wicked woman's shelter, but a secure haven of refuge, as the sea was running high. We posted our sentries on shore and, without dropping our oars, ate the renegade's provisions, and fervently prayed God and Our Lady to aid and favour us with a happy ending to our adventure which had begun so prosperously. At Zoraida's entreaty I gave orders that her father and the other Moors, who were still bound, should be put ashore; for her courage failed her, and her tender heart grieved at the sight of her father bound and those countrymen of hers prisoners. We promised her to free them at the moment of our departure, since we should incur no danger by leaving them in that uninhabited spot. Our prayers were not in vain, for Heaven answered them. The wind presently changed in our favour, and the sea grew calm, inviting us to resume our voyage with joyful hearts. At this we unbound the Moors and put them ashore one by one, to their great astonishment. But when we came to land Zoraida's father, who had entirely regained consciousness, he said:

'"Why do you think, Christians, that this wicked woman is glad you have set me free? Do you think that it is out of pity for me? Not at all. But because my presence would hinder her in the gratification of her wicked desires. Do not imagine that she has been moved to change her faith out of a belief that your religion is better than ours. No, it is because she knows that immorality is more freely practised in your country than in ours."

'And turning to Zoraida, with myself and another Christian holding him by both arms in case he might do something desperate, he cried: "Infamous and misguided girl! Where are you going in your blind frenzy, in the power of these dogs, our natural enemies? Accursed be the hour in which I engendered you, and accursed the pleasure and delight in which I brought you up!"

'But when I saw that he was not likely to end quickly, I hurriedly put him ashore; and from there he went on calling out his curses and lamentations, praying to Mahomet to beseech Allah to destroy us, confound us, and annihilate us. And when we had hoisted sail and could no longer hear his words, we saw his actions, and watched him plucking his beard, tearing his hair, and rolling on the ground. Once indeed he strained his voice so loud that we could hear him cry: "Come back, beloved daughter – come back to land! I forgive you everything! Give those men the money, for it is theirs; and come and comfort this wretched father of yours, who will lose his life in the sands of this desert if you forsake him."

'Zoraida listened to all this, and felt it all, and wept, not knowing what else to say in reply but: "May it please Allah, dear father, that Lela Marien, who has been the cause of my becoming a Christian, may console you in your grief. Allah well knows that I could have done nothing but what I did, and that these Christians owe me nothing for my goodwill. For even if I had wanted not to come with them, but to stay at home, it would have been impossible. So fast did my soul hurry me towards a deed which I know to be good, beloved father, though it appears wicked to you."

'This she said at a time when her father could not hear it, and we could no longer see him. I comforted Zoraida, and we all attended to our ship, which was so speeded by a favourable wind that we fervently expected to be on the Spanish coast at dawn next day.

'But as good seldom or never comes pure and unadulterated, accompanied or followed by no alarming evil, our fortune, or perhaps the curses the Moor cast on his daughter – for a father's curses are always to be feared – so willed it, I say, that when we were well out to sea, and almost three hours of the night had gone by, just as we were scudding before the wind under full sail with oars shipped – for the favourable wind relieved us of the labour of using them – we made out, by the light of a clear moon, a square-rigged ship close by us, with her sails spread, steering with the wind on her quarter and standing across our bows. She was so near that we had to lower our sail so as not to collide with her, and they had to put their helm hard up to give us room to pass. They had gathered on the deck to ask us who we were, where we came from, and where we were sailing for. But as they asked us in French, our renegade said: "Do not reply. They are no doubt some of those French pirates who take everything as a prize."

'At this warning no one said a word. But when we had got a little ahead and the ship was already on our lee, they suddenly let off two cannon, both loaded, it appeared, with chainshot, for with one shot they cut our mast in half and blew it and our sail overboard. A moment later they fired off another, and the ball hit us amidships, laying the vessel's side entirely open, though it did no other damage at all. But we saw that we were sinking, and all began to shout for help, imploring the men in the ship to take us aboard, for we were drowning. Then they put to, and launched their skiff or ship's boat; and a full dozen well-armed Frenchmen got in, with their arquebuses, and their matches lighted, and drew alongside us. Then, seeing how few we were and that our ship was sinking, they picked us up, saying that they had served us in that way for our discourtesy in not replying to them. Meanwhile our renegade took the box with Zoraida's treasures and threw it into the sea, without anyone noticing what he was doing.

'Finally we got aboard among the Frenchmen, who when they had found out all they wanted to about us, robbed us of everything we possessed, as if they were our mortal enemies, stripping Zoraida even of the anklets on her feet. But I was not so much disturbed at Zoraida's distress as at my own fear that, after they had stolen her rich and precious jewels, they would proceed to rob her of the most valuable of all, which she prized the most highly. But these people's desires do not extend beyond money, though of this their lust is insatiable; and on that occasion it was so extreme that they would have stripped us even of our slave's uniforms, if these had been of any use to them. Some of them even wanted to throw us all into the sea, wrapped in a sail, for they meant to pretend to be Bretons and to trade with some Spanish ports; and if they were to take us into harbour, their robbery would be discovered and they would be punished. But the captain – it was he who had robbed my beloved Zoraida – said that he was content with the booty he had, and that he did not want to touch at a Spanish port; but to slip through the Straits of Gibraltar by night, or in any way he could, and make for La Rochelle, which was the place they had sailed from. So they agreed to let us have their ship's boat and all that was necessary for the short voyage we had still to make. This they did next day, close to the Spanish coast, the sight of which made us forget all our troubles and hardships so completely that they might never have occurred: such is man's joy at regaining lost liberty.

'It must have been about midday when they put us into the boat, giving us two barrels of water and some ship's biscuit. And just as the lovely Zoraida was going, the captain was seized with some sort of pity and gave her some forty crowns; and he refused to let his men rob her of the clothes which she is wearing now. We got into the boat, thanking them for this last kindness and displaying gratitude rather than resentment. They then stood out to sea on a course for the Straits, and we set about rowing most vigorously without looking to any guiding star but the shore, which we could see ahead; and at sunset we were so near that we thought we might make land before the night was far spent. But as there was no moon and the sky looked black, it did not seem safe to us to make for the coast, not knowing just where we were. Yet many of us wished to, even though it were among the rocks and far from any inhabited spot. For, as we said, in that case we need have no fear of the Tetuan pirates, who leave Barbary at night and are on the Spanish coast by dawn, where they generally pick up a prize and have got back home by nightfall. But after a great deal of discussion we decided to approach the land slowly, if the sea was calm enough to allow it, and to put ashore wherever we could. This we did; and it must have been a little before midnight when we arrived at the foot of a great hill, which stood back sufficiently from the sea to leave a little space suitable for our landing. We grounded on the beach, leapt ashore, and kissed the earth. With tears of the greatest joy we gave thanks to the Lord God for His incomparable goodness to us. Then, taking out of the boat such provisions as were in it, we dragged it ashore and climbed a good way up the hillside. But although we stood on Christian soil, we could not assure ourselves or really believe that it was so.

'Dawn came, I thought, more slowly than we could have wished. We climbed the hill to the top to see if we could make out a village or shepherd's huts. But though we strained our eyes, we could see no house or person, no path or road. So we decided to push on inland, for we could hardly fail to find someone soon who could tell us where we were. What distressed me most was to see Zoraida on foot in this rough country. For though at times I carried her on my shoulders, she was too distressed by my weariness to be refreshed by the rest it gave her. So she made me put her down and walked patiently on with a great show of cheerfulness, holding me by the hand. We must have gone something less than a mile when the tinkle of a little sheep-bell came to our ears, a sure sign that there was a flock somewhere near. We all looked carefully round to find it, and saw a shepherd lad at the foot of a cork-tree, comfortably and idly whittling a stick with his knife. When we called, he looked up and got briskly to his feet. But, as we afterwards learnt, the first of us he caught sight of were the renegade and Zoraida; and at the sight of their Moorish dress he thought that all the hosts of Barbary were upon him and, running at a surprising speed towards the wood ahead of us he began to bawl at the top of his voice: "Moors! The Moors are ashore! Moors! Moors! To arms! To arms!"

'We were all bewildered by this outcry, and did not know what to do. But realizing that the shepherd's cries would rouse the countryside, and that the mounted coastguards would soon come to see what was the matter, we decided that the renegade should take off his Turkish robes and put on a jacket, or slave's coat; which one of our party gave him at once, though it left him in his shirt. So, commending ourselves to God, we took the path we had seen the shepherd take, expecting every moment that the coastguards would be upon us. And we were not wrong. For two hours had not gone by when, as we left the heath for the plain, we saw about fifty horsemen riding towards us at a very fast half-gallop. At the sight of them we halted and waited. But when they came up and saw a group of wretched Christians instead of the Moors they were expecting, they were puzzled; and one of them asked us if we by chance were the cause of the shepherd's hue and cry. I answered Yes. But as I was going to tell him my story and who we were, one of the Christians in our party recognized the horseman who had asked us the question and, without giving me a chance to speak, cried out: "Thanks be to God, gentlemen, for bringing us to so good a place. For, if I am not deceived, the soil we are treading is close to Velez Malaga. And if my years of captivity have not blotted your image from my mind, you, sir, who are asking us who we are, are my uncle, Pedro de Bustamante."

'The Christian prisoner had no sooner spoken than the horseman jumped from his mount and ran to embrace the young man, crying: "My beloved nephew, I do recognize you now. We mourned you for dead, I and my sister – your mother – and all your family, who are still living. For God has been pleased to spare our lives to enjoy the sight of you. We had learnt that you were at Algiers and, to judge by your clothes and the clothes of your whole party, you have had a miraculous deliverance."

'"That is so," replied the young man, "and we shall have time enough to tell you the whole story."

'Immediately the horsemen realized that we were Christian captives they dismounted, and each one of them offered us his horse to ride to the city of Velez Malaga, which was about four and a half miles away. We told them where we had left the boat, and some of them turned back to get it and bring it along to the city. Others took us up behind them, and Zoraida rode behind our Christian's uncle. The whole town came out to greet us. For they had already had the news of our arrival from one of the guards, who had ridden ahead. They were not at all surprised at seeing escaped slaves or captured Moors, because all the people of that coast are used to seeing both; but they were astonished at Zoraida's beauty, which was at its height at that moment, by reason of the exertion of the journey and of her joy at finding herself on Christian soil, with no more to fear. This had brought such colour to her cheeks that, unless I was then much deceived by my love, I dare swear that there was no more beautiful creature in the world; at least none that I had ever seen.

'We went straight to the church to thank God for mercies received; and the moment Zoraida went in, she exclaimed that there were faces there which looked like Lela Marien's. We told her that those were her images, and the renegade made her understand, as best he could, what they signified, and that she could worship them as she would the true Lela Marien who had spoken to her. She has a good intelligence and an easy and clear intuition, and so she understood what he said about the images at once. They took us from there, and divided us among several houses in the town, but our companion from that place took the renegade, Zoraida, and myself to the house of his parents, who were tolerably well provided with this world's goods, and treated us with as much affection as they did their son.

'We stayed in Velez six days, at the end of which the renegade, having lodged his statement in due form, went off to the city of Granada, to be reconciled to the bosom of Mother Church by means of the Holy Inquisition. The rest of the freed captives went each where he pleased. Only Zoraida and I remained with nothing but the crowns which the Frenchman in his kindness had given her. With these I bought the beast she rides. So I am travelling with her as her father and squire, but not as her husband, with the object of learning whether my father is alive, or if either of my brothers has had better fortune than I; though as Heaven has given me Zoraida as a companion, I do not think that the best lot that can befall me will seem better. Zoraida's patience in bearing the discomforts of poverty, and her desire to become a Christian, fill me with admiration, and bind me to serve her all the days of my life. But my happiness in knowing that I am hers and she is mine is troubled and spoilt by my uncertainty whether I shall find any corner of my country to shelter her. For I fear that time and death may have worked such changes in the fortunes and lives of my father and brothers that, failing them, I shall scarcely find anyone who knows me.

'There is no more of my story to tell you, gentlemen. I leave it to you to judge whether it is strange and entertaining. I can only say that I wish I had told it you more briefly, though fear of boring you has caused me to omit a great number of details.'

Chapter XLII. *Of further events at the Inn, and many other note-worthy matters.*

THE Captive was silent after telling his tale, and Don Ferdinand observed: 'I assure you, Captain, that the way in which you have told your strange adventure has been as remarkable as the strangeness and novelty of the events themselves. It is a curious tale and full of astonishing incidents. In fact we have enjoyed listening so much that we should be glad to have it all over again, even if it took till tomorrow morning to tell it.'

On his saying this, Cardenio and all the others offered him their utmost services, in such warm and sincere language that the captain was thoroughly convinced of their goodwill. Don Ferdinand, in particular, offered to make his brother the Marquis stand godfather at Zoraida's baptism if he would return with him, and himself to provide him with enough money to appear in his own country with suitable dignity and decency. The Captive thanked him courteously for all this, but would not accept any of his generous offers.

By this time night had fallen, and when it was quite dark a coach came up to the inn with some men on horseback, who asked for accommodation. But the landlady answered that there was not an inch unoccupied in the whole inn.

'However that may be,' said one of the horsemen, who had come in, 'room must be found for my lord Judge, who is approaching.'

At this title the landlady grew confused, and said: 'Sir, the trouble is this: I have no beds. If his worship the Judge brings one with him, as I suppose he does, let him come in and welcome. My husband and I will give up our room to accommodate his worship.'

'That will do,' said the squire.

By this time there had alighted from the coach a man whose dress proclaimed his high office; for his long robe with ruffled sleeves proved that he was a judge, as his servant had said. He led by the hand a young lady of about sixteen in travelling dress, so gay, striking, and beautiful that the sight of her impressed them all; and so vividly that, if they had not already seen Dorothea, Lucinda, and Zoraida at that inn, they would have doubted whether she had her match for beauty.

Don Quixote was present at the entrance of the judge and the young lady; and as soon as he saw them, he said: 'Your worship may certainly enter and take your ease in this castle. For, though it is narrow and uncomfortable, there is no place in the world so narrow and uncomfortable that it does not allow room for arms and learning. Especially if arms and letters bring beauty as their pilot and guide, as your worship's learning does in the person of this fair maiden, before whom not only should castles open and reveal themselves, but rocks split and mountains cleave and bow down to give her entertainment. Come into this paradise, I say, your worship, for here there are stars and suns to attend the heaven your worship brings with you. Here you will find arms at their zenith and beauty in its prime.'

The judge was astounded at Don Quixote's speech, and after gazing at him attentively, was no less astounded at his appearance. But finding no words with which to reply, he fell into a fresh amazement at the sight of Lucinda, Dorothea, and Zoraida, who had heard of the new guests and of the young lady's beauty from the landlady, and had come out to see her and welcome her. Don Ferdinand, Cardenio, and the priest, however, gave the judge a simpler and more courteous greeting. That dignitary was indeed confused, both at what he saw and at what he heard, but the beauties of the inn made the lovely girl welcome. Presently the judge perceived that all the people there were people of quality, though he was bewildered at Don Quixote's figure, face, and air. But when they had all exchanged polite greetings and carefully considered the accommodation of the inn, everything was arranged as before. All the women were to share the attic already described, and the men to stay outside, on guard as it were. So the judge was satisfied that his daughter – for such the young lady was – should lodge with the other ladies, which she was delighted to do; and with part of the landlord's narrow bed and half of the one the judge had brought, they managed better that night than they had expected.

Now the first moment he saw the judge the captive felt his heart leap with the idea that this was his brother. So he asked one of the servants to tell him his master's name, and the district he came from, if he knew it. The squire replied that he was the Licentiate Juan Perez de Viedma, and that he had heard that he came from a little place in the mountains of Leon. This information, together with what he had seen, finally confirmed him in the belief that this was his brother who by their father's advice had followed the profession of learning. The excited and delighted Captive then called Don Ferdinand, Cardenio and the priest aside to tell them, assuring them that the judge really was his brother. What is more, the servant had told him that he was going to take up the post of judge in the Indies, in the High Court of Mexico; also that the young lady was his daughter, whose mother had died at her birth, and that he had become very rich from the dowry left him with the child. The captain asked them to advise him how to reveal himself, or how to find out first whether his brother would be ashamed to discover him poor, or would acknowledge him with open arms, were he to do so.

'Leave it to me to make the experiment,' said the priest. 'I will gladly do so, for there is no reason to think that you will not be very well received, Captain. Your brother shows every sign of goodness and good sense, and his behaviour does not suggest that he is arrogant or ungrateful, or does not know how to assess the accidents of fortune at their true value.'

'All the same,' said the captain, 'I should like to reveal myself in a roundabout way, and not suddenly.'

'I promise you,' said the priest, 'that I will manage it in such a way that we shall all be satisfied.'

By this time supper was ready, and all sat down to table except the captain and the ladies, who were supping on their own in their room. Then in the middle of the meal the priest remarked: 'I had a comrade of your name, Sir Judge, at Constantinople, where I was a slave for several years. That man was one of the bravest commanders in all the Spanish infantry; but, brave and enterprising as he was, he was unfortunate.'

'What was this captain's name, sir?' asked the judge.

'His name,' replied the priest, 'was Ruiz Perez de Viedma, and he came from a place in the mountains of Leon. He told me of an incident that had happened to him and his brothers, which I should have taken for an old wives' tale told over a winter fire, if it had not been related by so truthful a man. What he told me was that his father had divided his property among his three sons, and had given them some advice which was better than Cato's. By his father's advice, anyhow, he went into the army; and in a few years, by his cour-

age and application, he rose to be an infantry captain, by his own
merits alone, and was on the way to be a colonel very soon. But fortune went against him. For when he might have expected things to
be good his luck broke, and he lost his liberty as well, on that most
happy day when many recovered theirs, at the battle of Lepanto. I
lost mine at the Goletta, and afterwards, by various accidents, we
found ourselves comrades in Constantinople. From there he went to
Algiers, where, as I learnt, one of the strangest accidents in the
world happened to him.'

From there the priest went on, and briefly told him the story of
Zoraida and his brother, which the judge heard with greater attention than he had ever given to a case before. The priest stopped at
the point when the French robbed the Christians in the boat, and
ended with a description of the poverty in which they had left his
comrade and the fair Moorish lady. He said that he had not heard
what had become of them since, whether they had reached Spain or
if the Frenchmen had carried them off to France.

The captain listened to all that the priest said, standing some way
off and noting all his brother's movements. And when he saw that
the priest had come to the end of his tale, the judge gave a deep
sigh and exclaimed, with his eyes filling with tears, 'Oh, sir, if you
knew what news you had given me, and how nearly it touches me!
But I cannot help showing it by the tears which spring to my eyes
in spite of all my fortitude and self-control! This brave captain you
speak of is my eldest brother. He was stronger and more courageous than my other brother or I, and chose the honourable and
worthy profession of arms – one of the three courses our father
proposed to us, as your comrade told you in that tale of his which
you thought was a fiction. I followed the career of learning, in
which God and my own hard work have raised me to the rank you
see. My younger brother is in Peru, and so rich that, with what he
has sent to my father and me, he has more than made up for the
capital he took away. He has even given my father enough to satisfy
his natural prodigality; and thanks to him, I have been able to follow my studies in a very fitting and creditable fashion, and to reach
my present position. My father is still alive, though dying with desire for news of his eldest son, and praying God night and day not
to let death close his eyes before he has seen him alive. I am aston-

ished that such a sensible fellow could have failed to send my father news in his great troubles and afflictions, or in his times of prosperity. Had our father or either of us been informed, he would not have had to wait for that miraculous cane to get his ransom. But it troubles me now not to know whether those Frenchmen set him free or killed him to cover up their robbery; and for that reason I shall not continue my journey joyfully as I began it, but in sadness and melancholy. Oh, my dear brother, who can tell where you are now? How gladly I would seek you and relieve you of your hardships, even at the cost of hardships to myself! Who will bear the news to our father that you are still alive, though perhaps in the deepest dungeons of Barbary? But even from there his riches, my brother's, and mine will rescue you. Oh lovely, generous Zoraida, who could ever repay you the good you have done my brother? Who will be present at your soul's rebirth, and at that wedding which would give us all such happiness?'

These were the judge's words, and he said more to the same effect, full of emotion at this news of his brother; and all the rest of the party too showed their compassion for his anxiety. The priest, however, seeing that he had succeeded by his trick in carrying out the captain's wishes, did not want to keep them any longer in sadness. So, getting up from the table and going into the room where Zoraida was, he led her out by the hand, followed by Lucinda, Dorothea, and the judge's daughter. The captain stood waiting to see what the priest would do; and what he did was to take him by the other hand, and lead them both up to the place where the judge and the rest of the gentlemen were sitting.

'Cease your tears, Sir Judge,' said he, 'and your wish shall be crowned with all happiness. For here you have your dear brother and your dear sister-in-law before you. Here is Captain Viedma, and this is the lovely Moorish lady, his benefactress. The Frenchmen, as I told you, reduced them to their present plight only so that you might show them the generosity of your noble heart.'

The captain started forward to embrace his brother, but the judge held him off awhile, with his arms on his shoulders, to look at him from a little farther off. Once he had recognized him, however, he embraced him so warmly and shed such tender tears of happiness, that most of the company had to weep as well. The words the two

N

brothers uttered and the feelings they displayed can hardly be conceived, still less written down. First they exchanged brief accounts of their adventures; then they displayed the warmth of brotherly love; next the judge embraced Zoraida; then he offered her all his possessions; then he made her embrace his daughter; then the lovely Christian girl and the most lovely Moor moved everyone to fresh tears. And there stood Don Quixote, listening and speechless, pondering on these extraordinary events and attributing them all to the chimaeras of knight errantry.

Soon they arranged that the captain and Zoraida should return with his brother to Seville and advise their father of his finding and deliverance, so that the old man might be able to come and be present at Zoraida's marriage and baptism. For it was not possible for the judge to abandon his present voyage, as he had news that the fleet was leaving Seville in a month's time for New Spain, and it would be most inconvenient for him to lose his passage.

The whole company was more than delighted at the captain's good fortune; and as by now almost two-thirds of the night was gone, they agreed to retire and spend the rest of it in sleep. Don Quixote took it on himself to mount guard over the castle, in case they might be attacked by some giant or unscrupulous villain, greedy for the great treasure of beauty which lay therein. Those who knew him thanked him, and gave the judge an account of the knight's strange humour, which delighted him more than a little. Only Sancho Panza was annoyed at the delay in going to bed; and he made himself more comfortable than any of them, throwing himself down on his ass's harness – which cost him very dear, as shall be told by and by. The ladies then having retired to their apartment, and the others accommodating themselves with the least discomfort possible, Don Quixote went out of the inn to be sentinel of the castle, as he had promised.

Now a little before dawn there reached the ears of the ladies a voice so sweet and musical that it compelled them all to listen, especially Dorothea, who was awake, though Doña Clara de Viedma – for this was the name of the judge's daughter – was asleep at her side. No one could imagine who it could be that sang so well; it was a single voice without instrumental accompaniment. At times it sounded as if the singing came from the yard, at times from the stable; and, while they were listening thus undecided, Cardenio came to the door of the room and said:

'If anyone is awake, listen and you will hear a mule-lad singing. As he chants, he enchants.'

'We can hear him, sir,' replied Dorothea. At which Cardenio departed, and Dorothea, listening with great attention, heard the words that he was singing. They were these:

Chapter XLIII. *The charming story of the Mule Lad, with other strange happenings at the Inn.*

> I am a mariner of love,
> And in his depths profound
> Sail on, although without a hope
> Ever to come to ground.
>
> My eyes are on a distant star,
> Which serves me for a guide,
> More beautiful and bright than all
> That Palinurus spied.
>
> I know not where it's leading me;
> And so, confused, I steer,
> My heart intent on watching it,
> Careless, yet full of care.
>
> And her unkindly shyness,
> And too much modesty
> Are clouds that shroud her from my eyes,
> Whom most I long to see.
>
> My Clara, clear and shining star,
> I fade beneath thy light,
> And when you hide your beams from me
> For me it's darkest night.

When the singer had reached this point in his song, Dorothea thought it would be a pity if Clara did not hear such a lovely voice, and so she shook her until she woke her up, saying:

'Forgive my waking you, child. But I want you to enjoy the finest voice you will ever hear in all your life.'

Clara woke up very drowsy, and did not understand at first what Dorothea was saying, but asked her to tell her again. She then repeated her words, upon which Clara began to listen. But scarcely had she heard two verses of the song than she **was** seized with a violent trembling, as if she had been taken with a serious attack of the quartan ague, and hugged Dorothea tightly, crying:

'Oh, my dear, dear lady, why did you wake me up? For the greatest good that Fortune could do me now would be to keep my eyes and ears shut, so that I should neither see nor hear that unhappy musician.'

'What is that you say, girl? They tell me that the singer is a mule-lad.'

'No, he is not,' replied Clara, 'but a lord of many estates, and one he holds in my heart so firmly that, unless he wishes to quit his tenure, it will be his for ever.'

Surprised at the girl's passionate words, which seemed to her much in advance of her apparent youth, Dorothea then said: 'You speak so obscurely that I cannot understand you. Explain yourself more clearly. Tell me what you mean by heart and estates, and about this singer whose song disturbs you so. But do not tell me anything now. I do not want your transports to rob me of the pleasure of hearing the singer, for I think he is going to sing again, with new words and to a new tune.'

'Let him by all means,' replied Clara. But she put her hands over both her ears to avoid hearing him, which surprised Dorothea once more. But she listened to the song, which ran like this:

> Sweet hope of mine,
> That break'st impossibilities and briars,
> And down that path dost run
> Which thou thyself didst make for thy desires,
> Be not dismayed to see
> At every step thyself nigh death to be.
>
> Sluggards do not deserve
> The glory of triumphs or of victory;
> Good luck will never serve
> Those who resist not fortune manfully,
> But weakly fall to ground,
> And in soft sloth their senses all confound.
>
> That love his glories holds
> At a high rate is reasonable and best;
> No precious stones nor gold
> Excel those pledges by love's hand impressed;
> And 'tis a thing most clear,
> Nothing is worth esteem that costs not dear.

> An amorous persistence
> Will often win things most impossible;
> So though I find resistance
> To my soul's deep desires, in her stern will,
> There's not a fear denies
> That I shall climb from earth to her fair skies.

Here the voice ceased, and Clara broke into fresh sobs; all of which excited Dorothea's desire to know the cause of the sweet singing and the mournful tears. So once more she asked Clara what it was she had meant to say before. Then, out of fear that Lucinda might hear her, Clara hugged Dorothea tightly and put her mouth so close to her ear that she could safely speak without being overheard:

'The singer, my lady,' she said, 'is the son of a gentleman of the Kingdom of Aragon, the lord of two villages, who used to live opposite my father's house in Madrid. And although my father has the windows of his house covered with canvas in the winter and with blinds in summer, I do not know how it was, but this young student saw me, either in church or somewhere else. He fell in love with me, in fact, and gave me to understand so from the windows of his house, so emphatically and with such tears that I had to believe him, and love him too, though I did not know what it was he wanted of me. One of the gestures he made me was to clasp his two hands together as a sign that he wanted to marry me; and although I should have been very glad for that to be, as I was alone and motherless I did not know whom to tell about it. So I let things be, and showed him no favour; though, when my father was out of the house and his father too, I did lift the curtain or the blind a little and let him see all of me; and he was so enraptured that he seemed almost beside himself. Then the time came for my father's departure; and he learnt of it, though not from me, for I could never tell him. He fell ill of grief, I understand, and so on the day we left I could not see him to say good-bye, not even by a glance. But when we had been two days on the road, as we were riding into an inn in a village a day's journey from here, I saw him at the door of the house, dressed as a mule-lad; and so much like one that if I had not borne his portrait in my heart, I should have found it impossible to recognize him. I knew him; I was amazed; I was delighted. He stole a look at me, undetected by my father, from whom he always hides his face when he passes in front of us on the roads, and as we come to the inns. But knowing who he is, and reflecting that it is for love of me that he travels on foot and endures all these hardships, I am dying of grief, and I follow his every step with my eyes. I do not know his purpose in coming, nor how he managed to escape his father, who loves him extremely, both because he has no other heir and because he deserves it; as you will find when you see him. What is more, let me tell you that all that he sings comes out of his own head, for I have heard that he is a very great scholar and poet. And there is another thing: each time I see him or hear him sing, I tremble all over, for fear my father will recognize him and come to know of our feelings. I have never spoken a word to him in my life, but, all the same, I love him so much that I cannot live without him. That is all that I can tell you, dear lady, about the musician whose voice has pleased you so; but from that alone you can clearly tell that he is no mule-lad, as you say, but a lord of hearts and lands, as I have told you.'

'Say no more, dear Doña Clara,' said Dorothea at this point, kissing her countless times. 'Say no more, I tell you, but wait till the day dawns. For I hope, with God's help, to set your affairs on the way towards the happy ending such a good beginning deserves.'

'But what ending can we expect, dear lady,' asked Doña Clara, 'seeing that his father is so rich and important that he will not think me fit to be his son's servant, much less his wife? Then, I would not marry without my father's knowledge for anything in the world. I only want the young man to go back and leave me. Perhaps with not seeing him, and with the great distance we are going to travel, the pain I feel now might grow less; though I must say that I do not think this remedy I am imagining can be of much use to me. I do not know what witchcraft there has been, nor how this love I feel for him has entered into me, since we are both so young – for I really believe we are of the same age, and I am not quite sixteen yet, nor shall be, my father says, till Michaelmas day.'

Dorothea could not prevent herself from laughing at Doña Clara's childish way of talking, and said: 'Let us sleep, dear lady, for a little of the night is still left, I think. God will send us morning, and things will go well if my skill does not fail me.'

With this they fell asleep, and the whole inn lay in deep silence. Only the innkeeper's daughter and her maid Maritornes were not asleep. For, knowing the ideas that possessed Don Quixote, and that he was outside the inn, mounted on guard, the pair of them decided to play him a trick, or at least to get some amusement by listening to his nonsense.

Now there was not a single window in the whole inn that opened on to the fields, but only a hole in a loft, used for throwing out the straw. At this hole the two demi-virgins placed themselves, and espied Don Quixote on his horse, leaning on his lance and, at intervals, heaving such mournful and deep sighs that each one of them seemed to tear out his soul. At the same time they heard him speak in soft, delicate and amorous tones:

'O my lady Dulcinea del Toboso, sum of all beauty, summit and crown of discretion, treasury of grace, store of virtue and, lastly, pattern of all that is beneficent, modest and delightful in the world! What is your grace doing at this moment? Can it be that you are mindful of your captive knight, who has submitted himself freely to so many perils, only to serve you? Let me have news of her, O three-faced luminary, Diana! Perhaps you are gazing on her now in envy of her looks, and see her pacing some gallery of her sumptuous palaces, or leaning with her breast upon some balcony rail, considering how, without danger to her modesty or greatness, she may alleviate the torment my aching heart suffers for her sake; with what glory she may crown my labours; what assuagement she may give to my anxiety; and lastly, what life to my death, and what reward to my services. And you, sun, who must even now be saddling your steeds in haste to rise and see my lady, I pray you, when you see her, salute her from me! But beware, when you gaze on her and salute her, not to kiss her on the face, or I shall be more jealous of her than you were of that wanton and fickle maid who made you sweat and run across the plains of Thessaly, or by the banks of Peneus; – for I do not well remember where you ran then in your jealous passion.'

When Don Quixote had reached this point in his mournful harangue the innkeeper's daughter began to call to him softly: 'Dear sir, come this way, if you please.'

At this sound Don Quixote turned his head, and saw by the light of the moon, which was then at its brightest, that someone was beckoning him from the hole, which seemed to him to be a window, and even to have gilded bars, which are proper to such rich castles as he imagined that inn to be. Instantly he conceived in his wild imagination that once again, as before, that beauteous damsel, the daughter of the warden of that castle, had come, overwhelmed by love of him, to ask for his favours. With this thought, not wishing to show himself discourteous or ungrateful, he turned Rocinante's head and went up to the window. Then, when he saw the two wenches there, he said:

'I pity you, beautous lady, for fixing your amorous desires where it is impossible for you to find a response befitting your great merit and breeding; for which you must not blame this wretched knight errant, whom love makes incapable of engaging his heart to any but that maiden whom, from the first moment his eyes lighted on her, he made absolute lady of his soul. Pardon me, kind lady, and retire to your room. Please do not reveal your desires to me further, that I may not appear yet more thankless. Though if, of the love you bear me, you can discover in me anything other than love itself by which I may satisfy you, demand it of me; and I swear to you, by that sweet and absent enemy of mine, to bestow it upon you out of hand, even if you should demand of me a lock of Medusa's hair, which was all snakes, or even the very rays of the sun enclosed in a flask.'

'My lady needs none of that, Sir Knight,' put in Maritornes at this juncture.

'What then does she need, discreet lady?' asked Don Quixote.

'Only one of your beautiful hands,' replied Maritornes, 'with which to appease the great desire which has brought her to this window, at such risk to her honour that if my lord, her father, came to know of it, the least slice he would cut off her would be her ear.'

'I should like to see him do that!' answered Don Quixote. 'But he will take good care not to, if he does not wish to come to the most disastrous end that ever a father met in all the world, for laying his hands on the delicate limbs of his enamoured daughter.'

Maritornes had now no doubt that Don Quixote would give her the hand she had asked him for and, turning her plan over in her mind, got down from the hole and went to the stable, from which

she fetched the halter of Sancho Panza's ass. Then she hastily returned to the hole, just as Don Quixote was standing up on Rocinante's saddle to reach the barred window at which he imagined the
love-lorn lady was standing. And, as he gave her his hand, he said:

'Take this hand, lady, or rather this scourge of the world's malefactors. Take this hand, I say, which no other woman's has touched,
not even hers who has complete possession of my whole body. I
do not give it to you to kiss, but that you may gaze on the structure
of its sinews, the interlacement of its muscles, the width and capacity
of its veins; from all of which you may judge what strength must be
in the arm to which such a hand belongs.'

'We shall see that presently,' said Maritornes, and making a running knot in the halter, she threw it over his wrist. Then, as she
came down from the hole, she tied the other end very firmly to the
bolt of the hay-loft door. At which Don Quixote exclaimed, feeling
the roughness of the cord on his wrist:

'Your ladyship seems to be grating my hand rather than fondling
it. Do not ill-treat it so. It is not to blame for the ill my heart does
you, nor is it right that you should avenge your whole displeasure
on so small a part of me. Consider, one who loves so well should
not take such ill vengeance.'

But no one was listening to this speech of Don Quixote's. For as
soon as Maritornes had tied him up the two of them went off, dying
of laughter, and left him so secured that it was impossible for him to
free himself. He was, as we have said, standing upon Rocinante,
with his arm thrust through the hole and attached by the wrist to
the bolt of the door, in the greatest fear and anxiety that he would be
left hanging by the arm, if Rocinante were to stir to one side or the
other. So he dared not make any movement; though, to judge from
Rocinante's patience and quietness, he might well have expected
him to stand there motionless for a whole century. In the end, finding that he was tied up and that the ladies had vanished, Don Quixote began to imagine that all this was a matter of enchantment, as
on the previous occasion when the enchanted Moor of a carrier had
mauled him in that same castle. And in his heart he cursed his lack
of sense and judgement in venturing to enter it a second time after
coming off so badly the first. For it is a rule among knights errant
that their having once attempted an adventure and failed in it is a

sign that it is not reserved for them but for others, and that they are therefore under no necessity of making a second attempt. However, he pulled his arm to see if he could get free, but he was so fast tied that all his endeavours were in vain. It is true that he pulled cautiously, for fear that Rocinante might move; but though he longed to sit down on the saddle, he could do nothing but remain standing or tug off his hand.

At times he longed for Amadis' sword, which was proof against any kind of enchantment; at others he cursed his fortune; then he dwelt upon the loss the world suffered through lack of him all the while he remained there enchanted, as he had no doubt at all he was. Then once more he remembered his beloved Dulcinea del Toboso; then he started calling for his good squire Sancho Panza, who lay drowned in sleep, stretched on his ass's pack-saddle, and oblivious at that moment even of the mother who bore him; then he called on the sages Lirgandeo and Alquife to help him; then he invoked his good friend Urganda to come to his rescue; and in the end morning found him there, despairing, bewildered and bellowing like a bull. For he had no hope that day would relieve his plight, which he believed to be eternal, since he imagined he was bewitched. This belief was strengthened when he found that Rocinante did not move or stir; from which he concluded that he and his horse would have to remain like that, without eating, drinking, or sleeping, until that malign influence of the stars should pass, or until another more learned enchanter should break the spell.

But in these beliefs he was much mistaken. For it was no sooner dawn than four well-dressed and equipped horsemen rode up to the inn with their firelocks on their saddle-bows. They called and thundered at the inn doors, which were still shut; and when Don Quixote saw them from the position in which he was still on guard, he cried out to them in loud and commanding tones:

'Knights, or squires, or whoever you may be, you have no right to knock on the doors of this castle; for it is abundantly clear that at such an hour those within are either asleep or, at least, unaccustomed to opening their fortress until the sun has covered the whole land. Retire without, and wait till day grows bright, and then we shall see whether it be right or not to open to you.'

'What the devil's this fortress or castle,' cried one of them, 'to keep us standing on these ceremonies? If you're the landlord, have the doors opened for us. We are travellers, and all we want is to bait our horses and ride on, for we are in a hurry.'

'Do I seem to you, knights, to have the air of an innkeeper?' asked Don Quixote.

'I don't know what you look like,' replied the traveller, 'but I know you're talking nonsense when you call this inn a castle.'

'A castle it is,' replied Don Quixote, 'one of the finest in the whole province, and there are people within who have carried a sceptre in their hands and a crown on their heads.'

'It would be better the other way round,' said the traveller; 'a sceptre on their heads and a crown branded on their hands. Though perhaps what you mean is that there's some company of actors inside; they often wear these crowns and sceptres you talk of. For I can't think that people good enough to have crowns and sceptres are lodging in a little inn like this one, and where it's so quiet too.'

'You know little of the world,' replied Don Quixote, 'since you are ignorant of the events which occur in knight errantry.'

The questioner's companions, growing impatient at his conversation with Don Quixote, began to knock furiously again, and so hard that the innkeeper and everyone else in the inn woke up. The host then got up to enquire who was knocking.

In the meanwhile one of the four travellers' horses happened to smell Rocinante, who was standing motionless, melancholy and sad, with drooping ears, bearing up his outstretched master; and being, after all, of flesh and blood, though he seemed of wood, he could not resist showing some feeling and smelling back at the creature who was making these endearing advances. But no sooner did he make the slightest movement than Don Quixote's feet, which were close together, slipped and, sliding from the saddle, would have landed him on the ground, had he not been hanging by his arm, which caused him so much pain that he felt as though his wrist were being cut off or his arm torn from its socket. For he was hanging so near the ground that he could touch it with the tips of his toes; which made his plight worse because, when he felt what a little way the soles of his feet were from the earth, he struggled and stretched his utmost to get them down. In fact, he was very like someone put to the torture of the 'strappado', in which the victim's feet neither quite touch nor quite fail to touch the earth, and so he increases his own agony in his anxiety to stretch himself, in the delusory hope that with a little more stretching he will reach the ground.

Chapter XLIV. *Of more extraordinary adventures at the Inn.*

FINALLY Don Quixote raised such a clamour that the inn doors were suddenly opened, and the innkeeper came out in a fright to see who it was shouting so loud. Maritornes too was awakened by his cries and, guessing what it was, went to the hay-loft where, unobserved, she untied the halter which held Don Quixote up. The knight then fell to the ground in front of the innkeeper and the travellers, and they went up to him to ask him what it was that made him shout so loud. He did not reply, but slipped the cord from his wrist and rose to his feet. Then, mounting Rocinante, he braced his shield, couched his lance and, making a wide sweep round the field, came back at a canter, exclaiming:

'Should anyone affirm that I have been rightfully enchanted, if I have the leave of my lady, the princess Micomicona, I will give him the lie, and challenge and defy him to single combat.'

The new arrivals were astounded at Don Quixote's speech; but the landlord relieved their surprise by telling them who he was, and that they need pay no attention to him, for he was out of his mind.

They then asked the innkeeper whether a lad of about fifteen, dressed as a mule-lad, had by any chance come to his inn, and gave a description of him which tallied with the appearance of Doña Clara's lover. The landlord answered that there were so many people in the inn that he had not noticed the person they were asking for. But when one of them saw the coach in which the judge had come, he exclaimed:

'He must be here. There can be no doubt of it, for this is the coach they say he was following. Let one of us stay at the door, and the rest go in and look for him. No, it might be as well if one of us were to ride round the inn, in case he should get away over the yard walls.'

'Let's do as you say,' replied another of them. Then two of them went in, one stayed at the door and the fourth started riding round the inn. The landlord watched all this, and could not conceive what they were taking these precautions for, though he knew quite well that they were looking for the lad whom they had described to him.

By now it was broad daylight; and for that reason, and because of the noise Don Quixote had made, everyone was awake and getting up, particularly Doña Clara and Dorothea, who had been able to sleep very little that night; one of them from excitement because her lover was so near, the other from eagerness to see this lad. Now Don Quixote felt near to bursting with rage, anger and fury when he found all four travellers ignoring him, and not one of them replying to his challenge; and could he have found it in his code of chivalry that a knight may lawfully undertake another enterprise despite his plighted word first to complete the one he is pledged to, he would have attacked them all and forced an answer out of them. But as it did not seem to him right or proper to begin a new undertaking till he had established Micomicona on her throne, he had to hold his tongue, keep quiet, and wait to see the result of the travellers' searching. It ended by one of them finding the young gentleman he was looking for sleeping beside a mule-lad, and little dreaming that anyone was looking for him or still less that he was found. The man, however, pulled him by the arm, and said:

'Really, Don Louis, the clothes you are wearing are *most* suitable to your rank, and the bed I find you on accords *in every way* with the luxury your mother brought you up in!'

The lad rubbed his sleepy eyes and, staring for a while at his captor, finally recognized him as a servant of his father's. This gave him such a surprise that for some time he could not manage to speak a word. And so the servant went on: 'There is nothing else for it now, Don Louis, but to be patient, and give in, and come back home, if you don't want your father, my master, to take a journey to the other world. For it's very much to be feared he will, he's so upset at your absence.'

'Why, how did my father know,' asked Don Louis, 'that I had come this way and in this disguise?'

'There was a student you told your plan to, and he was so upset at your father's grief when he missed you that he gave you away. So our master sent off four of us servants to look for you; and here we all are at your service, more delighted than you can think that we can go back so quickly and restore you to the sight of your very loving father.'

'That shall be as I wish, or as Heaven decrees,' replied Don Louis.

'What can you wish or Heaven decree, except that you agree to come back with us? There is no other course possible.'

All these arguments were overheard by the mule-lad lying next to Don Louis, who got up to tell Don Ferdinand, Cardenio, and the rest, who were now dressed, what was happening. He reported that the man was calling the lad '*Don*', and repeated their conversation, saying that the man wanted the boy to go back to his father's house, but that he would not. This and so much as they already knew of him – the fine voice Heaven had blessed him with – made them all most anxious to learn more about him, and even to help him, should the men try to do him any violence. So they went to the spot where he was, and found him still protesting to his servant. At the same moment Dorothea came out of her room, and Doña Clara after her in great alarm. Dorothea called Cardenio aside and told him very briefly the story of the singer and of Doña Clara; and he told her what had happened when his father's servants had come to look for him. But he did not speak quite quietly enough, for Doña Clara overheard him, and got into such a state, that she would have fallen down if Dorothea had not managed to catch her. Then Cardenio told Dorothea to take the girl back to their room, and promised to try and set everything to rights. So back they went.

Now all four of Don Louis' pursuers had entered the inn, and were standing round him, urging him to come back instantly, without losing a moment, and console his father. He replied that on no account could he do so until he had completed a matter on which depended his life, his honour and his heart. The servants then insisted, saying that under no circumstances would they return without him, and that they would take him whether he agreed or not.

'That you will not do,' replied Don Louis, 'unless you take me dead; although whatever way you take me, I shall be lifeless.'

Now by this time everyone else in the inn had come up to hear the argument, in particular Cardenio, Don Ferdinand, his companions, the judge, the priest, the barber and Don Quixote, who now thought that there was no more need to guard the castle. Cardenio, who knew the boy's story already, asked the servants what motive they had for wishing to take the lad against his will.

'Our reason,' replied one of the four, 'is to save his father's life, for he's in danger of losing it through this gentleman's absence.'

To which Don Louis replied: 'There is no reason why I should give an account of my business here. I am free. I shall go back if I please; and if I do not, none of you shall compel me.'

'Reason will compel you to,' replied the man, 'and if that's not enough for your worship, it's enough to make us do our duty, which is what we came for.'

'Let us know what is at the bottom of this,' put in the judge at this point.

But the man, who recognized him as a neighbour, replied: 'Do you not know this gentleman, my Lord Judge? He is your neighbour's son, and he has run away from his father's house in a disguise most unbecoming to his quality, as your worship can see.'

The judge then looked at the lad more closely, recognized him, and embraced him, saying: 'What childishness is this, Don Louis? What mighty reason can you have had for coming out in this fashion, and in a dress so unfitting to your rank?'

Tears came into the lad's eyes, and he could not answer a single word. But the judge told the four servants to rest assured that everything would be all right. Then, taking Don Louis by the hand, he drew him aside and demanded his reasons for coming.

While the judge was asking him various questions, a great uproar was heard at the inn door. The cause of it was that two guests who had stayed the night there had seen that everyone was busy enquiring about these four men, and had tried to get away without paying their reckoning. But the innkeeper was more attentive to his own business than to other people's and, laying hold of them as they were going out of the door, demanded his money. He called them such names, too, for their dirty trick that they were moved to reply with their fists, and had begun to do so with such vigour that the poor innkeeper had to shout for help. The landlady and her daughter could see no one who was not too busy to help him except Don Quixote, and it was to him the daughter shouted: 'Help, Sir Knight, by the power God gave you, help my poor father; for here are two wicked men thrashing him like corn.'

To which Don Quixote replied slowly and with great composure: 'Beauteous damsel, your petition is ill-timed, for I am prevented from embarking on any other adventure until I have brought the one to which I have pledged myself to a successful conclusion. But what I can do to serve you I will inform you now. Run and tell your father that he must hold his own in the battle as best he can, and on no account let himself be conquered, whilst I beg Princess Micomicona's permission to help him in his distress; and if she gives it to me, you may be assured that I shall rescue him.'

'Sure as I'm a sinner,' said Maritornes, who was standing near, 'before your worship gets this permission of yours, my master will be in the other world.'

'Allow me, lady, only to get this permission,' replied Don Quixote. 'For once I have got it, it will matter very little if he is in the other world. I will fetch him out of it, if the whole of that world oppose me. Or, at least, I will wreak such vengeance for you on those who sent him there that you will be more than moderately satisfied.'

Then without another word he went down on his knees in front of Dorothea, begging her in knightly and errant-like words that her Highness would be pleased to give him permission to help and succour the warden of that castle, who was in a grievous pass. The Princess gave it him most readily, and he instantly buckled his shield, grasped his sword, and ran to the inn door, where the two guests were still pounding the landlord. But no sooner did he get there than he wavered and stood still, although Maritornes and the landlady demanded what it was that prevented him from helping their master and husband.

'I delay,' said Don Quixote, 'because it is not lawful for me to draw my sword against squires and the like. Call my squire Sancho here, for this defence and vengeance properly concerns him.'

In the meantime the fight at the inn door was reaching a climax, and the landlord was getting the worst of it, which infuriated the landlady, her daughter and Maritornes, who were beside themselves at the sight of Don Quixote's cowardice and the damage their husband, father, and master was sustaining.

But let us leave him there, for someone is bound to help him; or, if no one does, let him suffer in silence for his rashness in taking on more than his strength warrants; and let us go back fifty paces and see how Don Louis answered the judge, whom we left asking him privately the reason for his travelling on foot in such poor clothes. The boy, then, clasped him tightly with both hands, in sign that his heart was oppressed by some great sorrow and, shedding copious tears, answered: 'My dear sir, the only thing that I can tell you is that from the moment when Heaven fated us to be neighbours and I saw Doña Clara, your daughter and my lady, I made her mistress of my heart; and if your wishes, my true lord and father, do not hinder me, she shall be my wife this very day. For her I left my father's house; for her I put on these clothes, to follow her wherever she went, as the arrow does the mark, or the sailor the pole-star. She knows no more of my passion than she has been able to learn on the few occasions when she has seen from a distance the tears in my eyes. Now you, sir, know that my family is rich and noble, and that I am their only heir. If these seem to you sufficient advantages, venture to make me completely happy and accept me now as your son. For though my father may be intent on other plans of his own, and may not approve the blessing I have found for myself, yet time has more power to undo and alter things than has human will.'

With this the enamoured youth fell silent. The judge was astonished, perturbed and perplexed, as much by Don Louis' sensible way of revealing his feelings as at finding himself in such a predicament. In fact he did not know what line to take in this sudden and unexpected situation. His only reply, therefore, was to ask Don Louis to keep calm for the time being and arrange with his servants not to go back that day. Then he would have time to consider what was best for everybody. At this Don Louis seized and kissed his hands, bathing them with tears, which would have melted a heart of stone, let alone the judge's. As a man of the world, he had already realized how good a match this would be for his daughter; though he hoped it would be possible for it to be concluded with the consent of Don Louis' father who, he knew, was aspiring to get a title for his son.

By this time the guests and the innkeeper had made their peace, for, through Don Quixote's persuasion and fair words rather than by threats, they had paid their full reckoning. Don Louis' servants, too, were waiting quietly for the judge to conclude his speech and for their master to make his decision, when the Devil, who never sleeps, ordained the sudden arrival at the inn of that barber from whom Don Quixote had taken Mambrino's helmet, and Sancho Panza the ass's harness which he had exchanged for his own. As this barber was taking his ass to the stable, he saw Sancho Panza mending some part of the pack-saddle; and as soon as he recognized him, he attacked him boldly, crying: 'I've got you now, master thief! Give me back my basin and my saddle with all the harness you robbed me of.'

Finding himself suddenly attacked, and hearing this abuse poured on him, Sancho grasped the saddle in one hand and gave the barber a punch with the other, which bathed his jaws in blood. But this did not make him leave go of the saddle; instead, he gave such a shout that everyone in the inn hurried towards the noise of this scuffle.

'Help, in the name of the King and of justice!' cried he. 'For I am taking back my property. This thief, this highwayman wants to kill me.'

'You're lying,' answered Sancho. 'I'm no highwayman, for my master Don Quixote won these spoils in fair fight.'

Don Quixote, who had now come up, was delighted to see his squire attacking and defending himself so well, and from then on he thought of him as a man of courage. He decided at that moment in his heart to knight him at the first available opportunity, confident that he was a fitting recipient of the order of chivalry. Now one of the things which the barber said in the course of the fight was:

'Sirs, this saddle is as much mine as the death I owe God. I recognize it as positively as if I had brought it into the world, and there is my ass in the stable who will not let me lie. Try it on him and see; if it doesn't fit just right, call me a liar. What is more, the same day they took it from me they took a new brass basin as well. It had never been used and was worth a good crown.'

Here Don Quixote could not refrain from answering him, and pushing himself between the pair to part them – the pack-saddle being laid on the ground for public inspection until the truth should be cleared up,

'Gentlemen,' he cried, 'you may clearly and manifestly see this good squire's error in calling that a basin which was, is, and shall

be Mambrino's helmet, that I won from him in fair fight, thus becoming its legitimate and lawful owner! In the matter of the pack-
saddle I will not interfere. All that I can say is that my squire Sancho
asked my permission to strip the trappings from the horse of this
vanquished coward and to adorn his own with them. I gave it him,
and he took them. As for their being changed from horse's harness to
pack-saddle, I can give no other explanation than the common one:
that these transformations occur in affairs of chivalry. To confirm
which, run Sancho my son, and bring the helmet which this good
fellow says is a basin.'

'Good Lord, sir,' said Sancho, 'if we've no better proof of our
case than what your worship's saying, Malino's helmet is as much a
basin as this good fellow's harness is a pack-saddle.'

'Do what I bid you,' replied Don Quixote, 'for it cannot be that
everything in this castle is governed by enchantment.'

Sancho went and fetched the basin and, as soon as Don Quixote
saw it, he took it in his hands and said: 'Look, your worships, how
can this squire have the face to say that this is a basin and not the
said helmet? I swear by the order of chivalry, which I profess, that
this was the same helmet I took from him, without addition or sub-
traction.'

'There is no doubt of that,' put in Sancho, 'for from the time my
master won it till now he has not fought more than one battle in it,
when he freed that unlucky chain-gang. And if it hadn't been for
this basin-helmet, things would have gone badly with him that time,
for there was a lot of stone-throwing in that engagement.'

Chapter XLV. *In which the question of Mambrino's Helmet and
the Pack-saddle is finally cleared up, with other Adventures
which most certainly occurred.*

'WHAT do you think about it, sirs,' asked the barber, 'when you
hear these gentlemen swearing and insisting that this isn't a basin
but a helmet?'

'Whoever says anything to the contrary,' said Don Quixote, 'if
he is a knight, I will teach him that he lies, and if he is a squire, that
he lies a thousand times.'

Our barber, who was looking on all the while and knew Don

Quixote's idiosyncrasies so well, decided to encourage his craziness and to give them all a laugh by carrying the joke further. So, addressing the other barber, he said:

'Sir barber, or whoever you are, learn that I am also of your profession, and have held a certificate for more than twenty years. I know all the instruments of the barber's art very well, without exception; and, what is more, I was a soldier for a while in my youth, and I also know what is a helmet, and what is a morion, and what is a closed casque, and other things concerning soldiering – I mean the different military arms. And I say, under correction, always submitting myself to better judgement, that this piece before us, which the good gentleman is holding, not only is not a barber's basin, but is as far from being one as black is from white, or the truth from a lie. But I do say that, though this is a helmet, it is not a complete helmet.'

'Certainly not,' said Don Quixote, 'because half of it – that is the beaver – is missing.'

'That is true,' said the priest, who had now grasped his friend the barber's purpose. Then Cardenio, Don Ferdinand and his comrades backed him up, and even the judge would have taken a hand in the joke if he had not been so concerned with the business of Don Louis; but the serious subject of his thoughts held him so engrossed that he paid little or no attention to these pleasantries.

'Good Heavens alive!' exclaimed the poor butt of a barber at this. 'Can so many honourable gentlemen possibly say that this is not a basin but a helmet? That's enough to surprise a whole university, be it ever so wise. Well, if this basin is a helmet, then, this pack-saddle must be a horse's harness as well, as this gentleman said.'

'It looks like a pack-saddle to me,' said Don Quixote, 'but, as I have already said, I am not interfering in that.'

'Whether it is a pack-saddle or a harness,' said the priest, 'Don Quixote has only to say; for in these matters of chivalry all these gentlemen and myself defer to him.'

'By God, sirs,' said Don Quixote, 'so many strange things have befallen me in this castle on the two occasions I have lodged here that I dare not give any positive answer to any question asked me concerning anything in it; for I imagine that whatever goes on here is by way of enchantment. The first time I was much annoyed by a

Moorish enchanter who dwells here, and Sancho fared rather badly at the hands of some henchmen of his; and last night I was suspended by this arm for almost two hours, without knowing either the means or the cause of my misfortunes. So to interfere now in so perplexed a matter and to give my opinion would be to make a rash judgement. Concerning their statement that this is a basin and not a helmet, I have already answered; but as to declaring whether that is a pack-saddle or a harness, I am not so bold as to give a definitive decision, but leave the matter to your worship's better judgement. Perhaps, since none of you are knights, as I am, the spells in this place will have no effect on you, your understanding will be free, and you will be able to judge of the affairs of this castle as they really and truly are, and not as they appear to me.'

'There is no doubt,' Don Ferdinand replied to this, 'that Don Quixote has spoken very wisely to-day in saying that the decision in this case lies with us; and so that it may rest on sounder foundations I will take the votes of these gentlemen in secret, and give you a clear and full account of the result.'

All this caused the greatest amusement to those who knew Don Quixote's idiosyncrasies; but it seemed the greatest nonsense in the world to those who did not, particularly to Don Louis' four servants, and to Don Louis himself, and to three more travellers who had happened to arrive at the inn and appeared to be troopers of the Holy Brotherhood, which indeed they were. But the most perplexed of all was the barber, whose basin had been turned into Mambrino's helmet before his eyes, and whose pack-saddle he fully expected to be transformed into a fine horse-harness. All of them, however, laughed to see Don Ferdinand go from one to another, taking their votes and whispering in their ears that they must declare in secret whether this pretty thing, which had been the subject of such fighting, was a pack-saddle or a harness. Then, after taking the votes of all those who knew Don Quixote, he loudly proclaimed:

'The fact is, my good fellow, that I am tired of taking so many opinions. For I find that everyone I ask declares that it is ridiculous to affirm that this is an ass's pack-saddle, for it is the harness of a horse, and of a thoroughbred horse at that. So you will have to be patient, for in spite of you and your ass, this is a harness and no pack-saddle, and you have stated and proved your case very badly.'

'May I never have a place in Heaven,' cried the poor barber, 'if your worships aren't all wrong; and may my soul as surely appear before God as this appears to me a pack-saddle and no harness. But might is right ... I say no more. But I promise you I'm not drunk, for I haven't broken my fast to-day, unless it be to sin.'

The barber's simple language caused no less laughter than the craziness of Don Quixote's, who remarked at this juncture: 'There is nothing more for it now but for each one to take his belongings, and what God gives may St. Peter bless.'

But one of the four servants observed: 'If this isn't a concerted joke, I can't understand how intelligent men can swear that these things aren't a basin and a pack-saddle. But you all seem intelligent enough, and yet you insist that you're right. So I suppose there must be some mystery about it all, for what you're saying goes clean against obvious truth and good sense, and I swear by' – and here he let out a round oath – 'that this is a barber's basin, and that's an ass's pack-saddle – and the whole world won't convince me to the contrary.'

'It might be a she-ass's,' observed the priest.

'It's all the same,' cried the servant, 'and that isn't the point. Either it's a pack-saddle or, as your worships say, it isn't.'

When he heard this one of the troopers, who had come in and listened to the argument, cried out angrily: 'It's as much a pack-saddle as my father's my father, and any one who says anything else must be drunk.'

'You lie like a base villain,' answered Don Quixote. And, raising his lance, which he had never let out of his hand, he aimed such a blow at the trooper's head that, unless he had dodged it, it would have left him stretched on the ground. The lance broke to pieces on the earth, and when the rest of the troopers saw their comrade assaulted they raised a shout for help for the Holy Brotherhood. The innkeeper, who was one of the fraternity, ran in an instant for his staff and his sword, and took his place beside his fellows. Don Louis' servants gathered round their young master, so that he should not escape in the scuffle. The barber, seeing the house in a turmoil, grasped his pack-saddle once more, and Sancho did the same. Don Quixote drew his sword and fell upon the troopers. Don Louis called to his servants to leave him and help Don Quixote–

and Cardenio and Don Ferdinand, who were on Don Quixote's side. The priest was shouting; the landlady screaming; her daughter wailing; Maritornes weeping; Dorothea was distracted; Lucinda in a flurry; and Doña Clara in a faint. The barber was mauling Sancho; Sancho pounding the barber; and Don Louis, whom one of his servants had been so bold as to seize by the arm to prevent his running away, had dealt the fellow a blow which bathed his jaws in blood; the judge was defending him; Don Ferdinand had one of the officers under his feet, and was trampling his carcass most heartily; and the innkeeper was straining his voice once more, shouting for help for the Holy Brotherhood. So the whole inn was full of tears, shouts, screams, amazement, fear, alarm, dismay, slashings, punches, blows, kicks and effusion of blood.

In the middle of this confused and chaotic tangle, the idea came into Don Quixote's head that he had been plunged head over heels into the discord in Agramante's camp, and so he cried in a voice which thundered through the inn: 'Hold, all! Sheathe your swords, all! Be calm, all! And listen to me, all of you, if all wish to remain alive!'

At this mighty voice they all stopped, and he continued, saying: 'Did I not tell you, gentlemen, that this castle is enchanted, and must be inhabited by some legion of demons? Behold the confirmation of my words, and gaze upon the discord in Agramante's camp transferred here and performed in our midst. See here they are fighting for the sword, yonder for the horse, here for the eagle, there for the helmet; we are all fighting and all at odds. Come then, Sir Judge, and you, Sir Priest; let one of you stand for King Agramante, the other for King Sobrino, and make peace amongst us. For, by God Almighty, it is a great villainy that people of such quality as we are here should slay one another for such trivial causes.'

The troopers, who did not understand Don Quixote's phraseology and found themselves roughly handled by Don Ferdinand, Cardenio and their companions, were unwilling to be pacified; but the barber was willing, for both his beard and the pack-saddle had been torn in the fight. Sancho, like a good servant, obeyed his master's slightest word. Don Louis' four servants grew calm, seeing how little they stood to gain by being otherwise. Only the innkeeper insisted that this madman's insolences must be punished, for he was always upsetting the inn. At last the uproar was quelled for a time, the pack-saddle remained a harness till Judgement Day, and in Don Quixote's imagination the basin remained a helmet and the inn a castle.

When, at the persuasion of the judge and the priest, everyone was pacified and had made friends, Don Louis' servants once more insisted that he must come with them at once; and whilst he was settling with them, the judge consulted Don Ferdinand, Cardenio, and the priest as to what he should do in the matter. He told them what Don Louis had said to him. It was finally agreed that Don Ferdinand should reveal himself to Don Louis' servants and say that it was his wish that Don Louis should come with him to Andalusia, where he would be received by his brother the Marquis in a manner suitable to his quality; for he knew that Don Louis was determined not to return to his father's presence even if they tore him to pieces. When the four of them were aware of Don Ferdinand's rank and Don Louis' obstinacy, they decided amongst themselves that three of them should return and give his father an account of events, and that the fourth should stay and wait on their young master, and not leave him till the others should return for him, or until he should learn what his father's orders were. Thus this tangle of quarrels was resolved by the authority of Agramante and the wisdom of King Sobrino.

However, the enemy of concord and adversary of peace, finding himself slighted and mocked, and seeing how little fruit he had reaped from plunging them all into this labyrinth of confusion, decided to try his hand again and bring some new quarrels and disturbances to life. It arose thus: the troopers calmed down when they overheard the rank of the men they had been fighting, and retired from the combat, it seeming to them that they would get the worst of the battle, whatever happened. But one of them – the one who had been pounded and trampled by Don Ferdinand – remembered suddenly that, among some warrants he was carrying for the arrest of various delinquents, was one for Don Quixote, whose seizure the Holy Brotherhood had ordered for his freeing the galley-slaves, as Sancho had had good reason to fear they would. When this occurred to him he decided to make certain that the description in the warrants tallied with the knight. So, taking a parchment from his breast, he lighted on what he wanted. Then he set himself to read it slowly – for he was no great reader – and at each word he read he clapped his eyes on Don Quixote, comparing the details in his warrant, one by one, with the knight's features, and found that beyond a doubt it was he that the warrant described. As soon as he had made certain of this, he folded up the parchment and, taking the warrant in his left hand, seized Don Quixote so firmly by the collar with his right that he could not breathe. Then he shouted:

'Help for the Holy Brotherhood! And to prove that I'm serious, read this warrant where it's written that this highway robber must be arrested.'

The priest took the warrant, and saw that all that the trooper said was true and that the description tallied with Don Quixote. But the knight was infuriated at finding himself roughly handled by this base scoundrel, and every bone in his body creaked as he clasped the trooper with all his might, with both hands round his throat. And if the fellow had not been rescued by his companions he would have breathed his last there and then, before Don Quixote would have let go his hold. The innkeeper, who was bound to help his fellow troopers, immediately ran to his aid. The landlady, seeing her husband in a fight once more, screamed again, and was instantly joined by Maritornes and her daughter, all three calling on Heaven and the company for help. And Sancho, seeing what was going on, remarked: 'By the Lord, all that my master says about the enchantments in this castle is true, for it's impossible to stay quiet an hour here.'

Don Ferdinand parted the trooper and Don Quixote and, to the relief of both, unlocked their hands which were clenched fast, the trooper's on the knight's collar, and the knight's round his adversary's throat. But, nevertheless, the troopers persisted in claiming their prisoner and the company's help in delivering him bound at their disposal, for such help it was their duty to the King and the Holy Brotherhood to give. So they once more demanded aid and assistance in the arrest of this robber, brigand and highwayman. But Don Quixote laughed at this description and said very calmly:

'Come here, filthy and low-born rabble! Is it highway robbery you call it, freeing the enchained, releasing prisoners, succouring the unfortunate, raising the fallen, relieving the needy? You infamous brood whose low and vile intelligence deserves no revelation from Heaven of that virtue which lies in knight errantry, nor any knowledge of your sin and ignorance in not reverencing the shadow – how much more the actual presence – of a knight errant! Come here, you pack of thieves, for you are no troopers, but highwaymen licensed by the Holy Brotherhood! Tell me, who was the dolt who signed a warrant of arrest against such a knight as I am? Who was it who did not know that knights errant are exempt from all jurisdiction, that their law is their sword, their charters their courage and their statutes their own will? Who was the idiot, I repeat, who does not know that there is no patent of nobility with so many privileges and immunities as a knight errant receives on the day when he is knighted and undertakes the stern practice of chivalry? What knight errant has ever paid tax, duty, queen's patten money, statute money, customs, or toll? What tailor was ever paid by him for a suit of clothes? What warden who received him in his castle ever made him pay his score? What maiden was not in love with him, and did not give herself up to his will and pleasure? And, lastly, what knight errant has there been, is there, or will there ever be in the world, who has not courage enough, on his own, to deal four hundred beatings to four hundred troopers, should they dare confront him?'

Chapter XLVI. *Of the notable Adventure with the Troopers and the great ferocity of our good Knight Don Quixote.**

WHILE Don Quixote was making this proclamation the priest was persuading the troopers that the knight was out of his mind, as they could see by his deeds and his words, and that, therefore, they need carry the matter no farther. For even if they were to arrest him and take him away, they would have to release him as a madman. But the man with the warrant replied that it was not for him to judge of Don Quixote's madness, but to carry out his superior's orders; and that once he was arrested they could let him out three hundred times if they chose.

* This heading is really misplaced, for the adventure is over. The oversight is the author's.

'For all that,' said the priest, 'your must not take him this time; nor, so far as I can see, will he let you.'

In the end the priest thought of so much to say and Don Quixote of so many crazy things to do that the troopers would have to have been madder than he if they had not recognized Don Quixote's infirmity. So they judged it best to be quiet, and even to make the peace between the barber and Sancho Panza, who were still quarrelling with great bitterness. As officers of justice, therefore, they intervened in the case and arbitrated to such purpose that both parties remained, if not entirely content, at least partially satisfied; it being settled that they should exchange pack-saddles, but not girths or headstalls. In the matter of Mambrino's helmet, too, the priest, unknown to Don Quixote, paid eight *reals* for the basin, and the barber wrote him out a receipt, promising not to take action for fraud thenceforth and for ever more, amen.

These two disputes being settled – and they were the most serious and urgent – nothing remained but for Don Louis' servants to agree that three of them should go back, and one stay to accompany their master wherever Don Ferdinand might take him. And as by now good luck had begun to shift obstacles and smooth difficulties in favour of the lovers and the brave folk in the inn, so Fortune was pleased to complete the task and bring everything to a happy ending. For the servants fell in with Don Louis' request, which so delighted Doña Clara that no one who looked into her face at that time could fail to recognize the rejoicing in her heart. As for Zoraida, although she did not very clearly understand everything she had seen, she was sad or gay by turns, according to the expressions she saw on everyone's face; but it was on her Spaniard's that her eyes were always fixed, in absolute dependence. The innkeeper, who had not failed to note the gift in compensation which the priest had given the barber, demanded payment of Don Quixote's account, and for the damage to the wine-skins and his loss of wine, swearing that neither Rocinante nor Sancho's ass should leave the inn until he had been paid to the last farthing. All this the priest peacefully settled, and Don Ferdinand paid although the judge had also very generously offered to do so. And so they all remained in peace and quietness, so that the inn no longer recalled the discord in Agramante's camp, as Don Quixote had said, but the peace and quiet of the times of Octavian. And it was the general opinion that they owed thanks for all this to the priest's good sense and great eloquence and to Don Ferdinand's incomparable generosity.

Don Quixote, then, seeing himself free and quit of all quarrels, both his squire's and his own, thought it would be well to continue the journey he had begun, and complete the great adventure for which he had been called and chosen; and so, firm in his resolution, he went to kneel down before Dorothea, who refused to let him utter a word until he arose. So he obediently got upon his feet and said:

'It is a common proverb, beauteous lady, that diligence is the mother of good fortune; and in many grave matters experience has shown that the solicitude of the suitor brings a doubtful matter to a happy ending. But in no affairs is this truth more evident than in those of war, in which promptness and speed forestall the enemy's designs, and gain the victory before the adversary has established his defences. All this I say, exalted and precious lady, because it seems to me that our sojourn in this castle is now profitless, and may do us very great harm, too, as we may one day discover. For who knows if your enemy the giant has not learnt, by means of secret and diligent spies, that I am on my way to destroy him, and, taking advantage of this delay, may not be fortifying himself in some impregnable castle or fortress against which my endeavours and the might of my untiring arm may avail me little? So, my lady, let us forestall his designs, as I have said, by our diligence, and depart immediately while our fortune is good; for to keep it on our side, as your Highness will desire, you must wait no longer than I delay in facing your adversary.'

Don Quixote fell silent and said no more, but most calmly awaited the beautiful Princess's reply; and she, with a lordly air, adapted to the style of Don Quixote, answered him as follows:

'I thank you, Sir Knight, for the desire you display to aid me in my great distress, like a true knight whose function and concern it is to succour the orphan and the needy. Pray Heaven that your desire and mine may be fulfilled, and that you may learn that there are grateful women in the world. As for my departure, let it be immediate, for I have no other wish than yours. Dispose of me wholly at your will and pleasure, for she who has once entrusted the defence of her person to you, and put into your hands the restoration of her domains, must not dare to go contrary to what your wisdom shall ordain.'

'By God's hand,' cried Don Quixote, 'seeing a lady humble herself before me, I cannot forbear the opportunity of raising her and placing her on her hereditary throne. Let our departure be immediate; for the saying that there is danger in delay puts spurs to my desire to be on the way. And since Heaven has never created, nor Hell seen, anyone to daunt or intimidate me, saddle Rocinante, Sancho, and harness your ass and the Queen's palfrey. Let us take our leave of the warden and these gentlemen and be away from here immediately.'

But Sancho, who was standing by all the while, shook his head and answered: 'Oh, sir, sir, there are more tricks done in the village than make a noise – saving her ladyship's presence.'

'What nastiness can there be in any village, or in all the towns in the world, which can be noised to my discredit, peasant?'

'If you're getting annoyed, your worship, I'll hold my tongue and not say what it's a good squire's duty to say, and what a good servant ought to say to his master.'

'Say what you like,' replied Don Quixote, 'so long as your words are not intended to strike fear into me; for if you are afraid, you are acting true to your character, and if I am fearless, I am acting true to mine.'

'It's not that, I swear to God as I'm a sinner,' replied Sancho, 'but I'm positively certain that this lady, who calls herself Queen of the great Kingdom of Micomicon, is no more a queen than my mother; for if she was what she says she is, she wouldn't go kissing with somebody in this company every time anyone turns his head, and round every corner.'

Dorothea blushed at Sancho's remarks, because it was true that her husband, Don Ferdinand, had sometimes, when no one was looking, gathered from her lips some of the rewards his love had earned. This Sancho had seen; and such immodesty had seemed to him more fitting in a courtesan than in the queen of a great kingdom. But as she could not contradict Sancho, she had to let him go on with his observations:

'I'm saying this, sir, because if the gentleman who is enjoying himself in this inn is going to gather the fruit of our labours, when

we've travelled the highways and by-ways and passed bad nights
and worse days, I've got no reason to be in a hurry myself about
saddling Rocinante, or harnessing my ass, or getting the palfrey
ready. It will be better for us to stay quiet – and let every whore
spin and us eat.'

Goodness, what a fury Don Quixote flew into when he heard his
squire speak with such disrespect! So tremendous was it that, with a
trembling voice and stammering tongue, his eyes darting fire, he
exclaimed:

'Villainous peasant, unmannerly, disrespectful, ignorant, blasphemous, foul-mouthed, presumptuous, backbiting slanderer!
Dare you utter such words in my presence, and in the presence of
these illustrious ladies? How have you presumed to breed such in-
famies and effronteries in your muddled imagination? Begone from
my sight, unnatural monster, storehouse of lies, armoury of deceit,
sink of knavery, inventor of iniquities, publisher of ravings, foe to
the respect due to royal persons! Go, never appear before me again,
on pain of my wrath!'

As he spoke, he frowned severely, puffed out his cheeks, glared
in all directions, and stamped loudly on the ground with his right
foot in sign of the rage pent up in his heart.

His words and his furious gestures so terrified Sancho that he
would have been glad if the earth had opened at that instant before
his feet and swallowed him; and he could think of no other course
but to turn his back and quit his master's furious presence. But the
wise Dorothea, who was now so well schooled in Don Quixote's
idiosyncrasies, sought to mitigate his wrath by addressing him
thus:

'Do not be vexed, Sir Knight of the Sad Countenance, at the idle
words which your good squire has spoken, for perhaps he did not
speak them without good reason; nor can we suspect his good
understanding and Christian conscience of making false accusations
against anyone. So we must positively believe that, as everything in
this castle happens by way of enchantment, as you yourself say, Sir
Knight, – it may be, I say, that Sancho may have seen, by diabolical
illusion, what he says he beheld, so much to the prejudice of my
honour.'

'By the Almighty God,' cried Don Quixote at this point, 'I swear your Highness has hit the mark. Some wicked vision has risen before that sinner Sancho's eyes, and shown him what he could not possibly have seen by any other means than by sorcery. For I know the poor man's goodness and innocence too well to believe that he would make false accusations against anyone.'

'That is the truth, and so let it rest,' said Don Ferdinand. 'Therefore your worship must pardon him and receive him once more into the bosom of your favour "as it was in the beginning", before these visions distracted his senses.'

Don Quixote replied that he would pardon him, and the priest went for Sancho, who came in very humbly and, falling on his knees, begged for his master's hand. The knight gave it him, and let him kiss it, and then after bestowing a blessing on him, he said: 'Now you will be convinced, Sancho, my son, that what I have so often told you is true, and that all events in this castle are performed by way of enchantment.'

'Indeed, I believe it,' said Sancho, 'except for the matter of that blanket-tossing. That really happened in the ordinary way.'

'Do not you believe that,' replied Don Quixote, 'for if that had been the case I should have avenged you then, or would do so even now. But neither then nor now have I been able to take vengeance for your injury, nor to see anyone on whom I could take it.'

Everyone wanted to know what this business about a blanket was, and so the innkeeper gave them a circumstantial account of Sancho Panza's flight through the air, at which they all laughed not a little; and Sancho would have been not a little ashamed if his master had not assured him once more that it was enchantment. But for all that, Sancho's folly never reached such a pitch that he did not believe it was absolute and certain truth, without any shadow of illusion, that he had been tossed by creatures of flesh and blood, and not by any unreal or imaginary phantoms, as his master believed and affirmed.

Two days had now passed since that illustrious company had come to the inn; and thinking that the time for departure had come, they devised a plan which would spare Dorothea and Don Ferdinand the trouble of going back with Don Quixote to his village under pretence of restoring Queen Micomicona, and allow the priest and the barber to bear him off, as they wished, and try to get him

cured of his madness at home. And this was the scheme they contrived. They made a bargain with a waggoner, who happened to be
passing that way with a team of oxen, to take him in this way: they
made a sort of cage of criss-crossed poles, sufficiently large to hold
Don Quixote comfortably; then Don Ferdinand and his companions, with Don Louis' servants, the troopers and the innkeeper, all
under the orders and directions of the priest, covered their faces and
disguised themselves in various ways, so that Don Quixote should
take them for different people from those he had seen at the castle.
This done, in absolute silence they entered the room where he was
asleep, taking his rest after the late conflicts. They went up to where
he was sleeping peacefully, with no suspicion of any plot and, grasping him firmly, securely tied his hands and feet, so that when he
woke up with a start he could not stir or do anything but gaze in
wonder at the strange faces he saw before him. And at once he fell
into the illusion his wild imagination was continually suggesting to
him, and assumed that those figures were the phantoms of that enchanted castle, and that he was now positively under a spell, since
he could neither stir nor defend himself. All this was precisely what
the priest, the inventor of the scheme, had expected. Of all those
present only Sancho was in his right mind and undisguised; and
although he was not far from sharing his master's disease, did not
fail to recognize those disguised figures. But he did not dare to open
his mouth until he saw what this assault and seizure of his master
would lead to, and the knight did not speak a word either, waiting
also to see the issue of this disaster.

The issue was that they dragged him to the cage and shut him in,
nailing the bars so fast that they could not be knocked down in a
hurry. They then took him on their shoulders. But as they left the
room they heard a fearful voice, as awful as the barber could make
it – not the barber of the pack-saddle but the other one:

'O Knight of the Sad Countenance!' he cried, 'be not grieved at
your confinement. It is needful for the speedier conclusion of the
adventure to which your great courage has committed you. The
which shall be concluded when the furious Manchegan lion shall be
united with the white Tobosan dove, and after they have humbled
their lofty crests to the soft matrimonial yoke, from which miraculous mating shall issue to the light of the sun brave whelps, who will

emulate the ravaging talons of their valorous father. This shall come
to pass ere the pursuer of the fugitive nymph shall twice in his swift
and natural course have visited the bright constellations. And you,
most noble and obedient squire that ever bore sword in belt, beard
on chin, or smell in nose, be not dismayed or displeased to see the
flower of knight errantry thus borne away before your eyes. For
very speedily, if it please the Artificer of the world, you will find
yourself so exalted and ennobled that you will not know yourself,
nor shall you be defrauded of the reward your good master has promised you. I assure you, on behalf of the sage Mentironiana, that
your wages shall be paid you, as the proof will show. Follow then
in the footsteps of your valorous and enchanted lord, for it is fitting
that you should go to that place where you both will stay. And
now, as it is not lawful for me to say more, God be with you, for
I return, I well know whither.'

Towards the end of this prophecy the barber raised his voice to
such a pitch, and then lowered it to so quiet a tone, that even those
in the joke almost believed in the truth of what they heard. Don
Quixote was much consoled by this prophecy. For he immediately
grasped its whole meaning, and saw that it promised him union in
holy and lawful wedlock with his beloved Dulcinea del Toboso,
from whose happy womb would issue the whelps, his sons, to the
everlasting glory of La Mancha. So, believing all this sincerely and
firmly, he raised his voice and said with a deep sigh:

'You, whoever you may be, who have prognosticated such happiness for me, I pray you, beg in my name that sage enchanter who
has my affairs in his charge not to let me perish in this captivity in
which I am borne off, until I see the fulfilment of the joyful and incomparable promises that have just been made to me. But, however
that may be, I shall account the pains of my prison glory, these
chains which bind me comfort, and this litter upon which I am laid
no hard field of battle, but a soft couch and happy marriage-bed.
And regarding the consolation of my squire Sancho Panza, I trust
in his honesty and good conduct that he will not leave me in good
or evil fortune. For though it should not happen, from his ill luck
or mine, that I shall be able to bestow on him the isle or other
equivalent gift which I have promised him, at least he cannot lose
his wages, since in the will which I have made I have provided for

O

his payment, not in proportion to his many good services, but to
my means.'

Sancho bowed his head in deep respect and kissed both his hands,
for he could not kiss one alone, since they were tied together. Then
the phantoms lifted the cage on to their shoulders and placed it on
the ox-cart.

Chapter XLVII. *Of the strange way in which Don Quixote was
enchanted, and other matters.*

WHEN Don Quixote himself was thus caged and placed on the cart,
he said: 'I have read many serious histories of knights errant; but
I have never read, or seen, or heard of enchanted knights being carried in this fashion and at the pace which these slothful and lazy
animals promise. For they are generally borne through the air with
extraordinary speed, enclosed in some thick and dusky cloud, or on
some chariot of fire, or on some hippogriff or other such beast. But
to be carried as I now am on an ox-cart, God help me, it puts me to
confusion. But perhaps chivalry and magic in our day must follow
a different course from that pursued by the men of old; and it may
be, too, that as I am a new knight in the world, and the first to resus-
citate the long-forgotten profession of knight errantry, they have invented fresh kinds of enchantment and other methods of carrying
the enchanted as well. What do you think about it, Sancho, my
son?'

'I don't know what to think,' replied Sancho, 'not being so well
read as your worship in the errant writings. But, all the same, I'd
be prepared to swear that these apparitions here around us are not
altogether Catholic.'

'Catholic? Holy father!' replied Don Quixote. 'How should
they be Catholic, if they are all demons who have taken fantastic
bodies to come and throw me into this state? If you want to convince yourself of that, touch them and feel them, and you will see
that their bodies are only air, and are nothing but an outward
semblance.'

'By God, sir,' replied Sancho, 'I've touched them already, and
this devil bustling about here is plump and tender. He has another
property, too, very different from anything that devils are said to

have. They all stink of brimstone and other foul odours, but this one smells of ambergris from a mile off.'

This remark of Sancho's referred to Don Ferdinand who, being a gentleman, must have smelt as Sancho said.

'Do not be surprised at that, Sancho my friend,' replied Don Quixote, 'for I would have you know that devils are very crafty. But although they carry smells about them, they do not smell, because they are spirits; and if they do smell, they cannot smell of good things, but only of evil and stinking ones. The reason is that they carry hell with them wherever they are, and can receive no kind of relief from their torments. Now, a good smell is something to delight and please; so it is not possible for them ever to smell sweet; and if this demon of yours seems to you to smell of ambergris, either you are mistaken or he seeks to deceive you and make you think that he is not a devil.'

All this conversation passed between master and servant; and as Don Ferdinand and Cardenio were afraid that Sancho would tumble to the whole of their plot, which he had already come very near to doing, they decided to cut the parting short. So they called the innkeeper aside and ordered him to saddle Rocinante and harness Sancho's ass, which he very quickly did. In the meantime the priest had come to an arrangement with the troopers to escort him to his village for so much a day. Cardenio hung the knight's shield on one side of Rocinante's saddle and the basin on the other. Then in dumb show he bade Sancho mount his ass and take Rocinante by the reins, and posted the troopers with their firelocks on either side of the cart. But before it moved off, the landlady, her daughter and Maritornes came out to say good-bye to Don Quixote, pretending to weep with sorrow at his misfortune; and he said to them:

'Do not weep, good ladies, for all these mischances are incidental to the calling I profess; and if these calamities did not befall me I should not consider myself a famous knight errant. For such things never happen to knights of small name and fame, since there is no one in the world to cast them a thought. But to the brave they do, for many princes and other knights envy them for their virtue and their valour, and seek by evil ways to destroy these good men. But, for all that, virtue is so powerful that of itself alone it will emerge victorious from any trial, despite all the necromancy ever known to

Zoroaster, its first inventor, and will shed its light on the world as the sun does in heaven. Pardon me, fair ladies, if I have inadvertently done you any displeasure, for wilfully and consciously I have never done so to anyone. And pray God to deliver me from these chains, into which some ill-intentioned magician has cast me, for if ever I am free from them I will never forget the favours you have done me in this castle, but shall acknowledge them, requite them, and repay them as they deserve.'

Whilst this passage was taking place between the ladies and Don Quixote, the priest and the barber took leave of Don Ferdinand and his comrades, of the captain and his brother, and of all those happy ladies, of Dorothea and Lucinda in particular. They all embraced, and agreed to send one another their news. Don Ferdinand made a point of telling the priest where to write and let him know Don Quixote's fate. He insisted that nothing would give him more pleasure than to hear, and promised to let the priest have any news that might please him, about his own marriage and Zoraida's baptism, or Don Louis' affairs and Lucinda's homecoming. The priest promised to comply most punctually with his request. Once more they embraced, and once more exchanged compliments. Then the innkeeper went up to the priest and gave him some papers, saying that he had found them in the lining of the trunk in which he had discovered the *Tale of Foolish Curiosity*, and told him that he might take them all with him as its owner had never come that way again. For, as he could not read, he did not want them himself. The priest thanked him and, on opening the manuscript, saw written at the head: *The Tale of Rinconete and Cortadillo*, from which he assumed that this was another story; and he expected that it would be a good one, since *The Tale of Foolish Curiosity* had been, and it was probably by the same author. So he kept it, intending to read it when he had an opportunity.

Then he and his friend the barber, both wearing their masks so that Don Quixote should not recognize them, mounted and set out after the cart. The order of the procession was the following: first went the cart, driven by its owner; on either side, as we have said, went the troopers with their firelocks; then followed Sancho Panza on his ass, leading Rocinante by the rein; last of all came the priest and the barber on their heavy mules, their faces covered as before mentioned, riding with a grave and sober air as fast as the slow pace of the oxen permitted. Don Quixote travelled seated in his cage, with his hands tied and his feet stretched out, leaning against the bars, as silently and patiently as if he had been no flesh-and-blood man, but a stone statue. And so they rode slowly and silently for about six miles, until they came to a valley which the carter thought would be a convenient place for resting and feeding his oxen. He told his thought to the priest, but the barber was of the opinion that they should go on a little farther; for he knew that behind a hill which showed up not far away there was a valley with more and much better grass than there was there, where they wanted to stop. So the barber's advice was taken, and they resumed their way.

At this moment the priest looked round and saw six or seven horsemen behind them, well dressed and mounted, who soon overtook them. For they were not riding at the slow and leisurely pace of oxen, but as people mounted on canons' mules, and anxious to press on and take their siesta at the inn, which could be seen less than three miles ahead. The swift travellers overtook the slow and greeted them courteously. Now, when one of the newcomers, who proved to be a Canon of Toledo and the master of the rest, saw the orderly procession with the cart, the troopers, Sancho, Rocinante, the priest and the barber, and Don Quixote, in particular, imprisoned in his cage, he could not help asking the reason for their carrying a man in that manner; though he had already concluded from seeing the troopers' badges that he must be some habitual highwayman or other malefactor whose punishment was a matter for the Holy Brotherhood. But one of the troopers, to whom he had put the question, replied: 'Sir, we don't know what it all means. The gentleman must tell you himself why he is carried like this.'

Don Quixote heard this question and answer, and replied: 'Are you gentlemen, perhaps, versed and skilled in matters of knight errantry? For, if you are, I will communicate my misfortunes to you. But if you are not, there is no reason for my tiring myself by telling you.'

By this time the priest and the barber had seen that the travellers were in conversation with Don Quixote de la Mancha, and had come up to answer for him, in case their plot might be discovered. But the canon, whom Don Quixote had addressed, replied: 'Truly,

brother, I know more about books of chivalry than about Villal-
pando's Logic. So, if that is all, you can safely tell me whatever you
please.'

'Then, in God's name, I will,' replied Don Quixote. 'I would
have you know, sir, that I am travelling in this cage under a spell,
because of the envy and fraud of evil enchanters; for virtue is persecuted by the wicked more than it is loved by the good. I am a
knight errant – not one of those whose names Fame has never
thought to record in her memory, but one who, in despite and defiance of envy itself, and of all the Magi ever born in Persia, all the
Brahmans of India, all the Gymnosophists of Ethiopia, shall write
his name in the temple of immortality, to serve as a pattern and
example to future ages, wherein knights errant may see what steps
they should follow if they would climb to the honourable summit
and pinnacle of arms.'

'The knight Don Quixote de la Mancha is speaking the truth,'
put in the priest at this juncture, 'for he is travelling in this cart beneath a spell, not for his own faults and sins, but through the
malignity of those to whom virtue is loathsome and valour odious.
This, sir, is the Knight of the Sad Countenance – if you have ever
heard speak of him at any time – whose valorous achievements and
mighty deeds will be written on stubborn brass and eternal marble,
however tirelessly envy and malice may work to obscure and conceal them.'

When the canon heard both prisoner and free men talk in this
style he almost crossed himself with astonishment, unable to
imagine what had happened; while the same amazement struck all
his companions. At this Sancho Panza, who had drawn near to hear
the conversation, sought to make everything plain by remarking:
'Now, gentlemen, whether you like it or not, the fact of the matter
is that Don Quixote is no more enchanted than my mother. He is in
possession of all his faculties; he eats and drinks and does his business like other men, and just as he did yesterday before they put him
in the cage. As that's the case, how can they expect me to believe
that he's under a spell? For I've often heard it said that people
who've been bewitched don't eat, or sleep, or speak; while my
master will out-talk thirty lawyers, if they'll only let him alone.'
Then, turning to face the priest, he went on: 'Oh, Master Priest,

Master Priest! Do you think I don't recognize you? Do you imagine I don't see what you're up to? Do you think that I don't see through these new enchantments? Of course I know you, even though you've a mask on your face, and understand you, however much you disguise your tricks. In fact, where envy reigns virtue can't exist, and generosity doesn't go with meanness. Damn it all! If it wasn't for your reverence my master would be married to the Princess Micomicona at this very moment, and I should be a count at least, for I could have expected no less, considering the generosity of my master, the Knight of the Sad Countenance, and the greatness of my services. But I see now that it's true, as they say in these parts, that Fortune's wheel goes swifter than a mill wheel, and the man who was at the very top yesterday is on the ground to-day. It's my wife and my children I'm sorry for. For just when they might have expected to see their father come in at the door a governor or vice-roy of some isle or kingdom, they'll see him enter as a stable-boy. I'm saying all this, Master Priest, to urge you to have some conscience about ill-treating my master like this. You take care that God doesn't call you to account in the other life for imprisoning him like this. He'll make you answer for all these succours and benefits my master, Don Quixote, leaves undone all this time he's a prisoner.'

'Tell that to your grandmother!' put in the barber at this point. 'What, Sancho, are you of your master's fraternity, too? I swear to God I'm beginning to think you'll have to keep him company in his cage, and labour under the same spell as he does, for you've caught something of his humour and chivalry. It was an ill moment when you fell with child by his promises, and worse still when you got that isle you're so set on into your brain.'

'I'm not with child by anyone,' replied Sancho; 'and I'm not a man to let anyone get me with child, not the King himself. For though I'm poor, I'm an old Christian, and I owe nothing to any man. If I'm set on isles, other people are set on worse. Every man's the son of his own deeds; and since I'm a man, I can become pope, let alone governor of an isle, especially since my master's capable of winning so many that he may have no one to give them to. Mind how you talk, Master Barber, for shaving beards isn't everything, and there's some difference between Peter and Peter. I say this because we all know one another, and there's no passing false dice on me. As to this enchanting of my master, God knows the truth; so let it rest there, for it won't improve for stirring.'

The barber did not care to answer him, in case Sancho should let out in his simplicity what the priest and he were trying so hard to keep hidden. With the same fear in his mind the priest invited the canon to ride with him a little ahead, promising to reveal the mystery of the cage and other things which would amuse him. The canon agreed and, going ahead with his servants, listened attentively to all that the priest told him about Don Quixote's character, life, madness, and habits, to a brief account of the beginnings and cause of his distraction, to the whole course of his history up to his confinement in the cage, and finally, to their plan for getting him back to his own village to see whether they might find any sort of cure for his madness. The canon and his servants were amazed anew at hearing Don Quixote's strange history, and when it was finished he said:

'Truly, Sir Priest, my own experience tells me that so-called books of chivalry are very prejudicial to the commonwealth; and although, out of idleness and bad taste, I have read the beginnings of almost all that have been printed, I have never managed to read one right through. For they all seem to me more or less the same, and there is no more in one than in another. Besides, in my opinion this sort of composition falls under the heading of Milesian Fables, which are extravagant tales, whose purpose is to amaze, and not to instruct; quite the opposite of Moral Fables, which delight and instruct at the same time. And even though the principal aim of such books is to delight, I do not know how they can succeed, seeing the monstrous absurdities they are filled with. For the delight that the mind conceives must arise from the beauty and harmony it sees, or contemplates, in things presented to it by the eyes or the imagination; and nothing ugly or ill proportioned can cause us any pleasure. What beauty can there be, or what harmony between the parts and the whole, or between the whole and its parts, in a book or story in which a sixteen-year-old lad deals a giant as tall as a steeple one blow with his sword, and cuts him in two as if he were made of marzipan? And when they want to describe a battle, first they tell us that there are a million fighting men on the enemy's side. But if the hero of the book is against them, inevitably, whether we like it or not, we have to believe that such and such a knight gained the victory by the valour of his strong arm alone. Then what are we to say of the ease with which a hereditary Queen or Empress throws herself into the arms of an unknown and wandering knight? What mind not totally barbarous and uncultured can get pleasure from reading that a great tower, full of knights, sails out over the sea like a ship before a favourable wind, and that one night it is in Lombardy and by dawn next morning in the land of Prester John of the Indies, or in some other country that Ptolemy never knew nor Marco Polo visited? If you reply that the men who compose such books write them as fiction, and so are not obliged to look into fine points or truths, I should reply that the more it resembles the truth the better the fiction, and the more probable and possible it is, the better it pleases. Fictions have to match the minds of their readers, and to be written in such a way that, by tempering the impossibilities, moderating excesses, and keeping judgement in the balance, they may so astonish, hold, excite, and entertain, that wonder and pleasure go hand in hand. None of this can be achieved by anyone departing from verisimilitude or from that imitation of nature in which lies the perfection of all that is written. I have never seen a book of chivalry with a whole body for a plot, with all its limbs complete, so that the middle corresponds to the beginning, and the end to the beginning and middle; for they are generally made up of so many limbs that they seem intended rather to form a chimaera or a monster than a well-proportioned figure. What is more, their style is hard, their adventures are incredible, their love-affairs lewd, their compliments absurd, their battles long-winded, their speeches stupid, their travels preposterous and, lastly, they are devoid of all art and sense, and therefore deserve to be banished from a Christian commonwealth, as a useless tribe.'

The priest listened to him with great attention, for he found him a man of good sense, and approved all that he said. And so he told him that, being of the same opinion himself, and bearing a grudge against books of chivalry, he had burnt all Don Quixote's large library of them. Then he went on to tell the story of the inquisition he had held over them, and to say which he had condemned to the flames and which he had spared, at which the Canon laughed a great deal. Yet he continued that, for all that he had said against such books, he found one good thing in them: the fact that they offered a good intellect a chance to display itself. For they presented a broad and spacious field through which the pen could run without let or hindrance, describing shipwrecks, tempests, encounters and battles; painting a brave captain with all the features necessary for the part; showing his wisdom in forestalling his enemies' cunning, his eloquence in persuading or dissuading his soldiers, his ripeness in counsel, his prompt resolution, his courage in awaiting or in making an attack; now depicting a tragic and lamentable incident, now a joyful and unexpected event; here a most beautiful lady, chaste, intelligent, and modest; there a Christian knight, valiant, and gentle; in one place a monstrous, barbarous braggart; in another a courteous prince, brave and wise; representing the goodness and loyalty of vassals, and the greatness and generosity of lords. Sometimes the writer might show his knowledge of astrology, or his excellence at cosmography or as a musician, or his wisdom in affairs of state, and he might even have an opportunity of showing his skill in necromancy. He could portray the sublety of Ulysses, the piety of Aeneas, the valour of Achilles, the misfortunes of Hector, the treachery of Sinon, the friendship of Euryalus, the generosity of Alexander, the courage of Caesar, the clemency and truthfulness of Trajan, the fidelity of Zopyrus, the prudence of Cato and, in fact, all those attributes which constitute the perfect hero, sometimes placing them in one single man, at other times dividing them amongst many. 'Now,' he concluded, 'if all this is done in a pleasant style and with an ingenious plot, as close as possible to the truth, there is no doubt at all that the author will weave a beautiful and variegated fabric, which, when finished, will be perfect enough to achieve the excellent purpose of such works, which is, as I have said, to instruct and delight at the same time. For the loose plan of these books gives the author an opportunity of showing his talent for the epic, the lyric, the tragic and the comic, and all the qualities contained in the most sweet and pleasing sciences of poetry and rhetoric; for the epic may be written in prose as well as in verse.'

Chapter XLVIII. *In which the Canon pursues the subject of Books of Chivalry and other matters worthy of his genius.*

'WHAT you say is true, Sir Canon,' said the priest, 'and for that reason the writers of such books are most blameworthy, since up to now they have paid no attention to good sense or to the art and rules. For if they had been guided by them, they might have become as famous in prose as the two princes of poetry, Greek and Latin, are in verse.'

'For my part,' replied the canon, 'I have been somewhat tempted to write a book of chivalry, observing all the points I have mentioned. To tell you the truth, I have written more than a hundred pages, and to find out whether they came up to my opinion of them, I have shown them to learned and judicious men given to that kind of reading, and to other ignorant men who merely want the pleasure of listening to nonsense, and I gained flattering approval from them all. But, for all that, I have not continued, because it seemed to me a task unfitting to my profession, and because I found the ignorant were more numerous than the wise; and though it is better to be praised by the few wise and mocked by the many fools, I do not want to subject myself to the muddled judgement of the opinionated crowd, who are generally the most given to reading such books. But most instrumental in making me drop the task of finishing it, even from my thoughts, was an argument which I drew from the comedies that are being played nowadays. For I reflected: if those now in fashion, the fictitious ones and the historical as well, are all, or most of them, notorious nonsense, monsters without feet or head; and if, despite that, the crowd enjoy seeing them, and approve of them and reckon them good, when they are so far from being so; and if the authors who write them and the managers who put them on say that they must be good, because the crowd likes them like that and not otherwise, and that the authors who observe a plan and follow the story as the rules of drama require only serve to please the three or four men of sense who understand them, while all the rest are left unsatisfied and cannot fathom their subtlety; and since these managers add that it suits them better to earn their bread from the many than approval from the few – such would have been the fate of my book after I had scorched my eyebrows studying to keep the rules I spoke of: it would have been love's labour lost. Sometimes I have tried to persuade the managers that their judgements are false, and that they would draw a bigger audience and get better reputations by playing comedies that follow the rules, instead of these extravagant pieces; but they are so bound and wedded to their opinion that there is no argument or proof that can move them from it. I remember saying to one of these obstinate fellows one day: "Tell me, do you remember how a few years ago they were playing three tragedies in Spain by a famous native poet? They were so good that they delighted, surprised and amazed everyone who saw them, learned and simple, the best people and the crowd, and those three alone earned the players more money than thirty of the best produced since?"

'The manager I am speaking of replied: "Of course, your worship means *Isabella*, *Phyllis* and *Alexandra*." "Those it was I meant," I replied. "Now, did not they keep carefully to the rules of drama, and did that prevent their being the successes they were and pleasing everybody? So the fault is not in the public for demanding absurdities, but in people who cannot put anything else on the stage. For there is no absurdity in *Ingratitude Avenged* or in *Numancia*.* You will not find any in *The Merchant Lover*, nor yet in *The Friendly Enemy*, nor in quite a few others written by various good poets, to their own fame and glory, and to the profit of the players." I said a good deal else as well, and I think I left him in some confusion, but not so satisfied or convinced as to retract his mistaken opinions.'

'You have touched on a subject, Sir Canon,' said the priest at this, 'which wakes in me an old grudge I bear against the plays they act to-day. It is as great as my grudge against books of chivalry. For though Drama, according to Tully, should be a mirror to human life, a pattern of manners, and an image of truth, the plays that are performed nowadays are mirrors of absurdity, patterns of foolishness, and images of lewdness. For what greater absurdity can there be in our present subject than for a child to come on in the first scene of the first act in swaddling clothes, and in the second as a grown man with a beard? What could be more ridiculous than to paint us a valiant old man and a young coward, an eloquent servant, a statesmanlike page, a king as a porter, and a princess a scullery-

* By Cervantes himself.

maid? And they pay no more regard to the place or the time in which their action is supposed to occur. I have seen a play whose first act opened in Europe, its second in Asia, and its third ended in Africa. And if there had been four acts, the fourth no doubt would have finished up in America; and so it would have been played in all four quarters of the globe. If imitation is the chief aim of a play, how is it possible to satisfy any average intelligence, when an action pretends to take place in the time of King Pepin and Charlemagne, and yet they make the principal character in it the Emperor Heraclius, who enters Jerusalem bearing the Cross and wins the Holy Sepulchre, like Godfrey de Bouillon, though there was a whole age between the one event and the other? And when the comedy is based on a fictitious story, how can they introduce historical events into it, and mix in incidents that happened to different people at different times; and, even then, with no attempt at verisimilitude, but with obvious errors inexcusable on every count? The worst of it is that there are idiots who say that this stuff is perfect and to look for anything else is to fish for dainties.

'And when we come to sacred drama? What a multitude of false miracles they invent! What apocryphal and unintelligible plots – the miracles of one saint attributed to another! Even in their profane plays they make bold to introduce miracles without any more reason or consideration than because they think that some miracle – or effect, as they call it – will go well, and that the ignorant public will enjoy it and come to the play. But all this is prejudicial to truth, and to the detriment of history. It shames our Spanish wits before foreigners, who observe the rules of drama with great strictness and consider us ignorant barbarians when they see the absurdities and extravagances of the plays we write. It is not sufficient excuse to say that the principal purpose for which well-ordered states allow public plays to be acted is to give the common people a respectable entertainment, and to divert the ill-humours which idleness at times engenders; and that since any play can do that, whether it is good or bad, there is no reason to impose laws or compel writers and actors to compose their plays in the proper way, because, as I have said, they can achieve their purpose with any play at all. To this I should reply that their purpose could be incomparably better achieved by good plays than by bad ones; because the audience would come out from a well-written and well-constructed play entertained by the comic part, instructed by the serious, surprised by the action, enlivened by the speeches, warned by the tricks, wiser for the moral, incensed against vice, and enamoured of virtue. All these effects a good play can work in the mind of an audience, however rough and sluggish; and it is absolutely impossible for a play with all these qualities not to amuse and entertain, satisfy and please, much better than one that lacks them, as most of the pieces generally played nowadays do. It is not the fault of the poets who write them, for some of them know very well where they are wrong and are thoroughly conscious of what they ought to do. But as plays have become a marketable commodity they say, and say truly, that the players would not buy them if they were not of the usual kind. And so the poet tries to adapt himself to the requirements of the manager who pays him for his work. The truth of that can be seen by the infinite number of plays written by one most fertile genius of these kingdoms with so much splendour and so much grace, with such well-turned verses, such choice language, such serious thought, and lastly, with so much eloquence and in so lofty a style, that the world is full of his fame; and yet, because he wishes to suit the taste of the actors, not all his pieces have achieved, as some have, the perfection which art requires. Other authors pay so little attention to their task that when the play is over the actors have to run away and hide, for fear of being punished, as they have often been, for acting scenes offensive to some prince or libelling some family.

'Now, all these evils, and many more of which I will not speak, would cease, if there were some intelligent and judicious person at court to examine all plays before they are performed, not only those that are acted in the capital, but all that are to be played anywhere in Spain. Then no magistrate in any town would allow any play to be performed without this man's approbation, under his hand and seal; and so the comedians would take good care to send their plays to Madrid, and could then act them in safety. The writers, too, would take more pains with their work, out of fear of the rigorous examination they would have to pass at the hands of someone knowing the business. In this way good plays would be produced, and the purpose of such entertainment successfully achieved: which is not only popular amusement, but also the good reputation of Spanish genius, the profit and security of the actors, and the avoidance of the need to punish them. Now, if the same person or some other were entrusted with the task of examining newly written books of chivalry, no doubt some would be produced of the perfection your worship requires, thus enriching our tongue with the charming and precious treasure of eloquence, and causing the old books to be eclipsed in the bright presence of the new. They would provide honest amusement not only for the idle but for the busiest of men; for it is impossible for the brow to be always bent, nor can our frail human nature sustain itself without some lawful recreation.'

When the canon and the priest had reached this point in their conversation the barber rode forward, caught them up, and said to the priest:

'Here, Master Priest, is the place I told you of. We can take our siesta here, and the oxen will find plenty of fresh pasture.'

'It looks good to me,' replied the priest, and told their intentions to the canon, who was attracted by the sight of the lovely valley before them and decided to stay with them. And so as to enjoy the scene and the conversation of the priest, for whom he had taken a liking, and to hear Don Quixote's adventures in greater detail, he ordered some of his servants to go to the inn, which was not far away, and bring enough for them all to eat, as he had decided to rest there that afternoon. One of his servants replied, however, that the baggage-mule, which must be at the inn already, carried sufficient provisions, and that they would need nothing from there but barley.

'If that is so,' said the canon, 'take all our mounts there and bring the baggage-mule back.'

While this was going on Sancho saw an opportunity of talking to his master without the continual presence of the priest and the barber, whom he regarded with suspicion. So he went up to the cage, and said:

'Sir, I want to relieve my conscience, and tell you something about your enchantment; and that is, that those two with their faces covered are our village priest and the barber. I think they've played this trick of carrying you off like this because they're envious of your worship for beating them in doing famous deeds. Supposing, then, that I'm right. It follows that you're not under a spell, but humbugged and fooled. Now, to prove it to you, I want to ask you one question, and if you answer me as I think you will, you'll put your finger on this trick and see that you're not enchanted, but have had your wits turned upside down.'

'Ask what you like, Sancho my son,' replied Don Quixote, 'and I will satisfy you and answer you to your heart's content. But as to your saying that the men accompanying us are the priest and the barber, our friends and fellow-villagers, it may well be that they look the same, but you must not believe for a minute that they really and truly are so. What you must believe and understand is that if they are like them, as you say, it must be because my enchanters have taken on their likeness and semblance, for it is easy for magicians to take on any appearance they please. And they will have assumed the likeness of our friends to give you cause to think as you do, and to put you into a maze of conjectures, from which not even the clue of Theseus could extricate you. Their intention will also be to confuse my brain and make me incapable of guessing the cause of this disaster. For if you tell me, on the one hand, that our village priest and barber are travelling here beside me, and if, on the other, I find myself caged and know that only superhuman power could encage me – for no human strength would be sufficient – what would you have me say or think, except that the manner of my enchantment is stranger than any I have read of in any history that treats of the enchantment of knights errant? So do not be disturbed by supposing that they are whom you say, but rest assured that they are no more the priest and the barber than I am a Turk. But as for these questions you wish to ask me, speak, for I will answer you, even though you go on asking till to-morrow.'

'Holy Mother!' replied Sancho, raising his voice. 'Can you possibly be so thick-skulled and brain-sick, your worship, that you can't see it's the sober truth I'm telling you, and that there's more roguery than enchantment about this unfortunate confinement of yours? Anyhow, I'll clearly prove it to you that you're not enchanted. Now, tell me, as God shall deliver you out of this trouble, and as you would find yourself in the arms of my lady Dulcinea when least you expect it – '

'Stop your hocus-pocus,' cried Don Quixote, 'and ask what you will. I have promised already to reply faithfully.'

'That's what I want,' said Sancho; 'for you to tell me the *whole* truth, without additions or subtractions, as those, like your worship, who make a profession of arms under the title of knights errant are expected to do.'

'I tell you that I will not lie on any matter,' replied Don Quixote. 'Get on with your questions; for really, Sancho, you weary me with all your oaths, your supplications and preambles.'

'Well,' said Sancho, 'I'm confident that my master's a good man and truthful. And so, I'll ask you one question that's very much to the point. Speaking with all respect, your worship, since you've been cooped up and enchanted, as you think, in this cage, have you been taken with any desire or inclination to make either big or little waters, as the saying is?'

'I do not understand what you mean by making waters, Sancho. Be more explicit, if you want me to answer you fully.'

'Is it possible that your worship doesn't understand what making big or little waters is? Why, boys learn that when they go to school. But what I mean is, have you had no mind to do what nobody can do for you?'

'Oh, I understand you now, Sancho. Yes, very often. In fact I want to at this moment. Get me out of my plight, for things are none too clean.'

Chapter XLIX. *Of the shrewd Conversation between Sancho Panza and his master Don Quixote.*

'Ah,' said Sancho, 'now I've caught you. I was longing to know that with all my heart and soul. Come now, sir, can you dispute the saying that's in everyone's mouth when some one's in a bad way: "I don't know what's the matter with so and so. He doesn't eat or drink or sleep, or answer straight when you ask him a question; it really looks as if he's bewitched." – From which you may gather that people who don't eat or drink or sleep or perform the natural functions I mentioned are enchanted; but if they have the desire your worship has, and drink when it's given them, and eat when they have something to eat, and answer all the questions they are asked, then they are certainly not bewitched.'

'You are right, Sancho,' replied Don Quixote; 'but I have told you already that there are many kinds of enchantments; and time may have changed the fashion from one kind to another. It may be usual now for people under a spell to do all that I do, although they did not before; so that there is no arguing or drawing conclusions against the customs of the times. I most certainly know that I am enchanted, and that is sufficient to ease my conscience, which would be greatly burdened if I thought that I was not under a spell, and yet remained in this cage like an idler and a coward, defrauding the many distressed and needy of the succour I could give them. For there must be many at this hour in positive and urgent need of my help and protection.'

'But for all that,' replied Sancho, 'for your greater security and satisfaction, it would be well, I think, if your worship were to try to get out of your prison. I promise to help you with all my power, and even to release you. Then you could try to mount once again on your good Rocinante, who seems to be enchanted as well, he's so melancholy and sad. And when you've done that, we can try our luck and look for more adventures. If we don't succeed there'll still be time to come back to the cage. And I promise you, on the faith of a true and loyal squire, I'll shut myself up alongside your worship, if you should chance to prove so unlucky or I so stupid as not to bring off this plan of mine.'

'I am content to do as you say, brother Sancho,' replied Don Quixote, 'and when you see an opportunity of managing my deliverance, I will obey you absolutely. But you will see, Sancho, how mistaken you are in your opinion about my misfortune.'

Our errant knight and ill-errant squire entertained themselves with this conversation until they reached the place where the priest, the canon and the barber had dismounted and were awaiting them. The carter then unyoked his oxen from the cart and turned them loose in that green and pleasant place, whose freshness invited not only enchanted persons like Don Quixote, but also such a rational and sensible creature as his squire. Sancho begged the priest to let his master out of his cage for a while, for otherwise his prison would not be as clean as decency required the accommodation of such a knight as his master to be. The priest understood him, and said that he would gladly oblige him, if it were not for his fear that once Don Quixote found himself at liberty he would play them one of his tricks, and go off and never be seen again.

'I'll go bail for his not running away,' replied Sancho.

'And I, for any sum,' said the canon, 'particularly if he gives me his word as a knight not to leave us without our consent.'

'I give it,' answered Don Quixote, who was listening all the time, 'the more so because anyone enchanted, as I am, is not at liberty to dispose of his person as he will. For his enchanter can make him powerless to stir from one spot for three centuries; and if he were to escape he would be brought back flying through the air.' Since this was the case, he said, they could certainly release him, especially as it would be to everyone's advantage: in fact, if they did not let him out, he protested, he could not refrain from offending their noses, unless they were to retire to some distance.

The canon took him by one of his hands, although they were tied, and on his pledged word, they let him out of his cage, at which he was vastly delighted. The first thing he did was to stretch his whole body, and then he went over to Rocinante and gave him two slaps on the haunches, saying: 'I still trust in God and his blessed Mother, flower and mirror of steeds, that we two shall soon find ourselves in the state our hearts desire: you with your master on your back, and I on top of you, exercising the function for which God sent me into the world.'

After saying this Don Quixote went aside with Sancho Panza to a distant spot, from which he returned much relieved, and still more eager to put his squire's plan into execution.

The canon gazed at him, and wondered at the strangeness of his crazy humour and at the excellent sense he displayed in his conversation and in his answers, only losing his stirrups, as we have said before, on the subject of chivalry. And so, once they were all seated on the green grass waiting for the provisions, the canon was moved by compassion to ask him:

'Can the idle and unsavoury reading of books of chivalry, my good sir, possibly have had such an effect on you as so to turn your brain that you have come to believe that you are under a spell, and other things of that kind, which are as far from being so as falsehood itself is from the truth? How is it possible for human reason to persuade itself of the existence of all those countless Amadises, of that multitude of famous knights, and of so many Emperors of Trebizond? Who could really believe in Felixmarte of Hyrcania, and all those palfreys, all those wandering damsels, all those serpents, all those dragons, all those giants, all those extraordinary adventures, all those varieties of spells, all those battles, all those desperate encounters, all that fine raiment, all those love-lorn princesses, all those squires who became counts, all those facetious dwarfs, all those love letters, all that wooing, all those courageous ladies and, in fact, all those monstrous absurdities contained in books of chivalry? For myself I can say that they give me a certain pleasure when I read them – so long as I do not deliberately reflect that they are all triviality and lies. But when I consider what they are I throw the very best of them against the wall, and I would pitch them into the fire if I had one near at hand. For such a punishment they certainly deserve for being liars and impostors, beyond the realms of common sense, as founders of new sects and new ways of life, and for causing the ignorant crowd to accept all the nonsense they contain as gospel truth. They have even the audacity to confuse the minds of intelligent and well-born gentlemen, as is clear from their effect on your worship, whom they have reduced to the state of being shut in a cage and carried on an ox-cart, as they transport a lion or a tiger from town to town to exhibit it for money. Come, Don Quixote, take pity on yourself; return into the bosom of discretion, and learn to use the generous talents that Heaven has blessed you with, by applying your mind to some other course of study which may redound to the profit of your soul and to the increasing of your honour. But if your natural inclination is so strong that you must read books of adventures and chivalry, read the Book of Judges in Holy Scripture, where you will find grand and authentic exploits, which are both heroic and true. Portugal had its Viriatus, Rome had its Caesar, Carthage its Hannibal, Greece its Alexander, Castile its Count Ferdinand Gonzalez, Valencia its Cid, Andalusia its Gonzalo Fernandez, Estremadura its Diego Garcia de Paredes, Jerez its Garci Perez de Vargas, Toledo its Garcilaso, Seville its Don Manuel de Leon; and their valorous exploits will entertain, instruct, delight, and surprise the highest intelligence that reads them. They are certainly a study worthy of your excellent mind, my dear Don Quixote, and you will rise from reading of them learned in history, enamoured of virtue, instructed in goodness, improved in manners, valiant but not rash, bold and no coward; and all this to the honour of God, your own profit, and the glory of La Mancha, whence, as I have learnt, you derive your birth and origin.'

Don Quixote listened most attentively to the canon's arguments, gazed at him for some time when he saw that he had finished, and said: 'Sir, your discourse was intended, I think, to persuade me that there have never been knights errant in the world, that all books of chivalry are false, lying, hurtful, and unprofitable to the commonwealth, and that I have done wrong to read them, and worse to believe in them, and worst of all to imitate them in setting myself to follow the very hard profession of knight errantry they teach. And, what is more, you deny the existence of either Amadis of Gaul or of Greece, and of all those other knights of whom the writings are full.'

'I meant precisely what you say,' answered the canon at this. To which Don Quixote replied:

'You were pleased to add also that such books have done me much harm, that they have turned my brain, and caused my present imprisonment, and that it would be better for me to make some amendment, and change my reading to other books more truthful, enjoyable and instructive.'

'Just so,' answered the canon.

'Why then, in my opinion it is you,' replied Don Quixote, 'that are deranged and enchanted, for daring to blaspheme against an institution so universally acknowledged and so authenticated, that anyone denying it, as you do, deserves the very punishment you say that you inflict on certain books when you have read them and they displease you. For to attempt to convince anyone that there were no such persons as Amadis and the other knights errant of whom so many records remain, would be like trying to persuade him that the sun does not shine, nor the frost chill, nor earth yield sustenance. For what intellect could there be in the world capable of persuading another that the story of Princess Floripes and Guy of Burgundy was not true? Or the adventure of Fierabras at the Bridge of Mantible, which took place in the time of Charlemagne, and which, I swear, is as true as that it is now daylight? And if that is a lie, then it must follow that there existed no Hector, nor Achilles, nor Trojan War, nor Twelve Peers of France, nor King Arthur of England, who is still wandering about the world to this day transformed into a raven, and is hourly awaited in his kingdom. Yes, they will even say, no doubt, that the history of Guarino Mezquino is false, and the Quest of the Holy Grail as well, and that the loves of Sir Tristan and Queen Iseult, and of Guenevere and Lancelot are apocryphal, although there are persons who almost remember having seen the Lady Quintañona. She was the best wine-server Great Britain ever had, and her existence is so authentic that I remember my grandmother on my father's side saying, when she saw an old lady with a stately head-dress: "My boy, that woman is very like the Lady Quintañona." From which I conclude that she must herself have known her, or must have seen some portrait of her, at least. Then who can deny the truth of the story of Peter and the fair Magalona, since even to this day you can see in the King's armoury the peg with which the brave Peter guided the wooden horse on which he used to ride through the air, and which is a little bigger than the pole of a coach? And near this peg is Babieca's saddle, and at Roncesvalles is Roland's horn, which is the size of a great beam; from which it can be inferred that the Twelve Peers existed, and the Peters, and the Cids and other such knights, of the sort commonly termed adventurers. If that is denied I shall be told it is not true that the brave Lusitanian Juan de Merlo was a knight errant, who went to Burgundy and fought in the city of Arras with the famous Lord of Charny, called Monseigneur Pierre, and after that with Monseigneur Henri de Remestan in the city of Basle, coming off from both exploits victorious and crowned with honour and glory. They will also deny the adventures and challenges also performed in Burgundy by the valiant Spaniards, Pedro Barba and Gutierre Quixada – from whose stock I am descended in the direct male line – when they beat the sons of the Count St. Pol. Nor will they agree that Don Ferdinand de Guevara went to Germany in quest of adventure, and fought there with Messire George, a knight of the Duke of Austria's house. They will say, too, that the jousts of Suero de Quiñones of the Honourable Pass were a fable, and the exploits of Sir Luis de Falces against the Castilian knight Don Gonzalo de Guzman, and all the many deeds performed by Christian knights of these and foreign realms, so authentic and true, I repeat, that anyone denying them must be devoid of all reason and right understanding.'

The canon was amazed to hear Don Quixote so mingling truth and fiction, and at the knowledge he displayed of everything in any way concerning the exploits of his knight errantry. And so he replied: 'I cannot deny, sir, that some of what you say is true, especially what you say of the Spanish knights errant; and I would admit also the existence of the Twelve Peers of France, though I cannot believe that they performed all those deeds that Archbishop Turpin attributes to them. For the truth of it is that they were knights chosen by the Kings of France, and were called peers as being all equal in worth, in rank and in valour; or at least, if they were not, they should have been. They were an order like the present-day order of Santiago, or of Calatrava, whose professing knights are presumed to be, or should be, worthy, valiant and well born; and as we now speak of a Knight of St. John or of Alcantara, so they used to speak in those days of a Knight of the Twelve Peers, because they were twelve equals, chosen to be members of that military order. As for the Cid, there is no doubt about him, and even less about Bernardo del Carpio; but that they performed the deeds attributed to them is a very doubtful matter. As for that other matter you speak of, Count Pierre's peg and its standing near Babieca's saddle in the King's armoury, I must confess that I am so ignorant or so short-sighted that, although I have seen the saddle, I have never noticed the peg, big as you say it is.'

'Yet it is there without a doubt,' replied Don Quixote, 'and what is more, they say that it is kept in an ox-hide sheath, to save it from rusting.'

'That may well be so,' replied the canon, 'but I swear by my holy orders I do not remember having seen it. Though, supposing I grant that it is there, that is no reason for my having to believe the stories of all these Amadises, or of all that multitude of knights we are told about. Nor is it reasonable for a man like yourself, possessed of your understanding, your reputation and your talents, to accept all the extravagant absurdities in these ridiculous books of chivalry as really true.'

Chapter L. *Of the learned Arguments between Don Quixote and the canon, and other matters.*

'THAT is a good joke!' replied Don Quixote. 'Books which are printed by royal licence and with the approval of those to whom they are submitted, and which are read with universal delight and applause by great and small, poor and rich, learned and ignorant, plebeians and gentlefolk – in short, by all kinds of persons of every quality and condition – could they be lies and at the same time appear so much like the truth? For do they not specify the father, the mother, the family, the time, the place, and the actions, detail by detail and day by day, of this or that knight? Be silent, sir, do not speak such blasphemies; and, believe me, if you take my advice you will be acting like a man of sense. Only read these books, and you will see what pleasure you get from them. For, tell me, could there be anything more delightful than to see displayed here and now before our eyes, as we might say, a great lake of pitch, boiling hot, and swimming and writhing about in it a great number of serpents, snakes and lizards, and many other sorts of savage and frightful creatures; and then to hear issuing from the middle of that lake a most dismal voice crying: "You, Knight, whoever you may be, that gaze on this dreadful lake, if you would reach the treasure hidden beneath these black waters, show the valour of your dauntless heart and plunge into the middle of its dark, burning liquor; for if you do not do so, you will not be worthy to see the mighty marvels hidden within the seven castles of the seven witches who dwell beneath this gloomy water." No sooner has the knight heard this dreadful voice than he abandons all thought for himself, and without reflecting on the peril to which he is exposing himself, or even easing himself of the weight of his ponderous armour, he commends himself to God and his lady, dives into the middle of the boiling lake; and then unexpectedly, and when he least knows where he is going, he finds himself amidst flowery meadows, incomparably finer even than the Elysian fields. There the sky seems to him more transparent and the sun to shine with a new brightness. Before his eyes opens a pleasant grove of green and leafy trees whose verdure charms his vision, while his ears are ravished by the sweet, untaught song of innumerable little bright-coloured birds which flit about the interlacing branches. Here he discovers a small stream, whose fresh waters glide like liquid crystal over delicate sand and little white stones, which resemble sifted gold and purest pearl. There he spies a fountain made of mottled jasper and smooth marble; here another, roughly fashioned, where tiny mussel shells, mingled with the twisted yellow and white houses of the snails, lying in disordered order among pieces of glittering crystal and counterfeit emeralds, form so gracefully varied a composition that art, the imitator of nature, seems here to surpass herself. Then suddenly there appears in the distance a strong castle or handsome palace with walls of solid gold, with turrets of diamonds, and gates of jacinth; so admirably built, in fact, that though the materials of which it is constructed are nothing less than diamonds, carbuncles, rubies, pearls, gold and emeralds, the workmanship is still more precious. And after this, could there be a finer sight than a lovely troop of maidens coming out of the castle in such gay and gorgeous attire that, if I were to set out now to describe them as the stories do, I should never end? And then for the one who seems the chief of them all to take the bold knight who plunged into the burning lake by the hand, and silently lead him into the rich palace or castle, and strip him as naked as his mother bore him, and bathe him in warm water, and then anoint him all over with sweet-smelling ointments, and put on him a shirt of finest samite, all fragrant and perfumed? Then for another maiden to come and throw over his shoulder a mantle, reputed to be worth a city, at the very least, or perhaps more? What finer sight, then, than after all that, to see them take him to another room where the tables are laid so magnificently that he is speechless with amazement? And to watch him sprinkle on his hands water all distilled of ambergris and sweet-smelling flowers? And to see him seated on an ivory chair? And to see all the maidens serve him, still preserving their miraculous silence? And bring him such variety of dishes, so deliciously cooked that the appetite is at a loss to know where to direct the hand? How pleasant it must be to hear the music which sounds all the while, without his knowing who is singing or whence it comes? And when the feast is over and the tables are cleared, for the knight to stay reclining on his chair, perhaps picking his teeth as his custom is, when suddenly there enters through the door of the hall another maiden more lovely than any of the first, who sits down beside him and begins to tell him what manner of castle it is, and how she lives there under a spell, and other things which surprise the knight and astonish the readers of his story.

'I will enlarge on this no further, for you can gather from what I have said that any passage from any story of knight errantry is bound to delight and amaze a reader. Believe me, sir, I repeat, and read these books. You will see how they drive away the melancholy, and improve your temper if it happens to be bad. I can say of myself that since I became a knight errant I have been valiant, courteous, liberal, well-bred, generous, polite, bold, gentle and patient, and an endurer of toils, imprisonments and enchantments. And although for the last little while I have been imprisoned in a cage like a madman, I expect by the valour of my arm, if Heaven favours me and fate is not against me, to find myself in a few days king of some kingdom, in which I can display the gratitude and liberality enclosed in this bosom of mine. For, by my faith, sir, a poor man is incapacitated from showing the virtue of liberality towards anyone, even though he may possess it in the highest degree; and gratitude which consists only of desire is a dead thing, as faith is dead without works. For that reason I could wish that fortune would speedily offer me an opportunity of making myself Emperor, so that I might show my will to do good to my friends, especially to this poor Sancho Panza, my squire, who is the best man in the world; and I should like to give him the countship which I promised him a long while ago, were it not that I am afraid he will not have the capacity to govern his estate.'

At this Sancho, who had overheard these last words of his master's, exclaimed: 'Set to work, Don Quixote. Get me that countship you've promised me so often and I've waited for so long. I've no lack of capacity to govern, I assure you; and if I had, I've heard of men who take noblemen's estates in farm, giving them so much a year and looking after the management. Then the lord lies with his feet up, enjoying the rent they pay him without a care in the world; and that's what I'll do. I won't haggle over a few pence more or less. I'll give it all up at once, and enjoy my income like a duke. Then let the world go hang.'

'That, brother Sancho,' said the canon, 'applies to the enjoyment of the revenues. But there is the administration of justice, which the lord of the estate must attend to. That is where capacity and a sound judgement come in and, above all, an honest intention to do right; for if that is lacking in the beginning, everything will go wrong in the middle and the end, and Heaven usually assists the good intentions of the simple, and confounds the evil designs of the crafty.'

'I don't understand these philosophies,' replied Sancho Panza. 'I only wish I were as sure of the countship as of my ability to govern. For I've as large a soul as the next man, and as stout a body as the best of them, and I'd be as good a king of my estate as any other King; and being so, I should do as I liked; and doing as I liked, I should take my pleasure; and taking my pleasure, I should be contented; and when one's content, there's nothing more to desire; and when there's nothing more to desire, there's an end of it. So for Heaven's sake let me have the estate, and then we'll see, as one blind man said to the other.'

'These are not bad philosophies, as you say, Sancho,' put in the canon; 'but all the same there is a great deal to be said on this subject of countships.'

But Don Quixote answered his squire: 'I do not know what more there is to say. I am guided solely by the example of the great Amadis of Gaul, who made his squire Count of the Firm Isle. So I need have no scruple of conscience in making Sancho Panza a count, for he is one of the best squires that ever served knight errant.'

The canon was astonished at this well-reasoned nonsense of Don Quixote's, at his description of the adventure of the Knight of the Lake, and at the impression made on him by the deliberate lies in the books he had read. And he marvelled, too, at Sancho's foolishness in so ardently desiring the countship his master had promised him.

By this time the canon's servants, who had gone to the inn for the baggage-mule, had returned. So, making a carpet and the green meadow-grass their table, they sat down in the shade of some trees and took their meal there, so that the carter could profit from the pasture there, as has already been said. Now, whilst they were eating they suddenly heard a considerable noise and the sound of a little bell from some brambles and thick bushes which grew close by; and at the same moment they saw a fine she-goat speckled with black, white and grey, run out of the thicket. After her came a goatherd

calling to her in the language they use when they want their beasts
to stop and come back to the fold. But the truant goat ran up to
the company, scared and trembling, as if for their protection, and
there stayed still till the goatherd arrived and, catching her by the
horns, addressed her, as if she were capable of speech and reason:

'Oh, wild one, wild one! Speckle, Speckle, how you've gone
limping about these days! What wolves have scared you, little one?
Won't you tell me what it is, pretty one? But it can only be that
you're a woman and can't stay still! The Devil take your moods,
and the moods of all like you. Come back, come back, friend!
You'll be safer in your fold, or with your companions, even if
you're not so happy. For if you, who should guide them and lead
them, go unguided and astray, what will become of them?'

The goatherd's words amused his hearers, especially the canon,
who said to him: 'Come, come, do not be angry, brother, I beg
you, and do not be in such a hurry to drive this goat back to her
fold. For since she is a female, as you say, she must follow her
natural instinct, despite all your pains to stop her. Take a snack and
drink a drop with us; it will soothe you and the goat can rest a
while.'

As he said this he handed him the hindquarter of a cold rabbit on
the point of a knife. The goatherd took it and thanked him. Then
when he had drunk and rested, he said: 'I shouldn't like your worships to take me for a simpleton for talking to this animal so sensibly; for in truth my words are not without some meaning. I'm a
peasant, but not so much of one that I don't understand how to
converse with men and beasts.'

'I can very well believe that,' answered the priest, 'for I already
know by experience that the mountains breed scholars, and sheepcotes contain philosophers.'

'At least, sir,' said the goatherd, 'they house men who have
learnt by experience. And to convince you of that, and to give you
an example, too – though, being uninvited, I may seem to be ob-
truding myself – if it doesn't bore you, gentlemen, and you will
lend me your attention for a little, I'll tell you a true tale which will
confirm that gentleman's words' – pointing to the priest – 'and
mine.'

To which Don Quixote answered: 'Seeing that this matter has a slight tinge of knightly adventure about it, I will listen to you, for my part, brother; and so will all these gentlemen, who are men of good sense and fond of the curious, the entertaining and the marvellous, all of which, I have no doubt, your story contains. Begin, then, friend, and we will all listen.'

'Count me out,' said Sancho. 'I am off to the stream with this pie, and I'm going to fill myself with enough for three days. For I have heard my master, Don Quixote, say that a knight errant's squire must eat his fill when he gets the chance, since they may lose their way for six days together in some wood that's so thick they can't find a way out; and if a man doesn't go in with a full belly or a well-stored haversack, he may very well stay there, as very often he does, till he is turned into mummy flesh.'

'You are quite right, Sancho,' said Don Quixote. 'Go where you like and eat what you can; but I am satisfied already. All I need is refreshment for my mind, which I will now give it by listening to this good man's story.'

'And so will we all,' said the canon.

But before beginning the promised tale, the goatherd gave the goat, which he was holding by the horns, a couple of slaps on the back, and said: 'Lie down beside me, Speckle, for we shall have time enough to return to our fold.' The creature seemed to understand him, for when her master sat down, she stretched herself calmly beside him and, looking up into his face, signified that she was listening, as he began the following story:

Chapter LI. *What the Goatherd told Don Quixote's escort.*

'NINE miles from this valley is a town which, although small, is one of the richest in all this district. In it there lived a farmer greatly honoured, both for his native virtue and for the wealth he had acquired, though honour always goes with riches. But his greatest fortune in his own eyes was the possession of a daughter of such consummate beauty, rare good sense, charm and virtue, that everyone who knew her, or even set eyes on her, was amazed at the surpassing qualities with which Heaven and nature had endowed her. As a child she was pretty, and she went on increasing in loveliness until at the age of sixteen she was exceedingly beautiful. The fame

of her loveliness began to spread among all the near-by villages –
but why do I say near-by villages? It reached to distant cities, and
even entered the royal palace and came to the ears of many sorts of
people, who would come to see her from all parts, as if she were a
rare sight or a wonder-working image. Her father guarded her carefully, and she guarded herself; for there are no locks, bolts, or bars
which keep a maiden better guarded than does her own modesty.
The father's wealth and the daughter's beauty led many, both of
their own town and strangers, to ask for her hand. But, having so
rich a jewel to dispose of, he was much perplexed and unable to
decide upon which of her infinite number of wooers to bestow her.
Now, among the multitude who desired her I was one, and I derived very great hopes of success from her father's knowing me and
because I was a native of their town, of pure blood, in the flower of
my youth, rich in goods, and no less well endowed in mind. But a
fellow-townsman with all the same qualifications was also her suitor;
and this caused the father to put off his decision and keep things in
the balance, for it seemed to him that either of us would be a good
match for his daughter. To solve his difficulty, he decided to refer
it to Leandra – for that is the name of the rich maid who has plunged
me into such misery – thinking that, as we two were equal, it was
best to leave it to his beloved daughter to choose according to her
own liking, a course that should be imitated by all fathers with children to marry. I do not mean that they should leave them to make a
choice among bad or evil persons, but that they should put the
good before them, and let them choose among them according to
their taste. I do not know what choice Leandra made; I only know
that her father put us both off on the score of his daughter's youth,
in general terms which neither bound him nor dismissed us. My
rival's name is Anselmo, and mine Eugenio – for I would have you
know the names of the persons involved in this tragedy, the end of
which is still unresolved, though it is clear enough that it is bound
to be disastrous.

'At this time there came to our town one Vicente de la Roca, the
son of a poor local farmer, which Vicente had returned from Italy
and other places where he had been soldiering. He had been carried
off from our town as a lad of about twelve by a captain who happened to be passing through with his troop; and now, about twelve

years later, returned as a youth in a soldier's uniform, pranked out in countless bright colours, and hung with innumerable glass trinkets and fine steel chains. One day he would put on one bit of finery, the next another, but all of them flimsy, gaudy, weighing little, and worth less. The country people, who are malicious by nature – and when idleness gives them an occasion are malice itself – noted and reckoned up each one of his bits of finery and trinkets, and found that he had only three suits of different colours, with stockings and garters to match. But he made so many transformations and variations with them that, if no one had counted them, one would have sworn that he had shown off more than ten suits of clothes and more than twenty plumes of feathers. Now, do not presume that what I am telling you about his clothes is a digression or superfluous, for they play a principal part in my story.

'Now, he used to sit on a bench under a great poplar in our market-place, and there he would keep us all open-mouthed, hanging on the exploits he described to us. There was no country in the whole world he had not visited, and no battle he had not taken part in. He had killed more Turks than there are in Morocco and Tunis, and engaged in more single combats, according to his own story, than Gante and Luna, Diego Garcia de Paredes, and a thousand others whom he named, and from every one of them he had come off victorious, without losing so much as a drop of blood. Then, again, he would show us scars of wounds, and although we could not make them out, he would persuade us that they came from musket-shots received in various actions and skirmishes. What is more, he would have the unparalleled effrontery to patronize his equals, even those who knew him, and say that his right arm was his father, his deeds his lineage, and that, as a soldier, he owed nothing even to the King himself. In addition to these pretensions he was something of a musician and plucked the guitar to such effect that some people said he could make it speak. But his accomplishments did not stop here, for he had also a talent for poetry, and used to make up a ballad a mile and a half long on every trifling thing that happened in the town.

'This soldier, then, whom I have just described, this Vicente de la Roca, this braggart, this swaggerer, this musician, this poet, was often seen and admired by Leandra from a window of her house which looked on to the market-place. She was captivated by the bright tinsel of his clothes, enchanted by his ballads – for he would give away twenty copies of every one he composed – the exploits which he attributed to himself came to her ears and, in the end – for so the Devil must have decreed – she fell in love with him before the presumptuous idea of wooing her had come into his head. And as no love affair is more easily brought to fruition than one which is backed by the lady's desire, Leandra and Vicente came to an agreement without any difficulty; and before any one of her many suitors had realized her infatuation she had already satisfied it by running off from her dearly beloved father's house – she has no mother – and eloping from the village with the soldier, who came off from this enterprise more triumphantly than from all the many others he had laid claim to. This event filled the whole place with astonishment, and everyone else who heard of it, too. I was confounded, Anselmo thunderstruck, her father distressed, her relations ashamed, Justice aroused, and the troopers on the watch. They scoured the roads, searched the woods, and everywhere they could, and at the end of three days found the fickle Leandra in a mountain cave, clad only in her shift and without the store of money and the precious jewels which she had brought away with her. They took her back before her unhappy father and questioned her about her plight. And she confessed quite freely that Vicente de la Roca had deceived her, persuading her, under promise of marriage, to leave her father's house, and offering to take her to the richest and most delightful city in all the world – he meant Naples – and that she had been sufficiently ill-advised and deceived to believe him. For after robbing her father she had entrusted herself to him on the same night she had been missed, when he had taken her to a wild mountain and shut her in the cave where they had found her. She also affirmed that the soldier had not robbed her of her honour, though he had taken everything she had before going off and leaving her in the cave; a fact which astonished everyone afresh.

'It was difficult, sir, to believe in the youth's self-restraint, but she vouched for it with such persistence as partly to console her disconsolate father, who set no store by the valuables they had taken so long as his daughter was left in possession of that jewel which, once lost, is beyond all hope of recovery. The very same day that

Leandra appeared her father removed her again from our sight, taking her and shutting her up in a nunnery at a town not far from here, in the hope that time would work off some part of the disgrace she had brought upon herself. Leandra's youth served as some excuse for her wickedness, at least for such as had nothing to gain from proving her good or bad; but those who knew her intelligence and considerable shrewdness attributed her fault not to ignorance, but to frivolity and the failings natural to woman-kind, who are generally ill-balanced and unsteady.

'With Leandra put away, Anselmo's eyes became blind, or at least there was no sight that gave him any pleasure, and my own were in darkness, without a light to guide them towards joy. In Leandra's absence our sorrow increased, our patience diminished, and we cursed the soldier's finery and railed at her father's lack of precaution. In the end he and I agreed to leave the village and come to this valley, where we spend our lives among the trees, he grazing a large flock of his own sheep, and I a large herd of goats, also my own. Here we give vent to our passion, either singing together in praise or dispraise of the lovely Leandra, or sighing separately and alone, and confiding our complaints to Heaven. Many others of Leandra's suitors have followed our example, and come to these wild mountains to follow the same employment; so many that this place seems to have become the pastoral Arcadia, for it is so crammed with shepherds and sheep-folds that there is not a corner in it where you will not hear the fair Leandra's name. One man curses her and calls her fickle, inconstant and immodest; another denounces her as forward and light; yet another absolves and pardons her; one more tries her and condemns her; one celebrates her beauty; another execrates her character; in fact, all disparage her and all adore her; and the madness extends so far that some complain of her disdain without ever having spoken to her, and some bewail their fate and suffer the maddening disease of jealousy, for which she never gave anyone any cause. For, as I have said, her fault was discovered before her infatuation was known. There is not a hollow rock, nor river bank, nor shade of a tree, that is not occupied by some shepherd or other recounting his misfortunes to the winds; and echo repeats Leandra's name wherever it can sound; the hills ring with Leandra, the streams murmur Leandra, and Leandra

P

keeps us all distracted and enchanted, hoping against hope, and fearing without knowing what we fear.

'Among all these distracted men, the one who shows the least but has the most sense is my rival Anselmo who, having so many other things he might complain of, complains only of her absence, and sings his lament in verses which show his excellent talents, to the sound of a fiddle, which he plays admirably. I follow an easier and, in my opinion, a wiser path, which is to curse the fickleness of women, their inconstancy, their double-dealing, their unkept promises, their broken faith and, last of all, the lack of judgement they show in their choice of objects for their desires and affections.

'And that was the reason, gentlemen, for the words I addressed to this goat on my arrival here; for as a female I despise her, although she is the best of all my flock. This is the story I promised to tell you. If I have been tedious in my tale I will make amends. Near here is my cottage, where I have fresh milk and most delicious cheese, and various fruits now in season, no less pleasant to the sight than to the taste.'

Chapter LII. *Of the Quarrel between Don Quixote and the Goatherd, with the rare Adventure of the Penitents, which he successfully achieved by the sweat of his brow.*

THE goatherd's tale much delighted all who heard it, especially the canon, who was particularly interested in the manner of its telling, which made the narrator appear more like a polished courtier than a rustic goatherd. In fact he remarked that the priest was right when he said that the mountains bred scholars. The whole company complimented Eugenio, but Don Quixote showed himself the most liberal of all in this respect, and said:

'I promise you, brother goatherd, that were I in the position to be able to embark on any adventure, I would immediately set about bringing yours to a happy conclusion. I would deliver Leandra from the nunnery, where there can be no doubt she is kept against her will, in despite of the abbess and all who might oppose me. Then I should place her in your hands, to be dealt with according to your will and pleasure – observing, however, the laws of chivalry, which command that no violence be done to a damsel. Yet

I trust in our Lord God that one malicious enchanter may not be so powerful that another better-intentioned enchanter may not prevail over him. And when that time comes I promise you my favour and aid, as I am bound to do by my profession, which is none other than to succour the weak and the distressed.'

The goatherd stared at him and, seeing Don Quixote so ragged and ill-favoured, asked the barber in astonishment who his neighbour was: 'Sir, who is that man who looks so strange and talks so oddly?'

'Why, who should it be,' answered the barber, 'but the famous Don Quixote de la Mancha, the redresser of injuries, the righter of wrongs, the protector of damsels, the terror of giants, and the victor of battles?'

'That sounds to me like the stuff in books about knights-errant,' observed the goatherd. 'They did all these things you say this fellow does, though I take it that either your worship is joking, or the gentlemen must have some of the rooms in his brain vacant.'

'You are a very great rascal,' cried Don Quixote at this point, 'and it is you that is vacant and deficient. For I am a good deal fuller than ever that whore's daughter, the whore that bore you, was.'

As he spoke, he took up a loaf which lay beside him and hit the goatherd full in the face with it, with such force that he flattened his nose. But the goatherd did not see the joke and, finding himself thus damaged in good earnest, took no account of the carpet or the table-cloth or the diners round it, but jumped upon Don Quixote and, grasping him round the neck with both hands, would no doubt have choked him if Sancho Panza had not come up at this point. Seizing him by the shoulders, the squire threw him on to the tablecloth, breaking the plates, smashing the cups, and upsetting and scattering everything on it. Then Don Quixote, finding himself free, rushed to get on top of the goatherd who, with his face covered in blood from Sancho's kicks, was feeling about on all fours for a knife off the cloth to take some bloody vengeance. But this the canon and the priest prevented. However, with some help from the barber, the goatherd managed to get Don Quixote down, and rained such a shower of blows on him that the knight's face poured blood as freely as his. The canon and the priest were bursting with laughter; the troopers danced for joy, and everyone cheered them on, as men do at a dog-fight. Only Sancho Panza was in despair, because he could not get himself loose from one of the canon's servants, who was preventing him from helping his master. In the end when everyone was enjoying the sport except the two combatants, who were worrying one another, they heard the call of a trumpet, so mournful that they turned their faces in the direction from which it seemed to come. But the person was who most excited at the sound was Don Quixote who, although much against his will, lay underneath the goatherd, pretty well bruised and battered.

'Brother Demon,' he cried to his enemy; 'for it is impossible that you can be anything else, since you have the valour and strength to subdue mine – I pray you, let us call a truce, for just one hour. For the dolorous sound of that trumpet which reaches our ears seems to call me to some new adventure.'

The goatherd, who was now tired of pummelling and being pummelled, let him go at once; and Don Quixote stood up, turning his face too in the direction of the sound, and suddenly saw a number of men dressed in white after the fashion of penitents, descending a little hill.

The fact was that in that year the clouds had denied the earth their moisture, and in all the villages of that district they were making processions, rogations and penances, to pray God to vouchsafe His mercy and send them rain. And to this end the people of a village close by were coming in procession to a holy shrine which stood on a hill beside this valley. At the sight of the strange dress of these penitents Don Quixote failed to call to mind the many times he must have seen the like before, but imagined that this was material of adventure, and that it concerned him alone, as a knight errant, to engage in it. And he was confirmed in this idea by mistaking an image they were carrying, swathed in mourning, for some noble lady whom these villainous and unmannerly scoundrels were forcibly abducting. Now, scarcely had this thought come into his head, than he ran very quickly up to Rocinante, who was grazing nearby and, taking off the bridle and shield which hung by the pommel, he had him bitted in a second. Then, calling to Sancho for his sword, he mounted and, bracing on his shield, cried in a loud voice to everyone present:

'Now, valiant company, you will see how important it is to have knights in the world, who profess the order of knight errantry. Now, I say, you will see, by the freeing of this good lady who is being borne off captive, what value should be set on knights errant.'

As he spoke, he dug his heels into Rocinante, for he had no spurs, and at a canter – for we do not hear in all this authentic history that Rocinante ever went at a full gallop – rode to meet the penitents, although the priest, the canon, and the barber tried to stop him. But they could not do so, nor could even Sancho keep him back by calling:

'Where are you going, Don Quixote? What demons have you in your heart that incite you to assault our Catholic faith? Devil take me! Look, it's a procession of penitents, and that lady they're carrying upon the bier is the most blessed image of the spotless Virgin. Look out, sir, what you're doing, for this time you've made a real mistake.'

Sancho laboured in vain, for his master was so set on reaching the sheeted figures and freeing the lady in black, that he did not hear a word; and, if he had heard, he would not have turned back, even at the King's command. Coming up, then, to the procession, he halted Rocinante, who already wanted a little rest, and cried out in a hoarse and angry voice:

'You who, perhaps because you are evil, keep your faces covered, stop and listen to what I am going to say to you.'

The first to stop were the men carrying the image, and one of the four priests who were chanting the litanies, observing Don Quixote's strange appearance, Rocinante's leanness, and other ludicrous details which he noted in our knight, answered him by saying:

'Worthy brother, if you wish to say anything to us, say it quickly, for these brethren of ours are lashing their flesh, and we cannot possibly stop to hear anything, unless it is so brief that you can say it in two words.'

'I will say it in one,' replied Don Quixote, 'and it is this: Now, this very moment, you must set this beautiful lady free, for her mournful appearance and tears clearly show that you are carrying her off against her will, and that you have done her some notable wrong. I, who was born into the world to redress such injuries, will not consent to your advancing one step farther unless you give her the liberty she desires and deserves.'

At this speech all his hearers concluded that Don Quixote must be some madman, and began to laugh most heartily. Their laughter was like gunpowder thrown on to Don Quixote's anger. For, without another word, he drew his sword and attacked the litter. Then one of the bearers left the burden to his companions, and came out to meet the knight, brandishing a forked stick or pole, which they used to prop the litter up while they rested. And though Don Quixote dealt it a heavy sword stroke, which cut it in three, with the remaining third which remained in his hand he dealt the poor knight such a blow on the shoulder of his sword arm that his shield was powerless to protect him against the peasant's attack, and down he came to the ground in a sad state. Now when Sancho Panza, who came panting at his heels, saw him down, he called out to his assailant not to strike another blow, for his master was a knight under a spell and had done no harm to anyone in all the days of his life. But what stopped the countryman, however, was not Sancho's shouts, but his seeing that Don Quixote stirred neither hand nor foot; and so, in the belief that he had killed him, he hastily tucked up his robe into his belt and started to run across the country like a deer.

By this time all Don Quixote's company had reached the place where he lay; but when the men in the procession saw them come running up, and with them the troopers with their cross-bows, they were afraid of some mischief and made a ring round the image. Then raising their hoods and grasping their scourges, while the priests wielded their candlesticks, they awaited the assault, determined to defend themselves and even, if they could, to attack their assailants. But by good luck things turned out better than they expected, for all that Sancho did was to throw himself upon his master's body and break into the most doleful and ridiculous lament in all the world, in the belief that he was dead. Our priest was recognized by another in the procession; and this recognition calmed the apprehensions of both parties. The first priest gave the second a brief account of Don Quixote. Then he and the whole crowd of penitents went to see if the poor knight was dead, and heard Sancho Panza proclaim with tears in his eyes:

'O flower of chivalry, whose well-spent life one single blow of a stick has cut short! O glory of your race, honour and credit to all La Mancha, and to the whole world besides, which, now that you are here no longer, will be overrun by malefactors who will no longer fear chastisement for their iniquities! O liberal beyond all Alexanders, since for only eight months' service you have given me the best isle surrounded and encircled by the sea! O humble to the proud and arrogant to the humble, undertaker of perils, sufferer of affronts, enamoured without reason, imitator of the virtuous, scourge of the wicked, enemy of evildoers, in a word, knight errant, which is the highest that man can desire!'

Sancho's groans and lamentations brought Don Quixote back to consciousness, and the first words he uttered were: 'He who lives absent from you, sweetest Dulcinea, is subject to greater calamities than these. Help me, Sancho my friend, to get up upon the enchanted car, since I am not fit to burden Rocinante's saddle, for all this shoulder of mine is shattered.'

'I will, sir, with the greatest of pleasure,' replied Sancho. 'Let us return to our village with these gentlemen who wish you well, and there we'll plan another expedition, which may bring us more profit and fame.'

'You are right, Sancho,' replied Don Quixote. 'It will be highly prudent to wait till the malign influence of the stars, which now reigns, has passed over us.'

The canon, the priest and the barber commended him for this resolution, and when they had enjoyed Sancho Panza's simplicities to the full, they placed Don Quixote on the cart, as before. Then the procession formed up once more, and went on its way. The goatherd took his leave of the company, and when the troopers declined to go any farther, the priest paid them what he owed them. The canon then begged the priest to let him know what might happen to Don Quixote – whether he was cured of his madness or remained in it – and with this took his leave. Here in fact they all divided and went their several ways, there remaining only the priest and the barber, Don Quixote, Panza and the good Rocinante, who bore himself throughout all this experience as patiently as his master.

The waggoner yoked his oxen and settled Don Quixote on a truss of hay. Then he followed the priest's directions and took the road, travelling at his usual deliberate pace, till at the end of six days they reached Don Quixote's village. There they arrived at midday, and as it happened to be a Sunday all the people were in the market-place when Don Quixote's cart passed through. They all rushed to see what was in it and, when they recognized their fellow-townsman, they stood in amazement. Then a boy ran off to tell the knight's housekeeper and niece the news that their master and uncle had come back, lean and sallow, and lying on a pile of hay on an ox-wagon. It was pitiful to hear the cries that these two good ladies raised, the slaps they gave themselves, and the curses which they launched afresh against his accursed books of knight errantry; all of which were renewed when they saw the knight enter the house.

At the news of Don Quixote's arrival Sancho Panza's wife ran up, for she knew by this time that her husband had gone with him to serve as his squire. And as soon as she saw Sancho her first inquiry was after his ass, to which Sancho replied that he was in a better state of health than his master.

'Thanks be to God,' she replied, 'for His goodness. But tell me now, my friend, what profit have you got out of your squireships? Have you brought me a skirt? Or some pretty shoes for the children?'

'I haven't brought any of that, wife,' said Sancho, 'although I bring other things of greater value and importance.'

'I'm very glad of that,' replied his wife. 'Show me these things of greater value and importance, my friend. The sight of them would be a joy to this heart of mine, for I have been most sad and sorrowful all the ages you have been away.'

'I'll show you them at home, wife,' said Panza. 'Be satisfied for the present. But if God permits us to go on our travels again, in search of adventures, you will soon see me a count or governor of an isle – and not of one of these local isles, but the best that can be found.'

'Heaven grant you may, husband, for we're in great need of it. But tell me, what is this about isles? I don't understand you.'

'Honey is not for the ass's mouth,' replied Sancho. 'You will see in due course, wife, and you'll be surprised when you hear all your vassals calling you "Your Ladyship".'

'What's that you're saying, Sancho, about Ladyships, isles and vassals?' asked Juana Panza, for that was the name of Sancho's wife – not that they were related by blood but because it is usual in La Mancha for wives to take their husband's surnames.

'Don't fret yourself, Juana, and be in such a hurry to know everything. It's enough that I'm telling you the truth, so shut your mouth. But there's one thing I can say to you in passing, that there's nothing so pleasant in the world for an honest man as to be squire to a knight errant, that seeks adventures. It's true that most of them one finds don't turn out as much to one's liking as a man could wish, for out of every hundred you meet ninety-nine generally turn out cross and unlucky. I know it by experience, for I've come off blanket-tossed from some and bruised from others. But, for all that, it's a nice thing to be looking out for incidents, crossing mountains, searching woods, climbing rocks, visiting castles, and lodging in inns at your pleasure, with the devil a farthing to pay.'

While this conversation was taking place between Sancho Panza and Juana Panza his wife, Don Quixote's housekeeper and niece received him, undressed him, and laid him in his ancient bed, where he stared at them with eyes askance and could not understand where he was. The priest charged the niece to look after her uncle very carefully and to keep good watch that he did not escape again, telling her all the trouble they had had in bringing him home. At this, the two women set up their cries anew. Once more they burst out in abuse of his books of knight errantry and implored Heaven to plunge the authors of so many lies and absurdities into the bottomless pit. In fact they were distracted, and frightened that as soon as their master and uncle felt a little better they would find him missing once more. And events fell out as they feared.

But though the author of this history has anxiously and diligently inquired after Don Quixote's exploits on his third expedition, he has been able to discover no account of them, at least from any authentic documents. Though fame has preserved a tradition in La Mancha that the third time Don Quixote left his home he went to Saragossa, and took part in some famous jousts in that city, and that adventures there befell him worthy of his valour and of his sound intelligence. Our author, in fact, would have been able to learn nothing of his mortal end, nor would he even have learnt of it, if good fortune had not thrown an aged doctor in his path. This man had in his possession a leaden box which, so he said, he had found among the ruined foundations of an ancient hermitage, that was being rebuilt. In this box he had found some parchments written

in the Gothic script but in Castilian verse, which contained many
of the knight's exploits and dwelt upon the beauty of Dulcinea del
Toboso, the shape of Rocinante, the fidelity of Sancho Panza, and
the burial of this same Don Quixote, together with various epitaphs and eulogies on his life and habits. Such of these as could be
read and understood the trustworthy author of this original and
matchless history has set down here, and he asks no recompense
from his readers for the immense labours it has cost him to search
and ransack all the archives of La Mancha in order to drag it into
the light. All that he asks is that they shall accord it such credit as
intelligent men usually give to those books of chivalry which are so
highly valued in the world. With this he will feel both rewarded, and
satisfied, and will be encouraged to seek and discover other histories, perhaps less authentic than this one, but at least as ingenious
and entertaining.

The first words written on the parchment found in the leaden
box were these:

THE ACADEMICIANS OF ARGAMASILLA,
A TOWN OF LA MANCHA, ON THE LIFE AND DEATH OF
THE VALOROUS DON QUIXOTE DE LA MANCHA,
HOC SCRIPSERUNT.

MUMBO JUMBO, ACADEMICIAN OF ARGAMASILLA,
UPON THE TOMB OF DON QUIXOTE

Epitaph

The dunderhead who for La Mancha won
More trophies than did Jason for his Creta,
The wit whose weathercock was over-fine,
When something broad and blunter were far meeter;
    The arm which from Cathay to far Gaeta
Broadened the boundaries of his mighty reign;
The Muse, none dreadfuller and none discreeter,
That carved on brazen plate the poet's line;
    He that the Amadises far outstripped
And made the gallant Galaor look a fool,
Leaving them both in love and war well whipped,
    And made the Belianises to quail,
He who on Rocinante erring went
Lies now beneath this cold stone monument.

THE GOOD COMPANION, ACADEMICIAN OF ARGAMASILLA, IN LAUDEM DULCINEAE DEL TOBOSO

Sonnet

She that you see here, stout and heavy featured,
High-bosomed, with a rather martial mien,
Is Dulcinea, El Toboso's queen,
Of whom the great Don Quixote was enraptured.
   For her it was he travelled far and wide
Over the great Brown Hills to the renowned
Montiel plain, and down to the grass-crowned
Aranjuez gardens, wearily he trod.
   The fault was Rocinante's! O hard doom
Of this Manchegan dame and errant knight
Unconquered! Dying in her beauty's bloom,
   Of tender years, quenched is her beauty's light,
And he whose fame the inscribed marble proves
Could not escape the wrath and wiles of love.

WHIMSICAL WILL, A VERY WITTY ACADEMICIAN OF ARGAMASILLA, IN PRAISE OF ROCINANTE, DON QUIXOTE DE LA MANCHA'S STEED

Sonnet

Upon the lofty throne of adamant
Trodden by mighty Mars's bloody heel,
The mad Manchegan did his standard plant,
Hanging his arms and that sharp blade of steel,
   With which he hacked, wasted and cleft in twain.
New feats of arms, for which art must devise
A style to suit the newest paladin.
And if Gaul prides herself on Amadis,
   Whose brave descendants have ennobled Greece,
And filled it full of triumphs and of fame,
To-day Bellona crowns Don Quixote's brows.
   Let high La Mancha ne'er forget his name,
Who rode on Rocinante, braver far
Than gallant Bayard or steel Brillador.

THE JOKER, ACADEMICIAN OF ARGAMASILLA, TO SANCHO PANZA

Sonnet

Here Sancho Panza lies, in body small,
But yet, strange miracle, in valour great,
As guileless squire and simple, truth to tell,
As in this world, I swear, lived ever yet.
    Of being a count he came within an ace,
Had not this wicked century conspired
Malignantly to harm him; for an ass
Insults and injuries are never spared.
    An ass he rode – it shames me to record –
This meek squire meekly following behind
The mild steed Rocinante and his lord.
    How vain are all the hopes of humankind!
How sweet their promises of quiet seem,
And yet they end in shadows, smoke and dream.

THE HOBGOBLIN, ACADEMICIAN OF ARGAMASILLA, ON DON QUIXOTE'S TOMB

Epitaph

Here lies the knight in death.
Well bruised and ill errant, he
Was borne by Rocinante
O'er road and track and path.
    Beside him Sancho's laid,
The foolish Sancho Panza,
As faithful as e'er man saw
One of the squirish trade.

DING-DONG, ACADEMICIAN OF ARGAMASILLA, ON THE TOMB OF DULCINEA DEL TOBOSO

Epitaph

Here Dulcinea's laid,
Once of flesh so lusty.
Ashes now cold and dusty
By ugly death she's made.

> Of godly parentage
> And fairish stock she came.
> She was great Quixote's flame,
> And glory of her village.

These were such verses as could be deciphered. The rest, as the characters were worm-eaten, were entrusted to a university scholar to guess out their meaning. We are informed that he has done so, at the cost of many nights of study and much labour, and that he intends to publish them, which gives us hope of a third expedition of Don Quixote.

Forse altri cantera con miglior plettro.

END OF THE FIRST PART

THE ADVENTURES OF
DON QUIXOTE

THE SECOND PART

To the Count of Lemos

SOME *days ago, on sending your Excellency my Comedies, printed before they were played, I said, if I remember rightly, that Don Quixote was waiting with his boots ready spurred to go and kiss your Excellency's hands. Now I announce him booted and on the way, and if he arrives I think I shall have done your Excellency some service; for much pressure has been put on me from countless directions to send him out, in order to purge the disgust and nausea caused by another Don Quixote who has been running about the world masquerading as the second part.*

But the personage who has evinced the greatest longing for him is the Emperor of China, who sent me a letter by express a month ago, begging me, or more correctly imploring me, to send the knight to him, for he wanted to found a college for the teaching of Castilian, and intended The History of Don Quixote *to be the textbook used there. Furthermore he informed me that I was to be rector of the college. I asked the bearer whether his Majesty had given him anything for me by way of contribution to my expenses. He answered that His Majesty had not so much as thought of it. 'Then, brother,' I replied, 'you can go back to your China at ten o'clock or twenty o'clock or at whatever hour you can get away, for I am not in good enough health to undertake so long a voyage. What is more, as well as being in ill health, I am very short of money and, Emperor for Emperor and Monarch for Monarch, I hold by the great Count de Lemos in Naples; for, without all these petty diplomas and benefices, he keeps me, shelters me, and does me more favours than I can desire.'*

With this I dismissed him; and with this I take my leave, offering your Excellency The Travels of Persiles and Sigismunda, *a book which I shall finish within four months, Deo volente, and which is sure to be either the worst or the best written of book s of entertainment in our tongue — but I must say that I repent of having said the worst. For, according to the opinions of my friends, it will attain the highest possible excellence. Come, your Excellency, with all the health we can wish you; Persiles shall be ready to kiss your hands, and I your feet, as your Excellency's servant, which I am.*

   From Madrid.
     The last day of October 1615.
      Your Excellency's servant

       MIGUEL DE CERVANTES SAAVEDRA

The Adventures of Don Quixote

THE SECOND PART

PROLOGUE

G OD bless me, how eagerly you must now be awaiting this prologue, illustrious, or maybe plebeian reader, in the expectation
of finding in it vengeance, wranglings and railings against the author
of the second *Don Quixote* – I mean the one said to have been be-
gotten at Tordesillas and born at Tarragona. But, in truth, I am not
going to give you that satisfaction, for though injuries awaken
anger in the meekest hearts, in mine the rule must admit of an exception. You would like me to call him ass, fool and bully; but I have
not even a thought of doing so. Let his sin be his punishment – with
his bread let him eat it, and there let it rest. What I cannot help resenting is that he upbraids me for being old and crippled, as if it
were in my power to stop the passage of time, or as if the loss of
my hand had taken place in some tavern, and not on the greatest
occasion which any age, past, present, or future, ever saw or can
ever hope to see. If my wounds do not shine in the eyes of such as
look on them, they are at least respected by those who know where
they were acquired; for a soldier looks better dead in battle than
safe in flight. And so firmly am I of this opinion that even if now I
could bring about the impossible, I would still rather have taken
part in that prodigious action than be at present whole of my
wounds without ever having fought there. The wounds a soldier
shows on his face and on his breast are stars to guide others to the
heaven of honour and to create in them a noble emulation. Let it
be remembered that it is not with grey hairs that one writes, but
with the mind, which generally ripens with the years. I also resented his calling me envious, and explaining to me, as if I were
ignorant, what sort of thing envy is; though, in very truth, of the

two kinds of envy, I know only the righteous, noble and well-meaning sort. And that being the case I am not likely to persecute any priest, particularly if he is a familiar of the Holy Office to boot. And if it was on behalf of a certain person that he wrote what he did, he is absolutely mistaken; for I revere that man's genius, and admire his works and his virtuous and unceasing industry. I am indeed grateful, however, to this kind author for saying that my *Novels* are rather satirical than 'exemplary', though they are good – for they could not be good if they were not good in every respect.

You will agree, I think, that I am showing great restraint and keeping well within the bounds of modesty, out of a feeling that one should not heap affliction on the afflicted, and that the affliction from which this gentleman suffers must certainly be a great one, since he dare not appear in the open field and under a clear sky, but hides his name and disguises his country, as if he were guilty of the crime of high treason. If by any chance you come to know him, tell him from me that I do not consider myself aggrieved. For I know very well what the temptations of the Devil are, and that one of his greatest is to put it into a man's head that he can write and print a book, and gain both money and fame by it; to prove which I should like you, in your pleasant and witty way, to tell him this story:

There was a madman in Seville who was taken with the oddest and craziest notion that ever a madman had in all the world. It was this: he made a tube out of a cane, sharpened at the end, and catching a dog, in the street or elsewhere, he would hold down one of its hind legs with one foot and lift the other one up with his hand. Next, fitting his tube to the right place, he would blow into it, as best he could, till he had made the dog as round as a ball. Then, holding it up in this way, he would give it a couple of slaps on the belly and let it go, saying to the bystanders, – and there were always plenty: 'Your worships will perhaps be thinking that it is an easy thing to blow up a dog?' – Does your worship think it is an easy thing to write a book?

And if the story does not suit him, you can tell him this one, friendly reader, which is also about a madman and a dog:

In Cordova there was another madman, whose habit it was to carry on his head a piece of marble slab or a stone of considerable weight; and when he met with an unwary dog, he would go up

close behind it and drop the weight plump on top of it. The dog
would fly into a panic and bark and yelp up three streets without
stopping. Now it happened once that amongst his victims was a
hatter's dog, much beloved by its master. The stone came down and
struck its head, and the battered beast set up a howl. Its master,
however, saw the deed and flew into a great rage. He seized a yard
measure, came after the madman, and beat him till he had not a
whole bone in his body, crying out at every blow he gave him:
'You dog, you thief! My pointer! Didn't you see, you cruel wretch,
that my dog was a pointer?' And with frequent repetitions of the
word 'pointer' he sent the madman off beaten to a pulp. The idiot
learnt his lesson and went away, and did not show himself in public
for more than a month. But at the end of this time he reappeared
with an even heavier weight, and would go up to a dog and stare
at it most intently. Then, without the will or the pluck to drop his
stone he would say: 'It's a pointer. Look out!'

In fact, he called all the dogs he met pointers, whether they were
mastiffs or curs; and so he never dropped his stone on one again.
Perhaps the same thing may happen to this story-teller. He may
never venture again to discharge the load of his wit in the form of a
book, for bad books are harder than rocks.

Tell him too that I do not care a straw for his threat to deprive
me of my profit by means of his book. For to adapt the words of
the famous farce *La Perendenga*, my answer is: Long live my
master the alderman, and Christ for us all. Long live the great
Count de Lemos, whose Christian charity and famous generosity
keep me on my feet despite all the blows of my scant fortune. And
long live the supreme beneficence of His Eminence of Toledo, Don
Bernardo de Sandoval y Rojas, even though there may be no more
printing-presses in the world, and even though more books be
printed against me than there are letters in Mingo Revulgo's
couplets. These two princes have received no adulation nor other
kind of flattery from me, but out of their goodness alone have taken
on themselves to do me kindnesses and favours; by which I consider myself happier and richer than if fortune had placed me on
her pinnacle by the ordinary means. The poor man may attain to
honour, but not the wicked. Poverty can cloud nobility, but not
obscure it altogether. Let virtue but show some light of her own,

even though it be through the straits and chinks of penury, and it will come to be valued by lofty and noble spirits, and so win favour. Say no more to him, and I will say no more to you, but only ask you to notice that this second part of *Don Quixote*, which I place before you, is cut by the same craftsman and from the same cloth as the first, and that in it I present you with the knight at greater length and, in the end, dead and buried. Let no one, therefore, presume to raise fresh testimonies to him, for the past ones are sufficient. Suffice it that an honest man has told the story of his amusing follies, and has no wish to take the subject up again. For however good things are an abundance brings down the price, and scarcity, even in bad things, confers a certain value.

I forgot to tell you that you may look out for *Persiles*, which I am just finishing, and the second part of *Galatea*.

Chapter I. Of what passed between the Priest and the Barber in the matter of the Knight's illness.

CIDE HAMETE BENENGELI recounts, in the second part of this history concerning Don Quixote's third expedition, that the priest and the barber did not see him for almost a month, for fear of reviving past events and recalling them to his memory. But all the same, they did not give up visiting his niece and his housekeeper, and charged them to be careful to treat him well, and to give him such food as was comforting and good for his heart and his brain, from which organs they had good reason to believe all his misfortunes arose. The two women declared that they were doing so, and would lavish on their master every possible care and kindness, for they had noticed in him occasional signs of returning sanity. The two friends received this news with great satisfaction, for it seemed to prove that they had done right in bringing him back enchanted in the ox-waggon, as is related in the last chapter of the first part of this great and authentic history. So they decided to visit him and test his recovery, though they hardly expected to find him cured, and agreed not to touch in any way on knight-errantry, so as not to run the danger of bursting open wounds which were still so tender.

They paid him a visit at last, and found him sitting up in bed, dressed in a thick green flannel waistcoat with a red Toledo cap, and so lean and withered that he seemed to be nothing but mummy-flesh. They were very well received by him; and on their questioning him about his health, he gave them a most intelligent account of it in very well-chosen language. In the course of their conversation they happened to discuss the principles of statecraft – as they are called – and methods of government, correcting this abuse and condemning that, reforming one custom and abolishing another, each one of the three setting up as a fresh legislator, a modern Lycurgus or a brand-new Solon. To such a degree did they refashion the commonwealth that it was as if they had taken it to the forge and brought away a different one. And Don Quixote spoke with such intelligence on all the subjects they handled that the two examiners had no doubt whatever that he was quite recovered and in complete possession of his wits.

His niece and his housekeeper were present at this discussion, and could not thank God enough on seeing their master so sound in the head. But the priest changed his first plan, which was not to touch on the subject of chivalry, and decided to make a thorough test whether Don Quixote's recovery was real or false. So, gradually, he worked round to some news which had come from Madrid, and told the knight among other things that it was considered certain that the Turk was going to make a descent with a huge fleet, but that his purpose was obscure, and no one knew where this mighty storm would burst. All Christendom, he said, was in alarm from that same dread which almost every year calls us to arms; and His Majesty had fortified the coasts of Naples, Sicily and the island of Malta.

'His Majesty has acted like a most prudent warrior,' answered Don Quixote, 'in fortifying his Estates in time, so that the enemy may not find him unprepared. But if he were to ask my advice, I would counsel him to take one precaution which is far from occurring to His Majesty at present.'

And the moment the priest heard this he said to himself: 'God protect you, my poor Don Quixote; for you seem to me to be throwing yourself from the high peak of your madness into the deep abyss of your folly.'

But the barber, who had already had the same thought as the priest, asked Don Quixote the nature of the precaution which he proposed they should adopt; for perhaps it was suitable to be added to the long list of impertinent projects commonly set before princes.

'Mine, Master Shaver,' said Don Quixote, 'will not be impertinent, but most pertinent.'

'I don't say that it is,' replied the barber, 'but experience has shown that nearly all the plans presented to his Majesty are either impracticable or ridiculous, or would do positive harm either to the King or his kingdom.'

'But mine,' answered Don Quixote, 'is neither impracticable nor ridiculous, but the easiest, the most proper, and the subtlest and simplest that could occur to any planner's imagination.'

'Your worship is slow in telling it to us, Don Quixote,' said the priest.

'I do not wish to tell it here at present,' said Don Quixote, 'for it to reach the ears of the Lords of the Council to-morrow morning, and for someone else to get the thanks and reward for my pains.'

'For myself,' said the barber, 'I give you my word, here before God, not to repeat what your worship says to King or Rook or earthly man – an oath which I learned from the Ballad of the Priest, who warned the King in the prologue against the thief who had robbed him of a hundred doubloons and his ambling mule.'

'I do not know the story,' said Don Quixote, 'but I know that the oath is a good one, because I believe that the barber is an honest man.'

'Even if he were not,' said the priest, 'I will go bail for him, and guarantee that he will no more speak of this matter than if he were dumb, upon pain of whatever penalty the court may provide.'

'And for your worship? Who will vouch for you, Master Priest?' asked Don Quixote.

'My profession,' replied the priest, 'which is to keep secrets.'

'In Heaven's name, then!' exclaimed Don Quixote, 'what more is there for His Majesty to do but to command by public crier all the knights errant who are wandering about Spain to assemble at the capital on a fixed day. For if only half a dozen came, might there not be one amongst them who would be sufficient in himself to destroy all the power of the Turk? Listen, your worships, and follow me. Is it, by any chance, anything new for a single knight errant to slaughter an army of two hundred men, as if the whole lot of them had one single throat or were made of marzipan? Tell me, now, how many histories are there full of such marvels? If there were living to-day – to my misfortune, though I will not say to any one else's – the famous Don Belianis or any of the innumerable descendants of Amadis of Gaul! If a single one of them were alive to-day and were to confront the Turk, the infidel would come off pretty badly, I promise you. But God will take care of His people and send one, who may not be as manly as the knights errant of old, but at least will not be behind them in spirit. God understands me, and I say no more.'

'Oh dear!' cried the niece at this point, 'may I die if my master doesn't want to turn knight errant again.'

To which Don Quixote replied: 'A knight errant I shall die, and let the Turk make his descent or ascent whenever he will, and with whatever power he can. For I say once more, God understands my meaning.'

At this the barber put in: 'Permit me, your worships, to tell you a short tale about something that happened at Seville. It comes so pat to the point that I'm itching to tell it to you.'

Don Quixote and the priest consented, and the others paid attention as he began thus:

'In the madhouse at Seville was a man whose relations had put him there because he had gone out of his mind. He was a graduate in common law of Osuna, but even if he had been of Salamanca, as many think, he would have been just as mad. This graduate, at the end of some years of confinement, persuaded himself that he was sane and in his right mind, and in this conviction wrote to the Archbishop, imploring him earnestly and in well-chosen language to order his release from the misery in which he lived, since by the mercy of God he had recovered his lost wits; for his relations kept him there to enjoy his share of the estate and, despite the clearest evidence, would have him stay mad till his death. The Archbishop was impressed by his many sensible and intelligent letters, and ordered one of his chaplains to find out from the governor of the madhouse whether what the graduate wrote to him was true. He asked him to speak to the madman and, if he appeared to be in his senses, to set him at liberty. The chaplain called, and the governor informed him that the man was still mad; and that, though he often talked like a person of great intelligence, in the end he would break out into wild talk, just as crazy and as persistent as his previous conversation had been sensible. This he would discover by speaking to him. The chaplain decided to do so, and on visiting the madman, talked with him for an hour and more, and in all this time he never said anything crazy or queer. On the contrary, he spoke so soberly that the chaplain was forced to believe that he was sane. Among other things the madman said was that the governor was hostile to him because he did not want to lose the presents his relations made him for saying that he was still mad, though with lucid intervals. His greatest stumbling-block, he said, in his misfortune was his great wealth. For, to enjoy it, his enemies misjudged him, and threw doubt on the mercy our Lord had done him in restoring him from a beast to a man. In fact he spoke in such a way as to throw suspicion on the governor, and to make his relatives appear covetous and inhuman, and himself sane. So the chaplain decided to take him to the Archbishop, so that he could discover the truth of the matter for himself. In all good faith, then, the excellent chaplain begged the governor to give orders for the graduate to be given back the clothes in which he had arrived. But the governor once more bade him take care what he was doing, for there was no doubt at all that the graduate was still mad. However, the governor's warning could not prevail upon the chaplain to leave the madman behind. So, seeing that it was the Archbishop's order, the governor obeyed, and they dressed the madman in his own clothes, which were new and decent. Now, when he found himself stripped of his madman's dress and clothed in the garb of sanity, he begged the chaplain out of charity to let him go and take leave of his mad companions. The chaplain said that he would like to come with him and see the lunatics who were lodged there. So they went upstairs, accompanied by some other people who were about, and the madman went up to a cage in which was a raging lunatic, who was calm and quiet at the time, however, and addressed him thus:

'"My brother, think if you have any commands for me. I am going home. For God in His infinite goodness and mercy has been pleased to restore me to my senses, little though I deserve it. Now I am sane and in my right mind, for to God's power nothing is impossible. Put great hope and trust in Him; for, since He has restored me to my former state, He will restore you too, if you have faith in Him. I will send you some delicacies to eat, and be sure you eat them; since I must tell you that in my opinion our madness arises from our having our stomachs empty and our brains full of wind. Take heart! Take heart, for despondency in our miseries weakens our health and brings on death."

'Another madman in another cage opposite the raging lunatic's overheard all that the graduate said and, getting up from an old mat on which he was lying naked to the skin, asked in a loud voice who this man was who was going away sane and in his right mind.

The graduate replied: "It is I, brother, who am going. I have no need to stay here any more, for which I give infinite thanks to Heaven, which has done me this great favour."

'"Mind what you say, graduate, and don't let the Devil deceive you," answered the madman. "Rest your feet and stay nice and quiet at home, and you'll spare yourself the return journey."

'"I know that I am well," replied the graduate, "and shall not have to travel the rounds again."

'"You well!" cried the madman. "Good! we shall see. God be with you! But I vow to Jupiter, whose majesty I represent on earth, that for the single sin which Seville is committing to-day by releasing you from this house and treating you as a sane man, I shall inflict such punishment on her as shall be remembered to all eternity, Amen. Don't you know, paltry little graduate, that I have the power to do so? For, let me tell you, I am Jupiter Tonans, and hold in my hands the flaming thunderbolts with which I can and do menace and destroy the world. But with one punishment alone I mean to chastise this ignorant city: for three whole years I will not rain on it, nor on all the surrounding districts; which time is to be reckoned from the instant I utter this threat. You free, you sane, you in your right mind, and I mad, and sick, and in chains ...? I would as soon think of raining as hang myself."

'The madman's loud speech called the attention of the bystanders, but our graduate turned to our chaplain and, seizing him by the hands, reassured him: "Do not be concerned, my dear sir. Take no notice of what this madman says. For if he is Jupiter and will not rain, I am Neptune, the father and god of the waters, and I will rain as often as I please, and whenever it is necessary."

'To which the chaplain replied: "All the same, Lord Neptune, it would not be right to annoy Lord Jupiter. Your worship may remain at home, and we will come back for you another day, when we have more time."

'The governor and the bystanders burst out laughing, which made the chaplain rather ashamed. Then they stripped the graduate and he stayed behind. And that is the end of my story.'

'So that, Master Barber,' said Don Quixote, 'is the story which came so pat to the point that you had to tell it? O, Master Shaver, Master Shaver, how blind is the man who cannot see through a hair-sieve! Is it possible that your worship does not know that comparisons between wit and wit, valour and valour, beauty and beauty, birth and birth, are always odious and resented? I, Master Barber, am not Neptune, the God of the waters, and I am not trying to make anyone believe me wise when I am not. I am only at pains to convince the world of its error in not reviving that most happy age in which the order of chivalry flourished. But our depraved times do not deserve to enjoy so great a blessing as did those in which knights errant undertook and carried on their shoulders the defence of kingdoms, the protection of damsels, the succour of orphans and wards, the chastisement of the proud, and the rewarding of the humble. Most of our knights nowadays prefer to rustle in damasks, brocades, and other rich clothes that they wear, than in armoured coats of mail. There are no knights now to sleep in the open, exposed to the rigour of the skies, in full armour from head to foot. There is no one now to snatch a nap, as they say, leaning on his lance and with his feet in the stirrups, as knights errant did of old. There is no one now to come out of a wood and go into the mountains, and from there tramp a waste and desert shore, most often stormy and tempestuous, and to find there on the beach a little boat without oars, sail, mast, or tackle, and with undaunted heart to fling himself in and commit himself to the implacable waves of the deep sea, which sometimes toss him to the sky and sometimes cast him down to the abyss. Then, exposing his breast to the irresistible tempest, he finds himself, when he least dreams of it, more than nine thousand miles from the place where he embarked; and leaping on to a remote and unknown shore, he undergoes experiences worthy to be inscribed not on parchment but on brass. Now sloth triumphs over industry, idleness over labour, vice over virtue, presumption over valour, and theory over the practice of arms, which only lived and flourished in the golden age and among knights errant. If I am not right, tell me, who was more virtuous and more valiant than the renowned Amadis of Gaul? Who was wiser than Palmerin of England? Who more approachable and skilful than Tirante the White? Who more gallant than Lisuarte of Greece? Who gave and received more sword-thrusts than Don Belianis? Who was more dauntless than Perion of Gaul, or readier to face peril than Felixmarte of Hyrcania, or more sincere than Esplandian? Who was more impetuous than Don Cirongilio of Thrace? Who was more fearless than Rodamonte? Who was more prudent than King Sobrino? Who was bolder than Reynald? Who more invincible than Roland? And who gayer and more courteous than Ruggiero, from whom the present-day Dukes of Ferrara are descended, according to Turpin's *cosmography*. All these knights and many others I could mention, Master Priest, were knights errant, the light and glory of chivalry. These, or such as these, I should wish to take part in my project; and, if they did, His Majesty would find himself well served at great saving of expense, and the Turk would be left tearing his beard. Therefore I wish to remain at home, since the chaplain is not taking me out; and if Jupiter, as the barber has said, will not rain, here am I who will rain whenever I please. This I say so that Master Basin may see that I understand him.'

'Really, Don Quixote,' said the barber, 'that wasn't why I told you the tale. I meant well by it, so help me God, and your worship shouldn't take offence.'

'I know best whether I take offence or not,' replied Don Quixote.

At which the priest put in: 'Although I have hardly said a word up to now, I should like to relieve myself of a scruple which is gnawing and grating at my conscience, and which arises from Don Quixote's last remarks.'

'Master Priest has a licence for other graver matters,' replied Don Quixote. 'So he can declare his scruple; for it is not pleasant to go about with scruples on your conscience.'

'Well, with your permission,' replied the priest, 'I will reveal my scruple. It is this. I cannot by any means persuade myself, Don Quixote, that all this crowd of knights errant you have referred to have really and truly been people of flesh and blood living in this world. On the contrary, I think that it is all fiction, fable and lies – dreams told by men awake, or rather half asleep.'

'That is another mistake,' replied Don Quixote, 'into which the many have fallen, who do not believe that such knights have ever existed. Often with different people and at different times I have tried to expose this almost universal error to the light of truth. On some occasions I have not succeeded in my purpose; on others I have, by supporting my argument with evidence so infallible that I might say I have seen Amadis of Gaul with my own eyes. He was a man tall of stature and fair of face, with a well-trimmed black beard. His looks were half mild and half severe. He was short of speech, slow to anger, and quickly appeased. Now, in the same way as I have drawn Amadis, I could, I think, depict and describe all the knights errant in all the histories in the world. For my absolute faith in the details of their histories and my knowledge of their deeds and their characters enable me by sound philosophy to deduce their features, their complexions and their stature.'

'How big then, my dear Don Quixote,' asked the barber, 'would the giant Morgante have been in your worship's opinion?'

'About the existence of giants,' replied Don Quixote, 'there are different opinions. But Holy Scripture, which cannot depart from the truth by so much as an inch, proves that they existed, by telling us the story of that great Philistine, Goliath, who was seven cubits and a half tall – a prodigious height. Besides, in the island of Sicily shin-bones and shoulder-blades have been discovered of a size which shows that their owners were giants as tall as great towers; geometry proves it beyond a doubt. But, for all that, I could not say for certain how tall Morgante was, though I imagine that he could not have been very big. My reason for this opinion is that I find in the history particularly devoted to his exploits that he often slept beneath a roof; and since he found houses he could get into, it is clear that his size was not excessive.'

'That is true,' remarked the priest, delighted to hear him talk such nonsense. He then asked him what he felt about the looks of Reynald of Montalban, of Sir Roland and of the other Twelve Peers of France, since they had all been knights errant.

'Of Reynald,' replied Don Quixote, 'I make bold to say that he was broad-faced, red-complexioned, with rolling and rather prominent eyes, exceedingly touchy and irascible, and a friend to thieves and vagabonds. Of Roland, or Rotolando, or Orlando – for histories give him all these names – I am of the positive opinion that he was of middle stature, broad-shouldered, rather bow-legged, dark complexioned, and red-bearded, with a hairy body and a menacing appearance, short of speech but very well-bred and courteous.'

'If Roland was no more of a gentleman than your worship has said,' returned the priest, 'it was no wonder that the lady Angelica the Fair left him for the gaiety, the dash and the grace of the downy-cheeked little Moor to whom she gave herself. She showed good sense in falling in love with Medoro's smoothness rather than with Roland's roughness.'

'That Angelica, Master Priest,' replied Don Quixote, 'was a giddy, roving damsel and somewhat flighty, and left the world as full of her indiscretions as of her famous beauty. She spurned a thousand lords – a thousand brave and wise lords – and contented herself with a pretty little page, with no other wealth or fame than the reputation for gratitude he won by his loyalty to his friend. The great singer of her beauty, the renowned Ariosto, did not dare, or perhaps did not care, to sing of what happened to this lady after her base surrender – for no doubt her conduct was not over-chaste – and left her with these lines:

> "And how Cathaya's sceptre fell to her
> Someone perhaps will sing to a better lyre."

And no doubt that was a kind of prophecy; for poets are also called *vates*, which means diviners. The truth is plain to see, for since then a famous Andalusian poet has wept and sung her tears, and another famous and unique Castilian poet has sung her beauty.'

'Tell me, Don Quixote,' put in the barber, 'hasn't any poet written a satire on this lady Angelica, seeing that so many have praised her?'

'I certainly believe,' replied Don Quixote, 'that if Sacripante or Roland had been a poet, he would have given the maiden a trouncing. For it is proper and natural for poets who have been scorned or refused by their ladies – feigned or actually modelled on those they have chosen as mistresses of their thoughts – to avenge themselves with satires and lampoons, a vengeance most certainly unworthy of generous hearts. But up to now there has come to my notice no defamatory verse against the lady Angelica, who turned the world upside down.'

'A miracle!' exclaimed the priest. But at this point they heard the housekeeper and the niece, who had withdrawn from the conversation, making a great outcry in the front yard; and they all ran out to the noise.

Chapter II. *Of the notable Quarrel between Sancho Panza and Don Quixote's Niece and Housekeeper, with other delightful Incidents.*

OUR story tells that the voices Don Quixote, the priest and the barber heard were the niece and the housekeeper crying out at Sancho Panza, who was struggling to get in and see Don Quixote, while they were holding the door against him.

'What does the little monster want in this house? Go back to your own, brother, for it's you and no other that lead my master astray, and entice him, and take him rambling along the by-roads.'

To which Sancho replied: 'You old devil! It is I that am enticed and led astray and taken rambling over the by-roads, and not your master. It's he who led me all about the wilds, and don't you make any mistake about it. He wheedled me from home with his blarney, promising me an isle, and I'm still waiting for it.'

'May the foul isles choke you,' replied the niece. 'Damn you, Sancho. And what are isles? Are they something to eat, you glutton, you cormorant?'

'They are not anything to eat,' replied Sancho, 'but to govern and rule. They're better than any four cities, and richer than four judgeships at court.'

'You shan't come in here all the same,' said the housekeeper, 'you bundle of mischief, you bag of villainies! Go and govern your house, and till your plot, and give up trying for your isles and islets.'

The priest and the barber were highly delighted to hear this triangular conversation. But Don Quixote feared that Sancho would blurt out a whole pack of mischievous nonsense and touch on matters not wholly to his credit. So he called him, and forced the pair of them to be quiet and let him in. Sancho entered, and the priest and the barber took their leave of Don Quixote, despairing of his sanity, since they saw how fixed he was in his crazy ideas, and how steeped in the idiocy of his wretched knight errantry. And so the priest said to the barber: 'You will see, friend. When we least expect it, our knight will be off once more to range the bush.'

'I've no doubt of that,' replied the barber, 'but I'm less surprised at the knight's madness than at the squire's foolishness in believing

Q

the story of the isle. For I'm afraid that all the disillusionment you
can think of won't get it out of his head.'

'God cure them,' said the priest, 'and let us keep our eyes open.
We shall see where this precious knight's pack of nonsense will land
him, and his squire's too. For the pair of them seem to be cast in
one mould, and the master's madness would not be worth a farthing
without the squire's foolishness.'

'That's true,' said the barber. 'I should be very glad to know what
the two of them are talking about now.'

'His niece and the housekeeper will tell us afterwards, I promise
you,' replied the priest, 'for they aren't the sort to refrain from
listening.'

In the meantime Don Quixote had shut himself up in his room
with Sancho, and when they were alone he said: 'It grieves me
deeply, Sancho, to hear you say that it was I who took you from
your cottage, when you know that I did not stay at home myself.
We set out together, we lived together, and we wandered together.
One fortune and one destiny befell us both. If you have been tossed
in a blanket once, I have been beaten a hundred times; and that is
where I have the advantage of you.'

'That was only right,' replied Sancho, 'for, as your worship says,
disasters have more to do with knights errant than with their squires.'

'You are mistaken, Sancho,' said Don Quixote. 'Remember the
saying, *quando caput dolet*, etc.'

'I understand no language but my own,' replied Sancho.

'I mean,' said Don Quixote, 'that when the head aches, all the
limbs feel pain; and so, as I am your lord and master, I am your
head, and you are a part of me, since you are my servant; and for
that reason the ill that touches me, or shall touch me, should give
pain to you; and yours to me.'

'So it should be,' said Sancho. 'But when they tossed me, the
limb, in the blanket, my head was outside the wall, watching me fly
through the air and not feeling any pain. But since the limbs have
to suffer for the head's pain, the head should also be made to suffer
for the limbs.'

'Do you mean to suggest, Sancho,' replied Don Quixote, 'that
I felt no pain when they were tossing you? If that is what you say,
you are wrong. You should not even think such a thing. For I felt

more pain then in my spirit than you did in your body. But let us put that aside for the present, for there will be a time when we can consider the matter and come to a proper conclusion. Now, tell me, Sancho, my friend, what do they say about me in the village? What opinion have the common people of me, and the gentry and the knights? What do they say of my valour, and my deeds and my courtliness? How do they speak of the resolve I have taken to revive and restore to the world the forgotten order of chivalry? In brief, Sancho, I want you to tell me all that has come to your ears on this score. You must answer me without adding to the good or subtracting from the evil in the very slightest. For it is the duty of loyal vassals to tell their lords the truth in its proper shape and essence, without enlarging on it out of flattery or softening it for any idle reason. I would have you know, Sancho, that if the naked truth were to come to the ears of princes, unclothed in flattery, this would be a different age. Other ages would be held to be of iron in comparison with ours, for this in which we live now I reckon to be of gold. Take this warning, Sancho, and bring discreetly and faithfully to my ears the true answer to the questions I have asked you.'

'I'll do so gladly enough, sir,' replied Sancho, 'on condition that your worship does not get annoyed at what I say. For you want me to tell you the naked truth and not dress it in any clothes, except those I found it in.'

'On no account shall I be angry,' replied Don Quixote. 'You can speak freely, Sancho, without any beating about the bush.'

'Then first of all,' said he, 'let me say that the common people take your worship for a very great madman, and they think I'm a great simpleton too. The gentlemen say that you're not content with being a country gentleman, but must turn yourself into a Don and launch forth into knighthood, with no more than a paltry vineyard and two acres of land, and hardly a rag to your back. The knights say that they don't like the petty gentry to set up in competition with them, especially squires who black their own shoes, and mend their black knitted stockings with green silk.'

'That,' said Don Quixote, 'does not apply to me, for I am always well dressed and never patched. Frayed I may be, but frayed rather from my armour than from age.'

'On the subject of your worship's valour,' Sancho went on, 'of your courtliness, your deeds, and your undertaking, there are different opinions. Some call you mad but amusing. Others, valiant but unfortunate. Others, well-mannered but presumptuous. And so they go running on, till they don't leave a whole bone in your worship's body, nor in mine.'

'Observe, Sancho,' said Don Quixote, 'that virtue is persecuted wherever it exists to an outstanding degree. Few or none of the famous heroes of the past escaped the slander of malice. Julius Caesar, a most courageous, most wise and valiant captain, was branded as ambitious, and not over-clean either in his clothes or in his habits. Alexander, whose exploits won for him the title of the Great, was said to have been given to some measure of drunkenness. Hercules, the hero of the many labours, is said to have been lascivious and effeminate. Sir Galaor, the brother of Amadis of Gaul, is criticized for having been over lecherous, and his brother for being a blubberer. So, Sancho, among so much slander against good men, what they say against me may pass, if it is no more than you have told me.'

'Ah, there's the trouble, damn it,' replied Sancho.

'Is there anything more, then?' asked Don Quixote.

'There's still the tail to skin,' said Sancho. 'What I've said so far is tarts and gingerbread. But if your worship wants to know all the slander they speak of you, I'll bring you here presently some one who'll tell you the lot and not spare a crumb. For last night Bartholomew Carrasco's son arrived from studying at Salamanca, where they made him a bachelor. And when I went to welcome him home he told me that your worship's story is already in print under the title of *The Ingenious Gentleman Don Quixote de la Mancha*. He says that I'm mentioned too under my own name of Sancho Panza, and so is the lady Dulcinea del Toboso, and so are other matters which happened to us in private. It made me cross myself in wonder, to think how the story-writer could have learnt all that.'

'You may be certain, Sancho,' said Don Quixote, 'that the author of our history is some sage enchanter.'

'But if the author of this history was a sage enchanter,' answered Sancho, 'how can it be that, according to the bachelor Sampson Carrasco – for that's the man's name – he's called Cide Hamete Aubergine!'

'That is a Moor's name,' observed Don Quixote.

'So it may be,' replied Sancho, 'for I have heard that your Moors, for the most part, are very fond of aubergines.'

'You must be mistaken, Sancho,' said Don Quixote, 'in the surname of this Cide, which in Arabic means Lord.'

'Very likely,' replied Sancho, 'but if you would like to have me bring the Bachelor here, I'll go for him like a shot.'

'That would be doing me a great favour, friend,' said Don Quixote, 'for I am alarmed at what you have told me, and I shall not eat a mouthful that will do me good until I am informed on the whole subject.'

'Then I'll go for him,' replied Sancho. So leaving his master, he went to find the Bachelor, with whom he returned in a short while. And between these three there passed a most entertaining conversation.

Chapter III. *Of the ridiculous Conversation which passed between Don Quixote, Sancho Panza and the Bachelor Sampson Carrasco.*

DON QUIXOTE was very thoughtful as he waited for the Bachelor Carrasco, from whom he expected to hear how he had been put into a book, as Sancho had told him. He could not persuade himself that such a history existed, for the blood of the enemies he had slain was scarcely dry on his own sword-blade. Yet they would have it that his noble deeds of chivalry were already about in print. Nevertheless he imagined that some sage, either friendly or hostile, had given them to the Press by magic art; if a friend, to magnify and extol them above the most renowned actions of any knight errant; and if an enemy, to annihilate them and place them below the basest ever written of any mean squire – although, he admitted to himself, the deeds of squires were never written of. But if it were true that there was such a history, since it was about a knight errant it must perforce be grandiloquent, lofty, remarkable, magnificent and true. With this he was somewhat consoled; but it disturbed him to think that its author was a Moor, as that name of Cide suggested. For he could hope for no truth of the Moors, since they are all cheats, forgers and schemers. He was afraid too that his love affairs might have been treated with indelicacy, which would redound to the disparagement and prejudice of his lady, Dulcinea del Toboso. For he was anxious that it should be declared that he had always preserved his fidelity and reverence towards her, scorning Queens, Empresses, and damsels of all qualities, and curbing the violence of his natural appetites. And so Sancho found him, wrapt and involved in a thousand such fancies when he returned with Carrasco, whom the knight received with great courtesy.

The Bachelor was not very big in body, although his name was Sampson, but a great wag, of poor colour though of great intelligence. He must have been about twenty-four years old, with a round face, a flat nose, and a big mouth – all signs that he was of a mischievous disposition and fond of jokes and japes, as he showed, on seeing Don Quixote, by going down on his knees before him, and saying:

'Give me your hands, your Mightiness, Don Quixote de la Mancha. For by the habit of St. Peter, which I wear – although I have taken no more than the first four orders – your worship is one of the most famous knights errant there has ever been on all the rotundity of the earth. Blessed be Cide Hamete Benengeli, who has left us the history of your great deeds recorded, and thrice blessed the man of taste who took the pains to have it translated out of the Arabic into our vulgar Castilian, for the universal entertainment of mankind!'

Don Quixote made him get up and said: 'So it is true, then, that there is a history of me, and that he was a Moor and a sage who composed it?'

'So true is it,' said Sampson, 'that it is my opinion there are more than twelve thousand copies of this history in print to-day. If not, let Portugal, Barcelona and Valencia speak; for there they were printed. There is even a report that it is being printed at Antwerp too. In fact, I am pretty sure that there cannot be any nation into whose tongue it will not be translated.'

'One of the things,' said Don Quixote at this, 'which must give the greatest pleasure to a virtuous and eminent man is to see himself, in his life-time, printed and in the Press, and with a good name on peoples' tongues. I said a good name because, were it the opposite, no death could be so bad.'

'If it is a question of a good reputation and a good name,' said the Bachelor, 'your worship alone bears away the palm from all knights errant. For the Moor in his language, and the Christian in his, have carefully and accurately depicted for us your worship's gallantry, your great courage in confronting perils, your patience in adversity, your fortitude too under misfortune and wounds, and the chastity and continence of the most platonic loves of your worship and my lady, Doña Dulcinea del Toboso.'

'Never,' Sancho Panza broke in at this point, 'have I heard my lady Dulcinea called Doña, but simply The Lady Dulcinea del Toboso. There the history's wrong.'

'That is not an important objection,' replied Carrasco.

'No, surely,' replied Don Quixote; 'but tell me, Master Bachelor, which of my exploits are most highly praised in this history?'

'About that,' replied the Bachelor, 'there are different opinions, as there are different tastes. Some favour the adventure of the wind-mills which seemed to your worship Briareuses and giants. Others the adventure of the fulling mills. One man is for the description of the two armies, which proved afterwards to be two flocks of sheep. Another thinks most highly of the tale of the corpse which they were taking to Segovia for burial. Another says that the best of all is the freeing of the galley-slaves. And yet another that there is nothing equal to the two Benedictine giants and the combat with the valorous Basque.'

'Tell me, Master Bachelor,' put in Sancho, 'does the adventure with the Yanguesans come in, when our good Rocinante had a fancy to look for dainties at the bottom of the sea?'

'The sage left nothing in his ink-horn,' replied Sampson. 'He tells us everything and dwells on every point, even to the capers Sancho cut on the blanket.'

'I cut no capers on the blanket,' replied Sancho. 'But in the air I did, and more than I liked.'

'In my opinion,' said Don Quixote, 'there is no human history in the world which has not got its ups and downs, particularly those that treat of knight errantry. They can never be full of fortunate incidents.'

'For all that,' replied the Bachelor, 'some who have read your history say that they would have been glad if the authors had left out a few of the countless beatings which Don Quixote received in various encounters.'

'That's where the truth of the story comes in,' said Sancho.

'Yet they might in fairness have kept quiet about them,' said Don Quixote, 'for there is no reason to record those actions which do not change or affect the truth of the story, if they redound to the discredit of the hero. Aeneas was not as pious as Virgil paints him, I promise you, nor Ulysses as prudent as Homer describes him.'

'That is true,' replied Sampson; 'but it is one thing to write as a poet, and another as a historian. The poet can relate and sing things, not as they were but as they should have been, without in any way affecting the truth of the matter.'

'Well, if it's telling the truth this Moor's after,' said Sancho, 'and my master's beatings are all set down, then mine will be found amongst them. For they never took the measure of his worship's shoulders without taking it of my whole body. But that's not to be wondered at, for this same master of mine says the limbs have to take a share in the head's pain.'

'You are a sly fellow, Sancho,' answered Don Quixote. 'I swear your memory does not fail you when you want to remember anything.'

'Even if I'd a mind to forget the thrashings I got,' said Sancho, 'the marks wouldn't let me, for they're still fresh on my ribs.'

'Be quiet, Sancho,' said Don Quixote, 'and do not interrupt the Bachelor, whom I beg to proceed and tell me what is said of me in this history of his.'

'And of me,' said Sancho, 'for they say I'm one of the principal presonages in it.'

'Personages, not *presonages*, Sancho my friend,' said Sampson.

'So we have another vocabulary corrector!' said Sancho. 'If it goes on like this we shall never be done in this life.'

'Hang me, Sancho,' answered the Bachelor, 'if you are not the second person in the history. And there are some who think the parts where you talk are the best bits in the story; though there are others who say that you were excessively credulous in believing in the governorship of that isle Don Quixote here promised you.'

'There is still sun on the thatch,' said Don Quixote, 'and all the while Sancho is getting older. With the experience that years bring he will become more competent and fitter to be a governor than he is now.'

'By God, sir,' said Sancho, 'any isle I can't govern at my present age I shall never govern if I live to be as old as Methusaleh. The trouble is that this isle of yours is hidden away, I don't know where, and not that I haven't the brains to govern it.'

'Leave it to God, Sancho,' said Don Quixote, 'and all will be well. Perhaps better than you think, for not a leaf stirs on a tree without God's will.'

'That is the truth,' said Sampson; 'for if God wills, Sancho will not lack a thousand isles to govern, let alone one.'

'I have seen governors about here,' said Sancho, 'who, to my thinking, don't come up to the sole of my shoe. Yet for all that they're called *your worship*, and served off silver.'

'Those are not governors of isles,' answered Sampson, 'but of more manageable territories. Governors of isles must at least be grammarians.'

'The "*gram*" I can easily manage,' said Sancho, 'but the "*marians*" I pass, for I don't understand them. But leaving this matter of a governorship in God's hands – and may He place me where I may serve Him best – let me say, Master Bachelor Sampson Carrasco, that I'm extraordinarily glad that the author of this history has spoken of me so nicely that what he says gives no offence. For, as I'm a good squire, if he'd said things about me unbefitting the old Christian I am, the deaf would be hearing of it.'

'That would be working miracles,' said Sampson.

'Miracles or no miracles,' said Sancho, 'let everyone mind how he speaks or writes about *presons*, and not put down helter-skelter the first thing that come into his head.'

'One of the faults they find in this history,' said the Bachelor, 'is that the author inserted a novel called *The Tale of Foolish Curiosity* – not that it is bad or badly told, but because it is out of place and has nothing to do with the story of his worship Don Quixote.'

'I'll bet the son of a dog has made a fine mix-up of everything,' put in Sancho.

'Now I believe that the author of my story is no sage but an ignorant chatterer,' said Don Quixote, 'and that he set himself to write it down blindly and without any method, and let it turn out anyhow, like Orbaneja, the painter of Ubeda, who, when they asked him what he was painting, used to answer "Whatever it turns out." Sometimes he would paint a cock, in such a fashion and so unlike one that he had to write in Gothic characters beside it: *This is a cock*. And so it must be with my history, which will need a commentary to be understood.'

'No,' replied Sampson, 'for it's so plain that there is nothing in it to raise any difficulty. Children finger it; young people read it; grown men know it by heart, and old men praise it. It is so dog-eared, in fact, and so familiar to all sorts of people that whenever they see a lean horse go by, they cry: "There goes Rocinante." Those who are most given to reading it are pages; there is not a gentleman's antechamber in which you will not find a *Don Quixote*. When one lays it down, another picks it up; some rush at it; others beg for it. In fact, this story is the most delightful and least harmful entertainment ever seen to this day, for nowhere in it is to be found anything even resembling an indelicate expression or an uncatholic thought.'

'To write in any other way,' said Don Quixote, 'would be to write not the truth, but lies; and historians who resort to lies ought to be burnt like coiners of false money. But I do not know what induced the author to make use of novels and irrelevant stories, when he had so much of mine to write about. No doubt he felt bound by the proverb: "With hay or with straw, it is all the same." For really, if he had confined himself to my thoughts, my sighs, my tears, my worthy designs, and my undertakings, he could have made a volume greater than all the works of El Tostado, or at any rate as big. In fact my conclusion is, Master Bachelor, that to compose histories or books of any sort at all you need good judgement and ripe understanding. To be witty and write humorously requires great genius. The cunningest part in a play is the fool's, for a man who wants to be taken for a simpleton must never be one. History is like a sacred writing, for it has to be truthful; and where the truth is, in so far as it is the truth, there God is. But notwithstanding this there are some who compose books and toss them off like fritters.'

'There is no book so bad,' said the Bachelor, 'that there is not something good in it.'

'No doubt of that,' replied Don Quixote, 'but it very often happens that authors who have deservedly reaped and won great fame by their writings have lost it all, or somewhat diminished it, when they have given them to the Press.'

'The cause of that,' said Sampson, 'is that printed books are viewed at leisure, and so their faults are easily seen, and the greater the fame of their authors the more closely are they examined. Renowned men of genius, great poets and famous historians are always, or generally, envied by such as make it their pleasure and particular pastime to judge the writings of others, without having published any of their own.'

'That is not to be wondered at,' said Don Quixote, 'for there are many theologians who are not good in the pulpit, but excellent at recognizing the faults or excesses of those who preach.'

'All that is true, Don Quixote,' said Carrasco, 'but I should be glad if such censors would be more merciful and less scrupulous, and not scold at the specks in the bright sun of the work they review. For, though Homer sometimes nods, let them reflect how long he stayed awake to give us the light of his work with the least possible shadow. And it may well be that what seem faults to them are moles, which at times enhance the beauty of a face. In fact it is my opinion that an author runs a very great risk in printing a book. For it is the greatest of all impossibilities to write one that will satisfy and please every reader.'

'The one which treats of me,' said Don Quixote, 'must have pleased few.'

'Quite the opposite; for as there are an infinite number of fools in the world, an infinite number of people have enjoyed that history. But here are some who have found fault, and taxed the author's memory for forgetting who it was that robbed Sancho of his Dapple. For it is not stated there, but only from the context do we infer that it was stolen. Yet a little farther on we find Sancho riding on this same ass, and are never told how he turned up again. They also say that he forgot to put down what Sancho did with the hundred crowns he found in the leather bag in the Sierra Morena, for they were never mentioned again. Many people want to know what use he made of them, or what he spent them on – that is one of the essential points left out of the work.'

'I'm not prepared now, Master Sampson,' replied Sancho, 'to go into details or accounts, for I've got a stomach-ache, and if I don't cure it with two gulps of the old stuff, it will put me on St. Lucy's thorn. I have a drop at home, and my old woman is waiting for me. I'll come back when I've had my dinner, and answer all your worship's questions, and all the world's besides, whether it's about my losing the ass or spending the hundred crowns.'

Then, waiting for no reply, he went off home without another word. Don Quixote begged and prayed the Bachelor to stop and take pot-luck with him, and he accepted the invitation and stayed to the meal, at which a pair of pigeons were added to the ordinary fare. Over table they talked of knight-errantry, Carrasco following the knight's humour, and when the banquet was ended they slept through the heat of the day, till Sancho came back and their previous discussion was resumed.

Chapter IV. *In which Sancho Panza satisfies the Doubts and Questions of the Bachelor Sampson Carrasco, with other matters worthy of being known and related.*

SANCHO returned to Don Quixote's house and, resuming the previous conversation, said: 'As to Master Sampson's saying that he wanted to know who stole my ass, and how, and when, I should like to state in reply, that the same night the two of us were running from the Holy Brotherhood in the Sierra Morena, after the luckless adventure of the galley-slaves and the one with the corpse they were carrying to Segovia, my master and I got into a thicket. Don Quixote rested on his lance and I on my Dapple; and, bruised and wearied as we were, from our recent affrays, we settled down to sleep as soundly as if we had been on four feather beds. As for me, I slept so heavily that whoever it was had a chance to come and prop me up on four stakes, which he put under the four corners of my pack-saddle, in such a way that he left me in the air, and took my Dapple from under me without my feeling it.'

'That is an easy trick,' said Don Quixote, 'and nothing new. For the same thing happened to Sacripante at the siege of Albraca, when that famous thief Brunelo took his horse from between his legs by the same device.'

'Dawn broke,' continued Sancho, 'and I had scarcely stretched

myself when the stakes gave way and down I came with a great
tumble on to the ground. I looked for my ass, and didn't find him.
Then tears started to my eyes, and I set up a great wailing. And if
the author of our history didn't put that in, you can reckon he left
out a good thing. Then, at the end of I don't know how many days,
when we were travelling with the lady Princess Micomicona, I recognized my ass, and who should be riding on him but that notorious malefactor Gines de Pasamonte, disguised as a gipsy, the cunning cheat my master and I freed from the galley-chain.'

'The mistake is not there,' replied Sampson, 'but when the author
says that Sancho was riding on this same Dapple, before the ass
turned up again.'

'I don't know how to answer that,' said Sancho. 'All I can say is
that perhaps the history-writer was wrong, or it may have been an
error of the printer's.'

'That is it, no doubt,' said Sampson; 'but what became of the
hundred crowns? Were they spent?'

'I spent them on myself and on my wife and children. It was because of them that my wife was so patient about my travellings and
ramblings in the service of my master Don Quixote. For if I'd come
back home at the end of all that time ass-less and penniless, I should
have expected a black welcome. Now if there's anything else you
want to know, here I am, and I'll answer to the king himself in
preson, though it's nobody's business to pry into whether I took
them or I didn't, and whether I spent them or not. For if the blows
I got on that journey were to be paid for in money, even if they were
reckoned at no more than four farthings apiece, another hundred
crowns wouldn't pay me for half of them. Let every man lay his
hand on his heart, and not set himself up to call white black and
black white; for everyone is as God made him, and often a good
deal worse.'

'I will take care,' said Carrasco, 'to warn the author of this history not to forget what our good Sancho has said should he print it
again, for it would improve it by quite a tidy bit.'

'Is there anything else to amend in this legend, Master Bachelor?'
asked Don Quixote.

'Yes, no doubt there is,' replied he, 'but nothing as important as
the matters mentioned.'

'Does the author,' asked Don Quixote, 'by any chance promise a second part?'

'Yes, he does,' replied Sampson, 'but he says he has not found it, and does not know who has it. And so we are in doubt whether it will come out or not. Indeed, some say that second parts are never any good, and others say that enough has been written about Don Quixote. So it is doubtful whether there will be a second part. Though some, who are more of the jovial sort than the saturnine, cry out: – Let us have more Quixotries. Let Don Quixote charge and Sancho Panza talk, and come what may, we shall be content.'

'What is the author up to, then?' asked Don Quixote.

'What?' replied Sampson. 'As soon as he has found the history which he is taking extraordinary pains to search for, he will give it straight to the Press. For he is keener on the profit he will get from it than for any kind of praise.'

At which Sancho remarked: 'Does the author expect to make money by it? It'll be a marvel if he gets any, for it'll be nothing but hurry, hurry, like a tailor on Easter eve; and work that's done in haste is never finished as perfectly as it ought to be. Let this Master Moor, or whatever he is, take care and look what he is doing, for I and my master will provide him with enough rubble in the way of adventures and different things for him to be able to make up not only a second part but a hundred more. The good man imagines, no doubt, that we're asleep here in the straw; but let him lift up a foot for shoeing, and he'll see whether we're lame. What I mean to say is that, if my master would take my advice, we should be in the field by now, undoing injuries and setting right wrongs, as is the use and custom of good knights errant.'

Sancho had no sooner reached the end of this speech than Rocinante's neighing came to their ears. This Don Quixote took as a good omen, and so he decided to set out on another expedition in three or four days. Then, declaring his intention to the Bachelor, he asked for his advice in what direction to begin his journey. The Bachelor's opinion was they should go towards the city of Saragossa in the Kingdom of Aragon. For there in a few days' time they would be holding most solemn jousts in honour of the feast of St. George, in which, if he were to vanquish all the knights of Aragon, he would acquire an ascendancy over every knight in the world.

He commended Don Quixote's honourable and valiant resolution, yet warned him to be more wary in encountering dangers; for his life was not his own, but belonged to all those who had need of him to protect them and succour them in their misfortunes.

'That's where I cry off, Master Sampson,' said Sancho at this, 'for my master attacks a hundred armed men like a greedy boy falling on half a dozen water-melons. God's truth, Master Bachelor, there are times to attack and times to retreat, and it can't always be *Santiago and at 'em!* Besides, I've heard it said, and by my master himself, if I remember rightly, that between the extremes of cowardice and foolhardiness lies the middle course of bravery. And if that's true, I wouldn't have him run away for no reason, or attack when the odds demand the other thing. But I'd like to warn my master of one thing especially: if he's to take me with him, it must be on condition that he does all the fighting, and that I'm not obliged to do anything except look after his person so far as his cleanliness and his feeding go. There I'll serve him gladly, but if he expects that I'll put hand to sword, even though it's only against base rascals with axe and steel cap, he's imagining the impossible. I'm not thinking of gaining great fame as a fighting man, Master Sampson, but as the best and loyalest squire that ever served knight errant. And if, in return for all my good services, my master Don Quixote should wish to give me some isle of the many which his worship says he's sure to stumble across hereabouts, I shall be much obliged. But, if he shouldn't give me one, I am as I was born, and man mustn't live relying on man but on God. What's more bread will taste as good without a governorship as with one – and perhaps better. How am I to know if the Devil hasn't set a trap for me in these governorships, and if I mightn't trip and fall in and knock out my teeth? Sancho I was born, and Sancho I expect to die. But if, for all that, Heaven should present me with some isle, or something else of the kind, freely and easily and without much trouble or risk, I'm not so foolish as to throw it away. For, as the saying goes, when they give you the heifer run with the halter, and – when a good thing comes take it off home.'

'Brother Sancho,' said Carrasco, 'you have spoken like a professor. But put your trust in God all the same, and in your master, Don Quixote, for he will give you a kingdom – not just an isle.'

'It's all the same to me whichever it is,' replied Sancho, 'although I assure you, Master Carrasco, that my master won't be throwing the kingdom he gives me into a torn sack. For I've felt my own pulse, and I find I've the health to rule kingdoms and govern isles, as I've told my master before now.'

'Look out, Sancho,' said Sampson, 'for honours change manners, and perhaps if you were once a governor, you would not recognize the mother that bore you.'

'That may be true,' replied Sancho, 'of those who are born among the mallows, but not of men that have four inches of old Christian fat on their souls, as I have. Just look at my character, and see whether I could be ungrateful to anyone.'

'God grant you are right,' said Don Quixote. 'We shall see when the governorship comes, for I seem to have it before my eyes already.'

With these words he turned to the Bachelor and begged him, if he were a poet, to do him the favour of composing him some verses on the subject of his intended parting from his lady Dulcinea del Toboso, putting one letter of her name at the beginning of each line, so that when the poem was complete these first letters taken together might read *Dulcinea del Toboso*.

The Bachelor replied that, although he was not one of the most famous poets in Spain – of whom there were said to be no more than three and a half – he would not fail to write the verses. Though he found one very great difficulty in their composition, for the name contained seventeen letters, and if he were to make four stanzas of four lines each, there would be one letter over, and if he were to write five-line stanzas, which go by the name of '*decimas*' or roundelays, there would be three short. But, anyhow, he would try to squeeze one letter, somehow or another, so as to get the name of Dulcinea del Toboso into four stanzas.

'You must get it in, whichever way you do it,' said Don Quixote, 'because if the name is not there, plain and manifest, no woman will believe that the verses have been made for her.'

They agreed on this point, and also that they should set out within eight days. Don Quixote charged the Bachelor to keep his intention secret, especially from the priest and Master Nicholas, and from his niece and his housekeeper, in case they should hinder his honourable and valiant purpose. Carrasco gave his word, and with that took his leave, enjoining Don Quixote to keep him informed of all his successes and reverses, whenever he had an opportunity. And so they parted, and Sancho went to make all necessary preparations for the expedition.

Chapter v. Of the wise and humorous Conversation between San-cho Panza and his wife Teresa Panza, and other matters worthy of happy record.

WHEN the translator of this history comes to write this fifth chapter, he declares that he considers it apocryphal, because in it Sancho's style is much superior to what one would expect of his limited understanding, and his remarks so subtle that they seem beyond the range of his intelligence. But in order to fulfil his duty as a translator he is unwilling to omit it, and so proceeds as follows:

Sancho arrived home so jubilant and cheerful that his wife could observe his joy a bowshot off; so much so that she could not help asking: 'What's the matter with you, Sancho, my friend, that you're so cheerful?'

'If it pleased God,' he replied, 'I should be very glad, wife, not to be as happy as I seem.'

'I don't understand you, husband,' replied she. 'I don't know what you mean about being glad not to be happy, if it pleased God. I may be a fool, but I don't see who can be happy at not being happy.'

'Look, Teresa,' answered Sancho. 'I'm happy because I've decided to take service again with my master, Don Quixote, who is after setting out for a third time to search for adventures. I'm going off with him again, for my poverty demands it. And so does my hope of finding another hundred crowns like those I spent. And this cheers me now, though it makes me sad to have to part from you and the children. If God were pleased to give me food to eat dry-shod and at home, without dragging me over by-paths and cross-roads — which He could do very cheaply by merely wishing to — of course my happiness would be firmer and stronger, for the joy I feel now is mixed with sadness at leaving you. That's why I said truly that I should be glad, if God pleased, not to be happy.'

'See here, Sancho,' replied Teresa. 'Since you've been a limb of a knight errant you talk in such a roundabout way that no one can understand you.'

'It's enough that God understands me, wife,' replied Sancho, 'for He's the understander of all things. Let it rest there. But mind you, woman, you'll have to take good care of Dapple these next three days, so that he's fit to carry arms. Double his feeds, and look out his pack-saddle and the rest of his tackle. For we're not going to a wedding, but to roam the world and play at give-and-take with giants and dragons and hobgoblins, and to hear hissings and roarings, and bellowings and blusterings. And even all that would be flowers of lavender if we hadn't to deal with Yanguesans and enchanted Moors.'

'I can well believe, husband,' replied Teresa, 'that squires errant don't get their bread for nothing, and so I shall pray our Lord without stopping to deliver you quickly from all your misfortunes.'

'I tell you, wife,' replied Sancho, 'that if I didn't expect to be governor of an isle before long I should drop dead here on the spot.'

'Oh, no, husband,' said Teresa, 'don't kill the hen, even if she has got the pip. Live, and to the Devil with all the governorships in the world. Without a governorship you came out of your mother's womb, without a governorship you've lived to this day, and without a governorship you'll go – or they'll take you – to your grave, when it shall please God. There are plenty in the world without a governorship, who don't give up living and being counted in the number of the people for all that! Hunger's the best sauce in the world, and as the poor have no lack of it, they enjoy their food. But, look you, Sancho, if by chance you should come on a governorship, don't forget me and the children. Remember that young Sancho's just fifteen now, and ought to go to school, if his uncle the abbot means to make him a churchman. Don't forget either that your daughter Mari Sancha won't drop down dead if we find a husband for her. For I've a suspicion that she's as anxious to marry as you are to see yourself a governor. And, after all, a daughter's better ill married than well kept.'

'If God lets me have any sort of governorship,' answered Sancho. 'I mean to marry Mari Sancha off all right, wife, so high that no one'll get near her without calling her "*your ladyship*".'

'No, no, Sancho,' replied Teresa. 'Marry her to her equal. That's the best thing. If you raise her from clogs to high-heeled shoes, and from common grey serge to farthingales and silk skirts, and from *Moll* and *you* to *Doña so-and-so* and *your ladyship*, the girl won't know herself. Then she'll come a thousand croppers at every step, and they'll all see she's just coarse and homespun stuff.'

'Be quiet, silly,' said Sancho. 'All she needs is two or three years' practice. Then the grand manner will come to her as if she were born to it. And if not, what does it matter? Let her be *"her ladyship"*, come what may.'

'Keep to your own station, Sancho,' replied Teresa. 'Don't try to raise yourself higher, and remember the proverb: "take your neighbour's son, wipe his nose, and ask him home." It would be a fine thing indeed to marry our Maria to a great count or a fine gentleman. He might take another look at her when the fancy took him, and then call her a peasant, the daughter of clodhoppers and flax-spinners. Not at my time of life, husband! I didn't bring up my child for that. Indeed I didn't. You bring the money, Sancho, and leave marrying her to me. There is Lope Tocho now, Juan Tocho's son, a sound, sturdy lad. We know him, and I can see he doesn't dislike the girl. Now, she'll be well matched with him. He's our equal, and we shall always have her under our eye. Then we shall be all together, parents and children, grand-children and sons-in-law, and peace and God's blessing will go with us all. No, none of your marrying her in those courts and grand palaces of yours, where they won't understand her and she won't understand herself.'

'Come here, beast,' replied Sancho, 'wife of Barabbas. Why do you want to hinder me now, for no reason at all, from marrying my daughter to someone who will give me grandsons who'll be called *"your lordships"*? Look you, Teresa, I've always heard my elders say that anyone who doesn't know how to enjoy good luck when it comes shouldn't complain if it passes him by. And now that it's knocking at our door, it wouldn't be right to shut it out. Let's sail, seeing that there's a fair wind blowing.'

Now it was this turn of speech and Sancho's remarks farther down that made the translator of this history, so he says, regard this chapter as apocryphal.

'Don't you think, creature,' continued Sancho, 'that it'll be a good thing to rig myself out with some profitable government that'll lift our feet out of the mud? Let me choose a husband for Maria Sancha, and see how they'll call you Doña Teresa Panza and give you a seat in church on a rug with pillows and cushions, in spite of all the ladies in the town. No, you had rather stay always the same, neither more nor less, like a figure in a tapestry. Let us talk no more about it, for Sanchicha shall be a countess, whatever you say.'

'How you do go on, husband!' answered Teresa. 'All the same, I'm still afraid that this countessing of my daughter's will be her un-doing. But do as you like. Make her a duchess or a princess. But let me tell you that it won't be with my will and consent. I've always been a lover of equality, and I can't bear to see haughtiness with no foundations. Teresa they wrote me down at my baptism, pure and simple without additions or trimmings or ornaments of *"Dons"* or *"Doñas"*. Cascajo was my father's name, but as I'm your wife, they call me Teresa Panza, though by rights it should be Teresa Cascajo – but kings act as the laws will. I'm content with my name without having a *"Don"* put on top of it, too heavy for me to carry. I don't want to have people who see me go by dressed up like a countess or a governor's wife crying out: "Look what airs the pig feeder gives herself. Yesterday she wasn't too proud to pull out a lump of flax, and she went to mass with the skirt of her dress over her head for a cloak. And to-day she wears a farthingale and buckles, and she's as proud as if we didn't know her." If God keeps me in my seven, or my five senses, or however many I've got, I don't mean to give them a chance to see me in that scrape. Go off, brother, and be a government or an isle, and give yourself what airs you please. But I swear on my mother's life that neither I nor my daughter will stir a step from our village. An honest woman and a broken leg are best at home, and for an honest girl a job of work's her holiday. Go off on your adventures with your Don Quixote and leave us to our misadventures. God'll send us better luck if we're good. – But I'm sure I don't know who put a Don on him, for his father never had one, nor his grandfather either.'

'You have a devil in that body of yours, I tell you,' replied San-cho. 'Lord bless the woman, what a lot of rubbish you've strung to-gether, one thing on another, without head or tail! What have your Cascajo, your buckles, your proverbs, and your airs to do with what I'm saying? Listen, you silly fool – I've reason enough to call you that, for you don't understand what I say, and go running away from your good fortune – If I'd said that my daughter was to throw herself down from a tower, or go wandering through the world the way Doña Urraca wanted to, you would be right not to agree to my plans. But if in two twos, in less than the twinkling of an eye, I clap a "*Don*" and a ladyship on her shoulders for you, and fetch her out of the stubble and put her under a canopy, on a dais, and in an alcove with more velvet cushions than there were Moors in the Almohada family of Morocco, why won't you consent and fall in with my wishes?'

'Do you know why, husband?' replied Teresa. 'Because of that proverb that says: Who covers you discovers you. Nobody looks very hard at poor people, but they stare at the rich; and if some rich man was poor once, then it's all grumbling and abuse, and you're never done with slanderers, who are as thick in these streets as a swarm of bees.'

'Look here, Teresa,' replied Sancho, 'and listen to what I'm going to say. You'll never have heard the like, perhaps, in all the days of your life. I'm not speaking now just out of my own knowledge, for what I'm going to say is the opinion of the holy father who preached in this village last Lent. He said, if I remember rightly, that what we see present and before our eyes appears, stays and persists in our memories much better and much more vividly than things past.' – This is the second speech of Sancho's, says the translator, that makes him consider this chapter apocryphal, for it is beyond Sancho's capacity. – 'How comes it,' he continued, 'that when we see someone finely dressed, adorned with rich clothes, and with a train of servants, we seem to be moved and compelled involuntarily to pay him respect, even though at that very moment our memory may recall to us the low condition we once saw him in? For the disgrace of poverty or low birth, once it's in the past, is no more, and the only things which exist are what we see present. So if the man whom Fortune drew out of the obscurity of his low estate – these were the father's very words – to the height of prosperity, is well-bred, generous, and courteous to all, and doesn't set himself up as the equal of people who have been noble since olden times, you may be assured, Teresa, that no one will remember who he was, but everyone will respect what he is – except for the envious – and no good fortune is safe from them.'

'I don't understand you, husband,' replied Teresa. 'Do whatever you like, but don't break my head with your haranguing and fine words. If you are revolved to do what you say ...'

'Resolved you mean, wife,' said Sancho, 'not *revolved*.'

'Don't start arguing with me, husband,' replied Teresa. 'I speak as God would have me speak, and I don't meddle with grand words. What I say is, if you are set on having a governorship, take your son Sancho with you, and teach him how to govern now, for it's a good thing for sons to inherit and learn their fathers' trades.'

'When I get my governorship,' said Sancho, 'I'll send for him post haste, and I'll send you money too, for I shan't be short of it. There's always somebody about who'll make a loan to a governor if he hasn't any. Just you dress him so as to hide what he is and make him look like what he's going to be.'

'You send the money,' said Teresa, 'and I'll dress him like a palm branch in a procession.'

'Then we're agreed,' said Sancho, 'that our daughter is to be a countess.'

'The day I see her a countess,' replied Teresa, 'I shall reckon I'm laying her in her grave. But I say once more, do as you please. For with this burden are women born, to be obedient to their husbands, even if they're dolts.'

And at this she began to cry as bitterly as if she saw little Sancha dead and buried already. Sancho consoled her by saying that though he was bound to make her a countess, he would put it off as long as he could. With this the conversation ended, and Sancho went to visit Don Quixote once more, and to make preparations for their departure.

Chapter VI. *Of what passed between Don Quixote and his Niece and Housekeeper: one of the most important chapters in this whole History.*

NOW, whilst Sancho Panza and his wife Teresa were holding the absurd conversation just related, Don Quixote's niece and house-keeper were not idle, for they were beginning to guess from countless signs that their master and uncle was wanting to break away a third time and return to the practice of what was to them his ill-errant chivalry. They tried by all possible means to divert him from so evil a course, but it was like preaching in the wilderness and hammering cold iron. Though amongst the many arguments they used on him was one of the housekeeper's to this effect:

'Really, master, if you don't keep your feet still and stay quiet at home, and give up wandering up hill and down dale like a soul in torment, seeking what they call adventures but I call misfortunes, I'll have to go and make my complaint, and call on God and the King to put a stop to it.'

To which Don Quixote replied: 'I do not know, mistress, what answer God will give to your complaints; or His Majesty either. I only know that if I were King, I should refuse to reply to the numberless impertinent petitions presented to me every day. For one of the greatest among the many burdens kings bear is to be obliged to listen to everybody and reply to everybody. So I should not want him to be troubled by any affairs of mine.'

To which the housekeeper replied: 'Tell us, sir, are there no knights in His Majesty's court?'

'Yes,' answered Don Quixote, 'there are many. And so there should be, for they enhance the greatness of princes and increase the royal dignity.'

'Then couldn't your worship,' she replied, 'be one of those who serve their Lord and King in comfort as one of his Court?'

'Listen, friend,' answered Don Quixote. 'Not all knights can be courtiers, nor can all courtiers be knights errant, nor should they be. There must be some of all kinds in the world; and although we are all knights, there is a great deal of difference between one and another. For the courtiers do not stir from their rooms or beyond the threshold of their court, but travel over the whole world merely by looking at a map, without a farthing's cost or suffering heat or cold, hunger, or thirst. But we, the true knights errant, measure the whole earth with our own feet, in sun, in cold, and beneath the sky, exposed to the inclemencies of the heavens by night and day, on foot and on horse. We know our enemies, not only from portraits but in their real persons; and in all perils and on all occasions we meet them in fight, without regard for trifling points or for the laws of the duel: whether either party carries a shorter lance or sword or not; whether he has some charm on him or some hidden trickery; whether the sun is to be divided and portioned or not; and other ceremonies of this kind which are observed in single combats between man and man, matters of which I know but you do not. And I must tell you also that a good knight errant may see ten giants whose heads not only touch but overtop the clouds, each of them with two enormous towers for legs, and with arms like the masts of huge and mighty ships, and each eye like a great mill-wheel and blazing more fiercely than a glass furnace, yet he must not be in the least dismayed. But, on the contrary, he must meet them with a brave air and a fearless heart, and attack them and, if it is possible, conquer them and rout them in one brief moment, even though they may be armed with the shells of certain fish which are said to be harder than adamant, and bear instead of swords trenchant knives of Damascus steel or clubs spiked with this same metal, as I have seen them on several occasions. All this I have said, mistress, to prove to you the difference there is between some knights and others. It is only right, then, for every prince to think more highly of this last, or rather of this first species of knight errant. For, as we read in their histories, there have been some amongst them who have been the salvation, not only of one kingdom but of many.'

'Oh, sir,' interposed his niece, 'do remember that all you say about knights errant is fiction and lies. And if their histories aren't burnt, they each deserve to wear a penitent's coat, or a badge by which they can be recognized as infamous corrupters of good manners.'

'By God,' said Don Quixote, 'if you were not my lawful niece, being my own sister's daughter, I should give you such a chastisement for the blasphemy you have uttered that it would resound through the whole world. How is it possible for a young frippet who scarcely knows how to manage a dozen bobbins of lace to dare to disparage and censure the histories of knights errant? What would Sir Amadis say if he were to hear you? He would certainly pardon you, though, for he was the humblest and most courteous knight of his age, and a great protector of maidens as well. But one might have heard you who would have made you sorry: for they are not all courteous and considerate. Some there are that are unmannerly ruffians. Nor are all who style themselves so knights through and through. Some are of gold, others of alloy. All appear to be knights, yet not all can stand the test of the touchstone. There are base fellows who puff themselves up to seem like knights, and there are proud knights who seem to be dying with desire to appear base fellows. The first rise by ambition or by virtue; the second fall from slackness or vice. We need, therefore, to use careful discernment in distinguishing these two kinds of knights, so like in name and so unlike in deeds.'

'Good Heavens!' exclaimed his niece. 'What a lot you know, uncle! Why, at a pinch, you could get up in the pulpit or go and preach in the streets, and yet you're so blind and so palpably foolish that you'd have us think you're valiant when you are old; and strong when you're infirm; that you right wrongs when you're bent by age; and, worst of all, that you're a knight when you aren't, for though a gentleman can be one, a poor man can't!'

'There is much reason in what you say, niece,' replied Don Quixote, 'and I could tell you things about pedigrees that would surprise you. But not choosing to mix the sacred with the profane, I will refrain. Look, friends, and listen to me. All the pedigrees in the world can be reduced to four kinds. The first are those families which from humble beginnings have extended and expanded until they have reached supreme greatness; the second are those of high extraction who have preserved and maintained their original dignity; in the third sort are those who from great beginnings have gradually dwindled and decayed like a pyramid until, like the point of that pyramid, they end in nothingness – for compared with its base or seat, the point of a pyramid is nothing. The last sort – and these are the most numerous – have had neither good beginnings nor a respectable development, and consequently will end up without a name, with no better pedigree than ordinary plebeian folk. Of the first, who have risen from humble origins to their present greatness, let the Ottoman house serve as an example; for, sprung from a lowly and mean shepherd, it stands now at the height we see it. Of the second kind, which had its origins in greatness and preserved its state without increasing it, let many princes serve as example, princes by heredity who maintain their dignities without increasing or diminishing them, containing themselves peacefully within the

limits of their estates. Of those who began great and ended in a
point there are thousands of examples. For all the Pharaohs and
Ptolemies of Egypt, the Caesars of Rome, and all that countless
throng – if one may so call them – of princes, monarchs and lords –
Medes, Assyrians, Persians, Greeks and Barbarians – all those
lineages and lordships have ended in a point and in nothing – like
those who gave them birth. For it would be impossible now to find
any of their descendants, and if we were to find them, it would be
in a low and humble station. Of the plebeian stock all that I can say
is that it only serves to swell the numbers of living men whose
great deeds deserve no other fame or eulogy. From all this I wish
you to infer, my dear sillies, that the subject of genealogies is a most
confused one, and that the only families which have a claim to greatness and fame are those who show it by their virtue, by their riches,
and by the liberality of their members. I said virtues, riches and
liberality, because the great man who is wicked will only be a great
evil-doer, and the rich man who is not liberal will be a miserly
beggar. For the possessor of riches is not rendered fortunate by
having them but by spending them – and not by spending them as
he pleases, but by knowing how to spend well. The poor gentleman
possesses no other way of showing that he is a gentleman except
by virtue; by being affable, well-bred, courteous, polite and accommodating; not haughty, arrogant, or censorious; and above all
by being charitable. For by giving a poor man a halfpenny with a
cheerful heart he will show himself as liberal as the man who gives
alms to the pealing of bells. For there will be no one that sees him
adorned with these virtues I speak of, who will not take him for a
man of good stock, even though he does not know him – and it
would be a wonder if he were not so, since praise has ever been the
prize of virtue, and the virtuous cannot fail to be praised. There are
two roads, my daughters, by which men can come to honour and
riches. One is the way of Letters; the other the way of Arms. For
myself I have more arms than learning, and my inclination is to
Arms, for I was born under the influence of the planet Mars. So I am
almost compelled to follow that road, and must pursue it despite the
whole world; and it will be vain for you to weary yourselves in persuading me to go counter to the heavens' wishes, Fortune's decrees,
reason's demands and, more than that, against my heart's desires.

For knowing as I do the innumerable toils attendant upon knight errantry, I know as well the infinite benefits which can be attained by it. I know that the path of virtue is very narrow, and the road of vice wide and spacious. I know, too, that their final goals are different; for the wide and spacious road of vice ends in death, and the narrow and laborious path of virtue ends in life; and not in life which has an ending, but in life without end. I know, as our great Castilian poet says, that

> By these rough tracks we travel, on our way
> To the high seat of immortality
> Never attained by such as from it stray.'

'Oh dear! Oh dear!' cried his niece; 'my master's a poet too! He knows everything. He can do everything. I'll bet you that, if he chose to turn bricklayer, he would build a house as easily as a bird cage.'

'I promise you, niece,' replied Don Quixote, 'that if these knightly thoughts did not master all my senses there would be nothing I could not do, nor anything rare which my hands could not make, particularly cages and toothpicks.'

Just at that moment there was a knocking at the door, and when Don Quixote asked who was there, Sancho Panza replied that it was he. And no sooner did the housekeeper learn who it was than she ran to hide, so as to avoid seeing him, so much did she loathe him. But the niece opened the door to him, and his master Don Quixote went to receive him with open arms. Then the two of them shut themselves up in his room, where they held another conversation every bit as good as the last.

Chapter VII. *Of a Discussion between Don Quixote and his Squire; with other very notable incidents.*

THE housekeeper no sooner saw Sancho Panza locked in with her master than she began to smell their drift, suspecting that the result of this conference would be a third expedition. So, taking her cloak, she went, full of anxiety and distress, to find the Bachelor Sampson Carrasco, thinking that, as he was a nicely spoken man and her master's new friend, he might be able to persuade him to give up his wild project. She found the Bachelor walking in the courtyard of his house, and on seeing him fell at his feet in a cold sweat of dismay; at the sight of which demonstration of grief and distress Carrasco asked her:

'What is this, Mistress Housekeeper? What has happened to you, that you seem so heartbroken?'

'It's nothing, dear Master Sampson; only that my master is breaking out – breaking out, there's no doubt about it!'

'Where is he breaking out, then, lady?' asked Sampson. 'Has he ruptured any part of his body?'

'He's not breaking out really,' she replied, 'except by way of his madness. I mean, dear Master Bachelor, that he wants to set out again – it will be for the third time – to seek up and down the world what he calls adventures, though I can't understand why he gives them that name. The first time they brought him back to us laid across an ass and beaten black and blue. The second time he came on an ox-cart, sitting shut up in a cage, making believe he was enchanted. And he was in such a state, poor soul, that his own mother wouldn't have known him – thin and sallow, with his eyes sunk right into his skull. It cost me more than six hundred eggs to bring him round to something like himself, as God knows and everybody else too, not counting my hens that won't let me tell a lie.'

'I can well believe that,' replied the Bachelor, 'for they are good, plump and well-bred creatures, and they wouldn't say the wrong thing if they burst for it. But, Mistress Housekeeper, is there nothing else? Has anything awful happened, or is it just that you're afraid of what Don Quixote will be up to next?'

'No, sir,' she replied; 'nothing worse than that.'

'Then don't worry,' said the Bachelor, 'but go home in peace, and get me something warm cooked for breakfast. And on your way recite St. Apollonia's prayer, if you know it. I'll be there very soon, and then you'll see wonders.'

'Oh dear, dear!' replied the housekeeper. 'St. Apollonia's prayer is it your worship says I'm to recite? That would be all right if my master had toothache, but the trouble isn't there but in his brain.'

'I know what I am saying, Mistress Housekeeper. Get along, and don't start arguing with me. You know that I am a Bachelor of Salamanca, and there is no better bacheloring than that,' replied Carrasco. At that the housekeeper went off, and the Bachelor went straight to find the priest and discuss with him a matter which shall be related in due course.

Now, while Don Quixote and Sancho were shut up together, there passed between them a conversation recounted in this history with great precision and in faithful detail. It began by Sancho's saying to his master: 'Sir, I have concerted my wife to let me go with your worship wherever you wish to take me.'

' "Converted" you mean, Sancho,' said Don Quixote, 'not "concerted".'

'I've implored your worship once or twice, if I remember rightly,' answered Sancho, 'not to correct my words, if you understand what I mean by them, but just to say when you don't understand: *Sancho*, or *Devil*, I don't understand you. And if I don't make myself clear then you can correct me, for I am so *focile*.'

'I do not understand you, Sancho,' replied Don Quixote promptly. 'I do not know what so focile means.'

'So focile,' replied Sancho, 'means I am so – so!'

'Now I understand you even less,' said Don Quixote.

'Well, if you can't understand me,' replied Sancho, 'I don't know how to say it. I can't say any more, God help me.'

'Now, now I have got it!' cried Don Quixote. 'You mean to say that you are so *docile*, pliant and tractable that you will accept what I say to you and act on my instructions.'

'I'll bet you caught my meaning at the very beginning,' said Sancho, 'but you wanted to confuse me so as to hear me make another two hundred blunders.'

'Maybe,' replied Don Quixote. 'Well, now, what does Teresa say?'

'Teresa says,' answered Sancho, 'that I must keep a firm finger on your worship, and let writing speak and beards be silent, since a good bargain doesn't hold up the business, and one gift is worth two promises. But I say a woman's counsel is bad, and he who doesn't take it's mad.'

'And so I say too,' replied Don Quixote. 'Go on, Sancho, my friend, go on; you are speaking pearls to-day.'

'The case is,' replied Sancho, 'as your worship knows, that we are all subject to death, that we are here to-day and gone to-morrow, and the lamb goes as soon as the sheep, and no one can promise himself more hours of life in this world than God is pleased to grant him. For death is deaf, and when it comes to knock on our life's doors it's always in haste, and won't stop for prayers or struggles, or sceptres or mitres, as it's commonly reported, and as they tell us from the pulpits.'

'That is all true,' said Don Quixote; 'but I do not know what you are leading up to.'

'I am leading up,' said Sancho, 'to your worship's settling some fixed wages, which you'll give me each month all the time I serve you, and to this salary being paid out of your estate; because I don't like depending on favours, which come late, or at a bad time, or not at all. May God help me with my own, and I should like to know how much it will be, whether it's much or little, for the hen lays as well on one egg as on several, and many a mickle makes a muckle, and whilst you're earning you're losing nothing. If indeed it should happen (which I neither believe nor expect) that your worship should give me the isle you promised me, I'm not so ungrateful or so particular to a farthing, that I shan't consent to have the rent of the isle reckoned up, and let it be stopped from my wages, cat for quantity.'*

'Sancho, my friend,' replied Don Quixote, 'sometimes a cat is as good as a rat.'

'I see,' said Sancho. 'I'll bet I ought to have said "*rat*" and not "*cat*"; but it doesn't matter, because your worship understood me.'

'Yes, understood you so well,' replied Don Quixote, 'that I have penetrated to the bottom of your thoughts, and I know what target you are aiming at with the countless arrows of your proverbs. Look you, Sancho, I would willingly settle a wage if I had found in any of the histories of knights errant anything to show me what squires used to earn by the month or by the year, or even anything to throw the slightest chink of light on the subject. But I have read all, or the greater part, of these histories, and I never remember reading that any knight errant ever allowed his squire a fixed wage. All I know is that they all served on favour, and when they least expected it, if fortune had gone well with their lords, they found themselves rewarded with an isle, or with something else of equal value, or at the least came off with a title and a lordship. If with these expecta-

* He means 'rate for quantity,' *i.e.*, that the revenue from the isle shall be set against his wages.

tions and increments you, Sancho, are pleased to return to my service, come and welcome. But to think that I shall wrench the old customs of knight errantry off their posts and hinges is to imagine the impossible. So, my dear Sancho, go back home and declare my intention to Teresa; and if she is pleased and you are pleased for you to serve me on favour, well and good; but, if not, we are friends as before, for if the dovecot does not lack grain it will not lack pigeons. And remember this, my son, good hopes are better than poor possessions, and a good claim than bad pay. I speak in this way, Sancho, to show you that I can rain down proverbs as well as you. Finally I want to say, and I will say, that if you do not wish to come with me on favour and take the same chances as I take, God be with you and make you a saint, but I shall not be short of squires more obedient and more careful than you, and not so awkward and talkative.'

When Sancho heard his master's firm resolve his sky clouded over and the wings of his heart began to droop, for he had believed that Don Quixote would not go without him for all the treasure in the world. And there he was, confused and thoughtful, when Sampson Carrasco came in, followed by the housekeeper and the niece, who were eager to hear what arguments he would use to persuade their master not to go out again in search of adventures. Then Sampson, the great joker, went up to the knight and, embracing him as before, addressed him in a loud voice: 'O flower of knight errantry! O resplendent light of arms! O honour and mirror of the Spanish nation! May it please almighty God – and so forth as hereinafter set down – that the person or persons placing any impediment or hindrance in the path of your third expedition may find no way out of the labyrinth of their desires, and never accomplish their dearest wishes.'

Then, turning to the housekeeper, he said: 'You may as well give up reciting St. Apollonia's prayer, Mistress Housekeeper, for I know that it is the positive determination of the spheres that Don Quixote shall once more carry out his lofty and novel design, and I should much burden my conscience were I not to advise that knight most forcibly no longer to keep the strength of his mighty arm and the goodness of his most valiant heart under restraint and coercion. For by his delay he defrauds the wronged of their righting, orphans

of their protection, maidens of their honour, widows of their consolation, married women of their support, and other things of this
kind which touch, belong to, and are part and parcel of, knight
errantry. On, then, my good Don Quixote, handsome and brave!
Rather to-day than to-morrow should your worshipful Highness
take the road; and should any means be lacking for the execution of your resolve, here am I to provide it with my person and
from my estate; and were it necessary to serve your Magnificence as
your squire, I should count it the greatest of good fortune.'

At which point Don Quixote turned to Sancho and said: 'Did I
not tell you, Sancho, that I should have plenty of squires and to
spare? See who it is that offers himself for the post! None other
than that most rare bachelor Sampson Carrasco, the perpetual
entertainer and light of the courts of the Salamantine schools, sound
in person, agile of limb, silent, impervious to heat and cold, hunger
and thirst, and possessing all the virtues requisite in the squire of a
knight errant. But Heaven forbid that this pillar of learning, this
repository of science, should be hamstrung and broken for my
pleasure, and the lofty palm of the fair and liberal arts be felled. Let
this new Sampson stay in his own country, and in honouring it
honour the grey hairs of his aged parents as well, for I shall be content with any kind of squire, since Sancho does not deign to come
with me.'

'I do deign,' exclaimed Sancho, melted, with his eyes full of tears.
'It shall not be said of me, dear master, the bread eaten, the company forsaken. For I don't come from thankless stock, and all the
world knows – especially our villagers – what sort of people my ancestors, the Panzas, were. It's clear to me, besides, from your worship's good deeds and fair speeches how anxious you are to benefit
me, and if I went into the question of my wages, how much they
were to be, more or less, it was to please my wife. For when once
she sets her hand to persuading, there's no mallet so tightens the
hoops of a cask as she tightens on to getting her own way. But in
the end a man must be a man, and a woman a woman; and since I'm
a man anywhere, as I can't deny, I intend to be so in my own house,
in despite of everybody. So there's nothing more for it now but for
your worship to draw up your will with its codicil, so that it can't
be revolted; and then let's get on the road, so that master Sampson's

soul shan't suffer. For he says his conscience dictates that he must persuade your worship to go out into the bleak world a third time. And I offer once more to serve you faithfully and loyally, as well as and better than any squire has served knight errant in past or present times.'

The Bachelor was surprised to hear the style and manner of Sancho Panza's speech; for though he had read his master's first history, he had never believed that Sancho was as comical as he was described there. But when he heard him say the will and codicil that cannot be *revolted* instead of the will and codicil that cannot be *revoked*, he believed all that he had read, and set him down as one of the solemnest asses of our age, thinking to himself that two such madmen as master and man could never have been seen in the world before. Finally Don Quixote and Sancho embraced and made friends, and with the advice and approval of the great Carrasco, who was their oracle from that time on, it was decided that their departure should be in three days. In the interval they would have an opportunity of providing for the journey, and of looking for a complete helmet; for this Don Quixote said he must have at all costs. And Sampson offered him one, for he knew that a friend of his had one, and would not refuse it to him, though it was all dingy from rust and mould and had none of the brightness of polished steel.

Countless were the curses which the housekeeper and the niece hurled at the Bachelor. They tore their hair, scratched their faces, and raised such a lament as hired keeners used to, just as if it were their master's death, not his departure, they were mourning. Now the plan which Sampson was following when he persuaded Don Quixote to set out once again involved some action which will be described further on in our history. It was a design formed on the advice of the priest and the barber, with whom he had previously discussed it.

Well, in those three days Don Quixote and Sancho got together what seemed to them necessary. And when Sancho had placated his wife, and Don Quixote his niece and his housekeeper, they set out at nightfall on the road to El Toboso, unobserved by anyone but the Bachelor, who decided to accompany them for a mile or two from the village. Don Quixote jogged along on his good Rocinante, and Sancho on his old Dapple, his saddle-bags stored with

R

food and the like, and his purse with money, which Don Quixote
had given him for contingencies. Sampson embraced the knight and
begged him to let him know what his luck might be, so that he
might either rejoice or mourn, as the laws of friendship required.
This Don Quixote promised to do, and Sampson went back to the
village, while the two of them took the road to the great city of El
Toboso.

Chapter VIII. *In which we learn what happened to Don Quixote
on his way to see his Mistress, Dulcinea del Toboso.*

'BLESSED be Allah the mighty,' says Hamete Benengeli at the beginning of this eighth chapter. 'Blessed be Allah!' he repeats three
times, and declares that he utters these blessings on finding that he
has now got Don Quixote and Sancho Panza into the field, and that
the readers of his delightful history may reckon that from this point
the exploits and humours of the knight and his squire begin. He
begs them to forget the past knight errantries of the Ingenious
Gentleman, and fix their eyes on those which are to come and are
now beginning on the road to El Toboso, as the others began on
the plain of Montiel – and it is not much that he asks, considering
how much he promises. And so he goes on to say:

Don Quixote and Sancho were left alone. But scarcely had Sampson gone than Rocinante began to neigh and Dapple to bray, which
was taken by both knight and squire for a good sign and a most favourable omen. If the truth be told, however, the snorting and braying
of the ass was louder than the horse's neighing, from which Sancho
gathered that his luck would surpass and overtop his master's,
though whether he based his belief on any judicial astrology he had
learnt or not I do not know, for the history does not tell. Though he
had been heard to say when he fell or stumbled, that he would be
glad if he had never left home, for nothing was to be got from falling
and stumbling but a torn shoe or broken ribs; and in that, fool
though he was, he was not far out.

'Sancho, my friend,' said Don Quixote, 'the night is coming
down faster and darker than it should, if we are to get to El Toboso
by daybreak. For I am resolved to go there before undertaking any
other adventure. There I shall receive the blessing and the gracious

leave of the peerless Dulcinea, with which licence I think that I shall certainly bring to a happy conclusion the most perilous of adventures. For nothing in this life makes knights errant more valiant than the knowledge that they are favoured by their ladies.'

'So I believe,' replied Sancho, 'but I think that it'll be difficult for your worship to get a word with her alone, at least in any place where you can receive her blessing. Though she may throw it to you over the wall of the back-yard, where I saw her the first time, when I took her that letter that told her all about the crazy antics your worship was performing up there in the mountains.'

'Backyard walls did you fancy they were, Sancho,' asked Don Quixote, 'when you gazed over them at her never sufficiently praised grace and beauty? They must certainly have been the galleries, or corridors, or porticoes, or whatever they are called, of rich royal palaces.'

'That may all be so,' replied Sancho, 'but walls they seemed to me, if I remember rightly.'

'However that may be, let us go there, Sancho,' replied Don Quixote. 'For so long as I see her it is all the same to me whether it is over walls or through windows, or chinks or garden grilles. For any ray reaching my eyes from the sun of her beauty will illuminate my understanding and fortify my heart, so that I shall be unique and peerless in wisdom and valour.'

'But really, sir,' replied Sancho, 'when I saw this sun, the lady Dulcinea del Toboso, it wasn't bright enough to cast any rays at all. That must have been because her Grace was winnowing the wheat I told you of, and the great dust she raised must have gathered like a cloud about her face and darkened it.'

'What, do you still persist, Sancho,' cried Don Quixote, 'in saying, thinking, believing, and insisting that my lady Dulcinea was winnowing corn – that being a function and exercise far removed from the common practice of persons of rank, who are constituted and reserved for other employments and amusements, which reveal their quality a bow-shot off! You little remember, Sancho, those verses of our ingenious poet in which he describes to us the tasks which the four nymphs performed in their crystal dwellings, when they raised their heads from their beloved Tagus, and sat in the green meadow to work those rich clothes he there describes, which were all of gold, silk thread and pearls, plaited and interwoven. In such work must my lady have been employed when you saw her, were it not for the envy which some evil enchanter seems to display towards my affairs, in changing and turning everything which might give me pleasure into shapes other than their true ones. And so I am afraid that if the author of that history of my exploits, which they say is now in print, chanced to be some enchanter hostile to me, he has probably changed one thing into another, mingling a thousand lies with one truth, and digressed to narrate actions out of the sequence proper to a faithful history. Oh, envy, root of infinite evil and canker-worm of virtue! All the vices, Sancho, bring with them some manner of delight; but that of envy brings only pain, rancour and furious rage.'

'That's the very thing I say,' replied Sancho. 'And I think that in this legend or history which the Bachelor Carrasco said he had seen about us, my reputation must go jolting topsy-turvy, or helter-skelter, as the saying is. Yet I swear as an honest man I've never spoken ill of any enchanter, and I haven't enough wealth to be envied. True, I have a touch of malice in me and I'm a bit of a rogue, but that's all covered up and hidden under the broad cloak of my simplicity – which is always natural and never artificial. Yet the historians ought to take pity on me and treat me kindly in their writings, if only because I've always believed in God and in all the tenets of the Holy Roman Catholic Church, and because I'm a mortal enemy to the Jews. But let them say what they will; for naked I was born and naked I am now, I neither lose nor gain. And though I chance to be put in books and passed about the world from hand to hand, I don't care a fig – let them say what they like about me.'

'That, Sancho,' said Don Quixote, 'reminds me of what happened to a famous modern poet, who had composed a malicious satire against all courtesans, yet did not include in it the name of a certain lady, for there was some question whether she was one or not. Now, seeing that she was not in the list with the rest, she complained to the poet, asking him what fault he had seen in her that he had not included her with the others, and requesting him to enlarge his satire and put her in the supplement; and if he did not he had better look out for himself. The poet did as she asked, and made her something worse than a character in a waiting-lady's story, and she was satisfied to find herself famous, even if for nothing good. Another story that fits is the one about that shepherd who set on fire and burnt the famous temple of Diana, accounted one of the seven wonders of the world, only so that his name should survive to future ages; and though it was decreed that no one should speak of him, or make any mention of his name by word or in writing, so that he should not achieve his ambition, still it became known that his name was Erostratus. Also to the point is the tale of the great Emperor Charles V and a certain gentleman in Rome. The Emperor wanted to see the Rotunda, a famous temple which in ancient days was called the *Temple of All the Gods*, and is now known by the better name of *all the Saints*. It is the most complete building surviving of all those which heathendom raised in Rome, and the one which best preserves its founders' reputation for grandeur and magnificence. It is in the shape of half an orange, magnificent in the extreme and very well lit, although the only light which enters is through one window, or rather through a round lantern at the top, from which the Emperor was gazing down on the building. With him, standing by his side, was a Roman gentleman, who was pointing out the beauties of this famous masterpiece of architecture. Then, after they had come down from the lantern, he remarked to the Emperor: "A thousand times, most sacred Majesty, the desire seized me to clasp your Majesty and throw myself down from that lantern so that I might win myself eternal fame in the world." "I thank you," replied the Emperor, "for not having put so bad a plan into execution. But henceforth I will give you no further opportunity of putting your loyalty to the proof; and so I command you never to speak to me or to appear where I am." – And with these words he gave him a handsome present. My meaning is, Sancho, that the desire of winning fame is in the highest degree active with us. What was it, do you think, cast Horatius down from the bridge, clothed in his full armour, into the Tiber? What burnt Mutius' arm and hand? What drove Curtius to throw himself into the deep, flaming gulf which opened in the centre of Rome? What made Caesar cross the Rubicon in the face of all the omens which had shown themselves adverse? And, to take more modern examples, what scuttled the ships and left the valiant Spaniards, led by the most courteous Cortes, stranded and isolated in the New World? These and a multitude of other great exploits are the effects of the love of fame, which mortals desire to win by mighty deeds as their portion of immortality. While we, Christians, Catholics and knights errant, have more to expect from future and everlasting glory enjoyed in the ethereal and celestial regions than from the vanity of fame achieved in this present transient life; which fame, however long it lasts, must finally end with the world itself, which has its fixed term. So, Sancho, our works must not transgress the bounds set us by the Christian religion which we profess. It is for us to slay pride by slaying giants; to slay envy by our generosity and nobility; anger by calmness of mind, and serenity of disposition; gluttony, and drowsiness by eating little and watching late into the night; indulgence and lust by preserving our loyalty to those whom we have made ladies of our hearts; and sloth by travelling through all parts of the world in quest of opportunities of becoming famous knights as well as Christians. Such, Sancho, are the means by which we must win that high praise which a good name confers.'

'All that your worship has said to me so far,' said Sancho, 'I've understood very well. Yet I should like you to resorb me one doubt, which has just now come into my head.'

'"*Resolve*", you mean, Sancho,' said Don Quixote. 'Speak up and welcome, for I will answer as well as I can.'

'Tell me, sir,' continued Sancho, 'these Julys and Augusts and all these heroic knights you spoke of, who are now dead, – where are they now?'

'The heathens,' replied Don Quixote, 'are no doubt in Hell. The Christians, if they were good Christians, are either in Purgatory or in Heaven.'

'That's all right,' said Sancho. 'But now tell me this. These tombs where the bodies of these great lords lie – have they silver lamps in front of them, or are the walls of their chapels adorned with crutches, winding-sheets, wigs, legs and wax eyes? If not, how are they adorned?'

'The tombs of the heathens,' replied Don Quixote, 'were for the most part sumptuous temples. The ashes of Julius Caesar were placed in a stone pyramid of extraordinary size, which is now called St. Peter's Needle. The Emperor Hadrian's sepulchre was a castle as big as a fair-sized village and was called *Moles Hadriani*. It is to-day the castle of St. Angelo at Rome. Queen Artemisia buried her husband Mausolus in a tomb which was reckoned one of the seven Wonders of the World. But none of these tombs, nor those many others which the pagans built, were adorned with winding-sheets, nor with any other offerings or signs to show that those buried in them were saints.'

'I'm coming to that,' said Sancho. 'Tell me now, which is the greater thing: to raise a dead man to life or to kill a giant?'

'The answer is obvious,' replied Don Quixote. 'It is a greater thing to bring a dead man to life.'

'I've caught you now,' said Sancho. 'The fame then of those who bring the dead to life, give sight to the blind, cure the lame, and restore the sick to health, before whose tombs lamps burn, and whose chapels are full of devout people kneeling and adoring their relics, will be a better fame, in this life and in the other, than the fame of all the heathen emperors and knights errant in all the world.'

'I grant you that too,' replied Don Quixote.

'Well, this fame,' continued Sancho, 'these favours, these prerogatives, or whatever they're called, rest in the bodies and relics of the saints, who, with the approval and licence of our Holy Mother Church, receive lamps, candles, winding-sheets, crutches, paintings, wigs, eyes, legs, whereby they increase people's devotion and spread abroad their Christian fame. Kings carry the bodies or relics of the saints on their shoulders, kiss the pieces of their bones, and deck and enrich their private chapels and favourite altars with them.'

'What do you mean to infer, Sancho, from all this you are saying?' asked Don Quixote.

'I mean to say,' replied Sancho, 'that we should set about turning saints. Then we shall get the good name we're aiming at rather sooner. Think, sir, yesterday or the day before – it's so lately that we can speak like that – they canonized or beatified two little friars, and now people think it very lucky to kiss and touch the iron chains they bound and tortured their bodies with. They are held in greater veneration, they say, than Roland's sword in our Lord the King's armoury, God bless him! So, dear master, it's better to be a humble little friar, of any order you like, than a valiant and errant knight. A couple of dozen lashings have more effect with God than a couple of thousand lance-thrusts, even against giants, or hobgoblins, or dragons.'

'All that is so,' replied Don Quixote, 'but we cannot all be friars, and many are the ways by which God bears His chosen to heaven. Chivalry is a religion, and there are sainted knights in glory.'

'Yes,' replied Sancho, 'but I have heard it said that there are more friars than knights errant in Heaven.'

'That,' replied Don Quixote, 'is because the number of religious is greater than the number of knights.'

'There are plenty of the errant sort,' said Sancho.

'Many,' replied Don Quixote, 'but few are those deserving the name of knights.'

In this and other such conversations they spent that night and the following day, without meeting with anything worth mentioning, which grieved Don Quixote not a little. Finally, on the next day, at nightfall, they made out the great city of El Toboso, at the sight of which Don Quixote's spirits rose and Sancho's sank, for he did not know which was Dulcinea's house, having never seen it in his life, and no more did his master. So they were both troubled, one with the desire to see her and the other because he had never seen her. And Sancho could not imagine what he should do when his master sent him into El Toboso.

Eventually Don Quixote decided to enter the city once the night had closed in. So until the hour approached they stayed among some oaks which grew around El Toboso, and when the appointed time came they entered the city, where things befell them that were things indeed.

Chapter IX. *The Contents of which will be seen as the Chapter progresses.*

IT was on the stroke of midnight, more or less, that Don Quixote and Sancho left the wooded hill and entered El Toboso. The village lay in a deep silence, for all the inhabitants were asleep, sleeping like logs, as the saying goes. It was a fairly clear night, though Sancho wished it had been quite dark, so that the darkness might cover up his roguery. In the whole village there was no sound to be heard but the barking of dogs, which deafened Don Quixote's ears and alarmed Sancho's heart. From time to time an ass brayed, pigs grunted, and cats mewed; which various-sounding cries were heightened by the stillness of the night. All this the enamoured knight took for a bad omen. But, for all that, he said to Sancho: 'Sancho, my son, lead on to the palace of Dulcinea. It may be that we shall find her awake.'

'Great heavens! what palace am I to lead on to?' asked Sancho. 'For where I saw her Highness was no palace but a very small house.'

'She must have been in retirement then,' replied Don Quixote, 'in some little apartment of her castle, solacing herself alone with her maidens, as is the use and custom of high ladies and princesses.'

'Sir,' said Sancho, 'since your worship will have it, in spite of me, that my Lady Dulcinea's house is a royal castle, is this a likely hour to find the gate open? And would it be right for us to start knocking till they hear us and open for us, and put all the people into uproar and confusion? Is it to our wenches' houses we're going, like their keepers, who come and call and enter at all hours of the day and night?'

'Let us find the castle anyway, first,' replied Don Quixote. 'Then I will tell you what we ought to do, Sancho. But look, either my eyes fail me, or that vast mass of shadow looming up over there must be Dulcinea's palace.'

'Then you lead, your worship,' replied Sancho. 'Perhaps it may be so, though if I were to see it with my eyes and touch it with my hands, I should no more believe it than I'd believe that now it's daylight.'

Don Quixote led on, and when he had gone about two hundred yards forward came to the mass which was throwing the shadow and, seeing a great tower, realized immediately that the building was no royal castle, but the parish church of the place. 'It's the church we have come upon, Sancho,' he said.

'So I see,' replied Sancho, 'and please God we haven't come for our burial. For it's not a good sign to be wandering about grave-yards at this time of night. Besides, if I remember rightly, I told you that the lady's house is in a blind alley.'

'Be damned to you, Sancho, you idiot!' cried Don Quixote. 'Where have you found royal castles and palaces built in blind alleys?'

'Sir,' replied Sancho, 'every land has its own customs. Perhaps it's the custom here in El Toboso to build palaces and great buildings in blind alleys. So I beg your worship to let me search in these streets and alleys here in front of me. I might possibly run across that castle in some corner – and may I see it eaten by dogs for dragging us on such a weary chase!'

'Speak respectfully, Sancho, of what belongs to my lady,' said Don Quixote, 'and let us keep our feast in peace, and not throw away the rope after losing the bucket.'

'I'll control myself, replied Sancho, 'but how can I bear it in patience when your worship wants me, when I've only seen our lady's house once, to recognise it again and find it in the middle of the night? For you can't find it yourself, though you must have seen it thousands of times!'

'You will drive me to despair, Sancho,' cried Don Quixote. 'Look you, heretic, have I not told you a thousand times that I have never seen the peerless Dulcinea in all the days of my life, nor ever crossed the threshold of her palace, and that I am only enamoured of her by hearsay, and because of the great reputation she bears for beauty and wisdom.'

'I hear it now,' replied Sancho, 'and since you say that you have never seen her, neither have I.'

'That cannot be,' said Don Quixote, 'for you told me, at any rate, that you saw her winnowing wheat, when you brought me an answer to the letter I sent to her by you.'

'Don't depend on that, sir,' answered Sancho, 'for I would have you know that my seeing her and the reply I brought back were by hearsay too; for I no more know who the lady Dulcinea is than I can punch the sky.'

'Sancho, Sancho,' cried Don Quixote, 'there are times for joking and times when jokes are out of place and unseemly. Because I say that I have neither seen nor spoken to the lady of my heart there is no reason for you to say that you have not spoken to her or seen her either; the contrary being the case, as well you know.'

While the pair of them were engaged in this argument, they saw a man approaching them with a couple of mules; and from the noise made by the plough, which he was dragging along the ground, they judged that he was a labourer who had got up before daybreak to go to his ploughing, as was the case. The ploughman came along, singing that doleful ballad which runs:

'It was an ill day for Frenchmen,
The rout of Roncesvalles.'

'Hang me, Sancho,' said Don Quixote, as he heard him, 'if we have any good fortune to-night. Do you hear what that peasant is singing?'

'Yes, I can hear,' replied Sancho. 'But what has the rout of Roncesvalles to do with us? He might just as well be singing the ballad of Calainos; it would be all the same so far as our good or ill luck goes.'

At this point the labourer came up, and Don Quixote asked him: 'Could you tell me, my friend – and may God give you good fortune – where hereabouts are the palaces of the peerless princess, Dulcinea del Toboso?'

'Sir,' replied the lad, 'I'm a stranger, and have only been a few days in this place, working in the fields for a rich farmer. In that house in front of you live the village priest and the sacristan, and both or either of them will be able to inform your worship about this princess, for they have a list of all the inhabitants of El Toboso. Though for myself, I don't believe there's any princess living in the whole place, although there are many ladies, and such fine ones that any one of them may be a princess when she's at home.'

'Well, friend,' said Don Quixote, 'among them must be the lady I am asking for.'

'That may be,' replied the youth. 'Good-bye, for the day's breaking now.' And urging on his mules, he waited for no more questions. Then said Sancho, seeing his master perplexed and somewhat out of humour: 'Now, sir, day's coming on apace, and it won't be wise to let the sun find us in the streets. It'll be better for us to go out of the city, and for your worship to hide in some bushes somewhere near. I will return by day and not leave a corner of this whole place unsearched for the house, castle or palace of my lady; and I shall be very unlucky if I don't find it. And when I find it I will speak to her Grace, and tell her where and how your worship is waiting and expecting her to give you orders and instructions how you may see her without damage to her honour and reputation.'

'Sancho,' said Don Quixote, 'you have uttered a thousand words of wisdom in the short space of a few brief sentences. The advice which you have just given me I welcome, and accept with very good will. Come, my son, let us find somewhere for me to hide, and you shall return, as you say, to see and speak with my lady, of whose discretion and courtesy I expect favours more than miraculous.'

Sancho was racked with desire to get his master out of the village, so that he should not detect his lie about the reply he had brought to the Sierra Morena on Dulcinea's behalf. So he hurried their departure, which was immediate. They found, two miles out of the place, a forest or thicket, where Don Quixote hid while Sancho returned to the city to speak with Dulcinea, in which embassy there happened to him things which call for renewed attention and fresh powers of belief.

Chapter X. *In which is related the device Sancho adopted to enchant the Lady Dulcinea, and other incidents as comical as they are true.*

WHEN the author of this great history comes to recount the contents of this chapter, he says that he would have liked to pass it over in silence, through fear of disbelief. For Don Quixote's delusions here reach the greatest imaginable bounds and limits, and even exceed them, great as they are, by two bow-shots. But finally he wrote the deeds down, although with fear and misgivings, just as our knight performed them, without adding or subtracting one atom of truth from the history, or taking into account any accusations of lying that might be laid against him. And he was right, for truth, though it may run thin, never breaks, and always flows over the lie like oil over water. So, continuing his history, he says that as soon as Don Quixote had hidden himself in the thicket, or oak wood, or forest, beside great El Toboso, he ordered Sancho to go back to the city, and not return to his presence without first speaking to his lady on his behalf, and begging her to be so good as to allow herself to be seen by her captive knight, and to deign to bestow her blessing on him, so that he might hope thereby to meet with the highest success in all his encounters and arduous enterprises. Sancho undertook to do as he was commanded, and to bring his master as favourable a reply as he had brought the first time.

'Go, my son,' said Don Quixote, 'and do not be confused when you find yourself before the light of the sun of beauty you are going to seek. How much more fortunate you are than all other squires in the world! Bear in your mind, and let it not escape you, the manner of your reception; whether she changes colour whilst you are delivering her my message; whether she is stirred or troubled on hearing my name; whether she shifts from her cushion, should you, by chance, find her seated on the rich dais of her authority. If she is standing, watch whether she rests first on one foot and then on the other; whether she repeats her reply to you two or three times; whether she changes from mild to harsh, from cruel to amorous; whether she raises her hand to her hair to smooth it, although it is not untidy. In fact, my son, watch all her actions and movements; because, if you relate them to me as they were, I shall deduce what she keeps concealed in the secret places of her heart as far as concerns the matter of my love. For you must know, Sancho, if you do not know already, that between lovers the outward actions and movements they reveal when their loves are under discussion are most certain messengers, bearing news of what is going on in their innermost souls.   Go, friend, and may better fortune than mine guide you, and send you better success than I expect, waiting between fear and hope in this bitter solitude where you leave me.'

'I'll go, and come back quickly,' said Sancho. 'Cheer up that little heart of yours, dear master, for it must be no bigger now than a hazel nut. Remember the saying that a stout heart breaks bad luck; and where there are no flitches there are no hooks; and they say, too, where you least expect it, out jumps the hare. This I say because now that it's day I hope to find my lady's palaces or castles where I least expect them, even though we didn't find them last night: and once found, leave me to deal with her alone.'

'Indeed, Sancho,' said Don Quixote, 'you always bring in your proverbs very much to the purpose of our business. May God give me as good luck in my ventures as you have in your sayings.'

At these words Sancho turned away and gave Dapple the stick; and Don Quixote stayed on horseback, resting in his stirrups and leaning on his lance, full of sad and troubled fancies, with which we will leave him and go with Sancho Panza, who parted from his master no less troubled and thoughtful than he. So much so that scarcely had he come out of the wood than he turned round and, seeing that Don Quixote was out of sight, dismounted from his ass. Then, sitting down at the foot of a tree, he began to commune with himself to this effect:

'Now, let us learn, brother Sancho, where your worship is going. Are you going after some ass you have lost? No, certainly not. Then what are you going to look for? I am going to look, as you might say, for nothing, for a Princess, and in her the sun of beauty and all heaven besides. And where do you expect to find this thing you speak of, Sancho? Where ? In the great city of El Toboso. Very well, and on whose behalf are you going to seek her? On behalf of the famous knight Don Quixote de la Mancha, who rights wrongs, gives meat to the thirsty, and drink to the hungry. All this is right enough. Now, do you know her house? My master says it will be some royal palace or proud castle. And have you by any chance ever seen her? No, neither I nor my master have ever seen her. And, if the people of El Toboso knew that you are here for the purpose of enticing away their Princesses and disturbing their ladies, do you think it would be right and proper for them to come and give you such a basting as would grind your ribs to powder and not leave you a whole bone in your body? Yes, they would be absolutely in the right, if they did not consider that I am under orders, and that

> You are a messenger, my friend
> And so deserve no blame.

'Don't rely on that, Sancho, for the Manchegans are honest people and very hot-tempered, and they won't stand tickling from anyone. God's truth, if they smell you, you're in for bad luck. Chuck it up, you son of a bitch, and let someone else catch it. No, you won't find me searching for a cat with three legs for someone else's pleasure. What's more, looking for Dulcinea up and down El Toboso will be like looking for little Maria in Ravenna, or the Bachelor in Salamanca. It's the Devil, the Devil himself who has put me into this business. The Devil and no other!'

This colloquy Sancho held with himself, and it led him to the following conclusion: 'Well, now, there's a remedy for everything except death, beneath whose yoke we must all pass, willy-nilly, at the end of our lives. I have seen from countless signs that this

master of mine is a raving lunatic who ought to be tied up – and
me, I can't be much better, for since I follow him and serve him,
I'm more of a fool than he – if the proverb is true that says: tell me
what company you keep and I will tell you what you are; and that
other one too: not with whom you are born but with whom you
feed. Well, he's mad – that he is – and it's the kind of madness that
generally mistakes one thing for another, and thinks white black
and black white, as was clear when he said that the windmills were
giants and the friars' mules dromedaries, and the flocks of sheep
hostile armies, and many other things to this tune. So it won't be
very difficult to make him believe that the first peasant girl I run
across about here is the lady Dulcinea. If he doesn't believe it I'll
swear, and if he swears I'll outswear him, and if he sticks to it I shall
stick to it harder, so that, come what may, my word shall always
stand up to his. Perhaps if I hold out I shall put an end to his sending
me on any more of these errands, seeing what poor answers I bring
back. Or perhaps he'll think, as I fancy he will, that one of those
wicked enchanters who, he says, have a grudge against him, has
changed her shape to vex and spite him.'

With these thoughts Sancho quieted his conscience, reckoning
the business as good as settled. And there he waited till afternoon,
to convince Don Quixote that he had had time to go to El Toboso
and back. And so well did everything turn out that when he got up
to mount Dapple he saw three peasant girls coming in his direction,
riding on three young asses or fillies – our author does not tell us
which – though it is more credible that they were she-asses, as these
are the ordinary mounts of village women; but as nothing much
hangs on it, there is no reason to stop and clear up the point. To
continue – as soon as Sancho saw the girls, he went back at a canter
to look for his master and found him, sighing and uttering countless
amorous lamentations. But as soon as Don Quixote saw him, he
cried: 'What luck, Sancho? Shall I mark this day with a white stone
or with a black?'

'It'll be better,' replied Sancho, 'for your worship to mark it in
red chalk, like college lists, to be plainly seen by all who look.'

'At that rate,' said Don Quixote, 'you bring good news.'

'So good,' answered Sancho, 'that your worship has nothing
more to do than to spur Rocinante and go out into the open to see

the lady Dulcinea del Toboso, who is coming to meet your worship
with two of her damsels.'

'Holy Father! What is that you say, Sancho my friend?' cried
Don Quixote. 'See that you do not deceive me, or seek to cheer my
real sadness with false joys.'

'What could I gain by deceiving your worship?' replied Sancho.
'Especially as you are so near to discovering the truth of my report.
Spur on, sir, come, and you'll see the Princess, our mistress, coming
dressed and adorned – to be brief, as befits her. Her maidens and
she are one blaze of gold, all ropes of pearls, all diamonds, all rubies,
all brocade of more than ten gold strands; their hair loose on their
shoulders, like so many sunrays sporting in the wind and, what's
more, they are riding on three piebald nackneys, the finest to be seen.'

'Hackneys you mean, Sancho.'

'There is very little difference,' replied Sancho, 'between nackneys and hackneys. But let them come on whatever they may, they
are the bravest ladies you could wish for, especially the Princess
Dulcinea, my lady, who dazzles the senses.'

'Let us go, Sancho my son,' replied Don Quixote, 'and as a reward for this news, as unexpected as it is welcome, I grant you the
best spoil I shall gain in the first adventure that befalls me; and, if
that does not content you, I grant you the fillies that my three mares
will bear me this year, for you know that I left them to foal on our
village common.'

'The fillies for me,' cried Sancho, 'for it's not too certain that the
spoils of the first adventure will be good ones.'

At this point they came out of the wood and discovered the three
village girls close at hand. Don Quixote cast his eye all along the
El Toboso road, and seeing nothing but the three peasant girls,
asked Sancho in great perplexity whether he had left the ladies outside the city.

'How outside the city?' he answered. 'Can it be that your worship's eyes are in the back of your head that you don't see that these
are they, coming along shining like the very sun at noon?'

'I can see nothing, Sancho,' said Don Quixote, 'but three village
girls on three donkeys.'

'Now God deliver me from the Devil,' replied Sancho. 'Is it
possible that three hackneys, or whatever they're called, as white

as driven snow, look to your worship like asses? Good Lord, if that's the truth, may my beard be plucked out.'

'But I tell you, Sancho my friend,' said Don Quixote, 'that it is as true that they are asses, or she-asses, as that I am Don Quixote and you Sancho Panza. At least, they look so to me.'

'Hush, sir!' said Sancho. 'Don't say such a thing, but wipe those eyes of yours, and come and do homage to the mistress of your thoughts, who is drawing near.'

As he spoke he rode forward to receive the three village girls, and dismounting from Dapple, took one of the girls' asses by the bridle and sank on both knees to the ground, saying: 'Queen and Princess and Duchess of beauty, may your Highness and Mightiness deign to receive into your grace and good liking your captive knight, who stands here, turned to marble stone, all troubled and unnerved at finding himself in your magnificent presence. I am Sancho Panza, his squire, and he is the travel-weary knight, Don Quixote de la Mancha, called also by the name of the Knight of the Sad Countenance.'

By this time Don Quixote had fallen on his knees beside Sancho, and was staring, with his eyes starting out of his head and a puzzled look on his face, at the person whom Sancho called Queen and Lady. And as he could see nothing in her but a country girl, and not a very handsome one at that, she being round-faced and flat-nosed, he was bewildered and amazed, and did not dare to open his lips. The village girls were equally astonished at seeing these two men, so different in appearance, down on their knees and preventing their companion from going forward. But the girl they had stopped broke the silence by crying roughly and angrily: 'Get out of the way, confound you, and let us pass. We're in a hurry.'

To which Sancho replied: 'O Princess and world-famous Lady of El Toboso! How is it that your magnanimous heart is not softened when you see the column and prop of knight errantry kneeling before your sublimated presence?'

On hearing this, one of the two others exclaimed: 'Wait till I get my hands on you, you great ass! See how these petty gentry come and make fun of us village girls, as if we couldn't give them as good as they bring! Get on your way, and let us get on ours. You had better!'

'Rise, Sancho,' said Don Quixote at this; 'for I see that Fortune,

unsatisfied with the ill already done me, has closed all roads by
which any comfort may come to this wretched soul I bear in my
body. And you, O perfection of all desire! Pinnacle of human gentleness! Sole remedy of this afflicted heart, that adores you! Now that
the malignant enchanter persecutes me, and has put clouds and
cataracts into my eyes, and for them alone, and for no others, has
changed and transformed the peerless beauty of your countenance
into the semblance of a poor peasant girl, if he has not at the same
time turned mine into the appearance of some spectre to make it
abominable to your sight, do not refuse to look at me softly and
amorously, perceiving in this submission and prostration, which I
make before your deformed beauty, the humility with which my
soul adores you.'

'Tell that to my grandmother!' replied the girl. 'Do you think
I want to listen to that nonsense? Get out of the way and let us go
on, and we'll thank you.'

Sancho moved off and let her pass, delighted at having got well
out of his fix. And no sooner did the girl who had played the part of
Dulcinea find herself free than she prodded her nackney with the
point of a stick she carried, and set off at a trot across the field. But
when the she-ass felt the point of the stick, which pained her more
than usual, she began to plunge so wildly that my lady Dulcinea
came off upon the ground. When Don Quixote saw this accident he
rushed to pick her up, and Sancho to adjust and strap on the pack-
saddle, which had slipped under the ass's belly. But when the saddle
was adjusted and Don Quixote was about to lift his enchanted mistress in his arms and place her on her ass, the lady picked herself up
from the ground and spared him the trouble. For, stepping back a
little, she took a short run, and resting both her hands on the ass's
rump, swung her body into the saddle, lighter than a hawk, and sat
astride like a man.

At which Sancho exclaimed: 'By St. Roque, the lady, our mistress, is lighter than a falcon, and she could train the nimblest Cordovan or Mexican to mount like a jockey. She was over the crupper
of the saddle in one jump, and now without spurs she's making that
hackney gallop like a zebra. And her maidens are not much behind
her. They're all going like the wind.'

And so they were, for once Dulcinea was mounted, they all

spurred after her and dashed away at full speed, without once looking behind them till they had gone almost two miles. Don Quixote
followed them with his eyes, and, when he saw that they had disappeared, turned to Sancho and said:

'Do you see now what a spite the enchanters have against me,
Sancho? See to what extremes the malice and hatred they bear me
extend, for they have sought to deprive me of the happiness I
should have enjoyed in seeing my mistress in her true person. In
truth, I was born a very pattern for the unfortunate, and to be a
target and mark for the arrows of adversity. You must observe also,
Sancho, that these traitors were not satisfied with changing and
transforming my Dulcinea, but transformed her and changed her
into a figure as low and ugly as that peasant girl's. And they have
deprived her too of something most proper to great ladies, which is
the sweet smell they have from always moving among ambergris
and flowers. For I must tell you, Sancho, that when I went to help
my Dulcinea on to her hackney – as you say it was, though it seemed
a she-ass to me – I got such a whiff of raw garlic as stank me out and
poisoned me to the heart.'

'Oh, the curs!' cried Sancho at this. 'Oh, wretched and spiteful
enchanters! I should like to see you strung up by the gills like pilchards on a reed. Wise you are and powerful – and much evil you
do! It should be enough for you, ruffians, to have changed the
pearls of my lady's eyes into corktree galls, and her hair of purest
gold into red ox tail bristles, and all her features, in fact, from good
to bad, without meddling with her smell. For from that at least we
have gathered what lay concealed beneath that ugly crust. Though,
to tell you the truth, I never saw her ugliness, but only her beauty,
which was enhanced and perfected by a mole she had on her right
lip, like a moustache, with seven or eight red hairs like threads of
gold more than nine inches long.'

'To judge from that mole,' said Don Quixote, 'by the correspondence there is between those on the face and those on the body,
Dulcinea must have another on the fleshy part of her thigh, on the
same side as the one on her face. But hairs of the length you indicate
are very long for moles.'

'But I can assure your worship,' replied Sancho, 'that there they
were, as if they had been born with her.'

'I believe it, friend,' said Don Quixote, 'for nature has put nothing on Dulcinea which is not perfect and well-finished. And so, if she had a hundred moles like the one you speak of on her, they would not be moles, but moons and shining stars. But tell me, Sancho, that which appeared to me to be a pack-saddle and which you set straight – was it a plain saddle or a side-saddle?'

'It was just a lady's saddle,' replied Sancho, 'with an outdoor covering so rich that it was worth half a kingdom.'

'And to think that I did not see all this, Sancho!' cried Don Quixote. 'Now I say once more – and I will repeat it a thousand times – I am the most unfortunate of men.'

And that rascal Sancho had all he could do to hide his amusement on hearing this crazy talk from his master, whom he had so beautifully deceived. In the end, after much further conversation between the pair, they mounted their beasts once more, and followed the road to Saragossa, where they expected to arrive in time to be present at a solemn festival which is held every year in that illustrious city. But before they got there certain things happened to them, so many, so important, and so novel that they deserve to be written down and read, as will be seen hereafter.

Chapter XI. *Of the strange Adventure which befell the valorous Don Quixote with the Car or Waggon of the Parliament of Death.*

VERY much downcast Don Quixote went on his way, pondering on the evil trick the enchanters had played on him in turning his lady Dulcinea into the foul shape of a village girl, and he could think of no remedy he could take to restore her to her original state. These thoughts took him so much out of himself that he gave Rocinante the reins without noticing it. And his horse, feeling the liberty he was given, lingered at each step to browse the green grass, which grew thickly in those fields. But Sancho roused his master from his musing by saying:

'Sir, griefs were not made for beasts but for men. Yet if men feel them too deeply they turn to beasts. Pull yourself together, your worship, and come to your senses and pick up Rocinante's reins. Cheer up and wake up, and show that gay spirit knights errant should have. What the devil is it? What despondency is this? Are we here or in France? Let all the Dulcineas in the world go to Old Nick, for the well-being of a single knight errant is worth more than all the enchantments and transformations on earth.'

'Hush, Sancho,' replied Don Quixote with more spirit than might have been expected. 'Hush, I say, and speak no more blasphemies against that enchanted lady. For I alone am to blame for her misfortune and disaster. From the envy the wicked bear me springs her sad plight.'

'And so say I,' answered Sancho, 'who saw her and can still see her now. What heart is there that would not weep?'

'You may well say that, Sancho,' replied Don Quixote, 'since you saw her in the perfect fullness of her beauty, for the enchantment did not go so far as to disturb your vision or conceal her beauty from you. Against me alone, against my eyes, was directed the power of their venom. But for all that, Sancho, one thing occurs to me: you described her beauty to me badly. For, if I remember rightly, you said that she had eyes like pearls, and eyes like pearls suit a sea-bream better than a lady. According to my belief, Dulcinea's eyes must be green emeralds, full and large, with twin rainbows to serve them for eyebrows. So take these pearls from her eyes and transfer them to her teeth, for no doubt you got mixed up, Sancho, taking her teeth for her eyes.'

'Anything's possible,' replied Sancho, 'for her beauty confused me, as her ugliness did your worship. But let's leave it all in God's hands. For He knows all things that happen in this vale of tears, in this wicked world of ours, where there's hardly anything to be found without a tincture of evil, deceit and roguery in it. But one thing troubles me, dear master, more than all the rest: I can't think what we're to do when your worship conquers a giant or another knight and commands him to go and present himself before the beauteous Dulcinea. Where is he to find her, that poor giant or that poor miserable conquered knight? I seem to see them wandering about El Toboso, gaping like dummies, in search of my lady Dulcinea; and even if they meet her in the middle of the street they won't know her any more than they would my father.'

'Perhaps, Sancho,' answered Don Quixote, 'the enchantment will not extend so far as to deprive vanquished and presented giants and knights of the power to recognize Dulcinea. But we will make the experiment with one or two of the first I conquer. We will send them with orders to return and give me an account of their fortunes in this respect, and so discover whether they can see her or not.'

'Yes, sir,' said Sancho; 'that seems a good idea to me. By that trick we shall find out what we want to, and if it proves that she is only disguised from your worship, the misfortunes will be more yours than hers. But so long as the lady Dulcinea has her health and happiness, we in these parts will make shift to put up with it as best we can. We'll seek our adventures and leave Time to look after hers; for Time's the best doctor for such ailments and for worse.'

Don Quixote was about to reply to Sancho, but he was interrupted by a waggon, which came out across the road loaded with some of the strangest shapes imaginable. Driving the mules and acting as carter was an ugly demon, and the waggon itself was open to the sky, without tilt or hurdle roof. The first figure which presented itself before Don Quixote's eyes was Death himself with a human face. Beside him stood an angel with large painted wings. On one side was an Emperor with a crown on his head, apparently of gold. At the feet of Death was the God they call Cupid, without his bandage over his eyes, but with his bow, his quiver and his arrows. There was also a knight in complete armour, except that he wore no helmet or headpiece, but a hat instead adorned with multi-coloured plumes. And there were other personages differing in dress and appearance. The sudden vision of this assembly threw Don Quixote into some degree of alarm, and struck fear into Sancho's heart. But soon the knight's spirits mounted with the belief that there was some new and perilous adventure presenting itself; and with this idea in his head, and his heart ready to encounter any sort of danger, he took up his position in front of the cart, and cried in a loud and threatening voice:

'Carter, coachman, devil, or whatever you may be, tell me instantly who you are, where you are going, and who are the people you are driving in your coach, which looks more like Charon's bark than an ordinary cart.'

To which the Devil, stopping the cart, politely replied: 'Sir, we're players of Angulo El Malo's company. We've been acting this morning in a village which lies behind that hill – for it's Corpus

Christi week. Our piece is called *The Parliament of Death*; and we have to perform this evening, in that village which you can see over there. So because it's quite near, and to spare ourselves the trouble of taking off our clothes and dressing again, we are travelling in the costumes we act in. That young man there plays Death. The other fellow's the Angel. That lady, who is the manager's wife, is the Queen. This man plays the Soldier. That man's the Emperor. And I'm the Devil and one of the chief characters in the piece, for I play the principal parts in this company. If your worship wants to know anything more about us, ask me. I can tell you every detail, for being the Devil I'm up to everything.'

'On the faith of a knight errant,' answered Don Quixote, 'when I saw this cart I imagined that some great adventure was presenting itself to me. But now I declare that appearances are not always to be trusted. Go, in God's name, good people, and hold your festival; and think whether you have any request to make of me. If I can do you any service I gladly and willingly will do so, for from my boyhood I have been a lover of pantomimes, and in my youth I was always a glutton for comedies.'

Now, whilst they were engaged in this conversation, as Fate would have it, one of the company caught them up, dressed in motley with a lot of bells about him, and carrying three full blown ox-bladders on the end of a stick. When this clown came up to Don Quixote, he began to fence with his stick, to beat the ground with his bladders, and leap into the air to the sound of his bells; and this evil apparition so scared Rocinante that he took the bit between his teeth, and started to gallop across the field with more speed than the bones of his anatomy promised; nor was Don Quixote strong enough to stop him. Then, realizing that his master was in danger of being thrown off, Sancho jumped down from Dapple and ran in all haste to his assistance. But when he got up to him he was already on the ground, and beside him lay Rocinante, who had fallen with his master – for such was the usual upshot of the knight's exploits and Rocinante's high spirits.

But no sooner had Sancho left his own mount to help Don Quixote than the dancing devil jumped on to Dapple, and dealt him a slap with the bladders, whereat, startled by the noise rather than by the pain of the blows, the ass went flying off across country towards

the village where the festival was to take place. Sancho watched
Dapple's flight and his master's fall, undecided which of the two
calls to attend to first. But finally, good squire and good servant
that he was, love of his master prevailed over affection for his ass,
though each time he saw the bladders rise in the air and fall on his
Dapple's rump, he felt the pains and terrors of death, for he would
rather have had those blows fall on his own eyeballs than on the
least hair of his ass's tail. In this sad state of perplexity he arrived
where Don Quixote lay in a great deal worse plight than he cared
to see him in and, helping him on to Rocinante, he said: 'Sir, the
Devil's carried Dapple off.'

'What Devil?' asked Don Quixote.

'The one with the bladders,' replied Sancho.

'Then I shall get him back,' said Don Quixote, 'even if he were
to lock him up in the deepest and darkest dungeons of Hell. Follow
me, Sancho. For the waggon goes slowly, and I will take its mules
to make up for the loss of Dapple.'

'There's no need to go to that trouble, sir,' said Sancho. 'Cool
your anger, your worship, for it looks to me as if the Devil has let
Dapple go and is off to his own haunts again.'

And so indeed he was. For when the Devil had given an imitation of Don Quixote and Rocinante by tumbling off Dapple he set
off to the village on foot, and the ass came back to his master.

'All the same,' said Don Quixote, 'it will be as well to visit that
demon's impoliteness on one of those in the waggon, perhaps on
the Emperor himself.'

'Put that thought out of your head, your worship,' answered
Sancho. 'Take my advice and never meddle with play-actors, for
they're a favoured race. I've seen an actor taken up for a couple of
murders and get off scot-free. As they're a merry lot and give pleasure, I would have your worship know that everybody sides with
them and protects them, aids them, and esteems them, particularly
if they belong to the King's companies and have a charter. And all
of them, or most of them, look like princes when they have their
costumes and make-up on.'

'For all that,' answered Don Quixote, 'that player devil shall not
go away applauding himself, even if the whole human race favours
him.'

And as he spoke, he turned towards the waggon, which was now very close to the village, calling out loudly, as he rode: 'Halt! Stop, merry and festive crew! For I would teach you how to treat asses and animals which serve as mounts to the squires of knights errant.'

So loudly did Don Quixote shout that those in the waggon heard and understood him; and judging from his words the purpose of their speaker, Death promptly jumped out of the waggon, and after him the Emperor, the Demon-driver, and the Angel; nor did the Queen or the god Cupid stay behind. Then they all loaded themselves with stones and took up their positions in a row, waiting to receive Don Quixote with the edges of their pebbles. But when he saw them drawn up in so gallant a squadron, with their arms raised in the act of discharging this powerful volley of stones, he reined Rocinante in, and began to consider how to set upon them with least peril to his person. While he was thus checked Sancho came up and, seeing him drawn up to attack that well-ordered squadron, said:

'It would be the height of madness to attempt such an enterprise. Consider, your worship, that there is no defensive armour in the world against the rain of these fellows' bullets, unless you could ram yourself into a brass bell and hide. And you must consider too, master, that it is rashness and not valour for a single man to attack an army with Death in its ranks, Emperors in person fighting in it, and assisted by good and bad angels. What's more, if this isn't reason enough to persuade you to stay quiet, consider that it's a positive fact that although they look like Kings, Princes and Emperors, there isn't a single knight errant among the whole lot of them there.'

'Now, Sancho,' said Don Quixote, 'you have certainly hit on a consideration which should deflect me from my determination. I cannot and must not draw my sword, as I have told you on many occasions before now, against anyone who is not a knight. It rests with you therefore, Sancho, if you wish to take revenge for the injury done to your Dapple; and I will help you from here with words of salutary counsel.'

'There's no reason, sir, to take revenge on anyone,' replied Sancho, 'for it's not right for a good Christian to avenge his injuries. What's more I shall persuade Dapple to leave his cause in my hands, and it's my intention to live peacefully all the days of life that Heaven grants me.'

'Since that is your decision,' answered Don Quixote, 'good Sancho, wise Sancho, Christian Sancho, honest Sancho, let us leave these phantoms and return to our quest for better and more substantial adventures. For I'm sure that this is the sort of country that can't fail to provide us with many and most miraculous ones.'

Then he turned Rocinante, Sancho went to catch his Dapple, and Death and all his flying squadron returned to their waggon and continued their journey. And this was the happy ending of the encounter with the waggon of Death, thanks to the healthy advice which Sancho Panza gave his master, to whom on the next day there came another adventure, with an enamoured knight errant, which proved no less exciting than the last.

Chapter XII. *Of the strange Adventure which befell the valorous Don Quixote with the brave Knight of the Mirrors.*

DON QUIXOTE and his squire passed the night following the day of this encounter with Death beneath some tall and shady trees, where, on Sancho's persuasion, the knight ate some food from the store which Dapple carried. And during their supper Sancho observed to his master: 'Sir, what a fool I should have been if I'd chosen the spoils of your worship's first adventure as my reward, instead of the three mares' foals. Indeed, indeed, a bird in the hand's worth two in the bush.'

'For all that,' replied Don Quixote, 'if you had let me attack, Sancho, as I wanted to, at least the Empress's golden crown and Cupid's painted wings would have fallen to you as spoils, for I should have pulled them off in spite of their struggles, and placed them in your hands.'

'The sceptres and crowns of player-emperors have never been pure gold,' replied Sancho, 'but tinsel or brass foil.'

'That is true,' replied Don Quixote. 'It would not be right for the finery in plays to be real; it should be counterfeit and illusory, as the play is itself. To which plays, Sancho, I would have you favourably disposed, and therefore, to the actors and authors as well, for they are all instrumental in conferring a great benefit on the commonwealth, holding up to us at every step a mirror in which the actions of human life are vividly portrayed. Indeed there is no comparison which presents to us more truly what we are and what we ought to be than the play and the players. Now, tell me, have not you seen a play acted with Kings, Emperors and Popes, knights, ladies and various other personages brought on to the stage? One plays the ruffian, another the cheat; here is a merchant, there is a soldier; one is the wise fool, another the foolish lover. But when the play is over, and they have taken off their dresses, all the actors are equal.'

'Yes, I have indeed,' replied Sancho.

'Now the same thing,' said Don Quixote, 'happens in the comedy and traffic of this world, where some play Emperors, others Popes and, in fact, every part that can be introduced into a play. But when we come to the end, which is when life is over, Death strips them of all the robes that distinguished them, and they are all equals in the grave.'

'A fine comparison,' said Sancho, 'although not so new that I haven't heard it on various occasions before – like the one of the game of chess, where each piece has its particular importance while the game lasts, but when it's over they're all mixed up, thrown together, jumbled, and shoved into a leather bag, which is much like shovelling life away into the grave.'

'Every day, Sancho,' said Don Quixote, 'you grow less simple and wiser.'

'Yes,' replied Sancho, 'for some of your worship's wisdom must stick to me. Since lands of themselves barren and dry, with mucking and tilling come to yield good fruit. I mean that your worship's conversation has been the muck, which has been cast upon the sterile ground of my dry wit, and the time of my service and communion with you has been the tillage. And so I expect to bear fruit of my own, which may be a blessing, and won't disgrace me, I hope, or slither off the paths of good breeding you have beaten in this parched understanding of mine.'

Don Quixote laughed at Sancho's affected language, but what he had said about his improvement seemed to him true. For from time to time he spoke in a way that surprised his master, although on all, or almost all, the occasions when Sancho tried to dispute in a grand style, his argument ended by tumbling from the heights of simplicity into the depths of ignorance. But where he showed his wit and his memory to best effect was in his use of proverbs, whether they applied to the subject or not, as will have been seen and noted in the course of this history.

In this and suchlike conversation they spent a great part of the night, till a desire came on Sancho to drop the hatches of his eyes, as he used to say when he wanted to sleep. So, unharnessing Dapple, he turned him over to graze freely and abundantly. But he did not take off Rocinante's saddle, it being his master's express command that, during such time as they should be in the field or not sleeping beneath a roof, he should not unsaddle his steed – for it was an ancient custom established and preserved by knights errant, to take off the bridle and hang it on the saddle-bow; but to unsaddle the horse – Never! This law Sancho obeyed and gave Rocinante the same freedom as Dapple. Now the friendship between the pair was so rare and so strong that there is a tradition handed down from father to son that the author of this true history devoted some special chapters to it, but, to preserve the propriety and decorum proper to so heroic a story, omitted to put them in. Though at times he forgets this purpose of his, and writes that as soon as the two beasts were together they would start scratching one another, and that once they were tired and contented, Rocinante would cross his neck over Dapple's – and it would stick out by more than half a yard. Then the two of them would gaze fixedly on the ground and stand in that position for three days, or at least for so long as they were left, or hunger did not compel them to seek for sustenance. The tradition is, I repeat, that the author left in writing a comparison between their friendship and that of Nisus and Euryalus, and of Pylades and Orestes. And if this is true, it can be deduced how strong the friendship between these two pacific animals must have been, to the wonder of the world and to the shame of humankind, who are so little able to preserve friendships for one another. Hence the saying:

> 'There is no friendship between friends ;
> Men's sparring canes are turned to lances'

and that is the reason for that other song:

> 'Twixt friend and friend the bug creeps in.'

But let no one suppose that the author digressed in comparing the friendship of these animals to that of men. For men have received many lessons from the beasts and learnt many important things from them, for example: from storks, the enema; from the dog, vomiting and gratitude; from cranes, vigilance; from ants, thrift; from elephants, chastity, and loyalty from the horse.

At length Sancho fell asleep at the foot of a cork-tree, and Don Quixote into a doze at the foot of a stout oak. But very little time had elapsed before the knight was awoken by a noise which he heard behind him. Thereupon he started up and began to look and to listen whence the noise proceeded. He soon made out two men on horseback, and heard one of them say to the other, as he dropped from his saddle: 'Get down, friend, and unbridle the horses, for this place seems to me both rich in grass for them, and in the silence and solitude my amorous meditations require.'

Saying this and stretching himself on the ground were the action of a moment; and as he threw himself down, the armour he was wearing made a clatter, a clear proof to Don Quixote that he must be a knight errant. So, going up to Sancho, who was still asleep, he pulled him by the arm, and with no little labour brought him to his senses, telling him in a whisper: 'Brother Sancho, we have an adventure.'

'God make it a good one!' answered Sancho. 'And where is she, dear master, her Grace Madam Adventure?'

'Where, Sancho?' replied Don Quixote. 'Turn your eyes and look, and you will see a knight errant lying down over there. It looks to me as if he is not any too cheerful, for I have just watched him leap from his horse and throw himself on the ground with some display of dejection. And when he fell his armour clattered.'

'But how does your worship make out,' asked Sancho, 'that it's an adventure?'

'I do not mean to say,' replied Don Quixote, 'that this is a complete adventure, but the beginning of one. For this is the way adventures start. But listen. It looks as if he is tuning up a lute or a viol, and by the way he is spitting and clearing his throat, he must be getting ready to sing something.'

'Yes indeed, so he is,' replied Sancho. 'Then he must be a knight in love.'

'There is no knight errant who is not,' said Don Quixote. 'Let us listen to him; for, if he does sing, from that thread we shall gain a clue to his thoughts, since out of the abundance of the heart speaks the tongue.'

Sancho was going to reply to his master, but he was prevented by the voice of the Knight of the Wood, which was neither very bad nor very good; and the pair of them listened attentively while he sang the following song:

> Mistress, prescribe a law whereby
>   I may obey your sovereign heart.
> I'll follow it unswervingly
>   And from its precepts ne'er depart.
>
> If you would have me die of pain
>   In silence, then account me dead,
> But if you'd have the ancient strain
>   Ring out, then Love himself shall plead.
>
> Proof against contraries I'm made,
>   Of softest wax and diamond hard.
> Beneath love's rule my heart is laid
>   And for its laws my soul's prepared.
>
> Or soft or hard, my breast is thine.
>   Imprint what characters you will.
> To all eternity, divine
>   Mistress, I'll do your bidding still.

With a sigh, fetched apparently from the depths of his heart, the Knight of the Wood ended his song, and a little later cried in a sad and sorrowful voice:

'O most beautiful and ungrateful woman in all the world! How can it be possible, most serene Casildea de Vandalia, for you to allow your captive knight to be consumed and to perish in perpetual wanderings and in hard and harsh labours? Is it not enough that I have made all the knights of Navarre acknowledge you the most beautiful lady in the world, and all the Knights of Leon, of Tartesia and of Castile, and all the Knights of La Mancha as well?'

'Not so,' remarked Don Quixote at this point, 'for I am of La Mancha, and have acknowledged no such thing. Nor could I, nor should I acknowledge anything so prejudicial to the beauty of my mistress. You can see now, Sancho, that this knight is raving. But let us listen; perhaps he will reveal himself further.'

'Yes, he will,' replied Sancho, 'for he looks the kind to complain for a month on end.'

But it was not so. For, overhearing this talk so near him, the Knight of the Wood proceeded no further with his lamentation, but got on to his feet and called out in loud but courteous tones: 'Who goes there? Who are you? Do you chance to be of the number of the happy or of the afflicted?'

'Of the afflicted,' replied Don Quixote.

'Then come to me,' answered the Knight of the Wood, 'and you will find sorrow and misery itself.'

Then finding himself so delicately and politely answered Don Quixote went over to him, as did Sancho as well, on which the plaintive knight took Don Quixote by the arm and said: 'Sit down here, Sir Knight, for to be assured that you are a knight and profess the order of knight errantry, it is sufficient that I have found you in this spot encompassed by solitude and the dews of night – the natural bed and proper habitation for a knight errant.'

To which Don Quixote replied: 'I am a knight, and of the order you name; and although sorrows, misfortunes, and disasters have their very seat in my soul, the compassion I feel for the misfortunes of others is not therefore banished from my heart. From what you have just sung I gathered that yours are misfortunes of love – I mean of the love you have for that ungrateful beauty whom you named in your lament.'

Now during this conversation they were seated together on the hard ground in peace and comradeship, as if they had not to break each other's heads at break of day.

'Are you, Sir Knight,' the Knight of the Wood asked Don Quixote, 'by any chance in love?'

'By ill chance I am,' replied Don Quixote, 'although the sufferings which arise from well-placed affections should rather be considered benefits than calamities.'

'That is true,' replied the Knight of the Wood, 'if disdain did not confuse the reason and the understanding. For when it is excessive it looks like revenge.'

'I have never been disdained by my mistress,' answered Don Quixote.

'No, certainly not,' said Sancho, who was near them, 'for our lady is as meek as a yearling ewe and softer than butter.'

'Is this your squire?' asked the Knight of the Wood.

'It is,' answered Don Quixote.

'I have never met a squire,' said the Knight of the Wood, 'who dared to speak when his master was speaking. At least there stands that man of mine, who is as big as his father, and it cannot be proved that he ever opened his lips when I was speaking.'

'Well,' said Sancho, 'I've talked right enough, and I can talk before another as ... But let it be; it'll be the worse for stirring.'

Then the Squire of the Wood grasped Sancho's arm and said: 'Let us two go where we can talk squire-like about anything we choose, and let's leave these gentlemen, our masters, to set to and tell one another the stories of their loves. For the morning'll catch them at it, I promise you, and they won't have finished then.'

'That suits me,' said Sancho, 'and I'll tell your worship who I am. Then you'll see whether I can compete with your most talkative of squires.'

At this the two squires drew aside, and the conversation between them was as comical as their masters' was serious.

Chapter XIII. *In which is continued the Adventure of the Knight of the Wood together with the wise, novel and agreeable Conversation between the two Squires.*

THE knights and their squires were separated, the squires telling the stories of their lives, the knights of their loves. But history recounts the servants' conversation first, and then follows the talk between their masters. And so it relates that when they had drawn a little aside the Squire of the Wood said to Sancho: 'It's a wearisome life we have, sir, we that are squires to knights errant. Indeed we eat our bread in the sweat of our brows, which is one of the curses God laid on our first parents.'

'It may be said too,' added Sancho, 'that we eat it in the chill of our bodies, for who suffers the heat and the cold worse than the miserable squires of knight errantry? It wouldn't be so bad if we could eat, for good fare lessens care. Yet sometimes we spend a whole day, or even two, without breaking our fast except on the winds that blow.'

'All that can be borne and put up with,' said the Squire of the Wood, 'seeing what hope we have of reward. For unless the knight errant he is serving is excessively unfortunate a squire will at least find himself rewarded in a little while with the handsome government of some isle, or with a respectable countship.'

'I,' replied Sancho, 'have already told my master that I shall be content with the government of an isle; and so noble and generous is he that he's promised me it on several occasions already.'

'I,' said the Squire of the Wood, 'shall be satisfied with a canonry for my services; and my master has already reserved one for me – and what a one!'

'Then, of course,' said Sancho, 'your worship's master must be a knight in the ecclesiastical line, that he can grant his worthy squire a favour of that kind. But mine is only a layman, though I remember that there was a time when some clever persons – they were rather malicious, I thought – were advising him to try and become an Archbishop. But he was set on becoming an Emperor, though I was trembling at the time for fear he might take it into his head to be a churchman, not feeling myself capable of holding a church benefice. For I would have you know that, though I seem a man, if it's a question of going into the Church I'm a very beast.'

'But indeed your worship is wrong,' said the Squire of the Wood, 'for your insular governments are not all of the right kind. Some are crooked, some poor, and some depressing; and, what's more, the stateliest and best of them brings a heavy load of cares and discomforts with it, and the unlucky man it falls to must bear them on his shoulders. It would be a great deal better for us who profess this accursed service to retire to our homes, and there employ ourselves in more agreeable exercises, as in hunting perhaps or in fishing. For what squire in the world is there so poor that he hasn't a horse and a couple of greyhounds and a fishing-rod to amuse himself with in his own village?'

'I'm not short of any of those things,' answered Sancho, 'though it's true that I haven't a horse. But I have an ass worth twice as much as my master's horse. God send me a bad Easter and may it be

S

the next one, if I would swap with him, even if I got four bushels of barley thrown in. Your worship may think I'm joking when I put that price on my Dapple – for dapple is my ass's colour. But I shan't be short of greyhounds, for there are enough and to spare in my village; and hunting is all the pleasanter when it's at someone else's expense.'

'To tell you the truth, Master Squire,' replied the Squire of the Wood, 'I've made up my mind, and I'm determined to quit the drunken goings-on of these knights of ours, and retire to my village and bring up my children; for I have three of them, lovely as three orient pearls.'

'I have two,' said Sancho, 'fit to be presented to the Pope himself, one girl especially whom I'm bringing up to be a countess, please God – though in spite of her mother.'

'And what's the age of the young lady who is being brought up to be a countess?' asked the Squire of the Wood.

'Fifteen, more or less,' answered Sancho, 'but she's as tall as a lance, as fresh as an April morning, and as strong as a porter.'

'Those are qualities,' said the Squire of the Wood, 'that fit her not only to be a countess, but to be a nymph of the green wood. Oh, the little whore, the whore, what muscles the rogue must have!'

To which Sancho replied rather peevishly: 'She's no whore, nor was her mother, and neither of them ever will be, God willing, whilst I'm alive. Speak rather more politely, for seeing that your worship was brought up amongst knights errant, who are politeness itself, these words of yours don't seem very well chosen.'

'Oh, how little your worship understands the play of compliments, Master Squire,' replied the Squire of the Wood. 'Why, don't you know that when a horseman deals the bull in the square a good lance-thrust, or when anyone does a thing really well the crowd always shout: "Oh, the whore, the little whore, that was nicely done!" And what seems abuse in that term is really notable praise. You should disown, sir, any sons or daughters who don't perform deeds that earn their parents praise like that.'

'Yes, I disown them,' answered Sancho, 'and since you mean so well by it, your worship may clap a whole brothel on top of me, my children and my wife, for everything they do and say is highly deserving of such praise. I'm longing to see them again, and therefore

I pray God to deliver me out of mortal sin – that's to say to deliver me from this perilous office of squire, into which I've run for a second time, through being enticed and deceived by a purse of a hundred ducats which I found one day in the heart of the Sierra Morena. For the Devil's always dangling a bag full of doubloons before my eyes here, there and everywhere. At every step I seem to be laying my hands on it, hugging it, and taking it home, then making investments and settling rents, and living like a prince. And while this runs in my head all the toils I endure with my idiot of a master become light and bearable, though I know he's more of a madman than a knight.'

'That's why they say that greed bursts the bag,' replied the Squire of the Wood. 'But, talking of madmen, there's no greater idiot in the world than my master. There's a proverb that just fits him: other men's cares kill the ass. For to restore another knight his lost wits he's making a madman of himself, and goes about looking for something which may hit him on the snout when he finds it.'

'And is he by any chance in love?'

'Yes,' said the Squire of the Wood, 'with a certain Casildea de Vandalia, the rawest and best-cooked lady to be found in the whole world. But that's not the foot he limps on at present, for there are greater tricks rumbling in his stomach, which he will speak of before many hours have passed.'

'There's no road so smooth,' replied Sancho, 'that it hasn't some obstruction or hole. In other houses they cook beans, but whole cauldrons full in mine. Madness needs more companions and messmates than wisdom. But if it's true, as it's commonly said, that to have companions in your troubles generally helps to relieve them, I can draw comfort from your worship since you serve another master as foolish as mine.'

'Foolish but valiant,' said the Squire of the Wood, 'and more of a rogue than either foolish or valiant.'

'That my master isn't,' replied Sancho. 'I mean there's nothing of the rogue in him. His soul is as clean as a pitcher. He can do no harm to anyone, only good to everybody. There's no malice in him. A child might make him believe it's night at noonday. And for that simplicity I love him as dearly as my heart-strings, and can't take to the idea of leaving him for all his wild tricks.'

'All the same, sir and brother,' said the Squire of the Wood, 'if the blind lead the blind, both will be in danger of falling into the ditch. It would be better for us to go back pretty quick and retire to our lairs, for seekers after adventures don't always find good ones.'

All this while Sancho was spitting frequently a kind of dryish gluey saliva; and when the kind Squire of the Wood noticed it, he observed: 'All this talk seems to be making our tongues stick to our palates. I carry a pretty good loosener, though, here hanging at my saddle-bow.'

And, getting up, he came back a moment later with a large leather bottle of wine and a pie half a yard long – which is no exaggeration, for the white rabbit it contained was so large that when Sancho felt it he thought it was a goat, and no kid either. And at this sight our squire exclaimed: 'Do you carry this around with you, sir?'

'Well, what do you think?' replied the other. 'Do I look like a wool and water squire? I carry a better meal on my horse's crupper than a general takes with him when he goes on a march.'

Sancho fell to without invitation and swallowed great shovels-ful in the dark, saying: 'Your worship is certainly a loyal and law-ful squire, good and proper, magnificent and grand, as this banquet shows. For if it hasn't come here by way of enchantment, at least it looks as if it has. You're not like me, poor and unlucky, with only a bit of hard cheese in my saddle bag, that you could break a giant's head with, and four dozen carob beans to bear it company, and about the same number of filberts and nuts. I've my master's mean-ness to thank for that, and his ideas and rules about knights errant keeping body and soul together on nothing but dry fruits and the herbs of the field.'

'My stomach isn't made for your thistles or your wild pears or your forest roots, I promise you, brother,' replied the Squire of the Wood. 'Let our masters have them, with their ideas and their laws of chivalry, and let them eat what they order others to. I carry my panniers and this bottle hanging on my saddle-bow, just in case; and I'm so devoted to it and love it so dearly that seldom an hour passes without my kissing it and hugging it once or twice.'

And so saying, he gave it to Sancho, who tilted it, put it to his mouth and gazed at the stars for a quarter of an hour on end. Then, when he had finished drinking, he let his head fall to one side, and remarked with a deep sigh:

'O the little whore, the rogue! What grand stuff it is!'

'Now see,' said the Squire of the Wood, hearing Sancho's '*little whore*', 'how you praised that wine by calling it a whore.'

'Yes, I confess that it's no dishonour to call anyone a whore, when you mean it for praise,' replied Sancho. 'But, tell me, sir, on your Bible oath, is this wine from Ciudad Real?'

'A rare judge!' answered the Squire of the Wood. 'From no other place, that's a fact, and it's a good few years old too.'

'Trust me for that,' said Sancho. 'Don't suppose that I wasn't up to recognizing its quality. Isn't it good, Sir Squire, that I have such a fine and natural instinct for this wine-judging? You've only to give me a drop to smell and I can hit upon the place, the grape, the savour, and the age; and the changes it'll go through, and every other point to do with wine. But there's nothing surprising in that, for I had in my family, on my father's side, the two best judges of wine that La Mancha has known for many a long year. And to prove it to you I'll tell you a story about them. They gave the pair of them some wine from a cask to try, and asked them their opinion of its condition, its quality, its goodness or badness. One of them tried it on the tip of his tongue, the other did no more than lift it to his nose. The first said that the wine tasted of iron; the second said that it had rather the flavour of leather. The owner said that the cask was clean, and that the wine had no blending from which it could have taken the flavour of iron or of leather. For all that the two famous judges persisted in their opinions. Time went on; the wine was sold; and when they came to clean the cask, they found a little key in it hanging on a leather thong. So your worship can see that a man of a breed like that has a right to give an opinion in such-like cases.'

'That's why I say,' said the Squire of the Wood, 'that we should give up going after adventures, and since we have loaves not seek for cakes, but go back to our cottages, for God will find us there if He wants to.'

'Until my master gets to Saragossa I'll serve him, and after that we'll come to some arrangement.'

At length the two good squires had talked and drunk so much

that they had need of sleep to tie their tongues and allay their thirst, for to quench it would have been impossible. So grasping the almost empty bottle between them, with their meat half chewed in their mouths, they fell asleep; where we will leave them for now, to relate what passed between the Knight of the Wood and the Knight of the Sad Countenance.

Chapter XIV. *In which the Adventure of the Knight of the Wood is continued.*

AMONG the many speeches which passed between Don Quixote and the Knight of the Wood, our history tells us that the latter addressed our knight to this effect:

'To be brief, Sir Knight, I would have you know that my destiny or, to be more exact, my choice led me to fall in love with the peerless Casildea of Vandalia. I call her peerless because she has no equal either in the greatness of her stature or in the perfection of her rank and beauty. Now this Casildea I am telling you of repaid my honest affections and courteous desires by employing me, as his stepmother did Hercules, in many and various labours, promising me at the end of each one that with the conclusion of the next I should attain the goal of my hopes. But in that way my toils have been increased link by link, till they are countless, and I still do not know which is to be the last, and to lead to the fulfilment of my honest desires. Once she commanded me to go and challenge that famous Seville giantess, the Giralda, who is as valiant and strong as if she were of brass, and without stirring from one place, is the most changeable and volatile woman in the world. I came, I saw, I conquered her. I forced her to stay still and keep to one point, for none but the north-wind blew for more than a week. There was a time too when she commanded me to go and weigh those ancient stones, the brave Bulls of Guisando, an exploit fitter to be entrusted to a porter than to a knight. Another time she commanded me to plunge headlong into the cavern of Cabra – a fearful and unheard-of peril – and bring her back a detailed account of what lay concealed in those dark depths. I stayed the motion of La Giralda; I weighed the Bulls of Guisando; I plunged into the cavern and brought to light what lay hidden in its depths; but my hopes are more dead than ever, and her commands and scorn more living. Finally, at long last, she has commanded me to travel through all the provinces of Spain and make all knights errant wandering there confess that she alone surpasses in beauty all ladies to-day living, and that I am the most valiant and the most enamoured knight in the world. In which task I have already travelled through the greater part of Spain, and there conquered many knights who have dared to gainsay me. But the deed I most pride and value myself for is that I vanquished in single battle that most famous knight Don Quixote de la Mancha, and made him confess that my Casildea is more beautiful than his Dulcinea; for by this victory alone I consider that I have conquered all the knights in the world, because this same Don Quixote I speak of has conquered them all; and since I have conquered him, his glory, his fame and his honour are transferred and have passed to my person:

> The victor's honour is increased
> By all his conquered enemy had.

So the innumerable exploits of the said Don Quixote fall to my credit and are mine.'

Don Quixote was amazed to hear the Knight of the Wood, and was a thousand times on the point of telling him that he lied. In fact, he had the word '*liar*' on the very tip of his tongue; but he restrained himself as best he could, so that he might later make him confess out of his own mouth that he lied. And so he calmly replied: 'Of your worship's having conquered most of the knights errant in Spain, Sir Knight, and even in the whole world, I say nothing. But that you have conquered Don Quixote de la Mancha, I beg leave to doubt. It may be that it was some other resembling him, although there are few like him.'

'What?' replied the Knight of the Wood. 'By the heavens above us, I did fight with Don Quixote and conquered him and forced him to yield. He is a man tall of stature, withered of face, lanky and shrivelled of limb, grizzled, with an aquiline and rather crooked nose, and great moustaches, black and drooping. He takes the field under the name of the Knight of the Sad Countenance, and has for his squire a countryman called Sancho Panza. He oppresses the back and guides the reins of a famous steed called Rocinante and, lastly, has for the mistress of his affections a certain Dulcinea del Toboso, formerly called Aldonza Lorenzo – as I call mine, since her name is Casildea and she comes from Andalusia, Casildea de Vandalia. If all these marks are not sufficient to confirm the truth of my words, here is my sword, which shall make incredulity itself give me credence.'

'Calm yourself, Sir Knight,' said Don Quixote, 'and listen to what I shall say. You must know that this Don Quixote you speak of is the best friend I have in this world. So much so that I can say I have the same regard for him as for myself, and by the very exact and precise description of him you have given me I cannot doubt that he is the same whom you conquered. On the other hand, I have the evidence of my eyes and hands that it could not possibly have been the same knight; were it not that he has many enchanters as his enemies – especially one who habitually persecutes him. For one of them may have taken his shape and allowed himself to be defeated so as to defraud him of the renown which his high deeds of chivalry have acquired and reaped for him over the whole known world. And, to confirm this, I would have you also know that it is not two days ago that those enchanters, his adversaries, transformed the shape and person of the fair Dulcinea del Toboso into a base and vile village girl. In just such a way they must have transformed Don Quixote. And if all this is not enough to convince you of the truth of my words, here is Don Quixote himself, who will maintain them with his arms, on foot or on horse or in what manner you please.'

As he spoke he got on to his feet and grasped his sword, awaiting the decision of the Knight of the Wood, who replied in an equally calm voice:

'A good paymaster doesn't worry about sureties. He that could once conquer you, Don Quixote, when you were transformed, may very well hope to overcome you in your proper person. But as it is not becoming for knights to perform their feats of arms in the dark, like highwaymen and ruffians, let us wait for day, so that the sun may look upon our deeds. And it shall be a condition of our battle that the vanquished shall be at the disposal of the victor, to do as he will with him, so long as he commands him to do nothing unbefitting a knight.'

'I am more than satisfied with this condition and I agree,' replied Don Quixote.

At these words they went over to their squires, and found them snoring in the attitudes in which sleep had overcome them. They awoke them and ordered them to get the horses ready, for at sunrise the two knights must engage in bloody and perilous single combat. At which news Sancho was stupefied with amazement, fearing for his master's safety by reason of the Knight of the Wood's valiant deeds, of which he had heard from his squire. But without speaking a word the two squires went to look for their cattle, for by this time all three horses and the ass had smelt one another out and were together. And by the way the Squire of the Wood observed to Sancho: 'You must know, brother, that when fighting men of Andalusia are seconds in any battle, it is not their custom to stand idly with their hands clasped while their principals are in combat. This I say to warn you that, while our masters are battling, we must have a fight as well and shiver one another to splinters.'

'That custom, Sir Squire,' replied Sancho, 'may obtain and hold good amongst the ruffians and fighting men you speak of. But amongst squires of knights errant – not a bit of it! At least I've never heard my master speak of any such custom, and he knows all the rules of knight errantry by heart. But even suppose I agreed that it's true, and that there's an express ordinance that squires must fight when their masters do, I still would not conform to it. I would rather pay such penalty as may be imposed on peaceful squires like myself; for it can't cost me more than two pounds of wax. I'd rather pay that, for I'm sure it will be less expensive than the lint I should need for healing my head, which is as good as split in two at the mere thought of fighting. There's another thing: fighting's quite out of the question, for I haven't a sword and I've never worn one in all my life.'

'I know a good remedy for that,' said the Squire of the Wood; 'I've here two linen bags of the same size. You shall take one and I the other, and we'll fight a pillow fight with equal arms.'

'With those weapons I'll gladly fight,' replied Sancho. 'For that kind of battle's more likely to dust us down than to wound us.'

'No, that shan't be,' answered the other, 'for we'll put in half a dozen nice smooth stones of equal weight. Then the wind won't catch them, and in that way we shall be able to thump one another and do no hurt or damage.'

'Good heavens!' exclaimed Sancho. 'So that's the sort of sable skins or carded cotton balls he's going to put into the bags, to save us bashing our skulls in and grinding our bones to powder! No, I tell you, sir, I'm not fighting, not even if they're filled with silk cocoons. Let our masters fight and good luck to them, but let us drink and eat. For time takes care enough to rob us of our lives, without our going out to look for ways of ending them off before their due time and season. They'll drop off when they're ripe.'

'All the same,' replied the Squire of the Wood, 'we must fight, if only for half an hour.'

'No, no!' answered Sancho. 'I shan't be so discourteous or ungrateful as to begin even the smallest quarrel with a man I've eaten and drunk with. Besides, how could I possibly fight in cold blood, without being provoked to it?'

'I'll provide a sufficient remedy for that,' said the Squire of the Wood. 'Before we begin the fight I'll go up to your worship and deal you three or four neat blows that'll lay you out at my feet. That will rouse your anger, even if it's sleeping sounder than a dormouse.'

'Against that trick,' answered Sancho, 'I know another, every bit as good. I'll take a thick stick, and before your worship starts rousing my anger, I'll thrash yours to sleep so soundly that it'll only wake up in the other world, where I'm known as a man who won't allow any one to pull his nose. Let every man look out for his own arrow; although it would be best for everyone to let his anger sleep. For no one knows another man's heart, and some come for wool that go away shorn, and God blessed peace and cursed quarrels. Because if a hunted cat, shut in and hard pressed, turns into a lion, God knows what I, who am a man, might turn into. So, from now on, I give you notice, Sir Squire, that I shall lay all the harm and damage that may result from our quarrel to your account.'

'That's right,' replied the Squire of the Wood. 'God send us day and all will be well.'

And now a thousand kinds of little painted birds began to warble in the trees, and with their various joyful songs seemed to welcome and salute the fresh Dawn, who was now showing her lovely face through the portals and balconies of the East, shaking from her locks an infinite number of liquid pearls, bathed in whose soft liquor the plants seemed also to bud, and to rain their small white pearls. The willows distilled sweet manna, the springs laughed, the brooks murmured, the woods rejoiced, and all the meadows were enriched by her coming.

But no sooner did the light of day allow him to see and distinguish objects than the first thing which presented itself to Sancho Panza's eyes was the nose of the Squire of the Wood, which was so large as almost to overshadow his whole body. The story goes, indeed, that it was of an extraordinary size, bent in the middle, covered with mulberry-coloured warts like an aubergine, and coming down two inches below his mouth. Its size and colour, its warts and its crookedness, made its owner's face so hideous that when Sancho saw it, his hands and feet began to quake like an epileptic child's, and he resolved in his heart to put up with two hundred blows rather than rouse his temper to fight with that demon.

Don Quixote too surveyed his adversary, but found that his helmet was already on with the vizor down, so that he could not see his face. He observed, however, that he was a well-built man, though not very tall in stature. Over his armour he wore a surcoat or cassock, of a material which seemed like finest gold, sprinkled with a great number of little disks of shining looking-glass, which made him appear exceedingly gallant and splendid. Over his helmet waved a great number of green, yellow and white feathers, while his lance, which was leaning against a tree, was very long and thick, and shod with more than a foot of steel.

Don Quixote observed all this and took it in, judging from what he saw, and noted that this knight must be of great strength. However, unlike Sancho Panza, he was not frightened by this, but politely and courageously addressed the Knight of the Mirrors: 'If your eagerness to fight, Sir Knight, has not exhausted your courtesy, I beg you of that courtesy to raise your vizor a little, so that I may see whether the splendour of your face corresponds to that of your carriage.'

'Whether you emerge vanquished or victor from this enterprise, Sir Knight,' replied the Knight of the Mirrors, 'you will have more than enough time and opportunity for gazing on me. And if I do not now satisfy your request, it is because I feel that I should be doing grievous wrong to the fair Casildea de Vandalia by wasting time in stopping to raise my vizor before forcing you to confess what you know I demand.'

'Well, while we are mounting our steeds,' said Don Quixote, 'you might tell me whether I am that Don Quixote whom you said you had conquered.'

'To that we make answer,' replied the knight, 'that you are as like to that knight I conquered as one egg is to another. But as you say that he is persecuted by enchanters I dare not affirm whether you are the aforesaid or not.'

'That is sufficient reason for me to believe you were deceived,' answered Don Quixote. 'However, to deliver you altogether from your error, let our horses be brought. For in less time than you would waste in raising your vizor – if God, my lady and my right arm avail me – I shall see your face, and you shall see that I am not the vanquished Don Quixote you imagine ...'

With that they cut short their speeches and mounted. Then Don Quixote turned Rocinante's rein to take so much of the field as was necessary for running a course with his adversary, while the Knight of the Mirrors did the same. But Don Quixote had not gone twenty paces when he heard the Knight of the Mirrors call him, whereat he returned half way to hear his adversary say: 'Remember, Sir Knight, that the condition of our combat is that the vanquished, as I have said before, must remain at the discretion of the victor.'

'That I know already,' replied Don Quixote, 'but only on condition that what is commanded and imposed on the vanquished does not transgress the bounds of chivalry.'

'That is understood,' replied the Knight of the Mirrors. At this moment the squire's extraordinary nose presented itself to Don Quixote's view, and he was no less astonished at the sight than Sancho. So much so that he judged him some monster, or a new kind of man, uncommon in the world. Sancho saw his master go off to make his charge, and did not care to remain alone with Big Nose. For he feared that with one flick of that nose his own fight would be over, and he would lie stretched on the ground either from the blows or the fright. So he ran after his master, holding on to one of Rocinante's stirrup leathers, and when it seemed to him time for him to turn round, said to him:

'I beseech you, dear master, to help me get up into that cork-tree before you turn and charge. From there, sir, I shall be able to see the gallant encounter you are going to have with this knight more comfortably and better than from the ground.'

'On the contrary, Sancho,' said Don Quixote, 'I think you want to climb up on to the platform to see the bulls from out of danger.'

'To tell you the truth,' answered Sancho, 'I'm so astounded and terrified by that squire's monstrous nose that I daren't stay near him.'

'So outrageous is it,' said Don Quixote, 'that, were I not the man I am, it would frighten me too. So, come, I will help you up into the spot you suggest.'

While Don Quixote stopped to help Sancho get up into the cork-tree, the Knight of the Mirrors fetched the circuit of the field that seemed to him necessary; and supposing that Don Quixote had done the same, waited for no trumpet sound or other signal to start them, but turned the head of his horse, which was no swifter nor better-looking than Rocinante, and rode forward to encounter his opponent at his full speed, which was a moderate trot. Seeing him, however, occupied with Sancho's ascent, he checked his rein and halted in mid-career, for which his horse was most grateful, being incapable of further movement. But Don Quixote imagined that his enemy was now flying down on him, and dug his spurs stoutly into Rocinante's lean flanks, which made him leap forward in such a fashion that, the history relates, on this single occasion in his life he went at something like a gallop – for at all other times his pace was a plain trot; and with this unspeakable fury the knight came down upon his opponent of the Mirrors, who drove his spurs rowel-deep into his horse, without being able to make him budge a single inch from the place where he had come to a halt in his career.

At this fortunate juncture Don Quixote found his adversary embarrassed by his horse and concerned with his lance, which he either could not, or had not time to, put into its rest. Taking no heed of his embarrassments, however, Don Quixote attacked the Knight of the Mirrors, in complete safety and without the slightest risk, and with such force that, almost unintentionally, he threw him over his horse's crupper to the ground, giving him such a fall that he moved neither hand nor foot, but gave every appearance of being dead.

No sooner did Sancho see him down than he slid from the cork-tree and ran at full speed to his master, who dismounted from Rocinante, and stood over the Knight of the Mirrors. Then, unlacing his helmet to see whether he was dead, or to give him air if he was alive, he saw ... Who without striking amazement, wonder and awe into his hearers could say what he saw? He saw, our history relates, the very face, the very physiognomy, the very image, the very picture of the bachelor Sampson Carrasco. And when he saw him he shouted loudly: 'Come here, Sancho, and see what you will not believe when you see it! Quick, my son, and take note what magic can do. Mark what wizards and enchanters are capable of.'

Sancho ran up, and when he saw the face of the Bachelor Sampson Carrasco he began to cross himself and bless himself a thousand times over. All this while the fallen knight showed no signs of life. And so Sancho said to Don Quixote: 'It's my opinion, sir, that your worship should thrust your sword right into this man's mouth, whichever way it is. He certainly looks like the Bachelor Sampson Carrasco, but perhaps if you kill him you'll be killing one of your enemies the enchanters.'

'That is not bad advice,' said Don Quixote, 'for the less enemies the better.' But as he was unsheathing his sword to put Sancho's suggestion into effect, the Mirror Knight's squire ran up, but without the nose which had so disfigured him, and cried out loudly: 'Take care what you're doing, sir. For that man at your feet is your friend the Bachelor Sampson Carrasco, and I'm his squire.'

'And your nose?' cried Sancho, on seeing him without his previous deformity.

And the squire replied: 'I have it here in my pocket.' And putting his hand into his right pocket, he drew out a pasteboard nose, shaped and painted in the manner described. Then, after staring at him more and more attentively, Sancho exclaimed in loud tones of wonder: 'God bless my soul! If it isn't Thomas Cecial, my friend and neighbour!'

'And what if it is?' replied the now un-nosed squire. 'Thomas Cecial I am, Sancho old friend, and I'll tell you presently the means, the tricks, and the schemes that brought me here. Meanwhile, beg and pray his worship your master not to touch, maltreat, wound, or kill the Knight of the Mirrors, who lies at his feet, for beyond any shadow of doubt he's the bold and ill-advised Bachelor Sampson Carrasco, our fellow-countryman.'

At this the Knight of the Mirrors came to himself, and Don Quixote at once put his naked sword point to his face, saying:

'You are dead, knight, if you do not confess that the peerless Dulcinea del Toboso surpasses your Casildea de Vandalia in beauty. What is more, you must promise, if you would survive this combat and defeat, to travel to the city of El Toboso and present yourself before her from me, so that she may do with you what she may best please. Then, if she leaves you to your own devices, you must return to seek me – for the trail of my exploits will serve you for guide and bring you to where I am – and tell me what has passed between her and you; – which conditions, in accordance with those fixed before our combat, do not transgress the rules of knight errantry.'

'I confess,' said the fallen knight, 'that the torn and soiled shoe of the lady Dulcinea del Toboso is worth more than the ill-combed, though clean beard of Casildea; and I promise to go and to return from her presence to yours, and to give you a complete and detailed account of all that you ask.'

'Also you must confess and believe,' added Don Quixote, 'that the knight you conquered was not, and could not have been, Don Quixote de la Mancha, but was another resembling him, as I confess and believe that you, although you resemble the Bachelor Sampson Carrasco, are not he, but another of like appearance, whom my enemies have set before me in his shape, so that I may restrain and moderate the force of my wrath and use the glory of my victory with moderation.'

'All this I acknowledge, hold and think, as you acknowledge, hold and think it,' answered the crippled knight. 'Let me get up, I pray you, if the shock of my fall will allow me, for it has left me in a pretty bad way.'

Don Quixote helped him to rise, with the aid of Thomas Cecial, his squire, from whom Sancho could not take his eyes. He asked him many questions, the replies to which gave him absolute proof that he really was Thomas Cecial, as he said. But the fear which had been aroused in him by his master's story that the enchanters had changed the Knight of the Mirrors into the shape of the Bachelor Carrasco prevented his believing the truth that he saw with his own eyes. In the end both master and man remained in their delusion, and the Knight of the Mirrors and his squire, gloomy and disgruntled, parted with Don Quixote and Sancho, with the intention of looking for a place where the knight's ribs could be plastered and strapped. Don Quixote and Sancho, for their part, resumed their road to Saragossa, where this history leaves them, to give an account of the identity of the Knight of the Mirrors and his big-nosed squire.

Chapter xv. *In which we are told who the Knight of the Mirrors and his Squire were, and given some account of them.*

EXTREMELY joyful, proud and vainglorious Don Quixote was at having subdued so valiant a knight as he imagined the Knight of the Mirrors to be, from whose knightly word he expected to learn whether the enchantment of his mistress still obtained. For the said vanquished knight was obliged to return, under pain of ceasing to be such, and give him an account of what might pass between himself and her. Don Quixote, however, thought one thing and the Knight of the Mirrors another. For, as we have said, he had nothing else in his mind just then but to find somewhere where he might be plastered.

Now our history tells us that when the Bachelor Sampson Carrasco counselled Don Quixote to return to the pursuit of his abandoned chivalries, it was after he had held a conference with the priest and the barber to decide on a means of inducing the knight to stay quietly and safely at home, without exciting himself with his wretched quests for adventures. At this consultation it was decided by unanimous vote, and with the particular approval of Carrasco, that they should let Don Quixote set out, since it seemed impossible to keep him back, and that Sampson should take the road as a knight errant and join battle with him — a pretext would not be lacking — and so vanquish him — which they reckoned an easy matter — and that there should be a covenant and agreement between them that the vanquished should be at the mercy of the victor. So that, Don Quixote being thus overthrown, the Bachelor Knight could command him to return home to his village, and not to leave it for two years, or until he should be commanded otherwise. For it was clear that Don Quixote would indubitably comply with these conditions, in order not to contravene and break the laws of chivalry. And it might so happen that during the time of his seclusion either he would forget his vain notions, or means might be found of curing his madness.

Carrasco accepted this task, and Thomas Cecial, a friend and neighbour of Sancho Panza's and a cheerful, hare-brained fellow, offered to be his squire. Sampson armed himself as has been recorded, and Thomas Cecial fitted over his natural nose the false one mentioned, as a mask, so that he should not be recognized by his friend when they met. So they followed the same road as Don Quixote took, very nearly caught them up during the adventure of the Waggon of Death – and at last lighted on them in the wood – the scene of the action of which the attentive reader has just read. And had it not been for Don Quixote's extraordinary opinions and his belief that the Bachelor was not the Bachelor, that worthy Bachelor would have been for ever incapacitated from proceeding to his Licentiate, all through finding no nests where he expected to find birds. And afterwards, seeing how badly their plans had turned out and the unfortunate end their journey had come to, Thomas Cecial said to the Bachelor:

'We have most certainly got what we deserved, Master Sampson Carrasco. It's easy enough to plan and set about an enterprise, but it's very often difficult to come well out of it. Don Quixote's mad, and we're sane. Yet he gets off sound and smiling, while your worship comes out bruised and sorrowful. So, let's consider now which is the madder, the man who's mad because he can't help it, or the man who's mad by choice?'

To which Sampson replied: 'The difference between these two is that the madman of necessity will be so for ever, but the madman by choice will cease to be so when he will.'

'Very well then,' said Thomas Cecial, 'I was mad by choice when I consented to be your worship's squire, and for that reason I wish to resign the post and go back home.'

'That is all right for you,' replied Sampson, 'but it would be folly to suppose that I shall go back home till I have thrashed Don Quixote. And it will not be the desire to restore him to his senses that will drive me after him, but the desire for revenge; for the pain in my ribs will not allow me to entertain a more charitable purpose.'

The two of them went on talking in this way until they came to a town, where they had the luck to find a bone-setter, who attended to the unfortunate Sampson. Then Thomas Cecial went home, and left the Bachelor behind brooding on his vengeance. Our history will speak of him again when the time comes, but now it must make merry with Don Quixote.

Chapter XVI. *Of Don Quixote's meeting with a Sensible Gentleman of La Mancha.*

JOYFUL, contented and proud, as we have said, Don Quixote pursued his journey, imagining himself from his late victory the most valiant knight errant the world contained in that age, and taking all adventures that might henceforth befall him as already achieved and brought to a successful conclusion. He despised spells and enchanters, and no more remembered the innumerable beatings he had received in the course of his chivalries, nor the stoning which had knocked out half his teeth, nor the ingratitude of the galley-slaves, nor the insolence of the Yanguesans and their shower of stakes. In fact he said to himself that, could he but find an art, means, or device for disenchanting his lady Dulcinea, he would not envy the best of good fortune that the most fortunate knight errant of past ages ever attained or could attain. And he was riding along completely absorbed in these fancies when Sancho addressed him:

'Isn't it odd, sir, that I've still got that monstrous, disproportionate nose of my neighbour, Thomas Cecial, before my eyes?'

'But can you possibly believe, Sancho, that the Knight of the Mirrors was the Bachelor Carrasco, and his squire your neighbour, Thomas Cecial?'

'I don't know what to answer to that,' replied Sancho. 'I can only say that the details he gave me of my house, of my wife and my children no other could have given me but he. And the face, less the nose, was Thomas Cecial's own. I've seen him very often in the village, for there's only a wall between his house and mine. And the tone of his voice was exactly the same.'

'Let us be reasonable, Sancho,' said Don Quixote. 'Think now, how is it conceivable that the Bachelor Sampson Carrasco should have come to fight with me as a knight errant, armed with offensive and defensive arms? Have I ever, by any chance, been his enemy? Have I ever given him reason to bear me a grudge? Am I his rival,

or does he make profession of arms, that he should envy the fame
that I have won by arms?'

'But what shall we say, sir,' replied Sancho, 'about this knight,
whoever he may be, looking so much like the Bachelor Carrasco,
and his squire like my neighbour, Thomas Cecial? Now if that's
enchantment, as your worship has said, weren't there any other two
in the world for them to take the likeness of?'

'It is all an artifice,' answered Don Quixote, 'and a trick of those
malign magicians that persecute me. Foreseeing that I should
emerge victorious from the combat, they provided that the vanquished knight should reveal the face of my friend the Bachelor, so
that the friendship I have for him should come between the edge of
my sword and the rigour of my arm, and moderate the just wrath of
my heart; by which means he might escape with his life, though he
sought by trickery and fraud to rob me of mine. For proof of which,
you know, Sancho, from your experience, which will not let you lie
or be deceived, how easy it is for enchanters to change one face for
another, transforming the beautiful into the ugly and the ugly into
the beautiful. Not two days ago you saw with your own eyes the
peerless Dulcinea's beauty and grace in all the perfection of their
natural proportions, and I saw her in the vile and ugly shape of a
coarse country wench, with bleary eyes and a stinking breath in her
mouth. So, it is no great matter for the perverse enchanters who
dared to make so wicked a transformation to have made another
with Sampson Carrasco and your neighbour, to snatch the glory of
my victory out of my hands. Even so, however, I am consoled; for,
after all, whatever shape he may have taken, I have vanquished my
enemy.'

'God knows the truth about everything,' answered Sancho.
Though since he knew that Dulcinea's transformation had been his
own fraudulent trick, his master's wild theories did not satisfy him.
But he did not care to reply, for fear of saying something which
would reveal his imposture.

While they were engaged in this conversation they were overtaken by a man who was riding on their road behind them, mounted
on a very handsome grey mare, and dressed in a fine green cloth
overcoat slashed with tawny velvet, and wearing a hunting cap of
the same material. The trappings of his mare were countrified, fit

for riding with short stirrups and of the same purple and green colours. He wore a Moorish scimitar, hanging on a broad green and gold sword-belt, and his leggings were of a similar make. His spurs were not gilt but covered with a green lacquer, so glossy and burnished that, since they matched the rest of his dress, they looked better than if they had been pure gold. Now when the traveller caught them up, he greeted them politely and, pricking his mare, was going to pass on ahead, had not Don Quixote addressed him, saying:

'Gallant sir, if your worship is taking the same road as we are, and haste is not important to you, I should esteem it a favour if we could ride together.'

'Really,' replied the man on the mare, 'I should not have pressed on ahead of you if I had not been afraid that your horse would be disturbed by my mare's company.'

'Sir,' broke in Sancho, 'you can safely, very safely, rein in your mare, for our horse is the chastest and best-behaved in the world. He has never done anything unmannerly on such an occasion as this, and the only time he transgressed my master and I paid for it sevenfold. Your worship may pull up, indeed, if it pleases you, for even if your mare were brought him between two plates, our horse wouldn't so much as look her in the face, I assure you.'

The traveller drew in his rein, gazing in astonishment at the figure and the face of Don Quixote, who was riding without his helmet, which Sancho carried like a bag, on the pommel of Dapple's saddle. And the more the man in green stared at Don Quixote, the more did Don Quixote stare at the man in green, who seemed to him a man of substance. His age appeared to be about fifty; his grey hairs few; his face aquiline; his expression between cheerful and grave – in short, from his dress and appearance he gave the impression of a man of good parts. But what the man in green thought of Don Quixote was that he had never seen anyone of that kind or anyone looking like him before. He was amazed at the length of his neck, the tallness of his body, the thinness and sallowness of his face, his armour, his gestures and his carriage – for his was a shape and figure not seen for many a long year in that country. Don Quixote observed the attention with which the traveller gazed at him and from his amazement assumed his curiosity. So, being so courteous and anxious to please everybody, before the other could ask him a question he met him half-way by saying:

'I should not wonder if your worship were surprised at this appearance of mine, for it is both novel and out of the common. But you will cease to be so when I tell you, as I now do, that I am a knight

> Of that breed that, the people say,
> After adventures ride.

I have left my native country; I have pledged my estate; I have given up my comfort and entrusted myself to the arms of Fortune, to take me where she will. I have sought to revive the now extinct order of knight errantry, and for a long while, stumbling here, falling there, flung down in one place and rising up in another, I have been carrying out a great part of my design, succouring widows, protecting maidens, and relieving wives, orphans and wards – which is the proper and natural office of knights errant. So, on account of my many valiant and Christian exploits I have been found worthy to appear in print in almost every country in the world. Thirty thousand volumes of my history have been printed, and it is on the way to be printed thirty thousand thousand times more, if Heaven does not prevent it. In fact, to sum everything up in a few words – or in one only – let me tell you that I am Don Quixote de la Mancha, otherwise called the Knight of the Sad Countenance. And, though praise of self is degrading, I am compelled sometimes to sound my own, though naturally only when there is no one present to sound it for me. So, noble sir, neither this horse, this lance, this shield, nor this squire, nor all these arms together, nor the sallowness of my face, nor my attenuated limbs should henceforth amaze you, now that I have made known to you who I am and the profession I follow.'

After this speech Don Quixote fell silent, and the man in green took a long time to reply, for he seemed unable to find words. But after a while he said: 'You guessed my thoughts, Sir Knight, when you observed my surprise; but you have not succeeded in dispelling my amazement at the sight of you. For though, as you say, sir, knowing who you are should dispel it, it has not done so. On the contrary now that I know, I am the more astounded. What! Is it possible that there are knights errant in the world to-day, and histories printed about real knight errantries? I cannot convince myself that there is anyone on earth to-day who favours widows, protects maidens, honours wives, or succours orphans, and I should not have believed it if I had not seen the proof in your worship with my own eyes. Heaven be praised, for that history of your noble and authentic chivalries, which your worship says is printed, will consign all the innumerable stories of imaginary knights errant, of which the world is full, to oblivion, such harm they do to good manners, and such damage and discredit to genuine history.'

'There is much to be said,' replied Don Quixote, 'on this question of whether the histories of knights errant are fictions or not.'

'But is there anyone,' asked the man in green, 'who doubts their falsehood?'

'I doubt it,' answered Don Quixote, 'but let the matter rest there. For if our journey is long, I trust to God I shall convince your worship that you have done wrong in going with the stream of those who affirm that they are not true.'

From this last speech of Don Quixote's the traveller suspected that he must be an idiot, and waited for some further remarks to confirm his suspicions. But before they could turn to any other subject, Don Quixote begged his fellow-traveller to tell him his name, since he had already told him something of his own condition and way of life.

To which the man in green replied: 'I, Sir Knight of the Sad Countenance, am a gentleman and native of a village where, please God, we shall dine to-day. I am more than moderately rich, and my name is Don Diego de Miranda. I spend my life with my wife, my children and my friends. My pursuits are hunting and fishing, though I keep neither hawk nor hounds, but only a quiet pointer and a good ferret or two. I have about six dozen books, some in Spanish and some in Latin, some historical and some devotional, but books of chivalry have never so much as crossed the threshold of my door. I read profane books more than devotional, since they give me honest entertainment, delighting me by their language, and arresting and startling me by their inventions – though there are very few of this kind in Spain. Sometimes I dine with my neighbours and friends, and very often I entertain them.

My fare is good and well served, and never stinted. I do not enjoy scandal, and do not allow any in my presence. I do not pry into my neighbours' lives, nor do I spy on other men's actions. I hear Mass every day. I share my goods with the poor, without boasting of my good works for fear of letting into my heart hypocrisy and vain-glory, enemies that subtly seize upon the wariest heart. I try to make peace between those I know to be at odds. I am devoted to Our Lady, and always trust in the infinite mercy of our Lord God.'

Sancho listened most attentively to this account of the gentle-man's life and occupations; for it seemed to him that this was a good and holy life, and that the man who led it must be able to work miracles. So, flinging himself off Dapple and hastily seizing his right stirrup, with devout heart and almost in tears he kissed the gentle-man's foot again and again. At which their fellow traveller ex-claimed: 'What are you doing, brother? Why these kisses?'

'Let me kiss you,' answered Sancho, 'for I think your worship's the first saint I've ever seen riding with short stirrups in all the days of my life.'

'I am no saint,' replied the gentleman, 'but a great sinner. Now you, brother, you must be good; your simplicity proves it.'

After this remark, which forced a laugh out of the depths of his master's melancholy and aroused fresh wonder in Don Diego, Sancho climbed once more into the saddle. Don Quixote then asked the man in green how many children he had, and observed that the ancient philosophers, who lacked the true knowledge of God, assumed the highest good to consist in the gifts of nature, in the gifts of Fortune, and in abundance of friends and good children.

'I, Don Quixote,' answered the gentleman, 'have one son and, but for him, perhaps I should count myself more fortunate than I do: not that he is wicked, though, but he is not as good as I should like. He is eighteen years old and has been for six years in Sala-manca studying the Latin and Greek tongues. But when I wished him to pass on to the study of other sciences I found him so soaked in that of Poetry – if it can be called a science – that it is impossible to make him take cheerfully to Law, which I should like him to study, or to the queen of all sciences, Theology. I would have him be an honour to his family, since we live in an age when our princes give high reward to virtuous and deserving scholarship; for learn-

ing without virtue is like pearls on a dunghill. He spends the whole
day in his criticisms, whether Homer expressed himself well or ill
in such a verse of the *Iliad*; whether Martial was indecent or not in
some epigram; whether such and such verses of Virgil are to be
understood in one way or another. In fact all his conversation is
about the books of these poets, and of Horace, Persius, Juvenal and
Tibullus; for by modern writers in the vernacular he sets little store.
But for all the dislike he seems to have for Spanish poetry, his
thoughts are now entirely taken up with making a gloss on four
lines they have sent him from Salamanca. It has to do, I think, with
some literary competition.'

To all this Don Quixote replied: 'Children, sir, are part of the
very bowels of their parents; and so we must love them, whether
they are good or bad, as we love the souls that give us life. It is the
parents' duty to guide them from childhood along the paths of
virtue, of good breeding, and of good and Christian manners, so
that when they are grown up, they may be the staff of their parents'
old age and a glory to their posterity. But as to forcing them to this
or that science, I do not think that it is right, although to persuade
them will do no harm; and if they have no need to study to earn
their bread – the student being so lucky as to be endowed by
Heaven with parents to spare him that – my opinion is that they
should be allowed to follow that branch of learning to which they
seem most inclined. And although that of Poetry is rather pleasur-
able than useful, it is not such as generally to do dishonour to its
votaries. Poetry, my dear sir, in my opinion is like a tender, young
and extremely beautiful maiden, whom other maidens toil to enrich,
to polish and adorn. These maidens are the other sciences; and she
has to be served by all, while all of them have to justify themselves
by her. But this maiden does not care to be handled, or dragged
through the streets, nor to be shown at the corners of the market
place, or in the antechambers of palaces. She is formed of an
alchemy of such virtue that anyone who knows how to treat her
will transform her into purest gold of inestimable price. Her possessor must keep her within bounds, not letting her run to base
lampoons or impious sonnets. She must be exposed for sale only in
the form of heroic poems, piteous tragedies, or gay and artificial
comedies. She must not let herself be handled by buffoons, nor by

the ignorant vulgar, who are incapable of recognizing or appreciating her treasures. Now do not imagine, sir, that by vulgar I mean only the common and humble people; for all who are ignorant, even if they are lords or princes, can rightfully be included under the name of vulgar. So anyone with the qualities I have named who takes up and handles Poetry will become famous, and his name will be treasured among all the civilized nations of the world. Now as to what you say, sir, about your son not greatly valuing Spanish poetry, I hold that he is wrong there, and the reason is this: great Homer did not write in Latin, because he was a Greek, nor Virgil in Greek, because he was a Latin. In fact all the ancients wrote in the tongues they sucked with their mother's milk, and did not go out to seek strange ones to express the greatness of their conceptions. And, that being so, this custom should rightfully be extended to all nations, and the German poet must not be despised for writing in his language, nor the Castilian, nor even the Basque, for writing in his.

'But your son, sir, as I imagine, does not dislike vernacular poetry, but poets who are merely vernacular and know no other tongues nor sciences to adorn, stimulate and help out their natural inspiration. Yet even in this he may be in error. For, according to true belief, the poet is born – I mean the natural poet comes out of his mother's womb a poet and, with that impulse which Heaven has given him, without further study or art, composes things which prove the truth of the saying: "There is a god in us ..." etcetera. Let me say also that the natural poet who makes use of art will improve himself and be much greater than the poet who relies only on his knowledge of the art. The reason is clear, for art is not better than nature, but perfects her. So nature combined with art, and art with nature, will produce a most perfect poet. To conclude my speech then, my dear sir, you should let your son travel where his star calls him; for if he is as good a scholar as he should be, and if he has successfully mounted the first step of learning, which is that of languages, he will ascend on his own to the summit of humane letters, which are so proper a pursuit for a gentleman of leisure, and adorn, honour and exalt him as mitres do bishops, or robes learned doctors of law. Scold your son, sir, if he writes lampoons to the detriment of other men's honour; punish him and tear

them up. But should he write satires after the manner of Horace for
the correction of vice in general, and as elegantly as he did, praise
him. For a poet may lawfully write against envy, and inveigh
against the envious in his verses, and against other vices too, so
long as he does not aim at any particular person. Though there are
poets who would run the risk of banishment to the Isles of Pontus
for the sake of uttering one piece of malice. If the poet, however, is
decent in his habits he will be so in his verses too. The pen is the
tongue of the soul; and as ideas are there engendered, so will his
writings be. And when kings and princes behold the miraculous
science of Poetry in some wise, virtuous and grave subject, they
honour, esteem and enrich him, and even crown him with the leaves
of that tree which the lightning never strikes, as if to show that men
whose temples are honoured and adorned by such crowns should
be attacked by no one.'

The man in green was lost in amazement at Don Quixote's
reasonings, so much so that he had begun to alter his previous
opinion that he was an idiot. In the middle of this conversation,
however, which was not much to his liking, Sancho had wandered
from the road to beg for a little milk from some shepherds who
were milking their ewes near by. And just as the gentleman was
about to renew the discussion, highly delighted by the knight's
sagacity and good sense, Don Quixote raised his head and saw a
cart decorated with the King's colours coming along the road by
which they were travelling. Believing that this must be some new
adventure, he shouted to Sancho to come and bring him his helmet,
and Sancho, hearing his name called, left the shepherds, and spurred
Dapple hurriedly towards his master, whom a stupendous and
desperate adventure now befell.

Chapter XVII. *In which is shown the highest point which Don
    Quixote's unparalleled Courage ever achieved, with the happy
    conclusion of the Adventure of the Lions.*

OUR history tells that when Don Quixote shouted to Sancho to
bring his helmet he was buying some curds of the shepherds. His
master's hurried call perturbed him, and he could neither think
what to do with them, nor what to put them in. So in order not to

lose them – for he had already paid for them – he decided to tip them into his master's helmet. After taking this precaution he turned back to see what Don Quixote wanted and, on approaching, heard him say: 'Give me that helmet, friend, for either I know very little of adventures, or what I see yonder is one which should, and does, require me to take to arms.'

The man in green heard this, and gazed in all directions without discovering anything but a cart coming towards them hung with two or three small flags, which made him think that it was carrying the King's treasure; and so he told Don Quixote. The knight, however, did not credit it, always firmly imagining that everything which befell him must be adventures and still more adventures. So he replied: 'Forewarned is forearmed. Nothing is lost by taking precautions. For I know by experience that I have enemies visible and invisible, and I do not know when or where, nor at what time or in what shape they will attack me.'

And turning to Sancho, he asked him for his helmet, which, having no opportunity of taking out the curds, the squire was compelled to give him as it was. Don Quixote took it and hurriedly clapped it on his head without noticing what was inside. But as the curds were squeezed and pressed, the whey began to run all over the knight's face and beard, which gave him such a shock that he cried to Sancho:

'What can it be, Sancho? My skull seems to be softening or my brains melting, or else I am bathed in sweat from head to foot. But if I am sweating, indeed it is not out of fear, though I most certainly believe it is a terrible adventure that is now going to befall me. Give me something to wipe myself with, if you have anything; for this copious sweat is blinding my eyes.'

Sancho kept quiet and gave him a cloth, at the same time thanking God that his master had not tumbled to the truth. Don Quixote wiped himself and took off his helmet to see what it was that seemed to be freezing his head. Then seeing the white clots inside his helmet, he put them to his nose and smelt them. At which he cried out: 'By the life of my lady Dulcinea del Toboso, these are curds you have put here, you treacherous, brazen-faced, unmannerly squire!'

To which Sancho replied with great calmness and hypocrisy: 'If they're curds give them to me, your worship, and I'll eat them. But let the Devil eat them, for it must be he who put them there! Should I dare to soil your worship's helmet? You must know who the villain is! I swear, sir, by the wits God gave me, I must have enchanters persecuting me too, since I'm your worship's creature and limb. They must have put that filth there to move your patience to anger, and make you baste my ribs as you often do. But this time truly they've leapt wide of the mark; for I trust in my master's good sense, since he will surely reflect that I've no curds, nor milk, nor anything of the sort, and that I'd rather put them in my stomach than in the helmet, if I had.'

'All that may be true,' said Don Quixote. Now the gentleman had watched this performance with amazement, especially when, after wiping his head, his face, his beard and the helmet, Don Quixote put it on again, steadied himself in his stirrups and, reaching for his sword and grasping his lance, cried: 'Now come what may, for here I stand ready to do battle against Satan in person.'

At this moment the cart with the flags arrived, and with it was nobody but the carter on one of the mules, and a man seated in front. Don Quixote, however, took up his stand before it and called out: 'Where are you going, brothers? What cart is this? What have you in it? And what flags are these?'

To which the carter replied: 'The cart's mine. In it are two fierce lions in a cage, which the General is sending from Oran to the capital as a present for his Majesty. The flags are the King's our master's, for a sign that there's something of his in my cart.'

'And are the lions big?' asked Don Quixote.

'Very big,' replied the man at the door of the cart. 'There have never been any so large that have ever crossed from Africa to Spain. I'm the lion-keeper, and I've brought over others, but none like these. There's a lioness and a lion. The lion's in this front cage, and the lioness in the rear one. They're very hungry at present, for they've had nothing to eat to-day. So will your worship please stand aside, for we're in a hurry to get to a place where we can feed them.'

To which Don Quixote replied with a slight smile: 'Lion cubs to me? To me lion cubs, and at this time of day? Then I swear to God the gentlemen who have sent them here shall see if I am a man to be frightened by lions. Get down, my good fellow, and if you are the lion-keeper, open these cages and turn out these beasts for me. For in the middle of this field I will teach them who Don Quixote de la Mancha is, in despite and defiance of the enchanters who have sent them to me.'

'Dear, dear!' muttered the gentleman in green at this juncture. 'Our good knight is giving us a proof of his nature. The curds, no doubt, have softened his skull and ripened his brains.'

At this point Sancho came up to him and cried: 'Sir, for God's sake do something to stop my master fighting with these lions. If he does, they'll tear all of us here to pieces.'

'Is your master so crazy then,' answered the gentleman, 'that you're afraid he will really fight these savage beasts?'

'He's not crazy,' replied Sancho, 'but foolhardy.'

'I will see that he does not,' promised the gentleman. And going up to Don Quixote, who was pressing the keeper to open the cages, he said: 'Sir Knight, knights errant should engage in adventures which offer a prospect of success, and not in such as are altogether desperate. For valour which verges on temerity is more like madness than bravery. What is more, these lions have not come against you, nor do they dream of doing so. They are going to be presented to his Majesty, and it would be wrong to stop them or to hinder their journey.'

'Pray go away, my dear sir, and see to your quiet pointer and your good ferret,' replied Don Quixote, 'and leave every man to do his duty. This is mine, and I know whether they are coming against me or not, these noble lions.' Then, turning once more to the lion-keeper, he said: 'I swear, Sir Ruffian, that if you do not open these cages this very moment I will pin you to your cart with this lance.'

The carter saw the armed phantom's determination, and said: 'Sir, for pity's sake, please let me unyoke the mules, and put myself and them into safety before the lions are let out. For if my beasts are killed I shall be ruined for ever, as I've no other property but my cart and my beasts.'

'O man of little faith!' replied Don Quixote. 'Get down, unyoke them, and do what you will. But you will soon see that you are labouring in vain, and might as well have spared yourself the trouble.'

The carter got down and very hurriedly unyoked, while the lion-keeper cried out loudly: 'Let everyone here be my witness that I'm opening these cages and letting the lions out against my will and under compulsion, and that I protest to this gentleman that all the harm and damage that these beasts may do will fall to his account, and so will my wages and dues. Sirs, take cover before I open, for I'm sure they'll do me no harm.'

Once more the gentleman implored Don Quixote not to do anything so mad, saying that to engage in such a wild freak was to tempt Providence. But Don Quixote replied that he knew what he was doing, and the gentleman warned him once more to look out, for he knew that he was mistaken.

'Now, sir,' replied Don Quixote, 'if you do not want to be a spectator of what in your opinion is going to be a tragedy, spur your grey mare and get into a safe place.'

When Sancho heard this he implored his master with tears in his eyes to desist from this enterprise, compared to which the adventure of the windmills and the fearful one of the fulling-mills and, in fact, every exploit he had attempted in the whole of his life, were tarts and gingerbread.

'Look, sir,' said Sancho, 'here's no enchantment or any such thing, for I've seen the claw of a real lion through the bars and cracks in the cages. And I'm sure that a lion with a claw like that must be bigger than a mountain.'

'Fear, at least,' answered Don Quixote, 'will make it seem bigger to you than half the world. Retire, Sancho, and leave me; and if I die here, you know our old agreement. You will repair to Dulcinea – I say no more.'

And he went on to make further declarations which removed all hope that he would desist from his insane purpose. The man in green would have resisted him, but not being as well armed, he thought it unwise to fight with a madman, for the knight now seemed to him completely mad. Don Quixote then began once more hurrying the lion-keeper and repeating his threats, which gave the gentleman a chance to spur his mare, Sancho to prod Dapple, and the carter his mules, all of them endeavouring to get as far away from the cart as they could before the lions broke loose. Sancho wept for his master's death, for this time he really believed he would perish at the claws of the lions. He cursed his luck and the fatal hour when he first thought of returning to his service. But for all his weeping and lamentations he did not cease from flogging Dapple to get him farther from the cart. Then, when the keeper saw that the fugitives were well away, he repeated his entreaties and warnings to Don Quixote. The knight, however, replied that he heard him, but that he would listen to no more warnings or entreaties, for they would be quite fruitless, and bade him make haste. Now whilst the keeper was opening the first cage, Don Quixote was considering whether it would be better to do battle on foot or on horseback, and finally decided to fight on foot, fearing that Rocinante would take fright at the sight of the lions. Therefore he leapt from his horse, threw away his lance and, buckling his shield and unsheathing his sword, with marvellous bravery and a bold heart took up his position in a leisurely way in front of the cart, commending himself to God with all his soul, and then to his lady Dulcinea.

And here it is to be noted that when the author of our true history came to this passage he exclaimed and cried: ' O brave and incomparably courageous Don Quixote de la Mancha! True mirror to all valiant knights in the world! Thou new and second Don Manuel de Leon – honour and glory of Spanish knights! In what words shall I recount this most fearful exploit, or with what arguments make it credible to future ages? What praises can there be unfitting and unmeet for you, hyperbole upon hyperbole though they be? You on foot, you alone, you bold, you brave-hearted, with only a simple sword and no trenchant Toledo blade, with a shield of not very bright and shining steel, you watching and waiting for the two fiercest lions ever bred in African forests! Let your deeds themselves praise you, valorous Manchegan, for here I leave them in all their glory, lacking words to extol them.'

Here this exclamation of our author's ended, and he went on to knit up the thread of his story, saying:

When the keeper saw Don Quixote firm in his position, and knew that he could not avoid letting the lion out without incurring the displeasure of the bold and angry knight, he flung open the door of the first cage, in which, as we have said, was the beast, which seemed to be of extraordinary size and of a fearful and hideous aspect. The lion's first action, however, was to turn round in his cage, extend his claws, and stretch his full length. Then he opened his mouth and yawned very leisurely, and sticking out almost two foot of tongue, licked the dust out of his eyes and washed his face. This done, he put his head out of his cage and looked in all directions with eyes blazing like live coals, a sight to strike terror into the bravest heart. Alone Don Quixote watched him attentively, hoping that he would now jump out of the cart and come within reach of his hands, for he intended to tear him to pieces. To such a height of extravagance was he transported by his incredible madness. But the noble lion, more courteous than arrogant, took no notice of this childish bravado, and after looking in all directions, as we have said, turned his back and showed Don Quixote his hindquarters. Then he lay down again in his cage with great calmness and composure. At this sight Don Quixote ordered the keeper to beat him and tease him into coming out.

'I won't do that,' answered the keeper, 'for if I excite him I shall be the first to be torn to pieces. Be content, Sir Knight, with the day's work, which is all that could be desired so far as valour goes. Do not seek to tempt Fortune a second time. The lion has his door open. It rests with him whether he comes out or not. But as he has not come out till now, he will not come out the whole day. The greatness of your worship's courage is now proved. No brave champion, as I understand it, is obliged to do more than challenge his enemy and await him in the field. If his opponent does not appear the disgrace lies on him, and the challenger wins the crown of victory.'

'That is true,' replied Don Quixote. 'So shut the door, my friend, and give me a sworn statement of what you have seen me do here, in the best form you can: to wit, that you opened for the lion; that I awaited him; that he did not come out; that I waited for him still; that he still did not come out, but turned and lay down. That is all my duty. Enchantments, away! And God prosper justice and truth and true chivalry. Shut the door, I repeat, while I signal to the fugitive and the absent that they may learn of this exploit from your lips.'

The keeper did as he was told, and putting the cloth with which he had wiped the shower of curds off his face on to the end of his lance, Don Quixote began to call to the others, who had never stopped running away and looking behind them at every step, riding all in a troop driven on by the gentleman in green. But when Sancho chanced to notice the signal of the white cloth, he exclaimed: 'May I die, if my master has not conquered the savage beasts, for he is calling us.'

They all stopped, and seeing that it was Don Quixote making these signals, they lost some part of their fear, and little by little drew nearer, till they could plainly hear him calling them. Finally, they came back to the cart, and when they arrived Don Quixote said to the carter:

'Yoke your mules again, brother, and go on your way; and you, Sancho, give him two gold crowns, for him and for the lion-keeper, in recompense for their having stopped for me.'

'I'll pay them with a very good will,' answered Sancho. 'But what has happened to the lions? Are they dead or alive?'

Thereupon the lion-keeper recounted the result of the encounter, minutely and at his leisure, extolling to the best of his power and skill the valour of Don Quixote, at the sight of whom the cowed lion would not, and dared not, come out of his cage, although he had held the door open for a considerable time. Then when he had told the knight that it would be tempting Providence to excite the lion into going out, as he wished him to, Don Quixote had most grudgingly and unwillingly permitted him to shut the door.

'What do you think of that, Sancho?' asked Don Quixote. 'Do any enchantments prevail against true valour? The enchanters may indeed be able to rob me of good fortune; but of resolution and courage, that is impossible!'

Sancho paid the two crowns; the carter yoked up; the keeper kissed Don Quixote's hands for the favour received, and promised to recount his valorous exploit to the King himself, when he saw him at court.

'If by chance, then, his Majesty should ask who performed it, you will tell him it was "*The Knight of the Lions*", for I am resolved that the title I have hitherto borne of "*The Knight of the Sad Countenance*" shall henceforward be so transformed, altered, varied and changed. And herein I follow the ancient custom of knights errant, who changed their names when they pleased or as the occasion required.'

T

The cart continued on its journey, and Don Quixote, Sancho and the gentleman in the green overcoat continued on theirs. In all this while Don Diego de Miranda had not spoken a word, so carefully was he watching and noting every word and action of Don Quixote, who seemed to him a sane man turned mad or a madman verging on sanity. The first part of this history had not yet come to his notice; for if he had read it he would have ceased to be surprised at the knight's behaviour, since he would then have known the nature of his madness. But as he did not know it, he sometimes took him for sane, sometimes for mad. For Don Quixote's words were consistent, elegant and well put, though his actions were wild, rash and foolish. 'What could be more insane,' he reflected, 'than to put on a helmet full of curds and imagine that the enchanters are softening your skull? And what could be rasher or more idiotic than to insist on fighting with lions?' But from this soliloquy Don Quixote drew him by saying:

'No doubt, Don Diego de Miranda, your worship considers me both foolish and mad. And it would be no marvel if you did, for my deeds testify no less. But, for all that, I wish your worship to take note that I am not so mad or so lacking as I must have seemed to you. It is a brave sight to see a gallant gentleman, beneath the eyes of his King, deliver a well aimed lance-thrust against a brave bull in the midst of a great square. It is a brave sight to see a knight, armed in shining armour, pace the lists in merry jousts before the ladies. And it is a brave sight to see all those knights, in military exercises or the like, entertain, cheer and, if one may say so, grace the courts of their princes. But braver than all these it is to see a knight errant travelling through desert and waste, by cross-roads, forests and mountains, to seek perilous adventures, in order to bring them to a fortunate and happy conclusion only for the sake of glory and lasting renown. It is a braver sight, I say, to see a knight errant succouring a widow in some lonely spot than a courtier knight wooing a maiden in the cities. All knights have their particular offices. Let the courtier serve ladies, lend splendour to the King's court with his liveries, support poor knights at his splendidly appointed table, arrange jousts, maintain at tourneys, and show himself grand, liberal, magnificent and, above all, a good Christian; for in this way he will comply with his precise obligations. But let the knight errant search the corners of the world, penetrate the most intricate labyrinths, at every step encounter the impossible, at midsummer brave the burning rays of the sun on high and desert wastes, and in winter the harsh inclemency of winds and frosts. Let no lions alarm him, nor hobgoblins daunt him, nor dragons affright him; for to seek them, attack them and conquer them all are his chief and proper exercises. I, since it has been my lot to be of the number of knights errant, cannot, then, fail to attempt everything which seems to me to fall within the bounds of my duty. And so to attack these lions whom I just now attacked was my rightful concern, although I knew it to be an excessive temerity. For I well know what valour is – a virtue placed between the two extremes of vice, cowardice and foolhardiness. But it is better for the brave man to rise to the height of rashness than to sink into the depths of cowardice. For just as it is easier for the spendthrift to be liberal than for the miser, so it is easier for the rash than for the cowardly to climb to true valour. And in this matter of encountering adventures, believe me, Don Diego, it is better to lose the game by a card too many than by a card too few, for *such a knight is rash and foolhardy* sounds better in the hearer's ears than *such a knight is timid and cowardly.*'

'I must say, Don Quixote,' answered Don Diego, 'that all that your worship's words and deeds are measured on the scales of reason itself; and I believe that if the ordinances and laws of knight errantry were lost they would be found in your worship's breast, as in their proper repository and archive. But let us hurry on to my village, for it is getting late. At my house your worship can rest from your recent labours. For though they were not of the body, they were of the spirit, and those too sometimes conduce to the body's weariness.'

'I accept your offer as a great favour and kindness, Don Diego,' replied Don Quixote. And spurring on faster than before, at about two o'clock in the afternoon they arrived in the village, at the house of Don Diego, whom Don Quixote called '*The Knight of the Green Coat*'.

Chapter XVIII. *What happened to Don Quixote in the Castle,
or House of the Knight of the Green Coat, and other very
strange matters.*

DON QUIXOTE found Don Diego de Miranda's house spacious
after the country fashion, with his arms, though in coarse stone,
above the street door; the provision store in the front yard; the
wine cellar in the porch, and several earthenware jars around, which,
being of El Toboso make, revived his memories of his enchanted
and transformed Dulcinea. Whereat, regardless of what he said or
before whom he said it, he exclaimed with a sigh:

> 'O lovely pledges, to my woe discovered,
>   Joyful and sweet when it was Heaven's will!

O Tobosan jars, how you bring to my memory the sweet pledge of
my great bitterness!'

The student poet, Don Diego's son, who had come out with his
mother to receive the knight, heard him speak these lines. And both
mother and son stood amazed at his strange appearance, as he dismounted from Rocinante and went with great politeness to beg for
her hands to kiss, while Don Diego said: 'Pray, wife, receive Don
Quixote de la Mancha with your usual hospitality. Here he is before
you, a knight errant, and the most valiant and wisest the world contains.'

The lady, whose name was Doña Christina, received him with
marks of great affection and politeness, and Don Quixote greeted
her with an abundance of judicious and polite phrases. He also addressed much the same compliments to the student, who judged
Don Quixote from his speech to be a man of wit and intelligence.

Here the author paints all the details of Don Diego's home, describing the contents of a rich gentleman farmer's house. But it
seems right to the translator of this history to pass over these and
other such particulars in silence, for they do not suit the principal
purpose of this history, which derives its strength rather from truth
than from dull digressions.

They led Don Quixote into a hall, where Sancho took off his
armour, leaving him in his Walloon breeches and chamois leather

jerkin, all stained with the grime of his armour. He wore a Vandyke collar like a student's, unstarched and without lace, date-coloured leggings and waxed shoes. He carried his good sword slung over his shoulders on a sealskin strap, he having, it is believed, a long-standing weakness of the kidneys; and over all this he wore a cloak of good grey cloth. But first of all he had washed his face and head with five or six buckets of water – there is some difference of opinion as to the number – the water remaining always the colour of whey, thanks to Sancho's gluttony and his purchase of those foul curds that turned his master so fair. In the garb we have described, and with a charming and gallant air, Don Quixote walked into another hall, where the student was waiting to entertain him while the table was being laid; for on the arrival of so noble a guest Doña Christina wanted to show that she knew how to entertain all visitors. Now whilst Don Quixote was taking off his armour, Don Lorenzo – for this was the name of Don Diego's son – had an opportunity of saying to his father: 'Who can this knight be, sir, whom you have brought home? For his name, his appearance, and his calling himself a knight errant puzzle my mother and me.'

'I don't know what to say, son,' answered Don Diego. 'I can only tell you that I have seen him act like the greatest madman in the world, and yet make such wise speeches as to blot out and efface his deeds. Speak to him yourself and feel the pulse of his understanding. Then, as you are a shrewd fellow, come to what conclusions you can as to his sense or lack of it; though, to tell you the truth, I think he is more mad than sane.'

At this Don Lorenzo went to meet Don Quixote, as has been said, and during their conversation Don Quixote said to him: 'Sir, Don Diego de Miranda, your father, has informed me of your rare abilities and subtle talents and, what is more, that you are a great poet.'

'Poet maybe,' answered Don Lorenzo, 'but by no means a great one. It is true that I am rather given to poetry, and to reading the good poets; but not to such an extent that I can give myself the title of great, as my father does.'

'I do not dislike this humility,' said Don Quixote, 'for there is no poet who is not arrogant, and does not think of himself as the best in the world.'

'There is no rule without exceptions,' answered Don Lorenzo;
'and there may be some who are, and yet do not think so.'

'Few,' said Don Quixote; 'but tell me, sir, what are these verses
that you have in hand at present, which your father has told me
make you rather restless and thoughtful? If it is a gloss, I understand something of this art of glossing, and I should like to hear
them. If they are for a literary competition, try to win the second
prize, for the first is always awarded by favour or to some person
of quality. The second goes for pure merit. So the third is really the
second, and on this reckoning the first should be third. It is just the
same with university degrees. Though, for all that, the nominal first
cuts a fine figure.'

'Up to now,' said Don Lorenzo to himself, 'I cannot consider
you a fool. Let us go on.'

'Sir,' he then said, 'you seem to have frequented the schools.
What sciences did you study?'

'Knight errantry,' replied Don Quixote, 'which is as good as
poetry, and even two inches better.'

'I do not know what that science is,' observed Lorenzo. 'I have
never heard of it till now.'

'It is a science,' replied Don Quixote, 'that comprises all or most
of the sciences in the world, since he who professes it must be a
jurist and know the laws of justice concerning persons and property,
so that he may give to everyone what is his own and his due. He
must be a theologian, so that he may give reasons for the Christian
rule he professes, clearly and distinctly, wherever he may be asked.
He must be a physician, and especially a herbalist, so that he may
recognize in the midst of deserts and wildernesses those herbs
which have the virtue of healing wounds, for the knight errant cannot go looking at every step for someone to cure him. He must be
an astronomer, to know by the stars how many hours of the night
are passed, and in what part and climate of the world he is. He must
know mathematics, for at any time he may find himself in need of
them. Not reckoning that he must be adorned with all the virtues,
theological and cardinal, I will descend to other small details and
say that he must be able to swim as they say Fish Nicholas or
Nicolao did. He must know how to shoe a horse and mend a saddle
and bridle. Also, to return to higher matters, he must keep faith with

God and his lady; he must be chaste in his thoughts, straightforward in his words, liberal in his works, valiant in his deeds, patient in his afflictions, charitable towards the needy and, in fact, a maintainer of truth, although its defence may cost him his life. Of all these parts, great and small, a good knight errant is composed. So you may see, Don Lorenzo, whether it is a snivelling science that chivalry teaches those who study and profess it, and whether the loftiest taught in colleges and schools are the equal of it.'

'If that is so,' replied Lorenzo, 'I agree that this science is superior to any.'

'How, if that is so?' demanded Don Quixote.

'What I mean to say,' said Don Lorenzo, 'is that I doubt whether there are, or ever have been, knights errant with so many virtues.'

'What I now say I have said many times before,' replied Don Quixote. 'The majority of people in this world are of the opinion that knights errant have never existed; and I hold that unless Heaven miraculously convinces them to the contrary, any labour undertaken for that purpose must be in vain, as experience has many times shown me. So I will not stop now to deliver your worship from the error you hold in common with the multitude. What I mean to do is to pray Heaven to deliver you from it, and make you see how beneficial and necessary knights errant were to the world in past ages, and how useful they would be in the present, if they were in fashion. But now, for the peoples' sins, sloth, idleness, gluttony and luxury triumph.'

'Our guest has broken out,' said Don Lorenzo to himself at this point. 'But for all that he is a brave madman, and I should be a poor fool not to see that.'

Here their conversation ended, as they were called to dinner. So when Don Diego asked his son what he had made of their guest's wits, he replied: 'All the physicians and authors in the world could not give a clear account of his madness. He is mad in patches, full of lucid streaks.'

They went to dinner, and the food was good, abundant and tasty; it was in fact the fare that Don Diego had said on the road he generally gave to his guests. But what most delighted Don Quixote was the marvellous silence throughout the whole house, which seemed like a Carthusian monastery. So, when the cloths had been removed, a grace said, and their hands washed, he earnestly begged Don Lorenzo to recite to him his verses for the literary competition; to which the young man replied:

'So that I may not seem to be one of those poets who refuse when they are asked to read their verses, but spew them up when they are not asked, I will recite my gloss, for which I expect no prize, as I have written it only to exercise my wits.'

'A wise friend of mine,' said Don Quixote, 'was of the opinion that no one should weary himself by writing glosses; and the reason, he said, was that the gloss could never come near to the text; and that often, or most times, the gloss was a long way from the intention and purpose of the theme set; and, furthermore, that the rules for glossing were too stringent, for they allowed no interrogations, nor "*said he*" nor "*shall say*", nor making verbs of nouns, nor changing the sense; with other restrictions and limitations by which glossers are bound, as your worship must know.'

'In truth, Don Quixote,' said Don Lorenzo, 'I should like to catch your worship out in some serious blunder. But I cannot, for you slip through my hands like an eel.'

'I do not understand what you say, sir,' replied Don Quixote, 'or what you mean about this slipping of mine.'

'I will make myself clear later,' answered Don Lorenzo. 'But, for the present listen, please, to the gloss and to the theme, which go like this:

> If but my 'was' might turn to 'is';
> I look for it, then it comes complete.
> Oh, might I say 'Now, now it is',
> Our after-griefs may be too great.

The Gloss

> As everything passes away,
> So Fortune's goods, that once she gave,
> Passed, and would not with me stay,
> Though she gave once all I could crave.
> Fortune, 'tis long since thou hast seen
> Me at thy feet, long centuries;
> I shall be glad, as I have been,
> If but my 'was' be turned to 'is'.

Unto no glory am I bent,
No prize, honour, or victory,
But to return to my content,
Whose thought afflicts my memory.
If only that you will restore,
Fortune, the vigour of my heat
Is calmed; but let it come before
I look for it, then it comes complete.

Impossible do I desire,
To make the past return, in vain;
No power on earth can so aspire
To call a past state back again.
Time passes on, time runs and flies
Swiftly, and never turns his face.
He is in error then that cries,
'Oh, might I say, "Now, now it is."'

I live in great perplexity,
Sometimes in hope, sometimes in fear,
Which is a death. Better to die
That of my griefs I might get clear;
For me to die were better far.
But fear repeats more soberly:
'Better to go on living, for
Our after griefs may be too great.'

When Don Lorenzo had finished reciting his poem, Don Quixote got upon his feet and grasped the young man's right hand, crying in a loud voice which sounded like a shout:

'Praise be to High Heaven, noble youth, but you are the best
poet in the world, and deserve to be crowned with laurel, not by
Cyprus or Gaeta, as the poet said, whom God forgive, but by the
Academies of Athens, were they surviving to-day, and by those
still in existence at Paris, Bologna and Salamanca. Would to
Heaven that the judges who would deny you the first prize might
be shot to death by the arrows of Phoebus, and that the Muses
might never cross the thresholds of their homes. Read me, sir, if
you will be so good, some of your greater poems; for I should like
to feel the pulse of your admirable genius in all its parts.'

Is it necessary to say that Don Lorenzo was delighted to be
praised by Don Quixote, although he considered him mad? O
power of flattery! How far you extend, and how wide are the fron-

tiers of your pleasing realm! This truth Don Lorenzo proved by acceding to Don Quixote's request and reciting to him this sonnet on the legend or story of Pyramus and Thisbe:

Sonnet

> The wall was broken by the maiden fair,
> Which cleft the gallant heart of Pyramus;
> Love flies from Cyprus that he may declare,
> Once seen, the narrow breach prodigious.
> There only silence speaks; no voice will dare
> Into so very strait a strait to pass;
> Let their souls speak, Love's nature is so rare
> That he makes easy things most arduous.
> Desire in her grows violent, and haste
> In the rash maid instead of heart's delight
> Calls down her death. See now the story's passed:
> Both of them in a moment – O strange sight! –
> One sword, one sepulchre, one memory
> Kills, covers, crowns with immortality.

'Heaven be praised,' cried Don Quixote, when he had heard Don Lorenzo's sonnet, 'that among an infinite number of rhymers I have seen one as accomplished as you are, my dear sir!'

Don Quixote was very well entertained at Don Diego's for four days; at the end of which he asked leave to depart, and thanked his host for his favours and the kind welcome he had received in his house. For since it was not right for knights errant to give up many hours to ease and luxury, he wished to go and fulfil his duty, seeking those adventures with which he was told that land abounded. In this way he hoped to pass the time till the day of the jousts at Saragossa, to which he would take the straight road; though first he must enter the Cave of Montesinos, of which so many amazing stories were told in those parts, and also investigate and discover the origin and true source of the seven lagoons commonly called the Lakes of Ruidera. Don Diego and his son commended his noble purpose, and bade him take all that he pleased from their house and farm, for they would most gladly serve him, as they were bound by his personal worth and his honourable profession to do.

Finally the day of his departure arrived, bringing joy to Don Quixote but sadness and melancholy to Sancho Panza, who had very much enjoyed the plenty in Don Diego's house and was loth to return to the hunger prevalent in forests and deserts, and to the scantiness of his ill-stored saddle-bags. He did not omit, however, to stuff them full of everything that seemed to him most necessary. Then, as he took his leave, Don Quixote said to Don Lorenzo: 'I do not know whether I have told your worship before, but if I have I will repeat it, that if you would save labour and pains in climbing to the inaccessible peak of the temple of Fame, you have only to quit the rather narrow road of poetry and follow the narrowest path of all, that of knight errantry, which is capable of making you an Emperor in a brace of shakes.'

With these words Don Quixote finally settled the question of his madness, the more so by adding: 'God knows I should like to take Don Lorenzo with me to teach him how to spare the humble and subdue and trample the proud under foot; accomplishments proper to the profession I follow. But since his youth does not demand it, nor his praiseworthy pursuits permit of it, I content myself by advising him that, as a poet, he will be able to win fame if he is guided rather by the opinion of others than by his own. For there is no father or mother to whom their children seem ugly; and this delusion is even more prevalent in respect of the children of the brain.'

Father and son were once more amazed at Don Quixote's mixture of wise and foolish arguments and at his tenacity in devoting himself to the search for his luckless adventures, which were the whole aim and object of his desires. So they repeated their offers and their compliments; and then, taking leave of the lady of the castle, Don Quixote and Sancho departed upon Rocinante and the ass.

Chapter XIX. *Of the Adventure of the Enamoured Shepherd, with other truly pleasant incidents.*

DON QUIXOTE had not left Don Diego's village far behind him when he met with two men, who seemed to be priests or students, and two peasants, the four of them riding on four asses. One of the students was carrying what looked like a piece of fine scarlet cloth and two pairs of knitted stockings, wrapped up in a piece of green buckram, which served him for a bag, while the other bore only a new pair of black fencing-foils with their buttons on. The peasants were carrying other things which showed that they had been making purchases in some big town and were bringing them back to their village. Now both students and peasants were as astounded as everyone usually was at the first sight of Don Quixote, and longed to know who this extraordinary man might be. The knight greeted them and asked what road they were taking. Then, on learning that it was the same as his own, he offered them his company, asking them to slacken their pace, for their ass-fillies went faster than his horse. Next he obligingly gave them a brief account of himself, his office and his profession of knight errant travelling in search of adventure in all parts of the world, saying that his proper name was Don Quixote de la Mancha, and his title *The Knight of the Lions*.

All this was like Greek or gibberish to the two peasants; but not to the students, who immediately realized that Don Quixote was weak in the head. But, for all that, they looked at him with wonder and respect, and one of them said:

'If, Sir Knight, your worship is taking no fixed road, as is the way of those in search of adventure, come with us, and you will see as fine and rich a wedding as has ever been celebrated in La Mancha or for many miles round.'

Don Quixote asked if it was some prince's nuptials, that he spoke so highly of it.

'No,' answered the student. 'It is the wedding of a farmer and a farmer's daughter. He is the richest man in the whole country, and she the most beautiful girl man ever saw. The arrangements they are making for the wedding are most strange and original, for it is to take place in a meadow close to the bride's village. She is always spoken of as Quiteria the fair, and her bridegroom as Camacho the rich. She is eighteen and he twenty-two, and they are well matched, although some curious people who know the pedigrees of all the world by heart are pleased to say that the fair Quiteria's is better than Camacho's; but we do not take notice of that nowadays, for riches can solder a great many cracks. To be brief, this Camacho is generous, and has taken it into his head to have the whole of this meadow covered in with boughs, so that the sun will have to take some pains if he wants to get in to visit the green grass which covers its soil. He has also got up some sword-dances and some morris dances, for there are many in the village who can jingle and shake the bells to perfection. Of the shoe-clatterers I say nothing, for he has invited a pack of them. But none of the things I have mentioned, nor many others which I have left out, will make this wedding more memorable than the actions I expect the desperate Basilio will perform there. This Basilio is a shepherd of Quiteria's own village, who has a house next to her parents, where Love took occasion to revive in the world the now-forgotten loves of Pyramus and Thisbe. For Basilio loved Quiteria from his earliest and tenderest years, and she answered his desires with a thousand innocent favours, so much so that the love between the two children, Basilio and Quiteria, was a source of amusement to the village. Now as they grew older, Quiteria's father decided to deny Basilio his former free access to his house and, to save himself from a life of suspicion and mistrust, arranged to marry his daughter to the rich Camacho, as he did not care to match her with Basilio, who is not so well favoured by fortune as by nature. But, to tell you the truth without envy, he is the most active lad we know, a great pitcher of the bar, a fine wrestler and a great ball-player. He runs like a deer, jumps better than a goat, and bowls down the ninepins like magic. He sings like a lark, and when he plays a guitar he almost makes it speak. What is more, he fences with the best of them.'

'For that accomplishment alone,' put in Don Quixote, 'this youth not only deserves to marry the fair Quiteria, but Queen Guenevere herself, if she were alive to-day, in spite of Lancelot and all who might try to stop him.'

'Tell that to my wife!' said Sancho Panza, who had been listening in silence hitherto. 'She doesn't like people marrying any but their equals, sticking to the proverb that says, every ewe to her mate. What I should like is for this good Basilio – I seem to love him already – to marry this lady Quiteria. – And may all those who hinder folks from marrying the ones they love have eternal salvation and sweet repose – I was going to say the opposite.'

'If all lovers were to marry,' said Don Quixote, 'parents would lose their right of marrying their children when and to whom they choose. And if the choice of husband were left to the daughter's pleasure, there would be one who would pick her father's groom, and another some passer-by in the street, whom she might fancy a brave and fine fellow though he might be a debauched swashbuckler. For love and fancy easily blind the eyes of the understanding, which are so necessary for choosing one's estate. The state of matrimony is in great danger from errors, and it needs much circumspection and the particular favour of Heaven to make a good choice. For if a prudent man wants to take a long journey he seeks a safe and peaceful companion to go with him, before setting out on the road. Why then should not he do the same when he has to travel all his life, right up to the resting-place of death; all the more so since his companion must be with him at bed and at board and everywhere, as the wife is with her husband. The companionship of one's own wife is not merchandise which, once bought, can be returned or bartered or exchanged; for marriage is an inseparable condition which lasts as long as life endures. It is a noose which becomes a Gordian knot once you put it round your neck, for if Death's scythe does not cut it, there is no untying it. I could say much more on this subject, if I were not prevented by my desire to know whether Master Licentiate has anything more to say about the story of Basilio.'

To which the student, whether bachelor, or licentiate as Don Quixote called him, replied: 'There is nothing more to say whatever, except that from the moment Basilio learnt that the fair Quiteria was to marry Camacho the rich he has never been seen to laugh or talk sensibly. He always goes about thoughtful and sad and talking to himself – a clear and certain sign that he has lost his wits. He eats little and sleeps little; and all he does eat is fruit, and if he does sleep he sleeps in the open, on the hard ground like a wild animal. From time to time he gazes at the sky, and at other times fixes his eyes on the earth in such distraction that he looks like nothing so much as a clothed statue with its garments blown about by the wind. Indeed he shows such signs of a heart torn by passion that all of us who know him are afraid that to-morrow the fair Quiteria's *Yes* will be his sentence of death.'

'God will find a cure,' said Sancho. 'For God, who gives the wound, gives the remedy. No one knows what's to come. There are many hours between now and to-morrow, and in one of them – even in a minute – the house falls. I have seen rain and sunshine together at the same moment. A man lies down sound at night and next day he can't move. Now, tell me, can there possibly be anyone who flatters himself that he has put a spoke into the wheel of Fortune? No, of course not. I wouldn't dare to put a pinpoint between a woman's yes and no, for there would be no room. Let them just tell me that Quiteria loves Basilio with all her heart and soul, and I'll give him a bag full of good luck. For love, as I have heard tell, looks through spectacles that make copper seem like gold, poverty like riches, and eye-rheum like pearls.'

'Will you never stop, Sancho, confound you?' exclaimed Don Quixote. 'Once you begin to string proverbs and old tales together, no one but Judas himself – may he take your soul – can follow you. Tell me, animal, what do you know about spokes or wheels or anything else?'

'Oh, if you don't understand me,' replied Sancho, 'it's no marvel my opinions are taken for nonsense. But no matter, I understand myself, and I know there wasn't much foolishness in what I said, though your worship's always such a cricket of my sayings, and of my doings too.'

'Critic, you should say,' said Don Quixote, 'not "*cricket*", you perverter of good language, confound you.'

'Don't turn sour on me, your worship,' replied Sancho. 'You know I wasn't brought up at the Court, and never studied at Salamanca to learn whether I'm putting a letter too many or too few into my words. Good Lord! You mustn't expect a Sayagan to speak like a chap from Toledo, and there may be Toledans who aren't so slick at this business of speaking pretty either.'

'That is so,' said the licentiate. 'Men bred in the tanneries and in Zocodover cannot speak as well as those who spend most of their day strolling in the cloisters of the Cathedral; and yet they are all Toledans. You will find the pure, correct, elegant and clear language among educated people at Court, even though they may have been born at Majalahonda. I said educated because there are many courtiers who are not so, and education is the grammar of good speech, which comes with practice. I, sirs, for my sins have studied canon law at Salamanca, and rather pride myself on expressing my meaning in clear, plain and forcible terms.'

'If you had not prided yourself more on knowing how to manage the foils you carry than your tongue,' said the other student, 'you would have come out first in your degree examination instead of last.'

'Look you, Bachelor Corchuelo,' replied the licentiate, 'if you consider skill in swordsmanship useless you hold the most erroneous opinion possible on the subject.'

'It is no mere opinion of mine,' answered Corchuelo, 'but a well-founded truth. And if you want me to prove it by experiment, you are carrying the swords. Here is a convenient spot. I have muscles and strength, and with my spirit, which is no poor one, I will make you admit that I am not in the wrong. Dismount, and make use of your measured paces, your circles, your angles and your science. Raw and clumsy and unskilled though I am, I hope to make you see stars at noonday. For I trust to God that the man is yet unborn who will make me turn my back, and there is no one on earth I will not force to give ground.'

'As to your turning your back or not,' replied the swordsman, 'it is no affair of mine, although your grave may well open for you on the spot where you first plant your foot – I mean that you will be struck dead there by the skill you despise.'

'We shall see now,' replied Corchuelo. And dismounting briskly from his ass, he snatched one of the swords the licentiate was carrying.

'That is not the way,' broke in Don Quixote. 'For I will be umpire of this duel, and see that this long unsettled question is fairly decided.' Then, alighting from Rocinante and grasping his lance, he took up his position in the middle of the road, at the moment when the licentiate was advancing gracefully and with measured steps against Corchuelo, who rushed at him, his eyes darting fire, as the saying is. The two peasants with them did not dismount from their fillies, but looked on as spectators of the mortal tragedy. Corchuelo's thrusts, lunges, down-strokes, back-strokes and double strokes were innumerable and thicker than hail. He rushed like an angry lion, but was met at full tilt by a blow on the mouth from the button of the licentiate's foil, which stopped him in the midst of his fury. In fact he had to kiss it as if it were a relic, although not with as much devotion as relics generally and rightfully receive. In the end the licentiate's lunges accounted for every one of the buttons of the short cassock his opponent was wearing, and cut his skirts to ribbons like the arms of cuttle-fish. Twice he knocked off his opponent's hat, and so wore him out that, in his vexation, anger and fury, he took his sword by the hilt and flung it into the air with such force that one of the peasant spectators, a clerk, who went for it afterwards, stated on oath that it had travelled a good two miles – which testimony has served, and still serves, to show and prove that, in very truth, brute strength is conquered by skill.

Corchuelo had sat down exhausted, when Sancho approached him and said: 'My goodness, Master Bachelor, if you'll take my advice, you won't challenge anyone to fence after this. Choose wrestling or pitching the bar instead, for you have the youth and strength for that. But as for these crack fighters, I've heard they can put a swordpoint through the eye of a needle.'

'I am satisfied,' replied Corchuelo, 'to have been tumbled off my hobby-horse, and to have learnt by experience a truth I was far from believing.'

So, getting up, he embraced the licentiate, and they remained better friends than before. Then, not caring to wait for the clerk who had gone for the sword, as they thought it would hold them back too long, they decided to push on, so as to arrive in good time at Quiteria's village, to which they all belonged.

During the remainder of the journey the licentiate expatiated on the excellencies of the sword, using such conclusive arguments, and so many instances and mathematical proofs, that they were all convinced of the virtue of the art, and Corchuelo was cured of his obstinacy.

Night was just beginning to fall, but as they arrived the village looked to them all as if it was surrounded by a sky filled with countless shining stars. They heard too the sweet confused sounds of various instruments, such as flutes, little drums, psalteries, recorders, tambourines and timbrels; and when they got near they saw that an arbour of trees, which had been put up by hand at the entrance to the village, was all full of little lights, which the wind did not disturb, for it was blowing so softly just then that it had not the strength to stir the leaves on the trees. The musicians were the merry-makers at the wedding, who were wandering about that pleasant spot in bands, some singing, others dancing, and yet others playing the diversity of instruments named. Indeed, it looked as though joy and gladness themselves were leaping and dancing all over that meadow. There were many others busily raising plat-

forms, from which next day they would be able to see in comfort
the plays and dances which were to be performed in that spot,
dedicated to the celebration of the rich Camacho's wedding and
Basilio's funeral. Don Quixote refused to enter the village, although
both the peasant and the student begged him to, giving what seemed
to him a most sufficient excuse: that it was the custom of knights
errant to sleep in the fields and woods rather than in towns or villages, even though it were under gilded roofs. Therefore he went a
little way off the road, much against Sancho's will, for the good
lodging he had had in Don Diego's castle or house was still fresh
in the squire's memory.

Chapter XX. *A description of the Wedding of Camacho the rich
and the Adventure of Basilio the poor.*

SCARCELY had the fair Aurora given shining Phoebus time to dry
the liquid pearls of her golden hair with the ardour of his hot rays,
when Don Quixote, shaking sloth from his limbs, stood up and
called his squire Sancho, who was still snoring. Seeing which, he
remarked before waking him:

'O you, fortunate above all who dwell on the face of the earth,
for without envy or being envied you sleep with a quiet mind,
neither persecuted by enchanters, nor alarmed by enchantments!
Sleep, I say again and a hundred times more, sleep; for no jealousy
of your lady holds you in perpetual vigil, nor do thoughts of how
to pay your debts keep you awake; nor of what you must do to feed
yourself and your little straitened family on the morrow. Ambition
does not trouble you, nor the vain pomps of the world worry you,
for the limits of your desires extend no further than care for your
ass. The care of your own person you have laid on my shoulders,
a compensatory burden which nature and custom have ever imposed upon masters. The servant sleeps and the master watches, reflecting on means of sustaining, bettering and favouring him. Anguish at seeing the sky turn to brass and shed no needful dew on the
earth does not afflict the servant but the master, who in barrenness
and famine must support him that served him in festivity and
abundance.'

To all this Sancho made no reply, since he was asleep; nor would he have woken so soon if Don Quixote had not brought him to with the butt-end of his lance. In the end he awoke, drowsy and slothful, and looking all around observed: 'There's a good smelling steam coming out of that arbour. If I'm not mistaken it smells more like broiled rashers than thyme and rushes. A wedding that begins with odours like that should be a liberal and generous one, I'll be bound.'

'Stop that, glutton,' said Don Quixote. 'Come, let's go and watch this ceremony, and see what the rejected Basilio does.'

'Let him do what he likes,' answered Sancho. 'He would be poor, and he would marry Quiteria. Isn't it enough not to have a farthing and to want to marry in the clouds? Really, sir, it's my opinion that the poor fellow should be content with what he finds and not go looking for dainties at the bottom of the sea. I'd bet one arm that Camacho could cover Basilio in gold pieces; and if that's so, as it must be, Quiteria would be a fine fool to throw away all the jewels and finery Camacho must have given her, and choose Basilio's bar-pitching and foil-play. They won't give you a pint of wine in a tavern for a good throw of the bar or a clever trick with a sword. Skills and graces that aren't saleable are all right for Count Dirlos, but when these talents fall to someone with good money I'd like to be in his shoes. On a good foundation you can build a good house, and the best foundation and bottom in the world is money.'

'For God's sake, Sancho,' cried Don Quixote at this point, 'be done with this speech of yours. For it is my belief that, if you were left to follow up every idea you start, you would have no time left to eat or sleep. You would waste it all in talking.'

'If your worship had a good memory,' replied Sancho, 'you'd remember the articles of our agreement, made before we left home this last time. One of them was that I should be allowed to talk as much as I pleased, so long as I didn't speak against my neighbour or your worship's authority. And I don't think I've violated that article so far.'

'I do not remember any such article, Sancho,' answered Don Quixote; 'but supposing you are right, I now wish you to be quiet and come. For the instruments we heard last night are once more delighting the valleys, and no doubt the wedding will be celebrated in the freshness of the morning, and not in the afternoon heat.'

Sancho obeyed his master, and saddled Rocinante and Dapple. Then they both mounted and rode leisurely towards the arbour. There the first thing that met Sancho's gaze was a whole steer spitted upon a whole elm, and for the fire over which it was to roast a pretty mountain of wood burning. The six earthen pots which stood around this blaze were not made in the common mould of ordinary pots, but were six medium-sized wine-jars, each one of which could hold a slaughter-house full of meat. Whole sheep were swallowed up in them and vanished from view like so many pigeons. There were numberless skinned hares and plucked chickens too, hanging on the trees, ready for burial in these pots. Countless also were the birds and game of all kinds hanging from the branches to cool in the air. Sancho counted more than sixty wine-skins of more than eight gallons each, and all full, as it after-wards proved, of choice wines. There were also piles of the whitest loaves, heaped up like mountains of wheat on the threshing-floor, and cheeses built up like bricks made a wall, while two cauldrons of oil, larger than dyers' vats, served for frying puddings, which they drew out ready and plunged into another cauldron of warmed honey, which stood alongside. There were more than fifty cooks, male and female, all clean, all busy and all jolly. In the distended belly of the steer were two dozen delicate little sucking-pigs, sewn up inside to make it tasty and tender. The spices of various sorts seemed to have been bought, not by the pound, but by the quarter, and were all displayed in a great chest. To conclude, the provision for the marriage was rustic, but plentiful enough to feed an army.

Sancho Panza gazed at all this, and as he contemplated it he grew to love it. The first things to captivate him and seize on his desires were the pots, from which he would have been glad to take a good dishful. Then the wine-skins captured his fancy, and last the products of the frying-pan, if such bloated vessels could be called pans. And so, unable to bear it any longer, he went up to one of the busy cooks, and in courteous and hungry terms prayed to be allowed to dip a crust of bread into one of the pots. To which the cook answered: 'Thanks to the rich Camacho, brother, hunger holds no sway to-day. Dismount and see if there's a ladle around. Then skim off a hen or two, and may they do you good.'

'I can't see one,' replied Sancho.

'Wait,' said the cook. 'Goodness, what a finnicking faint-hearted fellow you are!' So saying, he took a large cooking-pot and, dipping it into one of the jars, brought out with it three hens and a couple of geese, remarking to Sancho: 'Eat. Take your breakfast off these skimmings, my friend. They'll stay your hunger till dinner time.'

'I've nothing to put them in,' replied Sancho.

'Then take them, ladle and all,' said the cook. 'Camacho's rich enough and generous enough for anything.'

Whilst Sancho was thus occupied Don Quixote was watching the entrance of some dozen peasants on one side of the arbour. All were dressed in their holiday best, and each mounted on a fine mare in rich and splendid country trappings with many bells hanging from the harness. These ran in an orderly troop, not once but many times, up and down the meadow, cheering and shouting: 'Long live Camacho and Quiteria. He is rich and she is fair, the fairest maid in all the world!'

When Don Quixote heard them he said to himself: 'It is clear that they have not seen my Dulcinea del Toboso, for if they had seen her they would be more sparing in their praises of this Quiteria of theirs.'

Shortly afterwards several different teams of dancers began to march into various parts of the arbour, among them a band of sword-dancers, some two dozen shepherds of gallant looks and bearing, all dressed in the finest and whitest of linen, with multi-coloured headdresses worked in fine silk. One of those on horse-back asked their leader, a sprightly youth, whether any of the dancers had hurt himself.

'None of us has been hurt, up to now, thank Goodness,' said he. 'We are all fit.' And presently he began to wind his way among his companions, twisting and turning with such skill that, used as Don Quixote was to seeing such dances, this one seemed better than any he had ever beheld.

He was delighted too with a dance performed by a troop of lovely girls of between fourteen and eighteen, all dressed in green. Their hair, which they wore half plaited and half loose, was of such bright gold that their heads, wreathed with jasmine, roses, amaranth and honeysuckle, seemed to rival the very sun. They were led by a venerable old man and an ancient matron, both more active and nimbler than might have been expected from their years. They danced to the sound of a Zamora bagpipe, and with their modest looks and nimble feet, showed themselves the best dancers in the world.

After them came another set piece, called a speaking masque. It was made up of eight nymphs, divided into two files, one of them led by the god *Love* and the other by *Interest : Love* adorned with wings, a bow, quiver, and arrows, and *Interest* in rich coloured silks and gold. The nymphs led by *Love* had their names on their shoulders written in great letters on white parchment. *Poetry* was the first, *Good Sense* the second, *Good Family* the third, and *Valour* the fourth. Those that followed *Interest* were distinguished in the same way. The first was *Liberality*, the second *Gifts*, the third *Treasure*, and the fourth *Peaceful Possession*. They were preceded by a wooden castle drawn by four savages, all clad in ivy and hemp dyed green, so life-like that for a moment they quite frightened Sancho. On the front of the castle and on each of its four sides was written *The Castle of Caution*. Four skilful musicians struck up for them on the flute and drum. Then *Love* began to dance, and after two turns he raised his eyes and bent his bow against a maiden standing on the battlements of the castle, whom he addressed after this fashion:

> I am the powerful deity
> In Heaven above and earth beneath,
> In sea's and hell's profundity,
> Over all that therein live and breathe.
> What fear is I never knew;
> I can perform all that I will;
> Nothing to me is strange or new;
> I bid, forbid, at pleasure still.

The verse ended, he shot an arrow over the top of the castle and returned to his position. Then *Interest* came out and made two turns. The drums stopped and he spoke:

> I am one can do more than Love,
> Yet it is love that is my guide.
> My strain's the greater, for to Jove
> Above I nearest am allied.

> I Interest am, with whom but few
> Perform the honest deeds they should,
> Yet 'twere a miracle to view
> If without me they could do good.

Then *Interest* retired, and *Poetry* came forward and, after doing her turns like the others, fixed her eyes on the maiden in the castle and said:

> Lady, to thee, sweet Poetry
> Her soul in imagery sends,
> Wrapped up in sheaves of sonnetry,
> Whose pleasing strain commends.
> If with my earnestness I thee
> Do not annoy, fair damsel, soon
> Your envied fortune shall, by me,
> Mount to the Circle of the Moon.

Poetry retired, and from *Interest's* side *Liberality* danced out and, after her turns, spoke:

> To give is Liberality
> In him that shuns two contraries;
> The one is prodigality,
> The other hateful avarice.
> I'll be profuse in praising thee,
> For though profuseness is a sin,
> It smacks of love and honesty,
> And most in gifts is seen.

In this way all the figures in the two bands came forward and retired, each one making her turns and speaking her verses, some of which were charming and some ridiculous, though Don Quixote only retained in his excellent memory those which have been quoted. Soon they all mingled, making and breaking circles, gaily, easily and gracefully; and when *Love* passed in front of the castle he shot his arrows into the air, but *Interest* broke gilded balls against it. Then, in the end, after a long dance *Interest* took out a big purse, made of a great striped cat-skin, which seemed to be full of money, and flung it at the castle, whose boards fell apart and tumbled down at the shock, leaving the maiden exposed and defenceless. *Interest* then came up with the figures in his train, and throwing a great golden chain around her neck, made show of capturing her and leading her away a prisoner. When *Love* and his party saw this they tried to rescue her, making all their motions to the sound of the drums, they and the musicians playing and dancing in harmony. The savages then pacified the two parties, very speedily setting up and re-fixing the boards of the castle. The maiden shut herself up in it once more, and with this the dance concluded to the great pleasure of the spectators.

Don Quixote asked one of the nymphs who had composed and directed the show, and she replied that it was a clergyman of that village, who was a great hand at these productions.

'I would wager,' said Don Quixote, 'that he is more friendly to Camacho than to Basilio, that bachelor or clergyman, and a better hand at satire than at vespers. How cleverly he introduced Basilio's accomplishments and Camacho's riches into the dance!' Then Sancho Panza, who was listening, put in: 'The King's my cock. I'm for Camacho.'

'Indeed,' said Don Quixote. 'You seem to be the sort of yokel, Sancho, who always shouts "*Long live the conqueror*".'

'I don't know what sort I am,' answered Sancho, 'but I know I shall never get such elegant skimmings from Basilio's pots as I got from Camacho's.' And showing his cooking-pot full of geese and pullets, he pulled one out and began to eat with great zest and appetite, saying: 'Hang Basilio's accomplishments! You're worth as much as you've got, and you get as much as you're worth. There are only two families in the world, my old grandmother used to say, the *Haves* and the *Have-nots*. She was always for the *haves*, and to this very day, my lord Don Quixote, the doctor would rather feel the pulse of a *Have* than a *Know*. An ass covered with gold looks better than a horse with a pack-saddle. So I say again, I'm for Camacho. The skimmings from his pots are geese and pullets, hares, and rabbits in plenty; but Basilio's, if they ever come to hand, will be cask-rinsings.'

'Have you finished your speech, Sancho?' asked Don Quixote.

'I'll get it over,' answered Sancho. 'For I see it offends your worship. But if this hadn't come to interrupt it, I had enough to say to last three days.'

'Pray God, Sancho,' said Don Quixote, 'I may see you dumb before I die.'

'At the rate we're going,' replied Sancho, 'I shall be chewing clay before your worship dies. Then perhaps I shall be so dumb that I shan't speak a word till the end of the world, or at least till Dooms-day.'

'Even though that should happen, Sancho,' said Don Quixote, 'your silence would never balance all your talking, past, present and future; especially as in the course of nature I suppose I shall die before you, and so I can never hope to see you dumb, not even when you are drinking or sleeping, which is the least I might have hoped for.'

'Really, sir,' answered Sancho, 'there's no trusting the fleshless woman – I mean Death. She devours the lamb as well as the sheep. And I've heard our priest say that she tramples equally on the high towers of kings and on the humble cottages of the poor. That lady is more powerful than dainty. She's not a bit squeamish. She eats of all and does for all, and fills her bags with all sorts of people, of all ages and conditions. She's no reaper who sleeps in the mid-day heat. She reaps at all hours, and cuts the dry grass as well as the green. She doesn't seem to chew, but gobbles and gulps down every-thing that's put before her; for she has a dog's appetite and nothing satisfies it. And although she has no belly, she seems to have a dropsy and a thirst to drink the lives of all living beings, as you drink a jug of cold water.'

'No more, Sancho,' Don Quixote broke in. 'Stop your fine phrases, and do not risk a fall. For really, in your country language you have said as much about death as any good preacher could. I tell you, Sancho, if your learning were equal to your natural wits you could take to the pulpit and go about the world preaching the prettiest sermons.'

'He preaches well that lives well,' replied Sancho, 'and I know no other *thologies*.'

'You have no need of them,' said Don Quixote. 'But I have not yet managed to understand or grasp how you know so much, see-ing that fear of God is the beginning of wisdom, and you fear a lizard more than you fear Him.'

'Judge of your chivalries, your worship,' answered Sancho, 'and don't meddle with other men's fears or courage, for I've as pretty a fear of God as any neighbour's son. Now leave me to gobble up these skimmings, for all the rest are but idle words, of which we must give account in another life.'

And so saying, he began a fresh assault on his cooking-pot with such appetite as to arouse Don Quixote; and no doubt his master would have helped him, if he had not been hindered by an event which must be told further on.

Chapter XXI. *A continuation of Camacho's wedding, with other delightful Adventures.*

WHILE Don Quixote and Sancho were engaged in the conversation set down in the last chapter they heard loud shouts and a great uproar, which came from the men on horseback, who rode out, galloping and shouting, to meet the bride and bridegroom. The pair were approaching, surrounded by countless different musical instruments and inventions, and accompanied by the priest, the kinsfolk of both, and the most important people from the neighbouring villages, all dressed in their holiday best. And when Sancho saw the bride, he said:

'Well I never! She isn't dressed like a farmer's daughter, but like a fine palace lady! Heavens alive! That necklace of hers looks like fine coral, and she isn't wearing Cuenca cloth but thirty pile velvet! And her trimmings aren't white linen, but I swear they're satin! Then look at her hands! Is it jet rings she's wearing? No, I'll be blowed if they're not gold, and very much so, set with pearls as white as curds, each one of them worth the eye out of my head. Oh, the little whore! And what hair! If it isn't false, I've never seen longer or redder in my life! Then can you find fault with her air or her figure? Wouldn't you say she is like a palm-tree loaded with bunches of dates? For that is what they look like, those jewels she's got hanging from her hair and at her throat. My Lord, she's a fine strapping girl, and could sail through the shoals of Flanders.'

Don Quixote laughed at Sancho Panza's rustic praise; but he thought that, except for his lady Dulcinea del Toboso, he had never seen a more beautiful woman. The fair Quiteria looked rather pale, which might have been from the bad night that brides always have, getting themselves ready for their coming wedding-day. They marched up to a theatre standing on one side of the meadow, decorated with carpets and branches. For there it was the ceremony was to take place, and there they were to sit, looking on at the dances and masques. But just as they arrived at this spot they heard a great outcry behind them, and a voice shouting: 'Wait a little, thoughtless and hasty people!'

At this loud interruption everyone turned round, and saw that the speaker was a man dressed in a black coat, trimmed with crimson patches in the shape of flames. He was crowned, they presently saw, with a wreath of funereal cypress, and carried a stout staff in his hand. When he got closer, everyone recognized him as the gallant Basilio, and all waited in suspense to see what would come of his interruption, fearing some evil consequences from his arriving at such a moment. He came up at last, weary and breathless, and taking up his position in front of the bride and bridegroom, dug his steel-tipped staff into the ground. Then, changing colour and fixing his eyes on Quiteria, he spoke these words, in hoarse and trembling tones:

'Well you know, ungrateful Quiteria, that by the sacred law which binds us, you can take no other husband whilst I live. Nor are you unaware that, while I waited for time and my efforts to increase my fortune, I did not fail to observe the respect due to your honour. But you turn your back on all the obligations you owe my love, and wish to make lord of what is mine another, whose riches not only bring him good fortune but great happiness as well. So, to fill his fortune to the brim – not because I think that he deserves it, but because Heaven has been pleased to give it to him – I will destroy with my own hand such obstacle or impediment as might hinder him, by removing myself from his path. Long life, then, to the rich Camacho with the ungrateful Quiteria! Long and happy years! And let poor Basilio die, for poverty has clipped the wings of his happiness and laid him in his grave.'

And so saying, he grasped his staff, which he had dug into the earth and, breaking it in half on the ground, showed that it served as the sheath for a medium-sized dagger, which was concealed in it. Then, planting what might be called the hilt in the ground, he threw himself nimbly and resolutely upon it, and in an instant the bloody point appeared out of his back with half the steel blade – the unhappy wretch lying stretched on the ground, bathed in his blood, and transfixed by his own weapon. His friends at once ran up to help him, appalled at his miserable and piteous plight. Don Quixote too left Rocinante and, hurrying to his aid, took him in his arms and found that he had not yet breathed his last. They would have drawn out the dagger, but the priest, who was present, was of the opinion that they should not do so till he had made his confession, for he would certainly die the moment they did. Coming a little to himself, however, Basilio cried in a faint and doleful voice:

'If, cruel Quiteria, in my last and fatal agony you would give me your hand as my bride, I should think that my rashness had some excuse, since by it I should attain the bliss of being yours.'

Hearing this, the priest bade him attend to the salvation of his soul rather than to the pleasures of the body, and earnestly to implore God's pardon for his sins and for his desperate deed. To which Basilio replied that he would on no account make his confession unless Quiteria would first give him her hand in marriage, for that happiness would strengthen his heart and give him breath for confession. When Don Quixote heard the wounded man's petition, he cried aloud that Basilio's request was very just and reasonable and, what was more, very practicable, and that Sir Camacho would be as honoured by receiving the lady Quiteria as the widow of the valorous Basilio as if he were to receive her from her father's side.

'There is no need of anything more here than one *Yes*,' said he, 'for it can have no sequel, since the bridal bed of this marriage must be the grave.'

Camacho listened to all this in bewilderment and confusion, not knowing what to do or say. But so many were the voices of Basilio's friends, beseeching him to permit Quiteria to give him her hand — so that his soul should not be lost by his desperate end — that he was moved, or even forced, to say that if Quiteria was willing he was content, since it was only delaying for a moment the fulfilment of his desires. Then they all ran up to Quiteria and, some with prayers, others with tears, and yet others with persuasive arguments, implored her to give her hand to poor Basilio. But she was harder than marble and more immovable than a statue, and appeared to be unable and unwilling to reply with so much as a word. Nor would she have done so, if the priest had not told her to make up her mind quickly, for now Basilio's soul was in his teeth, and there was no time to wait for irresolute minds.

The fair Quiteria answered never a word, but seemingly in a fluster of grief moved to where Basilio lay with his eyes turned up, breathing short and painfully, and muttering her name between his teeth, apparently about to die like a heathen and no Christian. At length she reached him, fell on her knees and, rather by signs than by words, besought his hand. Then Basilio opened his eyes and, staring fixedly at her, said: 'Quiteria, you have come to relent at a time when your pity can only serve as a knife to finish off my life. For I have no more strength to bear the honour you are giving me by choosing me as yours, nor will it ease the pain which is so rapidly filming my eyes with the dread shadow of death. I implore of you, my fatal star, not to give me your hand out of mere complaisance nor to deceive me once more, but to confess and declare that you give it to me freely and unconstrainedly, as to your lawful husband; since it would be wrong to deceive me in the condition I am in, or to deal falsely with one who has dealt so truly with you.'

As he was speaking he fainted, and all the bystanders thought that each convulsion would carry his soul away. Then Quiteria, all modest and bashful, took Basilio's right hand in hers, and said: 'No force would be sufficient to constrain my will. With all the freedom in the world I give you my hand as your lawful wife and accept yours, if it is freely given, and your mind is not clouded and changed by the calamity you have rashly brought upon yourself.'

'Yes, I give it,' replied Basilio, 'undisturbed and unchanged, and with the clear understanding that Heaven has granted me. So I give and deliver myself to you as your husband.'

'And I as your wife,' replied Quiteria, 'whether you live many years, or are borne from my arms to the grave.'

'The lad talks a great deal for one so gravely wounded,' remarked Sancho at this point. 'They should make him stop his love-talk and attend to his soul, for to my mind it's nearer to his tongue than to his teeth.'

So Basilio and Quiteria clasped hands, and the priest tenderly and tearfully gave them his benediction, begging God to give good repose to the soul of the bridegroom. But the moment he received the blessing, Basilio jumped briskly to his feet, and with unexpected deftness wrenched out the dagger which was sheathed in his body. All the bystanders were amazed, and some of them, more credulous than curious, began to cry out: 'A miracle, a miracle!'

But Basilio answered: 'No miracle, no miracle; but a trick, a trick!' The priest ran up in confusion and astonishment to feel the wound with both his hands, and found that the knife had not passed through Basilio's flesh and ribs, but through a hollow iron tube, which he had fitted into position, filled with blood so prepared, as it afterwards came out, as not to congeal. In fact the priest, Camacho and all the spectators had been tricked and fooled. The bride, however, showed no signs of resenting the ruse. On the contrary, when she heard that the marriage, being fraudulent, was invalid, she said that she reconfirmed it. From which everyone concluded that the affair had been planned with her agreement and connivance. This so enraged Camacho and his supporters that they took their vengeance into their own hands, and many of them drew their swords and attacked Basilio, in whose defence almost as many swords were unsheathed in an instant. At the head of them Don Quixote on horseback, with his lance on his arm and well covered by his shield, forced everyone to give way before him. But Sancho, who never got any pleasure or solace from such doings, took refuge among the pots from which he had extracted his welcome skimmings, regarding that spot as sacred and certain to be respected. Then Don Quixote cried out in a loud voice:

'Hold, sirs, hold! We have no right to take vengeance for the wrongs love does us. Consider that love and war are one; and as in war it is legitimate and customary to use artifices and stratagems to conquer the enemy, so in contests and rivalries of love deceits and plots practised to attain the desired end are justifiable, so long as they are not to the detriment and dishonour of the loved object. Quiteria was Basilio's, and Basilio Quiteria's, by Heaven's just and favourable decree. Camacho is rich and can buy his pleasure when, where and how he will. Basilio has only this one ewe-lamb, and no one, however powerful, shall take her from him; for whom God hath joined let no man put asunder. And whoever attempts will first have to pass by the point of this lance.' With this he brandished his weapon so stoutly and deftly that he struck fear into all who did not know him.

So deeply did Quiteria's disdain fix itself into Camacho's mind that she was instantly blotted from his memory; and consequently the persuasions of the priest, who was a wise and well-meaning man, prevailed with him, and left him and his partisans appeased and quieted. In sign of which they sheathed their swords, rather blaming Quiteria for her lightness than Basilio for his trick, and Camacho arguing to himself that if Quiteria loved Basilio as a maiden she would still love him after her marriage, and so he must give Heaven greater thanks for losing her than for getting her.

So, Camacho and his supporters being consoled and pacified, all Basilio's party were quiet, and Camacho the rich proved that he did not resent the trick, or take it to heart, by desiring that the entertainment should proceed as if he were really being married. However, neither Basilio nor his wife nor his followers would take part, but went off to Basilio's village. For just as the rich have their flatterers and their train; so even the poor, if virtuous and sensible, have also followers to honour and uphold them.

They took Don Quixote with them, esteeming him a man of worth and valour. Sancho alone was filled with gloom, when he saw himself dragged away from Camacho's splendid feast and entertainment, which lasted till night. Dejectedly and sorrowfully he followed his master, who rode with Basilio's party, and left behind him the flesh-pots of Egypt, though he bore them with him in his heart; their skimmings in the cooking-pot, although almost consumed to the last, representing for him the glory and plenty of the good things he had lost. So, pensive and brooding though hungerless, without alighting from Dapple, he followed in Rocinante's tracks.

Chapter XXII. *Of the great Adventure of Montesinos' Cave in the heart of La Mancha, which the valorous Don Quixote brought to a happy ending.*

MANY and great were the compliments which the newly-married couple paid Don Quixote, being grateful for the readiness he had shown to defend their cause, measuring his wit by his valour, and accounting him a Cid in arms and a Cicero in eloquence. The good Sancho was entertained for three days at the expense of the bridal

couple, from whom he learnt that the pretended wounding was not
a plot pre-arranged with the fair Quiteria, but a trick of Basilio's,
from which he had expected the very result they had witnessed.
Though it is true that he confessed he had let some of his friends
into his secret, so that they might support his plans and back up his
deceptions at the needful moment.

'Deceptions they could not and should not be called,' said Don
Quixote, 'seeing that they were designed for a good purpose. For
the marriage of two lovers was a project of the highest excellence.'
He warned them, however, that love's greatest adversary is hunger
and continued poverty. For love is all gaiety, rejoicing and happiness, particularly when the lover is in possession of the beloved,
against whom want and poverty are open and declared enemies. All
this he said to persuade Basilio to give up practising his arts, for although they brought him fame they earned him no money, and to
apply himself to increasing his wealth by lawful and industrious
means, which the prudent and hard-working never lack. The poor,
honourable man – if it is possible for a poor man to be honourable –
in possessing a lovely wife, has such a jewel that if he is robbed of it
his honour is lost and slain. The lovely and honourable wife whose
husband is poor deserves to be crowned with laurels and palms of
victory and triumph. Beauty alone attracts the desires of all who
gaze on it and recognize it, and princely eagles and high-soaring
birds swoop down upon it as on a dainty lure. But if to this beauty
are joined want and necessity, the crows, the kites and all the other
birds of prey attack it as well, and the wife who remains constant
against all such assaults well deserves to be called her husband's
crown.

'Consider, my wise Basilio,' added Don Quixote; 'it was the
opinion of I do not remember what sage that there has been only
one good woman in the whole world, and he advised everyone to
think and believe that his wife was she; for thus would he live content. I am not married myself, nor till now have I had any thought
of being so; but, nevertheless, I would be so bold as to give counsel
to anyone who might ask me for it as to the way in which he should
seek the woman to marry. First I should advise him to consider
reputation more than wealth. For the good woman gets a good
name not solely by being good, but by appearing so; and looseness

and free behaviour in public damage a woman's honour more than secret sinning. If you bring a good woman home it will be easy to preserve her or even increase her in her goodness; but if you bring home a bad one, it will put you to some labour to mend her, for it is not very practicable to pass from one extreme to another. I do not say that it is impossible, but I regard it as difficult.'

Sancho listened to all this, and said to himself: 'When I speak of matters of pith and substance, this master of mine's in the habit of telling me that I ought to take a pulpit in hand and go about the world preaching pretty sermons. But, as for him, it's my opinion that once he begins to string sentences and give advice, it's not only one pulpit he should take in hand, but two on every finger, and go through the markets crying: "Who buys my wares?" The devil take him for a knight errant, so many things he knows. I was thinking to myself that he only knew about these chivalries of his, but there isn't a subject he doesn't pick at and dip his spoon into.'

Sancho muttered this so loud that his master overheard him and asked: 'What are you grumbling at, Sancho?'

'I'm not speaking and I'm not grumbling,' answered Sancho. 'I was only saying to myself that I wish I'd heard what your worship has just said before I got married. Then perhaps I should be saying now that the loosed ox enjoys licking himself.'

'Is your Teresa so bad, Sancho?' asked Don Quixote.

'She's not very bad,' answered Sancho. 'But she's not very good; at least, she's not as good as I should like.'

'You do wrong, Sancho,' said Don Quixote, 'in speaking evil of your wife, for, after all, she is the mother of your children.'

'We owe one another nothing,' answered Sancho, 'for she slanders me when she fancies, especially when she's jealous. And then Satan himself wouldn't be able to bear with her.'

Three days they stayed with the newly married pair, and were regaled and treated like princes. Then Don Quixote asked the skilful licentiate to give him a guide to lead him to the cave of Montesinos, for he had a great desire to explore it and see with his own eyes whether the marvels related about it thereabouts were true. The licentiate suggested a cousin of his, a famous scholar much given to the reading of books of chivalry, who would gladly take him to the mouth of this cave and show him the Ruidera Lagoons, which

U

were also famous throughout La Mancha, or rather throughout the whole of Spain. He went on to say that Don Quixote would enjoy his cousin's company, as he was a lad who knew how to make books for the press and to dedicate them to princes.

By and by the cousin appeared riding an ass in foal, with a pack-saddle covered with a multi-coloured rug or sack-cloth. Sancho saddled Rocinante, bridled Dapple, and filled his saddle-bags, with which the cousin's kept company, being also well provided. Then, after commending themselves to God and bidding everyone fare-well, they set out on their way, taking the road to the famous cave of Montesinos. On the ride Don Quixote asked the cousin the nature or character of his pursuits, his profession and studies. To which he replied that by profession he was a humanist, and that his pursuits and studies were to compose books for the press, all of great profit and entertainment to the commonwealth. One, he said, was entitled *The Book of Liveries*, in which he described seven hun-dred and three devices with their colours, mottoes and ciphers. From these the gentlemen of the court could extract and use what-ever they pleased at festival times and celebrations, and would then have no need to beg their liveries from anybody, or to rack their brains, as they say, to invent them to suit their desires and purposes.

'For,' said he, 'I give suitable devices to the jealous, the scorned, the forgotten and the absent, and fit them out neat as a new pin. I have another book as well, which I mean to call *Metamorphoses, or the Spanish Ovid*, a new and rare invention. In it, parodying Ovid, I give an account of the Giralda of Seville and the Angel of the Magdalen, the Gutter of Vecinguerra at Cordova and the Bulls of Guisando; the Sierra Morena; the fountains of Leganitos and Lava-pies in Madrid, not omitting those of the Piojo, of the Golden Gutter, and the Priora; all this with such allegories, metaphors, and transformations as will delight, surprise and instruct at the same time. I have another book that I call the *Supplement to Polydore Virgil*, which treats of the invention of things. It is a work of great erudition and research, for I elucidate and set out in an elegant style matters of great importance omitted by Polydore. He forgot to tell us who was the first man in the world to have catarrh, and the first to use ointments to cure himself of the French pox; but all these points I set out with the utmost precision on the testimony of twenty-five authorities. So your worship can judge whether I have not worked well, and whether this book will not be useful to the whole world.'

Then Sancho, who had listened very attentively to the cousin's narrative, inquired of him: 'Tell me, sir – good luck to you with the printing of your books – but can you say – though I know you can, for you know everything – who was the first man to scratch his head? For it's my opinion that it must have been our father Adam.'

'Yes, of course,' replied their guide, 'for there is no doubt Adam had a head and hair; and that being so, and he being the first man in the world, he must sometimes have scratched himself.'

'Yes, so I thought,' answered Sancho; 'but tell me now, who was the first tumbler in the world?'

'Really, brother,' replied their guide, 'I cannot decide that now. I have not gone far enough in my studies. I will look it up when I get back to my books, and satisfy you when we meet again, for this must not be the last time.'

'Now, look you, sir,' answered Sancho. 'Don't put yourself to any trouble about it, for I've hit on the answer to my question. The first tumbler in the world was Lucifer; for when they threw him or flung him out of Heaven, he went tumbling down to the abyss.'

'You are right, my friend,' said their guide.

'That question and answer are not yours, Sancho,' said Don Quixote. 'You have heard them from somebody.'

'Hush, sir,' replied Sancho, 'for if I take to questioning and answering I shan't be done by to-morrow morning, I promise you. Indeed, if it's a matter of asking stupid questions and giving foolish answers I've no need to go looking for help from the neighbours.'

'You have said more than you know, Sancho,' said Don Quixote, 'for there are some who tire themselves out learning and proving things which, once learnt and proved, do not concern either the understanding or the memory a jot.'

That day they spent in such-like pleasant conversations, and at night they lodged in a little village which the scholar told Don Quixote was no more than six miles from Montesinos' cave. If, however, he was resolved to explore it, he would need to provide himself with ropes, by which he might let himself down into its depths. Don Quixote replied that he must see the bottom, even if it reached to the pit of hell. So they bought some hundred and fifty feet of rope, and the next day at two in the afternoon came to the cave, whose mouth is wide and spacious but choked with box-thorn and wild fig-trees, brambles and briars, so thick and intertwined that they entirely mask and cover it. When they found it, the scholar, Sancho and Don Quixote dismounted, and the first two presently tied the knight very firmly with the ropes. And whilst they were swathing and binding him, Sancho said: 'Consider what you are doing, your worship. Don't bury yourself alive, and don't put yourself where you will be like a bottle hung down a well to cool. Indeed, it's no concern of yours, sir, to explore this place. It's probably worse than a dungeon.'

'Bind me and be silent,' answered Don Quixote, 'for such an enterprise as this, Sancho my friend, was reserved for me.'

Then said their guide: 'I beseech your worship, Don Quixote, to be observant and to examine with the eyes of a lynx what lies below. Perhaps there may be things for me to put into my book of transformations.'

'The drum is in hands that knows well how to beat it,' observed Sancho Panza.

When this was said and Don Quixote's fastenings, which went about his doublet and not over his armour, secured, the knight exclaimed: 'We have been careless in not providing ourselves with a little bell to be tied beside me on this rope. For by my sounding it you might have known that I was still descending and still alive. But since that is not possible now, let it be in God's hands to guide me.'

Then he knelt down and said a prayer to Heaven in a low voice, begging God to aid him and give him good fortune in this seemingly novel and perilous adventure. After which he said aloud: 'O mistress of my actions and movements, most illustrious and peerless Dulcinea del Toboso! If it is possible for the prayers and requests of your venturesome lover to reach your ears, I implore you by your incomparable loveliness to listen to them, for their only purpose is to beg you not to deny me your favours and protection now that I have so much need of them. I am about to cast myself, to plunge and bury myself, in the abyss which opens here before me, solely that the world may know that with your favour there is nothing so impossible that I cannot undertake and accomplish it.'

As he said this he drew near to the chasm, and saw that it was not possible to let himself down or make a way to the entrance unless by force of arms or by cutting a way through. So he drew his sword and began to hack and slash at the briars growing at the mouth of the cave. At this frightful clatter a huge number of great crows and jackdaws flew out, so thick and fast that they swept Don Quixote to the ground; and, had he been superstitious, which as a good Catholic he was not, he would have taken them as a bad omen and given up the idea of immuring himself in such a place.

At length he stood up, and seeing no more crows come out, nor any other birds of night, such as bats, which had flown out with the crows, with Sancho and the scholar paying out the rope he let himself down to the bottom of the dreadful cave. And as he descended, Sancho threw him his blessing and made countless signs of the cross over him, saying:

'May God guide you, and the Rock of France, together with the Trinity of Gaeta, O flower, cream, and skimming of knights errant! There you go, braggart of the world, heart of steel, and arm of brass! Once more, God guide you and bring you back, safe, sound and unharmed to the light of this world which you have forsaken to bury yourself in that darkness you're seeking.'

The scholar offered almost the same prayers and entreaties, but Don Quixote went on calling out for rope and more rope, and they paid it out little by little. But when his shouts, which came up from the cave as through a funnel, were heard no more, they had already paid out the hundred and fifty foot and were thinking of hoisting Don Quixote up again, as they could give him no more. Nevertheless they waited for about half an hour, at the end of which they began to hoist the rope, which came easily and without any weight on it, which made them suppose that Don Quixote had stayed below. In this belief Sancho Panza began to weep bitterly and hauled away hurriedly, anxious to learn the truth. But when little more than thirty foot seemed to be left they felt a weight, of which they were extremely glad. Finally at fifteen foot they made Don Quixote out distinctly, and Sancho called to him: 'Welcome back to you, your worship, for we were thinking you had stayed there to found a family.'

But Don Quixote did not reply a word, and when they had drawn him completely out, they saw that his eyes were shut, as if in sleep. They laid him out on the ground and untied him; but for all that he did not wake. Then they turned him over and over, and stirred him and shook him so heartily that after some time he came to himself, stretching his limbs as if waking from a deep sleep. Then gazing in all directions, as if in alarm, he said:

'God pardon you, my friends, for you have robbed me of the sweetest existence and most delightful vision any human being ever enjoyed or beheld. Now, indeed, I positively know that the pleasures of this life pass like a shadow and a dream, and wither like the flowers of the field. Oh, unhappy Montesinos! O gravely wounded Durandarte! O luckless Belerma! O tearful Guadiana, and you, unfortunate daughter of Ruidera, who show by your waters what tears your fair eyes have wept!'

The scholar and Sancho listened most attentively to Don Quixote's words, which he uttered as if wrenching them with immense pain from his bowels. They begged him to explain what he meant, and to tell them what he had seen in that hell.

'Hell you call it?' said Don Quixote. 'Do not call it that. For it does not deserve that name, as you will presently see.'

He begged them for something to eat, for he was very hungry. Then they spread the scholar's saddle-cloth on the green grass and set about emptying the saddle-bags; and all three in love and good fellowship ate their lunch and their supper in one. Then, when the cloth was lifted, Don Quixote de la Mancha said: 'Let no one arise. Listen to me, my sons, all of you!'

Chapter XXIII. *Of the Amazing Things which the consummate Don Quixote related that he had seen in the deep Cave of Montesinos, whose Impossibility and Immensity has caused this Adventure to be considered Apocryphal.*

IT was about four in the afternoon when the sun, obscured by clouds, showed but a dim light, and with his tempered rays gave Don Quixote the opportunity to relate to his two illustrious

auditors without heat and discomfort what he had seen in Montesinos' cave. He began as follows:

'About eighteen or twenty feet down in the depths of this dungeon, on the right-hand side, there is a concave space capable of
containing a large cart with its mules. A little light comes into it
from far off through some chinks or holes opening to the earth's
surface. This concave space I saw the while I passed, weary and sad
at finding myself hanging and dangling by the rope, journeying
through that obscure nether region on no assured or charted road;
and so I determined to go in there and rest a little. I called out to
ask you not to let out any more rope till I bade you, but you could
not have heard me. I gathered up the rope you had let down and,
rolling it into a coil or pile, sat down on it, most thoughtfully considering how I could reach the bottom without anything to support
me. In this perplexed meditation, suddenly and involuntarily I was
overcome by a deep sleep, and when I least expected it, not knowing
how or why, I woke up to find myself in the middle of the most
beautiful, pleasant and delightful meadow nature could create or
the liveliest human imagination conceive. I opened and rubbed my
eyes, and saw that I was not asleep but really awake. For all that, I
felt my head and my bosom to make certain whether it was my very
self who was there, or some empty and counterfeit phantom; but
touch, feeling and the coherent argument I held with myself assured me that I was there then just as I am here now. Soon there
appeared before my eyes a royal and sumptuous palace or castle,
whose walls and battlements appeared to be formed of clear transparent crystal; and when two great doors opened in them I saw
coming out towards me a venerable old man, in a cloak of purple
serge which trailed on the ground. Across his shoulders and breast
he wore collegians' bands of green velvet. His head was covered by
a black Milan cap, and his hoary beard reached to his waist. He carried no arms at all, but a rosary in his hands of beads larger than
fair-sized walnuts, every tenth one the size of an ordinary ostrich
egg. His bearing, his gait, his solemnity and his ample presence,
each separately and all together, struck me with wonder and admiration. When he came up to me the first thing he did was to embrace
me warmly. Then he said:

'"It is many centuries, valorous knight, Don Quixote de la

Mancha, that we who dwell in these enchanted solitudes have been waiting to see you, so that you may inform the world of what is contained here, buried in this deep cave you have entered, which is called Montesinos' cave: an exploit reserved to be attempted only by your invincible heart and your stupendous courage. Come with me, illustrious sir, for I would show you the marvels concealed in this transparent castle, of which I am the governor and perpetual chief warden; for I am Montesinos himself, from whom the cave takes its name."

'Scarcely had he said that he was Montesinos when I asked him whether it was true, as it was reported in the world up here, that he had cut the heart of his great friend Durandarte out of his breast with a little dagger, and carried it to the lady Belerma, as Durandarte had bidden him at the point of death. He replied that the whole story was true, except as regards the dagger, for it was neither a dagger nor small, but a thin stiletto sharper than an awl.'

'That stiletto,' put in Sancho, 'must have been made by Ramon de Hoces of Seville.'

'I do not know,' continued Don Quixote. 'But it could not be that stiletto-maker, because Ramon de Hoces was living yesterday, and the fight at Roncesvalles, where this tragedy occurred, was many years ago. But inquiry into that is of no importance, for it does not disturb or alter the truth and sequence of the history.'

'That is true,' said the scholar. 'Please continue, Don Quixote, for I am listening with all the pleasure in the world.'

'I take no less pleasure in telling my tale,' answered Don Quixote. 'So the venerable Montesinos, I say, brought me into the crystalline palace, where in a low hall of extreme coolness and all of alabaster stood a marble sepulchre made with great craftsmanship, on which I saw a knight lying at full length, wrought not in brass, nor marble, nor carved jasper, as is usual on other tombs, but of pure flesh and bone. He had his right hand – which seemed to me somewhat hairy and muscular, a sign of great strength in its owner – resting beside his heart; and before I could ask Montesinos any question, he saw me gaze with amazement at the figure on the sepulchre, and said:

' "This is my friend Durandarte, flower and mirror of all true lovers and valiant knights of his age. He is kept here enchanted, as

I am, and many more knights and ladies, by Merlin, the French
wizard, who, they say, was the Devil's son. Though it is my belief
that he was no Devil's son, but knew, as the saying is, one trick
more than the Devil. How or why he enchanted us no one knows,
but that will be told in the course of time, and before very long now,
I imagine. What astonishes me is that I know, as surely as that it is
now day, that Durandarte ended his life in my arms, and that after
his death I cut out his heart with my own hands. In truth it must
have weighed two pounds, and according to natural philosophers a
man with a large heart is endowed with greater courage than one
with a small. And yet despite my knowing that this knight really
died, how is it that ever and anon now he complains and sighs as
if he were alive?"

'At those words the wretched Durandarte cried out in a loud voice:

> ' "Oh, my cousin Montesinos!
> It was the last thing I asked you,
> That as soon as I was dead
> And my spirit had departed,
> You should bear my heart to where
> Fair Belerma dwelt and waited,
> Cutting it from out my chest
> With a sword or with a dagger."

'When the venerable Montesinos heard this he threw himself on
his knees before the afflicted knight and cried, with tears in his
eyes: "Long ago, Sir Durandarte, my dearest cousin – long ago I
did what you bade me on that bitter day of our defeat. I tore out
your heart as best I could, and left not a fragment of it in your
bosom. I wiped it with a lace handkerchief. I set out with it on the
road to France, having first laid you in the bosom of the earth, with
enough tears to wash my hands clean of the blood-stains they had
got from groping in your entrails. And for further proof, beloved
cousin, at the first place I came to after leaving Roncesvalles, I
threw a little salt on your heart so that it should not smell bad, but
should come, if not fresh, at least dry, into the presence of the lady
Belerma, whom the sage Merlin has kept here many years enchanted
with you and me, your squire Guadiana, Mistress Ruidera, her
seven daughters and two nieces, and many others of your acquaintances and friends. Yet, though five hundred years have passed, not

one of us has died; only Ruidera, her daughters and nieces are missing, whom out of the compassion he must have had for their tears, Merlin turned into as many lagoons, which are now known in the world of the living and in the province of La Mancha as the Lagoons of Ruidera. The seven belong to the Kings of Spain, and the two nieces to the knights of a most holy order, that of St. John. Guadiana, your squire, also bewailed your sad fate, and was converted into a river called by his name. But when he reached the earth's surface and saw the sun of another sky, so great was his grief at finding he had abandoned you that he plunged into the bowels of the earth. Yet as it is not possible for him to cease flowing in his natural course, from time to time he emerges and shows himself where the sun and mankind may see him. The lagoons I have spoken of minister their waters to him, and with these and many others he enters Portugal in pomp and grandeur. But, for all that, wherever he goes he shows his sorrow and melancholy, and takes no pride in breeding savoury and valuable fish in his waters, but unlike the golden Tagus bears only coarse and tasteless ones. And what I am telling you now, my dear cousin, I have told you many times; but as you do not reply, I imagine either that you do not believe me or do not hear me, which – God knows – pains me greatly. Now, however, I want to give you some news which may not serve to assuage your grief, but will in no way increase it. Learn that you have here in your presence – open your eyes and see him! – that great knight of whom the sage Merlin has prophesied so much, that Don Quixote de la Mancha, I tell you, who has revived and improved on the ancient art of chivalry, which is now forgotten. Through his mediation and favour, too, we ourselves may perhaps be disenchanted, for great deeds are reserved for great men."

'"And if that should not be," replied the afflicted Durandarte in a faint whisper; "if that should not be, cousin, I say: patience and shuffle the cards." And turning upon his side he resumed his customary silence and said not a word more.

'At this moment loud screams and cries were heard, accompanied by deep groans and anguished sobs. I turned my head and saw through the crystal walls a procession of most lovely maidens passing in two files through another hall, all dressed in mourning, with white turbans on their heads after the Turkish fashion. At the tail end of the files came a lady – as by her gravity she seemed – also dressed in black, with a white veil so ample and long that it kissed the ground. Her turban was twice as large as the greatest of the others. She was beetle-browed and somewhat flat-nosed, with a large mouth and red lips. Her teeth, which she sometimes bared, appeared to be few and not very well placed, although they were as white as peeled almonds. She bore in her hands a fine cloth, and in it, as far as could be made out, a heart of mummy flesh; so dry and shrivelled was it. Montesinos told me that all those in the procession were servants of Durandarte and Belerma enchanted there with their master and mistress, and that the last one, carrying in her hands the heart in its cloth, was the lady Belerma, who with her maidens formed that procession on four days in the week, and sang, or rather wept, dirges over his cousin's body and afflicted heart. If she appeared to me somewhat ugly, or not as beautiful as fame reported, he said the reason lay in the bad nights and worse days she spent under that spell, as could be seen from the great rings round her eyes and from her sickly complexion.

'"Do not suppose," he added, "that her sallowness and the rings round her eyes spring from the monthly disorders common to women, for it is many months, or even years, since these have even appeared at her gates. They arise from the grief in her heart for the object she perpetually holds in her hands, which ever renews and brings to her memory the misfortune of her ill-fated lover. For, were it not for this, scarcely would the great Dulcinea del Toboso, so celebrated in all these parts and even throughout the whole world, equal her in beauty, grace and spirit."

'"Not so fast, Sir Montesinos," said I then. "Tell your story properly, sir, for you will know that all comparisons are odious, and so there is no reason to compare anyone with anyone. The peerless Dulcinea is who she is, and the lady Doña Belerma is who she is, and was – and there let it rest."

'To which he replied: "Pardon me, Don Quixote; I confess that I was wrong, and spoke ill in saying that the lady Dulcinea del Toboso would hardly have equalled the lady Belerma. It has been enough for me to learn by certain inductions that your worship is her knight to make me bite my tongue rather than compare her to anything but Heaven itself."

'With this satisfaction which the great Montesinos gave me my heart was quieted from the shock I received at hearing my mistress compared with Belerma.'

'I'm amazed, though,' said Sancho, 'that your worship didn't spring on the old dodderer, and kick his bones to pulp, and pull out his beard till there wasn't a hair left.'

'No, Sancho my friend,' replied Don Quixote, 'it would not have been right in me to do that. For we are all obliged to respect the aged, even if they are not knights, but all the more so when they are such and under enchantment. I know well enough that I was not behind-hand with him in the long conversation which passed between us.'

'I do not know, Don Quixote,' observed the scholar at this point, 'how your worship could have seen so many things and heard and said so much in the short space of time you were down below.'

'How long was I down?' asked Don Quixote.

'A little more than an hour,' answered Sancho.

'That cannot be right,' said Don Quixote, 'for night fell there and morning rose, and three more nights and mornings; so that, by my reckoning, I must have stayed three days in those remote and secret regions.'

'My master should be speaking the truth,' said Sancho, 'for as everything that has happened to him is by way of enchantment, perhaps what seems to us an hour may seem three days and nights down there.'

'That will be right,' answered Don Quixote.

'And did your worship eat anything in all that time, sir?' asked the scholar.

'I did not break my fast with even a mouthful,' answered Don Quixote. 'I had not so much as a thought of hunger.'

'And the enchanted, do they eat?' asked the scholar.

'No, they do not,' answered Don Quixote, 'nor do they defecate, although it is believed that their nails grow, and their beards and hair.'

'And do the enchanted sleep by any chance, sir?' asked Sancho.

'No, certainly not,' answered Don Quixote, 'at least in those three days that I was with them none of them closed an eye, and neither did I.'

'Here's where the proverb fits,' said Sancho; 'tell me what company you keep and I will tell you who you are. Your worship goes about with the enchanted who watch and fast. It's no wonder, then, that you didn't eat or sleep whilst you were in their company. But pardon me if I say, your worship, that of all you have said, God help me – I was going to say the Devil – if I believe one word.'

'Why not?' asked the scholar. 'Would Don Quixote lie? Why, even if he had wanted to he had not time to compose and invent such a multitude of fictions.'

'I don't believe that my master's lying,' answered Sancho.

'Then what do you believe?' asked Don Quixote.

'I believe,' answered Sancho, 'that this Merlin or these enchanters, who bewitched that whole crowd your worship tells us you saw and talked with down below, crammed all that rigmarole you've told us into your head, and what remains to be told as well.'

'All that could be so,' replied Don Quixote, 'but it is not. For what I told you of I saw with my own eyes and touched with my own hands. But what will you say when I tell you now, that among the countless marvellous things that Montesinos showed me – which I shall proceed to tell you of at leisure and in due course during our journey, for they do not all belong here – were three peasant girls, leaping and frisking like she-goats in those pleasant fields, and no sooner did I see them than I realized that one of them was the peerless Dulcinea del Toboso, and the other two those same country girls who were with her when we met them on their way out of El Toboso? I asked Montesinos whether he knew them. He answered no, but that he thought they must be some enchanted ladies of quality, for they had only appeared in those fields a few days before. But I need not be surprised at that, for there were many other ladies of past and present times there, transformed into different strange shapes, and among them he had recognized Queen Guenevere and her attendant Quintañona, who poured out the wine for Lancelot *when from Britain first he came.*'

On hearing this Sancho thought he would go out of his wits or die of laughing. For knowing as he did the truth about Dulcinea's pretended enchantment, and that he had been her enchanter and the inventor of the story, he finally realized, beyond all doubt, that his master was out of his mind and mad on all counts. And so he said to him:

'At an evil time, in a worse season, and on a bitter day did your worship descend to the other world, dear master, and it was an unlucky moment when you met with Sir Montesinos, who has so changed you for us. You were all right up here with your wits whole, as God gave them to you, uttering judgements and offering counsel at every step, and not, as you now are, talking the greatest nonsense imaginable.'

'As I know you, Sancho,' said Don Quixote, 'I take no notice of your words.'

'Nor I of yours either,' answered Sancho, 'though you may beat me or kill me for what I've said, and for what I mean to say, if you don't correct and mend your own. But tell me, your worship, now that we're at peace, how or by what signs did you recognize the lady our mistress? And, if you spoke to her, what did she say and how did you reply?'

'I recognized her,' said Don Quixote, 'because she had on the same clothes as she was wearing when you pointed her out to me. I spoke to her, but she did not answer a word. On the contrary, she turned her back and ran away so fast that an arrow would not have caught her. I made to follow her, and would have done so if Montesinos had not advised me not to tire myself in that way, for it would be in vain; and, what was more, it was high time for me to return out of the cave. He also told me that in course of time he would advise me of a means of disenchanting him, and Belerma and Durandarte and everyone there. But what distressed me most of all I saw and noted was that just as Montesinos was speaking one of the luckless Dulcinea's two companions drew near to my side, without my seeing her come, and with her eyes full of tears said to me in low and troubled tones: "My lady Dulcinea del Toboso kisses your worship's hands and implores you to let her know how you are, and as she is in great want, she also begs your worship most earnestly to be so good as to lend her half a dozen *reals* on this new cotton skirt I have here, – or as many as your worship has about you. She promises to pay you back in a very short time."

'Such an errand surprised and amazed me, and I turned to Montesinos to ask him: "Is it possible, Sir Montesinos, for people of quality when enchanted to be in want?" to which he replied: "Believe me, Don Quixote, what they call want is usual everywhere, extends to all regions, reaches everyone, and does not even spare the enchanted. So, as the lady Dulcinea del Toboso has sent to ask you for these six *reals*, and the security is apparently good, there is nothing for it but to give them to her, for no doubt she must be in some difficulty."

'"A pledge I will not take," I replied, "nor can I give her what she asks, for all I have got is four *reals*."

'Those I gave her. They were the ones you gave me, Sancho, the other day to give in alms to any poor we might meet on the roads. And I said to her:

'"Friend, tell your mistress that I am grieved in the spirit at her troubles, and that I wish I were Fugger that I might relieve them. Say that I would have her know that I neither can nor may have health, lacking her pleasing company and her wise conversation, and that I beg her with all possible earnestness to be so good as to allow her captive servant and travel-weary knight to see and address her. You will say to her also that, when least she expects it, she will hear that I have made an oath and vow, like that which the Marquis of Mantua made to avenge his nephew Baldwin when he found him on the point of death in the midst of the mountains – which was to eat no bread off table-cloths and sundry additional trifles till he had obtained his revenge. So too shall I swear; not to rest, and to travel the seven portions of the earth more diligently than did Don Pedro of Portugal, until I have released her from her enchantment."

'"All that and more your worship owes my lady," replied the maiden. And taking the four *reals*, instead of making me a curtsey, she cut a caper, and leapt two yards, by measure, into the air.'

'Holy Father!' Sancho broke in at this point in a loud voice. 'Are such things possible in the world? Can there be enchanters and enchantments so strong as to have changed my master's sound wits into this raving madness? Oh, sir, sir, in God's name, look out for yourself! Think of your good name, and don't believe in these bubbles that have spoilt and crazed your wits!'

'It is because you love me, Sancho, that you talk like this,' said Don Quixote, 'and as you are not experienced in the affairs of this world, anything that has any difficulty about it seems to you impossible. But the time will come, as I have told you already, when I shall relate to you some of the things I saw down there; and they will make you believe what I have said, for their truth admits of no reply or controversy.'

Chapter XXIV. *In which a Thousand Trifles are recounted, as nonsensical as they are necessary to the True Understanding of this great History.*

THE translator of this great history from the original written by its first author, Cide Hamete Benengeli, says that when he reached the chapter relating the adventure of Montesinos' cave he found written in the margin in the hand of this same Hamete these words:

'I cannot persuade myself that all that is written in the previous chapter literally happened to the valorous Don Quixote. The reason is that all the adventures till now have been feasible and probable, but this one of the cave I can find no way of accepting as true, for it exceeds all reasonable bounds. But I cannot possibly suppose that Don Quixote, who was the most truthful gentleman and the noblest knight of his age, could be lying; for even if he were riddled with arrows he would not tell a lie. Besides, if I consider the minute and circumstantial details he entered into, it seems an even greater impossibility that he could have manufactured such a great mass of extravagance in so short a time. So if this adventure seems apocryphal, it is not I that am to blame, for I write it down without affirming its truth or falsehood. You, judicious reader, must judge for yourself, for I cannot and should not do more. One thing, however, is certain, that finally he retracted it on his death-bed and confessed that he had invented it, since it seemed to him to fit in with the adventures he had read of in his histories.' With that the author continued, saying:

The scholar was astonished alike at Sancho Panza's boldness and at his master's patience, and concluded that the placid disposition he then displayed arose from his pleasure at seeing his lady Dulcinea del Toboso, even though enchanted. For were it not the case, Sancho's speeches and arguments would have earned him a thrashing, since really, thought the scholar, he had been a little too saucy with his master, whom he thus addressed:

'Don Quixote de la Mancha, I reckon this day I have spent with you very well spent, for in it I have gained four things. First, my acquaintance with your worship, which is a great pleasure to me. Secondly, a solution of the secret of Montesinos' cave, of the metamorphoses of Guadiana, and of the lagoons of Ruidera, all of which will serve me for the *Spanish Ovid* I have in hand. Thirdly, to have discovered the antiquity of playing cards, which were in use as far back as the time of the Emperor Charlemagne, as can be deduced from the words you attribute to Durandarte, when, at the end of Montesinos' great speech, he woke up and said: "Patience and shuffle the cards." He cannot have learnt that expression or turn of phrase under a spell, but must have done so before he was enchanted, in France and in the time of the aforesaid emperor. Now this discovery comes just right for the other book I am compiling, which is the *Supplement to Polydore Virgil on the Inventions of Antiquity*, for I believe that he forgot to include the invention of cards, as I shall now do, for it is of great importance, particularly as I shall be able to quote so serious and truthful an informant as Sir Durandarte. Fourthly, to have learnt for certain the source of the river Guadiana, until now unknown to men.'

'You are right,' said Don Quixote, 'but I should like to know to whom you intend to dedicate them – supposing by God's favour you are granted a licence to print these books of yours, which I doubt.'

'There are lords and grandees in Spain to whom they might be dedicated,' replied the scholar.

'Not many,' replied Don Quixote. 'Not because they do not deserve the dedications, but because they do not like to accept them in case they may be under the obligation of making the authors the return to which they are entitled for their labour and courtesy. But I know a prince who can supply the defects of all the rest, with such advantages that if I made bold to mention them I should perhaps awaken the jealousy of more than one generous soul. But let the matter rest here until a more opportune time, and let us go and look for somewhere to lodge to-night.'

'Not far from here,' said their guide, 'is a hermitage where dwells a hermit, who is said to have been a soldier once, and has the reputation of being a good Christian, and very wise and charitable as well. Beside his hermitage he has a little house, which he has built at his own cost; but though it is small, it is big enough to receive guests.'

'Does this hermit happen to keep chickens?' asked Sancho.

'Few hermits are without them,' answered Don Quixote, 'for those you find to-day are not like the anchorites in the Egyptian deserts, who used to wear palm-leaves and eat the roots of the earth. It must not be supposed that because I speak well of the ancients it is at the expense of the hermits of to-day. I only mean to say that present-day penances do not equal the rigours and austerities of olden times; but they are all good, nevertheless. At least I consider them good; and, if the worst comes to the worst, the hypocrite who pretends to be good does less harm than the public sinner.'

Whilst they were talking they saw a man on foot overtaking them, walking fast and prodding with his stick a mule loaded with lances and halberds. On coming up he greeted them and passed. Don Quixote, however, called out: 'Stop, my good fellow! You seem to be going faster than your mule wants to.'

'I can't stop, sir,' replied the man, 'for these weapons you see me carrying are needed for to-morrow. So I'm compelled to press on. Good-bye. But if you want to know the reason why I'm carrying these things, I mean to put up to-night at the inn beyond the hermi-tage. If you're travelling the same way you'll find me there, and I'll tell you some wonders. So good-bye once more.'

And he prodded his mule on so fast that Don Quixote had no time to ask him what wonders he had to tell them. But as he was rather curious and always possessed by the desire to learn something new, he decided that they should press on that moment so as to spend the night at the inn, and not stop at the hermitage where the scholar wanted them to stay. So all three mounted and took the straight road to the inn, which they reached a little before nightfall. On the way the scholar suggested to Don Quixote that they should call at the hermitage to get a drop to drink; and when Sancho heard him he turned Dapple in that direction, Don Quixote and the scholar taking the same way. But, as Sancho's ill-luck would have it, the hermit was not at home, as they were told by an under-hermitess, whom they found in the hermitage. They asked for a drop of the real stuff, but she replied that her master did not keep it, though if they would like water for nothing, she would give it them with pleasure.

'If I had a water thirst,' replied Sancho, 'there are wells on the road where I could have quenched it. O, Camacho's wedding and the plenty at Don Diego's, how often I miss you!'

Now they left the hermitage and spurred towards the inn, and a little farther on they fell in with a lad, who was strolling along in front of them at so slow a pace that they overtook him. He was carrying a sword on his shoulder and, slung on it, a bundle or package, apparently containing clothes, his breeches, cloak and shirt probably, for he had on a short velvet jacket, in places rubbed shiny as satin, and his shirt hung out. His stockings were silk and his shoes square-toed after the court fashion. He must have been eighteen or nineteen, and he had a merry face and an agile-looking body. As he went along he sang scraps of songs to relieve the tediousness of the road, and when they caught him up he had just ended one, which the scholar got by heart, and which went:

> To the wars I am driven by lack of pence,
> If I had them, nothing would get me hence.

The first to speak to him was Don Quixote, who said: 'You travel very light, Sir Gallant. Whither bound? Tell us, if you please.'

To which the lad replied: 'Heat and poverty are my reasons of my travelling so light, and it's the wars I am bound for.'

'How poverty?' asked Don Quixote. 'Heat is a likely enough reason.'

'Sir,' replied the lad, 'in this bundle I have a pair of velvet breeches, the fellows to this jacket. If I wear them out on the road, I shan't be able to cut a dash in them in the city, and I've no money to buy others. So, for that reason and to cool myself, I'm travelling like this until I catch up with some companies of infantry, which are less than forty miles from here. I shall enlist with them, and there'll be no lack of baggage-wagons to travel on from there to the port of embarkation, which is said to be Cartagena. For I'd rather have the King for my lord and master and serve him in the wars than some frayed fellow at Court.'

'Do you get an allowance by any chance?' asked the scholar.

'If I'd served a grandee of Spain or an important personage,' replied the lad, 'I should most certainly have one, for that is what comes of serving good masters. Their men generally rise from the servants' hall to be ensigns or captains, or to some other good appointment. But I, poor wretch, have always served adventurers and hangers-on whose pay and rations were so miserably short that they'd be half spent on starching one ruff. It'd be a miracle indeed for a page to an adventurer to get a stroke of luck.'

'But tell me honestly,' asked Don Quixote, 'is it possible that in all the years you served you were not even able to lay hands on a livery?'

'I've had two given me,' answered the page, 'but just as, if a man leaves a monastery without taking his vows they strip him of his habit and give him back his clothes, so my masters returned me mine. For when the business they came to Court for was done they returned home and took back the liveries, which they had only given out for show.'

'A notable *spilorceria*, as the Italians say,' remarked Don Quixote, 'but count yourself lucky, all the same, to be coming away from Court with so laudable an intention. For there is nothing on earth more honourable or more profitable than to serve God first, and then your king and natural lord, especially in the profession of Arms, which may not gain you more riches than Letters, but wins you more honour, as I have very often said. For though Letters may have been the foundation of more estates than Arms, still soldiers have an indefinable superiority over men of letters, and a certain splendour about them which puts them above everybody. Bear in mind what I am now going to say to you, for it will be of great profit and comfort to you in your hardships. It is that you should dismiss from your mind all thought of possible disasters, for the worst of them is death; and to die an honourable death is the best fortune of all. The brave Roman emperor, Julius Caesar, when asked which was the best death, replied the unexpected, the sudden and the unforeseen; and although this was the reply of a heathen, ignorant of the true God, yet considering human infirmity, he was right. For supposing you are killed in the first engagement or skirmish, or by a cannon shot or the springing of a mine, what does it matter? It is but death and there is an end. And, as Terence says, a soldier looks better slain in battle than alive and safe in flight, and the more obedient he is to his captains and commanders the higher does the good soldier rise in fame. Mark, my son, that gunpowder is a more pleasing smell to a soldier than civet; and if old age overtakes you in this honourable profession, though you may be full of wounds, crippled and lamed, at least it will not find you without honour, and honour such as poverty will not be able to diminish. What is more, it is now being enacted that old and crippled soldiers are to be maintained and relieved, for it is not right that they should be treated like blacks, whose masters release them and grant them their liberty when they are old and cannot work, and by casting them out of the house with the title of free men make them the slaves of hunger from whom they can only hope to be freed by death. I will say no more for the present. But get you up on the haunches of this steed of mine as far as the inn. There you will dine with me and continue your journey to-morrow. And may God speed you according to your merit.'

The page refused his invitation to ride behind, but he accepted the supper at the inn, and Sancho is said to have muttered to himself at this point: 'God bless you, what a master he is! Is it possible for a man who can say all the good things he's just said, to swear that he saw all the absurd impossibilities he has told us about Montesinos' cave? Well, well, we shall see!'

At this they reached the inn, just as night was falling; and it was no small pleasure to Sancho to find that his master took it for a real inn and not, as usual, for a castle. And no sooner had they gone in than Don Quixote asked the innkeeper for the man with the lances and halberds; and he replied that he was in the stable attending to his mule. The scholar and Sancho then looked to their asses, and Sancho gave Rocinante the best rack and the best stall in the stable.

Chapter XXV. *Of the adventure of the Braying and the Entertaining Meeting with the Puppet-Showman, together with the memorable Prediction of the Prophetic Ape.*

DON QUIXOTE stood upon thorns, as the saying is, to hear the wonders which had been promised him by the arms-carrier. So he went to the stable to look for him, and on finding him demanded that he should immediately give them the promised answer to their questions on the road.

'I can't tell you the tale of my wonders, standing up,' replied the man, 'I must have leisure. Let me finish giving my beast his fodder, good sir, and I'll tell you something that will astonish you.'

'Do not let that hinder you,' answered Don Quixote, 'for I will help you.'

And so he did, sifting the barley and cleaning out the rack, a humble service which induced the man the more willingly to tell him what he wanted to hear. So, sitting down on a stone bench with Don Quixote beside him, and with the scholar, the page, Sancho Panza and the innkeeper for senate and audience, he began after this fashion:

'Your worships must know that in a place about fourteen miles from this inn it happened that an alderman lost an ass, through a deceitful trick of a servant-maid of his – but that's a long story – and although this alderman made every possible effort to find him, he could not. A fortnight must have gone by, so the story goes, since the ass was missed, when, as the unfortunate alderman was standing in the market-place, another alderman of the same town came up to him and said: "Reward me for my good news, friend. Your ass has turned up."

'"That I will and gladly, friend," replied the other, "but tell me where he's turned up."

'"I saw him this morning on the mountain," answered the finder, "without a pack-saddle or gear of any kind, and so lean that he was a pitiful sight. I wanted to catch him and bring him to you; but he is so wild and shy now that when I got up to him he ran off into the thickest part of the wood. We'll go back together to look for him, if you like. Just let me take this she-ass home, and I'll come straight back."

'"That will be doing me a great kindness," said the man who had lost his ass. "I'll try to repay you in the same coin."

'Everybody who knows the truth of the matter tells the story with these details, just as I'm telling it to you now. To be brief, the two aldermen went off to the mountain on foot and hand in hand, but when they got to the exact spot where they expected to see the ass they couldn't see him, and they couldn't discover him anywhere in those parts for all their searching. Seeing, then, that he was not to be found, the alderman who had seen him said to the other:

"'Look, my friend, I've just thought of a plan, by which we shall certainly discover the animal, even if he's hidden in the bowels of the earth, not to mention the mountain, and it's this: I can bray to perfection, and you can do a little in that line. Why, it's as good as done."

"'A little, you say, friend?" said the other. "Goodness me, I'll take odds of nobody, not even of the asses themselves."

"'Now we'll see," replied the second alderman, "for my plan is that you shall take one side of the mountain and I the other. We'll make a complete circuit of it, and every few yards you'll bray and I'll bray. The ass can't fail to hear us and answer us if he is on the mountain."

"'I think that's an excellent plan," replied the owner of the ass, "and worthy of your great mind."

'Then they separated, as agreed and, as chance would have it, both brayed almost at the same time. Now each of them was taken in by the other's bray, and ran to look, thinking that the ass had just turned up. But when they met, the owner of the lost beast said: "Is it possible, friend, that it wasn't my ass that brayed?"

"'It was only I," answered the other.

"'Then let me tell you, friend," said the owner of the beast, "that in the matter of braying there's nothing to choose between you and an ass; for I've never seen or heard anything more natural in my life."

"'Such praise and such compliments," replied the inventor of the plan, "apply more fittingly to you than to me, friend. For, by God my Maker, you can give odds of two brays to the best and most skilled brayer in the world. Your tone's loud, your time correct, your note well sustained and your cadences thick and fast. In fact I acknowledge myself beaten, hand you the palm and award you the colours for this rare accomplishment."

"'I declare," replied the owner, "that I shall think more highly of myself from now on, and reckon I know a thing or two, seeing that I have a talent; for though I thought that I could bray well, I never supposed that I did it as perfectly as you say."

'"Let me tell you, too," said the other, "that there are rare talents in this world wasted on the wrong men, who don't know how to make use of them."

'"Ours," replied the owner, "are not of much service to us except in such a case as we now have on our hands; but now, please God, they may come in useful."

'At which they separated once more and resumed their braying, but at every pace they made a fresh mistake and came back to one another, until finally they agreed on a counter-sign and uttered their brays two at a time, so that each might know that it was the other and not the ass. In this way, giving a double bray at every step, they made a complete circuit of the mountain without the lost ass replying by so much as a sign. But how could the poor ill-fated beast have replied? For they found him in the thickest part of the wood, eaten by wolves. And at the sight of him, his master exclaimed:

'"I was astonished myself that he did not reply. For, had he been alive, he would have brayed if he'd heard us, or he would have been no ass. But I'm well rewarded for my labours in looking for him, even though I found him dead, by hearing you bray so gracefully, friend."

'"We're a fine pair," replied the other, "for if the abbot sings well the little monk isn't far behind."

'With this they returned to their village, disconsolate and hoarse; and there they told their friends, their neighbours and acquaintances their adventures in search of the ass, each exaggerating the other's gift for braying; and the story leaked out and spread to the neighbouring villages. Now the Devil, who never sleeps, and loves to sow heart-burnings and discord broadcast, raising calumnies on the wind and grand chimaeras out of nothing, so ordered it that the people of the other villages, at the sight of anyone from ours, would immediately begin to bray as if to throw our alderman's notable accomplishment in our faces. When the boys took to it all the demons in hell seemed to have joined in the sport, for the braying went on spreading from one village to another, till now the natives of our braying village are as well known and as easily distinguished as Negroes from whites. And this unlucky jest has gone so far that very often the mocked have gone forth with arms in their hands and in regular formation to do battle with the mockers, and King or

Rook, fear nor shame, has been strong enough to prevent it. To-morrow or the next day, I believe, the people of my village, the brayers, are to take the field against another village about six miles from ours, one of our worst persecutors; and to be well prepared for them, I have bought the lances and halberds you saw. These are the marvels I promised to tell you, and if they don't seem wonderful to you, I know no others.'

With that the good fellow ended his tale, and just then there came through the outer door of the inn a man all dressed in chamois-leather, hose, breeches and doublet, crying in a loud voice: 'Master landlord, have you any room? For here come the fortune-telling ape and the puppet show, "The Releasing of Melisendra."'

'Good Heavens!' exclaimed the landlord. 'Here's Master Peter. We shall have a great night of it.'

(I forgot to say that this Master Peter had his left eye and almost half his cheek covered with a green silk patch, which showed that there was something wrong with all that side of his face.)

'Your worship is welcome, Master Peter,' the innkeeper went on to say. 'But where are the ape and the puppets? I don't see them.'

'They're not far off,' replied the man in chamois leather, 'but I came ahead to find out if there was room.'

'I would turn out the Duke of Alba himself to make room for Master Peter,' said the innkeeper. 'Bring the ape and the puppets, for there are people in the inn to-night who'll pay to see the show, and the ape's talents as well.'

'Very good,' answered the man with the patch. 'I'll reduce the price and be content with my bare expenses. And now I'll go back and bring in the cart with the ape and the show in it.'

Then Don Quixote enquired of the innkeeper who this Master Peter was, and what the show and the ape were he brought with him. And the landlord replied: 'He's a very famous puppet-player, and he's been travelling about this Aragonese side of La Mancha for some time, showing a play about the releasing of Melisendra by the renowned Sir Gaiferos. It is one of the finest and best acted shows we've seen in this part of the kingdom for many a year. He has an ape with him too, with the rarest talents an ape ever had or man imagined. If you ask him anything he listens to what you say and then jumps on to his master's shoulder and tells him the answer in his ear, and Master Peter repeats it at once. He says more about what's happened than about what's to come; and although he isn't always right in everything, in most cases he's not mistaken; which makes us believe he has the Devil inside him. He charges two *reals* a question, if the ape replies – I mean if his master replies for him, after he's whispered in his ear. So Master Peter's generally supposed to be extremely rich. He's a gallant man, as they say in Italy, and a boon companion, and he leads the grandest life in the world. He talks more than six men and drinks more than twelve, all at the expense of his tongue, his ape and his puppet show.'

At this moment Master Peter came back, and in the cart came the show and the ape, which was big and tailless with buttocks like felt, but not ugly in the face. As soon as Don Quixote saw him, he asked: 'Tell me, you, Master Fortune-teller, what fish do we catch? And what is to become of us? See, here are my two *reals*.'

And he bade Sancho give them to Master Peter, who replied for the ape: 'Sir, this animal doesn't answer or give information about things to come. About the past he knows something, and about the present a little.'

'I swear I wouldn't give a farthing to be told what's happened to me in the past,' cried Sancho. 'For who could know it better than I do myself? And for me to pay to be told what I know already would be mighty foolish. But seeing that he knows the present, here's my two *reals*. Tell me, excellent ape, what my wife Teresa Panza is now doing, and how she's amusing herself.'

Master Peter refused to take the money, saying: 'I don't want to receive payment till the service has been rendered.'

Then he slapped his left shoulder twice with his right hand, and with one spring the ape jumped up. Next, putting his mouth to his master's ear, he gnashed his teeth very rapidly together, and after keeping up this chattering for the length of a *Credo*, jumped with another spring to the ground. And then without a moment's delay Master Peter hastily threw himself on his knees in front of Don Quixote and embraced his legs, exclaiming:

'I embrace these legs as I would embrace the twin pillars of Hercules, O illustrious reviver of the now-forgotten order of knight errantry! O never sufficiently praised Don Quixote de la Mancha, raiser of the faint-hearted, prop of those about to fall, arm of the fallen, staff and consolation of all the unfortunate!'

Don Quixote was astounded; Sancho bewildered; the scholar amazed; the page astonished; the bray-townsman foxed, and the landlord perplexed. In short, all his hearers were dumbfounded at the words of the puppet-showman, who continued:

'And you, good Sancho Panza, the best squire of the best knight in the world, be of good cheer, for your good wife Teresa is well, and at this very hour she's combing a pound of flax, and to prove what I say, on her left she has a broken-mouthed pot, which holds a good drop of wine to cheer her at her work.'

'I can well believe that,' replied Sancho, 'for she's a blessing and, if she weren't jealous, I wouldn't swap her for the giantess Andandona, who was a very excellent and worthy woman according to my master. My Teresa is of the sort who don't go short of anything, even if their heirs have to pay for it.'

'Now I declare,' exclaimed Don Quixote at this point, 'that he who reads much and travels much, sees much and learns much. What amount of persuasion it would have taken to convince me that there are apes in the world with the power to divine, as I have just seen with my own eyes there are. For I am the same Don Quixote de la Mancha that this good animal has spoken of, though he has been somewhat too liberal in my praise. But whatever I may be, I thank Heaven for endowing me with a mild and compassionate nature, always inclined to do good to all and ill to none.'

'If I had money,' said the page, 'I would ask Master Ape what will happen to me on the journey I am taking.'

To which Master Peter, who had got up from Don Quixote's feet, replied: 'I've already said that this little beast doesn't foretell the future. But if he could, your not having money wouldn't matter, for to serve Don Quixote, who is here present, I would forego all the profit in the world. And now, because I am in his debt, and to give him pleasure, I will set up my puppet-show and give everyone in the inn a performance free of charge.'

The innkeeper was immeasurably delighted at this offer, and pointed out a place for him to set up his show, which he did in a moment. Now Don Quixote was not very satisfied with the ape's prophesyings, for he did not think it right for an ape to divine either future or past events. So, whilst Master Peter was arranging his puppets, he took Sancho aside into a corner of the stable, out of the hearing of the company, and said to him:

'Listen, Sancho. I have thoroughly pondered that ape's extra-ordinary talents and, as I see it, there is no doubt that this Master Peter, his master, must have made a pact, implicit or explicit, with the Demon.'

'If the pack's explosive and with the Demon,' said Sancho, 'it'll certainly be a very dirty pack. But what's the use of the packs to this Master Peter?'

'You do not understand me, Sancho. I only mean to say that he must have made some bargain with the Devil, who has infused this talent into the ape so that he can gain his living by it; and when he is rich, he will give him his soul; for that is what the universal enemy is after. This I conclude from the fact that the ape only an-swers questions concerning things past or present, for the Devil's knowledge extends no further; he only knows the future by guess-work, and not always then. For to know the times and the seasons is reserved to God alone; for Him there is no past or future, for all is present. And that being so, as it is, it is clear that this ape speaks in the style of the Devil, and I am astonished that he has not been denounced to the Holy Office, and examined, and had it squeezed out of him by whose virtue he divines. For it is certain that this ape is no astrologer, and neither he nor his master casts, or knows how to cast horoscopes, though they are so fashionable in Spain nowa-days that there is not a servant-maid or a page or an old cobbler who does not presume to cast a nativity as easily as pick up a knave of cards from the floor, perverting the amazing truth of the science with their ignorant lying. I know of a lady who asked one of these horoscope-casters whether a little lap-dog bitch she had would fall with pup and bear, and how many pups she would have and of what colour. To which Master Astrologer replied, when he had cast the figure, that the bitch would fall and bear three puppies, one green, one scarlet and one speckled, always providing that she were covered between eleven and twelve o'clock of the day or night, either on a Monday or a Saturday. And what happened was that two days later the bitch died of over-eating, and Master Astrologer gained the reputation in the town of being a very accurate caster of a horoscope, a reputation which they mostly have.'

'All the same,' said Sancho, 'I wish, sir, that you'd ask Master Peter to ask his ape whether it's true what happened to you in Montesinos' cave. For it's my opinion, begging your worship's pardon, that it was all fraud and fictions, or at least that you dreamt it.'

'Everything is possible,' answered Don Quixote. 'I will do as you advise, though I have certain scruples about it.'

Here Master Peter came to look for Don Quixote, and telling him that his puppet-show was now up, begged him to come and see it, for it was worth seeing. Don Quixote informed him of what was in his mind, and begged him first to ask his ape to say whether certain happenings in Montesinos' cave were imaginary or real; for to him they seemed to partake of both.

So without a word Master Peter went to fetch his ape and put him before Don Quixote and Sancho, saying: 'Look you, Master Ape, this gentleman wants to know if certain things which happened in a cave called Montesinos' were false or true.'

Then, at the customary sign, the ape leapt on to his left shoulder and apparently spoke in his ear. Whereupon Master Peter immediately answered: 'The ape says that part of what your worship saw or experienced in the said cave is false and part true, and that's all he knows about this question. But if your worship wants to learn more he'll reply to any inquiries made of him on Friday next. For his virtue is now exhausted, and won't return to him till Friday, as he has said.'

'There now,' exclaimed Sancho, 'Didn't I say you'd never make me believe all you told us about the happenings in that cave, or even a half of it?'

'Events will show, Sancho,' answered Don Quixote; 'for time, which reveals all things, leaves nothing that it does not drag into the light of day, even things hidden in the bosom of the earth. But let this suffice for now, and let us go and see good Master Peter's show, for I think there will be some novelty in it.'

'How "*some*"?' demanded Master Peter. 'This show of mine contains sixty thousand novelties. I tell your worship, Don Quixote, that it's one of the rarest spectacles in the whole world. But deeds, not words! Let's set to work, for time's drawing on, and we have a great deal to do, to say and to show.'

Don Quixote and Sancho complied and went to the show, which was now set up and uncovered; and they found it looking gay and resplendent, being lit all round by a multitude of wax tapers. On their arrival Master Peter got inside, as it was he who had to work the puppets in the play; and outside stood a boy, Master Peter's servant, to serve as interpreter and announcer of the mysteries of the show, holding in his hand a wand with which he pointed out the figures as they appeared.

When everyone in the inn was in his place, some standing in front of the show, and Don Quixote, Sancho, the page and the scholar in the best positions, the interpreter began to announce what the hearer or the reader of the following chapter will hear or see.

Chapter XXVI. *A continuation of the Delightful Adventure of the Puppet-Showman, and other matters sufficiently entertaining.*

HERE Tyrians and Trojans, all were silent: that is, all the spectators of the show were hanging on the lips of the interpreter of its wonders, when they heard a number of kettle-drums and trumpets strike up inside the puppet theatre, and a sudden volley of artillery, whose noise as suddenly ceased. Then the boy lifted his voice and announced:

'This true story, here presented to your worships, is taken word for word from the French chronicles and the Spanish ballads, which are in everyone's mouth and sung by the boys about the streets. It treats of the lord Sir Gaiferos' freeing of his wife Melisendra, who was a prisoner in Spain, in the hands of the Moors, in the city of Sansueña, now known under the name of Saragossa. And there you may see Sir Gaiferos playing at backgammon according to the song:

> Gaiferos is playing at the tables,
> and now his Melisendra is forgotten.

And that personage, who appears there with a crown on his head and a sceptre in his hand, is the Emperor Charlemagne, reputed father of the said Melisendra, who is vexed at his son-in-law's idleness and negligence, and comes out to scold him. Notice the vehemence and earnestness with which he rates him. It looks as if he has a mind to deal him a knock or two with his sceptre; and there are even authors who say he did so – good and hard. Then after a long speech in which he said that Sir Gaiferos was imperilling his honour by not rescuing his wife, the emperor went on – so the story goes: "Look to it now, sir: I have said enough." And see, the Emperor, sirs, turn his back and leave Sir Gaiferos in a rage. Now you see him, impatient with anger, flinging away the board and the pieces, calling in haste for his armour and begging his cousin Sir Roland for the loan of his sword Durindana. Sir Roland, however, will not lend it to him, but offers him his company in the difficult enterprise he is undertaking. This the angry warrior refuses, saying that he is capable of rescuing his wife alone, even though she were imprisoned in the deepest bowels of the earth. At that he departs to put on his armour, so that he can set out on his journey immediately. Now turn your eyes, sirs, to that tower yonder, which is supposed to be one of the towers of the castle of Saragossa, now called the Aljaferia. The lady appearing on that balcony dressed in the Moorish fashion is the peerless Melisendra, who has often stood gazing from there down the road to France, solacing herself in her captivity by thinking of Paris and her husband. Now behold a new incident, the like of which you have probably never seen before. Do you observe that Moor stealing up on tiptoe, with his finger to his lips, behind Melisendra's back? Now see him give her a kiss full on the mouth, and see her spit and wipe it from her lips with the white sleeve of her smock. See how she wails and tears her lovely hair in grief, as if she were to blame for his crime. Observe, too, that grave Moor standing in the gallery. He is King Marsilio of Sansueña. Now, when he saw this Moor's insolence, although the man was a relative of his and a great favourite, he had him taken and given two hundred lashes. And here he is led through the chief streets of the city with criers before and officers of justice behind. See, here they come to execute his sentence, almost immediately after his crime, for among the Moors there are no indictments or remands, as there are with us.'

'Boy, boy,' interrupted Don Quixote in a loud voice, 'go straight ahead with your story, and do not go curving off at a tangent; for it requires much proof and corroboration to bring a truth to the light.'

'Boy,' cried Master Peter also, from within, 'don't go in for flourishes, but do what this gentleman says. That'll be best. Go on with your plain-song, and don't stray off into counterpoint, for that's the way the strings get broken.'

'Very good, sir,' answered the boy, and resumed his story. 'This figure here on horseback in a Gascony cloak is this same Sir Gaiferos. And there is his wife, now avenged for the amorous Moor's insolence, better and calmer in demeanour, standing on the battlements of the tower and talking to her husband, whom she takes for a traveller. The words of the conversation that passed between them are given in the ballad:

> Sir knight, if it is to France you are going,
> Ask for Gaiferos when you are there.

'But I will not repeat it now, for prolixity often breeds boredom. Enough to see Sir Gaiferos reveal himself, and Melisendra's joyful looks as she recognizes him. Now we see her let herself down from the balcony to get up on to the crupper of her good husband's horse. But, unlucky lady, see, she is caught by the lace of her skirt on one of the balcony spikes, and is hanging in the air, unable to reach the ground. But see how merciful Heaven sends aid in her sorest need, for Sir Gaiferos comes up and, never pausing to see whether her fine skirt is torn or not, grasps her and brings her forcibly to the ground. Then, in one leap, he sets her on the crupper of his horse, astride like a man. Bidding her hold on tight, he puts her arms over his shoulders and crosses them over his chest, so that she shall not fall; for the lady Melisendra was not used to this manner of riding. Hear too how the horse neighs with delight at the brave and lovely burden he is bearing, his own lord and lady. See how they turn round and leave the city, and happily and joyfully take the road to Paris. Go in peace, O peerless pair of true lovers! May you safely reach the land of your desires, and may Fortune not impede your happy journey! May your friends and relations see you enjoying the remainder of your life in calmness and peace, and may your days be as many as Nestor's!'

Here Master Peter raised his voice once more and cried: 'Plainness, boy! Don't soar so high, for all affectation's bad.'

The announcer made no reply, but went on: 'There was no lack of idle spectators, who pry into everything. They observed Melisendra's descent and her mounting on horseback. They informed King Marsilio, and he ordered the alarm to be sounded immediately. See how quickly it is done. Now the city is drowned in peals of bells ringing from all the towers of the mosques.'

'That is not right,' interrupted Don Quixote. 'In this matter of the bells Master Peter is much mistaken, for they do not use bells among the Moors, but kettle-drums and a kind of trumpet like our clarion; and this about ringing the bells in Sansueña is most certainly complete nonsense.'

When he heard this Master Peter stopped ringing and said: 'Don't worry about trifles, Don Quixote, or expect perfection, for you never find it. Don't they perform countless comedies in these parts almost every day, full of innumerable improbabilities and absurdities? But, for all that, they have a successful run and are greeted, not only with applause but with admiration and all. Go on, boy, and let them speak, for so long as I fill my bag they can act as many improbabilities as there are motes in the sun.'

'That is right,' replied Don Quixote. And the boy went on.'See what a numerous and resplendent cavalcade rides out of the city in pursuit of the pair of Christian lovers! How many trumpets sound, how many clarions blow, how many drums and kettle-drums beat! I am afraid they will catch them and bring them back tied to their own horse's tail. That would be a dreadful spectacle.'

Now seeing this pack of Moors and hearing such an alarm, Don Quixote thought it only right to help the fugitives. So, rising to his feet, he cried aloud:

'Never while I live shall I permit an outrage to be done in my presence on so famous a knight and so bold a lover as Sir Gaiferos! Stop, low-born rabble! Neither follow nor molest him, or you must do battle with me.'

Matching his actions to his words, he unsheathed his sword, and at a single bound planted himself in front of the show. Then with swift and unparalleled fury he began to rain blows upon the puppet-heathenry, knocking down some, beheading others, maim-

X

ing one, and destroying another; and, among other thrusts, he delivered one down-stroke that would have sliced off Master Peter's
head as easily as if it had been made of marzipan, had he not ducked
and crouched and made himself small.

'Stop, your worship!' he kept shouting. 'Reflect, Don Quixote,
that these are not real Moors you're upsetting, demolishing and
murdering, but only little pasteboard figures! Look out, you're destroying me, poor sinner that I am, and ruining my whole livelihood!'

But this did not make Don Quixote stop raining down his cuts,
his two-handed blows, his forestrokes and his backstrokes. In fact,
in less time than it takes to say a couple of *Credos* he had brought the
whole show to the ground, and hacked all its fittings and puppets to
bits. King Marsilio was gravely wounded, and Charlemagne had his
crown and his head cut in two. The crowd of spectators were in an
uproar; the ape fled up to the inn roof; the student was frightened;
the page in a panic; and even Sancho Panza himself in a terrible
alarm. For, as he affirmed after the storm had passed, he had never
before seen his master in so outrageous a temper. But when the
general destruction of the show was complete, Don Quixote grew
rather calmer and said:

'I should like to have before me at this moment all who do not
believe, and do not wish to believe that knights errant are useful in
the world. Consider what would have happened to the good Sir
Gaiferos and the fair Melisendra, if I had not been present here.
Assuredly by this hour those dogs would have caught them and
wrought them some outrage. When all is done, long live knight
errantry, before everything else in the world to-day!'

'A long life and welcome,' put in Master Peter in a weak voice;
'and let me die, for I am so unfortunate that I can say with King
Roderick:

> Yesterday I was Lord of Spain,
> But to-day I have not a tower
> That I can say is mine!

Not half an hour ago, indeed not half a minute ago, I was the master
of Kings and Emperors. My stables, my coffers and my bags were
full of countless horses and fine dresses without number, and now I

am desolate and abject, a poor beggar and, worst of all, I've lost my ape, for before I have him in my possession again I shall have to sweat blood for it, I swear. And all because of the inconsiderate fury of this Sir Knight, who is said to protect wards and redress wrongs and perform other works of charity. It's only in my case his generous purpose has come to grief. God bless my soul! He's rightly called the Knight of the Sorrowful Countenance, for he's discountenanced my puppets.'

Sancho Panza was moved by Master Peter's complaint, and said to him: 'Don't weep, Master Peter. Don't moan, or you'll break my heart. I assure you that my master Don Quixote's a good scrupulous Christian and a Catholic, and if he reckons he's done you any wrong he'll admit it and gladly pay you. He'll satisfy you too, and more so.'

'Provided Don Quixote will pay me some part of the damage he has done me I shall be satisfied, and his worship will be quiet in his conscience. For there's no salvation for a man who holds another's property against its owner's will, and does not restore it.'

'That is so,' said Don Quixote, 'but so far I am not aware that I have anything of yours, Master Peter.'

'What?' answered Master Peter. 'Look at these relics lying on this hard and barren ground. How were they scattered and annihilated but by the invincible strength of that powerful arm? And whose were their bodies but mine? And how did I support myself if not by them?'

'Now I am finally convinced,' said Don Quixote at this, 'of what I have very often believed: that these enchanters who persecute me are always placing before my eyes shapes like these, and then changing and transforming them to look like whatever they please. I assure you gentlemen that all that has passed here seemed to me a real occurrence. Melisendra was Melisendra; Sir Gaiferos, Sir Gaiferos; Marsilio, Marsilio; and Charlemagne, Charlemagne. Therefore I was stirred to anger and, to comply with my profession of knight errant, I sought to give aid and protection to the fugitives, with which proper intention I did what you have seen. If things have turned out contrariwise the fault is not mine, but lies with my wicked persecutors. But all the same, I am willing to mulct myself the costs of this error, although it did not arise from malice. Let

Master Peter consider what he wants for the puppets destroyed, and I will pay him for them now in good and current Castilian coin.'

Master Peter bowed and replied: 'I expected no less from the unparalleled Christian spirit of the valorous Don Quixote de la Mancha, true succourer and protector of all needy and distressed vagabonds. Master Landlord here and the great Sancho shall be arbiters and assessors between your worship and myself, as to the probable value of the damaged figures.'

The landlord and Sancho consented to act, and Master Peter then picked up off the ground King Marsilio of Saragossa, less his head, and said: 'Now you can see how impossible it is to restore this king to his former state; and so, to my mind, and subject to your better judgment, I should receive four and a half *reals* for his death, end and extinction.'

'Go on,' said Don Quixote.

'Now for this gash from top to bottom,' Master Peter went on, picking up the cleft Emperor Charlemagne, 'it wouldn't be much if I asked five *reals* and a quarter.'

'That is no small amount,' said Sancho.

'And no great one,' replied the landlord. 'Let's split the difference and say five *reals*.'

'Give him the whole five and a quarter,' said Don Quixote, 'for in such a notable mischance as this we will not stand out for a quarter more or less. But let Master Peter finish quickly, for it's nearly supper time, and I feel certain twinges of hunger.'

'For this figure,' said Master Peter, 'which has lost its nose and one eye and is the fair Melisendra, I want — and I'll be moderate — two *reals* and twelve *maravedis*.'

'Well, the devil is in it,' said Don Quixote, 'if Melisendra and her husband are not over the French border, at least, by now. For the horse they were on seemed to me to fly rather than gallop. So you cannot sell me a cat for a hare by confronting me with a noseless Melisendra when, if all goes well, she is now with her husband in France, taking her pleasure for all she is worth. God help every man to his own, Master Peter. Let us have plain dealing and honest intentions. Now proceed.'

Master Peter saw that Don Quixote was rambling back to his old theme. So, not wanting to let him get away with it, he said: 'It can-

not be Melisendra, then, but one of her serving-maids. So if I have
sixty *maravedis* for her I shall be well paid and content.'

In this way he went on putting prices on the many other puppets
destroyed, and afterwards the two assessors adjusted them to the
satisfaction of both parties. The total amounted to forty *reals* and
three-quarters; and over and above this sum, which Sancho paid
over at once, Master Peter asked two *reals* for the trouble of catching his ape.

'Give them to him, Sancho,' said Don Quixote, 'not to catch his
ape but to get a "skinfull". And I would give two hundred more as
a gift to anyone who could tell me for certain that the lady Melisendra and her lord Sir Gaiferos were now in France and among
their own people.'

'No one could tell us that better than my ape,' said Master Peter,
'but there's no devil could catch him now; though I imagine that
affection and hunger will force him to look for me to-night. God
will send the morrow and we shall see.'

Finally the storm over the puppet-show died down, and they all
supped in peace and amity at the expense of Don Quixote, who was
liberal in the extreme.

Before dawn broke the man with the lances and halberds was off,
and shortly after daybreak the student and the page came to bid
Don Quixote farewell, the one to return home and the other to continue on his way, to help him on which Don Quixote gave him a
dozen *reals*. Master Peter did not care to get involved in any more
arguments with Don Quixote, for he knew him too well, and so he
got up before the sun and, taking up the remains of his show and
his ape, also went off to seek adventures. The innkeeper, who did
not know Don Quixote, was amazed at his liberality and at his
madness, when, last of all, Sancho paid him very well on his
master's orders. Then, taking their leave of him, they left the inn at
almost eight in the morning and got on their road, where we will
leave them, for this is a fitting opportunity for relating other
matters pertinent to the telling of this famous history.

Chapter XXVII. *In which we are told who Master Peter and his Ape were, with Don Quixote's ill-success in the Braying adventure, which did not terminate as he wished or expected.*

CIDE HAMETE, the chronicler of this great history, introduces the present chapter with these words: '*I swear as a Catholic Christian,*' on which his translator observes that Cide Hamete's swearing as a Catholic Christian, he being a Moor, as he doubtless was, meant only that as a Catholic Christian, when he swears, swears, or should swear the truth, and observe it in all he says, so he would tell the truth, as if he had sworn like a Christian Catholic, in writing of Don Quixote; especially in his statement regarding who Master Peter was, and about his ape that amazed the whole countryside with its prophesyings. He remarks then that any reader of the first part of this history will clearly remember Gines de Pasamonte, whom Don Quixote set free with the other galley-slaves in the Sierra Morena – a benefit for which he was later ill requited by that malignant and unmannerly crew. That Gines de Pasamonte, whom Don Quixote called Ginesillo de Parapilla, was the man who stole Dapple from Sancho Panza; though the time and the manner of the theft having been omitted from the First Part of this history through the neglect of the printers, many have attributed the omission to the author's faulty memory. But, to be brief, Gines stole the ass while Sancho Panza was asleep on its back, using the cunning method Brunelo practised when he got Sacripante's steed from between his legs at the siege of Albraca. And how Sancho recovered his beast has already been related. This Gines, then, was afraid of being discovered by the officers of the law, who were seeking after him to punish him for his villainies and crimes, which were so numerous and so heinous that his own account of them filled a large volume. So he decided to cross into the kingdom of Aragon and, putting a patch over his left eye, took up the trade of puppet-showman, for at this and at sleight-of-hand he was extremely adept. Later he bought the ape from some released Christian who had come over from Barbary, and taught it to jump on to his shoulder at a certain signal, and whisper, or appear to whisper, in his ear. Thus prepared, before going into a village with his beast and his puppet-show he would collect information in the next place, or from anyone he could, about local events and the people concerned in them. This he would commit to memory. Then the first thing he would do was to show his puppet play, sometimes playing one story, sometimes another, but all gay, amusing and familiar. Then, once the performance was over, he would announce the ape's accomplishments, telling the villagers that he could divine all the past and the present, but that he had no skill in things to come. For an answer to each question he asked two *reals*, though for some he made it cheaper, according as he felt the pulse of his questioners. Sometimes he would put up at the houses of people whose stories he knew, and if he found them unwilling to pay him the price of a question he would merely sign to his ape, and then say that the beast had told him such and such, giving an exact account of actual happenings. In this way he gained an incredible reputation, and everyone followed him. At other times he was shrewd enough to shape his answers to fit the questions; and as no one examined him or pressed him to say how his ape did his divining, he made apes of them all and filled his money bags. Thus, as soon as he came into the inn he knew Don Quixote and Sancho, and this made it easy for him to astonish the knight, the squire and everyone in the place. But it would have cost him dear if Don Quixote's hand had descended a little lower when he cut off King Marsilio's head and destroyed all his chivalry, as has been related in the previous chapter. This is the whole story of Master Peter and his ape.

But to return to Don Quixote de la Mancha – after he had left the inn he decided first to view the banks of the river Ebro and all that district, and then to go on to the city of Saragossa, for there was enough time for all this before the jousts. With this intention he pursued his journey and travelled for two days without meeting with anything worthy of recording. Then on the third day, as he was mounting a slope, he heard a great din of drums, trumpets and musketry. At first he thought that a regiment of soldiers was passing that way, and spurred Rocinante up the hill to get a sight of them. But when he reached the top he saw below him more than two hundred men, by his reckoning, armed with different sorts of weapons, such as spears, crossbows, partisans, halberds and pikes, as well as some muskets and plenty of shields. Then he came down the hillside, and drew so near to the band that he distinctly saw their

banners, distinguished their colours, and made out the devices they
bore. One of them in particular, on a standard or pennon of white
satin, was a life-like painting of an ass of the little Sardinian breed,
with its head up, its mouth open, and its tongue out, in the very act
and posture of braying, and round it were written in large letters
these two lines:

> They did not bray in vain,
> Our worthy bailiffs twain.

From this device Don Quixote concluded that these must be the
people of the braying village, and so he said to Sancho, reading out
to him what was written on the standard. He also remarked that the
man who had given them an account of the affair had been mistaken
in saying that it had been two aldermen who had brayed, because
according to the verses on the standard they were bailiffs. To which
Sancho Panza replied:

'There's nothing in that, sir. It's perfectly possible that the aldermen who brayed have come in course of time to be bailiffs of their
village, and so they can be called by either title. What's more, it
doesn't affect the truth of the story whether the brayers were bailiffs
or aldermen, since they brayed anyway; for a bailiff's as good a
brayer as an alderman.'

In short, they realized that the mocked village was coming out
to fight with another, which had mocked it more than was reasonable or neighbourly. Don Quixote rode up to them, to Sancho's no
small annoyance; for he was never fond of finding himself mixed up
in these affairs. The men in the squadron received him in their
midst, thinking that he was one of their party. Don Quixote then
raised his vizor with a graceful air and deportment, and went up to
the ass-standard, where all the chiefs of their army gathered round
to look at him, being struck with the same astonishment that the
first sight of him usually excited. And seeing them gaze at him so
intently, without anyone speaking or asking him a question, our
knight tried to make use of the silence and, breaking his own, raised
his voice to say:

'My good sirs, I beg you in all earnestness not to interrupt a
speech which I wish to make you, until you find it either annoying
or wearisome. But if this happens, at your slightest signal, I will put
a seal on my mouth and a gag on my tongue.'

They all bade him say what he would, for they would most gladly listen to him. Then, with their permission, Don Quixote continued:

'I, my dear sirs, am a knight errant, whose exercise is arms and whose profession it is to succour those who need succour and to relieve the distressed. Some days ago I learnt of your misfortune, and the reason which moves you so often to take up arms in order to avenge yourselves on your enemies; and having pondered your affairs in my mind not once but many times, I find that, according to the law of duelling, you are mistaken in regarding yourselves as insulted, for no individual can insult a whole village, except by charging it collectively with treason, not knowing who in particular committed the treason which is the subject of the charge. We have an example of this in Don Diego Ordoñez de Lara, who accused the whole town of Zamora since he did not know that Vellido Dolfos alone had committed the treason of killing his king. So it was that he challenged them all, and the vengeance and the answer concerned all, though it is true that Don Diego went a little too far, and even considerably exceeded the just limits of a challenge, for he had no need to challenge the dead, the waters, the corn, the unborn children, or other objects therein mentioned. But let that pass; for when anger overflows its bed there is no father, governor, or bridle can restrain the tongue. This being so, then, that one man alone cannot insult a kingdom, a province, a city, a commonwealth, or a whole population, there is clearly no need to go out and take up the challenge for such an insult, for it is not one. It would be a fine thing for the people of the *Clock Town* to be perpetually at drawn swords with anyone calling them by that name, or for the *Heretics* either, or the *Aubergine-eaters*, the *Whalers*, the *Soap-boilers*, or others whose names or nicknames are for ever on the tongues of the boys and the riff-raff! It would be a fine thing, indeed, for all these famous towns to be enraged, and take vengeance, and perpetually go about with their swords out like gutting-knives in every petty quarrel. No, no! God does not permit or desire that. Prudent men and well-ordered states must take up arms, unsheathe their swords, and imperil their persons, their lives and their goods for four causes only. Firstly, to defend the Catholic faith; secondly, in self-defence, which is permitted by law natural and divine; thirdly, in defence of honour, family and estates; fourthly, in their king's service in a just war; and if we wish to add a fifth count, which can be reckoned as part of the second, in defence of one's country. To these five principal causes can be added some others which are just and reasonable, and compel one to take up arms. But whoever takes them up for trifles or for matters laughable and amusing rather than insulting is, in my opinion, lacking in all common sense. Besides, the taking of unjust vengeance – and no vengeance can be just – goes directly against the sacred law we profess, by which we are commanded to do good to our enemies and to love those who hate us, a commandment which may seem rather difficult to obey, but which is only so for those who partake less of God than of the world, and more of the flesh than of the spirit. For Jesus Christ – God and true man – who never lied, nor could, nor can lie, being our law-giver, said that His yoke was gentle and His burden light, and therefore He could not have commanded us to do anything impossible to perform. So, my dear sirs, you are bound to keep the peace by law divine and human.'

'The devil take me,' said Sancho to himself at this point, 'if this master of mine isn't a thologian; and if he isn't one, he's as like one as makes no odds.'

Don Quixote took a little breath and, seeing that they were still giving him their attention, decided to go on with his speech. This he would have done, had not Sancho with his usual sharpness interposed and, seeing his master pause, spoken up for him:

'My master, Sir Don Quixote de la Mancha, formerly called *the Knight of the Sad Countenance* and now *The Knight of the Lions*, is a very sensible gentleman who knows both Latin and the vernacular like a Bachelor, and in all he handles or counsels acts like a very good soldier. He has all the laws and ordinances of what they call the duel at his finger-tips, and so there's nothing else for it but to be guided by his advice, and on my head be it if you go astray; the more so since it's said that it's folly to fly into a rage merely at hearing one bray. For I remember that when I was a boy, I brayed whenever I fancied, without any suggestion from anyone, and I did it so gracefully and naturally that when I brayed all the asses in the village brayed too. But I didn't cease on that account to be the son of my parents, who were very honest people; and though quite a

few of the most stuck-up people in my village envied me my talent,
I didn't care a farthing. And to prove that I'm speaking the truth,
wait and listen, for this trick's like swimming, once learnt never forgotten.'

Then, clapping his hand to his nose, he began to bray so stoutly
that all the neighbouring valleys rang. But one of the villagers standing near him thought that he was making fun of them and, raising
the pole he was carrying, dealt him such a blow with it that Sancho
was knocked to the ground unconscious. On seeing his squire so
maltreated, Don Quixote made for his assailant with his lance in his
hand, but so many of them interposed that it was impossible to
avenge him. On the contrary, finding a shower of stones raining
down on him and a thousand levelled crossbows and no less a number of muskets threatening him, he turned Rocinante's head and departed from them as fast as he could gallop, praying to God with all
his heart to deliver him from that peril, and fearing at every step
that a bullet would enter his back and come out through his chest;
and each moment he fetched a breath to see whether he could still
breathe. But the band of villagers were content to see him fly and
did not shoot at him. As for Sancho, they put him on his ass, hardly
yet conscious, and left him to follow his master; not that he had the
sense to guide the beast, but Dapple followed in Rocinante's tracks,
for he could not bear to be separated from him for a moment. When
Don Quixote had gone a considerable distance he turned his head
and saw Sancho coming. Then, finding that he was unpursued, he
waited for him.

The band of villagers stayed there till night, and then, since their
enemies had not come out to battle, went back to their village, rejoicing and happy; and had they known the ancient custom of the
Greeks, there on that spot they would have raised a trophy.

Chapter XXVIII. *Of things which Benengeli says the reader will
learn if he reads them with attention.*

WHEN the valiant man flies it is clear that there is foul play; and
it is a wise man's duty to reserve himself for a better occasion. This
truth was verified in Don Quixote who, yielding before the fury
of the village and the wicked designs of that angry band, could not

be seen for dust. For, oblivious of Sancho and the peril he had left
him in, he put himself sufficiently far off to feel safe. Sancho followed him, lying across his ass, as has been said, and caught up with his
master at last, having now come to himself. And when he overtook
him he let himself fall at Rocinante's feet, sore all over, bruised and
beaten, and Don Quixote dismounted to search his wounds; but
finding him sound from head to foot, he said to him in some anger:

'It was an evil hour when you learnt to bray, Sancho! For when
did you find it a good thing to mention rope in the hanged man's
house? What counterpoint but blows could you get to your braying music? Give thanks to God, Sancho, that instead of blessing
you with a stick they did not make the sign of the cross over you
with a sword.'

'I'm in no state to answer you now,' replied Sancho, 'for my
shoulders ache with every word. Let us mount and get away from
here, and I'll bray no more. But I can't refrain from saying that
knights errant run away and leave their good squire to be ground
like privet or wheat at the hands of their enemies.'

'Retreat is not flight,' said Don Quixote. 'For you must know,
Sancho, that valour which is not founded upon the basis of prudence is called temerity, and the successes of the rash are rather to
be ascribed to good luck than to courage. So I confess that I retired,
but I did not fly; and in this I imitated many valiant men who have
reserved themselves for better times. History is full of such examples, which I shall not cite now, for they would be of no profit
to you and tedious to me.'

By now Sancho had remounted, with the help of Don Quixote,
who in his turn climbed on to Rocinante; and at a leisurely pace
they made their way towards the shelter of a grove of poplars which
was visible as much as a mile away. From time to time Sancho
uttered deep sighs and painful groans; and when Don Quixote
asked him the cause of his bitter grief he replied that from the base
of his spine to the nape of his neck he was in such pain that it was
driving him out of his senses.

'The cause of that pain,' said Don Quixote, 'must undoubtedly
be that the staff with which they beat you was long and slender, and
so caught the whole of your back where the aching parts lie. But if
it had caught more of you, the aches would have been worse.'

'Lord love me!' said Sancho. 'Your worship has solved a great mystery and cleared it up most prettily! 'Struth! Was it so difficult, then, to find the cause of my pain, that you must tell me that the aching parts are just the ones the staff hit? If it was my ankles that were sore there might be some doubt about the reason; but that I should ache where they thrashed me – there's not much mystery about that. Honestly, my dear master, another man's hurts are easy to bear; and every day I see more clearly how little I can expect from keeping company with your worship. For since you let me be thrashed this time we shall come back again and again to the blanketings of old and other such pranks; and if it's my back that gets it this time, it'll be my eyes next time. I should do much better – only I am a clod and shan't get any wiser in all the days of my life – I should do better, I say, to go back home and support my wife and bring up my children with whatever God may be pleased to give me than go traipsing after your worship over trackless roads and non-existent paths and rides, drinking poorly and eating worse. Then, take sleeping! Count out seven feet of earth, brother squire, and if you want more, count as many again. Take as much as you like and stretch yourself out to your heart's content. May I see the man who first started knight errantry burning in Hell and ground to dust, or at least the first who was willing to be squire to such a parcel of idiots as the knights errant of old must have been. About present-day ones I say nothing, for since your worship's one of them I hold them in respect, because I'm sure you know a point more than the Devil about all you talk of and think about.'

'I would lay a good bet with you, Sancho,' said Don Quixote, 'that now you are talking without interruption there is no ache in the whole of your body. Say everything that comes into your mind and into your mouth, my son, for if it relieves you of your pain I will willingly control the vexation your impertinences cause me. And if you so much desire to return home to your wife and children, God forbid that I should hinder you. You have money of mine. Reckon how long it is since we left our village on this third expedition, reckon how much is due to you every month, and pay yourself out of hand.'

'When I worked for Thomas Carrasco,' replied Sancho, 'the father of the Bachelor Sampson Carrasco, whom your worship knows well, I got two ducats a month besides my food. I don't know what I should earn with your worship, but I know that a knight errant's squire has more work to do than a farmer's man. For the fact of the matter is that we who work for farmers have a stew for supper at night and sleep in our beds, however much we have to toil by day, and whatever ill may befall us. But I haven't slept in a bed since I've been in your worship's service. And except for the short while we stayed at Don Diego de Miranda's, and the picnic I had with the skimmings from Camacho's pots, and the time I ate and drank and slept at Basilio's, all the rest of the time I've slept on the hard ground under the open sky, subject to what they call the inclemencies of heaven, living on scraps of cheese and crusts of bread, and drinking water from brooks, or sometimes from the springs we find in these by-roads we travel.'

'I confess, Sancho,' said Don Quixote, 'that all you say is true. How much more then do you consider I should give you than Thomas Carrasco did?'

'I think,' said Sancho, 'if your worship were to give me two *reals* more a month I should be satisfied. That is so far as wages for my work go. But in the matter of your solemn promise to grant me the governorship of an isle, you should rightly add another six *reals* for compensation, which would make thirty *reals* in all.'

'Very good,' replied Don Quixote. 'Now, to work out the wages you have allotted to yourself, it is twenty-five days since we left the village. Reckon proportionately, and see what I owe you. Then pay yourself, as I have said, from your own pocket.'

'O my Lord!' cried Sancho. 'Your worship's a long way out in your reckoning; for in the matter of the promised isle you must count from the day your worship promised it me to this present hour.'

'Well, how long is it since I made the promise, Sancho?' asked Don Quixote.

'If I remember rightly,' answered Sancho, 'it must be more than twenty years, to within three days more or less.'

Don Quixote gave himself a great slap on the forehead and began to laugh very heartily, saying: 'But I hardly travelled for two months in the Sierra Morena or in the whole course of our expeditions, and you say, Sancho, that it is twenty years since I promised you the isle? I think you want to absorb all the money of mine you have in your wages. Though if that is so and it gives you pleasure I grant it you from now on, and much good may it do you; for rather than have so bad a squire I shall be glad to be left poor and penniless. But tell me, perverter of the squirely ordinances of knight errantry, where have you ever seen or read of any knight errant's squire bargaining with his master, with "So much a month you will have to give me for serving you"? Embark, embark, scoundrel, villain, fiend — you seem to be all three — embark I say on the wide seas of their histories, and if you find that any squire has said or thought as you have spoken, you may nail it on my forehead and plant your four fingers in my face to boot. Turn your rein, or your ass's bridle, and go back home, for you shall not take one step further with me. O bread ill-requited! O promises ill-placed! O man more beast than human! Now, when I was intending to establish you in state, and in such a state that they would call you Lord, despite your wife, now do you leave me? Are you going now, when I had come to the firm and mighty resolve to make you lord of the best isle in the world? Well, as you have said again and again, the honey is not ... etcetera. An ass you are, and an ass you must be, and an ass you will end when the course of your life is run. For it is my opinion that it will reach its final term before you realize and acknowledge that you are a beast.'

Sancho looked fixedly at Don Quixote whilst he was uttering these reproaches, and was so stricken with remorse that the tears came into his eyes and he cried in a weak and sorrowful voice: 'Master, I confess that all I need to be a complete ass is a tail. If your worship would care to put one on me, I should reckon I had deserved it, and would serve you as an ass for all the remainder of my life. Pardon me, your worship, take pity on my youth, consider that I know but little, and that if I talk a lot it proceeds rather from weakness than from malice. But who errs and mends, himself to God commends.'

'I should have been surprised, Sancho, if you hadn't mixed some little bit of a proverb into your speech. Well, I pardon you, on condition that you mend your ways and show yourself henceforth not quite so greedy in your own interests, but try instead to broaden your mind, and take courage and spirit to hope for the fulfilment of my promises, for though it may be delayed yet it is not impossible.'

Sancho promised compliance, though it meant drawing strength out of weakness. Then they entered the wood, where Don Quixote settled himself at the foot of an elm and Sancho at the foot of a beech; for such-like trees have feet but no hands. Sancho spent the night in pain, for his beating made itself more felt with the night dew. But Don Quixote passed it in his everlasting meditations, though, for all that, they both closed their eyes in sleep, and when dawn broke pursued their journey in search of the banks of the famous Ebro, where an adventure befell them which will be related in the coming chapter.

Chapter XXIX. *Of the famous Adventure of the Enchanted Boat.*

TWO days, by their reckoning, after they left the poplar grove Don Quixote and Sancho came to the river Ebro, the sight of which was a great delight to Don Quixote, as he contemplated and gazed upon the charms of its shores, the clearness of its waters, the smoothness of its stream, and the abundance of its liquid crystal. In fact this cheering sight recalled a thousand amorous thoughts to his mind. Especially he dwelt on his vision in the cave of Montesinos, for although Master Peter's ape had told him that part of it was true and part false, he leaned rather to its being true than false: the very opposite view to Sancho's, who considered it all one great lie. Well, as they were riding along in this way, there hove in sight a little boat without oars or any sort of gear, made fast to the trunk of a tree which grew on the bank. Don Quixote looked in all directions, but could see no one. So without more ado he dismounted from Rocinante, and bade Sancho get down from Dapple and tie the two beasts close together to the trunk of a poplar or willow growing there. And on Sancho's enquiring the reason for this sudden dismounting and tethering, Don Quixote answered:

'I must tell you, Sancho, that this boat, deliberately and beyond all possibility of error, summons me to embark, and travel in it to succour some knight or other person of rank in distress; and he must be in very great trouble. For this, as we read in histories of chivalry, is the practice of the enchanters whose actions and speeches they describe. When a knight is placed in some peril from which he can only be delivered by the hand of another knight, though they may be six or eight thousand, or even more, miles apart, they either snatch the second knight up in a cloud or provide him with a boat to board, and in less than the twinkling of an eye they take him, through the air or over the sea, where they will and where his aid is needed. So, Sancho, this boat is put here for that very purpose, and that is as true as it is now day. But, before this happens, tie Dapple and Rocinante together, and may God's hand guide us, for I would not fail to embark were barefoot friars to entreat me.'

'Well, as it's like that,' replied Sancho, 'and your worship will run at every step into these follies – I don't know what else to call them – there's nothing for it but to obey and bow my head, according to the proverb: Do what your master orders and sit down with him at his table. But for all that, for my conscience' sake I must warn your worship, that I don't think this said boat belongs to any of your enchanted folk, but to some fishermen of this river, for they catch the best shad in the world here.'

This Sancho said as he was tying up the beasts, leaving them to the care and protection of the enchanters, with great grief in his heart. But Don Quixote bade him not to worry about abandoning the animals, for He who was to lead them through such longinquous ways and regions would take care to provide for them.

'I don't understand this logiquous of yours,' said Sancho. 'I have never heard such a word in all the days of my life.'

'*Longinquous*,' replied Don Quixote, 'means remote; and it is no wonder you do not understand it, for you are not obliged to know Latin, like some who claim to know it and do not.'

'Now they're tied up,' said Sancho, 'what have we to do next?'

'What?' answered Don Quixote. 'Cross ourselves and weigh anchor. I mean embark and cut the ropes by which this boat is fastened.' Then, jumping in, with Sancho after him, he cut the boat adrift, and it was carried little by little from the bank. When Sancho found himself some two yards off shore he began to tremble, fearing that he was lost; and nothing caused him more pain than to hear Dapple braying and to see Rocinante struggling to break loose.

'The ass is braying,' he said to his master, 'for grief at being deserted, and Rocinante's trying to get free to rush after us. O my dearest friends, stay there in peace, and may the madness that takes us from you turn to disappointment and bring us back to your company!'

At this he began to weep so bitterly that Don Quixote asked peevishly and testily: 'What are you afraid of, cowardly beast? What are you weeping at, butter-heart? Who is pursuing you or harassing you, soul of a town mouse? What do you lack, always in need amidst the bowels of abundance? Are you perchance travelling barefoot over the Riphaean mountains? No, you are sitting on a bench, like an archduke, on the calm current of this delightful river, from which we shall emerge in a short while into the wide sea. But we must have come out already and have travelled at least two thousand miles – or more. If I had only an astrolabe here with which I could take the height of the pole, I would tell you how far we have gone; though if I know anything we have passed, or soon shall pass, the equinoctial line which divides and cuts the opposing poles at equal distance.'

'And when we get to this noxious line your worship speaks of,' asked Sancho, 'how far shall we have gone?'

'A long way,' replied Don Quixote, 'for we shall have covered the half of the three hundred and sixty degrees of earth and water the globe contains according to the computation of Ptolemy, who was the best cosmographer known, when we come to the line I mentioned.'

'By God,' said Sancho, 'but your worship has got me a pretty fellow for a witness of what you say, this same Tolmy or whatever you call him, with his amputation.'

Don Quixote burst out laughing at the interpretation Sancho had put on the name, the computation and the reckoning of the cosmographer Ptolemy, and said:

'You must learn, Sancho, that according to the Spaniards and those who embark at Cadiz to go to the East Indies, one of the signs by which they know that they have passed the equinoctial line I mentioned is that the lice die on everyone aboard ship. Not one remains alive, and you could not find one in the whole vessel if you were to be paid its weight in gold. So, you might pass a hand over your thigh; if you catch anything living, we shall have no doubts on that score; and if not, then we have passed.'

'I don't believe a word of that,' answered Sancho, 'but I'll do what your worship orders all the same, though I don't know why we need to make these experiments, for I can see with my own eyes that we haven't moved more than five yards from the bank. We haven't drawn two yards off from where the animals are, for there are Rocinante and Dapple in the very place we left them; and, taking our bearings as I do now, I swear we aren't stirring or moving at an ant's pace.'

'Make the investigation I asked of you, Sancho, and do not worry about any others, for you know nothing about the colures, lines, parallels, zodiacs, ecliptics, poles, solstices, equinoxes, planets, signs of the zodiac and points, which are the measures of which the celestial and terrestrial spheres are composed. But if you had that knowledge, or part of it, you would clearly see how many parallels we have cut, how many signs seen, and what constellations we have left behind and are now leaving. Once more I ask you, feel and fish, for I believe you are as clean as a sheet of smooth white paper.'

Sancho felt himself and, reaching his hand gently and cautiously behind his left knee, raised his head and looked at his master, saying: 'Either the test's false or we haven't got where your worship says, not by many a long mile.'

'Well, why?' asked Don Quixote. 'Have you found anything?'

'More than somewhat,' answered Sancho. And shaking his fingers, he washed his whole hand in the river, down which the boat was softly gliding in midstream, without any occult intelligence to move it, or any hidden enchanter, but only the current of the water, which was calm there and smooth.

At that moment they caught sight of two great water-mills in the middle of the river, and no sooner did Don Quixote view them than he exclaimed to Sancho in a loud voice: 'Do you see? There, my friend, stands the city, castle, or fortress. In it must lie the persecuted knight, or the Queen or Princess in distress, for whose succour I have been brought here.'

'What the devil does your worship mean by city, fortress, or castle?' asked Sancho. 'Can't you see that those buildings in the river are water-mills, where they grind the corn?'

'Hush, Sancho!' said Don Quixote. 'They may seem to be water-mills, but they are not. I have already told you that spells transform all things and change them from their natural shapes. I do not mean that they actually change them, but they appear to, as we learnt by experience in the transformation of Dulcinea, sole refuge of my hopes.'

By this time the boat had got into the middle of the stream and had begun to travel rather less slowly than before. And when the millers saw it drifting down the river and on the point of being dragged under by the mill-stream, a number of them rushed hurriedly out with long poles to stop it. And when they came, all floury, with their faces and clothes covered with meal, they presented an ugly appearance, as they shouted out: 'Where are you going, you devils? Are you out of your senses? What are you after? Do you want to drown or be dashed to pieces on these wheels?'

'Did I not tell you, Sancho,' exclaimed Don Quixote at this, 'that we had reached a place where I have to show the strength of my arm? Look what scoundrelly villains have come out to encounter me! Look what fiends are opposing me! Look at those ugly faces grimacing at us! Now then, you shall see, rogues!'

And standing up in the boat he began to threaten the millers, crying out loudly: 'Ugly and ill-advised rabble, set free and deliver him whom you keep under duress in this fortress or prison of yours, be he of high or low or of whatever degree! For I am Don Quixote de la Mancha, otherwise called *the Knight of the Lions*, for whom by Heaven's high destiny the happy accomplishment of this adventure is reserved.'

As he spoke he grasped his sword, and began to make passes in the air against the millers who, hearing but not understanding these ravings, wielded their poles to stop the boat, which was now entering into the rapids of the mill-race. Sancho went down on his knees, devoutly praying Heaven to rescue him from his imminent peril; which it did, thanks to the prompt efforts of the millers, who planted their poles against the boat and stopped it, but not so skilfully as to prevent its overturning and throwing Don Quixote and Sancho head over heels into the water. Fortunately for the knight, he could swim like a duck, though the weight of his armour took him twice to the bottom; and if it had not been for the millers, who plunged into the water and dragged them both out bodily, it would have been good-bye to the pair of them. Then, when they were brought to land, drenched and far from dying of thirst, Sancho went down on his knees and, with hands joined and eyes fixed to Heaven, implored God in a long and devout prayer to deliver him from all his master's rash plans and enterprises in future.

By this time the fishermen had arrived, who owned the boat, which had been broken to pieces by the mill-wheels; and when they saw it smashed, they set about stripping Sancho and demanding payment of Don Quixote, who told the millers and the fishermen very calmly, as if nothing had happened, that he would pay for the boat with the best will in the world, providing they would set free the person or persons who were oppressed in that castle, without ransom.

'What persons and what castle are you talking of, madman?' asked one of the millers. 'Can it be the people who come to this mill to have their corn ground that you want to carry off?'

'Enough,' said Don Quixote to himself. 'It would be preaching in the wilderness to try and induce this rabble by prayers to do any virtuous act. Two powerful enchanters must have met in opposition in this adventure, the one frustrating the other's designs. One provided me with the boat, and the other threw me out. God help us, but this whole world is tricks and devices, one against the other. I can do no more.' And raising his voice, he went on, gazing all the while at the water-mills: 'Friends, whoever you are, who lie locked up in this prison, pardon me. For unfortunately for myself and for you, I cannot deliver you from your affliction. This adventure must remain reserved for another knight.'

Saying this, he compounded with the fishermen, and paid them fifty *reals* for the boat, and Sancho handed the money over with very ill grace, saying:

'Two boat trips like this will sink our whole fortune to the bottom.'

The fishermen and the millers gazed in astonishment at those two figures, so unlike other men, and were quite unable to make out what Don Quixote was driving at. But, concluding that both knight and squire were mad, they left them, the millers returning to their mill and the fishermen to their huts. Don Quixote and Sancho went back to their beasts, and to their beast-like existence; and such was the end of the adventure of the enchanted boat.

Chapter XXX. *Don Quixote's meeting with a fair Huntress.*

KNIGHT and squire were sufficiently depressed and out of humour when they reached their animals – especially Sancho. Indeed it grieved him to the soul to have touched their stock of money, for with every penny taken he seemed to be robbed of his very eyeballs. At length they mounted in silence and left the famous river, Don Quixote deep in thoughts of his love, and Sancho of his preferment, which at that time seemed to him very far from his grasp. For, fool though he was, he was well enough aware that all, or most, of the knight's actions were extravagant, and he was looking for an opportunity of escaping and going home without entering into any reckonings or farewells with his master. But Fortune was kinder to him than he had feared.

It fell out, then, that the next day at sunset, as they were emerging from a wood, Don Quixote cast his eyes about a green meadow, and saw some people on the further side, whom, when he drew near, he recognized to be a hawking party. He rode closer, and saw among them a gallant lady on a palfrey or milk-white hack decked with green trappings and with a silver side-saddle. The lady herself was in green, so bravely and richly attired that she looked the very soul of bravery. On her left wrist she bore a hawk, from which Don Quixote concluded that she was a great lady, and probably the mistress of all the hunters, as was the fact; and so he said to Sancho:

'Run, Sancho my son, and tell that lady with a hawk on the palfrey that I, the *Knight of the Lions*, salute her great beauty, and that if Her Magnificence gives me leave, I will go and kiss her hands, and serve her to the uttermost of my strength in all that her Highness may command me. And mind, Sancho, how you speak. Take care not to mix any of your proverbs into your embassage.'

'What sort of mixer do you take me for!' answered Sancho. 'To tell me that! As if this was the first time in my life I've taken messages to high and mighty ladies.'

'Except for the one you took to the lady Dulcinea,' replied Don Quixote, 'I do not know of any you have ever carried, at least in my service.'

'That's right,' answered Sancho, 'but a good paymaster doesn't worry about sureties, and in a well-stocked house the supper's soon cooked. I mean that there's no need to tell me anything or give me any sort of advice, for I'm ready for anything and I can manage a bit of everything.'

'Indeed I believe you,' said Don Quixote. 'Go then and God guide you!'

Sancho went off at a trot, urging Dapple out of his usual pace and, coming up to the fair huntress, dismounted and went down on his knees before her, saying: 'Beautiful lady, that knight you see yonder, the *Knight of the Lions* by name, is my master, and I am one of his squires, called at home Sancho Panza. This same *Knight of the Lions*, who was known not long ago as the *Knight of the Sad Countenance*, sends by me to ask for your Highness's permission to come, with your approval, goodwill and consent, and put his desire into effect; which is no other, as he says and I confirm, than to serve your lofty haughtiness and beauty. In giving your permission your ladyship will be doing something which will redound to your fame, and he will receive a most signal favour and happiness.'

'Indeed, good squire,' answered the lady, 'you have delivered your message with all the ceremony that such messages demand. Rise from the ground; for it is not right for the squire of so great a knight as he of the *Sad Countenance*, of whom we have already heard a great deal here, to remain on his knees. Rise, friend, and tell your master that he is most welcome to come and serve me and the Duke my husband, in a country house of ours near here.'

Sancho got up, impressed alike by the great lady's beauty and by her good breeding and courtesy, but even more so by her saying that she had knowledge of his master, the *Knight of the Sad Countenance* – and if she did not call him the *Knight of the Lions*, it could only be owing to his having taken the name so recently. The Duchess – whose title is unknown – then asked him:

'Tell me, brother squire, about this master of yours. Is he not one about whom a history has been printed called *The Ingenious Gentleman Don Quixote de la Mancha*, and has he not for the lady of his heart a certain Dulcinea del Toboso?'

'That's the man, my lady,' answered Sancho, 'and his squire, Sancho Panza by name, who is, or should be in that history, is myself, unless I was changed in my cradle – I mean changed in the press.'

'All this is most delightful,' said the Duchess. 'Go, brother Panza, and tell your master that he is heartily welcome on my estates, and that nothing would give me greater pleasure than his visit.'

Sancho returned to his master, overjoyed at this most agreeable answer, and repeated all that the fine lady had said to him, lauding her great beauty, her charm and her courtesy to the skies in his country language. Don Quixote preened himself in his saddle, set his feet firmly in the stirrups, adjusted his vizor, gave the spur to Rocinante, and advanced with a graceful bearing to kiss the Duchess's hands. And she meanwhile called the Duke, her husband, and repeated the whole of Sancho's message to him while Don Quixote was on the way. The pair of them had read the first part of this history, and consequently knew of Don Quixote's extravagances. So they awaited him with the greatest delight and were most anxious to make his acquaintance, their intention being to fall in with his whimsies, to agree with him in all he said, and to treat him like a knight errant for so long as he would stay with them, observing towards him all the ceremonies usual in books of knight errantry, which they had read and were very fond of.

Now Don Quixote rode up with his vizor raised and made as if to dismount, whereat Sancho hurried to hold his stirrup. But the squire was so unlucky as to catch one foot on a cord of the pack-saddle as he was dismounting from Dapple, and was unable to disentangle himself; so that he remained dangling with his face and his chest on the ground. Don Quixote was not accustomed to dismounting without someone to hold his stirrup, and thinking that Sancho had already caught hold of it, threw his body off with a jerk, carrying Rocinante's saddle, which must have been badly girthed, after him, so that he and the saddle fell to the ground together, to his no small discomfiture, and to the accompaniment of a volley of curses which he uttered between his teeth at the unfortunate Sancho, who still had his foot in the noose. The Duke ordered his huntsmen to go to the assistance of the knight and the squire, and they raised Don Quixote, who was in an ill plight from his fall and went limping to kneel as best he could before the Duke and Duchess. But the Duke would on no account permit this; instead he dismounted from his horse and went to embrace Don Quixote, saying:

'I am grieved, Sir Knight of the Sad Countenance, that the first step your worship has taken upon my land has been as unlucky as we have seen; but the carelessness of squires is often the cause of even worse accidents.'

'The moment of my first meeting with you, valorous Prince,' answered Don Quixote, 'could not possibly be unlucky, even had my fall been to the centre of the deep abyss; for even from there the glory of seeing you would have raised and rescued me. My squire – God's curse on him – is better at loosening his tongue to utter malice than at securing a saddle firmly. But wherever I may be, prostrate or upright, on foot or horse, I shall always be at the service of yourself and of my lady the Duchess, your worthy consort, the sovereign mistress of beauty and universal princess of courtesy.'

'Gently, my dear Don Quixote de la Mancha,' said the Duke, 'for where my lady Doña Dulcinea del Toboso is no other beauties should be praised.'

By this time Sancho Panza was free from the noose and, being close at hand, anticipated his master's reply by saying: 'It cannot be denied – in fact it must be declared that my lady Dulcinea del Toboso is very beautiful. But the hare starts up when least you expect it, and I've heard say that what's called Nature is like a potter who makes vessels of clay, and if a man makes one fine pot he can also make two, three or a hundred. This I say because my Lady the Duchess is every bit as fine as the lady Dulcinea del Toboso, I swear.'

Don Quixote turned to the Duchess and said: 'Your Highness can imagine that never in the world has knight errant had a more garrulous or a droller squire than mine, and he will prove my words if your great Sublimity will accept my service for a few days.'

To which the Duchess replied: 'I am most heartily glad that Sancho is droll, for it is a sign that he is wise. Since jokes and humour, Don Quixote, as you very well know, do not go with sluggish wits. So, as the good Sancho is droll and humorous, from now on I'll affirm he is wise.'

'And garrulous,' added Don Quixote.

'So much the better,' said the Duke. 'For much humour cannot be expressed in few words. But let us not waste our time in talk. Come, great Knight of the Sad Countenance ...'

'Of the Lions, your Highness should say,' interrupted Sancho, 'for there's no *Sad Countenance* now.'

'*Of the Lions*, be it,' continued the Duke, 'Come, Sir Knight of the Lions, I say, to a castle of mine not far from here. There you will be entertained as so exalted a personage should be, and as the Duchess and I are accustomed to entertain all knights errant who come here.'

While they were speaking Sancho had adjusted and girthed Rocinante's saddle. So, Don Quixote mounting on him, and the Duke on a fine horse, they put the Duchess between them and took the road for the castle, the Duchess commanding that Sancho should ride beside her, for she found infinite delight in listening to his wise sayings. Sancho did not require pressing, and working his way in among the three of them, made a fourth in the conversation, to the great pleasure of the Duke and Duchess, who counted it great good fortune to receive in their castle such a knight errant and so itinerant a squire.

Chapter XXXI.   *Which treats of many great matters.*

GREAT was Sancho's delight at finding himself, as he thought, in the Duchess's favour, for he figured it out that he would find in her castle all that he had found at Don Diego's and Don Basilio's. For he was always fond of good living, and so seized any opportunity of regaling himself by the forelock, whenever it occurred.

Now our history recounts that on their way to the country-house or castle the Duke rode ahead and gave his servants orders as to their behaviour towards Don Quixote. For when he reached the gates of the castle with the Duchess, two lackeys or grooms promptly ran out, clothed down to their feet in what they call morning-dress of finest crimson satin, and almost before he had heard or seen them caught Don Quixote in their arms, saying: 'Go, your Highness, and help my lady the Duchess to dismount.'

Don Quixote did so, and high compliments passed between the two on the subject. But at length the Duchess's insistence triumphed, and she refused to get down from her palfrey except into the Duke's arms, saying that she did not consider herself worthy of

laying so useless a burden on so great a knight. In the end the Duke
came out to help her down, and as they entered a great courtyard,
two beautiful maidens came up and threw a huge mantle of the
finest scarlet over Don Quixote's shoulders. Then in an instant all
the galleries of the court were crowded with the Duke and Duchess's
men and women servants, crying loudly: 'Welcome to the flower
and cream of knights errant.' And all, or most of them, sprinkled
flasks of scented waters over Don Quixote and the ducal pair, all
to the great astonishment of the knight. And this was the first time
that he was positively certain of being a true and no imaginary
knight errant, since he found himself treated just as he had read
these knights were treated in past ages.

Sancho abandoned Dapple and, tacking himself on to the
Duchess, went into the castle. But, his conscience pricking him at
leaving the ass alone, he went up to a reverent waiting-woman who
had come out with the others to receive the Duchess, and said in a
low voice: 'Mistress Gonzalez, or whatever your worship's name
may be!'

'Doña Rodriguez de Grijalba is my name,' answered the waiting-
woman. 'What are your orders, brother?'

To which Sancho replied: 'I wish your worship would be so
kind as to go out to the castle gate, where you'll find a dapple ass
of mine. Please put him, or have him put, in the stable; for the poor
beast is rather nervous, and can't endure being left alone on any
account.'

'If the master has no better manners than his man,' answered the
waiting-woman, 'we've struck a fine bunch! Get away, fellow, and
ill luck to you and the man who brought you here! Look after your
own ass, for we waiting-women in this house aren't accustomed to
such offices.'

'But indeed,' replied Sancho, 'I've heard my master – and he is a
dowser for histories – tell the story of Lancelot:

> When he from Britain rode,
> Ladies attended him
> And waiting-maids his steed;

and as for my ass, I wouldn't change him for Sir Lancelot's horse.'

'Fellow, if you're a jester,' said the waiting-woman, 'keep your jokes for those that like them and will pay you for them. You'll get nothing but a fig from me.'

'Very well,' answered Sancho, 'so long as it's a good ripe one, and if years count for anything you won't lose the trick by a pip too little.'

'Son of a whore!' exclaimed the waiting-woman, now incensed with rage. 'Whether I'm old or not, my account is with God and not with you, you garlic-stuffed rogue.'

She said this so loudly that the Duchess heard her and, turning round to find her waiting-woman so excited and her eyes so furious, asked her with whom she was having words.

'Here,' answered she, 'I'm having them with this good fellow, who has asked me in all seriousness to go and stable an ass of his which is at the castle gates, raking up as example something about some place or other where ladies waited on a certain Lancelot and waiting-women on his horse – and what's more, he ended up by calling me an old woman.'

'That I should consider an insult,' replied the Duchess, 'the greatest possible insult.' Then, taking Sancho aside, she said: 'Take notice, Sancho, that Doña Rodriguez is quite a girl, and that she wears that headdress for authority and out of habit, not on account of her years.'

'Bad luck follow me for the rest of my days,' answered Sancho, 'if I meant any harm. I only spoke because I'm very fond of my ass, and I thought I couldn't entrust him to a kindlier person that the lady Doña Rodriguez.'

Then Don Quixote, who had overheard all this, demanded: 'Is this fit talk, Sancho, for this place?'

'Sir,' answered Sancho, 'everyone must speak of his needs where-ever he is. Here I was when I remembered my Dapple, and here I spoke of him; and if I had thought of him in the stable I would have spoken of him there.'

On which the Duke remarked: 'Sancho is very right, and there's no reason to blame him. Dapple shall have as much fodder as he can eat. Sancho need not worry, for the ass shall be treated as well as he would be himself.'

After this conversation, pleasing to all but Don Quixote, they went upstairs and showed the knight into a hall hung with the rich-

est cloth of gold and brocade. Six maids took off his armour and
acted as pages, all of them trained in their parts by the Duke and
Duchess, and instructed in their behaviour towards Don Quixote,
for his hosts were anxious that he should really believe that they
were treating him as a knight errant. When the knight's armour
was off he was left in his tight-fitting breeches and his chamois
leather doublet. Withered, tall and lank, with his jaws that kissed
one another inside his mouth, he was a figure at which the maids
would have burst out laughing, if they had not been at pains to disguise their smiles – which was one of the special orders they had received from their master. They begged to be allowed to strip him
so as to put a clean shirt on him, but he would not consent, saying
that modesty was as necessary in a knight errant as valour. He
asked them, however, to give the shirt to Sancho and, shutting
himself up with him in a room where there was a rich bed, he
stripped and put it on. Then, finding himself thus alone with
Sancho, he said to him:

'Tell me, you old clown, to-day promoted to jester, do you
think it right to dishonour and insult that venerable and dignified
waiting-woman? Was this the time to remember Dapple? Are these
the gentlemen to leave animals neglected, seeing how grandly they
treat their owners? In God's name, Sancho, control yourself. Do
not show the yarn you are woven of, or let them see what gross and
peasant stuff you are. Reflect, you sinner, that the more honourable
and well bred the servant, the higher the master is esteemed, and
that one of the greatest advantages of princes over other men is that
they are waited on by servants as good as themselves. Do you not
see, obstinate fellow that you are and unlucky man that I am, that if
they discover that you are a coarse boor or a simple idiot, they will
take me for a charlatan or for some swindling knight? No, no,
Sancho, my friend, avoid, avoid these pitfalls, for once you fall into
being a babbler and a droll, you have only to stumble and you will
descend to the state of a disgraced buffoon. Restrain your tongue.
Consider and ruminate upon your words before they leave your
mouth, and observe that we have now come to a place which, by
God's aid and the valour of my arm, we must leave with our fame
and wealth increased to the uttermost.'

Sancho promised most earnestly to obey and to sew up his

mouth or bite his tongue before uttering a single unfitting or ill-considered word. He assured Don Quixote that he might rest easy on that score, for their identity should never transpire through him.

Don Quixote then dressed himself, put on his shoulder-strap with his sword, threw the scarlet mantle over his shoulders, put on a green satin hunting-cap which the maids had given him and, thus adorned, walked out into the great hall, where he found the maidens lined up in two equal rows and each one of them holding some requisite for his ablutions, which she handed him with great courtesies and formalities. Next there came forward twelve pages with the butler to take him to dinner, where the Duke and Duchess were already waiting for him. They put him between them and led him with great pomp and majesty into another hall in which a rich table was laid with only four covers. The Duke and Duchess came to the door of the hall to receive him, and with them one of those grave ecclesiastics who rule the houses of princes; of those who, not being born princes themselves, do not succeed in teaching those who are how to behave as such; who would have the greatness of the great measured by the narrowness of their own souls; who, wanting to show those they rule how to be frugal, make them miserly; such a man, I mean, was this grave ecclesiastic who went out with the Duke and Duchess to receive Don Quixote. After exchanging innumerable courtly compliments, they concluded by taking Don Quixote between them and going to take their seats at the table. The Duke invited our knight to take the head, and although he at first refused his host pressed him so hard that he had to give in. The ecclesiastic sat opposite him, and the Duke and Duchess on either side.

Sancho watched all this ceremony, gaping with astonishment to see the honour these princes were paying his master; and when he saw the many compliments and entreaties which passed between the Duke and Don Quixote on the subject of his sitting at the head of the table, he said: 'If your worships will give me leave I will tell you a story of an incident in my town concerning this business of seats.'

The moment Sancho opened his mouth Don Quixote trembled, in fear that his squire would certainly utter some absurdity. But Sancho read his anxiety from his face and said: 'Have no fear, dear master, of my going astray or saying anything off the point, for I haven't forgotten the advice you gave me just now about speaking much or little, well or ill.'

'I remember nothing about it, Sancho,' answered Don Quixote. 'Say what you like so long as you say it quickly.'

'Well, what I want to say,' said Sancho, 'is quite true, for my master, Don Quixote here, won't let me lie.'

'So far as I am concerned, Sancho,' answered Don Quixote, 'lie as much as you like. I shall not stop you. But be careful what you say.'

'I have so considered it and reconsidered it that I am as safe as the man in the tower who sounds the alarm, as you shall see by the tale.'

'It would be as well,' said Don Quixote, 'if your Highnesses would order this fool to be turned out from here, or he will be uttering a thousand idiocies.'

'But they must not take Sancho away, I declare, not by so much as an inch,' exclaimed the Duchess. 'I love him dearly, for I know he is very wise.'

'A wise life to your Holiness,' exclaimed Sancho, 'for your good opinion of me, although I don't deserve it. Now this is my tale: There was a gentleman of my town who sent out an invitation. He was very rich and important, as he came of the Alamos of Medina del Campo, and was married to Doña Mencia de Quiñones, who was the daughter of Don Alonso de Marañon, Knight of the Order of Santiago, who was drowned in the Herradura. It was about him that the quarrel was years ago in our town – and, as far as I can make out, my master Don Quixote took part in it – I mean when young Thomas, the scamp, the son of Balbastro the smith, got wounded. Isn't this all true, master? Say it is, for goodness' sake, or these gentlefolk may take me for a lying babbler.'

'So far,' said the ecclesiastic, 'I think you are a babbler but no liar. Though I do not know what I shall take you for later.'

'You call on so many witnesses, Sancho,' said Don Quixote, 'and cite so many proofs that I cannot help agreeing that you must be speaking the truth. Go on and cut your story short, for at the rate you are going you will not be done in two days.'

'He must not cut it short,' said the Duchess, 'to please me. No, he must tell it in his own way, even if it takes him six days to finish; for even if it took so long, those would be the best days of my life.'

'Well, good sirs,' Sancho proceeded, 'this same gentleman, whom I know as well as my own hands – for it is only a bowshot from my house to his – sent an invitation to a poor but honest farmer.'

'Go on, brother,' said the ecclesiastic at this point. 'At the rate you are going you will not be done with your tale till the next world.'

'I'll stop short of half-way there, please God,' answered Sancho Panza. 'Well, this same farmer arrived at the house of the gentleman who had invited him – God rest his soul, for he's dead now and, what's more, they say he died an angel's death, though I wasn't there, as I had to go to Tembleque at the time, harvesting ...'

'On your life, son,' broke in the priest, 'do not wait to bury the gentleman but come back quickly from Tembleque, and finish your story, unless you have a mind for more funerals.'

'Well, the fact is,' Sancho resumed, 'that just as the pair of them were going to sit down to table – I seem to see them now better than ever ...'

The Duke and Duchess greatly enjoyed the good priest's evident disgust at Sancho's prolixity and at the frequent pauses in his story, but Don Quixote was consumed with anger and vexation.

'Well, then,' said Sancho, 'just as the two of them, as I have said, were going to sit down to the meal, the farmer insisted on the gentleman's taking the head of the table, and the gentleman likewise insisted on the farmer's taking it, for a man's wishes should be obeyed in his own house. But the farmer, who prided himself on his courtesy and good breeding, steadfastly refused, until the gentleman angrily put his hands on his shoulders and sat him down by force, saying: "Sit down, blockhead, for wherever I sit shall be head of the table for you." Now that's the story, and I really don't think I've brought it in out of place.'

Don Quixote flushed and his brown face was veined with red, while the Duke and Duchess, perceiving Sancho's malice, concealed their smiles for fear that Don Quixote should end by losing his temper. Then, to change the subject and prevent Sancho from proceeding to further impertinences, the Duchess asked Don Quixote what news he had of the Lady Dulcinea, and whether he

had sent her any presents of giants or malefactors recently, since he
could not have failed to overcome plenty. To which Don Quixote
replied: 'My lady, though my misfortunes had a beginning they will
never have an end. Giants I have conquered, and rogues and malefactors I have sent her. But where should they find her, seeing that
she is enchanted and transformed into the ugliest peasant girl
imaginable?'

'I don't know,' said Sancho. 'She seems the loveliest beautiful
creature in the world to me. I'm quite sure, at least, that no tumbler
could give her odds for nimbleness or frisking. She can spring from
the ground on to an ass as sprightly as a cat, I promise you, lady
Duchess.'

'Have you seen her enchanted, Sancho?' asked the Duke.

'Have I seen her!' answered Sancho. 'Why, who the devil was it
but I that first thought of this enchantment business? She's as much
enchanted as my father!'

When the ecclesiastic heard speak of giants, rogues and enchantments, he reckoned that this must be Don Quixote de la Mancha,
whose history was the Duke's ordinary reading, for which he had
often taken him to task, saying that it was folly to read such follies.
And now that he was convinced that his suspicions were correct, he
turned on the Duke in great anger:

'Your Excellency, sir, will have to account to our Lord for this
good man's doings. This Don Quixote, or Don Fool, or whatever
you call him, cannot be such an idiot, I imagine, as your Excellency
would have him be, seeing the opportunities you put in his way of
carrying on with his fooleries and nonsense.'

Then, turning to address Don Quixote, he said: 'And you,
simpleton, who has driven it into your brain that you are a knight
errant and conquer giants and capture malefactors? Get along with
you, and take my advice: go back to your home, and bring up your
children, if you have any. Look after your estate, and stop wandering about the world, swallowing wind and making yourself a
laughing-stock to all who know you and even to those who do not.
Where, in the name of mischief, have you ever learnt that knights
errant exist to-day, or ever did? Where would you find giants in
Spain, or malefactors in La Mancha, or your enchanted Dulcineas,
or all that pack of nonsense that figures in your story?'

Y

Don Quixote listened attentively to the venerable man's words, and when he saw that he had done, regardless of the Duke and Duchess, he got on to his feet with an angry expression and excitement in his face, and said:

But his reply deserves a chapter to itself.

Chapter XXXII. *Of Don Quixote's Reply to his Censor, and other incidents serious and entertaining.*

So, springing to his feet and trembling from head to foot like a man filled with mercury, Don Quixote stammered out hastily: 'The place where I am, the presence I am in, and the respect I have, and have always had, for the calling your worship professes, hold and tie the hands of my just indignation. And so, for those reasons and because I know, as everyone knows, that the weapons of gownsmen are the same as women's, the tongue, I will enter with the same weapon into equal battle with you, though I might have expected good counsel from you instead of infamous reproaches. Charitable and wholesome reproof requires different behaviour and different language. But harsh and public reproach exceeds the bounds of just censure; for well-meaning rebukes are better uttered with gentleness than with asperity, and it is wrong, without knowledge of the sin, to proclaim the sinner bluntly a blockhead and a fool. Now tell me, your worship, for what follies that you have seen in me do you condemn and reproach me, and tell me to go home and attend to my household, and to my wife and children, though you do not know if I have any or not? Is it enough to enter other men's houses by hook or by crook and rule their owners, and after a narrow upbringing – without more knowledge of the world than the district sixty or seventy miles around – roundly to lay down the law to chivalry and judge of knights errant? Is it, perchance, idleness and waste of time to wander through the world, seeking no pleasures but the austerities by which the virtuous ascend to the seat of immortality? If knights, grandees, noblemen, or the high-born were to consider me a fool, I should take it as an intolerable affront; but that scholars who never entered or trod the paths of chivalry should set me down as a madman does not affect me a jot. A knight I am and a knight I shall die, if it please the Most High. Some travel over the broad field of proud ambition; others by way of base and servile adulation; others again by way of deceitful hypocrisy, and a few by way of the true religion. But beneath the influence of my star I journey along the narrow path of knight errantry, in which exercise I despise wealth, but not honour. I have redressed grievances, set right wrongs, punished insolences, conquered giants, and trampled down fiends. I am in love, only because knights errant are obliged to be so; and, being so, I am not one of those depraved lovers, but of the continent and platonic sort. I always direct my purposes to virtuous ends, and do good to all and ill to none. Whether he who so purposes, whether he who so labours, whether he who so acts, deserves to be called a fool, let your Highnesses decide, excellent Duke and Duchess.'

'By God, that's good!' cried Sancho. 'Say no more for yourself, my dear master. For there's nothing more in the world to be said, thought, or done. Besides, since this gentleman denies the very existence of knights errant, is it surprising that he doesn't know anything of what he is talking about?'

'Are you perhaps, brother,' asked the priest, 'that Sancho Panza they speak of, to whom your master promised an isle?'

'I am,' answered Sancho, 'and I deserve it as much as anyone on earth. I'm one of your – keep company with good men and you'll be one of them – yes, and of your – not with whom you're bred, but with whom you're fed – and of your – lean against a good tree and you'll get good shelter. – I've leant on my good master, and I've been going about in his company for many months and, God willing, I shall come to be like him. And if he lives and I live he'll have no lack of empires to rule, nor I of isles to govern!'

'No, of course not, Sancho my friend,' interposed the Duke, 'for in Don Quixote's name I can offer you the government of an odd one of mine, and no poor one either.'

'Go down on your knees, Sancho,' cried Don Quixote, 'and kiss his Excellency's feet for the favour.'

Sancho obeyed, and at the sight of him the priest got up from table, exclaiming in a great fury: 'By this habit I wear, I must protest that your Excellency is as stupid as these two sinners. They may well be mad if the sane sanction their insanity! Your Excellency may keep them company, but so long as they stop in this house I shall stay in mine, and refrain from reproving what I cannot remedy.'

And without another word or another mouthful he went off, and the Duke and Duchess's entreaties were powerless to stop him; not that the Duke said much to him, for laughter at his foolish burst of anger. But when he had stopped laughing he said to Don Quixote: 'You have answered so nobly for yourself, Sir Knight of the Lions, that you can require no further satisfaction of him; since, though this appears an offence, it is not one at all, for as women cannot give offence, neither can ecclesiastics, as your worship knows better than I.'

'That is true,' answered Don Quixote, 'and the reason is that one who cannot be offended can offend nobody. As women, children and ecclesiastics cannot defend themselves, even if they are attacked, they cannot be affronted. For between an offence and an affront there is this difference, as your Excellency knows better than I. An affront comes from one who is capable of giving it, gives it, and maintains it, but an offence can come from anyone without carrying an affront with it. Let us take an example: a man is standing carelessly in the street; ten men with arms in their hands come up and strike him; he draws his sword and does his duty; but the number of his opponents is against him and prevents his fulfilling his purpose, which is to avenge himself. This man is offended but not affronted. And this can be confirmed by another example. A man's back is turned; another man comes up and strikes him, and after striking him, does not wait, but runs away; the other follows him, but does not catch him. The man who was struck suffered an offence but no affront; for an affront has to be maintained. If the striker, even if he struck foully, had drawn his sword and stayed facing his enemy, the man who was struck would be offended and affronted at the same time; offended because he had been treacherously hit, and affronted because his assailant maintained his action, holding his ground without turning his back. And so, according to the laws of the accursed duel, I may be offended, but am not affronted. For children cannot wound and women do not generally do so, and so they have no call to maintain their position. The same applies to men of religion, for these three classes of people lack arms offensive and defensive; and so, although naturally they are compelled to defend themselves, they have not the power to offend anyone. But although I just said that I might have been aggrieved, now I say no. That is impossible. For one who cannot receive an affront can still less give one. For which reasons I should not resent, and do not resent, what that good man said to me. I only wish he had stayed a little longer, so that I could have convinced him of his error in supposing that knights errant have never existed in the world. For if Amadis had heard him, or one of his countless lineage, it would have gone badly with his worship, I assure you.'

'I'll swear to that,' said Sancho. 'They would have given him a slashing that would have split him from top to toe like a pomegranate or an over-ripe melon. They were fine lads at putting up with such jests! My goodness, I'm sure that if Reynald of Montalban had heard that little man's words, he would have given him a slap on the mouth that would have kept him quiet for more than three years. No, he should have picked a quarrel with them, and seen what he was like when they'd done with him.'

The Duchess was dying with laughter at Sancho's remarks, considering him madder and more entertaining than his master; and there were many at that time who shared her opinion. At last Don Quixote was calm and the meal finished; and as they were removing the table-cloths four maids came in, one with a silver basin, a second with a jug also of silver, a third with two very fine rich towels on her shoulder, and the fourth with her arms bare to the elbow, bearing in her white hands – and white they were indeed – a round ball of Naples soap. The one with the basin went up and, gracefully and without embarrassment, placed it under Don Quixote's chin. He, wondered at the ceremony, but silently assumed that it must be a custom of that country to wash the beard instead of the hands, and stretched his chin out as far as he could. At that same moment the jug began to rain on it, and the maid with the soap to set about it with such vigour that she raised snowflakes – for the lather was as white as snow – not only on his beard, but over the docile knight's whole face and his eyes – so much so that he was forced to shut them. The Duke and the Duchess, who had been informed of none of this, were waiting to see how the extraordinary ablutions would end. Now when the barber-maid had raised a handful of lather she made believe that she had used up the water, and bade the maid with the jug fetch more, for Don Quixote would wait; on which the second maid departed, and Don Quixote remained the strangest and most ludicrous figure imaginable. All the spectators, and they were many, gazed at him and, seeing him with half a yard of neck more than commonly brown, his eyes closed, and his beard full of soap, it was a great wonder that they were discreet enough to conceal their laughter. The maids who were playing this trick kept their eyes lowered and dared not look at their master and mistress, who were moved to anger and laughter at the same time, and did not know what to do, whether to punish the girls' presumption or reward them for the pleasure of seeing Don Quixote in that state. Finally the girl with the jug came back, and they finished washing Don Quixote. The girl with the towels very deliberately wiped him dry and, making him a low obeisance and curtsey, all four of them together were about to leave the hall. But in case Don Quixote should tumble to the joke, the Duke called to the girl with the basin: 'Come and wash me too, and see that you have enough water.'

The maid, who was shrewd enough, came and offered the basin to the Duke as she had done to Don Quixote, and they hastily soaped him and washed him thoroughly, leaving him dry and clean. Then they curtseyed and departed. It came out afterwards that the Duke had sworn to punish their sauciness if they did not wash him as they had Don Quixote, but they cleverly made amends by soaping him in the same manner.

Sancho paid great attention to these ceremonial ablutions, and said to himself: 'Bless me! What if it's the custom in this country to wash squire's beards as well as knights'? For, upon my soul, I've need of it, and if they were to shave me I should take it for a still greater favour.'

'What are you saying to yourself, Sancho?' asked the Duchess.

'I was saying, lady,' answered he, 'that I've always heard how at other princes' courts they give you water for your hands when they clear away the table-cloths, but not lather for your beard. So a long life's a good thing, for you see a great deal. Yet they say too that those who live long have plenty of ill to suffer, though to suffer one of these washings is more like pleasure than pain.'

'Don't you worry, friend Sancho,' said the Duchess. 'I will have my maids wash you, and scrub you if need be.'

'I'll be content if they do my beard,' answered Sancho, 'at least for the present; but for the rest Heaven will provide in due course.'

'Butler,' said the Duchess, 'see what the good Sancho wants, and comply with his wishes in all respects.'

The butler replied that Sancho should be served in every way, and with that went off to dine, taking Sancho with him, while the Duke, the Duchess and Don Quixote remained at table, talking of many different matters, all touching the profession of arms and of knight errantry. The Duchess asked Don Quixote, since he seemed to have a good memory, to delineate and describe the features of the lovely lady Dulcinea del Toboso who, according to fame's report of her charms, should certainly be the most beautiful creature in the world, even in all La Mancha. Don Quixote sighed on hearing the Duchess' request, and said: 'If I could pluck out my heart and place it before your Highness's eyes on this table in a dish, I should relieve my tongue of the toil of expressing what is almost inconceivable, for in it your Excellency would see her completely portrayed. But why should I set out to describe and delineate the beauty of the peerless Dulcinea, exactly and feature by feature? That is a burden fitter for other backs than mine, an enterprise which should occupy the pencils of Parrhasius, of Timanthus and of Apelles, and the chisels of Lysippus, to paint and to carve her on wood, on marble and in bronze. It would require the Ciceronian and Demosthenian rhetoric as well to praise her.'

'What does Demosthenian mean, Don Quixote?' asked the Duchess. 'It is a word I have never heard in all the days of my life.'

'Demosthenian rhetoric,' answered Don Quixote, 'is as much as to say the rhetoric of Demosthenes, as Ciceronian is Cicero's, which two were the greatest rhetoricians in the world.'

'That is so,' said the Duke, 'and you have shown your ignorance by asking such a question. But, all the same, Don Quixote would give us great pleasure if he would paint her for us, for I am sure that even in rough sketch and outline she will come out so fair that the fairest will envy her.'

'I certainly would,' replied Don Quixote, 'if the misfortune which recently befell her had not blotted her from my mind. So bad was it that I am readier to weep her than to describe her. For I would have your Highness know that when I went some days ago to kiss her hands and receive her blessing, consent and licence for this third expedition, I found a different person from the one I sought. I found her enchanted and transformed from a princess into a country-girl, from beauty to ugliness, from angel to devil, from sweet-smelling to pestiferous, from eloquent to rustic, from gentle to skittish, from light to darkness and, to conclude, from Dulcinea del Toboso to a Sayagan peasant girl.'

'God bless me!' exclaimed the Duke in a loud voice at this moment. 'Who can it have been that did the world such wrong? Who was it that robbed it of the beauty which delighted it, of the grace which charmed it, and the modesty which honoured it?'

'Who?' answered Don Quixote. 'Who can it have been but some malign enchanter, one of the many that envy and persecute me? That accursed race, born into the world to obscure and obliterate the exploits of the good, and to light up and exalt the deeds of the wicked. Persecuted I have been by enchanters. Enchanters persecute me, and enchanters will persecute me till they sink me and my high chivalries into the profound abyss of oblivion. They damage and wound me where they see I feel it most. For to rob a knight errant of his lady is to rob him of the eyes with which he sees, of the sun by which he is lighted, and of the prop by which he is sustained. Many other times I have said it, and now I say it again: a knight errant without a lady is like a tree without leaves, a house without foundations, and a shadow without a body to cast it.'

'There is no more to say,' said the Duchess, 'but yet, if we are to give credit to the history of Don Quixote, which has lately been given to the world to the general applause of mankind, we gather from it, if my memory is correct, that your worship never saw the lady Dulcinea, and that this same lady does not exist on earth, but is a fantastic mistress, whom your worship engendered and bore in your mind, and painted with every grace and perfection you desired.'

'There is much to say on that score,' replied Don Quixote. 'God knows whether Dulcinea exists on earth or no, or whether she is fantastic or not fantastic. These are not matters whose verification can be carried out to the full. I neither engendered nor bore my lady, though I contemplate her in her ideal form, as a lady with all the qualities needed to win her fame in all quarters of the world.

These are: spotless beauty, dignity without pride, love with modesty, politeness springing from courtesy, courtesy from good breeding and, lastly, high lineage, for with good blood beauty shines and glows with a degree of perfection impossible in a humbly born beauty.'

'That is true,' said the Duke, 'but Don Quixote must give me permission to say what the history of his exploits, which I have read, compels me to say. For though it is to be inferred that there is a Dulcinea, in El Toboso or out of it, and that she is beautiful in the highest degree, as your worship paints her, even then it does not appear that she compares in the matter of high lineage with the Orianas, the Alastrajareas, the Madasimas and others of that breed of whom the histories your worship knows so well are full.'

'As to that I may say,' answered Don Quixote, 'that Dulcinea is the daughter of her works, that virtues improve blood, and that the virtuous and humble are to be more highly regarded and prized than the wicked and exalted. All the more so since Dulcinea has a vein in her which may raise her to be a queen with a crown and sceptre, for the merit of one lovely and virtuous woman is sufficient to perform even greater miracles; and if not formally, at least virtually, she has greater fortune stored within her.'

'It's my opinion, Don Quixote,' said the Duchess, 'that you proceed with great caution in all you say, and proceed, as they often say, with plummet in hand. Henceforth I shall believe, and make my whole household believe – and my lord the Duke too, if it is necessary – that there is a Dulcinea in El Toboso, and that she lives to-day, and is beautiful, nobly born and deserving that such a knight as Don Quixote should serve her; which is the highest compliment I know how to pay her. But I cannot help entertaining one scruple, and bearing a certain grudge against Sancho Panza. This is my scruple: the aforesaid history relates that the same Sancho Panza, when he took her a letter on your worship's behalf, found the said Dulcinea winnowing a sack of corn and, to be more exact, they say that it was red wheat. Now, that detail makes me doubt the greatness of her lineage.'

To which Don Quixote replied: 'My lady, your Highness should know that all or most of the things which happen to me are out of the ordinary course of things which befall other knights errant, whether they be directed by the inscrutable will of the fates or by the malice of some envious enchanter; it being a thing now proved that of all the famous knights errant, one has the gift of being immune from enchantment and another has flesh so impenetrable that he cannot be wounded; as had the famous Roland, one of the twelve Peers of France, of whom it is told that he could only be wounded on the sole of his left foot, and even so only with the point of a stout pin and with no other kind of weapon at all. So when Bernardo del Carpio killed him at Roncesvalles, seeing that he could not wound him with his sword he lifted him from the ground in his arms and strangled him, thus recalling the death that Hercules dealt Antaeus, the fierce giant who, they said, was a son of Earth. I mean to infer from what I say that I might possibly have one of these gifts, not of invulnerability, for experience has often taught me that my flesh is soft and by no means impenetrable; nor of immunity from enchantment, for I have known myself to be put into a cage, in which the whole world would not have been strong enough to imprison me had it not been by virtue of enchantment. But since I freed myself from that spell I am inclined to believe that there is no other which can harm me. So that these enchanters, seeing that they cannot use their evil practices on me, avenge themselves on the objects I love best, and seek to take my life by ill-treating Dulcinea by whom I live. So, therefore, I believe that when my squire bore her my message they turned her into a peasant girl employed in the mean occupation of winnowing wheat, though I have affirmed that this wheat was neither red nor wheat, but grains of orient pearl. And to prove the truth of this, I should like to tell your Highness that, coming a little while since by El Toboso, I could never find Dulcinea's palace, and the other day, though Sancho my squire saw her in her proper shape, which is the most beautiful in the world, she appeared to me as a coarse and ugly peasant girl and not at all well spoken, though she is the world's paragon of wisdom. Now, since I am not enchanted and cannot be, according to sound judgment, it is she who is enchanted, injured, changed, altered and transformed. Through her my enemies have avenged themselves upon me, and for her I shall live in perpetual tears till I see her in her pristine state.

'All this I have told you so that no one may heed Sancho's words about Dulcinea's sifting or winnowing. For since they transformed her for me, it is no wonder that they changed her for him. Dulcinea is noble and well-born, springing from one of El Toboso's gentlemanly families, which are many, old and most noble; and no doubt the peerless Dulcinea has no small share of their blood, for through her her town will be famous and memorable in future ages, as Troy has been for Helen and Spain for La Cava, though hers will be a worthier title to fame.

'On the other hand, I would have your Lordships understand that Sancho Panza is one of the drollest squires that ever served knight errant. Sometimes his simplicities are so shrewd that it gives me no small pleasure to consider whether it is simplicity or shrewdness that prevails. Some rogueries in him convict him of knavery, and his indiscretions confirm him a fool. He doubts everything and believes everything. When I think he is going to tumble into folly he comes out with clever sayings which exalt him to the sky. In fact I would not exchange him for any other squire, even if I were to receive a city to boot; and therefore I am in doubt whether it would be right to send him to that governorship with which your Highness has favoured him, although I see in him a certain aptitude for this governing business, and with a slight trimming of his understanding he would do as well with some governorship as the King with his taxes. Particularly as we know now through long experience that there is no need of great ability or much learning to be a governor, for there are a hundred round here who can scarcely read, and yet govern like so many goshawks. The whole point is to have good intentions and to desire to do right in everything. For they will never lack some one to advise and guide them in their actions, like those unlettered military governors who have an assessor to pronounce sentence. I would advise him not to take bribes or forsake justice, and on certain other little matters which are lying on my chest and will come off in due course for Sancho's benefit and to the advantage of the isle he will govern.'

The Duke, the Duchess and Don Quixote had arrived at this point in their conversation when they heard many voices and a great noise of people in the palace. And suddenly Sancho came into the hall in a great scare with a linen-strainer for a bib, and after him a number of lads, or rather kitchen-boys and other underlings, one of whom was carrying a little bowl of water, which from its colour and uncleanliness appeared to be dish-water. The boy with the bowl was following him, and teasing him by trying most persistently to push it right beneath his beard, which another boy made as if to wash.

'What is this, fellows?' asked the Duchess. 'What is this? What are you trying to do to this good man? What, do you not realize that he is a governor elect?'

To which the barber-scullion replied: 'This gentleman won't let himself be washed, as the custom is and as the Duke, my master, was washed and the gentleman, his master.'

'Yes, I will,' answered Sancho, in a great rage, 'but I should like it to be done with cleaner towels, with whiter soap, and less dirty hands; for there's not so much difference between me and my master that he should be washed with angel's water and I with devil's lye. The customs of countries and princes' palaces are only good so long as they give no offence, but the washing custom here in use is worse than the flogging penitents'. My beard's clean, and I've no need of such refreshings. And if anyone comes to wash or touch a hair of my head – I mean of my beard – speaking with all due respect, I'll give him such a punch as will leave my fist embedded in his skull, for these *cirimonies* and soapings seem to me more like practical jokes than hospitable civilities.'

The Duchess was dying with laughter at Sancho's angry protest. But it did not give Don Quixote much pleasure to see him so ill-adorned in a streaked towel and surrounded by so many of the kitchen underlings. Making a deep bow, therefore, to the Duke and Duchess, as if asking for permission to speak, he calmly addressed the rabble: 'Ho there, knights and gentlemen! Leave this lad alone and go back whence you came, or wherever else you please! For my squire is as clean as another, and these bowls are no more fitting for him than your little narrow-mouthed drinking cups. Take my advice and leave him, for neither he nor I will abide this jesting business.'

But Sancho caught his words out of his mouth and went on: 'No, let them come and make a mock of the stupid yokel! I'll stand for it, as sure as it's now night! Let them bring a comb here, or what ever they like, and curry this beard of mine, and if they get anything out of it which, offends against cleanliness let them give me a convict's crop.'

Here the Duchess remarked, still laughing: 'Sancho Panza is absolutely right, and will speak nothing but the truth. He is clean and, as he says, has no need to wash. And if our custom does not please him, his soul is his own. What is more, you ministers of cleanliness have been exceedingly remiss and careless – I do not know whether I should not say presumptuous – in bringing before such a personage and such a beard your wooden troughs and bowls and your dish cloths, instead of jugs and basins of pure gold and holland towels. But, indeed, you are a sorry low-born crew and, like the scoundrels you are, cannot help showing the envy you bear to knight errant's squires.'

The roguish servants, and even the butler who was with them, thought that the Duchess was speaking seriously. So they took the strainer off Sancho's chest, and slunk away abashed and left him. Whereat seeing himself relieved from what had seemed to him extreme peril, he threw himself on his knees before the Duchess, crying: 'Great ladies can do great kindnesses, and I don't know how to repay the one your Highness has just done me except by having myself knighted, so that I may spend all the days of my life in the service of so exalted a lady. I'm a peasant; Sancho Panza is my name; I'm married; I have children and serve as a squire. If in any respect I may serve your Highness, I shall be no slower in obeying than your ladyship in commanding.'

'It is evident, Sancho,' replied the Duchess, 'that you have learnt to be courteous in the school of courtesy itself. It is evident, I mean, that you have been reared in Don Quixote's bosom, who must needs be the cream of courtesy and the flower of ceremonies, or "*cirimonies*" as you call them. Good luck to such a master and such a servant, one the pole-star of knight errantry and the other the star of squirely fidelity. Arise, Sancho my friend, for I will reward your courtesy by making the Duke, my lord, fulfil his promise to favour you with a governorship as speedily as he can.'

With this the conversation ceased, and Don Quixote retired to take his siesta. But the Duchess begged Sancho, if he had no great desire for sleep, to come and spend the afternoon with her and her maidens in a very cool room. Sancho replied that, although it was true that it was his custom to sleep for four or five hours on summer afternoons, he would, to serve her Excellency, try with all his might to take no sleep at all that day, and would come in obedience to her command; and so he left the hall.

Then the Duke renewed his orders to his servants to treat Don Quixote as a knight errant, and to adhere scrupulously to the style in which it is recorded that the knights of old were entertained.

Chapter XXXIII. *Of the Delightful Conversation between the Duchess, her Maidens and Sancho Panza, which deserves to be both read and noted.*

WELL, the story goes that Sancho did not sleep that afternoon, but kept his promise, and went after dinner to visit the Duchess, who for the pleasure of listening to him made him sit beside her on a low chair, although Sancho was so well bred that he was reluctant to sit down. But the Duchess bade him seat himself like a governor and talk like a squire, because under either head he deserved the very throne of the Cid Ruy Diaz, the Campeador. Sancho shrugged his shoulders, obeyed and sat down, and all the Duchess's maids and waiting-women surrounded him eagerly, keeping perfect silence to hear what he would say. But it was the Duchess who spoke first, saying:

'Now that we are alone and no one can overhear us here, I should like the noble governor to resolve certain doubts of mine arising from the history of the great Don Quixote, now in print. One of these doubts is this: since the good Sancho never saw Dulcinea, I mean the lady Dulcinea del Toboso, nor took her Don Quixote's letter, for it was left in the note-book in the Sierra Morena, how did he venture to forge her reply and all that story about finding her sifting wheat, since it was all a mock and a lie, prejudicial to the peerless Dulcinea's reputation and ill-suited to the quality and fidelity of a good squire?'

At these words Sancho got up from his chair and, without a word of reply, quietly made a circuit of the room, his body bent and one finger on his lips, lifting up the hangings as he went. Then, when he had done, he returned to his seat and said:

'Now, my lady, that I'm sure that nobody's eavesdropping and that only these ladies can hear me, I will reply to your question without fear or alarm, and to anything more I may be asked. Now the first thing I say is that I reckon my master Don Quixote's stark crazy, although sometimes he will talk in a way which, to my thinking and in the opinion of all who hear him, is so wise and leads down so good a track that Satan himself could not speak better. But, all the same, to my mind he's really and truly a madman, an idiot. So, seeing that I've tumbled to that, I don't mind making him believe things without rhyme or reason in them, like that about the reply to his letter, and the business six or eight days ago which I'd like you to know though it's not in the history: the matter of my lady Dulcinea's enchantment. For I made him believe that she's enchanted, which is no more true than the moon's a green cheese.'

The Duchess begged him to tell her about this enchantment or trick, and Sancho related it all just as it had happened, to the no small pleasure of his hearers. Then, pursuing her remarks, the Duchess observed:

'From what the good Sancho has told me there is a doubt leaping up in my mind, and a little whisper comes to my ears and says to me: "Since Don Quixote de la Mancha is a crazy fool and a madman, and Sancho Panza, his squire, knows it, yet, for all that, serves and follows him, and hangs on these empty promises of his, there can be no doubt that he is more of a madman and a fool than his master; and that being so, as it is, you will be criticized, lady Duchess, if you give the said Sancho Panza an isle to govern; for if a man cannot govern himself, how will he know how to govern others?" '

'By God, lady,' said Sancho, 'but this doubt was born in the nick of time. Tell it, your worship, to speak clearly or any way it will, for I know it speaks the truth and that I should have left my master days ago if I had been wise. But that was my lot and my ill-luck. I can do nothing else; I have to follow him; we're of the same village; I've eaten his bread; I love him dearly; I'm grateful to him; he gave me his ass-colts; and, what is more, I'm faithful; and so it's impossible for anything to part us except the man with the pick and shovel. And if your Highness doesn't wish them to give me the promised governorship, God made me without it, and perhaps my not getting it may redound to the good of my conscience. For though I'm a fool, I understand the proverb which says: for his own hurt the ant sprouted wings. And it may well be that Squire Sancho may get to Heaven quicker than Governor Sancho. They bake as good bread here as in France; and in the night all cats are grey; and a man's pretty unlucky if he hasn't broken his fast by two in the afternoon; and there's no stomach a hand's breadth bigger than another, that can be filled, as the saying goes, with straw and hay; and the little birds of the field have God to provide for them and feed them; and four yards of Cuenca shoddy will warm you more than any four of Segovia broadcloth; and when we leave this world and go into the ground below the prince's path is as narrow as the labourer's, and the Pope's body takes up no more feet of earth than the sexton's, though one's higher than the other; for when we go down the pit we all have to shrink and fit, or they make us shrink and fit whether we like it or not – and good night! And I say once more that if your ladyship doesn't wish to give me the isle because I'm a fool, I shall be wise enough not to care. And I've heard say that behind the cross lurks the devil; and all is not gold that glitters; and from among oxen, ploughs and yokes they took Wamba to be King of Spain; and from among silks, entertainments and riches they took Roderick to be eaten by snakes, if the verses of the old ballads don't lie.'

'How not lie!' put in the waiting-woman Doña Rodriguez at this point, she being one of the listeners. 'For there's a ballad that says that they put King Roderick, all alive, into a tomb with toads, snakes and lizards, and that two days later the King cried from inside this tomb in low and doleful tones:

Now they eat me, now they eat me
In the part where most I sinned.

and, according to that, this gentleman's quite right when he says that he would rather be a peasant than a king, if he is to be eaten by reptiles.'

The Duchess could not restrain her laughter at her waiting-woman's simplicity, or withhold her astonishment at Sancho's reasonings and proverbs; and she said to him: 'Now the good Sancho knows that once a knight makes a promise he tries to fulfil it, even if it costs him his life. The Duke, my lord and master, al-

though he is no knight errant, is none the less a knight, and so he
will keep his word about the promised isle, despite the envy and
malice of the world. Let Sancho be of good heart, for when he least
expects it he will find himself seated on the throne of his isle, invested in his dignity, and grasping his governorship, which he will
fling aside in time for another of brocade three inches thick. But I
charge him particularly to look to the government of his vassals,
remembering that they are all loyal and well born.'

'About the matter of governing them well,' answered Sancho,
'there's no need to urge me, for I'm charitable by nature and have
compassion on the poor; and from him who cooks and kneads you
must not steal his bread, and I swear they shan't throw me false dice.
I'm an old dog and understand their calls, and I can snuff myself at
the right time, and won't let them put cobwebs over my eyes, because I know where the shoe pinches. I mean to say that the good
shall have entrance and inflammation with me, and the wicked
neither foot nor fellowship. And I think that in this matter of a
governorship the beginning's everything, and that, maybe, when I
have been governor a fortnight I shall take to it like a duck to water,
and know more about it than about the field-work I was brought
up in.'

'You are right, Sancho,' said the Duchess, 'for no one is born
with knowledge, and bishops are made from men, not from stones.
But to come back to the conversation we were having just now
about the lady Dulcinea's enchantment, I consider it absolutely certain and proved beyond a doubt that Sancho's scheme of tricking
his master and making him believe that the peasant girl was Dulcinea, and that if his master did not recognize her it was because she
was enchanted – that all that, I say, was the invention of one of those
enchanters who persecute Don Quixote. Because I know that the
peasant girl who skipped on to the she-ass really and truly was and is
Dulcinea del Toboso, and that it was the good Sancho who was deceived, though he may think he is the deceiver; and there is no more
doubt about that than about anything else we have never seen. And
I would have Master Sancho know that we also have enchanters
here who love us well and tell us what is happening in the world,
plainly and simply, without tricks and tangles. And believe me,
Sancho, the frisky peasant girl was and is Dulcinea del Toboso, and

she is as enchanted as the mother that bore her; and when least we expect to we shall see her in her proper shape, and then Sancho will be disabused of the delusion under which he labours.'

'All that may well be,' said Sancho Panza, 'and now I'm prepared to believe my master's story about his vision in Montesinos' cave; where he says he saw the lady Dulcinea del Toboso in the same dress and looking just as I said I had seen her when I enchanted her just for my own amusement. But it must all have been contrariwise, as your worship says, my lady, because it can't and mustn't be presumed that I could invent such a shrewd trick on the spur of the moment with my poor wits, and I don't believe that my master's so mad as to accept anything so far beyond all the bounds of probability on such weak and feeble persuasion as mine. But you shouldn't reckon me ill-natured on that score, my lady, because a stupid like me isn't bound to tumble to all the malicious plots of these vile enchanters. I made that story up to escape my master Don Quixote's scoldings, and not meaning to harm him; and if things have turned out otherwise, God's in Heaven and judges our hearts.'

'That is true,' said the Duchess; 'but tell me now, Sancho, what is this you say about the cave of Montesinos? I should like to hear about it.'

Then Sancho Panza told her, detail by detail, all that has already been related about this adventure. And when she had heard it the Duchess said: 'Now since the great Don Quixote says he saw the same peasant girl there that Sancho saw on the way out of El Toboso, there is no doubt that we must infer from this incident that it is Dulcinea, and that there are some very active and exceedingly meddling enchanters about here.'

'I agree,' said Sancho Panza, 'but if my lady Dulcinea del Toboso's enchanted, so much the worse for her; for I don't have to take on my master's enemies, who must be plentiful and wicked. The truth may be that it was a peasant girl I saw. I took her for a peasant girl, and a peasant girl I judged her to be. But if it was Dulcinea it can't be laid to my account; they can't run to me about it, or start a scrap with me on the subject. No, I won't have them coming to me every moment with their argy-bargying: "*Sancho said it, Sancho did it, Sancho went, and Sancho came*", as if Sancho were some what's-his-name, and not the same Sancho Panza who is going all about the world now in books, as Sampson Carrasco told me. For he's a person bachelored by Salamanca, at the very least, and the likes of him can't lie excepting only when they've a fancy to, or when it's greatly to their advantage. So there's no reason for anyone to blame me; and since I have a good reputation and, as I have heard my master say, a good name is worth more than great riches, let them fit this governorship on me and they'll see marvels; for one who has been a good squire will be a good governor.'

'All that the good Sancho has just said,' observed the Duchess, 'are Catonian sentences, or at the least drawn from the very heart of Michael Verino himself – *florentibus occidit annis*. Well, well, to speak in Sancho's own fashion, beneath a bad cloak there is often a good drinker.'

'Really, my lady,' replied Sancho, 'I've never drunk out of vice in my life. Out of thirst very possibly, for there's nothing of the hypocrite about me. I drink when I've a fancy, and when I haven't and I'm offered drink, I take it so as not to seem finicky or ill-bred. For a toast to a friend – what marble heart is there that won't pledge a friend? But although I wear shoes I don't soil them, especi- ally as the squires of knights errant almost always drink water, be- cause they're for ever travelling through forests, woods and mea- dows, by mountains and crags, without finding a merciful drop of wine, even if they'd give one eye for it.'

'So I believe,' answered the Duchess. 'And now let Sancho go and rest. By-and-by we will talk at greater length, and we will give orders for him to be fitted, as he put it, with this governorship.'

Once more Sancho kissed the Duchess's hands, and begged her to be so kind as to see that good care was taken of his Dapple, who was the light of his eyes.

'What Dapple is this?' asked the Duchess.

'My ass,' answered Sancho, 'for not to call him by that name I generally call him Dapple. I asked this waiting-woman here to take care of him when I entered the castle, and she couldn't have got angrier if I'd called her old or ugly, though it should be more proper and natural for waiting-women to look after asses than to lord it in halls. Good Heavens, what a dislike a certain gentleman of my vil- lage had for these ladies.'

'He must have been a yokel,' said Doña Rodriguez the waiting-woman, 'for if he were a well-born gentleman he would rate them higher than the horn of the moon.'

'Now, now!' said the Duchess. 'Let us have no more of that. Be quiet, Doña Rodriguez, and be calm, Master Panza, and leave me to see that Dapple is looked after. For if he is a jewel of Sancho's I will place him in the apple of my eye.'

'It will be all right if he's in the stable,' answered Sancho, 'for in the apple of your Highness's eye neither he nor I are worthy to stay for a single moment; and I would no more consent to that than to stab myself all over. For although my master says that in courtesies one should rather lose by a card too many than a card too few, in matters of donkeys and asses you have to go with compass in hand and warily.'

'Let Sancho take him to his government,' said the Duchess. 'There he can tend him as he will and even exempt him from labour.'

'Don't think, lady Duchess, that your Grace has said anything remarkable,' said Sancho, 'for I've seen more than a few asses go to governorships, and my taking mine will be no novelty.'

Sancho's words started the Duchess laughing with delight once more; and sending him to rest, she went to give the Duke an account of her conversation with him. Then, between the two of them, they planned and arranged a new trick to play on Don Quixote, a rare one and well suited to his style of chivalry. And indeed they invented many of that kind, which were both ingenious and appropriate, and are some of the best adventures contained in this great history.

Chapter XXXIV. *Of the Instructions received for the Disenchantment of the peerless Dulcinea del Toboso, which is one of the most famous Adventures in this Book.*

GREAT was the pleasure the Duke and Duchess received from their conversation with Don Quixote and Sancho Panza; and being resolved in their intention of playing some tricks on them which should bear some appearance or semblance of adventures, they took an idea from Don Quixote's account of the cave of Montesinos, and from it prepared a famous one. What most astonished the Duchess, however, was the greatness of Sancho's simplicity. For he had now come to believe that Dulcinea's enchantment was the infallible truth, although he had himself been the enchanter and the trickster in that business. So, having given their servants directions as to their behaviour, some six days later they took Don Quixote on a hunting-party with an array of huntsmen and beaters worthy of a crowned king. They gave him a hunting-suit, and Sancho another of the finest green cloth. But Don Quixote refused to put his on, with the excuse that he had to return next day to the stern exercise of arms, and that he could not carry wardrobes or stores with him. Sancho, however, took what they gave him, with the intention of selling it at the first possible opportunity.

Then, when the appointed day came, Don Quixote put on his armour and Sancho his new suit and, the squire riding on Dapple, whom he would not leave behind even though they offered him a horse, joined the troop of beaters. The Duchess came out magnificently dressed, and Don Quixote, out of pure courtesy and good manners, took the rein of her palfrey, although the Duke tried to prevent him. After some time they reached a wood lying between two very high hills, where they took up their positions, laid their ambushes, arranged their beats, and distributed the huntsmen to their various stations. Then the hunt began with such a great noise of shouting and hallooing that, what with the barking of the dogs and the sound of the horns, they could not hear one another speak.

The Duchess dismounted and took up her station with a sharp spear in her hands in an ambush where she knew the wild boar generally passed. The Duke and Don Quixote also dismounted and placed themselves on either side of her, while Sancho assumed a position at the extreme rear, without getting off his Dapple, whom he dared not abandon for fear that some accident might befall the beast. But scarcely had they alighted and put themselves in a line with a great number of their servants, when they saw a huge wild boar rushing towards them, hard pressed by the hounds and pursued by the huntsmen, gnashing its teeth and tusks, and spraying foam from its mouth. At which sight Don Quixote braced his shield and advanced to encounter it, sword in hand. The Duke also advanced with his spear, but the Duchess would have been ahead of them all if her husband had not prevented her. Only Sancho, at the sight of the valiant beast, abandoned Dapple and started running as fast as he could. He tried to climb a tall oak, but could not; for when he was half way up, as his ill-luck would have it, a bough which he had grasped in his endeavour to get to the top broke and, falling to the ground, left him in the air, caught on a fork of the oak and unable to get down. Finding himself in this plight with his green suit tearing, and thinking that if the fierce beast were to come that way it would be able to reach him, he began to shout so loud and persistently for help that everyone who heard him but did not see him supposed that some wild animal was devouring him. At last the tusked boar was run through by the many javelin points which the hunters levelled against him; and Don Quixote, turning his head at the shouts, which he had already recognized for Sancho's, saw him hanging head down from the oak, and beside him Dapple, who did not abandon him in his calamity — and Cide Hamete says that he seldom saw Sancho without seeing Dapple, or Dapple without seeing Sancho: such was the friendship and loyalty between them. Don Quixote went up and released Sancho who, once free and on the ground, looked at the tear in his hunting-suit and grieved in his soul, for he thought that in that suit he possessed an inheritance.

Meanwhile they laid the mighty boar on a baggage-mule and, covering it with sprigs of rosemary and branches of myrtle, bore it away as the spoils of victory to some large field-tents, which were pitched in the middle of the wood. There they found the tables set and a dinner prepared, a grand and sumptuous spread which clearly displayed the greatness and magnificence of the host. And as Sancho showed the Duchess the rents in his torn coat, he observed: 'If this had been a hunting of the hare or of small birds, my coat would have been in no danger of getting into this state. I don't know what pleasure's to be got from lying in wait for an animal who can kill you, if he catches you on his tusk. I remember hearing an old ballad once which says:

> By the bears you may be eat,
> As was Favila the great.'

'That was a Gothic King,' said Don Quixote, 'who went out hunting and was eaten by a bear.'

'What I mean,' replied Sancho, 'is that I wouldn't have princes and kings putting themselves in such-like perils for the sake of a pleasure that should really not be a pleasure, for it consists in killing an animal which has not committed any offence.'

'But you are quite mistaken,' answered the Duke, 'for the exercise of hunting is the most essential of all sports for kings and princes. Hunting is war on a small scale; in it there are stratagems, artifices and ambushes for the safe conquest of the enemy. In hunting one suffers extremes of cold and intolerable heats; idleness and sleep are cut short; the bodily strength is increased; the hunter's limbs are made nimble. In short, it is an exercise which can be followed without prejudice to anyone and with pleasure to many; and the best thing about it is that it is not for everyone, as other kinds of sport are, except for hawking which is also reserved for kings and great lords. So, Sancho, you must change your mind, and when you are a governor follow the chase. You will see that you will be a hundred times the better for it.'

'No, indeed,' answered Sancho, 'a good governor and a broken leg are best at home. It would be a fine thing if people came wearied out to look for him on some business, and he was amusing himself in the forest. The government would go to the devil at that rate. Indeed, sir, hunting and pastimes are better suited to idlers than to governors. The way I mean to take my pleasure is in a game of cards at Easter, and skittles on Sundays and holidays; for these huntings and the like don't go with my temper or my conscience.'

'Pray God, Sancho, that you prove as good as your word,' said the Duke, 'though there's a gap indeed 'twixt word and deed.'

'Be that as it may,' replied Sancho, 'a good paymaster doesn't worry about sureties; and God's help's better than early rising; and belly carries legs and not legs belly. I mean that if God helps me and I do my duty with a good heart, there's no doubt that I shall govern better than a goshawk. So let them put a finger in my mouth and see if I bite or not.'

'God and all His saints confound you, Sancho you wretch!' cried Don Quixote. 'When will the day come, as I have often asked before, when I shall hear you utter a continuous and connected sentence without proverbs? Let this fool be, your Highnesses, for he will grind your souls, not only between two but between two thousand proverbs, dragged in as fittingly and as much to the point as – God bless him, and me too, if I have patience to listen to them!'

'There may be more of Sancho Panza's proverbs,' said the Duchess, 'than the Greek Commander's, yet they are no less valuable for the pithiness of their expression. I can say for myself that they give me more pleasure than others that are better applied and more seasonably introduced.'

With this and similar entertaining talk they left the tent for the wood, and passed the day visiting the hunters' posts and ambushes. Here they were overtaken by night, which was neither so clear nor so calm as was usual at that season of the year, it being about midsummer. But a certain half-light that obtained was of great assistance to the plans of the Duke and Duchess. For as soon as it was dusk and night was beginning to fall, it suddenly appeared as if the whole wood in all directions was burning, and presently they heard from here, there and everywhere, countless trumpets and other martial instruments, as if several troops of cavalry were passing through the forest. The light of the fires and the sound of warlike instruments almost blinded the eyes and deafened the ears of the spectators, and of everyone in the wood as well. Presently they heard a great shouting of *Lelili*, which is the Moors' battle-cry. Trumpets and clarions blared, kettle-drums rattled, fifes shrilled, almost all together and so continuously and rapidly that any one with any senses at all must have lost them at the confused din of all those instruments. The Duke was struck dumb, the Duchess astonished, Don Quixote amazed, and Sancho trembling; in fact even those who were in the secret were seized with alarm. Fear held them silent when a postilion dressed as a demon passed in front of them, blowing instead of a bugle a huge hollow ox-horn, which emitted a hoarse and fearful sound.

'Hie, there, brother courier!' cried the Duke. 'Who are you? Where do you come from? And what men of war are these who appear to be passing through this wood?'

To which the courier replied in bold and horrific tones: 'I am the Devil. I have come to seek Don Quixote de la Mancha. The people approaching are six troops of enchanters, bearing the peerless Dulcinea del Toboso on a triumphal car. Here she comes enchanted, with the gay Frenchman Montesinos, to give Don Quixote instructions how the said lady is to be disenchanted.'

'If you were the Devil, as you say you are and as your appearance suggests, you would have recognized the said knight Don Quixote de la Mancha, for you have him before you.'

'By God and my conscience,' answered the Devil, 'I was not looking at him; for my mind is distracted by so many matters that I was forgetting the principal purpose I had come for.'

'This Devil must certainly be an honest fellow,' said Sancho, 'and a good Christian. For if he weren't he wouldn't swear by God and his conscience. So I suppose that there must be some good people even in Hell.'

Then the Demon, without dismounting, directed his gaze on Don Quixote and said: 'To you, Knight of the Lions – and may I see you between their claws – I am sent by the unhappy but valiant knight Montesinos, who commanded me to bid you on his behalf await him on the spot where I should meet you, since he brings with him her whom they call Dulcinea del Toboso, for the purpose of giving you instructions as to her disenchantment, and as my coming here was for no other reason I need stay no longer. May demons like myself have you in their keeping, and the good angels preserve this noble pair.' Then, when he had spoken, he blew his enormous horn, turned his back and departed without waiting for a reply.

This produced further amazement in everyone, especially in Sancho and Don Quixote; in Sancho at their insistence, in defiance of the truth, that Dulcinea was enchanted; and in Don Quixote since he could not be certain whether what had happened in Montesinos' cave was true or not. But while he was deep in these thoughts, the Duke asked: 'Does your worship intend to wait, Don Quixote?'

'Why not?' answered he. 'I shall stay here, fearless and strong, though all Hell should come to assail me.'

'But if I see another devil and hear another horn like the last one I'll no more stay here than I'd stay in Flanders,' said Sancho.

By this time the night had grown darker, and numerous lights began to flit about the wood, much as the dry exhalations of the earth flit about the sky and appear to our vision as shooting stars. At the same time a frightful noise was heard, like the rumbling of the ponderous wheels of ox-waggons, from whose harsh and continuous creaking wolves and bears, if there are any around, are said to fly. The turmoil, however, continued to increase, and it actually sounded as if four separate skirmishes or battles were being fought in the four quarters of the wood. Close by there pealed the harsh thunder of dreadful artillery; further off countless musket-shots rang out; almost at hand resounded the shouts of the combatants; afar off the Moslem war cries were repeated; in fact the cornets, horns, bugles, clarions, trumpets, drums, cannons and guns, and, above them all, the fearful creakings of the waggons, made together so confused and horrible a din that Don Quixote had to avail himself of all his courage to endure it. But Sancho's heart fell into his boots and sent him fainting to the skirts of the Duchess, who received him in them, and promptly ordered water to be thrown in his face. This was done, and he returned to his senses just as the waggon with the creaking wheels came up to where they stood. It was drawn by four ponderous oxen, all swathed in black trappings, with a flaming wax torch tied to each horn. On top of the waggon was placed a high seat, on which was seated a venerable old man, dressed in a long robe of black glazed buckram, with a beard whiter than snow and so long that it fell below his waist; for the waggon was full of lights and it was easy to distinguish everything in it. It was driven by two ugly demons dressed in the same buckram, with such hideous faces that once Sancho had seen them he closed his eyes for fear of seeing them again. Then, when the waggon came up opposite the place where they were standing, the venerable old man rose from his high seat and, standing up, called in a loud voice: 'I am the sage Lirgandeo.' Then the waggon passed on without another word. Behind it came another of the same kind, with another old man on a throne, who made the waggon stop and in a voice no less solemn than the first cried: 'I am the sage Alquipe, close friend of Urganda the Unknown.' He passed on, and immediately yet another waggon of the same kind appeared, though the man seated on the throne was not old like the others, but a very stout fellow of an evil appearance who, on coming up, arose like the others, and proclaimed in harsher and more devilish tones: 'I am Arcalaus the enchanter, the mortal enemy of Amadis of Gaul and all his kin'; and passed on. The three waggons halted a little way off, and the deafening din of their wheels ceased. After that there was no further noise but the sound of soft and harmonious music, which delighted

Sancho, who took it for a good omen, and said to the Duchess, from whom he had not stirred by so much as an inch: 'Lady, where there's music there can be no mischief.'

'Nor where there are lights and brightness,' replied the Duchess.

To which Sancho answered: 'Flame may give light and bon-fires brightness, as we can see, but they may very well scorch us. But music is always a sign of feasting and merriment.'

'That remains to be seen,' said Don Quixote, who was listening. And he was right, as the following chapter will show.

Chapter XXXV. *A Continuation of Don Quixote's Instructions for the Disenchantment of Dulcinea, and other wonderful things.*

IN time to the delightful music they saw a triumphal car approaching, drawn by six grey mules and covered in white linen; and on each beast rode a penitent, also dressed in white, with a great lighted wax torch in his hand. This waggon was twice, or even three times, bigger than the previous ones. On the front of it and at the side were twelve other penitents, white as snow, all with their torches alight, a sight both marvellous and terrifying. On a raised throne was seated a nymph swathed in countless veils of gold tissue, which made her appear, if not richly, at least gorgeously apparelled. Her face was covered with a delicate and transparent veil, in such a way that its folds did not prevent them from making the features of a lovely maiden; and the multitude of lights made it possible to distinguish her beauty and her youth, for she seemed to be neither more than twenty nor less than seventeen. Beside her came a figure swathed to the feet in a trailing robe which brushed the ground, with his head covered by a black veil. At the moment when the waggon arrived opposite the Duke and Duchess and Don Quixote the music of the oboes ceased, and soon the harps and lutes which were being played in the waggon ceased also. Then, rising to his feet, the figure in the robe threw its folds aside and, stripping the veil from his face, revealed plainly the very shape of Death, fleshless and hideous, which caused Don Quixote some disturbance and Sancho some alarm, while the Duke and Duchess assumed an appearance of fear.

This living Death rose upon his feet, and began to speak in a drowsy voice and with a sleepy articulation, after this manner:

> I Merlin am who, as the histories say,
> Had for my father even the Devil himself
> (A lie by lapse of time now authorized),
> Prince of the Magic Art, repository
> And monarch of the Zoroastrian science.
> Jealous I am of ages and of times
> Which seek to cloak the exploits of the brave
> Knights errant, whom I loved in ancient days,
> And still do love with deep affection.
> Although the nature of enchanters and
> Those that are wizards and magicians is
> Perpetually hard and harsh and stern,
> Yet mine is tender, soft and amorous,
> Loving to do good deeds to one and all.
>   Into the murky caverns of black Dis,
> Where my soul was, fast occupied in drawing
> Certain rhomboids and mystic characters,
> There came the piteous voice of that fair maid,
> The peerless Dulcinea del Toboso.
> I learnt of her enchantment and mischance,
> And transformation from a highborn lady
> Into a rustic village wench. I grieved,
> And caged my spirit in the hollow shell
> Of this most dreadful and fierce skeleton.
> But after searching through ten thousand books
> Of this, my devilish and my vile craft,
> I come to bring the fitting remedy
> To such a grief and to so great an ill.
>   O you, glory and pride of all who wear
> The coat of steel and hardest adamant,
> O Light, O lantern, path, pole-star and guide
> Of those who, casting off their sluggish sleep
> And feather beds, make themselves strong to endure
> The intolerable use and exercise
> Of sanguinary and laborious arms,
> To you I say, great Hero never praised
> Enough, yet ever praised, most valiant
> And at the same time most wise Don Quixote,
> La Mancha's splendour and the star of Spain,
> That to restore into her pristine state
> The peerless Dulcinea del Toboso,
> Needful it is that your squire, Sancho Panza,

Shall deal himself three thousand and three hundred
Lashes upon his two most ample buttocks,
Both to the air exposed, and in such sort
That they shall smart, and sting and vex him sorely.
This is the universal resolution
Of all the authors of her sad misfortunes;
And therefore, lords and ladies, have I come.

'My goodness!' exclaimed Sancho. 'Three thousand lashes! But I'd as soon give myself three stabs as three lashes. The devil take this way of disenchanting! I don't see what my buttocks have got to do with these enchantments. By God, if Master Merlin doesn't find another way of disenchanting the lady Dulcinea del Toboso, she may go enchanted to her grave!'

'I will take you,' said Don Quixote, 'Don Yokel, stuffed with garlic, and I will bind you to a tree, naked as your mother bore you, and not only will I give you three thousand three hundred, but six thousand six hundred lashes, so well laid on that it will take more than three thousand three hundred tugs to pull them off. Do not answer me a word, or I will tear your soul out.'

But on hearing this Merlin observed: 'It must not be done that way. The lashes the good Sancho is to get must not be applied by force, but must be of his own free will; and at such time as he pleases, for there is no date fixed. But it is permitted him, if he wishes to cut this whipping down by half, to receive it at the hand of another, though it must be a fairly weighty hand.'

'At no one else's, nor at my own. Nor shall it be a weighty one, nor one that can be weighed,' replied Sancho. 'No hand whatever shall touch me. Was it I that bore the lady Dulcinea del Toboso, that my buttocks shall pay for the sins of her eyes? My master, now, he's a part of her; for every moment he's calling her *his life* and *his soul* – his support and his prop. He can whip himself for her – and he should – and do all that's needful for her disenchantment. But me whip myself? I bernounce.'

Scarcely had Sancho finished speaking when the silvery nymph who rode beside Merlin rose to her feet and, flinging the thin veil from her face, revealed a countenance which seemed to all excessively lovely. Then, with a masculine assurance and in no very lady-like tones, she addressed Sancho Panza directly: 'O wretched squire with no more soul than a pitcher, with heart of cork, and bowels of flint and pebble! If you were commanded, shameless thief, to cast yourself to the ground off a huge tower; if they bade you, enemy of the human race, to eat a dozen toads, two dozen lizards and three dozen snakes; if they entreated you to kill your wife and children with a fierce and sharp scimitar, it would be no wonder were you to appear squeamish and reluctant. But to make a to-do about three thousand three hundred lashes, when the most wretched charity scholar gets as many every month; that amazes, astonishes and affrights the compassionate bowels of all who hear of it, and of everyone too who may come, in the course of time, to hear of it. Cast, you miserable, hard-hearted animal, cast, I say, those startled owl's eyes of yours upon these pupils of mine, which have been compared to glittering stars, and see them weep thread by thread and skein by skein, making furrows, tracks and channels down the fair fields of my cheeks. Let it move you, knavish and malevolent monster, that my blooming youth – for I am still in my teens: I am nineteen and not yet twenty – is being consumed and withered beneath the skin of a rustic peasant girl; and if I do not look like one now, that is a particular favour that the lord Merlin, here present, has done me, solely in order that my features may soften you; that the tears of a distressed beauty may turn rocks into cotton and tigers into sheep. Lash, lash that thick hide of yours, you great untamed beast; raise up from sloth that spirit which inclines you to eating and still more eating, and set at liberty the smoothness of my skin, the meekness of my temper and the beauty of my countenance. But if you will not relent for me or submit to any reasonable terms, do so for the sake of that poor knight there at your side; for your master, I say, whose soul I can now see stuck in his throat, not ten inches from his lips, only awaiting your answer, harsh or kind, to issue through his mouth or return to his breast.'

On hearing this, Don Quixote felt his throat and said, turning to the Duke: 'By God, sir, Dulcinea has spoken the truth, for here is my soul sticking in my throat like the nut of a crossbow.'

'What do you say to that, Sancho?' asked the Duchess.

'I say, lady,' replied Sancho, 'what I've said already, that as for the lashes I bernounce them.'

'*Renounce* you should say, Sancho, and not what you said,' observed the Duke.

'Let me alone, your Highness, I'm in no state now to look into subtleties or to consider a letter or two more or less; for these lashes I'm to get, or I'm to give myself, have so upset me that I don't know what I'm saying or doing. But I should like to hear from the lady, from my lady Doña Dulcinea del Toboso, where she learnt her way of begging. She comes to ask me to tear my flesh open with lashes and calls me *pitcher-soul* and *great untamed beast*, and a string of other bad names – may the Devil bear them! Is my flesh, by chance, brass? And does it matter to me whether she's disenchanted or not? What hamper of fine linen, shirts, kerchiefs and socks – though I don't wear them – does she bring with her to soften me? None, but just one piece of abuse on top of another, though she knows the local proverb, that an ass loaded with gold goes lightly up a mountain; and that gifts break rocks; and praying God and wielding the hammer; and a bird in the hand is worth two in the bush. Then my lord and master, who should be stroking my neck and wheedling me to make myself soft as wool or carded cotton, says that if he catches me he'll bind me naked to a tree and double the dose of lashes. These compassionate gentlemen should consider that they're not just asking a squire to whip himself, but a governor, which is, as you might say, gilding the lily. Let them learn, let them learn – the devil take them – how to ask, and how to beg, and how to show their breeding; for all times are not the same, and men are not always in a good humour. Now I'm ready to burst with grief because of the tear in my green coat, and they come and ask me to whip myself of my own free will, which I'd as soon do as turn Red Indian.'

'Then, truly, friend Sancho,' said the Duke, 'if you do not get yourself softer than a ripe fig, you shall not set a hand on the government. It would be a fine thing if I were to send my islesmen a cruel governor with bowels of flint, who would not bow to the tears of distressed maidens nor to the petitions of wise, haughty and ancient enchanters and sages. To be brief, Sancho, either you shall be whipped, or you shall whip yourself, or you shall not be governor.'

'Sir,' answered Sancho, 'won't they give me two days to consider what is best for me?'

'No, on no account,' said Merlin. 'Here, at this instant and on this spot the issue of this business must be settled. Either Dulcinea shall return to the cave of Montesinos and to her former state of peasant girl, or she shall be carried in her present shape to the Elysian fields, where she will wait till the number of lashes is complete.'

'Come, good Sancho,' said the Duchess, 'be of good heart, and show your gratitude to Don Quixote for his bread that you have eaten, for we are all bound to serve him and to please him for his worthy character and his high chivalry. Accept this lashing, my son, and let the devil go to the devil and fear to the faint-hearted, for a good heart breaks bad luck, as you well know.'

To this advice Sancho replied by addressing Merlin with an inquiry well off the point: 'Tell me, your worship, Sir Merlin; when the courier-devil came here, he gave my master a message from Sir Montesinos, bidding him wait for him here, since he was going to give him instructions for the disenchantment of the lady Doña Dulcinea del Toboso. Yet so far we haven't seen Montesinos or anyone like him.'

To which Merlin replied: 'The Devil, friend Sancho, is an ass and a very great scamp. I sent him to seek your master with a message not from Montesinos but from me. For Montesinos is in his cave awaiting his disenchantment, or rather hoping for it, for there is still the tail to skin. If he owes you anything, or you have any business to do with him, I will bring him to you, and put him wherever you like. But now make up your mind to accept this penance and, believe me, it will be of great advantage to you, both to your soul and to your body; to your soul because of the charity with which you do it, and to your body because you are of a sanguine temperament, I know, and it can do you no harm to lose a little blood.'

'Many doctors there are in the world – even enchanters are doctors,' replied Sancho, 'but since they all tell me so – though I don't see it myself – I agree to give myself the three thousand three hundred lashes, on condition that I can do it whenever I choose, without any fixing of times and seasons. I'll try to wipe off the debt as soon as possible, so that the world may enjoy the beauty of the lady Doña Dulcinea del Toboso, for it appears that she's really beautiful, though I never thought she was. But there must be one other condition, that I shan't be obliged to draw blood with this whipping, and if any of the lashes are only fly-teasers they must be reckoned in. Also if I make a mistake in the number Sir Merlin, since he knows everything, shall take care to keep count and advise me of the number too many or too few.'

'There will be no need to advise you of any too many,' answered Merlin. 'For the lady Dulcinea will be disenchanted at the very moment when you reach the exact number, and will come in gratitude to look for the good Sancho to give him thanks and a reward too for his good deed. So there is no need to be scrupulous about a few lashes too many or too few, and Heaven forbid that I should deceive anyone, even by so much as a hair's breadth.'

'Well, then, in God's hands be it!' said Sancho. 'I accept my bad luck ... I say that I agree to the penance with the conditions noted.'

No sooner had Sancho pronounced these last words than the music of the oboes struck up once more, and a great number of muskets were fired. Don Quixote hung on Sancho's neck, giving him countless kisses on his forehead and his cheeks. The Duchess and the Duke and all the spectators showed signs of the greatest satisfaction, and the waggon began to move off. As the fair Dulcinea passed she bowed her head to the Duke and Duchess and made a deep curtsey to Sancho.

And now the gay and smiling dawn came on apace; the little flowers of the fields raised their heads and stood erect; and the liquid crystals of the brooks, murmuring over the white and grey pebbles, went to pay tribute to the expectant rivers. The merry earth, the clear sky, the pure air, the serene light, each and all together gave manifest signs that the day, which came treading on the skirts of the dawn, would be calm and bright. Delighted with the chase and at the skill and success of their plans, the Duke and Duchess returned to their castle with the intention of following up their joke, for nothing promised them greater pleasure.

Chapter XXXVI. *Of the strange and inconceivable Adventure of the Afflicted Waiting-woman, alias the Countess Trifaldi, with a letter which Sancho Panza wrote to his wife, Teresa Panza.*

IT was a steward of the Duke's, a very comical and nimble-witted fellow, who had played the part of Merlin and arranged all the details of the last adventure. He had composed the verses and made a page play Dulcinea, and now with the collaboration of his master and mistress he contrived another plan, the most amusing and the strangest imaginable.

Next day the Duchess enquired of Sancho whether he had begun upon the penance he had undertaken for the disenchanting of Dulcinea; and he replied that he had, for on the night before he had given himself five strokes. But when the Duchess asked with what instrument he replied that it was with his hand.

'That,' said the Duchess, 'is more like a slapping than a whipping. It is my opinion that the sage Merlin will not be content with such softness. The good Sancho will have to get a whip with prickles or a cat o'nine tails, that can be felt; for learning must be beaten in, and the release of a great lady like Dulcinea must not be sold so cheap. Remember, Sancho, that works of charity which are performed feebly and half-heartedly have no merit and are worth nothing.'

To which Sancho replied: 'Give me a whip or a proper rope's end, your ladyship, and I'll use it, so long as it doesn't hurt me too much. For I would have your Grace know that, peasant though I am, my flesh is more like cotton than rushes, and it would not be right for me to destroy myself for someone else's good.'

'Very well,' answered the Duchess. 'To-morrow I will give you a whip which will just suit you, and agree with the tenderness of your flesh like its own sister.'

To which Sancho replied: 'I must tell you, your Highness, dear lady of my heart, that I've written a letter to my wife, Teresa Panza, giving her an account of everything that's happened to me since I left her. I have it here inside my shirt. There's nothing lacking but the signature. I wish that your Wisdom would read it, for I think it's written in a governor's style – I mean in the way that governors should write.'

'And who dictated it?' asked the Duchess.

'Who should have dictated it but myself, poor sinner that I am?' answered Sancho.

'And did you write it yourself?' asked the Duchess.

'Not a bit of it,' answered Sancho, 'for I can't read or write, though I can make my mark.'

'Let us see it,' said the Duchess, 'for no doubt it will display the quality and aptness of your wit.'

On which Sancho drew from his breast an unsealed letter, which the Duchess took, and saw that it ran like this:

Sancho Panza's letter to Teresa Panza, his wife.

If it is a good whipping they gave me it is a fine mount I have now; if I have a good governorship it cost me a good whipping. You will not understand this now, dear Teresa, but one day you will. I must tell you, Teresa, that I am determined you shall ride in a coach, for that is the proper thing; every other way of travelling is like going on all fours. Wife of a governor you are; see if anyone will tread on your heels. I am sending you herewith a green hunts-man's suit, which my lady the Duchess gave me. Turn it into a bodice and skirt for our daughter. Don Quixote, my master, as I have heard tell in these parts, is a sane madman and a droll idiot, and they say I am just as bad. We have been in Montesinos' cave; and the Sage Merlin has got me to help in the disenchantment of Dul-cinea del Toboso, whom you at home call Aldonza Lorenzo. With three thousand three hundred lashes – less five – which I am to give myself, she will be as disenchanted as the mother that bore her. You will tell nobody about this; for take your business to court and some will say it is white and some black. In a few days I shall leave for my governorship, to which I go very anxious to make money, and I am told that all new governors go in the same frame of mind. I will take its pulse and advise you if you are to come with me or no. Dapple is well, and sends his greetings; I do not intend to leave him behind, even if I am taken to be made Grand Turk. My lady the Duchess kisses your hands a thousand times. Send her two thousand kisses in return, for there is nothing that costs less or goes cheaper,

*as my master says, than fair compliments. God has not been pleased
to furnish me with another bag of another hundred crowns like the
last time, but do not let that worry you, Teresa dear, for the man
who sounds the alarm is safe, and it will all come out in the wash – I
mean the governorship. Only one thing troubles me: they say that
once I taste it I shall eat my hands after it, and if that is so I shall
not get off very cheap, although the maimed and handless find begging alms as good as a canonry. So, one way or another, you will be
rich and fortunate. God grant it you, as he can, and preserve me to
serve you. From this castle, the 20th of July 1614.*

> *Your husband the governor*
> *Sancho Panza.*

When she had finished reading the letter, the Duchess said to
Sancho: 'There are two small matters in which the worthy governor
is a little astray. The first is in saying, or leaving it to be understood,
that he has been given this governorship in return for the whipping
he has to take, though he knows, as he cannot deny, that when my
lord the Duke promised it to him no one dreamt that there was such
a thing as a whipping in the world. The other is that he reveals considerable covetousness, and I would not like him to turn out badly,
for covetousness burst the bag, and the greedy governor does ill-
governed justice.'

'I don't mean all that, lady,' answered Sancho; 'and if your worship thinks that this letter doesn't go as it should, I've only to tear
it up and write a new one, though maybe it'll be a worse one, if it's
left to my poor brain.'

'No, no,' replied the Duchess. 'It is a good one, and I want the
Duke to see it.'

Upon this they went out into a garden, where they were to dine
that day, and the Duchess showed Sancho's letter to the Duke, who
was highly delighted with it. They dined, and when the cloths had
been removed and they had amused themselves for a good while
with Sancho's savoury conversation, they suddenly heard the doleful sound of a fife and the harsh beating of an untuned drum. Everyone seemed disturbed by this confused, warlike and melancholy
music, especially Don Quixote, who could not sit still for pure excitement. Of Sancho it can only be said that fear took him to his ac-

customed refuge, which was at the Duchess's side or in her skirts; for in sober earnest the sound they heard was most doleful and melancholy. Then, while they were all waiting in suspense, they saw coming down the garden before them two men clad in mourning robes so long and flowing that they trailed on the ground; and as they came they beat two great drums also swathed in black. By their side walked the fifer, pitch black like them, and these three were followed by a personage of gigantic size, bemantled rather than clad, in the blackest of cloaks with a monstrously long train. Over his cloak he wore a broad shoulder-strap, black as well, from which hung a huge scimitar with black hilts and sheath. His face was covered by a transparent black veil, through which could be seen a very long and snow-white beard, and he kept step to the drum-beats with great gravity and composure. To be brief, his size, his solemn gait, his blackness and his escort were sufficient to produce the amazement they did in all who saw him and did not know who he was. Thus he approached in slow and ceremonious state and knelt before the Duke, who with everyone else present awaited him standing, and would not allow him to speak until he had risen up. This the prodigious scarecrow did and, once on his feet, raised the mask from his face to reveal the most horrid, long, white, thick beard ever till then beheld by human eyes. Then from his broad and swelling chest he strained and forced out a grave and sonorous voice, fixing his eyes on the Duke as he spoke:

'Most high and powerful lord, my name is Trifaldin of the White Beard. I am squire to the Countess Trifaldi, otherwise called the Afflicted Waiting-woman, on whose behalf I bring your Highness a message. It is that your Magnificence should be pleased to grant her faculty and licence to enter and tell you of her plight, which is one of the strangest and most amazing that any troubled mind in all the world could imagine. But first she wishes to know whether in this castle of yours there is staying the valorous and unconquered knight Don Quixote de la Mancha, to seek whom she has come on foot and fasting from the kingdom of Candaya to this your realm, a journey which should rightfully be reckoned miraculous or performed by force of enchantment. She is waiting at the door of this fortress or country-house, and only awaits your good pleasure to enter. I have spoken.'

Then he coughed and stroked his beard from top to bottom with both hands, in great composure awaiting the Duke's reply, which was: 'Many days ago, good squire Trifaldin of the White Beard, we heard of the distress of my lady Countess Trifaldi, whom enchanters have caused to be called the Afflicted Waiting-woman. You may gladly tell her to enter, stupendous squire, and that the valiant knight Don Quixote de la Mancha is here, from whose generous nature she may safely expect every protection and aid. You may tell her also on my behalf that if she is in need of my help it shall not fail her, for I am bound to aid her by my knighthood, which compels me to favour every sort of women, in particular widowed matrons in distress and affliction – for such her ladyship must be.'

On hearing this Trifaldin bent his knee to the ground and, motioning the fife and drums to strike up, quitted the garden to the same music and at the same pace as he had come in, leaving everyone amazed at his presence and gravity. Then the Duke turned to Don Quixote and said: 'To be sure, renowned knight, neither the darkness of malice nor of ignorance can cover and obscure the light of valour and virtue. This I say because, virtuous sir, you have hardly been six days with us in this castle, and already the sorrowful and afflicted come from far-off and distant lands to seek you; and not in coaches or on dromedaries, but on foot and fasting, confident of finding in that mighty arm the remedy for their distresses and hardships, thanks to your great deeds which cover and circle the whole of the known world.'

'I wish, Sir Duke,' replied Don Quixote, 'that blessed man of religion were here, who showed at table the other day so great a distaste for knights errant and so malignant a grudge against them, so that he might see with his own eyes whether such knights are necessary in the world. He would at least have certain evidence that your extraordinarily afflicted and disconsolate in harsh predicaments and appalling misfortunes do not go to seek their remedy at the houses of scholars, nor at the village sexton's, nor to the knight who has never ventured beyond the boundaries of his town, nor to the slothful courtier, who had rather look for news to tell and repeat than attempt to perform deeds and exploits for others to relate and write down. Remedy for distresses, relief in hardship, succouring

of maidens and consoling of widows are nowhere so readily to be obtained as from knights errant. I give infinite thanks to Heaven that
I am one, and I do not repine at whatever trouble or hardship may
befall me in this most honourable exercise. Let the waiting-woman
come in and ask what she will; for I will work her relief by the
strength of my arm and the dauntless resolution of my courageous
spirit.'

Chapter XXXVII. *The famous Adventure of the Afflicted Wait-ing-woman continued.*

THE Duke and Duchess were highly delighted to see how well Don
Quixote responded to their plan. But at that point Sancho exclaimed: 'I shouldn't like this lady to lay any stumbling-block in the
way of my promised government, for once I heard a Toledo
apothecary say – and he talked like a linnet – that where waiting-
women meddled no good could come of it. Heavens alive, how that
apothecary disliked them! Now since, as far as I can make out, all
waiting-women are meddlers and trouble-makers, whatever their
quality or condition, what will they be like when they're afflicted,
as they say this Countess Three Skirts or Three Tails is? – for in
my country skirts and tails, tails and skirts, are all the same.'

'Be quiet, Sancho my friend,' said Don Quixote, 'for since this
waiting-lady comes from such distant lands to seek me, she cannot
be one of those in the apothecary's reckoning. Particularly since she
is a countess; and when countesses serve as waiting-women it
will be in the service of Queens and Empresses, for in their own
houses they are high ladies, and are served by other waiting-
women.'

At which Doña Rodriguez, who was present, spoke up: 'My
lady the Duchess has waiting-women in her service who might
have been countesses in their own right, if Fortune had been kind.
But laws go as kings will. Let no one speak ill of waiting-women,
particularly when they are old and unmarried; for though I am not
one, yet I can easily see and appreciate the advantage that a maiden
waiting-woman has over a widow; and the man who clipped us still
has the shears in his hand.'

'All the same,' replied Sancho, 'there's so much to shear in these waiting-women, according to my barber, that it would be better not to stir the rice, even though it cakes.'

'Squires are always our enemies,' replied Doña Rodriguez. 'For, seeing that they are the imps of the antechambers and watch us at every turn, such times as they are not praying – and those are many – they spend in gossiping about us, disinterring our bones and interring our good names. But let me tell those animated logs that we shall live in the world in spite of them – and in the houses of the great – though we die of hunger and cover our bodies, delicate or otherwise, with black weeds like a nun's, as a dung-hill is sometimes covered up with a sheet on the day of a procession. I can assure you that if I were allowed, and the time were right, I would let them know – not only those present but the whole world – that there is no virtue that you will not find in a waiting-woman.'

'I believe,' said the Duchess, 'that my good Doña Rodriguez is right, very right. But she must wait for a fitting time to defend herself and other waiting-women, to refute the bad opinion of that evil apothecary and to uproot it entirely from the breast of the great Sancho Panza.'

To which Sancho replied: 'Since I've had a sniff at a governorship all squirely vapours have left me, and I don't give a wild fig for all the waiting-women in the world.'

They would have continued with the waiting-woman controversy, had they not heard the fife and drums strike up again to announce the approach of the Afflicted One. The Duchess then asked the Duke whether it would be right to go and receive her, since she was a countess and a lady of rank.

'In so far as she's a countess,' observed Sancho, before the Duke could reply, 'I'm for your Highness's going out to receive her; but in so far as she's a waiting-woman I'm of the opinion you shouldn't stir a step.'

'Who asked you to meddle in this, Sancho?' asked Don Quixote.

'Who, sir?' answered Sancho. 'I meddle, and I've a right to meddle, as a squire who has learnt the laws of courtesy in your worship's school. For you're the most courteous and well-bred knight there is in all courtship; and in these matters, as I've heard your worship say, you may lose as much by a card too many as by a card too few, and good ears need few words.'

'It is as Sancho says,' said the Duke. 'We will see the shape of the countess, and measure by that the courtesy due to her.'

At this the drums and fife came in as before – and here the author ended this brief chapter and began the next, pursuing the same adventure, one of the most notable in the story.

Chapter XXXVIII. *The Afflicted Waiting-woman relates her Misfortune.*

BEHIND the melancholy musicians there began to enter the further part of the garden some waiting-women to the number of twelve, divided into two files, all dressed in ample nuns' habits, seemingly of milled serge, with white stoles of fine Indian muslin, so long that only the edge of their habits showed. Behind them came the Countess Trifaldi, whom the squire Trifaldin of the White Beard led by the hand, she clothed in finest black blanket-cloth, unnapped – for had it been napped every grain would have shown up the size of a good Martos chick-pea. Her tail or skirt, or whatever they call it, fell in three trains, which were borne by three pages, also dressed in mourning and forming a handsome mathematical figure with the three acute angles formed by the three trains, whence it was concluded that she got her name of the Countess Trifaldi, as one might say the *Countess with the Three Skirts*. This, Benengeli says, was correct, for her proper title was the Countess *Lobuna*, from the many wolves bred in her country; and if they had been foxes instead of wolves she would have been the Countess *Zorruna*, it being a custom in those parts for owners to take their titles from the thing or things most abundant on their estates; but to celebrate the novelty of her skirt, this countess dropped *Lobuna* and took the name of *Trifaldi*.

The lady and her twelve waiting-women advanced at a processional pace, their faces covered with black veils, which were not transparent like Trifaldin's, but so thick that nothing showed through them. As soon as this squadron of waiting-women appeared, the Duke, the Duchess and Don Quixote stood up, as did everyone else who was watching the slow procession. The twelve waiting-women stopped and made a passage, through the middle of which the Afflicted One advanced without letting go of Trifaldin's hand. At this the Duke, the Duchess and Don Quixote advanced a matter of a dozen paces to receive her. Then, sinking on to her knees on the ground, she cried in a voice rather coarse and rough than subtle and delicate:

'May it please your Highnesses to show less courtesy to this your waiting-man – I should say waiting-woman. For, as I am the Afflicted One, I shall not be able to reply to you as I ought, since my strange and unparalleled misfortune has carried off my wits I know not where, – but it must be a long way, for the more I seek them the less I find them.'

'He would lack wits, lady Countess,' replied the Duke, 'who did not from your person discover your worth, which, without further examination, is deserving of all the cream of courtesy and all the flower of courtly ceremony.'

And, raising her by the hand, he took her to sit in a seat beside the Duchess, who also received her with great politeness. Don Quixote was silent, and Sancho was dying to see the faces of the Countess and of some of her many ladies; but this was not possible till they uncovered themselves of their own will and accord. All were calm and stood in silence, waiting for someone to break it, which the Afflicted Lady did with these words:

'I am confident, most powerful lord, most lovely lady and most wise company, that my extreme affliction will find in your most valiant breasts a reception no less assured than generous and compassionate. For such it is that it could melt marble, soften adamant, and mollify the steel of the most hardened hearts in the world. But, before it is published in your hearings, not to say in your ears, I should like to be made cognizant whether there is in this body, circle and company that most stainless of knights, Don Quixote de la Manchissima, and his most squirely Panza.'

'The Panza,' said Sancho, before any one else could reply, 'is here, and the Don Quixotissimo as wellissimo; and so, most Afflicted and most Waiting-ladylike of Ladies, you may say whatever you wishimo, for we are all ready and most prepared to be your servitorissimos.'

At this Don Quixote got up and, addressing himself to the Afflicted Lady, said: 'If your distresses, anguished lady, can promise you any hope of relief through any valour or prowess of any knight errant, here is my arm which, short and feeble as it is, shall be wholly employed in your service. I am Don Quixote de la Mancha, whose function it is to succour the necessitous of all sorts; and that being so, assuredly you have no need, lady, to sue for favours, nor to hunt for preambles, but only to state your grievances plainly and without circumlocutions, for your hearers will know how, if not to relieve them, at least to commiserate with them.'

At these words the Afflicted Lady seemed about to fling herself at Don Quixote's feet. Indeed she did throw herself down, and struggled to embrace them, saying: 'Before these feet and legs I throw myself, unconquered knight, for they are the bases and pillars of knight errantry. I would kiss these feet, on whose steps hangs and depends the whole remedy of my misfortune. O valorous knight errant, whose veritable deeds outdistance and obscure the fabulous exploits of the Amadises, Esplandians, and Belianises!'

Then, leaving Don Quixote, she turned to Sancho Panza and, seizing him by the hands, exclaimed: 'O loyalest squire that ever served knight errant in ages present or past, whose goodness is greater than the beard of Trifaldin, my attendant here present! Well may you pride yourself that in serving the great Don Quixote you are serving, symbolically, the whole troop of knights who have ever handled arms in all the world. I conjure you by all you owe to your great benevolence and fidelity to be my kind intercessor with your master that he may immediately favour this most humble and most afflicted Countess.'

'As to my goodness, my lady,' answered Sancho, 'being as long and as large as your squire's beard, that means very little to me. Let me have my soul bearded and whiskered when I quit this life: that's what matters. For the beards of this world I care little or nothing. But without these wiles and prayers I will ask my master – and I know he loves me well, especially now that he has need of me in a certain business – to favour and aid your grace in whatever he can. Unload your distress, relate it to us, and leave the rest to us, for we shall all understand one another.'

The Duke and Duchess were bursting with laughter at this passage, and so was everyone else who had taken the measure of the adventure. And in their hearts they praised the shrewdness and cunning of the Trifaldi, who returned to her seat and said: 'Of the

famous kingdom of Candaya, which lies between the great Tapro-
bona and the Southern Sea, six miles beyond Cape Comorin,
Queen Doña Maguncia was mistress. Widow she was of King
Archipiela, her lord and husband, by which marriage they got and
procreated the Princess Antonomasia, heiress of their kingdom.
Which said Princess Antonomasia was bred and grew up under my
tutelage and teaching, since I was her mother's most ancient and
chiefest waiting-lady. It happened then that, in the course of time,
the girl Antonomasia reached the age of fourteen in such perfection
of beauty that nature could not raise her a point higher. Her wits,
too, were far from contemptible. She was as intelligent as she was
lovely. She was the most beautiful creature in the world; and is so
yet, if the envious fairies and hard-hearted Fates have not cut the
thread of her life. But that they will not have done, for Heaven could
not permit such evil to be done on earth, and a cluster from the fairest
vine in the vineyard to be carried off unripe. Her beauty, insufficiently praised by my dull tongue, caused an infinite number of
princes, both native and foreign, to fall in love with her; and among
those who dared to raise his thoughts to the heaven of so much
loveliness was a knight of low degree there was at court, who relied
on his youth and gallantry, his many accomplishments and graces,
and the ease and brilliance of his wit. And I would have your Highnesses know, if I am not boring you, that he could play a guitar so
well that he made it speak; and, what is more, he was a poet and a
great dancer, and was so good at making bird-cages that he could
have earned his living by their manufacture if he had been in extreme need. Now all these talents and graces would have been
sufficient to move a mountain, let alone a delicate maiden. But all
his graces and charms, all his endowments and accomplishments,
would have been ineffectual against the fortress of my child's
virtue, if the shameless thief had not resorted to the expedient of
winning me first. First the cursed, godless vagabond set about gaining my goodwill and buying my consent to hand over to him,
like a bad custodian, the keys of the fortress I was guarding. In
short he wheedled me and forced my agreement with all manner of
toys and trifles that he gave me. But what chiefly overthrew me and
brought me to the ground were some verses which I heard him sing
one night, from a barred window which gave upon the narrow

street where he was standing. If I remember rightly they ran like this:

> " An ill doth wound me to the soul,
> Struck by my sweetest enemy,
> Yet what most tormenteth me
> Is that my hurt I must conceal."

'The song seemed to me pearls and his voice syrup, and from that time till now, let me tell you, considering the harm I fell into through these and other such verses, I have been of opinion that poets should be banished from good and well ordered states, as Plato counselled; – at least the lewd ones – for the verses they write are not like the poem about the Marquis of Mantua, which delights and brings tears to the eyes of women and children, but are barbed couplets, which like smooth thorns pierce your soul and wound you there like lightning, leaving your clothes untouched.

'Another time he sang:

> "Come death quietly, without pain.
> Let me not thy coming know,
> That the pleasure to die so
> Make me not to live again."

And many other little verses and refrains of this kind, which enchant when sung, and surprise when read. Then what if they stoop to compose a kind of poem which was then in fashion in Candaya called a roundelay? That makes your soul leap up and laughter tickle in your throat; it fills your body with unease and, in short, is like mercury to all the senses. So, I tell you, my lords, such minstrels ought to be exiled to the islands of lizards. It is not they that are to blame, however, but the simpletons who praise them and the foolish women who believe them. If I had been the good waiting-woman I should have been, his stale conceits would not have moved me, and I could not have believed that he was speaking the truth when he said: "*Dying I live, in frost I burn; In fire I tremble; I hope without hope, I go and stay;*" with other impossibilities of that stamp, of which their writings are full. Then, when they promise the Phoenix of Arabia, Ariadne's crown, the horses of the Sun and the pearls of the South, the gold of Tibar, the balsam of Pancaya! That is where they stretch their pens farthest, for it costs them little to promise what they never intend to, nor can perform. But, where am I digressing to? Alas, I am a luckless creature! What madness or what folly leads me to recite the faults of others, having so much to say of my own? O unlucky I am, I repeat, for it was not the verses that conquered me, but my own guilelessness. It was not the music, but my own lightness which seduced me. My great ignorance and lack of foresight opened the road and freed the path for the passage of Don Clavijo – for that is the name of the gentleman I mentioned. And so I was the go-between, and he found his way, not once but many times, to Antonomasia's room, though under the promise of marriage. By me she was beguiled and not by him, for, sinner that I was, I would not have consented to his approaching the edge of her slipper-sole without swearing to be her husband. No, no, not that! Marriage must always be the condition of any business of that kind I manage. There was only one difficulty in this affair, disparity of rank, since Don Clavijo was a private gentleman and Princess Antonomasia the heiress, as I have said, of the kingdom. For some time this intrigue was hidden and cloaked by my cunning precautions, till it became clear to me that it was speedily being revealed by a certain swelling of Antonomasia's belly, fear at which made the three of us take counsel together. And we decided that before the mischief came to light Don Clavijo should ask for Antonomasia's hand before the vicar, on the strength of a written promise of marriage which the Princess had made him, framed by my ingenuity in such strong terms that Samson himself could not have broken it. Our plan was put into effect, and the vicar examined the contract and took the lady's confession. She confessed openly, and he ordered her to be put under the care of a very honourable sergeant of the court.'

'So there are sergeants of the court and poets and roundelays in Candaya too,' interrupted Sancho. 'I swear it makes me think the world's the same everywhere. But pray hurry up, my lady Trifaldi; for it's late, and I'm dying to know the end of your long story.'

'Indeed I will,' answered the Countess.

Chapter XXXIX. *The Trifaldi continues her Stupendous and Memorable Story.*

EVERY word Sancho spoke delighted the Duchess as much as it vexed Don Quixote. But, commanding him to be silent, the Afflicted One went on: 'At length, after a great number of questions and answers, since the Princess persisted in her resolve without departing or wavering from her first declaration, the vicar pronounced in favour of Don Clavijo and entrusted her to him as his lawful wife, which so annoyed the queen, Doña Maguncia, Princess Antonomasia's mother, that within three days we buried her.'

'She'll have died, no doubt,' exclaimed Sancho.

'That is obvious,' replied Trifaldin, 'for in Candaya we do not bury the living but the dead.'

'There have been cases, Sir Squire,' retorted Sancho, 'when they have buried someone who has fainted in the belief that he was dead. And it seemed to me that Queen Maguncia would have done better to swoon than to die, for with life much can be remedied, and the Princess's slip wasn't so great that they had to take it all that hard. Now if this lady had married one of her pages, or some other servant of the house, as many others have done, so I have heard tell, the damage would have been irreparable. But to have married a well-bred and clever knight, as you have just described him to us, really, really, though it was folly, it was not as bad as they think. For according to my master's rule, and he's here and won't let me lie, just as they make bishops of scholars, they can make Kings and Emperors of knights, especially if they're errants.'

'You are right, Sancho,' said Don Quixote, 'for a knight errant, if he has two grains of luck, has every potentiality for becoming the greatest lord in the world. But let the Afflicted Lady continue; for it is evident to me that the bitter part of this story – so far so sweet – remains to tell.'

'Indeed the bitter part is to come,' replied the Countess. 'And so bitter that bitter-apple is sweet and oleander savoury in comparison. The Queen was dead, not fainting, and we buried her. But no sooner had we covered her with earth and said our last farewell to her than – who but must weep to tell such grief? – on top of the Queen's grave appeared the giant Malambruno, mounted on a wooden horse.

He was first cousin to Maguncia, and not only cruel but an enchanter. Then, in revenge for his cousin's death and Don Clavijo's audacity, and to punish Antonomasia's boldness, by his magic arts he put the pair of them under a spell on top of the very grave itself. She was turned into a brass monkey, and he into a dreadful crocodile of an unknown metal; and between them stands a post, also of metal, with some characters written in the Syriac tongue, which, trans-lated into Candayesque and then into Castilian, make up this sen-tence:

"These two bold lovers will not regain their former shape until the valorous Manchegan comes to fight me in single combat; since for his great valour alone the Fates reserve this unparalleled ad-venture."

"The enchantment done, he drew from its sheath a broad and tre-mendous scimitar and, seizing me by the hair, made a feint of cut-ting my windpipe and shearing off my head at a blow. I was dis-traught; my voice stuck in my throat; I was terrified in the extreme. But, for all that, I mastered myself as best I could, and in trembling and piteous tones made him such a copious confession that he sus-pended the execution of that cruel punishment. Finally he had all the waiting-women in the palace brought before him, all these who are now present and, after enlarging on our fault and abusing the characters of our kind, their evil practices and wicked schemings, and loading on all of us the guilt which was mine alone, he said that he would not inflict capital punishment on us, but other protracted pains which would be a perpetual social death. Then the very in-stant he finished speaking we all felt the pores of our faces open, and a sensation as if we were being pricked all over them with needle-points. At once we clapped our hands to our cheeks and found our-selves in the state that you will now see.'

Then the Afflicted One and the other waiting-women lifted the veils which covered them and revealed their faces, all thick with beards, some fair, some black, some white and some grizzled, at the sight of which the Duke and Duchess made show of amazement, Don Quixote and Sancho were stupefied, and all the spectators aghast.

'In this way,' the Trifaldi proceeded, 'that wicked and evil-minded Malambruno punished us by covering the softness and smoothness of our skins with the roughness of these bristles. Would to Heaven he had cut off our heads with his enormous scimitar, instead of darkening the light of our faces with this fleece which covers us. For if we examine the matter, dear gentlemen – and what I am going to say now I should say with my eyes running a fountain of tears; though the thought of our misfortune and the seas which they have wept already keep them moistureless and dry as ears of corn, and therefore I shall speak without tears – where, I ask you, can a waiting-woman go with a beard? What mother or father will take pity on her? Who will give her aid? For even when she has a soft skin and tortures her face with a thousand sorts of lotions and cosmetics, she can scarcely find anyone to like her. So what shall she do when she reveals a face like a forest? O waiting-women, my companions, in an unlucky moment were we born; in an evil hour our parents begot us!' And as she spoke she gave a show of fainting.

Chapter XL. *Of Matters touching and pertaining to this Adventure and this memorable History.*

IN very truth, all who enjoy stories like this should show their gratitude to Cide Hamete, its first author, for his meticulousness in recording its minutest details, leaving nothing, however trivial, which he does not bring clearly to light. He depicts thoughts, reveals intentions, answers unspoken questions, clears up doubts, resolves objections; in fact elucidates the slightest points the most captious critic could raise. O most renowned author! O fortunate Don Quixote! O famous Dulcinea! O droll Sancho Panza! May you live, jointly and separately, for infinite ages, to the delight and general amusement of mankind!

The history goes on to tell that when Sancho saw the Afflicted Lady in a faint, he said: 'On the faith of an honest man and the memory of all my ancestors, the Panzas, I swear I've never heard or seen, nor has my master ever related to me, nor so much as imagined, an adventure like this. May a thousand devils take you – I would not abuse you, Malambruno – for the enchanter and giant you are! Could you find no other sort of punishment to inflict on these sinners except bearding them? Wouldn't it have been better and more fitting to their case to have cut off half their noses from the middle upwards, even if it had made them talk with a snuffle, rather than to have clapped beards on them? I'll bet they haven't enough money to pay for being shaved.'

'That is the truth, sir,' replied one of the twelve. 'We have not the means to cleanse ourselves. So, as an economical remedy, some of us have taken to using pitch or sticking plasters, applying them to our faces and pulling them off with a jerk, which makes us as bare and smooth as the bottom of a stone mortar. For although in Candaya there are women who go from house to house removing body-hairs, plucking eyebrows, and mixing various lotions of use to women, we, being my lady's waiting-women, would never let them in, for most of them smell of your go-betweens who have ceased to be principal parties. So, if we are not relieved by Don Quixote, with beards we shall be carried to the grave.'

'I would pluck mine out,' said Don Quixote, 'in the land of the Moors, if I could not relieve you of yours.'

At this point the Trifaldi recovered from her faint and said: 'The tinkling of that pledge, valorous knight, reached my ears in the midst of my swoon, and was instrumental in bringing me round and restoring my senses. So, once more I beg you, illustrious Errant and indomitable Sir, to put your gracious promise into effect.'

'There will be no delay on my account,' replied Don Quixote. 'Think, lady, what it is I am to do. For my courage is very ready to serve you.'

'The case is this,' answered the Afflicted One. 'From here to the Kingdom of Candaya, if you go by land, it is fifteen thousand miles to within half a dozen. But if you go by air and in a straight line it is nine thousand six hundred and eighty-one. You must also know that Malambruno told me that when Fortune should provide me with a knight to deliver us he would send him a mount, much better than your hired hacks, and with less vices; for it will be the same wooden horse on which the valiant Pierres carried off the fair Magalona. Which horse is guided by a peg in his forehead, which serves for a bridle, and he flies through the air with such speed that the devils themselves seem to be moving him. This same horse, according to ancient tradition, was made by the sage Merlin. He lent it to Pierres, who was his friend and made long journeys on him, and as I have said, stole the fair Magalona and bore her on his crupper through the air, leaving all who watched them from the earth staring like fools. He lent him only to those he liked or who paid him best, and from the great Pierres' time till now we know of nobody who has ridden him. Since then Malambruno has captured him by his arts, holds him in his power, and uses him on the voyages which he takes at times through different parts of the world – to-day he is here, to-morrow in France, and the day after in Potosi. And the good thing is that this horse does not eat or sleep or cost anything to shoe, but ambles at such a pace through the air, though he has no wings, that his rider may carry a cup full of water in his hand without spilling a drop, so smoothly and easily does he travel; for which reason the fair Magalona greatly enjoyed riding him.'

'For smooth and easy going,' interrupted Sancho, 'give me my Dapple. True, he does not go through the air, but on land I'll back him against any ambler in the world.'

Everyone laughed, and the Afflicted Lady went on: 'Now this same horse, if Malambruno intends to put an end to our trouble, will be here in our presence within half an hour of nightfall. For he informed me that the sign by which I should know that I had found the knight I was seeking would be his sending me the horse with all convenience and speed to the place where that knight might be.'

'How many, now, does this horse take?' asked Sancho.

'Two persons,' answered the Afflicted One, 'one on the saddle and the other on the crupper. Generally these two are knight and squire, when there is no stolen maiden.'

'I should like to know, Afflicted Lady,' said Sancho, 'what this horse is called.'

'His name,' replied the lady, 'is not that of Bellerophon's horse, who was called Pegasus; nor of Alexander the Great's, Bucephalus; nor of the furious Roland's, whose name was Brillador; nor yet Bayard, who belonged to Reynald of Montalban; nor Frontino like Ruggiero's; nor Bootes, nor Pirithous, which they say were the names of the horses of the Sun. Nor is he called Orelia either, like the horse on which the unfortunate Roderick, last king of the Goths, rode into the battle in which he lost his life and his kingdom.'

'I'll bet,' said Sancho, 'that seeing they haven't given him any of these famous names of well-known horses, they haven't given him the name of my master's mount, Rocinante, either, though it would fit a great deal better than any of those you've mentioned.'

'You are right,' replied the bearded Countess, 'but yet his name suits him well, for he is called Clavileño the Swift, which name fits him because he is wooden, because of the peg he has in his forehead and because of the speed at which he travels. So, as far as his name goes, he can easily compete with the famous Rocinante.'

'I don't dislike the name,' replied Sancho, 'but what sort of bridle or halter do you have to guide him by?'

'I have already told you,' answered the Trifaldi. 'By the peg. For by turning it in one direction or the other the rider can make him go where he will, either through the air, or brushing and, as it were, sweeping the earth, or by a middle course, which is the proper one for all well-ordered actions.'

'I should like to see him,' said Sancho, 'but to imagine that I'll ride him, either on saddle or crupper, is to want pears from an elm-tree. A fine thing indeed for them to ask me, who can scarcely keep on my Dapple and on a pack-saddle softer than silk itself, to get up on a wooden crupper, without so much as a pillow or a cushion. Lord bless me, I don't intend to bruise myself to take off anyone's beard. Let everyone be shaved as best he can. Nor do I propose to accompany my master on this long journey. Besides I've got nothing to do with the shaving of those beards, as I have with the disenchantment of Dulcinea.'

'Oh yes, you have, friend,' replied the Trifaldi, 'so much so that without your presence I understand we shall achieve nothing.'

'In the name of all the saints,' cried Sancho, 'what have squires to do with their master's adventures? Are they to get the renown for their successes and we to bear the burden? Oh no, no! Supposing now the historians were to say: such a knight achieved such and such an adventure, but with the help of so-and-so, his squire, without whom it would have been impossible to complete it. But they write baldly: Don Paralipomenon of the Three Stars brought off the adventure of the six spectres, no more giving the name of his squire who was present all through, than if he hadn't existed. Now, gentlemen, I say once more that my master can go alone, and much good may it do him. But I shall stay here in the company of my lady the Duchess, and maybe when he comes back he'll find the lady

Dulcinea's case in a very much better way. For I intend, in my idle and leisure moments, to give myself a bout of whipping without a stitch to cover me.'

'All the same, good Sancho,' observed the Duchess, 'you must go with him if it is necessary; for they are good people who are asking you, and these ladies' faces must not be left bristly for your idle fears. That would certainly be a shame.'

'In the name of all the saints, once more!' replied Sancho. 'If this charity were to be done for some modest maidens or foundling girls a man might take some risks, but to endure them to rid waiting-women of their beards. Damn it! I would rather see them all bearded, from the tallest to the shortest, from the nicest to the neatest.'

'You are bitter against waiting-women, Sancho my friend,' said the Duchess. 'You are very much of the opinion of that Toledan apothecary. But you are unfair, I promise you. There are waiting-women in my house who might serve as a model to all their sort; for here is my Doña Rodriguez who will not allow me to say otherwise.'

'Say it, your Excellency,' said the Rodriguez, 'for God knows the truth about everything, and good or bad, bearded or beardless though we be, yet our mothers bore us waiting-women like the rest of our sex. Since God cast us into the world, He knows the reason why; and I hold by His mercy and by no one's beard.'

'That is enough, Lady Rodriguez,' said Don Quixote. 'Lady Trifaldi and company, I wait for Heaven to look with kindly eyes on your distresses. Sancho shall do what I bid him. Now let Clavileño come and let me find myself facing Malambruno, for I know there is no razor could shave your graces more easily than my sword will shave Malambruno's head from his shoulders. For God suffers the wicked, but not for ever.'

'Ah,' exclaimed the Afflicted One, 'may all the stars of the celestial regions look down on your greatness with benignant eyes, valorous knight, and infuse into your spirit all prosperity and valour to be a shield and protection to the down-trodden race of waiting-women, abhorred by apothecaries, slandered by squires and tricked by pages! Woe betide the wretch who in the flower of her years did not prefer to be a nun rather than a waiting-woman! What an unhappy lot we waiting-women are, for even though we were descended in the direct male line from Hector of Troy himself, our mistresses would not leave off calling at us *you there* and *you*, as if they thought that made them queens. O giant Malambruno, although you are an enchanter your promise can be relied on. So send us now the peerless Clavileño so that our misfortunes may be ended, for if the heat comes on and these beards of ours remain we shall be out of luck!'

The Trifaldi spoke with such feeling that she drew tears from the eyes of all the spectators, and even filled Sancho's to the brim, so that he resolved in his heart to follow his master to the very ends of the earth, if it depended on that to rid those venerable faces of their fleeces.

Chapter XLI. *Of the coming of Clavileño and the end of this protracted Adventure.*

BY this time night had come on, and with it the moment fixed for the arrival of the famous horse Clavileño, whose failure to appear troubled Don Quixote. For he thought that Malambruno's delay in sending him meant either that he was not the knight for whom that adventure was reserved, or that the giant dared not meet him in single combat. But all of a sudden there entered through the garden four savages, all dressed in green ivy, bearing a great wooden horse on their shoulders. This they put on its feet on the ground, and one of them cried: 'Let the knight who has courage enough climb upon this machine.'

'I shan't mount it then,' said Sancho, 'for I've no courage and I'm no knight.'

But the savage went on to say: 'Let the squire, if there is one, take the crupper and trust the valiant Malambruno, for except by his sword he will be injured by no other, nor by the malice of any other person. There is no more to do than to turn this peg upon the horse's neck, and he will bear them through the air to where Malambruno awaits them. But for fear the height and distance from the earth should cause them giddiness they must keep their eyes covered till the horse neighs, which will be a sign that they have completed their journey.'

This said, they left Clavileño and retired with a graceful movement in the direction they had come from. And at the sight of the horse the Afflicted One said to Don Quixote, almost in tears: 'Valiant Knight, Malambruno has kept his word. The horse is here, our beards are growing, and each one of us implores you by every hair to shave and shear us, for nothing remains to do but for you to mount with your squire and make a happy start on your strange journey.'

'That I will do, lady Countess Trifaldi,' said Don Quixote, 'with a strong and resolute heart. I will not even wait to find a cushion or put on spurs, for fear of delay, such is my desire to see you, lady, and all these waiting-women smooth and clean.'

'That I will not do,' said Sancho, 'neither with good nor ill will, nor in any way. And if this shaving can't be done without my climbing on the crupper, my master may look for another squire to go with him, and these ladies another way of smoothing their faces, for I'm no sorcerer to enjoy travelling through the air. And what will my islesmen say when they learn that their governor goes roaming down the winds? And another thing: it is nine thousand and odd miles from here to Candaya, and supposing the horse should tire or the giant be in a bad mood, we might be half a dozen years before we got back, and then there would be no isle or islesmen in the world to recognize me. Now since the saying is that there's danger in delay, and when they give you the calf run with the halter, with all due respect to these ladies' beards St. Peter's all right at Rome. I mean that I'm all right in this house, where they have done me such favours, and from whose master I expect the great benefit of seeing myself governor.'

Upon which the Duke replied: 'Sancho, my friend, the isle which I have promised you is neither movable nor fugitive. It has such deep roots struck into the abysses of the earth that it will not be tugged or budged from where it is with three pulls. And I am aware, as you must realize, that there is no kind of position of the first rank that is not gained by some sort of bribe, some more, some less. So the price I mean to exact for this governorship is that you shall go with your master Don Quixote to complete and crown this memorable adventure. For whether you return on Clavileño with the speed his swiftness promises, or adverse fortune befalls you and you return

on foot like a pilgrim, from tavern to tavern and inn to inn, whenever you return you will find your isle where you left it, and your
islesmen longing as they have always been to receive you as their
governor. My goodwill also shall be constant. Do not doubt the
truth of this, Master Sancho, for that would be grievously to mis-
understand my desire to serve you.'

'No more, sir,' cried Sancho. 'I'm a poor squire and can't carry
all these favours on my back. Let my master mount; let them bind
these eyes of mine, and commend me to God; and let me be informed whether I shall be able to commend myself to our Lord or invoke
the angels to favour me, when we pass through those altitudes.'

To which the Trifaldi replied: 'Sancho, you may safely commend yourself to God, or to whom you will; for though Malambruno is an enchanter he is a Christian, and performs his enchantments with great sagacity and caution, meddling with nobody.'

'Well then,' said Sancho, 'God help me, and the Holy Trinity of
Gaeta!'

'Since the memorable adventure of the fulling-mills,' said Don
Quixote, 'I have never seen Sancho in such a fright as now; and if
I were as superstitious as some, his pusillanimity would cause me
some tremors of heart. But come here, Sancho, for with these gentlemen's permission I should like to say a word or two to you in
private.'

Then, leading Sancho among some of the garden trees and grasping him by both hands, he said: 'Now you see, Sancho, what a long
journey awaits us, and God knows when we shall return, or what
opportunities or leisure our business will afford us. Therefore I
would have you now retire to your room, as if you were going to
look for something needed for the journey, and give yourself in a
brace of shakes, say five hundred on account of the three thousand
and three hundred lashes promised. They will stand to your credit,
for a thing well begun is half done.'

'By God,' said Sancho, 'but your worship must be out of your
wits. You might just as well say: you see me in difficulties and ask
me for a maidenhead. Now that I've to be sitting on a bare board,
does your worship want me to flay my bum? Really and truly, it
isn't right of you. Let's go now and shave these waiting-women,
and when we get back I promise you, upon my soul, I'll be so quick

to redeem my debt that your worship'll be content. I say no more.'

'Well, with that promise, good Sancho,' replied Don Quixote, 'I am comforted; for indeed, though you are foolish you are a veracious man.'

'My complexion's not verdigris but brown,' said Sancho, 'but even if I were a mixture I would keep my word.'

With that they came back to mount Clavileño and, as he climbed on, Don Quixote said: 'Blindfold yourself, Sancho, and mount, Sancho! For whoever sends for us from such distant lands will not deceive us, seeing how little glory would redound to him from defrauding one who trusts him. But supposing everything to turn out contrary to my expectation, no malice can obscure the glory of our having undertaken this exploit.'

'Let's go, sir,' said Sancho, 'for these ladies' beards and tears are sticking into my heart, and I shan't get any nourishment out of my food till I see them in their first smoothness. Get on, your worship, and blindfold yourself beforehand, for if I have to go on the crupper it's clear that the rider in the saddle mounts first.'

'That is true,' replied Don Quixote and, taking a handkerchief from his pocket, he begged the Afflicted One to cover his eyes carefully. But after they were bandaged he uncovered them again to say: 'If I remember rightly, I have read in Virgil of the Trojan Palladium, which was the wooden horse the Greeks presented to the goddess Pallas, and which was pregnant with armed knights who afterwards worked the total ruin of all Troy. So first it would be well to see what Clavileño carries in his stomach.'

'There is no need,' said the Afflicted One. 'I will answer for him, for I know that Malambruno has nothing malicious or treacherous about him. You may mount, Don Quixote, without any fear, and on my shoulders be it if any harm befalls you.'

It seemed to Don Quixote that anything he might say in reply concerning his own safety would be to cast a slur on his valour. So, without further discussion, he mounted Clavileño and tried the peg, which turned easily; and as he had no stirrups and his legs hung down, he looked like nothing so much as a figure in a Flemish tapestry, painted or woven, riding in some Roman triumph. Grudgingly and slowly Sancho also managed to get up and, making himself as comfortable as he could on the crupper, found it rather hard and not at all pleasant. So he begged the Duke, if it were possible, to oblige him with a cushion or pillow, even one from his lady the Duchess's couch or from a page's bed; for the crupper of that horse felt more like marble than wood. To which the Trifaldi objected that Clavileño would suffer no sort or kind of trappings on him, but what he could do was to sit side-saddle like a woman, as he would not feel the hardness so much that way. This Sancho did and, taking his farewell, allowed them to bind his eyes, though after they were bound he uncovered them again and, looking tenderly and tearfully on everyone in the garden, begged them to aid him in his peril with a couple of Paternosters and as many Ave Marias, that God might provide someone to say the same for them when they were in a like predicament. On which Don Quixote said:

'Scoundrel, are you on the gallows, perhaps, or at your last gasp, to resort to prayers of this kind? Are you not, soulless and cowardly creature, in the same seat the fair Magalona occupied, and from which she climbed down, not to her grave but to be Queen of France, if the histories do not lie? And I, who am beside you, cannot I compare with the valiant Pierres, who rested on the same spot where now I rest? Blindfold yourself, blindfold yourself, spiritless beast, and do not let the fear which possesses you issue from your mouth, at least not in my presence.'

'Let them blindfold me,' replied Sancho, 'but since they won't let me commend myself or be commended to God, is it surprising that I'm afraid there may be some region of devils hereabouts, who will bear us off to Peralvillo?'

They were now blindfolded, and Don Quixote, feeling that all was in order, touched the peg; and no sooner did he set his fingers on it than the waiting-women and everyone else present raised their voices and cried: 'God guide you, valorous knight!' 'God be with you, dauntless squire!' 'Now you are in the air already, cleaving it more swiftly than an arrow.' 'Now you are beginning to mount and soar to the astonishment of all of us below;' 'Hold on, valorous Sancho, you are swaying. Be careful not to tumble. For your fall would be worse than that rash youth's who sought to drive the chariot of his father the sun.'

Sancho heard their shouts and, pressing closer to his master, with his arms around him, asked: 'Sir, how can they say we're flying so high when their voices reach us here, and they seem to be speaking just beside us?'

'Pay no attention to that, Sancho. For as these matters of flights are out of the ordinary course of things, you will see and hear what you please a thousand miles away. And do not press me so tight or you will upset me. Indeed I do not know what is so troubling and frightening you, for I dare swear that never in all the days of my life have I ridden an easier-paced mount. We seem not to be moving from one spot. Banish fear, my friend; for really this business is going as it should, and we have the wind astern.'

'That's true enough,' replied Sancho. 'On this side there's such a breeze striking me that it might be a thousand bellows blowing.'

And Sancho was right, for they were giving him air from several large bellows. Indeed so well had the Duke, the Duchess and their steward planned the adventure that no detail was lacking to make it perfect. And when he felt the wind blow on him, Don Quixote said: 'There can be no doubt, Sancho, that we have come to the second region of the air, where the hail and snow are born. Thunder, lightning and thunderbolts are engendered in the third region. If we go on climbing at this rate we shall soon strike the region of fire, and I do not know how to manage this peg so as not to mount so high that we shall scorch.'

Here, with some pieces of tow hanging from a stick and easily lit and quenched, they warmed the riders' faces from the distance. At which Sancho, who felt the heat, exclaimed: 'May I die if we're not in the fiery place already, or very near it, for a great piece of my beard has been singed. And, sir, I'm for taking off the bandage and seeing where we are.'

'Do no such thing,' replied Don Quixote. 'Remember the true story of Doctor Torralva, whom the devils took flying through the air riding on a broomstick, with his eyes shut. In twelve hours he reached Rome and got down at the Torre di Nona, which is a street in that city, and saw all the turmoil, and the attack and the death of Bourbon, and by morning he was back in Madrid, where he gave an account of all he had seen. He also said that, as he was going through the air, the Devil bade him open his eyes, which he did and found himself, it seemed to him, so near the body of the moon that he could have taken hold of it with his hands; and he dared not look down to the earth for fear of turning giddy. So, Sancho, there is no need for us to unbind our eyes; for he in whose charge we are will take care of us. Now perhaps we are fetching round and climbing so that we can swoop down on the kingdom of Candaya, like a hawk or a falcon on a heron, to seize it the better for mounting. And although it seems to us not half an hour since we left the garden, believe me, we must have gone a long way.'

'I know nothing about that,' answered Sancho Panza. 'I can only say that if the lady Magallanes or Magalona was happy on this crupper her flesh couldn't have been very tender.'

All this conversation between the two heroes was overheard by the Duke, the Duchess and those in the garden, and gave them extraordinary delight. But, desiring to bring this strange and well-contrived adventure to an end, they set light to Clavileño's tail with some tow, and suddenly the horse, which was stuffed with crackers, flew into the air with a tremendous bang and threw Don Quixote and Sancho Panza to the ground, half scorched.

By this time the whole troop of bearded waiting-women had disappeared from the garden, the Trifaldi and all; and those who remained lay stretched on the earth as if in a faint. Don Quixote and Sancho rose up in a sorry state and, looking in all directions, were surprised to find themselves in the same garden they had started from, and to see such a number of people lying on the ground. But their wonder grew greater when they saw a tall lance planted in one corner of the garden, and hanging from it by two green silk cords a smooth white parchment on which was written in large gold letters: *'By the mere attempting of it the illustrious Don Quixote de la Mancha has finished and achieved the adventure of the Countess Trifaldi, otherwise called the Afflicted Waiting-woman. Malambruno is completely content and satisfied. The chins of the waiting-women are now smooth and clean, and their Majesties Don Clavijo and Antonomasia are in their pristine state. Now once the squirely whipping is completed, the white dove will be free from the pestiferous goshawks which pursue her, and in the arms of her loving mate; for so it is ordained by the sage Merlin, proto-enchanter of enchanters.'*

When Don Quixote read the letters on the parchment, he clearly understood that they referred to Dulcinea's disenchantment, and giving deep thanks to Heaven for the achievement of so great a deed with so little peril, and for restoring to their former bloom the faces of the venerable waiting-women, who were now nowhere to be seen, he approached the Duke and Duchess, who had not yet come to their senses and, grasping the Duke by the hand, said to him:

'Well, my good lord, courage, courage! It is all nothing. The adventure is achieved, with no harm to anyone, as the words on that parchment clearly show.'

The Duke came to himself gradually, like someone waking from a heavy sleep, and so did the Duchess and all the others who were lying about the garden; and with such signs of wonder and alarm as almost to convince one that what they had learnt so well to act in jest had happened in earnest. The Duke read the scroll with his eyes half closed, and then went with open arms to embrace Don Quixote, telling him that he was the bravest knight ever seen in any age. Meanwhile Sancho went to look for the Afflicted One, to see what her face was like without her beard and whether she was as beautiful without it as her brave appearance promised. But they told him that as soon as Clavileño came down burning through the air and struck the ground, the whole troop of waiting-women, and the Trifaldi with them, had disappeared, and that they had gone shaved clean and without their bristles. The Duchess asked Sancho how he had fared in that long journey, and he replied:

'I felt, lady, that we were going, as my master said, flying through the region of fire, and I wanted to uncover my eyes a bit. But when I asked my master's leave to take off the bandage he wouldn't allow me. But as I have some sparks of curiosity in me, and want to know what is forbidden and denied me, softly and stealthily I pushed the handkerchief that covered my eyes just a little bit up up on my nose and looked down towards the earth. And the whole of it looked to me no bigger than a grain of mustard seed, and the men walking on it little bigger than hazel-nuts. So you can see how high we must have been then.'

At which the Duchess remarked: 'Sancho my friend, reflect what you are saying. For seemingly you did not see the earth but the men going about on it, since it is clear that if the earth appeared to you like a grain of mustard seed and each man like a hazel nut, one man alone would have covered the whole earth.'

'That's true,' replied Sancho, 'but, all the same, I looked through one little corner and saw the whole of it.'

'Mind, Sancho,' said the Duchess, 'for we do not see the whole of what we look at from one little corner.'

'I don't understand these lookings,' answered Sancho. 'I only know that your ladyship would do well to realize that as we flew by enchantment, by enchantment I could see the whole earth and all men on it from wherever I looked. And if you don't believe this, your Grace won't believe that when I moved the bandage up by my eyebrows I saw myself so near the sky that there wasn't a hand's breadth and a half between me and it; and I can swear to you, my lady, it was mighty big too. We happened to be going by the place where the seven little she-goats are and, by God, as I was a goat-herd in my country when I was young, as soon as I saw them I felt a longing to play with them for a bit. And if I hadn't done so I think I should have burst. So, quick as a thought, what do I do? Saying nothing to anyone or to my master either, softly and gently I got down from Clavileño and played with the kids – which are sweet as gillyflowers – for almost three-quarters of an hour, and Clavileño didn't stir from the spot nor move on.'

'And while the good Sancho was playing with the goats,' asked the Duchess, 'how was Don Quixote amusing himself?'

To which Don Quixote replied: 'As all these matters and all such happenings are out of the order of nature, it is no wonder Sancho says what he does. I can only answer for myself that I did not slip the bandage either up or down, nor did I see sky, earth, sea or sands. It is true that I felt myself passing through the regions of air, and even touching the region of fire, but that we passed beyond it I am unable to believe. The region of fire being between the atmosphere of the moon and the farthest region of air, we could not have reached the sky, where the seven kids are that Sancho speaks of, without being scorched. So, seeing that we are not burnt, either Sancho is lying or Sancho is dreaming.'

'I'm neither lying nor dreaming,' answered Sancho. 'Just you ask me the marks on those same goats, and you will see by that whether I'm telling the truth or not.'

'Tell me them, then, Sancho,' said the Duchess.

'Two of them,' answered Sancho, 'are green, two scarlet, two blue and one mottled.'

'That is a new kind of goat,' said the Duke, 'for in this our region of the earth such colours are not usual – I mean she-goats of such colours.'

'That's clear enough,' said Sancho, 'for there certainly should be a difference between the she-goats of heaven and of earth.'

'Tell me, Sancho,' asked the Duke, 'did you see any he-goats there amongst the she-goats?'

'No, sir,' answered Sancho. 'But I've heard tell that not one has passed the horns of the moon.'

They were in no mind to ask him anything more about his journey, for Sancho seemed to be in the mood to roam through all the heavens and give an account of everything in them, although he had not stirred from the garden. In fact this was the end of the adventure of the Afflicted Waiting-woman, which gave the Duke and Duchess cause for laughter, not only at the time but for all their lives, and Sancho a subject of talk for ages, if he should live so long.

But Don Quixote went up to Sancho and whispered in his ear: 'Sancho, if you want me to believe what you saw in the sky, I wish you to accept my account of what I saw in the Cave of Montesinos. I say no more.'

Chapter XLII. *Of Don Quixote's advice to Sancho Panza before he went to govern his Isle, and other grave matters.*

THE Duke and Duchess were so delighted with the entertaining results of the adventure of the Afflicted One, that they decided to carry on with their jests, seeing how apt a subject they had to take them in earnest. So having outlined the plot and given their servants and tenants instructions how they were to act towards Sancho in the matter of the governorship of the promised isle, the day after Clavileño's flight the Duke told Sancho to prepare and put himself in readiness to go and be governor, for his islesmen were longing for him as for water in May. Sancho made his bow and said:

'Ever since my journey through the sky, when from its lofty height I gazed on the earth and saw it so small, my very great desire to be a governor has partly cooled. For what greatness is there in governing on a mustard seed? What dignity or power in commanding half a dozen men the size of hazel nuts – for as far as I could see there were no more on the whole earth? If your Lordship would be so kind as to give me ever so small a bit of the sky, even a mile would do, and I would rather have it than the best isle in the world.'

'See here, friend Sancho,' answered the Duke. 'I cannot give anyone a portion of the sky, not even so much as a finger-nail of it, for such favours and rewards are in God's hands alone. What I can give you I will, and that is an isle, right and straight, round and well proportioned, exceedingly fertile and fruitful; and there, if you know how to manage things, from the riches of earth you can gain the riches of heaven.'

'Well now,' replied Sancho, 'let the isle come. For I'll try to be such a governor that I'll get to Heaven, despite all rogues. And it's not out of greed that I want to leave my poor huts and rise to greater things, but from my desire to find out what it tastes like to be a governor.'

'If once you try it, Sancho,' said the Duke, 'you will take to governing like a duck to water, for it is the sweetest thing to give orders and be obeyed. I am pretty sure that when your master comes to be an Emperor – which no doubt he will, by the way his affairs are going – they will not tear his office away from him at their pleasure, and he will be vexed and grieved from the bottom of his heart for the time lost before he became one.'

'Sir,' replied Sancho, 'it's a good thing to command, I imagine, even if it's only a herd of cattle.'

'Let me be buried alongside you, Sancho,' said the Duke; 'you know everything, and I expect you will be just such a governor as your wisdom promises. But here let it rest. Remember that to-morrow, for certain, you are to go to the governorship of the isle, and this evening you shall be fitted with suitable dress and everything necessary for your departure.'

'Let them dress me as they will,' said Sancho, 'for whatever way I go dressed I shall be Sancho Panza.'

'That is true,' said the Duke, 'but clothes have to suit the office or dignity occupied. It would not be right for a lawyer to be dressed like a soldier, nor a soldier like a priest. You will go, Sancho, dressed as part lawyer, part captain, because in the isle I am giving you arms are as necessary as learning and learning as arms.'

'Learning,' answered Sancho, 'I've little of that, for I don't even know my A.B.C., though I have the big Christ-cross in my memory, and that's enough to make me a good governor.'

'With a memory like his,' said the Duke, 'Sancho cannot go wrong.'

At this moment Don Quixote came up, and when he learned what was happening and how soon Sancho was to leave for his governorship, by the Duke's permission he took his squire by the hand and led him to his apartment to give him advice as to his behaviour in office. Then, having entered, he shut the door after him and, almost forcing Sancho to sit down beside him, addressed him with great deliberation:

'I give infinite thanks to Heaven, Sancho my friend, that first and foremost, before I strike any good luck myself, prosperity has come out to meet and receive you. I who had staked the payment for your services on my own success find myself at the beginning of my advancement; while you find yourself rewarded with your heart's desire before your time and contrary to all reasonable expectations. Some bribe, importune, solicit, rise early, entreat, pester, and yet fail to achieve their aims; then there comes another, and without knowing how or why he finds himself with the place and office which many others have sought for. Here the proverb comes in pat, that there is good and bad luck in petitionings. You are, in my opinion, most certainly a dullard. Yet without rising early or working late or putting yourself to great pains, with only the breath of knight errantry which has touched you, you find yourself without more ado governor of an isle, as if that were nothing. I say all this, Sancho, so that you shall not attribute this favour to your own merits, but shall give thanks to God, who disposes things so kindly, and afterwards to the greatness implicit in the profession of knight errantry.

'With your heart disposed to believe my words, be attentive, my son, to this your Cato, who will advise you and be the pole-star and guide to direct you and bring you to a safe port, out of this stormy sea in which you are likely to drown. For offices and great places are nothing but a deep gulf of confusion.

A A

'Firstly, my son, you must fear God; for in fearing Him is wisdom and, being wise, you can make no mistake.

'Secondly, you must consider what you are, seeking to know yourself, which is the most difficult task conceivable. From self-knowledge you will learn not to puff yourself up, like the frog who wanted to be as big as an ox. If you achieve this, the memory that you kept hogs in your own country will come to be like the peacock's ugly feet to the tail of your folly.'

'True enough,' answered Sancho, 'but that was when I was a boy. Afterwards, when I was more of a man, it was geese I kept, not hogs. But this doesn't seem to me to the point, for not all governors come from royal stock.'

'True,' replied Don Quixote, 'and therefore those who are not of noble origin must accompany the gravity of the office they exercise with a mild suavity which, guided by prudence, may save them from malicious slanderers, from whom no station is free.

'Rejoice, Sancho, in the humbleness of your lineage, and do not think it a disgrace to say you come of peasants; for, seeing that you are not ashamed, no one will attempt to shame you. Consider it more meritorious to be virtuous and poor than noble and a sinner. Innumerable men there are, born of low stock, who have mounted to the highest dignities, pontifical and imperial; and of this truth I could weary you with examples.

'Remember, Sancho, that if you take virtue for your means, and pride yourself on performing virtuous deeds, you will have no reason to envy those who were born princes and lords. For blood is inherited but virtue acquired, and virtue has an intrinsic worth, which blood has not.

'This being so, if any of your relations should chance to come and visit you when you are in your isle, do not reject them or insult them. On the contrary, you must receive them, make much of them and entertain them. In that way you will please God, who would have no one disdain His creation; and what is more, you will be complying with your duty to the order of nature.

'If you should take your wife with you – for it is not right that those engaged in government should be for long without wives of their own – instruct her, indoctrinate her and pare her of her native rudeness; for often everything a wise governor gains is lost and wasted by an ill-mannered and foolish wife.

'If you should chance to be widowed – a thing which may happen – and wish to make a better match to suit your office, do not choose a wife to serve you as a bait and a fishing-rod and take bribes in her hood; for I tell you truly that whatever a judge's wife receives her husband will have to account for at the Last Judgment, where he will have to pay fourfold in death for the statutes of which he has taken no account in his lifetime.

'Never be guided by arbitrary law, which has generally great influence with the ignorant who set up to be clever.

'Let the poor man's tears find more compassion in you, but not more justice, than the pleadings of the rich.

'Try to discover the truth behind the rich man's promises and gifts, as well as behind the poor man's sobbings and importunities.

'Where equity may justly temper the rigour of the law do not pile the whole force of it on to the delinquent; for the rigorous judge has no higher reputation than the merciful.

'If you should chance to bend the rod of justice, do not let it be with the weight of a bribe, but with that of pity.

'When you happen to judge the case of some enemy of yours, turn your mind away from your injury and apply it to the truth of the case.

'Do not let personal passion blind you in another's case, for most of the errors you make will be irremediable, and if you should find a remedy it will cost you your reputation, or even your fortune.

'If a beautiful woman comes to beg you for justice, turn your eyes from her tears and your ears from her groans, and consider the substance of her plea at leisure, if you do not want your reason to be drowned in her sobs and your honour in her sighs.

'Do not revile with words the man you must punish with deeds, since the pain of the punishment is sufficient for the wretch without adding ill-language.

'Consider the culprit who comes before you for judgment as a wretched man, subject to the conditions of our depraved nature, and so far as in you lies without injury to the contrary party, show yourself pitiful and lenient; for although all godlike attributes are

equal, mercy is more precious and resplendent in our sight than
justice.

'If you follow these precepts and rules, Sancho, your days will
be long, your fame eternal, your rewards abundant, your happiness
indescribable. You will marry your children as you wish to; they
and your grandchildren will have titles; you will live in peace and
good-will among men, and in your life's last stages you will arrive
at the hour of death in a mild and ripe old age, and the tender
and delicate hands of your great-grandchildren will close your
eyes.

'The instructions I have so far given you are for the embellish-
ment of your soul. Listen now to some which will serve you for the
adornment of your body.'

Chapter XLIII. *Of Don Quixote's further Advice to Sancho Pança.*

COULD anyone hear this last discourse of Don Quixote's and not
take him for a person of singular intelligence and excellent intentions? For as has often been said in the course of this great history,
he went astray only in the matter of chivalry, but in the rest of his
talk showed a clear and unbiassed understanding, so that his acts
discredited his judgment and his judgment his acts at every step.
But in this matter of the second set of precepts which he gave
Sancho, he showed himself possessed of a very nice humour and
displayed both his sense and his madness to an exalted degree.
Most attentively did Sancho listen to him and endeavour to commit
his counsels to memory, resolved to observe them and thereby to
bring the pregnancy of his government to a happy delivery. Don
Quixote then went on to say:

'So far as concerns the government of your person and your
house, Sancho, my first charge to you is to be clean, and to pare
your nails and not let them grow as do some, who are ignorantly
persuaded that long nails beautify the hands; as if that excrescence
and appendage which they omit to cut were merely nail, whereas it
is like the claws of a lizard-catching kestrel – a foul and unsightly
object.

'Do not go unbelted and loose; for disorderly clothes are the indication of a careless mind, unless this disorderliness and negligence falls under the head of cunning, as it was judged to do in the case of Julius Caesar.

'Discreetly take the measure of your office's value; and if it will allow you to give your servants liveries, let them be modest and useful, not gaudy and grand, and divide them between your servants and the poor – I mean that if you have six pages to dress, dress three of them and three poor men. Then you will have pages both for heaven and earth. Your vainglorious have not attained to this new fashion of giving liveries.

'Do not eat garlic or onions; for their smell will reveal that you are a peasant.

'Walk leisurely and speak with deliberation; but not so as to seem to be listening to yourself, for all affectation is bad.

'Eat little at dinner and less at supper, for the health of the whole body is forged in the stomach's smithy.

'Be temperate in drinking, remembering that excess of wine keeps neither a secret nor a promise.

'Take care, Sancho, not to chew on both sides of your mouth nor to eruct in anyone's presence.'

'This about *eruct* I don't understand,' said Sancho.

'Eruct, Sancho,' said Don Quixote, 'means belch, and that is one of the coarsest words in the Castilian language, though it is very expressive; and so refined people have resorted to Latin, and instead of *belch* say *eruct* and for *belches eructations*; and if some people do not understand these terms it is of little consequence, for they will come into use in time, and then they will be generally understood; for that is the way to enrich the language, which depends upon custom and the common people.'

'Indeed, sir,' said Sancho, 'I shall bear your counsel about belching in mind, for I generally do it very often.'

'*Eructing*, Sancho, not *belching*,' said Don Quixote.

'Eruct I shall say from now on,' replied Sancho, 'and I swear I won't forget.'

'Also, Sancho, you must not interlard your conversation with the great number of proverbs you usually do; for though proverbs are maxims in brief, you often drag them in by the hair, and they seem more like nonsense.'

'Let God look after that,' answered Sancho, 'for I know more proverbs than a book, and so many of them come all together into my mouth when I speak that they fight one another to get out; and the tongue seizes hold of the first it meets with, even though it mayn't be just to the point. But from now on I'll take care to bring in only those that suit the gravity of my office. For in a well-stocked house the supper is soon cooked; and a good bargain doesn't hold up the business; and the man who sounds the alarm is safe; and giving and taking need some sense.'

'Go on, Sancho,' said Don Quixote. 'Cram them in, thread and string your proverbs together; no one will stop you. My mother scolds me and I whip the top. I tell you to refrain from proverbs, and in one moment you have brought out a whole litany of them which have as much to do with what we are discussing as have the hills of Ubeda. Look you, Sancho, I do not find fault with a proverb aptly introduced, but to load and string on proverbs higgledy-piggledy makes your speech mean and vulgar.

'When you are riding horseback do not throw your body all on the crupper, nor carry your legs stiffly stuck out from the horse's belly; and do not go so slackly either, and look as if you were riding Dapple; for horse-riding makes horsemen of some and stable boys of others.

'Be moderate in your sleeping, for he that does not rise with the sun does not enjoy the day; and remember, Sancho, that industry is the mother of good fortune, and slothfulness, its opposite, never yet succeeded in carrying out an honest purpose.

'This final precept I am going to give you does not concern the adornment of the body, but I would have you keep it carefully in your memory, for I believe that it will be of no less service to you than those I have just given you. It is never to engage in disputes about lineage, or at least never to compare one family with another; for one of the two must necessarily be the better, and you will be hated by the one you set lower and get no sort of reward from the one you place higher.

'Let your clothing be full breeches, a long coat and a cloak a little longer; on no account tight-fitting breeches, for they do not suit either gentlemen or governors.

'This, Sancho, is all the advice that occurs to me for the present.

In the course of time my instructions will suit occasions as they arise, if you take care to inform me of your circumstances.'

'Sir,' replied Sancho, 'I can see very well that all you have told me is good, godly and profitable. But of what use will it be to me if I remember none of it? True enough, that about not letting my nails grow, and about marrying a second time if I have a chance, I shan't easily forget. But as for your other bits and pieces, they're already gone out of my head as clean as last year's clouds. So I shall have to have them in writing; for though I can't read or write I can give them to my confessor, and he'll ram them in and refresh my memory in time of need.'

'Oh, sinner that I am!' said Don Quixote. 'How wrong it is for a governor not to be able to read and write! For you must know, Sancho, that for a man to be illiterate or left-handed argues one of two things: either he is the son of exceedingly poor and base parents, or so perverse and wicked himself that neither good example nor good teaching have been able to penetrate him. It is a great defect in you, and so I should like you to learn at least to sign your name.'

'I can sign my name very well,' replied Sancho. 'For when I was warden of a brotherhood in my village I learnt to make some letters, like they put on bales of goods, and they said they spelt my name. But I'll tell you what, I'll pretend that my right hand is paralysed, and have someone else sign for me. For there's a remedy for everything except death, and as I wield the power and the staff I'll do as I like; the more so because he that has the mayor for his father ... And I being a governor, which is higher than a mayor, let them come on and play at bo-peep with me. Let them flout me and slander me; let them come for wool and they'll go away shorn; and whom God loves, his house knows it; and the rich man's foolishness passes for wisdom in the world; and since I shall be rich, and a governor and liberal as well, which I intend to be, no one will see a fault in me. Make yourself honey and the flies will suck you; you're worth as much as you've got, as my old grandmother used to say; and there's no getting revenge on a well-rooted man.'

'Confound you, Sancho!' interrupted Don Quixote. 'Sixty thousand devils take you and your proverbs! You have been stringing them together for a whole hour and giving me the pangs of tor-

ture with each one. Mark my words, those proverbs of yours will
bring you to the gallows one day. Your vassals will take away your
government for them, or break into revolts. Tell me, nit-wit,
where do you find them? And how do you apply them, stupid? For
to utter one and apply it well makes me sweat and labour as if I
were digging.'

'Goodness me, my dear master,' answered Sancho, 'you complain
about very small matters. Why the devil do you fret yourself because I make use of my wealth? For I have no other. My only fortune is proverbs and still more proverbs. Why, four of them occur
to me now, that come in slick to the point or like pears in a basket.
But I won't say them, for Sage Silence is Sancho's name.'

'You are not that Sancho,' said Don Quixote. 'You are not
Sage Silence, but wicked chatter and perverse obstinacy. But all
the same I should like to know what four proverbs come to your
mind just now so slick to the point; for I have been racking mine –
and it is a good one – and I cannot think of one.'

'What better,' said Sancho, 'than – don't put your thumbs between two back teeth, and – "Get out of my house, what do you want
with my wife?" admits of no answer – and whether the pot strikes
the stone or vice versa, it's a bad look-out for the pot – every one of
which fits to a hair. For no one should meddle with his governor
nor with those in authority, for he will come off second best, like
the man who puts his finger between the back-teeth – and whether
they're back-teeth or not doesn't matter so long as they're molars.
And there's no answering the governor any more than there's a reply to "Get out of my house! What do you want with my wife?"
As to the one about the stone and the pot, a blind man can see that.
So he who sees the mote in the other man's eye must see the beam in
his own, so that it shan't be said of him that the dead woman was
frightened by the one with her throat cut. And your worship's well
aware that the fool knows more in his own house than the wise man
in another's.'

'No, no, Sancho,' replied Don Quixote, 'the fool knows nothing
in his own house nor in anyone else's, since no edifice of wisdom can
rest on a foundation of folly. But let us leave the matter here, Sancho, for if you govern badly the fault will be yours, and the shame
mine. But it consoles me that I have done my duty in advising you as

truly and wisely as I can. For that absolves me of my obligation and my promise. God guide you, Sancho, and govern you in your government, and deliver me from my suspicion that you will turn your whole isle upside down, a thing which I could prevent by informing the Duke of your character, and telling him that all that fat little body of yours is nothing but a sackful of proverbs and mischief.'

'Sir,' answered Sancho, 'if I don't seem to your worship worthy of this governorship, I give it up from this moment. For I love a single black nail's breadth of my soul more than my whole body, and plain Sancho can live just as well on bread and onions as Governor Sancho on partridges and capons. What's more we're all equal while we're asleep, great and small, poor and rich alike; and if your worship reflects, you'll see that it was only you who put this business of governing into my head, for I know no more of governing isles than a vulture; and if anyone thinks that the Devil will get me for being a governor, I had rather go to Heaven plain Sancho than to Hell a governor.'

'By God, Sancho,' said Don Quixote, 'if only for those last words of yours, I consider you worthy to be governor of a thousand isles. You have a good instinct, without which all knowledge is of no avail. Commend yourself to God and try not go astray in your main resolution. I mean that you must always maintain your unshaken purpose and design to do right in whatever business occurs, for Heaven always favours honest intentions. Now let us go to dinner, for I think that my Lord and Lady are waiting for us.'

Chapter XLIV. *How Sancho Panza was taken to his Governorship, and of the strange Adventure which befell Don Quixote in the Castle.*

THEY say that in the real original of this history it states that when Cide Hamete came to write this chapter his interpreter did not translate it as it was written, for it was in the form of a complaint addressed by the Moor to himself for having undertaken so dry and cramped a story; since he seemed always to be restricted to Don Quixote and Sancho, not daring to launch out into digressions and episodes that would have yielded both pleasure and profit. He said that to have his mind, his hand and his pen always confined to a single subject and to so scanty a list of characters was an unbearable hardship, in no way fruitful for the author; and that to avoid this inconvenience in the first part he had resorted to short tales, like 'The Foolish Curiosity' and 'The Captive Captain', which are, in a sense, separate from the story, though the rest of the tales concern the adventures which befel Don Quixote himself, and could not well be omitted. He also thought, as he says, that many would have all their attention engrossed by the claims of Don Quixote's exploits, and would have none left for the tales. In fact they would hurry through them in haste or disgust and fail to notice the delicacy and ingenuity of their construction, which would have shown up well if they had been published on their own and not tied to Don Quixote's craziness and Sancho's fooleries. So he decided not to insert any tales, either detached or connected, in this second part, but to include some similar episodes arising out of the actual happenings themselves; and even these should be sparing and no longer than their bare narration required. So, being confined and enclosed within the narrow limits of the story, though he has the skill, the knowledge and the capacity for dealing with the whole universe, he begs that his pains shall not be under-valued, and that he shall be praised not for what he writes, but for what he has refrained from writing.

The author then goes on to say that after supper on the evening of the day when Sancho received his instructions Don Quixote handed him a written copy, so that he might get someone to read them to him. But no sooner had he given them to Sancho than they fell into the hands of the Duke, who showed them to the Duchess, and the pair of them were again surprised at Don Quixote's madness and good sense. So, to continue with their jest, they sent Sancho that evening with a great escort to the village which was to serve as his isle. Now the man who had charge of the matter happened to be a steward of the Duke's, a very shrewd and humorous fellow – for there can be no humour without shrewdness – and it was he who had played the part of the Countess Trifaldi so gracefully, as has been already described. With this to his credit and carefully coached by his master and mistress as to his conduct towards Sancho, he was miraculously successful in his design.

Though it must be confessed that the moment Sancho set eyes on this steward, he fancied he was gazing on the very countenance of the Trifaldi; and turning to his master, he said: 'Sir, may the Devil fly away with me here where I stand, a true man and a Christian, if your worship doesn't agree that this steward of the Duke's here is exactly like the Afflicted One.'

Don Quixote examined the steward carefully, and said to Sancho after his inspection: 'There is no call for the Devil to fly away with you, Sancho, either as true man or Christian – though I do not know what you mean – for the Afflicted One's face is just like the steward's. Yet for all that the steward is not the Afflicted One, for that would imply a very palpable contradiction. But this is no time to make these investigations, for that would be to plunge ourselves into inextricable labyrinths. But believe me, friend, we must pray very earnestly to our Lord to deliver us from wicked wizards and enchanters.'

'It's no joke, sir,' replied Sancho. 'I heard him speak just now, and I thought it was the very voice of the Trifaldi sounding in my ears. Well, I'll be quiet; but I shall keep my eyes open in future all the same, and see if I can discover any other sign to confirm or dispel my suspicion.'

'So you must, Sancho,' said Don Quixote, 'and inform me of all you discover about the matter, and of everything that befalls you in your government too.'

At length Sancho set out, accompanied by a great number of people, dressed as a lawyer in a very broad overcoat of tawny watered camlet and a hunting-cap of the same material, and riding with short stirrups on a mule. Behind him, by order of the Duke, went Dapple with brand-new harness and silk trappings. From time to time Sancho turned back to gaze on his ass, in whose company he rode so contentedly that he would not have changed places with the Emperor of Germany. On taking leave of the Duke and Duchess he kissed their hands and begged his master for his blessing, which Don Quixote gave him with tears and Sancho received with blubberings.

Let the good Sancho go in peace, amiable reader, and God speed him. Expect two bushels of laughter when you learn how he behaved in his government. Meanwhile mark what befell his master that night, and if you do not laugh at that, at least you will spread your lips in a monkey grin; for Don Quixote's adventures must be honoured either with wonder or with laughter.

The story goes, then, that no sooner had Sancho departed than Don Quixote felt his loneliness and, had it been possible to revoke his squire's commission and take away his governorship, he would have done so. The Duchess observed his melancholy and asked him why he was sad, saying that if it were for Sancho's absence, she had squires, waiting-women and maids in her house who would serve him to his complete satisfaction.

'It is true, my lady,' answered Don Quixote, 'that I grieve for Sancho's absence. But that is not the principal cause of my seeming sad; nor the reason why of the many offers your Excellency makes me I can only accept the goodwill with which they are made. For the rest I entreat your Excellency to give me leave to wait upon myself within my own apartment.'

'Indeed, Don Quixote,' said the Duchess, 'that must not be. You shall be served by four of my maids, as beautiful as flowers.'

'To me,' replied Don Quixote, 'they will not be like flowers, but like thorns pricking me to the soul. They shall no more come into my room, or anywhere near it, than fly. If your Highness will continue your undeserved favours towards me, suffer me to enjoy them alone and to wait on myself within my own doors, so that I may put a wall between my desires and my virtue. I am unwilling to forego this practice for all your Highness's liberality towards me. In fact I would rather sleep in my clothes than allow anyone to undress me.'

'No more, no more, Don Quixote,' replied the Duchess. 'I promise to give orders that not even a fly shall enter your room, let alone a maid. For myself, I am not one to infringe Don Quixote's sense of decency, for, by what I can perceive, the most resplendent of his many virtues is his modesty. You may undress and dress yourself, your worship, alone and in your own fashion, how and when you will, and no one shall hinder you. In your own room you will find all the utensils needed by one sleeping behind locked doors, so that no call of nature will oblige you to open them. May the great Dulcinea del Toboso live a thousand ages, and may her name travel round the whole earth, for meriting the love of so valiant and modest a knight. And may kind Heaven infuse into the heart of our

governor Sancho the desire to finish off his whipping speedily, so
that the world may once more enjoy the beauty of so great a lady.'

To which Don Quixote made answer: 'Your Highness's words
are true to your character; for in the mouths of virtuous ladies there
can be no evil. Dulcinea will be the more fortunate and the more
famous in the world for your Highness's commending her than for
all the praises the most eloquent in the land could bestow on her.'

'Well now, Don Quixote,' replied the Duchess, 'it is supper-
time, and the Duke must be waiting. Come, your worship, let us
sup, and you shall retire early, for the journey you took yesterday to
Candaya was not so short as not to have caused you some chafing.'

'No, I feel none, lady,' answered Don Quixote, 'for I dare swear
to your Excellency that never in all my life have I ridden a quieter
or better-paced beast than Clavileño. I do not know what could
have induced Malambruno to dispose of so swift and mild a creature, and to burn him like that for no reason at all.'

'We may well imagine,' replied the Duchess, 'that repentance
for the wrong he had done the Trifaldi and company and other persons, and for the crimes he must have committed as sorcerer and
enchanter, decided him to destroy all the instruments of his art; and
as Clavileño was the chief of them and caused him most disquiet in
his wanderings from land to land, he burnt him, so that his ashes
and the trophy scroll might immortalize the valour of the great Don
Quixote de la Mancha.'

Once more Don Quixote gave thanks to the Duchess, and after
supper he retired to his room alone, refusing to allow anyone to
come in and wait on him, so great was his fear of encountering
temptations which might induce him, or compel him, to forget the
proper chastity he reserved for his lady Dulcinea, having ever present in his imagination the virtue of Amadis, flower and mirror of
knights errant. Closing the door behind him then, he undressed by
the light of two candles. But as he took off his stockings – oh
disaster unworthy of such a personage! – there burst, not sighs, nor
anything else to discredit the purity of his breeding, but about two
dozen stitches of one of his stockings, which made it look like a
window-lattice. The good gentleman was extremely distressed, and
would have given an ounce of silver to have there a sixteenth of an
ounce of green silk, for his stockings were green. Here Benengeli

exclaims in his writing: 'Oh, poverty, poverty! I do not know why the great Cordovan poet was moved to call you

Holy and misvalued gift!

For, Moor though I am, I know very well by the commerce I have had with Christians that holiness lies in charity, humility, faith, obedience and poverty. But, for all that, I declare that anyone who grows content with poverty must have much of God in him, unless it is that kind of poverty of which one of His greatest saints says: *"Possess all things as if you possessed them not"*, and this they call poverty in spirit. But you, secondary poverty – for it is of you I speak – why do you chose to break in upon gentlemen and men of birth rather than upon other people? Why do you compel them to shine up their shoes, and to have the buttons of their coats some of silk, some of hair and some of glass? Why must their ruffles be generally crumpled and not spread in a smooth pattern?' – which shows the antiquity of starch and smooth ruffs. 'How wretched,' he went on, 'is the man of birth who is always regaling his honour with chicken-broth while he dines poorly behind closed doors, making a hypocrite of his toothpick by going out into the street with it, though he has eaten nothing which obliges him to clean his teeth! How miserable is he, I repeat, whose honour is terrified at the thought that someone may discover from a mile off the patch on his shoe, the sweat marks on his hat, the threadbareness of his coat, and the hunger in his stomach!'

All these reflections were revived in Don Quixote by the breaking of his stitches. But he was comforted by seeing that Sancho had left him some riding-boots, which he decided to put on next day. At length he lay down again, brooding and dispirited, as much for lack of Sancho as for the irreparable disaster to his stockings, which he would have darned up, even though with silk of another colour – the most expressive token of a gentleman's penury. He put out the candles, but it was hot and he could not sleep. So he got out of bed and slightly opened a window with an iron grille which looked out on a beautiful garden, and as he opened it, he perceived people walking and talking among the greenery. As he set himself to listen attentively and the voices from below were fairly loud, he heard these words:

'Do not press me to sing, Emerencia, for you know that from the moment this stranger entered the castle and my eyes fell upon him, I have been unable to sing, and can only weep. Besides, my mistress's sleep is rather light, and I would not have her find us here for all the treasure in the world; and even supposing she slept and did not wake, my singing would be in vain should he sleep and not wake to hear it, this new Aeneas who has come into my land to abandon me in scorn.'

'Do not mind that, friend Altisidora,' came the answer, 'for no doubt the Duchess and everyone in this house are asleep, except for the lord of your heart and disturber of your soul. For I heard him open the window of his apartment just now. So no doubt he is awake. Sing, poor grieved one, softly and gently to the sound of your harp, and if the Duchess hears us we can blame the heat of the night.'

'That is not the point, Emerencia,' replied Altisidora. 'I do not wish my song to reveal my heart, for I should be taken for a light and capricious girl by those ignorant of the mighty force of love. But, come what may, better a shamed face than a sore heart.'

Then someone began to play most softly on the harp, and Don Quixote marvelled as he heard it. For at that instant there arose in his memory an infinity of similar adventures – of windows, bars and gardens, serenades, love-songs and swoonings, which he had read of in his airy books of chivalry. He immediately imagined that one of the Duchess's maidens had fallen in love with him, and that her modesty compelled her to keep her feelings secret. He trembled at the thought that he might yield, but resolved in his mind not to let himself be conquered. Then, commending himself with good heart and will to his lady Dulcinea del Toboso, he decided to listen to the music and, to let them know that he was there, he gave a pretended sneeze, which considerably delighted the maids, for they wanted nothing better than for Don Quixote to hear them. Then, after running over and tuning her harp, Altisidora struck up this ballad:

> Thou that in thy bed dost lie
> Between the Holland sheets,
> Sleeping with thy legs outstretched
> All night long till morn,

O thou knight, the valiantest
All La Mancha has produced.
More modest and more blessed, thou,
Than finest gold of Araby.

Hear a damsel sorrowful,
Nurtured well but thriven ill,
Who with light of thy two suns
Feels her soul scorched and ablaze.

Thou thine own adventures seekest,
Other's misadventures findest,
Dealest wounds and yet refusest
To give healing remedy.

Tell me, O thou valiant youth
– May God prosper thy desires! –
Wert thou born in Lybia,
Or in Jaca's mountains?

Whether serpent gave thee suck,
Or perhaps thy nurses were
The uncouth wildness of the woods
And the mountains horrible.

Dulcinea well may boast,
That most plump and healthy maid,
Conquering a tiger's heart
And taming a most savage beast.

For which famous she shall be
From Henares to Jarama,
From Tagus to Manzanares,
From Pisuerga to Arlanza.

If I could but change with her,
I would give a skirt to boot
Of the gayest that I have,
Hung about with golden fringe.

Oh, that I were in thy arms,
Or, if not, beside thy bed,
That I might but scratch thy head
And of dandruff rid thy hair.

Much I ask, but am not worthy
Of a favour so outstanding,
Let me then but stroke thy feet;
That is enough for one so humble.

What fine night-caps I would give thee,
And what silver socks I'd work thee,
Breeches of the finest damask,
And what Holland cloaks as well!

And how many rarest pearls,
Each as big as an oak-gall,
Which, if it had no companions,
Might be called the only pearl.

Gaze not then from thy Tarpeian
Rock upon this fire that burns me.
Manchegan Nero of the world,
Do not revive it with thy harshness.

Young I am, a tender pullet,
My age is not yet past fifteen.
Fourteen I am and three months over,
I swear by God and by my soul.

I do not limp, I am not lame,
Nothing in me is misshapen,
And my hair is like the lilies;
When I stand it sweeps the ground.

Though my mouth is like an eagle's
And my nose is rather flat,
With my topaz teeth my beauty's
Raised as high as Heaven above.

My voice will prove, if thou but listen,
Equal to the very sweetest,
And thou'lt find my form and figure
Something more than middling too.

These and all my other graces
Are the spoils fall to thy quiver,
I am a maiden of this house,
And my name's Altisidora.

Here ended the song of the sore stricken Altisidora, and here began the fright of the courted Don Quixote, who said to himself, heaving a deep sigh: 'What an unhappy errant I am, that there is no maiden sets eyes on me but is enamoured! How sad is the fate of the peerless Dulcinea del Toboso that she cannot be left alone to enjoy my incomparable constancy! What do you want of her, Queens? Why do you persecute her, Empresses? Why do you bait her, fourteen and fifteen-year-old maidens? Leave, leave the miserable lady to triumph, rejoice and glory in the lot which Love has chosen to bestow on her in rendering her my heart and delivering her my soul. Reflect, enamoured crew, that for Dulcinea alone am I dough and sugar paste, but for all others I am flint. For her I am honey, but for you aloes. For me Dulcinea alone is beautiful, wise, modest, gay and well-born, and the rest ugly, stupid, fickle and base-born. To be hers and no other's nature cast me into the world. Let Altisidora weep or sing; let that lady despair for whose sake I was beaten in the castle of the enchanted Moor; for I must be Dulcinea's – roasted or boiled, clean, well-born and chaste – in despite of all the powers of sorcery in the world.'

With this he banged the window to and, fretful and heavy-hearted, as if some great disaster had befallen him, lay down on his bed, where we will leave him for the present, since the great Sancho Panza is calling us, being desirous of making a beginning of his famous government.

Chapter XLV. *Of how the great Sancho Panza took possession of his Isle and of the fashion in which he began to govern.*

O perpetual discoverer of the Antipodes! Torch of the world! Eye of Heaven! Sweet stirrer of wine coolers! Here Thymbrius, there Phoebus, now archer, now physician! Father of Poetry, inventor of Music, you who always rise and – though you seem to – never set! On you I call, sun, by whose aid man engenders man. On you I call to favour me and to light the darkness of my mind, that I may be scrupulous in the narration of the great Sancho Panza's government; for without you I feel myself timid, faint-hearted and confused.

I must tell you then that Sancho Panza with all his escort arrived at a village of about a thousand inhabitants, which was one of the best in the Duke's dominions. They gave him to understand that this was called the Isle Barataria, either because the town's name was *Baratario*, or because of the '*barato*', or low price, at which he had got the government. When they reached the gates of the place, which was walled, the town-council came out to receive him. They rang the bells, and all the inhabitants demonstrated their general rejoicing and conducted him in great pomp to the principal church to give thanks to God. Then with some comical ceremonies they delivered him the keys of the town, and admitted him as perpetual governor of the Isle Barataria. The new governor's apparel, his beard, his fatness and his smallness surprised everyone who was not in the secret, and even those many who were. Next they bore him from the church to the judge's throne and seated him upon it, where the Duke's steward thus addressed him:

'It is an ancient custom in this famous isle, Lord Governor, that everyone who comes to take possession of it is obliged to reply to a question, and this must be a rather intricate and difficult one. By this reply the town touches and feels the pulse of its new governor's understanding and, accordingly, is either glad or grieved at his coming.'

Whilst the steward was thus addressing him, Sancho was gazing at a number of large letters inscribed on the wall facing his seat. Now, as he could not read, he asked what those paintings were on that wall, and the answer came: 'Sir, yonder is written and recorded the day on which your Lordship took possession of this isle, and the inscription says: "*This day, such a date of such a month in such a year, there took possession of the isle the Lord Don Sancho Panza; may he enjoy it for many years.*"'

'Who are they calling Don Sancho Panza?' asked Sancho.

'Your Lordship,' answered the steward, 'for no other Panza has entered this isle but the one seated on that seat.'

'Then take notice, brother,' said Sancho, 'that I'm no Don, and there has never been a Don in my whole family. Plain Sancho Panza's my name, and Sancho my father was called, and Sancho my grandfather, and they were all Panzas without the addition of Dons or Doñas. I fancy there are more Dons than stones in this isle. But enough. God knows my meaning, and perhaps if my government lasts four days I may weed out these Dons, for judging by their numbers they must be as tiresome as gnats. Go on with your question, Master Steward, for I'll reply as best I can, whether the town be sorry or rejoice.'

At this moment two men came into the judgment-hall, one dressed as a labourer and the other as a tailor with scissors in his hand, the latter crying:

'My lord Governor, here's why I and this countryman have come before your worship. That fellow came to my shop yesterday – I, saving your presence, am a licensed tailor, God be praised! – and put a piece of cloth into my hands, and asked me:"Would there be enough here, sir, to make a cap?" I measured the stuff and answered him yes. I suppose he must have suspected that I intended to rob him of part of the cloth, basing his belief on his own roguery and the bad reputation of tailors. And he was quite right. Then he asked me to examine it again and see if there was enough for two. I guessed his drift, and said yes. Then, persisting in his damned idea, he went on adding caps, and I added more yeses till we came to five. And he has just come this very moment for his caps, and I've offered them to him. And he won't pay me for the making, but demands that I shall pay him instead or return him his cloth.'

'Is all this true, brother?' asked Sancho.

'Yes, sir,' answered the fellow, 'but make him show you the five caps he has made me, your worship.'

'With pleasure,' said the tailor.

And taking his hand suddenly from under his cloak, he displayed five caps, one on the tip of each finger, and said: 'Here are the five caps this good man ordered and, by God and my conscience, there wasn't a scrap of cloth over, and I'll submit the work to be examined by the inspectors of the trade.'

Everyone present laughed at the number of caps and the novel nature of the case. But Sancho set himself to consider a little and said: 'There seems to me no need for long delays in this suit; it can be decided on the spot by a wise man's judgment. My sentence, therefore, is that the tailor shall lose his making and the countryman his cloth, the caps to be given to the prisoners in the jail, and let that be an end of the matter.'

This judgment moved the audience to laughter, but the governor's orders were carried out.

Next there came before him two old men, one of them carrying a cane for a walking stick. 'Sir,' said the one without the stick, 'Some time ago I lent this fellow ten crowns in gold, as a favour and a service to him, on condition that he should repay me on demand. I didn't ask him for them for a long time, so as not to put him into greater difficulties through repaying than he was in when I lent him them. But as he didn't seem to me to be troubling about his debt, I asked him for them, not once but many times. Now not only does he not repay me but he denies the debt, saying that I never lent him these ten crowns, or that if I did he has returned them. I have no witnesses of the loan – nor he of the repayment, for he never made it. So I want your worship to put him under oath, and if he swears that he has repaid me I will let him off the debt here, before God.'

'What do you say to this, you fellow with the stick?' asked Sancho.

'I confess that he lent them to me, sir,' answered the old man. 'Hold down your wand of justice, your worship, and since he leaves it to my oath, I'll swear that I really and truly returned them to him.'

The Governor lowered his wand, and at the same time this old man gave his stick, as if it were very much in his way, to the other old man to hold whilst he took his oath. Then he put his hand on the cross of the wand and declared that he had truly borrowed the ten crowns demanded of him, but that he had returned them into the plaintiff's own hands, and that it was only the other man's forgetfulness that made him continually demand them back.

At this the great Governor asked the creditor what answer he had to give to his adversary. For beyond all doubt the debtor must be speaking the truth since, in his opinion, he was an honest man and a good Christian. It must, in fact, have been the plaintiff who had forgotten how and when the money had been returned, and thenceforward he must never ask for repayment again. The debtor took back his stick, bowed and went out of the court. Now when Sancho saw the defendant also depart without more ado and observed the plaintiffs' resignation, he bowed his head on his breast and, placing the first finger of his right hand over his brows and his nose, remained as if in thought for a short while. Then he raised his head and ordered the old man with the stick, who had already left the building, to be recalled; and when he was brought back into his presence, Sancho said: 'Give me that stick, my fellow. I've need of it.'

'With great pleasure,' replied the old man, putting it into Sancho's hand. 'Here it is, sir.' Sancho then took it and, handing it to the other old man, said to him: 'Go, in God's name. You're repaid now.'

'What, sir?' replied the old man. 'Is this stick worth ten gold crowns then?'

'Yes,' said the Governor. 'If it isn't I'm the greatest dolt in the world. And now you'll see whether I haven't the gumption to govern a whole kingdom.'

Then he ordered the cane to be broken open in the presence of everyone; and when this was done they found ten gold crowns inside. Whereupon everyone expressed astonishment, and hailed the governor as a new Solomon. And when asked how he had deduced that the ten crowns were inside the cane, he answered that he had watched the defendant give the stick to the plaintiff whilst he took his oath that he had really and truly returned the money; and when the fellow had completed his oath and asked for the stick back, it had occurred to him that the sum in dispute must be inside. From this, he added, they might see that sometimes God directs the judgments of governors, even if some of them are fools. Besides, he had heard the priest of his village tell of a similar case, and he had so good a memory that, if it weren't that he forgot everything he wanted to remember, there would not be a better in the whole isle. Finally they departed, one abashed and the other satisfied. The audience was flabbergasted, and the secretary who noted down Sancho's words, acts and gestures was unable to decide whether to write him down a wise man or a fool.

But no sooner was this case over than a woman came into the court, stoutly clinging to a man dressed like a rich herdsman, and crying out loudly as she came: 'Justice, Lord Governor! Justice! If I don't find it on earth, I'll go and seek it in Heaven! Sweet governor, this wicked man sprang on me in the middle of a field, and abused my body like a dirty dish-rag and, poor wretch that I am, he robbed me of a treasure I've kept for more than twenty-three years, and defended from Moors and Christians, natives and foreigners. I've always been as resistent as a cork-tree and preserved myself as pure as the salamander in the fire, or as wool on the briars, for this fellow now to come and handle me with his clean hands!'

'We have still to discover whether this fine fellow has clean hands or not,' said Sancho.

Then, turning to the man, he asked him what answer he had to offer to the woman's complaint. And the man replied in great confusion: 'Sirs, I am a poor herdsman with a herd of swine, and this morning I left this place to sell — saving your presence — four pigs, and what with dues and exactions they took from me very nearly their full value. Now as I was coming back to my village I met this good woman on the way, and the Devil, the author of all mischief, made us couple together. I paid her sufficient, but she wasn't content and caught hold of me and wouldn't let me go until she had dragged me to this place. She says I forced her, and that's a lie, as I'll swear on oath; and that's the whole truth, to the last crumb.'

Then the Governor asked him if he had any silver money on him, and he replied he had about twenty ducats inside his shirt in a leather purse. This the governor ordered him to take out and hand over to the plaintiff just as it was. He obeyed trembling, and the woman took it, making a thousand curtseys to the company, and praying God for the life and health of the good governor, who thus looked after needy orphans and maidens. With this she left the court, grasping the purse tightly with both hands, although she looked first to see if the money in it was really silver. Then, no sooner was she gone than Sancho said to the herdsman, who was on the point of tears, for his eyes and his heart yearned after his purse, 'Run after that woman, my good fellow, and take the purse away from her, whether she likes it or not. Then come back here with her.'

It was not a fool or a deaf man he spoke to, for the man dashed out at once like lightning and ran to obey. All the audience were in suspense as they awaited the outcome of the case. Then shortly afterwards the man and woman came back, more closely entwined and locked together than before, she with her skirt tucked up and the purse in the fold, and the man struggling to get it away from her. But it was impossible, so stoutly did she defend it, crying out loudly: 'Justice, in God's name! Justice! See, Lord worshipful Governor, the shamelessness of this bold, godless fellow. In the middle of the town, in the middle of the street, he's been trying to rob me of the purse your worship made him give me.'

'And did he rob you?' asked the Governor.

'How rob me?' replied the woman. 'I had rather lose my life than this purse. A pretty babe I should be! You must set other cats at my chin than this miserable, filthy fellow. Pincers and hammers, mallets and chisels, won't be enough to get it out of my clutches, nor lion's claws either. They shall sooner have my soul from the very heart of my body!'

'She's right,' said the man. 'I'm beaten, I admit, and tired out. I confess I haven't the strength to take it from her. I give up.'

Then the Governor said to the woman: 'Show me that purse, honest and valiant woman.'

She gave it to him at once, and the Governor returned it to the man, saying to the forcible but unforced woman: 'Sister, if you'd shown the same valorous spirit you've displayed in defending that purse, or even half as much, in defending your body, the strength of Hercules couldn't have forced you. Get out, confound you, and ill luck go with you. Don't stay anywhere in this isle, nor within twenty miles of it, under pain of two hundred lashes. Get out at once, I say, you loose-tongued, shameless swindler.'

The woman was thrown into confusion, and went off hanging her head, in high dudgeon, and the Governor said to the man: 'Good fellow, go back home, in God's name, with your money, and in future, if you don't want to lose it, try not to get a fancy for coupling with anyone.'

The man thanked him with the worst possible grace and departed, and the audience were once more astonished at their new governor's judicious decisions. All this, duly recorded by his chronicler, was straightway written down for the Duke, who was most eagerly waiting for news. But here let good Sancho rest. His master is clamouring for our attention, being disturbed by Altisidora's music.

Chapter XLVI. *Of the fearful Fright Don Quixote received from certain Cats and Bells in the course of his Wooing by the enamoured Altisidora.*

WE left the great Don Quixote wrapt in the imaginations aroused in him by the music of the enamoured maiden Altisidora. He carried them with him to bed where, like fleas, they would not let him sleep or rest a moment, but mingled in his brain with thoughts of his torn stockings. However, as time is swift and no barrier will stay it, he rode the hours apace, and the morrow speedily arrived. When he saw the dawn he quitted his soft feather-bed, and, casting aside sloth, dressed himself in his chamois suit, and put on his riding boots to hide the disaster to his stockings. He threw his scarlet cloak over him and put on his head a green velvet cap trimmed with silver lace; hung his sword-belt over his shoulders with its trusty, trenchant blade; picked up a great rosary which he always carried with him, and with great gravity strutted into the antechamber, where the Duke and Duchess, already dressed, appeared to be expecting him. But as he passed through a gallery he found Altisidora there waiting for him with the other maid, her friend. And the moment she saw him she pretended to faint, and dropped into the arms of her companion, who began to unlace her bodice in a great hurry. This Don Quixote observed and, going up to them, said: 'Now I know the cause of these attacks.'

'I'm sure I don't,' replied the friend, 'Altisidora is the healthiest girl in this whole house, and I've never heard her so much as sigh so long as I've known her. Ill luck to all knights errant in the world, if they're all so ungrateful! Now get along, Don Quixote, for this poor girl won't come to herself so long as you stay here.'

To which Don Quixote replied: 'Kindly have a lute put into my room to-night, and I will console this afflicted maiden to the best of my powers. For in the beginnings of love a prompt undeceiving is generally an effective remedy.'

With this he departed for fear of being observed there. But he was no sooner gone than the fainting Altisidora came to her senses and said to her companion: 'We must put a lute there for him indeed. No doubt Don Quixote means to give us some music, and if it is his own it won't be too bad.'

When they related this last incident to the Duchess, and told her of Don Quixote's request for a lute, she was exceedingly delighted, and planned with the Duke and her maids a new trick which would afford them some harmless amusement. So they looked forward with great pleasure to the night, which was not long in falling. But the Duke and Duchess whiled away the interval in delightful conversation with Don Quixote; and it was on this same day that the Duchess actually sent off one of her pages – the one who had played the part of the enchanted Dulcinea in the wood – to Teresa Panza, with her husband Sancho Panza's letter and the bundle of clothes he had

left to be forwarded to her; and she sent him off with injunctions to
bring back a faithful account of his conversation with her. After
this – it was eleven at night by then – Don Quixote found a guitar
in his room. He strummed it and opened the window. Then, hearing
people moving in the garden, he ran his fingers over the strings,
tuned it as well as he knew how, and after spitting and clearing his
throat began to sing in a hoarse but not unmusical voice the following ballad which he had composed himself:

> The powerful force of love
> Doth oft unhinge the soul,
> Taking for instrument
> Unthinking idleness.
>
> Sewing and useful work
> And ceaseless occupation
> Are a sure antidote
> To the poison of love's grief.
>
> Modest and prudent maids,
> Whose longing is to wed,
> Chastity is their dower;
> There is no higher praise.
>
> Those that knight errants be
> And those that haunt the court
> Woo the loose sort of maid,
> But wed the modest ones.
>
> Loves in the East arise
> Between a host and guest,
> But they soon reach their West:
> At parting they are done.
>
> Love that's so newly come,
> Now here, to-morrow gone,
> Never leaves images
> Deep printed in the soul.
>
> Picture on picture drawn
> Leaves neither sign nor mark.
> Where there's one beauty, the
> Second won't win the trick.
>
> On my soul's canvas is
> Painted indelibly
> Peerless Dulcinea.
> Nothing can blot her out.

In lovers constancy's
The most prized quality.
Love can work miracles,
And raise up lovers too.

Don Quixote had come to this point in his song, which was heard by the Duke and Duchess, Altisidora and almost all the people in the castle, when suddenly, from a balcony which directly overhung his window, a rope was let down with more than a hundred sheepbells fastened to it and, immediately afterwards, a great sack, full of cats with smaller bells tied to their tails, was flung after it. The jingling of the bells and the squawking of the cats made such a din that even the Duke and Duchess, who had contrived the joke, were aghast, while Don Quixote was dumbfounded with fear. Now two or three of the cats, as fate would have it, got through the window, and as they rushed about the room it was as if a legion of devils had broken in. They knocked over and put out the candles burning there, and ran about trying to find a way of escape. And all the while the rope with the great sheep-bells on it continued to rise and fall, and the majority of the people of the castle, not being in the secret, remained speechless with astonishment. Finally Don Quixote rose to his feet and, drawing his sword, began to make stabs through the window, crying loudly:

'Avaunt, evil enchanters! Avaunt, crew of sorcerers! For I am Don Quixote de la Mancha, against whom your wicked plots are powerless and of no avail.'

Then, turning round upon the cats, who were running about the room, he dealt them many blows. And all of them rushed to the window and jumped out, except one which, finding itself hard pressed by Don Quixote's sword-thrusts, jumped at his face and dug its claws and teeth into his nose, whereupon Don Quixote began to roar his very loudest in pain. Now when the Duke and Duchess heard him, realizing the probable cause, they ran in great haste to his room and, opening the door with the master-key, found the poor knight struggling with all his might to tear the cat from his face. They went in with lights, and when he saw the unequal struggle the Duke ran up to disengage them, although Don Quixote cried out:

'Let no one pull him off! Leave me to deal with this devil, this wizard, this enchanter, hand to hand. For I will teach him myself what it is to deal with Don Quixote de la Mancha.'

But the cat snarled and held on, heedless of his threats. At last, however, the Duke pulled it off and threw it out of the window, Don Quixote coming off with a scratched face and not too whole a nose. But he was much annoyed at not being left to finish the battle he was fighting so stoutly against that perverse enchanter. Then they sent for oil of Hypericum, and that same Altisidora with her whitest of hands put bandages on all his wounds, saying to him in a soft voice, as she bound them up:

'All these misfortunes befall you, flinty-hearted knight, for your sin of hardness and obstinacy. May it please God that your squire Sancho shall forget to whip himself, so that this beloved Dulcinea of yours may never emerge from her enchantment, and you may never enjoy her nor come to the bridal bed with her, at least while I, who adore you, am alive.'

To all this Don Quixote gave no word of reply, but heaved a deep sigh, and presently lay down on his bed, after thanking the Duke and Duchess for their kindness, not because he had been in any fear of that cattish and bellish rabble of enchanters, but because he realized their good intentions in coming to his rescue. The noble pair left him to rest and went away concerned at the unfortunate result of their joke, for they had not thought the adventure would have proved so tiresome and costly to Don Quixote. But it kept him confined to his room for five days, and there another adventure befell him, more pleasant than the last. His historian will not relate it now, however, having to visit Sancho Panza, who was proceeding very busily and very drolly with his government.

Chapter XLVII. *The account of Sancho Panza's Behaviour in his Government, continued.*

THE history tells that Sancho Panza was taken from the court of justice to a sumptuous palace, where a royal and most spotless table was laid in a great hall. Immediately upon his entrance into this room the clarions sounded and four pages came in to bring him water for his hands, which Sancho received with great gravity. Then the music stopped and he took his seat at the head of the table, for there was no other seat besides and no other place laid. At his side there stood a personage with a little whalebone wand in his hand, who afterwards proved to be a physician. Then they lifted up the very rich white cloth which covered the fruit and a great variety of dishes of different foods. A person looking like a student pronounced the blessing, and a page tucked a lace bib under Sancho's chin, while another, who performed the office of butler, put a plate of fruit in front of him. But scarcely had he eaten a mouthful when the physician touched the dish with his little wand, and it was whisked from in front of him at top speed. The butler, however, brought him another dish of different food, which Sancho was just going to try. But before he could reach it to taste it the wand touched it, and a page whipped it off as quickly as the other had taken the fruit. Sancho was amazed at this performance and, looking at each one of them, asked whether he was supposed to eat his dinner like a conjuring trick. And the man with the wand replied:

'It must merely be eaten, Lord Governor, according to the manner and custom of other isles where there are governors. I, sir, am a physician, and I am salaried to act as doctor to the Governors of this isle. I am much more careful of their health than of my own, studying day and night and sounding the Governor's constitution to find means of curing him if he should fall ill. My principal duty is to be present at his dinners and suppers, to let him eat what seems to me fitting, and to take away from him what I presume may do him harm and be injurious to his stomach. That is why I ordered that dish of fruit to be removed, it being far too moist; and the other dish I had removed because it was too heating, containing many spices which increase the thirst; for one who drinks much kills and consumes the radical humour wherein life consists.'

'At that rate,' said Sancho, 'the dish of roast partridges over there won't do me any harm. They look very tasty to me.'

To which the physician replied: 'The Lord Governor shall never eat of them whilst I live.'

'Why not?' asked Sancho.

'Because our master Hippocrates,' answered the physician, 'the pole-star and light of medicine, says in one of his aphorisms: "*Omnis saturatio mala perdicis autem pessima*"; which means all surfeit is bad, but that of partridges is worst.'

'If that's so,' said Sancho, 'pray see, Master Doctor, which of all the dishes on the table will be most wholesome for me and do me least harm, and let me eat of it without your tapping it. For, by the life of the Governor and in true earnest, I'm dying of hunger, and to deny me my victuals is more likely to rob me of my life than to lengthen it, whatever you may say, Master Doctor.'

'Your worship is right, Lord Governor,' replied the physician, 'and therefore, in my opinion, you should not eat of those stewed rabbits there, for they are a furry food. You might have tried that veal if it had not been roasted with a pickle sauce; but as it is, it is out of the question.'

'That great smoking dish further over,' said Sancho, 'looks to me like a mixed stew, and seeing what a lot of different things there are in these stews, we can't fail to find something in it tasty and wholesome for me.'

'*Absit!*' cried the physician, 'far from us be such an evil thought! There is nothing in the world less nourishing than a mixed stew. Leave your stews for canons or rectors of colleges, or for country weddings. And let them be banished from Governors' tables, at which every delicacy and refinement must preside. And the reason is that always, everywhere, and by everybody, simple medicines are more highly prized than compounds. For in simple ones there is no danger that one may make a mistake, while in the compounds one may err by varying the proportions of the ingredients. But it is my certain opinion that to conserve and improve his health, my Lord Governor should now eat a hundred wafer rolls and some thin slices of quince flesh, which will sustain his stomach and help his digestion.'

When he heard this Sancho leant against the back of the chair and stared intently at the doctor, demanding in grave tones what his name was and where he had studied.

'My name, Lord Governor,' replied the physician, 'is Doctor Pedro Recio de Aguero, and I am a native of a village called Tirteafuera, which lies on the right of the road from Caracuel to Almodovar del Campo; and I hold the degree of doctor from the university of Osuna.'

To which Sancho replied in a great rage: 'Then, Doctor Pedro Recio de Aguero, native of Tirteafuera, which lies on the right of the road from Caracuel to Almodovar del Campo, graduate of Osuna, get out of here at once! Or if you don't, I swear by the sun I'll take a stick and, beginning with you, I'll beat every doctor out of the isle; every one of them at least that I find to be ignorant, though your learned, prudent and sensible physician I'll raise above my head and honour as a god. And I say again, get out of here, Pedro Recio, or if you don't I'll take this chair I'm sitting on and smash it over your head. And let me answer for it at Doomsday. For I will justify myself by swearing it was a good and godly deed to kill a bad doctor. Bad doctors are the curse of the state. Let me have something to eat, or else you can take away my governorship, for a post that won't find a man in food isn't worth two beans.'

The doctor was alarmed at the Governor's violent outburst, and tried to make his get-away. But at that moment a post-horn sounded in the street, and the butler looked out of the window and turned to say: 'Here's a messenger from my master the Duke. He must be bringing some despatch of importance.'

The courier entered, sweating and flurried, and drawing a sealed envelope from under his shirt, placed in in the Governor's hands. Whereat Sancho gave it to the butler, and ordered him to read the address, which ran as follows: 'To Don Sancho Panza, Governor of the Isle Barataria, into his own hands or those of his secretary.'

Hearing which, Sancho asked: 'Who here is my secretary?'

And one of those standing by answered: 'I, sir, for I can read and write, and I'm a Basque.'

'With that last qualification,' said Sancho, 'you could well be secretary to the Emperor himself. Open this envelope and see what it says.'

The newly-made secretary did so and, having read the contents, pronounced that it was a matter to be discussed in private. Sancho then ordered the room to be cleared, and no one to remain but the steward and the butler; on which the doctor and the rest departed. After which the secretary read the letter, which ran as follows:

'*It has come to my knowledge, Don Sancho Panza, that some enemies of mine and of this isle will deliver a furious assault upon it, though on what night is uncertain. You must keep watch and be on the alert for fear of surprise. I have also learnt by trustworthy spies that four per-*

sons have entered the place in disguise to take your life, for they are
afraid of your abilities. Keep your eyes open, watch who comes to
speak to you and eat nothing that is set before you. I will be sure to aid
you if you find yourself in difficulties. Whatever happens I rely on your
acting with your accustomed intelligence.

From this place, the sixteenth of August at four in the morning.

Your friend,
The Duke.'

Sancho was astonished, and his companions pretended to be so
as well. Then turning to the steward, he said:

'What we must do now – and immediately – is to put Doctor
Recio in the lock-up; for if anyone may kill me it will be he, and
that by the most lingering and worst of all deaths, hunger.'

'Yet,' said the butler, 'it is my opinion that your worship ought
not to eat anything that is on this table, for it has been prepared by
nuns and, as the saying goes, behind the cross stands the devil.'

'I don't dispute it,' replied Sancho. 'So for the moment let me
have a piece of bread and some four pounds of grapes. There can
be no poison in them. For really I can't hold out without eating, and
if we have to be ready for these battles they threaten us with we
must be well nourished, since guts carry heart and not heart guts.
You, secretary, reply to the Duke, my Lord, and say that all his
orders shall be carried out exactly and most faithfully. You will
salute my lady the Duchess on my behalf, and say that I beg her not
to forget to send my letter and my bundle by messenger to my wife,
Teresa Panza. Tell her that I shall consider it a great favour, and
will be sure to serve her to the uttermost of my power. And, by the
way, you can put in a greeting to my master, Don Quixote de la
Mancha, that he may see I'm grateful and, being a good secretary
and a good Basque, you may add anything you please that's to the
point. Now let them clear away the cloth and give me something to
eat, and then I'll deal with all the spies and murderers and enchanters
that may set upon me or on my isle.'

At this point a page came in and said: 'There's a countryman here
on business who wants to speak to your worship on a matter which
he says is of great importance.'

'It's very odd,' said Sancho. 'Can these businessmen really be so

stupid that they can't see this is no time to come about their business?
Are we governors and judges not men of flesh and blood? Don't we
need to rest awhile like other men? Or do they expect us to be made
of marble stone? Upon my soul, if this governorship of mine lasts –
and I've an inkling it won't – I'll lay into some of these businessmen. Now tell that fellow to come in; but make sure first that he
isn't one of these spies or one of my murderers.'

'He isn't, sir,' answered the page. 'He seems a harmless sort. Indeed, if I'm not mistaken he's as harmless as a crust of bread.'

'There's nothing to fear,' said the butler, 'for we're all here.'

'Wouldn't it be possible, steward,' asked Sancho, 'for me to eat
something of weight and substance now Doctor Pedro Recio has
gone, even if it were only a bit of bread and an onion?'

'To-night at supper we will make up for the shortcomings of
your dinner, and your Lordship shall be amply satisfied,' declared
the steward.

'God grant it,' replied Sancho.

At this the peasant came in. He was a man of very good appearance, a decent honest soul as you could see from a thousand miles
off, and his first words were: 'Who here is the Lord Governor?'

'Who should it be,' replied the secretary, 'but the one seated in
the chair?'

'Then I humble myself in his presence,' said the countryman.
And going down on his knees, he begged the Governor for his hand
to kiss. But Sancho refused it, and bade him get up and tell him what
he wanted. And the countryman obeyed, saying: 'I'm a labouring
man, sir, a native of Miguelturra, a village six miles from Ciudad
Real.'

'Here's another Tirteafuera!' exclaimed Sancho. 'But go on,
brother, for I can tell you I know Miguelturra very well. It's not
very far from my own village.'

'The matter is this, sir,' continued the countryman. 'I, by the
mercy of God, am married with the licence and blessing of the Holy
Roman Catholic Church. I have two sons, both students, the
younger studying for a bachelor and the elder for a licentiate. I am
a widower, for my wife died, or rather a wicked doctor killed her by
purging her when she was pregnant; and had God allowed her child
to see the light and it had been a boy I would have put him to study

B B

for a doctor, so that he might not be envious of his brothers, the bachelor and the licentiate.'

'So,' said Sancho, 'if your wife hadn't died, or been killed, you wouldn't be a widower now.'

'No, sir, certainly not,' replied the countryman.

'We're getting on famously,' said Sancho. 'Go ahead, brother; this is a time for sleep rather than for business.'

'Let me tell you, then,' said the countryman, 'that this son of mine, who is to be a bachelor, fell in love with a young lady in our village, called Clara Perlerino, daughter of Andrew Perlerino, a very rich farmer; and this name of Perlerino doesn't come to them by descent or ancestry, but because everyone in the family is paralytic and, to make it sound better, they call themselves Perlerinos. Though, to tell you the truth, the young lady seems an orient pearl, and looked at from the right hand side is like a flower of the field. From the left she isn't so good, for she's short of that eye she lost from small-pox. But although she has a great number of large pits in her face, her admirers say that they aren't pits, but graves in which the souls of her lovers lie buried. She's so clean that her nose is cocked right up, as they say, to avoid soiling her face, and looks as if it's running away from her mouth. But she is extremely handsome all the same, and has a big mouth, that would figure among the shapeliest of its kind, if she wasn't short of ten or a dozen teeth. I don't know what to say about her lips, for they're so thin and delicate that they might be wound into a skein, if it were usual to wind lips. They look marvellous, for they are a different colour from the ordinary run of lips, being mottled blue, green and purple. Pardon me, Lord Governor, for painting the young lady's features in such detail, but she'll be my daughter some day, for I like her, and she doesn't seem bad to me.'

'Paint what you like,' said Sancho. 'Your picture refreshes me; and if I had dined this portrait would be the best dessert in the world.'

'I've still to serve you with that,' answered the countryman, 'but the time may come when we may be acquainted if we aren't now. And I tell you, sir, that if I could paint her elegance and the height of her body it would be something to marvel at. Yet that I can't do because she's bent and shrunken, and her knees meet her mouth.

But it's clear enough, all the same, that if she could stand upright her head would touch the ceiling. She would have given my bachelor her hand in marriage by now, only she can't stretch it out because it's withered; but even then you can tell how fine and shapely it is from her long furrowed nails.'

'So far, so good,' said Sancho. 'Take it, brother, that you've painted her from head to foot. What is it you want now? Come to the point without all these twistings and windings, and trimmings and additions.'

'I should like your worship to do me a favour,' answered the countryman, 'and give me a letter of recommendation to the girl's father, begging him to be so kind as to let this marriage take place, since we're not unequal in fortune's gifts or in nature's. For, to tell you the truth, my Lord Governor, my son's bewitched, and not a day passes that the evil spirits don't torment him three or four times; and from falling into the fire once, his face is crinkled like parchment and his eyes are rather moist and running. But he has a temper like an angel's and, if it weren't that he bangs and punches himself, he would be a saint.'

'Do you want anything else, my good fellow?' asked Sancho.

'There's one other thing I should like,' said the countryman, 'only I daren't mention it. But let it come out; it mustn't go bad inside me, come what may. So I'll tell you, sir, I'd like your worship to give me three hundred or six hundred ducats to help towards my bachelor's dowry. I mean, sir, to help him set up house; for, after all, they'll have to live on their own, and not be subject to the interference of their parents.'

'Think if there's anything else you'd like,' said Sancho, 'and don't let shame or bashfulness prevent your mentioning it.'

'No, nothing at all,' answered the countryman.

But no sooner did he answer than the Governor rose to his feet, and seizing the chair on which he had been sitting, cried out: 'I swear to God, Don lubberly, boorish Lumpkin, that if you don't get out of my sight this instant I'll break your head open with this chair! You villainous son of a whore! You devil's own painter! Is this the time to come asking me for six hundred ducats? And where have I got them, stinker? And why should I give them to you, even if I had them, rogue and idiot? What are Miguelturra and the whole family of Perlerinos to me? Get out, I say, or if you don't, I swear by the Duke, my master, I'll do as I said. You can never be from Miguelturra; you are some scoundrel sent here by Hell to tempt me. What, you godless wretch? I haven't held the governorship a day and a half, and you expect me to have six hundred ducats, do you?'

The steward signed to the countryman to leave the room, which he did, hanging his head, and apparently terrified that the Governor might carry out his threat; for the rogue was an excellent actor.

But let us leave Sancho in his rage – and peace to the whole company – and return to Don Quixote, whom we left with his face bound up and dressed for his cattish wounds, which took more than a week to heal. And on one of these days there occurred an incident which Cide Hamete promises to recount as truthfully and exactly as he always relates every minutest detail of this history.

Chapter XLVIII. *Of Don Quixote's Adventure with Doña Rodriguez, the Duchess's Waiting-woman, and other incidents worthy of record and of eternal remembrance.*

THE sore-wounded Don Quixote was exceedingly fretful and melancholy, with his face bandaged and marked, not by the hand of God but by the claws of a cat – such are the misfortunes incidental to knight errantry. For six days he did not appear in public, but on one of those nights, lying awake and watchful, brooding on his misfortunes and on Altisidora's persecution, he heard someone opening the door of his room with a key, and immediately imagined that the enamoured maiden was coming to surprise his chastity and overcome the fidelity he owed his lady Dulcinea del Toboso.

'No,' said he, in an audible voice, believing in his imaginary picture, 'the greatest beauty on earth shall not prevail upon me to cease my adoration of the lady I hold engraved and imprinted in the centre of my heart and in my innermost entrails, whether you are transformed, my lady, into an onion-eating country girl or a nymph of the golden Tagus, weaving tissues of twisted silk and gold, or if Merlin or Montesinos holds you where he will; for wherever you may be you are mine, and everywhere I have been or shall be I am yours.'

As he concluded this speech the door opened. He stood up on the bed, enveloped from head to foot in a yellow satin quilt, a nightcap on his head, and his face and moustache in bandages – his face because of his scratches, and his moustaches to keep them from drooping and falling; and in this costume he appeared the strangest phantom imaginable. He riveted his eyes on the door, but where he expected to see the love-lorn and distressed Altisidora come in, he saw a most venerable waiting-woman, with a white pleated veil, so long that it covered and swathed her from head to foot. In the fingers of her left hand she carried a burning half-candle, and with her right she shaded her face to keep the light from her eyes, which were covered by a pair of enormous spectacles. She advanced with noiseless tread, moving her feet very softly. Don Quixote gazed at her from his vantage point and, imagining from her dress and her silence that this was some witch or sorceress coming to do him a mischief, began to cross himself most energetically. The apparition drew nearer, and when it reached the middle of the room it raised its eyes and observed Don Quixote's frantic exercise. Now if he was frightened at the sight of such a figure, she was equally startled by his appearance, for the moment she saw him so tall and yellow, in his quilt and his disfiguring bandages, she screamed out loudly: 'Jesus! What's that?'

With the sudden fright the candle fell from her hands; and finding herself in the dark, she turned to go. But in her alarm she tripped over her skirt and came down with a great thud. Then the terrified Don Quixote began to speak:

'I conjure you, phantom or whatever you are, to tell me your name and to say what you want of me. If you are a soul in torment, say so, and I will do everything in my power for you, for I am a Catholic Christian and love to benefit all mankind. It was with that end I took up the order of knight errantry which I profess, the exercise of which extends even to relieving souls in purgatory.'

The bewildered waiting-woman, hearing herself thus exorcised, judged Don Quixote's fright by her own, and answered in low and plaintive tones: 'Don Quixote – if, perhaps, your worship is Don Quixote – I am no phantom or apparition or soul in purgatory, as your worship seems to think, but Doña Rodriguez, maid-of-honour to my lady the Duchess, and I come to you in such a distress as it is your custom to remedy.'

'Tell me, Doña Rodriguez,' asked Don Quixote, 'do you come to me, perhaps, on a mediation of love? For I must inform you that I am good for no one, thanks to the peerless beauty of my lady Dulcinea del Toboso. To be plain, Doña Rodriguez, if you will omit and lay on one side all love messages you may go and relight your candle and come back. Then we will talk of anything you may ask or desire, saving, as I say, all incitements to love.'

'I bring a message from anyone, sir!' answered the waiting-woman. 'Little does your worship know me. Indeed, I am not so extremely old as to resort to such child's tricks. God be praised, I have my soul in my body and all my teeth and molars in my mouth, except for a few that I have lost to the catarrh, which is so common in this land of Aragon. But wait for me a moment, your worship. I will go out and light my candle, and come quickly back to recount my griefs to the reliever of all griefs in the world.'

And without waiting for a reply, she went out of the room, leaving Don Quixote calmly and thoughtfully awaiting her return. But a thousand thoughts soon crowded into his mind on the subject of this new adventure, and it occurred to him that he had judged and acted improperly in putting himself in danger of breaking his pledged faith to his lady. 'Who knows,' he said to himself, 'whether the Devil, who is subtle and crafty, is not trying to deceive me now with a waiting-woman, though he has not been able to do so with Empresses, Queens, Duchesses, Marchionesses, or Countesses? For I have very often heard very wise men say that, if he can, he will rather give you a flat-nosed than a hawk-nosed woman. And who knows whether this solitude, this opportunity, and this silence may not arouse my sleeping desires and cause me, after all these years, to fall where I have never stumbled? In such cases it is better to fly than to await battle. Yet I cannot be in my senses to be thinking and talking such nonsense; for it is impossible for a white-veiled, fat, bespectacled waiting-woman to move or arouse any lecherous thought in the most depraved breast in the world. Can there possibly be a waiting-woman on earth with wholesome flesh? Is there one of them in the world who is not impertinent, affected and prudish? Avaunt then, you rabble of waiting-women, useless for any human pleasure. How wise was that lady who, they say, had two dummy ones beside her couch, with spectacles and sewing-cushions as if they were working, and found them as good as the real thing for sustaining the dignity of her hall.'

At this he leapt out of bed with the intention of closing the door and preventing Doña Rodriguez' entrance. When he got there, however, to shut it, the lady was already returning with a lighted white wax candle. But when she saw Don Quixote near-to, wrapped in his quilt with his bandages and his night-cap or bonnet, she was once more seized with fright and, retreating two paces, asked: 'Am I safe, Sir Knight? For I do not take it as a sign of modesty that your worship has got out of bed.'

'I would ask you that same question, lady,' replied Don Quixote. 'Tell me whether I shall be safe from assault and ravishment.'

'From whom or of whom do you ask for this assurance, Sir Knight?' asked the waiting-woman.

'From you and of you,' replied Don Quixote, 'for I am not made of marble nor you of brass, nor is it now ten o'clock in the morning, but midnight, or even a little after, I imagine; and besides, we are in a room more close and secret than that cave can have been where the bold, treacherous Aeneas enjoyed the lovely and gentle Dido. But give me your hand, lady, for I desire no greater security than my continence and modesty and the assurance offered by that reverend hood.'

Saying which, he kissed his right hand, and with it seized hers, which she gave him with the same ceremony.

Here Cide Hamete puts in a parenthesis, and swears by Mahomet that he would give the better cloak of two he had to have seen those two walk from the door to the bed, thus entwined and linked.

Finally Don Quixote got into bed, and Doña Rodriguez remained sitting in a chair a little way from his bedside, without taking off her spectacles or putting down her candle. Don Quixote muffled and covered himself completely, leaving no more than his face revealed, and when the two were settled, the first to break the silence was the knight, who said:

'Now, Doña Rodriguez, you may unburden yourself and disclose all the contents of your sorrowful heart and afflicted bowels. It shall be heard by me with chaste ears and remedied by compassionate deeds.'

'That I believe,' replied the waiting-woman, 'for no less Christian an answer could be expected from your worship's gentle and agreeable appearance. The case is, Don Quixote, that although you see me seated in this chair in the middle of the kingdom of Aragon and in the habit of a decayed and forlorn waiting-woman, I am a native of the highlands of Oviedo and of a family which is allied with many of the best in that province. But my ill luck and the improvidence of my parents, which led to their untimely impoverishment, brought me, I do not know how or why, to the Court of Madrid, where, for the sake of peace and to avert greater misfortunes, my parents put me in service as waiting-maid to a noble lady; and I would have your worship know that no one ever surpassed me at back-stitch and plain work in the whole of my life. My parents left me in service and returned to their country, and a few years afterwards they departed this life – it must have been to Heaven, for they were very good people and Catholic Christians. I was left an orphan depending on the miserable salary and scanty favours of such court servants. About that time a squire of the house fell in love with me, without my giving him the least cause for it, a man already advanced in years, bearded and personable and, what is more, as well-born as the king, for he came from the mountains. We did not manage our affair so secretly as to keep it from the notice of my lady who, to save us from scandalmongers, had us married with the licence and approbation of Holy Mother Church, from which marriage was born a daughter, to put an end to my good fortune, such as it was – not that I died in childbed, for I was delivered safely and in due time, but because shortly afterwards my husband died of a shock he received, which would much astonish your worship if I had time now to tell you of it.'

At this she began to weep piteously, and said: 'Pardon me, your worship, Don Quixote, I cannot help it. Every time I remember my unfortunate husband my eyes fill with tears. God help me! With what dignity he used to carry my lady behind him on the crupper of a stout mule, black as jet itself! For they did not use coaches or chairs in those days, as they say is the fashion now, and ladies rode behind their squires. So much at least I cannot refrain from telling you, so that you may be aware of my husband's fine breeding and manners. A judge of the court happened to be coming out of the

Santiago street in Madrid, which is rather narrow, with two of his officers riding before him, and as soon as my good squire saw him, he turned his mule's rein, as if meaning to wait upon him. Then my lady, who was riding behind, whispered in his ear: "What are you doing, you blockhead? Are you forgetting that I am here?"

'The judge, out of politeness, pulled up his horse and said: "Go on your way, sir, for it is I who should wait upon the lady Casilda" – that was my mistress's name.

'However, my husband, cap in hand, insisted on waiting for the judge. At this my mistress, full of rage and spite, drew a stout pin – or I think it was a bodkin – out of its sheath and ran it into his loins, whereupon my husband gave a loud cry and writhed his body so that both he and his mistress fell to the ground. Two of her grooms ran to pick her up, and the judge and his officers ran to her too. The Guadalajara gate was in an uproar – I mean the idlers who were around. My mistress came away on foot, and my husband ran into a barber's shop, crying that his bowels were pierced right through. After that his courteousness became a subject of gossip, so much so that the boys used to chase after him in the street; and for that reason and because he was rather short-sighted my lady dismissed him; and I am perfectly certain that the grief of it brought on his calamitous death. I was left a widow and unprotected, with a daughter on my hands who went on increasing in beauty like the foam of the sea. At length, as I had the reputation of being a fine needle-woman, my lady the Duchess, who had recently married my lord the Duke, offered to bring me with her to this kingdom of Aragon, and my daughter with me. Here in course of time she grew up, with all the graces in the world. She sings like a lark, dances like a thought, capers in the country-dance like a wild thing, reads and writes like a schoolmaster, and reckons like a miser. Of her cleanliness I say nothing, for running water is not cleaner, and now she must be sixteen, five months and three days, more or less, if my memory does not fail me. To be brief, this girl of mine fell in love with the son of a very rich farmer, who lives in one of my master the Duke's villages, not very far from here. In short, I don't know how it happened, but these two came together. He deceived her under the promise of marriage, and now he refuses to keep his word; and although the Duke my master knows it, because I have complained to him not once but many times and implored him to command this farmer to marry my daughter, he turns a deaf ear and will hardly listen to me. And the reason is that this trickster's father is very rich and lends him money and sometimes goes surety for him in his scrapes, and so he does not like to displease him or worry him in any way. So, my dear sir, I should like your worship to undertake the redressing of this wrong, either by entreaty or by arms; for, as all the world says, your worship was born to right wrongs, to redress injuries, and to protect the unfortunate. Reflect on my daughter's orphan state, your worship, her breeding, her youth, and all the virtues I have told you she possesses; for by God and on my conscience, of all my lady's maids there is not one who reaches up to the sole of her shoe. And as for that Altisidora, whom they reckon the liveliest and the freest, if you compare her with my daughter, she doesn't come within six miles of her. For I must say, my dear sir, that all is not gold that glitters; and that Altisidora has more boldness than beauty about her and more freedom than modesty. Besides which she is not very wholesome, for she has a certain taint in her breath, and one cannot bear to be near her for a moment. And even my lady the Duchess ... But I must be silent, for they say that walls have ears.'

'On my life, Doña Rodriguez, what is the matter with my lady the Duchess?' asked Don Quixote.

'Thus pressed,' replied the waiting-woman, 'I cannot refuse to answer your question with the whole truth. Do you observe, Don Quixote, the beauty of my lady the Duchess, the bloom of her complexion, that is like nothing so much as a smooth and burnished sword; those twin cheeks of milk and carmine, which hold the sun in one and the moon in the other, and the graceful way she treads, as if she scorns the ground? Doesn't she seem to dispense health wherever she goes? But let me tell your worship that she may thank God for it in the first place, and in the next two issues that she has, one on each leg, through which she discharges all the ill humours of which the doctors say she is full.'

'Holy Virgin!' exclaimed Don Quixote. 'Can my lady the Duchess possibly have two such drains? I should not have believed it if the barefoot friars had told me; yet since Doña Rodriguez says so, it must be so. But such issues and in such places must distil not humours but liquid ambergris. Truly, I believe that this opening of issues must be an important matter for the health.'

Scarcely had Don Quixote finished this sentence when the doors of the room burst open with a great bang, and with the shock the candle fell out of Doña Rodriguez' hand, leaving the room dark as the wolf's maw, as the saying is. Then the poor waiting-woman felt her throat so tightly gripped by two hands that she could not squawk; and someone else, without a word, very nimbly lifted her skirts and began to give her a pitifully hearty slapping, apparently with a slipper. And though Don Quixote felt this he did not budge from his bed, having no idea what was the matter, but stayed quiet and still, fearing that it might soon be his turn for a beating. It was no idle fear; for leaving the belaboured waiting-woman, who dared not cry out, the silent executioners fell on Don Quixote and, pulling off his sheet and his quilt, pinched him so hard and so often that he was driven to defend himself with his fists; and all this in a bewildering silence. The battle lasted almost half an hour. Then the phantoms departed. Doña Rodriguez gathered up her skirts and went out of the door, bemoaning her disaster, but without saying a word to Don Quixote. He, mournful and pinched, perplexed and thoughtful, remained alone; where we will leave him, longing to know who was the malign enchanter that had dealt him such a trick. But that will be told in good time. For Sancho Panza calls us, and the order of this history demands that we go to him.

Chapter XLIX. *What happened to Sancho Panza on the Rounds of his Isle.*

WE left the great Governor vexed and angry with that portrait-painting rogue of a peasant, who had been tutored by the steward, as the steward was by the Duke, to make sport of him. But he held his own against them all, ignorant, coarse and clumpish though he was, and said to those with him and to Doctor Pedro Recio, who had come back into the hall once the private matter of the Duke's letter had been disposed of:

'I now plainly understand that judges and governors ought to be, and must be, made of brass, to endure the importunities of your men of business, who expect to be listened to and attended to at all

hours and seasons, and are intent only on their own affairs, come
what may. And if the poor judge doesn't hear them and attend to
them, either because he can't or because it isn't the regular time for
giving them audience, they immediately curse him and slander him
and bite at him and even pull his family to pieces. Foolish man of
business, stupid man of business, don't be in such a hurry! Wait for
the proper time and season for your affairs. Don't come at dinner
time, nor at bed time; for judges are flesh and blood and must give
to their nature what nature requires; excepting only me, who give
mine nothing to eat, thanks to the worthy Doctor Pedro Recio
Tirteafuera there, who would have me die of hunger, and declares
that death is life. God give the same fate to him and all his breed –
I'm speaking of quacks, for good doctors deserve palms and laurels.'

All who knew Sancho Panza were amazed to hear him speak so
elegantly, which they could not account for, unless it be that offices
and serious duties quicken some intellects as they deaden others.
Finally Doctor Pedro Aguero of Tirteafuera promised to allow him
some supper that night, even though it might mean transgressing
all the rules of Hippocrates. With this promise the Governor was
satisfied, and looked forward with great impatience to nightfall
and meal-time; and even though time seemed to him to be standing
still, at length the long wished for moment arrived, and they gave
him for his supper a hash of beef and onions and some boiled calves'
feet, rather stale from keeping. But he fell to it all with more pleasure
than if he had been given Milan game, Roman pheasants, Sorrento
veal, Moron partridges, or Lavajos geese; and during his supper he
turned to the doctor and said:

'Look here, Master Doctor, you needn't trouble in future to give
me choice things and delicate dainties, for that would mean wrenching my stomach off its hinges. It's used to kid, beef, bacon, salt
meat, turnips and onions, and if it's given palace food by chance, it
takes it with queasiness and sometimes with loathing. I'd like the
butler to bring me mixed stews – as they call them; and the stronger
they are the higher they smell. He can shove in anything he likes so
long as it's good to eat, and I'll thank him for it, and pay him one
day. But let no one fool me; for either we are or we aren't. Let's all
live and eat in peace and friendship, for when God sends daylight
it's dawn for all. I shall govern this isle without waiving a right or

taking a bribe; and let everyone keep his eyes open and mind his own business; for I would have them know that the devil is loose in Cantillana, and if they give me cause they'll see wonders. Just you make yourselves honey and the flies'll eat you.'

'Truly, Lord Governor,' said the butler, 'your worship is very right in all you say, and I offer in the name of all the islesmen of this isle to serve you with all diligence, love and goodwill; for the mild manner of government which your worship has shown us in these beginnings leaves us no room to do or think anything which may redound to your disservice.'

'I believe you,' answered Sancho, 'and you would be a set of fools if you did or thought otherwise. Let them look after my feeding and my Dapple's, I say once more, which is the main point of the matter, and the most important. And when the time comes let us make the rounds; for I intend to cleanse this isle of every sort of impurity, and of your vagabond, idle and ill-conditioned persons. For I should like you to know, friends, that your vagrant and lazy sort are the same thing in a state as drones are in the hive, eating up the honey the workers make. I intend to favour labouring men, preserve gentlemen's privileges, reward the virtuous, and above all respect religion and honour the clergy. What do you think of that? Am I saying something or cracking my brains for nothing?'

'You are saying so much, Lord Governor,' said the steward, 'that I am amazed to find a man of so little learning as your worship – for I believe you have none – say so many things that are full of judgment and good counsel. For those that sent you here and we that came with you were far from expecting anything of the sort from you. But every day we see something new in the world; jokes are turned to earnest and mockers find themselves mocked.'

Night had now come on, and the Governor, having eaten his supper by leave of Doctor Recio, prepared to make his rounds, accompanied by the steward, the secretary, the butler, the chronicler, whose duty it was to record his deeds, and enough constables and clerks to make up a fair-sized battalion. Sancho walked in the middle with his wand of justice, a grand sight to see. Now when they had patrolled a few of the town streets they heard the clashing of knives and, running to the spot, found no more than two men fighting. These broke off when they saw the law approaching, one of them crying: 'Here, in the name of God and the King! What! Are people to be attacked here and robbed and assaulted in the open streets?'

'Be calm, my good fellow,' said Sancho, 'and tell me the cause of this quarrel, for I'm the Governor.'

At that his adversary put in: 'My Lord Governor, I will tell you very briefly. Your worship must know that this gentleman has just won more than a thousand *reals* here in this gambling house opposite, God knows how. And I, who was a spectator, decided several doubtful throws in his favour, against all the dictates of my conscience. He got up with his winnings, and when I expected him to give me a crown at least as a fee – such as it's usual and customary to pay men of quality like myself, who stand by to judge fair play, and back up malpractice and prevent quarrels – he pocketed his money and left the house. I came after him in a rage, and requested him in fair and civil words to give me some eight *reals*, for he knows that I am an honourable man and have no profession or place, since my parents neither taught me a trade nor bequeathed me a post. But the rogue – he's a greater thief than Cacus and a greater cheat than Andradilla – wouldn't give me more than four *reals*. So you see, my Lord Governor, what a shameless, conscienceless fellow he is. But I swear, if your worship hadn't come, I would have made him cough up his winnings and taught him how to balance accounts.'

'What do you say to this?' asked Sancho.

The other replied that his adversary was speaking the truth but that he had not intended to give him more than four *reals*, because he was continually giving him something; and that men who expect tips must be polite and take what they get with a smile on their faces, and not haggle with winners unless they know for certain that they are sharpers and that their gains are unfairly got. But there was no better proof of his honesty and that he was no thief, as the other suggested, than his refusal to pay; for sharpers must always pay tribute to their accomplices.

'That's right,' said the steward. 'Now consider, my Lord Governor, what should be done with these men.'

'This is what shall be done,' answered Sancho. 'You, master winner, fair, foul, or indifferent, must pay your knifer a hundred *reals* here and now, and disburse thirty more for the poor in the prisons. And you, who have neither place nor profession and go idly about this isle, must take these hundred *reals* at once, and to-morrow and no later get out of this isle for ten years' banishment, on pain of finishing your sentence in the next life if you break the ban; for I'll hang you on a gallows – or at least the hangman shall do it for me – and let no one reply or he shall feel the weight of my hand.'

The one disbursed, the other took the money; the one left the isle, the other went home; and the Governor went on to say: 'Now if I'm good for anything I'll put down these gambling houses, for I strongly suspect that much harm comes of them.'

'This one at least,' said one of the clerks, 'your worship won't be able to put down, because it's kept by a great personage, and his losses at cards every year are incomparably greater than his winnings. Your worship can show your power against other gambling dens of lower degree, for it's those which do the greatest harm and harbour the worst abuses. But the notorious sharpers dare not practise their tricks in gentlemen's and lords' houses. And since the vice of gambling has become a common habit, it's better for it to be practised in houses of quality than at some tradesmen's, where they catch a wretch after midnight and flay him alive.'

'Yes, Master Clerk, I know there's much to be said on that score,' replied Sancho.

At this moment there came up a constable, who had hold of a youth, and he said: 'Lord Governor, this young man was coming our way, but as soon as he spied the law he turned round and began to run like a stag, a sure sign that he's a criminal. I went off after him, but if it hadn't been that he tripped and fell I should never have caught him.'

'Why did you run away, man?' asked Sancho.

'Sir, to avoid answering all those questions the constable asks,' replied the youth.

'What is your trade?'

'A weaver.'

'And what do you weave?'

'Iron heads for lances, so please your worship.'

'So you choose to be funny? Is it a buffoon you are? Very well. And where were you going just now?'

'To take the air, sir.'

'And where do you take the air in this isle?'

'Where it blows.'

'Good, you answer to the point. You're a clever one, my lad, but kindly reckon that I'm the air, and blow astern of you and drive you into jail. Hold him there, and take him away, for I'll make him sleep there to-night out of the air.'

'By God,' said the lad, 'your worship can no more make me sleep in prison than make me king!'

'Well, why can't I make you sleep in prison?' asked Sancho. 'Haven't I power to arrest and discharge you whenever and as often as I please?'

'However much power your worship may have,' said the youth, 'won't be enough to make me sleep in prison.'

'Why not?' demanded Sancho. 'Take him at once where he'll see his mistake with his own eyes, and in case the jailer should use his interested liberality on his behalf, I'll make him go bail for two thousand ducats that he won't let you stir a step out of prison, my man.'

'This is all ridiculous,' answered the youth. 'The point is that no man living shall make me sleep in the jail.'

'Tell me, devil,' demanded Sancho, 'have you an angel to release you and free you from the fetters that I shall have put on you?'

'Now, my Lord Governor,' answered the youth with a charming smile, 'let us reason together and come to the point. Suppose your worship orders me to be taken to prison, and has me loaded with fetters and chains there and put in a cell, laying the jailer under heavy penalties to carry out your orders, and not let me out; all the same if I don't wish to sleep, and stay awake all night without closing an eyelid, will your worship with all your power be able to make me sleep if I don't choose to?'

'No, of course not,' said the secretary, 'the man has made out his case.'

'You would stay awake then,' asked Sancho, 'only because it's your own will, and with no intention of crossing me?'

'None, sir,' said the youth, 'none at all.'

'Then go, in Heaven's name,' said Sancho. 'Go and sleep at home and God give you sound sleep. I don't want to rob you of it. But

I warn you not to make a mock of the law in future, for you may meet someone who'll return you the joke on your skull.'

The youth went off, and the Governor continued his rounds. Then shortly afterwards two constables came up, grasping a man, and said: 'Lord Governor, this person looks like a man but isn't. She's a woman, and no plain one, dressed up in a man's clothes.'

They raised two or three lanterns to her face, and their light revealed the features of a girl of sixteen or so, with her hair gathered into a little net of gold and green silk, and lovely as a thousand pearls. They looked her up and down, and saw that she was wearing flesh-coloured silk stockings with white taffeta garters edged with gold and seed-pearl. Her breeches were of green cloth of gold, her jacket or coat of the same cloth hung loose, and beneath it she wore a doublet of the finest white and gold material. Her shoes were white and like a man's. She wore no sword on her belt but a jewelled dagger, and on her fingers several very fine rings. In short, everyone thought the girl handsome, but not one of them recognized her, the natives of the place saying that they could not think who she was. But most surprised of all were those who were in the secret of the tricks which were being played on Sancho, because this meeting had not been contrived by them, and so they awaited its upshot with some excitement. Sancho was struck by the girl's beauty, and asked her who she was, where she was going, and what reason she had for wearing those clothes. And she answered with honest shame, her eyes fixed on the ground: 'Sir, I cannot reveal in public what it is so important for me to keep secret. One thing I want to be understood is that I am not a thief or a wicked person, but a poor young lady driven by jealousy to forget my modesty.'

Hearing this, the steward said to Sancho: 'Make your attendants retire, my Lord Governor, so that this lady can say what she will with less embarrassment.'

The Governor gave orders to that effect, and everyone drew aside except the steward, the butler and the secretary. Then, when they were alone, the young lady went on to say: 'Gentlemen, I am the daughter of Pedro Perez Mazorca, who farms the wool in this place and often comes to my father's house.'

'That won't pass, lady,' said the steward, 'for I know Pedro Perez very well, and I know that he has no children, male or female.

What's more you say that he's your father, and then add that he often comes to your father's house.'

'I'd already seen that,' said Sancho.

'Indeed, gentlemen, I'm confused and I don't know what I'm saying,' answered the young lady, 'but the truth is that I am the daughter of Diego de la Llana, whom your worships must all know.'

'Now that'll pass,' said the steward, 'for I know Diego de la Llana and I know that he's an important and rich gentleman, and that he has a son and a daughter, and since he has been left a widower there has been no one in this whole place who can say that he has seen his daughter's face, for he keeps her so confined that he doesn't even let the sun look on her. But, for all that, it's rumoured that she's extremely beautiful.'

'That's the truth,' replied the young lady. 'I am that daughter. Whether rumour lies or not about my beauty, you gentlemen will have discovered, for you have seen me.'

At this she began to weep piteously, and at the sight of her tears the secretary put his lips to the butler's ear and said to him very quietly: 'Something serious must certainly have happened to this poor young lady for her to be wandering from her home in this disguise and at such an hour, she being of such quality too.'

'There's no doubt of that,' answered the butler, 'and besides, her tears confirm the suspicion.'

Sancho comforted her with the best arguments he knew, and begged her to tell him what had happened to her without any fear; for they would all try most earnestly to help her in every possible way.

'This is the case, gentlemen,' she replied. 'My father has kept me confined for the last ten years, that is ever since my mother was laid in the earth. Mass is said at home in a fine chapel, and in all that time I've seen nothing but the sun by day and the stars and the moon by night. I don't know the look of streets, or market-places, or churches, or even men, except my father and my one brother, and Pedro Perez, the wool-farmer, who visits the house so often that it came into my head to call him my father so as not to mention my real one. This confinement, and his refusal to let me leave the house even to go to church, have made me very unhappy these many days and months. I longed to see the world, or at least the village where

I was born, and this wish didn't seem to me to infringe the modesty proper to young ladies of my birth. Now when I heard them talk of bull-fighting and cane-throwing and play-acting, I asked my brother, who is a year younger than I, to tell me about it all, and about many other things I hadn't seen; and he explained them to me in the best way he could, but it only inflamed my longing to see them. In the end, to shorten the tale of my undoing, let me say that I begged and entreated my brother – oh, I wish I had never begged and entreated him ...'

And she burst into tears once more. At which the steward said to her: 'Proceed, lady, and finish telling us what happened to you, for your words and your tears are keeping us all on tenterhooks.'

'There's little more to tell,' replied the young lady, 'though there are still many tears to be shed, for there's no other way of atoning for sinful wishes.'

The young lady's beauty had sunk into the butler's very soul, and as he held up his lantern once more to look at her again, it seemed to him that they were not tears she wept but seed-pearl or meadow dew; and he even raised them a point higher and compared them to orient pearls, hoping all the while that her misfortunes were not as great as her tears and sobs suggested. The Governor was out of all patience at the girl's slowness in telling her story, and bade her put them out of their suspense; for it was late and there was much of the town still to cover. Then, between sobs and half-breathed sighs, she went on:

'My misfortune and misery is no other than this: that I entreated my brother to disguise me as a man in one of his suits, and take me out one night to see all the town, while our father was asleep. He gave in to my entreaties, put these clothes on me, and dressed himself in some of mine, which suited him as if he were born for them, for he has no down on his chin and looks like nothing so much as a lovely girl. To-night – it must be an hour or so ago – we left the house, and our young and unruly fancies sent us wandering all round the town. But just as we were going to return home we saw a great troop of people coming, and my brother said to me: "Sister, this must be the watch. Fly like the wind, and follow me. If we are recognized, it'll be the worse for us." And as he spoke he turned round and set off running, though it was more like flying. Before I had gone six paces I fell down from fright, and then the officers of justice came up and brought me before your worships. And here I am shown up for a wicked, capricious girl before all these people.'

'So that's all your trouble, young lady,' said Sancho, 'and it wasn't jealousy that brought you from your home, as you told us at the beginning of your tale?'

'Yes, that's all, and it wasn't jealousy that brought me out, but just a wish to see the world; and that didn't go further than seeing the streets of this place.'

And the truth of the young lady's story was confirmed by the arrival of two constables with her brother as their prisoner, for one of them had caught him when he ran away from his sister. He wore a rich skirt and a blue damask cloak with fine gold lacings; his head had no covering or adornment except his hair, which was as red and curly as rings of gold. The Governor, the steward and the butler took him on one side out of his sister's hearing, and asked him how he came to be so dressed; and he, with no less shame and embarrassment, told the same tale as she had told, to the great pleasure of the love-stricken butler. The Governor, however, addressed them: 'This has been a very childish prank indeed, and there was no need of all this sighing and sobbing over the telling of your rash and stupid escapade. For if you had said, "we are so-and-so and so-and-so and we left our parents' house in this disguise to amuse ourselves, and we only did it out of curiosity and for no other reason," the story would have been done without all this moaning and weeping and the rest of it.'

'That's quite true,' replied the young lady, 'but I must confess, your worships, that I was in such a confusion that I couldn't decide what to do.'

'Nothing has been lost,' said Sancho. 'Let us go and leave you both at your father's house; perhaps he won't have missed you. But don't behave so childishly in future, or be so anxious to see the world; for an honest maid and a broken leg are best at home, a woman and a hen are soon lost by gadding, and the girl who's anxious to see also longs to be seen. I say no more.'

The youth thanked the Governor for the favour he proposed to do them by escorting them home, which was not far. So they set out. On their arrival the brother threw a pebble at a window, whereat a maid-servant who was waiting for them immediately came down and opened the door; and they went in, leaving everyone wondering at their beauty and good breeding, and at their desire to see the world by night without going further than their village. But they put everything down to their tender years.

The butler was left with his heart transfixed, and at once resolved to ask the young lady's father for her hand next day, feeling quite certain that he would not be refused, as he was a servant of the Duke's. The thought even came into Sancho's head of marrying the youth to his daughter Sanchica, and he decided to put his plan into practice at the proper time, believing that no husband could be refused to a governor's daughter.

This was the end of that night's rounds and, within two days, of the governorship, by which end all Sancho's designs were cut short and obliterated, as shall later be seen.

Chapter L. *Which reveals who the Enchanters and Executioners were that beat the Waiting-woman and pinched and scratched Don Quixote, with the Adventure of the Page who bore the letter to Teresa Panza, Sancho Panza's wife.*

CIDE HAMETE, that most meticulous investigator of every detail of this true history, says that at the moment when Doña Rodriguez left her room to go to Don Quixote's apartment another waiting-woman, who slept with her, heard her; and as all waiting-women are fond of prying, listening and sniffing, she went after her so silently that the good Rodriguez did not notice her. Now as soon as this waiting-woman saw the other enter Don Quixote's room, for fear of failing in the waiting-woman's custom of tale-bearing she went to inform her mistress the Duchess that Doña Rodriguez was in Don Quixote's bedroom. Whereat the Duchess told the Duke, and asked his permission for herself and Altisidora to go and see what that lady wanted with Don Quixote. The Duke agreed, and the two of them very warily and silently crept step by step and took up their position behind the door of the room, so close that they overheard every word spoken inside. And when the Duchess heard the Rodriguez expose the secret of her garden of fountains, neither she nor Altisidora could bear it; and so they burst into the room, in a great fury and spoiling for revenge, to pinch Don Quixote and slap the waiting-woman in the manner described. For affronts directed against the beauty and pride of women awake in them a high degree of anger, and kindle their desire for revenge. And when the Duchess told the Duke what had happened, he was greatly amused.

Then, in pursuance of her plan for amusing herself at Don Quixote's expense, the Duchess sent the page who had played the part of Dulcinea in the performance of her disenchantment – which Sancho had clean forgotten in his occupation of governing – to his wife, Teresa Panza, with her husband's letter and another from herself, also a great string of fine corals as a present.

Now the history tells that this page was very shrewd and sharp, and out of eagerness to serve his master and mistress set out with a very good will for Sancho's village. And just as he entered it he saw a great number of women doing their washing in a stream, and asked them if they could tell him whether there was a woman called Teresa Panza living there, the wife of a certain Sancho Panza, squire to a knight called Don Quixote de la Mancha. And a girl stood up from her linen and answered him: 'Teresa Panza's my mother, and Sancho's my father, and the knight's our master.'

'Then come, young lady,' said the page, 'and take me to your mother. For I bear a letter and a present for her from that father of yours.'

'That I will, and gladly, my dear sir,' replied the girl, who seemed to be fourteen or so.

And leaving the clothes she was washing to one of her companions, she did not wait to put on a hat or shoes, for she was bare-legged and dishevelled, but ran skipping along before the page's horse, crying: 'Come, your worship, our house is at this end of the village, and my mother's at home, in a great state because she hasn't heard from my father for so long.'

'Well, I bring her such good news,' said the page, 'that she'll have to thank God for it.'

At length, jumping, running and skipping, the girl came to the village, but before she entered the house she called from the door: 'Come out, mother Teresa, come out, come out! For here's a gentleman bringing letters and other things from my good father!'

At this call her mother, Teresa Panza, came out spinning a bunch of flax, and wearing a grey skirt, so skimpy that it looked as if it had been cut short as a mark of shame, a grey bodice and a shirt. She was not very old, although she looked more than forty, but strong and tough, vigorous and wizened. When she caught sight of her daughter, and the page on horseback, she said: 'What's this, child? Who's this gentleman?'

'A servant of my Lady Teresa Panza,' answered the page. And with these words he leapt from his horse and went up to kneel most humbly before the Lady Teresa, saying: 'Give me your hands, my Lady Doña Teresa, which you are as the lawful and particular wife of the Lord Don Sancho Panza, own Governor of the Isle Barataria.'

'O my dear sir, get up from there. Don't do that,' replied Teresa. 'I'm none of your palace ladies, but a poor working woman, daughter of a ploughman, and wife of a squire-errant and no governor.'

'Your worship,' answered the page, 'is the most worthy wife of a most arch-worthy Governor, and to prove it true, receive this letter and this present.' And he whipped out from his pocket a string of corals with gold beads between them, and threw them round her neck, saying: 'This letter is from the Governor, and another which I bring and these corals are from my lady the Duchess, who has sent me to your worship.' Teresa was thunderstruck, and her daughter no less so.

'May I die if our master Don Quixote isn't in this,' cried the girl. 'He must have given father the governorship or countship he promised him so often.'

'That's right,' answered the page, 'for it is on account of Don Quixote that Lord Sancho is now governor of the Isle Barataria, as can be seen by this letter.'

'Read it me, your worship, Master Gentleman,' said Teresa, 'for although I can spin I can't read a word.'

'No more can I,' put in Sanchica, 'but wait for me here, and I'll go and call someone to read it, either the priest himself or the Bachelor Sampson Carrasco. They'll be very glad to come and have news of my father.'

'There's no need to call anyone,' said the page, 'for though I can't spin I can read, and I will read it.' And so he read it all, though it is not printed here, as it has been set down already. Then he took out another letter, from the Duchess, which went like this:

'*Friend Teresa,*

Your husband Sancho's excellent qualities of goodness and wit have moved me to beg my husband the Duke to confer on him the governorship of one of his many isles. I am informed that he governs like a goshawk, at which I am much pleased, as, of course, is my lord, the Duke. Wherefore I give great thanks to Heaven that I was not mistaken in choosing him for this governorship. For I would have the Lady Teresa know that it is hard to find a good governor in the world, and may God be as good to me as Sancho is in his governing.

I send you herewith, my dear, a string of corals with golden beads between them. I should have been glad if they had been orient pearls, but one who gives you a bone does not wish you dead. The time will come when we shall know one another and converse together; and God knows what will come of that. I send my regards to Sanchica, your daughter. Tell her from me to be prepared, for I mean to make a fine match for her when she least expects it.

They tell me that there are fat acorns in your village. Send me some couple of dozen, for I shall value them most highly, coming from your hand. Write me a long letter, advising me of your health and prosperity, and if you need anything you have only to open your mouth and it shall be filled to full measure. God keep you. From this place.

Your loving friend,
The Duchess.'

'Ah!' cried Teresa, on hearing the letter, 'what a good, simple, humble lady! Let me be buried with such ladies, I say, and not the madams we're used to in this place, who think that because they're gentry the wind mustn't touch them; and go to church in such finery as if they were real Queens, and seem to think they're demeaning themselves by looking at a peasant woman. And here you see where this good lady calls me friend and treats me like her equal, although she's a Duchess; and may I see her equal to the highest steeple in all La Mancha. As to the acorns, my dear sir, I'll send her ladyship a peck, so fat that people will come from far and near to admire them. But for the present, Sanchica, mind and make a fuss of this gentleman. Look after his horse, get some eggs out of the stable, and cut plenty of bacon. Let's give him a dinner fit for a prince; he deserves it for the good news he's brought us and for his handsome face. In the meantime I'll go and tell my neighbours about our good luck, and the Holy Father too, and Master Nicholas the barber. For they're always been such friends to your father.'

'Yes, I'll do that, mother,' answered Sanchica, 'but you'll have to give me half that necklace, mind, for I don't think my lady the Duchess is so silly as to have sent it all to you.'

'It's all for you, daughter,' cried Teresa, 'but let me wear it round my neck for a few days; for truly it seems to make my heart glad.'

'You'll both be glad too,' said the page, 'when you see the parcel I've got in this bag. It's a suit of the finest cloth which the Governor only wore for one day's hunting, and he's sent it all to the lady Sanchica.'

'May he live a thousand years,' exclaimed Sanchica, 'and the bearer no less – and two thousand more if need be.'

At this Teresa left the house with the letters, and with the necklace round her neck, beating the letters as she went along, as if they were tambourines; and chancing to meet the priest and Sampson Carrasco, she began to dance, crying:

'There's no poor relation about us now, I promise you! We've got a little government! And if your gay gentlewomen meddle with me, I'll take them down a peg or two.'

'What's this, Teresa Panza? Are you crazy? What are those papers?'

'I'm not crazy; but these are letters from Duchesses and Governors, and the beads round my neck are fine corals, and the Ave Marias and Paternosters are of beaten gold, and I'm a Governor's lady.'

'Heaven help us, we don't know what you mean, Teresa. What is it you're saying?'

'There, look,' replied Teresa, and gave them the letters. The priest read them aloud to Sampson Carrasco, and they looked at one another in astonishment at the news they read. Then the Bachelor asked who had brought the letters, and Teresa replied that they should come to her house and see the messenger, who was a youth as handsome as a gold brooch, and had brought another present worth twice as much. The priest took the corals from her neck and examined them; and being convinced of their value, he wondered afresh, and said: 'By my cloth, I don't know what to make of these letters and presents. On the one hand I can see and feel that these are fine corals, and on the other I read that a Duchess sends to ask for two dozen acorns.'

'Let us strike a balance between the two,' said Carrasco; 'and let us go now and see the bearer of this packet, for he may solve the mystery.'

This they did, and Teresa returned with them. They found the page sifting some barley for his horse, and Sanchica cutting a rasher to pave it with eggs for the page's dinner. They were both taken by his looks and his grand appearance, and after they had exchanged courteous salutations, Sampson asked him for news of Sancho Panza and Don Quixote, for though they had read Sancho's letter and the Duchess's they were still perplexed and could not make out all this about Sancho's governorship, especially about its being an isle, seeing that nearly all the islands in the Mediterranean sea belong to His Majesty.

'There's not the slightest doubt that Sancho Panza is a governor,' replied the page. 'But whether it's an isle or not he governs is no concern of mine. Enough that it's a place of more than a thousand inhabitants. But as to my lady the Duchess sending to beg for a few acorns, if you knew how simple and humble she is you wouldn't be surprised, for she has even on occasions sent to borrow a comb from a neighbour. Indeed, I would have your worships know that although the ladies of Aragon are as high in rank as the ladies of Castile, they're not so haughty and ceremonious, but much more affable with the people.'

While they were in the middle of this conversation Sanchica burst in with her apron full of eggs and asked the page: 'Tell me, sir, does my father wear laced breeches since he's a governor?'

'I have not noticed,' answered the page, 'but he certainly should wear them.'

'Oh, my Lord,' exclaimed Sanchica, 'what a sight it must be to see my father in tights! Isn't it odd that I have longed to see him in laced breeches ever since I was born?'

'Well, your Grace will see him in just such clothes if you live,' answered the page. 'If his government lasts two months he'll be wearing a travelling hood, I promise you.'

The priest and the barber clearly saw that the page was pulling their legs; but the quality of the corals and the hunting-suit Sancho had sent — for Teresa had by now shown them the clothes — spoke on the other side. However, they could not forbear laughing at Sanchica's wish, especially when Teresa said: 'Master Priest, inquire about here if there's anyone going to Madrid or Toledo who could buy me a hooped farthingale, a good, proper, fashionable one, and of the best quality; for I must certainly do my husband's government all the credit I can. They may tease me but I'll go to Court, and buy a coach like the rest of them, for she that has a governor for husband can afford to keep a coach.'

'And why not, mother?' said Sanchica. 'And the sooner the better, please God. Though people may call after us when they see me riding in a coach beside my lady mother: "Look at that good-for-nothing, old Garlic Gut's daughter. See her sitting there in that coach leaning back like Pope Joan." But let them tread in the mud, and me ride in my coach with my feet off the ground. Bad luck to every scandalmonger in the world! Let them laugh so long as I go warm! Aren't I right, mother dear?'

'Oh, how right you are, daughter!' answered Teresa. 'All this good fortune, and even better, my good Sancho foretold me. And you'll see that he won't stop till he has made me a Countess, my girl, for with luck it's the beginning that counts; and I've often heard your dear father say — and he's got more proverbs than children — when they give you the calf run with the halter; when they give you a governorship, hold on to it; when they give you a countship, grip it tight; and when they whistle you with something good to give you, gulp it down. Or else sleep on and don't answer, when luck and good things come knocking at your door.'

'And what do I care,' added Sanchica, 'if some of them say: "Look at the dog in linen breeches"? — and all the rest, when they see me stuck-up and high falutin.'

And the priest observed when he heard her: 'I cannot help thinking that every one of this Panza family was born with a sack of proverbs inside him. I have never known one of them who does not spill them out at all times and in every conversation he takes part in.'

'That's the truth,' said the page, 'for Lord Governor Sancho spouts them at every turn, and although many of them are off the point, still they give pleasure, and my lady the Duchess and the Duke are highly delighted with them.'

'But do you still affirm that it's true, sir,' asked the Bachelor, 'this about Sancho's governorship, and that there is really a Duchess who sends him presents and writes to him? Because we can't believe it, even though we've handled the presents and read the letters. We reckon it's one of our neighbour Don Quixote's inventions, for he thinks that everything is done by enchantment. So I'm afraid we shall have to touch you and feel you, to see if you are an imaginary ambassador or a flesh-and-blood man.'

'Sirs,' answered the page. 'All I know of myself is that I'm a real ambassador, that my Lord Sancho Panza is in fact a governor, that my master and mistress, the Duke and Duchess, can give and have given him that government, in which I've heard the said Sancho Panza performs most admirably. Whether there are enchantments in this or not your worships may settle between yourselves; for that's all I know, as I will swear you an oath on the life of my parents, who are now living and whom I love and honour exceedingly.'

'That may be,' replied the Bachelor, 'but "*dubitat Augustinus*".'

'Let him doubt who will,' said the page, 'but I've told you the truth, and truth will always rise above a lie, like oil on water; and if not, "*operibus credite et non verbis*". Let one of you come with me and he shall see with his own eyes what he does not believe when he hears it.'

'That journey's for me,' exclaimed Sanchica. 'Take me on your horse's crupper, sir. I should love to go and see my father.'

'Governors' daughters,' replied the page, 'mustn't travel the highways on their own. They must be attended by coaches and litters and a great crowd of servants.'

'Good Heavens,' replied Sanchica, 'I can go as easily on an ass as in a coach. Do you take me for one of your squeamish ones?'

'Quiet, girl,' said Teresa, 'you don't know what you're saying. This gentleman's right, for circumstances alter cases. When it was

Sancho, it was Sancha; when it's Governor, it is my Lady. Aren't I right, sir?'

'The Lady Teresa says more than she imagines,' said the page. 'Now let me have my dinner and send me off, for I want to get back this evening.'

'Your worship shall come and do penance with me,' said the priest, 'for Lady Teresa has more goodwill than good cheer to welcome so worthy a guest.'

The page declined, but in the end had to give in, to his own advantage; and the priest bore him off, highly delighted at the opportunity of questioning him at his leisure about Don Quixote and his doings.

The Bachelor offered Teresa to write answers to her letters; but she did not want him meddling in her affairs, as she took him for a bit of a joker; and so she gave a roll and a couple of eggs to a young friar who could write, and he penned two letters for her, one to her husband and the other to the Duchess, dictated out of her own head, and by no means the worst quoted in this famous history, as will be seen later.

Chapter LI. Of the progress of Sancho Panza's Government and other matters such as they are.

DAWN broke after the night of the Governor's rounds, which the butler had passed without sleep, his thoughts dwelling on the face, the charm and the beauty of the disguised young lady, while the steward spent what remained of it writing down for his master and mistress all Sancho's sayings and doings, in considerable amazement at both, for his speeches and his actions were such a mixture of shrewdness and simplicity.

At length the Lord Governor rose and, by order of Doctor Pedro Recio, they made him breakfast on a little preserved fruit and four gulps of cold water. Sancho would willingly have exchanged the meal for a bit of bread and a bunch of grapes. But, finding that it was a matter rather of compulsion than of choice, he submitted with much grief of heart and mortification of stomach, Pedro Recio making him believe that scanty and delicate fare sharpened the intellect, as was most necessary for persons appointed to authority

and high employment, which required strength of mind rather than
bodily vigour. By this sophistry Sancho was induced to bear such
keen hunger that in his secret heart he cursed his government and
even the giver of it. However, with his hunger and his preserved
fruit, he sat in judgment that day; and the first case that came before
him was a question submitted by a stranger in the presence of the
steward and the rest of the fraternity. It was this:

'Sir, a deep river divides a certain lord's estate into two parts ...
Listen carefully, your worship, for the case is an important one and
rather difficult. I must tell you, then, that over this river is a bridge,
and at one end a gallows and a sort of courthouse, in which four
judges sit to administer the law imposed by the owner of the river,
the bridge and the estate. It runs like this: "Before anyone crosses
this bridge, he must first state on oath where he is going and for
what purpose. If he swears truly, he may be allowed to pass; but if he
tells a lie, he shall suffer death by hanging on the gallows there displayed, without any hope of mercy." Though they know the law and
its rigorous conditions, many people cross the bridge and, as they
clearly make true statements the judges let them pass freely. Now
it happened that they once put a man on his oath, and he swore that
he was going to die on the gallows there – and that was all. After
due deliberation the judges pronounced as follows: "If we let this
man pass freely he will have sworn a false oath and, according to the
law, he must die; but he swore that he was going to die on the gallows, and if we hang him that will be the truth, so by the same law
he should go free." We ask your worship, Lord Governor, what
the judges ought to do with this man; for they are still perplexed
and undecided; and when they heard of your worship's great wisdom
and acuteness, they sent me to beg you for your opinion of this
intricate and doubtful case.'

'Really these worthy judges who sent you to me might have
saved themselves the trouble,' replied Sancho. 'There's a good deal
more dullness than acuteness in me. But repeat the matter to me, all
the same, so that I may understand it; and then perhaps I shall hit
the nail on the head.'

The questioner repeated what he had said at first, and Sancho observed: 'I think I can resolve this business in a brace of shakes. It's
like this: The man swears that he is going to die on the gallows, and

if he does die his oath was true, and by the law as it stands he deserves to go free and cross the bridge. But if they don't hang him,
he swore to a lie and by that same law deserves to be hanged.'

'The Lord Governor is quite correct,' said the messenger, 'and
as regards his judgment and his interpretation of the case, there is
no more question or doubt.'

'But let me continue,' replied Sancho. 'They must let that part of
the man which swore truly cross the bridge, and hang the part that
swore to a lie; and in that way the conditions of passage will be fulfilled to the letter.'

'Then, Lord Governor,' said the questioner, 'this man will have
to be divided into two parts, the lying part and the truthful part;
and if he's divided, he's bound to die. Thus no part of the law's demands is fulfilled, and it's absolutely necessary for us to comply
with it.'

'Look here, my good fellow,' replied Sancho, 'either I'm a dolt
or there's as much reason for this passenger of yours to die as to
live and cross the bridge; for, if the truth saves him, the lie equally
condemns him; and this being so, which it is, I think you should tell
those gentlemen who sent you to me that since the reasons for condemning him and acquitting him are equally balanced they must let
him pass freely, for it's always more commendable to do good than
to do ill. This decision I would give signed with my name if I knew
how to sign. And in this case I have not spoken out of my own head,
for there came to my mind one of the many precepts my master Don
Quixote gave me the night before I came to be made Governor of
this isle; which was that when justice was in doubt I should incline
to the side of mercy; and God has been pleased to bring it to my
mind now, for it fits the case to a T.'

'That's so,' said the steward, 'and I don't believe that Lycurgus
himself, who gave laws to the Lacedaemonians, could have given a
better decision than the great Panza has done. And now let the
session be closed for this morning, and I'll order the Governor a
dinner that will more than satisfy him.'

'That's what I want, and fair play,' said Sancho. 'If I have some
dinner it may rain cases and decisions. I'll polish them off as they
fall.'

The steward kept his word, for it weighed on his conscience to be

killing so wise a governor by hunger. Besides, he intended to finish
with him that same night by playing him the last trick he was commissioned to play. So it was that the Governor dined that day in defiance of all Doctor Tirteafuera's rules and aphorisms, and when the
cloths were lifted a courier came in with a letter for him from Don
Quixote. Sancho bade the secretary read it to himself, and then if
there was nothing in it that should be kept secret, to read it aloud.
The secretary obeyed and, after glancing it over, he said: 'It can
certainly be read aloud. What Don Quixote has written to your
worship deserves to be stamped and written in letters of gold. This
is what he says:

*Letter of Don Quixote de la Mancha to Sancho Panza, Governor
of the Isle Barataria.*

*Where I expected, friend Sancho, to hear news of your negligence and
folly, I have had accounts of your wise actions, for which I return
especial thanks to Heaven, which can raise the poor from the dunghill
and make wise men of fools. They tell me you govern like a man; yet as
a man you are scarcely more than a brute creature, so humbly do you
behave. But I would have you take note, Sancho, that it is often fitting
and necessary for the authority of office to go counter to the heart's
humility. For the due state of a person appointed to an important office
must conform to the requirements of that office, and not to the moderation natural to his humble disposition. Dress well, for a stick well decorated seems more than a stick. I do not mean that you should wear finery
or trinkets, or that, being a judge, you should clothe yourself as a soldier,
but that you should wear the dress your office requires, so long as it is
clean and neat.*

*To gain the goodwill of the people you govern you must do two things
amongst others; the first is to be civil to everyone – though I have told
you this once already – and the other, to provide an abundance of the
necessities of life, for there is nothing which distresses the hearts of the
poor more than hunger and want.*

*Do not make many statutes, but if you make them, try to make good
ones and, particularly, see that they are kept and fulfilled; for if statutes are not kept they might as well not exist. Besides, they show that
though the prince had the wisdom and authority to make them, he had
not the courage to see that they were observed. And laws which threaten*

but are not carried out come to be like that log which was king of the frogs. He frightened them at first; but in time they despised him and climbed upon his back.

Be a father to virtues and a step-father to vices. Do not always be harsh or always mild; choose the mean between the two extremes, for here lies the point of wisdom.

Visit the prisons, the slaughterhouses and the markets, for the governor's presence in such places is of much importance. It comforts the prisoners, who expect a speedy release; it is a bugbear to the butchers, who for a time, have to use accurate weights; and it scares the market-women for the same reason.

Do not show yourself greedy – even if you are so perhaps, which I do not believe – or given to women or gluttony; for if the people and such as have dealings with you discover your dominant inclination they will open battery-fire on you in that quarter, until they bring you down to the depths of perdition. Consider and reconsider, view and review, the counsels and instructions I gave you in writing before you left here for your government, and you will see that you will find in them, if you observe them, an additional help to ease you over the troubles and difficulties which governors meet at every turn.

Write to your Lord and Lady and show them your gratitude; for ingratitude is the daughter of pride and one of the greatest sins known, and the person who is grateful to his benefactors gives assurance that he will be so to God also, who has done him, and continues to do him, so many benefits.

The Duchess has sent off a messenger with your suit and another present to your wife Teresa Panza. We expect an answer at any moment. I have been a little indisposed from a certain cat-clawing that befell me, somewhat at the expense of my nose. But it was nothing, for if there are enchanters who persecute me, there are also some who defend me.

Let me know whether the steward who is with you had anything to do with the business of the Trifaldi, as you suspected; and you should keep me advised of everything which happens to you, for the distance is short; more particularly as I intend soon to leave this idle life I am living at present, for I was not born for it.

There is a matter which has arisen, and which I believe will put me into disgrace with the Duke and Duchess. But though it concerns me much it does not affect my decision at all. For, when it comes to the point,

C C

I must comply with my profession rather than with their pleasure, according to the saying: amicus Plato, sed magis amica veritas. *I give you this in Latin, for I suppose that you have learnt it since you have become Governor.*

So farewell, and God keep you free from all harm.

Your friend,

Don Quixote de la Mancha.

Sancho listened most attentively to the letter, which was praised for its wisdom by all who heard it. He then rose from table and, calling the secretary, shut himself up in his room with him, intending to reply to his master Don Quixote at once and without more delay. So he instructed the secretary to write from his dictation without adding or omitting a word – which he did – and the answering letter was to this effect:

Sancho Panza's Letter to Don Quixote de la Mancha.

The pressure of my business is so great that I have not time to scratch my head, or even to cut my nails, and so I wear them very long, Heaven help me. This I say, beloved master, so that your worship may not be surprised that I have not given you an account till now of my good or ill fortune in this government, in which I suffer from worse hunger than when we two were roaming the woods and wilds.

The Duke my master wrote to me the other day, informing me that certain spies had come into this isle to kill me. But so far the only one of them I have discovered is a certain doctor in this town, who gets a salary for killing all the governors who come here. His name is Doctor Pedro Recio, and he is a native of Tirteafuera. And your worship can see from that name whether I have not reason to fear death at his hands! This same doctor boasts that he does not cure existing maladies, but prevents them from arising. And the remedies he uses are diet, diet, and still more diet, till he has reduced his patient to skin and bone, as if leanness were not a worse evil than fever. In short he is killing me of hunger, and I am dying of annoyance; and instead of coming here, as I expected, to get warm food and cool drink, and to lay my body between holland sheets and on feather pillows, I have come to do penance like a hermit; and as I am not doing it willingly I think that the Devil will get me in the end.

Up to now I have not touched a fee or taken a bribe, and I cannot imagine where this will end; for they have told me here that most of the governors who come to this isle take a great deal of money either in gifts or in loans from the people of the town before entering, and that this is the ordinary custom among newly created governors, and not only here.

Going the rounds the other night, I came across a most lovely young lady in men's clothes, and a brother of hers dressed as a woman. My butler fell in love with the girl, and has thoughts of making her his wife, so he says, and I have chosen the boy for my son-in-law. To-day the two of us are going to make our intentions known to the father of the pair, a certain Don Diego de la Llana, who is as perfect a gentleman and an old Christian as you could desire.

I visit the markets, as your worship advised me, and yesterday I found a market-woman pretending to sell fresh hazel-nuts, and discovered that she had mixed one bushel of fresh nuts with one of old, worthless, rotten ones. I impounded them all for the charity boys, who will know how to pick the good from the bad, and forbade her to enter the market for a fortnight. The people said that was a good sentence, for it is a common opinion in this town, your worship, that there is not a worse sort of people than your market-women. For they are a shameless, godless, brazen lot, as I can well believe from my experience of other places.

I am very glad that my lady the Duchess has written to my wife Teresa Panza and sent her the present your worship speaks of, and I will try to show myself grateful in due course. Kiss her hands on my behalf, your worship, and tell her I say that she has not thrown it into a torn sack, as the end will show. I should not like you to have any unpleasant disputes with my Lord and Lady, sir, for if you quarrel with them I shall certainly suffer for it; and it would not be right, seeing that you gave me the advice to be grateful, not to be grateful yourself for all the favours they have done you and the hospitality they have given you in their castle.

The cat-clawing business I do not understand; but I imagine it must be one of those tricks the wicked enchanters are always playing on your worship. I shall learn about it when we meet.

I should like to send your worship something; but I do not know what to send, unless it is some enema tubes to be used with bladders. They are very curious things, and made in this isle. But if my office lasts I will find something to send you, by hook or by crook.

If my wife Teresa Panza writes to me, please pay the carriage and

send me the letter; for I am longing to hear how things are with my
house, my wife and my children. And so may God deliver your worship
from evilly disposed enchanters, and bring me safe and sound out of this
government – which I doubt, for from the way Doctor Pedro Recio is
treating me I do not expect to leave with more than my life.

> *Your worship's servant,*
> *Sancho Panza the Governor.*

The secretary sealed the letter and despatched the courier at once,
and Sancho's tormentors assembled and planned together the means
of making an end of his government. That evening Sancho spent
drawing up some ordinances touching the good government of what
he supposed to be his isle. He decreed that there must be no corner-
ing of provisions in the state, and that wine could be imported from
anywhere at all, on condition that its place of origin was declared, so
that it could be priced according to its value, goodness and reputation; and anyone watering it or changing its name should pay for it
with his life. He lowered the price of all footwear, especially of
shoes, the current price seeming to him exorbitant. He fixed the rate
of servants' wages, which were mounting unchecked at a headlong
pace. He imposed the heaviest penalties on singers of lewd and disorderly songs, either by night or by day. He decreed that no blind
man should sing miracles in rhyme unless he could bring unquestionable evidence that they were true, as most of their tales were,
in his opinion, fictitious and brought discredit upon the genuine
ones. He created and selected an inspector of the poor, not to persecute them but to examine whether they were genuine; for under the
disguise of poverty and counterfeit sores go sturdy thieves and hale
drunkards. So good, in fact, were the laws he ordained that they are
kept in that place to this day under the name of '*The Constitutions
of the great Governor Sancho Panza.*'

Chapter LII. In which is recorded the Adventure of the second
  dolorous or distressed Waiting-woman, otherwise called Doña
  Rodriguez.

CIDE HAMETE relates that once Don Quixote was healed of his
scratches, the life he led in that castle seemed to him clean contrary
to the rule of knighthood which he professed; and so he determined

to beg the Duke and Duchess's leave to depart for Saragossa, as the festival was drawing near at which he hoped to win the armour usually jousted for. But as he was at table one day with his hosts, and on the point of carrying out his intention and asking their permission, suddenly there entered through the door of the great hall two women – as they afterwards proved – swathed in mourning from head to foot. One of them ran up to Don Quixote and threw herself flat on the ground with her lips pressed to his feet, uttering all the while the deepest, saddest and most melancholy groans. All the spectators were in a consternation and even the Duke and Duchess, though they suspected that this was some new trick which their servants had prepared for Don Quixote, were puzzled at the earnestness of the lady's demonstrations of grief until the compassionate Don Quixote prevailed upon her to rise from the ground and remove her cloak from her tearful visage. The face revealed, however, was the cause of even greater astonishment, for they beheld the waiting-woman Doña Rodriguez, and the other mourning figure proved to be her daughter who had been deceived by the rich farmer's son. All who knew her were astonished, and the Duke and Duchess most of all, for though they considered her rather a silly creature, they did not think her so far gone as to perform these crazy tricks.

After a while Doña Rodriguez turned to her master and mistress and said: 'May it please your Excellencies to give me leave to retire a little with this knight, for that I must do if I am to escape from a situation into which I have come through the impudence of an ill-conditioned villain.'

The Duke gave her leave to retire with Don Quixote for as long as she pleased; and she then turned her face to that knight, and said: 'Some days ago, valiant knight, I related to you the treacherous wrong a wicked farmer has done to my dear beloved daughter, who is the unfortunate lady here before you; and you promised me to take up her cause and right the injury she has suffered. But now it has come to my knowledge that you desire to leave this castle in search of good ventures – may God send you them! Therefore I wish you to challenge this stubborn rustic before you slip off into the highways, and force him to marry my daughter, in fulfilment of his promise of marriage made previously to his lying with her. For to expect justice from the Duke, my master, is to ask for pears off an elm tree, for the reason I have declared to your worship in private. So, may our Lord give you good health and not leave us unprotected.'

To this plea Don Quixote replied with great gravity and circumstance: 'Good lady, moderate your tears, or rather dry them, and be sparing of your sighs, for I take upon me the charge of seeing your daughter's wrong redressed; though it would have been better for her not to have been so easy in believing lovers' promises, for most of them are quick to promise but very slow to perform. So, by leave of my Lord the Duke, I will set out immediately to search for this profligate young man, and find him, challenge him and kill him, should he refuse to fulfil his pledged word. For the principal purpose of my order is to spare the humble and punish the proud; – I mean to succour the wretched and to destroy the cruel.'

'There is no need,' replied the Duke, 'for your worship to put yourself to the trouble of searching for the rustic of whom this good lady complains, nor have you any need either to ask my permission to challenge him. I grant him duly challenged and take it upon myself to inform him of this defiance and make him accept it, and come to answer for himself at this castle of mine, where I will give you both a fair field, observing all the conditions proper to such affairs, and securing impartial justice to you; for all princes are obliged to grant a free field to those who do battle within the bounds of their dominions.'

'Then with that assurance and your Highness's good leave,' replied Don Quixote, 'I hereby declare that for this occasion I waive my gentry, lower myself to the meanness of the offender, and reduce myself to his level, thus granting him the right of combat with me; and so I defy and challenge him, though absent, by reason of the wrong he did in defrauding this poor girl, who was a maid and now by his fault is one no longer; and he shall fulfil the promise he gave her to be her lawful husband, or he shall die in the ordeal.'

Then, stripping off a glove, he threw it into the middle of the hall, and the Duke picked it up, repeating that he accepted the challenge in his vassal's name, and fixing the date at six days hence, and the place in the castle courtyard, and the arms those customary among knights – lance and shield and complete armour with all the other pieces, without deceit, trickery, or any supernatural charm, inspected and examined by the judges of the lists. 'But first of all,' said the Duke, 'this good lady and this bad maiden must place the right of their cause in the hands of Don Quixote; for in no other manner can anything be done or this same challenge be brought to due execution.'

'Yes, I do place it there,' answered the waiting-woman.

'And I too,' added the daughter, all tearful, ashamed and confused.

These provisions being settled, and the Duke having made the necessary arrangements, the ladies in mourning departed, and the Duchess commanded that henceforth they should not be treated as her servants, but as ladies errant, who had come to her house to sue for justice. So they were given private quarters and waited on like strangers, much to the astonishment of the other servants, who could not imagine where the folly and presumption of Doña Rodriguez and her unfortunate daughter would stop.

At this point, to crown the feast and bring the meal to a fine conclusion, there suddenly entered the hall the page who had taken the letters and presents to Teresa Panza, the wife of Governor Sancho Panza, which arrival delighted the Duke and Duchess, who were longing for news of his journey. The page replied to their questions by saying that he could not answer publicly or briefly, but he begged their Excellencies to wait until they were alone. In the meantime they might amuse themselves with certain letters, two of which he brought out and put in the Duchess's hands. One was headed 'Letter for my lady the Duchess of I do not know where,' and the other 'To my husband Sancho Panza, Governor of the isle Barataria, whom may God prosper more years than me.'

The Duchess's cake would not bake, as the saying is, until she had read her letter. She opened it, glanced through it and, finding that she could read it aloud to the Duke and the bystanders, did so, to this effect:

Teresa Panza's Letter to the Duchess.

I was delighted, your Highness, with the letter you wrote me, for truly my dear lady, I had greatly longed for it. The string of corals is very fine, and my husband's hunting-suit is every bit as good. All this village is glad that your ladyship has made my consort Sancho a governor, though everyone disbelieves it, particularly the priest, Master Nicholas the barber, and Sampson Carrasco the Bachelor; but that does not worry me. So long as it is true — which it is — they can say what they like; though, to tell you the truth, I should not have believed it myself but for the coming of the corals and the suit; for they all take my husband for a dolt in this village, and cannot imagine he can be fit to govern any thing except a herd of goats. Heaven be his guide, and put him in the way he should go to suit his children's needs.

My dearest lady, I am determined, by your leave, to make hay whilst the sun shines, and go to Court and lean back in my coach, to spite the thousands that envy me already. So please, your Excellency, bid my husband send me a bit of money, and let it be quite a bit, for expenses are enormous in the capital. It is amazing, but bread costs a real there and meat thirty maravedis a pound. But if he wishes me not to come, let him advise me in time, for my feet are itching to get on the road. My friends and neighbours tell me that if my daughter and I cut a grand and stately figure at Court, my husband will get more honour by me than I by him, since many people are sure to ask: 'Who are the ladies in that coach?', and one of my servants will answer: 'The wife and daughter of Sancho Panza, Governor of the Isle Barataria'; and in this way Sancho will get known and I shall be highly thought of — and you can get any thing in Rome! I am as sorry as can be that they have not harvested acorns in our village this year. However, I am sending your Highness about half a peck, which I went to the woods myself to gather and pick over, one by one. I could find none bigger, though I wish they were the size of ostrich eggs.

Do not forget to write to me, your Pomposity, and I will be sure to answer and inform you of my health and of all there may be to tell you about this place, where I remain, praying our Lord to preserve your Highness and not to forget me. My daughter Sancha and my son kiss your Grace's hands.

Your servant, whose desire is to see your ladyship rather than to write,

Teresa Panza.

Everybody was highly delighted at Teresa Panza's letter, most of all the Duke and the Duchess, who asked Don Quixote's opinion whether it would be right to open the letter addressed to the

Governor, which she imagined must be excellent. Don Quixote said that, to please them, he would open it, which he did, and it ran in this fashion:

Teresa Panza's Letter to Sancho Panza her husband.

I received your letter, my beloved Sancho, and I swear to you as a Catholic Christian I was within an inch of going off my head with delight. Yes, indeed, when I learnt that you are a Governor I thought I should fall dead on the spot from pleasure; for they say that sudden gladness kills like a great grief, you know. And your daughter Sanchica wetted herself without noticing it, out of pure joy. I had the suit you sent me before me, and the corals my lady the Duchess sent me round my neck, and the letters in my hands, and the bearer of them standing there; but for all that it really seemed all to be a dream. For who could have thought that a goatherd would come to be a Governor of Isles? You remember, my dear, how my mother used to say that to see much you must live long? I think she was right, for I expect to see more if I live longer, and I do not mean to stop till I see you a rent-farmer or a tax-gatherer, for in those trades you certainly do have and handle money, though the Devil carries off those that abuse them. My lady the Duchess will tell you how I long to go to Court. Consider the matter and let me know your pleasure; for I will try and do you honour there by going about in a coach.

Neither the priest, the barber, the Bachelor, nor even the sexton, can believe that you are a Governor. They say that it is all humbug or a matter of enchantment, like all your master Don Quixote's affairs; and Sampson says that he is going to look for you, and knock the governorship out of your head and the madness out of Don Quixote's skull. But I do nothing but laugh and look at my necklace, and plan how to make up that suit of yours for our daughter. I sent some acorns to my lady the Duchess. I wish they had been gold. Send me some strings of pearls, if they are in fashion in your isle.

The news in this village is that Berrueca has married her daughter to a wretched sort of painter, who came here to do any sort of painting jobs. The council commissioned him to put His Majesty's arms over the doors of the Council House. He asked for two ducats, which they gave him in advance. He worked for eight days, and at the end of that time he had done nothing and said that he could not manage to paint such trumpery. He returned the money, but all the same he posed as a good workman and got married. The truth is he has given up the pencil and taken to the spade, and now he goes to the fields like a gentleman. Pedro de Lobo's son has taken orders and shaved his head, meaning to be a priest. When Minguilla, Mingo Silvato's grand-daughter, heard of it she sued him for breach of promise. Malicious tongues are pleased to say that she is with child by him, but he denies it stoutly.

This year there are no olives, and there is not a drop of vinegar to be found in the whole village. A company of soldiers passed through here, and took three local girls away with them. I will not tell you their names, for they may come back; and they will be sure to find men to marry them, with all their blemishes, good and bad.

Sanchica is making bone-lace; she earns eight clear maravedis a day, which she is putting by in a money-box to help towards her wedding portion. But now that she is a governor's daughter you will give her a dowry without her working for it. The fountain in the market-place has dried up. A thunderbolt fell on the pillory — may they all fall there!

I await an answer to this and a decision about my going to Court; and with this, may God preserve you more years than me — or as many, for I should not like to leave you in this world without me.

Your wife,

Teresa Panza.

These letters called forth applause, laughter, approval and wonder; and, to crown everything, the courier arrived bearing Sancho's letter to Don Quixote, which was also read in public and aroused some doubts as to the Governor's foolishness. The Duchess retired to hear from the page what had happened to him in Sancho's village; and he told her in great detail without omitting any relevant circumstance. He gave her the acorns and also a cheese which Teresa had given him, a very good one, and better than those of Tronchon. The Duchess accepted it with the greatest pleasure; and there we will leave her, to tell of the end of the government of the great Sancho Panza, flower and mirror of all Governors of Isles.

Chapter LIII. *Of the troubled conclusion of Sancho Panza's Government.*

'IT is idle to think that things in this life will last for ever in one state. On the contrary, everything seems to go in cycles, or rather round-about. Summer follows on spring, autumn on summer, winter on autumn, and spring on winter, and so time revolves in this continuous wheel. Only human life speeds to its end faster than the wind, without hope of renewal, except in that other life which has no bounds to limit it.' So says Cide Hamete, the Mohammedan philosopher; for many, by the light of nature and without the illumination of the faith, have come to understand the brevity and instability of our present existence and the everlastingness of the eternal life to come. In this place, however, our author alludes only to the swiftness with which Sancho's government ended, was consumed and undone, and vanished into shadow and smoke.

On the seventh night of his governorship he was lying in bed, sated not with bread or wine but with judging, giving opinions, and making laws and decrees, when just as, despite his hunger, sleep was beginning to close his eyes he heard a great noise of bells and shouting, which sounded as if the whole isle were foundering. He sat up in bed and listened, trying to make out the cause of this mighty uproar; but far from his discovering it, his confusion and terror were only augmented by the sound of countless trumpets and drums, which came on top of the din of voices and bells. So, getting up, he put on his slippers, because of the dampness of the floor, and without a dressing-gown or anything of that sort went to the door of his room, just in time to see more than twenty persons with lighted torches in their hands and swords unsheathed, some crying at the tops of their voices: 'Arm! Arm! Lord Governor. Arm! for countless enemies have invaded this isle, and we are lost if your skill and valour do not succour us!'

Raising this tremendous noise they rushed tumultuously to the place where Sancho was standing, stupefied, and fascinated at what he heard and saw. And when they reached him one of them cried: 'Arm yourself at once, your Lordship, if you do not want to be lost and all the isle with you.'

'What have I to do with arming?' replied Sancho. 'What do I

know of arms or succour? It would be better to leave these matters to my master Don Quixote. He will despatch them and put them right in a flash. For, sinner that I am before God, I don't understand anything about these hurly-burlys.'

'Oh, Lord Governor,' cried another, 'what weakness is this? Arm yourself, sir! For here we bring you arms of offence and defence. Come out to the market square, and be our leader and captain; for that is your duty as our Governor.'

'All right, let me be armed,' answered Sancho.

Instantly they brought him two large and ancient shields with which they had come provided, and clamped them over his shirt, without leaving him time to put on any other clothing, one shield in front and the other behind. They pushed his arms through some holes they had made in them, and bound him very tightly with cords, so that he found himself walled in and boarded up, upright as a spindle and unable to bend his knees or stir a step. Then they put a spear into his hand, and he had to lean on it to keep on his feet. When they had got him trussed up they told him to march and lead them, and put courage into them all; for with him as their pole-star, their lantern and light, all would be well.

'How can I march, poor wretch that I am?' answered Sancho. 'I can't bring my knee-joints into play, for these boards which are clamped to my flesh get in my way. What you must do is to take me up in your arms and lay me, crosswise or standing, at some postern, and I will guard it either with this spear or with my body.'

'Go on, Lord Governor,' cried another. 'It's fear, not the boards, that prevents your walking. Hasten and stir yourself, for it's late. Our enemies are increasing, their cries grow louder, and danger presses.'

Thus urged and abused, the poor Governor attempted to move, but came down on the ground with such a bump that he thought he must be broken to bits. He lay like a tortoise enveloped in its shell, or like a side of bacon clapped between two boards for salting, or like a boat upside-down on the beach. But though they saw him fall, those playful rogues had no compassion on him. Instead, they put out their torches, and began to repeat their urgent call to arms, trampling over poor Sancho, and dealing him repeated bangs on his shield. Indeed, if he had not made himself small and shrunk his head in between them things would have gone very badly with the poor governor, who being thus contracted in that narrow space, sweated copiously, and petitioned God with all his heart to deliver him from his danger. Some stumbled and others fell over him; and there was one who stood on top of him for a good while, and from there, as from a watch-tower, directed the armies, shouting loudly: 'Here, you on our side, here! The enemy is pressing harder over here! Guard that postern! Keep that gate shut! Down with those scaling ladders! Bring up the grenades, the pitch and resin, and the kettles of boiling oil! Barricade the streets with mattresses!'

In fact in a fine frenzy he named every appurtenance, implement and weapon of war used for the defence of a city; and the battered Sancho, who heard and suffered it all, said to himself: 'Oh, if only the Lord would be pleased to make an end of my losing this isle, and I might find myself dead, or out of this great affliction!' Heaven heard his petition, and when least he expected it he heard voices crying: 'Victory! Victory! The enemy are beginning to fly! Here, Lord Governor, arise, enjoy your conquest, and divide the spoils taken from the enemy by the valour of your invincible arm!'

'Lift me up,' moaned the sorrowful Sancho in a woe-begone voice. So they helped him up and, once on his feet, he said: 'I would have you nail to my forehead the enemy I conquered. I will divide no spoils of enemies, but I beg some friend, if I have one, to give me a drink of wine, for I am dry, and to wipe off my sweat, for I'm turning to water.'

They wiped him down, brought him his wine, and untied the shields; and when seated on his bed he fainted away, such had been his fatigue, agony and terror.

The jokers were now sorry they had carried things so far, but were consoled on seeing him recover. He asked them the time, and they replied that it was now daybreak. He said no more, but began to put on his clothes, in deep silence, without another word, while everyone gazed at him, waiting to see what this sudden dressing portended. At length, having slowly put on his clothes, for he was bruised and could not move very fast, he went towards the stable, followed by everyone present. And when he came to Dapple he embraced him, giving him the kiss of peace on his forehead, and said to him with moist eyes: 'Come here, dear companion and friend of mine, my fellow-partner in my trials and sorrows. When I went along with you and had no other thought but the mending of your harness and the feeding of your little carcase, happy were my hours, my days and my years! But since I left you and climbed the tower of ambition and pride a thousand miseries have pierced my soul, a thousand troubles and four thousand tribulations.'

And all the while he was speaking he went on saddling his ass, and no one said a word. When Dapple was ready, he mounted him with great pain and difficulty and, addressing himself to the steward, the secretary and the butler, and to Pedro Recio the doctor, and the many others present, said: 'Make way, gentlemen, and let me return to my old freedom. Let me go and seek the life I left, and rise again from this present death. I was not born to be a governor, nor to defend isles or cities from the enemies who choose to attack them. I understand more about ploughing and digging and the pruning and gathering of vine-shoots than of law-giving or defending provinces or kingdoms. St. Peter is well at Rome: I mean that everyone is best practising the trade for which he was born. A reaper's hook comes better to my hand than a governor's sceptre. I prefer stuffing myself with salad to being at the mercy of a meddling doctor who kills me by hunger; and I had rather lie down under the shade of an oak-tree in summer and wrap myself in a shepherd's cloak of two skins in winter, with my liberty, than lie between holland sheets and dress in sable skins under the burden of a governorship. God be with your worships. Tell the Duke my master that naked I was born and naked I am now; I neither lose nor gain. I mean that I came into this government without a farthing, and I leave it without one, contrary to the way of the governors of other isles. Make way for me and let me go and plaster myself, for I believe that all my ribs are broken, thanks to the enemies who have been trampling me this night.'

'You must not do that, Lord Governor,' said Doctor Recio, 'for I will give your worship a potion that is good against falls and bruises, and which will immediately restore you to your former health and vigour. As for your dinners, I promise to reform my ways, and let you eat abundantly of everything you like.'

'Too late,' answered Sancho. 'I would as soon turn Turk as stay. These tricks aren't to be played twice. I swear I'd as soon fly to

Heaven without wings as remain in this government or accept another, even if it were presented to me between two dishes. I am a Panza, and we are all stubborn. If once we cry odds, odds it must be, even though it's evens, and in spite of all the world. Here in this stable I will leave the ant wings that carried me up into the air for the martins and other birds to peck at. Let us come back to earth and steady walking, for if I'm not to look smart in slashed Cordova shoes I shan't be short of rough hemp sandals. Every ewe to her mate, and let no one stretch his leg more than the length of his sheet. Let me go now, for it's getting late.'

To which the steward replied: 'Lord Governor, we will most willingly let your worship go, though we shall be very sorry to lose you, for your wit and Christian behaviour make us love your presence. But it is common knowledge that every governor is obliged to go into residence before absenting himself from the place where he has governed. Do so, your worship, for the ten days you have held the government. Then go, and God's peace be with you.'

'No one can ask an account of me,' answered Sancho, 'except someone appointed by the Duke, my lord. I am going to see him and I shall give him an exact report. Besides, coming out naked as I do, there is no need of any other evidence to prove that I governed like an angel.'

'By God, the great Sancho is right,' cried Doctor Recio, 'and it is my opinion we should let him go, for the Duke will be infinitely glad to see him.'

To this they all agreed, and they allowed him to depart, first offering him their company and anything he might desire for the comfort of his person and the convenience of his journey. Sancho answered that he wanted no more than a little barley for Dapple, and half a cheese and half a loaf for himself; for the journey was short, and he had no need of more or better provisions. They all embraced him, and he embraced them all with tears in his eyes, and left them wondering, both at his words and at his very determined and sensible resolution.

Chapter LIV. *Concerning matters relating to this History and to no other.*

THE Duke and the Duchess were resolved that Don Quixote's challenge to their vassal in the above-mentioned cause should go forward, and as the youth was in Flanders, where he had fled in order to avoid having Doña Rodriguez for his mother-in-law, they arranged to substitute for him a Gascon lackey called Tosilos, first priming him thoroughly in his part. So two days later the Duke told Don Quixote that his opponent would arrive in four days' time, to present himself in the field, armed as a knight, and maintain that the maiden lied by half a beard – or even by a whole beard – if she affirmed that he had given her a promise of marriage. Don Quixote received this news with great satisfaction and flattered himself that he would perform wonders in this business, counting himself most fortunate to have an opportunity of displaying the power of his mighty arm before the Duke and Duchess; and so he waited most contentedly for the four days which, measured by his impatience, seemed like four hundred centuries.

Now letting them pass, as we let other things, let us go and accompany Sancho, who was riding on Dapple between mirth and mourning, in search of his master whose company gave him more pleasure than the governorship of all the isles in the world. Now it happened before he had gone far from the isle of his governorship – he had never set out to discover whether it was an isle, a city, town, or village he was governor of – that he saw coming along the road he was travelling on six pilgrims with staves, foreigners of the sort that sing for alms. Now when they came up to him they spread out in a row and, raising their voices all together, began their song in a language which Sancho could not understand, except for one word which clearly stood for alms; whence he concluded that it was alms they were asking for in their song. And being extremely charitable, as Cide Hamete tells us, he took the half loaf and the half cheese with which he was provided out of his saddlebag and offered it to them, telling them in dumb show that he had nothing else to give. They received his gift most gratefully, but cried: '*Geld! Geld!*'

'I don't understand what you want of me, good people,' answered Sancho.

Then one of them took a purse from under his shirt and held it up, giving Sancho to understand that it was money they were begging for. So, putting his thumb to his throat and extending his hand upwards, he signed to them that he had not a halfpenny; and spurring Dapple, he broke through their ranks. But as he passed, one of them, who had been staring fixedly at him, rushed up and, flinging his arms round his waist, addressed him loudly in Castilian: 'Good Lord! What's this I see? Can it possibly be my good friend here in my arms, my dear neighbour Sancho Panza? Yes, there can be no doubt of it, for I'm not dreaming, and I'm not drunk – as yet.'

Sancho was astonished to hear himself called by his name and to find a foreign pilgrim embracing him, and hard though he stared at him without saying a word he was unable to recognize him. Seeing his puzzlement, however, the pilgrim exclaimed: 'What! Is it possible, brother Sancho Panza, that you don't recognize your neighbour, Ricote the Moor, your village shopkeeper?'

At this Sancho stared at him more intently still, and beginning to recall his features, in the end recognized him perfectly. Then, without dismounting from his ass, he threw his arms round his neck and cried: 'Who the devil could have recognized you, Ricote, in that clown's dress you're wearing? Tell me, who has frenchified you, and how have you dared return to Spain. You'll get very short shrift if they catch you and recognize you.'

'If you don't give me away, Sancho,' answered the pilgrim, 'I'm sure that no one will know me in this dress. But let's go off the road to that poplar grove over there, where my companions intend to dine and rest. You shall eat there with them, for they're very pleasant folk, and I will have a chance of telling you what's happened to me since I left our village in obedience to His Majesty's proclamation, which threatened the unfortunate people of my nation with so much rigour, as you have heard.'

Sancho complied, and after Ricote had spoken to the rest of the pilgrims they went off to the poplar grove, which showed up some distance from the highway. Here they threw down their staves and took off their capes or pilgrim's cloaks, remaining in their jackets. They were all handsome young fellows except for Ricote, who was well on in years. Each carried a haversack, apparently well stored, at least with those spicy foods that call up the thirst from a mile off.

They lay on the ground and, using the grass for tablecloth, spread out on it bread, salt, knives, onions, walnuts, hunks of cheese and clean hambones, which had nothing on them to gnaw yet were not past sucking. They also produced a black dish, which goes by the name of caviare and is made of fishes' roe – a great rouser of thirst. There was no shortage of olives either, though they were dry and without any pickle, yet tasty and pleasant enough. But the chief glory of that banquet-field was six bottles of wine, each of the men fetching his own out of his haversack. Even the worthy Ricote, who had transformed himself from a Moor into a German or a Dutchman, produced his, which could compare with the other five in size. Then they began to eat with great appetite, most leisurely savouring every mouthful, which they took from the point of the knife – a very little of each thing – and then, all together at one moment, they raised their arms and bottles in the air, and put their own mouths to the bottles' mouths, their eyes as firmly fixed on the sky as if they were taking aim at it. And in this way they continued for some time, shaking their heads from side to side to show their pleasure at emptying the bowels of those vessels into their stomachs. Sancho looked on at all this 'and was in no wise grieved'. On the contrary, remembering the familiar proverb – When at Rome, do as the Romans do – he asked Ricote for his bottle and took his aim with the rest, with no less pleasure than they.

Four times the bottles suffered themselves to be tipped, but the fifth time it was impossible, for they were as sapless and dry as a rush, which rather dampened the spirits of the party. From time to time one of them would thrust his right hand into Sancho's and say: '*Spaniard and Dutchman, all one – goot gombanion*,' and Sancho would reply, '*Goot Gompanion, I swear by Gott*,' and burst into a laugh which lasted an hour, forgetting for the time being all that had befallen him in his governorship; for cares have generally but little sway over the time when men are eating and drinking. At length the wine was finished, and such a drowsiness began to seize them all that they fell asleep on the very table-cloth. Only Ricote and our squire stayed awake, for they had eaten more and drunk less. The Moor drew Sancho aside, and they sat down at the foot of a beech, leaving the pilgrims buried in sweet sleep, and without once stumbling into his Moorish jargon, Ricote spoke as follows in pure

Castilian: 'Well, you know, Sancho Panza, my neighbour and friend, what a terror and dismay the proclamation and edict which His Majesty commanded to be published against those of my nation struck into us all. At least it had that effect upon me, so much so that I almost imagined its dreadful penalty already inflicted upon my own family, even before the time allowed us to leave Spain had expired. So I arranged – sensibly I think – as a man does who knows that on a certain date he will lose his home and so provides himself with another to move to – I arranged, I say, to leave my village, alone and without my family, and to go and look for a place to take them to in comfort and without that haste which generally prevailed. For I saw very well, as all our elders saw, that those proclamations were not just threats, as some said, but would certainly be put into effect at the time appointed. I could not help believing this, knowing as I did our people's desperate and foolish intentions; which made me think it was divine inspiration that had moved His Majesty to adopt such wise measures. Not that we were all guilty, for some of us were steadfast and true Christians. But we were so few that we could not make head against those who were not; and it is no good thing to nourish a snake in your bosom and have enemies within your own house. In fact it was with good reason that all of us were punished with exile; a mild and merciful penalty in the opinion of some, though to us it was the most terrible that could be inflicted. Wherever we are we weep for Spain; for, after all, we were born here and this is our native country. Nowhere do we find the reception our misery requires. In Barbary and in all those parts of Africa where we hoped to be received, entertained and welcomed we are worst treated and abused. We did not know our good fortune till we had lost it, and so ardently do almost all of us long to return to Spain that most of those – and there are plenty – who know the language, as I do, return and leave their wives and children over there unprotected; such is our love for Spain. For now I know by experience the truth of the saying, that the love of one's country is sweet.

'I left our village, as I told you, and went to France, but though they made us very welcome there I wanted to see other lands. I crossed into Italy and reached Germany, where it seemed to me I could live in greater freedom, for its inhabitants do not look into fine points: everyone lives as he pleases, and over the greater part of the country there is liberty of conscience. I took a house in a town near Augsburg, but left it to join with these pilgrims, whose custom it is to come to Spain in some numbers each year to visit its holy places, which they regard as their Indies, where they will get a sure harvest and certain profit. They wander over almost the whole country, and there is no village they do not leave with meat and drink, as you would say, and a *real*, at least, in money. And at the end of their journey they come off with more than a hundred crowns over, which they get out of this country into their own in gold coin, hidden either in the hollows of their staves, or in the patches of their cloaks, or by any device they can contrive, despite the guards at the posts or ports where they are searched. Now it is my intention, Sancho, to dig up the treasure which I left buried, for as it is outside the village I can do so without risk; and then to write, or go myself, from Valencia to my wife and daughter, who I know are in Algiers, and contrive a means of bringing them to some port in France, and of getting them from there to Germany, where we shall await whatever God may please to do with us. For, truly, Sancho, I am certain that Ricota, my daughter, and Francisca Ricota, my wife, are Catholic Christians; and though I am not much of one myself, still there is more Christian than Moor in me, and I always pray to God to open the eyes of my understanding and make me know how to serve Him. But what astonishes me, and what I do not understand, is why my wife and daughter went to Barbary rather than to France, where they could live like Christians.'

To which Sancho replied: 'Look you, Ricote, perhaps it wasn't their choice, for Juan Tiopieyo, your wife's brother, took them away; and as he must be a rank Moor, he would go to the safest place for him. And one more thing I can tell you: I think you've come for nothing, if you're seeking your buried hoard, for we had news that they took a large number of pearls and a great deal of gold coin from your brother-in-law and your wife, who had it on them when they were searched.'

'That may well be,' replied Ricote; 'but I know that they did not touch my hoard, Sancho, for I did not tell them where it was, being afraid of some calamity. So, if you'll come with me, and help me get it up and conceal it, I'll give you two hundred crowns, which will relieve your wants; for, as you know, I'm well aware you have plenty.'

'I would do it,' answered Sancho, 'but I'm not at all greedy. If I had been, I laid down a post this morning where I might have lined the walls of my house with gold, and eaten off silver plate before six months were out. So for that reason, and because to my mind it would be treason against my king to favour his enemies, I would not go with you even if you were to give me four hundred crowns down in cash, instead of a promise of two hundred.'

'And what post is it that you left, Sancho?' asked Ricote.

'I gave up the governorship of an isle,' replied Sancho, 'and such an isle that you won't easily find one like it, I swear.'

'And where is this isle?' asked Ricote.

'Where?' replied Sancho. 'Six miles from here, and it's called the Isle Barataria.'

'Nonsense, Sancho!' said Ricote. 'Isles are out at sea. There are no isles on the mainland.'

'How not?' replied Sancho. 'I tell you, Ricote my friend, that I left it this morning, and yesterday I was governing there at my ease like a sagittary; but I gave it up all the same, for a governor's seems to me a dangerous post.'

'And what did you gain from your government?' asked Ricote.

'I gained,' replied Sancho, 'the knowledge that I'm no good at governing anything but a herd of cattle, and that the wealth that's won from such governments is earned at the price of your rest and sleep, and even of your food. For in isles governors may eat very little, especially if they have doctors to look to their health.'

'I don't understand you, Sancho,' said Ricote. 'All you say seems nonsense to me. For who would give you isles to govern? Was the world short of men more capable of being governors than you? Stop talking, man, and come to your senses. Think whether you won't come with me, as I asked you, and help me get up the treasure I left hidden – for really there's so much of it that I can call it a treasure – and I will give you something to live on, as I said.'

'I've already told you, Ricote,' answered Sancho, 'that I won't. Be satisfied that I shan't betray you. Go your way, in God's name, and leave me to go mine. For I know that well-gotten gains may be lost, and ill-gotten gains may bring down the gainer too.'

'I don't want to press you,' said Ricote. 'But tell me, were you in our village when my wife and daughter and brother-in-law left?'

'Yes, I was,' answered Sancho, 'and I can tell you that your daughter looked so beautiful when she went that everyone in the place came out to see her, and they all said she was the loveliest creature in the world. She departed weeping, and embraced all her friends and acquaintances and all who came to see her, begging everyone to commend her to Our Lord and Our Lady His Mother; and all this with such feeling that it brought tears to my eyes, and I'm not generally much of a weeper. There were many in fact who wanted to go out and capture her on the road and hide her away, but fear of breaking the King's decree prevented them. The person who seemed most affected of all was Don Pedro Gregorio – the rich young heir, you know. They say he loved her dearly. He has never appeared in our village again since she went off, and we all think that he followed after her to steal her away, though we've heard nothing more of it till now.'

'I always had a shrewd suspicion,' said Ricote, 'that that gentleman loved my daughter; but I trusted in my Ricota's virtue, and it never worried me to know he wanted her. For you must have heard, Sancho, that Moorish women seldom or never have affairs with Old Christians, and my daughter, who, in my belief, cared more for her religion than for love, would not pay any attention to the young heir's attentions.'

'God grant you're right,' replied Sancho, 'for it would be bad for both of them. Now let me go off, Ricote my friend, for I want to come to-night to the place where Don Quixote my master is.'

'God be with you, brother Sancho, for now my companions are stirring, and it's time to be on our way.'

Then these two embraced. Sancho mounted Dapple, Ricote seized his staff, and they parted.

Chapter LV. *Of what happened to Sancho on the road and other matters, the best in the world.*

SANCHO's long stay with Ricote prevented his arriving at the Duke's castle that day, though he had got within a mile and a half of it when night overtook him. It was rather dark and cloudy, but as it was summer that did not trouble him much, and he left the road with the intention of waiting till morning. But as his ill luck would have it, just as he was looking for a place where he could settle most comfortably, he and Dapple fell into a deep and very dark pit, which lay amongst some very old buildings. As he fell he commended himself to God with all his heart, thinking that he would not stop short of the bottom of the abyss. But it was not so, for a little more than eighteen feet down Dapple touched ground, and Sancho found himself still on his back, quite unwounded and undamaged. He felt himself all over his body and drew in his breath to see if he was sound or had a hole in any part of him; but finding himself well and whole and sound in health, he could not give the Lord God sufficient thanks for His mercy He had done him; for he had thought that he was most certainly broken into a thousand pieces. He also groped with his hands over the walls of the pit to see if it was possible for him to get out without anyone's aid, but he found them all smooth and offering no hold, which grieved him deeply, especially when he heard Dapple piteously and dolefully lamenting. And it was no wonder, nor was he complaining for nothing, for he was truly in a sad way.

'Oh,' cried Sancho Panza then, 'what unexpected accidents do happen at every turn to those that live in this miserable world! Who would have said that the man who saw himself yesterday enthroned as the Governor of an isle, commanding his servants and his vassals, would find himself to-day buried in a pit without a soul to relieve him, or a servant or vassal to come to his aid? Here we shall perish of hunger, my ass and I, if we don't die before that, he from his bruises and broken bones, and I from grief. At least I shan't be as lucky as my master Don Quixote de la Mancha when he went down into the cave of that enchanted Montesinos, where he found someone to entertain him better than if he'd been at home: for it seems he found the cloth laid and his bed made. There he saw beautiful and delightful visions, but here I truly believe I shall see toads and snakes. What a poor wretch I am! Look where my follies and fantasies have brought me! They'll dig my bones out of here, clean and white and scraped, when it's Heaven's will that they find me, and my good Dapple's with them – and from them perhaps they'll discover who we are, those at least who have been told that Sancho

Panza never parted from his ass, nor his ass from Sancho Panza. Once more I say, what wretches we are that our ill-luck hasn't allowed us to die in our own country and among our own people. There, if there was no relief to be found for our calamity, at least there would be no lack of someone to bewail it, and to close our eyes in the last hour of our sojourn on earth. O my companion and friend, what ill payment I have given you for your good services! Pardon me, and beg Fortune in the best way you know to get us out of this miserable plight into which we two are cast, and I promise I'll put a laurel crown on your head, like any poet laureate's, and give you double feeds.'

In this fashion Sancho Panza lamented, and his ass listened to him without answering a word, such was the distress and anguish the poor creature was in. At last, when he had spent all that night in piteous complaints and lamentations, the day came, and by its clarity and splendour Sancho saw that it would be the greatest of all impossibilities to get out of that pit without assistance. So he began to wail and shout, to see if anyone could hear; but all his cries were wasted on the wilderness, for in all the country round there was no one within hearing; and so he ended by giving himself up for dead. Dapple was lying on his back, but Sancho did manage to get him upon his feet, though he could hardly stand. Then taking a piece of bread out of the saddle-bags, which had shared their unfortunate fall, he gave it to his ass, who did not dislike it. And his master said to him, as if he could understand: 'Bread is relief for all grief.'

And now Sancho discovered a hole in one side of the pit, capable of containing one person if he stooped and shrank. This he made for, and squeezing himself into it found that it was large and spacious inside, as he could see by a shaft of sunlight which entered through what might be called the roof and lit up everything. He saw also that it opened and widened into another huge vault, and when he had discovered this he went out again to his ass, and began to break away the earth from the hole with a stone, so that in a little while he had made a passage through which the beast could easily enter, which he did. Then, taking him by the halter, he began to travel onwards through that cavern in search of a way out on the other side. Sometimes he went in the dark and sometimes without much light, but never without fear.

'Help me, almighty God!' he muttered. 'This, though a misadventure for me, would be an adventure to my master Don Quixote. For he would certainly take these depths and dungeons for flowery gardens and palaces of Galiana, and would expect to emerge from this dark and narrow place into flowering meadows. But poor me, ill-advised and fainthearted, at every step I expect another pit deeper than this one to open and swallow me up. O welcome the evils that come singly!'

Thus he went on, and when he had gone, as he supposed, a little more than a mile and a half, he made out a dim light, which looked like the light of day, entering from somewhere; and this seemed to him a sign of an opening into some road, which he expected to lead into the other world.

Here Cide Hamete Benengeli leaves him, and returns to Don Quixote, who was looking forward with joy and contentment to the time of the battle which he was to fight with the ravisher of the honour of Doña Rodriguez' daughter, for whom he intended to right the wrong and injury so foully done her. Now he happened to be riding out one morning to exercise and practise for the combat in which he expected to be engaged next day; and as he put Rocinante into a charge or short gallop, the horse chanced to plant his feet so near to a hole that if Don Quixote had not tugged hard at the reins he must inevitably have fallen in. He pulled him up, however, and did not fall. Then, approaching rather nearer but not dismounting, he looked into the depths, and as he peered down he heard loud shouts within; and when he listened attentively he was able to distinguish and understand the shouter's words: 'You up there! Is there any Christian can hear me, or any charitable gentleman to take mercy on a sinner buried alive, on an unhappy Governor without a government?'

It seemed to Don Quixote as if he heard Sancho Panza's voice; and this puzzled and amazed him. But raising his own as high as he could, he called: 'Who is that down there? Who is it crying out?'

'Who else could it be crying out,' came the answer, 'but the forlorn Sancho Panza, Governor, for his sins and misfortune, of the Isle Barataria, once squire to that famous knight, Don Quixote de la Mancha?'

When Don Quixote heard this his amazement was redoubled and

his alarm increased, for it occurred to his mind that Sancho Panza must be dead and his soul be there in purgatory. So, prompted by this thought, he cried: 'I conjure you by all that is holy to tell me as a Catholic Christian who you are. And if you are a soul in purgatory tell me what you wish me to do for you. For since it is my profession to favour and aid those in this world who are in need, it shall also be so to aid and relieve the distressed in the other world who cannot help themselves.'

'That sounds as if it's my master Don Quixote de la Mancha speaking,' came the reply, 'for to judge by the voice it can certainly be no one else.'

'Don Quixote I am,' replied Don Quixote, 'whose profession it is to aid and succour in their needs the living and the dead. Therefore tell me who you are, for you hold me rapt with amazement. If you are my squire Sancho Panza and are dead, since the devils have not got you and, by God's mercy, you lie in purgatory, there are ceremonies of our Holy Mother Church capable of delivering you from your torments, and I will intercede with her, for my part, in so far as my wealth will allow. So declare yourself, and say who you are.'

'I vow by all that's holy and by any oath your worship likes, Don Quixote de la Mancha,' replied the voice, 'that I'm your squire Sancho Panza, and that I've never been dead in all the days of my life. But having left my government for matters and causes that it would take a long time to tell you of, I fell last night into a pit where I'm now lying, and Dapple with me, who will not let me lie – for, to prove it to you, here he is with me.'

What is more, it seems as if the ass understood Sancho's words, for at that moment he began to bray so loudly that the whole cave resounded.

'A famous witness!' cried Don Quixote. 'I recognize that bray as if it were my own child, and I know your voice, dear Sancho. Wait for me. I will go to the Duke's castle, which is nearby, and bring someone to get you out of that pit, where your sins must have cast you.'

'Go, your worship,' said Sancho, 'and come back quickly, for God's sake. I can't bear being buried alive here, and I'm dying of fear.'

Don Quixote left him and went to the castle to tell the Duke and Duchess of Sancho's plight, which astonished them not a little, though they well understood how he must have fallen, knowing as they did that the cavern had existed there from time immemorial. But they could not imagine how he had left his government without their having advice of his coming. At last, it is said, they brought ropes and cables, and by dint of many hands and hard work Dapple and Sancho Panza were dragged out of their darkness into the light of the sun, where a certain student saw the squire and observed: 'This is the way all bad governors should leave their governments, just as this sinner comes out of the depths of the abyss, perishing of hunger, pale and probably without a farthing.'

And Sancho said when he heard him: 'It's eight or ten days, brother sharp-tongue, since I went to govern the isle they gave me, and all that while I've never had my belly full even for an hour. During that time doctors have persecuted me and enemies have trampled my bones. I've had no chance of taking bribes or of collecting dues, and since that's the case, I don't think I deserved to come out like this. But man proposes and God disposes; and God knows what's best and fittest for everyone; and circumstances alter cases; and let no one say: this water I won't drink; for where you think there are flitches, there aren't even hooks. God understands me, and that's enough. I say no more, though I could.'

'Do not be angry, Sancho, or vexed at what you may hear,' said Don Quixote, 'otherwise you will never be at peace. Come with a clean conscience, and let them say what they will; for you may as well try to put doors to an open field as tie up the tongues of slander. If the Governor leaves his government a rich man they say that he has been a thief; and if he comes away poor that he is a good-for-nothing and a dolt.'

'Well this time,' answered Sancho, 'they'll surely take me for a fool, but not for a thief.'

Deep in this conversation they reached the castle, surrounded by boys and a great number of other people; and there the Duke and Duchess were waiting for them in a gallery. But Sancho would not go up to see the Duke without first putting Dapple up in the stable; for the ass, he said, had passed a very bad night in their lodging. Then he went up to see his lord and lady, before whom he went down on his knees and said: 'I, my Lord and Lady, because your Highnesses would have it so and without any merit of mine, went to govern your Isle Barataria, which I entered naked, and naked I am now: I neither lose nor gain. Whether I have governed well or ill, witnesses of my conduct over there will say as they please. I have settled questions and decided lawsuits, perishing of hunger all the time, since Master Pedro Recio – native of Tirteafuera, insular and governmental doctor – would have it so. We were attacked by enemies at night, and though they pressed us very hard the islemen say that we came off free and victorious by the valour of my arm, and may God save them if they speak the truth. In short, during that time I have measured the burdens and obligations that government entails, and find them, by my reckoning, more than my shoulders can carry. They are no load for my ribs nor arrows for my quiver. And so before the government flung me up I decided to fling up the government; and yesterday morning I left the isle as I found it, with the same streets, houses and roofs that it had when I went into it. I have exacted no loans from anyone, nor taken a share in any profits; and although I intended to make some useful laws I didn't make one, for fear they shouldn't be kept; for in that case one might as well not make them. I left the isle, as I said, with no other company than my Dapple. I fell into a pit and crept along it, till this morning, by the light of the sun, I saw a way out, but no easy one; for if Heaven hadn't sent me my master Don Quixote, I should have been there till the end of the world. So, my lord Duke and my lady Duchess, here's your governor, Sancho Panza, who in those eight days that he has held his governorship has gained this knowledge, that he would not give a farthing to be a governor, not just of one isle but even of the whole world. And that being so, embracing your worship's feet and imitating the boys' game which goes "*you jump and give me one*", I give the government a jump and pass into the service of my master Don Quixote. For with him at least I get my bellyful, although I eat my bread in bodily fear; and it's all one to me whether it's carrots or partridge, so long as I'm full.'

With this Sancho brought his long speech to an end, Don Quixote dreading all the while that he would utter thousands of absurdities; and when he heard him finish with so few, he gave thanks to

Heaven in his heart. The Duke embraced Sancho and said that it grieved him to the heart that he had left his government so soon, but that he would soon manage to give him some other less onerous and more profitable post on his estate. And the Duchess embraced him too, and ordered them to look after him well, for he showed signs of having been badly bruised and worse treated.

Chapter LVI. Of the prodigious and unparalleled Battle which took place between Don Quixote de la Mancha and the lackey Tosilos, in defence of the daughter of Doña Rodriguez, the Waiting-woman.

THE Duke and Duchess did not repent of the trick they had played on Sancho Panza by giving him his governorship; especially as the steward came that same day and related to them minutely all the speeches Sancho had made and all the actions he had performed during his term of office. And in conclusion he gave an exaggerated account of the assault on the isle, of Sancho's fear, and of his departure, from all of which they got no small enjoyment. After this our history relates that the time appointed for the battle arrived. Now as the Duke had instructed his lackey Tosilos over and over again how he was to deal with Don Quixote so as to overthrow him without killing or wounding him, he ordered the steel heads to be taken off the lances, telling Don Quixote that his Christian feeling, on which he prided himself, forbade their imperilling their lives in this battle. He was content, he said, to give them a fair field on his ground – although he was breaking a decree of the Holy Council which prohibits such duels – but he did not desire the affair to be carried to the extremity. Don Quixote said that his Excellency might make whatever dispositions in the matter he pleased, and that he would obey him in every detail. So, when on the dreaded day the Duke had ordered a spacious platform to be erected facing the castle square, on which the judges of the lists and the appellants, mother and daughter, might take their places, a countless troop of people came in from all the towns and villages of the neighbourhood to witness this novel battle; for none like it had been seen or heard of in that country within the memory of living man.

The first to enter the lists was the master of ceremonies, who surveyed the ground and paced it all over, in case there might be any foul play there or any hidden object over which one of them might stumble and fall. Next entered the waiting-women, who sat down on their seats, hooded to their eyes and even to their breasts; and they showed signs of no small concern when Don Quixote appeared in the lists. A little later, heralded by many trumpets, there appeared on one side of the square the great lackey Tosilos, with his vizor down and wholly encased in stout and shining armour. His horse was clearly a Friesland, huge and grizzled, with a quarter of a hundredweight of hair hanging from each fetlock. The valiant combatant came on, well instructed by the Duke his master how to behave towards the valiant Don Quixote de la Mancha, and warned on no account to kill him, but to try and avoid his first onset for fear of meeting his death, which he would certainly do if they were to meet head-on. He paced the square, and when he arrived in front of the waiting-women stood for a while to look at the lady who sought him in marriage. Then the marshal of the field called Don Quixote, who had already presented himself in the lists, and side by side with Tosilos he addressed the ladies, asking if they consented to Don Quixote's undertaking their cause. They assented, saying that they would accept his judgment in the case as right, final and valid. By this time the Duke and Duchess had taken their places in a gallery that overlooked the lists, which were swarming with people waiting to see the merciless and unparalleled battle. A condition of the combat was that if Don Quixote conquered his antagonist must marry Doña Rodriguez' daughter, and if he were conquered his opponent was free of the promise exacted of him and need give no further satisfaction.

The master of ceremonies divided the sun between them, and set each of them in the place where he was to stand. The drums struck up, the air was filled with the sound of trumpets, the earth shook beneath their feet. The hearts of the gazing crowd were in suspense, hanging on the issue of the affair, some in hope and others in fear. At length Don Quixote, recommending himself with all his heart to our Lord God and to the Lady Dulcinea del Toboso, stood waiting for them to give the agreed signal for the onset. Our lackey, however, had other thoughts; and what preoccupied him I will now tell you. It seems that as he gazed upon his fair enemy she appeared to him the most beautiful woman he had seen in all his life; and the little blind boy, who is generally called Love in these parts, could not lose this opportunity of triumphing over a lackeyish soul and placing it upon the list of his trophies. And so, coming up to him softly and unseen, he ran a six foot dart into the poor lackey's left side and pierced his heart through and through; which he could do in safety, for Love is invisible and comes and goes where he will, without anyone calling him to account for his deeds.

So, when the signal for the charge was given, our lackey was in transports at the beauty of the lady whom he had made mistress of his heart. And so he took no notice of the trumpet's sound; unlike Don Quixote, who charged as soon as he heard it, and rushed against his enemy at the utmost speed that Rocinante would permit. And when his good squire Sancho saw him attack, he called out loudly: 'God guide you, cream and flower of knights errant! God give you victory, for the right is on your side!'

Now although Tosilos saw Don Quixote coming at him, he did not stir a step from his position, but instead called loudly to the marshal of the lists; and when that official came up to see what he wanted he asked him: 'Sir, isn't this a battle to decide whether or not I'm to marry that lady?'

'That is so,' was the reply.

'Then,' said the lackey, 'My conscience pricks me, and it would be a sin if I went on with this battle. So I declare myself beaten, and I'm willing to marry the lady at once.'

The marshal of the lists was amazed at Tosilos' speech, and being in the secret of the plot did not know how to reply to him with so much as a word. Don Quixote drew up in mid-career, seeing that his adversary was not attacking. The Duke could not conceive why they were not going on with the battle, but the marshal of the lists went to tell him what the lackey had said, which left him astonished and extremely angry. Whilst this was going on Tosilos went up to where Doña Rodriguez was sitting and said in a loud voice: 'Madam, I wish to marry your daughter, and I do not want to use strife and contentions to gain what I can have in peace and without peril to my life.'

When the valorous Don Quixote heard this, he said: 'Well, in that case I am free and absolved from my promise. Let them marry, and good luck to them! And since the Lord God has given her to him, may Saint Peter bless her.'

The Duke came down to the castle square, and went up to Tosilos to ask him: 'Is it true, knight, that you yield yourself vanquished, and that your timorous conscience prompts you to marry this lady?'

'Yes, sir,' replied Tosilos.

'He's acting very wisely,' put in Sancho Panza at this point, 'for if you give the cat what you have to give the mouse you'll be out of your trouble.'

Tosilos went off to unlace his helmet, begging for prompt assistance since his breath was failing him, and he could not bear being shut up so long in that narrow lodging. They took it off quickly, and the lackey's face was plainly revealed, at which sight Doña Rodriguez and her daughter cried out aloud: 'It's a cheat! It's a cheat! They've put Tosilos, my master the Duke's lackey, in place of my real husband! Justice from God and the King for this trickery – or this villainy rather!'

'Do not be grieved, ladies,' said Don Quixote, 'for it is neither trickery nor villainy. Or if it is, it is not the Duke who is the cause, but those wicked enchanters who persecute me, and who, jealous of my gaining glory from this victory, have transformed your husband's face into this man's, who you say is the Duke's lackey. Take my advice and marry him, despite the malice of my enemies, for there is no doubt that he is really the man you desire for your husband.'

The Duke, who heard this, was on the point of dispersing all his anger in laughter, and said: 'Such extraordinary things happen to Don Quixote that I am inclined to think this is not my lackey. But here is a plan for us: let us put the marriage off a fortnight, if they will, and keep this personage about whom we are doubtful locked up; in which time perhaps he will return to his original shape. For the spite these enchanters entertain against Don Quixote cannot last as long as that, especially as these deceptions and transformations avail them so little.'

'Oh, sir,' cried Sancho, 'it's the usual practice of these malefactors to change anything my master has to do with from one shape into another. A knight he conquered a long while ago, called the Knight of the Mirrors, they turned into the shape of the Bachelor Sampson Carrasco, a native of our village and a great friend of ours, and my lady Dulcinea del Toboso they turned into a rustic peasant-girl; and so I imagine this lackey will die and live a lackey all the days of his life.'

At which the voice of Doña Rodriguez' daughter put in: 'I don't care who he may be that asks for my hand, I'm grateful to him. I had rather be a lackey's lawful wife than a gentleman's cast-off mistress, though my deceiver's no gentleman.'

The final upshot of all this was that Tosilos was locked up, to see what would come of his transformation. Everyone adjudged the victory to Don Quixote, but most of the spectators remained depressed and sad because the long expected combatants had not hacked one another to pieces; much like boys who are sorry when the man they are expecting to be hanged does not appear because he has been pardoned, either by the injured party or the judge. The people went off; the Duke and Duchess returned to the castle; Tosilos was locked up; Doña Rodriguez and her daughter were very glad to know that in one way or another the matter would end in matrimony; and as for Tosilos, he was of a like mind.

Chapter LVII. Which tells how Don Quixote took leave of the Duke, and of his adventure with the witty and wanton Altisidora, the Duchess's Maid.

Now it seemed right to Don Quixote for him to quit the lazy life he was leading in that castle; for he thought himself guilty of a great fault in permitting himself to be shut up in idleness amidst the countless luxuries and delights which the Duke and Duchess lavished on him in his character of knight errant; and it seemed to him that he would have to render a strict account of his indolence and seclusion to Heaven. So one day he asked the Duke and Duchess for permission to depart. This they granted him, though showing their extreme sorrow at his departure. The Duchess gave Sancho Panza his wife's letters, and he shed tears over them, saying: 'Who would have thought that these great hopes the news of my governorship raised in the breast of my wife Teresa Panza would needs end in my

D D

returning to the draggled adventures of my master Don Quixote de la Mancha? I'm glad all the same to see that my Teresa behaved in her true character by sending the acorns to the Duchess. For if she had not sent them she would have shown herself ungrateful, and I should have been vexed. It comforts me that this gift can't be called a bribe, because I already had the governorship when she sent them, and it's right and proper for those who receive a kindness to show themselves grateful even if only in trifles. After all, naked I went into the government, and naked I left it; and so I shall be able to say with a clean conscience, which is no small matter: "Naked I was born, naked I am now; I neither lose nor gain."'

This Sancho said to himself on the day of their departure; and Don Quixote, having taken leave of the Duke and Duchess the night before, presented himself in the morning in the courtyard of the castle fully armed. All the people of the house gazed on him from the galleries, and the Lord and Lady came out to see him as well. Sancho was mounted on Dapple, with his saddle-bags, his clothes-bag and his provisions, very pleased because the Duke's steward – the one who had played the Trifaldi – had given him a little purse with two hundred gold crowns to supply the needs of the road. Of this Don Quixote as yet knew nothing.

Now whilst everyone was gazing on him, as has been said, among the Duchess's other waiting-women and maids who were watching him the witty and wanton Altisidora raised her voice and began in piteous tones:

> 'Hear then, O you wicked knight,
> Check your reins a little:
> Do not so bestir the flanks
> Of your most ill-governed beast.
> Think, false one, you are not flying
> From some dreadful serpent,
> Only from a lambkin
> Still not grown to sheep.
> Horrid monster, you have tricked
> The most lovely damsel
> Diana on her hills has seen,
> Or Venus looked on in her woods.
>   Cruel Vireno, fugitive Aeneas,
>   Go off and join up with your mate Barabbas.

Wickedly you're bearing off
In your wicked clutching paws
The heartstrings of a humble maid
Tender and enamoured.
Three kerchiefs you have lifted
And some garters, black and white,
From such legs as equal
Marble in their smoothness.
Two thousand sighs you've taken,
Which, if they were fire, could
Set two thousand Troys alight,
If there were two thousand Troys.
  Cruel Vireno, fugitive Aeneas,
  Go off and join up with your mate Barabbas.

Of your squire, that Sancho,
May his bowels grow tough
And hard, that Dulcinea,
Left in her enchantment,
For the crime that you have done
May sadly bear the penalty.
For sometimes in my country
The just for sinners pay.
May your best adventures
Into misadventures turn,
All your pleasures to a dream,
Firmness to forgetfulness.
  Cruel Vireno, fugitive Aeneas,
  Go off and join up with your mate Barabbas.

And may you be known for false
From Seville to Marchena,
From Granada to Loja,
From London into England.
If you ever play at trumps
At piquet or primera,
May you never have a king,
Never see a seven or ace.
When you cut your corns
May the place be bloody,
If they pull your teeth out,
May the stumps remain!
  Cruel Vireno, fugitive Aeneas,
  Go off and join up with your mate Barabbas.'

And all the while the pitiable maid Altisidora was uttering her lament Don Quixote kept his eyes on her. Then, without a word of reply, he turned his face to Sancho and said: 'By the life of your ancestors, Sancho, I conjure you to answer me truly. Tell me, have you by any chance got the three kerchiefs and the garters this love-sick maiden is talking about?'

To which Sancho replied: 'Yes, I have got the three kerchiefs, but the garters – they are over the hills and far away.'

The Duchess was astonished at Altisidora's effrontery. For although she knew that she was bold, merry and not too moral, she would not have thought her so far gone as to proceed to such freedoms; and as she was not informed of this joke her wonder increased.

But the Duke wanted to carry the sport further, and said: 'It seems wrong to me, Sir Knight, that after the hospitable entertainment you have received in this castle of mine you should make bold to carry off at least three kerchiefs belonging to my maid, if not a pair of garters as well. These are indications of a false heart, and ill become your fair name. Return her garters or I defy you to mortal combat, without any fear that your scoundrelly enchanters may change or transform my face, as they did for Tosilos, my lackey, who entered into battle with you.'

'God forbid,' replied Don Quixote, 'that I should unsheathe my sword against your most illustrious person, from whom I have received such favours. The kerchiefs I will return, since Sancho says he has them. As for the garters it is impossible, for I have never had them, nor he either; and if this maid of yours will look in her hiding-places she will find them, I promise you. I, my Lord Duke, have never been a thief, nor do I ever mean to be one as long as I live, unless God lets me out of His care. This maid speaks, as she admits, like one love-sick, for which I am not to blame. And so I have not to ask pardon of her or of your Excellency, whom I implore to have a better opinion of me, and once more to give me leave to pursue my way.'

'May God send you a good journey, Don Quixote,' said the Duchess, 'and may we always have good news of your exploits. Go, and God bless you, for the longer you delay the greater the fire you kindle in the breasts of the maidens who look upon you. As for this maid of mine, I will punish her so that she shall not transgress in future, either in looks or in deeds.'

'Hear only one word more, valorous Don Quixote,' put in Altisidora. 'I beg your pardon for saying that you had stolen my garters for, by God and my soul, I have them on. I have fallen into the error of the man who went searching for the ass he was riding on.'

'Didn't I say so?' exclaimed Sancho. 'A great hand I am at hiding stolen things! For if I had wanted to I should have had a splendid opportunity in my government.'

Don Quixote bowed his head, and made obeisance to the Duke and Duchess and to all the bystanders. Then, turning Rocinante's rein, with Sancho following him on Dapple, he left the castle, taking his way towards Saragossa.

Chapter LVIII. *Of adventures that poured on Don Quixote so thick and fast that they trod upon each other's heels.*

WHEN Don Quixote found himself in open country, free and disembarrassed of Altisidora's attentions, he felt himself in his element, with his spirits reviving for the fresh pursuit of his scheme of chivalries. And, turning to Sancho, he said: 'Liberty, Sancho, is one of the most precious gifts Heaven has bestowed upon man. No treasures the earth contains or the sea conceals can be compared to it. For liberty, as for honour, one can rightfully risk one's life; and, on the other hand, captivity is the worst evil that can befall men. I say this, Sancho, because you have witnessed the luxury and abundance that we have enjoyed in this castle which we are now leaving. Yet in the midst of those highly-spiced banquets and snow-cooled drinks I seemed to be confined within the straits of hunger, since I did not enjoy them with the same liberty as if they had been my own; for obligations to return benefits and favours received are bonds that curb a free spirit. Happy is he to whom Heaven has given a crust of bread, without the obligation of offering thanks for it to any but Heaven itself!'

'For all that your worship says,' answered Sancho, 'it isn't right for us to be ungrateful, on our side, for two hundred gold crowns which the Duke's steward gave me in a little purse that I'm carrying, as a plaster and comforter next to my heart against emergencies. For we shan't always find castles to be entertained in. Sometimes we shall strike inns where they may beat us.'

The knight and squire errant were engaged in such conversations as this when, after riding for more than three miles, they saw about a dozen men dressed like labourers taking their dinner in a little green meadow, and sitting on their cloaks which were spread on the grass. Beside them they had what looked like white sheets, which covered certain objects underneath, some of which stood upright and some of which lay flat at short distances apart. Don Quixote rode up to the diners and, after first saluting them courteously, asked them what lay under their linen covers. To which one of them replied: 'Sir, beneath these sheets are some images, sculptured in relief, for a show we're presenting in our village. We carry them covered up so that they shan't get soiled, and on our shoulders so that they shan't break.'

'If you would be so kind,' said Don Quixote, 'I should like to see them, for images that are carried with such care must certainly be good ones.'

'Yes, that they are,' said the other, 'considering their price, for there's not one of them that didn't cost more than fifty ducats. And to prove that it's true, your worship, wait and see with your own eyes.'

Then, getting up, he left his dinner and went to take the cover off the first image, which proved to be of St. George, mounted on horseback with his lance thrust through the mouth of a serpent, coiled at his feet and represented with all its usual fierceness. The whole image looked a blaze of gold, as they say, and when Don Quixote saw it he said: 'This knight was one of the best errants in all the Heavenly Host. His name was St. George, and he was an especial defender of maidens. Let us see this other one.'

The man uncovered it, and it proved to be St. Martin, mounted on a horse, dividing his cloak with the poor man. And the moment Don Quixote saw him he exclaimed: 'This knight too was one of the Christian adventurers, and I believe he was even more generous than valiant; as you can see, Sancho, by his dividing his cloak with the poor man and giving him half. And no doubt it must have been winter at the time; for if it had not been he would have given him the whole, since he was so charitable.'

'That couldn't have been the reason,' said Sancho. 'He must have been following the old proverb that says, to give and to keep has need of brains.'

Don Quixote laughed and begged them to take off another of the cloths, beneath which was revealed the image of the patron of Spain on horseback with bloody sword, trampling down Moors and treading on their heads. And when he saw him Don Quixote said: 'This is a knight indeed, and of Christ's squadrons. He is called Don Saint James the Moor-killer, one of the most valiant saints and knights the world ever possessed or Heaven possesses now.'

Then they took off another cover, which revealed St. Paul fallen from his horse, with all the details usual in a picture of his conversion. On seeing it so life-like that you might have said that Christ was speaking and St. Paul replying, Don Quixote said: 'This was the greatest enemy our Lord God's church had in his time, and the best defender it will ever have – a knight errant by his life and a peaceful saint in his death, a tireless labourer in the vineyard of the Lord and teacher of the Gentiles. He had Heaven for his school and Jesus Christ Himself for his professor and master.'

There were no more images, and so Don Quixote bade them be covered up again, saying to those who were carrying them: 'I reckon it a good omen, brothers, that I have seen what I have seen, for these saints and knights professed, even as I do, the calling of arms. But the difference between us is that they were saints and fought in the heavenly fashion, and I am a sinner and fight in the human way. They conquered Heaven by force of arms, because Heaven suffers violence, but up till now I do not know what I am conquering by the force of my labours. But should my Dulcinea del Toboso be released from the pains she suffers, my fortune being improved and my mind righted, it may be I shall direct my steps along a better path than I am now following.'

'May God hear you and sin be deaf,' put in Sancho at this point.

The men were as astonished at Don Quixote's appearance as at his words, and did not understand the half of his meaning. They finished their dinner, lifted up their images and, bidding the knight farewell, went on their way. And Sancho was astonished afresh at his master's knowledge, as if he had never known him before, for it seemed to him that there could be no history or event in the world that he had not got written on his nails and imprinted in his memory.

'Truly, my lord and master,' he said to him, 'if what has happened to us to-day can be called an adventure, it has been one of the mildest and sweetest that has befallen us in all the course of our wanderings. For we have come out from it without a beating or bodily fear; and we haven't so much as put hand to sword, or thumped the earth with our bodies, or even been left hungry. Heaven be praised that I have seen all this with my own eyes!'

'You are right, Sancho,' replied Don Quixote, 'but you must consider that times are wont to vary and change their course. And what the common people generally call omens, being founded on no cause in nature, should be taken by a wise man for happy accidents. One of these omen-watchers may get up early one morning, and as he leaves his house meet a friar of the order of the blessed St. Francis; then he will turn round and go back home, as if he had encountered a griffin. Another, a Mendoza, spills the salt on his table, and melancholy spills on his heart, as if nature were obliged to give signs of approaching disasters by things as unimportant as these. The wise Christian should not pry too curiously into the counsels of Heaven. Scipio lands in Africa and stumbles as he leaps ashore; his soldiers take it for a bad omen, but he embraces the ground and cries: "You cannot escape me, Africa, for I have you clasped in my arms." So, Sancho, my meeting with these images has been for me a most happy event.'

'I can well believe it,' answered Sancho, 'and I should like your worship to tell me the reason why Spaniards, when they're going into battle, call on that St. James, the Moor-killer: "*St. James and close, Spain!*" Is Spain perhaps open, that she has to be closed? Or what is this ceremony?'

'You are very simple, Sancho,' answered Don Quixote. 'See here. God has given Spain for her patron and protector this great knight of the Red Cross, especially in those desperate conflicts the Spaniards have fought with the Moors; and so they invoke and call upon him as their defender in all their battles, and often they have seen him there, visibly overthrowing, trampling, destroying and killing the hosts of Hagar, and I could give you many examples of this recorded in authentic Spanish histories.'

Sancho changed the subject, and said to his master: 'I am amazed, sir, at the brazenness of the Duchess's maid, Altisidora. The creature they call Love must have wounded her and pierced her cruelly. They say that he's a little blind boy, and yet though he's blear-eyed, or rather has no sight, if he takes ever such a little heart for his target he hits it and pierces it through with his arrows. I've heard tell too that Love's darts are blunted and dulled by a maiden's reserve and modesty; but in this Altisidora they seem to have been whetted rather than blunted.'

'Take note, Sancho,' said Don Quixote, 'that Love observes no restraints and keeps no rules of reason in his proceedings. He is of the same temper as Death, who attacks the lofty palaces of kings as well as the humble cottages of shepherds; and when he takes possession of a heart the first thing he does is to remove fear and shame from it. And so, being shameless, Altisidora proclaimed her desires, which roused more confusion than pity in my breast.'

'Shocking cruelty!' exclaimed Sancho. 'Monstrous ingratitude! I can say for myself that I should have surrendered and become her vassal at her slightest word of love. The Devil! What a marble heart! What bowels of brass, and what a rough-cast spirit! But I can't think what that maiden can have seen in your worship to make her yield and submit like that. What grace was it, what dash, what charm, what looks? which of all these was it, or was it all of them together that captivated her? For really and truly, often I stop and look at your worship from your feet to the last hair of your head, and I find more about you to scare me than to charm me. And as I've heard too that beauty is the first and principal quality that breeds love, I don't know what the poor creature fell in love with, since your worship has none.'

'Consider, Sancho,' replied Don Quixote, 'that there are two kinds of beauty, one of the soul and the other of the body. The spiritual is displayed and shown in intelligence, in chastity, in good behaviour, in generosity and in good breeding; and all these qualities may fittingly exist in an ill-favoured man. Then when the gaze is fixed on that beauty, and not on the physical, love generally arises with great violence and intensity. I am well aware, Sancho, that I am not handsome; but I also know that I am not deformed; and it is enough for a man of worth not to be a monster for him to be dearly loved, provided he possesses those spiritual endowments I have mentioned.'

Whilst engaged in this talk they strayed into a wood which lay off the road, and suddenly and unexpectedly Don Quixote found himself entangled in some nets of green thread which were stretched from tree to tree; and unable to imagine what they could be he said to Sancho: 'In my opinion, Sancho, the matter of these nets must be one of the strangest adventures imaginable. May I die if the enchanters who persecute me are not trying to enmesh me and stop my journey, as if to revenge the cruelty I showed to Altisidora. But I will teach them that, though these nets were made of hardest adamant instead of green thread, or were stronger than that in which the jealous God of blacksmiths entangled Venus and Mars, I would break them as easily as I would rushes or cotton yarn.'

But as he was trying to push on and break through, there suddenly appeared ahead from between some trees two most lovely shepherdesses. At least they were dressed like shepherdesses, although their jackets and skirts were of fine brocade, and their skirts, I declare, were petticoats of rich watered gold silk. The gold of their hair, too, which was loose on their shoulders, could compete with the rays of the very sun, and they were crowned with garlands of green laurel and red amaranth. In age they appeared not less than fifteen nor more than eighteen. This was a sight to dazzle Sancho, astonish Don Quixote and make the sun stop in its course to watch them; and so all four remained in wondering silence. At length the first to speak was one of the two shepherdesses, who said to Don Quixote: 'Stop, Sir Knight, and do not break these nets, which are not stretched here to hurt you but for our amusement; and since I know that you will ask why they are placed here and who we are, I will tell you in few words. In a village about six miles away live many people of quality, gentlefolk and rich, several of whom have made up a party, of friends, neighbours and relations, to come and take our pleasure at this spot, which is one of the most charming in all the district. Here we have formed amongst ourselves a new pastoral Arcadia, the girls dressing as shepherdesses and the lads as shepherds. We have learnt two eclogues by heart, one by the famous poet Garcilaso and the other by the most excellent Camoens in his own Portuguese tongue, neither of which have we played till now.

Yesterday we came here. We have pitched our tents – field tents they call them – among these saplings on the banks of a flowing stream which waters all these meadows. And last night we stretched these nets among the trees to catch the silly little birds, meaning to drive them into the snare by our noise. If you please, sir, to be our guest you will be liberally and courteously entertained, for no care or sadness shall be of our party.'

She stopped, and said no more. Then Don Quixote replied: 'Truly, fairest lady, Actaeon could have been struck with no greater wonder or amazement when he spied Diana unawares bathing in the waters, than I am at the sight of your beauty. I commend the scheme of your entertainments, and thank you for your invitation; and if I can serve you, you may command me in the certainty of being obeyed. For my profession is no other than to show myself a grateful benefactor to all kinds of people, especially to those of the rank you seem to be; and if these nets, which can occupy only a small space, were to fill the whole rotundity of the globe I would seek new worlds to pass through so as to avoid breaking them. And so that you may give some credence to this hyperbole of mine, learn that it is Don Quixote de la Mancha – no less – who makes you his promise, if by chance this name has reached your ears.'

'Oh, my dear friend,' the other shepherdess then cried, 'what very good luck! Do you see this gentleman here before us? Well, I would have you know that he is the most valiant, the most enamoured and the most courteous knight in the whole world, unless the history of his exploits, which I have read in print, lies and deceives us. I will wager that this good fellow with him is a certain Sancho Panza, his squire, whose drolleries none can equal.'

'That's quite right,' said Sancho, 'I am the droll fellow and the squire your Grace speaks of, and this gentleman's my master, the same Don Quixote de la Mancha historified and aforesaid.'

'Oh!' cried the other shepherdess. 'Let us beg him to stay, dear, for our families will be overjoyed to have him. I have also heard tell of this valour and charm of his. He is especially famous for being the most steadfast and constant lover known, and they say his lady – a certain Dulcinea del Toboso – bears away the palm from all the beauties in Spain.'

'And she has the right to it,' said Don Quixote, 'unless, indeed your peerless beauty may put the matter in doubt. But do not endeavour to detain me, ladies, for the urgent obligations of my profession leave me in no condition to rest.'

At this moment there came up to them the brother of one of the two shepherdesses, also dressed in shepherd-fashion, and every bit as rich and splendid as his sister, who informed him that the gentleman with them was the valorous Don Quixote de la Mancha, and the other his squire Sancho, of whom he would know, since he had read their history. The gay shepherd paid his compliments, and begged the knight to accompany him to their tents; and Don Quixote had to give in and do so. Then the beaters came up, and the nets were filled with different kinds of birds which, deceived by the colour of the meshes, fell into the peril they were trying to avoid. More than thirty people had assembled in that spot, all extravagantly dressed as shepherds and shepherdesses, and in a moment they were informed who Don Quixote and his squire were; and they were no little delighted, for they knew him already from his history. Then they repaired to the tents, where they found the tables richly, abundantly and elegantly laid, and honoured Don Quixote by placing him at the head; and all gazed at him in wonder. At length when the cloth was removed the knight sonorously and very gravely observed: 'Though some say that man's greatest sin is pride, I say that it is ingratitude, and I base my belief on the common saying that Hell is full of the ungrateful. This sin I have endeavoured to avoid, in so far as I have been able, ever since I have had the use of reason; and if I cannot repay the benefits done me with equal benefits, I substitute my desire to repay them, and when that is not enough I proclaim them abroad. For he that declares and proclaims the benefits he receives would likewise repay them if he could, but for the most part receivers have not the resources of givers. Thus God is above us all, for He is a greater giver than any, and man's gifts cannot equal the beneficence of God because of the infinite distance between them. This poverty and deficiency, however, is to some extent compensated for by gratitude. I, therefore, grateful for the favours here done me, and unable to respond in like measure, being restricted by the narrow limits of my means, offer what little is in my power. I, therefore, engage to maintain, for two whole days, in the middle of this high road which leads to

Saragossa, that these two ladies here disguised as shepherdesses are the most beautiful and the most courteous maidens in the world, excepting only the peerless Dulcinea del Toboso, sole mistress of my heart, without offence be it said to all of either sex who hear me.'

At these words Sancho, who had been listening with great attention, cried out loudly: 'Is it possible that anyone in the world could be bold enough to say and swear that this master of mine is mad? Tell me, your worships, gentlemen shepherds, is there a village priest living, though ever so wise and learned, who could speak as my master has just done? Or is there any knight errant, though ever so renowned for bravery, who could make such an offer as he has made?'

Then with a flushed and angry face Don Quixote turned on Sancho and cried: 'Could there possibly be anyone, Sancho, on the whole face of the earth who would not say that you are a dolt, lined with knavery and fringed with unspeakable mischief and roguery? Who set you meddling with my affairs, and enquiring whether I am a man of sense or crazy? Be quiet! Say no more, but saddle Rocinante, if he is unsaddled, and let us go and put my offer into effect, for seeing that right is on my side you can reckon all who dare gainsay me as vanquished already.'

Then with a great demonstration of furious indignation he rose from his seat, leaving the astonished company wondering whether to reckon him mad or sane. They, however, tried to dissuade him from his challenge, protesting that they were sufficiently assured of his grateful nature and that there was no need of fresh demonstrations to prove his valour, for those related in his history were sufficient. But Don Quixote, all the same, persisted in his resolution and, bracing his shield and grasping his lance, took up his position on Rocinante in the middle of a highway, not far from that green meadow. Sancho followed him on Dapple with all the people of the pastoral flock, curious to see the upshot of his arrogant and extraordinary challenge.

Then, planted, as we have said, in the middle of the road, Don Quixote wounded the air with such words as these: 'You, passengers and wayfarers, knights, squires, travellers on foot and horse, passing along this road or about to pass in the next two days! Learn that Don Quixote de la Mancha, knight errant, is posted here to maintain that there is no beauty or courtesy in the world greater than that of the nymphs inhabiting these meadows and woods, setting on one side the mistress of my soul, Dulcinea del Toboso. So let anyone of the contrary opinion come on. I await him here.'

Twice he repeated these same words, and twice they were unheard by any adventurer. But by a stroke of Fortune, which continued to advance his affairs from success to success, there soon appeared on the road a crowd of men on horseback, many of them with lances in their hands, riding all bunched together and at a great pace. And no sooner did they come into view than they turned and got out of the road, perceiving that they might run into danger if they stayed. Only Don Quixote remained still with undaunted heart, while Sancho Panza shielded himself behind Rocinante's hindquarters. The troop of spearmen came up, and one of them who rode somewhat ahead began to bawl at Don Quixote: 'Get out of the way, you silly devil, or these bulls will trample you to pieces.'

'Ho, rabble!' replied Don Quixote. 'I care for no bulls, not for the fiercest ever bred on the banks of Jarama. Confess, scoundrels, the whole lot of you together, that what I have proclaimed is the truth; otherwise, do battle with me.'

The herdsman had no time to answer, nor had Don Quixote a second to get out of the way, even if he had wanted to; and so the troop of wild bulls and tame bullocks, and the crowd of herdsmen and others, who were taking them to a nearby town where they were to be baited next day, passed over Don Quixote and over Sancho, Rocinante and Dapple, overthrowing them all and tumbling them along the ground. Sancho lay there bruised, Don Quixote was stunned, Dapple trampled, and Rocinante not too sound. But at length they all got up, and Don Quixote set off in great haste, stumbling and falling, as he pursued the herd, shouting: 'Halt! Stop, you scoundrelly rabble! For but a single knight awaits you, one who scorns the coward's maxim: build a bridge of silver for a flying enemy!'

But the runaways did not stop for this, and took no more notice of his threats than of last year's clouds. Weariness halted Don Quixote; and more enraged than revenged he sat down on the road, waiting for Sancho, Rocinante and Dapple to come up. They arrived;

master and man remounted; and without turning to take leave of
the pretence or counterfeit Arcadia, they went on their way with
more shame than satisfaction.

Chapter LIX. *Of an extraordinary accident which befell Don
Quixote and might be considered an adventure.*

IN a clear and limpid spring, which they found in a shady clump of
trees, Don Quixote and Sancho removed the dirt they had got from
the unmannerly behaviour of the bulls; and there beside it the woe-
begone pair sat down to rest from their fatigue, leaving Dapple and
Rocinante loose without headstall or bridle. Sancho had recourse to
the larder in his saddle-bags, and brought out what he was pleased to
call his fodder. He rinsed his mouth, and Don Quixote washed his
face, from which refreshment their jaded spirits regained some
courage. But Don Quixote ate nothing, out of pure vexation, nor,
out of pure courtesy, did Sancho venture to touch the food before
him, waiting for his master to take the first bit. Seeing him so deep
in thought, however, that he forgot to raise the bread to his mouth,
the squire silently, and in defiance of all the rules of good breeding,
began to cram the bread and cheese into his mouth.

'Eat, Sancho, my friend,' said Don Quixote. 'Sustain life,
for you have more need than I; and let me die a victim of my
thoughts and of the force of my misfortunes. I was born, Sancho,
to live dying, and you to die eating; and to prove the truth of my
words gaze upon me. Printed in histories, famous in arms, courteous in my actions, respected by Princes, courted by maidens; yet
after all, when I expected palms, triumphs and crowns, earned and
merited by my valorous exploits, I have seen myself this morning
trampled, kicked and pounded by the feet of unclean and filthy
animals. This reflection blunts my teeth, dulls my grinders, numbs
my hands, and completely robs me of appetite, so that I think I may
let myself die of hunger, the most cruel of all deaths.'

'At that rate,' said Sancho without ceasing his rapid munching,
'your worship will not approve of the proverb which says: — Let
Martha die, but die with her belly full. As for me, I'm not thinking
of killing myself. I prefer to do like the cobbler, who stretches the
leather with his teeth till he makes it reach where he wants. I will

lengthen my life with eating till it reaches the end that Heaven has fixed. For I tell you, sir, that there's nothing crazier than to think of dying of despair, as you do. Take my word for it, and have something to eat. Then lie down to sleep a bit on the green cushions of this grass, and you'll find yourself feeling quite a bit soothed when you wake up.'

Don Quixote complied, thinking that Sancho reasoned more like a philosopher than a fool, and remarked: 'If you could do something for me, Sancho, which I will explain to you, my relief would be more certain and my anxieties less great; and it is this: While I follow your advice and sleep go you a little way off from here and, baring your flesh to the air, give yourself three or four hundred lashes with Rocinante's reins on account of those three thousand and odd you have incurred for Dulcinea's disenchantment; for it is no small pity that the poor lady remains enchanted through your forgetfulness and negligence.'

'There's a great deal to be said on that score,' said Sancho. 'Let us sleep, both of us, for the present; and afterwards God knows what will happen. I tell you, your worship, this whipping a man in cold blood is a hard matter, and harder still if the lashes fall upon a body ill-nourished and underfed. Let my lady Dulcinea have patience, and she'll see me riddled with lashes when she least expects it; and till death all is life – I mean that I'm still alive, and still anxious to perform what I have promised.'

Don Quixote thanked him and ate a little, while Sancho ate a good deal; and the two of them threw themselves down to sleep, leaving those two constant companions and friends, Rocinante and Dapple, to graze unrestrained and at their will on the rich grass, which was plentiful in that meadow. And rather late they awoke, remounted, and continued their journey, pressing on to reach an inn which lay in sight, apparently some three miles away. I say that it was an inn because Don Quixote called it one, contrary to his usual habit of calling all inns castles.

When they arrived he asked the landlord if there was lodging, and received the answer that there was, and as comfortable and luxurious as they could find in Saragossa. So they dismounted, and Sancho put his provisions away in a little room of which the host gave him the key. Then he took the beasts to the stable, gave them their fodder, and came out to see what orders Don Quixote had for him. He found him sitting on a stone bench, and gave especial thanks to Heaven that this inn had not seemed to his master a castle. Now when supper time came they retired to their room, and Sancho asked the landlord what he had to give them to eat. The host replied that they could have as much as they could eat of anything they liked to ask for, as the inn was stocked with the birds of the air, the fowls of the woods and the fish of the sea.

'There's no need of all that,' replied Sancho. 'We shall be satisfied with a couple of chickens roasted for us, for my master is weak in the stomach and eats little, and I'm no enormous glutton.'

The landlord replied that he had no chickens, for the kites had devoured them.

'Then, Master Host,' said Sancho, 'have a pullet roasted for us, so long as it's a tender one.'

'A pullet! Good heavens!' replied the landlord. 'Indeed, I sent more than fifty to town only yesterday to be sold. Ask for anything else you like, your worship, but not for pullets.'

'Well,' said Sancho, 'there'll be no shortage of veal or goat, surely.'

'We've none in the house just now,' replied the landlord, 'for they're all finished up, but next week we shall have plenty.'

'That'll do us a lot of good!' replied Sancho. 'But I'll bet you can make up for everything with lashings of bacon and eggs.'

'My Lord!' exclaimed the landlord. 'He's a fine one, this guest of mine. I've just told him I've got no pullets or hens, and he expects me to have eggs! Discuss some other delicacies, if you like, but stop asking for rarities.'

'Let's decide on something, for goodness' sake,' said Sancho. 'Tell me, once and for all, what you have got, Master Host, and stop your discussions.'

'What I have actually got,' said the innkeeper, 'is two cow heels that might be taken for calves' feet, or two calves' feet that are like cow heels. They are stewed with chick-peas, onions and bacon, and at this very minute they're crying out "*Eat me! Eat me!*"'

'I mark them for mine from this moment,' said Sancho, 'and let no one touch them. I'll pay more than anyone else for them, for there's nothing tastier in the world, to my mind. Just give me cow heels and I don't care a fig whether they're like calves' feet or not.'

'No one shall touch them,' said the landlord, 'for the other guests I have, being people of quality, have their own cook and steward and provisions with them.'

'If you go in for quality,' said Sancho, 'there's none better than my master; but the office he professes doesn't allow of larders and butteries. We just stretch out in the middle of a field and stuff ourselves with acorns or medlars.'

Such was Sancho's conversation with the innkeeper, which he now decided to break off, without answering the host's enquiries regarding his master's office or profession.

Supper-time arrived. The host brought in the stew, such as it was, and Don Quixote went to his room and sat down very comfortably to his meal. He seems, however, to have heard some talking in the next room, which was divided from his own by no more than a thin partition: 'I beg you, Don Jeronimo,' exclaimed a voice, 'till they bring in the supper let us read another chapter of the second part of *Don Quixote de la Mancha.*'

The moment Don Quixote heard his name he stood up and listened, all ears, to what they were saying about him. Then he heard this Don Jeronimo, who had been addressed, reply: 'Why, Don Juan, do you want us to read this nonsense? Can anyone who has read the first part of the history of Don Quixote de la Mancha possibly take any pleasure in reading the second?'

'All the same,' said Don Juan, 'it would be well to read it, for there's no book so bad that there isn't something good in it. But what most displeases me in this one is that it depicts Don Quixote out of love with Dulcinea del Toboso.'

On hearing these words Don Quixote was filled with furious indignation, and called out at the top of his voice: 'Whoever says that Don Quixote de la Mancha has forgotten, or can forget, Dulcinea del Toboso, I will teach him with equal arms that he is a long way from the truth; for the peerless Dulcinea del Toboso can never be forgotten, nor is Don Quixote capable of forgetting. His motto is constancy, and his profession to preserve it with gentleness and without violence.'

'Who is it answering us?' came a voice from the other room.

'Who should it be,' answered Sancho, 'but the same Don Quixote de la Mancha, who will make good all he has said now and in the future; for a good paymaster doesn't worry about sureties.'

As soon as Sancho had spoken two gentlemen – for so they appeared – rushed in through the door of the room, and one of them flung his arms round Don Quixote's neck, crying: 'Your presence cannot belie your name, nor can your name do otherwise than give credit to your person. No doubt, sir, you are the real Don Quixote de la Mancha, pole-star and morning star of knight errantry, in despite of him that sought to usurp your name and annihilate your exploits, as the author of this book has done, which I here deliver to you.'

And he put into his hands a book which his companion had been carrying. Don Quixote took it and without a word began to turn over the pages. Then after a while he returned it, saying: 'In the little that I have seen I have found three things in this author deserving rebuke. The first is some words I have read in the prologue; the second that the language is Aragonese, for he often writes without articles; and the third, which most confirms him an ignoramus, is that he stupidly wanders from the truth in the most essential point in the whole history. For he says here that the wife of Sancho Panza, my squire, is called Mari Gutierrez, and that is wrong, for her name is Teresa Panza; and it is much to be feared that anyone who is mistaken on so important a point will be mistaken throughout the history.'

At which Sancho put in: 'A pretty thing in a historian. He must be very well acquainted with our affairs indeed, if he calls my wife Teresa Panza Mari Gutierrez. Take the book again, sir. See if I'm in it, and whether they've changed my name.'

'From your words, friend,' said Don Jeronimo, 'you must certainly be Sancho Panza, Don Quixote's squire.'

'Yes, I am,' answered Sancho, 'and proud of it.'

'Then I will swear,' said the gentleman, 'that this modern author does not treat you with the decency which your appearance seems to deserve. He depicts you as a guzzler and a fool, with no humour at all, very different from the Sancho described in the first part of your master's history.'

'Heaven forgive him,' said Sancho. 'He should have left me for-

gotten in my corner. For let him play who knows the strings, and
St. Peter is well at Rome.'

The two gentlemen begged Don Quixote to come into their
room and sup with them, for they were sure that there was no food
fit for him in the inn. And the knight, ever polite, acceded to their
request and took supper with them, while Sancho remained in
supreme and absolute dominion over the stew. He sat at the head of
the table, and with him the innkeeper who was no less devoted
than Sancho to cow heel and calves' foot.

During the course of the meal Don Juan asked Don Quixote
what news he had of the lady Dulcinea del Toboso; whether she
had married, whether she had been brought to bed or was pregnant,
or whether she was still a virgin and mindful, saving her chastity
and good name, of Don Quixote's amorous addresses. To which he
replied: 'Dulcinea is a virgin, my desires more constant than ever,
our intercourse as fruitless as of old, and her beauty transformed
into that of a coarse peasant girl.'

And then he proceeded to relate to them, in great detail, the lady
Dulcinea's enchantment, the events in Montesinos' cave, and the
instructions of the sage Merlin for her disenchantment – the affair
of Sancho's flagellation. Great was the pleasure the two gentlemen
received from hearing Don Quixote relate his extraordinary adventures, and they were alike surprised at his extravagancies and at his
elegant manner of recounting them. One moment they thought him
a man of sense, and the next he slipped into craziness; nor could
they decide what degree to assign him between wisdom and folly.

Sancho finished his supper and, leaving the innkeeper sozzled,
went to his master's room, saying as he entered: 'Hang me, gentlemen, if the author of that book you've got there has any wish to
be on good terms with me. But though he calls me a guzzler, you
tell me, I hope he doesn't call me a drunkard.'

'He does,' said Don Jeronimo, 'though I do not remember his
exact words. But I know they were ugly ones, and false as well, as I
can plainly read on the physiognomy of honest Sancho here before
me.'

'Take my word for it, gentlemen,' said Sancho, 'the Sancho and
Don Quixote of that history must be different people from those
who figure in the one composed by Cide Hamete Benengeli; for

they are truly we two: my master valiant, wise and a true lover, and myself, simple, droll, and no guzzler nor a drunkard.'

'I believe you,' said Don Juan, 'and were it possible, there should have been a law that no one should dare to write of the affairs of the great Don Quixote except Cide Hamete, his first historian; just as Alexander decreed that no one should dare paint him except Apelles.'

'Let anyone portray me who will, but let him not abuse me,' said Don Quixote; 'for patience will very often trip when overloaded with injuries.'

'No injury can be done to Don Quixote,' said Don Juan, 'which he cannot avenge, if he does not ward it off with the shield of his patience, which seems to me both strong and great.'

In such conversation they passed a great part of the night, and although Don Juan would have liked Don Quixote to read more of the book to see what subjects it dwelt on, they could not prevail upon him to do so. He said that he took it as read, and concluded that it was all nonsense. What was more, he did not wish its author to flatter himself with the thought that he had read it, even should he chance to learn that he had had it in his hands; for our thoughts should be kept from filthy and obscene subjects, and much more so our eyes.

They asked him in what direction he had decided to travel. He replied to Saragossa, to take part in the jousts for the suit of armour which are held in that city every year.

Don Juan told him that the new history related how Don Quixote – or whoever it was – had been there, running at the ring – of which the author gives a wretched account, barren of invention, poor in style, and miserably poorest in descriptions, though rich in absurdities.

'For that reason,' replied Don Quixote, 'I will not set foot in Saragossa. Thus I will publish this modern historian's lie to the world, and people shall see that I am not the Don Quixote he writes of.'

'You will do wisely in that,' said Don Jeronimo, 'for there are jousts at Barcelona too, in which Don Quixote will be able to prove his valour.'

'That I intend to do,' said Don Quixote, 'but give me leave to retire, for it is time for bed, and be pleased to count me in the number of your best friends and servitors.'

'And me too,' said Sancho; 'for you may find me good for something.'

With this they took their leave, Don Quixote and Sancho retiring to their room and leaving Don Juan and Don Jeronimo amazed at the spectacle of mingled wisdom and folly they had witnessed. But they were now quite certain that these were the authentic Don Quixote and Sancho, and that those the Aragonese author had described were not.

Don Quixote rose early, and rapped at the partition of the next room to bid his new friends farewell. Then Sancho paid the innkeeper munificently, but advised him either to make less boast of the provisions at his inn or to keep it better provided in future.

Chapter LX. *Don Quixote's adventure on the way to Barcelona.*

THE morning was cool, and the day gave promise of being so too, when Don Quixote rode out of the inn, having first informed himself which was the most direct way to Barcelona, avoiding Saragossa – for he was determined to prove the falsehood of the new history which he understood had so greatly maligned him. Now it chanced that nothing worth recording befell him for more than six days. But at the end of that time he strayed from the road, and night overtook him among some thick trees – oaks or perhaps cork trees, for on this point Cide Hamete does not observe his usual meticulousness. Master and man dismounted and leant against the tree-trunks, where Sancho, who had taken lunch that day, rushed headlong into the arms of sleep. Don Quixote, however, not from hunger but from his restless imagination, was unable to close his eyes, and let his thoughts wander here and there and in a thousand different places. First he imagined himself in Montesinos' cave; then he saw Dulcinea, transformed into a peasant girl, leap upon her ass-colt; then there rang in his ears the sage Merlin's words, repeating to him the conditions to be observed and the means to be taken for Dulcinea's disenchantment. He was in despair at his squire Sancho's negligence and lack of charity; for to his knowledge he had only given himself five lashes, a poor and disproportionate sum compared to the infinite number outstanding. This thought roused him to such grief and rage that he argued thus with himself: 'If the Great Alexander cut the Gordian knot with the sword, to cut is as good as to untie, yet, nevertheless, became universal lord of all Asia, exactly the same might happen now in the disenchantment of Dulcinea, were I to lash Sancho against his will; for if the virtue of this remedy consists in Sancho's receiving the three thousand and odd stripes, what does it matter to me whether he applies them himself or someone else gives him them, since the efficacy lies in his receiving them, from whatever hand they may come?'

With this idea he went up to Sancho, having first taken Rocinante's reins and arranged them for use as a whip, and began to untie his laces – though it is thought that he had only the one, in front, which kept up his breeches. But no sooner did his master approach than Sancho started up wide awake and cried: 'What is it? Who is touching me and pulling at my clothes?'

'It is I,' answered Don Quixote, 'come to make good your negligence and remedy my own troubles. I have come to whip you, Sancho, and to discharge in part the debt to which you are pledged. Dulcinea is perishing; you are living in idleness; I am dying of desire; so pull down your breeches of your own free will, for it is my intention to give you at least two thousand lashes in this lonely spot.'

'Oh no!' said Sancho. 'Keep off, your worship, or I swear by the true God the deaf shall hear us. The lashes I am pledged to must be applied voluntarily and not by force, and at present I've no desire to whip myself. Enough that I gave your worship my word to flog and flap myself as soon as I feel like it.'

'It cannot be left to your good feeling, Sancho,' said Don Quixote, 'for you are a hard-hearted peasant, although your flesh is tender.'

And so he struggled with him and tried to pull his laces loose. Upon which Sancho jumped to his feet, closed with his master and, gripping him by main force, gave him a back trip which threw him face upwards upon the ground. Then setting his right knee on his chest, he held his master's hands down so tightly that he could not stir and could scarcely breathe.

'What, traitor?' cried Don Quixote. 'Do you rebel against your master and natural lord? Do you presume against your bread-giver?'

'I depose no King, I make no King,' answered Sancho, 'but help myself who am my own lord. Promise to let me alone, your worship, and not try and whip me for the present, and I'll let you go free. But if you don't

> Here and now thou diest, traitor,
> Enemy of Doña Sancha.'

Don Quixote passed his word, and swore on his life not to touch a thread of Sancho's clothing and to leave it to his free will and pleasure to whip himself when he would. Sancho then got up and went some distance off, but just as he was going to lean against another tree he felt something touching his head and, putting up his hands, grasped a man's feet in shoes and stockings. He trembled with fear, and ran to another tree, where the same thing happened. Then he shouted to Don Quixote to come to him. This his master did, asking him what was the matter and what he was afraid of; to which Sancho replied that all the trees were full of human feet and legs. Don Quixote felt them and, immediately guessing the cause, he said: 'You have nothing to be frightened of, Sancho. These are no doubt the legs of robbers and bandits who have been hanged on these trees; for in these parts Justice usually hangs them when it catches them, often in batches of twenty or thirty; by which I conclude that I must be in the neighbourhood of Barcelona.' And he was perfectly right, for when the morning dawned they looked up and saw that the clusters in the trees were bandits' bodies.

But if they were alarmed at those dead bandits they were even more terrified at the sight of more than forty live ones, who suddenly surrounded them and commanded them in Catalan to stay still, and not to move till their captain came up. They found Don Quixote on foot, his horse unbridled and his lance resting against a tree; in short, being utterly defenceless, he thought it best to fold his hands, bow his head, and reserve himself for a better occasion. The robbers immediately fell to work upon Dapple, and quickly emptied the saddle-bag and the clothes-bag; and it was a good thing for Sancho that he carried the Duke's ducats, with his own money, tied in a belly-band. But, for all that, these good folks would have stripped him and searched him, even to see what was hidden between his skin and his flesh, if their captain had not come up at that juncture. He was apparently about thirty-four, stout, of more than medium height, of a stern appearance and swarthy complexion. He rode a powerful horse and wore a coat of mail, with four pistols by his side, of the sort known in those parts as petronels. Seeing that his squires – for that is what they call men of that trade – were going to strip Sancho Panza, he commanded them to stop, and was immediately obeyed: and so it was that the belly-band escaped. But he was surprised to see a lance resting against the tree, a shield on the ground, and Don Quixote in armour and deep in thought, with the gloomiest and most melancholy expression that sadness itself could assume. He therefore approached him, and said: 'Don't be so sad, my good fellow, for you have fallen into the hands of no cruel Osiris, but of Roque Guinart, who is more compassionate than cruel.'

'My sadness,' replied Don Quixote, 'is not on account of falling into your power, valorous Roque, whose fame has no bounds on the whole earth, but that I was so negligent as to let your soldiers catch me unbridled, although I am obliged by the order of knight errantry I profess to live continually on the alert and to be at all hours my own sentinel. For I would inform you, great Roque, that if they had found me on my horse with my lance and shield, it would have been no easy task for them to force me to yield, for I am Don Quixote de la Mancha, with whose exploits the whole world resounds.'

Roque Guinart perceived at once that Don Quixote's infirmity was nearer to madness than to valour, but although he had heard him spoken of at times he had never considered his adventures real, nor been able to persuade himself that such a humour could reign in any man's heart. But he was extremely delighted at this meeting, for he could now prove for himself the truth of the stories he had heard. And so he said to him: 'Valorous knight, do not be vexed or account your present fortune sinister. Perhaps by this stumbling your crooked lot will be set straight, for Heaven frequently raises the fallen and enriches the poor in strange, unheard of and circuitous ways, inconceivable by man.'

Don Quixote was just going to thank him when they heard behind them a noise as of a troop of horse, though it proved to be only one, ridden at full gallop by a youth of apparently twenty, dressed in green damask breeches and a loose coat braided with gold, with a hat turned up in the Walloon fashion, tight-fitting boots, and gilt spurs, dagger and sword. He carried a small firelock in his hand and two pistols by his sides. At the noise Roque turned his head and saw this handsome figure, who cried as he drew near to him: 'I was coming to look for you, valorous Roque, to find in you, if not a cure, at least a relief for my affliction. And not to keep you in suspense, for I see that you have not recognized me, I will tell you who I am. I am Claudia Jeronima, daughter of Simon Forte, your particular friend, and the sworn enemy of Clauquel Torrellas, who is also yours, as he is one of the opposite faction. Now you know that this Torrellas has a son called Don Vicente Torrellas, or at least he was so called two hours ago. He, then – to cut short the tale of my misfortunes I will tell you briefly what he has brought upon me – he saw me and courted me; I listened to him and fell in love with him, unknown to my father; for there is no woman, however secluded or reserved, who has not time enough to carry her unruly desires into effect. In short, he promised to be my husband and I gave him my word to be his wife, though we went no further than that. But yesterday I learnt that he had forgotten his obligations to me and was going to marry another, and that the ceremony was to take place this morning. The news confused my senses and I lost all patience. So, as my father was not in town, I found means of putting on the dress you see and, spurring on my horse, overtook Don Vicente about three miles from here. Then without stopping to make him reproaches or to listen to excuses I fired this gun at him and these two pistols into the bargain, and I believe I must have lodged more than two bullets in his body, thus washing my honour clean in his blood. And there I left him surrounded by his servants, who dared not or could not interfere in his defence. Now I have come to ask you to pass me over into France, where I have relations with whom I can live, and also to beg you to defend my father, so that Don Vicente's many friends may not venture to take their cruel revenge on him.'

Struck with the fair Claudia's gallantry and boldness, with her handsome figure and strange story, Roque said: 'Come, lady, and let us see if your enemy is dead. Then afterwards we will see what we can best do for you.'

But Don Quixote, who had been listening eagerly to Claudia's words and Roque Guinart's reply, broke in: 'No one need trouble himself to defend this lady, for I take it upon myself. Give me my horse and my arms, and wait for me here. I will go and seek this knight and, dead or alive, I will make him keep his pledged word to this beauty.'

'Let no one doubt that,' said Sancho, 'My master's a very good hand at match-making, for it's not many days ago that he made another man marry, who'd also refused to keep his promise to a maiden. And if it hadn't been for the enchanters who persecute him, changing his true shape into a lackey's, that maiden would have been one no longer by this time.'

Roque, who was more concerned with the fair Claudia's adventure than with the speeches of master and man, paid no attention to them, but commanded his squires to return to Sancho all that they had taken off Dapple, and to withdraw to the place where they had been quartered the night before. Then he set out with Claudia in great haste to look for the wounded or dead Don Vicente.

They came to the spot where Claudia had met him, but found nothing there but recently spilled blood. Gazing in all directions, however, they made out some people on a hillside, and concluded rightly that this must be Don Vicente, whom his servants were carrying, alive or dead, to cure him or to bury him. They hurried to catch them up; and as the procession was going slowly, they easily did so, finding Don Vicente in the servants' arms, begging them in a weak and weary voice to leave him to die, for the pain of his wounds would not allow of his going any further.

Claudia and Roque jumped down from their horses and went to him. The servants were frightened at Roque's presence, and Claudia was disturbed at the sight of Don Vicente. So that it was half compassionately and half severely that she went up to him and said, taking him by the hands: 'Had you but given me these hands and kept our compact, you would not have come to this pass.'

The wounded gentleman opened his almost closed eyes and, recognizing Claudia, replied: 'Now I see, fair and deluded mistress, that it was you who killed me, a punishment I never deserved nor earned, for neither in my desires nor in my actions have I ever so much as wished to do you wrong.'

'Then it is not true,' cried Claudia, 'that you were going this morning to marry Leonora, rich Balvastro's daughter?'

'No, certainly not,' answered Don Vicente. 'It must have been my ill-luck that brought you that news, so that you might bereave me of my life out of jealousy. But I count my lot fortunate since I die in your arms. And, to prove to you that this is true, hold my hand and take me for your husband, if you will; for I can give you no other satisfaction for the injury you imagine you have received from me.'

Claudia wrung his hand and was herself wrung to the heart, falling in a faint upon Don Vicente's bloody breast, as the death spasm seized him. Roque was perplexed and did not know what to do. The servants ran for water to throw in their faces, and returned to sprinkle them with it. Claudia recovered from her faint, but not Don Vicente from his paroxysm, for his life was done. When Claudia saw this and realized that her sweet husband no longer lived, she rent the air with her sobs, wounded the Heavens with her lamentations, tore her hair, tossing it to the winds, disfigured her face with her hands, and showed all the signs of grief and sorrow that could be expected from a wounded heart.

'Cruel and unthinking woman,' she cried, 'how easily were you moved to carry out your evil purpose! Jealousy, you raging fury, to what a desperate end you bring her that harbours you in her bosom! O my husband, whose luckless fate has brought you from the bridal bed to the grave, because of your pledge to me!'

So piteous, indeed, were Claudia's plaints that they brought tears to Roque's eyes, though he was not used to weeping. The servants wept; Claudia swooned again and again; and all around seemed a scene of grief and misfortune. At length Roque Guinart ordered Don Vicente's servants to take his body to his father's place, which was near, to give him burial. Claudia told Roque that she would retire to a nunnery where an aunt of hers was abbess, and there she meant to end her days in the company of a better and more eternal spouse. Roque commended her pious resolution, offering to accompany her wherever she pleased, and to defend her father from Don Vicente's relations and from all the world, if they should seek to injure him. Claudia would on no account accept his company, however, but, thanking him for his proposal in the best words she could find, took her leave of him in tears. Don Vicente's servants lifted the body, and Roque returned to his men. So ended the loves of Claudia Jeronima. But was it surprising, seeing that the cruel and invincible hands of jealousy wove the web of her lamentable story?

Roque Guinart found his squires where he had ordered them to be, and Don Quixote among them, mounted on Rocinante and making them a speech, to persuade them to give up their style of life, as perilous for the soul as for the body. But as most of them were Gascons, a wild and unruly people, Don Quixote's address did not affect them much. When Roque got back he asked Sancho Panza whether his men had restored to him the jewels and property they had taken from Dapple. Sancho replied that they had, but that three kerchiefs were missing, worth three cities.

'What's that you say, man?' cried one of them. 'I have them, and they're not worth three *reals*.'

'That is right,' said Don Quixote, 'but my squire values them at the price he said on account of the person who gave me them.'

Roque Guinart ordered them to be immediately restored; then, commanding his men to form a line, he bade them produce before him all the clothing, jewels and money, and everything else that they had stolen since the last share-out. Then, making a quick estimate and reducing whatever could not be divided into its money value, he shared it all out among his band with such careful impartiality that there was not one of them who got a farthing more or less than another. And after this share-out, which left everyone satisfied and pleased, Roque said to Don Quixote: 'If I were not so scrupulous with these men, it wouldn't be possible to live with them.'

Whereupon Sancho remarked: 'Well, justice must be a very good thing, for here I see that it has to be practised even among thieves.'

Now this remark of his was overheard by one of the squires, who raised the butt of his gun, and would no doubt have split Sancho's skull with it if Roque Guinart had not called to him to stop. Sancho was scared and decided not to open his lips again so long as he was in that company. At that moment there ran up one or more of the squires who had been posted as sentinels on the roads to observe all travellers and to keep their chief informed of all that passed.

'Sir,' said this scout, 'there's a great troop of people not far away, coming on the Barcelona road.'

'Have you made out whether they are coming to look for us, or whether they're the sort we look for?' asked Roque.

'They're the sort we seek, every one of them,' answered the squire.

'Then out, all of you,' commanded Roque, 'and bring them here to me. Don't let one escape.'

They obeyed, leaving Don Quixote, Sancho and Roque on their own, anxious to see what would follow. And meanwhile Roque said to Don Quixote: 'This life of ours must seem novel to Don Quixote: strange adventures, strange incidents, and all of them perilous. And I don't wonder if it appears so to him, for I truly admit that there's no way of life more disturbed and full of alarms than ours. I was driven to it by certain desires for revenge, powerful enough to disturb the calmest minds. By nature I am compassionate and good-natured; but, as I have said, the thirst to revenge an injury has so overborne all my good resolutions that I continue in this career despite my conscience. And as deep calls to deep and one sin to another, one feud has linked on to the next until I am involved not only in my own but in those of others. But God is so good that, although entangled in the labyrinth of confusions, I have not lost hope of escaping to a safe harbour.'

Don Quixote was surprised to hear this good and sensible statement, for he had not expected to find a man of such understanding among thieves, murderers and highway robbers. 'Sir Roque,' he replied, 'the beginning of health lies in the knowledge of the disease, and in the sick man's willingness to take the medicines the doctor prescribes. You are sick; you know your complaint, and Heaven, or rather God, who is our doctor, will apply medicines to cure you, medicines which generally cure slowly, not suddenly and by a miracle. What is more, wise sinners are nearer to a cure than foolish ones, and since you have shown your good sense in your speech, you have only to keep up your courage, and hope for an improvement in the sickness of your conscience. But if you would shorten the journey and set yourself easily on the path of your salvation, come with me, and I will teach you to be a knight errant, a calling beset with such toils and misfortunes as, taken as a penance, will carry you to Heaven in a twinkling.'

Roque laughed at Don Quixote's advice and, changing the subject, related Claudia Jeronima's tragic adventure, which moved Sancho deeply, for he had been no little attracted by the girl's beauty, boldness and spirit.

By this time the squires had arrived with their capture, bringing with them two gentlemen on horseback, two pilgrims on foot, and a coach full of women, with some half a dozen servants mounted and on foot, who were of their company, and two muleteers, who followed the gentlemen. The squires were all round them, and victors and vanquished alike kept a profound silence, waiting for the great Roque Guinart to speak. First he asked the gentlemen their names, where they were going and what money they were carrying, to which one of them replied: 'Sir, we are two captains in the Spanish infantry. Our companies are at Naples, and we are going to embark on one of four galleys, which are said to be at Barcelona under orders to sail for Sicily. We have two or three hundred crowns with us, and account ourselves rich. For such is the habitual poverty of soldiers that we are content with a little wealth.'

Roque asked the pilgrims the same questions as the captains, and their reply was that they were going to take ship and cross to Rome, and that between the two of them they might have about sixty *reals*. He also desired to learn who was travelling in the coach, to what place, and with what money, and one of the horsemen replied: 'My mistress, Doña Guiomar de Quiñones, wife of the President of the Naples Tribunal, with a small daughter, a maid and a waiting-woman, travel in this coach. There are six of us servants attending her, and our money is six hundred crowns.'

'So,' said Roque Guinart, 'we have here nine hundred crowns and sixty *reals*. My soldiers must be about sixty in number. Reckon out how much this comes to for each, for I am bad at figures.'

On hearing this the robbers raised a shout of: 'Long live Roque Guinart, and to hell with the villains who seek his ruin!'

The captains showed their distress; the President's lady looked sad; and the pilgrims were not too cheerful at seeing their goods confiscated. Roque kept them for a while in suspense, but he had no mind to prolong their suffering, which could be seen from a mile off. So, turning to the captains, he said: 'Have the kindness, Master Captains, to lend me sixty crowns, and you, Lady President, eighty to satisfy this troop that attends me, for the abbot must eat that sings for his meat. And then you can go your ways free and un-molested, with a safe conduct which I will give you so that if you meet another of my bands which are scattered about these parts they may do you no harm; for it is not my desire to injure soldiers, nor ladies, especially no lady of quality.'

The captains were liberal and eloquent in their acknowledgments of Roque's courtesy and generosity, for so they regarded his leaving them their own money. The lady, Doña Guiomar de Quiñones, wanted to jump out of the coach and kiss the great Roque's hands and feet; but he would not allow her to do so on any account. On the contrary, he begged her pardon for the injury he was forced to do her, to comply with the strict obligations of his wicked calling. The President's lady ordered one of her servants to give him at once the eighty crowns which had been assessed as her contribution, and the captains had already paid out their sixty. The pilgrims were go-ing to hand over their little all, but Roque told them to wait, and turned to his men, saying: 'Two of these crowns go to each of you, and there are twenty men. Let ten be given to these pilgrims, and the other ten to this good squire, so that he may be able to speak well of us and our doings.'

Then bringing out writing materials, with which he always kept himself provided, Roque gave them a written safe-conduct for the chiefs of his bands and, taking leave of them, let them go free, all admiring his generosity, his gallant bearing and strange conduct, and regarding him rather as an Alexander the Great than as a notorious robber.

Then one of his squires said in his Catalan dialect: 'This captain of ours is more like a friar than a highwayman. But if he wants to show himself generous in future, let it be with his own possessions, not with ours.'

The unfortunate fellow did not speak softly enough for his words to escape Roque, who drew his sword and almost cut the man's head in two, saying: 'That's how I punish mutinous babblers.'

Everyone was terror-stricken, and no one dared say a word, such was the awe they held him in.

Roque then drew to one side and wrote a letter to one of his friends at Barcelona, informing him that he had with him the famous Don Quixote de la Mancha, the knight errant of whom there had been such reports; and that he was the most entertaining and sensible fellow in the world. In four days' time, he continued, on St. John the Baptist's day, he would present himself in the middle of the city Strand, in full armour, on his horse Rocinante, with his squire Sancho on an ass; and he bade him advise his friends the Niarros of this, so that they might amuse themselves at his expense. But he wanted his enemies the Cadells to miss that pleasure, though that would be impossible because Don Quixote's deeds, both crazy and sensible, and the drolleries of his squire, Sancho Panza, could not fail to afford general amusement to all the world. This letter Roque despatched by one of his squires, who changed his highwayman's dress for a peasant's, and went into Barcelona to deliver it to the person to whom it was addressed.

Chapter LXI. *What happened to Don Quixote on his entering Barcelona, with other matters containing more truth than wisdom.*

THREE days and three nights Don Quixote stayed with Roque, and if it had been three hundred years he would still have found new matter for observation and wonder in his mode of life. They began the day in one place; they dined in another; sometimes they fled and did not know from whom; at other times they waited for whom they knew not. They slept on their feet, interrupting their sleep to move from one spot to another. It was all sending out spies, listening to scouts, and blowing the matches of fire-locks, though they had only a few of these, for almost all of them used flint-locks. Roque would spend the night away from his men, they had no idea where, for the numerous proclamations which the Viceroy of Barcelona had published against him, setting a price on his head, kept him in continual apprehension. He could trust

E E

nobody, and even feared that his own men would kill him or hand him over to justice; a truly miserable and wearisome life.

Finally by unfrequented roads, by cross-ways and secret paths, Roque, Don Quixote and Sancho set out with six squires for Barcelona. They reached the Strand on St. John's Eve at night, and Roque embraced Don Quixote and Sancho – to whom he gave the ten crowns he had promised, but not handed over till then – and left them with countless offers of service made on both sides. Roque turned back, and Don Quixote remained waiting for day, mounted and just as he was; and it was not long before the fair face of dawn began to peep from the balconies of the East, cheering the grass and the flowers. And their ears were regaled at the same instant by the sound of countless oboes and kettledrums, the ringing of morrice-bells, and the '*Tramp, tramp! Make way, make way!*' of people, who appeared to be coming from the city. Dawn gave way to the sun, whose face broader than a shield gradually rose from below the horizon. Then Don Quixote and Sancho gazed in all directions, and saw the sea, which they had never seen before. It appeared to them very broad and spacious, and a good deal bigger than the lagoons of Ruidera, which they had seen in La Mancha. They saw the galleys lying off the Strand, which, with their awnings down, appeared decked with streamers and pennants that fluttered in the wind and kissed and swept the water. From on board there rang out clarions, trumpets and oboes which filled the air near and far with sweet martial music. Then they began to move, and carry out a kind of mock skirmish on the calm waters; and a crowd of gentlemen, riding out from the city, on fine horses and magnificently attired, seemed to be carrying out corresponding movements. The soldiers in the galleys fired countless pieces of artillery, to which those on the city walls and in the forts replied, and the heavy artillery rent the air with its dreadful roar, to be answered by the cannon on board the galleys. The cheerful sea, the joyous land, and the sky, clear though sometimes clouded by the smoke of the artillery, seemed to rouse and spread a sudden gaiety among all the people. Sancho could not imagine how those great bulks he saw moving on the sea could have so many feet.

By this time the gaily clad horsemen had galloped up with cries, cheers and shouts to the place where Don Quixote was standing in amazement and stupefaction; and one of them, the recipient of

Roque's letter, addressed the knight in loud tones: 'Welcome to our city, mirror, beacon, star and pole-star of all knight errantry,' – and so on and so forth. 'Welcome, I say, to the valorous Don Quixote de la Mancha! – not the false, not the fictitious, not the apocryphal Don who has lately been shown us in false histories, but the true, the legitimate and genuine knight, described to us by Cide Hamete Benengeli, flower of historians!'

Don Quixote replied never a word, nor did the gentlemen expect him to answer; but, wheeling about with all their followers, they began to execute a complicated curvet around Don Quixote, who turned to Sancho and said: 'These people have clearly recognized us. I will wager they have read our history, and the lately printed Aragonese one as well.'

Then the gentleman who had spoken to Don Quixote addressed him once more: 'Come with us, Don Quixote, for we are all your servants and true friends of Roque Guinart.'

To which Don Quixote replied: 'If courtesies breed courtesies, yours, Sir Knight, is a daughter or a very close relation of the great Roque's. Take me where you please, for I am wholly at your disposal, especially if you wish to employ me in your service.'

The gentleman replied in no less polite terms and, clustering round him, they all set out for the city to the sound of the oboes and kettle-drums. But as they entered the Evil One, who is master of all mischief, and the boys, who are wickeder than the Evil One – or two mischievous, insolent lads at least mingled with the crowd, and one of them lifting Dapple's tail and the other Rocinante's, fastened a bunch of furze to each. The poor animals felt these strange spurs, and by swishing their tails aggravated their pain to such an extent that with a thousand capers they threw their riders to the ground. Insulted and furious, Don Quixote ran to rid his old horse's tail of its plumage, and Sancho did the same for Dapple. Don Quixote's escort had a mind to punish the boys' insolence, but that was impossible, for they had worked themselves in among the thousands who were following. So Don Quixote and Sancho remounted and, amidst the same acclamations and music, reached their guide's house, a large and important one, which proclaimed the wealth of its owner. And there we will leave them for the present, for Cide Hamete would have it so.

Chapter LXII. *The adventure of the Enchanted Head; with other childish matters which cannot be omitted.*

DON QUIXOTE'S host was called Don Antonio Moreno, a rich and intelligent gentleman and very fond of honest and decent entertainment. So when he found the Knight in his house he cast about for innocent ways of bringing out his eccentricities, for the jest that wounds is no jest, and amusements are worth less if they involve injury. The first thing he did was to make Don Quixote take off his armour and show himself in his tight chamois-skin doublet – which has been mentioned and described already – on a balcony giving on to one of the principal streets of the city in sight of the populace and the boys, who gazed at him as though he had been a monkey. The horsemen in their gala dress began to career before him once more, as though they had put on their finery for him alone and not to celebrate the festival; and Sancho was highly delighted, imagining that somehow or other he had stumbled on another Camacho's wedding, another house like Don Diego Miranda's, another castle like the Duke's.

Don Antonio had some of his friends dining with him that day, and they all did Don Quixote honour, treating him like a knight errant, at which he was puffed up with vainglory and could not contain himself for pleasure. And such were Sancho's droll sayings that all the servants of the house and everyone who heard him hung on his lips. And when they were at table Don Antonio addressed Sancho: 'We have heard here, honest Sancho, that you are so fond of minced chicken blancmange and forcemeat balls that if you have any left you stuff them into your shirt for another day.'

'No, sir, that's not true,' answered Sancho, 'for I'm more cleanly than greedy, and my master Don Quixote, who is here present, knows very well that the pair of us often go for eight days together on a handful of acorns or nuts. It's true that sometimes if they happen to give me the heifer I run with the rope; I mean to say that I eat what I'm given, and use my opportunities as I find them; but you can take it from me that if anyone says I'm an inordinate and dirty eater he's wide of the mark; and I would say it in another way but for my respect for the honourable beards here at table.'

'I assure you,' said Don Quixote, 'that the frugality and cleanliness with which Sancho eats might be written and engraved on sheets of brass, to remain as an everlasting memorial for future ages. It is true that when he is hungry he appears something of a gobbler, for he eats fast and chews on both sides of his mouth. But in cleanliness he is most punctilious, and at the time when he was governor he learnt to eat delicately; so much so that he used to eat grapes, and even the seeds of the pomegranate, with a fork.'

'What!' exclaimed Don Antonio, 'has Sancho been a governor?'

'Yes,' answered Sancho, 'of an isle called Barataria. Ten days I governed it as well as you could ask, and in that time I lost my rest and learnt to despise all the governorships in the world. I ran away from it, and fell into a cave, where I gave myself up for dead and escaped alive only by a miracle.'

Don Quixote related in detail the whole episode of Sancho's government, which afforded his hearers the greatest amusement. Then, when the cloths were removed, Don Antonio took the knight by the hand and led him into a private room, where there was no other furniture but a table, apparently of jasper, supported on a stand of the same material on which stood a bust, seemingly of bronze, in the style of the heads of Roman emperors. Don Antonio paced up and down the room with Don Quixote, taking several turns round the table, and after some time observed: 'Now that I am certain, Don Quixote, that no one is listening or can hear us, and the door is shut, I will tell you of one of the extraordinary circumstances, or rather wonders, imaginable, on condition that what I shall communicate be deposited in the inmost, secret recesses of your heart.'

'I swear it shall,' replied Don Quixote; 'and I will even throw a flagstone over it, for greater security. Since I would have you know, Don Antonio' – for by now he had learnt his host's name – 'that you are talking to one who, though he has ears to hear, has no tongue to betray. Therefore you may safely convey what lies in your breast into mine, and be assured it is cast into the abysses of silence.'

'Trusting in that pledge,' replied Don Antonio, 'I will at once strike you with amazement, and somewhat relieve myself from the discomfort of having no one to communicate my secrets to; for they are not fit to be entrusted to all.'

Don Quixote waited in bewilderment for the outcome of all these precautions. Then Don Antonio took hold of his hand and passed it over the bronze head, along the table, and down the jasper stand on which it stood, and then said: 'This head, Don Quixote, was made by one of the greatest enchanters and sorcerers the world has ever known. I believe he was a Pole by race and a disciple of the famous Escotillo, of whom so many wonders are told. He was here in my house, and at the price of a thousand crowns constructed this head, which has the virtue and property of answering any questions spoken into its ear. He took the bearings, drew the figures, observed the stars, marked the seconds, and completed his work as we shall see tomorrow. For on Fridays it is silent and, today being Friday, we shall have to wait until tomorrow. During that time you will be able to decide on your questions, and I know by experience that its answers will be the truth.'

Don Quixote was amazed at this description of the head, and inclined to disbelieve Don Antonio; but, seeing how little time he had to wait before making a trial, he preferred to say nothing, but only to thank his host for revealing so great a secret to him. They then left the room, Don Antonio locked the door, and the two of them went into the hall where the other gentlemen were sitting. In the meanwhile Sancho had told them many of the adventures and incidents which had befallen his master.

That afternoon they took Don Quixote through the city, clad not in armour but in street dress, a long overcoat of tawny cloth which would have made the very ice sweat at that season. They gave their servants orders to keep Sancho entertained, and not to let him leave the house. Don Quixote rode, not on Rocinante but on a big, easy-paced mule with very fine trappings, and when they put on him his overcoat they stitched a parchment to his back, without his noticing it, on which they had written in large letters: '*This is Don Quixote de la Mancha.*' Now as soon as they began their tour the scroll attracted general attention, and as a great number of passers by read it Don Quixote was astonished to find that many people recognized him and greeted him by name. So much so that he turned to Don Antonio, who was riding at his side, and observed: 'Great is the prerogative that lies in knight errantry, since it makes its professors known and famous through all the ends of the earth. For look, Don Antonio, even the boys of this city know me, though they have never seen me before.'

'That is so, Don Quixote,' replied Don Antonio, 'for just as fire cannot be hidden and confined, virtue cannot fail to be recognized; and that virtue which is achieved by the profession of arms outshines and excels all others.'

Now, as Don Quixote was riding along amidst the acclamations described, a certain Castilian happened to read the scroll on his back and exclaimed very loudly: 'The devil take Don Quixote de la Mancha! How have you got here alive after all the beatings you've received? You're a madman. If you had been mad in private and behind closed doors you would have done less harm. But you have the knack of turning everyone who has to do with you into madmen and dolts. Just look at these gentlemen riding with you! Go back home, idiot, and look after your estate and your wife and children, and quit this nonsense that worm-eats your brain and skims the cream off your intellect.'

'Get along with you, fellow,' said Don Antonio, 'and don't offer advice where it isn't asked for. Don Quixote de la Mancha is a man of good sense, and we that ride with him are no fools. Virtue must be honoured wherever it's found. Go away and bad luck to you, and don't meddle where you aren't wanted.'

'Indeed you're right, your worship,' replied the Castilian, 'for to offer this fellow advice is to kick against the pricks. But it distresses me all the same that this idiot's reputed good sense should waste away along the channel of knight errantry. But bad luck to me and all my descendants if from now on, should I live more years than Methusaleh, I offer advice to anyone, even though he asks me for it.'

The counsellor then departed and the tour continued; but so great was the crush of boys and people reading the scroll that Don Antonio had to take it off, under the pretence of doing some other thing. When night fell they returned to the house, where a ball took place; for Don Antonio's wife, who was a lady of rank, gay, good-looking and intelligent, had invited some of her friends to come and honour her guest and enjoy his strange humours. Quite a few came, and after a splendid supper the dance began about ten o'clock. Among the ladies were two of a roguish and jocose disposition, who, although very modest, were rather free in devising jokes to afford harmless amusement. These two were so insistent on getting Don Quixote out to dance that they tired him out, body and soul. It was a sight indeed to see the knight's form, tall, lanky, lean and sallow, tightly encased in his clothes, so awkward and, even worse, by no means nimble. These ladies made up to him on the sly, and he repulsed them also surreptitiously; but, finding himself hard pressed by their advances, he raised his voice and cried: '*Fugite, partes adversae!* Leave me in peace, unwelcome thoughts. Away, master your desires, ladies, for she that is my queen, the peerless Dulcinea del Toboso, will allow no thoughts but of her to enslave and subdue me!'

So saying, he sat down on the floor in the middle of the room, wearied and shaken by the exercise of so much dancing. Don Antonio had him taken up bodily and carried to bed, and the first to lay hands on him was Sancho, who asked: 'What the devil did you mean by dancing, master? Do you think that all brave men must be dancers, and all knights errant skip around? If so you're much mistaken. I can tell you there are men bolder at killing a giant than at cutting a caper. If you had been for the clog-dance I would have taken your place, for I can do it like a goshawk, but as for dancing I can't work a stitch at it.'

The company were highly amused at Sancho's observations, and he put his master to bed, covering him up with clothes so that he should sweat out the chill he had taken from his dancing.

The next day Don Antonio decided to make the experiment with the enchanted head, and with Don Quixote, Sancho, two other friends and the two ladies who had tormented the knight at the dance and who had stayed that night with Don Antonio's wife – he locked himself up in the room that contained the head. After explaining its properties he pledged them to secrecy, saying that this was the first time the virtue of this enchanted head was to be put to the test. Now only Don Antonio's two friends knew the trick of this enchantment; and if Don Antonio had not first revealed it to them they would have been as astonished as the rest; for it was impossible not to be impressed by so ingenious and cunning a contrivance.

The first who approached the head was Don Antonio himself,

who whispered in its ear, though not so softly as not to be over-heard by everyone: 'Tell me, head, by the virtue inherent in you, what am I thinking of now?'

And the head replied without moving its lips, in a clear and distinct voice: 'I have no knowledge of thoughts.'

These words struck everyone with amazement, the more so as there was no human being in the neighbourhood of the table or in the whole room who could have spoken the reply.

'How many are we here?' asked Don Antonio again.

And the answer came in the same quiet tone: 'There are you and your wife, two friends of yours and two of hers, a famous knight called Don Quixote de la Mancha, and his squire, Sancho Panza by name.'

Here indeed was fresh cause for astonishment, and everyone's hair stood on end in pure horror. Then Don Antonio moved away from the head and said: 'This is enough to convince me that I was not cheated by the man who sold you to me, learned head, talkative head, answering head, wonderful head! Let someone else come and ask his question.'

And as women are generally impatient and inquisitive, the first to go up was one of Don Antonio's wife's two friends, and her question was: 'Tell me, head, what shall I do to be very beautiful?'

And the reply was: 'Be very chaste.'

'I have no more to ask,' said the questioner.

Then her companion went up and said: 'I should like to know, head, if my husband loves me or not.'

And the answer was: 'Think what he does for you, and you will know.'

The married woman moved away, and said, 'I might have spared it that question, for a man's actions certainly proclaim his feelings.'

Then one of Don Antonio's two friends went up and asked: 'Who am I?'

And the reply came: 'You know.'

'That doesn't answer my question,' replied the gentleman. 'I asked you to tell me whether you knew me.'

'Yes, I know you,' answered the voice. 'You are Don Pedro Noriz.'

'I don't want to know any more, for that's enough to convince me, head, that you know everything.'

Then he moved away, and the other friend went up and asked: 'Tell me, head, what are the desires of my son and heir?'

'I have already said,' came the answer, 'that I have no knowledge of wishes; but I can tell you all the same that your son would like to bury you.'

'That,' said the gentleman, 'is only too plain and palpable.' And he asked no more. Then Don Antonio's wife went up and said: 'I don't know what to ask, head. I should only like to learn from you whether I shall enjoy my dear husband for many years.'

And the answer came: 'Yes, you will, for his good health and temperance promise him long years of life, which it is the habit of many to cut short by intemperance.'

Then Don Quixote approached and asked: 'Tell me, you that reply, was it truth or a dream, the account I gave of my experiences in the cave of Montesinos? Will my squire Sancho's whipping be completed? Will Dulcinea's disenchantment come to pass?'

'As for the matter of the cave,' came the answer, 'there is much to say: it has something in it of both. Sancho's whipping will go on slowly. Dulcinea's disenchantment will be duly accomplished.'

'I wish to know no more,' said Don Quixote, 'for when I see Dulcinea disenchanted I shall reckon that all the good fortune I can desire has come to me at one fell swoop.'

The last to ask was Sancho, and his question was: 'Shall I ever get another governorship? Shall I quit this hungry squire's life? Shall I see my wife and children again?'

To which the answer came: 'You will govern in your own house; and if you go home you will see your wife and children; and by giving up service you will cease to be a squire.'

'By God, that's rich!' exclaimed Sancho Panza. 'I could have told myself all that; the prophet Perogrullo couldn't do better.'

'Animal!' cried Don Quixote. 'What answer do you expect? Is not it enough that the replies this head gives correspond to the questions asked it?'

'Yes, it's enough,' answered Sancho. 'But I wish it would be less sparing of its knowledge and tell me more.'

The questions and answers were now at an end, but there was no end to the amazement of everyone except Don Antonio's two friends who were in the secret. But Cide Hamete Benengeli would at once explain the trick for fear that the astonished world might believe that there was some magic or strange mystery in this head. So he declares that Don Antonio Moreno had it devised at home, in imitation of a head he had seen at Madrid, which was manufactured by an engraver for his own amusement and to puzzle the ignorant. Its construction was like this: the top of the table was of wood painted and varnished to look like jasper, and the stand on which it stood was of the same material, with four eagle's claws projecting from it to support the weight more firmly. The head, which looked like a bronze portrait bust of a Roman emperor, was all hollow, and so was the top of the table, into which it fitted so neatly that no sign of a joint could be seen. The stand of the table was also hollow, to correspond with the throat and head of the bust, and the whole was made to communicate with another room beneath the one where the head stood. Through all the hollows in the stand, the table, the throat and breast of the portrait bust described, ran a metal pipe, so well fitted as to be completely concealed. In the room below, corresponding to the one upstairs, stood the man who was to make the answers, with his mouth to this same pipe, so that the voice from above came down and the voice from below sounded up, clearly and articulately as through an ear trumpet, and so it was impossible to discover the trick. The answerer was a nephew of Don Antonio's, a quick and intelligent student; and as his uncle had told him who would come into the room with him that day, it was easy for him to reply promptly and correctly to the first question, and to answer the others by guesswork and, as he was a clever lad, cleverly. And Cide Hamete goes on to say that this oracular machine continued to exist for ten or twelve days, but when the rumour spread through the city that Don Antonio had in his house an enchanted head which answered all questions asked it, he was afraid that its fame might reach the ears of those watchful sentinels of our faith, so he gave an account of the matter to the Inquisitors, who ordered him to dismantle it and use it no further, for fear the ignorant rabble might be corrupted. But in Don Quixote's opinion and Sancho Panza's, the head remained enchanted and oracular, which pleased Don Quixote more than it did Sancho.

The gentlemen of the city, for Don Antonio's pleasure and to entertain Don Quixote and give him an opportunity of displaying his eccentricities, arranged a tilting at the ring for six days later, but it failed to take place through an accident which shall be described later.

Don Quixote had a desire to stroll about the city without ceremony and on foot, for he feared that the boys would bother him if he went on horseback. So he and Sancho went out for a walk with two servants whom Don Antonio lent him. Now, as they were going down a street, Don Quixote happened to raise his eyes, and saw written over a door in very large letters: '*Books printed here*', which greatly pleased him, for he had never before seen any printing and longed to know how it was done. So he went in with all his followers, and saw them drawing off the sheets in one place, correcting the proofs in another, setting up the type in a third and revising in yet another – in fact he saw all the processes of a large printing-house. Don Quixote went up to one compartment and asked what they were doing there. The workmen explained to him; and he watched in wonder and passed on. Then he went up to another man and asked him what he was doing, and the workman replied: 'Sir, that gentleman you see there –' and he pointed out a handsome, important looking fellow with a serious air – 'has translated an Italian book into our Castilian tongue, and I am setting it up for the press.'

'What is the title of the book?' asked Don Quixote.

'Sir,' replied the author, 'the book in Italian is called "*Le Bagatelle*."'

'And what corresponds to *Le Bagatelle* in our Castilian?' asked Don Quixote.

'*Le Bagatelle*,' said the author, 'is, one might say, *The Trifles* in Castilian; but though this book is humble in its title it has good solid things in it.'

'I know a little Italian,' said Don Quixote, 'and pride myself on singing some of Ariosto's stanzas. But tell me, sir – and I do not ask because I wish to test your knowledge, but out of simple curiosity – have you ever found the word "*pignata*" in your reading?'

'Yes, often,' replied the author.

'And how do you translate it into Castilian, sir?' asked Don Quixote.

'How else,' replied the author, 'but by "*stew*"?'

'Good Heavens!' exclaimed Don Quixote, 'how advanced you are in the Italian tongue! I will lay a firm wager that where the Italian has "*piace*" you say in Castilian "*please*", and where it has "*piu*", you say "*more*", and "*su*" you translate "*above*" and "*giu*" "*beneath*".'

'Yes, of course I do,' replied the author, 'for these are their proper equivalents.'

'Yet I dare swear,' said Don Quixote, 'that you are not appreciated by the world, which is always loath to reward intellect and merit. What abilities are lost here! What talents neglected! What virtues unappreciated! But yet it seems to me that translating from one tongue into another, unless it is from those queens of tongues Greek and Latin, is like viewing Flemish tapestries from the wrong side; for although you see the pictures, they are covered with threads which obscure them so that the smoothness and gloss of the fabric are lost; and translating from easy languages argues no talent or power of words, any more than does transcribing or copying one paper from another. By that I do not mean to imply that this exercise of translation is not praiseworthy, for a man might be occupied in worse things and less profitable occupations. I except from this observation two famous translators: the first Doctor Cristobal de Figueroa for his *Pastor Fido*, and the other Don Juan de Jáuregui for his *Aminta*, which leave you in doubt which is the translation and which the original. But tell me, sir, is this book printed on your own account or have you sold the copyright to a bookseller?'

'I am printing it on my own account,' replied the author, 'and I expect to gain a thousand ducats at least from this first edition of two thousand copies. They will sell like hot cakes at six *reals* apiece.'

'You are very good at figures,' said Don Quixote, 'but it is very clear that you do not know the tricks of the printing trade or the arrangements printers make with one another. When you find yourself saddled with two thousand copies of a book you will find your back so sore that it will frighten you, I promise you, particularly if the book is a little out of the way and not a bit spicy.'

'What then?' exclaimed the author. 'Would you have me give it to a bookseller, who will pay me three farthings for the copyright and even think he's doing me a kindness by giving me that? I don't print my books to win fame in the world, for I am already known by my works. I want profit, for fame isn't worth a bean without it.'

'God send you good luck,' replied Don Quixote. And he passed on to another compartment where he found them correcting a sheet of a book called *Light of the Soul*, on seeing which he said: 'Books like this, numerous though they are, are the kind that ought to be printed, for there are many sinners nowadays, and there is need of infinite light for so many in the dark.'

He went on farther and saw them also correcting another book; and when he asked its title they replied that it was the *Second part of the Ingenious Gentleman Don Quixote de la Mancha*, composed by someone or other, native of Tordesillas.

'I have heard of this book already,' said Don Quixote, 'but truly, on my conscience, I thought it had been burnt by now and reduced to ashes for its presumption. But it will get its Martinmas like every hog. Works of invention are only good in so far as they adhere to truth or verisimilitude; and general history is the better for being well authenticated.'

With these words he left the printing-house, with some signs of annoyance. That same day Don Antonio arranged for him to be taken to see the galleys lying off the Strand, which delighted Sancho greatly because he had never seen any in all his life. Don Antonio informed the commodore that he was going to bring him a guest that afternoon – the famous Don Quixote de la Mancha, of whom he and all the inhabitants of the city had heard. But what happened then shall be told in the next chapter.

Chapter LXIII. *Of the Disaster that befell Sancho Panza on his visit to the Galleys, and the strange adventure of the fair Moorish girl.*

PROFOUND were Don Quixote's reflections over the enchanted head's reply, but none of them hit on the trick, and all centred on Dulcinea's promised disenchantment, which he regarded as certain. To that he returned again and again, and rejoiced in his heart in the belief that he would speedily see its accomplishment. As for Sancho, although he loathed being a governor, as has been said, he still longed to rule again and be obeyed; for such are the evil effects of authority, even of mock authority.

That afternoon Don Antonio Moreno, their host, and his two friends accompanied Don Quixote and Sancho to the galleys. The commodore had been warned of their coming, and as soon as the famous pair reached the shore all the galleys struck their awnings and sounded their clarions. Then they immediately launched a pinnace covered with rich carpets and cushions of crimson velvet, and the moment Don Quixote set foot aboard the captain's galley all the rest discharged their midship guns. Then as Don Quixote climbed the starboard ladder, the whole crew saluted him with three cheers, as is the custom when an important person boards a galley. The General, for so we shall call him, who was a Valencian gentleman of quality, gave Don Quixote his hand, and embraced him, saying: 'I shall mark to-day with a white stone – for I do not expect to spend a better one in all my life than this day of my meeting with Don Quixote de la Mancha – as a sign that in him is contained and epitomised all the valour of knight errantry.'

Don Quixote replied to him in no less courteous terms, immeasurably delighted to find himself treated in so lordly a fashion. They all went on to the poop, which was very well decorated, and sat down on the side benches. Then the boatswain passed along the gangway and gave a signal on his whistle for the crew to strip off their shirts, which they did in a second. Sancho was startled to see so many men bare to the skin, and even more so when he saw them set the awning so quickly that it looked to him as if all the devils were at work there. But this was tarts and gingerbread to what came next. Sancho was sitting on the captain's stand, beside the last oarsman on the starboard side, who following his instructions seized Sancho and lifted him up in his arms. Then, all the crew standing ready, starting from the starboard side they sent him flying along from hand to hand and from bench to bench, so fast that poor Sancho lost the sight of his eyes, and imagined no doubt that the devils of hell were bearing him off; and they did not stop until they had sent him up the larboard side and put him down again in the poop. The poor fellow was left battered, panting and all in a sweat, unable to imagine what had happened to him. Don Quixote, who had witnessed Sancho's wingless flight, asked the general if those were the ceremonies usually practised upon persons coming aboard the galleys for the first time; for if they happened to be, he had no desire to be initiated, and would perform no such exercises; and he swore to God that if anyone presumed to lay hold on him to toss him in that manner, he would kick his soul out of his body. And as he spoke he stood up and grasped his sword.

At that very moment they struck the awning and lowered the lateen-yard from the top of the mast to the bottom with a tremendous noise. Sancho thought that the sky was coming off its hinges and was going to fall on his head, which he ducked in great fear and tucked between his legs. Don Quixote did not find it much to his liking either, for he too began to tremble, hunching his shoulders and visibly blanching. The crew hoisted the yard with the same speed and clatter with which they had lowered it, and all this in silence, as if they had neither voice nor breath. The boatswain gave the signal to weigh anchor and, leaping into the middle of the gangway, began to tickle the crew's backs with his whip or hide-strap; and gradually they put out to sea. When Sancho saw so many red feet – for such he thought the oars to be – moving as one, he said to himself: 'Here are things really and truly enchanted, as the things my master talks of are not. What have these wretches done that they flog them so? And how does this single man, who goes about whistling, have the audacity to whip all these people? Surely this is hell, or at least purgatory.'

Seeing with what attention Sancho was watching events, Don Quixote said to him: 'O friend Sancho, how quickly and at how little cost you could strip yourself to the waist, if you would, and

take your place among these gentlemen to complete Dulcinea's
disenchantment. For with so many companions in torment you
would not feel much yourself; besides, the sage Merlin might perhaps reckon each of these lashes, being well laid on, as ten of those
you will have to give yourself in the end.'

The General was going to enquire about those lashes and about
Dulcinea's disenchantment, when a sailor cried out: 'Montjuich is
signalling that there's a vessel with oars on the coast along the
western shore.'

When he heard this the General leapt into the gangway and
cried: 'Pull, my lads! Don't let it get away! It must be an Algerian
pirate brigantine the watch tower is signalling.'

The other three galleys then caught up the flagship for orders.
The General commanded two of them to stand out to sea, intending to keep along the coast himself with the third, for then the vessel
could not escape them. The crew plied their oars, driving the
galleys forward with such fury that they seemed to be flying.
When the galleys that had put out to sea were about two miles off,
they sighted a vessel which they judged to be of fourteen or fifteen
banks or oars – and so it proved. When this vessel made out the
galleys she took to flight, in the hope of getting away by her speed.
But things went badly for her, as the flagship was one of the fastest
craft sailing the seas, and gained on her so rapidly that the crew of
the brigantine plainly realised that they could not escape. Therefore their commander would have had his men abandon their oars
and surrender, for fear of exasperating the captain commanding
the galleys. But Fortune ordained otherwise, and so it was that when
the flagship had got near enough for those aboard the pirate ship
to hear the shouted summons to surrender, two Toraquis – that
is to say two drunken Turks – out of the fourteen in the brigantine
fired their muskets and killed two soldiers who were posted on our
forecastle. At this sight the General swore not to leave a single man
in the vessel alive, but as he began to attack with extreme fury she
slipped away under the flagship's oars. The galley shot some distance ahead, and when the pirates saw that they had escaped they
made sail while the galley was turning, and once more set off with
sail and oar. But this rash attempt only led to their undoing, for the
flagship overtook them within little more than half a mile and,

clapping her oars on them, caught them all alive. The two other galleys had come up by this time, and all four returned with their prize to the shore, where a vast crowd was waiting for them, eager to see their capture. The General cast anchor near the land, and sent a pinnace for the Viceroy of the city, whom he had recognized on the Strand. Then he ordered the lateen-yard to be lowered so as to hang the commander out of hand, and the rest of the pirates he had caught in the vessel, about thirty-six in number, all stout fellows, and most of them Turkish musketeers. The General asked who was master of the brigantine, and he was answered in Castilian by one of the captives, who afterwards proved to be a Spanish renegade: 'This young man here, sir, is our master.'

And he pointed to a lad who seemed to be hardly twenty, one of the handsomest and gallantest youths imaginable. Then the General questioned him: 'Tell me, rash dog, what made you kill my soldiers, for you saw it was impossible for you to escape. Is this the respect due to a captain's galley? Do you not know that temerity is not valour? Faint hopes should make men bold but not rash.'

The master would have replied, but the General could not for the moment attend to his answer, having to go and receive the Viceroy, who was just coming aboard the galley, and with him some of his attendants and several people of the city.

'It has been a fine chase, Sir General,' said the Viceroy.

'How good,' replied the General, 'your Excellency will presently see hanging on this yard-arm.'

'How so?' asked the Viceroy.

'Because,' replied the General, 'they have killed two soldiers of mine against all law and against all right and usage of war, two of the best soldiers sailing on these galleys; and I have sworn to hang every man I have captured, and this youth in particular, who is master of the brigantine.' And he pointed him out, with his hands tied and the rope round his neck, awaiting death.

The Viceroy looked at him, and when he saw him so handsome, so gallant and so resigned, the youth's beauty gave him an instant letter of recommendation, and the Viceroy felt a great desire to save him from death. 'Tell me, captain,' he asked him, 'are you a Turk by race, or a Moor, or a renegade?' And the youth replied in the same Castilian tongue: 'I am neither Turk, Moor, nor renegade.'

'Then what are you?' asked the Viceroy.

'A Christian woman,' answered the youth.

'A woman, and a Christian? In such a dress, and such a plight? This is marvellous but hardly credible.'

'Suspend my execution, gentlemen,' said the youth, 'for you'll not lose much by deferring your vengeance while I tell you my life's story.'

Could anyone be so hard-hearted as not to be mollified by these words, or as not at least to listen to what that sad, pitiable youth had to tell? The General bade him say what he would, but not hope to be pardoned for his notorious offence. With this permission the youth began to speak as follows: 'I was born of that nation, unhappy and unwise, on which a sea of misfortune has lately fallen. I was born of Moorish parents, and in the course of their misfortune carried to Barbary by two of my uncles. For though I protested that I was a Christian, which indeed I am, and no pretended and feigned one but a true Catholic, it was in vain. It had no influence on the officers responsible for our miserable banishment, nor would my uncles believe it either. They took it for a fiction I had invented so as to stay in the land where I was born; and so against my will they forced me to go with them. I had a Christian mother and a wise and Christian father too. I sucked the Catholic faith with my mother's milk. I was brought up with good principles, and neither in my language nor in my customs, I think, did I show any signs that I was a Moor. And with my virtues, for so I think them to be, grew such beauty as I have; and although I was very reserved and secluded, that was not enough to prevent my being seen by a young gentleman called Don Gaspar Gregorio, the eldest son of a gentleman whose estate adjoins our village. How he saw me, how we conversed, how he lost his heart to me, and I gained very little by him, would be a long story, particularly at this time when I am afraid that the cruel rope which threatens me may cut short my narrative. So I will only tell you that Don Gregorio wished to accompany me in our exile. He mingled with the Moors from other places, for he knew the language very well, and on the journey made friends with my two uncles with whom I was travelling; for my prudent and far-sighted father had left the place as soon as he heard the first proclamation of our banishment, and gone to look for some spot in foreign lands that would receive us. He left a quantity of pearls and stones of great value, with some money in Portuguese coin and gold doubloons, buried in a hiding place known only to me. He ordered me, in the event of our being expelled before his return, on no account to touch the treasure he was leaving. I obeyed him, and with my uncles, as I have said, and other relatives and friends, crossed over to Barbary. The place where we settled was Algiers – and we might as well have chosen Hell itself. The king got news of my beauty, and rumour told him of my wealth, which proved in some ways to my advantage. He summoned me before him, and asked me from what part of Spain I came, and what money and jewels I had with me. I told him the place, and that the jewels and money were still buried there, but could easily be recovered if I were to go back for them myself. All this I said in hopes that his greed might be more effective in blinding him than my beauty. But whilst he was talking to me news reached him that one of the handsomest and most gallant youths imaginable had come with me. I immediately realized that they were speaking of Don Gaspar Gregorio, whose good looks exceed all possible exaggeration. I was alarmed at the thought of Don Gregorio's danger, for among those barbarous Turks a handsome boy or youth is more highly prized than the most beautiful woman. The king immediately commanded him to be brought before him so that he might see him, and asked me whether what they said of this lad was true. Then, inspired as I believe by Heaven, I assented, but informed him that he was no man, but a woman like myself, and I begged him to let me go and dress this girl in her proper garb, so that she might display her full beauty and appear in his presence without embarrassment. He agreed, and deferred till next day the discussion of my return to Spain to bring out the hidden treasure. I talked with Don Gaspar and told him what danger he ran in appearing as a man. Then I dressed him as a Moorish woman, and that same evening brought him into the presence of the king, who was struck with admiration by the sight of him and decided to keep this maiden as a present for the Great Turk; and to avoid the danger she might run in his own women's seraglio, and out of self-distrust, he had her put into the house of some Moorish ladies of rank, who were to guard and wait on her. There they immediately took Don Gregorio. What the pair of us felt – for I cannot deny that I love him – I leave to the imagination of all parted lovers. The king presently devised a scheme for my returning to Spain in this brigantine, accompanied by two Turks – they were the ones that killed your soldiers. This Spanish renegade came with me as well' – she pointed to the man who had first spoken – 'and I know for certain that he is secretly a Christian, and set on remaining in Spain and not returning to Barbary. The rest of the brigantine's crew are Moors and Turks, who are there only to serve at the oars. But so greedy were these insolent Turks that they violated their orders that as soon as we touched Spain this renegade and I should be put ashore in Christian dress – with which we came provided. They decided first to sweep the coast and take a prize, if they could, fearing that if they landed us first we might meet with some accident which would reveal that the brigantine was at sea, and then they might be taken, if there chanced to be any galleys on that coast. Last night we sighted this shore and, not suspecting these four galleys, were discovered: you have seen our fate. The end of it is that Don Gregorio remains in woman's dress among the Moors, in manifest peril of his life, and I am here with my hands bound, expecting, or rather fearing, to lose my life, of which I am already weary. This, gentlemen, is the conclusion of my lamentable story, as true as it is wretched. But I beg of you to let me die like a Christian, since, as I have told you, I am perfectly guiltless of my nation's crime.'

There she ceased, and the tears which filled her lovely eyes drew many from those of her auditors. Then the Viceroy, who was much moved, went up to her without speaking a word, and with his own fingers untied the rope binding the Moorish girl's fair hands.

Now all the while this Christian Moor told her strange story an ancient pilgrim who had boarded the galley with the Viceroy kept his eyes fixed on her; and no sooner did she end her tale than he threw himself at her feet and embraced them, addressing her in words broken by countless sobs and sighs: 'O Anna Felix, my unhappy daughter! I am your father Ricote, returned to seek you, for I cannot live without you, who are my soul.'

At these words Sancho opened his eyes and raised his head, which he had kept lowered, brooding on his unfortunate handling. And when he looked at the pilgrim he recognized that same Ricote whom he had met on the day he left his government, and he was convinced that this was his daughter. For when she was unbound she embraced her father, mingling her tears with his. Then, turning to the General and the Viceroy, the pilgrim said: 'This, gentlemen, is my daughter, less happy in her fate than in her name. She is called Anna Felix, with the surname of Ricote, and is as famous for her beauty as for her father's riches. I left my country to seek some place in foreign parts to shelter us and take us in, and when I found it in Germany I came back in this pilgrim's habit with other Germans, to look for my daughter and dig up the great riches I had left buried. I did not find my daughter, though I did find my treasure, which I have with me. But now by the strange turn you have seen I have found a treasure which makes me still richer, my beloved daughter. If strict justice can allow the gates of mercy to be opened to our guilelessness and our united tears, extend it to us who have never thought of wronging you or in any way partaken of the designs of our people, who have rightly been expelled.'

Then Sancho spoke: 'I know Ricote well, and I'm sure it's quite true that Anna Felix is his daughter. Though as to the tale of his comings and goings and his good or bad intentions I've nothing to say.'

Everyone present was struck by this strange incident, and the General declared: 'Your tears, let me assure you, will prevent my fulfilling my oath. May you live, Anna Felix, all the years which Heaven has allotted you. But the rash and insolent men who committed the crime must pay the penalty.'

Then he immediately ordered the two Turks who had killed his soldiers to be hanged from the yard-arm. But the Viceroy earnestly entreated him not to hang them, for their action arose rather from frenzy than from design. The General acceded to the Viceroy's plea, for cold-blooded vengeance is never good. They then set about devising a plan for delivering Don Gaspar Gregorio from his peril, and Ricote offered to contribute more than two thousand ducats which he had in pearls and jewels. They discussed many schemes, but the best proposal came from the Spanish renegade, who proposed to go back to Algiers in a small vessel of about six banks of oars manned by Christian rowers, for he knew where, how, and when he could disembark, and was also acquainted with the house where Don Gaspar was kept. The General and the Viceroy were doubtful whether to rely on the renegade, or if they dare trust him with a Christian crew. But Anna Felix answered for him, and her father Ricote promised to pay the Christians' ransoms, if by chance they were captured.

When they had agreed on these plans the Viceroy returned on shore, and Don Antonio Moreno bore the Moorish girl and her father off with him, with the Viceroy's injunctions to receive them and make as much of them as he could. And for his own part that dignitary offered anything in his house for their entertainment, such kindness and goodwill did Anna Felix's beauty inspire in his breast.

Chapter LXIV. *Of an adventure which gave Don Quixote more pain than any which had befallen him before.*

OUR HISTORY tells us that Antonio Moreno's wife received Anna Felix into her house with very great pleasure. She welcomed her with considerable kindness, being attracted both by her beauty and her intelligence, for the Moorish girl was remarkable for both; and all the people of the city crowded to see her, as if they had been brought together by the ringing of bells. Don Quixote told Don Antonio that their scheme for rescuing Don Gregorio was not a good one, for there was more danger than advantage in it. It would be better, he thought, for them to put him ashore in Barbary with his horse and his arms, for he would deliver him in spite of the whole breed of Moors, as Don Gaiferos had done his wife Melisendra.

'Consider, your worship,' said Sancho on hearing this, 'that when Don Gaiferos rescued his wife and took her to France it was all done on dry land; but here, if we do perhaps deliver Don Gregorio, we have no way of bringing him to Spain, for there's the sea in between.'

'There is a remedy for everything except death,' replied Don Quixote. 'We only need a vessel off the shore, and the whole world shall not prevent our boarding it.'

'Your worship paints a good picture and makes it sound easy,' said Sancho, 'but there's many a slip 'twixt cup and lip, and I'm all for the renegade. He seems a stout and likely fellow to me.'

Don Antonio replied that if the renegade did not succeed in his plan they would adopt the expedient of the great Don Quixote's passing over into Barbary. Two days later the renegade left in a light vessel of twelve oars with a very resolute crew; and after another two days the galleys sailed for the Levant, the Viceroy having promised the General to send him an account of the fortunes of Don Gregorio and Anna Felix.

Now one morning Don Quixote was riding out to take the air on the Strand, in complete armour – for, as he often said, his ornaments were arms, his rest the bloody fray, and he was never a moment without them – when he saw coming towards him a knight, also in full armour, with a shining moon painted on his shield, who, when he came near enough to be heard, cried in a loud voice, addressing his words to Don Quixote: 'Illustrious knight and never-sufficiently-praised Don Quixote de la Mancha, I am the knight of the White Moon, whose unparalleled deeds may perhaps recall his name to your memory. I have come to do battle with you and to try the strength of your arms, with the purpose of forcing you to acknowledge and confess that my mistress, let her be who she may, is incomparably more beautiful than your Dulcinea del Toboso; which truth, if you confess it fairly, will save you from death, and me from the pains of killing you. But if you fight and I vanquish you I desire no other satisfaction than that you shall forsake arms, abstain from seeking adventures, and withdraw to your own village for the period of a year, which you must pass without putting hand to sword, in profound peace and profitable ease, such as will contribute to the increase of your estate and the profit of your soul. But if you conquer me, my head shall be at your mercy, the spoils of my armour and horse shall be yours, and the renown of my deeds shall be transferred to you. Consider which is your better course, and reply quickly, for to-day is the only day I have for the despatch of this business.'

Don Quixote stood confounded and amazed, as much at the Knight of the White Moon's arrogance as at the reason for his challenge. But he replied calmly and with a severe demeanour: 'Knight of the White Moon, whose exploits have not till now come to my notice, I will make you swear that you have never seen the illustrious Dulcinea. For had you seen her I know you would have taken care not to engage in this enterprise, since the sight of her must have cured you of all belief that there has been or ever could be any beauty comparable with hers. Therefore, without giving you the lie, but merely saying that you are incorrect in your statement, I accept your challenge upon the conditions you have named, here and now, so that we shall not lose the day to which you are confined. I only except from your conditions the transfer of your renown. For I do not know what your deeds may be, and I am content with my own, such as they are. Take, then, whichever side of the field you wish, and I will do the same; and whom Heaven favours may St. Peter bless.'

The Knight of the White Moon had been observed from the city, and the Viceroy was informed that he was in conversation with Don Quixote de la Mancha. That dignitary supposed that this was some new adventure devised by Don Antonio Moreno or by some other gentleman of the city, and so rode at once to the Strand with Don Antonio and other gentlemen in attendance, just as Don Quixote was wheeling Rocinante round to take the necessary ground for his charge. Whereat, seeing that they were both just on the point of turning for the encounter, the Viceroy interposed, demanding the reason for their sudden battle. The Knight of the White Moon replied that it was a matter of pre-eminence in beauty, repeated to him shortly his challenge to Don Quixote, and informed him of the acceptance of the conditions by both parties. The Viceroy then went up to Don Antonio and asked him quietly whether he knew who this Knight of the White Moon was, or if it was some trick they were playing on Don Quixote. Don Antonio replied that he did not know who he was, nor if the challenge was in jest or earnest. This reply left the Viceroy in doubt whether to let them proceed with the battle or not; but he could not persuade himself that it was anything but a joke and so drew aside, saying: 'Sir Knight, if there is nothing else for it but to confess or die, and Don Quixote swears black and the Knight of the White Moon white, in God's hands be it, and fall to!'

The Knight of the White Moon thanked the Viceroy for his licence in polite and well-chosen terms, and Don Quixote did the same. Then, commending himself to Heaven with all his heart and to his Dulcinea – as was his custom at the outset of battles – he wheeled round to take a little more ground, for he saw that his adversary was doing the same. Then, without any sound of trumpet or other warlike instrument to give them the signal for the charge, they both turned their horses at the same moment. But as the Knight of the White Moon was the nimbler, he met Don Quixote two-thirds down the course and hurtled into him with such tremendous force that, without touching him with his lance – which he seemed to be deliberately holding up – he brought Rocinante and Don Quixote to the ground with a terrible fall. Then immediately springing upon the knight, he put his lance to his vizor and cried: 'You are vanquished, knight, and if you do not acknowledge the conditions of our challenge, you die.'

Then, battered and stunned, without lifting his vizor Don Quixote proclaimed in a low and feeble voice, as if he were speaking from inside a tomb: 'Dulcinea del Toboso is the most beautiful woman in the world, and I am the most unfortunate knight on earth; nor is it just that my weakness should discredit that truth. Drive your lance home, knight, and rid me of life, since you have robbed me of honour.'

'That I will not do, I swear,' said the Knight of the White Moon, 'Let the renown of the lady Dulcinea del Toboso's beauty live unimpaired; for all the satisfaction I ask is that the great Don Quixote de la Mancha shall retire to his village for a year, or until such time as I please, as was agreed between us before entering upon this battle.'

The Viceroy and Don Antonio heard all this, and so did many others who were there; and they also heard Don Quixote reply that, as his victor asked nothing of him to the prejudice of Dulcinea, he would comply with all the rest like a true and scrupulous knight.

After this acknowledgment the Knight of the White Moon turned rein and, bowing his head to the Viceroy, entered the city at a canter. The Viceroy ordered Don Antonio to go after him and find out by any means possible who he was. Then they lifted Don Quixote up and, uncovering his face, found him pale and bathed in sweat, nor could Rocinante move for some time, so severe was his fall. Sancho, very sad and downcast, did not know what to say or do, for all this episode seemed to him to be happening in a dream,

and the whole business to be a matter of enchantment. He saw his
master overthrown and bound to lay aside his arms for a year. The
glorious light of his exploits seemed to him darkened, and Sancho's
own hopes from his recent promises scattered as the wind scatters
smoke. He was afraid that Rocinante might be crippled for ever
and his master's bones be permanently knocked out of joint, though
it would hardly be a pity if his madness had been knocked out of
him too. In the end they carried Don Quixote into the city in a
sedan-chair, which the Viceroy sent for, and that functionary himself rode back as well, eager to know who this Knight of the White
Moon was that had left Don Quixote in so sad a plight.

Chapter LXV. *Which reveals who the Knight of the White
Moon was, with Don Gregorio's deliverance and other events.*

DON ANTONIO MORENO followed the Knight of the White
Moon; and a great number of boys followed him too, and pestered
him until he took refuge in an inn inside the city, which Don Antonio entered also in his anxiety to make his acquaintance. A squire
came out to receive and disarm him, and he then shut himself up in
a lower room, where Don Antonio followed him, standing upon
thorns to know who he was. Then, when the Knight of the White
Moon saw that this gentleman would not leave him, he said: 'I
know very well, sir, what you have come for: to find out who I am
– and as I know no reason to hide my identity from you, while my
servant here is taking off my armour I will tell you the whole truth
of the matter, omitting nothing. My name, sir, is Bachelor Sampson
Carrasco, and I come from the same village as Don Quixote de la
Mancha, whose madness and folly have excited the pity of all who
know him. I have felt particularly concerned and, believing that his
health depends on his resting at home on his own land, I devised a
trick to make him stay there. Some three months ago I went out
on to the roads after him, disguised as a knight errant, styling myself *The Knight of the Mirrors*, and intending to fight with him and
conquer him without hurting him, and to make it a condition of our
combat that the vanquished should be at the disposal of the victor.
What I intended to require of him – for I had no doubt of my
success – was that he should go home and not leave his village for

a whole year, during which time he might be cured. But Fate ordained otherwise, for he conquered me and tumbled me off my horse; and so my plan failed. He continued on his way, and I went home, vanquished, ashamed and shaken by my fall, which was rather a severe one. However, I did not relinquish my project of seeking him once more and beating him, as you have seen to-day. And as he is so scrupulous in observing the ordinances of knight errantry there is no doubt that he will keep the conditions I have laid on him, as he has promised. This, sir, is the whole story, and I have nothing more to tell you. I implore you not to give me away or tell Don Quixote who I am, so that my good plan may work, and his understanding be restored to him; for he has an excellent brain, if he can only be freed from the follies of chivalry.'

'Oh, sir,' said Don Antonio, 'may God pardon you the injury you have done the whole world in your attempt to restore the most amusing of all madmen to his senses. Don't you see, sir, that no benefit to be derived from Don Quixote's recovery could outweigh the pleasure afforded by his extravagances? However, I fancy that all the worthy Bachelor's arts will not be sufficient to restore so completely crazy a man to sanity. And if it were not a sin against charity, I should say that I hope Don Quixote may never be cured, for with his recovery we not only should lose his pleasantries but his squire Sancho Panza's as well; and either of them can turn melancholy itself to mirth. I will keep quiet, all the same, and tell him nothing, to see if I prove right in suspecting that all Master Carrasco's efforts will be in vain.'

The Bachelor replied that anyhow the business was now well on the way, and that he hoped for a favourable result. Upon which Don Antonio offered to follow his instructions, and the Bachelor took his leave, had his armour tied on a mule, mounted the horse on which he had done battle and left the city that same day, returning home without any incident worthy of recording in this true history. Don Antonio repeated all that Carrasco had told him to the Viceroy, who was not over pleased, for with Don Quixote's retirement there was an end of all the entertainment his mad exploits afforded everyone who heard of them.

Don Quixote stayed six days in bed, melancholy, sorrowful, brooding and in a bad way, turning over and over in his mind the misfortune of his defeat. Sancho comforted him, however, saying amongst other things: 'Raise up your head, sir, and cheer up, if you can. Thank Heaven that although you were tumbled to the ground you got off without a single rib broken, for there's give and take in everything, you know, and there aren't always flitches where there are hooks. A fig for the doctor; you've no need of him to cure you of this complaint. Let's go back to our homes, and give up wandering in search of adventures in lands and places we don't know. But when you come to think of it, I'm the greater loser by this, although your worship's in the worse state. For though with my government I gave up all desire to be a governor again, I've never lost my longing to be a count. But that will never come to anything, if your worship gives up trying to be a king, and abandons the profession of chivalry. So my hopes are all going up in smoke.'

'Be quiet, Sancho. Do you not see that my seclusion and retirement need last no more than a year? After that I will return to my honourable calling, and I shall not fail to win a kingdom, and a countship to give you.'

'God grant you may,' said Sancho, 'and may sin turn a deaf ear, for I've always heard that a good hope is better than poor possessions.'

Here their conversation was interrupted by Don Antonio, who entered crying out joyfully: 'A reward for good news, Don Quixote! Don Gregorio and the renegade who went for him are in harbour. In harbour, do I say? They're already at the Viceroy's, and will be here in a moment.'

At this Don Quixote was somewhat cheered, and said: 'Indeed I was just going to say that I should have been delighted if everything had turned out otherwise, for then I should have had to cross to Barbary, where by the force of my arm I should have liberated not only Don Gregorio but all the Christian captives in Barbary. But what am I saying, poor wretch? Have not I been conquered? Have not I been overthrown? Am I not forbidden to take up arms for a year? Then what am I promising? What am I boasting of, seeing that I am fitter to handle a distaff than a sword?'

'No more of that, sir,' said Sancho; 'let the hen live, even if she's got the pip. It's your turn to-day, mine to-morrow. There's no need to worry about all these clashes and knocks, for the man who's down to-day may be up to-morrow, unless he prefers to stay in bed; to lose his pluck I mean, instead of gathering fresh courage for fresh fights. Now, get up, your worship, to receive Don Gregorio, for it sounds to me as if everyone's excited, and he must be in the house by now.'

And he was right, for Don Gregorio and the renegade had already given the Viceroy an account of their journey there and back, and in his eagerness to see Anna Felix Don Gregorio had rushed to Don Antonio's with his rescuer. Although he had been in woman's dress when they got him away from Algiers, he had exchanged clothes in the boat with a slave who had escaped with him. But whatever dress he had worn, his appearance would have commanded respect, admiration and envy, for he was exceedingly handsome and apparently about sixteen or seventeen years old. Ricote and his daughter went out to receive him, the father in tears, the daughter blushing, but they did not embrace, for where there is great love there is not usually overmuch freedom. Their beauty was universally admired, and though they did not speak to one another their eyes revealed their modest and joyful thoughts. The renegade recounted his plan and the means he had employed for Don Gregorio's rescue, and Don Gregorio told of the dangers and difficulties he had been in among the women with whom he had stayed, telling no long story, but showing by his brevity that his discretion outran his years. Finally Ricote liberally rewarded the renegade as well as the men who had rowed the rescue boat. The renegade was reconciled and restored to the Church, and from a rotten limb was made clean and sound again through penance and repentance.

Two days later the Viceroy discussed with Don Antonio how permission might be obtained for Anna Felix and her father to stay in Spain; for it did not seem to them unreasonable that so Christian a daughter and a father apparently so right-minded should be allowed to remain. Don Antonio offered to go to the capital to arrange the matter, having necessarily to go on other business, and intimated that many difficulties could be overcome by means of favours and bribes.

'No,' said Ricote, who was present at this conversation. 'There's nothing to hope from favours or bribes, for no prayers, promises, gifts or compassion can avail with the great Don Bernardino de Velasco, Count de Salazar, to whom his Majesty has entrusted our expulsion. For though it is true that he tempers justice with mercy, since he sees that the whole body of our race is contaminated and rotten he applies to it the burning cautery and not the soothing ointment. And so by prudence, sagacity and diligence, as well as by terror, he has borne the weight of his vast project on his strong shoulders to its due execution; and our arts, stratagems, pleadings and frauds have had no power to dazzle his Argus eyes, which are ever on the watch to see that not one of us remains or lies concealed, to sprout like a hidden root in times to come and bear poisoned fruit in Spain, which is now clean and free from the fears with which our numbers inspired her. What an heroic resolve of the great Philip the Third, and what unheard-of wisdom in entrusting its execution to this Don Bernardino de Velasco!'

'At any rate,' said Don Antonio, 'when I am there I will make every possible effort, and leave the rest to Providence. Don Gregorio shall come with me to relieve the anxiety his parents must feel at his absence. Anna Felix shall stay in my house with my wife, or in a nunnery, and I know that the Viceroy will be glad to have the good Ricote staying with him till we see how I manage.'

The Viceroy consented to all that was proposed; but when Don Gregorio heard what had passed he said that on no account could he, or would he, leave Doña Anna Felix. At length, however, he fell in with the arrangements, reflecting that he might contrive to come back for her when he had seen his parents. So Anna Felix stayed with Don Antonio's wife, and Ricote in the Viceroy's house.

The day came for Don Antonio's departure, and two days later for Don Quixote's and Sancho's, for the knight's fall would not allow of his taking the road any sooner. There were tears, there were sighs, sorrowings and sobbings when Anna Felix took her farewell of Don Gregorio, to whom Ricote offered a thousand crowns, if he wanted them. But he would take no more than five, which he borrowed from Don Antonio, promising to repay them in the capital. With this the pair departed, and afterwards Don Quixote and Sancho, as we have said – Don Quixote unarmed and in travelling clothes, and Sancho on foot, for Dapple was loaded with the armour.

Chapter LXVI. *Which treats of what the reader shall see or the listener hear.*

As THEY left Barcelona Don Quixote turned to gaze on the spot where he had fallen and said: 'Here stood Troy. Here my ill-luck, and not my cowardice, despoiled me of the glory I had won. Here Fortune practised her shifts and changes upon me. Here my exploits were eclipsed. Here, in short, my happiness fell, never to rise again.'

Hearing which, Sancho said: 'Great hearts, my dear master, should be patient in misfortune as well as joyful in prosperity. And this I judge from myself. For if I was merry when I was Governor now that I'm a squire on foot I'm not sad, for I've heard tell that Fortune, as they call her, is a drunken and capricious woman and, worse still, blind; and so she doesn't see what she's doing, and doesn't know whom she is casting down or raising up.'

'You are very philosophical, Sancho,' replied Don Quixote, 'and you talk most wisely. I do not know how you have learnt to. All I can tell you is that there is no such thing in the world as Fortune, and that events here, whether good or ill, do not fall out by chance but by a particular providence of Heaven, from which comes the saying that every man is the architect of his own destiny. I have been so of mine, but have failed in the necessary prudence, and so my presumption has brought me to disaster, for I should have reflected that the feeble Rocinante could never withstand the mighty bulk of the White Moon Knight's horse. However, I stood up to him; I did what I could; I was overthrown; and though I lost my honour I did not lose, nor could I lose, the virtue of keeping my word. When I was a knight errant, daring and valiant, my arms brought credit to my exploits, and now that I am a common squire I will bring credit on my words by fulfilling the promise I made. Trudge on then, friend Sancho, and let us go and spend our year of probation in our own land, and in our seclusion we will gather new virtue to return to that profession of arms which I can never forget.'

'Sir,' answered Sancho, 'trudging on foot is not so pleasant a thing that I feel spurred to make long marches. Let us leave these arms hung up on some tree, to dangle like those thieves we saw.

Then, if I'm on Dapple's back with my feet off the ground, we'll make whatever journeys may please and suit your worship; but if you imagine that I can travel long stages on foot you're expecting the impossible.'

'You have spoken well, Sancho,' replied Don Quixote. 'Let my armour be hung up as a trophy, and beneath it, or somewhere near, let us carve on the trees what was written on the trophy of Roland's arms –

> ... Let no one move them
> But one who dares his prowess against Roland.'

'That seems to me very much to the point,' answered Sancho, 'and if it weren't that we should feel the want of Rocinante on the road, it would be a good thing to leave him hanging there as well.'

'No,' replied Don Quixote. 'I would not have him or the armour hung up, for fear they might say: There is a bad reward for good service.'

'Your worship's quite right,' answered Sancho, 'for wise men say that the ass's fault shouldn't be laid on the pack-saddle; and since you are to blame for this business you should punish yourself and not vent your anger upon your armour, which is battered and bloody already, nor upon poor meek Rocinante, nor upon my tender feet, asking them to travel more than is proper.'

All that day they spent in these arguments and discussions, and the next four as well, without anything arising to hinder their journey. But on the fifth day, as they were coming into a village, they found a crowd of people round the inn door amusing themselves, for it was a holiday. And as Don Quixote approached them a countryman raised his voice and said: 'One of these two gentlemen coming this way shall decide our wager, for he doesn't know the parties.'

'That I will, with pleasure,' answered Don Quixote, 'and with complete impartiality, if I can manage to understand it.'

'The case is this, then, good sir,' said the countryman. 'A man of this village, who is so fat that he weighs twenty stone, has challenged a neighbour of his, who only weighs nine, to run a hundred yards' race with him, upon condition that they run at even weights. Now when the challenger was asked how the weights were to be

F F

made even, he said that the challenged man, who weighs nine stone, must carry eleven stone of iron on his back, and so they would both be equal at twenty stone.'

'That's wrong,' broke in Sancho before Don Quixote could reply. 'It's my job to settle this question and give a decision on the whole case, as it is only a few days since I gave up being a governor and a judge, as all the world knows.'

'Do so and welcome, friend Sancho,' said Don Quixote, 'for I am not fit to give crumbs to the cat, my wits are so shaken and shattered.'

With this permission Sancho addressed the countrymen, who were standing round him in mute and open-mouthed expectation of his decision.

'Brothers, the fat man's demand is unreasonable, and has not a shadow of justice in it. For if what they say is true, that the man challenged may choose the weapons, it isn't right for his opponent to choose for him weapons which would hinder him and prevent his gaining the victory. Therefore my decision is that the fat challenger should prune, pare, scrape, trim and shave away eleven stone of his flesh, from whatever part of his body may seem best to him, and so, reduced to nine stone in weight, he will be on level terms with his adversary at nine: and then they will be able to run even.'

'God's truth,' exclaimed one of the countrymen who heard Sancho's decision, 'this gentleman has spoken like a saint and given sentence like a canon! But I'm pretty sure the fat fellow has no mind to part with an ounce of his flesh, let alone eleven stone.'

'The best way will be for them not to run at all,' put in another. 'Then the thin chap won't break down under his load, nor the fat fellow lose his flesh. Let half of the wager go in wine, and let's take these gentlemen to the tavern that has the best. And the blood be on my head.'

'I thank you, gentlemen,' replied Don Quixote, 'but I cannot stop a moment, for sorrowful thoughts and disastrous events force me to appear discourteous and to travel in haste.'

And so, spurring Rocinante, he pressed on, leaving them all astonished at the appearance of this strange figure and at the wisdom of his servant, for such they judged Sancho to be. And another of the countrymen said: 'If the servant is so wise, what must the master be? If they're going to study at Salamanca, I bet they'll be judges at court in a twinkling. It's all a game. A man studies and studies. Then with favour and good luck he finds himself with a wand in his hand or a mitre on his head, when he least expects it.'

That night master and man spent in the open field under the bare and naked sky, and when they pushed on next day they saw a man coming towards them on foot with a haversack round his neck and a javelin or pike in his hand, a foot-courier to the life. Now as this figure drew near to Don Quixote, he quickened his pace and, coming up to him half running, embraced him round the right thigh, for he could reach no higher, and exclaimed with signs of great pleasure: 'Oh, my lord Don Quixote de la Mancha, how glad my lord the Duke, my master, will be, when he hears that your worship is returning to his castle, for he is still there with my lady the Duchess.'

'I do not recognize you, friend,' replied Don Quixote, 'and I shall not know who you are unless you tell me.'

'I am Tosilos, Don Quixote,' replied the courier, 'my lord the Duke's lackey, who would not fight with your worship about marrying Doña Rodriguez' daughter.'

'God defend me!' exclaimed Don Quixote. 'Is it possible that you are the man whom my enemies the enchanters turned into a lackey to defraud me of the honour of that battle?'

'Gently, my good sir,' replied the messenger. 'There was no enchantment nor any transformation. I was as much the lackey Tosilos when I went into the lists as I was Tosilos the lackey when I came out. I meant to marry without fighting, for I liked the look of the girl; but my plan turned out otherwise, for as soon as you left our castle the Duke my master had me given a hundred strokes for disobeying the orders he had given me before going into the battle; and it all ended with the girl turning nun and Doña Rodriguez going back to Castile. Now I'm on my way to Barcelona to deliver a bundle of letters from my master to the Viceroy. If your worship would like a little drink clean though a bit warm, I've a gourd full of good stuff and a few slices of Tronchon cheese, which will serve to raise your thirst if it happens to be sleeping.'

'I like your offer,' said Sancho. 'Drop the rest of the compliment, and pour out, my good Tosilos, and be damned to all the enchanters in the Indies.'

'Truly,' said Don Quixote, 'you are the greatest glutton in the world, 'and the greatest simpleton on earth if you cannot be persuaded that this courier is enchanted and this Tosilos counterfeit. But stay with him and drink your fill. I will go on slowly, and wait for you to come up with me.'

The lackey burst out laughing, unsheathed the gourd and unpacked the cheese from his haversack. Then he took out a little loaf, and he and Sancho sat down on the green grass, and in peace and good fellowship quickly despatched the haversack's complete contents, with such a hearty appetite that they even licked the packet of letters, only because it smelt of cheese. And after which Tosilos said to Sancho: 'There's no doubt, friend Sancho, that this master of yours ought to be counted a madman.'

'Why ought?' replied Sancho. 'He owes nothing to anyone, for he pays his debts, especially where madness passes for coin. Plainly I see it, and plainly I tell him; but what's the use? Particularly now that he's done for, for he's been conquered by the Knight of the White Moon.'

Tosilos asked him to relate what had happened, but Sancho replied that it would be uncivil to keep his master waiting for him, for there would be time for the story some other day, if they met. So, getting up and shaking the crumbs from his beard and his clothes, he said goodbye to Tosilos and left him. Then, driving Dapple before him, he overtook his master, who was waiting for him in the shade of a tree.

Chapter LXVII. *Of Don Quixote's resolution to turn Shepherd and lead a pastoral life till the year of his pledge had expired, with other incidents truly good and entertaining.*

IF Don Quixote was much troubled in mind before his overthrow he was much more so after it. He was lying in the shade of a tree, as we have said, and there his thoughts, like flies round honey, set upon him and stung him. Some of them dwelt on Dulcinea's disenchantment and others on the life he must lead in his enforced retirement. Then Sancho came up, loud in his praises of the lackey Tosilos' liberality.

'Is it possible, Sancho,' asked Don Quixote, 'that you still think he is a real lackey? You seem to have forgotten how you saw Dulcinea del Toboso converted and transformed into a country girl, and the Knight of the Mirrors into the Bachelor Carrasco, all the work of the enchanters who persecute me. But tell me now; did you ask that Tosilos, as you call him, what has been the fate of Altisidora; whether she has wept for my absence or already consigned to oblivion those amorous desires which tormented her in my presence?'

'I was too well employed,' answered Sancho, 'to have time to ask such silly questions. Heavens alive, sir! Is your worship now in a fit state to enquire about other people's desires, especially amorous ones?'

'Look you, Sancho,' said Don Quixote, 'there is a great deal of difference between acts done out of love and those done out of gratitude. A knight may very well not be in love; but ungrateful, to speak in all strictness, he must not be. Altisidora, to all appearances, loved me deeply; she gave me the three kerchiefs you know of; she wept at my departure; she cursed me; she abused me and, regardless of shame, complained of me publicly: all certain proofs that she adored me, for lovers' anger usually vents itself in such maledictions. I had no hopes to offer her, nor treasures to give her, for my hopes are pledged to Dulcinea, and the treasures of knights errant are illusory and false as fairy gold. I can only devote to her the memories I have of her, without prejudice, however, to those I have of Dulcinea, whom you wrong by your delay in scourging yourself and castigating that flesh of yours – may I see the wolves devour it! – which you would rather preserve for the worms than apply to the relief of that poor lady.'

'Sir,' answered Sancho, 'to tell you the truth, I can't persuade myself that the flogging of my posterior has anything to do with the disenchanting of the enchanted. For you might as well say: If your head aches, anoint your knees. I'm pretty certain, at least, there isn't a single instance of disenchantment by lashes in all the histories of knight errantry your worship has read. But whether there is or not, I'll lash myself when I've a mind to punish myself and time serves.'

'God grant you may,' replied Don Quixote, 'and Heaven give you grace to recall and acknowledge your obligation to aid my lady, who is yours too since you are my servant.'

Deep in these conversations, they were pursuing their journey when they came to the very spot where they had been trampled by the bulls. Which Don Quixote recognised, saying to Sancho: 'This is the field where we met the gay shepherdesses and gallant shepherds, who here proposed to revive another pastoral Arcadia. The project was both new and ingenious, and if you think well of it, Sancho, we will follow their example and turn shepherds, at least for the time I have to live in retirement. I will buy some sheep and everything needful for the pastoral vocation. I will call myself the shepherd Quixotiz and you the shepherd Panzino, and we will wander through the mountains, woods and meadows, singing here, lamenting there, drinking of the liquid crystals of the springs, or of the limpid streams, or the mighty rivers. The oaks shall give us of their sweetest fruit with generous hands; the trunks of the hard cork-trees shall offer us seats; the willows, shade; the roses, perfume; the broad meadows, carpets of a thousand blended colours; the clear, pure air shall grant us breath; the moon and the stars their light, despite the darkness of the night; song shall afford us delight, and tears gladness; Apollo verses, and love a theme, whereby we shall be able to win eternal fame, not only in the present age but in those to come.'

'God's truth!' exclaimed Sancho. 'But that kind of life squares with me exactly – and corners too. What's more, no sooner will the Bachelor Sampson Carrasco and Master Nicholas the barber get a sight of us than they'll want to follow it too and turn shepherds with us. But God grant it mayn't come into the priest's head to enter the fold as well – he's so gay and fond of his amusements.'

'You have spoken very well,' said Don Quixote, 'and the Bachelor Sampson Carrasco, if he comes into the pastoral company, as no doubt he will, could call himself the shepherd Samsonino or the shepherd Carrascon. Barber Nicholas might call himself Nicholoso, as old Boscan called himself Nemoroso. I do not know what name we could give the priest, unless it be one deriving from his calling, the shepherd Curiambro perhaps. As for the shepherdesses whose lovers we are to be, we can pick and choose their names like pears; and as my lady's name would suit a shepherdess as well as a Princess, there is no need for me to tire myself out seeking another to suit her better. You, Sancho, shall call your shepherdess by whatever name you please.'

'The only name for mine,' replied Sancho, 'will be Teresona, it'll suit her fatness well, and her name's Teresa. It'll sound well when I sing of her in my verses and reveal my chaste desires, for I'm not one to go to other men's houses seeking better bread than is made of wheat. The priest had better not go taking a shepherdess, for good example's sake, but if the Bachelor decides to have one his soul's his own.'

'God bless me,' exclaimed Don Quixote, 'what a life we shall lead, Sancho my friend! What pipes will ring in our ears! What hurdy-gurdies, what tambourines, what timbrels, and what fiddles! Perhaps then all the *albogues* may sound! Then almost all the pastoral instruments will be there.'

'What are *albogues*?' asked Sancho. 'I've never heard of them or seen one in all my life.'

'*Albogues*,' answered Don Quixote, 'are thin brass plates like candlesticks, which are struck against one another on the concave or hollow side, and make a sound which may not be very agreeable or harmonious, but is not unpleasing and blends well with the rustic quality of the hurdy-gurdy and the tambourine. This word *albogue* is Moorish, like all words beginning with *al* in our Castilian language: for instance *almohaza*, *almorzar*, *alhombra*, *alguacil*, *alhucema*, *almacén*, *alcancía* and a few others like them. Our language contains only three words from the Moorish which end in "*í*"; they are *borceguí*, *zaguizamí* and *maravedí*. *Alhelí* and *alfaquí* can be recognised as Arabic both by their initial "*al*" and by their final "*í*". This I mention by the way, since it has come to my mind through my chancing to mention the *albogue*. One circumstance will greatly contribute to make us perfect in our new profession. I am, as you know, something of a poet, and the Bachelor Sampson Carrasco too is a good one. I do not mention the priest; but I will wager he has a smack and touch of the poet about him, and Master Nicholas has it as well, I have no doubt, for all or most barbers are guitarists and rhymers. I will mourn absent beauty; you shall celebrate yourself as the constant lover; the shepherd Carrascon shall complain of scorn, and the priest Curiambro of whatever he likes; and so we shall go on to our hearts' content.'

'But I'm so unlucky, sir,' replied Sancho, 'that I'm afraid I shall never see the time when I can follow this calling. Oh, what smooth spoons I shall make when I'm a shepherd! What fried breadcrumbs and cream cheeses and garlands and shepherds' nick-nacks! They may not win me a reputation for wisdom, but they won't fail to get me a name for cleverness. My daughter Sanchica shall bring us our dinner to the fold. But, mind out! For she's good-looking, and shepherds are not all simple. There are rogues amongst them, and I wouldn't like her to go for wool and come back shorn. For your lovings and wicked desires are as common in the fields as in the cities, and you find them in shepherds' huts as well as in royal palaces. So take away the opportunity and you take away the sin; and what the eye doesn't see the heart doesn't grieve for; and a leap over the hedge is better than good men's prayers.'

'No more proverbs, Sancho,' said Don Quixote, 'for any one of those you have cited is enough to explain your thought. Often I have advised you not to be so prodigal of proverbs and to restrain yourself from introducing them, but it seems to me like preaching in the desert, and my mother beats me and I whip the top.'

'Your worship reminds me of the saying that the pot called the kettle black. You scold me for quoting proverbs, and string them together in pairs yourself.'

'Observe, Sancho,' answered Don Quixote, 'that I bring my proverbs in to the purpose, and when I quote them they fit like a ring on a finger. But you bring them in by the hair. You drag them instead of guiding them. And if I remember rightly I have told you before that proverbs are brief maxims drawn from the experience and observations of the wise men of old, and a proverb ill applied is not wisdom but stark nonsense. But let us leave the subject and, as darkness is coming on, go a little off the highway to some place where we can spend the night, and God knows what tomorrow will bring.'

They left the road and supped poorly and late, much to the displeasure of Sancho, who was reminded of the hardships of knight errantry suffered among woods and forests, though sometimes plenty reigned in castles and houses, as at Don Diego de Miranda's and at the rich Camacho's wedding, and at Don Antonio Moreno's. But he reflected that neither day nor night could last for ever, and so he spent that night in sleep and his master in watching.

Chapter LXVIII. *Of the bristling adventure which befell Don Quixote.*

THE night was rather dark, for though the moon was in the sky she was in no part where she was visible. For sometimes the lady Diana goes for a trip to the Antipodes and leaves the mountains dark and the valleys gloomy. Don Quixote yielded to nature and slept his first sleep, but he did not give way to a second. It was quite the opposite with Sancho, who had no second because his first lasted him from night till morning, which showed his sound constitution and freedom from care. But Don Quixote's cares kept him so wide awake that he finally roused Sancho by saying: 'I am amazed, Sancho, at the insensibility of your nature. I believe you are made of marble or brass, and have no emotion or feeling in you. I watch while you sleep; I weep while you sing; I faint from fasting while you can hardly move or breathe from pure gluttony. It is the duty of good servants to share their masters' pains and feel their griefs, even if only for appearance's sake. Observe the serenity of this night and the solitude of the place, which invites us to mingle some watching with our slumber. Get up, in Heaven's name! Go a little way off, and with a willing heart and thankful spirit give yourself three or four hundred lashes upon the score of Dulcinea's disenchanting. This I implore you as a favour, for I do not want to come to grips with you as I did last time, since I know you have a heavy hand. When you have done we will spend the rest of the night singing, I of separation, and you of constancy, embarking this moment upon the pastoral calling we are to follow in our village.'

'Sir,' replied Sancho, 'I am no monk to get up and scourge myself in the middle of my sleep, nor do I think it would be an easy matter to suffer the pain of a whipping one moment and to be singing the next. Allow me to sleep, your worship, and don't worry me about this scourging business, or you'll make me swear an oath never to touch a hair of my coat, much less my flesh.'

'Heart of flint,' cried Don Quixote. 'Remorseless squire, ungrateful for my bread and thankless for my favours past and future! Through me you became a governor, and through me you are now in close expectation of being a count, or of getting some equivalent title. Nor shall the fulfilment be longer delayed than for this one year, for "*post tenebras spero lucem*" – After darkness I expect light.'

'I don't understand that,' replied Sancho. 'I only know that while I sleep I have no fear, nor hope, nor trouble, nor glory. God bless the inventor of sleep, the cloak that covers all man's thoughts, the food that cures all hunger, the water that quenches all thirst, the fire that warms the cold, the cold that cools heat; the common coin, in short, that can purchase all things, the balancing weight that levels the shepherd with the king and the simple with the wise. There's only one bad thing about sleep, as I have heard say, and that is that it looks like death; for there's but little difference between a sleeping man and a dead one.'

'Sancho,' said Don Quixote, 'I have never heard you speak so eloquently as now; which makes me realise the truth of that proverb you sometimes cite: "Not with whom you are bred but with whom you are fed."'

'Devil take it, dear master!' exclaimed Sancho. 'It isn't I that am stringing proverbs this time; for they fall from your worship's mouth also, two by two, faster than from mine. Only there is this difference between yours and mine, that yours come in season and mine out of place; but they're all proverbs all the same.'

They had reached this point when they heard a harsh, deafening din spreading through all the valleys around. Don Quixote rose to his feet and put his hand to his sword. Sancho crouched beneath Dapple, setting the bundle of armour on one side of him and the ass's pack-saddle on the other, and trembling as much from fear as Don Quixote from excitement. The din was gradually getting louder and drawing nearer to the trembling pair, or to one trembler at least, for the other's valour is well known by now. The cause was this – some hog-dealers happened to be driving some six hundred swine or more at that early hour to sell them at a fair; and this herd made such a noise with their grunting and squeaking that both Don Quixote and Sancho were deafened, and utterly at a loss to account for it.

The straggling swine came snorting on pell-mell, and regardless of all respect for Don Quixote's dignity or Sancho's passed over them both, demolishing Sancho's entrenchments, and not only tumbling Don Quixote over but sweeping Rocinante along into the bargain. On went the unclean beasts at headlong speed, overthrowing as they went the pack-saddle, the armour, Dapple, Rocinante, Sancho and Don Quixote.

Sancho got up as best he could, and asked his master for his sword, saying that he would like to kill half a dozen of those unmannerly and swinish gentry, for now he had realised what they were.

'Let them be, friend,' said Don Quixote, 'for this outrage is the penalty for my sin, and it is Heaven's just chastisement on a conquered knight errant, that jackals shall devour him, wasps sting him and hogs trample him down.'

'And it's Heaven's chastisement too, I suppose,' replied Sancho, 'that flies shall sting the squires of vanquished knights errant, that lice shall eat them and hunger assail them. If we squires were the sons of the knights we serve or their very close relatives, it would be no great mattter if the penalties for their faults lighted on us unto the fourth generation. But what have the Panzas to do with the Quixotes? Well, let's get ourselves comfortable again, and sleep through what little remains of the night, and God will send us day and perhaps better luck.'

'You may sleep, Sancho,' replied Don Quixote, 'for you were born to sleep; but I was born to watch, and in the little time that is left till day I will give rein to my thoughts and vent them in a little madrigal, which, unknown to you, I have composed in my head to-night.'

'To my mind,' replied Sancho, 'thoughts that yield to verse can't be very troublesome. Rhyme it as much as you please, your worship, and I'll sleep as long as I can.'

Then, taking up as much ground as he wanted, he curled himself up and slept a sound sleep, undisturbed by bonds, debts, or cares. And Don Quixote, leaning against a beech or cork tree – Cide Hamete Benengeli does not specify what tree it was – sang in this strain to the accompaniment of his own sighs:

> Love, when I dwell upon
> The wounds you deal me, terrible and fierce,
> I run to death apace
> In hopes that there my great pains will be gone.

But when I reach that place,
The harbour in this sea of my sad ills,
Such joy my bosom feels
That life grows stronger and I cannot pass.

And so by life I'm slain,
Unwelcome state that mingles life and death!
Living I die, and as my breath
Dies, death recalls me into life again.

With each line he sighed and shed some tears, groaning as if his
heart were pierced through by grief at his overthrow and by his
absence from Dulcinea.

And now day appeared, the sun darting his beams full on
Sancho's eyes. He uncurled and awoke, shaking and stretching his
drowsy limbs. Then, viewing the havoc the hogs had wrought on
his stores, he cursed the herd and more besides. At length the pair
resumed their journey, and at dusk saw some ten horsemen coming
towards them with four or five men on foot. Don Quixote's heart
leapt and Sancho's quailed with terror, for the people approaching
carried lances and shields and were advancing in very warlike formation. Whereupon Don Quixote turned to Sancho and said: 'Ah,
Sancho, if I could use my arms, and my promise had not tied my
hands, I should reckon this array coming against us no more than
tarts and gingerbread. Perhaps, however, it may not be as we fear.'

By this time the horsemen had come up and, raising their spears,
surrounded Don Quixote without a single word, pointing them at
his back and breast and threatening him with death. Then one of
those on foot, putting a finger to his lips as a sign to him to be
silent, seized Rocinante's bridle and led him off the road. The rest
of the men on foot followed in the steps of Don Quixote's captors,
driving Sancho and Dapple from behind, and all preserving an
amazing silence. Two or three times the knight was on the point of
asking where they were taking him and what they wanted, but no
sooner did he begin to open his lips than they made as if to close
them with the points of their spears; and the same thing happened
to Sancho, for as soon as he made to open his mouth one of the
footmen pricked him with a goad, serving Dapple in the same way,
as if he too wanted to speak. Night closed in; they quickened their
pace; the fears of the two prisoners increased; all the more so when

hey heard their captors cry from time to time: 'Get on, Trog-
odytes!' 'Silence, barbarians!' 'Pay up, Anthropophagi!' 'Don't
complain, Scythians!' 'Don't open your eyes, murderous Poly-
phemuses, man-eating lions!' and many other such names with
which they tormented the ears of the wretched master and man.
Sancho went along muttering to himself: 'What, call us ortolans!
Us, barbers and Andrew popinjays? And silly 'uns and Polly
amouses? I don't like any of those names. It's an ill wind blowing
this grain. All our troubles are coming together like kicks on a dog,
and pray God it may stop at threats, this ill-venturous adventure!'

Don Quixote rode on in a daze, unable to guess the purpose of
these abusive epithets addressed to them for all the thought he put
to it, though he gathered that he could expect no good from them
and must fear much evil. About an hour after dark they arrived at a
castle, which Don Quixote recognised as the Duke's where he had
been staying a little while ago.

'God bless me!' he exclaimed, as soon as he made out the buildings. 'What can this be? In this house, indeed, all is courtesy and
kindness; but for the vanquished good turns to evil, and evil to
worse.'

And when they came into the main court of the castle they saw it
decorated and set out in a manner which increased their astonishment and redoubled their fears, as will be seen in the following
chapter.

Chapter LXIX. *Of the rarest and strangest adventure that befell
Don Quixote in the whole course of this great history.*

THE horsemen dismounted, and with those on foot caught Don
Quixote and Sancho violently and bodily in their arms and brought
them into the courtyard, around which blazed about a hundred
torches set in their sconces, while around the galleries of the court
were more than five hundred lamps, so that despite the night, which
was rather dark, the scene was as bright as day. In the centre of the
yard was raised a bier some six foot above the ground, completely
covered with a broad canopy of black velvet, around which, ranged
along the steps, there burnt more than a hundred white wax tapers
in silver candlesticks; and lying on this bier was displayed the corpse

of a maiden so lovely that her beauty seemed to make Death itself
beautiful. On a brocade pillow lay her head, crowned with a garland woven of various sweet-smelling flowers; her hands were
crossed on her breast, and between them was a branch of yellow
victor's palm. On one side of the court a stage had been erected
with two seats on which were sitting two persons, who by the
crowns on their heads and the sceptres in their hands appeared to be
kings, either real or pretended. By the side of this stage, which was
approached by steps, were two other seats on which their captors
seated Don Quixote and Sancho, still in complete silence and giving
the pair to understand by signs that they must keep silent too. But
they would have done so without any signs, for amazement at
what they saw kept their tongues tied. Then there mounted upon
the stage two principal personages, whom Don Quixote recognized as the Duke and Duchess, his hosts, and they took their
places on two richly ornamented seats beside the pair who appeared
to be kings. Who would not have been amazed at this, when, in
addition, Don Quixote recognized the corpse lying on the bier as
the fair Altisidora's? As the Duke and Duchess mounted the platform Don Quixote and Sancho rose and made them a deep bow
which they returned by a slight nod of the head. Then an officer
came across the court and, going up to Sancho, threw over him a
robe of black buckram all painted with fiery flames and, snatching
off his victim's cap, put on his head a pasteboard mitre like those
worn by the penitents of the Inquisition, whispering in his ear that
if he opened his lips they would gag him or take his life. Sancho
surveyed himself from head to foot and saw that he was ablaze
with flames, but as they did not burn him he did not care two pins
for them. He took off the mitre and saw that it was painted with
devils. Then he put it on again, saying to himself: 'Well, well, the
flames don't burn and the devils don't carry me off.'

Don Quixote also gazed at Sancho, and though fear kept his
senses numbed he could not forbear smiling at his squire's appearance. And now, apparently from beneath the bier, a soft and pleasant music of flutes began to rise, which sounded soft and amorous,
though unbroken by any human voice, for in that place silence
itself was mute. Then there suddenly appeared beside the pillow
of this seeming corpse a handsome youth in Roman dress, who sang

n a sweet and clear voice to the sound of a harp, which he played
himself, these two stanzas:

> Until Altisidora shall return
> To life, she that Don Quixote's cruelty slew,
> And all the while that at the fairy court
> In robes of sackcloth the court ladies mourn,
> And whilst my lady clothes her waiting-maids
> In sombre serge and heavy baize of grief,
> So long in sweeter tones than his of Thrace
> Shall I lament her beauty and disgrace.
>
> Nor do I think that at my dying day
> This, my most mournful duty, will be done,
> For still with tongue struck dead and mouth a-cold
> I mean to pay my debt to you in song.
> And when my soul from prison is released
> And led beside the mournful Stygian lake,
> 'Twill celebrate you as it goes, and sing
> Until the waters of oblivion ring.

'No more,' exclaimed one of the two seeming kings at this
point; 'No more, divine singer. It would be an endless task to recall to us the death and charms of the peerless Altisidora, not dead,
as the ignorant world thinks, but living on the tongues of fame and
in the penance which Sancho Panza, here present, must undergo to
restore her to the light. Therefore, O Rhadamanthus, you who
judge with me in the gloomy caverns of Dis – for you know all
that the inscrutable fates have decreed concerning the restoration of
this damsel to life – speak and declare it now, so that the happiness we expect from her return may be delayed no longer.'

Scarcely had Minos, his fellow judge, so spoken when Rhadamanthus rose to his feet and said: 'Here, officers of this house, high
and low, great and small! Come here, one and all, and mark
Sancho's face with twenty-four slaps. Give him a dozen pinches and
six pinpricks on his arms and loins, for on this ceremony depends
Altisidora's restoration.'

On hearing this Sancho broke his silence and cried out: 'By my
life! I'd as soon turn Moor as let my face be marked or my cheeks
be fingered. God's truth! What has the handling of my face to do
with this young lady's resurrection? The old woman so enjoyed the
spinach that she didn't leave any, green or dry. They enchant

Dulcinea and whip me to disenchant her. Altisidora dies of some disease God chose to give her, and to revive her I am to have twenty-four slaps in the face, my body riddled with pins and my arms black and blue with pinches. Try those jokes on your brother-in-law. I'm an old dog and don't answer to every whistle.'

'You shall die,' proclaimed Rhadamanthus in a loud voice. 'Relent, tiger! Humble yourself, proud Nimrod! Suffer in silence, for nothing impossible is asked of you. And do not start raising difficulties in this business. Smacked you must be; pricked you shall be, and pinched till you groan. Ho, there! Officers, obey your orders. Or, on the word of an honest man, you will see what you were born for.'

At this point there appeared some six waiting-women crossing the court in a procession, one behind the other, four of them with spectacles and all with their right hands raised and four inches of wrist bare to make their hands appear longer, as is the present fashion. And the moment Sancho saw them he bellowed like a bull: 'I'd let the whole world handle me, but to be touched by waiting-women – never! Let the cats scratch my face, as they did my master's in this very castle. Let them run me through the body with sharp dagger points. Let them tear my arms with red hot pincers. I'll bear it all in patience to oblige these gentlemen. But the devil may carry me off before I'll consent to be touched by a waiting-woman.'

Then Don Quixote also broke the silence and observed to Sancho: 'Patience, my son. Oblige these gentlemen and render deep thanks to Heaven for having endowed your person with such virtue that by its martyrdom you can disenchant the enchanted and bring the dead to life.'

By this time the waiting-women had drawn close to Sancho and, quietly now and more resigned, he settled himself squarely in his chair, presented his face and beard to the first one, who dealt him a very well placed slap, and then made him a deep curtsey.

'Less courtesy and less paint, Mistress Waiting-woman,' said Sancho, 'for I'll be blowed if your hands don't smell of vinegar wash!'

To be brief, all the waiting-women slapped him, and many others of the household pinched him. But what he could not stand was the pin-pricking, and so he leapt up from his chair in a visible rage and, seizing a lighted torch from beside him, went after the waiting-women and the rest of his tormentors, crying: 'Get away, monsters of hell! Do you suppose that I'm made of brass that I can't feel your damned torments?'

At this Altisidora, who must have been tired from having lain flat so long, turned on her side, at which sight the whole assembly cried almost with one voice: 'Altisidora is alive! Altisidora is living!'

Rhadamanthus then bade Sancho calm his rage, for their purpose was now achieved. Then as soon as Don Quixote saw Altisidora begin to stir he went down on his knees before Sancho, saying: 'Now is the time, son of my loins – no more my squire! – to give yourself some of those lashes to which you are pledged for Dulcinea's disenchantment. Now, I say, is the time when your virtue is seasoned and effective for the working of the good that is expected of you.'

To which Sancho replied: – 'This is more like plot upon plot than honey upon pancakes. A fine thing it would be to have lashes following on pinches, slaps and pricks. After that there'll be nothing for it but to take a great stone and tie it round my neck and throw me down a well – which I wouldn't much mind if I'm to be made the whipping-boy to cure other folks' ailments. Leave me alone or, by God, I'll fling you all out, thirteen at a time, even if it spoils the market.'

Here Altisidora sat up on her bier, and at the same moment the clarions sounded, accompanied by flutes and by a general shout of: 'Long live Altisidora! Long live Altisidora!'

The Duke and Duchess and the kings, Minos and Rhadamanthus, got up and, all in a body, with Don Quixote and Sancho too, went to receive Altisidora and help her down from the bier. And she, pretending to be faint, bowed to the Duke and Duchess and to the kings and, looking across at Don Quixote, addressed him thus: 'God forgive you, loveless knight, for because of your cruelty I have spent more than a thousand years, as it seems to me, in the other world. But you, most compassionate squire in all the world, you I thank for the life which is restored to me. From this day forth, friend Sancho, dispose of six of my smocks which I bequeath

GG

to you to make you six shirts; and if they are not all whole at least they are all clean.'

Sancho kissed her hands for the gift, kneeling on the ground with the mitre in his hand. The Duke ordered that this should be taken from him and his cap returned, and that his overcoat should be put on him in place of the robe of flames. But Sancho begged the Duke to leave him the robe and the mitre, which he would like to take with him to his own country as a keepsake to remind him of that amazing adventure. The Duchess replied that he should certainly keep them, he must know already how dearly she loved him.

Then the Duke ordered the courtyard to be cleared, all the people to retire to their rooms, and Don Quixote and Sancho to be taken to the apartments they knew from of old.

Chapter LXX. *Which follows the sixty-ninth and deals with matters indispensable for the clear understanding of this history.*

SANCHO slept that night on a truckle-bed in the same room with Don Quixote, an honour he would have avoided if he could, for he knew very well that, what with questions and answers, his master would never let him sleep. And he was in no mood for much talking, for he was still smarting from the pain of his recent martyrdom, which paralyzed his tongue. In fact he would rather have slept alone in a hovel than in that rich room in company. His fears and suspicions were only too well-founded, for the moment his master got into bed he demanded: 'What do you think, Sancho, of this night's events? Great and powerful are the effects of love disdained, for with your own eyes you have seen Altisidora dead, slain by no other arrows, by no other sword, by no other warlike weapon or lethal poison than the cruelty and scorn with which I have always treated her.'

'She might have died and welcome, when she liked and how she liked,' replied Sancho, 'and left me alone, for I never enamoured her nor slighted her in all my life. I don't know, and I can't think, what the health of that capricious, silly young lady Altisidora has to do with the torture of Sancho Panza. I've told you that already. Now indeed I do plainly see that there are enchanters and enchantments in the world, from whom may God deliver me, for I can't deliver myself. All the same I beg your worship to let me sleep and ask me no more questions if you don't want me to throw myself out of the window.'

'Sleep, Sancho, my friend,' replied Don Quixote, 'if the pin-pricks and pinches and face-slappings you have received will allow you.'

'No pain,' answered Sancho, 'equals the insult of that face-slapping, if only because I suffered it at the hands of waiting-women, confound them! But I beg your worship once more to let me sleep. Sleep is the remedy for all our waking miseries.'

'So be it,' said Don Quixote, 'and God be with you.'

The two of them fell asleep, and in the interval Cide Hamete, the author of this great history, wishes to relate the Duke and Duchess's reasons for devising the elaborate contrivance just described. He says that the Bachelor Sampson Carrasco, mindful how as the Knight of the Mirrors he was beaten and overthrown by Don Quix-ote – which defeat and overthrow spoilt and undid all his schemes – decided to try his hand again, hoping for better success than the last time. So, having learnt where Don Quixote was from the page who brought the letter and present to Sancho's wife, Teresa Panza, he looked out new armour and a fresh horse, and painted a white moon on his shield, loading it all on a mule which was led by a country man – not by Thomas Cecial, his old squire, for fear Don Quixote or Sancho might recognise him. He came, then, to the Duke's castle, and that nobleman informed him of Don Quixote's departure, of the road he had chosen and of his intention of taking part in the jousts at Saragossa. The Duke also described their jests at the knight's expense and the scheme for Dulcinea's disenchantment at the cost of Sancho's posterior. Last of all he gave him an account of the trick Sancho had played on his master by giving him to un-derstand that Dulcinea was enchanted and transformed into a peasant girl, and how the Duchess, his wife, had convinced Sancho that it was he that was mistaken, and that Dulcinea really was en-chanted. All this considerably amused and surprised the Bachelor, as he pondered on Sancho's cunning and simplicity and on Don Quix-ote's extreme folly. The Duke begged him, should he find the knight, to return that way, whether he beat him or not, and give him an account of events. The Bachelor promised that he would

and departed on his quest, but not finding Don Quixote at Saragossa, went on – with what success we know. Then he returned to
the Duke's castle and told him the whole story with the conditions
of the combat, and said that Don Quixote was already on his way
back to fulfil his pledge like a good knight errant, and retire to his
village for a year, during which time, said the Bachelor, he might
possibly be cured of his madness. It was that in fact which had
caused him to assume his disguise, for it was a pitiful thing that a
gentleman of Don Quixote's intelligence should remain a lunatic.
With this he took leave of the Duke and went back to his village,
to wait there for Don Quixote, who was following him. Hence it
was that the Duke had a chance to play this last trick, such pleasure
did he take in the humours of Sancho and Don Quixote. He posted
a number of his servants, on foot and on horseback, on all the roads
round the castle, far and near, in every direction by which he
thought Don Quixote might return, to bring him to the castle,
willingly or by force, should they find him. And when they did they
advised the Duke, who had already arranged what was to be done.
As soon as he got word of Don Quixote's arrival he had the torches
and the lamps lit in the court, and Altisidora placed on her bier with
all the accessories described, the whole farce so well and convincingly contrived that the play was but little removed from reality.
In fact Cide Hamete says that he considers the mockers were as mad
as their victims, and the Duke and Duchess within a hair's breadth
of appearing fools themselves for taking such pains to play tricks
on a pair of fools.

Day surprised that pair, one of them sleeping soundly and the
other wakefully indulging his unbridled fancies, and with it came
the desire to rise; for the feather-bed of sloth never pleased Don
Quixote, whether victor or vanquished. Then Altisidora – returned
in Don Quixote's opinion from death to life – following up her
master's and mistress's humour, came into Don Quixote's room,
crowned with the same garland she had worn on the bier, and
dressed in a loose gown of white taffeta flowered with gold, her
hair loose on her shoulders, and leaning on a black stick of finest
ebony. Disturbed and abashed by her entrance, Don Quixote
shrank down and almost completely covered himself under the
sheets and quilts of his bed, tongue-tied and unable to offer her a

single word of greeting. So Altisidora sat down in a chair beside the head of his bed, and after heaving a deep sigh said in a tender and feeble voice: 'When women of rank and reserved maidens tread honour under foot and permit their tongues to break down all impediments and give public notice of their hearts' secrets they are indeed in desperate straits. I, Don Quixote de la Mancha, am one of these, distressed, vanquished and love-lorn, yet still patient and modest; so excessively patient and modest indeed that my heart burst for my silence and I lost my life. For two days ago, through grief at your cruel treatment – oh, harder than the marble to my plaints, thou stony-hearted knight! – I lay dead, or at least was held to be so by all who saw me; and were it not that Love took pity on me and entrusted my cure to the sufferings of this good squire, there I should have stayed in the other world.'

'Love might just as well have entrusted it to my ass,' said Sancho. 'I should have thanked him for it. But tell me, lady – and may Heaven fix you up with a kinder lover than my master! – what did you see in the other world? What's it like in Hell? For if you die in despair you're sure to end up there.'

'To tell you the truth,' replied Altisidora, 'I couldn't have been dead outright, for I never went to Hell. Once I had entered there indeed I shouldn't have been able to get out at my pleasure. The truth is that I arrived at the gate, where something like a dozen devils were playing at tennis, all in their breeches and doublets, with their collars trimmed with Flanders lace and with ruffles of the same that served them for cuffs, with four inches of arm bare to make their hands look longer. They were holding rackets of fire, and what most astonished me was that, instead of balls, they used what looked like books stuffed with wind and fluff – a most amazing thing! But that didn't astonish me so much as seeing that all the players were grumbling and snarling and cursing, though it's usual in games for the winners to be gay and the losers gloomy.'

'That's no wonder,' observed Sancho, 'for whether they're players or not, devils can't be content, winning or losing.'

'That's probably so,' replied Altisidora, 'but there's another thing that astonishes me too – I mean, which astonished me then – and that was that after the first volley there wasn't a ball left whole or of any use for the next time; and so they whirled through books old and new at a wonderful rate. One of them they dealt such a whack – a brand-new one it was and smartly bound – that they knocked its guts out and scattered the leaves. Then one devil said to another: "Look what book that is." And his mate replied: "It's the second part of the History of Don Quixote de la Mancha, not composed by Cide Hamete, its original author, but by an Aragonese who styles himself a native of Tordesillas." "Away with it, out of here," cried the other devil. "Throw it into the pit of hell, and never let me set eyes on it again." "Is it so bad?" asked the other. "So bad," replied the first, "that if I were to set myself deliberately to make it worse I couldn't!" They went on with their game, tossing other books about, but as I had heard the name of my beloved and adored Don Quixote I endeavoured to retain this vision in my memory.'

'A vision it must have been, beyond a doubt,' said Don Quixote, 'for there is no other person of that name in the world; and that history is passing from hand to hand even now, though it stays in none, for they all kick it on. But I have not been disturbed to hear of myself passing like a phantom body through the shades of Hell, nor through the light of earth either, for I am not the person this history is concerned with. If it were good, faithful and true it would have centuries of life; but if it is bad, its passage will be short from its birth to its burial.'

Altisidora was on the point of proceeding with her complaint against Don Quixote when the knight addressed her: 'I have told you many times, lady, how distressed I am that you have fixed your affections on me; for I can only acknowledge them, not relieve them. I was born to belong to Dulcinea del Toboso. The Fates, if they exist, have dedicated me to her, and to think that any other beauty can occupy the place she holds in my heart is to imagine the impossible. This should be sufficient to make you retreat within the limits of your chastity, for no one can be bound to perform the impossible.'

At this Altisidora pretended to be angry and upset, crying: 'My God, Don Stock-fish, Brazen Soul, Date Stone, more obstinate and hard-hearted than a peasant courted when he is aiming at the butts, I'll tear your eyes out if I get at you. Do you really imagine, Don Vanquished, Don Cudgelled, that I died for you? All you've seen to-night has been pretence. I'm not the sort of woman to let myself grieve by so much as the dirt in one finger-nail for such a camel, much less to die for one!'

'That I can well believe,' put in Sancho, 'for this dying for love's a joke. They may talk about it, but as for doing it – believe it, Judas!'

While they were deep in this discussion the musician and poet who had sung the two stanzas already noted came in and said to Don Quixote with a deep bow: 'Number me among your most faithful servants, Sir Knight, for I have been deeply devoted to you for a long time, both on account of your fame and of your deeds.'

'Tell me, sir,' Don Quixote replied, 'who you are, that my courtesy may respond to your deserts.' The lad replied that he was the musician and panegyrist of the previous night.

'Truly,' replied Don Quixote, 'you have a perfect voice, though what you sang did not seem much to the purpose to me; for what have Garcilaso's stanzas to do with that lady's dying?'

'Do not wonder at that,' replied the singer, 'for among the unshorn poets of our age it is the custom for each to write as he will, and to steal from whomever he likes, whether it is much to the point or not; and there is nothing they sing or write so stupid that they do not put it down to poetic licence.'

Don Quixote was about to reply, but he was prevented by a visit from the Duke and Duchess, with whom he had a long and charming conversation, during which Sancho displayed such drollery and such shrewdness that he left his hosts more astonished than ever at his mixture of simplicity and acuteness. Don Quixote begged them for leave to depart that same day, since it was more fitting for a vanquished knight like himself to live in a pigsty than in a royal palace. They gladly granted him his request, and the Duchess asked him whether Altisidora remained in his good graces. 'Madam,' he replied, 'your ladyship must learn that all the evil in that maiden arises from idleness, the remedy for which is honest and continuous occupation. She has just now informed me that they wear lace in Hell, and since she must certainly know how to make it let it never be out of her hands; for when she is busy working the bobbins the image or images of her desires will not work in her imagination. That is the truth, and that is my opinion and advice.'

'And mine too,' added Sancho, 'for never in all my life have I seen a lacemaker who died for love. Maidens who have work to do spend more thought on finishing their jobs than on thinking of their loves. I speak from experience, for while I am digging I don't think of my poppet, I mean my Teresa Panza, though I love her better than my eyelashes.'

'That is well said, Sancho,' exclaimed the Duchess, 'and I will see that my Altisidora is kept busy in future with some kind of needlework, for she does it extremely well.'

'There is no reason, my lady, to resort to that remedy,' said Altisidora, 'for the thought of the cruelty with which this vagabond scoundrel has treated me will blot him from my memory without any other help. And now, with your Highness's permission, I will retire from here, so as no longer to have before my eyes his sad countenance – I mean his ugly, abominable face.'

'That,' said the Duke, 'reminds me of the saying: He that flings insults will soon forgive.'

Altisidora made a pretence of wiping her tears with her handkerchief, and with a curtsey to her master and mistress left the room.

'Poor girl,' exclaimed Sancho. 'It's ill-luck you have, very ill luck, for his soul's as dry as rushes and his heart's as tough as oak. Now if it was me you'd had to deal with your pigs would have been brought to a better market, I promise you.'

The conversation ended. Don Quixote dressed himself, and dined with the Duke and Duchess; and that afternoon he departed.

Chapter LXXI. *Of what befell Don Quixote and Sancho, his Squire, on the way to their village.*

THE vanquished and travel-worn Don Quixote rode along, very melancholy on one score and very cheerful on another. His sadness arose from his defeat, and his gaiety from the consideration of Sancho's virtue, as he had shown it in the resurrection of Altisidora; although it was with some reservations that he convinced himself that the lovelorn maiden had really died. But Sancho was by no means cheerful. He was sad because Altisidora had not kept her promise to give him her smocks. And, turning this over and over in his mind, he said to his master: 'Really, sir, I'm the most unfortunate doctor in the whole world. There are physicians who kill their patients and get paid for their trouble, though they do no more than sign a slip of paper for medicines which the apothecary makes up for them, and the trick's done. Yet though bringing that maiden to life has cost me drops of blood, slaps, pinches, pricks and whippings, I don't get a farthing. I swear here and now, though, that if they put another sick person on my hands they'll have to grease them before I cure him. For the abbot must eat that sings for his meat, and I won't believe that Heaven has endowed me with the virtue I have for me to communicate it to others free, gratis and for nothing.'

'You are right, Sancho my friend,' answered Don Quixote, 'and Altisidora has acted very wrongly in not giving you the promised smocks; though your virtue was given you gratis and has cost you no study, unless it be a study to learn to suffer tortures on your person. For myself I can say that if it is payment you want for your whipping on account of Dulcinea's disenchantment, I would long ago have given you what was fair. But I do not know whether payment will sort well with the cure, and I should not wish the reward to hinder the medicine. All the same I think that nothing would be lost by trying. So consider, Sancho, how much you want and whip yourself presently. You may pay yourself cash down with your own hand, for you carry my money.'

Sancho opened his eyes and ears a foot wider at this offer and, consenting in his heart to take a hearty whipping, said to his master: 'Well now, sir, I'm ready to put myself at your disposal and satisfy your worship's desires, for my own advantage. If I appear mercenary it's my love for my wife and children that makes me so. Tell me, your worship, how much a stroke will you give me?'

'Were I to pay you, Sancho,' replied Don Quixote, 'in proportion to the magnitude and importance of the service, the treasure of Venice or the mines of Potosi would be a small recompense. Reckon up what you have of mine, and put a price upon each stroke.'

'The number,' replied Sancho, 'is three thousand three hundred odd, and I have given myself about five of them. The rest are to come. Let those five count as the odd ones, and let us come to the three thousand three hundred which at a quarter of a *real* apiece –

and I won't take less to oblige anyone – come to three thousand three hundred quarter *reals*, and that three thousand makes one thousand five hundred half *reals*, which come to seven hundred and fifty *reals*; and the three hundred make a hundred and fifty half *reals*, which comes to seventy-five *reals*; and adding these to the seven hundred and fifty, it comes to eight hundred and twenty-five *reals*. These I will subtract from the money of your worship's I have, and I shall go home rich and contented, though soundly whipped, for you don't catch trout ... I say no more.'

'O blessed Sancho! O kindly Sancho!' cried Don Quixote. 'How deeply we shall be bound to serve you, Dulcinea and I, all the days of our lives that Heaven shall grant us. If she is returned to her former state – and it is impossible she should not be – her misfortune will have proved good fortune, and my defeat a most happy triumph. Now look, Sancho, when will you begin the scourging? For if you will make it quick, I will add a hundred *reals*.'

'When?' replied Sancho. 'To-night, without fail. See, your worship, that we spend it in the fields, under the open sky, and I will lay my flesh open.'

At last night came, night for which Don Quixote had longed with all the impatience in the world, for it seemed to him that the wheels of Apollo's car had broken and that the day was of more than its customary length; just as lovers feel, who can never adjust time to their desires. At length they went in among some pleasant trees which stood some way off the road; and there, emptying Rocinante's saddle and Dapple's pack-saddle, they lay down on the green grass and supped off Sancho's stores. Then, making a strong and flexible whip out of Dapple's halter and headstall, Sancho retired some twenty paces from his master among some beeches. Whereat Don Quixote remarked, seeing him depart with such spirit and resolution: 'Mind you do not cut yourself to pieces, friend. Let there be a pause between the strokes. Do not rush headlong forward and have your breath fail you in the middle. Do not lay it on so strong, I mean, that your life fails you before you reach the required number. And for fear you lose by a card too many or too few, I will stand close by and count the lashes on this rosary of mine. May Heaven favour you as your good purpose deserves!'

'A good payer doesn't worry about sureties,' replied Sancho. 'I mean to lay it on so that it hurts without killing, for that's where the whole point of this miracle lies.'

Then he stripped himself to the waist and, seizing the whip, began to lay it on, while Don Quixote counted the strokes. Now Sancho must have given himself six or eight when the joke began to appear tiresome, and very dear at the price; so stopping awhile, he informed his master that he had made a mistake, for each stroke was worth half a *real*, not a quarter.

'Go on, Sancho my friend, and do not be faint-hearted,' said Don Quixote, 'I will double the stakes.'

'In that case,' replied Sancho, 'in God's hands be it. Let it rain lashes.'

But the rogue gave up lashing his own shoulders, and belaboured the trees, uttering such deep groans from time to time that with each one it sounded as if his spirit were being torn from his body. Don Quixote, being naturally humane, and much afraid besides that Sancho might put an end to his life and he through Sancho's imprudence not attain his purpose, now cried out: 'On your life, friend, let the matter rest here. For this seems a rough sort of physic to me, and it would be well to take it gently. Zamora was not won in an hour. You have given yourself a thousand lashes, if I have not miscounted. Let that do for now, for the ass, to use a homely phrase, will carry a load, but not a double load.'

'No, no, sir,' replied Sancho, 'It must not be said of me – the money paid, the work delayed. Stand aside a little longer, your worship, and let me give myself another thousand lashes at any rate. Then in two such bouts we shall have finished this job, and even have something to spare.'

'Well, since you are so well disposed,' said Don Quixote, 'may Heaven help you. Stick to it, and I will stand aside.'

Sancho returned to his task so furiously that he had soon stripped a number of trees of their bark, so severely did he lash himself. And once, raising his voice and dealing one of the beeches a tremendous stroke, he cried: 'Here dies Sampson and all with him.'

Don Quixote ran up at once at the sound of that piteous cry and the crack of the merciless lash and, seizing the twisted halter which served Sancho for a whip, exclaimed: 'Heaven forbid, Sancho my friend, that you should lose your life for my pleasure, for it must serve to support your wife and children. Let Dulcinea await another opportunity, and I will contain myself within the bounds of proximate hope until you gain new strength to conclude this matter to everyone's satisfaction.'

'As your worship would have it so, master,' replied Sancho, 'I'll stop, and gladly. Throw your cloak over my shoulders, for I'm sweating and don't want to catch cold, which is a danger your new flagellants run.'

Don Quixote did as he was asked and, himself remaining in his doublet, covered Sancho, who slept till the sun woke him. Then they resumed their journey, which they concluded for the day in a village nine miles further on. There they dismounted at an inn, which Don Quixote recognized as such, and did not take for a castle with a deep moat, towers, portcullises and a drawbridge, for since his defeat he spoke on all subjects with a sounder judgment, as will now be shown. They lodged him in a lower room, which was hung with some old painted cloths such as you find in small villages, instead of with leather hangings. On one of them some wretched dauber had depicted the rape of Helen at the moment when the bold guest stole her from Menelaus; and on another was the history of Dido and Aeneas – she on a high tower in the act of signalling with half a sheet to her fugitive guest, who was in full flight over the sea in a frigate or brigantine. One noticeable difference between the two pictures, however, was that Helen went with no very ill grace, for she was slyly smiling to herself, but the fair Dido was shown dropping tears as big as walnuts from her eyes. Now when Don Quixote saw this he observed: 'Those two ladies were most unfortunate not to have been born in the present age, and I even more unfortunate not to have been born in theirs. Had I encountered those gentlemen, Troy would not have been burnt nor Carthage destroyed; for all those calamities would have been avoided simply by my killing Paris.'

'I'll bet,' said Sancho, 'that before long there won't be a wine-shop or tavern, an inn or a barber's shop, where the history of our exploits won't be painted up. But I should like them to be painted by a better hand than painted these.'

'You are right, Sancho,' said Don Quixote, 'for this artist is like Orbaneja, the painter of Ubeda, who used to answer when they asked him what he was painting, "whatever it turns out". And if he happened to paint a cock, he would write under it: "This is a cock", in case anyone might think it was a vixen. That is the sort of person, it seems to me, the painter or writer – for it is all one – must have been who published the history of this new Don Quixote that has come out. Or he must have been like a certain poet who hung about the court years ago, by the name of Mauleon, who used to answer any question he was asked offhand. When someone inquired of him the meaning of "*Deum de Deo*", he replied "*Do as you like*". But enough of that. Tell me, Sancho, if you have a mind to give yourself another bout to-night, and whether you had rather be under a roof or beneath the open sky.'

'Indeed, sir,' Sancho replied, 'for the whipping I intend to give myself a house is as good as the fields. But I should like to be among trees, all the same, for they seem to have a fellow feeling and help me marvellously to bear my troubles.'

'No, no, friend Sancho, that shall not be,' replied Don Quixote. 'You must get your strength back, and we shall have to wait till we get to our own village; for we shall be there the day after to-morrow at the latest.'

Sancho replied that it should be as his master pleased, but that he would like to finish the matter off quickly in warm blood and while the mill was grinding. 'For there is often danger in delay, and pray to God and wield the hammer, and one gift is better than two promises, and a bird in the hand is worth two in the bush.'

'No more proverbs, Sancho, in God's name,' exclaimed Don Quixote. 'You seem to be returning to *as it was in the beginning*. Speak plainly, simply and without complications, as I have often asked you before, and you will see how one loaf becomes as good for you as a hundred.'

'I don't know why I'm so unlucky,' replied Sancho, 'but I can't utter a sentence without a proverb, nor utter a proverb that doesn't seem to the point. Still I'll amend if I can.'

And with that their conversation ended for the time being.

Chapter LXXII. *How Don Quixote and Sancho arrived at their village.*

ALL that day Don Quixote and Sancho stayed in that village, waiting in the inn for night, the one to make an end of his flagellation in open country, and the other to witness its completion and with it the accomplishment of his desires. Meanwhile a traveller arrived at the inn on horseback with three or four servants, one of whom said to the man, who was apparently his master, 'Here, Don Alvaro Tarfe, your worship can pass the heat of to-day. The lodging looks clean and cool.'

And overhearing this remark Don Quixote observed to Sancho: 'If I remember rightly, Sancho, I came upon the name of Don Alvaro Tarfe as I was turning over the pages of that second part of my history.'

'That may be so,' answered Sancho. 'Let's let him dismount, and then we'll ask him.'

The horseman dismounted, and the hostess gave him a room on the ground floor opposite Don Quixote's, hung with more painted cloths like those in the knight's apartment. The new arrival changed into light summer clothes and, strolling to the wide cool porch of the inn, where Don Quixote was pacing up and down, asked him: 'Which way are you travelling, my dear sir?'

'To a village nearby,' replied Don Quixote, 'where I live. And where is your worship bound for?'

'I am going to Granada, sir,' replied the gentleman, 'which is my native district.'

'And a good district!' said Don Quixote, 'But be so courteous as to tell me your name, for I am more concerned to know it, I think, than I can well tell you.'

'My name is Don Alvaro Tarfe,' replied the guest.

'Then I take it,' said Don Quixote, 'that you are no doubt that Don Alvaro Tarfe who features in the second part of the History of Don Quixote de la Mancha, recently printed and published by a modern author.'

'I am he,' replied the gentleman, 'and this same Don Quixote, the principal subject of that same history, was a very great friend of mine. It was I who drew him from his home or, at least, persuaded him to go to some jousts which were being held at Saragossa, where I was going myself. And to tell you the truth, I did him many kindnesses and saved him from having his back tickled by the hangman for his foolhardiness.'

'And tell me, Don Alvaro, do I in any way resemble this Don Quixote you speak of?'

'No, certainly not,' replied the guest, 'not at all.'

'And this Don Quixote,' said our one, 'did he have a squire with him called Sancho Panza?'

'Yes, he had,' replied Don Alvaro, 'and though he had the reputation of being a comical fellow I never heard him say anything at all funny.'

'I can very well believe that,' broke in Sancho Panza, 'for it's not everyone that can say good things, and this Sancho Panza you mention, sir, must be a very great knave and a dolt and a thief, all rolled into one. For I'm the true Sancho Panza, and I have more wit than ever rained from the sky. Only put me to the test, your worship. Walk behind me for a year or so, and you'll see what good things fall from me at every step. So many and so good they are that often when I don't know what I'm saying everyone who hears me bursts out laughing. And the true Don Quixote de la Mancha, the famous, the valiant and the wise, the enamoured, the righter of wrongs, the guardian of minors and orphans, the protector of widows, the slayer of maidens, he that has the peerless Dulcinea for his sole mistress, is this gentleman here, my master. Any other Don Quixote whatsoever, and any other Sancho Panza, are a mockery and a dream.'

'By God, I believe you,' replied Don Alvaro, 'for you've said more good things in the four sentences I've heard you utter than the other Sancho Panza in all I heard him say, which was a great deal. He was more of a guzzler than a wit. In fact there's no doubt in my mind that the enchanters who persecute Don Quixote the Good have been trying to persecute me with Don Quixote the Bad. But I don't know what I'm saying, for I dare swear that I left him shut up in the madhouse at Toledo for treatment, and here starts up another Don Quixote very different from mine.'

'I do not know,' said Don Quixote, 'whether I am good, but I can say that I am not "*the bad*". And to prove it I would have you know,

Don Alvaro Tarfe, that I have never been in Saragossa in all the days of my life. On the contrary, when I was told that the fictitious Don Quixote had taken part in the jousts in that city I decided not to go there, and so to proclaim his lie to the world. Instead I went openly to Barcelona, the treasure house of courtesy, the refuge of strangers, the hospital of the poor, the country of the valiant, the avenger of the injured, and the abode of firm and reciprocal friendships, unique in its position and its beauty. And although the adventures that befell me there occasioned me no great pleasure, but rather much grief, I bore them the better for having seen that city. In short, Don Alvaro Tarfe, I am Don Quixote de la Mancha, the same of whom fame speaks, and that miserable man who sought to usurp my name and take the credit for my designs is not he. I beg your worship, as you are a gentleman, to be so kind as to make a declaration before the mayor of this place that you have never seen me in all the days of your life till to-day, and that I am not the Don Quixote written of in the second part, nor is this Sancho Panza, my squire, the man your worship knew.'

'I'll do that with very great pleasure,' replied Don Alvaro, 'for it's very surprising to see two Don Quixotes and two Sanchos at the same time, alike in their names yet how different in their deeds. Let me affirm once more that I didn't see what I did see, and that what happened to me didn't happen.'

'No doubt,' said Sancho, 'your worship must be enchanted, like my lady Dulcinea del Toboso. Would to Heaven I could disenchant you by giving myself another three thousand three hundred lashes as I'm doing for her, for I would give them you without interest.'

'I don't understand what you mean by lashes,' said Don Alvaro.

Sancho answered that it was a long story, but he would tell it him if they chanced to be going the same way.

By now it was dinner time, and just as Don Quixote and Don Alvaro were eating together the mayor of the village happened to come into the inn with a clerk. Whereupon Don Quixote laid a petition before him, claiming as a matter of right that Don Alvaro Tarfe, the gentleman there present, should declare before him that he did not know Don Quixote de la Mancha, also there present, and that it was not he who was written of in a history entitled *The*

Second Part of the Exploits of Don Quixote de la Mancha, composed by a certain Avellaneda, native of Tordesillas. To be brief, the mayor complied in due form. The declaration was made judicially to the great satisfaction of Don Quixote and Sancho, as if such a declaration were of great importance to them, and the acts and deeds of the two Don Quixotes and the two Sanchos did not clearly show the difference between them. Many civilities and offers of service passed between Don Alvaro and Don Quixote, in which the great Manchegan showed so much good sense that Don Alvaro Tarfe was convinced that he had been deceived. He even suspected that he must have been enchanted, since he had touched two such different Don Quixotes with his own hands. As evening came on they left the village, and after about a mile and a half their two roads diverged, one leading to Don Quixote's village, and the other the way Don Alvaro had to take. In the short interval Don Quixote had told him of his disastrous defeat, and of Dulcinea's enchantment and relief, all of which amazed Don Alvaro afresh. However, he went on his way, first embracing Don Quixote and Sancho, and left Don Quixote to his.

That night they spent among some trees to give Sancho an opportunity of performing his penance, which he did in the same way as on the night before, damaging the beech trees' bark more than his shoulders, of which he took such care that the whipping would not have brushed off a fly, if there had been one there. The deluded knight did not miss a single stroke in the count, and found that with the last night's score they came to three thousand and twenty-nine. The sun seems to have risen early to see the sacrifice, and in its light they continued on their way talking, the two of them, about Don Alvaro's mistake, and what a good idea it had been to take his affidavit in due and authentic form before the justice. That day and that night they spent on the road without anything noteworthy befalling them, except that Sancho completed his task, to the inordinate delight of his master, who longed for daylight and to see whether he might meet his now disenchanted lady Dulcinea on the road. And as he travelled on he went up to every woman he encountered to see if she was not Dulcinea del Toboso, holding infallibly that the sage Merlin's promise could not prove false. So, full of hopes and expectations, they climbed to the top of a hill, and when they made out their village Sancho fell on his knees and cried: 'Open your eyes, my beloved country, and see your son Sancho Panza returning – if not rich yet well beaten. Open your arms and receive your son Don Quixote too, who, though conquered by another, has conquered himself – which, as I have heard him say, is the very best kind of victory. I bring money though, and if it's a good whipping they gave me it's a fine mount I have now.'

'Stop these fooleries,' said Don Quixote, 'and let us enter our village right foot foremost. Once there, we will give play to our imaginations and devise the scheme of the pastoral life we mean to follow.'

With this they rode down the hill and made for home.

Chapter LXXIII. *Of the omens Don Quixote met on entering his village, and other matters which adorn and confirm this great history.*

As they approached, Cide Hamete tells us, Don Quixote saw two boys quarrelling on the village threshing floor, and heard one of them say to the other: 'Don't worry, Periquello, you won't see it in all the days of your life.'

When Don Quixote heard this he said to Sancho; 'Did you not hear, friend, what that boy said: – "You'll never see it again, never."'

'Well,' replied Sancho, 'what does it matter what the boy said?'

'What?' exclaimed Don Quixote, 'Do you not see that if you apply that saying to myself, it means that I shall never see Dulcinea again?'

Sancho was just going to reply when he was prevented by the sight of a hare coursing over the fields followed by a number of greyhounds and hunters, and in her terror she ran to take shelter beneath Dapple's feet. Sancho took her up safe in his hands and presented her to Don Quixote, who immediately cried out: '*Malum signum! Malum signum!* A hare flies; the hounds pursue her; Dulcinea will not appear!'

'You're a strange one, your worship,' said Sancho. 'Let's suppose that this hare is Dulcinea del Toboso, and these hounds chasing her are the vagabond enchanters who transformed her into a peasant girl. She runs away; I pick her up and put her into your worship's charge; and you have her in your arms and caress her. Now, where's the bad sign in that, and what ill omen do you draw from it?'

The two boys who had been quarrelling came up to see the hare, and Sancho asked one of them what they had been wrangling about. The one who had said: *You will never see it again*, answered that he had taken a cage of crickets from the other boy and did not intend to give it back to him so long as he lived. Sancho took four quarter *reals* from his pocket and gave them to the boy in return for the cage, which he placed in Don Quixote's hands, saying: 'Here, sir, are these omens broken and destroyed. They have nothing more to do with our fortunes, to my mind, than last year's clouds. And if I'm not mistaken I have heard our parish priest say that Christians and sensible people should pay no attention to such nonsense. And even your worship has told me so in days gone by, and given me to understand that all Christians who heeded omens were fools. But there's no need to dwell on that; let's go on into the village.'

The hunters came up and demanded their hare, which Don Quixote gave them. Then he and Sancho passed on, and as they drew near the village they came upon the priest and the Bachelor Carrasco at their prayers in a meadow. Now it must be mentioned that Sancho had thrown over Dapple and the bundle of arms, by way of a cover, the buckram robe painted with flames of fire which they had put on him in the Duke's castle on the night when Altisidora rose from death. He had also squeezed the mitre on to Dapple's head, and this adornment transformed her as strangely as ever ass was transformed in all the world. The priest and the Bachelor recognised them immediately, and went up to them with open arms. Don Quixote dismounted and embraced them warmly; whilst the boys, whose lynx eyes nothing can escape, sighted the ass's mitre and rushed up to look at it, calling to one another: 'Come on, boys, and you'll see Sancho Panza's ass finer than Mingo, and Don Quixote's beast leaner than ever.'

At length, surrounded by boys, they entered the village in the company of the priest and the Bachelor and, going to Don Quixote's house, found his housekeeper and niece, whom the news of his coming had already reached. It had also reached Teresa Panza,

Sancho's wife, who ran out to see her husband, dishevelled and half naked, dragging her daughter Sanchica by the hand and, seeing him not so well got up as she thought a governor should be, she asked him: 'How is it you come like this, husband, on foot? You look footsore, too, and more like a misgoverned wretch than a governor.'

'Hush, Teresa,' answered Sancho, 'for often where there are hooks there's no bacon. Let's go home and you shall hear wonders. I bring money – and that's what counts – gained by my own industry and at no cost to anyone.'

'Bring your money, good husband,' said Teresa. 'I don't care where you gained it, for however you got it you won't have started up a new custom in the world.'

Sanchica kissed her father and asked him whether he had anything for her, for she was longing for him as they do for showers in May. Teresa then took him by the hand on one side and Sanchica held him by the belt on the other, at the same time pulling Dapple along behind, and they went to their house, leaving Don Quixote at his, in the care of his niece and his housekeeper and in the company of the priest and the Bachelor.

Then without waiting on time or season, Don Quixote took the priest and the Bachelor aside that very moment, and told them in few words of his defeat and the obligation he was under not to leave his village for a year; which he intended to observe to the letter, without infringing it by an atom, as befitted a knight errant bound by the rules and order of his profession. He told them also how he intended to turn shepherd for the year, and pass his time in the solitude of the fields, where he could give free rein to his amorous thoughts, whilst occupying himself in that pastoral and virtuous calling. He begged them to be his companions, if they had not much to do and were not prevented by more important business, and said he would buy sufficient sheep and stock to give them the name of shepherds. But, he informed them, the principal part of the business was already done, for he had fixed on names for them which would fit them to a T. The priest asked him for them, and Don Quixote replied that he was to call himself the shepherd Quixotiz, the Bachelor the shepherd Carrascon, the priest the shepherd Curiambro and Sancho Panza the shepherd Panzino. They were all astonished at Don Quixote's fresh craze. But to keep him from leaving the village again on his chivalries, in the hope that he could be cured in that year, they gave in to his new project, applauding his folly as wisdom and offering to join him in its pursuit.

'That is excellent,' said Sampson Carrasco, 'for, as all the world knows by now, I am a most famous poet. I will compose pastoral or courtly verses at every turn, or whatever best suits the case, to afford us some amusement in the lonely places where we shall have to wander. But what is most important of all, gentlemen, is for each one of us to choose the name of the shepherdess he means to celebrate in his verses, and not to leave the toughest tree without her name inscribed and cut into it, according to the use and custom of love-stricken shepherds.'

'That is quite right,' replied Don Quixote, 'though for myself I have no need to seek for the name of any imaginary shepherdess, since there is the peerless Dulcinea del Toboso, glory of these banks, ornament of these meadows, the prop of beauty, the cream of grace and, in short, a fitting object for all praise however hyperbolical.'

'That is true,' said the priest, 'but we must look around for accommodating shepherdesses, and trim their angles if they do not fit us square.'

'And if our invention fails,' added Sampson Carrasco, 'we will give them the names we see in print. The world is full of them, Phyllidas, Amaryllises, Dianas, Fleridas, Galateas and Belisardas; for as they sell them in the markets we can easily buy them and keep them for our own. If my lady – my shepherdess I should say – should happen to be called Anna, I will celebrate her under the name of Anarda; if she is Francesca, I will call her Francenia; if she is Lucia, Lucinda; for that is what it all comes to. And if Sancho Panza is to enter our confraternity, he can celebrate his wife Teresa Panza under the name of Teresaina.'

Don Quixote smiled at the application of the name, and the priest bestowed infinite praise on his chaste and honourable resolution, repeating his offer to bear him company for as long as he could spare from his unavoidable duties. With this they took their leave of him, begging him most urgently to take good care of his health and keep to a wholesome diet.

Now, as Fate would have it, his niece and his housekeeper had overheard the conversation of these three, and as soon as the two visitors were gone they both went in to Don Quixote, whom his niece addressed: 'What is this, uncle? Now that we were thinking that you had come back to stay at home and live a quiet and decent life here, you want to embroil yourself in fresh mazes. So now it's to be "*Are you coming, gentle shepherd, dearest shepherd, are you going?*" Really, uncle, that straw's too old to make pipes of.'

Whereupon the housekeeper added: 'And will your worship be able to stand the heat of the summer afternoons in the fields, and the night dews of winter, and the howling of the wolves? Of course not. For that's a life for stout men, hardened and reared for the work almost from their swaddling clothes. Of the two evils now, it would be the lesser to be a knight errant than a shepherd. Look, sir, take my advice, which I'm not giving you on a stomach full of bread and wine, but fasting and with the experience of my fifty years: — Stay at home, look after your property, confess frequently, be good to the poor, and on my soul be it if any harm come to you.'

'Be quiet, daughters,' replied Don Quixote. 'I know very well what I must do. Take me to bed, for I do not feel very well, and rest assured that, whether I am a knight errant now or a wandering shepherd, I shall never fail to provide for your needs, as you shall find by experience.'

And his good daughters — for such his niece and his housekeeper were — took him to bed where they gave him some food and what comfort they could.

Chapter LXXIV. *Of how Don Quixote fell ill, of the Will he made, and of his Death.*

As all human things, especially the lives of men, are transitory, being ever on the decline from their beginnings till they reach their final end, and as Don Quixote had no privilege from Heaven exempting him from the common fate, his dissolution and end came when he least expected it. Whether that event was brought on by melancholy occasioned by the contemplation of his defeat or whether it was by divine ordination, a fever seized him and kept him to his bed for six days, during which time he was frequently visited by his friends, the priest, the Bachelor and the barber, and his good squire Sancho Panza never left his bedside.

All of them believed that grief at his overthrow and the disappointment of his hopes for Dulcinea's deliverance and disenchantment had brought him to this state, and tried to cheer him in every possible way. The Bachelor bade him be of good heart, and get up and begin on his pastoral life, for which he had already composed an eclogue, which would knock out every one Sannazaro had ever written. He said that he had bought a couple of fine dogs with his own money from a herdsman from Quintanar to guard the flock, one called Barcino and the other Butron. But Don Quixote's dejection persisted all the same. His friends called in a doctor, who took his pulse and did not offer much comfort, saying that he should certainly attend to the salvation of his soul, for his body's was in danger. Don Quixote heard this with a quiet mind, but not so his housekeeper, his niece and his squire, who began to weep piteously, as if he already lay dead before their eyes. It was the doctor's opinion that melancholy and despondency were bringing him to his end. Don Quixote begged to be left alone, for he wanted to sleep a little. They obeyed him, and he slept for more than six hours, at a stretch as they say; so long, in fact, that his housekeeper and his niece thought that he would pass away in his sleep. But at the end of that time he woke and cried out loudly: 'Blessed be Almighty God, who has vouchsafed me this great blessing! Indeed his mercies are boundless, nor can the sins of men limit or hinder them.'

His niece was listening to her uncle, and these words seeming to her more rational than his general speech, at least during that illness, she asked him: 'What is it you say, sir? Is there anything new? What mercies are these, or what sins of men?'

'The mercies, niece,' answered Don Quixote, 'are those which God has shown me at this moment, mercies to which, as I have said, my sins are no impediment. My judgment is now clear and free from the misty shadows of ignorance with which my ill-starred and continuous reading of those detestable books of chivalry had obscured it. Now I know their absurdities and their deceits, and the only thing that grieves me is that this discovery has come too late, and leaves me no time to make amends by reading other books, which might enlighten my soul. I feel, niece, that I am on the point of death, and I should like to meet it in such a manner as to convince the world that my life has not been so bad as to leave me the character of a madman; for though I have been one, I would not confirm the fact in my death. Call my good friends, my dear, the priest, Bachelor Sampson Carrasco and Master Nicholas the barber, for I want to confess and make my will.'

But his niece was excused this task by the entrance of the three. And the moment Don Quixote saw them he exclaimed: 'Congratulate me, good sirs, for I am Don Quixote de la Mancha no longer, but Alonso Quixano, called for my way of life the Good. Now I am the enemy of Amadis of Gaul and of all the infinite brood of his progeny. Now all profane histories of knight errantry are odious to me. I know my folly now, and the peril I have incurred from the reading of them. Now, by God's mercy, I have learnt from my own bitter experience and I abominate them.'

When the three heard his words they believed that some fresh madness had certainly seized him, and Sampson said to him: 'Must you come out with that, Don Quixote, just now when we have news that the Lady Dulcinea is disenchanted? Now that we are just on the point of turning shepherds to spend our lives singing like any princes, do you want to turn hermit? No more of that, I pray you. Return to your senses and cease your idle tales!'

'Tales?' replied Don Quixote. 'Up to now they have been only too real, to my cost. But, with Heaven's aid, my death shall turn them to my profit. I feel, sirs, that I am rapidly dying. Stop your fooling, and bring me a priest to confess me and a clerk to make my will, for in such extremities as this a man must not jest with his soul. So send for a clerk, I beg of you, while my friend the priest confesses me.'

They looked at one another in amazement at Don Quixote's words and, though in doubt, were inclined to believe him. And one of the signs by which they concluded that he was dying was the ease with which he changed from mad to sane; for he said much more in the vein of his last utterances, so well spoken, so Christian and so connected, that they were finally resolved of all their doubts and convinced that his mind was sound. The priest made everyone leave the room, remained alone with him and confessed him. The Bachelor went for the clerk, and in a short time came back with him and with Sancho Panza, who had had news from Carrasco of his master's state and, finding the housekeeper and the niece in tears, began to blubber and weep himself. When the confession was ended the priest came out, saying: 'Truly he is dying and truly he is sane, Alonso Quixano the Good. We had better go in so that he can make his will.' This news gave a terrible start to the brimming eyes of his housekeeper, his niece and his good squire, Sancho Panza, causing them to break out into fresh tears and groans. For in truth, as has been said before, whether he was plain Alonso Quixano the Good, or Don Quixote de la Mancha, he was always of an amiable disposition and kind in his behaviour, so that he was well beloved, not only by his own household but by everyone who knew him.

The clerk went in with the others and, after he had drawn up the heads of the will, Don Quixote disposed of his soul with all the requisite Christian formalities and came to the bequests, saying:

'*Item*, *this is my will regarding certain moneys which Sancho Panza, whom in my madness I made my squire, retains, there having been between him and me certain accounts, receipts and disbursements. I wish him not to be charged with them, nor asked to account for them, but if there should be any surplus after he has paid himself what I owe him, the residue is to be his. It will be very little, and may it do him much good. And if when I was mad I was party to giving him the governorship of an isle, now that I am sane I would give him a kingdom, were I able, for the simplicity of his nature and the fidelity of his conduct deserve it.*'

Then, turning to Sancho, he said: 'Pardon me, friend, that I caused you to appear mad, like me, making you fall into the same sort of error as myself, the belief that there were and still are knights errant in the world.'

'Oh, don't die, dear master!' answered Sancho in tears. 'Take my advice and live many years. For the maddest thing a man can do in this life is to let himself die just like that, without anybody killing him, but just finished off by his own melancholy. Don't be lazy, look you, but get out of bed, and let's go out into the fields dressed as shepherds, as we decided to. Perhaps we shall find the lady Dulcinea behind some hedge, disenchanted and as pretty as a picture. If it's from grief at being beaten you're dying, put the blame on me and say you were tumbled off because I girthed Rocinante badly. For your worship must have seen in your books of chivalries that it's a common thing for one knight to overthrow another, and the one that's conquered to-day may be the conqueror to-morrow.'

'That's right,' said Sampson. 'Honest Sancho has hit the truth of the matter.'

'Let us go gently, gentlemen,' said Don Quixote, 'for there are no birds this year in last year's nests. I was mad, but I am sane now. I was Don Quixote de la Mancha, but to-day, as I have said, I am Alonso Quixano the Good. May my sincere repentance restore your former esteem for me. Now let the clerk go on.

'*Item, I bequeath all my estate, without reserve, to Antonia Quixana, my niece, here present, there being first deducted from it in the most convenient way all that is necessary for the fulfilment of my bequests. And the first payment to be made I desire to be the wages due to my housekeeper for the time she has been in my service, and twenty ducats besides for a dress. I leave as my executors Master Priest and Master Sampson Carrasco, here present. Item, it is my wish that, should my niece Antonia Quixana be inclined to wed, she should marry a man of whom she has first had evidence that he does not even know what books of chivalry are; and in case it shall be discovered that he does know, and my niece shall yet wish to marry him, and shall marry him, she shall lose all I have bequeathed her, which my executors may distribute in pious works as they think fit. Item, I beseech the said gentlemen, my executors, that if by good fortune they should come to know the alleged author of a history circulating hereabouts under the title of* The Second Part of the Exploits of Don Quixote de la Mancha, *they shall beg him on my behalf, with the greatest earnestness, to forgive the occasion I unwittingly gave him of publishing so many gross absurdities as are therein written; for I quit this life with an uneasy conscience at having given him an excuse for writing them.*'

With this he concluded his testament and, falling into a faint, lay stretched at full length on the bed. Everyone was alarmed and ran to his assistance, and during the three days that he lived after making his will he fainted very frequently. The house was in a turmoil. However his niece ate, his housekeeper drank and Sancho Panza was cheerful; for legacies tend to dull or moderate in the inheritor the grief that nature claims for the deceased.

At last Don Quixote's end came, after he had received all the sacraments and expressed his horror of books of chivalry in strong and moving terms. The clerk, who happened to be present, said that he had never read in any book of chivalries of a knight errant dying n his bed in so calm and Christian a manner as Don Quixote, who amidst the compassionate tears of all present gave up the ghost – that is to say, died.

When the priest saw that he was no more he desired the clerk to draw up a certificate that Alonso Quixano the Good, commonly called Don Quixote de la Mancha, had passed out of this present life and died a natural death; which testimonial he required in order to deprive any author other than Cide Hamete Benengeli of all excuse for falsely resuscitating him and writing interminable histories of his deeds.

Such was the end of the Ingenious Gentleman of La Mancha, whose dwelling Cide Hamete was unwilling to indicate exactly, so that every town and village of La Mancha might contend for the honour of fathering and possessing him, as the seven cities of Greece did for Homer. The tears of Sancho, of Don Quixote's niece and of his housekeeper are not here recorded, nor are the recent epitaphs upon his tomb; but this is what Sampson Carrasco put there:

> Here lies the gentle knight and stout,
> Who to such height of valour got
> That, if you mark his deeds throughout,
> Death over his life triumphed not
> With bringing of his death about.
>
> The world as nothing he did prize,
> For as a scarecrow in men's eyes
> He lived, and was their bugbear too;
> And had the luck, with much ado,
> To live a fool, and yet die wise.

And said the most prudent Cide Hamete to his pen: 'Here you shall rest, hanging from this rack by this copper wire, my goosequill. Whether you are well or ill cut I know not, but you shall live long ages there, unless presumptuous and rascally historians take you down to profane you. But before they approach you, warn them as best you are able:

> Beware, beware, you scoundrels,
> I may be touched by none:
> This is a deed, my worthy king,
> Reserved for me alone.

'For me alone Don Quixote was born and I for him. His was the power of action, mine of writing. Only we two are at one, despite that fictitious and Tordillescan scribe who has dared, and may dare again, to pen the deeds of my valorous knight with his coarse and ill-trimmed ostrich feather. This is no weight for his shoulders, no task for his frozen intellect; and should you chance to make his acquaintance, you may tell him to leave Don Quixote's weary and mouldering bones to rest in the grave, nor seek, against all the canons of death, to carry him off to Old Castile, or to bring him out of the tomb, where he most certainly lies, stretched at full length and powerless to make a third journey, or to embark on any new expedition. For the two on which he rode out are enough to make a mockery of all the countless forays undertaken by all the countless knights errant, such has been the delight and approval they have won from all to whose notice they have come, both here and abroad. Thus you will comply with your Christian profession by offering good counsel to one who wishes you ill, and I shall be proud and satisfied to have been the first author to enjoy the pleasure of witnessing the full effect of his own writing. For my sole object has been to arouse men's contempt for all fabulous and absurd stories of knight errantry, whose credit this tale of my genuine Don Quixote has already shaken, and which will, without a doubt, soon tumble to the ground. Farewell.'